"In this impressive volume Michael Horton takes the movement of confessing evangelicals to a new level. He reminds and rethinks the greatness of seventeenth-century Reformed theology and makes it accessible for readers today. Even those who cannot go along with some of his central positions will find them to be challenging and formidable. Horton has produced an up-to-date work that is well worth grappling with."

—*George Hunsinger, Hazel Thompson McCord Professor of Systematic Theology, Princeton Theological Seminary*

"The most authoritative systematic theologies must possess a range of qualities: a firm grasp of the overall shape and proportions of Christian teaching, an eye for its fine details, deep biblical and historical learning, conceptual prowess matched by descriptive power, and a sense of cultural occasion—all animated by humble delight in the inexhaustibility of God and the gospel. Michael Horton's presentation exhibits all these excellences. This is a work of outstanding theological and spiritual cogency and will command wide attention."

—*John Webster, King's College, University of Aberdeen*

"Horton's *The Christian Faith* has the great merit of never letting the reader forget that doctrine is for disciples who want to walk the way of Jesus Christ. Horton knows that the best systematic theology is a practical theology—one that helps us understand the ways of God, makes sense of life, and gives direction for God-glorifying living. He also knows that the best systematic theologies draw on biblical and historical theology. May many readers therefore take up this book, read, and walk!"

—*Kevin J. Vanhoozer, Blanchard Professor of Theology, Wheaton College and Graduate School*

"Michael Horton has done the Protestant church a profound service by bringing the theology of the Reformation forward to the twenty-first century. For decades there has been a need for Reformed dogmatics to tackle new questions in theology, philosophy, and culture. Horton's well-researched volume brings a rich theological heritage into conversation with ideas and thinkers shaping the future of our world. This volume demonstrates that Protestant orthodoxy is alive and active. Horton's precision is sure to initiate a new series of theological refinement in light of new global realities."

—*Anthony B. Bradley, associate professor of theology and ethics, The King's College*

"Michael Horton's awareness of modern theological and philosophical currents combines with his articulate commitment to historical orthodoxy to make this book one of the most significant voices to be heard in framing a systematic theology for this generation of the Reformed movement."

—*Bryan Chapell, president, Covenant Theological Seminary*

"*The Christian Faith* offers a fine, comprehensive companion to a number of recent systematic theologies. Crisply written, scripturally informed throughout, distinctively evangelical and Reformed, conversant with classic as well as contemporary Christian authors—Horton's study is an outstanding contribution that will richly nourish Christian pilgrims on their way toward the consummation of Christ's kingdom."

—*Cornelis P. Venema, president, Mid-America Reformed Seminary*

"A crisp, clear, and forceful new theology that is at once biblical and reverent, historical and contemporary, learned but accessible. What a great gift this is to the church!"
—*David F. Wells, Distinguished Research Professor, Gordon-Conwell Theological Seminary*

"*The Christian Faith* is impressively deep, immensely practical, and infinitely hopeful for us pilgrims on the Way. Michael Horton will sculpt your appreciation for theology and enhance your love for Christ crucified. Anyone wanting to impact this world effectively—pastors, missionaries, evangelists, church planters, lay leaders, and all other wayfarers—*must* read this book."
—*Pastor Fikret Böcek, The Protestant Church of Smyrna, Turkey*

"There has been a renaissance of theological writing in our day, but no one writes as carefully, cogently, and thoughtfully in the grand tradition of Protestant systematic theology as does Michael Horton. This work is a powerful reminder that theology ought to grow first from the soil of the biblical text; then, in conversation with the church across the ages, it ought to clarify conceptually the great truths of the gospel. Theology, as Horton has written it here in *The Christian Faith*, must always be cognizant of the challenges of the contemporary world, but it must finally belong to the church, which gives it voice in the first place. There is no one better at this task in our day than Michael Horton."
—*Richard Lints, Andrew Mutch Distinguished Professor of Theology, Gordon-Conwell Theological Seminary*

"This is a remarkable volume: lucid, insightful, learned, and faithful, *The Christian Faith* is that rare book that substantially contributes to *and* helpfully introduces Christian theology. I highly recommend it."
—*Kevin W. Hector, The University of Chicago Divinity School*

"*The Christian Faith* is a remarkable accomplishment—the most significant single-volume systematic theology to be written in decades! This book is written for the sake of the church, yet it also reflects a fresh engagement with a broad range of biblical and theological scholarship. *The Christian Faith* is an excellent resource for all who wish to engage classical Christian theology in a Reformed key."
—*J. Todd Billings, associate professor of Reformed theology, Western Theological Seminary*

"Dr. Horton has produced a remarkable work. His approach to systematic theology is fresh and critically needed in our time. Every pilgrim will profit from this work."
—*R. C. Sproul, chairman and president, Ligonier Ministries*

"Michael Horton has hit a home run: a narrative-shaped, comprehensive, one-volume systematic theology that is biblically grounded, warmly evangelical, confessionally Reformed in its angularity while catholic in its tone, and freshly contemporary. In the spirit of the Westminster Catechism, Horton directs to the glory of God and joy of doing theology."
—*John Bolt, professor of systematic theology, Calvin Theological Seminary*

Michael Horton

THE CHRISTIAN FAITH

A **Systematic Theology**
for Pilgrims On the Way

ZONDERVAN®

ZONDERVAN

The Christian Faith
Copyright © 2011 by Michael Horton

Requests for information should be addressed to:
Zondervan, 3900 *Sparks Dr. SE, Grand Rapids, Michigan 49546*

ISBN 978-0-310-40918-2 (ebook)

Library of Congress Cataloging-in-Publication Data

Horton, Michael Scott.
        The Christian faith : a systematic theology for pilgrims on the way / Michael S. Horton.
            p. cm.
        Includes bibliographical references and index.
        ISBN 978-0-310-28604-2 (hardcover)
        1. Theology, Doctrinal. 2. Reformed Church — Doctrines. I. Title.
BT75.3.H67 2010
230'.42 — dc22   2010019271

Cover design: Rob Monacelli
Interior design: Matthew VanZomeren

Printed in the United States of America

19 20 21 22 23 24 25 26 /DCI/ 28 27 26 25 24 23 22 21 20 19 18 17 16 15 14 13 12 11

CONTENTS

ACKNOWLEDGMENTS

Especially for a book like this one, it is impossible to list all of the names of those to whom I am indebted. Therefore, I will only express gratitude to those who provided direct input on this project.

In addition to my professors, colleagues, and students who have encouraged, refined, and corrected my thinking, I am grateful to my seminary research assistants over the past several years (now alumni), Ryan Glomsrud and Brannan Ellis, who have offered useful critiques. I owe a special debt to my current research assistant, Brian Hecker, as well as Jeff Eicher, for labors especially in correcting footnotes and compiling indexes, respectively. Keith Mathison generously read through the penultimate version, and I am grateful to him for his thorough evaluation and suggestions.

I also express thanks to Brett Watson, Eric Landry, and the team at White Horse Inn/*Modern Reformation* magazine, who have endured my lengthy preoccupation with this project. For constant sustenance and the opportunity to test this material on exceptional parishioners, I thank Christ United Reformed Church (Santee, California), and especially our gifted pastor, Michael Brown. I am grateful also to Zondervan's exceptional team, especially to Stan Gundry, who encouraged me to write this book, and to my editors, David Frees, Dirk Buursma, and Verlyn Verbrugge, for their expertise and support along the way.

For our entire marriage, I have tested my wife's patience in the process of writing, first, my four-volume dogmatics series and now this one-volume systematic theology. More than a decade (and four children) later, she is more precious to me than ever for her encouragement and support, as well as for her wisdom and insight into God's Word. It is to her and to our children—James, Olivia, Matthew, and Adam—that I dedicate this volume.

ABBREVIATIONS

ANF   *Ante-Nicene Fathers* (ed. Alexander Roberts and James Donaldson; Grand Rapids: Eerdmans, repr. 1976)

BDAG   Walter Bauer, Frederick W. Danker, et al., *A Greek-English Lexicon of the New Testament and Other Early Christian Literature* (3rd ed.; Chicago: Univ. of Chicago Press, 2000)

BSac   *Bibliotheca sacra*

Church Dogmatics   Karl Barth, *Church Dogmatics* (ed. G. W. Bromiley and T. F. Torrance; trans. G. W. Bromiley; Edinburgh: T&T Clark, 1956–1975)

CO   *Calvini opera*, 59 volumes. In *Corpus reformatorum* (ed. C. G. Bretschneider, H. E. Bindseil, et al., vols. 29–87; New York: Johnson, repr. 1964)

CTJ   *Calvin Theological Journal*

Elenctic Theology   Francis Turretin, *Institutes of Elenctic Theology* (ed. James T. Dennison Jr.; trans. George Musgrave Giger; Phillipsburg, N.J.: P&R, 1992)

HTR   *Harvard Theological Review*

Institutes   John Calvin, *Institutes of the Christian Religion* (ed. J. T. McNeill; trans. Ford Lewis Battles; Philadelphia: Westminster, 1960)

JAOS   *Journal of the American Oriental Society*

JETS   *Journal of the Evangelical Theological Society*

JR   *Journal of Religion*

LXX   Septuagint (Greek translation of the Old Testament)

m. Pesaḥ   Mishnah, *Pesaḥ*

NPNF1   *Nicene and Post-Nicene Fathers* (ed. Philip Schaff et al.; 1st series; Grand Rapids: Eerdmans, repr. 1982)

NPNF2   *Nicene and Post-Nicene Fathers* (ed. Philip Schaff et al.; 2nd series; Grand Rapids: Eerdmans, repr. 1982)

OS   Ioannis Calvini, *Opera Selecta* (ed. P. Barth and G. Niesel; 5 vols.; Munich: Kaiser, 1926–1936)

PG   Patrologia graeca (ed. J.-P Migne; 162 vols.; Paris, 1857–1886)

PL   Patrologia latina (ed. J.-P Migne; 217 vols.; Paris, 1844–1864)

PRRD   Richard Muller, *Post-Reformation Reformed Dogmatics* (2nd ed.; Grand Rapids: Baker, 2003)

SJT   *Scottish Journal of Theology*

SNTSMS Society for New Testament Studies Monograph series

TDOT   *Theological Dictionary of the Old Testament* (ed. G. Johannes Botterweck and Helmer Ringgren; Grand Rapids: Eerdmans, 1974–2006)

ThTo   *Theology Today*

TT   *Tracts and Treatises* (trans. Henry Beveridge; 3 vols.; Grand Rapids: Baker, repr. 1958)

WBC   Word Biblical Commentary

WTJ   *Westminster Theological Journal*

THE NICENE CREED[1]

We believe in one God, the Father Almighty,
    Maker of heaven and earth,
    of all things visible and invisible.
And in one Lord Jesus Christ, the only-begotten Son of God,
    begotten of his Father before all worlds,
    God of God, Light of Light,
    very God of very God,
    begotten, not made, being of one substance with the Father;
    by whom all things were made;
    who for us and for our salvation
    came down from heaven,
    and was incarnate by the Holy Spirit of the virgin Mary,
    and was made man;
    and was crucified also for us under Pontius Pilate;
    he suffered and was buried;
    and the third day he rose again according to the Scriptures,
    and ascended into heaven, and is seated at the right hand of the Father;
    and he shall come again, with glory, to judge both the living and the dead;
    whose kingdom shall have no end.
And we believe in the Holy Spirit, the Lord and giver of life,
    who proceeds from the Father and the Son;
    who with the Father and the Son together is worshiped and glorified;
    who spoke by the prophets;
    and we believe in one holy catholic and apostolic church;
    we acknowledge one baptism for the remission of sins;
    and we look for the resurrection of the dead,
    and the life of the world to come. Amen.

---

1. The Nicene Creed, in *Trinity Hymnal* (rev. ed.: Philadelphia:
Great Commission Publications, 1990), 846.

THE DOGMA IS THE DRAMA: A THEOLOGY FOR PILGRIMS ON THE WAY

In 1949, the English playwright and novelist Dorothy Sayers observed the common antipathy in her day toward doctrine: "'Dull dogma,' they call it." According to Sayers, however, Christianity is the most interesting story ever told. "And the dogma *is* the drama."[1] For many Christians, words such as *doctrine* and *theology*—and especially *systematic theology*—conjure up images of intellectual pride, divisiveness, and the presumption that we can put God in a box, neatly explained by our categories and formulations. Of course, we are nearly infinitely resourceful in using good things with corrupt motives and for less than noble ends. We can exhibit spiritual pride also in our experience or morality. However, it is the goal of good theology to humble us before the triune God of majesty and grace. As we will see more fully, the older theologians of the Reformation and Post-Reformation eras were so convinced that their interpretations fell far short of the majesty of God that they called their summaries and systems "our humble theology" and "a theology for pilgrims on the way."

I. WHY THEOLOGY? DRAMA, DOCTRINE, DOXOLOGY, AND DISCIPLESHIP

Theology simply means "the study of God," and *doctrine* means "teaching." Since the main message of Scripture is the unfolding mystery of Christ, who reveals his Father and reconciles us to him, theology is a central concern of every believer. It would be odd if we told our spouse or other loved ones that we wanted to spend time with them and experience their fellowship regularly but did not want to know anything about them—their characteristics, accomplishments, personal histories, likes and dislikes, and plans for the future.

Yet when it comes to God, people often imagine that it is possible to have a

---

1. Dorothy Sayers, *Creed or Chaos* (New York: Harcourt & Brace, 1949), 3.

personal relationship with God apart from theology. In fact, some Christians assume that knowing doctrine and practical living are competing interests. The modern dichotomy between doctrine and life, theology and discipleship, knowing and doing, theory and practice has had disastrous consequences in the life of the church and its witness in the world. I hope to change some readers' minds about systematic theology and its relevance by first changing our working assumptions about its nature, goals, and methods.

A. DRAMA: THE GREATEST STORY EVER TOLD

A modern myth is that we outgrow stories. When someone asks us to explain who we are, we tell a story. Furthermore, we interpret our personal narratives as part of a larger plot. Who are we? Why are we here? Where are we going? What's the point? Is there a God and if so can we know him? Why is there evil in the world? The biggest questions, demanding the most rigorous intellectual analysis, are really doctrines that arise from a particular story that we either assume or embrace with explicit conviction. The Christian answers these big questions by rehearsing the story of the triune God in creation, the fall of the creatures he made in his own image, the promise of a redeemer through Israel, and the fulfillment of all types and shadows in the incarnation, life, death, resurrection, ascension, and return of Jesus Christ. The Apostles' and Nicene creeds are not just a list of key doctrines; they are a confession in the form of a story, our shared testimony to the most significant facts of reality.

Modern secularists often imagine that their most deeply held beliefs are not really beliefs at all, but more like a simple acknowledgment of facts. They suppose that they are not personally involved, and certainly they have no sense of these "facts" being interpreted through a wider set of assumptions (i.e., narrative). In fact, "telling a story" is often classified with myths and fairy tales. Although the cure can be worse than the disease if taken in excessive doses, postmodern criticism of the "myth of neutrality" or "the view from nowhere" offers a powerful antidote to the hubris of modern reason. It is not only the remote tribe or religious enthusiast whose assumptions, convictions, and practices are shaped by a particular story; the modern ideas of "progress," "enlightenment," and "liberation" are also part of a shared narrative that has been assumed by Westerners since the Renaissance, but especially since the seventeenth and eighteenth centuries.

Of course, "reality" is not merely a construction of the will; "truth" is not just a useful lie or clever fiction, as Friedrich Nietzsche thought. However, our apprehension of the truth of reality is always interpreted. For example, at the graveside of a loved one, three people may be grappling with the same reality (i.e., death). However, the first person interprets the event within the narrative of being "dead in Adam" versus having everlasting "life in Christ," while the second person treats it as a liberation of the soul for a (hopefully) higher reincarnation, and the third person might interpret it as no more than the cessation of bodily functions.

For over three centuries now, atheists and skeptics have catechized the West in the belief that as cultures progress, belief in God or at least in extraordinary divine intervention in nature and history will wane. What proponents forget is that this concept of "progress" itself presupposes a certain kind of faith: an interpretation of reality that requires personal commitment. Among other things, it presupposes that reality is entirely self-creating and self-regulating (autonomous), such that the very idea of a personal God who enters into a world that we have defined as "without God" already precludes the possibility of entertaining specific claims to the contrary. The most rigorous physicist can become the most rigid dogmatist, closing his or her mind arbitrarily to every argument or evidence that might challenge such presuppositions. Narrative paradigms are resilient. They can be overthrown, but everyone works hard at preserving them from impeachment. Once upon a time in the West, one could become an atheist or deist only with considerable difficulty; the widespread narrative within which everyone operated rendered unbelief implausible. Today, it is exactly the opposite. To believe in the triune God of Scripture who speaks and acts in history requires an act of apostasy from the assumed creed of our age.

I say all of this to make the point that it's not only religion that needs stories. The inextricable connection of faith and practice in terms of drama, doctrine, doxology, and discipleship has evident corollaries in every philosophy, religion, and culture. The drama determines the big questions as well as the answers. The doctrines are convictions that arise in light of that drama. People do not collect their beliefs one at a time, stacking one on top of another. Rather, there is a certain limitation in the beliefs a particular person is likely to hold given the plausibility of the paradigm (or drama) that he or she currently assumes to be true. And then, no less than the most ardent believer does the religious skeptic live out these convictions. No less than Christianity, Marxism and capitalism, democracy and totalitarianism, feminism and fascism are stories that involve personal commitment. It's not that there are only interpretations (stories) and no facts (truths), but that there are no uninterpreted facts.

Since God is the author of reality, it is his interpretation that we must pursue. No one can actually live in the world that is imagined by secularism. Not even the most hardened nihilist can live in the world of pure meaninglessness that his or her narrative presupposes. In their daily practice, the most ardent religious skeptics have to presuppose a basic order and intelligibility in reality that contradicts the creed of self-creation through random chance.

Today a story (narrative) that pretends it isn't one is called a *metanarrative* (*meta* meaning "beyond"). Many of the most unquestioned presuppositions of modernity were simply taken as the deliverances of absolute and universal reason. For example, where progress meant for Christians both God's outworking of his redemptive plan in history and our growth in the grace and knowledge of Christ (defined by the biblical story), for modern secularists it meant outgrowing childhood superstition (i.e., belief in the miraculous intervention of a transcendent God within history and nature). Everything in religion—particularly biblical faith—that belonged to a narrative or story was dismissed as myth, and any truth contained in these stories had to be demonstrated by the canons of universal reason and morality. In its most authoritarian version, religion was considered "unscientific." In the middle of the twentieth century, theologian Rudolf Bultmann formulated a method of "demythologizing" the Bible, so that modern people could still find the gospel relevant to their existence in the world without having to accept its miracle-laden stories.

This is not the first time that philosophy attempted to translate myth into pure and timeless principles of reason, morality, or experience. In fact, the great figures of ancient Western philosophy—especially Socrates, Plato, and Aristotle—attempted to refine the gold of truth from the dross of the Greek myths of the gods. The result is a metanarrative—a story masquerading as a purely rational description of "the way things really are."

In a seminal essay, Jean-François Lyotard summarized postmodernism as "incredulity toward any metanarrative." As he defines it, a metanarrative is a "demythologized" story. By pretending to have transcended particular narratives and discovered the archetypal truth in itself, we forget that many of our most cherished values, expectations, and convictions are creations of a particular time and place rather than universal truths.[2]

In reaction against postmodernism, some Christians have insisted that Christianity is, in fact, a metanarrative. However, this is based on a misunderstanding. For Lyotard, a metanarrative is a certain way in which modernity has legitimized its absolutist discourse and originated or grounded it in autonomous reason. "In philosophical discourse," notes Merold Westphal, "*meta* signifies a difference of level and not primarily of size." Biblical faith, however, does not legitimize itself or ground itself in this way. "Now, undeniably Christianity is a *mega* narrative, a big story. But the story that begins with 'Let there be light' and ends with the 'Hallelujah Chorus' under the baton of the angel Gabriel is not a *meta* narrative. The recital of the *Heilsgeschichte* [history of redemption] in creed and in sermons belongs to first-order Christian discourse."[3] It is a confession of faith, a personal act of witness

---

2. Jean-François Lyotard, *The Postmodern Condition: A Report on Knowledge* (trans. Geoff Bennington and Brian Massumi; Minneapolis: Univ. of Minnesota Press, 1984), xxiv, xx, 34, 37. For a superb interpretation of Lyotard's intention, see

Merold Westphal, *Overcoming Onto-theology: Toward a Postmodern Christian Faith* (New York: Fordham Univ. Press, 2001), xiii–xv.

3. Westphal, *Overcoming Onto-theology*, xiii–xiv.

to the God who has entered our history in and through a particular narrative that cannot be "translated" or demythologized in secular terms. All of our worldviews are stories. Christianity does not claim to have escaped this fact. The prophets and apostles were fully conscious of the fact that they were interpreting reality within the framework of a particular narrative of creation, fall, redemption, and consummation, as told to a particular people (Israel) for the benefit of the world. The biblical faith claims that its story is the one that God is telling, which relativizes and judges the other stories about God, us, and the world—especially the ones that have assumed the shape of Promethean metanarratives. The modern (Enlightenment) narrative has given rise to a host of dogmas that have, in turn, generated a form of life—practices that we take for granted. As the wars of the last hundred years attest, these narratives and systems have literally moved armies.

The writing of metanarratives is precisely what many Western philosophers (and theologians) were up to when they tried to transpose the Christian story into symbols of supposedly higher truths. For example, even though to them Christ was not the incarnate God who died for our sins and was raised bodily on the third day, modernity allowed that his death and resurrection may still be important symbols of the universal kingdom of ethical duty, love, or religious experience.

Whenever the history of redemption is exploited for its symbolic potential in the cause of reason, religion, morality, Communism or democracy, capitalism or socialism, scientific progress, or imperial and national hubris, it is no longer Christianity. For the Greek philosophers, the myths of the gods were "just a story"—the dispensable husk that hides the kernel of timeless truth. The Enlightenment (and Protestant liberalism) followed the same course with Christianity, assuming that philosophy and science dealt with judgments of *fact* (what actually happened), while religion was concerned with judgments of *value* (the meaningfulness we find in the myth).

The prophets and apostles did not believe that God's mighty acts in history (*mega*narratives) were dispensable myths that represented universal truths (*meta*narratives). For them, the big story did not point to something else beyond it but was itself the point. God really created all things, including humans in his image, and brought Israel through the Red Sea on dry ground. He really drowned a greater kingdom than Pharaoh and his army in Christ's death and resurrection. God's mighty acts in history are not myths that symbolize timeless truths; they create the unfolding plot within which our lives and destinies find the proper coordinates.

Metanarratives give rise to ideologies, which claim the world's allegiance even, if necessary, through violence. The heart of the Christian narrative, however, is the gospel—the good news concerning God's saving love and mercy in Jesus Christ. It is the story that interprets all other stories, and the lead character is Lord over all other lords. However, the Christian story differs from such metanarratives also in origin and in legitimization, having "its origin in revelation, not in philosophy, and most especially not in modern philosophy, grounded in the autonomy of the human subject, whether that be the individual as knower (Descartes' *ego cogito*), the individual as bearer of inalienable rights (Locke, Jefferson), or modern humanity collectively as the fulfillment of history (Hegel, Marx, popular American self-consciousness as the city set on a hill)."[4]

Consequently, Westphal adds, "Christianity has at least as good grounds as Lyotard to be skeptical and suspicious, skeptical of claims to be the voice of pure reason on the grounds that human finitude and fallenness undermine this ideal, which goes back to Plato's notion of the soul as divine, and suspicious when (perhaps with Lyotard's help) modernity's metanarratives are seen for what they are, the self-congratulatory self-legitimation of modernity."[5] Metanarratives attempt to justify "us" and judge the rest of the world, while in biblical faith God judges us as well and justifies the ungodly.[6]

We do not have to say that Christianity is a metanarrative to affirm that it is *true*. C. S. Lewis pointed out that Christianity is the *true* myth — the myth that actually became fact. "It *happens* — at a particular date, in a particular place, followed by definable historical consequences. We pass from a Balder or an Osiris, dying nobody knows when or where, to a historical Person crucified (it is all in order) *under Pontius Pilate*. By becoming fact it does not cease to be myth."[7] In other words, it is still a story, even though it is true. Not even the resurrection is a metanarrative; its meaning cannot just be read off of the surface of historical events but is defined by its intratextual context as part of an unfolding plot.

The prophets, apostles, and evangelists of the Bible did not imagine that *story* and *fact* were somehow antithetical (equivalent to fiction and nonfiction). Nor did it occur to them that in order to offer testimony to actual historical events they had to occupy an ostensibly neutral, value-free vantage point. However, they also claimed that this was God's story and that they were both eyewitnesses of his acts and his appointed messengers who had received God's own interpretation of those acts. Unlike the idols of the nations that are the spitting image of their maker, the God of Israel is the Creator and Redeemer, Alpha and Omega, Lord and Consummator of history.

---

4. Ibid., xv.

5. Ibid.

6. Westphal notes that according to the Christian story there is only one absolute kingdom, and it progresses not by violent conquest but by the proclamation of the gospel. In the process, it relativizes every human kingdom and in fact delegitimizes every form of absolutism, "including democratic capitalism and the Christian church, just to the degree that they are not the full embodiment of God's kingdom." Westphal (ibid.) concludes, "Modernity's metanarratives legitimize 'us'; the Christian narrative places 'us' under judgment as well. In knowing how the story ends we do not know which aspects of our work will be burned as wood, hay, and stubble. Christianity is not Lyotard's target."

7. C. S. Lewis, "Myth Became Fact," in *God in the Dock* (ed. Walter Hooper; Grand Rapids: Eerdmans, 1970), 66–67.

While modernity built its empires on the basis of a metanarrative of progress and self-sufficiency and confidence in a destiny of perfectible humanity, the tendency in our postmodern times is to lose any conscious sense that our own lives are part of a larger plot. We become aimless drifters who come from nowhere special and have no divinely given destiny but are free to write our own individual scripts from the meaningless combinations of endless choice. In our day, the script is sold to us with persuasive advertising that promises health, wealth, and happiness here and now. Our daily experience is flooded with images of the successful person and the life story that we could have if we purchase the appropriate props. Even "God," "Jesus," and spirituality have their place, as long as they are merely tools or resources for our self-making and self-transformation. However, there is nothing especially *post*modern about this outlook. What we witness in our contemporary Western cultures is not so much a renunciation of metanarratives but the dominance of a new one, namely, the metanarrative of coming from nowhere and going nowhere but making things up as we go, in between birth and death. This nihilism (lit., "nothingness-ism") aspires to the status of absolute ideology just as surely as the triumphalistic crusades that preceded it.

However, the Christian faith is a counterdrama to all of the meganarratives and metanarratives of this passing age—ancient, medieval, modern, and postmodern. It speaks of the triune God who existed eternally before creation and of ourselves as characters in his unfolding plot. Created in God's image yet fallen into sin, we have our identity shaped by the movement of this dramatic story from promise to fulfillment in Jesus Christ. This drama also has its powerful props, such as preaching, baptism, and the Supper—the means by which we are no longer spectators but are actually included in the cast. Having exchanged our rags for the riches of Christ's righteousness, we now find our identity "in Christ." Instead of God being a supporting actor in our life story, we become part of the cast that the Spirit is recruiting for God's drama.

The Christian faith is, first and foremost, an unfolding *drama*. Geerhardus Vos observed, "The Bible is not a dogmatic handbook but a historical book full of dramatic interest."[8] This story that runs from Genesis to Revelation, centering on Christ, not only richly informs our mind; it captivates the heart and the imagination, animating and motivating our action in the world. When history seems to come to a standstill in sin, guilt, and death, the prophets direct God's people to God's fulfillment of his promise in a new covenant.

---

8. Geerhardus Vos, *Biblical Theology: Old and New Testaments* (Grand Rapids: Eerdmans, 1948), 17.

B. DOCTRINE: THE GRAMMAR OF FAITH

The great doctrines of the Christian faith arise out of this dramatic plot. "And the Word became flesh and dwelt among us, and we have seen his glory, glory as of the only Son from the Father, full of grace and truth" (Jn 1:14). Where the world's religions focus on timelessly eternal truths, the most important teachings of Christianity concern historical events. There once was a time when the Son was not incarnate and had not yet won our redemption at Golgotha. Yet we live on this side of that divine achievement. At the same time, Christ has not yet returned to consummate his kingdom. Much has already happened, but there is still more to come. That means we are different from what we were, but we are not yet what we will be; our identity is still being defined by the unfolding mystery of the gospel. The gospel is *good news*, not good instructions, good ideas, or good techniques. It announces the "new thing" that God has accomplished in history for us and for our salvation:

> Oh sing to the LORD a new song;
>> sing to the LORD, all the earth!
> Sing to the LORD, bless his name;
>> tell of his salvation from day to day. (Ps 96:1–2)

Doctrine simply means "teaching." God not only promises and fulfills a particular future; he explains the implications. So, for example, the Gospels focus on the dramatic narrative as Jesus Christ is actually winning our redemption, while the Epistles unpack the significance of those events. Not only was Jesus Christ crucified and raised on the third day; he "was delivered up *for our trespasses* and raised *for our justification*" (Ro 4:25, emphasis added). As an effective communicator, God tells us what he is going to do, does it, and then tells us what he did. Doctrine summarizes these divine accomplishments. As Paul Ricoeur noted, doctrine keeps the narrative from slipping into the past; it indicates the meaning of these events for us now and into the future.[9]

Especially as the purpose of his mission becomes more evident as the disciples approach Jerusalem, Jesus directs their attention to his crucifixion and resurrection. And yet, even after Peter offers his marvelous confession of Jesus as the Christ (Mt 16:13–20), he rebukes Jesus for bringing up his impending death (vv. 21–23). Only after the resurrection, when Jesus explained how he was the central character (Lk 24), did the disciples understand the story that their own Scriptures had anticipated. In his Great Commission, Jesus commanded the disciples to take this message to

---

9. Paul Ricoeur, *Figuring the Sacred: Religion, Narrative, and Imagination* (trans. David Pellauer; ed. Mark I. Wallace; Minneapolis: Fortress, 1995), 173.

everyone, baptizing and teaching in his name (Mt 28:18–20), and at Pentecost they were empowered as witnesses to proclaim that which they had seen and heard.

As we hear this story, the Spirit draws us in and casts us as characters in the unfolding drama. Along with the disciples on their journey from Galilee to Jerusalem, we find ourselves understanding the point of Jesus' mission, not really understanding it, and then really recognizing his person and work. Because of Pentecost, we understand the meaning of Christ's life, death, resurrection, and second coming even more than the disciples before the Spirit's descent.

In their epistles, the apostles unpack and interpret this drama under the Spirit's inspiration (2Ti 3:10–17; 2Pe 1:16–21), relating the various aspects of the gospel and explaining its implications for the new society inaugurated by Christ's resurrection. Now they see clearly what was less evident to them before, interpreting not only their own eyewitness experience of Christ's person and work but the Old Testament narrative that led up to it. Under this apostolic testimony, we too can discover the meaning of these events. It is the doctrine that defines and refines our understanding of the unfolding drama. When Philip was sent to the treasurer of the Ethiopian court, he joined him in his chariot as he was reading Isaiah 53. "Do you understand what you are reading?" Philip asked. The treasurer replied, "How can I, unless someone guides me?" After being invited to sit with him, "Philip opened his mouth, and beginning with this Scripture he told him the good news about Jesus" (Ac 8:30–31, 35). This is why Christ gave teachers to his church—first of all, prophets and apostles, and now pastors and teachers.

Separated from its dramatic narrative, doctrine becomes abstract, like mathematical axioms. However, if we focus only on the Christian story (the tendency of some narrative theologies), we miss crucial implications of that plot and the inner connections between its various sequences.

As Dorothy Sayers observed in *The Lost Tools of Learning*, we begin our educational development by parroting our parents, older siblings, and teachers. Children at this *grammar* stage delight in simple rhymes and repetitive phrases that increasingly become the stock of basic knowledge on which they will draw for the rest of their lives. Then, as we move into our teenage years, we like to argue. Beginning to think through the logical connections between the various facts of our knowledge and experience, we enter the *dialectical* stage, typically a period of questioning, testing, and thinking through why we believe what we believe. In the past at least, it was thought that the purpose of high school was to form our habits of thought and expression when we enter our *rhetorical* stage of development.

We pass through these stages in our Christian growth and discipleship as well. Whether as new converts or as children raised in the church, we are introduced to words such as *God, redemption, Trinity, image of God, means of grace, justification,* and *eschatology*. Eventually, we are competent enough with this new language to ask good questions—even to challenge our teachers to give us reasons for this faith that we profess and to show us how the various doctrines are related to each other in a system of truth. By questioning and testing our interpretation of God's Word, we come to know what we believe and why we believe it, so that the grammar of faith becomes our own language of worship through which we interpret all of reality and live in the world.

Theology is the concern of every believer because it is the *grammar* of the Christian faith. Imagine the response if elementary schools decided to eliminate the teaching of the alphabet, multiplication tables, or the difference between a noun and a verb simply because the children often found it irrelevant, boring, and rote. We know from experience how difficult it is to learn a new language as adults in comparison with childhood: whether the new grammar is French, Hebrew, Mandarin, or the language of a new vocation. Those of us raised on typewriters are often amazed at the superior skills our children have acquired with computers by learning the grammar of this recent technology at the stage when it is most easily acquired. If we decided we would never learn anything that is difficult, involved, and often tedious, the range of our human knowledge, emotions, and experience would become narrow. We would miss out on some of the most interesting and fulfilling aspects of reality.

In systematic theology, we are drawing together all three of these stages at once: teaching the vocabulary and rules of speech (grammar) of Christianity, investigating its inner consistency and coherence as well as comparing and contrasting it with rival interpretations (logic), so that we can defend our faith in an informed, compelling, and gentle manner (rhetoric) (1Pe 3:15–16). In his ascension to the Father's right hand in power and glory, Jesus Christ poured out gifts on his church, including shepherds whose ministry of preaching and teaching brings completion, edification, unity, and maturity to Christ's body so that we will "no longer be children, tossed to and fro and blown about by every wind of doctrine, by people's trickery, by their craftiness in deceitful scheming. But speaking the truth in love, we must grow up in every way into him who is the head, into Christ ... " (Eph 4:14–15 NRSV).

C. DOXOLOGY: SAYING "AMEN!"

When the doctrine is understood in the context of its dramatic narrative, we find ourselves dumbfounded by God's grace in Jesus Christ, surrendering to *doxology* (praise). Far from masters, we are mastered; instead of seizing the truth, we are seized by it, captivated by God's gift, to which we can only say, "Amen!" and "Praise the Lord!" This pattern can be discerned in the apostolic epistles. For example, after leading hearers along the Alpine summits of God's electing, justifying, regenerating, sanctifying, and preserving grace—with the consummation still up ahead—Paul breaks out in wonder at the vista: "What then shall we say to these things? If God is for us, who can be against us?" (Ro 8:31). After another excursus on God's electing purposes, Paul exclaims,

> Oh, the depth of the riches and wisdom and knowledge of God! How unsearchable are his judgments and how inscrutable his ways!
>
> > "For who has known the mind of the Lord,
> >   or who has been his counselor?"
> > "Or who has given a gift to him
> >   that he might be repaid?"
>
> For from him and through him and to him are all things. To him be glory forever. Amen. (Ro 11:33–36)

Without knowing the dramatic plot and its doctrinal significance, our doxology becomes unfocused. Our praise lacks not only depth but even its rationale: For what exactly are we praising God? Are we responding to God's character and works, or merely expressing ourselves?

At the same time, doxology challenges our intellectual pride and curbs our thirst for speculation. Sound doctrine fuels worship, not sectarian strife. When the apostle Paul reaches the threshold of God's majesty in these doxologies I have cited, he no longer asks and answers questions but worships the God who eludes comprehension.

The better theologians in history have evidenced a similar submission to mystery. For example, at numerous points in his *Institutes*, John Calvin summarizes his interpretation of a scriptural teaching and then exhorts us to adore the mystery rather than attempt to grasp it. Centuries before, Anselm of Canterbury wrote even his deepest theological investigations in the form of prayer, such as this famous one: "I do not endeavor, O Lord, to penetrate thy sublimity, for in no wise do I compare my understanding with that; but I long to understand in some degree thy truth, which my heart believes and loves. For I do not seek to understand that I may believe, but I believe in order to understand."[10]

D. DISCIPLESHIP: THE WAY OF CHRIST IN THE WORLD

Our minds transformed by God's Word so that we are grateful captives of praise to God, we become reshaped in Christ's image as new characters in his drama. Theology is inextricably tied to baptism. Upon taking their oath of citizenship,

---

10. Anselm, "Proslogion," in *St. Anselm, Proslogium and Monologium* (trans. Sidney Norton Deane; Chicago: Open Court, 1935), 6.

immigrants begin to learn the language and customs of their new country. In baptism, *God's* oath comes first. Yet when God claims us as the beneficiaries of his covenant mercies in Christ, we are relocated from the fading empire of sin and death to the kingdom of grace. As the visible sign and seal of God's saving promise, baptism also provokes our response of repentance and faith — not just once but throughout our pilgrimage. This is called *mortification* and *vivification*: recognizing that our "old self" (the dead-end character "in Adam") has been crucified and buried with Christ and that our "new self" has been raised with Christ. Learning God's Word — including its doctrine — is a nonnegotiable responsibility of our new citizenship. The baptized are privileged and obligated to learn the language of Zion.

Unless we are relocated from the stories of this fading age to our identity in Christ and begin to understand the implications of this new script, our discipleship will be little more than moralism. Merely imitating Christ's example is different from being united to Christ through faith, bearing the fruit of his resurrection life. It is the creed that gives rise to praise and therefore to informed and heartfelt love, service, and witness to our neighbors in the world. Doctrine severed from practice is dead; practice severed from doctrine is just another form of self-salvation and self-improvement. A disciple of Christ is a student of theology. Although the biblical concept of discipleship surely means more than study, it does not mean less. The common practice of following a rabbi (meaning "teacher") in order to receive formal and informal daily instruction was the pattern of Jesus' ministry. Our English word *disciple*, in fact, comes from the Latin noun *discipulus*, meaning "student."

Only after we have understood and experienced this astonishing gospel do we find the proper motivation for our *discipleship* in the world. Thus, Paul writes,

> I appeal to you therefore, brothers, *by the mercies of God*, to present your bodies as a living sacrifice, holy and acceptable to God, which is your spiritual worship. Do not be conformed to this world, but be transformed by the renewal of your mind, that by testing you may discern what is the will of God, what is good and acceptable and perfect. (Ro 12:1 – 2, emphasis added)

For the previous eleven chapters, Paul had explored the treacherous valley of our condemnation in Adam and the breathtaking heights of salvation in Christ. All throughout, doctrinal arguments were punctuated with doxological exclamation. Only now — in view of God's mercies — the call to discipleship becomes our "reasonable service" (KJV) of worship, and not mere duty. We can now offer ourselves not as dead sacrifices of atonement but as *living sacrifices* of thanksgiving. We cannot claim interest in God or the Bible while regarding doctrine as insignificant. The New Testament view of a disciple was not first of all a way of life that Jesus called the disciples to imitate but a unique messianic ministry that he called them to understand through his teaching and deeds. They were called, first and foremost, to be *witnesses*—pointing away from themselves to the Word made flesh for our salvation.

E. PUTTING IT ALL TOGETHER: GOD'S NEW ROLE FOR US IN HIS PLAY

This movement back and forth between the narrative drama, doctrine, doxology, and discipleship is evident throughout the New Testament epistles. It is also apparent in the Psalms—the hymnal of the Bible, where often we discover the dramatic account of God's mighty acts despite human sin, provoking the psalmist to grateful praise and then to the response of faith and obedience. This does not mean we always move in a straight line from drama to discipleship. Sometimes something that happens in our experience opens us up to a truth we had never really understood, and sometimes our practice shapes and misshapes our doctrinal convictions. Often, a half-learned doctrine or half-remembered episode in the redemptive drama becomes more fully realized in prayer and praise, especially in moments of crisis or delightful wonder. The traffic moves in all directions, back and forth, in between these coordinates, so that our faith is anchored in the work of the triune God and is reaching out to our neighbors in love.

Typically, periods of reformation in both individuals and the church corporately arise from rediscovering this sweeping pattern from biblical drama to doctrine to doxology to discipleship. Periods of decline usually work their way in reverse. First, *we begin to question the reliability of the narrative.* How can we find our own stories in the unfolding drama of God's miraculous intervention in history for sinners when our world seems to be governed by nothing more than natural or humanly devised processes and causes? The doctrines may be true, but their historical narrative becomes questionable. Second, *the doctrines come under criticism as people recognize that the doctrines depend on the narrative.* No one believes that Jesus rose from the dead because of any universal law of nature, reason, or morality. It is not a deliverance of universal religious experience. Therefore, if Christ was not actually raised bodily on the third day, then there is no basis for speculating about a "doctrine of resurrection." Third, *worship loses its rationale.* We may still express our inner experience or piety (at least for a while), but eventually this leads to burnout because it is self-referential. Our hearts are stirred by truth, not by vacuous exercises. Finally, *we become disciples more of the culture than of Christ.* Instead of being transformed by the renewing of our minds, we become conformed to the pattern of our non-Christian neighbors (Ro 12:1–2). In a last gasp for religious authenticity, the church tries to defend Judeo-Christian morality (discipleship), but it is a desperate attempt. The battle has already been lost at the earlier stages. Without the creeds, the deeds surrender to vague moralism.

As individual believers and as churches, we are always prone to fall away unless we are brought back by the Spirit to the Word. Therefore, we always need a theology grounded in that Word in dependence on the Spirit. The study of Christian doctrine is always an indispensable enterprise for the faith and practice of the whole church — not only for academics or even pastors, but for the whole communion of saints. Everyone who confesses the creed should always be growing in his or her understanding of its depth and implications.

The alternative to this growth in the knowledge and grace of Christ is not pious experience or good works but gradual assimilation to the powers of this passing evil age. The biblical drama plots our character "in Adam" by our natural birth in this present evil age. Nevertheless, "According to his great mercy, he has caused us to be born again to a living hope through the resurrection of Jesus Christ from the dead, to an inheritance that is imperishable, undefiled, and unfading, kept in heaven for you, who by God's power are being guarded through faith for a salvation ready to be revealed in the last time" (1Pe 1:3–5). Once strangers to God's promises, we are now rewritten into God's script. We should never lose our astonishment at the good news that in Christ even Gentiles can hear the divine playwright declare,

> You are a chosen race, a royal priesthood, a holy nation, a people for his own possession, that you may proclaim the excellencies of him who called you out of darkness into his marvelous light. Once you were not a people, but now you are God's people; once you had not received mercy, but now you have received mercy. (1Pe 2:9–10)

The key markers in this plot are not premodernity, modernity, and postmodernity but before and after Christ's resurrection from the dead. Because Christ has been raised as the firstfruits of the new creation, we are living in "these last days" (2Ti 3:1; Heb 1:2; Jas 5:3; cf. 1Pe 1:5) before "the last day" when Jesus returns in glory and judgment (Jn 6:40; 12:48). The Spirit creates the church at the intersection of "this age" and "the age to come" (Mt 12:32; 24:3; 1Co 2:6; Gal 1:4). It is therefore this unfolding drama that orients us as new characters who know where we have been, where we are, and where we are going.

Nobody has to be taught the world's story; we are born with it, as fallen children of Adam. However, we have to be taught *out of it* by persistent pastors and teachers who know that we prefer by nature to think differently of God and ourselves than the Scriptures require. "But understand this," Paul warned Timothy, "that in the last days there will come times of difficulty. For people will be lovers of self, lovers of money, proud, arrogant, abusive, disobedient to their parents, ungrateful, unholy, heartless, unappeasable, slanderous, without self-control, brutal, not loving good, treacherous, reckless, swollen with conceit, lovers of pleasure rather than lovers of God, having the appearance of godliness, but denying its power" (2Ti 3:1–5). It is the constant renewing of the mind by God's Word that reorients us away from this fading age with its aimless plot, its "empty words" (Eph 5:6) and "philosophy and empty deceit" (Col 2:8), toward the everlasting inheritance in Christ.

This happens first of all in the regular gathering of God's people—the casting call that transfers us from death to life through preaching and sacrament. We cannot take this new identity for granted, however. We must be renewed in this inheritance constantly, since our default setting is always the script that governs the idolatries of this present age. Furthermore, just as we were created by God as inherently covenantal creatures—in relationship with God and each other, and redemption restores this extroverted identity—theology is done best in community and conversation rather than in lonely isolation. Theology is always done for and by the church. Therefore, I have included discussion questions at the end of each chapter in the hope that they will encourage fruitful and lively interaction on the matters that concern us all.

II. WHY *SYSTEMATIC* THEOLOGY?

Every discipline or field of inquiry tries to draw together particulars into an integrated whole while allowing the whole to be determined by its parts. Systematic theology is like the box top of a jigsaw puzzle, and every believer is a theologian in the sense of putting the pieces together. If we fail to recognize there is a box top (i.e., a unified whole) to Scripture, we will have only a pile of pieces. Simplistic slogans, formulas, and catchphrases will not suffice in conveying the richness of the Scriptures.

Furthermore, to dismiss the importance of a systematic understanding of the faith is to deny, at least by implication, that the Bible is a *canon*—that is, a collection of varied texts that are united by their divine source (the Father's speaking), their content (the Son's work of redemption), and their power to generate the world of which they speak (the Spirit's work of inspiration, illumination, and regeneration). To assume that we cannot derive from Scripture a systematic teaching about God, creation, humanity, Christ's person and work, the application of redemption, the church, and our future hope is at least implicitly to assume that the Bible itself is self-contradictory or at least insufficient for providing a unified faith and practice.

Yet if we ignore the pattern that has been provided for us from Scripture itself, we will try to force the pieces to fit our preconceptions. We all have presuppositions when we come to a given biblical passage, doctrine, or practice. So we have a working systematic theology, whether we want to or not. By acknowledging that we do already have certain assumptions about the whole teaching of Scripture, we are better able to evaluate and critique them. Our goal at least must be to go back and forth between the whole and the parts. Just as the whole provides a context for understanding the parts, the parts can challenge our understanding of the whole. In other words, the system can change—which is exactly what happens in theological as well as social, political, and scientific revolutions.[11]

Drawing together the drama, the doctrine, the doxology, and the discipleship that recasts us as new characters in God's play, systematic theology works closely with its sister disciplines. Systematic theology relies on careful exegesis of Scripture, harvesting the fruit of the labors of *Old Testament* and *New Testament studies*. It also depends on *historical theology* and *church history* for its understanding of the way the church has interpreted God's Word, both faithfully and unfaithfully, in an effort to follow its wisdom and avoid its follies.[12] No more than other disciplines can theology advance by starting from scratch with each new era or profound thinker. We are always standing on the shoulders of those who have gone before us, taking for granted many conclusions that we have learned from a larger consensus. We are heirs of truth and error, clarity and confusion, faithfulness and folly. Only by engaging the past can we acquire the resources for interpreting Scripture in our own time and place.

Systematic theology also looks *to practical theology* (sometimes called pastoral theology), ethics, and apologetics in order to keep its reflection closely tied to the concrete welfare of Christ's body and mission in the world.

However, perhaps the closest subdiscipline to systematic theology is *biblical theology*. Like a topographical map, biblical theology draws all of the strands together to help us see the organic development of revelation and redemption from election to glorification. We see the high peaks, low valleys, rivers, and plains that lead from promise to fulfillment. Biblical theology rivets our attention to the historical development of various themes, pointing up discontinuities as well as continuities—the "many times" and "many ways" in which "God spoke to our fathers by the prophets, but in these last days ... by his Son" (Heb 1:1–2). There we discern not only the fresh stages of redemption in history but the eschatological, vertical disruption of history by God's descent. With each new era of redemptive history, we discern the "new thing" that God has done toward the furtherance of his purposes in Jesus Christ. We recognize Yahweh as our God, yet more fully known in Christ and by the Spirit as the triune God. As the plot unfolds, we can trace the growth of the

---

11. See, for example, Thomas Kuhn, *The Structure of Scientific Revolutions* (Chicago: Univ. of Chicago Press, 1996).

12. In many Protestant systems (and faculties of divinity),

there is also a subdiscipline known as symbolics or confessional theology, which focuses specifically on the creeds, confessions, and catechisms of a particular tradition or denomination.

church from the first human family to the nation of Israel and now to the uttermost parts of the earth.[13]

Yet it is systematic theology that puts all of these themes together in order to show their logical connections. Princeton's early twentieth-century biblical theologian Geerhardus Vos nicely explained this harmony between systematic theology and biblical theology, which is really what we mean when we speak of doctrine and narrative: "In Biblical Theology the principle is one of historical, in Systematic Theology it is one of logical construction. Biblical Theology draws a *line* of development. Systematic Theology draws a *circle*."[14] For example, the doctrine of the Trinity did not fall from heaven all at once but was revealed progressively as God's plan unfolded in history. Biblical theology follows that organic development, while systematic theology pulls together these insights in a formal dogma and relates the Trinity to other doctrines in Scripture. If biblical theology is a topographical map, systematic theology is more like a street map, pointing out the logical connection between various doctrines spread throughout Scripture. Without biblical theology, systematic theology easily surrenders the dynamism of revelation to timeless truths; without systematic theology, biblical theology surrenders the Bible's internal coherence — the relation of the parts to the whole.

By "system" or "systematic," we should not imagine a comprehensive chart that maps God's inner being, leaving no question unanswered. On the contrary, as in the natural sciences, the more that we understand God's truth, the more we are struck by the mystery. Instead of the image of a speculative system, we should think in more organic terms, like an ecosystem in which diversity and interdependent unity are equally important. To assume that the Bible itself gives us a system of doctrine and practice is simply to acknowledge its organic unity as a single canon: the interdependence and coherence of its various teachings.

There is also a difference between systematic theology and *dogmatics*, the latter engaging in a deeper analysis of Christian doctrines than a systematic summary can provide. I have followed this distinction in my own work. While this present volume seeks to offer a summary of Christian doctrine in its systematic relations, I have written a four-volume series in dogmatics in which I explore particular topics in greater detail, with more exegesis as well as engagement with alternative views.[15] My goal was to focus on specific topics in contemporary theology. I had a specific agenda, namely, to reflect on the potential of *covenant* not as a central dogma but

---

13. Like systematic theology, biblical theology takes different forms. The biblical theology movement associated with Oscar Cullmann, Gerhard von Rad, and G. E. Wright, for example, is more influenced by higher-critical assumptions than the biblical theology of Geerhardus Vos, Herman Ridderbos, and others.

14. Vos, *Biblical Theology*, 16.

15. The series is published by Westminster John Knox and includes *Covenant and Eschatology: The Divine Drama* (2004); *Lord and Servant: A Covenant Christology* (2005); *Covenant and Salvation: Union with Christ* (2007); *People and Place: A Covenant Ecclesiology* (2008).

as a framework that belongs to the integral structure of the Bible itself. However, a systematic theology is quite different. <u>It is more disciplined in the sense that all of the major topics of theology must be covered and displayed in their relations.</u> It is my goal in this present summary of Christian teaching to bring to bear all of these subdisciplines (biblical, historical, pastoral, and dogmatic theology).

III. BACK TO THE SOURCES!

We often speak of various theological schools—Franciscans and Dominicans, Calvinists and Arminians, Barthians and Baptists. There is nothing wrong with specifying particular circles of interpretation. In fact, honesty requires that we acknowledge our own confessional commitments instead of pretending that we are coming to the scriptures without prejudices. Nevertheless, theologians do not (at least, should not) write for schools but for the church and should therefore aim at "the faith that was once for all delivered to the saints" (Jude 3), which binds the whole family of Christ together in a common hope.

I am writing from the perspective of a Reformed Christian living in North America. I do not presume to speak *for* all Christians from a supposedly unbiased "view from nowhere," but I do hope to speak *to* all Christians from a Reformed perspective concerning the faith we hold in common. To put it differently, I do not believe there is any such thing as a "Reformed faith," any more than there is a "Lutheran faith" or "Baptist faith." There is *one faith*—the Christian faith—and this volume is an attempt to explore that faith as it is summarized in the confessions of Reformed Christianity.

Although there were important gains in the medieval period, Renaissance humanism recovered an interest in history and the original languages. *Ad fontes!* ("Back to the sources!") was the cry. Out of this movement the Reformation was born, returning to the original Hebrew and Greek texts of Scripture instead of relying on the Latin Vulgate and the commentaries. Since the church is created and sustained by the Word, it is not surprising that whenever the church returns to its original wells, fresh periods of reformation and renewal occur.

Like any science, theology is not free to determine its own content and shape but is constrained by reality. No less than genetics or astronomy, theology involves subjectivity (i.e., the act of interpreting from one's own background and presuppositions) while aiming at objective reality. The data (in this case, Scripture) can always overturn a theory or even an entire paradigm. In all disciplines, including theology, periods of discovery (or rediscovery) are usually followed by periods of refinement and systematization. The Copernican revolution in science generated a new paradigm, but its details were worked out over successive generations. As the theory had to stand up to impressive challenges, it ended up being vindicated, even though it had to be refined and adjusted in light of the available data and objections along the way.

Similarly, the Reformation produced the era of Protestant orthodoxy (also known as Protestant scholasticism). It was this age that refined the Reformation's insights and produced our evangelical confessions and catechisms, liturgies, church orders, and hymns. Older churches were reformed and newer churches were started. In fact, out of this confessional era, Protestant missions found its beginning. It was also an era of remarkable achievements in biblical scholarship and pastoral theology. Protestant orthodoxy was an ecumenical project, seeking refinement not only in criticism of other traditions but by drawing on the best of the East and the West as well as ancient, medieval, and contemporary theologies. In other words, it was an era not only of reformation but also of consolidation: going back to the original Scriptures and integrating the best of the past with the insights of the Reformation. Even when taking a polemical (i.e., critical) stance, these theologians were much more familiar with other Christian traditions than we tend to be today. Even when they were arguing, they were at least talking with those within and outside of their own confessional tradition, and wherever possible they stressed the continuity of the Christian faith instead of attempting radical revolutions and innovations.

Although he often stood in a critical relation to Reformed orthodoxy, Karl Barth expressed his debt to these theologians for introducing him to the richness and depth of the church's dogmatic reflection — in sharp contrast with Friedrich Schleiermacher and liberal theology. As Barth began to prepare his Göttingen lectures, he expressed wonder at how his training could have skipped over the rich heritage of Protestant orthodoxy. Neo-Protestantism (i.e., liberalism) sought to "push through" this period in ever-new proposals that were really little more than "a new mixture of Enlightenment and Pietism." However, Barth realized, "Success can come only if we have previously learned to read the Reformers as the Church's teachers and, with them, Scripture as the document for the Church's existence and nature, and therefrom to ask what Church science might be. That precisely may be learned, nay must be, from the early orthodox theologians."[16]

At a time when even certain streams of evangelical theology seem unaware of this important resource, Barth's caution to his own students is as valid today as it was in the early twentieth century: "Even though you may later decide to go along with the great Schleiermachian revolution which characterizes almost all modern dogmatics, my urgent recommendation is that you should know what you are doing when you take this course, having first learned and considered the unreconstructed

---

16. Karl Barth, "Foreword" to Heinrich Heppe's *Reformed Dogmatics: Set Out and Illustrated from the Sources* (trans. G. T. Thomson; London: Allen & Unwin, 1950), vi–vii.

dogmatics of the older writers."[17] By his own recollection, exposure to the Reformed scholastics gave Barth resources for reconceiving theology in a more God-centered and biblically grounded fashion.[18] Even the liberal existentialist theologian Paul Tillich felt compelled to defend Protestant scholasticism from the caricatures he encountered among American theologians.[19] Of course, these older systems were often polemical—defending one tradition over against others. However, in doing so, they were typically more conscious of the whole history of diverse biblical interpretations than we are today. Walking into the expansive hallways of these older systems, one discovers the insights of the ancient Christian East, the great Latin theologians of the ancient and medieval West, and the different rooms inhabited by various churches and traditions. One also discovers new treasures, mined by careful exegesis and more recent scholarship from a variety of disciplines.

There are no golden ages, and even if we might desire it, we cannot simply repeat the work of those who have gone before us. In fact, if we follow their example, we will be open to new insights from God's Word, always reforming our systems to conform to that rule. "Back to the sources!" in our day means a return not simply to these older systems but to the fountain of Scripture and the rich, deep, and broad streams of ecumenical reflection from which they so liberally drank.

This volume attempts to draw a circle (the street map) by closely attending to the broad and sweeping landscape of biblical theology (the topographical map). The goal is doctrine that can be not only understood, clarified, and articulated but also preached, experienced, and lived as "community theater" in the world today. So let us attend together to the greatest drama ever staged—to a script whose performance draws us in, not as the original characters themselves (as the masters of modernity would have it)—yet also no longer merely as spectators (like unscripted players)—but as a growing cast of pilgrims making their way together behind their royal Redeemer in a procession to the City of God.

---

17. Karl Barth, *Göttingen Dogmatics: Instruction in the Christian Religion* (trans. Geoffrey W. Bromiley; Grand Rapids: Eerdmans, 1991), 1:21.

18. See Barth's "Letter to Brunner, January 26, 1924," cited in Bruce L. McCormack, *Karl Barth's Critically Realistic Dialectical Theology: Its Genesis and Development, 1909–1936* (New York: Oxford Univ. Press, 1995), 332.

19. Paul Tillich, *A History of Christian Thought* (New York: Simon and Schuster, 1968), 276–77. "Orthodoxy," he explained, "is greater and more serious than what is called fundamentalism in America." Whereas fundamentalism is a reactionary movement with little depth or awareness of the resources of catholic Christianity, "classical Orthodoxy had a great theology. We could also call it Protestant scholasticism." He continued, "When I speak of Orthodoxy, I refer to the way in which the Reformation established itself as an ecclesiastical form of life and thought after the dynamic movement of the Reformation came to an end. It is the systematization and consolidation of the ideas of the Reformation.... Hence, we should deal with this period in a much more serious way than is usually done in America. In Germany, and generally in European theological faculties—France, Switzerland, Sweden, etc.—every student of theology was supposed to learn by heart the doctrines of at least one classical theologian of the post-Reformation period of Orthodoxy.... We should know these doctrines, because they form the classical system of Protestant thought. It is an unheard-of state of things when Protestant churches of today do not even know the classical expression of their own foundations in the dogmatics of Orthodoxy.... All theology of today is dependent in some way on the classical systems of Orthodoxy."

Part One

KNOWING GOD

The Presuppositions of Theology

Chapter One

DISSONANT DRAMAS: PARADIGMS FOR KNOWING GOD AND THE WORLD

Any genuine field of knowledge (the older meaning of *scientia* or "science") must have an object—in other words, a subject matter. Furthermore, that object must be knowable. Astronomy is a legitimate science because planets, stars, and other bodies in space actually exist and can be studied. *Theology* is "the study of God." For reasons explored later in the chapter, the object shifted in the modern era (with notable exceptions) from God and his works to humanity and its morality, spirituality, and experience. *Science* came to refer narrowly to the empirical sciences, and religion could only be a legitimate discipline only to the extent that it was studied as a natural phenomenon of culture. As a consequence, theology has become largely a subdiscipline of psychology, sociology, cultural anthropology, or history of religions, even in universities with a Christian past. As we will see, theologians themselves pioneered this turn to the self in the hope of making Christianity more relevant and acceptable in our world.

The opening claim of this systematic theology is that the triune God is the object of theology and that this God is knowable because he has revealed himself to us. To explore this claim, we will begin with the widest horizon. Although this is the most philosophical chapter in this volume, our discussion will draw on the content of the Christian faith itself in order to develop the basic presuppositions of our worldview. From this widest horizon, we will narrow our focus to the character of theology, revelation, and Scripture.

I. DISSONANT DRAMAS: THE NATURE OF REALITY

The widest horizon for theology—indeed for all of our knowledge—is the question of *ontology*: what is reality? Nothing is more central to our governing narratives than the God-world relation. In an important essay, existentialist philosopher and theologian Paul Tillich (1886–1965) suggested that all of the varied schools and theories in philosophy of religion can be grouped under two contrasting paradigms: *overcoming estrangement* and *meeting a stranger*.[1] Adding a third, which I will call *the stranger we never meet*, I will define these paradigms and then defend a version of meeting a stranger that fits with the biblical drama.

A. PANTHEISM AND PANENTHEISM: OVERCOMING ESTRANGEMENT

The first grand narrative erases (or tends to erase) the infinite-qualitative distinction between God and creatures. Narrated in myriad myths across many cultures, this is the story of the ascent of the soul—that divine part of us, which has somehow become trapped in matter and history. Although it originates in dualism—a stark (even violent) opposition between finite and infinite, matter and spirit, time and eternity, humanity and God, the goal is to reestablish the unity of all reality. In some versions, only that which is infinite, spiritual, eternal, and divine is real, so all else perishes or is somehow elevated into the upper world. Nevertheless, the goal is to lose all particularity and diversity in the One, which is Being itself.

If one begins with a story of the cosmos in which the divine is somehow buried within us, a sacred spark or soul trapped in a body, space, and time, then the ultimate source of reality is not outside of us but inside. God does not *enter into* the times and spaces that he has created; rather, all of reality *emanates* from this divine principle of unity like rays from the sun.

In Platonism, for example, spiritual/intellectual entities possess more "being," while aspects of reality that belong more to history and matter fall down the ladder in diminishing grades of being. To the "upper world" belong the eternal forms: unchanging, one, and real; the "lower world" consists of the realm of mere appearances: ever-changing, diverse, and shadowy in their existence. In the case of human beings, the mind or spirit is the immortal spark of divinity, while the emotions are slaves of the body and its bondage to the realm of mere appearances. We just need

---

1. Paul Tillich, *Theology of Culture* (New York: Oxford Univ. Press, 1959), 10. Tillich most frequently states this contrast in terms of the "ontological" versus the "cosmological" paradigms, but since every worldview includes an ontology and cosmology, I prefer his synonyms—"overcoming estrangement" versus "meeting a stranger."

to go deeper within to find the truth, overcoming our sense of estrangement from "being" by returning to the source of a single Light.[2]

In this perspective, if God is considered in personal terms at all, not just as a unifying principle (namely, The One, Ground of Being, Absolute Spirit, the Unity of All, etc.), he is certainly not viewed as someone other, standing over against the self, especially in judgment. In other words, divinity is domesticated, brought inside of the self, so that it can no longer threaten, judge, rule, or condemn. This type of deity does not offend, disrupt, command, or save; rather than a stranger, God, the gods, or the divine principle is the most immanent and personal aspect of one's own existence.

Although the confusion of the Creator with creation characterizes paganism generally, it formed the horizon for Greek philosophy. In the second century, a movement arose within esoteric Jewish and Christian groups that tried to reinterpret the biblical narrative in a basically Greek philosophical framework. Known as *Gnosticism*, this heresy was decisively challenged by Irenaeus (AD 115–202), bishop of Lyons.[3] In contrast to the biblical story of a good creation, the fall into sin through transgressing the covenant, and redemption through Christ's incarnate life, death, and resurrection, the Gnostics sought redemption from an evil creation through inner enlightenment (*gnosis*). Plundering the Bible for its material, Gnostic sects offered a radical reinterpretation. The God of creation (Yahweh), represented in the Old Testament, becomes the evil deity who imprisons divine souls in bodies, while the serpent in the garden sought to liberate Adam and Eve through inner enlightenment. The God of redemption (Christ), revealed in the Gnostic "gospels," is an avatar of sorts, leading initiates away from their bodily incarceration in history, toward their divine destiny.

While distancing himself from the Gnostics, Origen of Alexandria (AD 185–254) nevertheless tried to assimilate Christian doctrine to a fundamentally Platonist scheme. In this he was following Philo of Alexandria, who had developed a system of Jewish Platonism with great success a century earlier. Origen rejected the biblical doctrine of *ex nihilo* creation and downplayed the reality of Christ's physical

---

2. It is not an overstatement to suggest that pantheism/panentheism has, since antiquity, represented the most dominant rival to biblical faith in both the East and the West, and continues to do so today. According to the Hindu Vedas and Upanishads, the Atman (soul/self) of individuals is one with divinity (Brahman). For all of their differences, it was the ontological horizon of Thales, Parmenides, Heraclitus, and Stoicism. This paradigm was taken over by Plato and continued in Middle Platonism (through the first-century Jewish philosopher Philo of Alexandria) and (with some revision) in Neoplatonism. The key difference is that "the One" of Plato, from which all reality emanates, is for Plotinus and other Neoplatonists not only pure

being but "beyond being" and therefore also beyond rational knowledge.

3. The study of Gnosticism has become a cottage industry today, especially with many scholars advocating a recovery of Gnostic emphases. The vast secondary literature has highlighted the diverse schools of this movement, although Irenaeus (*Against Heresies*) has stood the test of time as an account (and Christian refutation) of the various types. See Hans Jonas, *The Gnostic Religion* (3rd ed.; Boston: Beacon, 2001); Kurt Rudolph, *Gnosis: The Nature and Structure of Gnosticism* (New York: Harper & Row, 1987); Birger A. Pearson, *Ancient Gnosticism: Traditions and Literature* (Minneapolis: Fortress, 2007).

embodiment in his incarnation, ascension, and return in the flesh. He also taught reincarnation and the final restoration of all spiritual entities, including Satan and the fallen angels. For these speculations, Origen was later judged heretical by the Christian East, but his Platonized version of Christianity remained powerful and long-lasting especially in monastic movements.

Within the history of Western Christianity there have been tendencies among some mystics to move in a pantheistic direction. An extreme example is the fourteenth-century mystic Meister Eckhart, who wrote in a characteristic sermon, "To the inward-turned man all things have an inward divinity.... Nothing is so proper to the intellect, nor so present and near as God."[4] The connection between rationalism and mysticism is as old as Platonism itself. This outer-inner dualism has characterized much of radical mysticism in the Middle Ages and the Renaissance, as well as in Sufi Islam and Jewish Kabbalism. This trajectory continued in radical Protestantism from the Anabaptists to the early Enlightenment. It is especially evident in the philosophy of Benedict Spinoza (1632-77), which was revived in German Romanticism and American Transcendentalism. Its influence is evident in the dominant forms of theological liberalism and especially today in New Age and neopagan spiritualities.[5]

Even in its dualism (for example, between spirit and matter), the pantheistic worldview is ultimately monistic. In other words, all of reality is ultimately one. There is no distinction, finally, between God and the world. While bodies may be lower than souls on the ladder of being, all of reality emanates from a single source to which it returns. In spite of the hierarchy of being, all distinctions—even between God and creation—become gradually lost. For example, theologian Rosemary Radford Reuther seeks to go back behind Christianity to ancient Near Eastern pagan myths and Gnosticism for a holistic (i.e., monistic) worldview.[6] "The visible universe is the emanational manifestation of God, God's sacramental body."[7]

---

4. Meister Eckhart, *Sermons and Treatises* (trans. Maurice O'Connell Walshe; Longmead, England: Element, 1987), 3:46. "And since likeness flows from the One," neither the seeking intellect nor the One itself (God) is satisfied "till they are united in the One" (78). The contemplative soul strives upward, "transformed in God and estranged from all multiplicity ... or shadow of difference," and together with "one God-Father-Son-and-Holy-Ghost loses and is stripped of all distinctions and properties, and is One alone" (85). J. Deotis Roberts (*A Philosophical Introduction to Theology* [London: SCM, 1991], 118) comments, "God appears to imply what Plotinus meant by 'Mind,'" while Godhead corresponds to the 'One' in Plotinus' Godhead; it is Being itself and not an individual being." Roberts further notes the similarities of this view to the Hindu idea of *Brahman*, although he tries to make these views consistent with Christianity. Everything "outer," even about Jesus Christ (his bodily

incarnation, life, suffering, pain, passions, etc.), is dispensable; the truth is "inner" unity with the divine. Like Mary, Jesus "inwardly was in a state of unmoved detachment" (Eckhart, *Sermons and Treatises*, 124).

5. Eckhart was also a personal favorite of Hegel. Ernst Benz (*The Mystical Sources of German Romantic Philosophy* [Allison Park, Pa.: Pickwick, 1983], 2) observes that the continuity between German medieval mysticism and German idealistic philosophy has been thoroughly recognized at least since Wilhelm Dilthey. For this connection especially between Hegel and Eckhart (as well as ancient Gnosticism), see also Cyril O'Regan, *The Heterodox Hegel* (Albany, N.Y.: SUNY Press, 1994).

6. Rosemary Radford Reuther, *Liberation Theology* (New York: Paulist, 1972), 118; *Sexism and God-Talk* (Boston: Beacon, 1993), 52, 60, 87.

7. Reuther, *Sexism and God-Talk*, 87.

Some have tried to blend pantheism ("all is divine") with belief in a personal God (theism).[8] Often identified as *panentheism* ("all-within-God"), this view holds that "God" or the divine principle transcends the world, although God and the world exist in mutual dependence.[9] In varying degrees of explicit dependence, panentheism is the working ontology of process theology and the theologies of Teilhard de Chardin, Wolfhart Pannenberg, and Jürgen Moltmann among many others, especially those working at the intersection of theology and the philosophy of science.[10] Some panentheists envision the world as the body of God.[11]

B. Atheism and Deism: The Stranger We Never Meet

At the other end of the spectrum from pantheism and panentheism are atheism and deism. Although Buddhism denies the existence of a personal God, Western atheism rejects any transcendent reality beyond the world of sense experience. Deism affirms the existence of a Creator God, but generally denies that this Architect of the Universe intervenes miraculously in nature or history.[12] Especially as formulated in the nineteenth and twentieth centuries by Ludwig Feuerbach, Karl Marx, Friedrich Nietzsche, and Sigmund Freud, modern atheism sees religion as arising from a psychological need to project something or someone to whom one can pray in the face of the threats and tragedies in a random and chaotic universe.[13]

Nietzsche advocated an "inverted Platonism," where the upper world is illusion and the lower world is real.[14] In fact, the dualism of two worlds is rejected as an illusion perpetuated by Christianity. Drawing on classical Greek myth, Nietzsche identifies Apollo (the god of order) with Plato's upper world and Dionysus (the god of pagan revelry and chaotic self-indulgence) with the lower world. Where the death of ultimate meaning led Schopenhauer to a state of depression — a passive resignation to fate — his disciple Nietzsche embraced it as a call to create meaning for ourselves. "That my life has no aim is evident from the accidental nature of its origin. That I can posit an aim for myself is another matter."[15] As Mark C. Taylor expresses it, "The lawless land of erring, which is forever beyond good and evil, is

---

8. The term *pantheist* seems to have originated with John Toland's *Socinianism, truly stated, by a pantheist* (1705). *Panentheism* was coined by Karl Christian Friedrich Karuse in 1828.

9. Charles Hartshorne, *Man's Vision of God and the Logic of Theism* (Hamden, U.K.: Archon, 1964).

10. See, for example, Philip Clayton and Arthur Peacocke, eds., *In Whom We Live and Move and Have Our Being: Panentheistic Reflections on God's Presence in a Scientific World* (Grand Rapids: Eerdmans, 2004).

11. Sallie McFague, *The Body of God: An Ecological Theology* (Minneapolis: Augsburg Fortress, 1993).

12. The term *deism* was apparently coined in 1564 by John Calvin's colleague Pierre Viret and is typically regarded as the religion of the Age of Enlightenment.

13. See Ludwig Feuerbach, *The Essence of Christianity* (trans. George Eliot; New York: Harper and Bros., 1957); Sigmund Freud, *The Future of an Illusion* (New York: Norton, 1989). More recently, the New Atheists have rehabilitated this theory. See, for example, Daniel C. Dennett, *Breaking the Spell: Religion as a Natural Phenomenon* (New York: Penguin, 2007).

14. Friedrich Nietzsche, *Twilight of the Idols* (trans. Duncan Large; Oxford: Oxford Univ. Press, 1998), 20.

15. Quoted in Mark C. Taylor, *Erring: A Postmodern A/Theology* (Chicago: Univ. of Chicago Press, 1984), 66.

the liminal world of Dionysus, the Anti-Christ, who calls every wandering mark to carnival, comedy, and carnality."[16]

Amid important differences, there are some surprising similarities between pantheism and atheism. In fact, they are two sides of the same coin. Both embrace the view that being is *univocal*: in other words, that there is only one kind of reality or existence. In this perspective, there is reality (that which exists) and then there are particular beings who exist, such as divine and non-divine entities. In the "overcoming estrangement" paradigm of pantheism, the physical world is a weak projection of an eternal (real) world. In the atheistic paradigm ("the stranger we never meet"), the projection is reversed; in fact, the longing for transcendent meaning and truth reflects a form of psychological neurosis, nostalgia for a nonexistent "beyond" that paralyzes our responsibility in the present. In other words, pantheism assumes that the upper world is real and this world is mere appearance, while atheism assumes that this world is real and the upper world is nonexistent. In their drive toward immanence, both paradigms locate the divine within the self (reducing theology to anthropology or psychology). When, under the influence of the pantheistic scheme, modern theologians emphasized religion as a purely inner affair of mystical experience or personal piety, the atheist was then quite warranted to regard God's existence as an entirely subjective claim with no bearing on actual reality.

In neither the pantheistic nor atheistic paradigm is God a personal being who transcends creaturely reality yet enters freely into relationship with it. Neither scheme allows for the personal intervention of God in nature and history. For pantheism, everything is "miraculous"; the divine is indistinguishable from nature or historical progress or at least the human soul. Yet "miracles" always happen within the self; they never happen in the external world, as disruptions of the ordinary process of nature. Religion or spirituality pertains exclusively to the inner or transcendent realm, beyond history and life in this world. Of course, naturalistic atheism has no place for the supernatural and deism excludes the possibility of miraculous divine intervention — either in judgment or grace. In both paradigms, nothing strange or unfamiliar is allowed to disrupt the sovereignty of the self, which is often identified as *autonomy*. As different as these paradigms are in many ways, they are co-conspirators in the suppression of the knowledge of God and his relationship with creatures.

To be sure, there has been a revival of deism and atheism in our culture, but these are largely modern (Enlightenment) heresies. In our postmodern environment, radical mysticism seems more pervasive. Turning inward for divine inspiration, many today say that they are "spiritual but not religious." Some writers today

---

16. Ibid., 157.

are announcing a shift in western culture from the Age of Belief to the Age of the Spirit. A revival of pantheistic and panentheistic worldviews (much like the ancient heresy of Gnosticism) is evident in academic as well as more popular circles.[17]

This spectrum, from pantheism and panentheism to deism all the way to atheism, plots the course of pagan ontologies (theories of reality) from primitive to postmodern cultures.

Worldview Paradigms	
Pantheism	All is divine.
Panentheism	All is within divinity; the divine and worldly principles are mutually dependent.
Deism	God created the world but does not intervene miraculously within it.
Atheism	God does not exist.

In sharp contrast, the biblical narrative tells the story of the triune God who created all of reality (visible and invisible) out of nothing for his own glory, the creation of humankind in his image and covenant, the transgression of that covenant, and the surprising announcement of his gracious promise to send a Savior. The "scarlet thread" of the promised Redeemer runs through every book of the Bible, from Genesis to Revelation: Jesus Christ is the unifying center of God's saving revelation.

II. A Covenantal Account of "Meeting a Stranger"

The biblical ontology is not a species of a larger genus. In other words, it does not fit into a generic paradigm but generates its own ontology.

A. Defining the Model

This model assumes that God and the world are distinct — Creator and creation. The world is dependent on God, but God is independent of the world. Precisely because the world is dependent at every moment on the word of the triune

---

17. Examples are too numerous to cite, as mysticism and technology, magic and science, spirituality and materialism merge. The second-century heresy of Gnosticism has enjoyed a renaissance ever since the Nag Hammadi discovery in 1945 and is especially popular today in academic circles. In some ways, contemporary advocacy of Gnosticism is the next stage of the New Age movement. Theologians like Harvey Cox, in *The Future of Faith* (New York: HarperOne, 2009), and popular writers like Brian McLaren, in *A New Kind of Christianity* (New York: HarperOne, 2010) defend this shift from Scripture and creeds to inner experience and deeds.

God, nothing in history or nature is ultimately self-caused. God is sovereign over and within every time and place. God is never "trespassing" on his own property and never "transgresses" natural laws, as if these stood above him. God is indeed a stranger, but one who has condescended to meet us in our own creaturely space, which we have in the first place because it is his gift.

From the biblical perspective, God is a stranger in two senses. First, *God is a stranger in a positive sense.* Intrinsically holy, God is *qualitatively* distinct from creation—not just more than, but different from, his creatures. There is no divine soul, preexisting throughout eternity, thrown mercilessly into the realm of time and matter. God breathed life into Adam in creation, and he "became a living being" (Ge 2:7 NIV)—an embodied soul and an animated body. And yet, God pronounced this creation good (Ge 1:10, 12, 18, 21, 25, 31). It is no crime to be different from God. Finitude is not a "falling away" from some primordial infinitude. There is no part of human nature that is higher, brighter, more infinite, or more real than another. This means that the only legitimate ontological distinction is between the uncreated God and the created world, not between spiritual and material realms. Ontological difference—the strangeness that makes us stand in awe of God's majesty—is good.

Second, *God is a stranger in a negative sense.* Whereas the *ontological* difference is a good gift of our creation, *ethical* difference came about as a result of the fall, when Adam transgressed the original covenant. In this sense, God is not only qualitatively *different* from us but morally *opposed* to us. We are estranged from God by sin. In his righteousness, goodness, justice, holiness, and love, God is outraged by our collective and personal rebellion. As human creatures, we are made in God's image; as sinners, we are "by nature children of wrath" (Eph 2:3). Salvation is achieved not by human ascent from the realm of shadows into the unity of divine being but by God's descent in our flesh. We are saved not from nature and history but from the bondage to both sin and death. The dilemma that this redemption solves is the reconciliation of sinners to God in Christ, not the reconciliation of infinitude and finitude, spirit and matter, universals and particulars. Thus, the history of the covenantal relationship of God and humanity rather than the metaphysics of being and becoming is the interest of this model.

B. DEFENDING THE MODEL

The biblical and pagan stories and consequent doctrines could not be more fundamentally opposed at the points I have mentioned. First, *the biblical God is personal, not an abstract principle.* There is no such thing as "the divine," "divinity," or a "divine realm." There is only the God who speaks and acts.

Second, *this personal God is the Trinity rather than "the One."* Especially in dominant Greek philosophy, the highest reality (i.e., that which possesses supreme being) is inherently one. Therefore, plurality must represent a falling away from that primordial unity, away from the fullness of being. In sharp contrast, the God of the Bible is not only one in essence but is also three in persons. Among other implications, this directly challenges philosophy's search — at least since the pre-Socratics — for the single unifying principle (logos) of reality, whether water (Thales), air (Anaximenes), a primordial and eternal chaos (Anaximander), number (Pythagoras), or mind (Parmenides). For the great Greek philosophers, the world came into being by the ministrations of semidivine entities (demiurges), through a unifying logos (rational principle). However, in the biblical worldview, the Logos is a person rather than a principle and is not semidivine, but is the eternally begotten Son of the Father, through whom all things were made (Jn 1:1–5; Col 1:15–17). The Father created the world with his "two hands": the Son and the Spirit.

Third, *the world has never been divine, even in its nonmaterial aspects, and therefore finitude is not a falling away from infinite being but belongs to the nature that God pronounced good.* Since "being" is not univocal, there is no place for a scale of being, with God at the top and rocks at the bottom, and human souls in between. Reality is not like the light controlled by a dimmer switch, with greater and lesser radiance. There is God and there is creaturely reality. The latter is utterly distinct from, yet created by, God, reflecting his character, and — in the case of humans — even bearing his likeness.

God alone *is* life: infinite, immortal, necessary, and sovereign existence; we *receive* a very different kind of creaturely life, as finite, mortal, contingent, and dependent image-bearers. Thus, even in those attributes that we share with God by analogy, God remains *qualitatively*, not merely *quantitatively*, different from creatures. It is not simply that God possesses more being, knowledge, power, love, and justice, but that God transcends all comparisons with us — even those that he reveals in Scripture.

Humanity was created by God's free decision and word — by the Father, in the Son, through the Spirit. The world is not an emanation of God's being, but a creation of his Word. It does not originate in a primordial violence between higher and lower realms, but in the eternal love of the persons of the Trinity for each other and their desire to share this love with creatures who are not and never will be divine. Since difference belongs to God's own existence, it is not surprising that the diversity and plurality of creation should be pronounced good by God (Ge 1:25, 31). Where the pagan worldviews locate evil somewhere in the essence of created, material, plural, finite, and embodied existence as such, the biblical worldview identifies evil with a historical violation of God's loving will and command by free creatures who demanded an autonomous existence that did not belong to them.

Fourth, *biblical faith does not begin with speculation about ostensibly universal truths but with the concrete context of a covenantal relationship.* In biblical faith, the relationship of the creature to its Creator is *contingent* and *covenantal* rather than natural, necessary, and essential — a relationship of giving and receiving; commanding and obeying. In other words, it is *communicative.* This covenantal ontology may be described as *liturgical*: God speaks, and creation responds, as each part of creation offers its own distinct voice in an antiphonal chorus of praise and thanksgiving. We are placed in the *ethical* sphere of historical, embodied, relational, and meaningful activity rather than in a sphere of emanating light cascading down silently along a ladder of being. The realm of history and matter is not a prison from which we must escape by contemplating unchanging reality, but the theater of God's glory.

C. THE HEART OF THE MODEL: A COVENANTAL RELATIONSHIP

The context that God created for this relationship is a *covenant.* Although qualitatively distinct from the world, God is not distant, aloof, and uninvolved. God created the world as the theater of his unfolding drama, at whose heart is a covenantal relationship. The triune God created us to share *in his drama,* not in his essence.

The religious and philosophical worldview of Israel's neighbors reflects a commitment to the "overcoming estrangement" paradigm. It was this idolatry that was strictly forbidden in Israel. However, the ancient Near Eastern world organized its international political life by making treaties. Having saved a lesser ruler (called a vassal) and his people from a foreign oppressor, the great king (called a suzerain) would issue a treaty or covenant with the terms of their new life under his protection and imperial governance. While Israel was strictly forbidden from adopting the religious beliefs and practices of its neighbors, this standard arrangement in secular politics was taken up by God as the heart of Israel's relationship to him. In Israel, Yahweh alone is the Great King.

A covenant is "a union based on an oath" (McCarthy) or, more specifically, "a relationship under sanctions" (Kline).[18] Under this broad definition existed a variety of treaty types.[19]

---

18. Dennis J. McCarthy, *Treaty and Covenant* (Rome: Pontifical Biblical Institute, 1963), 96; Meredith Kline, *By Oath Consigned* (Grand Rapids: Eerdmans, 1968), 16.

19. A growing number of ancient Near Eastern scholars have demonstrated the striking parallels between these ancient secular (especially Hittite) treaties and the covenants between Yahweh and Israel. For the connections to the ancient Near Eastern "suzerainty treaty," see G. E. Mendenhall, *Law and Covenant in Israel and the Ancient Near East* (Pittsburgh: The Biblical

Colloquium, 1955); Meredith G. Kline, especially *Treaty of the Great King* (Grand Rapids: Eerdmans, 1961); Delbert R. Hillers, *Covenant: The History of a Biblical Idea* (Baltimore: Johns Hopkins Univ. Press, 1969). While obvious differences between biblical covenants (especially those depending on Israel's obedience distinguished from those promising unilateral divine deliverance even beyond Israel) is widely recognized, some (following Moshe Weinfeld) argue that these differences find more formal classification in the contrast between suzerainty treaties and

With important antecedents in Irenaeus and Augustine among other formative theologians, Reformed theology discerned three overarching covenants in Scripture under which all sorts of other covenants were arranged.[20] The first is the *covenant of redemption* (also called the *pactum salutis* or covenant of peace). Entered into by the persons of the Trinity in the councils of eternity, with the Son as its mediator, the covenant of redemption is the basis for all of God's purposes in nature and history. The second is the *covenant of creation* between the triune Lord and humanity in Adam as its head or covenantal representative.[21] The third is the *covenant of grace*, which God made with his church after the fall, with Christ as its head, beginning with his promise of salvation to Adam and Eve and continuing through the family of faith leading from Seth to Noah and on to Abraham and Sarah all the way to the new covenant as inaugurated by Christ's death. In this covenant, God promises to be our God and to make believers and their children his own redeemed family, with Christ—the Last Adam—as its federal representative, head, and mediator. Therefore, the object of theology is not God in his hidden essence but, in the words of seventeenth-century Reformed theologian Francis Turretin, "God as he has covenanted with us in Jesus Christ."[22] Each of these covenants will receive their due attention and exegetical defense as this book unfolds.

The Bible gives rise to a sense of history, with its pattern of promise and fulfillment. This outlook contrasts sharply with the Platonic (and more generally pagan) conception of eternal realities and their temporal shadows. Our history is not an allegory of the music of the eternal spheres, but a real plot with genuine twists and turns whose ultimate pattern is known only to God.

Without losing any of its particularity, history is unified by God's eternal purposes in Christ. It moves forward toward that goal, but only because it is charged along that line at various points by God's miraculous intervention and sustained by

---

royal grants. The former is a conditional relationship, while the latter is an outright gift—an inheritance to be passed down in perpetuity to a loyal servant's descendants. For this distinction, see especially Moshe Weinfeld, "The Covenant of Grant in the Old Testament and the Ancient Near East," *JAOS* 90 (1970): 184–203. For more recent critical interaction with Weinfeld's thesis, see Walter Brueggemann, "A Shape for Old Testament Theology, I & II: Structure Legitimation," in *Old Testament Theology: Essays on Structure, Theme, and Text* (ed. Patrick D. Miller; Minneapolis: Augsburg Fortress, 1992); Gary N. Knoppers, "Ancient Near Eastern Royal Grants and the Davidic Covenant: A Parallel?" in *JAOS* 116 (1996): 670–97. I am grateful to Bryan Estelle for suggesting these last two references. Although I find Weinfeld's thesis compelling, it is probably unwise to make the law-covenant/promise-covenant too heavily dependent on formal similarities with ancient Near Eastern treaties. Regardless of parallels, only the exegesis of particular covenants in Scripture can determine its basis and terms. The Reformed (covenant) theologians of the sixteenth and seventeenth centu-

ries were able to see distinctions between various types of covenants in Scripture long before these comparisons in ancient Near Eastern studies. Nevertheless, such recent scholarship only serves to confirm their exegetical insights.

20. For example, the *Westminster Confession* includes the covenant of works and the covenant of grace in chapter 7, with the covenant of redemption at least assumed in chapter 8. For patristic sources, see Everett Ferguson, *Backgrounds to Early Christianity* (2nd ed.; Grand Rapids: Eerdmans, 2003), 92, 288, 292, 405, 425, 468–69, 507–8, 524–27, 547–50. See also Ligon Duncan, "The Covenant Idea in Melito of Sardis: Introduction and Survey," along with "The Covenant Idea in Irenaeus of Lyons: Introduction and Survey" (Greenville, SC: Reformed Academic Press, 1998).

21. Various synonyms are employed for the covenant of creation, such as the covenant of law, works, life, and nature.

22. François Turretin, *Institutes of Elenctic Theology* (Philadelphia P&R Publishing, 1992), 1:16–17.

God's gracious providence. Jesus Christ has undone Adam's treason and fulfilled the trial, winning the right for himself and for his posterity to eat freely from the Tree of Life.

Yet even in this covenantal unity of its consummated state, creation does not lose its bewildering diversity. Unlike the teaching of Eastern religions and Western Stoicism/Platonism, the individual is never absorbed like a drop of water in the ocean. The world retains its own inner quantitative differences and its qualitative difference from God. Even the Pauline contrast of *flesh* and *Spirit* is lifted out of its Greek meaning and is interpreted as the clash between "this age" under the dominion of sin and death and "the age to come" ruled by the risen Christ through the Holy Spirit. The biblical contrast, therefore, is between sin and grace, not nature and grace. In its totality, creation is good, fallen, redeemed, and it will be restored to glorify and to enjoy God forever.

In addition, this biblical paradigm offers a more paradoxical eschatology than the first two, neither of which has any place for the arrival of the Stranger in our history. In the first paradigm, "God" has always been with us, a part of us, one with us, eternally. At most, the incarnation may be a symbol of that which has always been true, namely, God's oneness with humanity. Thus, there is really nothing new in history; everything moves in an eternal cycle of birth, death, and rebirth. The second paradigm denies the possibility of the arrival of any particular Messiah. However, biblical eschatology affirms an "already and not yet" tension. Ultimate meaning is found within history, not beyond it, although salvation comes through God's intervention (promise and fulfillment) rather than through the powers inherent in history itself. The Stranger has arrived! There is no path from us to God, but God has blazed his own trail to us. Like the disciples on the Emmaus road, we are disoriented by the appearance of the Risen Christ whose recital of the biblical drama (with himself at its center) replots our own existence within history. He has met us along the way, in our own historical existence. And yet now is the hour of grace. He will return one day to bring a closure to history in the last judgment. The final meaning of history is disclosed in Christ's resurrection from the dead as the firstfruits of those who sleep, but for now history remains open and frequently ambiguous; Christ's kingdom remains largely hidden under suffering and the cross.

All of this is summarized in Paul's speech before the philosophers in Athens. Surrounded by Epicureans (ancient deists) and Stoics (ancient pantheists), Paul told a shockingly new story. Against both schools he spoke of a Creator God who, unlike their idols, made all things and rules all things. God is independent of the world. Though he needs nothing, he entered into an intimate relationship with his creatures and so cares for the particular lives that he has "determined allotted periods and the boundaries of their dwelling place" (Ac 17:26). While the philosophers were used to debating the latest *ideas* (v. 21), Paul concluded by announcing the latest historical *event* in God's redemptive work: "The times of ignorance God overlooked, but now he commands all people everywhere to repent, because he has fixed a day on which he will judge the world in righteousness by a man whom he has appointed; and of this he has given assurance to all by raising him from the dead" (vv. 30–31).

The response was no less mixed then than it usually is today: "Now when they heard of the resurrection of the dead, some mocked. But others said, 'We will hear you again about this,'" and several joined two of their leaders—a man named Dionysius and a woman named Damaris—to believe his message (vv. 32–34). Therefore, God is neither identified with the world (as in the pantheism of the Stoics) nor aloof from and uninvolved with the world (as in the deism of the Epicureans). Although God is indeed a stranger, he has condescended to relate us to himself.

In Christ we meet not only the divine Stranger but our human representative—the Lord and Servant of the covenant of grace, the one who commands and the one who fulfills, the one who judges and the one who undergoes our judgment and reconciles us to the triune God. Jesus himself taught that all of the Scriptures (then, of course, the Old Testament) speak concerning him (Lk 24:25–27; Jn 5:39–40), and his apostles emphasized this point in their sermons and in their teaching. Since this is the case, we cannot bring Christ into the picture merely at the stage of redemption. The same Word who became flesh was the one in whom and through whom all things were made—and are truly known (Jn 1:1–3; Col 1:15–20).

Against the image of either modern masters or postmodern tourists, the Bible identifies God's covenant people as *pilgrims*. Neither having arrived nor merely carried along by arbitrary whim, we are travelers who "seek the city that is to come" (Heb 13:14). The Creator is also the Consummator, as Jesus declared in his revelation to John: "'I am the Alpha and the Omega,' says the Lord God, 'who is and who was and who is to come, the Almighty'" (Rev 1:8).

III. EPISTEMOLOGY: KNOWING GOD

Epistemology follows ontology. In other words, our theory of how we know anything depends on what we think there is to be known. If our soul (or spirit/mind) has been alienated from its eternal home through bodily imprisonment, then our epistemological goal must be "the upward journey of the soul to the intelligible realm," beyond sense experience.[23] Consistent with its ontology, the "overcoming

---

23. Plato, *The Republic* 8:1135–36 (517b–18e), in *Plato: Complete Works* (ed. John M. Cooper; Indianapolis: Hackett, 1997).

estrangement" model typically understands knowing as a kind of intellectual seeing. The soul (or mind) remembers and seeks to recollect the vision of the eternal forms that it beheld before its imprisonment in time and matter. The principal metaphors for thinking are therefore *visual*. True knowledge is not acquired by learning new things but by remembering the eternal Truth that our souls enjoyed prior to embodiment. The objects of sense, belonging to the realm of shadows, are cloudy and always changing, while the objects of understanding, belonging to the eternal forms, are clear, distinct, fixed, and pure. In order to overcome our estrangement, "the whole soul" must be turned away from the shadows to behold the bright sun itself, namely, the Good.[24]

Plato's Socrates teaches, "While we live, we shall be closest to knowledge if we refrain as much as possible from association with the body and do not join with it more than we must, if we are not infected with its nature but purify ourselves from it until the god himself frees us."[25] Only by using "pure thought" does the philosopher try "to track down each reality pure and by itself, freeing himself as far as possible from his eyes and ears, and in a word, from the whole body, because the body confuses the soul and does not allow it to acquire truth and wisdom whenever it is associated with it."[26] Obviously, historical facts (contingent truths) are inferior to the eternal truths of pure thought (necessary truths). The former pertain to the realm of changing appearances and therefore cannot rise above mere opinion. In fact, the objects of historical study are violence, strife, and the daily business of the body that "makes us too busy to practice philosophy."[27]

The influence of Platonism on the church father Origen (AD 185–254) was so thorough that the early Christian theologian taught not only that the soul was the immortal part of human beings that preexisted eternally but also that this soul was often reincarnated in different bodies.[28] For Origen, Christ is primarily the soul's educator, who, by his moral example and teaching, leads us from the transitory realm of material things to the invisible realm that is the soul's true home. Hence, the historical incarnation, life, death, and resurrection of Christ are symbols of the eternal cycle of the soul's birth, rebirth, and return. Christ's ascension was "more an ascent of mind than of body," blazing the trail for contemplative disciples.[29] Echoing Plato, much of ancient and medieval Christian spirituality was characterized by this contemplative ascent toward the "beatific vision"—the direct sight of the

---

24. Ibid., 8:1136 (518d).

25. Plato, *Phaedo* 59 (66e–67a), in *Plato: Complete Works*: "I think the true philosopher despises them [the body with its senses].... So in the first place, such things clearly show that the philosopher more than other men frees the soul from association with the body as much as possible" (56 [65a]). Physical vision and hearing—the lower senses even more—because of their attachment to the body, deceive and confuse the soul (56 [65b]).

26. Ibid., 57 [66a].

27. Ibid., [66c–d].

28. Origen, *First Principles* 2.9.2, in *ANF*, 4:290.

29. Ibid., 23.2.

Good in itself.[30] Nietzsche and his heirs also applied their ontology to epistemology. If there is no transcendent Good from which being emanates or a God who has revealed himself in historical phenomena, then all that is left is the bare willing of the self. Reality is whatever one makes of it, and knowledge is power.

A. HOW CAN WE KNOW GOD?
POST-REFORMATION INTERPRETATION

From this brief survey, we can recognize there is no such thing as a neutral epistemological method. We always presuppose a certain view of reality before we ask how to investigate it. Why are we here? Is there a God and if so, what is his relationship to the world? Where is history going? The narrative we embrace (or at least assume), along with its attendant doctrines and practices, determines how we can know it. Whether we are explicitly aware of it or not, all of us think, experience, and live within the ambit of a particular story and its dogmas that answer those big questions.

According to the gospel, the divine Stranger has met us throughout our history in our own world and has even descended to us as our elder brother, reconciling us to his Father. In a covenantal perspective, we are no less dependent on God for our knowledge than for our existence. Given both the positive ontological difference and the negative ethical opposition between God and fallen humanity, we dare not attempt to ascend to heaven by our own reason, will, and works, but we must meet God where he has promised to descend to us, meeting us in grace. This is the covenant of grace, with Christ's mediation as the only basis for a safe conduct into God's presence. In contrast to the *visual* analogies that dominant our western intellectual heritage, its principal metaphors for knowing God are *oral/aural*—God's speaking and our hearing rather than our seeing and mastering reality. Hearers are never autonomous, but receive both their existence and their knowledge from the God who speaks.

Drawing heavily on the ancient Christian writers, the Protestant Reformers began with the recognition of God's transcendence and from there fixed their attention on God's accommodation to our weakness in revelation and redemption.

1. GOD'S INCOMPREHENSIBLE MAJESTY

Similar to our contrast between "overcoming estrangement" and "meeting a stranger," the sixteenth-century Reformers contrasted the *theology of glory* with the

---

30. The profoundly influential fifth-century writer known by the pseudonym Dionysius counseled his interlocutor "to leave behind everything you have perceived and understood, everything perceptible and understandable, all that is not and all that is, and, with your understanding laid aside, to strive upward as much as you can toward union with him who is beyond all being and knowledge" (Pseudo-Dionysius, *The Mystical Theology*, in *Pseudo-Dionysius: The Complete Works* [trans. Colm Luibheid; Mahwah, N.J.: Paulist, 1987], 135. Luther, who said of Dionysius that he "Platonizes more than he Christianizes," had this scheme especially in mind when he thundered against the theology of glory.

theology of the cross, beginning with Martin Luther's Heidelberg Disputation in 1518.[31] Instead of striving as masters of reality to behold God in his archetypal majesty, we must take our place as unfaithful servants and be addressed by him on his own terms, in judgment and grace. While the theology of the cross proclaims God's descent to sinners in the flesh, by grace alone in Christ alone, theologies of glory represent human attempts to ascend away from the flesh to union with God through mysticism, merit, and philosophical speculation. Ascending upward in proud pursuit of the beatific vision, away from a supposedly lower realm of bodies, history, and particulars, we miss in our self-righteousness and vaunted wisdom the saving descent of the majestic God in lowliness, bodily suffering, and the most concrete particular imaginable, namely, a Jewish baby lying in a manger who later was to hang on a cross. God does not invite us to discover him in his glory but to meet him where he has promised to be gracious.

God's majesty is not benign. A direct "beatific vision" of God in his glory is more likely a glimpse of hell rather than of heaven, of judgment rather than of grace. When Moses asked to see God's glory, Yahweh allowed his "back"—that is, his goodness and grace—to pass by while he sheltered the prophet behind a rock. "'But,' [the LORD] said, 'you cannot see my face, for man shall not see me and live'" (Ex 33:20). All that we know—or think we know—about God already within ourselves is a revelation of God's law—his majestic glory. However, in our fallen condition, the glorious righteousness of God can only condemn us. Only in the gospel is the gift of righteousness through faith in Christ disclosed to sinners, so that they can stand in God's presence without being consumed. This is the thrust of Paul's argument in Romans 3. In the first two chapters, he explained that we by nature suppress the truth of God in unrighteousness, distorting it in order to avoid the reality of God's wrath. We must learn to receive God's revelation and redemption where he has condescended to us, in the lowliness of a manger, on the cross, and in the baseness of ordinary human language.

Similarly, John Calvin explained that the attributes of God are set forth in Scripture. "Thereupon his powers are mentioned, by which he is shown to us *not as he is in himself, but as he is toward us*: so that this recognition of him consists *more in living experience than in vain and high-flown speculation*" (emphasis added).[32] Knowing God *as he is in himself* was the familiar refrain of mystics and other enthusiasts in all ages, but God's incomprehensible majesty is damning rather than saving. God cannot be directly known by our climbing the scale of being, but can only be known in and through the Mediator. Calvin explained:

---

31. See Walther von Loewenich, *Luther's Theology of the Cross* (Minneapolis: Augsburg, 1976); A. E. McGrath, *Luther's Theology of the Cross: Martin Luther's Theological Breakthrough* (Oxford: Basil Blackwell, 1985); B. A. Gerrish, "To the

Unknown God: Luther and Calvin on the Hiddenness of God," *JR* 53 (1973): 263–92.

32. Calvin, *Institutes*, 1.10.2.

> When faith is discussed in the schools, they call God simply the object of faith, and by fleeting speculations ... lead miserable souls astray rather than direct them to a definite goal. For since "God dwells in inaccessible light" (1Ti 6:16), Christ must become our intermediary.... Indeed, it is true that faith looks to one God. But this must also be added, "to know Jesus Christ whom he has sent" (Jn 17:3).[33]

While a theology of glory presumes to scale the walls of God's heavenly chamber, a theology of the cross will always recognize that although we cannot reach God, he can reach us and has done so in his preached and written Word, in which the Incarnate Word is wrapped as in swaddling cloths.

Treating "God" as an object of theology, Francis Turretin noted, is very different from the way metaphysics approaches God as an object—and different from the way "objects" are treated in other disciplines.[34] This is because God is different from other objects of study. Unlike planets, he is not simply "there" for our inspection. Nor can God be manipulated or dissected or subjected to repeatable experiments. If we are to know God—at least in a saving manner—he must condescend to reveal himself in terms we can understand and embrace by his grace. Therefore, this approach is opposed to rationalism on one hand and to post-Kantian moralism and mysticism on the other.[35]

No one finds God, but God finds us. Although they walked at Jesus' side for three years, the disciples did not understand his person or work until he opened their eyes, proclaiming himself from all the Scriptures and celebrating the Supper after the resurrection (Lk 24). Both for our finitude and for our sinfulness, our reconciliation with God requires revelation in the form of divine initiative and condescension. The highest wisdom and knowledge are found not in a grasping, seizing, ascending, mastering vision of pure ideas but in a receiving, welcoming, seated, and descending recital of God's works in history. Not only in the content of the gospel but in its very form, then, it is "folly to Gentiles" (1Co 1:23).

The Reformers' insistence on God's incomprehensible majesty had clear precedent in the ancient church, especially in the East. For example, after exploring various divine attributes, Gregory of Nyssa (335–394) cautions, "But in each of these terms

---

33. Ibid., 3.2.1.

34. Turretin, *Elenctic Theology*, 1:17–18.

35. Turretin, ibid.: "Reason is the instrument which the believer uses, but it is not the foundation and principle upon which faith rests" (1:33). Richard Muller summarizes the consensus of the Reformed orthodox: "Reason never proves faith, but only elaborates faith toward understanding" (*PRRD*, 1:34). Arminian and Socinian thinkers were hitching their wagons to Descartes, while French and Dutch Reformed theologians criticized the new system of rationalism. Even Roman Catholic theologians employed the Cartesian method against the Calvin-

ists (Richard H. Popkin, *Problems of Cartesianism: Cartesianism and Biblical Criticism* [ed. Thomas M. Lennon, John M. Nicholas, and John W. Davies; Montreal: McGill-Queen's Univ. Press, 1982], 71–72). The Reformed theologian Voetius went into direct combat with Descartes, and the former's disciple (Schook) wrote a critique that provoked a response from Descartes (Theo Verbeek, *Descartes and the Dutch: Early Reactions to Cartesian Philosophy 1673–1650* [Carbondadle and Edwardsville: Southern Illinois Univ. Press, 1992], 20). Consequently, there is no historical basis to the claim that Reformed orthodoxy was shaped by modern rationalism.

we find a peculiar sense, fit to be understood or asserted of the Divine nature, yet not expressing that which that nature is in its essence."[36] God's *essence* remains hidden to us, but his *energies* (i.e., workings or operations) are revealed. Gregory's brother Basil argued, "The energies are various, and the essence simple, but we say that we know our God from His energies, but do not undertake to approach near to His essence. His energies come down to us, but His essence remains beyond our reach."[37] These arguments were directed especially against Platonists like the Arian Eunomius, who insisted that we can know God as he is in himself, that is, in his essence.

Similarly, John of Damascus (d. AD 749) counsels, "He revealed that which it was to our profit to know; but what we were unable to bear He kept secret. With these things let us be satisfied, and let us abide by them, not removing everlasting boundaries, nor overpassing the divine tradition."[38] We know God by his works, not in his hidden essence.

We will return several times to this crucial distinction of Eastern theology between God's essence and energies. As I will argue more fully, Western theology—following Augustine and Aquinas—did not recognize this distinction and insisted that the only reason we do not behold God in his essence at present is our bodily form. Although the East was as susceptible as the West to the influences of Platonism, its essence-energies distinction reckoned more fully with the Creator-creature difference and often guarded against the pantheistic tendencies evident in Western mysticism.[39]

In this respect, the Reformers reflect the East's emphasis on God's incomprehensibility (in his essence) and God's self-revealing condescension (in his energies). As we know the sun only as we are warmed by its rays, we know God only in his activity toward us, not as he is in himself.[40] While medieval systems contained lengthy treatments of the divine essence, Calvin moves quickly through a necessary affirmation of God's spirituality and immensity to discuss the Trinity. "They are mad who seek to discover what God is," he says.[41] "What is God? Men who pose this question are merely toying with idle speculations.... What help is it, in short, to know a God with whom we have nothing to do?... The essence of God is rather to be adored than inquired into."[42]

36. Gregory of Nyssa, *On 'Not Three Gods,' To Ablabius*, in *NPNF2*, 5:333.

37. Basil, *Epistle 234*, in *NPNF2*, 8:274.

38. John of Damascus, *An Exact Exposition of the Orthodox Faith*, in *NPNF2*, 9:1.

39. See Vladimir Lossky, *The Mystical Theology of the Eastern Church* (Crestwood, N.Y.: St. Vladimir's Seminary Press, 1976), 65–89, 220.

40. B. B. Warfield, *Calvin and Augustine* (Philadelphia: Presbyterian & Reformed, 1956), 153. Warfield notes, "[Calvin] is refusing all a priori methods of determining the nature of God

and requiring of us to form our knowledge of Him a posteriori from the revelation He gives us of Himself in His activities." See further his excellent summary of this reticence in Calvin and the tradition generally to explore the "whatness" (139–40).

41. John Calvin, *Commentaries on the Epistle of Paul the Apostle to the Romans* (ed. John Owen; Grand Rapids: Baker, 1996), 69.

42. Calvin, *Institutes* 1.2.2. Early Reformed writers such as Musculus repeated this approach, launching their discussion of God with the question of *who* God is rather than *what* God is. See Muller, *PRRD*, 3:228.

Through this Word of reconciliation—the gospel—God becomes a stranger in a third sense: not only because he is our creator (ontological difference) and judge (ethical difference), but because he is our *redeemer*. This is a strange Word from a strange God because it contradicts our moral reasoning, which is captive to a theology of glory. Limited to "the moral law within" (the most certain universal truth, Kant observed), the gospel can only be dismissed as foolish superstition. Contrary to our distorted intuitions, the gospel does not encourage our conquest of heaven through intellectual, mystical, and moral striving. It announces that even while we were enemies, God reconciled us (Ro 5:10). While we were dead in sins, he made us alive in Christ (Eph 2:5). We are saved by God's good works, not our own (Eph 2:8–9). Because we are sinners, God's speech is disruptive and disorienting. It is not we who overcome estrangement, but God who heals the breach by communicating the gospel of his Son.

A God who eludes our comprehending gaze—who masters but is never mastered—is a terrifying prospect for the fallen heart until Christ steps forward as our mediator. This is not because we remain embodied creatures seeking to overcome estrangement, but because we are fallen from our original dignity, under God's wrath. Calvin reminds us:

> In this ruin of mankind no one now experiences God either as Father or as Author of salvation, or favorable in any way, until Christ the Mediator comes forward to reconcile him to us.... It is one thing to feel that God as our Maker supports us by his power, governs us by his providence, nourishes us by his goodness, and attends us with all sorts of blessings—and another thing to embrace the grace of reconciliation offered to us in Christ.[43]

Apart from the gospel we flee from God's self-revelation, dressing folly in the robe of wisdom and ungodliness in the garments of virtue. It is ultimately an ethical revolt against the God who made us.

It is this marvelous strangeness, both of God's ontological majesty and of God's amazing grace toward estranged sinners, that leads us to doxology:

> Oh, the depth of the riches and wisdom and knowledge of God! How unsearchable are his judgments and how inscrutable his ways!
>
> > "For who has known the mind of the Lord,
> >   or who has been his counselor?" [Isa 40:13].
> > "Or who has given a gift to him
> >   that he might be repaid?" [Job 35:7; 41:11].
>
> For from him and through him and to him are all things. To him be glory forever. Amen. (Ro 11:33–36)

---

43. Calvin, *Institutes* 1.2.1.

2. GOD'S CONDESCENDING GOODNESS

Created in God's "image" and "likeness" (Ge 1:26), we "live and move and have our being" in God (Ac 17:28). Only because God gives us life and truth are we capable of existing and knowing, but this means we are capable of true knowledge. Although we do not know anything exactly as God knows it, true human knowledge does not stand in contradiction to divine knowledge but depends on it. The essence of the sin of our first parents was that they wanted to have an independent, autonomous existence and knowledge, no longer depending on "every word that comes from the mouth of God" (Mt 4:4). In fact, this reference is taken from Jesus' temptation by the serpent in the wilderness, in which he undoes Adam's transgression by answering back properly.

Neither being nor knowledge is ever shared univocally (i.e., identically) between God and creatures. As God's being is qualitatively and not just quantitatively distinct from ours, so too is God's knowledge. God's knowledge is archetypal (the original), while ours is ectypal (a copy), revealed by God and therefore accommodated to our finite capacities.[44] Our imperfect and incomplete knowledge is always dependent on God's perfect and complete knowledge.

A covenantal ontology requires a covenantal epistemology. We were created as God's analogy (image bearers) rather than as self-existent sparks of divinity; therefore, our knowledge is also dependent rather than autonomous. So there is indeed such a thing as absolute, perfect, exhaustive, and eternal truth, but this knowledge is possessed by God, not by us. Rather, we have *revealed* truth, which God has accommodated to our capacity.

Following Thomas Aquinas (1225–74), our older theologians therefore argued that human knowledge is analogical rather than either univocal or equivocal (two terms are related *analogically* when they are similar, *univocally* when they are identical, and *equivocally* when they have nothing in common).[45] Take the word *ball*. There is no obvious connection between a formal dance and an object that I bounce. Thus, the use of the word "ball" in these different contexts is equivocal. However, in sports, "ball" is used analogically. Football and baseball are not the same games;

44. See Willem van Asselt, "The Fundamental Meaning of Theology: Archetypal and Ectypal Theology in Seventeenth-Century Reformed Thought," *WTJ* 64, no. 2 (2002): 319–35. According to the Lutheran scholastic J. A. Quenstedt, this distinction (carried over from medieval theology by the Reformed theologian Franciscus Junius) was also affirmed by Lutherans (Luther Poellot, ed., *The Nature and Character of Theology: An Introduction to the Thought of J. A. Quenstedt* [St. Louis: Concordia, 1986], 22–23; this is an abridged translation of the first chapters of the 1696 edition of Quenstedt's *Theologia didactio-polemica sive systema theologicum*; see also Heinrich Schmid, *The*

Doctrinal Theology of the Evangelical Lutheran Church [3rd ed.; Minneapolis: Augsburg, 1961], 16).

45. Thomas Aquinas, *Summa Theologica* I, Q. xiii, a.5, 10. For Aquinas's view of analogy, see David Burrell, "Analogy," in *The Westminster Dictionary of Christian Theology* (ed. Alan Richardson and John Bowdon; Philadelphia: Westminster, 1983). For the various subtleties of this position, see Ralph M. McInerny, *Aquinas and Analogy* (Washington, D.C.: Catholic Univ. Press, 1999); Bernard Montagnes, *The Doctrine of the Analogy of Being according to Thomas Aquinas* (Milwaukee, Wis.: Marquette Univ. Press, 2004).

even the balls they use are qualitatively different. Nevertheless, they are similar enough for them both to be called ball games. Only when I am comparing one baseball game to another is ball used univocally—referring to exactly the same thing.

When we say that God is good, we assume we know what *good* means from our ordinary experience with fellow human beings. However, God is not only *quantitatively better* than we are; his goodness is *qualitatively different* from creaturely goodness. Nevertheless, because we are created in God's image, we share this predicate with God analogically. *Goodness*, attributed to God and Sally, is similar but always with greater dissimilarity. At no point is goodness exactly the same for God as it is for Sally. The difference is qualitative, not just quantitative; yet there is enough similarity to communicate the point.

God reveals himself as a person, a king, a shepherd, a substitutionary lamb, and so forth. These analogies are not arbitrary (i.e., equivocal), but they are also not exact correspondence (i.e., univocal). Even when we attribute love to God and Mary, *love* cannot mean exactly the same thing for a self-existent Trinity and a finite person. In every analogy, there is always greater dissimilarity than similarity between God and creatures. Nevertheless, God judges that the analogy is appropriate for his self-revelation. We do not know exactly what divine goodness is like, but since God selects this analogy, there must be a sufficient similarity to our concept of goodness to justify the comparison.

This doctrine of analogy is the hinge on which a Christian affirmation of God's transcendence and immanence turns. A univocal view threatens God's transcendence, while an equivocal view threatens God's immanence. The former leads to rationalism, while the latter engenders skepticism.

Challenging the doctrine of analogy, Duns Scotus (1266–1308) held that at least some of our knowledge must coincide *univocally* with God's knowledge if there is to be any real knowledge of reality. At least *being* (existence) must mean the same thing for God as it does for us, Scotus argued; otherwise, the predicate is vacuous.[46] This displays once again the connection between ontology and epistemology. For Scotus, the univocity of being means that "the difference between God and creatures, at least with regard to the pure perfections, is ultimately one of degree"—quantitative rather than qualitative.[47] Scotus's demand for absolute

---

46. John Duns Scotus, *Opera Omnia* (Civitas Vaticana: Typis Polyglottis Vaticanus, 1950-), includes *Ordinatio* 1 and 2, where Scotus argues these positions against Aquinas. For an English translation, see Allan B. Wolter, trans., *Duns Scotus: Philosophical Writings* (Indianapolis: Hackett, 1987). Key interpreters of Scotus include Allan B. Wolter and Felix Alluntis, *John Duns Scotus: God and Creatures* (Washington, D.C.: Catholic Univ. Press of America Press, 1975); Richard Cross, *Duns Scotus* (Oxford: Oxford Univ. Press, 1999).

47. Cross, *Duns Scotus*, 39. This is an important recognition, since Cross is a formidable defender of Scotus against critics who suggest that he denied the Creator-creature distinction. See his essay "Idolatry and Religious Language," *Faith and Philosophy* 25, no. 2 (2008): 191–92. I am grateful to Brian Hecker for this reference.

certainty of truth, unaided by divine grace, drew him into conflict with the more Augustinian theologian Henry of Ghent (1217–1293).

Affirming God's incomprehensible majesty, the Reformers and their scholastic heirs embraced the doctrine of analogy but offered a critical revision. Instead of our speculative ascent from the familiar to the less familiar, choosing our own analogies, we must restrict our thinking to the analogies that God offers us by his condescending grace. God became human; humans do not rise up to God. Therefore, we do not use our own analogies to climb the ladder of contemplation; rather, God uses analogies from the world he created to communicate with us.[48] We know God not by contemplating and speculating (terms that derive from the verb "to see"), but from hearing God tell us how things are and how we can know them. There is a certain plausibility to the argument of modern atheists from Ludwig Feuerbach to Sigmund Freud that metaphysical reasoning attempts to project onto an imaginary Infinitude the superlatives (or negations) of finite human beings. "God" — the "Perfect Being" — becomes a mirror of our own prejudices: an idol created in the image of the worshiper. However, unlike metaphysics, theology begins with God's self-revelation and listens to God in his gracious condescension.

Like Scotus, however, many modern theologians (both conservative and liberal) have regarded the doctrine of analogy as a halfway house on the way to skeptical equivocity. If we cannot be sure that our predications correspond exactly to the inner being of God, then how can we claim true knowledge? This charge has been leveled in recent decades, for example, by writers as diverse as liberal theologian Langdon Gilkey and conservative evangelical Carl F. H. Henry.[49] According to Gordon Clark (Henry's mentor), truth is only given in the form of propositional statements and if our knowledge is only analogical of God's, we have no foundation for certainty.[50] "The main logical difficulty with the doctrine of analogy," writes Henry, "lies in its failure to recognize that only univocal assertions protect us from equivocation; the very possibility of analogy founders unless something is truly known about both analogates."[51] For a certain proposition to be true, according to this perspective, it must mean exactly the same thing for God as it does for us.

---

48. Cf. Poellot, ed., *Nature and Character of Theology*, 22–23: "Archetypal theology is essentially in God, and it is that very same infinite wisdom of God by which God knows Himself in Himself ... and outside of Himself all things through Himself by an indivisible and immutable act of knowledge. Ectypal theology is nothing else than a certain expressed or rather foreshadowed image and form of that infinite and essential theology, either shared in this world or to be communicated in that which is to come by God, graciously and out of pure goodness, with intelligent creatures, according to their ability. (Note: This distinction is not of a univocal in its one meaning, but of an analog in its counterpart.)"

49. Langdon Gilkey, "Cosmology, Ontology, and the Travail of Biblical Language," *JR* 41 (July 1961): 200; Carl F. H. Henry, *God, Revelation, and Authority* (Waco, Tex.: Word, 1976), 1:237–38. I interact with both figures on this point in *Covenant and Eschatology: The Divine Drama* (Louisville: Westminster John Knox, 2002), 189–91.

50. Cornelius Van Til led the defense of analogy, insisting against Gordon Clark that God's knowledge and our knowledge do not "coincide at a single point." See Herman Hoeksema citing Gordon Clark's "Answer," in Herman Hoeksema, *The Clark-Van Til Controversy* (Hobbs, N.M.: Trinity Foundation, 1995), 9.

51. Henry, *God, Revelation, and Authority*, 4:118.

Especially as refined by Protestant scholasticism, however, the doctrine of analogy affirms that finite and creaturely knowledge is nevertheless *true* knowledge because it has its ultimate source in God even though it is not identical with God's knowledge. God's existence is not a threat to but is the necessary precondition and source of our own. So why would not the same be true of God's knowledge and ours? Creatures can attain finite knowledge (dependent truth) because God possesses infinite knowledge (absolute Truth). Therefore, against certain forms of postmodern theory, Christian theology affirms that there *is* a God's-eye perspective from which genuine truth can be communicated, but, against the tendency of modern thought, it denies that anyone but God occupies this privileged perch. We must be satisfied with God's Word and leave God's sovereign knowledge to himself.

Although not all representatives (certainly not Carl Henry, for instance) would embrace an "overcoming estrangement" paradigm, univocity has been the characteristic ontological and epistemological presupposition of this scheme, just as equivocity is the ground of "the stranger we never meet." If univocity breeds rationalism, equivocity generates epistemological skepticism. Both positions presuppose human autonomy and are, therefore, unwilling to regard reality and access to that reality as a gift that comes to us from outside of ourselves. It is significant that Paul describes this perverse refusal to accept our role as covenant creatures as ingratitude (Ro 1:20–21). This refusal is not, therefore, simply an intellectual problem, but is rooted in an ethical rebellion that is willfully perpetuated. As Paul goes on to relate in that passage, the biblical term for this pursuit of autonomous metaphysics is *idolatry*.

B. THE SOVEREIGN SELF: VARIATIONS ON A THEME

In spite of itself, not even modernity can be entirely novel. Though considered the founder of modern philosophy, René Descartes (1596–1650) employed a system that was to a large extent another verse in the hymn of Western Platonism. If this rationalistic side of modernity extended the life of the "overcoming estrangement" paradigm, modernity's other side—"the stranger we never meet"—lives on in postmodernity. In both cases, the tie that binds is the univocity of being—the confusion of Creator and creature. Either all of reality is in some sense divine and infinite (pantheism/panentheism), or all of reality is material and finite (atheism). Even David Hume's skeptical empiricism (rejecting universals in favor of particulars) and Nietzsche's "will to power" represented the full flowering of seeds sown by late medieval nominalism. In fact, the postmodern theorist Gilles Deleuze declared, "There has only ever been one ontological proposition: Being is univocal. There has only ever been one ontology, that of Duns Scotus, which gave being a single voice.... From Parmenides to Heidegger it is the same voice which is taken up, in an echo which itself forms the whole deployment of the univocal. A single voice raises the clamor of being."[52]

What especially distinguishes modernity, however, is the rigor with which it pursued the project of absolute autonomy (self-creation and self-rule) over against all external authorities. Whether through reason, empirical investigation, ideas, or will, the individual will rise to the heavens in conquest over gods and mortals.

Especially in the shadow of the Wars of Religion, which engulfed most of Europe in a century of horrendous bloodshed between Roman Catholics and Protestants, many thinkers longed for universal foundations in reason and morality that could transcend confessional distinctives. How could Christianity serve as the common foundation of Western culture if "Christendom" was embroiled in wars over its proper interpretation? Descartes, a Jesuit polymath who saw the religious wars at first hand, even briefly as a soldier, tried his hand at discovering this universal foundation once and for all.

After demolishing the edifice of so-called knowledge that had been constructed over his lifetime from external instruction, authority, empirical observation, and opinions that he has acquired from tradition, Descartes erects a new skyscraper for himself and by himself on a perfect foundation that could never be shaken. Locking himself in his apartment, away from all human society, Descartes announces, "I have freed my mind of all kinds of cares; I feel myself, fortunately, disturbed by no passions; and I have found a serene retreat in peaceful solitude. I will therefore make a serious and unimpeded effort to destroy generally all my former opinions."[53] He will, for methodological purposes, imagine that the world he knows is an illusion created by a malignant demon. Furthermore, "I will consider myself as having no hands, no eyes, no flesh, no blood, nor any senses, yet falsely believing that I have all these things."[54] Appealing to the example of Archimedes' fulcrum, he writes, "I shall have the right to entertain high hopes if I am fortunate enough to find a single truth which is certain and indubitable."[55] Only by this method of absolute skepticism does Descartes think he can demonstrate the one thing that cannot be doubted: the "clear and distinct idea" that, it turns out, is his own existence as "a thing that thinks" (*res cogitans*).[56]

---

52. Gilles Deleuze, *Difference and Repetition* (trans. Paul Patton; New York: Columbia Univ. Press, 1994), 66–67.

53. René Descartes, *Meditations on First Philosophy* (trans. Laurence J. Lafleur; Indianapolis: Bobbs-Merrill, 1951), 17.

54. Ibid., 22.

55. Ibid., 23.

56. Ibid., 24–32. His own synopsis in *Meditations on First Philosophy* begins, "In the First Meditation, I offer the reasons why we can doubt all things in general, and particularly material objects.... In the Second, the mind, which in its intrinsic freedom supposes that everything which is open to the least doubt is nonexistent, recognizes that it is nevertheless absolutely impossible that it does not itself exist." This argument rests on "the clearest possible conception" of the immortality of the soul, "and one which is entirely distinct from all the conceptions one can have of the body" (13–14). The Third Meditation argues for God's existence, without "any comparisons drawn from physical things, in order that the minds of the readers should be as far as possible withdrawn from the use of and commerce with the senses" (15). "In the Fourth, it is proved that all things which we conceive or perceive

Ironically, from this autonomous epistemological method, Descartes seeks to demonstrate the necessity of God's existence. And finally, he argues that God is not a deceiver, but that the only reason for errors is the fact that the self is suspended between God (perfect being) and non-being (finitude).[57] Just as he promised, Descartes has argued for the indubitable foundation of knowledge in the existence of the soul and God by the light of nature alone, without any appeal to the biblical narrative of creation, fall, and redemption. However, the result is a "natural religion" that identifies truth with intellectual ascent rather than with the incarnation, sin with creaturely finitude, and redemption with enlightenment. He may arrive at God's existence; however, it is by a method of autonomous reason (which he assumes is neutral), starting with himself as an incorporeal mind—"a thing that thinks"—with no inherent relationship (covenantal or otherwise) to others, including the God whose existence he seeks to demonstrate. It is indeed lonely at the top. "The logic of Christian faith differs radically from this Cartesian logic in at least two respects," notes Daniel L. Migliore. "First, the starting point of inquiry for the Christian is not self-consciousness but awareness of the reality of God, who is creator and redeemer of all things. Not 'I think, therefore I am,' but 'God is, therefore we are.'.... Second, for Christian faith and theology, inquiry is elicited by faith in God rather than being an attempt to arrive at certainty apart from God."[58]

The earlier synthesis of Christianity and Platonism, which dominated medieval thought, leads to idolatrous projections—a "theology of glory"—but the modern turn to the subject actually makes the self the master of all reality. Contrary to popular assumptions, the Enlightenment was not antireligious, although it was critical of inherited orthodoxies.[59] In fact, its roots reached deeply into the soil of medieval and Renaissance mysticism, especially with the revival of Neo-Platonism, Kabbalism, and quasi-Gnostic esoteric speculations.

Joachim of Fiore (1135–1202), founder of the Spiritual Franciscans, had written a profoundly influential commentary on the book of Revelation that divided history into three ages: the Age of the Father (law: the order of the married); the Age of the Son (grace: the order of the clergy), and the Age of the Spirit (direct and intuitive experience of God: the order of the monks). In the third age, there would be no need for God to

---

very clearly and very distinctly are wholly true" (15). He explicitly excludes from consideration here errors produced by sin or "beliefs which belong to faith or to the conduct of life," focusing only on "those which pertain to speculative truth and which can be known by the aid of the light of nature alone" (16). The Fourth Meditation offers a new argument for God's existence as the basis for even the certainty of geometry, and the Fifth defends the distinction (emphasized by Plato) between genuine understanding and imagination or opinion. "All the errors which arise from the senses are here exposed, together with the methods of avoiding them" (16).

57. Ibid., 50–53.

58. Daniel L. Migliore, *Faith Seeking Understanding: An Introduction to Christian Theology* (2nd ed.; Grand Rapids: Eerdmans, 2004), 5.

59. See, for example, the well-researched and elegant work by David Sorkin, *The Religious Enlightenment: Protestants, Jews, and Catholics from London to Vienna* (Princeton: Princeton Univ. Press, 2008).

reveal himself through the veil of creaturely mediation. Everyone will know the truth inwardly, apart from Scripture, preaching, sacrament, and church.[60] The mystical ascent from the realm of appearances to the realm of spirit was transformed into a historical ascent that would become secularized as the modern idea of progress. In other words, the Platonic ladder of being was laid on its side: ascending horizontally rather than vertically.

Joachim's speculations shaped many of the apocalyptic movements of the late Middle Ages, including the early Anabaptists. In fact, although Joachim was hardly the only influence, a line may be drawn from him to Renaissance Neo-Platonists like Nicholas of Cusa, Giordano Bruno, and Pico della Mirandola, all the way to the sixteenth-century Anabaptists, and on to the Enlightenment.[61] In his *On the Peace of Faith* (1453), Nicholas of Cusa envisions a conference in heaven where the religions are finally reconciled, recognizing that they are one in their moral and spiritual core. Cusa's influence is obvious especially in Giordano Bruno and Gottfried Leibniz, as also in the German idealists and Romantics. Lessing, Kant, Hegel, Schelling, and Marx all refer to Joachim. Though secularized, the expectation of a new age of direct, immediate, and inward gnosis was indebted in no small measure to Joachim's millennial enthusiasm.

In *The Education of the Human Race* (1778), rationalist philosopher G. E. Lessing (1729 – 1781) announced that Joachim's Age of the Spirit had finally dawned. Sharply contrasting "necessary truths of reason" and "accidental [or contingent] truths of history," Lessing professed that he could not get across this "ugly ditch." In other words, he said, regardless of whether Christ literally rose from the dead, such facts of contingent history are insufficient to ground or to challenge eternal principles of reason.[62] On the basis of this Platonist prejudice, Lessing asserted that Christianity's supernatural claims are indemonstrable simply because they are historical. This "ugly ditch" between "necessary truths of reason" and "accidental truths of history" that Lessing said he could not get across was widely influential in modern thought.[63] Lessing says, "It follows that the religion of Christ and the

---

60. An abridgement of Joachim's commentary is found in Bernard McGinn, *Apocalyptic Spirituality: Treatises and Letters of Lactantius, Adso of Montier-en-Der, Joachim of Fiore, the Franciscan Spirituals, and Savonarola* (Classics in Western Spirituality; Mahwah, N.J.: Paulist, 1979).

61. Marjorie Reeves, *Joachim of Fiore and the Prophetic Future* (London: Sutton, 1999); idem, *The Influence of Prophecy in the Later Middle Ages* (South Bend, Ind.: Univ. of Notre Dame Press, 1993); Warwick Gould and Marjorie Reeves, *Joachim of Fiore and the Myth of the Eternal Evangel in the Nineteenth and Twentieth Centuries* (New York: Oxford Univ. Press, 2002); Bernard McGinn, *Visions of the End* (New York: Columbia Univ. Press, 1998), 126–60; Norman Cohn, *The Pursuit of the Millennium* (New York: Oxford Univ. Press, 1970).

62. Henry Chadwick, ed., *Lessing's Theological Writings* (Palo Alto, Calif.: Stanford Univ. Press, 1967), 53.

63. Ibid., 32: "Lessing's antithesis between the 'accidental truths of history' and the 'necessary truths of reason' foreshadows the language of German idealism. For Fichte (deeply influenced by Lessing), 'only the metaphysical can save, never the historical.' And for Kant before him, 'the historical can serve only for illustration, not for demonstration.' Lessing is preparing the way for the divorcing of the Gospel history from the 'eternal truths' of Christianity in D. F. Strauss (strikingly anticipated in Schleiermacher's *Christmas Eve*, 1806), and for the high valuation of idea and depreciation of past event which runs through [John Henry Cardinal] Newman's *Essay on Development.*"

Christian religion are two quite different things."[64] It may also be added that this trajectory leads to the theologian Rudolf Bultmann (1884–1976), who said, "The Jesus of history is of no concern to me…I am deliberately renouncing any form of encounter with a phenomenon of past history, including an encounter with the Christ after the flesh."[65]

So there is a basically "gnostic" contrast in modern theology between the outer and the inner, time and eternity, body and spirit, particular and universal. We know the infinite reality only within ourselves — immediately, directly, and intuitively. We meet the divine in our mind or spirit, or in our inner sense of morality, in the feeling of dependence on the Absolute, or in an existential encounter. Whatever the path inward, these philosophies agree in rejecting an external revelation that comes to us from a transcendent God who speaks and acts in concrete history, embodied in our flesh, publicly accessible in our phenomenal experience.

The central problem with this whole line of thinking, from a Christian perspective, is that the most important and interesting things the Bible says concern historical events rather than eternal truths. If we know God only according to his works, not in his essence, then the history of God's action — revealed and interpreted in Scripture — is our only access. The search for an inner core of pure morality, religion, and spirituality that unites humanity — over against the particular narratives, doctrines, and practices that distinguish Christians from others — is hardly a postmodern pastime. Religious pluralism and relativism lie at the heart of modernity, as is evident in Lessing's clever parable of *Nathan the Wise* (1778), which is similar to Nicholas of Cusa's *On the Peace of Faith* — not to mention, John Lennon's "Imagine."

In contrast to rationalism and idealism, the Scottish empiricist David Hume (1711–1776) argued that the phenomena of sense experience are the only objects of our knowledge. In radical opposition to rationalism, Hume argued that Descartes' "self" was an illusion and that our sense experience, passions, and social custom not only are unavoidable for apprehending what we call knowledge but provide our only access to it. In fact, "Reason is, and ought only to be the slave of the passions, and can never pretend to any other office than to serve and obey them."[66] In his essay "On Miracles," Hume buttressed deistic objections to miracles — even anticipating the atheistic critique that such claims in every religion are nothing more than an illusion, a coping mechanism in the face of overwhelming natural forces.[67]

---

64. Chadwick, ed., *Lessing's Theological Writings*, 106.

65. Bultmann, "Reply to Theses of J. Schniewind," in *Kerygma and Myth: A Theological Debate* (ed. Hans Werner Bartsch; trans. Reginald H. Fuller; London: SPCK, 1953), 117. Famous for his method of "demythologizing" (i.e., "translating" what he regarded as the myths of Scripture into truths of our contemporary existence), Bultmann distinguished sharply between the Jesus of History (of no significance to faith) and the Christ of Faith (known only in personal encounter here and now).

66. David Hume, *A Treatise of Human Nature* (New York: Dover, 2003), 295.

67. David Hume, "On Miracles," in *An Enquiry Concerning Human Understanding* (ed. Eric Steinberg; Indianapolis: Hackett, 1993), sec. 10.

I mentioned at the beginning of this chapter that knowing God became especially problematic in modernity—at least for philosophers and theologians. We have to assume that "God" exists, they have said, in order to acknowledge the laws of nature and morality, but we cannot know anything about this God. The necessity of God's existence may be deduced from our practical need for morality or from our experience of transcendence, but God cannot be an object of *knowledge.* Though associated more generally with deism, this approach was developed with rigor by Immanuel Kant (1724–1804), and it remains one of the most pervasive assumptions of our Western thought today. It was after reading Hume's *Enquiry* that Kant was awakened from his dogmatic slumbers in rationalism and thereafter set out to create a harmonization of reason and sense experience. "The world is tired of metaphysical assertions," he wrote.[68] Not only the univocal speculations of rationalism but also the analogical revelation of God in Scripture was ruled out of court as claiming the kind of knowledge ("metaphysical") that we cannot have.

Kant believed that the idea of God, like the concepts of time and space, structure our minds in their encounter with the phenomena of our otherwise chaotic sense-experience. Yet these concepts ("noumena") themselves can never be the object of our knowledge. Philosopher David Walsh observes:

> The distinction he sought to maintain between knowledge of appearances and the thing-in-itself could not be sustained once it was subjected to self-examination. To know appearances as appearance is already to go beyond mere appearance; it is already to know the thing-in-itself.... Without actually admitting it, Kant disclosed the extent to which reason rests on faith. The central question of his philosophy—"How are synthetic a prior judgments possible?"—is never and can never be answered.[69]

In *Critique of the Power of Judgment,* Kant says that the final purpose of human beings "is the value that he alone can give to himself, and which consists in what he does ... in the freedom of his faculty of desire; i.e., a good will is that alone by means of which his existence can have an absolute value and in relation to which the existence of the world can have a final end."[70]

It is this moral autonomy—free will and commitment to duty—that Kant regards as our link with divinity. Ironically for Kant, as Walsh notes, "It is our capacity to do without God that discloses our closeness to divinity. Not even the desire for union with God can deflect us from the severe path of duty for its own sake. What is right takes precedence over all else.... As moral beings we stand at

---

68. Immanuel Kant, *Prolegomena to Any Future Metaphysics* (ed. Lewis White Beck; Indianapolis: Bobbs-Merrill, 1950), 126.

69. David Walsh, *The Modern Philosophical Revolution: The Luminosity of Existence* (Cambridge: Cambridge Univ. Press, 2008), 30, 35.

70. Immanuel Kant, *Critique of the Power of Judgment,* Gesammelte Schriften, 5:443.

the summit of our existence, sharing the transcendence of God himself."[71] Thus, hypertranscendence came full-circle to hyperimmanence; from the abandonment of the self-revealing God came the enthronement of the autonomous (divine) self.

The implication, as Kant himself explicitly states, is that religion is founded on morality rather than vice versa. Furthermore, he says, "The right way to advance is not from grace to virtue but rather from virtue to grace."[72] So Kant reverses the order of dependence: morality is not grounded in God; the idea of God is inferred from the practical dictates of morality; our sense of justice depends not on a future judgment, but the idea of a future judgment is an inference drawn from the necessity of punishment in the case of moral failure.[73]

Kant was concerned that the flames of rationalism as well as Hume's skepticism threatened to destroy morality. That is why he said, "I have found it necessary to deny *knowledge*, in order to make room for *faith*."[74] Besides his unwarranted antithesis between faith and knowledge, Kant's definition of *faith* was no more than "a confidence in moral duty."[75] But, of course, this left the self to stew in its own juices, with the lid firmly set on top of the boiling cauldron of religious and moral enthusiasm. Without any supernatural in-breaking of communication from God to human beings, religion could occupy an island of irrational subjectivity, each spiritual person and religious community talking to itself about its own pious experience and duties. The outward forms that "pure religion" (morality) takes in various cultures ("ecclesiastical faiths") may be objects of study, but not God and his works. As a science, then, "theology" was reduced to "religious studies," with a concentration in ethics, psychology, and sociology.

It is worth noting that all of the paragons of the Enlightenment were reared in evangelical homes and churches. Unwittingly, pietism and rationalism conspired to drive out orthodoxy by pitting reason against faith, doctrine against practical experience and morality, and the external means of grace (the church and its formal ministry of Word and sacrament) against the inner life of the individual believer.[76]

If God transcends our rational investigation, the existence of "God" is predicated for Kant on the basis of *practical reason* (the focus of his second *Critique*).[77] At first, it sounds as if Kant is affirming the orthodox maxim that God is known by us not as he is in himself but as he reveals himself in his works. In fact, he even

---

71. Walsh, *The Modern Philosophical Revolution*, 41, 47.

72. Kant, *Religion within the Boundaries of Mere Reason*, Gesammelte Schriften, 6:202.

73. Lewis White Beck, *A Commentary on Kant's Critique of Practical Reason* (Chicago: Univ. of Chicago Press, 1960), 256.

74. Immanuel Kant, "Preface to Second Edition," in *Critique of Pure Reason* (trans. Norman Kemp Smith; 2nd ed.; New York: St. Martin's, 1965), 29.

75. Ibid.

76. The close connection between pietism and the German Enlightenment is often noted by historians. See, for example, Peter Gay, *The Enlightenment: The Rise of Modern Paganism* (New York: Norton, 1995), 62, 291, 326, 328–29, 348, 351.

77. Kant anticipates the arguments in the first Critique, *Critique of Pure Reason*, in his earlier work, *The One Possible Basis for a Demonstration of the Existence of God* (Lincoln: Univ. of Nebraska Press, 1979).

employs the distinction between archetypal and ectypal theology.[78] However, where orthodoxy grounded ectypal theology in historical revelation (viz., Scripture), Kant grounded it in autonomy: the self's inner sense of moral duty — "and it cannot first come to us either through inspiration or through tidings communicated to us, however great the authority behind them."[79] The moral law within, not the external gospel revealed miraculously from heaven, was normative for Kant. The only way forward is to presuppose God as a transcendental category necessary for moral action — practical reason, not pure reason. Typical of non-Christian thought, autonomous rationalism (certainty) is founded on an irrational leap, demanded by practical rather than rational necessity.

Kant was not consistent with his own method. "In a famous inconsistency," notes John E. Wilson, "Kant says that the (transcendent) 'thing in itself' is the unknown nonsensible 'cause' of an object."[80] How could Kant know that something possesses the capacity for *causing* things if it is inherently unknowable? In spite of the "learned ignorance" of this position, it turns out that Kant actually thought he knew a good deal more than his method allowed. Kant's transcendental method presupposed a host of doctrines that he believed *must* be true if we are morally responsible creatures. Besides God's existence, the immortality of the soul and the gradual moral improvement of humanity in this life and the next are (he thinks) necessary presuppositions of practical reason.

Kant also seems to know a lot about what cannot be true, given the presuppositions of moral reason. On this basis of practical reason, it cannot be true that humans are born in original sin, and there is no need for a divine Redeemer, his atoning sacrifice, justification by grace through faith, and gracious regeneration. In fact, these doctrines are subversive of moral (practical) reason.[81] The Christian teachings concerning Christ's bodily resurrection and ascension create enormous philosophical problems by claiming that, instead of being freed from material existence, the immortal soul is bound to its body forever. Again we are simply told

---

78. Immanuel Kant, *Lectures on Philosophical Theology* (ed. Allen W. Wood; trans. Gertrude M. Clarke; Ithaca, N.Y.: Cornell Univ. Press, 1986), 23.

79. Immanuel Kant, *Religion and Rational Theology* (ed. and trans. Allen W. Wood and George di Giovanni; Cambridge: Cambridge Univ. Press, 1996), 14.

80. John E. Wilson, *Introduction to Modern Theology: Trajectories in the German Tradition* (Louisville: Westminster John Knox, 2007), 29.

81. Kant, *Religion and Rational Theology*, 76–97, 104–41. The effects of grace, miracles, mysteries, and means of grace do not belong essentially to pure religion (96). Thus, "the *dogmatic* faith which announces itself to be a *knowledge* appears to reason dishonest and impudent ..." (96). Reason — including practical reason — cannot incorporate within it anything "supernatural," since this is beyond our concepts and experience (96). "It is totally inconceivable, however, how a rational human being who knows himself to deserve punishment could seriously believe that he only has to believe the news of a satisfaction having been rendered for him, and (as the jurists say) accept it *utiliter* [for one's advantage], in order to regard his guilt as done away with.... No thoughtful person can bring himself to this faith" (147). "Faith in a merit which is not his own, but through which he is reconciled to God, would therefore have to precede any striving for good works, and this contradicts the previous proposition" (148). Christ's example, rather than the dogmas concerning his unique person and work, is consistent with practical reason (149).

that this violates "the hypothesis of the spirituality of the rational beings of this world"—ironically, Kant's own ecclesiastical faith of the Enlightenment, which he universalizes as the metanarrative of pure reason.[82] These doctrines (i.e., the Christian gospel) belong to "the external cover" that should never be confused with the "pure religion" of inner morality.[83] The former are "based on faith in a particular revelation which, *since it is historical*, can never be demanded of everyone" (emphasis added).[84]

I have already referred to the tendency of modern thought to "demythologize" the Christian story in terms of nonhistorical principles (rational, ideal, ethical, or existential). Hans Georg-Gadamer goes so far as to suggest that modern hermeneutics arose out of an explicit concern for "the liberation of interpretation from [church] dogma."[85] Whatever we find in the Bible that comports with "pure religion" (universal morality) is acceptable, and whatever we find that speaks of God's miraculous intervention in history is merely the mythological husk of "ecclesiastical faith."

Reflecting this approach, Kant insists that even the Bible must be read "in a sense that harmonizes with the universal practical rules of a pure religion of reason."[86] Demonstrating once more the ironic similarity of mystical enthusiasm and rationalism, Kant says that this approach places the Spirit above the letter of Scripture.[87] This misreading of 2 Corinthians 3:6 pervades modern philosophy. It was already anticipated by Gnostics and radical mystics like Eckhart, whose Spirit–letter dichotomy was invoked directly by the radical Anabaptist leader Thomas Müntzer against Luther.[88]

Paul's contrast is between the written law that condemns us apart from Christ and the gospel that the Spirit reveals to us in Christ. By contrast, in the interpretation of the enthusiasts, "Spirit" refers to the inner core of religion: its morality

---

82. Ibid., 157.

83. Ibid., 123.

84. Ibid., 141.

85. Hans-Georg Gadamer, *Truth and Method* (2nd. ed.; trans. Joel Weisenheimer and Donald G. Marshal; New York: Continuum, 1994), 176.

86. Ibid., 142.

87. Ibid., 144, 284.

88. Thomas Müntzer, "The Prague Protest," in *The Radical Reformation: Cambridge Texts in the History of Political Thought* (ed. and trans. Michael G. Baylor; Cambridge: Cambridge Univ. Press, 1991): All the parsons have is "the mere words of Scripture" (2). God speaks to pure hearts "in his own person" and "this is then the paper and parchment on which God does not write with ink, but rather writes the true holy Scripture with his living finger, about which the external Bible truly testifies" (4). "I pledge on my highest honor that I have applied my most concentrated and highest diligence in order that I might have

or obtain a higher knowledge than other people of the foundations on which the holy and invincible Christian faith is based" (9). Lacking new revelations, ministers "gobble whole the dead words of Scripture and then spit out the letter and their inexperienced faith (which is not worth a louse) to the righteous, poor, poor people" (6). All believers should have new revelations: "The office of the true shepherd is simply that the sheep should all be led to revelations and revived by the living voice of God..." (6-7). The true, secret, and inborn "word" (in contrast to the "outer word" of Scripture and preaching) "arises from the abyss of the soul" and "springs from the heart" ("Sermon to the Princes," in *The Radical Reformation*, 20). According to Anabaptist scholar Thomas N. Finger, Müntzer proclaimed a higher (inner) spiritual authority, "surpassing even Scripture's" (Thomas N. Finger, "Sources for Contemporary Spirituality: Anabaptist and Pietist Contributions," *Brethren Life and Thought* 51, no. 1-2 [Winter/Spring 2006]: 37).

(Kant/Lessing), spiritual experience (Schleiermacher), and absolute reason (Hegel). As such "Spirit" is universal. "Letter," however, refers to the particular and historical expressions of religion, such as the Bible. Basically, "Spirit" and "letter" are interpreted in Platonic—even Gnostic—terms, associated with the upper world and lower world, respectively.

Routinely today, polls and surveys of contemporary religious views reveal the popularity of being "spiritual but not religious": believers in God—even in Jesus as supreme idea or example—but not committed to the "externals" of religion, such as church membership, creeds, preaching, and sacraments. True faith or spirituality is a private, inward, and moral disposition that lies at the core of every religion. This universal experience of the divine unity of all things cannot be identified with a particular revelation or creed or be put into words. Whenever we encounter these popular assumptions, they are in large measure the continuing legacy of Kant—which is itself an extension of a line of medieval and Protestant radicalism. The Reformers called this "enthusiasm" (God-within-ism).

The "one thing in our soul which, if we duly fix our eye on it," cannot help but instill wonder, says Kant, is "the moral law within."[89] Consequently, the chief end of humanity is the ethical kingdom of God, in which every person fulfills his or her moral duty.[90] He argued that whatever Jesus teaches that is in conformity with the moral law is acceptable to practical reason, but we would have known this without his life and ministry.[91] Everything in Christianity that pertains to supernatural revelation is but the outer garment that may be stripped from the inner core of universal morality that unites all genuine religious experience.[92]

Already the "demythologizing" project is well underway: that is, trying to interpret the miraculous accounts in the Bible as provoking a higher knowledge or way of being in the world rather than as referring to actual events in the past. In fact, in a famous interchange with Bultmann, Julius Schniewind posed exactly the right question: "Has the invisible ever been made visible, and if so, where?... And the only answer is the Christian answer—the invisible God has entered into our visible

---

89. Ibid., 93.

90. Ibid., 132–35.

91. Immanuel Kant, *Religion within the Limits of Reason Alone* (trans. Theodore M. Greene and H. H. Hudson; New York: Harper and Bros., 1960), esp. chs. 3–4. For a sympathetic—even laudatory—yet carefully researched treatment, see Allen W. Wood, *Kant's Moral Religion* (Ithaca, N.Y.: Cornell Univ. Press, 1970), esp. ch. 5.

92. The covenantal outlook of the Bible binds Jews and Gentiles together through faith in Christ. This covenant of grace runs through both Testaments. However, the Greek spirit triumphs over the "Jewish element" in Kant and in much of

philosophy and theology in his wake. Kant's judgment that the dogmatic and cultic elements of religion are the superstitions of "ecclesiastical faith" draws him into an explicit criticism of "Jewish faith," which he says "stands in no essential connection" with Christianity (*Religion and Rational Theology*, 154). Judaism only awakened from its own dogmatic slumbers "when much foreign (Greek) wisdom had already become available to this otherwise still ignorant people, and this wisdom presumably had had the further effect of enlightening it through concepts of virtue and, in spite of the oppressive burden of its dogmatic faith, of making it ready for revolutions which the diminution of the priests' power ... occasioned" (156).

world."[93] So even before tackling the question of *faith* and reason, the real problem for modernity is the relationship of *history* and reason. Like the thought of deists more generally, Kant's thought is simultaneously characterized by hypertranscendence (an unknowable God) and hyperimmanence (the divinity of the inner self as a moral legislator).[94]

G. F. W. Hegel (1770–1831) tried to resolve the inconsistencies in Kant's thinking, rejecting (among other things) Kant's distinction between unknowable noumena and knowable phenomena. For Hegel, everything that exists in reality is rational. Reason must draw itself away from the noisy clamor of historical particulars toward participation in the "passionless calm of purely thinking knowledge."[95] In the transition from Kant to Hegel we see the pendulum from dualism to monism in mid-swing.

Far from denying rational access to constitutive truth concerning God, Hegel regarded the Christian religion as the summit of *finite representations* of his own *infinite and absolute system*. For Hegel, "speculative" is the highest compliment, whereas for his Lutheran and Reformed forebears, it was a term of derision. He was convinced he knew the "absolute system" of knowledge that contained the whole and its parts.[96] Hegel believes that, far from being beyond rational access, his system makes it possible to know God as he is in his inner being, "no longer concealed and secret." "The development of the thinking spirit only began with this revelation of divine essence. It must now advance to the intellectual comprehension of that which originally was present only to the feeling and imagining spirit."[97]

It should be noted that the paragons of German idealism (such as Schelling, Schlegel, Hegel and Schopenhauer) were students of ancient Gnosticism, Kabbala, and radical mystics like Meister Eckhart (1260–1328) and Jacob Böhme (1575–1624), the latter of whom Hegel hailed as "the first German philosopher."[98]

---

93. Julius Schniewind, "A Reply to Bultmann," in *Kerygma and Myth: A Theological Debate* (ed. Hans Werner Bartsch; London: SPCK, 1953), 50. Schniewind points out that Bultmann's "demythologization" project is hardly new. "Modern man is by no means the first to feel the difficulty of accepting it [the gospel]. The great majority of mankind have always been ready and willing enough to accept a vague and general belief in God which makes no specific demands upon them, but the more definite Christian belief in Christ they prefer to reject as myth. The cultural scorn of a Celsus and the coarse ribaldry of the nineteenth and twentieth centuries are at one in this" (51).

94. See Allen W. Wood, "Kant's Deism," in *Kant's Philosophy of Religion Re-examined* (ed. P. Rossi and M. Wreen; Bloomington: Indiana Univ. Press, 1991), 1–21.

95. Karl Löwith, *From Hegel to Nietzsche* (trans. David E. Green; New York: Columbia Univ. Press, 1991), 28.

96. Hegel regarded Schleiermacher's "feeling of absolute dependence" as pure subjectivity—"the genuine objectivity of truth is annulled" (G. W. F. Hegel, *Lectures on the Philosophy of Religion* [ed. Peter C. Hodgson; New York: Oxford Univ. Press, 2008], 157). "As soon as mental content is placed into feeling, everybody is reduced to his subjective point of view" (G. W. F. Hegel, *Reason in History* [trans. Robert S. Hartman; New York: Macmillan, 1956], 17).

97. Hegel, *Reason in History*, 17.

98. There is perhaps no better study of Hegel's relationship to Gnosticism than Cyril O'Regan, *The Heterodox Hegel* (Albany, N.Y.: SUNY Press, 1994). See also Ernst Benz, *Mystical Sources of German Romantic Philosophy* (Pittsburg: Pickwick, 1983); Glenn A. Magee, *Hegel and the Hermetic Tradition* (Ithaca, N.Y.: Cornell Univ. Press, 2001).

In a further step toward Hegel, F. C. Oetinger (1702–1782), a pastor and devotee of Böhme, various Anabaptist mystics, and Emmanuel Swendenborg, wrote:

> The spirit contains all within itself; to a certain degree reason exalts the whole to the level of an abstract idea and at the time of the Golden Age one will find true to the highest degree what is, after so many false definitions, the true definition of knowledge, the true knowledge. The quintessence of divine things, the base of which is in the spirit and which then spreads into the reason. God buried it in the spirit. The seeker has with God's help to take it in to the reason. Reason must be in accord with the spirit, and the spirit by the same token must be in accord with God.[99]

Invoking Joachim of Fiore, Oetinger promises that in the third age, "analytic learning will be replaced by intuition."[100] Everyone will know the whole meaning of history intuitively rather than merely parts. In fact, all disciplines will become one and revelation will be the fountain of law, the arts, and the sciences.

To these indigenous Western resources were added generous doses of Indian Buddhism. Anonymous, but probably written by Hegel, "The Oldest Systematic Programme of German Idealism" anticipates the imminent dawn of the new age. The Age of the Spirit will bring "through reason itself the overthrow of all superstition, and the persecution of the priesthood, which recently pretends to reason."

> Then comes absolute freedom of all spirits, which carry the intellectual world in themselves, and which may not seek God or immortality *outside themselves*. Finally, the idea that unites all others, the idea of beauty, taking the word in a higher Platonic sense.... We must have a new mythology, but this mythology must be in service of the ideas; it must be a mythology of reason ... then will rule the universal freedom and equality of the spirits! A higher spirit sent from heaven must establish this new religion among us. It will be the last and greatest work of humanity.[101]

For Hegel, Absolute Spirit realizes itself in the historical process of thesis, antithesis, and synthesis. Thus, conflict is always the necessary passage to higher development. Nevertheless, the real winner is always infinite spirit over finite matter. The thesis (matter) is contradicted by its antithesis (spirit), and the latter goes on its way, fueled by its destruction of the particular.[102]

---

99. Quoted in Benz, *Mystical Sources of German Romantic Philosophy*, 40.

100. Ibid.

101. Anonymous, "The Oldest Systematic Programme of German Idealism," in *The Early Political Writings of the German Romantics* (ed. and trans. Frederick C. Beiser; Cambridge: Cambridge Univ. Press, 1996), 4–5. See also Beiser's masterful study, *German Idealism: The Struggle Against Subjectivism, 1781–1801* (Cambridge, MA: Harvard University Press, 2002).

102. Hegel, *Reason in History*, 20: "To begin with, we must note that world history goes on within the realm of Spirit.... Physical nature does play a part in world history.... But Spirit, and the course of its development, is the substance of history....

[Humanity] constitutes the antithesis to the natural world; he is the being that lifts itself up to the second world. We have in our universal consciousness two realms, the realm of Nature and the realm of Spirit... One may have all sorts of ideas about the Kingdom of God; but it is always a realm of Spirit to realized and brought about in man."

He adds, "The nature of Spirit may be understood by a glance at its direct opposite—Matter. The essence of matter is gravity, the essence of Spirit—its substance—is Freedom" (22). This writing may also be found in Hegel's *Lectures on the Philosophy of Religion*; Vol III: *The Consummate Religion* (ed. Peter C. Hodgson; trans. R. F. Brown, P. C. Hodgson, and J. M Stewart; Berkeley: Univ. of California Press, 1985).

For Hegel, religion is "the innermost region of spirit."[103] It is here where finite spirit realizes its unity with Absolute Spirit. Drawing inspiration for his pantheism from radical mystics, Hegel writes, "Master Eckhart, a Dominican monk, says in one of his sermons: 'The eye with which God looks at me is the eye with which I look at Him, my eye and His eye are identical. In justice, I am weighed in God and He in me. If God did not exist, I would not exist; and if I did not exist, He would not exist either.'"[104] "The Divine, and hence religion, exists for the Ego," so that Hegel can even say that "man is an end in himself," yet "only by virtue of the divine in him — that which we designated at the outset as Reason, or, insofar as it has activity and power of self-determination, as Freedom."[105] "Without the world," Hegel concluded, "God is not God," since God (Absolute Spirit) is identical with the process of history.[106] Once more we recognize the recurring pattern in the "overcoming estrangement" paradigm: a fundamental dualism striving toward an ultimate monism that brings the truest (inmost) self back home to its original unity with divinity.[107]

Because Hegel identified Absolute Spirit with the unfolding of history to ever-higher stages through thesis, antithesis, and synthesis, he was able to inspire contradictory programs. Robert S. Hartman summarizes the ironies of his influence:

> The influence of his philosophy confirms his thesis that universal Reason, through men, shapes history. The fate of this philosophy bears witness to its dialectical form. The most rational and religious philosopher, Hegel unchained the most irrational and irreligious movements — Fascism and Communism. Often regarded as the most authoritarian, he inspired the most democratic: Walt Whitman and John Dewey. The philosopher who equated what is with what ought to be, he released the greatest dissatisfaction with what is; and thus, as the greatest conservative, unchained the greatest revolution... [Some] became conservatives and so-called "Hegelians of the Right." Other thinkers accepted the form of his philosophy and opposed its content. They became revolutionaries and "Hegelians of the Left." The two opposing factions met finally in the mortal embrace of Stalingrad.[108]

Walsh explains concerning Hegel's interpretation of Christianity:

> His Jesus never even suggests that men and women believe in him, for he has come to invite them to believe in themselves. They are called to hearken to "the holy law of their reason, to pay attention to the inner judge of their hearts, to conscience, a measure that is also the measure of divinity" (*Theologische Jugendschriften*, 119).... Hegel reads the message of Jesus as salvation from the dead letter of the law to obtain the living reality of spirit, a perfect bond of friendship between those who

---

103. Hegel, *Reason in History*, 24.
104. Hegel, *Philosophy of Religion*, 17.
105. Hegel, *Reason in History*, 45.
106. Hegel, *The Christian Religion*, 235.
107. Hendrikus Berkhof comments, "One wonders whether

in the end Hegel's monism is a dualism of God and the historical world of human beings after all" (*Two Hundred Years of Theology* [Grand Rapids: Eerdmans, 1989], 54).
108. Robert S. Hartman, "Introduction" to G. F. W. Hegel's *Reason in History*, xi.

share the same spirit. "Faith is a knowledge of spirit through spirit, and only like spirits can know and understand one another" [*Early Theological Writings*], 239.... There can be no suggestion of Christ's actions as an external sacrifice for the sins of mankind.[109]

According to Hegel, "The infinite cannot be carried in this vessel."[110]

Following mystics and radical Anabaptists like Thomas Müntzer, Hegel contrasted the "Spirit" with the "letter" in terms reminiscent of Kant and Lessing. In fact, "The complaint against the dead letter of historical religion is at the core of the project in which Hegel is engaged," notes Walsh. Focusing on the person of Jesus Christ—his divinity—distracts the community from the pursuit of "spirit."

> Spirit cannot be manifest in the material, because it is the nature of spirit to be that which can be known only through itself. Clothing spirit in a miraculous display is really its concealment. Miracles are a forced conjunction of spirit and body that are essentially opposites.... Such a purely physical resurrection has now become an obstacle to the inner resurrection of his spirit within existence.... Spiritual union can occur only inwardly.[111]

Similar to Kant and Lessing, Hegel writes, "The series of different religions which will come to view, just as much sets forth again only the different aspects of a single religion, and the ideas which seem to distinguish one actual religion from another occur in each one."[112] The relation of spirit to spirit is "complete immediacy."[113] "The divine nature is the same as the human, and it is this unity that is beheld" in the revelation of Christ.[114]

If the object of theology is really ethics for Kant, and Absolute Spirit for Hegel, then for the father of modern theology, Friedrich Schleiermacher (1768–1834), it is universal religious experience, especially "the feeling of absolute dependence." The revolution in epistemology—the "turn to the self"—now dominated the theological academy, and increasingly the churches of Europe and eventually the West generally. As Idealism blended with Romanticism, *feeling and willing* replaced both Kantian *doing* and Hegelian *knowing*. Louis Dupré's verdict concerning Goethe could be as easily applied to Romanticism generally: It "epitomizes the Promethean attempt to create a cultural universe which would absorb transcendence itself to a point where the very distinction between immanent and transcendent ceased to make sense."[115] Courageous souls broke down Kant's barricade against the supposedly unknowable *noumena*, seeking not to know God according to his accom-

---

109. Walsh, *The Modern Philosophical Revolution*, 82, 85–86.

110. Ibid., 86.

111. Ibid., 89.

112. G. F. W. Hegel, *Phenomenology of Spirit* (trans. A. V. Miller; Oxford: Clarendon, 1977), 417.

113. Ibid., 459.

114. Ibid., 460.

115. Louis Dupré, *A Dubious Heritage: Studies in the Philosophy of Religion after Kant* (New York: Paulist, 1977), 9.

modated revelation but to discover their own unity with divinity. Neo-Platonist, Gnostic, and radical mystical speculations of a decidedly pantheistic tendency shaped the German idealists and Romantics in England (William Blake) and America (Transcendentalists like Emerson, Thoreau, Hawthorne, and Melville).

Yet none perhaps was more explicit in his debt to this "overcoming estrangement" paradigm than the German Romantic-Idealist Friedrich Schelling (1775-1854). In the conflict between darkness and light, divinity and humanity struggle together to emerge in moral struggle. God has fully overcome this antithesis (darkness or evil) in himself, but we haven't yet. Evil is the primordial chaos even from which God emerges as positive good, overcoming this dark side in his own nature.[116] God suffers with creation as spirit overcomes the strife of matter.

Behind Schelling's Romantic philosophy is the recurring pagan myth of primordial chaos (darkness, evil) being overcome by the higher gnosis. In fact, he realizes that this is "a concept which is common to all the mysteries and spiritual religions of ancient times."[117] "It is the path to glory. God leads human nature down no other path than that down which God himself must pass.... Spirit exists from that which it is not and can arrive there only by submitting to the pain of its incarceration. All creation arises from the unconsciousness whose bonds it must burst in a moment of 'divine and holy madness.'"[118] In *The Ages of the World*, he wonders, "Perhaps the one is still coming who will sing the greatest heroic poem, grasping in spirit something for which the seers of old were famous: what was, what is, what will be. But this time is not yet come."[119] When this day does dawn, we will know God not according to his works, but as he is in himself.[120]

The nineteenth century was characterized by a tug-of-war between neo-Kantians and neo-Hegelians. In between, there were occasionally alternative voices, such as Søren Kierkegaard (1813–1855), who wanted to turn thought back toward actual existence and to reaffirm the infinite-qualitative distinction between God and humans. However, the Kantian barricade against constitutive knowledge of God through revealed truth remained firmly in place. Reacting against a moribund state church as well as Hegelian rationalism, Kierkegaard lodged the essence of Christian faith in inwardness and subjectivity.[121] The criticism of orthodoxy by the pietists remained influential in the thinking of those who had been reared in it.

---

116. F. W. J. Schelling, *Philosophical Inquiries into the Nature of Human Freedom* (trans. James Gutmann; New York: Open Court, 2003), 373.

117. Ibid., 403–4.

118. F. W. J. Schelling, *The Ages of the World* (trans. Jason M. Wirth; Albany: SUNY Press, 2000), 101–2.

119. Ibid., xl.

120. Walsh, *The Modern Philosophical Revolution*, 165. See also Frederick C. Beiser, *German Idealism: The Struggle against Subjectivism (1781–1801)* (Cambridge, Mass.: Harvard Univ. Press, 2002), ch. 8 (esp. 588–95).

121. Søren Kierkegaard, *Concluding Unscientific Postscript* (trans. David E. Swensen and Walter Lowrie; Princeton, N.J.: Princeton Univ. Press, 1971), 201.

Kierkegaard spoke for many when he wrote, "There is only one proof of the truth of Christianity and that, quite rightly, is from the emotions."[122]

Criticism became the constant refrain of liberal neo-Kantian theologians, such as Albrecht Ritschl (1822–1889), who dismissed the most important Christian doctrines on the basis that they were metaphysical. Again the circularity of such reasoning is obvious, at least to us now in retrospect: *Christian doctrines make objective truth-claims about God; but God cannot be an object of our knowledge; therefore, such doctrines are unfounded speculations.*[123] Adolf von Harnack (1851–1930) sought a gospel "freed from all external and particularistic elements."[124] Rather, the gospel is for Harnack simply the law of love.[125] "How you are to maintain yourself in this life on earth, and in what way you are to serve your neighbor, is left to you and your own liberty of action. This is what the apostle Paul understood by the Gospel and I do not believe he misunderstood it."[126] Whatever the gospel is, it is definitely not a dogma.[127]

At most, said these theologians, these doctrines express, symbolize, or otherwise represent eternal truths about something else, a higher and more universal reality. In truth, such criticism is actually more metaphysical and more susceptible to critique as a metanarrative than is orthodox Christianity. That is because "Greeks"—ancient and modern—point away from God-in-the-flesh toward the unspoiled vision of eternal truths, while in the gospel the eternal Father focuses the world's attention on the eternal Word made flesh: "This is my beloved Son, with whom I am well pleased; listen to him" (Mt 17:5).

The liberal religion is subjective from beginning to end, whether this subjectivity is considered in individualistic or communal terms. Accordingly, the Bible is regarded as Holy Scripture because of the unique place given to it by the community. Jesus Christ is the "Son of God" for the same reason.[128] Sin is not objective guilt, provoking an objective wrath of God, but is a subjective experience of alienation and lack of dependence on God. Christ redeems us by the powerful impression of his personality, his sense of dependence on and nearness to God, and the persuasive force of his moral purpose. Is it any wonder that the modern atheists

---

122. Søren Kierkegaard, *The Journals of Søren Kierkegaard* (1849) (trans. and ed. Alexander Dru; New York: Oxford Univ. Press, 1938), 314.

123. Concerning Ritschl, Herman Bavinck offers this insightful observation: "His real intention, after all was no other than—following in Kant's footsteps—to make a complete separation between religion and science. But he failed to make the separation complete. In religion he continued to incorporate theoretical elements, bound it to history, adopted a biased viewpoint in favor of Christianity, made exegesis and the history of dogma subservient to a system, and fundamentally remained a dogmatician" (*Reformed Dogmatics*; Vol 1: *Prolegomena* (trans. John Vriend; Grand Rapids: Baker, 2003], 70).

124. Adolf Harnack, *What Is Christianity?* (trans. Thomas B. Saunders; New York: Harper Bros., 1957), 74.

125. Ibid., 70–77.

126. Ibid., 116.

127. Ibid., 146.

128. Albrecht Ritschl, "Instruction in the Christian Religion," in Ritschl, *Three Essays* (trans. Philip Hefner; Philadelphia: Fortress, 1972), 229.

from Feuerbach to Freud diagnosed religion as neurosis, an illusory projection of the self on the basis of wish-fulfillment?

Even more radical than Kant's system, a movement centered at Marburg known as Neo-Kantianism profoundly shaped a generation of thinkers, including theologians such as the liberal pietist Wilhelm Herrmann and especially his pupil, Rudolf Bultmann.

Another bright student of Herrmann's, who eventually broke more radically from his mentors, was Karl Barth (1886–1968). Barth recognized that the whole liberal program could only mean that theology is a species of comparative religion or anthropology. Unless God is the object of theology, and the self-revealing subject, Barth properly emphasized, theology cannot be considered a true science—that is, a field of genuine knowledge.[129] We will consider in later chapters whether Barth himself offers a coherent and scriptural account of this claim, but he decisively shifted the focus back to God as the revealed object and revealing subject.

In our own day, hypertranscendence (deism and atheism) continues its secret pact with hyperimmanence (pantheism and panentheism).[130] This is what happens when we refuse to receive our existence and knowledge as a gift and to be judged and justified by the Stranger who calls out, "Adam, where art thou?" Either we can know and master reality as gods, or our existence is nothing more than an illusion and our knowledge a collage of advertisements and slogans. However, Christianity teaches that because God exists, there is absolute (archetypal) truth, even if our knowledge of that truth is—and remains into eternity—finite, creaturely, and accommodated revelation from God.

In many ways, postmodern skepticism about the possibility of language conveying transcendent truth and meaning reflects the exhaustion of modern rationalism, a sense of having had high hopes dashed. If we cannot have absolute (archetypal) knowledge, then we cannot even have relative (ectypal) knowledge. If we cannot know as God knows, then we cannot even know as creatures. As a result, in Nietzsche's words, "'Interpretation,' the introduction of meaning—not 'explanation'.... There are no facts, everything is in flux, incomprehensible, elusive; what is relatively most enduring is—our opinions."[131] Modern philosophy merely mined Christian doctrines and transformed them into "concepts" and "categories." In truth, they are merely *metaphors*.[132] "Truths are illusions which we have forgotten

129. This emphasis especially dominates volume 1 of Barth's *Church Dogmatics*, on the doctrine of the Word of God (eds. G. W. Bromiley and T. F. Torrance [Edinburgh: T&T Clark, 1975]).

130. This analogy of a secret pact between irrationalism and rationalism is articulated by Cornelius Van Til in *The Defense of the Faith* (Phillipsburg, N.J.: P&R, 1979), 125–26.

131. Friedrich Nietzsche, *The Will to Power* (ed. Walter Kaufmann; trans. Walter Kaufmann and R. J. Hollingdale; New York: Random House, 1967), 327.

132. Friedrich Nietzsche, *Philosophy and Truth: Selections from Nietzsche's Notebooks of the Early 1870s* (ed. and trans. Daniel Breazeale; Atlantic Highlands, N.J.: Humanities Press, 1979), 83.

are illusions."[133] Metaphors do not refer to extralinguistic "reality" but merely to other metaphors.[134]

Nietzsche's vehement protest against Christianity as "Platonism for the masses" makes a certain kind of sense in the light of the modern forms of religion in his day. Scheiermacher had declared, "True religion is sense and taste for the Infinite."[135] Herrmann asserted, "Personal, living Christianity . . . is inaccessible to that method of knowledge which holds in material affairs."[136] Why wouldn't such a religion become irrelevant for those who lacked a sufficient appetite for "the Infinite"? Yet this is surely something other than the biblical faith, which sympathizes more with Nietzsche than with many modern theologians when he argues, "When one places life's center of gravity not in life but in the 'beyond'—in nothingness—one deprives life of its center of gravity altogether." If our goal is the flight of the soul from this world, "Why communal sense, why any further gratitude for descent and ancestors, why cooperate, trust, promote, and envisage any common welfare?" Nietzsche asks.[137]

Yet this confusion of Christianity with Platonism (and German idealism) Nietzsche never seems to have questioned. He could only offer sweeping generalizations, contrasted with his equally sweeping (and extreme) alternatives. "Christianity is the hatred of the senses, of joy in the senses, of joy itself."[138] He could even concede, "Oh, I understand this flight up and away into the repose of the One."[139] What kept him from making this move was his hatred for "that overleaping of this world" that occurs in religion.[140] Yet Nietzsche's own version of the apocalyptic dawn of the Age of the Spirit—the reign of Dionysus over Christ—became the inspiration of tyrants throughout the twentieth century.[141]

---

133. Ibid., 84.

134. Ibid., 87.

135. Friedrich Schleiermacher, *On Religion: Speeches to its Cultured Despisers* (trans. John Orman; London: Paternoster, 1893), 36.

136. Wilhelm Herrmann, *The Communion of the Christian with God* (New York: G. P. Putnam's Sons, 1913), 11.

137. Nietzsche, *The Antichrist* (trans. Walter Kaufmann, in *The Portable Nietzsche* [New York: Penguin, 1976], 618).

138. Ibid., 589. "This God has degenerated into a staff for the weak, the god of the poor, the sinners, the sick par excellence. The result of this is that the kingdom of God has been enlarged. Formerly it was only his chosen people . . . but now the kingdom has spread and is a ghetto kingdom" (585). Nietzsche celebrates the constant striving after nobility, strength, and superiority. The poor "Teuton" became a monk, "a 'sinner,' stuck in a cage, imprisoned among all sorts of terrible concepts . . . full of suspicion against all that was still strong and happy. In short, a 'Christian'" (*Twilight of the Idols*, in ibid., 502).

Instead of allowing the natural development of higher and nobler human life, it has encouraged sympathy for the weak and the suffering (ibid., 573). Michael Silk summarizes, "For Nietzsche, decadence is any kind of saying no to life; decadence is whatever defies and negates life, the real, and the world" (Michael Silk, "Nietzsche, Decadence, and the Greeks," *New Literary History* 35 no 4 [2004]: 594). Silk adds, "He regularly refers to the fondness for the "other world" as part of the emasculating of true existence. Freedom "means that the manly instincts which delight in war and victory dominate over other instincts, for example, over those of 'pleasure'" (*Twilight of the Idols*, in *The Portable Nietzsche*, 542).

139. Nietzsche, *Will to Power*, 112.

140. Ibid.

141. Harry Ausmus even includes Nietzsche in the line that leads from Joachim: "Although Nietzsche's language is different, he too believed in a three-stage view of history, consisting of the premoral, moral, and ultramoral ages." The third is the age of the Ubermensch, who "will complete the transvaluation of all values, by which the individual will arrive at a perfection which could not be otherwise achieved" ("Nietzsche and Eschatology," *JR* 58, no. 4 [1978]: 351–59).

However, at this point at least it was a Platonized form of religion that he was rejecting rather than the Bible's world-affirming narrative of creation, incarnation, redemption, resurrection, and the consummation of created reality. Not in a flight into a "beyond," away from the supposedly lower world, but in the arrival of the age to come; not in a renunciation of life here and now, but in the embrace of life as the anticipation of feasting with God and each other in joy, does Christian hope prove itself the only true rival of Platonism.[142]

From beginning to end, biblical faith is opposed to any notion of a world emanating from God's essence, with divine souls thrown mercilessly into bodies and the realm of appearances. God created a world distinct from himself out of loving freedom, not necessity. Sin is ethical (covenant-breaking), not ontological (a falling away from infinite Being). And redemption comes through this God's assumption of our humanity, fulfilling the covenant and bearing its sentence in our place, raised from death to the right hand of the Father, from which he will return to judge the living and the dead and make all things new. Gone, then, is Plato's "upper world" (as Nietzsche understands it), which forever consigns this "lower" world of embodied living nothing more than a shadowy realm. "God" is not an abstract, dualism-grounding principle, for God transcends even the highest heavens. Indeed, heaven itself is part of creation, and God is no less at home in the world that he made than in any other part of his creation.

Nietzsche loves the real world of ever-changing dynamism over Plato's realm of unchanging forms, but God loves this world more. In fact, in joy he created its diverse forms of life and his providence keeps history's ever-moving, ever-changing dynamism in play. It was not by the self's escape from this world and embodiment to achieve union with the upper world, but by God's becoming flesh that salvation has been brought to the earth.

Christianity can only concur with Nietzsche's insistence, against much of ancient and modern philosophy, that reason adheres in reality itself, not above it or in speculative reason. That which *actually happens* in this world, not what philosophers argue *must* be the case, should always take precedence.[143] For that very reason, the gospel's claims must be allowed to disorient and reorient our presuppositions about God and the world. However, Nietzsche's fondness for this world of genuine play is thwarted by his affirmation of the basically Buddhist "eternal recurrence of the same." Each cycle may have its own power, but it is always a repetition.By contrast, the Bible keeps pilgrims moving toward the "new thing" that God will do in history, something that has continuity with the past, yet is altogether different.

---

142. I engage Nietzsche's criticism of Christianity as "Platonism for the Masses" in *Covenant and Eschatology: The Divine Drama* (Louisville: Westminster John Knox, 2002), 20–46.

143. Nietzsche, *Twilight of the Idols*, in *The Portable Nietzsche*, 558.

By surrendering to the eternal cycle of nature, Nietzsche shows himself a greater disciple of Plato than of Paul. This world is affirmed, but at the expense of any transcendent source and meaning. Following in Nietzsche's wake, nihilism wants to affirm becoming over being, but there is no purposeful origin or goal in which "becoming" even makes sense. This world and its history are affirmed, but for what reason and with what practical effect, since it is simply the theater of competing wills to power? There is plurality, but it is random, lacking any ultimate unity or purpose that is willed by someone other than the sovereign self or the sovereign state.[144]

For all of his revolutionary flourishes, Nietzsche (and, hence, postmodernism) did not break with modernity but encouraged the consummation of the Enlightenment program. Mark C. Taylor writes, "The ceaseless play of opposites renders transition permanent and passage absolute."[145] Packed into this laconic statement is both the idea that there is a journey without origin or destination and that, despite his profession of atheism, "God" *is* this pointless becoming (rendering "passage *absolute*"). Following in Nietzsche's wake, this is but a small step beyond Hegel, who had already identified God with the process of history. All that was left was to remove Hegel's deterministic *telos*—that is, the inexorable destiny of a history that is already fully present (immanent) throughout its development.

However, neither Nietzsche nor his heirs have actually overthrown Platonism and Idealism; they have merely reversed its dichotomies and therefore continue to work within its ambit.[146] Nietzsche's preference for symbols and eternal truths over Christianity's historically based dogmas betrays the fact that he was the real Platonist. If Christianity were truly "Christian," he argued, it would join the Buddhist way of life: "it is a means to being happy."[147] "A god who died for our sins: redemption through faith; resurrection after death—all these are counterfeits of true Christianity for which that disastrous wrong-headed fellow Paul must be held responsible."[148] The Reformation was the consummation of this hatred for everything noble, meritorious, and praiseworthy in humanity.[149]

It is remarkable that in this vast and highly influential trajectory of idealism, from Kant to Nietzsche, the ontological source or principle of infinite reality behind the objects of sense remains invisible and unknowable. No more than

---

144. For a masterful treatment of the "one and many" problem in culture from a Trinitarian theological perspective, see Colin Gunton, *The One, The Three, and the Many: God, Creation and the Culture of Modernity* (Cambridge: Cambridge Univ. Press, 1993).

145. Mark C. Taylor, *Erring: A Postmodern A/Theology* (Chicago: Univ. of Chicago Press), 11.

146. Nietzsche, *Will to Power*, 98. For example, we may discern not only the dualism but the preference even for Plato's

"upper world" in Nietzsche's comment. Although he called Christianity "Platonism for the masses," Nietzsche asserts, "Precisely that which is Christian in the ecclesiastical sense is anti-Christian in its essence: things and people instead of symbols; history instead of eternal truths; forms, rites, dogmas instead of a way of life."

147. Ibid., 87.

148. Ibid., 101.

149. Ibid., 114.

the sovereign noumena (concepts) for Kant is the sovereign will visible to us for Nietzsche. The infinite principle on which our existence and knowledge depends is itself unknowable. Contemporary philosopher Hilary Putnam is exactly right when he says that "almost every philosopher makes statements which contradict his own explicit account of what can be justified or known."[150] Hegel asserts, "The spiritual as such cannot be directly confirmed by the unspiritual, the sensible [i.e., that which is known by the physical senses]."[151] Schleiermacher's universal "feeling" that grounds existence can only be experienced, never revealed once and for all in history. Nietzsche's "will" is absolute, but never visible.

In sharp contrast, the gospel tells us that "the Word became flesh ... and we beheld his glory." The one by whom the worlds were made has become one of us, yet without surrendering his transcendence. The Eternal Logos was apprehended by ordinary sense experience and his resurrection from the dead in history was a public event that secured the restoration of the fallen creation.

CONCLUSION

Central to a biblical worldview, over against its rivals, is the qualitative distinction between God and the world. This distinction holds with respect not only to ontology (reality), but to epistemology (how we know it). In his existence and knowledge, God transcends us. At no point do the lines intersect, not even "spirit to spirit." Our souls are no more divine than our bodies. Only the Triune God is eternal, infinite, and omniscient.

And yet, God is not only transcendent in majesty, but immanent in loving in his covenantal condescension. Just as his transcendence is not sacrificed to a supposedly direct and immediate relation of our spirit to divinity, God's immanence is more thorough than philosophical dualism allows. God did not merely assume a human soul, but our flesh in its entirety. God does not speak secretly in our spirits, but publicly in our human language, and the creaturely elements of water, bread and wine. Jesus Christ is not a symbol of the ontological unity of God and humans; he is the unique incarnation of God in our humanity—and retains the distinctness of his two natures in one person. Ever transcendent, he is nevertheless Immanuel, "God with us."

One implication of the Creator-creature (i.e., archetypal-ectypal) distinction is that although human beings, more than other creatures, strain naturally toward

---

150. Hilary Putnam, *Realism and Reason: Philosophical Papers* (Cambridge: Cambridge Univ. Press, 1983), 3:226.

151. Hegel, *The Christian Religion* (AAR Texts and Trans-lations 2; ed. and trans. Peter C. Hodgson; Atlanta: Scholars Press, 1979), 19.

transcendence, they, no less than other creatures, never know reality as pure object. Only God sees reality in independent objectivity. God alone knows things as they really are in themselves. Beyond time and space, though moving freely within both, God knows the world as other than himself—not as inherently antithetical, but as qualitatively different. There is no essential antithesis between spirit and matter or even between God and humanity, so there is no higher synthesis between them. There is *absolute difference* between Creator and creation and *relative difference* within creation itself. Neither divine nor demonic, creation is good even in its difference from God. We are worldlings. Whatever excellencies pertain to our nature and office as God's image-bearers, we know the world only as participants, never as detached observers.

The problem of relating subject and object, which in our Western culture goes all the way back to the Greeks and became especially acute in modernity, is aroused in the first place by a presupposition that at least in that supposedly divine part of us (the soul or mind) we transcend the world. Obviously, this means that although we are subjects and participants in the world with respect to our bodily and sensual constitution, we should aspire to rise above this realm of appearances and by this ascent of mind contemplate things as they really are in themselves. Pure objectivity is attained by the unity of our mind with divinity. This presupposition binds the otherwise disparate programs of modernity (as in ancient Greek philosophy), even where they disagree about how to attain this.

All of this symmetry is broken, however, with the biblical doctrine of *ex nihilo* creation, where the line is drawn not between spirit and matter, but between Creator and creature. If we are worldlings even in our intellectual and spiritual aspect, then we do not—in fact, cannot—transcend the world of phenomena. The world—even souls, minds, or wills—is not related naturally or necessarily to God. Yet God is free to relate the world—in all of its fullness—to himself. We swim in the world like fish in the sea, but of God we sing, "The sea is his, for he made it, and his hands formed the dry land" (Ps 95:5).

Only in biblical covenantalism is the God-world relation truly analogical. Especially in French poststructuralism (associated with Emmanuel Levinas and Jacques Derrida), the point has been well made that all of the philosophical systems we have considered contain with them the seeds of their own de(con)struction. As the Reformed apologist Cornelius Van Til recognized, modern rationalism is grounded in irrationalism.[152] Although at first blush antithetical, the two non-Christian paradigms we have considered share more in common than either does with "meeting a stranger." They are united by the view that *being and knowledge are univocal for God*

---

152. Van Til, *Defense of the Faith*, 123–31.

and creatures. In other words, they confuse the Creator with the creature, either by divinizing humanity or by humanizing deity. Whether by seeking to deepen Platonism or overturn it, modernity does not know how to treat a stranger, especially if that stranger is God. Thus, the liturgy of two voices — the speaking Lord and the answering servant — is aborted. And all we hear are the clashing voices of competing wills — humanity talking to itself, creating itself, and fulfilling itself through its own speech.

It is never a question of *whether*, but of *which* theology and metaphysics. The most dangerous metaphysics is one that pretends that it is not one. The demand for sovereignty, in whatever version it takes, lies at the heart of both of the alternatives to "meeting a stranger." Heralds of the first paradigm follow Apollo — the god of order — to ascend from the realm of shadows to the heights of spirit, while devotees of Dionysus — the god of pagan revelry — descend into the depths with Nietzsche to make their own fire.

Either way, we refuse to hear and receive our existence and knowledge from the Sovereign Creator who speaks. One is reminded of Paul's contrast in Romans 10 between "the righteousness that is based on the law" and "the righteousness based on faith": the one ascends to the heavens as if to bring God down; the other descends into the depths as if to bring Christ up from the dead — when all the while God is as near as the Word that is preached. In the Christian *ontology*, we are created and sustained by God's Word; in the Christian *epistemology*, we interpret God and the world through this same Word, either as rebels in the covenant of works or as children of God and co-heirs with Christ in the covenant of grace.

DISCUSSION QUESTIONS

1. Compare and contrast the three ontological paradigms explored in this chapter. Which is more consistent with a biblical worldview and why?
2. How does panentheism differ from pantheism?
3. How is Plato's epistemology an application of his ontology?
4. Discuss the importance of Kant's approach to the question of knowing God, especially as it influenced later thinkers. Can you recall conversations you have had with people who assume (perhaps unwittingly) Kant's approach?
5. What is the significance of the archetypal-ectypal distinction, as well as the doctrine of analogy, in Christian epistemology?

Chapter Two

THE CHARACTER OF THEOLOGY: A THEORETICAL OR A PRACTICAL SCIENCE?

Having articulated the broadest of our concentric circles—a Christian view of reality and knowledge in general—we are ready to move closer to our target by concentrating on the character of *theology* as a specific discipline.

In the sixth book of *Nicomachean Ethics*, Aristotle identified five intellectual habits. As the term is employed in philosophy and theology, a *habit* is a disposition or aptitude for a particular activity, even if one has never actually done anything with it. For example, a person might have a habit for music, while never having actually learned how to sing or to play an instrument. Each habit is suited to its own particular science, depending on the object that a given field investigates:

- *technē* (Latin, *ars*/English, art): used in making things
- *phronēsis* (*prudentia*/prudence): used in doing things (*phronēsis* is roughly equivalent to ethics)
- *epistēmē* (*scientia*/science): most characteristic of discursive (acquired) knowledge
- *nous* (*intellectus*/intellect): most characteristic of intuitive (innate) knowledge
- *sophia* (*sapientia*/wisdom): knowledge of highest objects (via contemplation)

These are not watertight compartments, of course. For example, an engineer or sculptor may be guided by various intellectual aptitudes (habits), but *technē* dominates. Discerning the dominant habit or way of knowing, one could then determine whether a given science was theoretical or practical. For example, Plato and Aristotle considered philosophy to be superior to other sciences because it was theoretical rather than practical.

Most Protestant scholastics held that theology was the most mixed of all the sciences, drawing on all of these ways of knowing, but that it was best characterized as *sophia*—wisdom from heaven. However, these theologians understood wisdom in terms that differed significantly at certain points from the classical (Greek) heritage. In pursuing a specifically biblical definition, they observed that theology cannot be easily classified as either a theoretical or a practical discipline. Before we can address this question, we need to reevaluate our Western assumptions that create this problem in the first place.

I. Seeing as Certainty: The Way of Vision

In addition to these five types of intellectual activity, Aristotle emphasized (like his mentor, Plato) that the highest—*sophia*, from which *philosophy* ("love of wisdom") is named—can only be attained through constant *theōria* (contemplation).[1] In the previous chapter, I noted in passing the dominance of visual metaphors for thinking in our Western heritage. For Greek philosophy generally, this contemplation is a vision of the eternal forms—not just gazing upon beautiful things (mere appearances), but the Beatific Vision of the Good in its essence.[2] *Contemplatio* is the Latin term for the Greek word *theōria*, and both come from verbs meaning "to see/behold." *Comprehend* is a transitive verb from Latin (*com + prehendere*), meaning "to grasp or seize with." Much like Eastern thought, our Western grammar for knowing is bound up with *seeing*, an intellectual vision that is clearer and more certain than the observation of realities available to physical sight.[3] In this way, knowing is an act of a subject seizing, grasping, dissecting, comprehending, mastering, and possessing its object.

Plato contrasted philosophers with "art fanciers and practical people," whose vocations keep them imprisoned in the realm of appearances. It makes sense in

---

1. Aristotle, *Nicomachean Ethics* (trans. Martin Ostwald; Englewood Cliffs, N.J.: Prentice Hall, 1962), 10.8.291–95.

2. This common assumption held, even though Plato and Aristotle diverged significantly on the "location" of the eternal forms. For Plato, the forms transcend the material world, while for Aristotle they are present in the matter itself. For example, an individual human being is such because the form of "humanness" determines the constitution of matter. The most obvious contemporary analogy would be the genetic code of particular species and individuals. In his famous painting *The School of Athens*, Raphael has Plato pointing up and Aristotle pointing outward. It is not surprising that Platonism generates rational-

ism and idealism while empiricists have favored Aristotle.

3. *Theory* is derived from the Greek *theōria* (seeing/looking). *Speculation* comes from the Latin *speculari*, "to look out" or "to examine." In fact, a *specula* was a watchtower. To be introspective is "to look within." The list of visual metaphors for knowing seems practically endless. When we understand something, we exclaim, "I see!" We speak of views, worldviews, outlooks, and inspection. Knowing is a kind of scrutinizing and observing. Even *contemplate* comes from the Latin verb *contemplari*, "to gaze attentively."

Plato's scheme: a botanist studies imperfect copies (trees) rather than eternal truth (Tree), but an artist is still further down the ladder, making copies of copies! And why would one want to be a historian, dedicating one's whole life to the realm of ever-changing shadows? For centuries of pagan and Christian thought, *theory* meant this understanding of knowledge as a kind of direct, immediate, and glorious vision of the Archetypal Truth in its very essence. And it stood in sharp contrast with practice, which belonged to the realm of embodied existence. *The problem of relating theory and practice is already provoked by this ontological dualism.*

Although there were movements in Second Temple Judaism that spawned ascetic groups (such as the Essenes), they were Torah centered and devoted to hearing the Scriptures and learning and following the wisdom of the Teacher of Righteousness. Whatever we may say about this group's beliefs, it is significant that Second Temple Judaism's most monastic community consisted of *hearers* rather than *seers*.

Changes came, however, through the influence of the first-century philosopher Philo of Alexandria, who attempted to blend Judaism with Platonism. The same influences shaped early Christian monasticism in both the East and the West—*theōria* as the highest form of union with God (*theōsis*) of which believers are capable. Obviously, this privileges the eye over the ear and intellectual union over the believer's union with Christ in the flesh. It is a testimony to the transforming power of the gospel that ancient Christian writers developed a richly incarnational theology in spite of the Platonic/Neoplatonic dualism that is evident throughout their spiritual writings.

The twentieth-century German philosopher Hans Blumenberg traced the genealogy of the metaphor of vision in Western philosophy back to "a dualistic conception of the world" found, for example, in Parmenides' poem *The Way of Opinion* but made common coinage by Plato.[4] In the Christian ascetic and mystical traditions of both the East and the West, the intellect (or soul) strives to attain "the Beatific Vision" by intense contemplation.[5] In the medieval West, monastic orders were divided between "the contemplative life" and "the active life," although some orders strove to keep them together. The same dualistic tendency may be discerned in Protestant history, with debates over the priority of faith and practice, doctrine and life, knowing and doing.

---

4. Hans Blumenberg, "Light as a Metaphor for Truth," in *Modernity and the Hegemony of Vision* (ed. David Michael Levin; Berkeley: Univ. of California Press, 1993), 32.

5. Rudolf Bultmann observes this connection in his discussion of revelation in medieval theology. "It is the ancient idea of *theōria*. Contemplation (*visio*) is not only the highest and authentic form of knowledge but the highest mode of existence.... The *visio* is pure contemplation, pure possession of what is present. Unlike willing, the attitude of contemplation does not point beyond itself but is fulfilled, whereas willing is unfulfilled. The Christian life is thus the *bios theōrētikos*.... God is construed as world, for God's existence is proved from the world, as in the Stoics. God is the rationally intelligible world-principle or world-all" (*What Is Theology?* [Fortress Texts in Modern Theology; ed. Eberhard Jüngel and Klaus W. Müller; trans. Roy A. Harrisville; Minneapolis: Fortress, 1997], 79). One need not adopt Bultmann's alternative (existentialism) in order to share his dubiousness about this approach.

Despite its Christian transformations and permutations, vision/light becomes the master metaphor for knowledge and experience from antiquity through the medieval era and on into the modern age, suitably named the Enlightenment.[6] The "inner light" draws together rationalists and mystics throughout history, including the modern age.[7] This inner light is more interior and autonomous and, therefore, considered more trustworthy and certain than any external source of truth.

As Blumenberg points out, the modern appropriation of the metaphor of light is in many respects indistinguishable from ancient Gnosticism, identifying "the inner light of the mind" with a primal divine light dispersed and trapped in matter.[8] Where Scripture uses the metaphor of light for an ethical, eschatological, covenantal, and historical transition from sin to redemption, Western philosophy interpreted light and darkness as referring to the upper world of mind/spirit and the lower world of matter/history. Redemption is assimilated to the idea of secret enlightenment (*gnōsis*) — a return of light to itself, the inner spirit's deliverance from its imprisonment in matter.[9]

This description seems to fit the pedagogical ascent of mind in Origen, where purgatory is regarded as a process of spiritual education and enlightenment through various reincarnations until finally every soul (including the devil) is united with God. Origen's teachings were rejected by the church, and in battles with the Gnostics, the second-century bishop Irenaeus was especially alert to the assimilation of the gospel to Greek philosophy in his confrontation with the Gnostics. Augustine also tried to transform this scheme by filling the categories with Christian content. However, the scheme itself remained deeply entrenched. Even for Augustine, the flight upward is also a flight inward.[10]

In the biblical creation account, the *word* comes before the *light*. In fact, the light is not eternal and the darkness is not a primordial chaos (dark matter), but both are created, material bodies (the sun to rule the day, moon and stars to rule the

---

6. Blumenberg reminds us of the significance of "the closed, medieval chamber in Descartes' portrayal of the turning point in his thinking: 'I remained for a whole day by myself in a small stove-heated room.'" "Here the relation of the room to the world is still completely medieval," says Blumenberg; [Descartes] had closed himself off from the outside in order to turn inward (Blumenberg, "Light as a Metaphor," 39).

7. Paul Tillich, *The History of Christian Thought* (ed. Carl E. Braaten; New York: Simon and Schuster, 1968), 317–18. Among the many historians pointing out this relationship, see Peter Gay, *The Enlightenment: An Interpretation* (New York: Norton, 1966), 1:62, 291, 326–29, 348, 350.

8. Transforming biblical stories and characters into something more palatable to Greek pagans, Gnosticism was a second-century heresy that taught salvation by inner enlightenment. Trapped in matter by an evil creator-god (identified as Yahweh),

the soul ascends from the realm of embodied "appearances," returning to its eternal home. There were several varieties of Gnosticism.

9. Blumenberg, "Light as a Metaphor," 40.

10. Paul Ricoeur, *History and Truth* (trans. Charles A. Kelbley; Evanston, Ill.: Northwestern Univ. Press, 1965), 111: "Let us think about the scope of the revolution in the history of thought that this text [Irenaeus's *Against Heresies*] represents in relation to that Neoplatonism in which reality is a progressive withdrawal, an ineluctable beclouding that increases as we descend from the One, which is formless, to the Mind, which is bodiless, to the World Soul, and to souls which are plunged into matter, which itself is absolute darkness." Ricoeur asks, "Are we sensitive to the distance between this text" and Neoplatonic speculations?

night). Augustine also transformed this metaphor, away from seeing *into* the light in the direction of seeing *in* the light. In other words, light illumines the word.[11] It is an act of grace experienced in conversion.[12] In fact, Blumenberg goes so far as to judge, "Never before and never since has the language of light been handled in such a subtle and richly nuanced way" as it is by Augustine.[13] However, Augustine still privileged the metaphor of vision/light over hearing/word, and therefore interior over exterior illumination.

Throughout the Enlightenment era, philosophers speculated that their own systems were evidence that the "third age" had arrived at last.[14] This Age of the Spirit became identified with the Age of Reason, and, as Paul Tillich observed, the inner light of mystics became the chief metaphor.[15]

Unlike thinking and seeing, communicating is an inherently social activity. The birth of modernity is symbolized by Descartes' lonely isolation in his apartment, meditating (contemplating) without conversing. He regarded every belief tainted by communally shared, historical, and embodied mediation as a toxic corruption of thought. Only by cleansing his thought of all such opinions, he imagined, could he enter the antiseptic purity of his inner chamber. Bizarrely, he assumed that through this self-imposed exile from reality he could master knowledge of it. "Inevitably, 'individualism' came into its own as the socializing effects inherent in voice as sound were minimized," notes Walter Ong. This is the "devocalization of the universe," reaching its apex in Isaac Newton.[16] Especially with the advent of deism, with the image of God as an architect rather than an actor and communicator in history, devocalization led to the impersonalization of the cosmos.

In an age of advertising and entertainment icons, as well as the Internet, treating knowledge as a kind of spatial-visual mapping and mastery of objects is only intensified. In addition, words are less trusted (and often less trustworthy), while we are perpetually tantalized by the icons that are "pleasing to the eye, and also desirable for gaining wisdom" (Ge 3:6 NIV).

---

11. Blumenberg, "Light as a Metaphor," 43.

12. Ibid., 44.

13. Ibid., 42.

14. For example, Lessing writes, "Perhaps even some enthusiasts of the thirteenth and fourteenth centuries had caught a glimmer of this new eternal gospel, and only erred in that they predicted its arrival as so near to their own time. Perhaps their 'Three Ages of the World' were not so empty a speculation after all.... Only they were premature. They believed that they could make their contemporaries, who had scarcely outgrown their childhood, without enlightenment, without preparation, at one

stroke men worthy of their third age." The path to maturity leads from "a sensual Jew" to "a spiritual Christian" (Gotthold Ephraim Lessing, "The Education of the Human Race," in *Lessing's Theological Writings* [trans. Henry Chadwick; Palo Alto, Calif.: Stanford Univ. Press, 1967], 97).

15. Tillich, *History of Christian Thought*, 317–18. The "inner light," Tillich suggests, binds disparate groups and movements: Platonism, Neoplatonism, Hinduism, medieval mysticism, radical Anabaptist sects, the Quakers, and the Enlightenment.

16. Ong, *Presence of the Word*, 72.

II. "Hear, O Israel …": Covenantal Speech

In Platonism, the world emanates eternally, necessarily, and silently from the One. In Genesis, however, the world comes into being at a definite point in (or with) time, freely, through God's speech. It is not only that human beings are created with the capacity for speech; they exist as those whom God has called into being and "worded" as his covenant creatures. The covenantal liturgy of hearing and answering is evident already in creation. Every creature knows itself as the being that the Great King has worded it to be. God prepares a place by speaking, "Let there be!" and even the "response" of inanimate creation can be correlated metaphorically with this antiphonal (speaking and response) liturgy of the covenant (Ps 19:1 – 4).

Yet it is only humans who, as God's royal image bearers, reply with specific intentionality and in fulfillment of their specific commission — "Here I am," a recurring Hebrew idiom.[17] The differences between "Here I am" and "I see" are obvious. In the one, I place myself at the disposal of the covenant Lord, submitting to his Word; in the other, I am in possession. In the "Here I am" of the covenant servant, one is no longer a detached spectator of the map, but is placed on the map — or rather, in the real world that is created by God's speech and filled with its own covenantal conversation — either as a faithful servant or as a treasonous rebel. After their disobedience, Adam and Eve tried in vain to flee God's presence. However, space is never neutral, as if anything could exist apart from God's Word, and the God of Scripture dwells *in the midst of* his people, *speaking,* not *in front of* them, as an *object of gaze.*

Blumenberg notes:

> For Greek thought, all certainty was based on visibility. What *logoi* referred back to was a sight with form …, i.e., *eidos* [idea]. Even etymologically, "knowledge" and "essence" (as *eidos*) are extremely closely related to "seeing." *Logos* is a collection of what has been seen. For Heraclitus, eyes are "more exact witnesses than ears"…. For the Greeks, "hearing" is of no significance for truth and is initially nonbinding. As an imparting of *doxa* [opinion], it represents an assertion that must always be confirmed visually.
>
> For the Old Testament literature, however, and for the consciousness of truth it documents, seeing is always predetermined, put into question, or surpassed by hearing. The created is based on the Word, and in terms of its binding claim, the Word always precedes the created. The real reveals itself within the horizon of its signification, a horizon allocated by hearing.[18]

---

17. I develop this point in *Lord and Servant: A Covenant Christology* (Louisville: Westminster John Knox, 2005), esp. ch. 4.

18. Ibid., 46.

The clash between these two worldviews is evident in Philo's attempt to "translate" the Jewish emphasis on *hearing* into the Greek category of *seeing*.[19]

Jewish scholar Jon Levenson observes that in contrast to the allegorizing ascent of mind practiced by Philo, the rabbinical tradition was committed to "the exposition of the plain sense of scripture."[20] Through this covenantal discourse, "God beckons with one hand and repels with the other."[21] He adds, "In its quality of indivisible charm and threat, [the Sinaitic experience] is eminently exotic, lying outside the boundaries of what is familiar."[22]

In other words, we might say that it is more like "meeting a stranger" than "overcoming estrangement." In the process of summoning us, the covenant Lord renarrates our lives, calling us away from our dead-end plots and casting us in his unfolding drama. Called by God to a destination that he does not yet know, Abraham does not *see* the truth; he *believes* the promise that he has *heard* and is justified. This same pattern is evident in the calling of the prophets and the apostles.

As Levenson points out, it is in telling and retelling this story of creation and exodus that Israel receives its identity and passes it down from generation to generation. "In the words of the rabbinic Passover liturgy (Haggadah), 'Each man is obliged to see himself as if he came out of Egypt.'" Far from Plato's exhortation to remember the eternal forms the mind has forgotten by its contamination with the body and time, biblical "remembering" is identifying one's own life story with the history of God's covenant with his people. Unlike the religions of the world, Israel derives meaning "not from introspection, but from a consideration of the public testimony to God."

> The present generation makes history their story, but it is first history. They do not determine who they are by looking within, by plumbing the depths of the individual soul, by seeking a mystical light in the innermost reaches of the self. Rather, the direction is the opposite. What is public is made private. History is not only rendered contemporary; it is internalized. One's people's history becomes one's personal history. One looks out from the self to find out who one is meant to be. One does not discover one's identity, and one certainly does not forge it oneself. He appropriates an identity that is a matter of public knowledge. Israel affirms the given. The given that is affirmed in the covenant ceremony is not a principle; it is not an idea or an aphorism or an ideal. Instead, it is the consequence of what are

---

19. Ibid., 46–47. Stephen H. Webb offers another example, from Philo's *Life of Moses*, which shifts the concentration from the voice to the burning bush and goes so far as to assert that the voice was seen. "Why is God's voice visible?" asks Webb, offering Philo's answer: "Because whatever God says is not words but deeds, which are judged by the eyes rather than the ears" (*The Divine Voice: Christian Proclamation and the Theology of Sound* [Grand Rapids: Brazos, 2004], 182). Evidently, words were not to be regarded as deeds. This is the danger of the hermeneutics of signification that we find not only in Philo but in Origen and Augustine. Whereas according to the biblical outlook we accomplish things by speaking, in this worldview words "stand for" or "re-present" (visual metaphors) the reality signified.

20. Jon D. Levenson, *Sinai and Zion: An Entry into the Jewish Bible* (San Francisco: HarperSanFrancisco, 1985), 7.

21. Ibid.

22. Ibid., 16.

presented as the acts of God.... Israel began to infer and to affirm her identity by telling a story.[23]

In this interpretation, genuine knowing—covenantal knowing—occurs not by looking away from history toward interior contemplation but by internalizing that very history so that it is part of one's own body and experience. (Circumcision in the old covenant and baptism in the new covenant literally mark this bodily-social character of knowing.) The "self"—understood as an autonomous individual—does not exist, but is already bound up with tradition, history, and community. "To be sure, the story has implications that can be stated as propositions," Levenson adds. "For example, the intended implication of the historical prologue is that YHWH is faithful, that Israel can rely on God as a vassal must rely upon his suzerain. But Israel does not begin with the statement that Yahweh is faithful; she infers it from a story," and one that depends on the particulars of time and place.[24]

This supports my contention in the introduction that theology is the lived, social, and embodied integration of drama (story), doctrine, doxology, and discipleship. *I am suggesting that hearing the covenantal Word of our Lord is the source of that dethronement of the supposedly sovereign self and of the integration that subverts the disintegrating logic of Western dualism and individualism.*

Obviously, receiving one's identity from one's God, through a story that one hears, is different from determining one's own identity through idols that the worshiper has created and therefore controls. Levenson says that "there is considerable truth" in the generalization that "whereas the Greeks thought with the eye, the Hebrews thought with the ear." In fact, he adds, in comparison with the Homeric epics, in the Hebrew Bible "visual description is usually of little account." "We do not know, for example, even the color of Abraham's hair or Moses' height. This is because in Israel, the focus is upon the word of God, not the appearance of man and his world (1Sa 16:7)." Although the other sense is involved, "the dominance of ear over eye does seem to be characteristic of ancient Israelite sensibility."[25] Significantly, especially in the prophets, even the exhortation to "see" or "behold" is a call from God to observe what he has done in history and to receive his interpretation of these acts.

Whereas intellectual vision draws thought away from history, Ong points out that historical truths must be told and the tellers are not private seers but public witnesses. Biblical religion is based on historical events: not on eternal principles or natural cycles, but on the report of God's mighty deeds in creation, providence, judgment, and redemption.[26] Instead of dividing the body of Christ into higher and

---

23. Ibid., 39.
24. Ibid.

25. Ibid.
26. Ong, *Presence of the Word*, 10.

lower realms, into those dedicated to the contemplative (theoretical) life in lonely isolation and those who pursue the active (practical) life in the world, covenantal knowing places all believers in the center of the action where God acts and interprets by his Word.

Whereas intellectual vision demands an ascent from worldly particulars to an eternal but impersonal "One," the interest in history arises in biblical faith out of the particular events of being summoned by a person:

> God calls to Abraham, "Abraham!" and Abraham answers, "Here I am" (Ge 22:1). A similar thing happens to Jacob ... (Ge 31:11). As Erich Auerbach has made clear in the first chapter of his *Mimesis*, this direct and unexplained confrontation—a verbal assault on a given person by God—is not the sort of thing one meets with in Greek or other nonbiblical tradition. God's word impinges on the human person as a two-edged sword.
>
> In the prophets, the sense of the word of God reaches particular intensity.... The word is not an inert record but a living something, like sound, something going on.[27]

Reflecting their origins in an oral culture, even Homer's epics were conveyed from generation to generation through social events of singing and play. The past was present not only in written records but in living speech. Paul's admonition to "let the word of Christ dwell in you richly" through "psalms and hymns and spiritual songs" (Col 3:16) reflects this social context. The goal of such singing in public worship was not individualistic, either in terms of mystical contemplation or self-expression, but the enveloping of the community in the gospel. Speech is always a happening, an event that not only unites the mind, heart, and body of individuals but also establishes a communion of hearers and speakers. It is not the eternal music of the spheres but the history of the covenant that God's people recite in their songs of praise.

"Abraham knew God's presence when he heard his 'voice,'" Ong notes, and the same could be said of Adam and Eve fleeing the voice of Yahweh. Although there may be presence without speech, there is no speech without presence. The voice "simply conveys presence as nothing else does." We might say that we are in someone's presence, but it would be odd to say that we are in front of someone's presence. Sight wanders and dissects, while hearing binds.

In short, nothing conveys personal presence and the command-response pattern of a covenantal relationship more than speech. The search for the "Beatific Vision" is a lonely pursuit, attempted only by the most serious philosopher or monk. However, the Beatific Word gathers a society of hearers who are redeemed and reshaped by their Master's utterance.

---

27. Ibid., 12.

Even when one reads a text that was originally a public and social event, the dynamics are different, allowing "withdrawal into oneself," which is why reading silently to oneself was virtually unheard of until quite recent times.[28] Private reading of Scripture, for example, is indispensable for meditating on certain passages and truths. Nevertheless, it is subordinate to the public preaching that socializes individual readers into a covenant community. Only then is the private reading held in check and informed by the hearing of the wider communion of saints. Bound by fewer rules than writing, oral speech is also more accessible to every class. Ong writes, "Sound unites groups of living beings as nothing else does."[29] This is not to marginalize the other senses, but our sense of sound requires "a certain distance" while inviting reciprocal communication. Real community comes into being with a common language.[30]

Where visual metaphors dominate, theologies of glory characteristically follow. The history of Western philosophy and its dominant visual metaphors privilege theologies of glory, ancient and modern.[31] Reason (theoretical contemplation) comprehends that which is certain through "clear and distinct ideas" (Descartes; see ch. 1, "The Sovereign Self," pp. 58–59), but practical questions provoked by our captivity to the realm of appearances distract us from this goal. We are most certain of what we grasp with intellectual vision (the necessary truths of reason), but beliefs derived from what we have heard (the accidental truths of history) are, at most, mere opinion. It is no wonder that autonomy is the correlate: I am certain of what I myself possess by intellectual vision, but I should not believe what I am told by someone else, even if that external authority happens to be God.

III. HEARING IS BELIEVING

Whether ideas or carved images of wood and stone, the idol is just "there," a given, crafted by its worshiper. By contrast, speech surprises—which is why the idols are often mocked in the prophetic literature for not being able to talk. The worshiper is in control; in fact, the idol is the worshiper's self-reflection. With idolatry, the object of worship is passive and the worshipers are active, but speech announces the presence of the other. When the king speaks, the kingdom falls silent. What will be said? What will be the consequences for us, good or bad? Does he come in peace or in judgment? We are put on the receiving end of knowledge—and therefore, of

---

28. Ibid., 126.

29. Ibid., 122.

30. Ibid., 123–24.

31. Although he does not refer specifically to the theological implications, Jacques Derrida explores this genealogy with remarkable skill, especially in *Margins of Philosophy* (Chicago:

Univ. of Chicago Press, 1982). Derrida does not overstate things when he suggests, "The entire history of our philosophy is a photology" (quoted in John McCumber, "Derrida and the Closure of Vision," in *Modernity and the Hegemony of Vision* [ed. David Michael Levin; Berkeley: Univ. of California Press, 1982], 235.)

our redemption. The object of our worship—the triune God—is alive, and we are mere recipients of his living and active Word. "So faith comes from hearing, and hearing through the word of Christ" (Ro 10:17)—specifically, the glad tidings, "the gospel of peace" (Eph 6:15).

Unlike an object on which we gaze, which is subject to our control and dissected by our probing, the voice of someone approaching affirms both absence and presence, the distance and the approaching nearness of the other. The stranger does not stand off in the distance but comes near and summons me. I am responsible for what I hear—a command or a promise; I am not a master.[32] I can no longer construct a theology, project my own experience, offer my own speculations about the nature of a perfect being, or present a critical reflection on praxis. Rather, I am *given* a theology. The Stranger speaks and, in doing so, judges and saves.

It is significant that when Adam and Eve hear God's approach in judgment, they do not offer the proper covenantal response, "Here I am," but instead flee from God's presence in dread. Just as they disobeyed God when the saw that the fruit was pleasing to the eye and desirable to make one wise, they fled from God when they saw that they were naked and were ashamed. In both cases, they refused to place themselves at the disposal of their covenant Lord, hearing and obeying his Word. When God calls Abram, he issues a faith-creating promise of a future that defies all that the patriarch already sees or knows as possible: "And he believed the LORD, and he counted it to him as righteousness" (Ge 15:6). When God calls to Moses from the burning bush, Moses answers, "Here I am" (Ex 3:4); and after forgiving Isaiah's sins, God calls the prophet to proclaim his Word. He responds, "Here am I! Send me" (Isa 6:8). Like Sarai and Abram, Moses and Isaiah, Mary of Nazareth finds no basis in her experience or reason to justify the astonishing announcement of the angel that she will bear the Savior of the world. God's Word has priority over any existing state of affairs that she can see either intellectually or empirically. She replies, "Behold, I am the servant of the Lord; let it be to me according to your word" (Lk 1:38).

"Here I am" corresponds to the Word of the covenant Lord; "I see!" expresses our possession of reality. We hear promises; we see their fulfillment. So there is no abstract contradiction in the Bible between hearing and seeing, but there is always a time and place for both. Seeing is not *believing*; it is *possessing*. The strict prohibition of visible representations of God was intended to save God's people for "the image [*eikôn*] of the invisible God" (Col 1:15) in the incarnation of the Son. However, when the Word became flesh in history, the disciples could recount their eyewitness testimony in the most vivid terms as the reality that they saw, heard, and

---

32. I treat this contrast more fully in *People and Place: A Covenant Ecclesiology* (Louisville: Westminster John Knox, 2008), 37–98.

touched with their hands (1Jn 1:1–4). This is not intellectual vision, but sensual vision: seeing with the bodily eye, not merely with the inner mind. Jesus invited doubting Thomas to inspect his hands and his side for proof that he had been raised, eliciting the response, "My Lord and my God!" But Jesus replied, "Have you believed because you have seen me? Blessed are those who have not seen and yet have believed" (Jn 20:28–29).

Yet there *will* be a time when we will no longer believe what we hear. Faith and hope will yield to sight—full possession of the promised reality—and only love will remain as we behold God face to face (1Co 13:8–12).

For us now, *hearing is believing* (Ro 10:17). God still ratifies his covenant through his visible Word—baptism and the Lord's Supper. Nevertheless, until Christ returns to raise our mortal bodies to immortality, along with the wider creation, "we wait eagerly" (Ro 8:23). "Now hope that is seen is not hope. For who hopes for what he sees? But if we hope for what we do not see, we wait for it with patience" (vv. 24–25). Paul's contrast between the righteousness that is by works and the righteousness that comes through faith (Ro 10) unfolds the following logic:

The Righteousness that is by Works	Seeing	Our Ascent	Vision of Glory
The Righteousness that is by Faith	Hearing	God's Descent	Word of Promise

The demand for absolute epistemic certainty not only is idolatrous in its illicit demand for archetypal knowledge that belongs to God alone; it also reflects an overrealized eschatology—that is, a premature announcement that the consummation has arrived. One day there will be no need for faith or hope, but for now, God is still "re-wording" creation. Even as God speaks this evangelical Word into this present age, the new creation dawns among us, but it is still largely hidden. For now, "we walk by faith, not by sight" (2Co 5:7).

This point is elaborated in the systems of Protestant orthodoxy. Not only is our knowledge of the truth always ectypal because we are creatures; in our current condition, these systems argued, it is the ectypal theology of *pilgrims on the way* (*theologia viatorum*), not yet the ectypal theology of *glorified saints* (*theologia beatorum*). It is no wonder they referred to this knowledge of pilgrims as "our humble theology."[33]

---

33. Quenstedt in Luther Poellot, ed., *The Nature and Character of Theology: An Introduction to the Thought of J. A. Quenstedt* (St. Louis: Concordia, 1986), 40. A Lutheran theologian, Quenstedt observed that this definition was largely drawn from Reformed systems: this theology of pilgrims (*theologia viatorum*) "by Franciscus Junius and Alsted is called humble theology and our [theology], by others the theology of the church militant." See also Herman Bavinck, *Reformed Dogmatics* (Grand Rapids: Baker, 2004), 28.

This faith is tested throughout our lives (Jas 1:3; 1Pe 1:7). As the object of our faith proves himself faithful throughout these trials, our faith grows. Even if we do not have God's personal revelation about why we are suffering or how he is weaving our trials into a hidden pattern, we do have the revelation of God's hidden purposes for us and for creation in Jesus Christ. God has demonstrated his faithfulness objectively, publicly, and finally in the resurrection of Jesus from the dead.

With the Reformation came a revolution from the dominance of Neoplatonist vision back to the biblical emphasis on the existence and knowledge of creaturely reality mediated by language. Whereas even Augustine subordinated hearing God speak to contemplative vision, Luther's *De servo arbitrio* (*On the Bondage of the Will*), Hans Blumenberg observes, "plays metaphors of the ear against those of the eye. The eye wanders, selects, approaches things, presses after them, while the ear, for its part, is affected and accosted. The eye can seek, the ear can only *wait*. Seeing 'places' things; hearing is placed.... That which demands unconditionally is encountered in 'hearing.' Conscience has a 'voice,' not light."[34]

Everything I have suggested thus far concerning the priority of hearing over seeing in this era of redemptive history was emphasized by the Protestant Reformers. In fact, Luther held closely to the biblical motif of all divine actions being mediated through God's Word. Oswald Bayer explains this view: "The new creation is a conversion to the world, as a conversion to the Creator, hearing God's voice speaking to us and addressing us through his creatures. Augustine was wrong to say that his voice draws us away from God's creatures into the inner self and then to transcendence."[35] In fact, the Westminster divines pointed out that God blesses the reading "but especially the preaching of the Word" of God as a means of grace since it is by this means that the Spirit confronts sinners in their self-enclosed existence, "driving them out of themselves, and drawing them unto Christ" (*Westminster Larger Catechism*, Answer 155). This Word calls us out of our subjectivity and renders us extrinsic, extroverted, and social creatures who hold fast to Christ in faith and to our neighbors in love.

Stephen Webb goes so far as to suggest that the Reformation represents "an event within the history of sound," an event of "revocalizing the Word."[36] Instead of a chiefly visual event—a theatrical display—that fills the spatial distance between transcendent Lord and the people separated by a screen, public worship became a verbal event. This ministry of the Word occurred not only in the sermon but in the public reading of Scripture, in the prayers and singing, in confession and absolu-

34. Hans Blumenberg, "Light as a Metaphor for Truth," in *Modernity and the Hegemony of Vision* (ed. David Michael Levin; Berkeley: Univ. of California Press, 1993), 48.

35. Oswald Bayer, *Living by Faith: Justification and Sanctification* (Grand Rapids: Eerdmans, 2003), 28.

36. Stephen H. Webb, *The Divine Voice: Christian Proclama-

tion and the Theology of Sound* (Grand Rapids: Brazos, 2004), esp. chs. 4 and 5. This is a superb treatment of the principal issues addressed in this chapter. See also Theo Hobson, *The Rhetorical Word: Protestant Theology and the Rhetoric of Authority* (Hampshire, U.K.: Ashgate, 2002).

tion—indeed, throughout the entire liturgy from God's greeting to the benediction. Even Communion was a vocal pledge from God which the whole covenant community received and to which it responded in celebration. "This follows," notes Webb, "from Calvin's belief that God's Word accomplishes what it commands. It is covenantal speech, active and full of life. Even in its stuttering, it has the power to give what it asks. God's Word called the world into being, and it continues to uphold the world through the speech of the Spirit-filled church."[37] Whereas medieval worship subordinated speech to sight, the Reformation (capitalizing on humanist concern for history and exegesis in the original languages) sought to expose the people to God's voice. "This was a verbosity caused not by the need to explain an image or to make a moral point. Rather, it was a verbosity intended to convey grace through sound."[38]

"Our Western philosophical tradition has given the intellect prominence among our human faculties," notes Oswald Bayer. "Luther, however, says that 'there is no mightier or nobler work of man than *speech.*' We are not rational beings first of all; we are primarily speaking beings."[39] This is not a slight point for Luther.[40] "For Luther everything depends upon the Bible; hearing, using, and preaching it as the living voice of the gospel (*viva vox evangelii*)."[41] This is in contrast to Augustine, for whom "the external Word is a sign (*signum*) that simply points us to the [thing itself] (*res*)."[42] Webb reminds us, "For Augustine … the Word that God speaks is heard internally before we give it an external voice.… Consequently, faith, like thought, begins in the interior recesses of the heart, where it is silent before it makes a sound."[43] Recall again Levenson's point above (see " 'Hear, O Israel,' " pp. 86–87) that for Judaism truth is public, coming to us from outside ourselves, and then affects us personally. The tendency of our Greek intellectual heritage is to reverse this movement, so that truth is first a silent, autonomous, and private thought or experience that we then express publicly through speech.

We may even detect in some of Augustine's reflections an anticipation of modern epistemology and hermeneutics, from Descartes to Schleiermacher. Yet for the Reformers, the relation is reversed: the Word is God's speech that comes from outside in, not from inside out. The external Word becomes internalized by the Spirit without ever losing its transcendent "otherness" as the voice of God rather than an echo of the inner self. This emphasis on the *verbum externum* (external Word) is simply a correlate of salvation by God in Christ *extra nos* (outside of ourselves).

---

37. Webb, *Divine Voice*, 159.
38. Ibid., 106.
39. Bayer, *Living by Faith*, 47.
40. See, for example, Martin Luther, *Luther's Works* (ed. and trans. Jaroslav Pelikan; St. Louis: Concordia, 1968), 35:117–24, 254, 359–60.
41. Bayer, *Living by Faith*, 45.
42. Ibid., 48.
43. Webb, *Divine Voice*, 131.

Whatever becomes visible *within* individuals and the community — repentance, faith, love, and other aspects of moral renewal — is the progressive result of this definitive declaration *outside* of them.

The Reformers regarded both Rome and the radical Protestants as "enthusiasts" because they tended to make the external Word subordinate to the internal word (inner light) of the believer. According to Luther:

> If you ask a Christian what the work is by which he becomes worthy of the name "Christian," he will be able to give absolutely no other answer than that it is the hearing of the Word of God, that is, faith. Therefore, the ears alone are the organs of a Christian man, for he is justified and declared to be a Christian, not because of the works of any member but because of faith.[44]

Therefore, preaching is not an indifferent medium but is deemed by God to be suitable to the delivery of a message that is itself saving news. Putting us on the *receiving* end of things, not only does justification come through faith alone; faith itself comes through hearing.[45]

"For Calvin as for Luther," John H. Leith observes, "'the ears alone are the organ of the Christian.'"[46] Calvin summarized, "When the Gospel is preached in the name of God, it is as if God himself spoke in person."[47] Leith elaborates, "The justification for preaching is not in its effectiveness for education or reform.... The preacher, Calvin dared to say, was the mouth of God." It was God's intention and action that made it effective. The minister's words, like the physical elements of the sacraments, were united to the substance: Christ and all of his benefits. Therefore, the word not only describes salvation but conveys it. "Calvin's sacramental doctrine of preaching enabled him both to understand preaching as a very human work and to understand it as the work of God."[48]

IV. THEORY AND PRACTICE

In view of this analysis so far, we may conclude that, strictly speaking, the Bible does not seek to integrate *theōria* and *praxis* but rather understands knowledge as an already integrated act of *acknowledgment* — thinking, feeling, and doing in one

---

44. Martin Luther, *Lectures on Titus, Philemon, and Hebrews* (vol. 29 of *Luther's Works*), 224, quoted in Webb, *Divine Voice*, 144.

45. This comparison between hearing and seeing is not meant to suggest that there is some magical quality to hearing or that God is bound by this medium. Rather, it is to say that God has bound himself to the spoken word as the *ordinary* method of self-communication. Like Augustine, many Christians would refer to their reading of Scripture as a moment of conversion. Furthermore, physical disabilities such as deafness are no obstacle to God's grace. Webb offers a well-informed treatment of this issue in *Divine Voice*, 51–55.

46. John H. Leith, "Calvin's Doctrine of the Proclamation of the Word," in *John Calvin and the Church: A Prism of Reform* (ed. Timothy George; Louisville: Westminster John Knox, 1990), 212.

47. Ibid., 211.

48. Ibid., 210–11.

simultaneous act. It is a covenantal act to acknowledge no other Lord and Savior but God in Christ. Faith is knowledge, but the sort of knowledge that is synonymously trust in a person through a report that this person has delivered through ambassadors. It is an act of putting oneself at the disposal of the speaker rather than of putting an object at the disposal of the examining subject. In biblical terms, to know God is to relate to God in faith as a covenant servant caught up in the drama and then in the doctrine, doxology, and discipleship that it generates. Theology is the "Amen!" of faith to God's character and his practical service to sinners in his redeeming grace.

In the light of these comparisons and contrasts, we are better able to address the question of this chapter. The dualism between practice and theory, faith and reason, pure religion and ecclesiastical faith, deeds and creeds, and countless other antitheses in modern thought is bound up with the fundamental dualism between the realm of spirit and the realm of matter, the intellectual ascent of vision versus the descent of God's Word to us in the flesh and in history. If we insist on the unwarranted presupposition that we can trust only that which we know as individuals immediately, intuitively, by an inner light, we will never believe that the highest truth can come to us as the telling of a story concerning particular historical events.

To put this point in more concrete terms, consider contemporary preaching. There is a tendency to subordinate the external Word to an inner vision in two directions. On one hand, preaching is considered by many (especially conservatives) to be a discourse *about* God and the teachings of Scripture. In this way, it is conceived primarily as theory. Speaking is merely a tool of intellectual reflection — teaching. On the other hand, preaching may be considered (especially by liberals) as an expression of inner experience and piety. In either case, the tendency is to place individuals in front of *their* inner ideas or experiences rather than in a community that is addressed by *God*.

In the Scriptures, however, *God* is the preacher, speaking through the mouth of his servants. Christ is not only the object about whom we speak but the subject who addresses us. Many of our translations of Romans 10:14 read, "And how are they to believe in him of whom they have never heard?" However, the sentence is better translated, "And how are they to believe *him whom* they have never heard?" We do not need to ascend to heaven to find Christ or bring him back from the dead; the resurrected and ascended Christ is as near as his voice in his Word (vv. 6–8). So when Paul says that "faith comes from hearing, and hearing through the word of Christ" (v. 17), he means nothing less than that Christ is the one speaking to us through "those who preach the good news" (v. 15). The proclamation of Christ, normed by his canonical Word, is itself nothing less than Christ himself addressing us here and now, creating the communion of the saints. In this way, God is not merely above us, but *in our midst* (in the Son) and *within us* (by his Spirit), gathering a society of hearers.

Not only the message but the method of preaching call us out of our subjectivity to hear and in hearing to receive a new identity that we could not have conceived, experienced, or achieved for ourselves. Beneath the pulpit and at the font and table, we are neither autonomous thinkers nor doers but are summoned in the totality of our existence and communion with the others whom the Spirit has gathered by this Word. As reflection on God's praxis in preaching and sacrament, theology cannot be reduced to theoretical contemplation. Nor can theology be set aside in favor of practical living, because intelligible communication includes revealed truths that must be understood.

A. THE THEORY-PRACTICE DEBATE IN THEOLOGY

On the question of whether theology is a theoretical or practical discipline, medieval theologians were divided, respectively, between the Dominicans (following Aquinas) and the Franciscans (following Scotus). On this point, the general consensus of Protestant scholastics favored some combination, while privileging the Franciscan view that the ultimate goal of theology is practical—namely, to reconcile sinners to God in Christ and to restore them to communion with God and each other in true worship.

First, Post-Reformation Lutheran and Reformed theologians affirmed the importance of theory but sharply contrasted revealed *doctrine* (and church dogmas interpreting it) and *speculation*. Although they criticized the attempt to scale ladders of merit, mysticism, and theoretical speculation to gaze on "the naked God" as a theology of glory, they taught that God had made himself an object of our analogical knowledge, and we would be ungrateful—indeed lost—if we ignored this condescending grace. Indeed, theology is the highest science because God is the source of all reality and redemption. *Theory,* for these writers, simply meant doctrine—revealed by grace, not attained by ascent—which was inseparable from doxology and discipleship.

The object of theology is not the self, religion, morality, or culture, but God. Therefore, even when thinking of theology as practical, these writers did not lose sight of God as the object: "Man's chief end is to glorify God, and to enjoy him forever" (*Westminster Shorter Catechism*, Answer 1). "Thus although theology treats of the same things with metaphysics, physics, and ethics, yet the mode of considering is far different," according to Francis Turretin (1623–1687).

> It treats of God not like metaphysics as a being or as he can be known from the light of nature, but as the Creator and Redeemer made known by revelation. It treats of creatures not as things of nature, but of God (i.e., as holding a relation and order

to God as their Creator, preserver, and Redeemer) and that too according to the revelation made by him. This mode of considering, the other sciences either do not know or do not assume.[49]

These other sciences may be helpful as servants, but hold no authority over theology and its task.

Second, in this context, *practical* did not mean what it typically signifies to us today. It was first of all *God's* practice that these theologians had in mind — namely, his creation of the world and redemption of sinners. Therefore, they did not begin with their autonomous reason or experience and then determine what parts of God's Word they found useful for human praxis (morality). Rather, they were convinced with Paul that everything that God had revealed was useful and sufficient for faith and practice precisely because it was "God-breathed" (2Ti 3:16 NIV). At the same time, the knowledge of God is not an end in itself; it is the knowledge of God's moral will for our lives (law) and his favor toward us in Christ (gospel).

No more than a patient should be content with a cardiologist who exhibits a comforting bedside manner and yet is ignorant of the circulatory system should parishioners settle for zeal without knowledge. However, the goal of theology is not to answer all of our questions and give us intellectual mastery of our object; rather, it is the practical reconciliation of sinners to God. Like medicine, Turretin argued, theology draws on a variety of different intellectual dispositions but with *an ultimately practical aim of healing*.[50] It is not metaphysicians and theoretical scientists we expect at our bedsides, but pastors and physicians. However, we expect both to know their discipline well. Toward the end of John's Gospel we read that Jesus did and taught many things "which are not written in this book; but these are written so that you may believe that Jesus is the Christ, the Son of God, and that by believing you may have life in his name" (Jn 20:30–31).

For the Reformers, theology was pursued in faith, founded and strengthened by the Spirit in Word and sacrament, and it required not only concentrated study but meditation and prayer. In fact, true to the theology of the cross, Luther added *suffering* as a necessary prerequisite for good theology. Believers who have experienced the anguish of God's wrath as well as the world's opposition know the sweetness of his gospel.[51] Similarly, Calvin judged that many theologians of his day who did not sense the importance of justification before a holy God had not yet sufficiently experienced the terrors of conscience that make the knowledge of God's truth such an urgent enterprise.[52] Thus, God's address envelops the whole person. It is *doctrine,*

---

49. Turretin, *Elenctic Theology*, 1:17, emphasis added.
50. Ibid.
51. John W. Doberstein, "Oratio, Meditatio, Tentatio: A Right Way to Study Theology," in *The Minister's Prayerbook* (ed. John W. Doberstein; Minneapolis: Augsburg, 1986), 276–89.

52. John C. Olin, ed., *A Reformation Debate: Sadoleto's Letter to the Genevans and Calvin's Reply* (Grand Rapids: Baker, 1966), 56.

not because it is theoretical rather than practical, but because it is *teaching that comes from God* rather than the ideas, experiences, or ethical ideals that arise from within us.

As has been often observed, Calvin's discussion of predestination in the *Institutes* follows his discourse on prayer, which is of comparable length. It is the singular privilege of God's children to be able to cry, "Abba! Father!" and to receive gifts from his hand by virtue of union with Christ. "So true is it that we dig up by prayer the treasures that were pointed out by the Lord's gospel, and which our faith has gazed upon."[53] The Puritans, perhaps those most Franciscan Protestants of all, explained the importance of theology in the most practical terms possible: learning to die well. Those who are prepared to die well in Christ are also better prepared to live in Christ, with faith toward God and love and good works toward their neighbors.

As the Enlightenment dawned, the definition of theology as a practical discipline became reduced to inner morality and experience. Already in the late sixteenth century, modern rationalism appeared, especially with the radical Protestant heresy known as *Socinianism*. Denying the Trinity, original sin, the deity of Christ, and his substitutionary atonement, as well as justification through faith alone, Socinianism anticipated the Enlightenment. *Arminianism*, while generally affirming the ecumenical creeds, downplayed the importance of doctrines it considered nonessential for practical morality and Christian experience.[54] Arminius himself asserted, "The proximate and immediate object of this doctrine or science is not God himself, but the duty and act of man which he is bound to perform to God."[55] Arminius's followers understood *practical* as basically synonymous with *ethical*. "What would Jesus do?" rather than "What has Jesus done?" became the focus.[56]

Pietism contributed to this human-centered tendency, focusing attention on the inner experience of the individual and in general downplaying the importance of doctrine. Its influence on the German Enlightenment has often been noted.[57] It is

---

53. Calvin, *Institutes* 3.20.2.

54. Concerning the great Arminian jurist and theologian Hugo Grotius, Peter Gay notes, "Grotius reduced Christianity to a few central tenets, rationalized the doctrine, and championed the freedom of the will against Calvinist Predestination, but the Resurrection of Jesus remained for him an undisputed, indisputable truth" (*The Enlightenment: An Interpretation*, 1:300). After discussing key features of the Enlightenment, Gay adds, "Meanwhile Dutch Arminians and French Jesuits offered similar doctrine on the Continent," with growing sympathy from "German Pietists" (326).

55. James Arminius, *The Works of James Arminius* (trans. James Nichols and William Nichols; Grand Rapids: Baker, 1986), 2:318.

56. Arminius himself challenged the view that the object of theology is "God and the church," "Christ," "a discourse

about God, the creatures, and principally about man and his fall, about his reparation through Christ, and about the sacraments and a future life" (*Works of James Arminius*, 320). Thus, for Arminius, treating theology as a practical rather than a theoretical science meant that *our duty* rather than God and his works must alone be the object.

57. F. Ernest Stoeffler, *The Rise of Evangelical Pietism* (Leiden: Brill, 1965); idem, *German Pietism during the Eighteenth Century* (Leiden: Brill, 1973); Gay, *The Enlightenment: An Interpretation*, 1:328–29. "Pietism, with its democratic confidence in religious experience, its impatience with doctrine and ratiocination, secured wide support, but it gradually hardened into an orthodoxy of its own: at the University of Halle the Pietists drove [Christian] Wolff from his chair into exile.... Kant, born into a Pietist household and instructed by some admirable Pietist teachers, testified that

not surprising, then, that most of the leading thinkers of the Enlightenment and Romanticism, including Kant and Schleiermacher, were reared in pietism. For both figures, faith and practice, doctrine and experience, can only be related equivocally. Doctrines express our practical needs and pious experience, but they do not reveal God's character, will, and works. Is it any surprise that the average Westerner today assumes that faith occupies an island of private irrationality, mysticism, morality, and subjective experience that it leases from the mainland of reason?

In our own day, this shift from God to the self and from doctrine to the subjective usefulness of religion and spirituality for private well-being is as evident in evangelical as in liberal circles. In fact, sociologist Christian Smith has characterized this spirituality as "Moralistic Therapeutic Deism."[58] Various movements (especially liberation theologies) have criticized these tendencies for their individualism and the reduction of faith to the inner realm rather than focusing on a more holistic redemption of the created order. Nevertheless, liberationism shares with bourgeois pietism a suspicion of doctrine (wisdom and knowledge) as a distraction from pragmatic needs and tools for transformation (technique).

Obviously, if the truth or importance of doctrine is determined by what we consider most useful for our moral improvement and religious experience, many of the most important Christian doctrines will lose their weight and eventually their saliency. If we imagine that we already know what we need to believe, experience, and pursue, then the doctrine of the Trinity, for example, will seem practically irrelevant. Only by beginning with the Trinity, reevaluating every topic in systematic theology and church practice, and reimagining our lives as the result of the distinct yet undivided work of the Father, the Son, and the Spirit does the doctrine prove its own practical value. Furthermore, modern atheism's critique of religion as nothing more than the projection of human longings and felt needs becomes more persuasive if we restrict the object of theology to whatever we happen to find useful.

As soon as reason was turned against the supernaturally revealed knowledge of God by the modern rationalists, Kant announced that rational knowledge of God was blocked. Kant "saved" religion from the jaws of a non-Christian idea of *theory* only to surrender it to an equally non-Christian idea of *practice*. He had already prepared for this move by having been reared in evangelical pietism, with its emphasis on the inner life and practical morality over doctrine. God cannot be the object of our theorizing but only the presupposition of our practice. This is not a universal

---

at its best Pietism gave its serious adherents 'that calm, that cheerfulness, that inner peace that is disturbed by no passion.'" Among the virtues that Kant praised in pietism was "its conviction that religion depends not on dogma or ritual or prayer but on experience" (329). Although Kant repudiated pietism as "enthusiasm," its influence is apparent throughout his work.

Other modern philosophers reared in pietism include Fichte, Hegel, Schelling, Schiller, Feuerbach, Schleiermacher, Kierkegaard, and Neitzsche.

58. Christian Smith and Melinda Lundquist Denton, *Soul Searching: The Religious and Spiritual Lives of American Teenagers* (New York: Oxford Univ. Press, 2005), 162.

truth of reason but a dogma derived from the story that the West has told itself since the Enlightenment.

In spite of preferring feeling over practical morality as the basis for theology, Schleiermacher ultimately follows Kant's human-centered and utilitarian orientation. Theology is a legitimate science not because it draws together the various elements that constitute a canonical unity in special revelation, "but only insofar as they [the scientific elements] are requisite for carrying out a practical task," which Schleiermacher defines later as "church leadership."[59] The minister is not so much a herald of Good News from the heavenly court as a leader, manager, and spokesperson for the community. In criticism of this view, Eberhard Jüngel and Klaus Müller comment, "Accordingly, the positive character of theology as science is in no way constituted by its object, but by its purpose."[60] This is the inevitable outcome of defining theology as exclusively practical and defining *practical* in terms of our activity (of acting and experiencing) rather than God's work of reconciliation.

Perhaps in our pragmatic, calculative, and scientific culture, it is praxis rather than theory that dominates and, among the intellectual virtues, *technē* (know-how for *making*) that reigns over wisdom, discursive and intuitive knowledge, and prudence. A crucial task before us today is to rediscover the power of God's creative and re-creative Word to restore the unity of thinking, feeling, and doing in the interaction between drama, doctrine, doxology, and discipleship.

B. FAITH AND REASON

"Faith seeking understanding" is not unique to Christians. Scientists pursue their hypotheses, some of which become established theories, by making certain claims. Of course, they test these claims, and their colleagues continue to verify or falsify them. However, in every pursuit of truth, an initial confidence in a particular interpretation of reality is presupposed.

Especially in the modern era there have been two extremes in treating the relationship between faith and reason: (1) *rationalism*, which attempts to base theological beliefs on universal principles of innate reason, [which absolute certainly as the only legitimate form of knowing;] (2) *fideism* (lit., "faith-ism"), which refuses to offer any arguments or evidence for Christian claims, usually on the suspicion that faith is intrinsically either opposed to or unrelated to reason. The first trajectory may be discerned especially in the heritage of Christian Platonism: from Clement of Alexandria to Pseudo-Dionysius to John Scotus Erigena. Modern rationalism

---

59. Friedrich Schleiermacher, *Brief Outline on the Study of Theology* (Richmond, Va.: John Knox, 1970), 19–20, quoted in the introduction to Rudolf Bultmann, *What Is Theology?* (Fortress Texts in Modern Theology; ed. Eberhard Jüngel and Klaus W. Müller; trans. Roy A. Harris; Minneapolis: Fortress, 1997), 26.

receive fresh impetus from Descartes, Leibniz, and Christian Wolff. Fideism may be discerned at least as a tendency in the thought of Tertullian, Pascal, Hamann, and Kierkegaard.

Rationalism and fideism continue to represent opposing extremes in our day. However, most Christian thinkers have held mediating views. According to the Protestant Reformers, reason—like every other human faculty—has been corrupted by the fall. Luther inveighed against "Whore Reason" and emphasized that our fallen reason is offended by every major Christian doctrine. Calvin also held that although unbelieving reason is still able to attain remarkable knowledge of "things below," it must be liberated from its hostility to God before it can rightly know "things heavenly." Anselm's dictum, "faith seeking understanding," represents the dominant view in church history. Daniel L Migliore observes, "Fideism says there comes a point when we must stop asking questions and must simply believe; faith keeps on seeking and asking."[61]

In a drunk-driving accident, blame falls on the driver rather than on the automobile. Similarly, God is the author of reality and the reason we employ to understand it, but we are inebriated, our power of reasoning being impaired by our willful "suppression of the truth in unrighteousness" (Ro 1:18–19). The Christian faith is not opposed to reason, but to this systematic misuse of reason that presupposes unbelief in the God who has revealed himself in Scripture and preeminently in his Son. While every major Christian doctrine transcends our rational ability to comprehend it (contra rationalism), none transcends our rational ability to apprehend it (contra fideism).

A *mystery* is inexhaustible, but a *contradiction* is nonsense. For example, to say that God is one in essence and three in persons is indeed a mystery, but it is not a contradiction. Believers revel in the paradox of the God who became flesh, but divine and human natures united in one person is not a contradiction. It is not *reason* that recoils before such miracles as *ex nihilo* creation, the exodus, or the virginal conception, atoning death, and bodily resurrection of Jesus Christ. Rather, it is the fallen heart of *reasoners* that refuses to entertain even the possibility of a world in which such divine acts occur.

So, on the one hand, we need to avoid a kind of positivism that make the act of faith dependent on the explicit awareness of reasons and evidence. William Lane Craig properly cautions against the unwarranted assumption of some critics and defenders that, "in the absence of positive evidence for Christian claims, faith is

---

60. Jüngel and Müller, eds., *What Is Theology?* 26.

61. Daniel L. Migliore, *Faith Seeking Understanding: An Introduction to Christian Theology* (2nd ed.; Grand Rapids: Eerdmans, 2004), 3.

62. William Lane Craig, "Faith, Reason, and the Necessity of Apologetics," in *To Everyone an Answer: A Case for the Christian Worldview* (ed. Francis J. Beckwith, William Lane Craig, and J. P. Moreland; Downers Grove, Ill.: InterVarsity Press, 2004), 19.

irrational for a normally functioning adult."[62] This is to confuse the rational defensibility of the Christian faith with the legitimacy of faith in spite of not having considered its apologetic arguments.

On the other hand, faith is not a subjective leap. Faithful reasoning neither enthrones nor avoids human questioning. Rather, it presupposes a humble submission to the way things actually are, not the way we expect them to be. Faithful reasoning anticipates surprise, because it is genuinely open to reality. If reality is always exactly what we assumed, then the chances are good that we have enclosed ourselves in a safe cocoon of subjective assertions. Unbelief is its own form of fideism, a close-mindedness whose a priori, untested, and unproven commitments have already restricted the horizon of possible interpretations. Whether that of the believer or that of the unbeliever, faith that no longer asks questions is no longer alive.

The dichotomy between faith and reason does not arise from the Christian claims or the question of their reliability per se but from philosophical presuppositions—which are ultimately ethical rather than intellectual—motivated by the refusal to occupy the created status of a covenant servant. Pantheism and panentheism ("overcoming estrangement") and deism and atheism ("the stranger we never meet") conspire in their attempt to drive out of the world any disruptive intervention by a sovereign God, either in judgment or in grace. Whether by identifying God with the world or by denying God's miraculous activity in the world, they deny that there can be any transcendent God who breaks into our history *from above*.

As the philosopher and scientist Michael Polanyi argued so persuasively, Anselm's dictum, "faith seeking understanding," does not distinguish religion from science or faith from reason. Rather, every act of knowing involves personal interest and commitment, our bodies and emotions as well as our minds, our hopes as well as our calculations.[63] The Enlightenment's neat compartmentalizing of faith and reason was simply a movement's way of demoting one set of beliefs in favor of a different set.

The most rigorous scientific theory involves personal subjectivity, and the most passionate commitment in faith demands an object. We fix our eyes on Christ, not on our believing. Every investigation, calculation, and experiment is motivated by an intellectual passion. Yet this intellectual passion involves a confidence that one is making contact with reality, something more than one's own inner hunches, experiences, or felt needs. It may be confidence in the triune God or in fairy godmothers or in the invisible hand of the market, but no one can live without confidence. If we doubted everything, we could never think, feel, or do anything. Christians have a reason for their confidence in exploration, and unbelievers must operate on

---

63. Michael Polanyi, *Personal Knowledge: Towards a Post-Critical Philosophy* (Chicago: Univ. of Chicago Press, 1958), 265.

"borrowed capital" in order to live with the tacit or subsidiary assumptions whose source they reject.

Although he was not a Christian, Polanyi came to conclude:

> Modern man is unprecedented; yet we must now go back to St. Augustine to restore the balance of our cognitive powers. In the fourth century AD, St. Augustine brought the history of Greek philosophy to a close by inaugurating for the first time a post-critical philosophy. He taught that all knowledge was a gift of grace, for which we must strive under the guidance of antecedent belief: *nisi credideritis, non intelligitis*. [Polanyi here provides a footnote to Augustine, *De libero arbitrio* 1.4: "The steps are laid down by the prophet, who says, 'Unless ye believe, ye shall not understand.'"] His doctrine ruled the minds of Christian scholars for a thousand years.[64]

However, "By the end of the seventeenth century Locke distinguished as follows between knowledge and faith: 'How well-grounded and great soever the assurance of faith may be wherewith it is received; *but faith it is still and not knowledge; persuasion and not certainty*'" (emphasis added).[65] According to this presupposition, faith accepts as true that which has been delivered to it by authority, while genuine knowledge can only be attained by autonomous investigation and proof. "All belief was reduced to the status of subjectivity: to that of an imperfection by which knowledge fell short of universality."[66]

Although rationalists, idealists, and empiricists differed among themselves, they were united by this fundamental dualism between faith and knowledge. And, like the theory/practice dilemma, this one is grounded in the deeper dualism between spirit and matter, higher and lower, eternal and historical, the inner knowledge of "clear and distinct ideas" (see pp. 57–59) within us that makes us masters and the unreliable opinions based on external testimony and authority concerning historical events that makes us servants.

C. Faith as Confidence in God's Promise: The Story Is the Point

When it comes to the gospel as it unfolds from Genesis to Revelation, there is no moral to the story, no higher truth that it symbolizes in its own mythical way. We have seen that the story of modern thought (we have not considered other important cultural factors) is largely the emancipation from the Christian story and from the doctrines and practices that arise from it. The problem is that Christianity cannot be "demythologized" or "translated" into alien stories, categories, or phi-

---

64. Ibid., 266.

65. John Locke, *A Third Letter for Toleration* (London, 1692), quoted in Polanyi, *Personal Knowledge*, 266.

66. Polanyi, *Personal Knowledge*, 266.

losophies. The key elements in its unfolding plot are not symbols or representations of a higher, purer, more universal truth. The Trinity; the creation of humanity in original righteousness and its fall through transgression of the covenant; the story of Israel from the call of Abram to the exile; the incarnation and saving work of Christ in his life, death, resurrection, and ascension; the descent of the Spirit at Pentecost; and Christ's return at the end of history to judge and consummate his kingdom — these are not dispensable narratives that express or conceptualize a deeper truth. They do not *make* a point; they *are* the point, and the point that others have wished to make of them — usually in the direction of ontological speculations — empties Christianity of its actual content and power.

Knowing is always a matter of growing in a relationship of trust — hence the frequent comparison of God's covenantal relationship to marriage in Scripture. Anomalies are recognized, but they do not bring down our fiduciary paradigm, because God has already demonstrated his reliability in spite of our confusion and piecemeal knowledge. We are all like the father of the child with seizures who told Jesus, "I believe; help my unbelief!" (Mk 9:24). "Now faith is the assurance of things hoped for, the conviction of things not seen," writes the author of Hebrews (Heb 11:1). Abraham followed God's call, "not knowing where he was going," but knowing the one who called him well enough to justify his confidence (vv. 8–12). And we have seen this same pattern of "faith seeking understanding" in the life of the disciples who followed Jesus. How much deeper is the conviction of believers today, as we stand on this side of the cross and resurrection, ascension and Pentecost. We could not have greater proof of God's faithfulness.

V. THEOLOGY AS WISDOM FOR INVOCATION

As noted earlier (p. 81), *philosophy* means "the love of wisdom." However, in contrast to the Greeks' concept of wisdom, the content and aim of wisdom in Scripture are neither theoretical contemplations of eternal forms nor practical rules for temporal success (i.e., the good life). Rather, God gives himself to us in a covenantal relationship. Knowing God *is* wisdom. By specifying theological knowing as a particular kind of wisdom for a particular kind of act — namely, calling on the name of the Lord — we reach the target of our concentric circles from broader to narrower definitions.

A. WISDOM

A covenantal epistemology resists the dualism between theory and practice because the knowledge that theology yields is oriented toward a proper *relation-*

ship—with God and with each other. Nevertheless, there can be no proper relationship without knowledge. Biblical wisdom is not simply a species of human wisdom. Scripture represents itself as both wisdom and knowledge. "The fear of the Lord is the beginning of wisdom" (Ps 111:10). As in the use of the general term *Torah*, there is no firm division between doctrinal and practical instruction. While more than information or knowledge, wisdom is surely not less.

Biblical wisdom resists our tendency to reduce the Christian faith to either theoretical contemplation or technical know-how. Knowledge of God's precepts and of the good news of God's saving work in Christ is a prerequisite of any genuine wisdom (see Ps 119). In fact, Paul lamented that his brothers according to the flesh did not lack zeal but rather knowledge—and specifically, that saving knowledge of the gospel (Ro 10:2–4). This Word comes to us from outside of ourselves but captivates our whole person. It is a knowledge that simultaneously informs our minds, melts our hard hearts, and animates our bodies to active service to our neighbor in love. If in certain cases " 'knowledge' puffs up" (1Co 8:1), so too can "wisdom"—in fact, Paul seems to use these terms interchangeably in reference to the superapostles (1Co 1:17; 2:1; 3:19), urging us instead to be "wise in Christ" (1Co 4:10).

Therefore, the wisdom that theology pursues is not a generic "practical living" or a form of "know-how." This would reduce the faith to moralism and technique— using the Bible to save ourselves and improve our lives. This is precisely the use to which Greeks would be willing to put religion—even Christianity perhaps, if it would settle for a general self-help kind of wisdom. After all, Paul reminds us in 1 Corinthians 1:22, "Greeks seek wisdom," but it is not the wisdom that comes from the gospel. In fact, it is precisely because the pagan search for wisdom is an autonomous quest for self-betterment rather than for salvation that "the word of the cross is folly to those who are perishing, but to us who are being saved it is the power of God" (1Co 1:18). The wisdom of the cross cannot be correlated with the wisdom of the world. In fact, through the cross God has exposed human wisdom and discernment as folly (vv. 19–21).

Although it certainly defines appropriate human praxis, theology is chiefly the wisdom *concerning Christ.* Theology is not "queen of the sciences." Although the topics it treats share overlapping interests with other disciplines, it does not offer an exhaustive account of reality and knowledge. Scripture does not deliver a normative theory of economics or politics, or even address every area of moral concern. These are hardly unimportant matters; in his common grace, God wisely gives wisdom to unbelievers as well as believers for these questions. Theology, however, is concerned with the highest wisdom, which the wise of this age could never attain. Although Scripture does not address every question or topic, its wisdom shapes our interpretation of every aspect of reality.

Paul especially highlights the concrete distinctiveness of biblical wisdom from all other forms of wisdom. The call to be "wise in Christ" is not a passing remark about letting Christ's moral instruction guide our daily living. It is much more than the secrets of how to live the good life, as Greek philosophy understood the purpose of wisdom. Evangelical wisdom is the knowledge of Christ, who *is* "wisdom from God, righteousness and sanctification and redemption" (1Co 1:30). We have a further indication of what this involves when Paul speaks of this wisdom as a mystery hidden from the philosophers but revealed to the world in these last days (1Co 4:1; 15:51; Eph 1:9; 6:19; Col 1:26–27; 1Ti 3:9). It becomes clear from these passages that *mystērion* ("mystery") has to do with both revealed doctrines (centering on God's purposes unveiled in Christ) and practices (the sacraments). Paul reminds Timothy of his early training in "the sacred writings, which are able to make you wise for salvation through faith in Christ Jesus," and adds that these inspired Scriptures are "profitable for teaching, for reproof, for correction, and for training in righteousness" (2Ti 3:15–16). They are inspired and therefore profitable, not profitable and therefore inspired.

Our theology is as definitively shaped by our participation in the public practices of baptism, Communion, fellowship, and prayer as by preaching and teaching. However, these are first and foremost *God's* faithful praxes. Unlike the Athenian philosophers, Jesus Christ did not offer himself merely as a teacher of the path to truth and happiness, but as "the way, and the truth, and the life" (Jn 14:6). He is not only the guide; he is the destination.

Theology, then, is both a practical wisdom (*sapientia*) and a knowledge of mysteries (*scientia*), both of which rest on Scripture. Zeal cannot compensate for ignorance, particularly ignorance of the gospel. In order to attain this knowledge, one must perform proper exegesis of the Scriptures, which is an *art* as much as a *science*. Furthermore, it requires *prudence*—interpreting Scripture in the light of Scripture, weighing difficult passages in the light of clearer passages, without jumping to conclusions too hastily. Prudence is involved also in evaluating the interpretations of Scripture in church history, through knowledge of its formulations and debates. Theology certainly involves *technical skill*, especially familiarity with the original languages. Indeed, theology does draw from all the habits or ways of knowing more comprehensively than any other science. However, it is principally a form of *wisdom*—the highest wisdom.

In this view of theology, knowing, doing, and feeling are not divorced as they usually are in modern thought. For Descartes, certainty turned on *knowing*; for Kant, on *doing*; and for Schleiermacher, on *feeling*. Much of recent theology has been a protest against knowing in favor of doing, as in liberation theology's definition of theology as "critical reflection on praxis"—that is, *our* praxis rather than

God's.[67] As we critique these human-centered approaches, we must observe that the importance of grounding our practice in doctrine is not determined by a preference for theory but by the priority of God's action over ours.

Where knowledge for someone like Descartes was aligned to seeing "clear and distinct ideas" in the mind (see pp. 58–59), the biblical concept of knowledge is the "Amen" of faith to God's Word. Geerhardus Vos fleshes this point out a bit:

> It is true, the gospel teaches that to know God is life eternal. But the concept of "knowledge" here is not to be understood in its Hellenic [Greek] sense, but in the Shemitic [Hebrew] sense. According to the former, "to know" means to mirror the reality of a thing in one's consciousness. The Shemitic and biblical idea is to have the reality of something practically interwoven with the inner experience of life. Hence "to know" can stand in the biblical idiom for "to love," "to single out in love." Because God desires to be *known* after this fashion, he has caused his revelation to take place in the milieu of the historical life of a people. The circle of revelation is not a school, but a "covenant." To speak of revelation as an "education" of humanity is a rationalistic and utterly unscriptural way of speaking. All that God disclosed of himself has come in response to the practical religious needs of his people as these emerged in the course of history.[68]

In a similar vein, the Jewish philosopher Abraham Joshua Heschel observes,

> Greek philosophy began in a world without God. It could not accept the gods or the example of their conduct. Plato had to break with the gods and to ask: What is good? Thus the problem of values was born. And it was the idea of values that took the place of God. Plato lets Socrates ask: What is good? But Moses' question was: What does God require of thee?[69]

Heschel points out the ethical implication of metaphysical and epistemological autonomy. Starting from the presupposition of a self-founding, the knower proceeds to make everything else a subject of his or her empire. Heschel's contrast also points out the difference once again between seeing and hearing. What characterizes this covenantal relationship is not abstract ideas we can master by our gaze but a personal Word we must heed.

In the biblical perspective, speaking is an action. It is not simply the externalization of internal thoughts but a praxis—God's praxis—that changes a certain state of affairs. God speaks a creative word and the world exists; a word of judgment and life withers; a word of redemption and faith is born; a word of forgiveness and sin-

---

67. Gustavo Gutiérrez, *A Theology of Liberation* (Maryknoll, N.Y.: Orbis, 1973), 4–11. Gutiérrez identifies what he takes to be three phases of theology's self-description. The first phase was "theology as wisdom"; the second, "theology as rational knowledge"; and what we now need, he says, is "theology as critical reflection on praxis."

68. Geerhardus Vos, *Biblical Theology: Old and New Testaments* (Grand Rapids: Eerdmans, 1948), 8–9.

69. Abraham Joshua Heschel, *God in Search of Man* (New York: Macmillan, 1976), 98.

ners are absolved; a word of new life and the dead are raised. God's speech—his Word—is not merely a collection of ideas but a "living and active" force with the most practical and concrete effects in our lives and world (cf. Heb 4:12). Words not only change minds; they change hearts and lives—indeed, the whole course of nature and history.

Paul Ricoeur writes,

> Saying and doing, signifying and making are intermingled to such an extent that it is impossible to set up a lasting and deep opposition between "theoria" and "praxis." The word is my kingdom and I am not ashamed of it.... As a listener to the Christian message, I believe that words may change the "heart," that is, the refulgent core of our preferences and the positions which we embrace.[70]

Finally, our working definition of wisdom (at least in its biblical context) is not complete apart from recognizing its aim. Our theological knowledge and wisdom are not techniques, theories, and observations by which we control the object of our gaze, but serve the most practical goal of *invoking the name of the Lord*. If our appropriate covenantal response to God's command is "Here I am!" the response to God's promise is "Amen!"—in other words, *faith*. Faith is not a general attitude, such as optimism. It has a specific object, namely, God. And saving faith is even more specific, as we have recognized above: it is faith in *the triune God as he is known in Jesus Christ, revealed in Scripture, according to the covenant of grace*. Therefore, the "faith seeking understanding" that accords with biblical (covenantal) epistemology is best defined as *invocation*.

Again, we obtain our proper coordinates here from the unfolding drama itself.

In the ancient Near East, a suzerainty treaty included the "invocation" clause, under which the lesser king could call on the name of the great king (suzerain) when in peril. This invocation formula is clearly present throughout the Bible's covenantal drama. Already in Genesis 4, the lines of Cain and Seth are compared and contrasted: the former is distinguished by cultural advances, while the latter is known by the announcement, "At that time people began to call upon the name of the Lord" (v. 26). We are meant to understand that beginning with Seth and his heirs, a church began to emerge, with Yahweh as its Great King and Redeemer.

Repeatedly in the Old Testament, the world is divided between God's people, who call on his name (Pss 80:18; 105:1; 145:18), and the foolish, who "do not call upon God" (Ps 53:4). Israel, too, follows the foolish nations when it turns from Yahweh and "there is no one who calls upon your name, who rouses himself to take hold of you" (Isa 64:7). We notice from this verse that just as God's Word seizes us, provok-

---

70. Paul Ricoeur, *History and Truth* (trans. Charles A. Kelbley; Evanston, Ill.: Northwestern Univ. Press, 1992), 5.

ing our response either of fearful flight or of answering, "Here I am," faith seizes God, but this time in a dependent, childlike, even helpless trust in the face of imminent danger instead of attempting to master. Invocation is not merely a form of thinking; it is a prayer—whether the cry of God's enslaved people in Egypt and Babylon or that of the tax collector: "God, be merciful to me, a sinner!" (Lk 18:13). Theology, more than anything else, is a human answer to a divine call, a summons that contains both command and promise, evoking danger and delight, fear and hope.

Joel prophesied that the liberation in the last days will involve a renewed invocation: Then "everyone who calls on the name of the Lord shall be saved" (Joel 2:32). And Paul quotes this verse in Romans 10: "For 'everyone who calls on the name of the Lord will be saved.' How then will they call on him in whom they have not believed? And how are they to believe in him of whom they have never heard?" (vv. 13–14).

This knowledge of God clearly comes from God, and it is mediated through human ambassadors. It is good *news*, not good *advice*. It will motivate us to follow God's commands, provoke experiences (terrifying as well as comforting), and yield doctrinal propositions. However, these other intellectual habits or ways of knowing ultimately serve the practical end of invoking and embracing Christ, "who became to us wisdom from God, righteousness and sanctification and redemption" (1Co 1:30). At the heart of the theological way of knowing, then, is the hearing of an announcement so that hearers may *call on the name of the Lord*. God's majestic face fills us with dread, but he allows the goodness and grace of his back to pass us by, hiding us in the shelter of his Son. Pulling us out of ourselves—our inner speculation and experience, felt needs, fears, and hopes—God gives us his name as the pledge of his whole person for our joy and security.

In order to display the harmony of theology (faith) and other sciences (reason), medieval scholasticism frequently offered various philosophical arguments for the existence of a supreme being and then deduced, "And this being we call God, don't we?" But this approach is exactly what Luther meant by a theology of glory: ascending to heaven in order to measure the immeasurable God rather than allowing him to condescend to us in humility and suffering. This means that theological science can begin not with speculation, morality, or religious experience but with God's revelation. Francis Turretin wrote, "But when God is set forth as the object of theology, he is not to be regarded simply as God in himself (for thus he is incomprehensible to us), but as revealed and as he has been pleased to manifest himself to us in his word."[71] Although a sympathetic interpreter of Aquinas, Turretin is simply following this Reformation insight when he adds, "*Nor is he to be considered exclusively under the*

---

71. Turretin, *Elenctic Theology*, 1:16–17.

relation of deity (according to the opinion of Thomas Aquinas and many Scholastics after him, for in this manner the knowledge of him could not be saving but deadly to sinners), but as he is *our* God (i.e., *covenanted in Christ as he has revealed himself to us in his word not only as the object of knowledge, but also of worship*)."[72]

Deity is not something that is available to us—and in any case, the God of Israel is not a species of a genus known as *God*. We have access to this particular God, who has "covenanted in Christ" and revealed himself in his Word, only to the practical end that we will know him in a saving rather than a deadly way. It is not the existence of a god that concerns theology, but the existence of the God who has defined himself for us as the one who created all things by his Word, led Israel through the Red Sea to the promised land, and in due time sent his Son to save the world.

Thus, theology is the wisdom that we need for invoking the Father, in the Son, and by the Spirit, for salvation and life. This contrasts sharply with the logic of modernity, which is more natural to us than we realize. For Kant—a thoroughgoing Pelagian—we do not need a miraculous revelation of the gospel because we do not need to be saved by grace. We only need "the moral law within"—deeds, not creeds. Kant wrote that the truly religious person does "not found his morality on faith, but his faith on morality: in such a case, however weak this faith may be, yet it alone is of a pure and true kind, i.e., the kind of faith that founds not a religion of supplication [invocation], but a religion of good life conduct."[73] Kant confesses that in reading the gospels he seeks moral imperatives rather than the good news of God's saving action: "in brief, ... *what is incumbent upon me*—clearly distinguished from *what God does for me*. Hence nothing new is imposed [by the gospel] upon me; rather (whatever the state of those reports) new strength and confidence is given to my good dispositions" (emphasis added).[74] Kant, therefore, saw with great clarity the correlation between one's presuppositions about the human predicament and religious epistemology. None of these Enlightenment figures wanted knowledge for invoking the name of God (i.e., the gospel), because they did not believe they needed to be saved. However, in the covenantal context of Scripture, morality is based on faith, and everything—including moral action—flows from this invocation of God for mercy, on the terms that he has announced in his peace treaty.

Because our God is an extrovert, an "outdoor" God who is always active and engaged with his creation, faith is never the kind of smug certainty that comes from ivory-tower contemplation on eternal ideas. Calvin emphasized with Luther this point that true and living faith is found in "a living existence." It is "not that knowledge which, content with empty speculation, merely flits in the brain, but that which

---

72. Ibid.
73. Immanuel Kant, *Religion and Rational Theology* (ed. Allen W. Wood and George di Giovanni; trans. Allen W. Wood,

George di Giovanni, et al.; Cambridge: Cambridge Univ. Press, 1996), 33.
74. Ibid., 50.

will be sound and fruitful if we duly perceive it, and if it takes root in the heart." Hence, we must seek for God in his works, revealed in his Word, not in his hidden essence.[75] "True acquaintance with God is made more by the ears than by the eyes."[76]

More provocatively, Luther wrote, "It is by living, no—more—by dying and being damned to hell that one becomes a theologian, not by knowing, reading, or speculating."[77] We learn on the road, as pilgrims making our way to the City of God through the trials, burdens, questions, and fears of our own hearts as well as the world around us. We learn truly of God's providence as we suffer, of God's forgiveness in our sins, of the resurrection of the dead as we lie dying. Luther's poignant but hyperbolic statement does not mean that we do not read or study, but that even as we do this, it is more like looking for urgently needed rescue than contemplating eternal truths. We do theology on our knees, calling on the name of our Redeemer. Yet precisely because our God is so great, our situation so dire, and our salvation so full and free, theology is indispensible to piety.

If we are rescued by invoking the Father, in the Son, by the Spirit, then getting God's name right is not merely the theoretical affair of scholars in an ivory tower but is a matter of life and death. We must know who God is, who we are, and what the covenantal stipulations and sanctions are under which we relate to this God, as well as what the history of God's works in judgment and deliverance is. Yet all of this is oriented toward the practical end that we will call on his name for salvation and worship. If there is "no other name" in heaven or on earth by which people may be saved than Jesus Christ (Ac 4:12; cf. Ac 2:21, 38; Ro 10:13; Php 2:9; Col 3:17; Heb 1:4), then the imperative of identifying the correct God (getting the name right) and invoking him in the terms that he has prescribed (understanding God's commands and promises) is of paramount importance for theology. In fact, it is the theological task par excellence. So theology is for prayer, and a particular kind of prayer— namely, invocation of the name of the Lord, on the basis of his covenant Word.

CONCLUSION

Theology serves the function of articulating the identity of this God so that he may be properly invoked. It is therefore critical for all aspects of the church's ministry—preaching, teaching, the sacraments, prayer, worship, evangelism, missions, diaconal care, and discipleship. With invocation of the triune God in the concrete context of an original covenant that we have transgressed and a covenant of grace

---

75. Calvin, *Institutes* 1.5.9.

76. John Calvin, *Commentary on the Four Last Books of Moses* (Edinburgh: Calvin Translation Society, 1870), 3:378.

77. Martin Luther, *Luthers Werke* (Weimar edition) 5.163.28,

as quoted by Jürgen Moltmann, *Experiences in Theology: Ways and Forms of Christian Theology* (trans. Margaret Kohl; Minneapolis: Fortress, 2000), 23–24.

that God pledges, even thinking becomes an act of faith, love, and obedience. Invocation draws our attention out and away from ourselves to God in faith and out to our neighbor in love.

Unlike Descartes, we are not left alone with our own thoughts but respond to the Stranger who beckons and before whom I become aware of my identity and responsibility. Beyond our own reconciliation with God, theology serves the practical aim of mission and witness, so that others too may call on the name of the Lord. "How then will they call on him in whom they have not believed?" Paul asks. "And how are they to believe in him of whom they have never heard? And how are they to hear without someone preaching? And how are they to preach unless they are sent? As it is written, 'How beautiful are the feet of those who preach the good news!'" (Ro 10:14–15). Because God is at work through the public ministry of the church and the daily witness of believers, raising for himself a congregation from the ruins of sin and death, theology is indispensable.

The knowledge such revelation yields is intended to lead us to faith in the Lord of the covenant and to our appropriate place within the covenant community as those who have been transferred from the domain of "not a people" to "God's people" (1Pe 2:10; Hos 1:9–10). Through this theology as prayerful meditation on God and his works, the Missionary God not only saves us but incorporates us into his missionary people. *Theology exists for this very purpose: to appeal to the God who has revealed himself and his redemptive purposes in Christ, so that he may be invoked in trouble, praised in deliverance, and obeyed in gratitude.*

DISCUSSION QUESTIONS

1. What are the five habits or dispositions of knowing that Aristotle identified?
2. Discuss the significance of the metaphor of vision in the history of Western thought. Make a list of familiar terms related to thinking or understanding that are visual metaphors. Is it just a metaphor, or does it shape (and reflect) a certain way of approaching knowledge?
3. Why did Martin Luther say "the ears are the organ of the Christian"? Discuss some of the ways in which hearing, rather than seeing, transforms our approach to theological truth.
4. How does the dichotomy between theory and practice play out in contemporary church life? How can a covenantal approach help us to overcome it?
5. What do you make of the definition of theological knowing (i.e., the *habitus* or disposition of this particular science) as "wisdom for invocation"?

Chapter Three

THE SOURCE OF THEOLOGY: REVELATION

God is the object of theology because he is also its self-revealing subject. Hidden in incomprehensible majesty, God reveals himself in a manner that is (1) accommodated to our capacities and (2) limited to that which God deems necessary for calling on his name, in Christ, within the context of the covenant of grace. This chapter fleshes out this claim by focusing directly on the doctrine of *revelation*. In his *Models of Revelation*, Avery Cardinal Dulles provides a useful typology that can be correlated with these paradigms.[1] After defining the models, I will suggest some critical features of a biblical theology of revelation.

I. MODELS OF REVELATION

Dulles offers the following models:

- Model 1: Revelation as Doctrine (God as Teacher)
- Model 2: Revelation as History (God as Actor)
- Model 3: Revelation as Inner Experience (God as Guest)
- Model 4: Revelation as Dialectical Encounter (God as Judge)
- Model 5: Revelation as New Awareness (God as Poet)

Identifying revelation chiefly (if not exclusively) with true propositions, model 1 is associated with conservative evangelicals and neo-Thomists.[2] In model 2, revela-

---

1. Avery Dulles, *Models of Revelation* (Garden City, N.J.: Doubleday, 1983).
2. Ibid., 39. Dulles cites Gordon Clark and Carl Henry for this view, quoting Clark's claim, "Aside from imperative sentences and a few exclamations in the Psalms, the Bible is composed of propositions" (39). According to Henry, theology "consists essentially in the repetition, combination, and systematization of the truth of revelation in its propositionally given biblical form" (47).

tion comes to us not in the form of doctrines but through God's mighty acts in history. Insofar as the Bible reliably reports these acts, it witnesses to revelation but is not itself the bearer of it. G. Ernest Wright and Wolfhart Pannenberg are among the many proponents of this view.[3] According to model 3, immediate (often mystical) experience "minimizes the need for mediation through created signs."[4] This view is especially identified with various strands of mysticism, pietism, and liberalism.[5] More than Christ's "external Word," the *indwelling* Christ is the highest authority in this model. Dulles observes that orthodox Calvinists and Lutherans stand most resolutely against such "enthusiasm."[6]

Critical of the first and second models as offering a false objectivism and the third for its false subjectivism, model 4 understands revelation as an event of personal encounter. With important differences in their formulations, Karl Barth, Rudolf Bultmann, and Emil Brunner, in their "dialectical" theologies, all reflect this basic approach.[7] "God, they insisted, could never be an object known either by inference from nature or history, by propositional teaching, or by direct perception of a mystical kind. Utterly transcendent, God encounters the human subject when it pleases him by means of a word in which faith recognizes him to be present."[8] Model 5 is similar to the third model (inner experience), except that it focuses more on revelation as "an expansion of consciousness or shift of perspective when people join in the movements of secular history."[9] According to one representative, Teilhard de Chardin, "It is no longer an act of cognition but of recognition.... God never reveals himself from outside, by intrusion, but from within, by stimulation and enrichment of the human psychic current," by bringing coherence to "our individual and collective being."[10]

---

3. G. E. Wright, *God Who Acts: Biblical Theology as Recital* (London: SCM, 1952); cf. Wolfhart Pannenberg, ed., *Revelation as History* (New York: Macmillan, 1968), esp. Pannenberg's introduction.

4. Dulles, *Models of Revelation*, 69.

5. Roman Catholic theologian Karl Rahner represents this approach in his account of "the experience of grace" (Dulles, *Models of Revelation*, 70). According to Rahner, there must be some experience of grace prior to and apart from the proclamation of the gospel, "for if faith were supported only by an external word, it could not rise above the level of human opinion" (72). In Protestant circles, "revelation as inner experience" can be identified with pietistic liberalism (represented especially by Friedrich Schleiermacher) and contemporary process theologians such as John Hick and John Cobb. According to the American philosopher of pragmatism William James, "The mystical feeling of enlargement, union, and emancipation has no specific content whatever of its own" (80). It is an experience that cannot be put into words.

6. Dulles, *Models of Revelation*, 76.

7. If Dulles's models stretch to the breaking point, it is most evident with the so-called "dialectical circle" (God as Judge), where significant tensions and divergences emerged. Barth grew

increasingly convinced that Bultmann had surrendered a Christian doctrine of revelation to the categories of existentialism. Brunner criticized Barth for allegedly becoming increasingly drawn too much toward "the orthodox teachers of the seventeenth century" and away from his earlier devotion to Kierkegaard. "For the Karl Barth of the *Church Dogmatics*, all this was pietism, a declension from pure doctrine," Brunner complains (*Truth as Encounter* [Philadelphia: Westminster, 1964], 43). Brunner's criticism of Bultmann's theology as "an idealistic philosophy with strong nihilistic traits" surely tested the limits of the label's usefulness (*Truth as Encounter*, 48). Yet all three figures held that revelation is always an event of personal encounter: an "I-Thou" relation that can never slip into an "I-It" relation (see Martin Buber, *I and Thou* [New York: Scribner, 1958], which they identified with the orthodox doctrine of revelation. Revelation, for Barth, is always an eschatological event that occurs in the eternal moment (God's time) and is synonymous with reconciliation.

8. Dulles, *Models of Revelation*, 28.

9. Ibid.

10. Ibid., 113. Karl Rahner was also influenced by Teilhard's thought. However, Barth dismissed Teilhard as "a giant Gnostic snake" (113).

Once again we may discern the broader shadows of the contrasting worldviews we have considered—"overcoming estrangement" being more consistent with revelation as inner experience and new awareness (models 3 and 5), while the other models are more favorable to "meeting a stranger" (but, I will argue, finally fall short).

II. TOWARD A BIBLICAL DOCTRINE OF REVELATION

"Long ago, at many times and in many ways, God spoke to our fathers by the prophets, but in these last days he has spoken to us by his Son" (Heb 1:1–2).

It is significant that neither the Old nor the New Testament yields a "theology of revelation" per se; we can only draw general conclusions from the specific instances of revelation "at many times and in many ways." Besides the diversity of genres and writers, there is a diversity of media.[11] Some of God's works are self-revealing simply by virtue of being his creations; others are his providential and miraculous actions in history whose purpose is disclosed to prophets and apostles. Sometimes God reveals himself directly (notwithstanding models 2 and 4), but at other times he reveals himself indirectly (notwithstanding models 1, 3, and 5). Even when this revelation is direct, it is mediated and never provides univocal description of God's inner being. None of these models, by itself, can account for the diversity of actual occurrences of revelation in Scripture.

Despite the variety, all revelation in Scripture shares certain basic characteristics. The Old Testament offers several terms for *revelation*, most frequently *gālâ*, from the root "to uncover," "to strip away."[12] Only in the New Testament is the verb given a nominal form (*apokalyptō*, "to unveil"; cf. *apokalypsis*, "revelation"). The human response is identified as knowing (*yādaʿ/ginōskō*), which is always more but certainly not less than intellectual apprehension. Furthermore, the goal is always God's communion with his covenant people.[13] The event of revelation was "inevitably a call from God; a call which had to be hearkened to, and obeyed (Isa 6)."[14] Neither the prophets nor the apostles are described as spiritually sensitive sages who were seeking this revelatory encounter. Rather, they were interrupted from their daily routine.

---

11. Among the many media of revelation, one could refer to the Urim and Thummim (Nu 27:21; Dt 33:8; 1Sa 28:6), prediction (Jer 28:16–17), teaching, proclamation, direct encounter (Ex 33:11; Am 7:8), and indirect media (Jos 24:25–26).

12. Dewey M. Beegle, "The Biblical Concept of Revelation," in *The Authoritative Word: Essays on the Nature of Scripture* (ed. Donald McKim; Grand Rapids: Eerdmans, 1983), 90.

Phaneroō/phanerōsis, "to manifest oneself"/"self-manifestation," also appears, for example, in 1 Timothy 3:16; 1 Peter 1:20; and 1 John 1:2.

13. James G. S. S. Thompson, *The Old Testament View of Revelation* (Grand Rapids: Eerdmans, 1960), 9.

14. Ibid., 10.

God addressed them. Across the diverse accounts of revelation in Scripture we can pull together various recurring threads to develop a satisfactory working definition.

A. REVELATION DEPENDS ON DIVINE INITIATIVE

Louis Berkhof reminds us, "It should be observed that in theology it [*revelation*] never denotes a mere passive, perhaps unconscious, becoming manifest, but always a conscious, voluntary, and intentional deed of God, by which he reveals or communicates divine truth."[15] In other words, human beings do not discover God; God reveals himself. God is never the revealed object without being the revealing subject.

It is clear from particular instances that revelation does not well up within a pious individual but comes to one from the outside. It is not a private intuition but a public truth. Not even the prophet or apostle is a recipient of revelation merely as a private person but as a public official of the divine court in covenantal history. They are not artists, poets, or ethicists. They are not even spiritual geniuses who operate on a higher wavelength. Rather, they are ordinary people who are called away from their ordinary vocations as ambassadors of the Great King. In fact, in the event of revelation, the one commissioned by God typically expresses a sense of unworthiness, distress, and hesitancy rather than a sense of absolute dependence, serenity, and pious delight. The communication was not merely a hunch, feeling, intuition, or mystical experience; the recipients of revelation give evidence of being "fully conscious of what was happening in the moment of encounter with the living God."[16]

From such examples we learn that revelation catches its human ambassadors by surprise. Rather than seizing, grasping, or mastering, they are claimed, summoned, and commissioned to speak God's words, and through their embassy God claims, summons, and commissions those who hear those words. God's transcendent otherness is the presupposition for this emphasis on the divine initiative, as Thompson notes: "God's dwelling is on high (Isa 33:5). God himself is high and lofty, and inhabits eternity, the realm to which man cannot penetrate (Isa 57:15; cf. Ecc 5:2). It is this hiddenness or transcendence of God that, on the one hand, makes man's unaided search for the Lord fruitless, and on the other, makes the self-disclosure of God absolutely necessary."[17]

The subjective models of revelation (3 and 5) are dominant in the trajectory that leads from radical forms of medieval mysticism to radical Protestantism all the way through the Enlightenment and Romanticism to liberalism. In these models (consistent with the paradigm of "overcoming estrangement"), revelation does not come to us from a personal God who initiates verbal communication but wells up

---

15. Louis Berkhof, *Introductory Volume to Systematic Theology* (Grand Rapids: Eerdmans, 1932), 117.

16. Thompson, *Old Testament View of Revelation*, 11.
17. Ibid.

within the pious soul. The Protestant Reformers identified the tendency to equate God's Word with inner experience and speculation as "enthusiasm" (from the Greek *enthousiasmos*—lit., God-within-ism). Such statements as this one from Meister Eckhart were taken up by radical Anabaptists and Enlightenment rationalists: "St. Paul said to Timothy, 'Beloved, preach the word!' Did he mean the audible word that beats the air? Certainly not! He referred to the inborn, secret word that lies hidden in the soul."[18] As Tillich observed, it is this doctrine of the "inner light" that unites rationalists and mystics of all ages.[19] It is this emphasis on religious subjectivity that unites otherwise disparate forms of modernity. If this is so, then the modern era should be regarded less as a period of increasing secularization and irreligion than as a period dominated by the autonomous mysticism of the inner self.[20]

Barth was right to stress, against this subjectivist view of revelation, that revelation is *God's personal summons* or call to his covenant servants—*here and now* as well as *then and there*. God is the initiator. Revelation cannot simply be revelation *about* God (as model 1 tends to assume); in revelation God is present in personal address, which creates a crisis and calls for a decision. At the same time, this dialectical view (model 4) goes too far in restricting revelation to an ever-new event of personal encounter.

B. REVELATION IS A SPEECH ACT

James G. S. S. Thompson observes concerning the Old Testament that this divine initiative in revelation takes the form of "Word":

> Everywhere in the Old Testament the activity of God as a medium of his self-disclosure is wedded to the Word of God. So closely connected are they that the act and the Word are sometimes synonymous; and if not identical, they are simultaneous. It would seem that often the activity without the Word could not be a medium of revelation. Even in the supreme self-revelatory act of God in the Old Testament—the Exodus—the Word was present throughout.... Along with every revelatory act there was the interpretative Word.[21]

Therefore, revelation cannot be reduced to doctrine (model 1); the exodus of Israel through the Red Sea is itself a revelation event (as model 2 underscores).

---

18. Meister Eckhart, "Sermon on the Eternal Birth," in *Late Medieval Mysticism* (ed. Ray C. Petry; Philadelphia: Westminster, 1942), 179.

19. Paul Tillich, *A History of Christian Thought* (ed. Carl E. Braaten; New York: Harper & Row, 1968), 286. Tillich adds (on the same page), "The subjective view of Pietism, or the doctrine of the 'inner light' in Quakerism and other ecstatic movements, has the character of immediacy or autonomy against the authority of the church. To put it more sharply, modern rational autonomy is a child of the mystical autonomy of the doctrine of the inner light."

20. The contrast between *enthusiasm* and the Reformation is similar to the contrast drawn by Nancey Murphy between Schleiermacher and Charles Hodge in terms of an inside-out epistemology versus an outside-in epistemology, respectively. See Nancey Murphy, *Beyond Liberalism and Fundamentalism: How Modern and Postmodern Philosophy Set the Theological Agenda* (Valley Forge, Pa.: Trinity, 1996), 28–35.

21. Thompson, *Old Testament View of Revelation*, 13.

Nevertheless, this event is not a brute fact whose significance and meaning is left to fallible human interpretation. God reveals his character, purposes, and accomplishments through his own interpretation of these mighty acts. In doing so, God reveals true propositions (emphasized by model 1) and his mighty acts (model 2), and he personally summons us to acknowledge his claim on us (model 4). This same act of revelation touches our inner experience (model 3) and provides a new awareness (model 5) — but in ways that radically challenge rather than simply confirm our assumptions, ideas, and experience.

Rooted in history rather than in timeless ideas or universal religious experience, God's self-revelation always involves new events and announcements that we could not have known apart from their being communicated to us. There are no uninterpreted facts, historical events, personal encounters, inner experiences, or states of awareness. The Bible knows nothing of the modern dichotomy between fact and value. The fact of the resurrection, for example, is inseparable from its interpretation as the fulfillment of God's promises to Israel. Jesus Christ "was delivered up for our trespasses and raised for our justification" (Ro 4:25). God's initiative in revelation is therefore present not only in the mighty acts of judgment and deliverance but in God's interpretation of these events.

Modern philosophy has been preoccupied with the relationship of language to reality. Assuming the long-standing view that our language and concepts provide pictures or representations of facts, logical positivists (1930s – 1950s) attempted to replace ordinary language with a nearly mathematical language of axiomatic propositions that could map the whole of reality. Only statements of fact (propositions) really counted as knowledge claims; statements of value were merely subjective and therefore meaningless. Ethical, aesthetic, and religious judgments were relegated to this latter sphere. "The cat is on the mat" counted as a reasonable proposition (a fact), while "The cat is beautiful" or "The cat is vicious" were merely subjective evaluations. Ironically, many conservative Protestant and Roman Catholic theologians (affirming model 1) have been shaped by this dichotomy as much as their rivals. The difference is that they believe that Christian doctrine belongs on the "fact" side of the ledger, while liberals accept the reduction of religion to subjective value. Conservatives have rightly challenged the demotion of religious claims to the "value" side of the ledger, highlighting the factual character of the Bible's miraculous claims. Nevertheless, they have often failed to challenge the dichotomy itself. Even a propositional claim like "Jesus rose from the dead" is a fact that is interpreted either in faith or in an evaluative paradigm that dismisses the possibility of miracles.

Challenging this fact-value dichotomy, contemporary communicative theory helps us to see the how language actually works in ways often overlooked in modernity. *We use words to get things done.* Of course, sometimes that includes referring, describing, proposing, and asserting, but we do a host of other things through speech, such as promising, warning, surprising, questioning, comforting, and so forth. The event of one's writing, uttering, or otherwise signifying something is called the *locutionary act*. What we do through such signifying is referred to as the *illocutionary act* (or force). That which is brought about in the hearer as a result is its *perlocutionary effect*.[22]

So, for example, to cry, "Fire!" in a crowded building is to engage in a threefold action: (1) uttering the word *fire*, (2) warning unsuspecting victims, and (3) causing the crowd to clear the building. It is clear enough that in this sort of speech act there is a personal encounter in which one is confronted with a decision, a historical-social context in which the exclamation is meaningful, and an inner experience of imminent danger. However, none of this would be possible apart from some propositional content. The assumed proposition is that there is a fire that is threatening the building, even if the speech act itself is more than a mere description of a state of affairs. Similarly, saying "I do" in the context of a wedding ceremony involves these three aspects as well: (1) speaking the words (locutionary act) and (2) promising (illocutionary act), which (3) brings about a new state of affairs—namely, marrying (perlocutionary effect). In each case, the speech act also depends on a context in which such an utterance *counts as* something that can actually create the intended state of affairs. Crying, "Fire!" creates the intended effect in the context of a crowded room. Likewise, the pronouncement of the couple as husband and wife can only effect a marriage when it is uttered by the appropriate person in the appropriate context. In the Bible, the *covenant* is the context in which the speech of prophets and apostles counts as God's judging and saving speech. "Calling on the name of the Lord" does not fit neatly into "fact" or "value"; it is something one does in the face of imminent threat, which achieves its perlocutionary effect in the context of God's covenant.

If we apply this approach to our doctrine of revelation, the false choices in the various models described above melt away. As an external Word that confronts—possibly even accosts—the hearer, this speech always arrives at the sovereign initiative of God. This is what the Reformers meant by their emphasis on the external Word. At the same time, they rejected the medieval definition of faith as mere assent to all of the doctrines taught by the church.

God's Word not only asserts truth; it creates and destroys, plants and uproots, judges and justifies, kills and makes alive: "The Lord has sent a word against Jacob, and it will fall on Israel" (Isa 9:8). Far from being a dead letter, the Word of God "gets around." It not only *sets* forth; it *brings* forth. The Word not only explains,

---

22. See J. L. Austin, *How to Do Things with Words* (ed. J. O. Urmsson and Marina Sbisàà (Cambridge, Mass.: Harvard Univ. Press, 1975); John R. Searle, *Speech Acts: An Essay in the Phi-* *losophy of Language* (Cambridge: Cambridge Univ. Press, 1969); Richard S. Briggs, *Words in Action: Speech Act Theory and Biblical Interpretation* (Edinburgh: T&T Clark, 2001).

describes, asserts, and proposes, but *arrives*. J. A. Motyer asks, "How did the prophet receive the message which he was commissioned to convey to his fellows? The answer in the vast majority of the cases is perfectly clear and yet tantalizingly vague: 'The word of the Lord came ...' "[23] Indeed, "the word of the LORD came to me, saying, ... " is also a common expression in the prophets. The Lord came in the energy of his speech, which was delivered through the prophets and has now been delivered consummately in the One who is the Word of God not only in energy but in essence (Heb 1:1–3). If we use language to get things done (and not simply to describe an existing state of affairs), then it is because we are God's analogues. The triune God is the archetypal poet (in the classical sense: *poieō* meaning "to make"), who creates reality by speaking.

The false choice between word-revelation and act-revelation that has been posed by twentieth-century debates is exposed by the recognition that speaking is itself an action and not only descriptive of acts. Communication is not limited to description, information, and instruction—as the propositional model implies.[24] "The word of God is living and active" (Heb 4:12). It comes not only with the authority of the Father as its source and the Son as its content but with the Spirit as its power (1Th 2:13; cf. Isa 49:2; Jer 23:29). As rain descends on the earth to yield a crop, "so shall my word be that goes out from my mouth; it shall not return to me empty, but it shall accomplish that which I purpose, and shall succeed in the thing for which I sent it" (Isa 55:11).

To be sure, we will be prone to our own version of reductionism if we force all instances of revelation into the prophetic pattern. God also reveals wisdom, laws, and doctrines; he reveals himself even by authorizing certain expressions of faith and experience as normative for his covenant people (as in the Psalms). Nevertheless, this arrival of the Word from outside of the prophet and apostle is characteristic of the Bible's historical narratives and its prophecies.[25] Even in visions, the spoken word remains dominant, as in Isaiah 6, where the action and dialogue keep us from fixing an idolatrous gaze on God in his naked majesty. Actually, dreams played a comparatively small role in Old Testament revelation.[26] In fact, although Zechariah's prophecies may have come to him through dreams (e.g., Zec 1:8–9; 4:1), in Jeremiah it is the false prophets who appeal to dreams as the principal vehicle of their so-called revelations (Jer 23:25–28, 32; 27:9; 29:8–9; cf. 23:16).[27] In Scripture,

---

23. J. A. Motyer, "Prophecy, Prophets," in *The New Bible Dictionary* (ed. J. D. Douglas; Grand Rapids: Eerdmans, 1962), 1039.

24. In fact, it is striking how many contemporary theologians observe the similarities between the Reformers' theology of the word and speech act theory; see esp. Austin, *How to Do Things with Words*; Oswald Bayer, *Theology the Lutheran Way* (ed. and trans. Jeffrey G. Silcock and Mark C. Mattes; Grand Rapids: Eerdmans, 2007), 126–38; Reinhard Hütter, *Suffering Divine Things: Theology as Church Practice* (Grand Rapids: Eerdmans, 2000), 82–94.

25. Claus Westermann, *What Does the Old Testament Say about God?* (Atlanta: John Knox, 1979), 20–21.

26. Thompson, *Old Testament View of Revelation*, 27.

27. Ibid.

the primary vehicle not only of revelation but of creation, providence, redemption, and consummation is God's speech. By his Word and Spirit, the Father summons the world into being out of nothing, calls Israel out of bondage into the Promised Land, and brings about a new creation within this present evil age.

The acts of God in history and in nature are essential bearers of revelation, as E. W. Heaton notes: "Beneath most of the nouns in the Old Testament there throbs a living verb," and, "Hebrew religion is a religion of the verb rather than the noun, because it finds its characteristic expression in action."[28] Thus, model 2 (revelation as a history of God's mighty acts) offers an important insight. However, lively verbs give rise to stable nouns, which a propositional view (model 1) highlights. Furthermore, God's speech acts generate observable events and their authoritative interpretation. Therefore, we cannot set "Word" and "Act" in opposition, as is the tendency in models 1, 2, and 4.

By themselves, historical events do not reveal God's mighty agency—precisely because we see their effects, which, far from revealing that agency, may even be astonishing and inexplicable;—rather, the divine cause must be revealed by God himself. In fact, this was why Barth was wary of identifying revelation directly with certain historical events. However, his own view (model 4) fails to adequately relate God's revelatory encounter here and now to the flow of history. Yet once we recognize that (1) God's speech itself is as much an action as the historical events it describes, and (2) his interpretation (which includes doctrinal description) is necessary in order for these momentous historical events to be revelatory, this becomes a false dilemma.

Our doctrine of revelation must be roomy enough to accommodate the variety of the forms of revelation and genres of its scriptural mediation that we encounter in the Bible. To borrow the insights of J. L. Austin, speech includes not only constatives (statements of fact) but performatives (statements that create a certain state of affairs). John Searle notes, "We tell people how things are (Assertives), we try to get them to do things (Directives), we commit ourselves to doing things (Commissives), we express our feelings and attitudes (Expressives), and we bring about changes in the world through our utterances (Declarations)."[29] Each of these types of illocutionary acts mentioned by Searle can be found throughout Scripture.[30] The covenant provides the broad context within which all of these speech acts count as divine revelation even when communicated through human agents.

---

28. E. W. Heaton, *The Old Testament Prophets* (New York: Penguin, 1958), 100.

29. John R. Searle, *Expression and Meaning: Studies in the Theory of Speech Acts* (Cambridge: Cambridge Univ. Press, 1985), viii.

30. Interestingly, the acts Searle calls "declaratives" are identified by Austin as "verdictives" (from "verdict"), which is precisely how Reformation theology understands the gospel.

Not only proposing doctrines to be believed and commands to be followed, God's revelation promises, threatens, creates, destroys, judges, liberates, comforts, confuses, and performs a host of other illocutionary acts, with many perlocutionary effects. Therefore, it addresses not only the intellect but the emotions—indeed, the whole person. It is not only the revelation *of God* (as personal encounter), but God's own revelation *concerning himself and everything else* in relation to him (as doctrine). *In short, the object of revelation—and thus of theology—is God and his works in the unfolding drama of redemption.* The variety and richness of God's manners of speaking elicit the many genres in which the Spirit brings about the appropriate response in narrative and praise, poetry and prose, wisdom and apocalyptic, prophecy and parable, law and doctrine.

C. REVELATION SERVES REDEMPTION

Revelation is not an act of downloading eternal information onto our noetic desktop. Revelation is not a catalog of timeless doctrines and morals. Nor is it a record of the inner experience or new awareness of a universal religious feeling that particular communities expressed in their own inadequate ways. Revelation is also not to be restricted to divine self-revelation (personal encounter), as if it were identical with redemption. Rather, as Geerhardus Vos observes, "Revelation is the interpretation of redemption."[31] In fact, as God's living and active speech, revelation does more than reveal; it creates the reality of which it speaks.

In this approach, revelation cannot be reduced to doctrine any more than to history or personal encounter. Here we are concerned with "the actual embodiment of revelation in history": "The process of revelation is not only concomitant with history, but it becomes incarnate in history. The facts of history themselves acquire a revealing significance. The crucifixion and resurrection of Christ are examples of this. We must place act-revelation by the side of word-revelation."[32] The last-quoted sentence is especially useful in challenging the false choice between act-revelation (highlighted by "Revelation as History") and Word-revelation (emphasized by "Revelation as Dialectical Encounter"). God's historical acts "are never entirely left to speak for themselves; they are preceded and followed by word-revelation. The usual order is: first word, then the fact, then again the interpretive word."[33] "For religion," Abraham Joshua Heschel notes, "is more than a creed or an ideology and cannot be understood when detached from acts and events."[34]

This process of God's self-revelation through historical events and interpretation

---

31. Geerhardus Vos, *Biblical Theology* (Grand Rapids: Eerdmans, 1948), 6.

32. Ibid., 6–7.

33. Ibid.

34. Abraham Joshua Heschel, *God in Search of Man* (New York: Macmillan, 1976), 7.

is never static. Rather, it occurs through history in the dynamic interplay between the covenant Lord and his servant people. A truly historical sense was born in Israel, while the nations were committed to cyclical patterns of cultic and cultural life. In nonbiblical religions, revelation most closely fits the "new awareness" model. The myths symbolize eternal truths that would be true regardless of whether the myths themselves narrate actual events in history. However, in Israel, revelation is inextricably connected to the "new thing" that God has done or will do in the future. The myth (or dramatic narrative) does not *reflect* the truth, as the lower world of appearances reflects the eternal principles of the upper world. Rather, the truth literally incarnates itself in history. Thompson notes, "Israel saw that there was a unity in all human experience, and that this was due to the rule of the Lord of history, who initiates and wills all history, and who directs all history.... Within that ancient Semitic world it is only in Israel that we have recorded history in the true sense."[35]

One weakness in all of the theories proposed above is the tendency to reduce God's communication to *revealing*. However, <u>God's speech does not merely interpret history; it creates it</u>. Revelation is not gnosis or enlightenment: a way of salvation by discovering God's hidden essence or will. It is never an end in itself, whether as supernatural information, existential encounter, or as inner experience and heightened awareness. God reveals himself only inasmuch and insofar as he deems necessary for our invocation of him for our salvation and life.

D. PROPOSITIONS WITHOUT PROPOSITIONALISM

Antipathy toward propositional revelation (model 1) is due to many factors. Suspicion of revealed doctrines or propositions is motivated in part by a general epistemological skepticism that reaches back at least to Kant and reaches its consummation in certain forms of postmodern theory (see ch. 1), and in part by a recognition of the inherent weaknesses of *reducing* revelation to doctrine. We have already seen the danger of reducing preaching to speech about God rather than seeing it also as God's own communication. God not only asserts the existence of a covenant that we might enter through our own intellectual assent and moral activity, but creates the reality of which he speaks by this same Word.

However, the opposite kind of reductionism is seen in Schleiermacher's denial of revealed doctrines: "But I am unwilling to accept the further definition that [revelation] operates upon man as a cognitive being. For that would make the revelation to be originally and essentially doctrine."[36] Revelation occurs exclusively as direct religious experience, while doctrine (even that which is found in the Bible)

---

35. Thompson, *The Old Testament View of Revelation*, 25.

36. Friedrich Schleiermacher, *The Christian Faith* (ed. and trans. H. R. Mackintosh and J. S. Stewart; Edinburgh: T&T Clark, 1928), 50.

is subjective human interpretation of that universal feeling. The result is that God can be considered the object of our *experience* but not of our *knowledge*.[37] Schleiermacher's view of revelation leaves no place for the concept of the "Word," since cognitive communication is inherent in the term.

Even those theories claiming to be more objective remain suspicious of propositional truth. At first, "Revelation as History" seems to hold great promise, but at the end of the day it collapses back into subjectivism. For instance, G. E. Wright speaks of the exodus as a paradigmatic "mighty act of God," but it turns out that the event acquires this status because Israel interpreted a plausibly natural phenomenon *as if* it were God's miraculous liberation of his people from Egypt.[38] The *fact* may have been purely natural, but the *value* is assigned by the subjective interpretation of a nomadic religious community.

For "Revelation as Dialectical Encounter" (model 4), reluctance to identify God's Word with human mediation in any direct way creates a chasm between the giver and receiver of revelation. Bultmann's nearly gnostic antithesis of the Jesus of History and the Christ of Faith, Brunner's antithesis of propositions and personal encounter, and Barth's declining to identify the revelation event directly with its creaturely forms of mediation perpetuate rather than transcend the subjectivist tendency of modern theology.

Faithful to neo-Kantian philosophy, much of twentieth-century theology has been united in its assault on the majesty of the doctrinal proposition. Whatever his differences with nineteenth-century liberalism, Bultmann speaks for the widest spectrum in modern theology when he speculates, "Above all, doctrines cannot be revelation."[39] After all, this would mean that revelation has happened; it lies in the past. "A revealed doctrine that is further handed on *is* no longer a revelation." It would be a salutary reminder if Bultmann had said that Jesus not only speaks the truth but is the Truth; however, he forces a choice: "Thus Jesus *is* the truth, he does not *speak* it. . . . And the believer does not *know* or *possess* the revelation. . . . Each generation has the same original relation to the revelation. Revelation thus remains revelation. It does not become something revealed. Otherwise God would become an idol."[40]

---

37. Ibid., 52.

38. Frank B. Dilley notes, "The modern 'Biblical Theologian' is in a quandary about what to say. His view of man and of history centers upon his assertion of a 'God Who Acts' [G. E. Wright], yet he seems unable to communicate what it is that he means by the actions of God. Unwilling to endorse the conservative view of a God Who Acts through outright miracles or the liberal doctrine of a God restricted to universal actions, he speaks about a God who acts specially in history, but without giving any concrete content to his assertions, and he seems unable to

distinguish his position from that of the liberalism he rejects." Wright places the whole weight of his proposal on the exodus and Sinai events, but "one searches [his work] in vain for any clear description of what God actually did" (Frank B. Dilley, "Does the 'God Who Acts' Really Act?'" in *God's Activity in the World* [ed. Owen C. Thomas; Chico, Calif.: Scholars Press, 1983], 47).

39. Rudolf Bultmann, *What Is Theology?* (Fortress Texts in Modern Theology; ed. Eberhard Jüngel and Klaus W. Müller; trans. Roy A. Harrisville; Minneapolis: Fortress, 1997), 82–83.

40. Ibid., 83.

This is not really a break with Schleiermacher and Romanticism, as Bultmann himself acknowledged.[41] Like his liberal pietist mentors, Bultmann affirms the subjective act of faith on the part of individual believers over against an objective faith that is believed (i.e., doctrine).[42] "What, then, has been revealed?" he asks. "Nothing at all, so far as the question about revelation asks for doctrines—doctrines, say, that no man could have discovered for himself—or for mysteries that become known once and for all as soon as they are communicated."[43]

Contrary to this claim, however, the New Testament declares that mysteries hidden in past ages have now been revealed for all time (1Co 2:6–10; Eph 3:8–12). The "already"—that is, past, completed events—indicated by the aorist active indicative in Greek includes the event of reconciliation and its interpretation together. The mystery of salvation has been accomplished and revealed once and for all. The "once and for all" (*hapax*) of Christ's completed work *and* its revelation are interdependent claims (Heb 1:1–2; 9:26–28; 10:2).

In an existentialist framework, the Event has always happened, always happens, and will always happen. Far from demythologizing, this is to fall back into the mythological imagination of paganism's eternal return. In Scripture, the gospel is something that was anticipated, has happened, and has its continuing effects through the Spirit's perfecting agency. When we hear the words, "Behold, the Lamb of God, who takes away the sin of the world" (Jn 1:29), God himself is here and now addressing us through the Baptist's words reported by John the evangelist. It is indeed a personal encounter. It is also "revelation as history," announcing the mighty act of God. Although it does not arise from inner experience as an eternal truth, it certainly generates experience as part of its perlocutionary effect: From now on, many of John's disciples will follow Jesus. *However, it can be none of these if it lacks any propositional content.* Whatever else he is doing by uttering these words, the evangelist is clearly proposing for our belief the fact that Jesus Christ is the promised sacrifice for sin.

In Bultmann's case (distinct from Barth's), the deeper motivation for opposing orthodoxy, including its doctrine of revelation, is simple: he does not expect modern people who use electric lights to believe in a world of angels and demons.[44] As different as their formulations are, Barth and Brunner share Bultmann's antithesis of

---

41. Ibid., 85. "Romanticism is aware that God is not possessed in doctrines that are intelligible or can be owned; it recognizes that revelation must remain revelation and that it is marked by its character as present" (85). "The historical pantheism of liberal theology is thus a murky mixture of romantic and idealistic motifs" (87). In fact, he adds, "There is precedent for the romantic concept in pietism, to the extent that in pietism 'religious inwardness' is a reaction to the dogmatic faith of orthodoxy." The problem with pietism and Romanticism,

he thinks, is that it reduces faith to experience (mysticism and irrationalism) just as orthodoxy reduces it to knowledge (89).

42. Ibid., 49.

43. Rudolf Bultmann, *Existence and Faith* (New York: World, 1969), 85.

44. Rudolf Bultmann, *Kerygma and Myth: A Theological Debate* (ed. Hans Werner Bartsch; London: SPCK, 1953), 5; cf. Peter Berger, *A Rumor of Angels: Modern Society and the Rediscovery of the Supernatural* (New York: Doubleday, 1960), 46–47.

personal encounter and propositional truth. Yet even the most emotive pledges of love or disappointment involve some propositional (designative) content.[45] Similarly, theologian Colin Gunton reminds us that even "I love you" contains some propositional content, even if it is more than that.[46] Friends and relatives would be justly offended if we abstracted a personal relationship from the details they reveal about themselves. Walther Eichrodt writes, "If what matters in both the Old and New Testaments is the existential understanding of the professing believer, and not the presuppositions or individual content of his belief, then obviously the relation of his convictions to history becomes immaterial."[47]

E. REVELATION AND MEDIATION: A WAY WITH WORDS

Beneath the tumultuous conflicts of liberals and conservatives are the various currents and countercurrents of modern epistemology. In spite of their great differences over the form that revelation takes, all of these models seem captive to a demand for revelational immediacy. R. S. Clark calls this the illegitimate demand for *religious certainty* and the illegitimate demand for *religious experience*.[48] We have already recognized this tendency in the first model, with the explicit denial of the doctrine of analogy in favor of univocity by conservative theologians like Gordon Clark and Carl F. H. Henry (see ch. 1, pp. 54–57). Yet this propensity for immediate knowledge or experience can be discerned across these models.

In various ways, we want to transcend our creaturely finitude and comprehend the naked God in a univocal (archetypal) gaze. Gunton blames much of the antipropositional tenor of modern theology on this demand for immediacy, which is finally a desire to transcend the Creator-creature divide. Hegel wrote, "The divine nature is the same as the human, and it is this unity which is intuitively apprehended (*angeschaut*)."[49] Gunton replies, "The first point is that for Hegel revelation is the function of an immediate relation of God to the mind, just as for Schleiermacher religion is a form of immediacy to experience." Barth, on the other hand, resisted the conflation of God and world but still argued for "a form of revelational immediacy."[50]

Gunton's inclusion of Barth seems unwarranted at first glance. After all, was Barth not the champion of God's "wholly otherness," emphasizing that God's self-revelation is never direct and that God reveals himself by concealing himself? How-

45. See Nicholas Wolterstorff, *Divine Discourse* (Cambridge: Cambridge Univ. Press, 1995), 211.

46. Colin Gunton, *A Brief Theology of Revelation* (Edinburgh: T&T Clark, 1995), 109.

47. Walther Eichrodt, *Theology of the Old Testament* (trans. J. A. Baker; Philadelphia: Westminster, 1951), 1:515.

48. R. S. Clark, *Recovering the Reformed Confession* (Phillipsburg, N.J.: P&R, 2008), chs. 1–2.

49. Cited in Gunton, *Brief Theology of Revelation*, 3.

50. Gunton, *Brief Theology of Revelation*, 3. Gunton adds, "While it would be ludicrous to tar all those whom I have mentioned with the Gnostic brush—though I would be prepared to have a good try with some of them—there is something suspicious about the kind of direct communication with God which experiential views of revelation, and sometimes even Barth's actualist conception, appear to presuppose" (10).

ever, Gunton's point may be justified. We may compare Pannenberg and Barth in this regard (representing models 2 and 3 above, respectively). In quite different ways, revelation in both Barth and Pannenberg seems to be understood as yielding archetypal knowledge. I will refer to this by using the uppercase R. In the eternal moment (Barth), or in the completed future (Pannenberg), Revelation pierces through the veil of Kant's thing-in-itself (*Ding-an-sich*). For Barth, whenever this Revelation occurs, it is nothing less than God's self-revelation of his inner being.[51] In fact, Revelation, properly speaking, *is* God.[52] In the revelatory event, we share in God's eternal self-knowledge.[53] Pannenberg agrees with Barth that in this self-revelation, God discloses nothing less than his essence.[54]

As a creaturely witness (indirect revelation), the Bible cannot reveal this essence, so Revelation itself must be located elsewhere—and this is where Pannenberg's path diverges significantly from Barth's. Historical events, for Pannenberg, are the site of the self-revelation of God's essence, rather than Barth's dialectical encounter in the Word-event.[55] Nevertheless, this Revelation can be comprehended only from the end of history.[56] Therefore, one might say that for Barth Revelation occurs "above" Scripture; for Pannenberg it happens "from the future," anticipated proleptically in Christ's resurrection.[57] Whether this Revelation is above us (Barth) or ahead of us (Pannenberg), its content is nothing less than God's immanent being. Both are wary of the traditional distinction of Reformation theology between the "hidden" and "revealed" God (another way of stating the archetypal-ectypal distinction), concerned that it might allow for a contradiction between "God in himself" and "God as he is toward us." Nevertheless, this univocal Revelation is related to its creaturely form here and now in a merely *equivocal* manner. On the side of Revelation-itself, this line of thinking is drawn toward rationalism; on the side of its mediated form, it tends toward irrationalism. This claim requires further argumentation.

Barth and Pannenberg agree that Scripture is a *witness* to revelation rather than Revelation-itself. Although there are, of course, propositional statements in

---

51. George Hunsinger, *Disruptive Grace: Studies in the Theology of Karl Barth* (Grand Rapids: Eerdmans, 2000), 338–60. In another essay in *Disruptive Grace*, Hunsinger cites Barth (*Church Dogmatics*) to this effect: "'Through God's revelation' we become 'participants' in this occurrence (II/1, 49), receiving and having a part in God's eternal self-knowledge (II/1, 68). For as 'God gives himself to us to be known in the truth of his self-knowledge' (II/1, 53), we receive a share in the truth of his knowledge of himself' (II/1, 51)." It is, however, "indirect," since it is mediated through Christ (170–71). Even granting Barth's veiling-unveiling dialectic, such quotes would seem to suggest a univocal view, although Hunsinger claims that Barth is more nearly identified with an analogical perspective. I would argue that even in our union with Christ, we do not share in God's self-knowledge. It is not simply the means (direct/indirect), but the content, that is in view in these distinctions. This is not to deny that what Christ mediates is real knowledge, but it is to assert that that knowledge is and always remains analogical and ectypal.

52. Barth, *Church Dogmatics*, vol. 1, pt. 1, 295–96.

53. Ibid., vol. 2, pt. 1, 53, 68.

54. Wolfhart Pannenberg, ed., *Revelation as History* (New York: Macmillan, 1968), 4.

55. Pannenberg, "The Doctrine of Revelation," in ibid., 125.

56. Ibid., 131.

57. Wolfhart Pannenberg, *Systematic Theology* (Grand Rapids: Eerdmans, 1991), 1:246.

Scripture, they are fallible human pointers to Revelation-in-encounter (for Barth) or Revelation-in-history (for Pannenberg). A *pointer to* Revelation is different from a *means of* Revelation. The subtle but important difference is seen, for example, in the way Daniel Migliore (following Barth) defines revelation as "God's free and gracious self-disclosure through particular events that are attested and interpreted by people of faith."[58] I would rewrite this sentence as follows: Revelation is "God's free and gracious self-disclosure through particular events *and* the words of the prophets and apostles through whom he communicates these events and their meaning." For Barth, the Word of God (i.e., the event of God's self-revelation) is always a new work, a free decision of God that cannot be bound to a creaturely form of mediation, including Scripture.[59] This Word never belongs to history but is always an eternal event that confronts us in our contemporary existence.[60] "If therefore we are serious about the fact that this miracle is an event," Barth writes, "we cannot regard the presence of God's Word in the Bible as an attribute inhering once and for all in this book as such and what we see before us of books and chapters and verses."[61]

Furthermore, Barth and Pannenberg share the Hegelian assumption that God's self-revelation is always indirect, which means that God's Word can never be identified directly with its mediated form (either Scripture or preaching). Until the end of history, all of our knowledge of God—including that communicated in Scripture—is equivocal, according to Pannenberg.[62] Although Barth draws attention to the personal encounter that is often undervalued in conservative evangelical treatments of revelation, even as sympathetic an interpreter as David Kelsey can conclude, "There is a convergence of critical judgment from otherwise different theological perspectives that the allegedly 'biblical' doctrines of 'revelation' developed in the neo-orthodox era were conceptually incoherent."[63]

Missing from all of the models of revelation that we have considered (at least in their dominant formulations) is an *analogical* account of revelation here and now.[64] Revelation is never immediate, univocal, or archetypal, whether in the form of reason, moral duty, experience, personal encounter, or historical events. Rather, it is always accommodated, mediated, analogical, and ectypal. Nowhere above the Scriptures, at the end of history, or even in Scripture do creatures transgress the barrier of finitude to gaze on God's essence. We are always hidden, like Moses

---

58. See Daniel L. Migliore, *Faith Seeking Understanding: An Introduction to Christian Doctrine* (2nd ed.; Grand Rapids: Eerdmans, 2008), 26.

59. Barth, *Church Dogmatics*, vol. 2, pt. 1, 527.

60. Ibid., vol. 2, pt. 1, 528.

61. Ibid., vol. 2, pt. 1, 530.

62. Wolfhart Pannenberg, "Analogy and Doxology," in *Basic Questions in Theology* (trans. H. G. Kehm; Philadelphia: Fortress, 1970), esp. 1:227.

63. David Kelsey, *The Uses of Scripture in Recent Theology* (Philadelphia: Fortress, 1975), 209.

64. Note that Pannenberg supports the equivocal view by accepting the criticism of analogy offered by proponents of univocity: "If our talk of God is only metaphorical, we can be assured of no ontological connection between our world and his existence" (*Basic Questions of Theology*, 1:238). (Analogy, however, is not the same as metaphor.)

behind the rock, as God's goodness and grace pass by. Yet because God condescends to bring us into his fellowship, an accommodated revelation can be given—and is given—through creaturely signs. *These creaturely signs are not mere witnesses to an archetypal knowledge of God in a revelation event, but are the means of an ectypal knowledge of God in Scripture and preaching.*

The reduction of revelation to inner experience or enlightenment reflects a hyperimmanence that places God under our control. However, Barth's emphasis on God's transcendence justifies Bonhoeffer's complaint that in this view God is never truly "haveable."[65] In his revelation, the God who cannot be possessed makes himself our richest treasure; the one who cannot be mastered makes himself the servant of our redemption; the one who is high and exalted makes himself lowly and the greatest sufferer of human injustice and hatred who ever lived. Yet, wonder of all wonders, even in loving us in this way, God remains transcendent, incomprehensible, and hidden. Revelation is accommodated discourse, even "baby talk," in which God "must descend far beneath his loftiness," as Calvin puts it.[66] Not even in revelation, according to Calvin, does the believer "attain to [God's] exalted state," but one *does* receive truth "accommodated to our capacity so that we may understand it."[67] "Better to limp along this path," Calvin cautioned, "than to dash with all speed outside it."[68]

In short, for the Reformers, revelation is never as lofty as univocal knowledge nor as inadequate as equivocal knowledge, and this accommodated revelation is given directly in Scripture. To put it crudely, God gets the job done. He displays his power in weakness and his wisdom in what Greeks consider folly. God is capable of revealing himself, his will and works, and his redemptive plans through creaturely mediation. The creatures themselves are not worthy, but God sanctifies them for his loving and sovereign purposes.

F. ESSENCE AND ENERGIES

If the reader will permit a tautology, God's communication—even through creatures—is divine. However, this does not permit us to worship burning bushes, budding rods, angels, prophets, or apostles. In the last chapter of the Bible, John reports, "I fell down to worship at the feet of the angel who showed [these things] to me, but he said to me, 'You must not do that! I am a fellow servant with you and your brothers the prophets, and with those who keep the words of this book. Worship God'" (Rev 22:8–9). Although the heavens declare God's glory, we do

---

65. D. Bonhoeffer, *Act and Being* (trans. Bernard Noble; New York: Harper & Bros., 1961), 90–91.

66. Calvin, *Institutes* 3.11.20; cf. 1.13.1.

67. Ibid., 1.17.13.

68. Ibid., 1.6.3.

not worship the celestial bodies. Nor do we offer worship to the Bible. But does this mean that the Bible is merely a human witness to revelation and not itself the medium of direct divine communication?

Part of the problem in answering this question is that our Western theology is usually restricted to the category of essence: either divine or nondivine. Eastern theology, however, introduced another category: *God's energies*. The sun's rays are not the sun itself, but they are also not the ground that is warmed by the sun. Rather, they are the shining forth or effulgence of the sun. Similarly, God's energies (*energeia*) are neither God's essence (*ousia*) nor a created effect but are God's knowledge, power, and grace directed toward creatures.[69] This view is analogous to the familiar formula in Protestant orthodoxy already mentioned, namely, that we come to know God in his works rather than in his essence. God's works are neither God's essence nor merely the created effect of his action, but God's effective agency, which I have elsewhere called God's workings.[70] God's act of creating the world by his Word is neither an emanation of God's being nor itself part of creation. Rather, it is God's activity. Presupposing this distinction, Calvin writes: "for the Spirit may be regarded as the essential power of God, whose *energy* is manifested and exerted in the entire government of the world, as well as in miraculous events" (emphasis added).[71]

Moses did not worship the burning bush, even though God had claimed it as the footstool of his heavenly throne in revealing himself to the prophet. God commanded Moses to make a bronze serpent and hold it up on a pole before Israel for healing, typologically signifying Christ's defeat of Satan at the cross (Nu 21:9; Jn 3:14). However, after generations of Israelites had made the bronze serpent an object of worship and offerings, King Hezekiah "broke in pieces the bronze serpent that Moses had made," destroyed the high places (2Ki 18:4), "and "trusted in the LORD, the God of Israel" (v. 5). We do not fall down before the Bible, because, unlike the hypostatic Word, it is not the site of God's essence but rather of his energies.[72] We worship God for, in, and through his actions, but never the actions themselves. The relationship between the Word of God and the words of prophets and apostles is analogical. Just as the ark of the covenant could be identified as the locus of God's presence in Israel's midst, even though God could not be contained in a box, Scripture is identified as the locus of God's revelation, even though he infinitely

---

69. Vladimir Lossky, *The Mystical Theology of the Eastern Church* (Crestwood, N.Y.: St. Vladimir's Seminary Press, 1976), 65–89, 220.

70. Michael Horton, *Covenant and Salvation: Union with Christ* (Louisville: Westminster John Knox, 2007), 211–15, 231, 268–70, 274–75.

71. John Calvin, *A Harmony of the Evangelists* (trans. William Pringle; Grand Rapids: Baker, 1996), 1:42.

72. Not even in their visions did the prophets see God's essence, but only representations that were overshadowed by his words. Only in Christ, the incarnate God, do we meet the physical presence of revelation worthy of worship, and still we see the person of the Son, who is God but not the divine essence itself.

transcends it. The patristic rule that the finite cannot comprehend (i.e., enclose) the infinite (*finitum non capax infiniti*) is applicable to every form of divine revelation.

Let us add to this category of divine energies the time-honored conviction that in every external work of the Trinity the Father is the origin and cause, the Son is the medium and content, and the Spirit brings about the work's intended effect within creation. Then, adapting this formulation to the categories of speech acts, we can say that in every external work of the Godhead—creation, providence, redemption, and consummation—the Father speaks his Word in the Son through the perfecting power of the Spirit. *To the Father is ascribed the locutionary act of speaking; to the Son the illocutionary act of command and promise, and to the Spirit the perlocutionary act of bringing about the appropriate response in creaturely reality.*[73]

In this model, there is no revelation of God's essence—direct, indirect, or otherwise. Nor is the medium of revelation (the Bible) either *God's essence* or merely a *creaturely witness*. Rather, as the canonical record of God's speech, it communicates to us here and now *God's powerful energies*. This vision of God's back is a revelation not of God's majesty but of his goodness and grace, as God proclaims his Word: "I will be gracious to whom I will be gracious, and will show mercy on whom I will show mercy" (Ex 33:19). God reveals his attributes (i.e., characteristics) rather than his hidden essence, what he is like rather than what he is in the inner depths of his hidden majesty.

Eastern Orthodoxy has appealed to Exodus 33 for its distinction between the revelation of God in his essence (inaccessible glory) and in his energies (gracious acts), just as the Reformers did for their contrast between a theology of glory and a theology of the cross, and as their heirs did for the further distinction between archetypal and ectypal theology. Notice further from this passage that God's gracious goodness is not a visual spectacle, but a covenantal pledge to invoke: "I ... will proclaim before you my name 'The LORD'" (v. 19). As Brunner recognized, "The 'vision' is rather the token of the reality of that which he 'hears,' the mysterious self-manifestation of the God who is 'present' in his mighty personal word."[74] In other words, God's revelation of his back is mediated through voice (proclamation) rather than a vision of his archetypal majesty. This proclamation is not merely Moses' expression of his religious experience, yet it is not God's glorious essence. Rather, it is his radiating energies—God's living speech, to which we have direct access in the Scriptures.

Mediation is not a *problem*; it is the *solution*—God's condescending mercy, in order to reveal himself without destroying us. In our predicament as covenant

---

73. See Kevin J. Vanhoozer, *The Drama of Doctrine: A Canonical-Linguistic Approach to Christian Theology* (Louisville: Westminster John Knox, 2005), 37–76.

74. Emil Brunner, *Revelation and Reason: The Christian Doctrine of Faith and Knowledge* (trans. Olive Wyon; Wake Forest, N.C.: Chanticleer, 1946), 91.

violators, our need is not for a naked revelation of God in his majesty but for God's revelation of his saving mercy in Christ. Our demand for archetypal knowledge of God's inner essence encourages us to try to go behind the concrete fact of God's accommodated revelation in Christ and in Scripture, whose humanity is treated as a barrier to revelation rather than as a medium of it. Instead, we must assume the posture of the covenant servant, like Mary at the angel's announcement: "'Behold, I am the servant of the Lord; let it be to me according to your word'" (Lk 1:38). This announcement was not merely new information; it created a new state of affairs in the world—namely, Mary's faith, through which she not only was redeemed but became the bearer of the world's Redeemer. Nevertheless, there was a definite propositional content to the announcement, enough in fact to provoke her experience of gratitude and expression of thanksgiving in the Magnificat (vv. 46–55).

God's sermon that he preaches to Moses has propositional content, yet it is not simply a propositional statement but is a world-generating, faith-creating, history-engendering pledge: "I . . . will show mercy on whom I will show mercy" (Ex 33:19). This is not just a proposition about God's attribute of freedom; it is a covenantal act in which God delivers himself over to his people, and they in turn deliver themselves over to God in faith. God conceals his glory under what Luther called *masks*. The masks are not identical with God's inner essence, but they are also not merely human responses to revelation; they are *the media of God's analogical revelation*. The creaturely form of God's self-revelation neither is transubstantiated into the divine essence nor remains a mere symbol or witness of his power, but is itself the medium of his divine energies. To the extent that it embraces univocity, the first model in Dulles's typology (revelation as doctrine) is no more satisfactory than the other forms of revelational immediacy.

G. TRIAL AND TESTIMONY

call for protection

In the covenantal economy, testimony is the correlate of invocation. Although the writings of the prophets and the apostles are more than witnesses to revelation, they are certainly that. The entire Bible can be construed as a long court case of Yahweh versus the Idols, with God's image bearers as his witnesses. This will become clearer as this unfolding story is recited in the following chapters of this volume. Just as the true prophets were distinguished from impostors by the fact that they had "stood in the council of the LORD to see and to hear his word" (Jer 23:18), the disciples became apostles based on their eyewitness testimony and commission (1Co 15:1–11; Gal 1:11–2:14; 1Jn 1:1–2; 2Pe 1:16–2:1). In this covenantal trial, they are not only witnesses but divine attorneys who have stood in his court and are authorized to bring the Word that they have heard to Israel and the world.

Through their unique witness, the Spirit creates a cloud of witnesses, testifying to the gospel throughout the world. Their testimony is that the Christ of Faith is the Jesus of History. Because the truths to which they bear witness occurred in history, the form that their witness takes is historical report. They are called by God to hear, see, report, and proclaim. They are evangelists. In fact, <u>*martyr* comes from the Greek word for "witness"</u> (*martys*).

Testimony cannot be reduced to either objectivism (fact) or subjectivism (value).[75] A covenant servant is not a dispassionate observer, standing on the fringes in neutral evaluation of the situation, nor merely a secretary taking divine dictation, but is already a part of the trial. At the same time, the witness cannot create the facts but can only testify to them. A false objectivism imagines that revelation is untainted by the subjectivity of the human witnesses. However, a false subjectivism imagines that human witness can only be an occasion for rather than the means of direct revelation. There is a vast difference between saying that revelation incorporates the interpretations of the prophets and apostles themselves and saying that it is simply a witness to their own inner experience of or encounter with revelation. Only because the Bible ultimately is *God's* testimony *through* human witnesses is it worthy of our complete confidence.

In spite of the centrality of testimony in revelation, its truth-conveying status is undervalued in all of the models of revelation that we have considered. In a propositionalist view, testimony easily loses its self-involving dimension: it is the *fact* that is revelation, not the *testimony* as such. However, this easily reduces faith to the level of mere assent. The apostles were not dispassionate historians (as if there could be such a thing), but *evangelists* commissioned by the risen Christ to speak his Word. Nevertheless, they testified to historical events that they did not themselves fabricate. In fact, they expressed surprise, confusion, and even fear in the face of these events.

At first glance, "revelation as history" seems best suited to employing the category of testimony. After all, this model concentrates its attention on "the mighty acts of God." Since the 1970s, a school known as *narrative theology* has emerged, influenced by this model of revelation. However, its leading proponents fall short of their own goal by placing revelation on the event side (fact) and testimony on the merely human (value) side of the ledger. If our only access to these events (human testimony) cannot be directly identified with revelation along with the events, then we only really know what the prophets and apostles experienced and attributed to God. In this case, who knows whether their evaluations are faithful interpretations

---

75. For this epistemology of testimony I am indebted especially to Paul Ricoeur, *Memory, History, Forgetting* (trans. Kathleen Blamey and David Pellauer; Chicago: Univ. of Chicago Press, 2004); Michael Polanyi, *Personal Knowledge: Towards* a *Post-Critical Philosophy* (Chicago: Univ. of Chicago Press, 1958); Walter Brueggemann, *Theology of the Old Testament: Testimony, Dispute, Advocacy* (Minneapolis: Fortress, 1997).

of the facts? However, faith is not believing *as if* God had acted in the exodus or the resurrection; it is a claim to facts as they are interpreted ultimately by God. As Dulles points out, the Hebrew term for "word" (*dābār*) is used for words *and* events.[76] God's acts *and* their interpretation are comprehended in Scripture under the category of Word. If "revelation as doctrine" cannot account for the rich variety of forms in which revelation arrives, then its reductionism is at least equaled by its rivals.

Is Barth's model of revelation a better fit with testimony? Although he emphasized Scripture's witnessing character, we are still left with the fact-value dilemma. In this case, the fact (or Fact) is Christ himself—the Word—who personally claims me here and now, but its interpretation (value) cannot be identified directly with divine revelation. Why should we privilege Scripture (as Barth—and for that matter, Schleiermacher—does) if it is merely a witness to revelation but not *itself* the authoritative deposit of God's definitive communication through human mediation?

In the subjectivist theories of revelation (inner experience and new awareness), the biblical idea of testimony (namely, witness to public and historical events) is exchanged for the testimony of the pious individual and community to their own religious experience. According to Schleiermacher, <u>faith cannot arise from the testimony of others; one's own personally felt experience is the only proper basis for faith—however the community (and its experience mediated through Scripture) may help to facilitate it.[77] The prophets and apostles testified to their personal experience, and we must testify to ours.</u>

It is certainly true, according to Scripture, that revelation touches us at the deepest levels of our experience (Heb 4:12–13). However, it does so precisely because it is an external Word that disrupts our natural reason and familiar experience. If its source were within the self, revelation would simply be a psychological projection of one's inner state of consciousness. Peter declares that apostolic testimony was not founded on "cleverly devised myths" but on eyewitness accounts, "knowing this first of all, that no prophecy of Scripture comes from someone's own interpretation. For no prophecy was ever produced by the will of man, but men spoke from God as they were carried along by the Holy Spirit" (2Pe 1:16, 20–21).

The sovereign self is dethroned rather than elevated, disoriented rather than

---

76. Dulles, *Models of Revelation*, 66–67: "Would it not be better to say that revelation is a complex reality consisting of the inspired word as the formal element and of the historical event as material element? This has been the opinion of many modern Catholic theologians, and seems to be favored by Vatican II.... 'This plan of revelation is realized by deeds and words having an inner unity: the deeds wrought by God in the history of salva-

tion manifest and confirm the teaching and realities signified by the words, while the words proclaim the deeds and clarify the mystery contained in them'.... The Hebrew term *dabar*, meaning both word and event, suggests this duality."

77. Friedrich Schleiermacher, *On Religion: Speeches to Its Cultured Despisers* (trans. John Oman; New York: Harper and Bros., 1958), 90.

self-certain, judged rather than judge. In this way, we know that we are not simply talking to ourselves, projecting our own experience onto the void, crafting idols of reason and experience. In revelation we do not experience our experience but are truly meeting a stranger who addresses us. C. S. Lewis expresses this well: "In all our joys and sorrows, religious, aesthetic, or natural, I seem to find things (almost incurably) thus. They are about something. They are a by-product of the (logically) prior act of attending to or looking towards something. We are not really concerned with the emotions: the emotions are our concern about something else."[78]

The gospel itself requires us to hold that testimony is not only one form but the most important form of revelation. We invoke the covenant Lord on the basis of the testimony of his prophets and apostles. Only a false objectivism and subjectivism keep us locked in a quandary over whether divinely commissioned human testimony, for all of its self-involving characteristics, can be a bearer of revelation.

Our legal system is based on the confidence in testimony yielding an account of historical events sufficient for a verdict, even though such testimony involves different perspectives from a variety of witnesses. This interplay of subjectivity and objectivity, this interpretation striving to conform to reality (or faith seeking understanding), is involved in every act of knowing to some extent.[79] Not only believers but also unbelieving Jews and Gentiles were witnesses *of* the empty tomb, but only believing Christians were witnesses *to* the risen Christ. Each group interpreted the evidence within the paradigm of its horizon of expectation. For example, Peter proclaims Christ's bodily resurrection as the fulfillment of Israel's narrative (Ac 2:14–36). Yet the objectivity of the event was sufficient to cause great disturbance in Jerusalem and to overthrow the unbelieving presuppositions of many. The facts constrained the horizon of their narrated interpretation. The biblical narrative involves human interpretation, but it is a divinely inspired interpretation of facts, and the covenant provides the context in which the authorized testimony, doctrine, and practical instruction of certain witnesses to those facts count as divine discourse.

III. THE WORD OF GOD

In keeping with the method stated above, it must be said first of all that *Word of God* is not a generic concept defined by the history of religions or abstract speculation, of which the Bible, for example, is a species. By this phrase we refer to three

---

78. C. S. Lewis, *Christian Reflections* (Grand Rapids: Eerdmans, 1995), 139.

79. On the role of passionate commitment in every intellectual pursuit, including the natural sciences, see Polanyi,

Personal Knowledge. A superb introduction to and elaboration of Polanyi's insights for Christian reflection is found in Esther Lightcap Meek, *Longing To Know: The Philosophy of Knowledge for Ordinary People* (Grand Rapids: Baker, 2003).

forms: (1) the hypostatic (i.e., incarnate) Word: Jesus Christ; (2) the sacramental Word: proclamation; (3) the written Word: the canon of Holy Scripture.[80]

First and foremost, not only in redemption but in creation and providence, the Father upholds all things in his eternal Word and by the power of the Spirit (Jn 1:1–3; Col 1:15–17; Heb 1:1–4; Rev 19:13). Of the same *essence* as the Father and the Spirit, the eternal Son is the original, archetypal, and hypostatic Word.

Second, participating in this eternal Light are the uncreated *energies* of God's living and active speech by which he creates, sustains, redeems, renews, and rules. In relation to the gospel, Reformed and Lutheran theologians often refer to this as "the sacramental Word": that is, the Word as a means of grace. Through this energetic divine speaking, God not only creates a community of redeemed sinners but constitutes it as his own covenant people by means of an authoritative canon — *Holy Scripture.*

In this way, God ensures that there is a normative *canon* (or constitution) on the basis of which contemporary *preaching* continues to be a medium of *Christ's* saving activity in the world. Since I treat the topic of preaching as a means of grace under ecclesiology, I will focus here on general revelation and, in the following chapter, on Scripture. Before considering the scope of revelation, it is important to distinguish the two parts of the Word of God.

A. THE WORD OF GOD AS LAW AND GOSPEL

Paul tells us that the law speaks "so that every mouth may be stopped, and the whole world may be held accountable to God." It can bring no justification; rather, "through the law comes knowledge of sin" (Ro 3:19–20). "But now," he adds, "the righteousness of God has been manifested apart from the law, although the Law and the Prophets bear witness to it — the righteousness of God through faith in Jesus Christ for all who believe" (vv. 21–22). Here the apostle uses "law" in two distinct senses: God's moral commands, which leave everyone condemned, and the Law and the Prophets as Scripture (i.e., the Old Testament).

Similarly, the Protestant Reformers sharply opposed law and gospel when it came to the covenantal principle by which one is justified, while affirming the unity of the Old and New Testaments in terms of promise and fulfillment. Both Testa-

---

80. Karl Barth is often credited with the development of this concept of the "threefold form" of the Word of God (*Church Dogmatics*, vol. 1, pt. 1, esp. 98–140). However differently Barth formulated the relation of Scripture and preaching to the hypostatic Word, the threefold form itself has been a staple of Reformed and Lutheran prolegomena ever since the Reformation. For example, according to Heinrich Bullinger, "For *verbum Dei*, 'the word of God,' doth signify the virtue and power of God: it is also put for the Son of God, which is the second person of the most reverend Trinity.... But in this treatise of ours, the word of God doth properly signify the speech of God, and the revealing of God's will; first of all uttered in a lively-expressed voice by the mouth of Christ, the prophets, and apostles; and after that again registered in writings, which are rightly called 'holy and divine scriptures'" (*The Decades* [ed. Thomas Harding; Cambridge: Cambridge Univ. Press, 1849], 1:37).

ments include both commands and promises. When we speak of the distinction between law and gospel, therefore, we are referring to different illocutionary stances that run throughout all of the Scriptures—everything in both Testaments that is in the form of either an *obligatory command* or a *saving promise* in Christ.[81] "Hence," wrote Luther, "whoever knows well this art of distinguishing between the law and the gospel, him we place at the head and call him a doctor of Holy Scripture."[82]

Calvin and his Reformed colleagues and theological heirs underscored this point as well.[83] Wilhelm Niesel observes, "Reformed theology recognizes the contrast between law and gospel, in a way similar to Lutheranism. We read in the Second Helvetic Confession: 'The gospel is indeed opposed to the law. For the law works wrath and pronounces a curse, whereas the gospel preaches grace and blessing.'"[84] Ursinus, chief author of the Heidelberg Catechism, called it "the chief division of Holy Scripture," and Beza insisted in his catechism that "ignorance of this distinction is one of the causes of the many abuses in the church" throughout history.[85] The great Elizabethan Puritan William Perkins taught that it was the first principle for preachers to learn in interpreting and applying passages.[86] More recently, Herman Bavinck and Louis Berkhof have observed the significance of this distinction for the whole Christian system of faith and practice.[87] J. Van Bruggen adds more recently, "The [Heidelberg] Catechism, thus, mentions the gospel and deliberately does not speak of 'the Word of God,' because the law does not work faith. The law (law and gospel are the two parts of the Word which may be distinguished) judges; it does not call a person to God and does not work trust in him. The gospel does that."[88]

From these two illocutionary stances assumed by the one Word of God as covenant canon—the stance of command and that of promise—the Word issues stipulations (things to be done) and tells the historical narrative of God's deliverance

---

81. See the apology to the *Augsburg Confession* (1531), art. 4. Article 5 of the *Formula of Concord* adds, "We believe, teach, and confess that the distinction between the law and the gospel is to be maintained in the church with great diligence" (F. Bente and W. H. T. Dau, eds. and trans., *Triglot Concordia: The Symbolical Books of the Evangelical Lutheran Church* [St. Louis: Concordia, 1921]).

82. Martin Luther, *Dr. Martin Luthers Sämmliche Schriften* (St. Louis: Concordia, n.d.), vol. 9, col. 802.

83. See Michael Horton, "Calvin and the Law-Gospel Hermeneutic," *Pro Ecclesia* 6, no. 1 (1997): 27–42.

84. Wilhelm Niesel, *Reformed Symbolics: A Comparison of Catholicism, Orthodoxy and Protestantism* (trans. David Lewis; Edinburgh: Oliver and Boyd, 1962), 217.

85. Zacharias Ursinus, *Commentary on the Heidelberg Catechism* (1616; trans. G. W. Willard in 1852; repr., Phillipsburg, N.J.: P&R, n.d.), 1; Theodore Beza, *The Christian Faith* (trans.

James Clark; Lewes, U.K.: Christian Focus Ministries, 1992), 41–43.

86. William Perkins, *The Art of Prophesying* (Edinburgh: Banner of Truth, 1996), 54–56.

87. See Herman Bavinck, *Reformed Dogmatics* (ed. John Bolt; Grand Rapids: Baker, 2008), 4:450; Louis Berkhof, *Systematic Theology: A New Combined Edition* (Grand Rapids: Eerdmans, 1996), 612, writes, "The churches of the Reformation from the very beginning distinguished between the law and the gospel as the two parts of the Word of God as a means of grace. This distinction was not understood to be identified with that between the Old and New Testament, but was regarded as a distinction that applies to both Testaments. There is law and gospel in the Old Testament, and there is law and gospel in the New."

88. J. Van Bruggen, *Annotations to the Heidelberg Catechism* (Neerlandia, Alberta: Inheritance Publications, 1998), 170.

(things to be believed). The law functions differently, depending on the covenant in which it is operative. In a covenant of works (a law-covenant), law prescribes what is to be performed, personally and perfectly, on penalty of death. "The promises of the law depend upon the condition of works," Calvin notes, "while "the gospel promises are free and dependent solely upon God's mercy."[89] In a covenant of grace, law has no power to condemn, since its stipulations have been fulfilled (personally and perfectly) and its penalties for violation have been borne in our place by our covenant head, Jesus Christ. As sacramental Word, the law kills, and through the work of the Spirit the gospel makes alive (2Co 3:6–11). Of course, the law also guides, as the gospel also instructs. However, it must first cut off all hope of life by our personal obedience. Hence, the Reformation churches affirmed a threefold use of the law: (1) to arraign us before God's judgment and prove the world guilty; (2) to remind all people, even non-Christians, of their obligations to the moral law written on their conscience, and (3) to guide believers in the way of gratitude.[90]

Once again the emphasis on God's Word as performative speech is highlighted. Not only proposing things to be believed and done, God in his Word actually himself brings about what is threatened in the law and what is promised in the gospel. Hardly an imposition of systematic categories on the biblical text, this crucial distinction is explicitly evident in the difference between the imperative and indicative moods in the Greek language.[91] The law's imperatives tell us what must be done; the gospel's indicatives tell us what God has done.

In the Reformed tradition, the law-gospel distinction was interpreted within the historical context of distinct covenants in history. The covenant of creation (also called the covenant of works or law) was based on the personal performance of all righteousness by the covenant servant. The covenant of grace is based on the fulfillment of all righteousness by our representative head and is dispensed to the covenant people through faith in him. There is still law in the covenant of grace. However, it is no longer able to condemn believers, but directs them in lives of gratitude for God's mercy in Christ.

Although the federal (covenant) theologians had been consigned to the dustbins of historical theology by neo-Protestantism, Karl Barth—mostly for other reasons than theirs—inherited many of the suspicions of his mentors concerning Protestant scholasticism. Citing the classic distinction between a covenant of works and a covenant of grace as the first "fatal historical moment" in Reformed theology, Barth

---

89. Calvin, *Institutes* 3.11.17.

90. The *Formula of Concord*, art. 6; Calvin, *Institutes* 2.7.6, 10, 12. It was Philipp Melanchthon who introduced the category of the "third use of the law" (a guide for Christian gratitude).

91. This distinction is standard in Greek grammars, includ-

ing H. E. Dana and J. Mantey, *A Manual Grammar of the Greek New Testament* (New York: Macmillan, 1943), 174–75; H. W. Smyth, *Greek Grammar* (Cambridge, Mass.: Harvard Univ. Press, 1976), 409–11.

and his students insisted on a single covenant of grace.[92] More recently, some within Reformed circles have criticized the covenant of works without necessarily denying the importance of the law-gospel distinction, though the denial of the former has often led to abandonment of the latter.[93] As we will see, Barth's criticism of a two-covenant scheme (as well as the distinction between law and gospel) is related to his denial of general revelation.

B. GOD'S REVELATION IN CREATION: GENERAL REVELATION

The context of God's Word in creation is the covenant of creation.[94] Adhering to the rule that revelation follows the historical economy of God's operations in creation, redemption, and consummation, it is important to observe that the Word spoken by God to our first parents before the fall differs from the Word later spoken to them and to heirs of the promise after them. <u>Love and law are an inseparable unity</u>, as Jesus teaches in his summary of the law as love of God and neighbor. Only after the fall was there an occasion for the surprising announcement of the gospel, establishing a covenant of grace.

1. SCRIPTURAL JUSTIFICATION FOR GENERAL REVELATION

The view that God has revealed himself through what he has made is as old as Genesis, interpreted through the poetry of the Psalms (especially Pss 8:1–9; 19:1–6; 102:25), widely attested in the prophets, confirmed by Jesus and the apostles, with the vision of the whole earth finally having its tongue loosed to sing God's praise. There is a divinely appointed order in creation that can be appealed to even in special revelation: "Consider the ravens.... Consider the lilies, how they grow" (Lk 12:24, 27). God is said to reveal himself in the thunder and lightning (Pss 18:9–15; 77:16–18, Ex 19:16–20), as in the natural processes of planting and harvest, in his command over the winds and the seas (Ex 14; Pss 93:3–4; 95:5; 107:23–30; 114:3, 5) and the sun, moon, and stars (Jdg 5:20; Jos 10:12–14; Isa 38:7–8), and in his care for his creatures (Pss 36:7; 147:9). "The heavens declare the glory of God, and the sky above proclaims his handiwork. Day to day pours out speech, and night to

92. See Daniel L. Migliore's introduction to *The Göttingen Dogmatics: Instruction in the Christian Religion*, by Karl Barth (ed. Hannelotte Reiffen; trans. Geoffrey W. Bromiley; Grand Rapids: Eerdmans, 1991), 1:xxxviii.

93. John Murray writes, "In the degree to which error is entertained at this point, in the same degree is our conception of the gospel perverted.... What was the question that aroused the apostle to such passionate zeal and holy indignation, indignation that has its kinship with the imprecatory utterances of the Old Testament? In a word it was the relation of law and gospel" (*Principles of Conduct* [Grand Rapids: Eerdmans, 1957], 181).

Renewed criticism of classic federal theology has been aided by the New Perspective on Paul—while, ironically, renewed appreciation for the distinction between law-covenants (suzerainty treaties) and gift-covenants (royal grants) in the biblical narratives is evident in Jewish and Roman Catholic biblical scholarship. This scholarship is summarized in Michael Horton, *Covenant and Salvation: Union with Christ* (Louisville: Westminster John Knox, 2007), part 1.

94. Reformed theologians employed various terms for this arrangement, including the covenant of works, law, nature, and life.

night reveals knowledge" (Ps 19:1–2). In fact, this praise "goes out through all the earth, and their words to the end of the world" (v. 4). Here we are directed by the psalmist to discover God's majesty, glory, and character in nature and history even beyond that special covenantal history with Israel.

Because of this, Paul can approvingly quote the pagan poet Epimenides and Cleanthes' "Hymn to Zeus" in his speech in Athens (Ac 17:28). Everyone is aware of God's existence, even of his moral will (Ro 2:14–15). Neither Jews, who have the written law, nor Gentiles, who have the law written on their conscience, can plead ignorance; yet it is this very fact that condemns us all (Ro 1:18–3:19). None of this includes any narration of God's saving purposes to fallen creatures, but it does testify to God's attributes expressed in his creative work and moral claim on creation in the original covenant.

2. Historical Interpretations of General Revelation

The ancient Greek school of Stoicism (founded by Zeno in the third century BC) taught that divinity permeates nature with its seminal reason (the *logos spermatikos*). The apologist Justin Martyr (AD 100–165) adapted this Stoic idea to Christianity by arguing that the divine spark or seed of rationality (the *logos spermatikos*) emanates from Christ throughout the world and can be found in the best philosophies of noble pagans. Just as Moses and the prophets prepared the Jews for Jesus Christ, Socrates, Plato, and Stoicism prepared the Gentiles for the gospel. Here we discover the seeds of the later Roman Catholic tendency to treat general and special revelation as different in *degree* rather than in *content*. Medieval theology increasingly developed a dualistic approach in which what we might call *secular* knowledge was attributed to nature, and *spiritual* knowledge to grace. Even in spiritual matters, however, the natural mind (weakened but not depraved by the fall) could discover truth. Consequently, medieval theology affirmed not only *natural revelation* but *natural theology*, on whose foundations the supernatural theology based on special revelation was erected.

In Western theology and philosophy, we may discern two broad approaches to general revelation, approaches that may be defined in terms of a recurring struggle over the relation of reason and revelation, nature and grace, logic and faith. Roman Catholic theology, on one hand, even when admirably defending the coinherence of faith and reason, typically assumes an underlying ontological dualism between nature and grace that provokes this problem in the first place. Roman Catholic theology teaches that grace *elevates* nature, orienting it to the supernatural, away from the lower self (the body and its passions). Grace is a substance that is added (infused) to nature in order to direct the aim of its gaze upward from material things to spiritual reality. For Lutheran and Reformed theologies, on the other hand, there is no such thing as a gift of grace superadded to nature (*donum superadditum*); creation itself is a gift (*donum concreatum*).[95] Grace, however, is a particular kind of gift: God's merciful favor toward sinners. The Reformers challenged the idea that there was some inherent tendency toward sin in God's creation. Grace is therefore not given to already good creatures in order to elevate them beyond nature, but to sinners in order to redeem and renew their nature so that it may be "created after the likeness of God in true righteousness and holiness" (Eph 4:24).

Just as grace is higher than nature in Roman Catholic teaching, special revelation is higher than general revelation. Just as the gospel is a clearer revelation of the law, Scripture is a clearer revelation of the truths of general revelation and adds to these general truths certain doctrines that cannot be known by the light of nature alone. Consequently, the tendency of such thinking is toward an ontology of *overcoming estrangement* and a view of revelation that corresponds to *new awareness*. So while it is possible to have a true natural theology, special revelation builds on natural revelation. That which is dimly sensed in nature is more clearly seen in supernatural grace.

Reformation theology, however, affirmed general revelation while dissenting from medieval interpretations. First, the Reformation's interpretation of general revelation differs from the Roman Catholic view with respect to its *content*. For the former view, the creation is founded in triune love, not grace. Although the gospel was already in God's heart in creation because of his eternal covenant of redemption (the pact between the persons of the Trinity), it was promulgated to creatures only after the fall. Only sinners need forgiveness; "good news" is given to those who are at fault. Consequently, what is required after the fall is not a *higher* revelation (fuller and more intense) but a *different* revelation (gospel rather than law). Nature does not need to be *elevated beyond itself* but to be *liberated to be itself*, glorifying and enjoying God.

As the created effect of God's speech, the natural world declares God's glory, and the natural law written on the conscience in the covenant of creation remains even after the fall.[96] However, there is no revelation of God's saving purposes in Christ that can be derived from this original revelation. This is why the passages I have cited in favor of general revelation mention God's glory, goodness, power, and justice but nothing of God's grace and mercy. Similarly, Paul says that in this general revelation God has clearly displayed "his invisible attributes, namely, his eternal power and divine nature" (Ro 1:20). From this original revelation in the covenant of creation, all people have an awareness of God's existence and know that they are morally accountable to him, but this natural revelation only obligates, rendering all

---

95. See, for example, in the *Book of Concord*, apology, arts. 2, 4 and *Formula of Concord*, solid declaration 1. This became a major concern in Reformed critiques, as we will see.

96. For a helpful introduction to natural law from a Reformed perspective, see David VanDrunen, *A Biblical Case for Natural Law* (Grand Rapids: Acton Institute, 2006).

people "without excuse" (Ro 1:20; cf. 2:12–16). As a form of law, it is the basis for any sense of relative justice, truth, and love in human society, but it is not a redemptive revelation: "Now we know that whatever the law says it speaks to those who are under the law, so that every mouth may be stopped, and the whole world may be held accountable to God. For by works of the law no human being will be justified in his sight, since through the law comes knowledge of sin" (Romans 3:19–20). Only after saying this does the apostle shift his focus to the gospel: "But now the righteousness of God has been manifested apart from the law, although the Law and the Prophets bear witness to it—the righteousness of God through faith in Jesus Christ for all who believe" (vv. 21–22).

Second, Reformation theology differs from the Roman Catholic view concerning the *status of the receiver* of general revelation. If there had been no fall, there would be no conflict between faith and reason, obedience to God's Word and sense experience, revelation and science. It is not *reason* that is opposed to faith but the *reasoner*. Just as Rome regards special revelation as differing only in degree, it sees human beings as standing in varying degrees of truth, righteousness, and grace. However, evangelical theology holds that all of those who are not yet united to Christ through faith are spiritually dead, unable to interpret reality in a consistently faithful manner because they willfully "by their unrighteousness suppress the truth" (Ro 1:18). Those who are spiritually dead do not need merely *more* revelation than is provided in nature, but *a different kind* of revelation, namely, good news. Because of God's faithfulness, there is still a natural revelation; because of our unfaithfulness, there can be no natural theology that is not a form of idolatry (Ro 1:18, 21–32). There may be civil virtue and justice that fellow humans recognize, but only Christ's righteousness can be sustained in the heavenly court, and this gift of righteousness to sinners is an external Word that no one knows apart from its being proclaimed (Ro 10:5–17).

Total depravity means that there was not any part of humanity left unsullied by the fall, not that human beings are as bad (or as ignorant) as they could possibly be. As Calvin recognized, the *sensus divinitatis* (sense of divinity)—the general awareness of God's existence and invisible attributes (Ro 1:19–20)—is common to all human beings as "the law of their creation."[97] Therefore, general revelation is indeed closely related to "revelation as inner experience." There is an intuitive, inward, and direct revelation in the human conscience, but it is an awareness of God's original relation to humanity in creation (the covenant of works), not a revelation of his free decision to have mercy on sinners (the covenant of grace).

Furthermore, our natural experience of God is itself an interpretation, and as

---

97. See especially Calvin, *Institutes* 1.3.1–3. The quotation is from 1.3.3.

the interpretation of our fallen hearts, it is corrupt. As soon as we see a glimmering ember of divine truth we smother it, and this is why there can be no true natural theology, even though we are swimming in general revelation.[98] For a true theology (even of nature), humanity needs another word, a revelation other than the *sensus divinitatis* (natural revelation) to announce God's free grace and reconciliation through the mediation of Christ. This revelation "alone quickens dead souls."[99] Natural theologies will always be some form of our native theology of glory, while the gospel reveals the theology of the cross.

Therefore, Calvin could speak almost glowingly of the "admirable light of truth shining in secular writers," teaching us that the human mind, "though fallen and perverted from its wholeness, is nevertheless clothed and ornamented with God's excellent gifts." He continues:

> What then? Shall we deny that the truth shone upon the ancient jurists who established civic order and discipline with such great equity?... Those men whom Scripture (1Co 2:14) calls "natural men" were, indeed, sharp and penetrating in their investigation of inferior things. Let us, accordingly, learn by their example how many gifts the Lord left to human nature even after it was despoiled of its true good.[100]

Like Augustine in *The City of God*, Calvin moves dialectically between an affirmation of the natural order *and* an insistence on its inability because of sin to generate an *ultimate* society.[101]

The goal of common grace is not to perfect nature but to restrain sin and animate civic virtues and arts, so that culture may fulfill its own important but limited, temporal, and secular ends, while God simultaneously pursues the redemptive aims of his everlasting city. With radical Anabaptists (such as Thomas Müntzer) especially in mind, Calvin—following Paul's claim that the moral law revealed in Scripture is the natural law revealed in creation—strongly opposed the idea that a valid civil order must be based on the Bible.[102] In addition to these natural remnants of the image of God in every person, Calvin speaks of God's common grace: "not such grace as to cleanse it [nature], but to restrain it inwardly." This common grace is tied to providence, to restraint; "but he does not purge it within."[103] Only the gospel can do this. Thus, common grace and natural law are complementary, not contradictory, concepts for Calvin.[104] Similarly, Jonathan Edwards wrote, "It

---

98. Ibid., 1.4.1–1.5.14
99. Ibid., 1.6.1.
100. Ibid., 2.2.15.
101. With Luther, he spoke of two kingdoms or "a twofold government." Christ rules creation in providence and common grace, but this heavenly kingdom of grace is different. These two kingdoms are "distinct," yet "they are not at variance" (4.20.2).

102. Calvin, *Institutes* 4.20.8, 14. The basic ligaments of Calvin's political theology can be found in 4.20.1–32.
103. Ibid., 2.3.3.
104. For precisely the same view, see Philipp Melanchthon, *Loci communes* (1543) (trans. J. A. O. Preus; St. Louis: Concordia, 1992), 70.

cannot be said that we come to the knowledge of any part of Christian divinity by the light of nature. The light of nature teaches no truth as it is in Jesus. It is only the Word of God, contained in the Old and New Testaments, which teaches us Christian doctrine."[105]

Because one cannot suppress everything at the same time, the ineradicable sense of justice (natural law) engenders secular community, while only the gospel can create a church. The internal word (*verbum internum*) will always be in the form of law (which is why religion is naturally associated with morality and eternal rewards), but the external Word (*verbum externum*) announced by a messenger creates saving faith. Hence, if we have only "revelation as inner experience," it will be something like Kant's "moral law within." Our inner experience may express revulsion at the Holocaust or other demonstrations of torture and violence. However, it will never express faith in Christ, because it knows nothing of the gospel until a herald brings the good news.

This distinction in content does not imply a dualism between creation (general revelation) and redemption (special revelation), since these are not separate spheres but distinct acts and covenants—and in both instances, they are the effect of the Father's speaking in the Son and by his Spirit.[106] Here dualism is vanquished, notes Herman Bavinck. "The foundations of creation and redemption are the same. The Logos who became flesh is the same by whom all things were made."[107]

From this summary we can recognize important continuities between medieval and Reformation theologies, especially with respect to the fact of general revelation and natural law. However, with respect to the content of general revelation and the moral capacity of sinners to rightly interpret it, these views differ sharply. As Karl Rahner and Joseph Cardinal Ratzinger (now Pope Benedict XVI) relate, modernist theology had reduced revelation to the "inevitable development, immanent in human history, of man's religious needs"—basically indistinguishable from the actual history of religions.[108] However, Rahner's own view seems hardly distinguishable from this perspective when he argues that God's grace is operative universally—even in atheists—as an "elevation of natural capacities toward the higher, supernatural sphere." When one applies this view of grace to the concept of revelation, Rahner argues, "It is quite possible, without falling into Modernism," to identify revelation with the "historical self-unfolding" of universal religious consciousness.[109]

Whereas Reformation theology understood general revelation as God's self-testimony as Creator and lawgiver, distinct from the special revelation of his

---

105. Jonathan Edwards, *Works of Jonathan Edwards* (ed. Harry S. Stout; New Haven, Conn.: Yale Univ. Press, 2003), 22:86.

106. On this point, see Herman Bavinck, *The Philosophy of Revelation* (Grand Rapids: Baker, 1979), 26–28.

107. Ibid., 28.

108. Karl Rahner and Joseph Ratzinger, *Revelation and Tradition* (trans. W. J. O'Hara; Freiburg: Herder, 1966), 10.

109. Ibid., 13.

salvation in Christ, Rahner sees revelation as an undifferentiated unity of content "with two sides." On one hand, revelation is subjective: a "supernaturally elevated transcendence" that is "always and everywhere operative" even when rejected. On the other hand, this revelation is also a historically mediated, "objective, explicit expression of the supernaturally transcendental experience." This history of revelation is always gracious and part of God's "saving providence."[110] In this conception, the law and the covenant of creation become assimilated to the gospel and the covenant of grace. The universal revelation of God's moral will is no longer seen as condemning humanity, "so that every mouth may be stopped, and the whole world may be held accountable to God" (Ro 3:19), but as gracious and saving revelation.

Not surprisingly, the history of redemption, as Rahner conceives it, is really "co-extensive with the spiritual history of mankind as such," as the Second Vatican Council affirmed.[111] The church's knowledge of this saving mystery is *higher* than this natural and universal knowledge but not qualitatively *different*. In fact, as Cardinal Dulles observed in referring to Rahner as a representative of "revelation as inner experience," the revelation of God's saving will elevates the soul within rather than coming to the person from outside. In this way, gospel is assimilated to law and law to gospel. Faith does not come by hearing the Word of Christ (Ro 10:17) but by responding obediently to the natural light that one already has within. Grace is simply God's supplemental assistance for these works.

Following the Council's argument, Rahner deduces this position from the thesis of God's universal saving will. If God has chosen to save everyone, then grace and revelation must be universally distributed. "It is only necessary to assume—and the data of present-day theology support this—that every human being is elevated by grace," so everyone participates in this divinization even if it is "not accepted freely in faith." Rahner does say that this divinization "can quite definitely be regarded as a word-revelation, provided the notion of word is not reduced to that of a phonetic utterance"—in other words, provided that the notion of word is no longer identified with verbal communication! "History in the concrete, both individually and collectively, is the history of God's transcendental revelation."[112] In this perspective, then, "the history of religion is at the same time the most explicit part of the history of revelation."[113] In its doctrine of implicit faith (*fides implicita*), Rome has held the possibility of salvation for those who "through no fault of their own" have embraced errors or failed to be adequately joined to the Roman Catholic Church. "On that basis it might become clear just what *fides implicita* is, which nowadays, unfortunately, plays a smaller part even in Catholic theology than it should."[114]

---

110. Ibid., 13–14.
111. Ibid., 16–17.
112. Ibid.

113. Ibid., 18.
114. Ibid., 20–21.

Christianity is not "a particular covenant of a particular people with God"; it is "the absolute religion of all."[115]

So this view of revelation can be seen as concentric circles. Just as grace is higher than nature, the church's special revelation is higher than general revelation. This revelation radiates outward to all Christian bodies, then next to the monotheistic religions, and finally to pantheists and even atheists (Rahner's "anonymous Christian").[116] That which distinguishes Christianity from other religions (and even atheism) is not the object of faith itself but the intensity and clarity with which it sees that object. This view is not new, as we have seen, but is the refinement of a Christian Platonism (and Stoicism) that runs from ancient theologians like Justin Martyr to the present. The paradigm is "overcoming estrangement" rather than "meeting a stranger."

3. Karl Barth's Rejection of Natural Revelation

Although the goal of the law, according to Paul, is to silence the world before God, modernity is one long filibuster in which the sovereign self refuses to yield even to the Speaker of the House. As Protestant liberalism increasingly assimilated revelation to the immanent development of human potential for morality and progress, the door opened for placing a natural theology alongside God's revelation in Christ. In the aftermath of the First World War, the German Christian movement argued that God had spoken most fully to our highest spiritual aspirations in Christ and to our highest cultural aspirations in German culture—specifically, in the führer.

It was against this backdrop that Karl Barth lodged his protest—his famous *nein!*—against natural theology. On this crucial point, Barth identified Protestant liberalism (or modernism) with Roman Catholicism. With exponents like Karl Rahner (not to mention the German Christian movement), Barth's wariness seems entirely reasonable. Once God's self-revelation can be identified with Christ in the realm of supernatural grace and with someone or something else in the realm of nature, the paganization of the church is inevitable.[117] Therefore, Barth's reaction is understandable—in many places prophetic—but it misunderstands the views and the distinctive contribution of Protestant orthodoxy on this question.

In his debate with Barth, Emil Brunner defended general revelation along the

---

115. Ibid., 21–22.

116. Karl Rahner, *Theological Investigations* (trans. David Bourke; London: Darton, Longman & Todd, 1976), 14:283. As the concentric circles extend outward, Judaism occupies the next ring, followed by Islam, then by other religions, reaching even those who, "through no fault of their own, do not know the gospel of Christ or his church, but who nevertheless seek God with a sincere heart, and moved by grace, try in their actions to do his will as they know it through the dictates of their conscience—those too may achieve eternal salvation" (U.S. Catholic Church, *Catechism of the Catholic Church* [2nd ed.; New York: Doubleday, 2003], 244; cf. 414).

117. Barth could draw a straight line, he thought, from Roman Catholic natural theology to evangelical pietism and liberalism, all the way to the "German Christian" ideology of the Nazi regime—that is, the declarations of church leaders on German culture and morality, "the 'common sense' of practically the whole of our positive and liberal ministry, and the prevailing tendency in the pietistic community-movement, which at this point is intimately bound up with the prevailing tendency in the church at large" (*Church Dogmatics*, vol. 1, pt. 1, 213). For his own part, Barth could only conceive of a radical break: "Let everyone make his choice and let none continue to look around for new and tiresome attempts at mediation!" (214).

usual Reformed lines I have summarized. Although Christ alone is the Logos of God, and all true knowledge—"even the perception of the simplest mathematical truth"—comes from the Son, "knowledge that comes *from* God is different from the knowledge *of* God.... Even the knowledge of the philosophical idea of the Logos or of truth is not yet the knowledge of God" (emphasis added).[118] By identifying the Logos of revelation—the eternal Son—with the logos of Greek thought (especially Stoicism and Platonism), medieval theology "identifies the immanent idea of *veritas* [truth], which our rational thought contains, with the Logos of revelation, and upon this bases its speculative doctrine of the 'Trinity' and of 'Christ.'" "It is here that the paths of medieval Catholic and Reformed theology diverge," says Brunner.

According to the Reformers, God's revelation in creation cannot be the basis for true theology, "because sin has perverted human reason." Following the light of nature—"abstract speculative thinking"—does not lead to God but to idols. "The ascent of the soul to God is a false path ... [that] does not end in the Living God, but in the abstract *ens realissimum* of Neoplatonist speculation; the true God can be known only by His coming down to us, in the revelation of Christ which is disclosed in faith."[119]

Brunner helpfully points out that whereas the Reformers understood the Logos of God as the eternal Son, Barth insists on identifying the Logos exclusively with the incarnate Christ. For the Reformers, the Logos *became* flesh in the fullness of time. Therefore, from this eternal Logos comes all truth, all rational knowledge, even prior to his incarnation for us and for our salvation.[120] Also with the Reformers, Brunner ties natural reason to law rather than gospel. The knowledge that reason has of God is a legal knowledge.[121] It rings in our conscience, commanding us to love God and neighbor, but it does not speak of redemption in Christ. Undoubtedly, Barth's restriction of revelation to the *incarnate* Christ is the corollary of his assimilation of law to gospel. Reason knows nothing of an incarnation, atonement, resurrection, new creation, and so forth, Brunner rightly contends. Furthermore, given our suppression of the truth in general revelation as well, sinful reason is not qualified to adjudicate divine action in history.[122]

As we can see clearly in Plato, Kant, and other philosophers, "The God whom the reason can grasp is actually the court which promulgates the law. Beyond that one may speculate or postulate, but beyond that, purely through the reason, man cannot discover any further certainty."[123] Nothing can be more universally and empirically demonstrated than the existence of moral reason (natural law) and original sin.[124] Kant recognizes the radical nature of evil, but this does not lead him "to break away from the 'Pelagian' point of view, namely, that man can at any time, from

118. Brunner, *Revelation and Reason*, 318.
119. Ibid., 318–19.
120. Ibid., 320.
121. Ibid., 322.

122. Ibid., 322–25.
123. Ibid., 326.
124. Ibid., 328.

his own inner core of goodness, free himself from evil, or can indeed 'pull himself together' to the good. . . . This would have meant a break with his philosophy of immanence as a whole, the renunciation of his transcendental Idealism; then Kant would have had to confess himself an adherent of the Christian faith. . . . In order to save his standpoint of immanence he finally abandons his concept of *radical* evil."[125]

In all of this we see that "legalism and rationalism are inseparable. . . . The rational ethic does not understand the other as the concrete 'thou,' just as it is, but as an ideal abstract 'value,' as a bearer of reason, as a 'something' to which there clings the value of reason or of mind, or as an occasion for acting according to one's duty."[126] The human being guided only by natural reason will always interpret the law of God "in a manner that permits him to believe that he can fulfill it in his own strength."[127]

But rightly interpreted, the law cuts off hope:

> For "through the law there comes knowledge of sin"—and indeed precisely through this law which has no "grace" in it, and is known as pure demand. Only when man is frightened to death by this ruthless "Thou shalt," and breaks down inwardly at this point, is he able to hear, or even want to hear, the message of forgiveness and of redemption. Until this takes place, indeed, he has no sense of need. . . . The dialectic of the law and the gospel, however, goes still deeper. Christ himself, as the Crucified, must fulfill the law, before, as the Risen Lord, he can give us the grace of God. Thus the revelation of grace is itself, from one point of view, the fulfillment of the law, in the sense that it takes the law seriously, and asserts its claims in no uncertain manner.[128]

<u>The Father's goal for Christ in his incarnation and ministry is not to do away with this law but to fulfill it—positively by loving and serving his neighbor even to the point of self-sacrifice, negatively by bearing God's legal wrath. In so doing, Jesus reveals the deeper meaning of both the law and the gospel—the good as more than fulfilling one's duty to commands but as self-giving, abundant, "fathomless love."[129]</u>

Paul says that by our unrighteousness we suppress or hold down the truth (Ro 1:18). "But we cannot 'hold down' something that does not exist," Brunner says.[130] Echoing his Reformed forebears, Brunner wrote that "natural man does not have half-truth so much as distorted truth. In Christ, one finds the truth of all philosophy and religion. In philosophy and religion there is only distorted truth."[131] We can appeal to unbelievers on the basis of the law, which they know even though they try to suppress it. Yet this does not mean, as Rome supposes, that this point of contact is an area of agreement to which we can then add the gospel.

The original, general revelation tells us what God requires but "provides no answer to the question, What does God intend to do with us—with us, sinful

---

125. Ibid., 329–30.
126. Ibid.
127. Ibid., 334.
128. Ibid., 335–36.

129. Ibid., 336–37.
130. Ibid., 63.
131. Eugene Heideman, *The Relation of Revelation and Reason in E. Brunner and H. Bavinck* (Assen: Van Gorcum, 1959), 38.

human beings?" "Hence this revelation still leaves us with the 'mystery of his will' (Eph 1:9), until, in the 'fullness of the time' (Gal 4:4), in the 'economy' of revelation which is called Jesus Christ, it is made known unto us 'according to his good pleasure, which he hath purposed in himself, that in the dispensation of the fullness of times, he might gather together in one all things in Christ'" (KJV).[132] General revelation displays God's power, wisdom, righteousness, goodness, and justice, as well as human responsibility, "but there it stops: it has no saving power."[133]

Therefore, Brunner affirms general revelation "because the Holy Scriptures teach it unmistakably, and we intend to teach it in accordance with Scripture."[134] If there were no general revelation, there would be no idolatry. It is not that people are not *religious* apart from Christ, but that they are not *evangelized*. "In short, biblical and natural theology will never agree; they are bitterly and fundamentally opposed."[135] However, Barth fails to recognize the proper distinction between God's revelation in creation and natural theology.[136] Brunner quotes Calvin: "For there are two different ways of working of the Son of God; the one, which becomes visible in the architecture of the world and in the natural order; the other, by means of which ruined nature is renewed and restored."[137] General revelation is a legal revelation. It faces people with their creator, lawgiver, and judge, but not with a savior. "Once more this is a point at which the theology of the Reformation diverges from that of the Catholic Church."[138]

If Roman Catholic theology teaches that grace elevates nature, Barth came close at times to suggesting that nature is opposed to grace — not only *morally*, because of the fall, but *ontologically*, simply as nature.[139]

Barth realized that Brunner was simply articulating the traditional Reformed view, but stated, "For my part, although I am Reformed, I want no part of it."[140] Whatever "revelation" might appear in the history of pagans, Barth insists, its

---

132. Brunner, *Revelation and Reason*, 97.
133. Ibid.
134. Ibid., 59.
135. Ibid., 61.
136. Ibid., 62.
137. Ibid.
138. Ibid., 70.
139. Ibid. Revelation is always gracious, with Christ and his redeeming work as the content, and it not only releases humans from moral bondage and creates faith in their heart but also creates the natural organs of reception. Brunner properly counters, "The Word of God does not have to create man's capacity for words. He has never lost it. It is the presupposition of his ability to hear the Word of God. But the Word of God itself creates man's ability to hear it in such a way as is only possible in faith."
140. Barth, *The Göttingen Dogmatics*, 91. Reacting to extremes, Barth refers to the bad example of Zwingli, who did

in fact argue (like Justin Martyr) that the great Greek philosophers prepared the way for the gospel; Socrates is a celebrated saint in heaven:

> Today many might be more inclined to think of Lao-Tse or Buddha. They recall the sayings that we have already quoted from Thomas and Zwingli about all who speak the truth speaking from God. And you perhaps know that to Luther's strong disapproval, and with much shaking of the head from Calvin, Zwingli was ready to people the Christian heaven with a whole series of noble pagans, including Hercules and Theseus, since as he saw it these pagans, like Abraham and his people, all knew and believed the one revelation. (149–50)

Barth is correct to join Luther and Calvin in rejecting the saving validity of general revelation, but his own assimilation of law to gospel disallows the Reformers' affirmation of a nonredemptive revelation.

content would have to include the Trinity, the cross, and the resurrection. In other words, it would have to be the gospel as well as law. Otherwise, it could not be a witness to God's one revelation.[141]

G. C. Berkouwer's analysis was similar to that of Brunner's outlined above: while Christ is certainly the mediator of every word from the Father, Barth's problem, Berkouwer concluded, was that he had collapsed law into gospel, the preincarnate into the incarnate Son, and therefore general revelation into special revelation.[142]

To conclude, we must resist the *Manichaean* temptation to divorce the God of creation from the God of redemption, as if the world did not reveal the goodness, kindness, power, and wisdom of God the Father, in the Son, and by the Spirit. <u>Law comes before gospel because creation comes before the fall. The gospel was announced to sinners as God's plan of redemption from the curse.</u> On the other hand, we must also resist the *Pelagian* temptation to view this general revelation as offering a path of salvation to fallen humanity. The problem is never on God's side but on ours. While creation continues to proclaim God's glory, we need Scripture to interpret even nature faithfully.[143]

DISCUSSION QUESTIONS

1. Summarize Avery Dulles's models of revelation. What are their strengths and weaknesses?
2. Identifying some of the unifying elements of revelation across the diverse genres of Scripture, discuss the place of propositions.
3. Define the three forms of the Word of God and the distinction between law and gospel. How do law and gospel function differently, depending on their covenantal context?
4. What is general revelation and how does it differ from special revelation?

---

141. Ibid., 150–51. "Revelation in the Bible, and whatever might be identical with it elsewhere, differs radically from all else that might be called revelation in religious history by reason of the fact that it is indirect communication. And indirect communication means God's incarnation."

142. G. C. Berkouwer, *General Revelation* (Grand Rapids: Eerdmans, 1955), 271–77.

143. Bavinck, *The Philosophy of Revelation*, 28. Therefore, as Colin Gunton has suggested, the church needs a biblical theology of nature rather than a natural theology, and this can be attained only by taking our bearings from explicitly Trinitarian coordinates. The Son and the Spirit, in Irenaeus's phrase, are the "two hands" of the Father, mediating his creating as well as his redeeming work. See Colin Gunton, *The Triune Creator* (Grand Rapids: Eerdmans, 1998), 2–20.

Chapter Four

SCRIPTURE AS COVENANT CANON

Like the ruins of a grand castle, human knowledge of God is grossly disfigured. For both a true interpretation of nature and any news of God's gracious gospel, we require *special* revelation. Theological knowledge, I have argued, can be best identified as a distinct form of wisdom oriented toward a practical end, namely, the proper invocation of God's name for salvation and true worship. If "faith comes from hearing, and hearing through the word of Christ" (Ro 10:17), we need a canon that delivers the authoritative teaching that we are to proclaim to the ends of the earth.

I. GOD'S RULING CONSTITUTION (WORD AS CANON)

Every covenant has a canon (meaning "rule"), and every community is defined by its constitution. As the word suggests, such a document actually *constitutes* a nation or company. In recent decades, parallels between ancient Near Eastern (especially Hittite) treaties and biblical covenants have been explored with remarkable results.[1] In many cases, the greater ruler (suzerain) would unilaterally impose conditions on the lesser ruler (vassal), and a copy of the treaty was deposited in the shrine of each capitol. Typically, these international treaties included a *preamble* that identified the treaty maker (the suzerain). The preamble of the United States

---

1. Among many others, the following should be mentioned: G. E. Mendenhall, *Law and Covenant in Israel and the Ancient Near East* (Pittsburgh: Biblical Colloquium, 1955); Delbert Hillers, *Covenant: The History of a Biblical Idea* (Baltimore: Johns Hopkins Univ. Press, 1969); M. G. Kline, *The Structure of Biblical Authority* (Grand Rapids: Eerdmans, 1975), esp. ch. 3.

Constitution begins, "We the people...." However, in these ancient treaties, it is the suzerain who creates the community that is called by his name. Following the preamble, a *historical prologue* justifies the suzerain's rights over the vassal. This is followed by a list of *stipulations* (commands) with attendant *sanctions* (life and death). The suzerain's act of liberation is the basis for his imperial rights, and he therefore annexes the vassal's kingdom to his own by giving him a written constitution.

With the preamble, "In the beginning, God ..." and the creation narrative as the historical prologue (Ge 1 and 2), the context is established for God's issuance of the stipulations (guarding and keeping the garden, refraining from eating from the Tree of Knowledge of Good and Evil) and the sanctions (death and life). Interpreted especially in the light of Romans 2, the canon of this original covenant is engraved on the conscience of every human being to this day—the canon of natural law.[2] The same pattern is explicit in the covenant at Sinai, with the historical books providing the dramatic prologue justifying Yahweh's suzerainty, stipulations (commands), and sanctions (threats for transgression). A condensed version appears in the Decalogue (Ex 20:2). Finally, the tablets were deposited in the ark of the covenant. With the historical books at the beginning and the announcement of the covenant curses in the prophetic books, this covenant and its canon were a temporary and typological economy leading Israel to its Messiah, the Savior of the world. A new exodus requires a new canon, and Exodus is the source of the New Testament's gospel genre.[3]

This close connection between canon and covenant is crucial for understanding the way in which the Bible regulates the faith and practice of the people of God. While the whole Bible is canonical in the broader sense (i.e., belonging to God's authoritative Word), the civil and ceremonial laws that constituted and governed the old covenant theocracy are no longer canonical in the narrower sense—that is, they are no longer in force; they are "obsolete" (Heb 8:13). As the writer to the Hebrews labors to point out, it would be tragic as well as regressive if God's people were to go back to the shadows of the law once the Reality (Christ) had arrived.

The one covenant of grace, which begins after the fall with God's promise of a

---

2. This identification of the moral law (summarized in the Ten Commandments) with the natural law that constituted humanity's original relationship to God is affirmed not only in Christianity but in Judaism and Islam. See, for example, David Novak, *Covenantal Rights: A Study in Jewish Political Theory* (Princeton, N.J.: Princeton Univ. Press, 2000).

3. Matthew begins by identifying the suzerain according to his human genealogy as the seed of the woman promised in Genesis 3:15. The first verse of Mark's Gospel reads, "The beginning of the gospel of Jesus Christ, the Son of God." The Gospel of Luke begins by explaining the author's historical method (eyewitness report). The preamble and historical prologue of John's Gospel most closely echo Genesis 1: "In the beginning was the Word, and the Word was with God, and the Word was God. He was in the beginning with God. All things were made through him, and without him was not any thing made that was made. In him was life, and the life was the light of men. The light shines in the darkness, and the darkness has not overcome it" (vv. 1–5). Next, we are introduced to John the Baptist's ministry and his testimony to the Messiah. See also Kline, *Structure of Biblical Authority*, 172–203.

Savior and continues through Abraham to David and finally to Christ, is administered differently in Old and New Testaments. The new covenant is constituted by its own canon (in the narrower sense of "canon"), the New Testament. This canon has its own historical prologue—the Gospels—which even begins by evoking parallels with Genesis and the history of Israel. It has its own stipulations (both doctrines and commands) and sanctions (life and death). It is not different in substance from the Abrahamic covenant, but it is distinguished from the covenant at Sinai that established what the New Testament calls the "old covenant."

From Mount Sinai Moses mediated God's law, but in person the Suzerain who prescribed the laws governing the typological theocracy now declares in his own Sermon on the Mount, "You have heard that it was said to those of old.... But I say ..." (Mt 5:21–48). Jesus does not set aside the law but fulfills it (Mt 5:17–20). The kingdom of God is no longer identified with any geopolitical kingdom on earth. It is no longer the era of driving the nations out of God's holy land but of living side by side with unbelievers in charity. It is the hour of grace, not of judgment. Instead of offering typological sacrifices, we receive the once-and-for-all guilt sacrifice.

Christ's death inaugurates the new covenant as a royal grant—that is, a last will and testament that dispenses an inheritance based on his perfect, personal, and perpetual obedience rather than our own (Mt 26:26–30 par.; Gal 3:10–29; 4:21–28; Heb 8:1–13; 9:15–28). The Epistles provide the apostolic interpretation of the new covenant, both its doctrines and its practices, and like the old covenant (the prophetic literature), the New Testament concludes with the ultimate covenant lawsuit (Revelation). The sanctions are also evident throughout—everlasting life through faith alone in Christ alone, everlasting death through unbelief. So although the new covenant is itself a last will and testament, those who spurn their inheritance (like Esau) must bear their own guilt and represent themselves in the covenantal courtroom. They place themselves back under a covenant of works, condemned as transgressors.

The New Testament makes much of the point that the Sinai covenant was delivered through a merely human mediator, was temporary, and could not bring everlasting life, while the covenant of grace has God incarnate for its mediator, is eternal, and brings justification of the ungodly (Gal 3:19–20; Heb 3:1–6). The whole point of the Sinai covenant that Moses mediated was to create a small-scale replica of the heavenly kingdom, with its types and shadows pointing Israel to the coming reality in Christ. However, Israel's national existence as this typological regime depended on its faithfulness to the covenant stipulations. Unlike the covenant that *Israel* swore at Sinai, "All that the LORD has spoken we will do" (Ex 19:8), this covenant of grace rests on *God's* oath and is therefore stable and unchanging (Heb 6:13–20; 8:1–10:18).

God's Word first creates the reality of which it speaks and then regulates it, as the Spirit brings about the proper effect and response within creation. As a nation first arises out of an event of liberation from enemies and then is organized officially by a written constitution, God's *sacramental* Word of judgment and grace creates the new exodus people and then constitutes them as God's own nation by the *canon* of Holy Scripture. Once again we discern the importance of locating our doctrine of Scripture in the drama of redemption. The Bible did not fall from heaven in one volume; rather, it is the deposit of an organic and unfolding canon: both the original Word that liberates and creates its own society and the rule under which that society flourishes.

In Scripture, there is a pattern of work (creating a people) and rest (ruling the kingdom). In Genesis 1–2, God creates and then enters his seventh-day rest in royal enthronement, ruling over the works of his hands. In Adam, humanity too, as God's image bearers, was to follow this pattern of work (trial) and sabbatical rest (enthronement). Similarly, God acted mightily in liberating his servant Israel from Egyptian bondage and then constituted them as his holy nation at Mount Sinai, delivering the terms of the treaty that would determine Israel's status in the land he was giving them. Israel was to guard, keep, and cultivate God's holy land. Living in strict observance of God's commands, Israel would enjoy long life, fruitfulness, and other temporal blessings in God's typological land of rest. In all of the biblical covenants, we see this working-resting pattern. By his energetic Word, God creates a people for himself and then establishes a written constitution by which he will structure his holy nation. The relationship between God's sacramental Word (oral proclamation) and his canonical Word (the biblical text) may therefore be correlated with this pattern of working and resting, subduing and ruling.

Peter speaks of the Word of God in both of these senses, as *sacramental* (means of grace) and as *regulative* (canon). In the first sense, he refers to creation as having come into being "by the word of God" and adds, "But by the same word the heavens and earth that now exist are stored up for fire, being kept until the day of judgment and destruction of the ungodly" (2Pe 3:7). Yet the prophetic Scriptures are also the deposit of revelation and are no less the product of divine speech, and so we must "pay attention [to them] ... knowing this first of all, that no prophecy of Scripture comes from someone's own interpretation. For no prophecy was ever produced by the will of man, but men spoke from God as they were carried along by the Holy Spirit" (2Pe 1:19–21). In First Peter there is a similar combination. The letter's recipients were "born again ... through the living and abiding word of God ...," which is "the good news that was preached to you" (1Pe 1:23, 25), in order to be saved and ruled by Christ. "For you were straying like sheep, but have now returned to the Shepherd and Overseer of your souls" (1Pe 2:25). Christ saves us in order to rule us and rules us in order to save us. It is through his Word and Spirit that Christ accomplishes both. His Word is both the rod that parts the waters of death so that we may pass through safely and the scepter or staff by which he keeps us under his care until we reach the other side.

There can be no covenant without a canon or canon without a covenant. In fact, the covenant *is* the canon and vice versa. Furthermore, like the ancient Near Eastern treaties, the old and new covenant canons include among their sanctions a death sentence for anyone who attempts even the slightest emendation (Ex 25:16, 21; 40:20; Dt 4:2; 10:2; 31:9–13; cf. Dt 27; Jos 8:30–35; Rev 22:18). The United States Constitution cannot be amended by the executive or judicial branch but only by the legislative, since this branch represents the people, who are its authors. However, God is the suzerain (or Great King) of his church, and he alone has the authority to determine its content. The canon is no more the creation of the church than a nation's constitution is the creation of its courts. The covenant Lord creates a people out of nothing by his speech and shapes, regulates, and defines the covenantal life of that people by his canon.

It is of great importance to observe that the same canon that rules also liberates. Tyrants simply overwhelm a weaker people, oppressing them with arbitrary laws and a capricious exercise of power. However, the triune God guards us in the salvation that he has won for us by the same Word. It is a power indeed—greater than all earthly powers, but it is "the power of God for salvation . . ." (Ro 1:16).

Although the prophets and apostles are clearly witnesses to God's Word and works, their *writings* are treated as nothing less than God's own testimony. God sent the Spirit to Ezekiel, causing him to stand on his feet to receive his commission: "You shall speak my words to them, whether they hear or refuse to hear, for they are a rebellious house" (Eze 2:7; cf. 2:1–4, 8–10). The Great King gives his servant a scroll, commanding him to eat it. Not only revealing the judgment that God will bring on Israel, the scroll that Ezekiel eats in this vision brings God's judgment to Israel (3:1–11). Note that (1) the prophet speaks God's words, and (2) they are God's words regardless of their effect—or rather, *because* they are God's words in human words, they will achieve their intended effect (Isa 55:10–11).

II. INSPIRATION: GOD'S WORD AND HUMAN WORDS

Jesus regarded the words of Scripture as his Father's own Word (Mt 4:4, 7, 10; 5:17–20; 19:4–6; 26:31, 52–54; Lk 4:16–21; 16:17; 18:31–33; 22:37; 24:25–27, 45–47; Jn 10:35–38). Peter insisted that the prophets did not speak from themselves, but as they "were carried along by the Holy Spirit" (2Pe 1:21), and in 3:15–16 refers to Paul's letters as "Scriptures" (*graphas*). Similarly, Paul refers to Luke's gospel as

"Scripture" in 1 Timothy 5:18 (cf. Lk 10:7). Paul calls Scripture "the sacred writings, which are able to make you wise for salvation through faith in Christ Jesus," and adds, "All Scripture is breathed out by God [*theopneustos*] and profitable for teaching, for reproof, for correction, and for training in righteousness, that the man of God may be competent, equipped for every good work" (2Ti 3:15–17). A doctrine of inspiration must take into account the "many times" and "many ways" that God has spoken in the past (Heb 1:1), which cannot be restricted to the prophetic model ("Thus says the LORD: '...'"). Nevertheless, "*All* Scripture is breathed out by God." As such, the Scriptures are not only a record of redemption but are themselves the primary means of grace, through which the Spirit applies redemption to sinners in the present.

A. TRINITARIAN COOPERATION IN INSPIRATION

In every external work of the Godhead, the Father speaks in the Son and by the perfecting agency of the Spirit. In salvation, the Father gives the Son, the Son gives the Spirit, and the Spirit gives the Son a bride. Not only because of its authoritative source (the Father's speaking) but also because of its saving content (the speech concerning his Son), Scripture is God's Word. Jesus himself taught that all of Scripture pointed to him. Its authority and its content are inextricably linked.[4] God does not need a house, but he created the world and even identified his home as a specific place (Jerusalem) in order to dwell with finite creatures he created in his own image. Similarly, God does not need a Bible, but he gave us one so that he might reconcile us to himself and expand his sanctuary to the ends of the earth.

So Scripture is the church's authoritative canon because it comes *from the Father*. In Peter Martyr Vermigli's words, "'Thus says the Lord' (*Dominus dixit*) ought to be held as a first principle (*primum principium*) into which all true theology is resolved."[5] Nevertheless, Scripture's authority also derives from *the Son as its content*. Theology is the highest science, adds Vermigli, "since it treats of nothing other than Christ"—even in the Old Testament.[6] These Reformers and their heirs regarded the characteristics of Scripture (namely, inspiration, authority, and sufficiency) as inseparable from its scope and content (law and gospel, with the unfolding plan of redemption in Christ through the covenant of grace).[7] "Thus, the scopus or center

---

4. Herman Ridderbos, *Studies in Scripture and Its Authority* (Grand Rapids: Eerdmans, 1978), 9–11.

5. Quoted in Muller, *PRRD*, 2:323.

6. Ibid., 2:352.

7. Ibid., 2:120. Against the charge that Protestant scholasticism separated the divine form of Scripture from its content (Christ), leading to an abstract theory of inspiration, Muller collects a host of citations affirming Christ as the scope of Scripture, which is intrinsic to its authority. Included are citations not only from Luther (Preface to James and Jude in *Luther's Works* [ed. and trans. Jaroslav Pelikan; St. Louis: Concordia, 1968], 35:396); *Schmalkald Articles* II.i (*Book of Concord* [2nd ed.; trans. James Schaffer; ed. Robert Kolb and Timothy Wengert; Minneapolis: Augsburg Fortress, 2001]), and Calvin, *Institutes* 2.6.2 (also commentary on 1Co 3:11), but from Reformed colleagues and successors, including Peter Martyr Vermigli, Theodore Beza, Edward Leigh, Zacharius Ursinus, and William Perkins (*PRRD*, 2:98, 198, 224, 227, 342, 367).

'toward which all the Scriptures tend … is Jesus Christ," wrote Jerome Zanchi.[8] "Scripture, argues [Edward] Leigh, is called the Word of God because of 'the matter contained within it.'"[9] Christ as mediator of the covenant of grace is the scope of all Scripture. Inspiration extends both to the form and the content, "law and gospel, and is wholly perfect in both," Edward Leigh observed.[10] These theologians did not therefore develop an abstract theory of biblical authority and inspiration, but recognized the interdependence of the source (the Father's utterance) and the content (the Son's person and work).

Yet our Trinitarian coordinates are not set until we have included in our focus *the perfecting agency of the Spirit. As the Spirit hovered over the waters in creation to prepare a place for the covenant partner, and "overshadow[ed]" Mary so that she would conceive the incarnate Son, the same Spirit breathed out these texts—and illumines hearers now to receive them as the Word of God.* Largely because of our Greek heritage, we tend to identify the Spirit's sphere of activity with that which is invisible, spiritual, and eternal. However, in the Bible, the Spirit is actively engaged in shaping matter and history according to the design of the Father in the Son. It is useful to recall the communicative categories to which I referred earlier. The locutionary act of speaking is the Father's; the Son is the content or illocutionary act that is performed by speaking, and the Spirit works within creation to bring about the intended effect. For example, the Father gives the gospel, the Son is the gospel, and the Spirit creates faith in our hearts to receive it.

If our doctrine of inspiration is concerned exclusively with the authoritative source (the Father's speaking), it will gravitate toward a mechanical view. We cannot develop an adequate doctrine of inspiration from an abstract concept of its supernatural origin independent of its content. Yet if it focuses exclusively on the saving content (Jesus Christ), it is likely to yield a canon-within-a-canon approach, limiting inspiration to that which explicitly preaches Christ (leaving such determination to exegetes). At the same time, focusing one-sidedly on the Spirit in our doctrine of inspiration typically generates various forms of mysticism and enthusiasm that separate the Spirit from the Word.

In 2 Timothy 3:15–17, this scope (content) and inspiration of Scripture converge. Timothy is reminded to digest "the sacred writings, which are able to make you wise for salvation through faith in Christ Jesus." Paul does not say "insofar as" they achieve this but simply states that they do. It is not the parts of Scripture that we find "profitable for teaching, for reproof, for correction, and for training in righteousness" that we regard as inspired. Rather, because all Scripture is breathed out by God, it is profitable for the purposes for which God intends it. This means

---

8. Muller, *PRRD*, 2:98.
9. Ibid., 2:198.

10. Ibid., 2:335.

that Scripture not only functions as the Word of God at various times, but it is the Word of God by virtue of its origin (from the Father), its content (in the Son), and its inspiration (by the Spirit).

As Colin Gunton writes, this Trinitarian character of divine communication is as crucial in general as in special revelation. Christ is the mediator even in creation (and is therefore the mediator of all creaturely knowledge). "But that point must be developed pneumatologically also, so that all rationality, truth, and beauty are seen to be realized through the perfecting agency of God the Spirit, who enables things to be known by human minds and made by human hands."[11] If this is true in general revelation, it is all the more obvious in special revelation.

The Trinitarian coordinates are evident in the following observation of the sixteenth-century Scottish divine Robert Rollock: "The sacred Scripture is the judge of all controversies" in religion.[12] "By the word Scripture, I mean not only the substance thereof, but also the form of revelation, which is also by divine inspiration." Yet Rollock is concerned not to raise the Bible above the Spirit, as though the former had an independent authority:

> Again, this manner of speaking is improper, when we say of the Scripture that it is the judge of controversies. For to speak properly, the Holy Ghost is the judge; for the judge must be a person, and the Holy Ghost is the third person in Trinity. The Scripture, therefore, is not properly said to be a judge; but it is the voice and sentence which the judge hath given, the principal instrument or means whereby the Spirit sets forth his judgment, and whereby he teacheth us, and worketh faith in our hearts.[13]

Although the Spirit is the judge of our faith and practice, he exercises this judgment through his Word, never apart from it. The Father speaks the Son through the perfecting agency of the Spirit. This quite typical presentation of inspiration from Reformed orthodox theologians can hardly be characterized as impersonal or mechanical.

Each of these points summarized thus far can be amply supported from Scripture, especially in John's Gospel. Throughout his ministry Jesus directs attention to the authoritative Word of the Father. Jesus does not speak on his own authority, but relates what he has heard. Nevertheless, this speech of the Father is concerning the Son. And then in the Upper Room Discourse, Jesus tells his disciples that he and the Father will send another witness from heaven, the Spirit, who will bring about within sinful human beings the conviction of sin and the "Amen!" of faith toward

---

11. Colin Gunton, *A Brief Theology of Revelation* (Edinburgh: T&T Clark, 1995), 125.

12. Robert Rollock, "A Treatise of Our Effectual Calling,"

in *Select Works of Robert Rollock* (ed. William M. Gunn; Edinburgh: Woodrow Society, 1869), 1:94.

13. Ibid., 1:94–95.

his Son. In John 1, the original creation serves as the backdrop of the new creation with the cooperation of the Father, the Son, and the Spirit.

In 2 Corinthians 1, the Father is the faithful promise maker, and "all the promises of God find their Yes in [Christ]." Yet we can only "utter our Amen to God for his glory" because he "has also put his seal on us and given us his Spirit in our hearts as a guarantee" (2Co 1:20–22).

B. GOD'S ENERGIES: FIAT AND FRUITFULNESS

an authoritative decree

God's energies are distinct from his essence yet are not simply a created artifact. In this context, I am focusing on God's energies in the form of communication. In some cases, this communication arrives in the form of a direct and immediate fiat, while in others it brings about within creatures a sanctified response. For example, in the creation account we encounter the fiat declaration "'Let there be ...'"— bringing a new state of affairs out of nothing ("And there was ..."). However, in the same narrative there are expressions that highlight God's indirect and mediated agency: "'Let the earth sprout ...' And the earth brought forth...." We often tend to identify God's action exclusively with the former—perhaps, at least in part, because of a weak pneumatology (doctrine of the Holy Spirit). In Genesis 1, creation is attributed not only to the Father's fiat utterance but to the Spirit's brooding over the waters to make that creative Word fruitful. God not only decrees things into existence directly; ordinarily the Spirit works within creation to draw out its own natural operations with which he has endowed it so that it properly fulfills its created ends.

Obviously, God is not the only speaker in Scripture. However, he is the original speaker, and his Word always comes before our response. His work in inspiration extends even to the praise offered by his creatures. The Psalms are the inspired hymnal, giving us our lines in the covenantal script, because not only does the Father speak directly in every case; the Spirit also brings about the intended response within creatures. Because the Spirit is at work in the process of inspiration, even the testimony of sinful creatures can be preserved from error, sanctified by God as the authorized paradigm for our own speech.

If we bear in mind our Trinitarian coordinates and the distinction between fiat (*ex nihilo*) utterances and indirect guidance of creaturely speech to its appointed end, we no longer have to choose between a *mechanical* view of inspiration and a *naturalistic* denial of inspiration. It is not a contradiction to say that divine speech comes *from* God *through* creaturely agency as it is made fruitful by the Spirit. The triune God is the ultimate source of both types of declarations: "'Let there be ...'" and "'Let the earth sprout....'" Even when the earth brings forth its fruit, it is because the Spirit is bringing about within it the potentialities given to it by the Father's Word.

C. VERBAL-PLENARY INSPIRATION

The common teaching of the East and West, Roman Catholics and classical Protestants, is that Scripture is not only in its content but also in its form the Word of God written. This consensus that Scripture is inspired *in its words as well as its meaning* is aptly summarized by the phrase *verbal-plenary inspiration*.[14] The common consensus of Christians is one reason why inspiration was not a special topic in theological systems until the dawn of the Enlightenment. Not even the confessions and catechisms of the Reformation offer a particular theory of inspiration; they simply identify God's Word with the words of Scripture.

It is important to note what is not meant by this formulation. First, *verbal-plenary inspiration does not mean that the prophets and apostles themselves were inspired in their persons, as if everything they believed, said, or did was God's Word*. Rather, it is their canonical writings that are inspired. In the passages cited above (pp. 155–66), Peter refers inspiration to the prophecies, and Paul attributes inspiration to the Scriptures. In fact, Paul says that "all Scripture is breathed out by God." Strictly speaking, then, Scripture is exhaled, not inspired.

Second, *this view does not assume that the prophets and apostles were merely passive in the process of inspiration*. Of course, there are visions, especially in the prophetic literature, but even dreams have to be interpreted, and it was the human agents who interpreted them. Yet it was the Spirit who ensured that their interpretations were from the Father and focused on the Son. "Concerning this salvation," Peter writes, "the prophets who prophesied about the grace that was to be yours *searched and inquired carefully*, inquiring what person or time the Spirit of Christ in them was indicating when he predicted the sufferings of Christ and the subsequent glories" (1Pe 1:10–11, emphasis added).

Third, *this formulation also does not suggest that inspiration pertains to the intention of the human authors, who prophesied more than they themselves knew*. An extreme example is Caiaphas the high priest, who, contrary to his intention, prophesied Christ's atoning sacrifice (Jn 11:49–53). His office, not his person, authorized him for this role, and it was God's intentions that were communicated. There is no reason to believe the apostles were aware that their letters would become part of the new covenant canon. Although they knew they were commissioned and authorized to speak for God, they could distinguish their own pastoral advice from divine command (1Co 7:6).

Fourth, *verbal-plenary inspiration does not collapse all events of inspiration into the prophetic mold*. Far from "Thus says the LORD," the speeches of Job's friends

---

14. This doctrine holds that Scripture is "God-breathed" (2Ti 3:16) both in its *words* and in its *meaning*. However, this in no way implies (much less requires) a "dictation theory" of inspiration. According to the common interpretation of this view, inspiration occurred organically—that is, through the distinct personalities and conceptualities of the human authors in their social-historical context.

are riddled with error, even if they are reliable reports of the dialogue. God even allows the sinful or erroneous responses of human beings to be included in his inspired canon. We must recall that the Bible was generated in the context of a covenantal drama. The script includes the speaking parts of unfaithful covenant servants, whose speech is nevertheless judged and corrected by the covenant Lord within the unfolding dialogue.

The prophetic "Thus says the LORD ..." or "The word of the LORD came to me, saying ..." corresponds to the fiat declaration, "'Let there be....'" In such instances, inspiration may even take the form of dictation. More characteristically, however, inspiration follows the "'Let the earth sprout ...'" pattern, with the obvious evidence of the text's human authorship.

Although inspiration pertains exclusively to the original speech acts that are included in the canon, God's extraordinary providence ensured the integrity of the process that led to inscripturation. We have no reason to deny that later redactors (editors) committed orally transmitted instances of revelation to textual form and collected them into what we now know as canonical books. In the words of the Reformed scholastic Johannes Wollebius, "God's word at first was unwritten, before Moses' time; but after Moses it was written, when God in his most wise counsel would have it to be sealed and confirmed by prophets and apostles."[15] Clearly, for example, Moses did not write his own obituary (Dt 34). In this interpretation of verbal-plenary inspiration, the original words of Scripture were given by the miracle of inspiration, and the process of compiling, editing, and preserving the text was superintended by God's providence.

D. DIVINE AND HUMAN AGENCY IN INSPIRATION

Verbal-plenary inspiration affirms, with Peter, that revelation does not arise within the prophet or apostle or within the community more generally but has its source in the triune God (2Pe 1:21). The biblical writers were *moved* to say certain things. God acted *upon* them, interrupting the ordinary course of their lives, thoughts, and expectations by his external communication. And yet, God was also acting by his Spirit *within* them to prepare them throughout their lives for their vocation and to make his Word fruitful in their own minds and hearts. In both of these ways—acting upon ("'Let there be ...'") and within his servants ("'Let the earth sprout ...'")—God communicated his will and works through ordinary human speech.

---

15. Johannes Wollebius, *The Abridgement of Christian Divinitie* (trans. Alexander Ross; London, 1656), 3.

1. Undervaluing the Humanity of Scripture: The Docetic Temptation

Similar to the early christological heresy of _Doceticsm, which denied the reality of Christ's full humanity,_ is a well-established historical tendency that one may discern in church history to downplay the humanity of Scripture. Some ancient theologians spoke of the biblical writers as mere "flutes" on which the Spirit played or "secretaries" through whom he dictated his revelation. Such analogies became literal theories in fundamentalism. J. I. Packer refers to the comment of J. W. Burgon: "Every book of it, every chapter of it, every word of it, every syllable of it, every letter of it, is the direct utterance of the Most High."[16] W. A. Criswell expressed the same view: "Each sentence was dictated by God's Holy Spirit.... Everywhere in the Bible we find God speaking. It is God's voice, not man's."[17] Fundamentalism and Protestant orthodoxy are distinct traditions, and nowhere can this be more clearly seen than in their differing emphases concerning biblical inspiration.

When evaluating the relationship of God's activity and that of creatures in the production of Scripture, the doctrine of analogy already proves its merits. If agency is univocal (the same thing) for God and for creatures, then the question is raised: Who acts _more_? Is God the author of Romans or is Paul? However, if agency is analogical, then God's activity in producing these texts is qualitatively different from human agency. In this way it may be seen that the role of human authors in producing the Scriptures is entirely their own activity and entirely God's. For example, Joseph could attribute the same act (his brothers' treachery) to different agents with different intentions: "As for you, you meant evil against me, but God meant it for good, to bring it about that many people should be kept alive, as they are today" (Ge 50:20). Scripture includes false utterances (namely, in the speeches of Job's friends, the psalmist's acknowledged misunderstandings of God and his ways—and those misunderstandings of the disciples in the Gospels—as well as the statements of pagan rulers and even Satan). Ascribing inspiration to Luke's account of Paul's speech in Athens in no way entails that the writings of pagan philosopher Epimenides or poet Aratus (the latter, in a hymn to Zeus) were inspired, even though Paul quoted them in Acts 17:28. Nor does it mean that their _words_ were inspired, but only that Paul's interpretation—his use of their words—shared in this inspired speech. Whatever these speakers intended, God's intention was to use these lines in the script of his unfolding drama, although these pagan sources are not treated as normative. Therefore, it is impossible to treat every word as normative, much less as the direct utterance of God. Yet the Bible as a whole is God's inspired script for the drama of redemption.

---

16. J. I. Packer, _Fundamentalism and the Word of God_ (Grand Rapids: Eerdmans, 1984), 180.

17. W. A. Criswell, _Why I Preach That the Bible Is Literally True_ (Nashville: Broadman, 1969), 68.

In its treatment of creation as well as inspiration, fundamentalism tends to collapse God's indirect speech act, "'Let the earth sprout...'" into God's direct fiat, "'Let there be'...." To the extent that the Bible is the Word of God, on this view, human mediation must be diminished or even denied. In this sense, fundamentalism shares with liberalism a univocal view of divine and human agency, leading the former to undervalue the Bible's humanity, while the latter interprets the obvious signs of the Bible's humanity as evidence of a merely natural process.

In contrast to *mechanical inspiration*, evangelical theology embraces a theory of *organic inspiration*.[18] That is, God sanctifies the natural gifts, personalities, histories, languages, and cultural inheritance of the biblical writers. These are not blemishes on or obstacles to divine inspiration but the very means that God employs for accommodating his revelation to our creaturely capacity. The christological analogy reminds us that the Word became flesh. The incarnation itself was a fiat declaration of the "'Let there be ...'" variety. Nevertheless, the Son's gestation and birth were part of a natural ("'Let the earth sprout ...'") process. Even his physical, intellectual, and spiritual maturation were gradual gains through ordinary means: "And the child grew and became strong, filled with wisdom" (Lk 2:40). His humanity was not charged with superhuman abilities but was like ours in all respects except for sin (Heb 4:15). "Although he was a son, he learned obedience through what he suffered" (Heb 5:8). If God can assume our full humanity without sin, then he can speak through the fully human words of prophets and apostles without error. As Herman Bavinck expressed the point, "Like Christ, [Scripture] considers nothing that is human strange."[19]

In spite of widely publicized exceptions (such as the Formula Consensus Helvetica's suggestion that the Hebrew vowel points were inspired), the older Protestant writers were fully appreciative of the diversity in Scripture and therefore in the forms of inspiration. This point is wisely elaborated, for example, by William Ames in his *Marrow of Theology* (1629):

> But divine inspiration was present among those writers in different ways. Some things were altogether unknown to the writer in advance, as appears in the history of past creation, or in the foretelling of things to come. But some things were previously known to the writer, as appears in the history of Christ written by the apostles. Some things were known by a natural knowledge and some by a supernatural.[20]

---

18. Mechanical inspiration is the belief that the biblical writers were merely passive in the process of inspiration. Often, this view represents the Bible as having been dictated entirely and directly by the Spirit. Organic inspiration is the belief that the biblical writers were fully involved in the process of inspiration, with their own distinctive intellectual, cultural, linguistic, and personality traits contributing to the text. This view also emphasizes the long historical process in which revelation was given and therefore the evident circumstances of the time and place of each book.

19. Quoted in Berkouwer, *Holy Scripture*, 27.

20. William Ames, *The Marrow of Theology* (ed. John D. Eusden; Durham, N.C.: Labyrinth, 1968), 186.

In some instances, supernatural inspiration operated by itself, Ames notes, while in other cases "knowledge was obtained by ordinary means," though guided by the Spirit's assistance so that "they might not err in writing.... But this was done with a subtle tempering so that every writer might use the manner of speaking which most suited his person and condition."[21]

Once again it is important to point out the difference between seeing the major problem to be overcome in terms of "nature and grace" and seeing it in terms of "sin and grace." Nature as such is finite, but finitude is not to be confused with sin and error. The preservation of human agents from error while their free agency remains intact is already presupposed in a biblical doctrine of God's sovereignty. God restrains sin and error in myriad ways every moment, yet without violence to creatures.

The Protestant scholastics were fully conscious of textual issues. "Much more than the Reformers," notes Muller, "they were aware of the edited nature of the text and the authorial anonymity of much of the material," and they pioneered historical-critical research without succumbing to the naturalistic presuppositions of higher criticism.[22] Given their high view of God's sovereignty in providence, signs of the Bible's humanity and historical conditioning, far from impeding, actually deepened their confidence in the inspiration of Scripture.

Once more we see the usefulness of the distinction between God's essence and his energies. The authorized words of commissioned agents are not transubstantiated into the Word of God. Not God's essence, but God's energies are communicated through these human agents. In the covenantal context, their words *count as* God's speech because these ordinary people are called to an extraordinary task. They do not speak in their own persons, but in their office as covenant attorneys or ambassadors. They are sent by the Father to proclaim the Son in the power of the Spirit. Thus, God's speech is neither simply a creaturely artifact nor an emanation of the divine essence. It is God's working, and the Bible is the authoritative deposit of that communicative agency.

As John Webster suggests, sanctification is an important category for understanding inspiration.[23] No more than pots, vessels, buildings, times, or places are human beings or their words intrinsically holy. Rather, it is God's calling and gift that sets the ordinary apart for his extraordinary use. It is not the essence of a human being's words but God's use of them in the service of his covenantal purposes that sets them apart from ordinary human speech.

When called by God, Moses protests his poverty of speech. Yet God replies,

---

21. Ibid.
22. Muller, *PRRD*, 406.

23. John Webster, *Holy Scripture: A Dogmatic Sketch* (Cambridge: Cambridge Univ. Press, 2003), 11–14.

"Now therefore go, and I will be with your mouth and teach you what you shall speak" (Ex 4:12). Moses asks God to send someone else, but God stands firm, conceding so far as to allow Aaron to assist him by speaking to the people on his behalf, but insisting that Moses is the one to communicate from God to Aaron: "You shall be as God to him. And take in your hand this staff, with which you shall do the signs" (4:16–17). Pharaoh responds by increasing the people's oppressive burden, yet God commands Moses to speak again to the king. "How then shall Pharaoh listen to me, for I am of uncircumcised lips?" (Ex 6:12). Yet again God commissions Moses to fulfill his task. God sanctifies his lips and attests to his commission by performing signs and wonders.

Similarly, when God reveals himself to Isaiah in his holiness, Isaiah does not respond to his vocation as one whose spiritual sensitivity has prepared him for this moment. Rather, the prophet senses his profound unsuitability: "Woe is me! For I am lost; for I am a man of unclean lips, and I dwell in the midst of a people of unclean lips; for my eyes have seen the King, the LORD of hosts!'" (Isa 6:5). Only when one of the seraphim touches a burning coal to his lips, forgiving him of his sin, is Isaiah able to say, "Here am I! Send me" (v. 8). The disciples were not waiting in the synagogue engaged in holy duties, preparing themselves for the Messiah's call, but were called away from their ordinary vocations. Similarly, Paul was accosted and called by the ascended Christ when he was on his way to another round of persecution of believers. Like these other servants, Paul always carried around with him a sense of his own unworthiness (1Ti 1:15) and also had to defend his apostleship over against the "superapostles" whose superior abilities in speech drew away disciples from Christ's flock (1Co 1:18–2:16; 14:19; 2Co 4:1–14; 10:1–12:21).

Sanctification falls on the "'Let the earth sprout...'" side of God's communicative energies. God not only creates, judges, and justifies human beings by direct fiat but claims such creaturely reality as the sphere and subject of his purifying action. The prophet's sins are forgiven—he is justified. Furthermore, his lips are healed—he is sanctified. The self-proclaimed "chief of sinners" (1 Tim 1:15 KJV) becomes the greatest missionary in church history. Sanctification is not the obliteration or even the alteration of nature, but God's act of claiming, redeeming, renewing, and commissioning nature for himself. The divine Word always remains *in and through* the human words, not just *alongside* them (as Barth's interpretation often suggests) or *overwhelming* them (as in the tendency of fundamentalism).

We should recall Mary's response to the annunciation. Troubled in heart, she asked, "How will this be, since I am a virgin?" After the most basic explanation ("the Holy Spirit will come upon you, and ... the child to be born will be called holy—the Son of God"), she replies, "Behold, I am the servant of the Lord" (Lk 1:34–35, 38). Mary was not a stone. She was indeed confused by the announcement and wondered how it could be possible, but it was enough to be assured that its possibility was not the point. God would do it. God establishes what is and is not possible. She believed the angel's assurance: "For nothing will be impossible with God" (v. 37).

2. THE GOSPEL AND THE PRIORITY OF GOD'S AGENCY IN INSPIRATION

As we have seen, revelation follows redemption, and both are *monergistic*. That is, God saves us without our help—in fact, while we are rebels. In the "overcoming estrangement" paradigm, it is the human search for the sacred that dominates; in the biblical account of "meeting a stranger," the focus is on God's seeking and saving the lost. Neither salvation nor revelation comes from within; they come to us from above.

If we tend to view our salvation as *synergistic* (i.e., cooperation between God and sinners), Berkouwer reminds us, we will likely "understand the God-breathed character as a sum of the divine and human, so that in fact we only have to deal partially with the divine voice in Scripture."[24] However, revelation and redemption are movements from God to us, not from us to God. Off of the table then are any romantic theories of inspiration in which revelation is a product of a religious genius, superior intellect, or eminent piety. Besides this theological rationale, we have the fact that the prophets and apostles are represented often in Scripture as weak servants.

The biblical writers are not simply expressing their religious experience in verbal form. They do not call and send themselves but are called and sent by God. In fact, the false prophets are contrasted with the true prophets by the fact that they have never stood in the Lord's council and therefore have not been sent with his words (Jer 23:9–40). The same criterion holds for the canonicity of New Testament texts: they must be identifiable within the circle of eyewitnesses who were directly called to their office by Jesus Christ. At the same time, those eyewitnesses are not inert, passive spectators of revelation but, like Mary, are taken up by the Spirit into his service along with the full range of their own characteristics. The triumphant declaration "Salvation belongs to the LORD!" (Jnh 2:9) is inextricably tied to the conviction that the gospel comes from God, not from the pious individual or community. It is because it is the Word of the Father concerning Christ brought to its perfect completion by the Spirit that Scripture conveys God's own authority both as "the power of God for salvation" (Ro 1:16) *and* the rule of God over all matters of faith and practice (2Ti 3:15–16). God not only saves us by his energetic Word so that he may rule us by his canonical Word; he rules us in order to keep us in his continually saving and sanctifying care.

---

24. Berkouwer, *Holy Scripture*, 172.

E. Inspiration and Illumination

Jesus Christ, by his own action, inaugurated the new creation, and by sending the Spirit, whom he promised in the upper room (Jn 14–16), he not only taught the disciples and made them witnesses, but designated their preaching and teaching as his written constitution. When that Word is read and preached today, it is Christ who speaks. However, the giving of that original canon deposit belongs to *revelation*; the subsequent work of the Spirit in the church belongs to *illumination*. The Scriptures are inspired regardless of human response, but in order to receive their teaching, hearts must be illumined by the Spirit who inspired the text (1Co 2:10–16). An analogy may be drawn from Jesus Christ as the hypostatic Word of God: "The light shines in the darkness, and the darkness has not overcome it. . . . He was in the world, and the world was made through him, yet the world did not know him" (Jn 1:5, 10). He is what he is regardless of human response. Nevertheless, revelation reaches its goal only when it is recognized as such. Only the Spirit can achieve this recognition (vv. 12–13).

Like the redemptive work that it proclaims, this revelation is past—already given, accomplished, and sealed once and for all, and now the Spirit effectually calls people to himself through that Word. Employing the building-erecting metaphor, Paul adds that the foundation-laying era of the new covenant came to a close with the apostolic era, and now the ordinary ministry of Word and sacrament builds on that foundation of the apostolic canon (1Co 3:9–17).

So inspiration is a characteristic of the biblical text, while illumination is the Spirit's subsequent work of bringing us to an understanding and acceptance of its meaning. This is the doctrine usually referred to as "the inner testimony of the Spirit." The Spirit's illumination is of two kinds, internal and external. The Spirit witnesses to the truth of Scripture and within us to win our consent. Rollock reminds us that illumination affects us, not the Scriptures themselves: "And the Holy Ghost also himself in this work gives no new light to the Scripture, which is clear and glorious in itself, as is aforesaid, but enlightens our minds, to this end, that we may see the great light of the sacred Scripture."[25] The Spirit brings forth the internal evidences of Scripture—its harmony, the grandeur of its message, the miracles, and the celestial doctrine.[26]

This inner witness of the Spirit was developed especially by Calvin as a way of answering the Roman Catholic claim that biblical authority rested on the testimony of the church.[27] Calvin's point is that "only God himself is a sufficient witness to himself."[28] In fact, Calvin compared Rome to the radical Protestants ("enthusiasts")

---

25. Rollock, "Effectual Calling," 70.
26. Ibid.

27. See Calvin, *Institutes* 1.7.
28. Quoted in Berkouwer, *Holy Scripture*, 41.

in their affirmation of continuing special revelation apart from and in addition to the canonical Word.[29] Divine revelation can only rest on a divine testimony. An infallible text can hardly be founded on a church that can err and in fact has often erred throughout its history.

Nevertheless, this testimony of the Spirit does not add a syllable to Scripture; rather, it convinces us of Scripture's truth.[30] The church is ordinarily the medium through which we become convinced of the truths of Scripture, but it is not the basis for our confidence in them. Only the Spirit can give us confidence in Scripture because it is the Spirit who inspired the sacred text and unites us to Christ, who is its content. Faith in Scripture rises and falls with faith in Christ, as Bavinck pointed out.[31]

Abraham Kuyper noted that the Spirit's inward witness "usually works 'gradually and unobserved.'"

> The Spirit's witness begins by binding us to the center of Scripture, namely, Jesus Christ. The extent of this authority is of no significance at first. Only by degrees does Scripture begin to fascinate us by its organic composition in a gradual assimilation process regarding its content and message.... Experiencing the *divinitas* [divinity] of Scripture takes place through experiencing God's *benevolentia* [benevolence].[32]

Once more we see the inextricable connection between the source, content, and perlocutionary effect of revelation. We cannot be convinced of the Bible's inspiration and authority as an independent or foundational theory of its origin abstracted from its content or from the Spirit's testimony. We become convinced of the divine authority of Scripture as we are persuaded by the Spirit of the glory of Christ and his gospel. At the same time, the Spirit is not involved in freelance missions. "The powerful operation of the testimony of the Spirit centers in the salvation that has appeared in Christ" and is therefore inseparable from the Bible.[33]

We receive the Scriptures as God's Word not because our reason judges it true and useful. Nor do we embrace them on the basis of the Spirit's inner testimony or our experience of new birth. Rather, through that testimony of the Spirit we come to understand and accept the *message* that Scripture communicates. As a result, Paul can say, "We also thank God constantly for this, that when you received the word of God, which you heard from us, you accepted it not as the word of men but as what it really is, the word of God, which is at work in you believers" (1Th 2:13). Notice

---

29. Calvin, *Institutes* 1.7.5.

30. D. F. Strauss called the *testimonium internum* "the Achilles' heel of the Protestant system," because it shifted objectivity away from external revelation to the human heart (*Die christliche Glaubenslehre* [1840], 1:136). However true this may be in the tendency of radical Protestantism, it misses the crucial point

that at least in its Reformed formulation, the internal witness was inseparable from the external Word.

31. Quoted in Berkouwer, *Holy Scripture*, 44.

32. Quoted in ibid., 49.

33. Ibid., 49.

too how this verse integrates the Word-as-canon ("you accepted it") and the Word-as-means-of-grace ("which is at work in you believers"). As Bavinck observes, "we believe Scripture 'not because of but through the Spirit's testimony.'"[34]

If we divorce illumination (the inner testimony of the Spirit) from inspiration, we easily fall into the impersonal view of Scripture as a dead letter, a view for which conservative Christians are often criticized and caricatured. However, the opposite danger is simply to collapse these categories.

F. Collapsing the Distinction between Inspiration and Illumination

The frequent judgment that Protestant liberalism is antisupernatural is in many cases wide of the mark, and Friedrich Schleiermacher is a good example. Deism denied God's miraculous intervention in nature and history, while Romanticism identified nearly anything and everything as a miracle. Schleiermacher had no difficulty accepting the Spirit's inspiration of Scripture, but he could not *limit* inspiration to Scripture, and it was in this too-broad understanding of inspiration that, from an orthodox perspective, he erred. "What is inspiration?" Schleiermacher answered, "It is simply the general expression for the feeling of true morality and freedom."[35] Elsewhere he wrote that since the Holy Spirit is "the common spirit of the church," all thinking concerning God's kingdom is "inspired by the Spirit."[36] Schleiermacher insists that not only the apostles' writings but their persons were inspired each and every moment.[37] So from his perspective, orthodoxy erred not in its supernaturalism but in its narrowing of inspiration to written texts. In fact, he calls this "an utterly dead scholasticism."[38] Ironically, Schleiermacher broadens the concept of inspiration to include the whole sweep of Christian history while excluding the Old Testament. The law, though divinely ordained, was not inspired in the same degree as the Christian Scriptures. How do we know this? Because "we have actual experience" and not mere "premonitions" of Christ.[39]

This more immanentistic way of conflating inspiration and illumination can be detected in the approach of some recent evangelical theologians, such as Stanley

---

34. Quoted in ibid., 52.

35. Friedrich Schleiermacher, *On Religion: Speeches to Its Cultured Despisers* (trans. John Oman; New York: Harper and Bros., 1958), 89.

36. Friedrich Schleiermacher, *The Christian Faith* (ed. trans. H. R. Mackintosh and J. S. Stewart; Edinburgh: T&T Clark, 1928), 598.

37. Ibid., 599.

38. Ibid., 600.

39. Ibid., 609–11. In fact, the prophets write within the context of "the legal dispensation," so that "only Messianic proph-

ecy would remain as capable of sharing in inspiration in our sense." "Further, the history of Christian theology shows only too clearly ... how gravely this effort to find our Christian faith in the Old Testament has injured our practice of the exegetical art." Schleiermacher recognizes that this figural interpretation of Old and New Testaments in terms of promise and fulfillment was exhibited in the preaching of Christ and his apostles and in the early church. Against this approach Schleiermacher suggests that the Old Testament be attached as an appendix to the New Testament.

Grenz. Since evangelicals are more closely related historically to Anabaptist and pietist traditions and, therefore, more experience based than doctrinal or sacramental, Grenz wonders why some evangelical theologians still hold to the scholastic-Calvinist "conviction that there is a deposit of cognitive revelation given once and for all in the Bible," together with that conviction's "combination of a material and a formal principle [*sola fide* and *sola scriptura*]."[40] Perhaps even more bravely than Schleiermacher (and certainly more radically than Barth), Grenz rejects a direct identification of revelation with Scripture.[41] He argues that "spirituality is generated from within the individual."[42] Consequently, Scripture is not God's Word, but "the foundational record of how the ancient faith community responded" to God.[43] Scripture discloses "the self-understanding of the community in which it developed."[44] Therefore, Scripture exists alongside experience and culture, and "these sources must be held in 'creative tension as responding in their different ways to the revelation of God.' "[45] In this way, inspiration is lowered to the level of illumination and therefore broadened to include the whole history of the people of God and their experience of this interplay between Scripture, tradition, and culture.

Similarly, John Franke argues that "the speaking of the Spirit through Scripture and through culture does not constitute two communicative acts but rather one unified speaking."[46] At this point, Franke seems to conflate inspiration with illumination—and beyond this, to conflate the Spirit's illumination of unbelievers and believers alike by common grace (through general revelation) with the illumination of believers to interpret special revelation faithfully. Our response to this formulation should be to point out that culture, though a theater of God's providence, is not a means of grace. The particular cultures that shape us are our *context*, but not our *authority* for faith and life. Therefore, we do not deny that we come to Scripture with certain cultural predispositions, but we do deny that they are normative or inspired by God. Sometimes the church is corrected even in its interpretation of Scripture through cultural insights and advances. This is because unbelievers, too, are created in God's image, and the Spirit provides illumination in earthly as well as heavenly matters.

---

40. Stanley Grenz, *Revisioning Evangelical Theology* (Downers Grove, Ill.: InterVarsity Press, 1993), 62.

41. Ibid., 76.

42. Ibid., 46.

43. Ibid., 77.

44. Ibid., 121.

45. Ibid., 91. In nineteenth-century christological debates, the Lutheran view that Christ's divine attributes were communicated to his humanity was reversed in what was called the "kenotic Christology." In this view, the Son emptied himself of his divine attributes in the incarnation. Something similar may be seen in recent debates over Scripture. On one hand, fundamentalism divinizes the human words, while "kenotic"

theories of Scripture empty Scripture of its divine character. As Donald Bloesch observes, referring especially to Ray Anderson, some evangelical theologians have also adopted this course. In addition to the dubious christological implications, Bloesch warns, "If the kenotic theory is carried too far, this means that the divine Word is transmuted into the human word of Scripture, and is thereby emptied of its divine content" (Donald G. Bloesch, "The Primacy of Scripture," in *The Authoritative Word: Essays on the Nature of Scripture* [ed. Donald McKim; Grand Rapids: Eerdmans, 1983], 150).

46. John Franke, *The Character of Theology* (Grand Rapids: Baker, 2005), 142.

However, inspiration is restricted to God's saving economy through special revelation. Like reason, tradition, and experience, culture can be a *servant* of ecclesiastical interpretation of the holy canon, but it cannot *reign* beside it. Franke does add that Scripture "functions as theology's norming norm" in its conversation with culture.[47] However, the crucial qualifier is *functions as*. Scripture functions normatively because of the decision of the community to regulate itself by this norm. This is rather different from saying that Scripture functions normatively because it is God's transcendent Word that creates the faith and therefore the community that acknowledges the Word.

Concerning 2 Timothy 3:16, Grenz and Franke suggest, "Through the rare use of *theopneustos* ... Paul declared that 'God breathes into the Scripture' thereby making it useful."[48] However, this verse does not say that God breathes *into* Scripture but that the Scriptures *are* "God-breathed" (*theopneustos*). They are not made useful whenever God breathes into them; they are useful because God exhaled them.[49]

At stake is an *ontological* view of biblical inspiration, which, if we accept the argument of Grenz and Franke, we are in danger of exchanging for a *functional* view. Is inspiration an attribute of the texts themselves, or is it something that happens in the individual or community through the use that the Spirit makes of them? In other words, is inspiration basically the same as illumination?

Grenz and Franke warn against "positing a simple, one-to-one correspondence between the revelation of God and the Bible, that is, between the Word of God and the words of scripture."[50] They argue that the community generated these texts as it sought to understand its relationship to earlier epochs and the relevance of its faith in the present.[51] It is no longer the text itself that stands as the church's norm, but "the message the Spirit declares through the text."[52] The Bible's authority seems thereby to become merely instrumental rather than intrinsic. They add:

> Consequently, we must never conclude that exegesis alone can exhaust the Spirit's speaking to us through the text. Although the Spirit's illocutionary act is to appropriate the text in its internal meaning (i.e., to appropriate what the author said), the Spirit appropriates the text with the goal of communicating to us in our situation, which, while perhaps paralleling in certain respects that of the ancient community, is nevertheless unique.[53]

In this account, the Word and the Spirit drift apart as inspiration is collapsed into illumination; the text (at least in its availability to us) becomes virtually indistinguishable from interpretation. While in some sense appropriating the scriptural

47. Ibid.

48. Stanley Grenz and John Franke, *Beyond Foundationalism: Shaping Theology in a Postmodern Context* (Louisville: Westminster John Knox, 2001), 65.

49. On the meaning of *theopneustos*, see the argument of A. A. Hodge and B. B. Warfield, *Inspiration* (Grand Rapids: Baker,

1979), 5.

50. Grenz and Franke, *Beyond Foundationalism*, 70–71.

51. Ibid., 72.

52. Ibid., 74.

53. Ibid., 74–75.

words, the Spirit may be actually saying something different to us today than he has said before. This move is highlighted by the identification of the Spirit's act as illocutionary (i.e., the stance or content of what is spoken) rather than perlocutionary (i.e., bringing about its intended effect). Therefore, this view risks substituting the Spirit not only for the written Word but also for the content, namely, Christ.

Anticipating objections, Grenz and Franke insist that "the problem of subjectivism arises only when we mistakenly place the individual ahead of the community."[54] Regardless of whether we hear the Spirit or not, the authors suggest, "the Bible remains objectively scripture *because it is the book of the church*" (emphasis added).[55] Whether individualistic or communal, however, this interpretation remains subjectivistic, treating Scripture merely as an inspiring record of Spirit-assisted ecclesial reflection rather than an inspired record of Spirit-breathed revelation from God. In short, God's agency is made subordinate to human agency, and this inevitably undermines *sola gratia* (grace alone). While affirming Scripture as a means of grace, this view has the unintended consequence of eliminating Scripture's status as a revealed canon that stands outside and above the pious individual and community.

Repeating a refrain that, despite its association with Counter-Reformation polemics, has become increasingly fashionable among Protestants, Grenz and Franke assert that the Bible is the church's book. "The [faith] community precedes the production of the scriptural texts and is responsible for their content and for the identification of particular texts for inclusion in an authoritative canon to which it has chosen to make itself accountable."[56] Such an assertion, at least as stated here, could give the impression that the church is sovereign in this matter: Scripture is authoritative canon because the church has decided to treat it as such. The authors admit that this "leads to a broader concept of inspiration."[57] On one hand, Scripture constitutes the church. "On the other hand, it is itself derived from that community and its authority."[58] The authors defend the same view of the relation between Scripture and tradition that was articulated at the Second Vatican Council.[59] However, lodging inspiration in the community rather than in Scripture itself, this position takes a step beyond the Roman Catholic view, closely approximating, if not repeating, the position of Schleiermacher.[60] By doing so, the view elides the qualitative distinction between inspiration (canon) and illumination (tradition); in

---

54. Ibid., 68.

55. Ibid.

56. Ibid., 115.

57. Ibid., 116.

58. Ibid., 117.

59. Ibid.: "Even though scripture and tradition are distinguishable, they are fundamentally inseparable. In other words, neither Scripture nor tradition is inherently authoritative in the foundationalist sense of providing self-evident, noninferential,

incorrigible grounds for constructing theological assertions. The authority of each—tradition as well as Scripture—is contingent on the work of the Spirit, and both Scripture and tradition are fundamental components within an interrelated web of beliefs that constitutes the Christian faith."

60. A similar view is articulated in Paul J. Achtemeier, *The Inspiration of Scripture: Problems and Proposals* (Philadelphia: Westminster John Knox, 1980), esp. 125–35.

fact, one can see in it an obvious distinction between the objective address of God and the internal word of the community. Beyond affirming that God acts through the church (by illumination), this view makes God's action and the church's action (by inspiration) indistinguishable.

The pendulum is swinging: reacting against the practical anarchy of Protestant individualism in our day, some Christians are assimilating Scripture to the church. Yet, as Calvin noted long ago, in spite of their obvious differences, radical Protestant "enthusiasm" and Roman Catholic theories of the church as the mother of Scripture share surprising similarities.[61] They are simply two ways of reducing God's speech to human speech, whether that of the pious believer or that of the holy church. "The description of the canon as a creation of the church is not in the least a uniquely Roman Catholic one," John Webster has noted. "For others besides [Adolf] Harnack have used the term [*creation*] to express the church's part in the formation of the canon."[62] Ever since Schleiermacher, many Protestant theologians have imbibed a romantic theory of "the community" that is much closer to a Roman Catholic position.

The Bible is not "the church's book" if by that one means that the community created its own canon—which is tantamount to saying that the vassal (servant) rather than the Suzerain (Lord) is the author of the covenant. To whatever extent "the people" create their constitution in modern states, the biblical canon must be defined by its own covenantal history, in which God's saving action and revelation create the community rather than vice versa. The positions I have criticized above can only yield what John Webster refers to as a "hermeneutical Pelagianism."[63] Against such views, he insists that we must see the Bible neither as the individual's book nor as the church's book, but as God's book. Without diminishing the human character of Scripture, Webster underscores the close connection between *sola gratia* (grace alone) and *sola scriptura* (Scripture alone). At issue in our doctrine of Scripture is the question not of what use we make of it (either communally or individually), but the use God makes of it within the economy of grace.[64]

III. THE TRUTHFULNESS OF SCRIPTURE

The historical facts of creation and redemption would be true regardless of whether God chose to report them through inspired Scripture. However, if God has in fact done so, then the Spirit's utterance cannot include error.

---

61. John Calvin, "Reply by Calvin to Cardinal Sadoleto's Letter," in *Tracts and Treatises of the Reformation of the Church* (ed. Thomas F. Torrance; Grand Rapids: Baker, 1958), 1:36.

62. John Webster, *Word and Church* (Edinburgh: T&T Clark, 2001), 77.

63. Webster, *Holy Scripture: A Dogmatic Sketch*, 100.

64. Ibid., 2, 19, 45.

Against the repeated claim that the doctrine of inerrancy arose first with Protestant orthodoxy, we could cite numerous examples from the ancient and medieval church.[65] Down to the Second Vatican Council, Rome has attributed inerrancy to Scripture as the common view of the church throughout its history.[66] Pope Leo XIII in 1893 went even further by espousing the dictation theory of inspiration, and successive popes during the twentieth century condemned the view that inerrancy was limited to that which is necessary for salvation.[67] Undoubtedly, this mechanical theory of inspiration is what most critics have in mind when they encounter the term *inerrancy*. Be that as it may, these examples do demonstrate that inerrancy is not an invention of Protestant orthodoxy.

Although higher-critical trends swept Roman Catholic biblical scholars—and Protestants too—into their wake, Rome remained committed at least formally to the verbal inspiration and inerrancy of Scripture. Quoting the Second Vatican Council, the most recent Catholic Catechism states, "Since therefore all that the inspired authors or sacred writers affirm should be regarded as affirmed by the Holy Spirit, we must acknowledge that the books of Scripture firmly, faithfully, and without error teach that truth which God, for the sake of our salvation, wished to see confided to the Sacred Scriptures."[68]

With equal clarity, Luther and Calvin can speak of Scripture as free from error.[69] However, it would be anachronistic to put post-Enlightenment questions to pre-Enlightenment figures. The Reformers could simultaneously affirm the inerrancy of Scripture—even to the point of using the unfortunate language of *dictation*—while pointing out apparent discrepancies in the text. Calvin believed that "the Scriptures should be read with the aim of finding Christ in them,"[70] and the truthfulness of Scripture was also for Protestant orthodoxy inseparable from its scope and

65. See Robert D. Preus, "The View of the Bible Held by the Church: The Early Church through Luther," and John H. Gerstner, "The View of the Bible Held by the Church: Calvin and the Westminster Divines," in *Inerrancy* (ed. Norman Geisler; Grand Rapids: Zondervan, 1980); John A. Woodbridge, *Biblical Authority: A Critique of the Rogers/McKim Proposal* (Grand Rapids: Zondervan, 1982); G. W. Bromiley, "The Church Fathers and Holy Scripture," in D. A. Carson and John A. Woodbridge, eds., *Scripture and Truth* (Leicester, U.K.: Inter-Varsity Press, 1983).

66. According to the First Vatican Council (1869–1870), the Old and New Testaments, "whole and entire," are "sacred and canonical." In fact, contrary to the tendency of some Protestants to lodge the nature of inspiration in the church's authority, this council added, "And the church holds them as sacred and canonical not because, having been composed by human industry, they were afterwards approved by her authority; nor only because they contain revelation without errors, but because, having been written under the inspiration of the Holy Spirit,

they have God for their Author" (First Vatican Council, ch. 3, "On Revelation," in *Sources of Catholic Dogma* [ed. Heinrich Denzmyer; Fitzwilliam, N. H.: Loreto, 2002], 3006).

67. In an 1893 encyclical, Pope Leo XIII asserted that the dictation view was "the ancient and unchanging faith of the church," held by all of the church fathers. Early in the twentieth century, Benedict XV said that it is "necessary to salvation" to affirm that the historical narratives as well as the doctrine are fully inspired and inerrant, and in 1943, Pope Pius XII condemned the view that limited inerrancy only to that which is necessary for salvation.

68. *Dei Verbum* [God's Word]: *Constitution on Divine Revelation*, art. 11, quoted in the *Catechism of the Catholic Church* (Liguori, Mo.: Liguori Publications, 1994), 31.

69. Klaas Runia, "The Hermeneutics of the Reformers," *CTJ* 19 (1984): 129–32.

70. John Calvin, *Commentary on the Gospel according to John* (trans. William Pringle; Grand Rapids: Baker, repr. 1996), 1:218.

content. <u>Scripture is the Word from the Father, through the Spirit, concerning the Son.</u> Wilhelm Niesel observes:

> Reformed theology, just like Lutheran, knows that it is God's Word which addresses us from the Bible and produces faith and that this Word is Christ himself. But this address does not become an experience within our control on the basis of which we can read through the Bible and test whether it "sets forth Christ." Calvin read the whole Bible expecting to find Christ there.[71]

There is therefore no "canon within a canon"; all Scripture is God-breathed and therefore useful (i.e., canonical) for norming the church's faith and practice.

With some notable exceptions, challenges to the church's historic doctrine of inspiration came from the quarters of radical Protestantism. Faustus Socinus (1539–1604) denied verbal inspiration (i.e., the inspiration of the words), and in the early eighteenth century Dutch Arminianism, under the influence of Hugo Grotius and Jean LeClerc, distinguished between inspiration (a pious motion of the soul) and revelation (divine communication), the latter pertaining only to the prophecies and the words of Jesus.[72] It was especially under LeClerc's influence that the concept of limited inerrancy arose.[73] As a child of the Enlightenment, higher-critical investigation in liberal circles began with the naturalistic presupposition that all claims of divine intervention in history were mythical. Liberals viewed such claims in the biblical text as evidence of a primitive and unscientific worldview and felt they must be treated as subjective claims of value rather than credible claims of fact. From this perspective, the question of the Bible's truthfulness was no longer a question, much less a problem.

A century later, Friedrich Schleiermacher, as we noted (see section F. above, p. 169), held to a Romantic concept of inspiration that is virtually identical to Grotius's pious motion of the soul.

In all of these ways, inspiration was treated as a subjective characteristic of individuals and the community rather than an objective property of the biblical text. It is no wonder that Albrecht Ritschl, Richard Rothe, F. D. Maurice, Matthew Arnold, and other Protestant liberals simply jettisoned the notion of inspiration.

---

71. Wilhelm Niesel, *Reformed Symbolics: A Comparison of Catholicism, Orthodoxy, and Protestantism* (trans. David Lewis; Edinburgh: Oliver and Boyd, 1962), 229.

72. Hugo Grotius, *Opera omnia theologica* (London: Moses Pitt, 1679), 3:672.

73. Louis Berkhof notes that this view was also held by some Protestant theologians under the influence of deism. He refers particularly to LeClerc (1657–1736), a Reformed theologian who embraced Arminianism and thereafter taught that inspiration was simply a spiritual enlightenment. LeClerc and others in his circle "distinguished between the doctrinal and the histori-cal portions of Scripture, and regarded the former, containing essential truths, with which the writers were made acquainted by revelation, as plenarily inspired; and the latter, containing nonessential truths, of which the writers had knowledge apart from revelation, as only partially inspired, and as marred by inaccuracies and mistakes" (*Systematic Theology* [Grand Rapids: Eerdmans, 1996], 154). Some argued that the thoughts were inspired while not necessarily the words, but Berkhof quotes Girardeau's objection: "Accurate thought cannot be disjoined from language" (155).

A. THE PRINCETON FORMULATION OF INERRANCY

Although inerrancy was taken for granted in church history until the Enlightenment, it was especially at Princeton Seminary in the late nineteenth and early twentieth centuries that it became a full-blown formulation. This view is articulated most fully in the book coauthored by A. A. Hodge and B. B. Warfield, *Inspiration*, published by the Presbyterian Church in 1881. Their argument deserves an extended summary, especially because it remains, in my view, the best formulation of inerrancy and challenges caricatures.

First, *they point out that a sound doctrine of inspiration requires a specifically Christian ontology*: "The only really dangerous opposition to the church doctrine of inspiration comes either directly or indirectly, but always ultimately, from some false view of God's relation to the world, of his methods of working, and of the possibility of a supernatural agency penetrating and altering the course of a natural process."[74] Just as the divine element pervades the whole of Scripture, so too does the human aspect. Not only "the untrammeled play of all [the authors'] faculties, but the very substance of what they write is evidently for the most part the product of their own mental and spiritual activities."[75] Even more than the Reformers, the Protestant orthodox were sensitive to the diverse means used by God to produce the Bible's diverse literature. This awareness has only grown, Hodge and Warfield observe, and should be fully appreciated.[76] God's "superintendence" did not compromise creaturely freedom. In fact, "it interfered with no spontaneous natural agencies, which were, in themselves, producing results conformable to the mind of the Holy Spirit."[77] Just as the divine element pervades the whole of Scripture, so too does the human aspect.

Far from reducing all instances of biblical revelation to the prophetic paradigm, as critics often allege, Hodge and Warfield recognize that the prophetic form, "Thus says the LORD," is a "comparatively small element of the whole body of sacred writing." In the majority of cases, the writers drew from their own existing knowledge, including general revelation, and each "gave evidence of his own special limitations of knowledge and mental power, and of his personal defects as well as of his powers." "The Scriptures have been generated, as the plan of redemption has been evolved, through an historic process," which is divine in its origin and intent, but "largely natural in its method."[78] "The Scriptures were generated through sixteen

---

74. Hodge and Warfield, *Inspiration*, 9.

75. Ibid., 12.

76. Ibid., 5. "Christian scholars have come to see that this divine element, which penetrates and glorifies Scripture at every point, has entered and becomes incorporated with it in very various ways, natural, supernatural and gracious, through

long courses of providential leading, as well as by direct suggestion — through the spontaneous action of the souls of the sacred writers, as well as by controlling influence from without."

77. Ibid., 6.

78. Ibid., 12–13.

centuries of this divinely regulated concurrence of God and man, of the natural and the supernatural, of reason and revelation, of providence and grace."[79]

Second, *Warfield and Hodge underscore the redemptive-historical unfolding of biblical revelation, defending an organic view of inspiration over a mechanical theory.* They note that many reject verbal inspiration because of its association with the erroneous theory of verbal dictation, which is an "extremely mechanical" view.[80] But since inspiration is not the same as dictation, theories concerning "authors, dates, sources and modes of composition" that "are not plainly inconsistent with the testimony of Christ or his apostles as to the Old Testament or with the apostolic origin of the books of the New Testament ... cannot in the least invalidate" the Bible's inspiration and inerrancy.[81] While higher criticism proceeds on the basis of antisupernatural and rationalistic presuppositions, historical criticism is a valid and crucial discipline.

Third, *the Princeton theologians faced squarely the question of contradictions and errors, noting problems in great detail.* Some discrepancies are due to imperfect copies, which textual criticism properly considers. In other cases, an original reading may be lost, or we may simply fail to find adequate data or be blinded by our presuppositions from understanding a given text. Sometimes we are "destitute of the circumstantial knowledge which would fill up and harmonize the record," as is true in any historical record. We must also remember that our own methods of testing the accuracy of Scripture "are themselves subject to error."[82]

Fourth, *because it is the communication that is inspired rather than the persons themselves, we should not imagine that the authors were omniscient or infallible.* In fact, the authors themselves seem conscious enough of their limitations. "The record itself furnishes evidence that the writers were in large measure dependent for their knowledge upon sources and methods in themselves fallible, and that their personal knowledge and judgments were in many matters hesitating and defective, or even wrong."[83] Yet Scripture is seen to be inerrant "when the *ipsissima verba* of the original autographs are ascertained and interpreted in their natural and intended sense."[84] Inerrancy is not attributed to copies, much less to our vernacular translations, but to "the original autographic text."[85]

Fifth, *the claim of inerrancy is that "in all their real affirmations these books are without error."*[86] The qualification "real affirmations" is important and deserves some elaboration. The scientific and cultural assumptions of the prophets and apostles were not suspended by the Spirit, and in these they were not necessarily elevated

---

79. Ibid., 14.
80. Ibid., 19
81. Ibid., 25.
82. Ibid., 27.

83. Ibid., 27–28.
84. Ibid.
85. Ibid., 42.
86. Ibid.

beyond their contemporaries. Nevertheless, that which they proclaim and affirm in God's name is preserved from error. For example, critics often point to Matthew 13:32, where Jesus refers to the mustard seed as "the smallest of all seeds." From the context it is clear that Jesus was not making a botanical claim but drawing on the familiar experience of his hearers, for whom the analogy would have worked perfectly well. A reductionistic view of language is implied at this point both in many of the criticisms and in many of the defenses of scriptural accuracy. It is unlikely that in his state of humiliation, in which by his own admission he did not know the day or hour of his return, Jesus had exhaustive knowledge about the world's plant life. Whatever contemporary botanists might identify as the smallest seed, if it were unknown to Jesus' hearers, the analogy would have been pointless. We have to ask what the biblical writers are *affirming*, not what they are assuming as part of the background of their own culture and the limitations of their time and place.

If we do not hold ourselves and each other to modern standards of specialized discourse in ordinary conversation, we can hardly impose such standards on ancient writers. Weather reports include the time of "sunrise" and "sunset," even though the reading public is no more likely than meteorologists to hold that the sun literally rises and sets. As Calvin observed, "Moses wrote in the manner of those to whom he wrote." If one wants to learn astronomy, Calvin adds, one must ask the astronomers rather than Moses, since his purpose was not to deliver supernatural information about the movement of planets.[87] Inerrancy requires our confidence not in the reliability of Moses and his knowledge of the cosmos but in the reliability of the historical narratives, laws, and promises that are disclosed in the Pentateuch. Even then, it is truthfulness, not exactness, that we expect when we come to the biblical text.[88]

To supplement the account of Warfield and Hodge, one could add that there are obvious discrepancies in biblical reports concerning numbers. However, these can be explained by recognizing the different methods of accounting, which are better known now than in the past. For example, on the basis of calculating the generations in Genesis, Archbishop Ussher concluded that the world was created on Sunday, October 23, 4004 BC. However, we know more now about ancient Near Eastern genealogies, which were not exhaustive but singled out significant and transitional figures. Similarly, Matthew's list is selective, highlighting the crucial (and sometimes surprising) links in the genealogy that led to Jesus Christ (Mt 1:1–17). Besides the sometimes sinful patriarchs (Abraham, Isaac, and Jacob), this gospel

---

87. John Calvin, *Commentary on Genesis* (trans. John King; Grand Rapids: Baker, 1981), 1:86.

88. Hodge and Warfield, *Inspiration*, 28–29. The Princeton theologians pointed out, "There is a vast difference between exactness of statement, which includes an exhaustive rendering of details, an absolute literalness, which the Scriptures never profess, and accuracy, on the other hand, which secures a correct statement of facts or principles intended to be affirmed.... It is this accuracy, and this alone, as distinct from exactness, which the church doctrine maintains of every affirmation in the original text of Scripture without exception."

includes Tamar (who disguised herself as a prostitute in order to conceive a child by Judah), Rahab (a prostitute who hid the messengers sent from Joshua to spy out the land of Canaan), Bathsheba (the victim of David's adultery, who bore Solomon), and Ruth (a Moabite). Before the account of Christ's birth in verses 18–25, the stage is already set for Jesus as the Savior. The goal (or scope) of such genealogies is to highlight the progress of redemption, not to provide general census data. It is impossible to know how many generations are missing from such genealogies, and therefore efforts at calculating human history from them are always bound to fail. The fact that evenhanded historical research has resolved apparent discrepancies such as this one cautions us against hasty conclusions. Many of the alleged conflicts between Scripture and science have turned out to be founded on flawed biblical exegesis. In every science, anomalies are frankly acknowledged without causing an overthrow of an entire paradigm or settled theory that enjoys widespread consensus on the basis of weightier confirmations.

On the one hand, we must beware of facile harmonizations of apparent contradictions. It is sometimes said that the Bible is not a book as much as it is a library. We have to resist the long-held assumption in our intellectual culture that plurality reflects a falling away from the oneness of being. God is three persons in one essence. Analogously, this triune God reveals the one truth of the gospel in a plurality of testimonies.

In fact, plurality and diversity are inherent in testimony, reflecting not only different personalities but different standpoints. In the field of law, there is a distinction between material and immaterial discrepancies.[89] The former refer to an actual contradiction between witnesses, while the latter are simply different accounts that nevertheless cohere, like pieces in a jigsaw puzzle. Even in the resurrection accounts, there are discrepancies, but far from undermining confidence in the facts that they report, these reflect different standpoints of the witnesses. They witnessed the same event, but at different points and from different perspectives. It is a sign of their authenticity that these gospels do not reflect the sort of collusion that might have produced a fully harmonized account. Furthermore, God spoke in many times and places through prophets and apostles, each of whom was shaped by various circumstances of God's providence, and the variations even between the four gospels enrich our understanding of the different nuances and facets of Christ's person and work.

On the other hand, we must beware of equally facile conclusions that depend on naturalistic presuppositions or our own incomplete knowledge. Like the biblical authors, we are not omniscient and must with patient reserve anticipate fuller

---

89. "Discrepancy," in *Bouvier's Law Dictionary and Concise Encyclopedia* (ed. John Bouvier; 4th ed.; New York: William S. Hein, 1984).

research and explanations. This does not require a dualistic distinction between concepts of "religious truth" (faith and practice) and "secular truth" (history and science), as theories of *limited inerrancy* hold.[90] If we cannot trust God as Creator, then we cannot trust God as Redeemer. Instead of this sort of a priori division, we must recall the purpose or intent of a biblical passage. Once again, it is a question of *scope*—what is being claimed rather than what is being assumed. As Warfield explains, "It is true that the Scriptures were not designed to teach philosophy, science, or ethnology, or human history as such, and therefore they are not to be studied primarily as sources of information on these subjects."[91]

The appeal to the *inerrancy of the original autographs* has been a bone of contention in this debate. After all, what does it matter if inerrancy is attributed only to the original autographs if we no longer have access to them? But this point is not as impertinent or speculative a point as it might first appear. We have to distinguish between the original autographs and their copies in any case, since the valid enterprise of historical-textual criticism presupposes it. The very attempt to compare textual variants assumes that there is an original body of documents that some copies and families of copies more or less faithfully represent. Errors in these myriad copies are a matter of fact, but they can only be counted as errors because we have ways of comparing copies in a manner that gives us a reasonable approximation of the original autographs.

Even if we do not have direct access to these original autographs, we do have criteria widely employed in all fields of textual criticism that give us a good idea of what was originally written.[92] However, the methodological assumptions of textual criticism are quite different from those of higher criticism, which as an apparatus of theological liberalism follows naturalistic presuppositions. Where real discrepancies and doubts remain as to the authenticity of certain sayings, on the basis of textual-critical rather than higher-critical analysis, they do not affect any point of the church's faith and practice.[93] The very fact that textual criticism is an ongoing enterprise yielding ongoing results demonstrates that reconstructing or approximating the content of the original autographs is a viable goal and that, for the most part, it has already achieved this goal.

---

90. Advocates of this position include James Orr, *Revelation and Inspiration* (Vancouver, B.C.: Regent College, 2002); G. C. Berkouwer, *Holy Scripture* (Grand Rapids: Eerdmans, 1975); Dewey Beegle, *The Inspiration of Scripture* (Philadelphia: Westminster, 1963); Jack Rogers and Donald McKim, *The Authority and Interpretation of the Bible: An Historical Approach* (San Francisco: Harper & Row, 1979); James Barr, *Fundamentalism* (London: SCM, 1977); Stephen T. Davis, *The Debate about the Bible: Inerrancy versus Infallibility* (Philadelphia: Westminster, 1977); Richard Coleman, "Reconsidering 'Limited Inerrancy,'" *JETS* 17 no. 2 (1974): 207–14. Although somewhat dated, the argu-

ments offered in Vern Poythress, "Problems for Limited Inerrancy," *JETS* 18, no. 2 (Spring 1975): 93–102, remain relevant.

91. Hodge and Warfield, *Inspiration*, 30.

92. For a careful analysis of this process, see esp. Bruce Metzger, *The Canon of the New Testament: Its Origin, Development, and Significance* (Oxford: Clarendon, 1987); F. F. Bruce, *The Canon of Scripture* (Downers Grove, Ill.: InterVarsity Press, 1988).

93. One example is the ending of the Lord's Prayer ("for yours is the kingdom and the power and the glory forever").

Sixth, *these theologians also denied that inerrancy was the foundation of our doctrine of Scripture, much less of the Christian faith*.[94] We must begin with the content and claims of Scripture, centering on Christ. Christianity is not true because it rests on an inspired and inerrant text, but vice versa. In fact, the redemption to which Scripture testifies and that it communicates would "be true and divine ... even if God had not been pleased to give us, in addition to his revelation of saving truth, an infallible record of that revelation absolutely errorless, by means of inspiration."[95]

B. INERRANCY AFTER BARTH

In view of the careful articulation of verbal inspiration by Hodge and Warfield, among others, it is surprising that as eminent a figure as the critical New Testament scholar C. H. Dodd could continue to misunderstand or misrepresent the concept of verbal-plenary inspiration.[96] The inerrancy debate in American Protestantism generally and evangelicalism specifically is largely a controversy between Old Princeton and Karl Barth. Both the identification of the former view with fundamentalism and of the latter with liberalism (or modernism) can only be considered caricatures. Nevertheless, both positions are quite different from Protestant orthodoxy.

First, Barth's criticism of the traditional accounts of biblical inerrancy arises from his distinctive *actualist* ontology. Therefore, his logic concerning Scripture might be put in the form of this syllogism: (1) God's being is in act; (2) revelation is identical with God and is therefore always an event (action), never a given deposit; (3) therefore, Scripture, as an object (i.e., written text), cannot be identified directly with revelation.

Against Tillich, Barth maintains that God genuinely speaks in Scripture and in preaching; "Speaking is not a 'symbol.'"[97] Nevertheless, as we have seen, for Barth, revelation is not only God's action, but is identical with God's essence (since God's being is in act). Thus, there is no tertium quid between God's essence and a creaturely artifact, as I have argued there should be by drawing on the essence-energies distinction. Since revelation simply is Jesus Christ, Barth argues, we may speak of "the Word of God not *as* proclamation and Scripture alone but as God's revelation *in* proclamation and Scripture ..." (emphasis added).[98]

---

94. Hodge and Warfield, *Inspiration*, 6–7.

95. Ibid., 8–9.

96. C. H. Dodd, *The Authority of the Bible* (London: Collins, 1960), 14–15: "The theory which is commonly described as that of 'verbal inspiration' is fairly precise. It maintains that the entire corpus of Scripture consists of writings every word of which (presumably in the original autographs, forever inaccessible to us) was directly 'dictated' by the Deity.... They consequently convey absolute truth with no trace of error or relativity." This follows from the use of the word *inspiration*, he suggests, in a grossly ahistorical fashion: "For primitive religious thought the 'inspired' person was under the control of a supernatural influence." In response I would say that the original autographs of the Bible are not "forever inaccessible to us" any more than those of other well-attested ancient texts with myriad copies that may be compared in order to arrive at the most likely original reading. Dodd reduces Warfield's and Hodge's account of verbal-plenary inspiration to "dictation" and a trancelike subversion of human agency in spite of their explicit rejection of such a mechanical view.

97. Barth, *Church Dogmatics*, vol. 1, pt. 1, 132–33.

98. Ibid., vol. 1, pt. 1, 132–37.

However, as Timothy Ward points out, "There seems to be a contradiction between this equation of revelation with the person of Jesus Christ and the earlier claim that revelation is speech 'in and of itself as such.'" How can revelation be *a person* and *speech*? Barth seems aware of the problem. He wants to affirm the "personalizing" of the Word of God without "deverbalizing" it. Yet his fear of making revelation into an "object or thing" seems to triumph over his concern to affirm it as speech.[99] Therefore, Barth concludes, "The Bible is not in itself and as such God's past revelation," but is a fallible, though normative, human witness to revelation.[100] Otherwise, we will make God (revelation) a human possession. "The Bible is God's Word to the extent that God causes it to be his Word, to the extent that He speaks through it."[101]

Ward replies that persons are no less susceptible to attempts to control and master than are words. Jesus was subjected to repeated attempts of the religious leaders and crowds to gain mastery over him—most notably, in the crucifixion.

Therefore, "possession is not a necessary corollary of reading and interpretation." One may read and hear Jesus Christ in faith and obedience, just as the disciples followed the Incarnate Word.[102]

Second, for Barth, the "veiled" (creaturely) form in which God addresses us in self-revelation is not only necessarily fallible but fallen. There is no room in Barth's theology for an unfallen human nature. In fact, he held that in order for Jesus' incarnation to be complete, the human nature that the Son assumed was inherently sinful, although Jesus was not guilty of any personal sins.[103] However, there is no necessary correlation in Scripture between Jesus' humanity—including weakness, suffering, and temptation—and sin. Jesus Christ "in every respect has been tempted as we are, yet without sin" (Heb 4:15). Sinfulness is accidental rather than essential to human nature. Consequently, there is no inherent relationship of humanity (as such) and error. God can reach us through frail, finite, limited creatures with ectypal truth accommodated to our capacity while preserving that revelation from error by his Spirit. Thus, we need not accept the false choice between an encyclopedia of propositions that correspond univocally to God's mind and a merely human testimony to Christ that is related only equivocally to God's Word. As with Christ, so also with Scripture: frailty does not entail failure. If the immortal God assumed our mortal humanity without surrendering to genuine temptation, then surely the same God knows how to reveal himself through sinful ambassadors,

99. Timothy Ward, "The Sufficiency of Scripture," in *Reformed Theology in Contemporary Perspective* (ed. Lynn Quickley; Edinburgh: Rutherford House, 2006), 15.

100. Barth, *Church Dogmatics*, vol. 1, pt. 1, 111–12.

101. Ibid., vol. 1, pt. 1, 109.

102. Ward, "Sufficiency of Scripture," 17–18.

103. Barth, *Church Dogmatics*, vol. 1, pt. 2, 510–12, 531. See Mark D. Thompson, "Witness to the Word: On Barth's Doctrine of Scripture," in *Engaging with Barth: Contemporary Evangelical Critiques* (ed. David Gibson and Daniel Strange; London: T&T Clark, 2008), 168–97.

preserving their sacred writings from error without diminishing their creatureliness in the slightest degree.

Third, as we have seen, Barth tends to collapse inspiration into illumination in a single event of revelation in which God addresses an individual personally. The Scriptures are for Barth the *normative* Christian witness to revelation, but it is difficult to see how in his view the Bible could be more than the first among equals—quantitatively but not qualitatively distinct from the church's interpretation. So, in spite of his noble labors to place the church back under the norm of Scripture (*Deus dixit!* ["God has said!"]), the ontological rationale for doing so remains questionable. Indeed, his refusal of any direct identification of God's Word with creaturely words of Scripture reflects the dualism of "Spirit" and "letter" that we discover in radical Anabaptist, pietist, and Enlightenment thinking.

There have been valiant attempts to reconcile Barth's doctrine of Scripture with the church's traditional view, among which that of Donald Bloesch is especially notable.[104] He allows that Barth's formulation too sharply separated the Word from the words, yet argues that "in his emphasis on the revealing work of the Spirit [Barth] is closer to the intention of the Reformers than is modern fundamentalism in this regard."[105] Bloesch realizes that Protestant orthodoxy "sought to maintain a dynamic view of both revelation and inspiration" and eschewed fundamentalism's tendency to deny its human aspect.[106] He correctly observes the correlation between fundamentalism's mechanical view and belief in "the univocal language of Scripture concerning God, which contravenes the position of most theological luminaries of the past who held that human language concerning God is either metaphorical or at the most analogical."[107]

Nevertheless, Bloesch repeats the prevalent caricature of Warfield's position when he suggests that the latter "is reluctant and often unwilling to affirm" the humanity of Scripture, including its "marks of historical conditioning."[108] More problematic is Bloesch's own attempt at reconciliation. On one hand, he writes, "Revelation includes both the events of divine self-disclosure in biblical history and their prophetic and apostolic interpretation." On the other hand, he adds, "At

---

104. Donald G. Bloesch, "The Primacy of Scripture," in *The Authoritative Word: Essays on the Nature of Scripture* (ed. Donald McKim; Grand Rapids: Eerdmans, 1983), 118. However, at several points his formulation succumbs to contradictions. On one hand, Scripture is "in its entirety the very Word of God," yet it is "not the revelation itself" (118). Potential for confusion mounts as Bloesch adds, "Yet we must go on to affirm that Scripture is more than a human witness to revelation: *it is revelation itself mediated* through human words" (emphasis added). Attempting to reconcile this contradiction, Bloesch turns to the concept of illumination: "It is not in and of itself divine revelation, but when illumined by the Spirit it becomes revelation to

the believer. At the same time, it could not become revelation unless it already embodied revelation, unless it were included within the event of revelation. Scripture is not simply a 'pointer to revelation' (as Brunner has asserted), but by the action of the Spirit it is a veritable bearer of revelation, a vehicle or 'conduit of divine truth' (Carl Henry)" (119).

105. Ibid., 120.

106. Ibid., 147.

107. Ibid. As we have seen, these theologians held that our knowledge of God is analogical, but I would disagree with Bloesch's characterization of their view as "metaphorical."

108. Ibid., 149.

the same time we must not infer that the propositional statements in the Bible are themselves revealed, since this makes the Bible the same kind of book as the Koran, which purports to be exclusively divine."[109] It is unclear to me how the inclusion of propositions among other speech acts as part of revelation necessarily entails an "exclusively divine" dictation, as Islam considers the Qur'an to be. How can we maintain coherently that *Scripture* is inspired—including "prophetic and apostolic interpretation" of divine acts—if we exclude propositional statements? If Scripture cannot be *reduced* to propositions, it is just as arbitrary to *exclude* such statements.

In evangelical circles generally, inerrancy was assumed more than explicitly formulated until it was challenged. Warfield and Hodge helped to articulate this position, which is more formally summarized in the "Chicago Statement on Biblical Inerrancy" (1978).[110] Like any formulation developed in response to a particular error or area of concern for faith and practice, the inerrancy doctrine invites legitimate questions and critiques. However, its alternatives are less satisfying. Whatever the holy, unerring, and faithful Father speaks is—simply by virtue of having come from him—holy, unerring, and faithful. In addition, the content of God's speech is none other than the gift of the eternal Son who became flesh for us and for our salvation. Revelation, therefore, is not merely an ever-new event that occurs through the witness of the Bible; it is a written canon, an abiding, Spirit-breathed deposit and constitution for the covenant community in every generation. Thus, the Christian faith is truly a "pattern of the sound words" and "the good deposit entrusted to you" that we are to "guard" by means of "the Holy Spirit who dwells within us" (2Ti 1:13–14; cf. 1Ti 6:20). It is an event of revelation that not only creates *our* faith (*fides qua creditor*, i.e., the personal act of faith) but, according to Jude 3, contains in canonical form "*the* faith that was once for all delivered to the saints" (*fides quae creditur*).

DISCUSSION QUESTIONS

1. What is the relationship between covenant and canon in a doctrine of Scripture? Discuss the relationship between God's sacramental Word (working) and God's canonical Word (resting/ruling). Is this formula validated by the biblical history of God's covenants?
2. Why is it important to think of inspiration in Trinitarian terms?
3. What is the essence-energies distinction, and why is it relevant to our understanding of inspiration?

---

109. Ibid.
110. Among other places, the "Chicago Statement" may be

found in R. C. Sproul, *Scripture Alone: The Evangelical Doctrine* (Phillipsburg, N.J.: P&R, 2005), 177–93.

4. Distinguish the organic conception of verbal-plenary inspiration from rival interpretations.
5. What is the "inner testimony of the Spirit," and what is its relationship to our doctrine of Scripture? Why is it important to distinguish inspiration and illumination without separating them?
6. Define the evangelical doctrine of inerrancy as formulated by Warfield and Hodge, especially in contrast to caricatures and rival positions.

Chapter Five

THE BIBLE AND THE CHURCH: FROM SCRIPTURE TO SYSTEM

A final attribute of Scripture to consider is its *sufficiency*, celebrated in the Reformation slogan *sola scriptura*. After developing and defending this important aspect of biblical authority, this chapter provides an account of how theology moves from the biblical text to church dogmas.

I. THE SUFFICIENCY OF SCRIPTURE: CANON AND COMMUNITY

In chapter 4, I underscored the connection between *canon* and *covenant* (see esp. "God's Ruling Constitution," pp. 151–55), but in considering the sufficiency of Scripture we now include *community*. As means of grace, the Word (particularly the gospel) preached creates the church; as normative canon (constitution), the Word as Scripture stands over the community. Through this Word, Christ not only creates a redeemed communion but governs it as Prophet, Priest, and King. The church is the recipient of God's saving revelation, never a source.

Before we survey the Roman Catholic-Protestant debate, it is helpful to refer briefly to the relation of tradition and Scripture in the Christian East. As on other points, the East is more fluid in its conception of this relationship. Some Orthodox theologians hold that the tradition of the first five centuries, particularly as enshrined in liturgical forms, belongs to the deposit of faith. Others, however, insist upon the qualitative distinction between Scripture and tradition. Sergius Bulgakov (1871–1944) affirmed the unique authority of Scripture "above all the sources of faith, especially of all tradition in all its forms,"[1] while Vladimir Lossky (1903–1958) regarded these as a unity.[2] Bulgakov held that Scripture is self-attesting, "an inherent witness to itself," while tradition depends on it.[3]

A. SOLA SCRIPTURA: THE REFORMATION DEBATE

We have seen that, at least in its official pronouncements, the Roman Catholic Church affirms the inspiration and inerrancy of Scripture. Among others, Heiko Oberman has pointed out that the nature of Scripture was not at issue in the Reformation dispute with Rome. Rather, differences emerged over the relationship between Scripture and tradition.[4] The Latin slogan *sola scriptura* means "*by* Scripture alone," not "Scripture alone".[5] For example, both Lutheran and Reformed churches regard the ecumenical creeds, along with their own confessions and catechisms, as authoritative and binding summaries of Scripture, to which they are all subordinate.

1. ROMAN CATHOLIC TEACHING

The emergence of parity between Scripture and tradition as two sources was due largely to the canon lawyers in the twelfth and subsequent centuries, yet still there were theologians of the stature of Duns Scotus and Pierre D'Ailly who insisted that Scripture was sovereign over tradition.[6] Only at the Council of Trent (1545–1563) was this view, defended by the Reformers, officially condemned. Augustine's famous statement that he would never have believed had he not been moved by the authority of the church was the touchstone for Rome's argument for the priority of the church over the Word.[7] Since the church preceded the canon and the latter evolved within and was finally authorized as such by the church, the conclusion seemed self-evident to Roman Catholic theologians that the church was the mother of Scripture. Furthermore, Scripture has to be interpreted. Would the Spirit inspire the canon without also inspiring its living interpreter, the church?

---

1. Sergius Bulgakov, *The Orthodox Church* (London: Centenary, 1935), 28.

2. Vladimir Lossky, *The Mystical Theology of the Orthodox Church* (Crestwood, N.Y.: St. Vladimir's Seminary Press, 1976), 25.

3. Bulgakov, *The Orthodox Church*, 22.

4. Heiko Oberman, *The Harvest of Medieval Theology: Gabriel Biel and Late Medieval Nominalism* (Grand Rapids: Eerdmans, 1967), 365–75.

5. A fruitful study of the Reformation's interpretation of this phrase is found in Keith Mathison, *The Shape of Sola Scriptura* (Moscow, Ida.: Canon, 2001).

6. Muller, *PRRD*, 1:41.

7. Augustine: "Ego vero evangelio non crederem, nisi me catholicae ecclesiae commoveret auctoritas" (*Contra epistulam Manichaei quam vocant Fundamenti*, I.v., in PL). Appeals were also made to Irenaeus, the second-century bishop of Lyons, who urged believers to recognize only interpretations of the Scriptures that are taught by the bishops. However, in both cases the context was the refutation of heresy (for Irenaeus, the Gnostics; for Augustine, the Manichaeans in particular). Motivated by pastoral concerns, these church fathers were intent on directing believers to authentic shepherds, because together they taught and pledged themselves to the rule of faith.

The Council of Trent established the view that Scripture and tradition are actually two forms of God's Word—"written" and "unwritten." Many unwritten (i.e., oral) traditions were passed around by the apostles and their circle and passed down by them to successive generations. Crucial to the development of this conception of tradition was the assumption that the apostolic office is still in effect, with the pope and magisterium as the successors to Peter and the other apostles.[8] However, it was not until the First Vatican Council (1870) that papal infallibility became a binding dogma for Roman Catholics.[9] According to this teaching, the pope, when speaking as Peter's successor (*ex cathedra* means "from the chair"), is preserved from error and may promulgate doctrines that are necessary to be believed for salvation.

The Second Vatican Council represents a more nuanced view of the relation of Scripture and tradition, thinking through the many variations that had been held before the arteries were hardened in the Counter-Reformation. However, this council repeated the dogma that Sacred Scripture and Sacred Tradition flow from the same source. "In order that the full and living gospel might always be preserved in the church the apostles left bishops as their successors. They gave them 'their own position of teaching authority.'"[10] One may discern in this statement a subtle form of the traditional Roman Catholic distinction between a *written canon* and a *living community*. Rome had made this a major argument in the Counter-Reformation, equating Paul's contrast between the "letter" and the "Spirit" (2Co 3:6) with the difference between Scripture and the living church.[11]

The council continues, "Sacred Tradition and sacred Scripture, then, are bound closely together, *flowing out from the same divine wellspring*, come together in some fashion to form *one thing*, and move toward the same goal" (emphasis added). In fact, it is Sacred Tradition that faithfully "transmits in its entirety the Word of God" in both its apostolic and postapostolic form.

> It *transmits it to the successors of the apostles* so that, enlightened by the Spirit of truth, they may faithfully preserve, expound, and spread it abroad by their preaching. Thus it comes about that the church does not draw her certainty about all revealed truths from the Holy Scriptures alone. Hence, both Scripture and Tradition must be accepted and honored with *equal feelings of devotion and reverence*. Sacred Tradition and Sacred Scripture make up *a single deposit of the Word of God*, which is entrusted to the church (emphasis added).[12]

---

8. Although episcopal (governed by bishops), the East was always suspicious of the hierarchicalism of the West and emphasized that the whole body of Christ is infused with the *charism* of the apostles—not that its members are apostles themselves, but that they are filled with the Spirit and led by the Spirit. According to the West, the idea gradually emerged that this *charism* was reserved for the priesthood, and especially for those who were part of the magisterium (cardinals and popes).

9. For a fuller treatment of this development, see Brian Tierney, *Origins of Papal Infallibility, 1150–1350* (Leiden: Brill, 1988).

10. Austin Flannery, OP, ed., *Vatican Council II: The Conciliar and Postconciliar Documents* (Northport, N.Y.: Costello, 1975), 754.

11. In 2 Corinthians 3, however, the letter/Spirit contrast is explicitly correlated with old/new covenants.

12. Flannery, *Vatican Council II*, 755.

Tradition is therefore the process of transmitting the Word of God. Although the magisterium is the servant of this Word, "whether in its written form or in the form of Tradition," the two "are so connected and associated that one of them cannot stand without the other."[13]

The magisterium (the teaching office, with the pope as primate) proposes or commands dogmas to be believed on the assumption that the apostolic authority that produced the New Testament continues in an unbroken succession through Rome's popes.[14] While Scripture and postcanonical tradition differ in degree of authority, they belong to the same genus, since they are both equally the offspring of divine revelation in the church. From this principle emerges Rome's dogma of implicit faith (*fides implicita*), which requires acceptance of all dogmas commanded by the church. The basis for this implicit faith is the church's own inherent authority. "Sacred theology relies on the written Word of God, taken together with Sacred Tradition, as on a permanent foundation."[15]

While some Roman Catholic theologians (especially Karl Rahner, Hans Küng, Yves Congar, and George Tavard) have tried to revive the view held by some medieval thinkers that Scripture is uniquely normative, Cardinal Ratzinger (now Pope Benedict XVI) replies that since there are many extrascriptural dogmas that such theologians must hold, "What sense is there in talking about the sufficiency of scripture?"[16] Once again we recognize the tendency of Rome to fall back on its scale-of-being ontology, with revelation consisting of different levels of intensity, conflating in its own way inspiration and illumination: "Scripture is not revelation but at most only a part of the latter's greater reality."[17]

Therefore, in spite of its high view of biblical inspiration, Roman Catholic teaching elides the important distinction between inspiration and illumination. Eliminating any qualitative distinction between apostolic and postapostolic offices and traditions, Rome denies the sufficiency of Scripture as the sole rule for faith and practice. Just as the New Testament supplements the Old Testament, Ratzinger argues, the church's ongoing interpretation supplements both.[18]

2. REFORMATION AND POST-REFORMATION INTERPRETATION

The crucial difference between Roman Catholic and confessional Protestant interpretations at this point is easily summarized. While the former treats the

---

13. Ibid., 755–56. Formally, Rome does not hold that private revelations can add anything to the deposit of faith: "Christian faith cannot accept 'revelations' that claim to surpass or correct the Revelation of which Christ is the fulfillment" (*Catechism of the Catholic Church* [Liguori, Mo.: Liguori Publications, 1994], 23). Nevertheless, we have seen that for Rome, revelation takes two forms — the written (Scripture) and the unwritten (tradition).

14. "The Roman Pontiff, head of the college of bishops, enjoys this infallibility in virtue of his office, when, as supreme pastor and teacher of all the faithful — who confirms his brethren in the faith — he proclaims by a definitive act a doctrine pertaining to faith or morals" (*Catechism of the Catholic Church*, 235, citing Vatican Council I).

15. Flannery, *Vatican Council II*, 763.

16. Karl Rahner and Joseph Ratzinger, *Revelation and Tradition* (trans. W. J. O'Hara; Freiburg: Herder, 1966), 29.

17. Ibid., 36–37.

18. Ibid., 44.

church's authority as *magisterial*, the latter treats it as *ministerial*.[19] Neither possessing absolute authority nor devoid of any authority, the church's role is that of a court rather than of a constitution. Christ has indeed established a teaching office in the church, but it depends on the illumination of the Spirit for its fallible interpretation of the infallible canon inspired by the Spirit.

A brief survey of Calvin's treatment in the *Institutes* (1.7–9) is instructive. Calvin challenges the idea that the church is the mother of Scripture: "[Paul] testifies that the church is 'built upon the foundation of the prophets and apostles' [Eph. 2:20]. If the teaching of the prophets and apostles is the foundation, this must have had authority before the church began to exist" (1.7.2). Augustine's famous maxim ("I would not have believed that the Scriptures are God's Word unless I had been taught this by the church") is nothing more than the relation of his own experience of *how he came to faith* rather than an assertion concerning the *source* of the faith's authority (1.7.3). Unless the credibility of doctrine is established by divine rather than human authority, our consciences will always waver. Those who seek to first prove the reliability of Scripture by appeals to an authority external to it (whether church or reason) are "doing things backwards" (1.7.4). "Scripture indeed is self-authenticated [*autopiston*]; hence, it is not right to subject it to proof and reasoning" (1.7.5). Once this divine authority is firmly established, we may certainly appeal to such external arguments, including the church's ministerial authority, as "very useful aids" (1.8.1). "In this way, we willingly embrace and reverence as holy the early councils, such as those of Nicea, Constantinople, Ephesus I, Chalcedon, and the like, which were concerned with refuting errors—in so far as they relate to the things of faith" (4.9.1).

Protestant orthodoxy followed in the same path as the Reformers. Rome had argued that even if the Scriptures had been lost, there would still be the living voice of the church. However, Robert Rollock responded, far from a dead letter waiting to be animated by a living church or apostle, Scripture is "most effectual, most lively, and most vocal, sounding to every man an answer of all things necessary unto salvation.... For the Scripture contains in it the word of God, which is lively and powerful (Heb 4:12)."[20] It is the Scriptures themselves that declare that they are living and active, Rollock adds.[21] "The voice of the church ... doth depend on the voice of the Scripture," since the church often errs.[22] After all, "the church is born and bred, *not of mortal, but of immortal seed, which is the word of God*, 1Pe 1:23."[23]

Rollock responded to the argument that it was tradition that preserved the cov-

---

19. From *master* and *servant*, this distinction refers to the normative (magisterial) authority of Scripture over reason, experience, tradition, and culture.

20. Quoted in Muller, *PRRD*, 1:85.

21. Ibid., 1:87.

22. Ibid., 1:88.

23. Ibid.

enant under the patriarchs by pointing out that "the *substance* of the Scripture was in those very traditions whereby the church was edified and kept" (emphasis added). Of course, the church came before the Scriptures as a completed canon, but a canon "was not then necessary, for that then the lively voice of God itself was heard." But now it is necessary.[24]

William Perkins wrote, "We hold that the very word of God hath been delivered by tradition."[25] In fact, Perkins adds, "This is true not only of the Old Testament, but of the New Testament as well, as some twenty to eighty years passed before the traditions were committed to writing.... And many things we hold for truth not written in the word, if they be not against the word."[26] William Ames makes the same point: In substance, the Word preceded and in fact created the church, although this oral tradition was later committed to textual form.[27]

Protestants had no trouble agreeing that there was a time when written Scripture and oral tradition were two media of a unified revelation, but they denied that this situation applies in the postapostolic era. The critical question for us is whether the noninspired traditions of ordinary ministers of the church can be equated with the revelation given through the extraordinary ministry of prophets and apostles.

Jesus excoriated the religious leaders for raising "the tradition of men" (Mk 7:8) to the level of God's Word. "So for the sake of your tradition you have made void the word of God" (Mt 15:6). On the other hand, Paul exhorts the Thessalonians to "stand firm and hold to the traditions that you were taught by us, either by our spoken word or by our letter" (2Th 2:15). A chapter later he warns them to keep away from those who are not walking "in accord with the tradition that you received from us" (2Th 3:6). In spite of their strife and immaturity, Paul commends the Corinthians "because you remember me in everything and maintain the traditions even as I delivered them to you" (1Co 11:2).

Jesus and Paul do not stand in contradiction on this point. The difference between "the tradition of men" and the tradition to which Paul refers is clear. Jesus recognized a qualitative difference between the inspired Scriptures (the Law and the Prophets) and the noninspired tradition of the elders. However, Jesus commissioned officers of the new covenant who stood on a par with the prophets. After the apostles, the church is served by ministers who are called not to lay the foundation but to build on it. When the traditions of the elders (in either covenant) are faithful interpretations of Scripture, they are valid, but when they raise themselves to the level of Scripture itself, they are invalid.

24. Ibid., 90.
25. William Perkins, "A Reformed Catholic," in *The Works of William Perkins* (ed. Ian Breward; Appleford, U.K.: 1970), 547.
26. Perkins, "A Reformed Catholic," 548–49.

27. William Ames, *The Marrow of Theology* (ed. John D. Eusden; Durham, N.C.: Labyrinth, 1968), 187.

Judicial decisions and the history of case precedent cannot be equated with the constitution itself. The new covenant had been inaugurated and now, by Christ's appointment, was receiving its constitution. While all apostolic pronouncements concerning faith and practice were to be received as God's Word ("either by our spoken word or by our letter"), the Spirit saw fit to commit the most necessary oral and written teaching to the New Testament Scriptures. Analogous to postprophetic traditions, then, postapostolic traditions have ministerial but not magisterial authority. The court is not the author of its own constitution.

Sound tradition is the effect of the Spirit's illumination rather than inspiration. Lutheran and Reformed churches do not regard creeds, confessions, and the decisions of councils and synods as compromising *sola scriptura*. Rather, they regard church dogmas as authoritative because they are "clearly revealed in the Word of God, formulated by some competent church body, and regarded as authoritative, because they are derived from the Word of God."[28] In its deliberative assemblies, the church has an ordained power to direct the confession and interpretation of the Word of God, but always in subservience to it. Where Rome holds that the faithful must believe everything that the church teaches (*fides implicita*), based on the authority of the church, Protestants maintain that we must believe everything that the Scriptures teach even if an angel or apostle were to bring a different gospel (Gal 1:6–9).

The distinction between the magisterial role of the Scriptures and the ministerial role of the church assumes a qualitative distinction between the *extraordinary* apostolic office and the *ordinary* offices of ministers and elders. Since there are no more apostles, there is no ongoing revelation. This is the argument that the Reformers made against both Rome and the radical Protestants.[29] The Scriptures are sufficient. If the ancient church recognized postapostolic tradition as an extension of apostolic tradition, why did their criteria for recognizing canonicity limit authorized texts to those of apostolic origin? Surely these ancient bishops did not regard tradition as a form of ongoing revelation; in fact, it was precisely against this view of the Gnostics that Irenaeus and others inveighed.

The church does indeed play an important role as a servant of the Spirit in *illumination*. Nevertheless, Johannes Wollebius asks,

> What can be more absurd than to make the words of the Master to receive their authority from the servant ... or that the Rule should have its dependence from the

---

28. Louis Berkhof, *Systematic Theology* (Grand Rapids: Eerdmans, 1996), 19.

29. In fact, Calvin wrote, "We are assailed by two sects," referring to Rome and the Anabaptists, even though they "seem to differ most widely from each other." "For when they boast extravagantly of the Spirit, the tendency certainly is to sink and bury the Word of God, that they may make room for their own falsehoods." "Reply by John Calvin to Cardinal Sadoleto's 'Letter,'" in *Calvin's Tracts and Treatises* (trans. Henry Beveridge; Grand Rapids: Eerdmans, 1958), 1:36.

thing ruled? . . . We know that the oracles of God are committed to the church, *Ro 3.2*, and that she is the pillar and ground of truth, *1Ti 3:15*. But as it is foolish to tell us that the candle receives its light from the candlestick that supports it, so it is ridiculous to ascribe the Scripture's authority to the church.[30]

We believe through the ministry of the church, not because of the church, Francis Turretin argued. He adds,

> We do not deny that the church has many functions in relation to the Scriptures. She is (1) the keeper of the oracles of God to whom they are committed and who preserves the authentic tables of the covenant of grace with the greatest fidelity, like a notary (Ro 3:2); (2) the guide, to point out the Scriptures and lead us to them (Isa 30:21); (3) the defender, to vindicate and defend them by separating the genuine books from the spurious, in which sense she may be called the ground (*hedraiôma*) of the truth (1Ti 3:15); (4) the herald who sets forth and promulgates them (2Co 5:19; Ro 10:16); (5) the interpreter inquiring into the unfolding of the true sense.[31]

These are weighty assignments. "But all these imply a *ministerial* only and not a *magisterial* power. . . . Through her indeed, we believe, but not on account of her" (emphasis added).[32]

No less than the ancient and medieval church did the Reformers view the ecumenical creeds as "the rule [*kanôn*] of faith." In fact, they appealed in painstaking detail to citations from the church fathers in support of their claim that the church has no intrinsic authority to prescribe articles of faith or commands to be followed. However, they held that creeds and councils have a secondary authority, binding believers only because they are summaries of Scripture as the final rule for faith and practice. Christ is the head who saves and rules his body. Therefore, the church is always put into question in its faith and life by the Word that created and preserves it, and it must always be ready to be reformed by it. Paul said that he had "laid a foundation, and someone else is building upon it" (1Co 3:10). That is the order: apostolic foundation followed by the ordinary ministry of the church on that basis. "For no one *can lay* a foundation other than that which *laid*, which is Jesus Christ" (v. 11, emphasis added). There is the foundation-laying period, and then the building phase.

If Paul could warn the Corinthians "not to go beyond what is written" (1Co 4:6), then surely those of us living in postapostolic times are no less obliged to this principle. Especially as the church was already being racked with internal division and errors, Paul in effect invoked the principle of *sola scriptura* in forbidding the saints from going beyond the written texts. Paul urges this in the context of his defense of his ministry against the charges of the "superapostles," who led many

30. Quoted in John W. Beardslee, *Reformed Dogmatics* (New York: Oxford Univ. Press, 1965), 5, 7, 9.

31. Turretin, *Elenctic Theology*, 1:87–90.
32. Ibid., 90.

Corinthians astray by their claim to extraordinary revelation that circumvented the apostolic circle. It is interesting that while Rome increasingly answered the heretics by appealing to its own authority (an ongoing apostolic authority), Paul himself, though indisputably an apostle, drew the Corinthians' attention to that which had been already committed to writing even while the apostles were living. There one could not go wrong. That Peter even refers to Paul's epistles as "Scripture" underscores just how early the apostles were talking about official pastoral letters as canonical (2Pe 3:16).

Ultimate authority always resides outside the self and even outside the church, as both are always *hearers* of the Word and *receivers* of its judgment and justification. The church is commissioned to deliver this Word (a ministerial office), not to possess or rule over it (a magisterial office). Thus, the authority is always transcendent. Even when it comes near us, it is never our own word that we hear (Ro 10:6–13, 17).

This sovereignty of Scripture over the church may be defended not only from the New Testament but secondarily from the actual process by which the postapostolic church arrived at the canon. Our twenty-seven books in the New Testament canon were first codified in an official list at the councils of Carthage (393) and Hippo (397).[33] However, two important facts need to be considered.

First, most of these texts were already widely recognized and employed regularly in public worship as divinely inspired. In fact, this was one criterion that was used for determining which texts were canonical. As we have seen, Peter refers to Paul's writings as Scripture. Tertullian was already quoting from twenty-three of these twenty-seven books by the late second and early third centuries. The wide use of these books (as well as the Old Testament) by the ancient Christian writers to judge all views and controversies testifies to the fact that they were already functioning as Scripture long before they were officially listed in a canon. In 367, Athanasius drew up the first list of all twenty-seven books, even identifying it as a canon, and maintained that "holy Scripture is of all things most sufficient for us."[34] Basil of Caesarea (330–379) instructed, "Believe those things which are written; the things which are not written seek not."[35] "It is a manifest defection from the faith, a proof of arrogance, either to reject anything of what is written, or to introduce anything that is not."[36]

Second, from these ancient Christian writers we can identify four main categories in which texts were to be placed: canonical, widely accepted, spurious, and

---

33. Bruce Metzger, *The New Testament: Its Background, Growth, and Content* (Nashville: Abingdon, 1965); D. A. Carson, Douglas Moo, and Leon Morris, *An Introduction to the New Testament* (Grand Rapids: Zondervan, 1992); Craig A. Evans, *Noncanonical Writings and New Testament Interpretation* (Peabody, Mass.: Hendrickson, 1992); Lee McDonald, *The Biblical Canon: Its Origin, Transmission, and Authority* (3rd ed.; Peabody, Mass.: Hendrickson, 2007); Craig A. Evans and Emanuel Tov, eds., *Exploring the Origins of the Bible: Canon Formation in Historical, Literary, and Theological Perspective* (Grand Rapids: Baker, 2008).

34. Athanasius, in *NPNF2*, 4:23.

35. Basil, "On the Holy Spirit," *NPNF2*, 8:41.

36. Ibid.

heretical.[37] There were criteria employed for determining canonical books, all of which had to do with the nature of the texts rather than with the authority of the church. These criteria included well-attested apostolic authorship or certification, wide acceptance and use as Scripture already in church practice, and consistency of content—or what became known in Reformation teaching as the "analogy of Scripture" (interpreting passages in the light of other passages, comparing the parts in the light of the whole, and vice versa). The canonicity of the letters of James, Jude, 2 Peter, 2 John, and 3 John, though they were widely accepted, was debated in the early church before they were recognized as belonging to the canon.

Both of these points underscore the fact that the church was recognizing, not creating, the canon. These leaders of the ancient church were engaged in historical criticism—determining which books *were* canonical, not *endowing* them with canonical authority. Athanasius, for example, rejected the Shepherd of Hermas because, though widely used, it did not have adequate evidence of apostolic origin and did not bear the marks of belonging to the circle of the apostles themselves.[38]

Finally, the sufficiency of Scripture is inseparable from both its scope and its *perspicuity* (or clarity).[39] Rome's contention has been that Scripture itself is difficult to understand, especially by laypeople, and that it therefore requires an infallible interpreter. Historically, it is difficult to justify the claim that Rome's teachings are clearer or more internally consistent than Scripture itself. In fact, the church's teachings—even those it requires belief in for salvation—fill a library of volumes, with pronouncements so detailed and technical that a layperson hardly knows where to begin. Doubtless, this fact contributed to the doctrine of implicit faith—believing *whatever the church teaches*, even if one is not aware of it. In fact, some views that were eventually settled upon as official church teaching had been previously condemned as heretical. In addition, for more than a century (1309–1437), there were four rival popes, each anathematizing the others' see. This division, known as the Western Schism, meant that all of Christendom lived under the condemnation of one or more popes, unsure of who had the real power of excommunication. In contrast, although the New Testament itself refers to internal debates even among the apostles, the canonical *texts* exhibit a striking clarity and unity.

From the evangelical perspective, Scripture is sufficient as the source of truth because Christ is sufficient as the basis, grace as the motive, and faith as the instru-

---

37. See Eusebius, "The Church History of Eusebius," in *NPNF2*, 1:155–57.

38. As Brunner notes, this process was far from an arbitrary exercise of ecclesiastical power: "If we compare the writings of the New Testament with those of the subapostolic period [e.g., Epistle of Clement, Shepherd of Hermas], even those which are nearest in point of time, we cannot avoid the conclusion that there is a very great difference between the two groups; which

was also the opinion of the fathers of the church" (Emil Brunner, *Reason and Revelation* [trans. Olive Wyon; London: SCM, 1947], 132).

39. For a recent account of Scripture's clarity, see Mark D. Thompson, *A Clear and Present Word: The Clarity of Scripture* (New Studies in Biblical Theology; Downers Grove, Ill.: InterVarsity Press, 2006).

ment of receiving everlasting salvation. In defending *sola scriptura*, Berkouwer reminds us, "The sharp criticism of the Reformers was closely related to their deep central concern for the gospel," which is evident in the other *solae*.[40] In this connection, the concept of canon is closely bound up with that of the covenant of grace. God is always the initiator, and we are the recipients. We are not first a certain kind of people who then create or adopt a certain constitution; we are constituted by the charter that defines us as those who belong to God in a covenant of grace. "The early church did not create the story," writes Herman Ridderbos. "The story created the early church!...Without the resurrection the story would have lost its power. It would have been the story of the life of a saint, not the gospel."[41]

The bewildering proliferation of denominations and sects seems to justify Rome's denial of Scripture's inherent clarity. However, as any parent can attest, children are often reprimanded for failing properly to hear or heed clear instructions. Furthermore, a student of church history will become increasingly sensitive to the complexity, ambiguity, crises, and even contradictions in church teaching. Although the divisions within Protestantism are a scandal, the histories of both Orthodox and Roman Catholic communions attest to similar strife — even if the institutions themselves have been held together by an implicit (and for much of their history, politically enforced) faith in bishops and popes.

Some of our differences in interpretation arise from the inherent richness and polyphonic voices of the human authors of Scripture. Even the four gospels reflect diverse interests, perspectives, accounts, and even theological emphases. Furthermore, there are different contexts, such as Paul's engagement with legalism and James's with antinomianism. While acknowledging the canonicity of Paul's writings, Peter could acknowledge that there are some things that are difficult to understand, which "the ignorant and unstable twist to their own destruction, as they do the other Scriptures" (2Pe 3:16). By laying the blame at the feet of false interpreters, Jesus and the apostles uphold the inherent clarity of Scripture. The church is not only *fallible*; it is *prone* to misinterpret God's Word apart from the constant faithfulness of the Spirit's illuminating grace. Even the gospel, which is as clear as the statement "Christ died for our sins and was raised for our justification" (cf. Ro 4:25), may be obscured, confused, distorted, or denied — again, partly because of its inexhaustible richness and partly because the gospel remains to a certain degree a stumbling block and foolishness even to Christians.

Finally, the clarity of Scripture is not uniform. There is a fundamentalist version of Scripture's perspicuity or clarity that undervalues its humanity, plurality, and

---

40. G. C. Berkouwer, *Holy Scripture* (Grand Rapids: Eerdmans, 1975), 302.

41. Herman Ridderbos, *Redemptive History and the New* *Testament Scriptures* (trans. H. DeJongste; Phillipsburg, N.J.: P&R, 1988), 42.

richness, treating the Bible as a collection of obvious propositions that require no interpretation. However, this is not the classic Protestant understanding of Scripture's clarity. The *Westminster Confession* (1.7) freely acknowledges that the Scriptures are "not alike plain in themselves, nor alike clear unto all." We must interpret obscure passages in the light of clearer ones, and we must do this together, not simply by ourselves. In doing so, we can discern the clear teaching of Scripture on the most important matters that it addresses.

Like its sufficiency, the clarity of Scripture is inseparable from its *scope*. If we come to the Bible looking for answers to our own questions that it does not address explicitly, treating it as an encyclopedia of general knowledge, we will draw from it conclusions that it does not intend. For instance, if we seek from Scripture infallible information concerning the age of the earth, we will miss the point of the passages we are citing. Passages of this kind require more interpretive skill than do the abundant and obvious declarations of the gospel. The tragic fact that Rome has condemned as heretical the clear teaching of the gospel is the most decisive challenge to its claim to be the church's infallible teacher of God's Word. The same must be said, also with great sorrow, for any Protestant body that strays from the clearest declarations of God's grace in Jesus Christ. If the gospel is not known and proclaimed in its purity and simplicity, it is the teacher rather than the text that is unclear.

The churches of the Reformation embrace ecumenical creeds and agree on specific confessions and catechisms. However, they do this not because they think that Scripture is insufficient, difficult, or inconsistent and required an infallible interpreter. Rather, they require communal subscription to these confessions precisely because they believe the Scriptures are so clear and consistent that their principal teachings can and should be summarized for the good of the whole community, children as well as adults.

Therefore, the Reformers rejected both the *magisterial* authority of the church defended by Rome and the denial of the church's *ministerial* authority that was often exhibited by radical Protestants. When Philip found an Ethiopian treasury secretary returning from Jerusalem reading Isaiah 53, he inquired, "Do you understand what you are reading?" "How can I, unless someone guides me?" the official replied (Ac 8:30–31). After Philip explained the passage in the light of its fulfillment in Christ, the official believed and was baptized and "went on his way rejoicing" (v. 39). Christ appointed the offices of teacher, pastor, and elder not to continue the extraordinary ministry of prophets and apostles but to preserve and proclaim the truth of Scripture. No one denies the need for interpretation, and, at least for the Reformers and their heirs, the church, through its representative synods, is given a ministerial authority to offer such communal interpretations. The question is whether ecclesial interpretations are always subject to revision by the light of Scripture or whether they are to be believed simply on the authority of the church itself.

Given the analysis above concerning the nature of God's Word as sacramental as well as canonically regulative, *sola scriptura* is not simply an affirmation of the unique authority of the Bible over tradition but a confession of the sovereignty of God's grace. Because God alone saves, God alone teaches and rules our faith and practice. Because the church is the creation of the Word (*creatura verbi*) rather than vice versa, "salvation belongs to the LORD!" (Jnh 2:9). Prior to becoming pope, Cardinal Ratzinger nicely summarized the difference between Rome and the Reformation churches on this point. According to the latter, the Word guarantees the ministry, whereas Rome holds that the ministry guarantees the Word. He adds, "Perhaps in this reversal of the relations between word and ministry lies the real opposition between the views of the church held by Catholics and Reformers."[42]

B. AUTHORITY AND SUFFICIENCY OF SCRIPTURE IN MODERN THEOLOGY

Protestantism has had its own challenges in retaining its confidence in the sufficiency of Scripture, especially in the wake of the Enlightenment. Modernity enshrined the self as the sovereign arbiter over Scripture and church, whether in the form of reason, duty, experience, pragmatic usefulness, or felt needs. In Anglicanism, a moderating ("Latitudinarian") position emerged, treating reason, tradition, experience, and Scripture as four legs of a stool of ecclesiastical authority. While insisting on the primacy of Scripture, John Wesley affirmed this fourfold authority. In 1965, Albert C. Outler coined the term *Wesleyan Quadrilateral* for this view that he discerned in Wesley's writings.[43]

With Schleiermacher, any qualitative distinction between the Bible and other media of revelatory experience was eroded. Ironically, it was in Protestantism, therefore, that even the Roman Catholic caveat that the authority of Scripture is intrinsic rather than given to it by the church was eliminated.[44] The Scriptures "must become the regulative type for our religious thinking, from which it is not of its own motion to depart," Schleiermacher argued. Nevertheless, the sufficiency of Scripture is lodged in the use we make of Scripture rather than in its nature as such: "And

42. Rahner and Ratzinger, *Revelation and Tradition*, 29.

43. Albert C. Outler, *John Wesley* (New York: Oxford Univ. Press, 1965); cf. Don Thorsen, *The Wesleyan Quadrilateral: Scripture, Tradition, Reason, and Experience as a Model of Evangelical Theology* (Lexington, Ky.: Emeth, 2005). The United Methodist Church's *Book of Discipline* (2004) identifies Scripture as primary.

44. Friedrich Schleiermacher, *The Christian Faith* (ed. and trans. H. R. Mackintosh and J. S. Stewart; Edinburgh: T&T

Clark, 1928), 594–95. According to Schleiermacher, the Scriptures are simply "the first member in the series" of "presentations of the Christian Faith" which have "ever since continued," though in some sense a norm for succeeding generations because of the uniqueness of Christ's degree of God-consciousness. Since Scripture gives expression to the common spirit of the community, "everything of the kind which persists in influence alongside of Holy Scripture we must regard as homogeneous with Scripture."

when the Holy Scripture is described as 'sufficient' in this regard, what is meant is that *through our use* of Scripture *the Holy Spirit can lead us into all truth*, as it led the apostles and others who enjoyed Christ's direct teaching" (emphasis added).[45] Therefore, in this view God's Word originates from within the individual or community (this is inspiration) and is expressed in ever-new variations within ever-new historical contexts.

It was against this departure from Christianity that Karl Barth launched his famous protest, recalling the decisive claim of the Reformers against the medieval church that God's Word comes to us from outside of the self and the community. Whatever objections we may have to some of Barth's views of revelation, he was emphatic on the point that the church always stands under the norm of Scripture alone.[46]

As I mentioned in the previous chapter (see "Collapsing the Distinction between Inspiration and Illumination," pp. 169–73), some evangelical theologians today are attracted to views of Scripture that repeat familiar trajectories of liberal Protestantism. Rather than faith being created by the Word of God, the Word itself is created by the experiences of the community, according to this perspective. Obviously this requires "a revisioned understanding of the *nature* of the Bible's authority," as Stanley Grenz suggests.[47] *Sola scriptura* has a noble history in evangelicalism. "The commitment to contextualization, however, entails an implicit rejection of the older evangelical conception of theology as the construction of truth on the basis of the Bible alone." Instead, Grenz suggests that we adopt "the well-known method of correlation proposed by Paul Tillich" and the "Wesleyan quadrangle."[48] The Bible's authority should be reciprocally rather than hierarchically related to our heritage and our contemporary context; and even here he adds, "the Bible *as canonized by the church*," as if the church authorized rather than received the canon (emphasis added).[49] Understandably, Grenz believes that this view will yield greater convergence between Protestant and Roman Catholic interpretations of Scripture and tradition, while also incorporating a Pentecostal and charismatic emphasis on continuing revelation.[50] However, each of these proposed media is itself relativized by yet another source of revelation: contemporary culture.[51]

From the foregoing summaries we can see that scholars across the ecclesiastical

---

45. Ibid., 606.

46. In addition to a host of citations one could draw from Barth's *Church Dogmatics* (vol. 1, pts. 1 and 2), see Karl Barth, *The Göttingen Dogmatics: Instruction in the Christian Religion* (ed. Hannelotte Reiffen; trans. Geoffrey W. Bromiley; Grand Rapids: Eerdmans, 1991), 1:273.

47. Stanley Grenz, *Revisioning Evangelical Theology* (Downers Grove, Ill.: InterVarsity Press, 1993), 88. A fine alternative to Grenz's interpretation of canon and covenant is Kevin J. Vanhoozer, *The Drama of Doctrine: A Canonical-Linguistic Approach to Christian Theology* (Louisville: Westminster John Knox, 2005), esp. 115–50, 211–42.

48. Grenz, *Revisioning Evangelical Theology*, 90–91.

49. Ibid., 93.

50. Ibid., 123, 130.

51. Ibid., 101–3.

spectrum have been domesticating God's sovereign voice to the voice of the church or the individual. John Webster reminds us that when God's speech acts and human speech acts become qualitatively indistinguishable, the church more easily indulges in the fantasy that it is already the fully realized kingdom of God, with "a broadly immanentistic ecclesiology" that lodges the church's visibility in its doing of its works rather than in its hearing of God's works. "Indeed, such accounts can sometimes take the form of a highly sophisticated hermeneutical reworking of Ritschlian social moralism, in which the center of gravity of a theology of Scripture has shifted away from God's activity toward the uses of the church."[52]

This process of shifting the weight from God's saving and ruling speech to that of the community happens in all sorts of ways—in the traditional Roman Catholic way, but also in the widespread interest among Protestants in "translating" and "applying" the Bible in ways that assume its inherent irrelevance for contemporary thought and life. In numerous variations, across the theological spectrum, we often imagine as believers and as churches that *our* speaking is more relevant for our contemporaries than *God's* speaking. Webster identifies this with a sort of Arminian or even Pelagian tendency to play down God's work and play up our work of "reading" and "interpreting." According to Webster, this risks surrendering not only *sola scriptura* but *sola gratia*.[53] "Scripture is not the word of the church; the church is the church of the Word." Therefore, "the church is the hearing church."[54] Only because the church passes on what it has heard is its authority something other than an arbitrary exercise of institutional power.

It is possible to hold a high view of biblical authority and sufficiency in theory while yielding a magisterial role in practice to sociology, politics, marketing, psychology, and other cultural authorities. Within evangelical circles, the decline of expository preaching in favor of topical speeches laced with personal anecdotes, insights, and examples drawn from cultural authorities communicates to God's people where we think the power and relevance of our speech really lies.

Similar to Tillich's method of correlation, the working assumption in much of contemporary evangelicalism seems to be that modern culture, whether identified with academic disciplines or with popular fashion, exegetes human identity and the ideals of proper human flourishing. According to this assumption, the culture shapes the horizon of our experience, expectations, and felt needs—determining what is relevant—and the Christian task is to apply the Bible to this already-defined "life" in relevant ways.

However, this is to invoke the Bible too late. When God breaks in on us through his Word, we are confronted with a series of contradictions. We learn that we do

---

52. John Webster, *Holy Scripture: A Dogmatic Sketch* (Cambridge: Cambridge Univ. Press, 2003), 43.

53. Ibid.
54. Ibid., 44.

not even know the meaning of our daily lives or the world, or human identity and flourishing, until God interprets us, our lives together, and our history in the light of his actions. "Popular education, the cultivation of morality and patriotism, the nurture of the emotions—none of these really need us theologians," Barth reminds us. "Others can do these and similar things much better than we can. The world knows this and acts accordingly. We are examined and rejected, and rightly so, before we become apprentices in such dilettante occupations." The church's activity, including its speech, is truly useful in the world only "when it stands under a norm."[55]

C. GOSPEL AND CULTURE

The missionary imperative has always called forth enormous energies in communicating the Christian faith in terms that can be understood by people in different times and places. Sometimes the ancient theologians accommodated too much to their philosophical and political milieu, but there are striking examples in which they subversively reinterpreted pagan categories in service to Christ.

However, the concern to relate the Bible to culture—displaying the relevance of Christianity for contemporary life—is a characteristically modern obsession. In the process, the definition of the gospel often broadens to include nearly anything that promotes the flourishing of humanity. Therefore, definitions are of first importance. By *gospel,* I mean *that specific announcement of redemption from sin and death in Jesus Christ, promised and fulfilled in history.* Also susceptible to varied definitions, *culture* may be understood (with Clifford Geertz) as *"webs of significance"—beliefs, practices, tools, habits, relationships, and artifacts—that are created by human beings in particular times and places.*[56] Of course, in this sense, the church is also a distinct culture. However, I am using the term here to refer to the common realm of social practices, vocations, beliefs, and assumptions that Christians share with non-Christians in a given time and place.

Of course, the sovereignty of God's speech in no way eliminates the significance of human utterances, whether in terms of culture, tradition, experience, or reason. Each of us is conditioned in our hearing and reading of God's Word by our cultural-linguistic location. Nevertheless, the most decisive cultural-linguistic location for the covenant people is "in Christ," under the normative authority of his Word. In theory at least, the classic Protestant position with respect to the sources of theology is simple, though somewhat clumsily expressed: the norm that norms but is not normed (*norma normans non normata est*). As with tradition, the

---

55. Barth, *Göttingen Dogmatics*, 1:273.
56. Clifford Geertz, *The Interpretation of Cultures* (New York: Basic Books, 1973), 5.

relationship of Scripture to culture, experience, and reason is *magisterial* and *ministerial*, respectively.

There is no such thing as culture, reason, tradition, or experience in the abstract. There are only cultures, reasoners, traditions, and people who experience reality. We cannot help but come to Scripture with these resources, but they are not neutral. We come either as covenant servants or as would-be masters. To the extent that we are able, we must make our tacit assumptions explicit. This is in part what it is intended in 2 Corinthians 10:5: "We destroy arguments and every lofty opinion raised against the knowledge of God, and take every thought captive to obey Christ." This can only be done if we acknowledge a normative authority standing above our tacit assumptions and recognized convictions drawn from our cultural conditioning.

No more than reason, experience, or tradition is culture itself to be viewed as inherently opposed to faith. Rather, it is our sinful condition that causes us to use these gifts as weapons against the sovereign God who gave them. God speaks providentially in his common grace through reason, experience, tradition, and culture, but he has only spoken miraculously and redemptively in his Word (Heb 1:1). To say that culture, reason, tradition, and experience are subordinate to Scripture is simply to assert that human beings are subordinate to God. A dialogue with culture may yield important formal agreements on universal human rights, stewardship of creation, and other dictates of the moral law inscribed on the human conscience. However, no more than reason, experience, or tradition does culture possess any inherent possibilities of discovering God's saving grace. On this point, Barth was correct to warn against turning culture into a source of gracious revelation alongside the Word of God.[57]

Descartes and Locke thought we should dispense with all external authorities, presuppositions, and inherited assumptions in order to arrive at incorrigible truths. However, this is a pretense—as impossible as it is unhelpful. Therefore, the popular assumption that people become Christians (or anything else) simply as an individual act of immediate intuition, unbiased investigation of the facts, or inner experience is more evidently modern than biblical. In the covenant of grace, God promises, "I will establish my covenant between me and you and your offspring after you throughout their generations for an everlasting covenant, to be God to you and to your offspring after you" (Ge 17:7).

God's mighty acts, celebrated in the great feasts and defined in the doctrines and commands of Torah, are to be "on your heart. You shall teach them diligently

---

57. Of relevance in this connection is my treatment of general revelation in ch. 3.

to your children, and shall talk of them when you sit in your house, and when you walk by the way, and when you lie down, and when you rise" (Dt 6:6–7). From circumcision to burial, each Israelite was shaped by the covenant. It was their environment, not simply a set of doctrines and ethical norms to which they yielded formal assent. It was not something that they knew about as detached observers, but a form of life that they indwelled, from which they interpreted all of reality. Israel's creed—the Shema (Dt 6:4–5)—was the summary of a whole network of narratives, practices, and texts they had absorbed into their bloodstream.

In its New Testament administration, this covenant of grace followed the same course. The narrative generates the doctrines and practices, evoking thanksgiving that then fuels discipleship. All of this is done in community. Even outsiders become insiders by hearing the same gospel, being baptized along with their household (Ac 16:15, 31–34), sharing in the Supper, being catechized in the same doctrine, and being shaped by a common fellowship of saints in local and broader assemblies. The covenant is the "form of life" or cultural-linguistic context that shapes Christian faith, practice, experience, witness, and service in the world. Yet even this ecclesial culture is corrupted by our sinful prejudices, errors, and practices. The covenant community itself remains simultaneously justified and sinful and must therefore always be transformed through the renewal of its mind by Scripture (Ro 12:2). This Word always stands above the world and the church because it is the voice of the Father; it alone is able to save us from lords that cannot liberate because its content is Christ; it always establishes its own relevance and creates its own form of life because its perlocutionary effect is produced within us by the Spirit.

When tradition and culture are given authoritative roles alongside Scripture, the church and the world are not able to be judged *or* redeemed by the voice of a stranger. In fact, the church easily becomes indistinguishable from the world instead of a witness to Christ in the power of the Spirit. The church cannot serve two masters. While God's general revelation may be evident in culture, it is only his special revelation that creates the church and keeps it from its constant tendency to be reabsorbed into this passing evil age. Because of God's common *grace*, no culture is entirely devoid of any sense of truth, justice, and beauty. Because of our common *curse*, no time, place, cultural movement, or civilization is capable of restoring paradise. There is indeed general revelation, which allows us to work with our unbelieving neighbors toward greater justice, charity, stewardship, and beauty in the world, but we must never forget that, apart from the gospel, this general revelation is always distorted by our ungodly hearts. Therefore, every natural theology will always evolve into a form of idolatry. The church is thus not a facilitator of a conversation between the gospel and culture, as if they were two sources of a single revelation.[58] Rather, it is that part of the world that lives—if it will live at all—by hearing God's announcement and binding address.

Of course, theological claims are always made from a particular cultural location.[59] However, precisely because the gospel functions as the primary entity in the conversation—even to the point of turning the dialogue into a divine monologue—the *relativity of our perspective* does not entail the *relativism of what is known*. Analogous to the hypostatic Word (Jesus Christ) and the written Word (Scripture), the church is the city of God descending from heaven (Rev 21:9–13). Christ assumed a human nature, not a human person. In other words, although he was a male Jew shaped by his own time and place, he is the "firstfruit" of a whole harvest and the head of his body because the nature that he assumed belongs to us all—in every place and time. In this way, he transcends all of our cultural differences and binds us into one people. This communion or society therefore transcends every cultural movement and every empire, ethnic group, economic class, and social demographic. As the sole head of his church, Jesus Christ alone establishes the catholicity of the church in the power of the Spirit through one faith and one baptism (Eph 4:5).

The kingdom of God is not a tower we are building to the heavens but a ladder that God has descended to reach us. The church originates not in human planning and organization but in God's eternal election. Nevertheless, it is also a human institution, reflecting the circumstances of its varied times and places. Because the city of God is a cultural-linguistic system descending from heaven through the work of the triune God, a third-century African Christian confesses the same faith as a twenty-first-century Asian or North American believer. This community is *constituted* by God's Word—"one Lord, one faith, one baptism" (Eph 4:5)—even while being *conditioned* (for better and for worse) by the distinct cultures and societies it inhabits. As Laura Smit reminds us, commenting on Calvin's view, "All of our knowledge of God is mediated, [but] he believes that it is mediated, not by our cultural context, but *to* our context by God himself."[60] The covenant of grace trumps all of the social contracts that vie illegitimately for our ultimate allegiance.

George Hunsinger reminds us that many of the recent attempts to find a "post-

---

58. Like Stanley Grenz, John Franke appeals to Tillich's method of correlation (with some modification), concluding, "Neither gospel nor culture can function as the primary entity in the conversation between the two in light of their interpretive and constructed nature; we must recognize that theology emerges through an ongoing conversation involving both gospel and culture" (*The Character of Theology* [Grand Rapids: Baker, 2005], 103). My concern is that post-conservatism, at least as Grenz and Franke delineate it, revives the experiential-expressivist side of pietism and, with it, some of the same liberal

presuppositions that defined a distinctively *modern* theology. See, for example, William Dyrness, "The Pietistic Heritage of Schleiermacher," *Christianity Today* 23:6 (Dec. 1978); cf. Barth's critique of Schleiermacher as a radical pietist in *The Theology of Schleiermacher: Lectures at Göttingen, Winter Semester of 1923/24* (ed. Dietrich Ritschl; Grand Rapids: Eerdmans, 1982).

59. Franke, *Character of Theology*, 90.

60. Laura Smit, "The Depth Behind Things," in *Radical Orthodoxy and the Reformed Tradition* (ed. James K. A. Smith and James Olthuis; Grand Rapids: Baker, 2005), 209.

modern" way of doing theology turn out to be little more than an echo of prominent themes in modernity.[61] He observes:

> The Christ of natural theology is always openly or secretly the relativized Christ of culture. The trajectory of natural theology leads from the Christ who is not supreme to the Christ who is not sufficient to the Christ who is not necessary.... "God may speak to us," wrote Barth, "through Russian communism or a flute concerto, a blossoming shrub or a dead dog. We shall do well to listen to him if he really does so" [*Church Dogmatics*, vol. 1, part 1, 60]. No such object, however, can ever be allowed to become a source of authority for the church's preaching, for no such object can have independent revelatory or epistemological status. Only by criteria derived from the one authentic scriptural voice of Christ can we know if God might be speaking to us in those ways or not.[62]

In every age, the gospel—as a surprising and offensive word that comes to us from outside of ourselves both as individuals and communities—radically disrupts the status quo of the church as well as the world.

Precisely because God's Word comes to the church and to the world from outside, to interrupt human conversation of religion, spirituality, and morality, they can be the theater of redemption. In spite of the genuine diversity of cultures and social locations, the Bible recognizes the solidarity of humanity in Adam under sin and death and the solidarity of the new creation in Christ.

Given the distinction between inspiration (Scripture) and illumination (tradition), how does theology move from the teachings delivered in the canon to its interpretations? What is the nature and role of church dogmas?

II. THE NATURE OF DOCTRINE: FROM SCRIPTURE TO SYSTEM

Working our way in concentric circles from the widest horizon—namely, ontology to epistemology and then to revelation and Scripture—we now arrive at the nature of Christian doctrine.

---

61. George Hunsinger, *Disruptive Grace: Studies in the Theology of Karl Barth* (Grand Rapids: Eerdmans, 2000), 76, referring to Harvey Cox: "One problem with Cox's analysis, which many will be sure to note, is that there really is nothing 'postmodern' about it. At best it simply rearranges the furniture in the old modernist room. Perhaps theology is just getting around to appropriating Marx's insights about how the poor are exploited and Lessing's insights in *Nathan the Wise* about the plurality and underlying unity of religions, but that hardly seems any reason to dignify the affair with an exalted term like 'postmodern.' After all, why have modern skeptics been so skeptical if not largely because their encounter with religious pluralism convinced them that all religious truth claims are arbitrary?"

62. Ibid., 80. "Certainly," Hunsinger adds, "one can only imagine Barth raising his eyebrows at the current crop of well-meaning enthusiasts who can think of no better way to promote his work than by extolling him as a 'postmodernist' before his time" (253). Referring to Jewish theologian Michael Wyschogrod, Hunsinger concludes, "Wanting to assimilate theology into the foreign mold of the surrounding culture ... is an essentially Gentile aspiration" (255).

A. GEORGE LINDBECK'S MODELS OF DOCTRINE

Once again we are assisted by an able typology, this time that of Yale's George Lindbeck (1923–), from his book *The Nature of Doctrine*.[63] Lindbeck's contrasting models are the *cognitive-propositional* and the *experiential-expressive*, to which he adds his own *cultural-linguistic* model as an alternative. With this section we bring together all of our reflections thus far in this chapter.

Lindbeck defines the cognitive-propositional theory of doctrine in roughly the same terms as Dulles' uses in his description of "revelation as doctrine" (model 1), which I delineated in chapter 3 (see "Models of Revelation," pp. 113–15). In fact, his examples are the same as Dulles's—namely, conservative evangelical Carl F. H. Henry and conservative neo-Thomist Catholic theologians. According to this perspective, doctrines are regarded as factual statements that correspond to reality. At the other extreme, the experiential-expressive theory treats doctrines as hypotheses that express religious experience. Naturally, this approach to doctrine is most consistent with Dulles's model of "revelation as inner experience" (or as new awareness). Simply put, these rival models represent modern conservative and liberal approaches, respectively.

Carl Henry, representing the cognitive-propositional model, followed Gordon Clark in endorsing a univocal rather than an analogical relationship between divine and human knowledge.[64] In *God, Revelation, and Authority*, Henry asserts that doctrines are "the theorems derived from the axioms of revelation."[65] Whereas Reformed theologian Geerhardus Vos (1862–1949) spoke of Scripture as an unfolding drama of redemption rather than merely a collection of timeless truths, Henry seems to have regarded propositions as the only conveyers of real truth.[66] Henry reflects an enormous debt to his mentor, who argued that biblical language is "inadequate" until distilled in propositional language.[67] Clark wrote, "Truth is a characteristic of propositions only. Nothing can be called true in the literal sense of the term except the attribution of a predicate to a subject."[68] In this way, language (specifically, Christian doctrine) is reduced to a single illocutionary stance—that of asserting and describing.

Navigating between these extremes, Lindbeck offers his own constructive proposal: a cultural-linguistic theory of doctrine that understands Christianity pri-

63. George Lindbeck, *The Nature of Doctrine: Religion and Theology in a Postliberal Age* (Louisville: Westminster John Knox, 1984).

64. See my interaction with Carl Henry on this point, with citations, in *Covenant and Eschatology: The Divine Drama* (Louisville: Westminster John Knox, 2002), 189–91.

65. Carl Henry, *God, Revelation, and Authority* (Waco, Tex.: Word, 1976), 1:234.

66. Carl Henry, "Narrative Theology: An Evangelical Appraisal," *Trinity Journal* 8 (1987): 3.

67. Gordon Clark, *Religion, Reason, and Revelation* (Nutley, N.J.: Craig Press, 1961), 143.

68. Gordon Clark, "The Bible as Truth," *BSac* 114 (April 1957): 158.

marily as a language and doctrine as its grammar. In this perspective, doctrines are neither propositional statements of external facts nor expressions of inner experience; they are rules developed by the church that govern the speech and practices that form people to have certain beliefs and experiences in the first place. Lindbeck argues that both conservatives and liberals assume a modern foundationalist epistemology, with doctrines arising either out of universal rationality or experience — which is one of the main reasons his position is identified as *postliberal*. Influenced especially by the later Wittgenstein and the cultural anthropology of Clifford Geertz, Lindbeck views the Christian faith as its own distinct *language game*.

Conservatives, Lindbeck maintains, cannot account for the truth of a religion apart from holding that its doctrines are without error, while liberals cannot account for the possibility that a given religion (such as Christianity) may be "unsurpassably true."[69] Lindbeck holds that a doctrine is true only when it is being "rightly utilized."[70] A crusader's cry, "Christ is Lord!" while cleaving the skull of an infidel, is categorically false.[71]

Lindbeck's model is superb at challenging the assimilation of the church's grammar to alien religious and secular grammars. Echoing Barth, Lindbeck insists, "It is the text, so to speak, that absorbs the world, rather than the world the text."[72] Christianity is not a species of religion but is its own language game. Statements such as "Jesus died for our sins and was raised for our justification" are meaningless simply as propositions abstracted from the narratives and the actual form of life that is engendered in the church through participation in preaching, sacrament, fellowship, prayer, praise, service, and witness. The drama must not only be explained, but performed in the "community theater" instituted by Christ and choreographed by the Word and Spirit. However, Lindbeck's model is not as successful in resisting the assimilation of revelation to the church's agency. Ultimately, in his model, it is the truthful praxis of believers that determines the truth value of Christian claims, and it is the church's use of Scripture that makes it authoritative. Is it the church's praxis that makes God's Word true, or vice versa?

Like Dulles's models of revelation, Lindbeck's models of doctrine — including his own — are richly suggestive but seem in the end to be too reductionistic. Lindbeck's description of the cognitive-propositionalist model draws on examples from Carl Henry, but he fails to distinguish these positions from the more nuanced perspectives of Protestant orthodoxy and its more recent proponents. In Lindbeck's own model, doctrine (like Scripture) appears to be authoritative because the church has determined its own grammar; the divine warrant beyond ecclesial sanction is as

---

69. Lindbeck, *Nature of Doctrine*, 49.
70. Ibid., 35.

71. Ibid., 64.
72. Ibid., 118.

bracketed from his account as it has been in modern liberalism since Kant. Where Paul teaches that all Scripture is "profitable" *because* it is "breathed out by God" (2Ti 3:16), Lindbeck seems to argue the reverse. A doctrine is "categorically true" when it is "rightly utilized."[73] And its ontological ("propositional") truth depends on its categorical truth.[74] Systematic theology, then, is the attempt "to give a normative explication of the meaning a religion has for its adherents."[75]

Yet how different is this really from Schleiermacher's famous definition: "Christian doctrines are accounts of the Christian religious affections set forth in speech"?[76] As appropriated by some evangelical theologians, Lindbeck's theory is taken to mean that the principal objective of Scripture is not to deliver true doctrine but to generate authentic religious experience and to offer practical imperatives for daily living.[77] At the end of the day, Lindbeck's proposal seems to share with the experiential-expressivist view an equivocal account of doctrine. In spite of certain affinities to Barth, Lindbeck seems no less reticent to identify God as the object of theology than Kant was. Furthermore, the tendency of his model (especially evident in his students, such as the often insightful and provocative Stanley Hauerwas) is to give priority to the *church's* practices rather than to *God's*—only when we use them properly in our daily practice do Scripture, baptism, and the Eucharist become means of grace. They seem to be in this view less God's objective means of salvation than occasions for communal self-description.

Cleavages have emerged on this issue within the Yale school itself. One of Hans Frei's students and leading interpreters, George Hunsinger, observes, "The cultural-linguistic pragmatism of [Lindbeck's] preferred type, however, raises a question of whether finally his proposal is not so much 'postliberal' as 'neoliberal,' since pragmatism has always been a routine liberal option."[78] Evangelical theologian Kevin Vanhoozer has noted that Lindbeck's cultural-linguistic method, at the end of the day, sounds like the experiential-expressivist view that he criticizes. He is especially concerned with the uses made of Lindbeck's theory by some evangelicals.[79]

Similarly, Colin Gunton judges, "So some kind of immediate experience appears in modern times to have replaced a traditional view of the mediation of the faith in propositional terms. George Lindbeck's critique of what he calls the cognitive-propositional conception of theology is in effect an attack on the notion of revealed

---

73. Ibid., 35.

74. Ibid., 52.

75. Ibid., 118.

76. Friedrich Schleiermacher, *The Christian Faith* (ed. and trans. H. R. Mackintosh and J. S. Stewart; Edinburgh: T&T Clark, 1928), 76.

77. Grenz, *Revisioning Evangelical Theology*, 18, 30, 32, 33–34, 48, 51–54, 57.

78. Hunsinger, *Disruptive Grace*, 11.

79. Kevin Vanhoozer, "Disputing About Words? Of Fallible Foundations and Modest Metanarratives," in *Christianity and the Postmodern Turn: Six Views* (ed. Myron Penner; Grand Rapids: Baker, 2005), 197–99. Vanhoozer suggests that, if taken to its logical conclusion, John Franke's version of constructivism is "devastating to biblical authority" (198). Cf. Vanhoozer, *Drama of Doctrine*, 10, 94–99, 175–84. In fact, Vanhoozer's elaboration of a "canonical-linguistic" model of doctrine appropriates Lindbeck's insights while making the appropriate corrections.

religion."[80] Gunton observes, "If it was once true that Jesus died for our sins on the cross, then it is always true."[81] Happily (for the world as well as for believers), the truth value of this proposition does not depend on how conformably to it we live or how faithfully we utilize it. Rather than determining its truth, our experiences and practices must be conformed to the reality of Christ's resurrection. "The heart of the problem is not the proposition, but our tenuous hold on the tradition," says Gunton. "Modernity has made doubters of us all, has appeared to cut such a breach between ourselves and our creedal past that we do not know whether there is a faith once delivered to the saints, or at least whether we may appeal to it." He concludes, "The problem is not that the propositions with which we are concerned are static; it is that they have been called into question."[82]

George Hunsinger argues that although Lindbeck's theological method remains more liberal than postliberal, and Carl Henry's model remains mired in a modernist epistemology, Hans Frei (Hunsinger's mentor and Lindbeck's colleague) and Reformed theologians like Kuyper and Bavinck are more promising conversation partners. "Other and very different formulations of Henry's concerns have standing within the evangelical community, formulations that uphold a strong doctrine of 'inerrancy' without Henry's modernist excesses." He adds, "In particular I will suggest that the views of Abraham Kuyper and Herman Bavinck offer a greater possibility for fruitful evangelical dialogue with postliberalism."[83] "The rejection of univocity separates them from someone like Henry, just as the affirmation of adequate and reliable reference separates them from modern skeptics."[84] "Whereas Henry seems to think the narratives are finally about the doctrines," notes Hunsinger, "for Frei it is just the reverse," and the same is true of Kuyper and Bavinck.[85] This volume, taking its bearings from Geerhardus Vos's insistence that doctrines arise out of the unfolding drama of redemption, is consistent with Hunsinger's conclusion.

Cognitive-propositionalist theories tend to reduce the faith to *doctrine*, understood as propositional statements. Experiential-expressivists tend to reduce the faith to *doxology*, which erupts from within the self's own religious experience. Similar in some ways to liberation theologies, the cultural-linguistic model gives pride of place to ecclesial praxis (*discipleship*). Narrative theologies focus on the unfolding *drama* of redemption.

What we desperately need in our day is a reintegration of these emphases. Abstracted from the drama of the biblical narrative, doctrines become timeless

---

80. Colin Gunton, *A Brief Theology of Revelation* (Edinburgh: T&T Clark, 1995), 7.

81. Ibid., 8.

82. Ibid., 12.

83. Hunsinger, *Disruptive Grace*, 340.

84. Ibid., 360.

85. Ibid., 349.

principles rather than explanatory notations in the script. At the same time, narratives need to be explained before their significance for us can be recognized. This recognition ordinarily yields an emotional response—fear, delight, sorrow, and thanksgiving—and motivates a certain way of being in the world as disciples of Christ.

Christian doctrine, in this view, is revealed by God and focuses especially on God's saving purposes in Christ. It is God's revelation of and the church's reflection upon God's works in history. Precisely because biblical doctrines are not the revelation of general, timeless truths, our inner experience, church practices, or God's commands for our daily lives, they decisively shape our experience and prepare us to follow God's commands in our daily living. Even in considering the church's practices, which Christ mandated, we must distinguish between those practices through which God himself ministers his grace (preaching and sacrament) and those practices that flourish among the saints as the fruit of this ministry (hospitality, generosity, service, justice, charity, and other acts of love).

B. A Covenantal Model of Doctrine: From Drama to Dogmatics

We may summarize the first part of this volume as an exposition of the principal elements of a covenantal approach to the theological task. *First, this task presupposes that God is qualitatively distinct from the creature.* Therefore, creaturely knowledge will always be revealed, dependent, accommodated, ectypal, and analogical rather than coinciding with God's archetypal knowledge at any point. *Second, this task presupposes that God's revelation comes to us from outside of ourselves.* Even the law, which is universally declared to the human conscience ever since creation, becomes a personal summons to judgment in our encounter with God in his self-revelation. The gospel is not buried deep within us but is known only in special revelation. *Third, every covenant has its canon—the historical prologue, stipulations, and sanctions that constitute and develop a norm for God's people.* The new covenant canon, therefore, constitutes and regulates the faith and practice of the covenant community, rather than being generated by it.

Just as God's revelation was not given all at once but developed organically, keeping up with the unfolding plot of redemptive history, the church's interpretation and formulations with respect to Scripture's sacred mysteries evolved over time, through conflict, refinement, and reformation. The church is a heavenly commonwealth created by the triune God, not by the people. Liberating his people, he gave them a *constitution*. Still, this constitution has to be interpreted and applied, not simply by individual citizens but by *church courts* with narrower and broader jurisdictions, as was the case at the Jerusalem Council in Acts 15 and in countless synods ever since. There is also a *tradition* of landmark cases with rulings that became established precedents for interpreting current laws—heresies that were resolved after prolonged conflict and a faithful interpretation of the ecumenical constitution that was distilled in creedal summaries.

Beyond these decisive cases that established the consensus of the whole church, particular traditions arose, elaborating this consensus in *confessions* and teaching them to new converts and their youth through catechisms. Finally, there are the individual *pastors* who must proclaim and teach God's Word and *theologians* who serve them, using all of these guardrails as they interpret the divine constitution, challenging the church to reflect more deeply and critically on its confession in the present. Recognizing the descending order of priority of these authorities—and the qualitatively distinct authority of the magisterial constitution over the ministerial authority of the church and its teachers—we are in a better position to avoid both ecclesial and individualistic hubris.

1. SCRIPTURE TO DOGMA

While they were still living, the apostles laid the foundation on which all subsequent ministers would build. The redemptive narrative surrounding Christ's person and work generated new doctrines—not wholly new, of course, because they were foretold by the prophets, but new in the sense that they were a change in covenantal administrations. Whereas Gentiles were once unholy, now believing Jews and Gentiles are one people in Christ (1Pe 2:9–10). Those who were far off have been brought near by Christ's blood (Eph 2:11–4:13). Yet precisely because the doctrine arises out of the unfolding narrative of redemption rather than as timeless concepts, it was difficult even for the apostles to get used to the new teachings and practices that were generated by the events of the new covenant.

After internal controversy even among the apostles, an overture was brought to the whole church through a representative assembly (Ac 15). There, "the apostles and the elders" concluded the matter by issuing a circular letter that was to be binding on all the churches. Gentile believers were not to be subservient or forced to become Jews in order to belong to the one people of God in these last days. Although the term *dogma* was first used in the Greek translation of the Old Testament and in the New Testament to refer to government edicts or the laws of Moses (Est 3:9; Da 2:13; Lk 2:1; Ac 17:7; Eph 2:15; Col 2:14), in Acts 16:4, *dogma* (derived from the verb *dokeô*) is used to refer to the "decisions" of the Jerusalem Council. Not even the apostles were delivering a new gospel, which neither they nor an angel from heaven were capable of doing (Gal 1:6–9), but they were interpreting the doctrine they had received (uniquely, by divine inspiration) in the promulgation of church dogma. We may rejoice in the fact that the gospel was a judge and liberator rather than a conversation partner with culture, tradition, reason, and experience. Though promised in the Old Testament, the revelation of the mystery hidden in past ages is a new doctrine, announcing that the dividing wall between Jew and Gentile has been dismantled. And it gives rise to a new praxis or discipleship, realized concretely in Christian community.

The era of *divinely revealed* dogmas as interpretations of the biblical narrative closes with the apostolic era. Correlative to the distinction between inspiration and illumination, the extraordinary ministry of the prophets and apostles is not in effect but has been succeeded by the ordinary ministry of pastors, teachers, and evangelists, as well as elders and deacons, and by the general sharing of gifts in the body of Christ. Christ's prophetic, priestly, and ruling ministry continues in the world today through his magisterial canon and the ministerial interpretations of the church's local and broader assemblies.

A constitution can be undermined as easily by undervaluing as by overvaluing the authority of the courts that it establishes for its interpretation. Like judicial precedents, tradition may err, but to dispense with its counsel is simply to shift the interpretive authority from the community to the private individual. We would find ourselves in a situation similar to the era between Joshua's death and the rise of the monarchy, when everyone did "what was right in his own eyes" (Jdg 17:6; 21:25), or in the condition of scattered sheep without a shepherd, the condition lamented in Jeremiah 23. The New Testament repeatedly calls us to submit to the magisterial authority of Scripture alone, guided by the ministerial authority of our pastors and elders. Nowhere in the New Testament is the authority for settling disagreements left to individual believers.

The church has no independent authority to create dogmas, but it does have a dependent and authorized role under Christ to arrive at Spirit-led decisions that serve the whole body. Since such teachings of the church (dogmas) are considered the teachings of *Scripture* (doctrines), they are binding; yet since the church in this present age remains simultaneously sinful and justified, they are always open to correction from the Word of God.[86]

Like the Jerusalem Council, where the apostles and elders together deliberated on the proper interpretation of God's Word, churches today — in their local and wider assemblies — have an obligation to confess the same faith together. Natural scientists formulate theories on the basis of their investigations of nature by drawing together various conclusions that are either explicitly or implicitly required from their data. Similarly, the church formulates its dogmas on the basis of Scripture, even if the formulas themselves are not expressed in Scripture directly. As Berkhof observes,

> The church does not find her dogmas in finished form on the pages of Holy Writ but obtains them by reflecting on the truths revealed in the Word of God. The Christian consciousness not only appropriates the truth but also feels an irrepressible urge to reproduce it and see it in its grand unity. While the intellect gives guidance and reflection, it is not purely an intellectual activity but one that is moral and emotional as well.[87]

---

86. Louis Berkhof nicely states this position: "There are no dogmas as such in the Bible, though the doctrinal teachings which they embody are found there. But these become dogmas only when they are formulated and officially adopted by the church. It may be said that religious dogmas have three charac-

teristics, namely, their subject matter is derived from Scripture; they are the fruit of the reflection of the church on the truth, as it is revealed in the Bible; and they are officially adopted by some competent ecclesiastical body" (*Systematic Theology*, 21).

87. Ibid., 23.

It is to be done by Christians "only in communion and in cooperation with all the saints. When the church, led by the Holy Spirit, reflects on the truth, this takes a definite shape in her consciousness and gradually crystallizes into clearly defined doctrinal views and utterances."[88] The church joins its fallible witness to the infallible witness of the prophets and apostles. Thus, for the definition of dogmas, "It is generally agreed that an official action of the church is necessary."[89] Christ gave pastors and teachers as gifts to the church, "so that we may no longer be children, tossed to and fro by the waves and carried about by every wind of doctrine" (Eph 4:14).

Heretics arise within the church, quoting Scripture in the solemn persuasion that they are properly interpreting it. Often, they reject church dogmas on the basis that those doctrines are not found directly and explicitly formulated in Scripture—and often employ extrabiblical terminology. However, every science seeks to interpret the whole in the light of its parts and vice versa and, especially in the face of challenges to a particular teaching, draws on precise terminology in order to more clearly state its faith and more sharply distinguish it from error. The *Westminster Confession* (1.6) points out that everything necessary for doctrine and life "is either expressly set down in Scripture, *or by good and necessary consequences may be deduced from Scripture*" (emphasis added). The Bible does not use terms like *essence* and *persons* (or even "trinity") to formulate its teaching on the Trinity, but the formula, "one in essence and three in persons," is an obvious example of a good and necessary consequence deduced from Scripture. The *Confession* (1.7) adds that although everything necessary for salvation may be understood by the unlearned as well as the learned, "All things in Scripture are not alike plain in themselves, nor alike clear unto all." Therefore, through the ministry of pastors and elders, Christ's body is built up, "until we all attain to the unity of the faith and of the knowledge of the Son of God," with Christ as the head and each part working properly (Eph 4:12–13, 15–16).

This affirmation of the church's ministerial authority is consistent with Christ's commission to the church to "make disciples of all nations, baptizing them in the name of the Father and of the Son and of the Holy Spirit, *teaching them to observe all that I have commanded you*" (Mt 28:19–20, emphasis added). The apostle Paul calls us to be "of the same mind, having the same love, being in full accord and of one mind" (Php 2:2). In fact, he exhorted Timothy to "follow the pattern of the sound words" that he had taught him (2Ti 1:13). Peter calls the church to "have unity of mind" (1Pe 3:8). In the Christian life as in any discipline, including the physical sciences, tradition is as valuable as it is inescapable; yet it must be always open to revision in the light of its source.

In church history, some dogmatic formulations have risen to the level of dogmas (namely, the Trinity, the two natures of Christ in one person, etc.), but they are never

---

88. Ibid.   89. Ibid., 24.

the work of any single theologian. They are the cumulative fruit of communal reflection and win the consent of the body of Christ. These different categories must be carefully distinguished. Some formulations of dogmas attain such credibility within a tradition that they are not—and should not be—easily challenged. Again, this is analogous to the natural sciences, where a widely approved paradigm is defended even when faced with unexplained anomalies. A paradigm only collapses when it becomes so overwhelmed by anomalies that it no longer is seen to account for the widest amount of data.[90] The Reformation may be seen as one such paradigm shift in the history of the church. Even so, the Reformers did not start over from scratch but incorporated their insights into the broader paradigm of catholic Christianity.

However, even the writings of a list of weighty theologians cannot be made confessionally binding. It is significant that Lutherans do not regard Luther's writings as ministerially binding. Lutherans subscribe to his *Small Catechism* and *Large Catechism* only because they were judged by a church body to reflect its consensus regarding scriptural teaching. None of Calvin's writings are included in the confessions and catechisms of Reformed and Presbyterian churches.[91] From a confessional perspective, whatever our churches do not publicly and corporately confess in our doctrinal standards cannot be required for subscription. Hardly legalistic, confessional subscription frees the Christian conscience on a host of issues, such as specific details of end-times eschatology, political agendas, distinctives of personal piety not addressed in Scripture, and many other issues that tend to divide churches in our day.

This course charted by the magisterial Reformation upholds the church's teaching ministry under the sovereign authority of Scripture. The seventeenth-century theologian Francis Turretin pointed out that while Rome fails this test by addition (making assent to all church teaching necessary for salvation), Arminians and especially Socinians fail the test by subtraction. For them, only those dogmas that are considered practically necessary for morality and religious experience are reckoned among the essentials.[92] Eventually, this subjective criterion led Schleiermacher to consider the dogma of the Trinity at best unimportant.

Ironically, as Berkhof notes, "the so-called fundamentalists of our day join hands with the liberals on this point with their well-known slogan, 'No Creed but the Bible.'"[93] If liberalism challenged creedal and confessional Christianity in the name of reason, *biblicism* rejects the legitimate authority of the church in drawing from Scripture "good and necessary consequences," assuming that its doctrines are

---

90. Michael Polanyi points out similar comparisons in *Personal Knowledge* (Chicago: Univ. of Chicago Press, 1958), 20. See also Thomas Kuhn, *The Structure of Scientific Revolutions* (Chicago: Univ. of Chicago Press, 1996).

91. Ironically, evangelical churches that do not subscribe to particular creeds and confessions are often more defined by the particular beliefs and writings of their leaders. For example, the doctrinal standards of Methodism include John Wesley's revision of the Thirty-nine Articles and his sermons.

92. Turretin, *Elenctic Theology*, 1:48.

93. Berkhof, *Systematic Theology*, 32.

taken directly from the words of the Bible. However, many of the fundamentals that it wishes to protect have been formulated by church courts by deducing necessary conclusions. When we lose our regard for the ministerial authority of the church to teach and confess the truths of God's Word, it is usually not long before we come to question the magisterial authority itself. The *Westminster Confession* nicely summarizes this conception of ecclesiastical authority:

> For the better government, and further edification of the church, there ought to be such assemblies as are commonly called synods or councils: and it belongeth to the overseers and other rulers of the particular churches, by virtue of their office, and the power which Christ hath given them for edification and not for destruction, to appoint assemblies; and to convene together in them, as often as they shall judge it expedient for the good of the church. It belongeth to synods and councils, ministerially to determine controversies of faith, and cases of conscience; to set down rules and directions for the better ordering of the public worship of God, and government of his church; to receive complaints in cases of maladministration, and authoritatively to determine the same: which decrees and determinations, if consonant to the Word of God, are to be received with reverence and submission; not only for their agreement with the Word, but also for the power whereby they are made, as being an ordinance of God appointed thereunto in his Word.[94]

The *Westminster Confession* adds the important caveat that such synods or councils "may err; and many have erred. Therefore they are not to be made the rule of faith, or practice; but to be used as a help in both." They are "to conclude nothing, but that which is ecclesiastical: and are not to intermeddle with civil affairs which concern the commonwealth, unless by way of humble petition in cases extraordinary."[95]

2. CREEDS AND CONFESSIONS

From the Latin *credo* ("I believe"), a creed is simply a summary of the church's faith. Sometimes *faith* is used in Scripture to refer to *the* faith that is believed (*fides quae creditur*, 1Co 16:13; 2Co 13:5; Eph 4:5, 13; Col 1:23; 2:7; 1Ti 4:1; 6:12; 2Ti 3:8; 4:7; 2Pe 1:1; Jude 3), while elsewhere it refers to the personal act of believing—the faith by which we believe (*fides qua creditur*). In its essence, faith is not a subjective experience or decision but a knowledgeable assent to and belief in Jesus Christ as he gives himself to us in the gospel.

As an apostle preparing for the post-apostolic era with the ordinary ministry of the Word, Paul commands Timothy to censure anyone who "teaches a different doctrine and does not agree with the sound words of our Lord Jesus Christ and

---

94. *The Westminster Confession of Faith*, ch. 31, in *The Trinity Hymnal* (Philadelphia: Great Commission Publications, 1990), 866–67.

95. *Westminster Confession*, ch 31.

the teaching that accords with godliness" (1Ti 6:3). Elders "must hold firm to the trustworthy word as taught, so that [they] may be able to give instruction in sound doctrine and also to rebuke those who contradict it" (Tit 1:9). "But as for you," Paul instructs Titus, "teach what accords with sound doctrine" (Tit 2:1). In fact, he tells Timothy, "Follow *the pattern of the sound words* that you have heard from me, in the faith and love that are in Christ Jesus. By the Holy Spirit who dwells within us, guard the good deposit entrusted to you" (2Ti 1:13–14, emphasis added). Not only sound words but the *pattern* of the sound words is enjoined by Paul. There is *a way of saying the faith* that is sound and that therefore guards "the good deposit entrusted to [us]."

We have seen that the apostolic generation represents the foundation-laying era of the New Testament church (1Co 3:10–11). The ordinary ministers like Timothy are to build on this foundation, to guard it, and to defend it. "Fight the good fight of the faith. Take hold of the eternal life . . . about which you made the good confession in the presence of many witnesses," Paul instructs Timothy (1Ti 6:12). Instead of exhorting his understudy to add to the deposit of apostolic truth, Paul urges him, "O Timothy, guard the deposit entrusted to you" (1Ti 6:20; cf. 2Ti 1:14). The apostles did not pass on their office to successors, but they did entrust the treasure to the office of the ordinary ministry. To borrow an illustration from U.S. history, the founders of the republic who achieved independence and drafted the Constitution are qualitatively distinct even from the greatest presidents who followed. Abraham Lincoln and John F. Kennedy occupy cherished positions, but as the first among equals who swear allegiance to the Constitution. They cannot add to or take away a single word from the Constitution, and their interpretations are subservient to the text and to the secondary (interpretive) ruling of the courts. Of course, the distinction between apostles and ministers is even more emphatic when we are talking about a divinely inspired constitution.

There is evidence that Paul himself was simply passing on (and lending his apostolic authority to) summaries that functioned as creedal formulas in the ancient church: "I delivered to you as of first importance what I also received: that Christ died for our sins in accordance with the Scriptures, that he was buried, that he was raised on the third day in accordance with the Scriptures" (1Co 15:3–4). In recalling the Corinthians to the proper celebration of the Lord's Supper, he declares, "I received from the Lord what I also delivered to you" (1Co 11:23). He also includes various "trustworthy sayings": "The saying is trustworthy and deserving of full acceptance, that Christ Jesus came into the world to save sinners" (1Ti 1:15; cf. 2Ti 2:11). The church is "a pillar and buttress of the truth," says the apostle, adding, "Great indeed, we confess, is the mystery of godliness: He was manifested in the flesh, vindicated by the Spirit, seen by angels, proclaimed among the nations, believed on in the world, taken up in glory" (1Ti 3:15–16).

Fragments of such early creedal summaries are found not only in the body of the apostolic letters but in their liturgical expressions found in the opening salutations and closing benedictions. Evidently, some of these creedal summaries were sung, and Paul incorporates them, for example, in praise of Christ's supremacy in Colossians 1:15–20 and in his summary of Christ's humiliation and exaltation in Philippians 2:6–11. It is no wonder, then, that Paul regarded singing as a means not only of thanking God but of making "the word of Christ dwell in [us] richly, teaching and admonishing one another in all wisdom" through such psalms and hymns (Col 3:16).

Of course, creedal formulas in the canon have normative status and magisterial authority, but postapostolic creeds possess a ministerial authority as consensual summaries of Scripture's central teachings. As the church grew not only numerically but geographically, its center of gravity shifted from the Jewish to the Gentile world. As Paul's own ministry demonstrates, mission always provokes conflict, even within the church. Getting the gospel *right* was as important as getting the gospel *out*. The church had to not only define its positions more carefully vis-à-vis these heresies; it had to formulate them in such a way that although they remained mysteries, they were not logical contradictions.

In all of these cases, the church's motivation was mission. How do we confess Christ in the light of the impressive challenges inside and outside of the church? Faithfulness to the message and the mission of Christ on the basis of his Word and in dependence on his Spirit led the postapostolic church to develop more refined creedal statements. The results of this era were the Nicene Creed (technically known as the Nicene-Constantinopolitan Creed, focusing on the dogma of the Trinity); the Chalcedonian Definition (concentrating on the person of Christ); and the Athanasian Creed (summarizing the catholic faith). Despite continued eruptions of discord through the centuries and widespread criticism in the modern era, these conclusions reached in the first five centuries created a consensus that has remained the touchstone of Christian confession to the present day.

It was precisely because of the enormous vitality and richness of its fresh encounter with Scripture (especially its translation from the original languages into the vernacular of the people) that the Reformation produced confessions and catechisms for building up the body of Christ in its common faith and practice. Far from proposing an alternative to either the Bible or the ecumenical creeds, the Reformers saw their confessions and catechisms as ways of reviving the significance of the Bible and the creeds in the life of the church. In fact, it was the renewal of catechetical instruction in the Reformation that provoked this practice in Roman Catholic circles. In the preface to his *Small Catechism*, Luther explains that he was motivated by a profound disappointment with the ignorance of most Christians he encountered even of the most basic elements of the Bible. He lamented that few even knew the Apostles' Creed, the Lord's Prayer, or the Ten Commandments. Confessions and catechisms are not academic treatises but expressions of the priesthood of all believers: the witness of the whole church to the whole world.

We do not believe the Bible's teachings *because* of the church's authority, but we do believe them *through* the church and its ministry. Children and theologians alike take their place under the magisterial norm of Scripture and its communal interpretation by the ministerial guidance of the church. Theological reflection must be aware of related disciplines, especially languages, philosophy, and history, but its primary calling is to the church rather than to the academy. Theologians find their proper place as servants of ministers of the Word and sacraments. This then is the proper order: (1) the Scriptures as the infallible canon, qualitatively distinct from all other sources and authorities; (2) under this magisterial norm, the ministerial service of creeds and confessions; (3) contemporary proclamation of God's Word in the church around the world; (4) long-standing interpretations in the tradition; (5) the particular nuances of individual theologians.

Conceived by the Spirit through Word and baptism, born in faith, sustained by Communion, and nurtured through prayer, fellowship, and discipleship, the church and every member of it always need theology because they always need God.

DISCUSSION QUESTIONS

1. Compare and contrast Roman Catholic and Reformation interpretations of the relationship between Scripture and tradition. What is the most critical question that distinguishes these positions?
2. What is the difference between magisterial and ministerial authority?
3. Describe and evaluate the "Wesleyan Quadrilateral" and Paul Tillich's "method of correlation."
4. Identify and evaluate George Lindbeck's "models of doctrine."
5. How would you describe a covenantal model of doctrine, especially in its relationship of individual and communal interpretation, as well as of the biblical canon and official church teaching?

COMPARATIVE CHART FOR PART 1

	Overcoming Estrangement	The Stranger We Never Meet	Meeting a Stranger
Ontology	"God" is the ultimate reality, of which our inmost self is a part, although estranged from its divine origin. Pantheism/panentheism. Divine immanence without transcendence.	"God" is the projection of the felt needs of the self. The finite particulars are the real; it is the "universal" that is a mere appearance. Deism/atheism. Divine transcendence without immanence.	Sharp Creator-creature distinction, yet also an affirmation of God's redeeming descent, assuming our flesh. Transcendence and immanence.
Epistemology	Inside-out. Recognizing eternal certainties within. Rationalism, idealism, Romanticism. Archetypal, univocal knowledge.	No distinction between inside and outside. Skepticism, pragmatism, nihilistic relativism. No transcendent signified beyond language. All knowledge is equivocal/constructed.	Outside-in. Dependent, ectypal, analogical knowledge mediated by God's Word.
Revelation	Inner experience/new awareness.	Natural or nonexistent.	Corrupted inner experience (of general revelation); external Word (of the gospel).
Scripture	Individual/communal reflection on pious experience.	Rejection of all claims that a text has ultimate authority, considering such claims violent and exclusive.	God's address and interpretation externally and objectively revealed as law and gospel through creaturely agency.
Doctrine	Theories expressing our experience.	Typically deployed as an instrument of social power and hegemony.	Truth revealed by God in Scripture, interpreted in church dogmas.

Part Two

GOD
WHO LIVES

Chapter Six

GOD: THE INCOMMUNICABLE ATTRIBUTES

We have seen that Christian orthodoxy has been wary of speculation concerning God's inner essence, focusing instead on God's characteristics as they have been revealed to us by God in his works, especially in Scripture, through the unfolding economy of the covenant of grace. One good place to begin is with the names of God. "As God's essence is hidden and incomprehensible," Calvin observes, "his name just means his character, so far as he has been pleased to make it known to us."[1]

I. Names, Narratives, and Nouns

The various cognates of the generic *El* (lordly/mighty one)[2] were in wide circulation already before the covenant at Sinai and are employed in the earliest biblical traditions the way English speakers use the words *God* and *gods*. *El* is combined with other descriptive terms to form such compounds as *El-Shaddai* (*shadad* = "powerful"), which are identified with specific acts in history. *Adonai* ("lord," "judge," "ruler") is also a common title. There are "names" and "*the* Name." It is only to Israel that God has given his personal name, *Yahweh*, which appears in our English translations in small capitals ("Lord") to distinguish it from the title *Adonai* ("Lord").[3]

---

1. Quoted in Louis Berkhof, *Systematic Theology* (Grand Rapids: Eerdmans, 1996), 47. Berkhof adds, "In the most general sense of the word, then, the name of God is his self-revelation. It is a designation of him, not as he exists in the depths of his divine Being, but as he reveals himself especially in his relations to man." These names "are anthropomorphic and mark a condescending approach of God to man."

2. *El*, *Elohim*, and *Elyon*. *El* = "lord." *Elohim* = "lordly/mighty ones"—plural of intensification.

3. Since the Hebrew texts were written before the advent of vowel points, we do not know the precise pronunciation of YHWH, although we can be certain it was not vocalized as "Jehovah" (as in the RV and ASV).

On one hand, the revelation of God's name is a sign of *transcendence*, measuring the gulf between God's majesty and the human servant. Misusing God's name required the death penalty under the old covenant (Ex 20:7; Lev 24:16). Nevertheless, this name is also a sign of God's *immanence*, having been given to his people as a pledge of his personal presence, to be invoked in danger and praised at all times.

The event in which God reveals this personal name to Moses (Ex 3) bears striking features of its covenantal context. Pharaoh is lord (suzerain) of Egypt, even an object of worship, at the time when Yahweh's children are under the heavy hand of oppression. God gives Moses his personal name to invoke as that of the covenant Lord who will liberate his people from Pharaoh's cruel suzerainty (Ex 3:4–15; 5:22–6:6). Each plague that God sends upon Egypt represents the defeat of one of the principal deities in the Egyptian pantheon. Israel's God, Yahweh, is Lord of all. The drama gives rise to the doctrine.

In sharp contrast with the names of pagan deities, therefore, God's name is not a secret password for manipulating the cosmic forces. Rather, it is a personal and covenantal guarantee. On the basis of this liberation, Israel is not to invoke any other gods or lords: "I am the LORD [Yahweh] your God, who brought you out of the land of Egypt, out of the house of slavery. You shall have no other gods before me" (Ex 20:2–3). The infinite and sovereign God over all condescends to identify himself as the God of Israel—the God of Abraham, Isaac, and Jacob. The point is frequently made that *the* Lord (*Adonai*) is *our* LORD (*Yahweh*) and vice versa.

The New Testament also shows a corresponding tendency to keep up with the unfolding plot of redemption by its names and titles for God. As with the Hebrew use of *El*, the New Testament writers had no trouble using the generic Greek word *theos* ("God")—already employed in the Greek translation of the Old Testament known as the Septuagint. And once again, the covenantal specificity of this God's identity is often expressed with a possessive genitive, expressed in English with *of*—for instance, the God of Abraham, Isaac, and Jacob; the God of Sinai; the God of Zion; the God of Israel; the God and Father of our Lord Jesus Christ; our great God and Savior, and so forth.[4] Thus, the God who is not intrinsically bound by any creaturely limit nevertheless binds himself freely to us in our times and places.

Invariably, God's self-identification with certain people, places, and things is connected with some significant event in which God acted. From these historical deeds recited especially in the narrative sections of the Old Testament and the New

---

4. Again with precedent in the Greek translation of the Old Testament (LXX), the New Testament employs *kyrios* for *Ado-* *nai*, "Lord," as a title in the covenantal relationship distinct from *Yahweh* as God's personal name.

Testament Gospels, strong verbs give rise to stable nouns.[5] This is another way of saying that the drama gives rise to particular doctrines. Not only are the people of Israel able to infer certain attributes or characteristics of their God from his mighty acts; God himself interprets these for them. Israel's lexicon of divine attributes does not come in the form of a systematic theology such as the present volume but in narrative, instruction, liturgy, and law.

The New Testament reveals a similar pattern. As the narratives generate doctrines, the doctrines give rise to doxology and are even expressed in the form of praise, as in 1 Timothy 1:17: "To the King of ages, immortal, invisible, the only God, be honor and glory forever and ever. Amen." As spirit (Jn 4:24), God is unavailable to human investigation apart from his own initiative and mediation. Further, again expressed doxologically, this God is identified as "the blessed and only Sovereign, the King of kings and Lord of lords, who alone has immortality, who dwells in unapproachable light, whom no one has ever seen or can see. To him be honor and eternal dominion. Amen" (1Ti 6:15–16). Only in such an attitude of prayer, praise, and reserved humility can we approach God's self-revelation.

God's attributes have often been distinguished as *incommunicable* and *communicable*, so called to distinguish those attributes that belong to God alone and those that may be predicated of God and humans (though only analogically; see pt. 1, ch. 1, "God's Condescending Greatness," p. 000). Consequently, the incommunicable attributes are especially identified by the way of negation (*via negationis*), by stating some of the respects in which God is *not* like us. Characteristically, these attributes are recognized by the alpha privative in Greek (the initial *a* of words such as *apatheia*, non-suffering) or a similarly negating prefix in Latin, which is taken over into English (for example, *immortal, invisible, immutable*).

The communicable attributes are typically identified by the way of eminence (*via eminentiae*), by highlighting attributes in which creatures share analogically but in a qualitatively inferior manner, often identified by the "omni-" prefix (for example, *omnipotent, omniscient*). While both of these ways are evident, implicitly and explicitly, in Scripture, in each case it is God who selects the appropriate analogies. Therefore, we must resist the temptation to deduce God's being from speculative arguments concerning a perfect being, either by negation or by comparison. Refusing to be an idolatrous projection of our own ideas of perfection, God infinitely transcends all comparisons (Isa 40:18–31). Nevertheless, out of love for his creatures, God condescends to our finite capacity by selecting analogies that are appropriate but nevertheless fall short of his majesty.

---

5. Walter Brueggemann, *Theology of the Old Testament: Testimony, Dispute, Advocacy* (Minneapolis: Fortress, 1997), 145–266.

II. INCOMMUNICABLE ATTRIBUTES

ATTRIBUTE	DESCRIPTION
Simplicity	As infinite spirit, God is not made up of different parts; his attributes are identical with his being
Aseity	Self-existence
Immutability	Unchangeableness
Impassibility	Incapacity for being overwhelmed by suffering
Eternity	God's transcendence of time

As we will see, it is these attributes of the way of negation that are most frequently challenged as a supposedly later corruption of biblical theology by pagan (Greek) metaphysics. However, it is not only later theologians but the apostle Paul as well who use the alpha-privative prefix, referring to God, for example, as immortal (*aphthartos*) and invisible (*aoratos*) (1Ti 1:17; cf. 6:15–16).

The seventeenth-century Genevan theologian Francis Turretin pointed out that the Socinians reproached the traditional doctrine of God on the basis that "the whole doctrine is metaphysical" (i.e., philosophical) rather than biblical.[6] Specifically, they charged that God's simplicity, aseity, immutability, and exhaustive foreknowledge originated in Stoic philosophy—a claim that has been repeated consistently down to our own day. In the same vein, Albrecht Ritschl attempted to eliminate all "metaphysical" ideas from Christian theology. The late nineteenth-century historical theologian Adolf von Harnack advanced his thesis that nearly everything we regard as Christian "orthodoxy"—"the Catholic element"—is in fact the result of "the acute Hellenization of the church."[7] Yet in all of these cases, it was not the elimination of metaphysical claims (an impossible goal in theology), but merely the exchange of one metaphysical system (Christian Platonism) for another (Hegelianism) that liberal theology achieved.

More recently, these criticisms have been repeated under the guise of a post-modern rebellion against *onto-theology* (literally, "being-theology" or "a theology of being").[8] Although contemporary critics often represent their accounts as post-

---

6. Turretin, *Elenctic Theology*, 1:191.

7. Adolph von Harnack, *History of Dogma* (Boston: Little, Brown, 1902), 1:48. This Arian polemic has been employed since the ancient church debates. See Jaroslav Pelikan, *The Emergence of the Catholic Tradition (100-600)* (vol. 1 of *The Christian Tradition: A History of the Development of Doctrine*; Chicago: Univ. of Chicago Press, 1971), 194–98.

8. First coined by Immanuel Kant, *onto-theology* became a broader shibboleth for metaphysics in general in the writings of Martin Heidegger. According to Kant, "transcendental theology" takes two forms with respect to identifying a Supreme Being: *cosmo-theology*, which is an attempt "to deduce the existence of the original being from an experience in general (without determining in any more specific fashion

modern, both the divine attributes that they reject and their arguments are often indistinguishable from those found in the work of nineteenth-century German liberalism and the Hegelian ("Mediating") school.

While encouraging us to take the postmodern critiques to heart, Merold Westphal correctly warns us against the tendency in current discourse to "identify the God of onto-theology simply as 'the omnipotent, omniscient and benevolent God'" who is in fact revealed in Scripture.[9] Even in evangelical theological circles today, it is simply assumed by many that the so-called incommunicable attributes for so long adduced by classical theism are suspect simply because of their philosophical associations and terminology. But this is a shortcut. After all, "the primary motivations for attributing omniscience, including foreknowledge, to God are biblical rather than philosophical, even if the vocabulary in which the matter gets discussed is, for better or worse, often Hellenic."[10]

On all of these historical fronts, the facile identification of orthodoxy with Greek philosophy has been unraveling in current scholarship.[11] Nevertheless, it has been rejuvenated, at least in evangelical theology, by Clark Pinnock and other advocates of open theism. In a chapter in *Most Moved Mover* titled "Overcoming a Pagan Influence," Pinnock dismisses the doctrine of God as formulated by ancient Christian theology all the way to current orthodoxy as hopelessly trapped in Greek

---

the nature of the world to which the experience belongs)" and *onto-theology*, which endeavors "to know the existence of such a being through mere concepts, without the help of any experience whatsoever" (*Critique of Pure Reason* [trans. Norman Kemp Smith; New York: St. Martin's, 1965], 525). For Heidegger (especially in *The End of Metaphysics* and *Identity and Difference*), onto-theology represents the age-old attempt to wed philosophy and theology, doing justice to neither by turning philosophy into an apologetic for God's existence and turning theology into a speculative enterprise that no longer relies on revelation. The result is a "god" to whom one cannot even pray. Heidegger properly saw that this onto-theological impulse (rationalistic theology) lies behind the modern desire for mastery through archetypal knowledge. Emmanuel Levinas, Jacques Derrida, and other postmodern thinkers continued and deepened Heidegger's critique of onto-theology. Basically, within this whole history of use, onto-theology represents the "overcoming estrangement" paradigm. The danger, however, lies in the naïve assumption that theology (and anti-theology or atheism) can escape metaphysical claims. Like Harnack's thesis, the onto-theology shibboleth may be used to mask a pietistic suspicion against definite doctrinal claims and refinements. We can avoid onto-theology *and* metaphysical agnosticism by recognizing that only ectypal, not archetypal, knowledge is available to us and that this comes from God in an accommodated and analogical form. A theology for pilgrims, not masters, is the goal of sound theology.

9. Merold Westphal, *Overcoming Onto-Theology* (New York: Fordham Univ. Press, 2001), 5.

10. Ibid.

11. On the biblical-theological side, James Barr led the way to its demise, and subsequent research has raised serious questions about its viability in relation to "Jesus(Hebrew) versus Paul (Greek)" and "the Reformers versus the Protestant scholastics." See James Barr, "The Old Testament and the New Crisis of Biblical Authority," *Interpretation* 26, no.1 (January 1971): 24–40; cf. Barr, *The Semantics of Biblical Language* (Oxford: Oxford Univ. Press, 1961); *Biblical Words for Time* (London: SCM, 1962). Against the application of the Harnack thesis to the so-called Jesus-versus-Paul antithesis, see Troels Engberg-Pedersen, ed., *Paul beyond the Judaism/Hellenism Divide* (Louisville: Westminster John Knox, 2001). For the criticism of the "Luther/Calvin versus Lutheranism/Calvinism" version, see Richard Muller, "Calvin and the 'Calvinists': Assessing Continuities and Discontinuities between the Reformation and Orthodoxy: Part 1," *CTJ* 30 (1995): 345–75; "Part 2," *CTJ* 31 (1996): 125–60; cf. Robert Preus, *The Theology of Post-Reformation Lutheranism* (2 vols.; St. Louis: Concordia, 1970–1972). Articles and monographs by Willem van Asselt, David Steinmetz, Susan Schreiner, Irena Backus, Robert Kolb, R. S. Clark, and Carl Trueman, among others, have contributed significantly to this field.

thought.[12] This does not keep Pinnock, any more than Harnack, from reading Scripture through the lens of modern thought, especially Hegel, in addition to Teilhard de Chardin and Alfred North Whitehead, a debt that Pinnock readily acknowledges.[13] In fact, he suggests that "modern culture ... is closer to the biblical view than classical theism."[14] With these challenges in mind, we take up the attributes in question.

A. SIMPLICITY (UNITY)

As human beings, we are complex and compound creatures. That is, we are made up of various parts. However, God is simple and spiritual. On the one hand, this means that God is not the sum total of his attributes but is simultaneously everything that all of the attributes reveal. On the other hand, each of these attributes identifies a different aspect of God's existence and character that cannot be reduced to the others. This latter point is especially important, given the tendency of recent critiques to identify this doctrine with an extreme view that denies any real difference between attributes.[15]

One implication is that we cannot rank God's attributes or make one more essential to God than another. God is love even when he judges; he is holy and righteous even in saving sinners; he is eternal even when he acts in time.

We may recall the distinction between God's essence and God's energies. The sun is one substance with many and various rays. In Basil's expression, "The energies are various, and the essence simple, but we say that we know our God from his energies, but do not undertake to approach near to his essence. His energies come down to us, but his essence remains beyond our reach."[16] God's simplicity in no way

---

12. Clark Pinnock, *Most Moved Mover* (Grand Rapids: Baker, 2001). First, Pinnock does not seem to grant that in the Hellenistic world are many mansions—not only Parmenidean stasis but Heracleitean flux. To reduce Hellenism to the Stoics and Plato is to ignore the fact that even Hegel and others appealed to important streams of Greek thought (especially Plato, Plotinus, and Aristotle). Reductionism is a glaring weakness of many aspects of the open theism proposal. Second, the early Reformed tradition has usually related to the classical theological tradition in a sympathetically critical manner, suspicious of the Stoicism of Justin Martyr and Origen, the Neoplatonism of Augustine, the Aristotelianism (alleged and real) of Aquinas, late medieval nominalism, and the rise of rationalism evident in Socinianism. This suspicion has been just beneath the surface throughout the movement's career, as is evident in the works not only of the scholastics but of their British and Continental heirs. C. Van Til, for example, in *A Christian Theory of Knowledge* (Phillipsburg, N.J.: P&R, 1969), 118–19, is sharply critical of Justin Martyr, Clement of Alexandria, Origen, and Augustine. He is able to show that while Augustine was "in some measure subject to the principles

of Platonism and particularly neo-Platonism," his writings display an irreducibly biblical interest. So Van Til can critique Augustine's philosophical framework while affirming the major thrust of his work as a distinctively Christian project. Cf. Clark Pinnock, "Theological Method," in *New Dimensions in Evangelical Thought: Essays in Honor of Millard J. Erickson* (ed. David S. Dockery; Downers Grove, Ill.: InterVarsity Press, 1998), 197–208.

13. Pinnock, *Most Moved Mover*, 142; cf. John Sanders, *The God Who Risks* (Downers Grove, Ill.: InterVarsity Press, 1998).

14. Clark Pinnock, "From Augustine to Arminius: A Pilgrimage in Theology," in *The Grace of God, the Will of Man* (ed. Clark Pinnock; Grand Rapids: Zondervan, 1989), 24.

15. For helpful clarifications of simplicity in Christian use, see Andrew Radde-Gallwitz, *Basil of Caesarea, Gregory of Nyssa, and Transformation of Divine Simplicity* (Oxford: Oxford Univ. Press, 2002); Stephen R. Holmes, "Something Much Too Plain to Say," *Neue Zeitschrift für systematische Theologie und Religionsphilosophie* 43 (2001): 137–54; cf. Richard Muller, *PRRD*, 3:38–67, 70–76.

16. Basil, "Epistle 234," *NPNF2*, 8:274.

limits the diversity evident in his works, but stipulates that in all of God's activity he is self-consistent. In every act, God is the being that he is and will ever be.

"Humanity" exists, and then there are particular attributes of this nature that I as an individual may or may not possess. However, God is different. There is no genus of "deity" of which the God of Abraham, Isaac, and Jacob is a species. Although we cannot help but talk about his immutability, then his goodness, then his love, we should not imagine that God is composed of these various attributes. Rather, God's existence is identical with his attributes. "For all the divine attributes, whether named or conceived, are of like rank one with another," notes Gregory of Nyssa.[17] God's goodness, love, omniscience, and holiness are simply who God is.[18] I would still be human even if I lacked judgment or enterprise, but God would not be God if he did not possess all of his attributes in the simplicity and perfection of his essence.[19]

Thus, whatever God gives is given out of abundance rather than lack. "It is not that God first lives and then also loves," notes Barth. "But God loves, and in this act lives."[20] This is true of all of God's attributes. Simplicity reminds us that God is never self-conflicted. In God's eternal decree, even in the most obvious example of possible inner conflict (namely, the cross), justice and mercy, righteous wrath and gracious love, embrace. Just where we would expect to see the greatest inner conflict within God, we read that "in Christ God was reconciling the world to himself" (2Co 5:19). At the place where the outpouring of his wrath is concentrated, so too is his love. Neither overwhelms or cancels out the other. God is "*just and the justifier* of the one who has faith in Jesus" (Ro 3:26, emphasis added). At the same time, simplicity does not (in the Reformed view, at least) eliminate the difference between attributes. Love, justice, goodness, and other attributes are not mere synonyms but are "conceptually different in God himself."[21]

We do not worship any divine attribute; we worship the personal God who is simultaneously the being that his attributes indicate. God is love, but love is not God. Nor does the doctrine of simplicity allow us to speak of God "limiting himself," as Arminian theology has held and various forms of Hegelian kenosis have emphasized.[22] Nor is God sovereign without also being at the same time good,

---

17. Gregory of Nyssa, "On the Holy Trinity and of the Godhead of the Holy Spirit, To Eustathius," *NPNF2*, 5:327 (PG 32, col. 689).

18. Turretin, *Elenctic Theology*, 1:187: "Attributes are not ascribed to God properly as something superadded to his essence (something accidental to the subject), making it perfect and really distinct from himself; but improperly and transumptively inasmuch as they indicate perfections essential to the divine nature conceived by us as properties." These attributes "can represent it [God's nature] only inadequately (i.e., not

according to its total relation, but now under this perfection, then under another)."

19. See Muller, *PRRD*, 3:281.

20. Barth, *Church Dogmatics*, vol. 2, pt. 1, 321.

21. Muller, *PRRD*, 3:292.

22. See John Cobb Jr. and Clark Pinnock, eds., *Searching for an Adequate God: A Dialogue between Process and Free Will Theists* (Grand Rapids: Eerdmans, 2000).

just, and loving. God is never free to be not-God. None of his attributes can be suspended, withdrawn, diminished, or altered, since his attributes are identical with his existence.

The denial of this attribute is often motivated by a broader criticism of God's immutability, impassibility, and eternity, as we will see.[23] It is not surprising that some critics of simplicity go on to deny God's spirituality. There is but a short step from the denial of at least this minimal affirmation of simplicity to the denial of God's infinity (i.e., divine transcendence).[24]

B. SELF-EXISTENCE (ASEITY)

Before we speak of God relating freely to creatures and entering into human history as Lord and Redeemer, our starting point is God's *aseity* ("from-himself-ness"), or independence from the world. It goes without saying that a dependent deity would be involved with the world. What is remarkable is that the triune God— self-existing, perfect, and independent—would nevertheless create and enter into covenantal relationships with creatures in freedom and love.

Karl Barth properly stressed the point that the God who is God without us has nevertheless determined to be God with us. Freedom *from* creation is the ground of God's freedom *for* creation.[25] Classical Christian theology has affirmed that God is *a-se*, which basically means independent of all external dependence. A similar term is *absolute*—literally, "without relation." This does not mean that God is incapable of relationship; it simply affirms that God relates creatures to himself but is not related to (i.e., dependent on) the world.

Clearly, the relationship between God and his creation is qualitatively different from any other. We naturally depend on others. Friendship exposes us to the joys and disappointments of life, and each day goes well or poorly in large measure because of what other people say, will, do, or feel in relation to us. Yet the psalmist exults, "Our God is in the heavens; he does all that he pleases" (Ps 115:3). We are told in Isaiah 40:

> The grass withers, the flower fades,
> but the word of our God will stand forever....

---

23. One of many instances of a denial of simplicity is that of Robert Jenson, *Systematic Theology* (New York: Oxford Univ. Press, 1997), 1:169; cf. George Hunsinger's critique in "Robert Jenson's *Systematic Theology*: A Review Essay," *SJT* 55, no. 2 (2002): 189–90.

24. In his passing reference to the being of God in the *Institutes*, John Calvin says, "The scriptural teaching concerning God's infinite and spiritual essence ought to be enough, not only to banish popular delusions, but also to refute the subtle-

ties of secular philosophy" (1.13.1). The latter would include, he says, Seneca's view of divinity as "poured out into the various parts of the world" (which anticipated Spinoza's pantheistic "substance"). "But even if God to keep us sober speaks sparingly of his essence, yet by those ... titles that I have used he both banishes stupid imaginings and restrains the boldness of the human mind" (1.13.1).

25. Barth, *Church Dogmatics*, vol. 2, pt. 1, 310.

Behold, the nations are like a drop from a bucket,
   and are accounted as the dust on the scales....
All the nations are as nothing before him,
   they are accounted by him as less than nothing and emptiness.
To whom then will you liken God,
   or what likeness compare with him? (Isa 40:8, 15, 17–18)

This question, "To whom then will you compare me, that I should be like him?" is repeated in verse 25 (by the way, again in 46:5), contrasting God's sovereignty, eternity, and unfathomable understanding with human weakness (vv. 26–31). No one can thwart God's ultimate designs (Da 4:34–37).

"Life" is predicated properly of God; only analogically can we say that God lives and we live. In other words, there is no such thing as *life* that can be predicated of God and humans univocally. God *is* life; he *gives* us life. God transcends heaven itself, which he has created (1Ki 8:27; Mt 24:35). As Paul explained to the Athenian philosophers, this is one of the attributes that highlight the contrast between God and the idols: "The God who made the world and everything in it, being Lord of heaven and earth, does not live in temples made by man, nor is he served by human hands, as though he needed anything, since he himself gives to all mankind life and breath and everything" (Ac 17:24–25). "'Or who has given a gift to him that he might be repaid?' For from him and through him and to him are all things. To him be glory forever" (Ro 11:35–36). God's independence from the world is a necessary correlate of his glory.

It is probably true, as many biblical scholars and theologians in recent decades have been eager to point out, that a primary text for God's aseity, Exodus 3:14, does not bear the weight that is placed on it.[26] "I am who I am" (from the verb "to be") may also be translated "I will be who I will be." However, the sermon that Yahweh preaches to Moses when he causes his glory to pass by suggests a connection to God's freedom: "I will be gracious to whom I will be gracious, and will show mercy on whom I will show mercy" (Ex 33:19). If this is at least a significant part of what is intended in Exodus 3:14, then God's independence from creation (aseity) is at least implied.

Walther Eichrodt observes that in Isaiah God's name becomes especially understood as referring to God's eternal and independent existence apart from the creation

---

26. Notoriously difficult to translate, this title (like the personal name *Yahweh*) is connected with the verb *hāyâ* ("to be"), which allows either "I am who I am" or "I will be who I will be." However we translate it, we must not make it say more than is intended. The traditional interpretation ever since Philo (that this personal name discloses God's immutability and aseity) is unlikely—even if such predicates can be inferred from other passages. "I am the Being" (*egō eimi ho ōn*) is the Septuagint translation of the Hebrew text, which, as a Greek expression, opened the door to some fanciful Jewish and Christian speculations on the being of God. More likely, however, this title combines God's complete freedom from the world and his freedom for it, as if to say, "Even though I do not need you, I will be there for you. I give you my name/word on it."

(e.g., Isa 40:28; 41:4; 43:10–20; 44:6; 48:12). God thereby reveals this name in the midst of demonstrating his eternal purpose and immutable nature. The Septuagint translated the phrase *egō eimi ho ōn* ("I am the Being") "to denote unalterable Being as the chief characteristic of the deity."[27] Jesus' statement in John 8:58 (cf. v 56), "Before Abraham was, I am [*egō eimi*]," adds credibility to this interpretation. Further support is found in Revelation 1:8, 17–18: "'I am the Alpha and the Omega,' says the Lord God, *who is and who was and who is to come*, the Almighty'.... 'I am the first and the last, and the living one.'" If we interpret the Old Testament (promise) in the light of the New (fulfillment), this statement is probably the best interpretation of Exodus 3:14.

Therefore, while Exodus 3:14 may not say everything that the tradition has supposed, it says a good deal more than many critics of aseity allow. Independent of the conditions of finitude appropriate to creaturely existence, Yahweh can be trusted to bring to pass everything that he has promised. His Name can be invoked with total confidence, both because he is faithful to his promise and because he is not dependent on creatures for realizing his purposes. Egypt's pantheon is the foil. In contrast to the various nature gods, limited by their specific areas of provenance, Yahweh is the Sovereign God (Dt 4:34–35). Precisely because God is not dependent on anyone or anything he has created, we are assured that nothing will keep him from being there for us.

God is no more dependent on human beings in salvation than in creation (see, e.g., Ro 9:15–16; Eph 1:5). Nothing but God's free decision is responsible for creaturely existence: "Worthy are you, our Lord and God, to receive glory and honor and power, for you created all things, and by your will they existed and were created" (Rev 4:11). One of Jesus' unmistakable references to his deity was that he, like the Father, has "life in himself" (Jn 5:26). The cosmos, the earth, and we ourselves exist for God. God does not exist for us, and even our existence is not necessary for God's existence or happiness.

Yahweh is the God who stands by his word, the one who will be faithful to his people. This is why the proclamation of the name is so closely associated with the proclamation of God's mercy and grace (Ex 33:17–20; 34:5–8). Moses responds to such proclamation with the recognition that he represents "a stiff-necked people" and that it is only because God is merciful and will "pardon our iniquity and our sin, and take us for your inheritance" that his presence can be regarded as a blessing rather than a curse (34:9). It is not claiming too much, therefore, to suggest that the gospel itself is embedded in the very name of Israel's God. The fact that God is incomparable and transcends the world—whose inhabitants are to him "like

---

27. Walther Eichrodt, *Theology of the Old Testament* (trans. J. A. Baker; Philadelphia: Westminster, 1951), 1:192.

grasshoppers" and whose "rulers of the earth [he makes] as emptiness"—brings delight to the weak: "He gives power to the faint, and to him who has no might he increases strength" (Isa 40:22–23, 29). Evil powers never have the last word, because although God enters into the matrix of creaturely powers, he is never simply one player among others. God remains qualitatively and not just quantitatively distinct from creation—and this is good news for those to whom the future seems destined to be controlled by oppressors.

We have seen that in the paradigm of "overcoming estrangement," God and the world are mutually (if asymmetrically) dependent. The world does not exist as a free choice and act of God but as the necessary emanation or aspect of his being, according to Platonism, Neoplatonism, Hegelian idealism, and process thought. According to the last two versions, the world needs God for its existence, but God also needs the world for the realization of his existence, happiness, and perfection: God's being is in becoming. However, God's aseity marks the chasm between biblical faith and pantheism/panentheism. At the same time, God's free decision to become the lead character in his own historical drama with creation marks the chasm between biblical faith and deism.

In Paul's Mars Hill speech, Paul points out that "in [God] we live and move and have our being" rather than vice versa (Ac 17:28). There is relatedness, but it is that of the world to God rather than of God to the world. Even in the incarnation, the eternal Son assumed our humanity rather than vice versa. It is precisely in God's independence and freedom from contingency that a habitable space is opened for the freedom of contingent reality. If the world is not God's body, it is nevertheless God's house. Yet it is a place for us to have fellowship with him rather than a temple that he needs or that can contain him (Ac 17:24–26).

Consequently, the extravagant variety in creation is an expression of God's lavish generosity. For example, think of the variety of colors in creation—and not only of colors but of shades. God could just as easily have created a simpler, more spartan and economical world, but he preferred to create a theater of abundance, beauty, and difference—sheer extravagance and liberality. There is no room in this view for fatalism. Our world is the result of God's freedom, not necessity.

Herman Bavinck notes that this "unbounded, limitless, absolutely undetermined, unqualified" view of God is irreconcilable with pantheism ancient and modern: "Babylonian, Hellenistic, Neo-platonist, kabbalistic and Spinozistic."[28] He adds, "Possessing every virtue in an absolute degree, perfectly, God's infinitude is qualitative, not quantitative; intensive and extensive; positive, not negative."[29] That

---

28. Herman Bavinck, *The Doctrine of God* (trans. William Hendriksen; Grand Rapids: Baker, 1977), 152.

29. Ibid. Karl Barth makes a similar point (perhaps in dependence on Bavinck) in *Church Dogmatics*, vol. 2, pt. 1, 263, 306.

last point—"positive, not negative"—is especially pertinent, since it affirms that although we use a negative predicate (in-finite), it is only to affirm a positive fullness and completeness of being. God's aseity is the infinite perfection of his greatness: "Great is the LORD, and greatly to be praised, and his greatness is unsearchable" (Ps 145:3).

The recurring charge against this traditional doctrine of God is that it is corrupted by Greek Stoicism, with God identified as the ideal Stoic sage (independent, self-sufficient, apathetic, and therefore untroubled). Many of the recent criticisms of traditional constructions have sought to recover the dramatic historical sense that one finds in the biblical text. However, we must beware of the temptation to quit ourselves of Parmenides (only "being" is real), only to rebound into the arms of Heracleitus (only "becoming" is real). There are at least *two* Greek traditions, after all. In our day, the pendulum has definitely swung in the latter direction.

Various theologians today across a broad spectrum have called into question any distinction between God's hidden essence (*deus in se*; "God in himself") and God's accommodated revelation (*deus pro nos*; "God in his relationship to us"), his archetypal and ectypal knowledge, God's mysterious transcendence and his marvelous immanence.[30] The result is a theology that identifies God's being with becoming, God's eternity with creaturely history, and God's working (energies) with God's being (essence). God's analogical self-revelation becomes a univocal description of God's inner being, as illustrated in Robert Jenson's statement, "The one God is an event; history occurs not only in him but as his being."[31]

God's independence from the world in no way restricts his freedom to relate creaturely reality to himself as he chooses, which he has done in creation and covenant and particularly in the person and work of Christ. God is more transcendent *and* more immanent than we can imagine. In the incarnation, the Son is free of the world even in his humiliation, part of the world even in his exaltation to the Father's right hand. As Karl Rahner reminds us, God neither keeps to himself nor loses himself in his freely chosen fellowship with creation.[32] It is not God's ability to enter into relationships that is in question, but the direction of dependence. Creatures *live*, but God *is life*—and he *has this life in himself.* God is always the donor; creatures the beneficiaries.

---

30. See, for example, Jenson, *Systematic Theology*, 1:66, where he argues, "The biblical God is not eternally himself in that he persistently instantiates a beginning in which he already is all he ever will be; he is eternally himself in that he unrestrictedly anticipates an end in which he will be all he ever could be. It holds also—or, rather, primally—with God: a story is constituted by the outcome of the narrated events."

31. Jenson, ibid., 1:221. As George Hunsinger points out, Jenson regularly attaches the shibboleth "abstract" to any notion

of divine simplicity and aseity. This is a typical red herring in recent criticisms of the tradition. Quoting Jenson's statement that "God's life is 'ordered by an Outcome that is his outcome, and so in a freedom that is more than abstract aseity' (1.160)," Hunsinger replies, "—as if God's aseity would necessarily be 'abstract' if it were fully actual in and for itself apart from history" (Hunsinger, "Robert Jenson's *Systematic Theology*," 182).

32. Karl Rahner, *The Trinity* (trans. Joseph Donceel; New York: Crossroad, 1997), 84.

This doctrine has tremendous practical value. If God were not free *from* creation, we might pray *for* him, but not *to* him. We would have no confidence that he could overcome evil or rescue us from death. Yet God's freedom *for* creation—even for those who are not only finite but sinful—is the presupposition of our hope in Christ. God does not need time, but he freely enters it; he does not need a house, but he builds one anyway. All of this is for our benefit, out of God's zeal to dwell together with finite, embodied creatures in covenant. That God freely does this in creation, without any inherent need, is a testimony to his unfathomable goodness. That he continues to do this even in relation to the unfaithful covenant partner is a measure of his unsearchable grace.

The Stoic sage is already related to the world but seeks to extricate himself even from allowing the world to have any relation to him. The reverse is true in the Christian doctrine of aseity. The God of Scripture is essentially independent yet freely chooses to bring creatures into fellowship and communion with himself—even though he already knows that his friends will become enemies. Even before he creates the world that he does not need, the Father, the Son, and the Spirit have covenanted in love for the salvation of sinners by the sacrifice of the incarnate Son. God's decision to do that which is necessary for our salvation but not for his perfect self-existence is the most obvious revelation of "the riches of his grace, which he lavished upon us, in all wisdom and insight" (Eph 1:7–8).

C. IMMUTABILITY

Another negation of finitude is *immutability* (nonchangeability). Building on the patristic consensus, Thomas Aquinas argued that God is *actus purus* ("pure act"), which means that there are no potentialities in God. Complete and perfect in himself from eternity to eternity, God has no potential that is not already fully realized. God cannot be more infinite, loving, or holy tomorrow than today. If God alone is necessary and independent of all external conditions, fully realized in all of his perfections, then there is literally nothing for God to *become.* For us, change might be for better or worse, but for a perfect God, change can only yield imperfection. The perfection of God's gifts depends on his own essential perfection. As James reminds us, "Every good gift and every perfect gift is from above, coming down from the Father of lights with whom there is no variation or shadow due to change" (Jas 1:17).

1. SCRIPTURAL SUPPORT

Just as the affirmation of God's independence from creation in no way excludes God's freedom to enter into relationships with creatures, Scripture clearly teaches that God changes creaturely reality but is not himself changed. Heaven and earth are "the work of your hands," the psalmist praises. "They will perish, but you will remain; they will all wear out like a garment. You will change them like a robe, and they will pass away, but you are the same, and your years have no end" (Ps 102:25 – 27).

God's immutability is hardly an irrelevant speculation; given the sinfulness of his human partner, it is a grand assurance: "For I the LORD do not change; therefore you, O children of Jacob, are not consumed" (Mal 3:6). <u>In Scripture, the virtue in God's changelessness lies in the assurance that God is reliable in his promises</u> — not only because he *wills* to be faithful to his word but because he *cannot* change his eternal counsels, regardless of what creatures do (Pss 16:8; 21:7). As the omniscient (all-knowing) God, who knows the end from the beginning, including the days he has allotted for us and even "the secrets of the heart" (Ps 44:21), there is no contingency that God's eternal decree has not taken into consideration. God knew that Adam would sin (Ro 8:20 – 21), plunging humanity into corruption, and he knew that Israel would fall as well (Dt 31:16 – 22). Nothing catches God by surprise, so that he would have to alter his revealed character or the predetermined course that is secret to us. Similarly, in Hebrews 6:17 – 18, God assures believers of the immutability of his promise by referring to "two unchangeable things": God's being and his oath to Abraham. Not only God's essence but his ultimate purposes and secret decrees do not change. Indeed, God works all things together for the good of his people (Ro 8:28). Believers were "predestined according to the purpose of him who works all things according to the counsel of his will" (Eph 1:11).

In all of these passages, God's unchangeable decree is presented as the basis for the believers' comfort that even "if we are faithless, he remains faithful — for he cannot deny himself" (2Ti 2:13). Above the vicissitudes of fluctuating circumstances and the ever-changing response of his covenant partners, there is the unchanging purpose of God — and in this, God's people can take immeasurable assurance. Even though the covenant of creation has been broken, and even Israel lies together in spiritual death with the world "in Adam" as transgressors (Hos 6:7; Ro 3), the eternal covenant of redemption remains inviolable because it is not conditioned on the human side but on the immutable will of the triune God.

Yet how do we square this with a host of passages that seem to suggest that God does adapt to new circumstances — at least in terms of changing his mind? Exodus 32:10 – 14 portrays God as relenting from destroying the Israelites because of Moses' intercession. In Jonah 3:10 we read, "When God saw what they did, how they turned from their evil way, God relented of the disaster that he had said he would do to them, and he did not do it." We will address these important passages after considering the historical development of this doctrine.

2. HISTORICAL DEFINITION

Thomas Wienandy explains that according to the patristic account, "God is unchangeable not because he is inert or static like a rock, but for just the opposite reason. He is so dynamic, so active that no change can make him more active. He is act pure and simple."[33] Once again, the essence-energies distinction was formative in ancient Christian reflection (especially in the East). God's essence is fully realized act. That is, there is no latent potential in God. He already is the God that he has always been and will always be—no more loving, wise, or omniscient tomorrow than he is today. Yet through his energies or operations in the world, he interacts with us—creating, sustaining, redeeming, and consummating.

The analogy is frequently drawn between the sun and its rays. We do not know God in himself but are warmed by the effulgence of his being. The "rays" are not an extension of God's being but of his power and activity. So, for example, Scripture says that God created and upholds all things "by the word of his power" (Heb 1:3), or the disciples are promised that they "will receive power" when the Holy Spirit comes at Pentecost (Ac 1:8), or the gospel is called "the power of God for salvation" (Ro 1:16; 1Co 1:18) and raises us from spiritual and, someday, physical death by his power (1Co 6:14). It is not God's immutable essence that emanates, is extended, or becomes fully realized in act; rather, it is God's powerful actions in time and space that achieve God's eternal purposes. God is never free to be someone other than God (i.e., to change in his essence), but God's workings (energies) are manifold and freely determined. God could have decided to create or not to create, for example; God realized his purposes but not his being in the act of creating the world. Eliminating this distinction leads logically to pantheism or panentheism, as is evident especially in modern theologies since Hegel. In this paradigm, the freedom, contingency, and changes evident in God's works are attributed to God's inner being.

If God is so self-complete and perfect, and has always been what he will always be, does this not mean that we worship the god of the Stoic sage, who in his undisturbed bliss has no relationship to creatures? "The objection here implied is based to a certain extent on misunderstanding," notes Louis Berkhof. "The divine immutability should not be understood as implying immobility, as if there were no movement in God."[34] For humans, of course, to exist "always in action" implies perpetual becoming. However, for God, who cannot become someone or something that he is not already, this means that God is *always active in the fullness and completeness of his own being*. Therefore, in contrast to Stoicism, the Christian doctrine of immutability does not deny God's ever-acting, ever-living, and ever-moving being. On the contrary, it reminds us that because God acts out of the unchanging perfection of

---

33. Thomas Weinandy, *Does God Suffer?* (Notre Dame, Ind.: Univ. of Notre Dame Press, 2000), 124.

34. Berkhof, *Systematic Theology*, 59.

his fully actualized being, such external works are always gratuitous, extravagant, and unnecessary expenditures that never diminish the inexhaustible riches of the giver. As Richard Muller points out, "The scholastic notion of God as immobile does not translate into English as 'immobile'—as one of the many cases of cognates not being fully convertible—but as 'unmoved.'"[35]

Responding to the Socinian, Turretin responded, "The necessity of the immutability we ascribe to God does not infer Stoic fate," since it neither imposes an internal necessity on God nor interferes "with the liberty and contingency of things."[36] Where the Stoic sage strives to realize perfection in apathetic detachment, the triune God already possesses a fully realized independence that is nevertheless living and active. Thus, each person of the Trinity goes out to the other in mutual joy and fellowship and in that complete fullness creates a nondivine world to share analogically in this extroverted communion. The immutable God is not the antithesis but the *source* of the mutable and ever-changing diversity of the world that he freely wills.

3. MODERN CHALLENGES

In the modern era, especially in the wake of Hegel, divine immutability was subjected to consistent rebuttals as an obstacle to the notion that the immanent Absolute Spirit realizes itself in—and in fact as—the unfolding of history. Bavinck notes that while Roman Catholic, Lutheran, and Reformed theologians affirm divine aseity and immutability, "According to Socinians, Pelagians, Arminians, and Rationalists, God is changeable not in his being but in his will." Taking a further step, "Gnosticism and Pantheism (Fichte, Hegel, Schleiermacher, Schopenhauer, Von Hartmann, etc.)" deny God's immutability in being, representing God "as eternally becoming."[37] This panentheistic paradigm has been revived more recently in various projects ranging from open theism and the work of such creative theologians as Jürgen Moltmann and Robert Jenson to process theology.

Such theologies have often appealed to the incarnation in their denial of immutability. The announcement that "the Word *became* [egeneto] flesh" (Jn 1:14, emphasis added) explicitly predicates change. How do we respond to this? First of all, we must test the premise on which this argument rests. As we will explore more fully in considering Christ's person, the creedal consensus affirmed that in the incarnation the eternal Son *assumed* our flesh, which involved no change to the divine person who assumed it. According to the Chalcedonian Christology affirmed by Christians of the East and West alike, the change is from *asarkos* ("not incarnate") to *ensarkos* ("incarnate"). If the incarnation implies change in the Son's *deity*, then the person who became flesh for our sake is not God but a humanized god or a deified human.

---

35. Richard Muller, "Incarnation, Immutability, and the Case for Classical Theism," *WTJ* 45, no. 1 (1983): 27.

36. Turretin, *Elenctic Theology*, 1:205–6.

37. Bavinck, *Doctrine of God*, 146–47.

Although he acknowledges the Hegelian influence in his formulations, Robert Jenson sometimes casts the debate in terms of the Lutheran-Calvinist debate — the former denying and the latter affirming that the finite cannot comprehend (i.e., enclose) the infinite (*finitum non capax infiniti*). However, Lutheran theologian Gerhard O. Forde has charged that Jenson is attempting to transform the theology of the cross into a theology of glory.[38] The incarnation does not cancel God's transcendent immutability, Forde argues. "When Martin Luther issued his frightening dictum to Erasmus and stated that God, hidden in majesty, has not bound himself to his word but kept himself free over all things, he was, I think, insisting on the impossibility of simply collapsing God into Jesus."[39] In other words, Jesus is indeed the revelation of God, but this does not eliminate the mystery; God remains hidden in majesty even as he reveals himself in grace.

> In Luther's theology the attributes of divinity such as divine necessity, immutability, timelessness, impassibility, and so forth, function as masks of God in his hiddenness.... Attempts to settle accounts with the immutability of God, for instance, are legion. Yet they never finally work.... Luther knew that no one can tear the mask from the face of the hidden God, but he also knew from the eschatological perspective that there was ultimate comfort in the divine names.... "If God were not immutable," Luther asks, "who can believe his promises?"[40]

Ultimately, a Hegelian theory of divine mutability does not really need the Christian story to make its point. God is already "incarnate" in his very being — changing, growing, living, dying, and rising again.

Yet the surprising announcement that we meet in the gospel is that the eternal Son became flesh without losing any of his divine transcendence in the process. This can happen because the God who truly transcends the world can freely enter into it and relate it to himself. Especially in Moltmann's theology, particularly the suffering and evil intrinsic (he thinks) to finite becoming belong to God's eternal being. Surely this underscores God's sympathy. However, like those trapped in a burning building, we need more than a rescuer who stands with us, experiencing our pain and fear; we need one who stands outside of us and can save us from the source of these symptoms. With the incarnation — divine and human natures united in one person — we have both. Forde adds, "If one simply erases the immutability systematically, the mutability flattens out to be self-evident. God threatens to become just a patsy who is enriched by sharing our misery."[41] Even from a practical perspective, says Forde, "God must be powerful and sweep all before him, else why do we need him?"[42] I would add, if God is already always realizing his being in

---

38. Gerhard O. Forde, "Robert Jenson's Soteriology," in *Trinity, Time, and Church* (ed. Colin Gunton; Grand Rapids: Eerdmans, 2000), 136.

39. Ibid.

40. Ibid., 137.

41. Ibid.

42. Ibid., 138, citing his *Systematic Theology*, 1:234.

becoming, then what is surprisingly wonderful and new about the Son's assumption of our humanity, subject to our weaknesses and suffering?

4. EXEGETICAL QUESTIONS

As with all of the divine attributes, it is crucial that we avoid two extremes, both of which presuppose a univocal rather than analogical view of the relation in comparisons between God and human beings. On one hand, the biblical testimony to a living history with a living God in a covenant with genuine interaction resists all Stoic and Platonic conceptions of a nonrelational and nonpersonal One. In the unfolding drama there are suits and countersuits, witnesses and counterwitnesses, and God is represented as repenting, relenting, and responding to creatures. On the other hand, we must always bear in mind that in revealing himself God hides himself. God explicitly forbids univocal comparisons (Nu 23:19; 1Sa 15:29; Isa 44:8–9; 46:4; Hos 11:9).

As the biblical drama unfolds, it is clear that although God represents himself as a genuine actor in the covenantal relationship, he cannot be *overwhelmed by surprise*. After all, his knowledge is perfect and encompasses the past, present, and future (Job 37:16; Ps 139:1–6, 16–18), including the free acts of human beings (Ex 7:1–7, 14; 8:15, 19; 9:12, 35; 10:1–2; 11:1–3, 9; 1 Sa 23:10–13; Isa 42:9; Ac 2:23; Ro 8:28; 9:16; Eph 1:11). Obviously, God is opposed by human beings, but he cannot be ultimately *overwhelmed by opposition* (Da 4:17–37; Ex 15:1–23; 8:11; Pss 22:28–31; 47:2–8; 115:3; 135:5–21; Jer 27:5; Ac 17:24–26; Ro 9:17–21; Rev 11:15–19). Accommodating himself to embodied and finite creatures, God appears in particular times and places—even though he cannot be circumscribed or overwhelmed by spatial limitation (Ps 139:7–12). All of this is simply to say that God always remains infinite and transcendent even in the finite and immanent forms of his self-revelation.

Among evangelical critics of these traditional attributes, open theists contend that the passages in Scripture depicting God as changing his mind, for example, must be taken seriously.[43] They cannot simply be dismissed as an anthropomorphism, while interpreting other passages (supporting divine immutability) as univocal truth. This is certainly true. The doctrine of analogy applies to *all* of the passages. There is no other way for God to enter into a covenantal relationship with finite creatures than to accommodate his self-revelation to our finitude. Only in this ongoing history do we have access to the threats and promises that are revealed, yet God's decree remains hidden to us (Dt 29:29). We do not know what God has

---

43. See Pinnock, *Most Moved Mover*; Sanders, *God Who Risks*; Gregory Boyd, *God of the Possible: An Introduction to the Open View of God* (Grand Rapids: Baker, 2000).

predetermined in his eternal counsels, but we do know that in his *conditional* promises (for example, to our first parents before the fall and to Israel at Sinai) there are changes in the course of God's dealings with his people. It is not with respect to God's being, character, or hidden decrees but with respect to the history in which these decrees are executed that we encounter instances of reversals in God's revealed plan.

Just as we must resist collapsing the distinction between God's essence (*ousia/dynamis*) and his energies (*energeia*), we must carefully distinguish God's hidden counsels from his revealed will. In 1 Samuel 15:11, for example, God regrets having made Saul king, and yet in verse 29 we read, "And also the Glory of Israel will not lie or have regret, for he is not a man, that he should have regret." Neither God's nature nor his secret plan changes. Rather, it is God's *revealed* plans that change. The judgment that he has warned that he will bring on the people is averted—precisely as God had predestined before the ages in his secret counsel. The dynamic give-and-take so obvious in the history of the covenant must be distinguished from the eternal decree that Scripture also declares as hidden in God's unchanging and inaccessible counsel (Eph 1:4–11).

These are not two contradictory lines of proof texts to be divided up between rival camps. Rather, there are two lines of analogy acting as guardrails to keep us on the right path. There is real change, partnership, and even conflict *in covenantal history* and therefore *between* God and human beings, but not *within* God's inner being. Just as God can assume our flesh without altering his divine nature, he can relate the world of becoming to himself without surrendering his fully complete and fully active being.

Critics of attributes such as immutability often reflect an impatience with mystery and analogical reserve that would caution against attempts to decode God's secrets.[44] According to Clark Pinnock, we worship either a God who does not want to "control everything, but to give the creature room to exist and freedom to love," or "an all-controlling despot who can tolerate no resistance (Calvin)," giving the false impression that Calvin actually held this position attributed to him.[45] Pinnock demands a choice between a God who is "immobile" (a "solitary monad") and the "Living God" who depends on the world for his happiness. The former he refers to as "the immobility package."

However, such objections rest on caricatures of traditional Christian theology. Charles Hodge reminds us that in the classical view God is immutable, "but

---

44. For example, Hunsinger notes concerning Jenson, "Again and again, throughout his career, he has vilified paradox as a 'pious mystery-mongering of the vacuity'; by means of paradox, he believes, 'we communicate nothing whatever.'... This criticism, it seems, underlies Jenson's resort to rationalistic metaphysics" ("Robert Jenson's *Systematic Theology*," 199).

45. Pinnock, *Most Moved Mover*, 4.

nevertheless that he is not a stagnant ocean, but ever living, ever thinking, ever acting, and *ever suiting his action to the exigencies of his creatures, and to the accomplishment of his infinitely wise designs*" (emphasis added). Far from speculating about *how* this is so, which extreme representations on both sides of this debate are often tempted to do, he adds,

> Whether we can harmonize these facts or not, is a matter of minor importance. We are constantly called upon to believe that things are, without being able to tell how they are, or even how they can be.... Theologians, in their attempts to state, in philosophical language, the doctrine of the Bible on the unchangeableness of God, are apt to confound immutability with immobility. In denying that God can change, they seem to deny that he can act.[46]

Reformed orthodoxy has been unanimous in observing the difference between immutability and immobility.

One of the advantages of the "way of negation" (as in *im*mutability) is that it halts before God's majesty, content to affirm God's infinite perfection without probing into the mysteries of God's hidden being. We do not know how God is immutable or how realistic the comparison is between his analogies and his essence. Yet God teaches us enough to enable us to know that he is infinitely other than we are and at the same time inseparably one with us — the object of our awe as well as our assurance.

D. IMPASSIBILITY

Impassibility means "immunity to suffering." Is God affected by us? Our answer to this question is already determined to a large extent by our view of God's simplicity, aseity, and immutability. Once we deny God's independence from the world (aseity), it is difficult to avoid the slide toward creating God in our own image. If God is dependent on the world, then it follows that, in principle at least, God can become overwhelmed and overcome by the world's opposition. All of the talk among open theists of God's infinite resourcefulness cannot eliminate the possibility that God's saving purposes will finally be thwarted on a grand scale, even as they are ostensibly in the case of those who do not share in the glory of the new creation.

1. DEFINING IMPASSIBILITY

First, it is important to define what we mean by *impassibility*. The Greek word *apatheia*, because it is used in Stoicism and Christian theology, may easily be misunderstood as referring to the same idea as *impassibility*.[47] However, the apathy or

---

46. Charles Hodge, *Systematic Theology* (New York: Scribner's, 1911), 1:390–91.

47. For a trenchant essay on the way in which the ancient theologians redefined impassibility, see David Bentley Hart, "No Shadow of Turning: On Divine Impassibility," *Pro Ecclesia* 11, no. 2 (2002): 184–206.

indifference at which the Stoic philosopher aimed—immunity to the harm or the delight that makes one's happiness dependent on others—is far from the Christian conception. This difference in meaning is further obscured by the fact that the Latin cognate, *passus*, is typically understood in the English word *passion* to refer to emotions generally. However, in its historical-theological context, *impassibility* is more specific. As Gerald Bray points out, the Greek theologian John of Damascus clearly defined God's *apatheia* as "suffering" (as in the passion of Christ). "The emphasis was not on tranquility in a state of indifference, but on the sovereignty of God."[48]

2. EVALUATING THE DOCTRINE OF IMPASSIBILITY

Deducing the attributes of the gods from their self-sufficiency, Plato taught that the gods cannot even love. Similarly, in our own day John Milbank argues that divine impassibility means that, strictly speaking, God is not offended by our sin and therefore does not require a satisfaction of his justice.[49] This eliminates even the possibility of forgiveness, as well as wrath. Obviously, this view could find no foothold in biblical revelation. So the problem inherited by Christian theologians, such as Augustine, was how to hold simultaneously to God's independence from the world and the central affirmation of God as love. Kevin Vanhoozer explains, "Augustine's solution to the paradox of God's love is to posit a properly divine kind of love, a gift-love: *agape*." In other words, God loves out of sheer abundance and self-sufficiency, not in order to receive anything in return.[50]

Following the Platonic rather than Stoic tradition, Augustine had no fear of *eros* ("desire out of need"), "tainting" love. It was perfectly natural and appropriate for human beings to exchange gifts out of self-interest *and* regard for the other. In any case, Augustine did not think it possible to eliminate self-interest from love in a pure kind of Stoic indifference that Kant and modern ethics imagine. Augustine argues that things are different when it comes to God, since all things exist from him, through him, and for him, and he stands in need of nothing.

---

48. Gerald Bray, *The Doctrine of God* (Downers Grove, Ill.: InterVarsity Press, 1993), 98. Open theists and other critics of impassibility confuse God's incapacity for being a passive victim with an inability to display emotion or to respond (either in wrath or in compassion) to creatures. Of course, this would not be a difficult position to refute from the scriptural evidence. However, it is a fundamental misunderstanding of what impassibility has meant in the broad history of Christian reflection. For example, the *Westminster Confession* says that God is "without parts or passions," but even in English, *passions* had for the writers of the confession a precise meaning consistent with its Greek and Latin origins (namely, uncontrollable rage or folly). When Wayne Grudem criticizes the confession at this point for teaching that this eliminates the possibility of God's expressing emotions, he overlooks this point (*Systematic Theology* [Grand

Rapids: Zondervan, 1994], 165–66). On this misunderstanding, Grudem concludes, "But the idea that God has no passions or emotions at all clearly conflicts with much of the rest of Scripture, and for that reason I have not affirmed God's impassibility in this book" (166). Paul Helm points out that even Aquinas allowed that God possessed affectional characteristics (analogically) with creatures, except any characteristic that would require God to be passive and temporal ("The Impossibility of Divine Passibility," in *The Power and Weakness of God: Impassibility and Orthodoxy* [ed. Nigel M. S. Cameron; Edinburgh: Rutherford House, 1990], 126).

49. John Milbank, *Being Reconciled: Ontology and Pardon* (New York: Routledge, 2003), 49–62.

50. Kevin J. Vanhoozer, *First Theology: God, Scripture and Hermeneutics* (Downers Grove, Ill.: InterVarsity Press, 2002), 74.

Plato's mistake was to think that a God who needs nothing cannot love; in my view, the mistake of contemporary critics of divine impassibility is to think that a God who loves must be needy. Before we criticize Augustine too quickly as mired in Greek rather than biblical presuppositions, we should recall again Paul's speech: "The God who made the world and everything in it, being the Lord of heaven and earth, does not live in temples made by man, nor is he served by human hands, as though he needed anything, since he himself gives to all mankind life and breath and everything" (Ac 17:24–25). In Romans, Paul cites Job 35:7 (cf. 41:11): "'Or who has given a gift to him that he might be repaid?' For from him and through him and to him are all things. To him be glory forever. Amen" (Ro 11:35–36). It *is* appropriate for humans (who are by nature needy) to offer gifts to each other for self-fulfillment and out of regard for the other. However, "Every ... *perfect* gift is from above, coming down from the Father of lights with whom there is no variation or shadow due to change" (Jas 1:17, emphasis added).

Although Augustine's interpretation of God's agape love reflects an insightful Christian alternative to Platonism and Stoicism, he could not see how God's bliss could be in any way affected by creatures. Of course, in his commentaries Augustine could affirm that God judged, had compassion, was roused to anger, and so forth. But such expressions are not only *affirmed analogically*; they are frequently *explained away* as unbefitting for a self-complete God. In my view, this tendency rests largely on the lack of any distinction between God's essence and energies. Yet with this important distinction, we are able to say that <u>while God's energies (acts) may sometimes be affected by creaturely action, God's essence and decree do not change.</u>

3. Recent Criticism of Impassibility

Criticism of divine impassibility has become something of a cottage industry in recent theology, standing as it does in the shadow of the Holocaust.[51] Jürgen Moltmann, for instance, especially in *The Crucified God* (1972) and *The Trinity and the Kingdom* (1981),[52] repeats the criticism that the traditional doctrine of God is the product of Greek philosophy more than of biblical teaching. Yet his own interpretation is a series of deductions from a central thesis of God's essential nature as "suffering love," which he develops by appealing to Jewish Kabbalism, Jakob Böhme, G. W. F. Hegel, and Friedrich Schelling, as well as more recent speculative thinkers.

---

51. T. E. Fretheim's *The Suffering of God: An Old Testament Perspective* (Philadelphia: Fortress, 1984) was formative in biblical-theological studies, and Brueggemann's *Theology of the Old Testament* articulates a highly anthropomorphic conception of God. An excellent contrast (and critique) of these views from a biblical-theological perspective is offered by Brevard Childs, *Biblical Theology of the Old and New Testaments: Theological Reflection on the Christian Bible* (Minneapolis: Fortress, 1993).

52. Jürgen Moltmann, *The Crucified God* (New York: Harper & Row, 1974); *The Trinity and the Kingdom: The Doctrine of God* (trans. Margaret Kohl; San Francisco: Harper & Row, 1981).

In this view, God is not Almighty, but cosufferer who transforms evil into good by suffering evil in his very being. Within God's essence, therefore, there is a tragic aspect that God must conquer through historical becoming.[53] Confusing God's essence with his energies as well as with the persons of the Godhead, Moltmann says that God "suffers from the love which is the superabundance and overflowing of his being."[54] After reducing all of God's attributes to "suffering love," he arrives at one characteristic that is finally descriptive (univocally) of the divine essence: "God's self-humiliation."[55] So where some nineteenth-century theologians advocated the concept of kenosis as a way of explaining the "self-emptying" of the eternal Son in the incarnation, Moltmann (much like Hegel) applies the concept to God's eternal being.[56] Analogy slips rather easily into univocity in Moltmann's theology of divine suffering. "The sole omnipotence which God possesses," he says, "is the almighty power of suffering love."[57] God is not only free to show compassionate love toward sinners; his eternal nature is suffering love.[58] God's compassion toward sinners is not, therefore, a free decision. Rather, "Self-sacrifice is God's very nature and essence."[59]

What happened to the freedom that Moltmann insisted on as the source of divine passion? In this suffering love, God is not merely working something out in the world (namely, the forgiveness of sins), but chiefly working something out in himself. Since suffering belongs to God's eternal being, he is overcoming it in himself and in the world simultaneously. "Suffering love overcomes the brutality of evil and redeems the energy in evil, which is good, through the fulfillment which it gives to this misguided passion."[60] Christ's incarnation and death appear to be, for Moltmann (like Hegel), a symbol of God's eternal being-in-becoming rather than a free decision of merciful love. In fact, not the cross but "the process of evolution is the process of redemption through suffering love."[61] The grip of theodicy (the problem of evil) in determining Moltmann's doctrine of God is particularly obvious in his speculation that "if God is already in eternity and in his very nature love, suffering love, and self-sacrifice, then evil must already have come into existence with God himself, not merely with creation, let alone with the fall of man."[62]

---

53. Moltmann, *The Trinity and the Kingdom*, 21. Confusing immutability with immobility, Moltmann also confuses impassibility with an inability to feel or respond to creaturely pain. We have seen that this is a recurring "straw opponent" in contemporary critiques.

54. Ibid.

55. Ibid., 27. "On the ground of the Jewish experience of God, [Abraham] Heschel developed a *bipolar theology* of the covenant. God is in himself free and not subject to any destiny; yet through his pathos God has at the same time committed himself in his covenant. He is the God of gods; and at the same time for his little people of Israel he is the God of the covenant.

He reigns in heaven; and at the same time dwells with the humble and meek." However, orthodoxy affirms this (as explained above), while Moltmann (unlike Heschel) simply collapses any distinction between God's essence and works.

56. Ibid., 28.

57. Ibid., 31.

58. Ibid., 32.

59. Ibid.

60. Ibid.

61. Ibid.

62. Ibid., 34.

While Manichaeism and other dualistic ontologies ground good and evil in two opposing gods, Moltmann seems to synthesize good and evil within the being of God. Thus Moltmann approves G. A. Studdert Kennedy's conclusion: "God, the Father God of Love, is everywhere in history, but nowhere is he Almighty."[63] Appealing to Böhme, Hegel, Schopenhauer, and more recent writers such as Miguel de Unamuno and Nicholas Berdyaev, Moltmann posits a contradiction in God's being—a "tragedy in God," that looks at times like a psychological Manichaeism.[64] God's "dark side" is sublated into a higher synthesis, just as it is in Hegel's speculative system. God cannot be conceived of as being "beyond history," since historical suffering (concretized in the history of Jesus) belongs to God's eternal nature.[65] Given the interdependence of God and the world via the history of suffering, "It is not only that we need God's compassion; God also needs ours.... The deliverance of the world from its contradiction is nothing less than God's deliverance of himself from the contradiction of his world."[66] The cross provokes the question, " 'Is this the atoning God, who wants to clear his conscience of the guilt, the reproach of having created man, and at the same time evil and suffering?' "[67]

Standing in what we have been calling the ontological ("overcoming estrangement") as opposed to the covenantal paradigm ("meeting a stranger"), Moltmann insists, "The incarnation of God's Son is not an answer to sin. It is the fulfillment of God's eternal longing to become man and to make of every man a god out of grace; an 'Other' to participate in the divine life and return the divine love."[68] Not surprisingly, then, Moltmann adds, "Perfection of Christ's cross makes 'the metaphysical historical' and 'the historical metaphysical.' "[69] Is not "suffering freedom" abstracted

---

63. Ibid., 35. Geoffrey A. Studdert Kennedy's *The Hardest Part* (London: Hodder and Stoughton, 1918) received more attention than Barth's *Epistle to the Romans*, which came out at the same time. "In fact," Moltmann judges, "it deserved even greater attention than Barth's book, for the theology of the suffering God is more important than the theology of the God who is 'Wholly Other' " (*The Trinity and the Kingdom*, 35).

64. Moltmann, *The Trinity and the Kingdom*, 40: Suffering and God's sorrow "is not merely the contradiction of God's world," Unamuno concluded. "It is bound up with that; but it is also a contradiction in God himself.... [Unamuno] contents himself with a pointer to Jakob Böhme's idea about there being a 'dark side' to God." Böhme's speculations are mediated to Moltmann especially, it seems, through Schelling. See F. Schelling, *The Ages of the World* (trans. Jason M. Wirth; Albany, N.Y.: SUNY Press, 2000).

65. Ibid., 45. Like many contemporary theologians, Moltmann does not seem to appreciate the nuances of classical Christian theology on these points. It is rather easy to prove from Scripture that God moves and that he is moved (for example, to compassion, to anger, etc.). However, the question must still be addressed: Does this refer to God's essence or God's ener-

gies? To the essence or the persons? (By definition, essences do not move and are not moved; "essence"—at least in Aristotle and Christian theology—simply means something that has predicable qualities. Even when I am moved to sorrow, it is not my humanity as such that is moved but I as a person.) Finally, is this language (like all of God's self-revelation) analogical or univocal? Moltmann never addresses these critical issues, but runs all of these distinctions together in a simplistic conclusion: "Anyone who denies movement in the divine nature also denies the divine Trinity. And to deny this is really to deny the whole Christian faith."

66. Ibid., 39.

67. Ibid., 40. Moltmann takes this question from Miguel de Unamuno's account of standing beneath Velázquez's crucifix, and he calls the question "an idea that reaches the limit of radical boldness."

68. Ibid., 46. Robert Jenson, by the way, suggests a similar move, treating the cross as a sublation of the "dark side" of reality (ontological fault) rather than an atonement for sin (ethical fault). I refer again to George Hunsinger's precise criticisms in "Robert Jenson's *Systematic Theology*," esp. 161–65.

69. Ibid., 47.

from God and divinized in this way when we read, "but freedom has no origin; it is an ultimate frontier. But because freedom exists, God himself suffers and is crucified"?[70] Reconciling "being"—inherently evil rather than created good—rather than reconciling sinners to God becomes the goal of such a system. For Moltmann, "God is not the Lord; he is the merciful Father."[71]

Instead of projecting a God who satisfies our existential interpretation of tragedy, we need to allow the biblical analogies to transform our reasoning. As David Bentley Hart observes, the patristic doctrine of God's *apatheia* nowhere suggests that God is incapable of loving or entering into relations with creatures. In fact, it is ironic that, "in our attempts to revise trinitarian doctrine in such a way as to make God comprehensible in the 'light' of Auschwitz, invariably we end up describing a God who—it turns out—is actually simply the metaphysical ground of Auschwitz."[72] In other words, if suffering—even evil—belongs to God's essential and eternal being, then does this not divinize horror? Furthermore, how could God be said to defeat evil and pain if these belong to his nature? In Moltmann, the staggering announcement that the God who is God without us nevertheless chose to be God with and for us surrenders to the nondoxological logic of a deity who can only allow for our existence by limiting himself and can only deal with our suffering by sharing it.

4. NAVIGATING BETWEEN SCYLLA AND CHARYBDIS

Neo-Hegelian theologies differ with Stoicism in their assumptions about what constitutes a perfect being, but ironically the two are closer to each other (especially in embracing a panentheistic ontology) than either is to biblical faith. The "god of the philosophers" is as easily the projection of Heracleitus and Hegel as of Plato and Plotinus. Vanhoozer is surely correct in concluding that panentheism appears to be the most popular paradigm in theology today.[73] "For classical theism," he points out, "God's love is a matter of his sovereign will, of benevolence: willing and acting for the other's good," whereas "the panentheist suggests that God's love is more a matter of affective empathy ('I feel your pain')."[74] At the same time, "A picture of God as causal agent holds classical theism captive," which makes it "difficult to reconcile divine love with the notion of personal relation."[75] How do we navigate between Stoicism and Hegelian panentheism?

On one hand, we must avoid the conclusion that God is untouched or unmoved by creaturely suffering. There is indeed a Stoic thread that runs from Origen to Maimonides to Spinoza and Kant that denies that God experiences joy or sorrow;

---

70. Ibid.

71. Ibid., 70.

72. David Bentley Hart, *The Beauty of the Infinite: The Aesthetics of Christian Truth* (Grand Rapids: Eerdmans, 2003), 160.

73. Vanhoozer, *First Theology*, 88.

74. Ibid., 89–90.

75. Ibid., 90.

he neither loves nor hates. In fact, traces of Stoicism are evident among Christian writers in the ancient, medieval, and modern period. However, the indifferent god of Stoicism is radically different from the living God of Scripture. How can one pray to this God or be personally related to him in any way?

On the other hand, God is the transcendent *Lord* of the covenant who is never a passive victim but is always the active judge and justifier. Even if God is revealed in Scripture (analogically) as responding to the world and especially to human beings in a covenantal relationship, it is not in the same way we respond to each other. Even when God hears the cry of his afflicted people in Egypt and delivers them, it is as the one who had already elected Israel and foretold to Abram the events that would lead up to their captivity and deliverance (Ge 15:13–21). Even as the Son became flesh and submitted to the cruelest injustice of human rebellion, he did so voluntarily: "No one takes [my life] from me, but I lay it down of my own accord. I have authority to lay it down, and I have authority to take it up again. This charge I have received from my Father" (Jn 10:18). God's merciful responsiveness to sinners is always a free act. To avoid the extremes of "Stoic" detachment and "Hegelian" dependence, we should bear a few points in mind.

First, the false choice to be avoided is that either God is related to the world (in the technical sense, as needing the world for his existence) or the world bears no relation to God. For open theists, a genuine God-world relationship must run in both directions: God must be *related to* (and therefore in some sense dependent on) the world, as well as vice versa. In this respect, ironically, it is closer to Stoicism than to classical Christianity. God's independence from the world was a distinctively Christian theme, designed to reorient our thinking away from such pagan assumptions. Thus, there is a relation, but we live and move and have our being in God rather than vice versa (Ac 17:28).[76] Because God has *related the world to himself*, even to the point of assuming our flesh, he can experience creaturely reality—and in fact does experience it more deeply than we. If the denial of impassibility represents the danger of making God dependent on (i.e., in the technical sense, related to) the world, we must also resist a defense of impassibility in which God's relating of the world to himself has no impact on his energies (i.e., his covenantal activity in the divine-human relationship).

God *delights* in the work of his hands, in our fellowship with him, in our worship, and in the love and service we render to our neighbor. Yet God *needs* none of this for his own fulfillment. In fact, it is because he needs nothing that the love he shows to creatures is creative. It is not because God lacks emotion that he loves in

---

76. On this point see Thomas Weinandy, *Does God Suffer?* (South Bend, Ind.: Univ. of Notre Dame Press, 2000), 113–46; Thomas Weinandy, ed., *Aquinas on Doctrine: A Critical Intro-* duction (Edinburgh: T&T Clark, 2004), 75–79; cf. David B. Burrell, *Aquinas: God and Action* (South Bend, Ind.: Univ. of Notre Dame Press, 1979), 84–87.

freedom, but because he does not lack anything. God does feel, but not as one who depends on the world for his joy. God responds to our sorrows with compassion, to our sin with anger, and to our obedience with delight. Yet he does so as a generous rather than as a needy lover.

God gives life but does not receive life; the world depends on God, but God does not depend on the world. Similarly, we can say that God is affected by us but is not determined in his being, will, or actions by us. God freely allows us to affect him, although even our affecting action is comprehended in God's eternal counsel. Even our prayers are means through which God works out in history that which he has already determined from the beginning. Similarly, God did not plan our redemption as a reaction to a fall that surprised him but as a self-determination prior to the act of creation. It is because God loves out of self-determining freedom rather than need that he can love in spite of the unresponsiveness of the human partner. After all, the gospel's astonishing revelation of God's grace reaches its climax in the announcement that God loved us while we were hostile toward him (Ro 5:10; 1Co 2:14; Eph 2:1–5). Our love for God is analogical of God's love for us; the latter remains qualitatively distinct, and therein lies the security of our hope in God (1Jn 4:10).

Second, it is crucial to bear in mind that impassibility refers to God's essence rather than to the particular persons who share it. It is the *persons* of the Trinity who are affected by creatures, not the divine *essence* itself. This is true even of human beings. Even in life-altering experiences of delight or despair, one's humanity is not altered; rather, the person is changed. Essences (or natures) cannot feel, will, or act. Only *persons* can love, be disappointed or delighted, angry or pleased, disturbed or satisfied. God's essence is not a person. It is only the persons who share this essence who can be affected. The Father, not the divine essence, so loved the world that he gave his Son and turned away from the sin-bearing Savior of sinners in wrath and judgment. Love is an attribute of the divine essence ("God is love" [1Jn 4:8, 16]), but only the divine *persons* love (verb).

Third, we must again recognize that God speaks to us in terms adequate to our understanding rather than adequate to his being. Just as open theism requires God's dependence on the world for genuine relationship, it tends to treat expressions of divine pathos in Scripture as univocal with human emotions. To repeat an earlier point, God's free decision to enter into creaturely history never threatens his essential transcendence. God is always "other" even when he is near. God shares in the joys and sorrows of his people, but he is never *overwhelmed by distress* (I develop this point further, in dependence on Vanhoozer, on p. 252). As the Covenant Lord, God is jealous and even filled with wrath when his covenant is violated, but is never *overwhelmed by emotion.* His anger is always consistent with justice, for example. God is never rash in his judgments, and this is good news for those who deserve his wrath: "I will not execute my fierce anger; I will not again destroy Ephraim; for I am God and no mortal, the Holy One in your midst, and I will not come in wrath" (Hos 11:9 NRSV; cf. Mal 3:6). And Scripture tells us repeatedly that God is longsuffering and slow to anger. Yet sometimes his wrath is aroused (something that arguments in favor of a univocal relation between divine and human feeling rarely include along with his love). In Psalm 2:12, for instance, God warns, "Kiss the Son, lest he become angry and you perish in the way, *for his wrath is quickly kindled*" (emphasis added). God is not a capricious tyrant whose tempers are easily flared; rather, those who are already under God's just condemnation continue to draw their breath only because of God's mercy. In all of these characteristics, God is qualitatively different from creatures.

The motivation to attribute human characteristics to God's essence is so determinative that theologians such as Moltmann and Pinnock even speculate that God cries real tears.[77] Pinnock cites Mormon theologian David Paulsen, among others, to challenge God's spirituality.[78] Adopting the presupposition that attributes of infinitude are always pagan distortions, one could even conceivably surrender Jesus' assertion that "God is spirit" (Jn 4:24) as one more incursion of Greek philosophy. This danger underscores the point that any attempt to bring God down from heaven or to rise up to God is merely a different side of the same coin: domesticating the transcendent God, confusing the Creator with the creature. At the heart of all theologies of glory, Luther warned, is the desire to ascend to God and strip off his self-chosen masks so that we are no longer restricted to his back but can behold his inner essence—the blinding glory of his face.

Confident in the sovereignty, goodness, and other attributes that they share as the one God, the persons of the Godhead enter freely into relationships with creatures in the full awareness that there will be a history of human failure, rebellion, and violence. The eternal covenant of redemption is the clearest evidence of this fact. Yet the divine persons open themselves up to this tragedy precisely because together they will overcome it. For God, unlike us, this confidence is not a possibility or even a probability but a certainty.

Scripture clearly represents the persons of the Godhead as involved in a covenantal relationship in which there is genuine give-and-take. God is pleased, angered, aroused to compassion and also to judgment. Yet in none of these cases can we conclude that God experiences things as we do. Even human sin is under God's ultimate control. God can take such "risks" because he is unfailing in his ability to work all things together for good according to his ultimate purposes (Ro

---

77. Moltmann, *The Crucified God*, 222; Pinnock, *Most Moved Mover*, 33–34.

78. Pinnock, *Most Moved Mover*, 35n31 and 68n11.

8:28). From the perspective of God's eternal decree, they are not risks at all—not because God is untouched by human failure but because he is never overwhelmed nor are his secret purposes ultimately thwarted. Yet from the perspective of God's unfolding covenantal history with us, there are risks involved on both sides. At this point, the appropriate move is not to identify either perspective with "how it really is" versus "how it seems to us," but to embrace both as analogical truth insofar as God has revealed it to us in Scripture.

The diversity of biblical analogies keeps us from being surrendered to an idolatrous gaze upon a single attribute. We do not worship love, but the loving God; nor do we worship sovereignty, but the sovereign God. Surely the dialectic play of analogies is comparable to the narrative representation of God as regreting and yet affirming that he is not a man that he should regret his decision (1Sa 15:29). We are not allowed to linger long, transforming accommodated communication to a form of idolatry. Jealousy is praised in God (Ex 20:5; 34:14; Dt 4:24), while it is condemned in creatures (1Co 3:3; Gal 5:20), so clearly *jealousy* cannot mean exactly the same thing in God and creatures. God is described as uprooting the Israelites "in anger and fury and great wrath" (Dt 29:28), and yet "his anger is but for a moment, and his favor is for a lifetime" (Ps 30:5).

All of these diverse analogies must be taken seriously within their specific redemptive-historical context and then interpreted in the light of the rest of Scripture. The anger that God condemns in us (Pr 29:11, 22; 22:24; 1Co 13:5) is different from the anger that fills him with holy wrath, whatever similarities there may be. Those who affirm the unity, coherence, and truthfulness of the biblical canon cannot be content with a theory that accounts for "passibility" passages or "impassibility" passages, but will find in the doctrine of analogy a way of accepting God's accommodated discourse across the wide, deep, luxuriant, and sometimes troubling expanse of revelation.

Fourth, a Christian doctrine of God must supplement causal with communicative analogies that are more in keeping with Scripture's own testimony to God's performative speech. Although traditional Christian theology has sharply distinguished its views from Aristotle's Unmoved Mover, I agree with Vanhoozer that the dominance of causal categories often perpetuates that caricature, and that communicative categories offer a better way of speaking about God's interaction with the world.[79] Vanhoozer makes this point by comparing God's impassibility to Jesus' impeccability (inability to sin):

> Jesus was sinless yet subject to real temptation in the same way that an invincible army is subject to attack. Something similar, I believe, may be said for divine impas-

---

sibility.... God feels the force of his people's suffering: "I have seen the affliction of my people who are in Egypt, and have heard their cry because of their taskmasters; I know their sufferings" (Ex 3:7). Yet as Jesus feels the force of temptation without sinning, so God feels the force of the human experience without suffering change in his being, will or knowledge. Impassibility means not that God is unfeeling but that God is never *overcome* or *overwhelmed* by passion.... God genuinely relates to human persons via his communicative action, but nothing humans do conditions or affects God's communicative initiatives and God's communicative acts.[80]

Evil and sin are also comprehended in God's eternal decree; therefore, not even these can be said to condition God's will or acts. Further, Vanhoozer's construction of this argument is Trinitarian: "the Son and Spirit are means of the Father's communicative action."[81]

Fifth, we must beware of allowing a theology of the cross to become a philosophy of glory. In neo-Hegelian theodicies, the particular person, Jesus of Nazareth, and the particular history in which he arrives are easily surrendered to a general principle. Colin Gunton points out concerning these formulations, "Their chief defect is that they turn Christ into a world principle at the expense of Jesus of Nazareth, and treat his cross as a focus for the suffering of God rather than as the centre of that history in which God overcomes sin and evil." The result of this separation of Trinity from atonement is the loss of the Christian Trinity and "an uncritical validation of modern culture."[82] In this scheme, God takes into his own being all suffering. "The objection to this is clear. To incorporate something into the divine life is to affirm it, and so to deny the central character of Christianity as a religion of redemption, in which evil is not affirmed but conquered, eschatologically and by anticipation, in the cross and resurrection of Jesus of Nazareth."[83]

At the cross, God did not affirm death and suffering; rather, he conquered it. He did not transform evil into good but vanquished evil forever. Precisely because suffering is not immanent to God's being, he can and will fulfill his promise to his suffering people that he "will wipe away every tear from their eyes, and death shall be no more, neither shall there be mourning, nor crying, nor pain anymore, for the former things have passed away" (Rev 21:4). Only God can wipe away our tears on that day, because he cannot be overwhelmed by suffering. He acts out of omnipotent, omniscient, and all-wise love, not out of eternal suffering.

Since many critics of impassibility associate the lingering influence of this doctrine with the tradition of Old Princeton, it is worth concluding our consideration of this attribute with a lengthy quote from the "lion of Princeton," B. B. Warfield.

80. Ibid., 93.
81. Ibid., 94.
82. Colin Gunton, *The Promise of Trinitarian Theology* (Edinburgh: T&T Clark, 1997), xx.
83. Ibid., xxi.

Philosophers of the Absolute tell us, Warfield says, "that God is, by the very necessity of his nature, incapable of passion, incapable of being moved by inducements from without; that he dwells in holy calm and unchangeable blessedness, untouched by human sufferings or human sorrows for ever."

Warfield replies to this contention:

> Let us bless God that it is not true. God can feel; God does love. We have scriptural warrant for believing that . . . God has reached out loving arms and gathered into his own bosom that forest of spears which otherwise had pierced ours. But is not this gross anthropomorphism? We are careless of names: it is the truth of God. And we decline to yield up the God of the Bible and the God of our hearts to any philosophical abstraction. . . . We may feel awe in the presence of the Absolute, as we feel awe in the presence of the storm or of the earthquake. . . But we cannot love it; we cannot trust it. . . . Nevertheless, let us rejoice that our God has not left us by searching to find him out. Let us rejoice that he has plainly revealed himself to us in his Word as a God who loves us, and who, because he loves us, has sacrificed himself for us.[84]

Although their common essence does not suffer, the Father, the Son, and the Spirit open themselves up to a covenantal relationship with free creatures. Affected by the world, they are not affected in the same way as we are because they are not the kinds of persons that we are.

E. ETERNITY AND OMNIPRESENCE

Since eternity and omnipresence refer to God's transcendence of time and space, respectively, it is worthwhile to treat them together. Various definitions of eternity have been articulated in the history of thought, with Plato holding that the One transcends time (i.e., is eternal) and Aristotle arguing that God is within time but without beginning or end (i.e., sempiternal). The fifth-century Christian thinker Boethius supplied perhaps the most favored definition of eternity among theologians for centuries: "the whole simultaneous and perfect possession of boundless life."[85] Augustine revised the Platonic concept of eternity: away from a simple negation of time, toward a more eschatological view of eternity as the fullness of time. In

---

84. B. B. Warfield, *The Person and Work of Christ* (ed. Samuel G. Craig; Philadelphia: P&R, 1970), 570–71.

85. Boethius, *The Consolation of Philosophy* (trans. V. E. Watts; London: Penguin, 1969), bk. 5 (see also Book 11 of Augustine's *Confessions*). For contemporary surveys of this debate as well as constructive proposals, many resources are available. On the more traditional side, see Paul Helm, *Eternal God* (Oxford: Clarendon, 1988); Brian Leftow, *Time and Eternity* (Ithaca, N.Y.: Cornell Univ. Press, 1991); Eleonore Stump and Norman Kretzmann, "Eternity," *Journal of Philosophy* 98 (1981): 429–58. Critical of "timeless eternity" are Anthony Kenny, *The God of the Philosophers* (Oxford: Clarendon, 1979);

Richard Swinburne, *The Christian God* (Oxford: Clarendon, 1994). A fine symposium of views on the subject is found in Gregory E. Ganssle and David M. Woodruff, eds., *God and Time: Essays on the Divine Nature* (Oxford: Oxford Univ. Press, 2002). I have excluded important philosophical debates, such as the vast literature interacting with J. M. E. McTaggart's important essay, "The Unreality of Time," in *Mind* 17 (1908): 457–74, although many of the works cited here engage McTaggart's schematization. One of the most illuminating discussions is offered by Wolfhart Pannenberg, whose interpretation I find most persuasive (see his *Systematic Theology* [Grand Rapids: Eerdmans, 1991], 1:401–9).

other words, eternity is God's gathering up of all of our times, healing and redeeming them from the sorrows of this present age. Advocates of *sempiternity* affirm that God had no beginning and will have no end, but they see this divine existence as *duration through all times* rather than an existence *above or beyond time*.[86] Therefore, they suggest, God is not eternal but everlasting.

If we knew exactly what eternity is, we would be eternal—in other words, God. Therefore, it is critical here to remain within the bounds of Scripture: its explicit statements, and legitimate inferences from those statements. God is praised because "from everlasting to everlasting you are God" (Ps 90:2), celebrated because he is "enthroned forever" in his Sabbath glory (Ps 102:12). Such passages, however, are indecisive for the present question, since at least evangelical critics of God's eternity do not deny God's "everlastingness" (sempiternity).[87] As Berkhof observes, "The form in which the Bible represents God's eternity is simply that of duration through endless ages, Pss 90:2; 102:12; Eph 3:21. We should remember, however, that in speaking as it does the Bible uses popular language, and not the language of philosophy."[88] Favoring sempiternity ("everlastingness"), Robert Reymond thinks Berkhof's last sentence too easily invokes mystery instead of squarely facing the problems he thinks are inherent in the classical Augustinian view of God as timelessly eternal.[89] However, I am inclined to interpret Berkhof as properly respecting the limitations inherent in our capacity to determine the nature of eternity by extrapolating from our experience of time.

At this point, our view of eternity may be illuminated by God's omnipresence. In dedicating the temple, Solomon prays, "Behold, heaven and the highest heaven cannot contain you; how much less this house that I have built!" (1Ki 8:27). Provoked by Israel's domestication of his transcendence, God declares, "Am I a God at hand, declares the LORD, and not a God far away? Can a man hide himself in secret places so that I cannot see him? declares the LORD. Do I not fill heaven and earth? declares the LORD" (Jer 23:23–24). Not even hell can be described as separation from God; rather, it is God's presence in wrath. The psalmist exclaimed, "Where shall I go from your Spirit? Or where shall I flee from your presence? If I ascend

---

86. Challenges to God's timeless eternity are found not only among those who also deny God's immutability, omniscience, aseity, and simplicity but also among some conservative evangelical (and Reformed) theologians, especially students of Gordon Clark, who favor univocity over analogy. See, for example, Ronald H. Nash, *The Concept of God* (Grand Rapids: Zondervan, 1983), 83. While Nash concludes that "the jury is still out" as to whether God is "a timeless or an everlasting being," Robert Reymond more emphatically rejects the traditional (Augustinian) arguments, concluding, "I am more inclined to view God's eternality in terms of everlastingness" (*A New Systematic Theology*

[Nashville: Nelson, 1998], 176n40). It is significant that Reymond argues, "If God's 'time-words' to us respecting his plans and actions do not mean for God the same as they mean for us, then for him the creation of the world may not have actually occurred yet.... In short, if God is timeless and if all of his acts are for him timeless acts, then we can have no true and certain knowledge of anything except perhaps pure mathematics" (175).

87. See Ganssle and Woodruff, *God and Time.*

88. Berkhof, *Systematic Theology*, 60.

89. Reymond, *New Systematic Theology*, 173.

to heaven, you are there! If I make my bed in Sheol, you are there!" (Ps 139:7–8). There is no day or night to God, no passage of days (vv. 11–12). Paradoxically, it is God's transcendence of time and place that brings the psalmist the deepest assurance of God's immanence in all of his times and places.

While omnipresence is an essential attribute, God's dwelling in the midst of his people is a prominent motif from Genesis to Revelation, creation to consummation. God's concrete presence among his people whom he liberated in the exodus, indicated by the pillar of cloud, was reckoned essential for proof of Israel's election (Ex 33:15–16). On the way to Canaan, God dwells with his people "outside the camp" (v. 7) in the tabernacle, through the priesthood and sacrifices. Given his holiness and Israel's sin, there must be a safe distance. Yet his goal is to dwell "in the midst of" his people, on Mount Zion, in the temple. Then in the ministry of Christ, the promise is given that he is God's temple (Jn 1:14), filled with the Glory-Spirit, forgiving sins, ascending to heaven to prepare a place for us (Jn 14:3), and sending his Spirit to make us living stones of his Spirit-filled temple-sanctuary (1Pe 2:4–5). In Revelation, God finally is seated "in the midst" of his elect. In the vision of the new Jerusalem coming down from heaven, John hears a voice declare, "Behold, the dwelling place of God is with man. He will dwell with them, and they will be his people, and God himself will be with them as their God" (Rev 21:2–3).

The question of God's presence and absence in the covenantal drama is equivalent to the question of salvation and judgment. In other words, we meet in Scripture both an *ontological omnipresence* and a *covenantal-judicial presence* in blessing or wrath. Of course, God is omnipresent in his essence, but the primary question in the covenantal drama is whether God is present for us, and if so, where, as well as whether he is present in judgment or in grace. Can we stand in his presence? Can we withstand his appearing?

God is omnitemporal in the way that he is omnipresent. As infinite spirit, God is not an infinitely extended body. He is present in every place because he transcends spatial categories. The same is true, I would argue, concerning time. God's transcendence of time is the very presupposition of his presence in every creaturely moment. Even when God is present in a particular place *for us*, in peace, he remains omnipresent *in his own essence*; the same is true of his eternity. The God who is eternal (essentially) is active within time (energetically).

Even descriptions of God's transcendence in terms of "above" in contrast to "below" (as in Ps 97:9; 108:5; Isa 57:15; Eph 4:6) are analogical. Heaven itself is part of God's creation, and God is no less present in the earth. As Francis Turretin explains, "God is said 'to be in heaven,' not exclusively of the earth, not as if he is included in heaven as to essence; but because in heaven as a royal palace, he displays his glory in an eminent manner." Thus, we are called to raise our eyes to heaven in order to direct our faith and prayers to God—specifically, placing them "upon our altar (Christ in heaven)" rather than looking to earthly idols.[90] Although God transcends time and space, he enters both freely as through an open door that he has created. More than this, even *enters* must be understood analogically, since God is already present in every moment and permeates every place.

To say that God is infinite is not to say that he is infinitely *extended throughout* time and space (the pantheistic view of ancient philosophers like Seneca and modern philosophers like Spinoza). Rather, it is to say that God *transcends the very categories of* time and space. Just as God can freely relate to the world without being conditioned by the world in his being, God can freely enter into time and space without being circumscribed or contained within either. To affirm God's infinite character is simply to witness once again to the marvelous truth that the difference between the Creator and creation is qualitative rather than quantitative.

Even if the ancient Hebrews did not understand *eternity* with the same philosophical conceptualities of classical Jewish and Christian theology, surely Paul was not afraid of the charge of Hellenizing when he endorsed a view of God as "the King eternal, immortal, invisible" (1Ti 1:17 NIV). It is significant that God's character as eternal is clustered here with his immortality and invisibility (or spirituality). It is not simply that God's duration, life, and being are *quantitatively* (even infinitely) greater but that he is *qualitatively* distinct from creatures to whom he has given the gift of time, space, and embodiment. In fact, eternity cannot refer to something that encompasses God. Indeed, not even the highest heavens are eternal. Only the triune God is eternal. The sempiternal view necessarily holds that there is at least one point at which God's being is univocal with creaturely being: namely, with respect to time. In this view, God may have more of it, but does not transcend this creaturely register.

As with the other incommunicable attributes we have considered, Scripture attests to God's eternity and omnipresence as a way of drawing the Creator-creature distinction. Besides Paul's doxology above (1 Ti 1:17), the Psalms often associate God's eternal nature with his other attributes of transcendence (including omnipresence):

> Lord, you have been our dwelling place
> > in all generations.
> Before the mountains were brought forth,
> > or ever you had formed the earth and the world,
> > from everlasting to everlasting you are God.

---

90. Turretin, *Elenctic Theology*, 1:199–200.

> You return man to dust
>   and say, "Return, O children of man!"
> For a thousand years in your sight
>   are but as yesterday when it is past,
>   or as a watch in the night. (Ps 90:1-4)

Regardless of whether eternity is to be understood here as beyond time or as infinitely extended time, it is obvious that God does not experience time as we do.[91] Even if God's eternity is not the simultaneity of past, present, and future, the reduction of a millennium to "a watch in the night" at least tends in that direction.[92] Precisely because God transcends time, he can be our dwelling place in all of our times. Just as God's aseity (self-existence) is the ground of his freedom for creation, his eternity is the presupposition of his freedom to relate temporal creatures to himself. He does not live in us; we live in him. We have time because God takes time to be with us.

I favor Augustine's conclusion that eternity transcends temporal categories—that time is a gift given with creation and for creation.[93] While God transcends time, redeemed creatures will experience a regathering of their times in perfect joy and fullness. Nevertheless, it is with the qualification that this "eternity" enjoyed by the saints is qualitatively distinct from God's eternal essence. Creatures (including their souls) are not by nature eternal, even though God *bestows immortality* on them in the resurrection. God alone "has immortality" (1 Ti 6:16). In the consummation, temporal creatures will remain temporal even in their experience of everlasting joy. For temporal and embodied creatures, analogies stretch to the breaking point. In light of this analogical approach, Louis Berkhof wisely cautions:

> We generally think of God's eternity in the same way, namely, as duration infinitely prolonged both backwards and forwards. But this is only a popular and symbolical way of representing that which in reality transcends time and differs from it essentially.... "Time," says Dr. [James] Orr, "strictly has relation to the world of objects existing in succession. God fills time; is in every part of it; but his eternity still is not really this being in time."[94]

This is not an intellectual cop-out but an entirely appropriate creaturely response

---

91. Once again, the doctrine of analogy proves its value. In his defense of God's temporality, Nicholas Wolterstorff concludes concerning the possibility of passages favoring God's eternal timelessness, "Of course if there were such passages, we would then be faced with the question of whether or not to take *these* passages as literally true." "The burden of proof, for Christians," he suggests, "lies on those who think that it [Scripture] should not be so taken" ("Unqualified Divine Temporality," in *God and Time: Four Views* [ed. Gregory E. Ganssle; Downers Grove, Ill.: InterVarsity Press, 2001], 189, 193). I take it that by *literal*, Wolterstorff means "univocal." However, according to an analogical account, *all* of the passages that disclose God's being and character are accommodated to our capacity rather than predicates that obtain univocally between God and creatures. As the Lord and creator of time, God cannot be made subject to it, even though he freely chooses to enter into it.

92. Of course, this is poetry, but it makes a theological claim.

93. Augustine, *Confessions* (trans. Henry Chadwick; Oxford: Oxford Univ. Press, 1991), bk. 11.

94. Berkhof, *Systematic Theology*, 60.

to the mystery of God's existence. "The relation of eternity to time constitutes one of the most difficult problems in philosophy and theology, perhaps incapable of solution in our present condition."[95]

DISCUSSION QUESTIONS

1. In exploring God's attributes in Scripture, what is the relationship between verbs and nouns—and beyond that, the relationship between narratives and names?

2. What do we mean by *incommunicable attributes*? With which way of investigating God's attributes are these most characteristically identified?

3. Do these attributes so stress God's transcendence that any genuine relationship between God and creatures is denied?

4. What biblical passages seem to challenge the idea that God is unchanging? How would you interpret them?

5. Identify and evaluate the various positions on God and time.

---

95. Ibid.

Chapter Seven

GOD: THE COMMUNICABLE ATTRIBUTES

The attributes treated in the previous chapter stress God's transcendent otherness from us: hence, the dominance of the negative prefix (e.g., God is *in*finite, *im*mutable, *in*visible, etc.). The attributes we consider in this chapter are called "communicable," because they are predicated of God and creatures, though always analogically.[1] Therefore, the way of eminence (*via eminentia*) takes center stage, with its *omni* (all) prefixes instead of negations. Especially in light of God's simplicity, the distinction between incommunicable and communicable attributes is merely a heuristic device. Some theologians treat God's omniscience and sovereignty under *incommunicable attributes*, but I am treating these attributes here because they are characteristics of God's knowledge and power.

infinite knowledge   *infinite power*

I. OMNISCIENCE AND OMNIPOTENCE: GOD'S KNOWLEDGE, WISDOM, AND POWER

Our knowledge is partial, ectypal, composite, and learned, but God's is complete, archetypal, simple, and innate. Hence, God is omniscient, that is, all-knowing (1Sa 23:10–13; 2Ki 13:19; Ps 139:1–6; Isa 40:12–14; 42:9; Jer 1:4; 38:17–20; Eze 3:6; Mt 11:21). God depends on the world no more for his knowledge than for

---

1. Turretin, *Elenctic Theology*, offers a typical scholastic definition: "The communicable attributes are not predicated of God and creatures univocally because there is not the same relation as in things simply univocal agreeing in name and definition. Nor are they predicated equivocally because there is not a totally diverse relation, as in things merely equivocal agreeing only in name. They are predicated analogically, by analogy both of similitude and of attribution.... Believers are said to be partakers of the divine nature (2Pe 1:4) not univocally (by a formal participation of the divine essence), but only analogically (by the benefit of regeneration ... since they are renewed after the image of their Creator, Col 3:10)" (1:190).

his being. Nor can his knowledge be any more circumscribed than his presence or duration. Even when we foreknow things hidden from others, our knowledge is finite and fallible. However, God's foreknowledge is qualitatively distinct. For us, knowing certain things is accidental to our nature; our humanity is not threatened by our ignorance of many things. However, God's simplicity entails that none of his attributes are added to his existence. It is impossible for God *not* to know everything comprehensively. Given his eternality, he knows the end from the beginning in one simultaneous act. God knows all things because he has decreed the end from the beginning and "works all things according to the counsel of his will" (Eph 1:11). This knowledge is inseparable from God's wisdom (Ro 8:28; 11:33; 14:7–8; 1Co 2:7; Eph 1:11–12; 3:10; Col 1:16).

In Scripture, God's knowledge and wisdom are closely related to veracity or truth (OT: ʾĕmet, ʾĕmûnâ, ʾāmēn; NT: alēthēs, alētheia, alēthinos, pistis). God *is* truth — in an ethical sense (i.e., fidelity: Nu 23:19; Jn 14:6; Ro 3:4; Heb 6:18) and in a logical sense (i.e., knowing how things really are). These characteristics converge in the prominent biblical theme of God's faithfulness (Heb. ḥesed), which is defined by his commitment to his covenant. It is this faithfulness that is on trial in covenantal history, involving Israel and Yahweh in the interchanging roles of judge, defendant, and witness — with testimony and countertestimony mediated by the prophets.

God's simplicity also cautions us against raising God's omnipotence above his other attributes. God always exercises his power in wisdom, knowledge, and truth. In fact, God is not able to exercise his power in a manner that is inconsistent with any of his other attributes.

A. FREE AGENTS AND THE INFINITE-QUALITATIVE DISTINCTION

Often, debates over divine and human freedom share a common misunderstanding of agency (willing and acting) as univocal for God and humans. *[handwritten: having only one meaning]* Therefore, the debate turns on who has *more* power over the other. Although open theism clearly constructs a straw opponent when it accuses Augustinian/Reformed theology of teaching that God is the only cause of all things (omnicausalism), there are extreme examples outside the mainstream that give life to the caricature.[2] Hyper-Calvinism shares with Arminianism (and especially open theism) a rationalistic tendency toward a univocal interpretation of the noun "freedom." The one begins with the central dogma of omnicausalism and the other with the central dogma of libertarian free will. However, if even freedom is predicated of God and humans analogically, then there is not a single "freedom pie" to be rationed (however unequally) between partners.

---

2. Against such extremes (and caricatures), the consistent teaching of Reformed theologians has affirmed God's sovereign decree concerning "whatsoever comes to pass," yet without coercion or directly causing every event (*Westminster Confession*, 3.1).

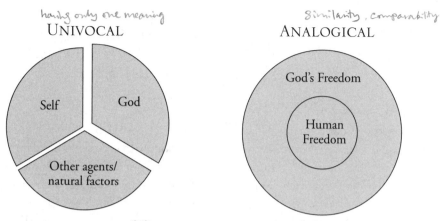

having only one meaning UNIVOCAL

similarity, comparability ANALOGICAL

<u>Human Freedom</u> (ectypal [*copy*]: "In him we live and move and have our being")
<u>God's Freedom</u> (archetypal [*original*]: God is the source of all creaturely freedom)

The reason that creatures possess any power and freedom at all is that they are created in the image of the God, whose sovereignty is qualitatively distinct and unique. Instead of being grateful for this vast creaturely (ectypal) liberty, Satan and human beings since the fall have longed for an independent and autonomous freedom grounded only in themselves. However, this craving to transcend creaturely existence is unreasonable. After all, "The earth is the LORD's and the fullness thereof" (Ps 24:1). God's omnipotence, as I. A. Dorner observed, is not set over against our freedom but is its necessary precondition.[3] Because God *is* freedom, such a thing as freedom exists and can be communicated to us in a creaturely mode.

Since all of our knowledge is analogical and accommodated, we can know only *that*, not *how*, God's sovereignty and human responsibility are perfectly consistent. Even when both agents are active in the same event, the terms *agents* and *active* are used analogically. Humans do not have *less* power than God but *all* of the power that is essential to their created nature. The "freedom pie" is God's. He does not surrender pieces but gives us our own pie that is a finite analogy of his own. "In him we live and move and have our being" (Ac 17:28). As God's image bearers, we *reflect* God's glory, but God does not give his own glory to a creature (Isa 48:11).

Tyrants stalk the earth devouring the freedom of their subjects. The flame of their power can burn only to the extent that it consumes the liberty of others. However, God "gives ... life and breath and everything" to us (Ac 17:25). God is a producer, not a consumer, of our creaturely freedom, and his presence fills our creaturely room with the air of liberty. Precisely because God alone is sovereign,

---

3. I. A. Dorner, *Divine Immutability: A Critical Reconsideration* (ed. Robert R. Williams and Claude Welch; Minneapolis: Fortress, 1994), 147.

qualitatively distinct in his freedom as Lord, creaturely freedom has its inexhaustible source in abundance rather than lack, generosity rather than a rationing or negotiation of wills.

B. SOVEREIGNTY AND OMNISCIENCE

God knows our thoughts exhaustively (Pss 44:21; 94:11), but God's thoughts are inaccessible to us apart from revelation. It is not simply that God has more thoughts, better thoughts, or deeper thoughts, but that his *way* of knowing is his own, never overlapping with creaturely knowledge. "For my thoughts are not your thoughts, neither are your ways my ways, declares the LORD. For as the heavens are higher than the earth, so are my ways higher than your ways and my thoughts than your thoughts" (Isa 55:8–9). In fact, Paul's excursus on God's freedom in election leads to the doxology,

> Oh, the depth of the riches and wisdom and knowledge of God! How unsearchable are his judgments and how inscrutable his ways!
>
> > "For who has known the mind of the Lord,
> >   or who has been his counselor?"
> > "Or who has given a gift to him
> >   that he might be repaid?"
>
> For from him and through him and to him are all things. To him be glory forever. Amen. (Ro 11:33–36)

In the great courtroom trial of the religions Yahweh declares,

> Who is like me? Let them proclaim it,
>   let them declare and set it forth before me.
> Who has announced from of old the things to come?
>   Let them tell us what is yet to be.
> Do not fear, or be afraid;
>   have I not told you from of old and declared it?
>   You are my witnesses!
> Is there any god besides me?
>   There is no other rock; I know not one. (Isa 44:7–8 NRSV)

God's knowledge can no more be confined to a temporal past than his presence can be confined to a spatial place.

God's knowledge and wisdom are particularly evident in the history of redemption, as the context of Paul's doxology (Ro 11:33) underscores. God's wisdom is seen in the revelation of the mystery of Christ in these last days, a wisdom that reduces human speculation and erudition to foolishness (1Co 2:7; Eph 3:10–11; Col 1:16). "In [Christ] we have obtained an inheritance, having been predestined according to the purpose of him who works all things according to the counsel of his will" (Eph 1:11). God's knowledge and wisdom, then, are not abstract concepts but are displayed characteristically in the service of God's covenant of grace—that is, in the unfolding mystery of God's purposes in Christ. It is this wisdom and knowledge that God reveals to his prophets (Isa 42:9; Am 3:7). In fact, Christ is himself the content of that wisdom and knowledge (1Co 1:30). God the Father has no higher or more prized knowledge than his knowledge of the Son—and vice versa.

On one hand, Scripture teaches that God has predestined the free acts of human beings; on the other hand, God represents himself as a genuine partner in history. God's revealed will is often disobeyed, but his sovereign will (i.e., that which he has predestined) is never thwarted. For example, Jesus proclaimed and offered himself to his people as the Messiah of Israel, even to the point of lamenting, "O Jerusalem, Jerusalem, the city that kills the prophets and stones those who are sent to it! How often would I have gathered your children together as a hen gathers her brood under her wings, and you would not!" (Mt 23:37). However, he also said, "No one can come to me unless the Father who sent me draws him" (Jn 6:44), and, "You did not choose me, but I chose you" (Jn 15:16).

In his Pentecost sermon, Peter expresses no fear of contradiction when in the same breath he blames human beings for Christ's crucifixion and says that Christ was "delivered up according to the definite plan and foreknowledge of God" (Ac 2:23). God's predestination in no way rendered the choices and actions of human beings illusory; rather, it was through such uncoerced responses that God fulfilled his secret plan. So God wills and acts, and humans will and act, but "will" and "act" are predicated analogically rather than univocally. In the familiar Joseph narrative, the same event—Joseph's cruel treatment by his brothers—has two authors with two distinct intentions: "You meant evil against me, but God meant it for good" (Ge 50:20).

Even in his revelation God remains transcendent and incomprehensible. God invites the whole world to salvation in his Son, yet effectually calls and gives faith to all whom he has elected from all of eternity. Our province is not God's secret counsels, but his revelation: "The secret things belong to the LORD our God, but the things that are revealed belong to us and to our children forever" (Dt 29:29). While God's secret plan does not change, his revealed plans often do. It is good news for us that the former is the basis for God's immutable commitment to our salvation, regardless of the obstacles we place in his path. God knows all things exhaustively because he has decreed all things exhaustively.

Open theists have recognized that even the traditional Arminian argument for predestination based on God's infallible foreknowledge renders those foreknown choices and actions certain. Therefore, open theists deny such exhaustive divine foreknowledge: God knows everything that he *can* know, but this excludes the free decisions of human beings.[4]

C. SOVEREIGNTY AND OMNIPRESENCE

Wolfhart Pannenberg draws together omnipotence, omniscience, and omnipresence, and he makes a good case for this. "No power, however, great, can be efficacious unless present to its object," he observes. "Omnipresence is thus a condition of omnipotence. But omnipotence shows what omnipresence by the Spirit actually means."[5] Pannenberg is not suggesting that only the Spirit possesses the divine attribute of omnipresence, but he underscores the important point that the Godhead exercises this omnipresence from the Father, in the Son, and by the Spirit. *Essences* do not will and act; only *persons* do. Because God is a Trinity, he acts sovereignly not only *on* creation but *in* it and *within* it, winning its consent rather than coercing or directly causing every decision and action. A Trinitarian perspective on God's sovereignty guards against Aristotle's mechanical concept of the Unmoved Mover.

John of Damascus seems to be thinking along similar lines when he relates God's omnipotence to his omniscience and omnipresence. First, he affirms that God knows all things, "holding them timelessly in his thoughts; and each one conformably to his voluntary and timeless thought, which constitutes predetermination and image and pattern, comes into existence at the predetermined time."[6] And then he adds, "For he is his own place filling all things and being above all things, and himself maintaining all things. Yet we speak of God having place and the place of God where his energy becomes manifest.... And his sacred flesh has been named the foot of God. The church, too, is spoken of as the place of God: for we have set this apart for the glorifying of God as a sort of consecrated place wherein we also hold converse with him."[7]

Therefore, a biblical view of God's sovereignty must always bear in mind the following correlatives. First, only when we recognize that *God is qualitatively distinct from creation* can we see that God is free to be the creator and redeemer, while we are free to be creatures and the redeemed. As Paul's citation of the Greek poet affirms,

---

4. See, for example, Clark Pinnock, "Systematic Theology," in *The Openness of God: A Biblical Challenge to the Traditional Understanding of God* (ed. Clark Pinnock et al.; Downers Grove, Ill.: InterVarsity Press, 1994), 121–23; Clark Pinnock, *Most Moved Mover* (Grand Rapids: Baker, 2001), 100; William Hasker, "An Adequate God," in *Searching for an Adequate God: A Dialogue between Process and Free Will Theists* (ed. John B. Cobb Jr. and Clark H. Pinnock; Grand Rapids: Eerdmans, 2000), 218–19. These writers insist that this view still affirms God's omniscience, but they fail to demonstrate how "all-knowledge" can exist when God is said to be ignorant of the

vast majority of future actions (namely, those brought about by human decision).

5. Wolfhart Pannenberg, *Systematic Theology* (Grand Rapids: Eerdmans, 1991), 1:415.

6. John of Damascus, "An Exact Exposition of the Orthodox Faith," in *NPNF2*, 9:12 (PG 94, col. 837).

7. Ibid., 9:15 (PG 94, col. 852). The same point was made in Paul's speech—namely, that it is precisely because God *transcends* time and space that he can *give* all places and times to creatures (Ac 17:24–27).

we live and move and have our being *in* God (analogically), not *with* or *alongside* God (univocally). It is not shared space but a lush garden of our own creaturely freedom that God has given to us.

Second, only when we understand God's sovereignty in the light of his *simplicity*—that is, the consistency of his willing and acting in accordance with his other attributes—can we avoid the notion of a divine despot whose sovereignty is unconditioned by his own nature. The idea of God's "absolute might" advocated by late-medieval voluntarism was judged by Calvin to be "profane." "We fancy no lawless god who is a law unto himself."[8]

Third, we must always bear in mind that in every exercise of his will and power, God is not a solitary monad but *the Father, the Son, and the Spirit.* The Father always wills and acts in the Son and by his Spirit, as well as through contingent agency. Therefore, God's sovereignty cannot be conceived as brute force or control.[9]

II. GOODNESS, LOVE, AND MERCY

God's knowledge, wisdom, and power are inseparable from his *goodness.* In fact, in the strict sense, Jesus said, "No one is good except God alone" (Mk 10:18). God's infinite goodness is the source of all creaturely imitations. Precisely because God does not depend on the world, his goodness is never threatened. God is good toward all he has made, even his enemies (Ps 145:9, 15–16; Mt 5:45). He can afford to be, because he is God with or without them.

Because God's attributes are identical with his essence, God not only loves; he *is* love (1Jn 3:1; 4:8, 16).[10] God loves absolutely and without any compulsion from the object of his love (Mt 5:44–45; Jn 3:16; 16:27; Ro 5:8). God takes delight in that which he does not need but nevertheless desires. Here, too, we must see that human love is not the measure of divine love, but vice versa. God is the original; we are the copy: "In this is love, not that we have loved God but that he loved us and sent his Son to be the propitiation for our sins" (1Jn 4:10).

Only God can love in absolute freedom, desiring the other without needing the other. It is not only impossible but is a cruel demand to expect human beings to love each other out of pure, disinterested benevolence. Even apart from sin, human beings were created in a web of relationships not only with each other but with

---

8. Calvin, *Institutes* 3.23.2. In his *Sermons on Job* (trans. Arthur Golding; Edinburgh: Banner of Truth Trust, 1993), Calvin writes, "And undoubtedly whereas the doctors of the Sorbonne say that God hath an absolute or lawless power, it is a devilish blasphemy forged in hell, for it ought not once to enter into a faithful man's head" (415).

9. As Stephen N. Williams observes in an essay ("The Sov-

ereignty of God," in *Engaging the Doctrine of God* [ed. Bruce L. McCormack; Grand Rapids: Baker, 2008], 175–78), this is a weakness in some defenses of God's sovereignty.

10. For an excellent biblical-theological treatment of this attribute, see especially D. A. Carson, *The Difficult Doctrine of the Love of God* (Wheaton: Crossway Books, 1999).

nonhuman creation. When these relationships are functioning properly, each has what he or she needs and loves out of gratitude and mutual dependence as well as simple desire for the other. However, God loves in perfect freedom. Therefore, he loves even those who do not return his love, and he loved us eternally even while we were enemies (Ro 5:10).

In the light of God's simplicity, we can never pit God's sovereignty against his love or his love against his sovereignty. It is especially in our day not a far stretch from "God is love" to "Love is God." However, as C. S. Lewis observed, when love itself becomes a god, it becomes demonic.[11] God always exercises his power, holiness, righteousness, and wrath—as well as his love and mercy—in conformity with his goodness. In fact, we could hardly affirm God's goodness if he did not uphold justice and the cause of his righteousness against sin and evil.

God's goodness is evident in creation and providence, of course, but <u>the clearest evidence of the complete consistency between God's goodness and his sovereignty, justice, wrath, and righteousness is Christ's cross.</u> There we behold the face of the God-Man who cries out, "It is finished." There, with unparalleled clarity, we see how far God is willing to go in order to uphold all of his attributes in the simplicity of his being. Human love is analogical of God's love, not vice versa. David Tracy reminds us that we must begin with the particular act of God in Jesus Christ rather than a "general conception" of love.

> [I]f this classic Johannine metaphor "God is love" is not grounded and thereby interpreted by means of the harsh and demanding reality of the message and ministry, the cross and resurrection of this unsubstitutable Jesus who, as the Christ, disclosed God's face turned to us as Love, then Christians may be tempted to sentimentalize the metaphor by reversing it into "Love is God." But this great reversal, on inner-Christian terms, is hermeneutically impossible. "God is love": this identity of God the Christian experiences in and through the history of God's actions and self-disclosure as the God who is Love in Jesus Christ, the parable and face of God.[12]

If God's love could trump his other moral attributes, then the cross represents the cruelest waste. The cross is the clearest testimony to God's simplicity—that is, his undivided and indivisible character.[13]

---

11. C. S. Lewis, *The Four Loves* (New York: Houghton Mifflin Harcourt, 1960), 22.

12. David Tracy, "Trinitarian Speculation and the Forms of Divine Disclosure," in *The Trinity* (ed. Stephen T. Davis, Daniel Kendall, SJ, Gerald O'Collins, SJ; Oxford: Oxford Univ. Press, 1999), 285–86. In a similar vein, J. Gresham Machen wrote, "It is a strange thing when men talk about the love of God, they show by every word that they utter that they have no conception at all of the depths of God's love. If you want to find an instance of true gratitude for the infinite grace of God, do not go to those

who think of God's love as something that costs nothing, but go rather to those who in agony of soul have faced the awful fact of the guilt of sin, and then have come to know with a trembling wonder that the miracle of all miracles has been accomplished, and that the eternal Son has died in their stead" (*Selected Shorter Writings* [ed. D. G. Hart; Phillipsburg, N.J.: P&R, 2004], 32).

13. One of many examples of attempting to decode the inner being of God (including the Trinity) by making God's love alone definitive of his inner being is Stanley Grenz, *Theology for the Community of God* (Grand Rapids: Eerdmans, 2000),

What makes God's love so comforting, therefore, is not only the obvious point that it has not been twisted into lust (which idolizes the other only to consume and dismember it as an object) but the more basic fact that this is so precisely because God's love is unconditioned by anything in the creature. Whenever God acts toward creatures, it is out of the complete satisfaction that he already enjoys as the Trinity. The eternally begotten Son lives from the love of the Father, but the Father is such because he has a Son, and in the Spirit the Father and the Son not only have a third person to love but one who loves them in return and brings sinful creatures into the circle of that loving fellowship. As Wolfhart Pannenberg observes, the Augustinian conviction that "God is he who eternally loves himself" can be maintained only when we understand this not only as the love of a solitary person for his own essence but as the love of the divine persons for each other.[14] In this eternal intratrinitarian exchange, no one is ever let down. There is no Stoic fear of entrusting one's happiness to the other.

Necessary rather than contingent, God's essential attributes would be expressed and manifested even if there were no fall into sin or even a creation external to the triune God. God would still be *gracious* and *merciful* in his essence even if there were no transgressors. In fact, God's gracious and merciful character does not require that he show mercy to anyone. Rebellion of such a high creature against such a holy God deserves everlasting punishment. God remains gracious and merciful in his essence, even though the exercise and objects of his mercy are determined in absolute freedom. In other words, God is not free to decide whether he will be merciful and gracious, but he is free to decide whether he will have mercy on some rather than others: "I will have mercy on whom I have mercy, and I will have compassion on whom I have compassion" (Ro 9:15, appealing to Ex 33:19). By definition, grace is undeserved, and mercy is the opposite of one's deserts.

Appealing to Reformed orthodoxy, Barth underscored the danger in treating grace merely as a gift, especially (as in Roman Catholic teaching) as an infused substance, abstracted from God in Christ. In grace, God gives nothing less than himself. Grace, then, is not a third thing or substance mediating between God

---

72–75. First, this move renders God's wrath merely a subjective experience of unbelievers rather than an objective divine stance (73), which eliminates any concept of propitiation. Second, this leads Grenz to assert that the essential unity of the Trinity is simply the love of each member for each other, since love "builds the unity of God" (72; cf. *The Named God and the Question of Being: A Trinitarian Theo-Ontology* [Louisville: Westminster John Knox, 2005], 336). This intratrinitarian love "describes God's inner life..." and offers "a direct insight" into his being (*The Named God*, 339). As a consequence of this elimination of the Creator-creature distinction, Grenz adds, "The Bible is the outworking of God's *essence* through the story of God's activity

in history in bringing about salvation" (397, emphasis added). Impatience with mystery and analogy seems to motivate these and similar attempts to unmask the hidden God. A different, but no less hazardous, speculation about the Trinity based on love may be found in Jonathan Edwards. See Oliver D. Crisp, "Jonathan Edwards' God: Trinity, Individuation, and Divine Simplicity," in *Engaging the Doctrine of God: Contemporary Protestant Perspectives* (ed. Bruce L. McCormack; Grand Rapids: Baker Academic, 2008), 91–105.

14. Pannenberg (*Systematic Theology*, 1:426) corrects Eberhard Jüngel on this point, citing Jüngel's *God as the Mystery of the World* (trans. Darrell L. Guder; Grand Rapids: Eerdmans, 1983).

and sinners, but is Jesus Christ in redeeming action. "God owes nothing to any counterpart." In short, "Grace means redemption," Barth adds.[15] Beyond the love and goodness that God shows to creation generally, grace "is always God's turning to those who not only do not deserve this favour, but have deserved the very opposite."[16] In fact, "Grace itself is mercy."[17]

The confidence of those who trust in God's promise is that "God is gracious and full of compassion" (Pss 86:15; 103:8; 116:5; 145:8). B. A. Gerrish points out that especially in Paul's eschatological thinking, "God's grace has *appeared* ... 'Grace,' for [Paul], means more than a divine attribute: it refers to something that has happened, entered into history," as in John 1:17: "Grace and truth came (*egeneto*) through Jesus Christ" (cf. 2Ti 1:9–10).[18] Grace is God's free favor toward sinners on account of Christ.

Similar to grace and mercy is God's *patience* toward transgressors (Ex 34:6; Ps 86:15; Ro 2:4; 9:22; 1Pe 3:20; 2Pe 3:15). Here, too, God is patient, but he is free to show his patience to whomever he chooses. Patience presupposes a situation in which God could justly respond in wrath. Grace, mercy, and long-suffering are the form that God's love and goodness take in relation to sinners.

III. HOLINESS, RIGHTEOUSNESS, AND JUSTICE

At the same time that God is kind, merciful, and long-suffering, he is also *holy*. The Hebrew word for "holy" (*qôdeš*) comes from the verb "to cut or separate," translated into Greek as *hagios* from the verb "to make holy" (*hagiazō*). In general terms, it underscores the Creator-creature distinction. God is majestic, glorious, beyond reproach. In a certain sense, holiness characterizes all of God's attributes. In his communicable and incommunicable attributes, God is qualitatively distinct from us. Beyond this ontological distinction, however, *holiness* typically refers in Scripture to God's ethical purity, which is especially evident against the backdrop of human sinfulness. God cannot be tempted nor tempt; he is ethically incapable of being drawn into evil (Jas 1:13). Thus, God's holiness especially marks the *ontological distinction* between Creator and creatures as well as the *ethical opposition* between God and sinners. However, because of God's mercy, God's holiness not only highlights his difference from us; it also includes his movement toward us, binding us to him in covenant love. In this way, God makes us holy. That holiness which is inherent in God alone comes to characterize a relationship in which creatures are separated

15. Barth, *Church Dogmatics*, vol. 2, pt. 1, 353–55. Barth quotes Polanus as follows: "Gratia in Deo residens est essentialis proprietas eius nimirum benignissima voluntas Dei et favor, per quem vere et proprie est gratiosus, quo favet et gratis benefacit creaturae suae" (353).

16. Ibid., 356.

17. Ibid., 369.

18. B. A. Gerrish, "Sovereign Grace: Is Reformed Theology Obsolete?" *Interpretation* 57, no. 1 (January 2003): 45.

unto God, *from* sin and death. Only in Christ can God's holiness be for us a source of delight rather than of fear of judgment.

Simply by creating the world in a state of rectitude as the space for fellowship with creatures, God hallowed the world. Yet after the fall, the holy becomes profane, subject to the curse. Nevertheless, God claims for himself certain places, peoples, and times as the sphere within which he will work out his redemptive purposes and even show his common grace to secular culture. When God elects Israel, calling Abram out of Ur, he makes holy that which is common, literally *cutting* Israel out of the nations by circumcision. While the nations inhabit an enchanted cosmos filled with gods and supernatural forces, Israel knows only Yahweh and its own election by Yahweh. Barth rightly comments, "The holy God of Scripture is certainly not 'the holy' of R. Otto, a numinous element which, in its aspect as *tremendum*, is in itself and as such divine. But the holy God of Scripture is the Holy One of Israel."[19]

The close proximity of God's holiness and glory (*kābôd*) is especially evident in Isaiah's vision (Isa 6), and both concepts are closely related to the Spirit as God's *Shekinah* presence among his people and, one day, throughout the earth. This holiness must be read by us through the lens of the gospel; otherwise, it becomes a blinding glory, an overwhelming presence that reduces sinful creatures to death, or to an idolatrous mysticism—a theology of glory. Only in Christ are the unholy made holy, elected, and separated out of the world as the temple that his glory fills.

The New Testament in no way contradicts this distinction between holy and profane, but rather God's holiness widens to include Gentiles, who are "cut out" of the perishing world through faith and receive the covenant sign and seal of baptism (Ac 10:9–48). Thus, as we have seen with other attributes typically associated with God's transcendence, God's holiness is a marker not only of God's distinction from the creation but also of God's driving passion to make the whole earth his holy dwelling. Although God alone is essentially holy, he does not keep holiness to himself but spreads his fragrance throughout creation. God *is* holy in his *essence*; people, places, and things are *made* holy by God's *energies*.

Righteousness (from the root *ṣdq*) in the Old Testament is a simultaneously forensic and relational term. It is a "right relationship" that is legally verified by obedience to the covenantal stipulations.[20] It is related closely to *mišpaṭ* (justice).[21] God's

---

19. Barth, *Church Dogmatics*, vol. 2, pt. 1, 360.

20. *Righteousness* has been one of the most widely debated terms in the Old Testament. Walther Eichrodt noted, "It is a decided obstacle to any attempt to define the concept of divine righteousness, that the original significance of the root *ṣdq* should be irretrievably lost." The predominant use is right behavior. "When applied to the conduct of God, the concept is narrowed and almost exclusively employed in a forensic sense.

God's *ṣedāqā* or *ṣedeq* is his keeping of the law in accordance with the terms of the covenant" (*Theology of the Old Testament* [trans. J. A. Baker; Philadelphia: Westminster, 1961], 1:240). This is not the distributive justice of Roman law, though, which is too formal and abstract to describe Israel's thought. Eichrodt follows the lead of Hermann Cremer, who interpreted righteousness as a right relationship between persons.

21. Ibid., 1:241.

righteousness is also connected with his mercy, especially in the Psalms. "*The maintenance of the fellowship now becomes the justification of the ungodly.* No manner of human effort, but only that righteousness which is the gift of God, can lead to that conduct which is truly in keeping with the covenant."[22] God has a moral vision for his creation, which is revealed in the various covenants that he makes with human beings in history, and his righteousness involves his indefatigable determination to see that vision through to the end for his glory and the good of creation.

At the same time, God's righteousness cannot simply be collapsed into his mercy (i.e., justification by grace through faith). As the revelation of God's moral will (i.e., law), God's righteousness condemns all people as transgressors; as the revelation of God's saving will (i.e., the gospel), God's righteousness saves all who believe (Ro 3:19–26). In both cases, God upholds his own righteousness. Against Albrecht Ritschl's view, which collapses righteousness into mercy, Barth affirms that God's righteousness includes the concept of distributive justice—"a righteousness which judges and therefore both exculpates and condemns, rewards and also punishes."[23] Yet for Barth, this condemnation turns out to be just another form of love and grace. According to Barth, God's wrath is always a form of mercy.[24] However, in Scripture, God's wrath is his righteous response to sin and his mercy is a free decicion to grant absolution to the guilty. As we have seen, God is free to show mercy on whomever he will and to leave the rest under his just condemnation. The righteousness that God discloses in the law brings condemnation, but the gift of righteousness that God gives brings justification and life (Ro 3:19–22). Once again, it is at the cross where we see the marvelous unity of divine attributes that might seem otherwise to clash. This paradox is lost if mercy, righteousness, and wrath are synonymous terms.

IV. JEALOUSY AND WRATH

Like mercy, grace, and patience, jealousy and wrath are aroused only in the context of an offense. God does not need to display these attributes in order to be who he is, but they are the response we would expect from the kind of God who is good, just, and holy. Just as God "has mercy on whomever he wills," he also "hardens whomever he wills" (Ro 9:18). *God must be just, but he is free to display his mercy toward some and his wrath toward others* (v. 22). Even when God expresses his wrath,

---

22. Ibid., 1:247.

23. Barth, *Church Dogmatics*, vol. 2, pt. 1, 391.

24. According to Barth's notion of universal election, every person is simultaneously condemned in himself or herself and justified in Christ. There can be no Easter Yes without the Good Friday No, but it is the Yes that wins out in the end, not only for all who believe but, at least in principle, for every person (ibid.,

394). Thus, condemnation and justification apply to all people, not to a race divided between righteous/unrighteous, sheep/ goats, saved/lost, justified/condemned, etc. In the contexts in which these contrasts appear in Scripture, however, there is no hint of these categories simply reflecting the dialectical truth about every person.

it is not the ill-tempered and irrational violence that is associated with the eruption of human emotion. God's wrath always expresses his wisdom and judgment—and even his love, which along with his other attributes has been accosted by those whom he created for love and to love. A being who is perfect in goodness and love *must* exercise wrath against sin, evil, hatred, and injustice.

Especially when considering God's jealousy, the doctrine of analogy proves its merits. We can be glad that whatever it is like for God to be jealous, it is qualitatively different from human jealousy—especially in our sinful condition. For example, as I. A. Dorner remarks, "The divine jealousy is one that is holy and not one that is envious."[25] Because God is righteous, holy, and just, and not a Stoic sage whose bliss is unaffected by evil actions, "his wrath is quickly kindled" (Ps 2:12). As with wrath, jealousy strikes most of us as unworthy of God particularly because of its associations in our own experience. As wrath generally connotes a thirst for revenge or brings to mind the temper tantrums of the powerful against the weak, jealousy is with good reason regarded universally as a negative human trait. But instead of jettisoning jealousy or attempting to "translate" it into (i.e., accommodate it to) our own experience, the biblical representation of God's jealousy can open us up to a new understanding of the term that challenges and potentially heals our experiences of corrupt human jealousy.

Robert Jenson is probably not saying too much when he suggests, "In the Scriptures … it is first among the Lord's attributes that he is 'a jealous God.'"[26] Yet once again this claim must be situated in its covenantal context. In the ancient Near Eastern treaties, the suzerain (great king) who liberated a lesser nation required the vassal to serve him only, refusing any backroom alliances with other suzerains. Jealousy, then, was the appropriate response of the suzerain to the treasonous conspiracy of the servant with his enemies. However, even this suzerain-vassal relationship is an analogy, and in Yahweh's unique performance the role of "jealous suzerain" is transformed.

The sole lordship of Yahweh, as we have seen, is the presupposition of biblical faith, and it is carried forward into the fuller revelation of God's identity as applied to Jesus Christ: "I am the way, and the truth, and the life. No one comes to the Father except through me" (Jn 14:6). "Therefore God has highly exalted him and bestowed on him the name that is above every name, so that at the name of Jesus every knee should bow, in heaven and on earth and under the earth, and every tongue confess that Jesus Christ is Lord, to the glory of God the Father" (Php 2:9–11). Therefore, "There is salvation in no one else, for there is no other name under heaven given among mortals by which we must be saved" (Ac 4:12 NRSV).

---

25. Dorner, *Divine Immutability*, 178.

26. Robert Jenson, *Systematic Theology* (New York: Oxford Univ. Press, 1997), 1:47, referring to Exodus 34:14.

God will not give his glory to another (Isa 42:8). God is jealous for his own name and for the people who call on his name and are called by his name.

Jealousy in humans is a perversion because it implies a right that does not belong to us. We hoard possessions, and to the extent that even relationships, creatures, and other people can become possessions rather than genuine others, our jealousy confirms our oppressive stance. However, the God who possesses creation already exercises his covenant lordship by giving rather than possessing, by sacrificing rather than hoarding, by spending rather than saving his wealth. It is God's jealousy for his people, in fact, that underscores his love and eventuates in their salvation. In us, jealousy is a form of coveting—claiming that which is not ours. In God, jealousy is a form of protecting—guarding that which is precious to God, both his character and his covenant people.

DISCUSSION QUESTIONS

1. Is it useful to think of God's omnipotence together with his omniscience, wisdom, and omnipresence? If so, why?
2. Discuss the significance of the doctrine of analogy for our understanding of the relationship between God's sovereignty and human freedom.
3. If God is essentially loving, good, gracious, and merciful, does that mean he is required to show his favor to everyone?
4. Discuss the relationship between God's holiness, righteousness, and justice. Are these attributes sometimes in conflict with God's love and grace? Where do we see their harmony most clearly?
5. How is the jealousy that Scripture attributes to God different from the jealousy that we judge immoral in human beings?

Chapter Eight

THE HOLY TRINITY

If covenantal thinking forms the architecture of Reformed faith and practice, the doctrine of the Trinity is the foundation.[1] The Trinity is not merely one doctrine among others; besides being proclaimed in Word and sacrament, this article of faith structures all the faith and practice of Christianity: our theology, liturgies, hymns, and lives. This is why so many references have already been made in this volume to the Trinity, to the Trinitarian shape of Christian ontology and epistemology, and to Christianity's doctrines of revelation and the divine attributes. "In the doctrine of the Trinity," wrote Herman Bavinck, "beats the heart of the whole revelation of God for the redemption of humanity." As the Father, the Son, and the Spirit, "our God is above us, before us, and within us."[2] After tracing the biblical-theological development of the dogma, I will turn to its historical-theological formulation and then to a systematic-theological summary.

I. BIBLICAL-THEOLOGICAL DEVELOPMENT OF TRINITARIAN DOCTRINE

Faith in the one God—Yahweh—arose not out of Greek speculation but out of God's self-revelation to Israel. The same God who forbade idolatry was addressed by Jesus as "Father." In fact, Jesus answered Satan's temptation by reasserting Israel's creed, the *Shema*: "You shall worship the Lord your God and him only shall you serve" (Mt 4:10, paraphrasing Dt 6:13). Jesus' acts of healing are pointers to this God and to no other: "And they glorified the God of Israel" (Mt 15:31). His will

---

1. A good example is the marvelous integration of covenant theology and the doctrine of the Trinity in Douglas F. Kelly, *Systematic Theology: The God Who Is: The Holy Trinity* (Ross-shire, Scotland: Mentor, 2008).

2. Herman Bavinck, *Reformed Dogmatics: God and Creation* (ed. John Bolt; trans. John Vriend; Grand Rapids: Baker, 2004), 2:260.

is the Father's will, and his works are "the works that the Father has given me to accomplish" (Jn 5:36). While there may be many so-called gods for the nations, "yet for us," says Paul, "there is one God, the Father, from whom are all things and for whom we exist, and one Lord, Jesus Christ, through whom are all things and through whom we exist" (1Co 8:6). Turning Gentiles "from idols to serve the living and true God" was as essential a part of the apostles' message as it had been for the prophets (1Th 1:9; cf. 1Pe 4:3).[3] Appearing before the Roman governor Felix, Paul entreated, "This I confess to you, that according to the Way, which they call a sect, I worship the God of our fathers, believing everything laid down by the Law and written in the Prophets, having a hope in God" (Ac 24:14–15). Included in that confession is "one God" (Eph 4:6).

If the New Testament affirms monotheism, however, it is also the Christian claim that the Old Testament already anticipates some sort of plurality when three distinct actors appear on the stage of Israel's history, sometimes even in the same scene, each identified as God. On the basis of the "new thing" that God had accomplished in Jesus Christ, the early Christians were directed by Jesus himself (especially in his postresurrection instruction reported in Lk 24) to reread the Old Testament texts with him at their center. Similar to the messianic passages in the Psalms and the Prophets, the "Angel of the LORD" theophanies simultaneously distinguish the Angel from and identify him with Yahweh (Ge 18; 22:11–18; 32:24–30; Ex 3:2–6). He is the Angel of God's Presence (Isa 63:9), which connects him to the Shekinah presence (the *kābôd* or Glory-Spirit) of God himself. An especially interesting scene opens up to us in Zechariah's vision of a courtroom scene, with Yahweh himself (the personal name, not just the title) identified with the Angel of the LORD (Zec 3:1–4).

To be sure, the New Testament is more redolent with passages elaborating this earlier revelation. This is for obvious eschatological reasons: the Son was not eternally incarnate, but was made human "when the fullness of time had come" (Gal 4:4; cf. Ro 1:1–6). Central to the early development of Trinitarian thought was the simple fact that faithful Jews had come to believe that God had acted just as he had promised, but that the events of the resurrection and the sending of the Spirit had shed new light not only on the ministry and teaching of Jesus but on the whole history of redemption. The confession "one God in three persons" arises naturally out of the triadic formulas in the New Testament in the context of baptism (Mt 28:19 and par.) and liturgical blessings and benedictions (Mt 28:19; Jn 1:18; 5:23; Ro 5:5–8; 1Co 6:11; 8:6, 12:4–6; 2Co 13:13–14; Eph 4:4–6; 2Th 2:13; 1Ti 2:5,

---

3. Brevard Childs, *Biblical Theology of the Old and New Testaments* (Minneapolis: Fortress, 1993), 362. "Paul even invokes the classic covenant formula, 'I will be their God, and they shall be my people,' when admonishing the Christians to lead a holy life separate from unbelievers (2Co 6.17)," Childs notes.

1Pe 1:2). Each person is equally worshiped as God—first by Jewish believers who stood as resolutely as ever against the pagan polytheism that surrounded them. Long before the dogma of the Trinity reached its formal refinement, believers were placing their faith in, worshiping, praying to, and being baptized into the reality of which it speaks.

In Jesus' own baptism, there are not simply three *names* but three *actors*—the Father who speaks ("This is my beloved Son"), the "beloved Son" who is baptized, and the dove who hovers above Jesus, suggesting reference to the Spirit hovering over the waters in creation and concurring with the benediction on all that God has made (Mt 3:13–17; Mk 1:9–11; Lk 3:21–22; Jn 1:32–34). Jesus also identifies himself as the Lord of the Sabbath (Lk 6:5). The Jews believed that the Messiah would be David's descendant, but Jesus points out to the religious leaders that David himself called this future son his Lord in Psalm 110:1 (Lk 20:41–44).

In John's Gospel, the self-identification of Jesus with God appears in the opening verses, as an intentional echo of the prologue in Genesis: "In the beginning was the Word, and the Word was with God, and the Word was God [*kai theos ēn ho logos*]. He was in the beginning with God. All things were made through him, and without him was not any thing made that was made" (Jn 1:1–3). He is "the only Son from the Father" (*monogenous para patros*, v. 14) and "the only begotten Son [*monogenēs theos*], who is in the bosom of the Father" (v. 18 NKJV).

The Word is simultaneously distinct from God the Father ("was with God") and one in essence with the Father ("was God"). Therefore, two crucial points are already made: The Word is a person distinct from the Father who is nevertheless identified also as God. This distinction of the Son from the Father and their unity in essence consistently reassert themselves throughout the fourth gospel, with Jesus' appropriation of God's personal name (Yahweh, I AM), existence, and attributes (Jn 6:35, 48, 51; 8:12, 58; 9:5, 28; 10:11, 14; 11:25; 14:6; 15:1, 5) and reach their climax in Jesus' Upper Room Discourse in chapters 14–16, where the Spirit's distinct person and unity with the Godhead are also underscored, and in Jesus' high priestly prayer in chapter 17. All of this provides the basis for the ancient doctrine of *perichōrēsis*—the interpenetration and communion of the Father, the Son, and the Spirit in, with, and through each other. After examining Jesus' scarred body after the resurrection, a doubting Thomas exclaims, "My Lord and my God!" (Jn 20:28), and Jesus declares his blessing on all who will come to share this confession (v. 29).

In the Apocalypse, Jesus appears to John as the "Alpha and the Omega ... who is and who was and who is to come, the Almighty" (Rev 1:8). "I am the First and the Last. I am the Living One; I was dead, and behold I am alive for ever and ever! And I hold the keys of death and Hades" (vv. 17–18 NIV). In fact, as Gerald Bray observes concerning this opening chapter of Revelation, we encounter both the voice of the Father (v. 8) and the voice of the Son (vv. 17–18), and John received his vision "in the Spirit" (v. 10). "In the famous letters to the seven churches (chs. 2–3), it is Christ who speaks, yet each letter concludes with the solemn command: 'He who has an ear, let him hear what the Spirit says to the churches.' "[4]

It was the teaching of Jesus himself, through his self-identification with the Father and the Spirit (Mt 22:44; Jn 5:19–47; 6:26–58; 7:28, 37–38; 8:12–38, 48–59; 10:1–18, 25–38; 11:25–26; 14:1–14, 20; 15:1–9, 26; 16:7, 14–15, 25–28; 17:1–26; 18:37; 20:22) that motivated the practice of Trinitarian faith even before the dogma was fully formulated, and this clear testimony of Jesus to his equality with the Father was not lost on the religious leaders (Jn 5:18). The christocentric reading of Israel's history is the most original and widely practiced way of interpreting the Old Testament, as when Paul treats the names *Yahweh* and *Jesus* as interchangeable: "We must not put *Christ* to the test, as some of them [the fathers in the wilderness] did and were destroyed by the serpents" (1Co 10:9, emphasis added).

Brevard Childs also notes that Jesus "assumes the titles of God by explicit reference to the Old Testament."[5] "In addition, Jesus shares or fully assumes the functions of the God of the Old Testament." Jesus takes Yahweh's judgment seat (2Co 5:10 with Ecc 12:14), at whose name "every knee shall bow ... and every tongue shall confess" his sovereign lordship (appropriating Isa 45:23, where Yahweh claims this worship for himself alone). "The Old Testament 'day of the Lord' is now identified with the coming of Jesus (1Th 5:2). Similarly, many of the liturgical forms of Israel's worship of God have been transferred to Christ. Christians now 'call upon the name' of Christ (Ac 19:13; Ro 10:14; etc.), and baptize 'in his name.' Angels worship him (Heb 1:6) and give praise to God and 'the Lamb' (Rev 5:13)."[6]

The fact that this son of Mary and Joseph has been demonstrated to be the "Son of God in power ... by his resurrection from the dead" (Ro 1:4) causes all of the canonical testimony to coalesce around him as the one who is named first in his works and only consequently in his person. Even the preexistence of the Son is clearly proclaimed in the Pauline corpus (Ro 8:3; 2Co 8:9; Gal 4:4; Php 2:6; Col 1:16–17). Christ is "the image of the invisible God," and "by him all things were created, in heaven and on earth, visible and invisible, whether thrones or dominions or rulers or authorities—all things were created through him and for him.... For in him all the fullness of God was pleased to dwell..." (Col 1:15–16, 19). Given the Jewish context, perhaps no stronger assertion of Christ's deity could be made than

---

4. Gerald Bray, *The Doctrine of God* (Downers Grove, Ill.: InterVarsity Press, 1993), 150.

5. Childs, *Biblical Theology*, 363: "In Heb 1:8 he is identified with the 'God' (*theos*) of Ps 45:7. He is 'Lord' (*kyrios*) in Ro 10:8–13 with reference to Dt 30:14. He is the 'first and last' of

Isa 44:6 in Rev 1:17; the 'I am He' of II Isaiah in Jn 8:28, and the 'one who is and was and who is to come' of Rev 1:8 with an allusion to Ex 3:14."

6. Childs, *Biblical Theology*, 363–64.

the announcement given by all of the apostles that there is no other name in heaven or on earth by which we may be saved (Jn 1:12; Ac 3:16; 4:12; 5:41; Ro 10:13; Php 2:9; 1Pe 4:14; Rev 2:13). This could mean only that Jesus of Nazareth was none other than Israel's Great King, Yahweh, whose name alone was to be invoked.

There are clear passages in the Old Testament that indicate also the distinct personality of the Holy Spirit (*rûaḥ*) and yet identify this distinct person as God. This is demonstrated with great narrative force in the creative brooding of the Spirit over the waters in the beginning, his "new creation" leading of the Israelites through the waters of baptism in the Red Sea, and his filling of the temple in the land of Canaan. In the Old Testament, we find numerous references to "the Spirit of God." Identified by the divine name (Ex 31:3; Ac 5:3–4; 1Co 3:16; 2Pe 1:21), the Spirit also has divine attributes ascribed to him (omnipresence, Ps 139:7–10; omniscience, Isa 40:13–14; 1Co 2:10–11), as well as divine works (creation, Ge 1:2; Job 26:13; 33:4; providential renovation, Ps 104:30; regeneration, Jn 3:5–6; Tit 3:5; resurrection of the dead, Ro 8:11). The Holy Spirit is also accorded divine homage (Mt 28:19; Ro 9:1; 2Co 13:14). The tandem "attorneys" (*paraklētoi*) from heaven who deliver Israel and lead the people to the Promised Land, witnessing to the covenant in blessing and curse, are now proclaimed in the upper room by Jesus (Jn 14–16) in terms of their respective missions of "coming" and "going," "sending," and "coming again."

This coming and going in and out of each other in the economy of redemption reveals the perichoretic relationship of these divine persons in their eternal fellowship. In Acts 5, Peter confronts Ananias and Sapphira by telling them that they have lied "to the Holy Spirit" (v. 3); in fact, they have "not lied to men but to God" (v. 4). We read in 2 Corinthians 3:17, "Now the Lord is the Spirit, and where the Spirit of the Lord is, there is freedom." Though distinct from the Father and Son, the Spirit "searches, speaks, testifies, commands, reveals, strives, creates, makes intercession, raises the dead," and engages in numerous other activities that identify him both as a distinct person (not just an influence) and as God.[7] These are indeed the *strong verbs* that identify the covenant Lord of Israel in the economy of creation, redemption, and consummation.

God reveals himself as the Trinity not only in the history of redemption, but in the personal experience of believers. This is a critical point, especially in view of Friedrich Schleiermacher's widely influential suspicion (treated below) that it makes no practical difference whether God is one or three since we experience God only as one person. Gordon Fee highlights the significance of the Trinity as an experienced reality in the New Testament, especially in Paul.[8] In fact, he develops his approach to the New

---

7. Louis Berkhof, *Systematic Theology* (Grand Rapids: Eerdmans, 1996), 98.

8. Gordon Fee, *God's Empowering Presence: The Holy Spirit in the Letters of Paul* (Peabody, Mass.: Hendrickson, 1994).

Testament exegesis of Trinitarian doctrine through the experience of the Spirit, "as the one who enables believers to confess the risen Christ as exalted Lord, and as the way God and Christ are personally present in the believer and the believing community."[9]

Fee later writes, "Thus, Paul's 'high christology' does not begin with doctrinal reflection but with experienced conviction. Those who have received the Spirit of God have been enabled to see the crucifixion in a new, divine light. Those who walk 'according to the Spirit' can no longer look on Christ from their old 'according to the flesh' point of view (2Co 5:15–16). They now know him to be their exalted Lord, ever present at the Father's right hand making intercession for them (Ro 8:34)."[10] Paul's encounter with the ascended Christ on the road to Damascus was decisive not only for his conversion and calling as an apostle but for his subsequent theological development.[11]

The doctrine of the Trinity is also evident in the new covenant worship instituted by Christ and his apostles, especially in the formula for baptism and the liturgical elements in public prayers, salutations, and benedictions. Rather than being regarded as a complex dogma with marginal practical significance, worship was a practice that called for further reflection and dogmatic formulation.[12] What were observant Jews doing praying and offering worship to Jesus as God and invoking the Father, the Son, and the Spirit for salvation? The friends and relatives of the earliest Christians knew what these practices intended, and it was enough to provoke the most serious charge of polytheistic idolatry.

One of the principal aims of traditional forms of worship and instruction throughout the history of the church (its liturgies, hymns, creeds, confessions, and catechisms) has been to integrate Trinitarian faith and practice into Christian worship and to pass this faith from generation to generation. In the rush to dispense with such formal structures, many churches today leave this central article out in the cold as an abstraction that fails to touch and shape their lives each week. However, if we return to the historical drama and the Trinitarian practices that gave rise to the dogma, its practical relevance for doxology and discipleship will be our presupposition rather than our goal.

II. HISTORICAL-THEOLOGICAL FORMULATION

Given the context of the New Testament, our focus so far has been on the difficulty that the Trinitarian confession presented in a Jewish milieu. However, subsequent refinement was provoked chiefly by encounters with Gentile (Greek) objections.

9. Gordon Fee, "Paul and the Trinity," in *The Trinity* (ed. Davis, Kendall, and O'Collins; Oxford: Oxford Univ. Press, 2002), 49.

10. Ibid., 62.

11. Seyoon Kim, *The Origin of Paul's Gospel* (Grand Rapids: Eerdmans, 1982).

12. On the link between Christology and worship in early Christianity, see Larry Hurtado, *Lord Jesus Christ: Devotion to Jesus in Earliest Christianity* (Grand Rapids: Eerdmans, 2005).

A. The Emergence of Christian Trinitarianism

The historical development of Trinitarian dogma is one of the best illustrations of the point that Christian theology is always done within a specific context yet with an overriding awareness of Scripture as its source and norm. Had the ancient church simply capitulated to the cultural categories that dominated the age, the dogma would have been aborted early on. Yet it was precisely by employing the categories and terminology available to them that they were able to press beyond the range of this philosophical inheritance and transform both philosophy and theology in the process.[13]

VIEWS OF THE TRINITY	
Modalism and Subordinationism	• God is one person (the Father), manifested to us sometimes also as "Son" and "Spirit." Subordinationists (and Arians) taught that the Son and the Spirit are inferior ontologically to the Father. • Founder of Modalism: Sabellius (3rd c. Roman presbyter). Later proponents: Socinians, Unitarians. Origen and Eusebius were subordinationists, as were the Arians.
Orthodox Trinitarianism	• God is one in essence, three in persons. • Hippolytus, Tertullian, Athanasius, Augustine, the Cappadocian Fathers, Council of Nicea (AD 325)
Tritheism	• God is three persons, with no unity of essence. • Founders: John Philoponus, Eugenius of Seleucia. Later proponents: Latter-day Saints (Mormons).

1. The Problem of Plurality in God

Both Platonism and Aristotelianism maintained the priority of the one over the many, although they parsed this differently. According to the former, mediated through Philo of Alexandria to early Christian theologians, such as Origen (185–254), the One, by definition, could not be divided.[14] Plurality itself is a fall from the unity of being. Consequently, Platonism would give rise to various forms of ontological subordinationism. While Origen sought to uphold a high Christology, there was a clear *ontological* subordination of the Son and the Spirit to the Father beyond the *economic* subordination of the Son in his redemptive mission.

---

13. For a superb treatment of these early developments, with particular attention to the ways in which the tradition redefined the language that it borrowed, see Jaroslav Pelikan, *Christianity and Classical Culture: The Metamorphosis of Natural Theology in the Christian Encounter with Hellenism* (New Haven, Conn.: Yale Univ. Press, 1995).

14. John Zizioulas, "The Doctrine of the Holy Trinity: The Significance of the Cappadocian Contribution," in *Trinitarian Theology Today* (ed. Christoph Schwöbel; Edinburgh: T&T Clark, 1995), 52–53.

A *substance* (or essence) is simply something about which something can be said.[15] Human beings share certain attributes that distinguish them from birds, for example. Those shared characteristics are the substance of humanity. According to Aristotle, the term *ousia* (substance or essence) referred both to the individual who bears an essence (*prōtē ousia*) and to the essence itself (*deutera ousia*). So, for example, Margaret (*prōtē ousia*) is a human being (*deutera ousia*). Essence was therefore the encompassing term for both species and individual. If we simply carry this over into Christian theology, we can see why using the same term for both *nature* and *persons* would make the debate more complicated and open to misunderstanding. How can we say that God is one *ousia* and three *ousiai* without contradiction?

The Aristotelian objection would encourage Arianism.[16] For Arius, a third-century Alexandrian presbyter, the Son was the first created being. "There exists a trinity (*trias*)," he said, "in unequal glories." The Father is "the Monad," so that "the Father is God [even] when the Son does not exist."[17] At this point, the line between heresy and Christianity was as thin as a vowel: Semi-Arians allowed that the Son and the Father were of a *similar* essence (*homoiousios*) but continued to deny that they were of the *same* essence (*homoousios*). Sabellius, a third-century presbyter in Rome, argued that the Father, the Son, and the Spirit are simply "masks" or modes in which the one person of God is experienced by believers. Although Sabellius was excommunicated by the bishop of Rome in AD 220, Sabellianism—also known as modalism—has remained a recurring challenge in church history.[18] The dominance of the one over the many, unity over plurality, is the common factor in all of these early departures from the Trinitarian faith.

2. ON THE WAY TO NICEA: "ONE IN ESSENCE, THREE IN PERSONS"

Arius did have logic on his side, but this logic was restricted to and defined by the conceptual category of essence. Of course, "one in essence, three in essence" is a contradiction that no one affirmed, but Christian pastors and theologians struggled for the right category. By the fourth century, the church had composed sophisti-

---

15. Aristotle defines *substance* (*ousia*) in chapter 5 of his *Categories*. Numerous unnecessary problems in contemporary theology result from erroneous conceptions of substance or essence. Often, it is assumed that a substance is a particular "stuff," but the term itself is much more limited and less metaphysically freighted. For an outstanding definition and its use in Trinitarian theology, see William P. Alston, "Substance and the Trinity," in *The Trinity* (ed. Davis, Kendall, and O'Collins), 179–202.

16. Bray, *Doctrine of God*, 127: "Origen, as a Platonist, had believed that an *ousia* which existed in one *hypostasis* could reproduce itself in a second, or even in a third.... Arius, however, was an Aristotelian who believed that if it was necessary to use a different name to describe an object, that object had to

be a different thing (*ousia*)." See also Lewis Ayres, *Nicaea and Its Legacy: An Approach to Fourth-Century Trinitarian Theology* (New York: Oxford Univ. Press, 2004); R. P. C. Hanson, *The Search for the Christian Doctrine of God: The Arian Controversy, 318–381* (Edinburgh: T&T Clark, 1988).

17. Quoted from Arius's poem "Thalia," in Rowan Williams, *Arius: Heresy and Tradition* (Grand Rapids: Eerdmans, 2002), 102.

18. Main lines of modalistic anti-Trinitarianism can be discerned in the teaching of Michael Servetus (sixteenth century), Emanuel Swedenborg (eighteenth century), Friedrich Schleiermacher (eighteenth-nineteenth centuries), and Oneness Pentecostals in our own day.

cated challenges to Arius, with Athanasius as the most notable spokesperson. Yet Athanasius, too, was still using the familiar terminology at hand, with *ousia* denoting both the essence and the persons.

The real innovation in the debate, with revolutionary implications in the history of both philosophy and theology, occurred when the fourth-century Cappadocian theologians (Gregory of Nyssa, Gregory of Nazianzus, and Basil of Caesarea) introduced a distinction between *ousia* and *hypostasis*, the former referring to Aristotle's *deutera ousia* and the latter to his *prōtē ousia*. "Persons" finally attained their own ontological status as something more than a subcategory of essence. Thus, faced with the fact of the incarnation, Christians could for the first time talk about persons as sharing in a common essence and yet related to each other as distinct individuals with their own properties of personal identity.[19] This breakthrough turned out to have tremendous significance not only for the doctrine of the Trinity but for the concept of human personhood as well. Thus, the formulation of the third-century Latin father Tertullian, "one in essence, three in persons," was given a deeper conceptual footing.[20]

However, the term *persons* generated another set of problems. Taken from the language of the stage, *prosōpon* in ordinary Greek usage as well as in its Latin form (*persona*) referred to a role that someone played—the connotation that *persona* has in English. This could be interpreted in a Sabellian (modalistic) manner, as if the persons are merely masks or roles played by one person.[21] Alert to these dangers, the Cappadocians rejected *prosōpon*, despite its time-honored usage since Tertullian (West) and Hippolytus (East), and stayed with *hypostasis*.[22] The Cappadocian theologians even risked language such as "three beings" on occasion ("three suns," "light from light," etc.), although they consistently qualified these analogies by affirming a single *ousia* shared by the three persons.[23]

---

19. Colin Gunton, *The Promise of Trinitarian Theology* (Edinburgh: T&T Clark, 1997), 9. As Gunton observes, the Aristotelian point motivated the Arian objection, namely, "that it violates sacred and traditional ontology and divides up the being of God.... By insisting, to the contrary, that God is eternally Son as well as Father, the Nicene theologians introduced a note of being in relation. Such is the impact of the doctrine of the incarnation on conceptions of what it is to be." Note that "being *in* relation," not being *as* relation, was the patristic doctrine of the East as well as the West.

20. This formula first appears in chapter 2 of Tertullian's *Against Praxeas*, ANF, 3:598. Furthermore, the fact that Tertullian was an early Latin theologian shows the danger in making sharp East-West antitheses.

21. Zizioulas, "Doctrine of the Holy Trinity," 46: "This modalistic interpretation made it impossible to understand how the Son, eternally or in the Incarnation had a relation of reciprocal dialogue with the Father, praying to him, etc., as the Gospel

stories require us to believe. It would also make it impossible for the Christian to establish a fully personal dialogue and relationship with *each* of the three persons of the Trinity."

22. Zizioulas, "Doctrine of the Holy Trinity," 46. By the way, the narrative thus far at least rules out the widely assumed antithesis between the East and the West, which Zizioulas encourages. Not only Jerome, and to a lesser extent Augustine, but Origen and Athanasius, too, just assumed the identity of *ousia* and *hypostasis*—even as, in the latter case, the goal was to refute subordinationism and Arianism. Furthermore, as even Zizioulas notes here, *hypostasis* had been regarded as synonymous with *prosōpon* by both Tertullian and Hippolytus. While the distinction between *ousia* and *hypostasis* would clear a path away from Arianism, and the refusal to identify *hypostasis* with *prosōpon* would offer a way out of modalistic tendencies, these are for the most part generational rather than geographical developments.

23. See, e.g., Gregory of Nyssa, *On "Not Three Gods," To Ablabius*, in *NNF2*, 5:330–36.

Pneumatology also played an important function in the development of Cappadocian formulations of the Trinity, as Basil's treatise on the Holy Spirit illustrates.[24] Furthermore, according to Basil, it is the persons rather than the nature (or essence) that we encounter in Christ and by the Spirit.[25] Thus, it does not make much difference whether one begins with the one God or the three persons. In the words of Gregory of Nazianzus, "No sooner do I conceive of the One than I am illumined by the Splendor of the Three; no sooner do I distinguish Them than I am carried back to the One."[26] Thinking of the one without the three leads to Arianism (or Unitarianism), and thinking of the three without the one leads to tritheism (or polytheism).

The catholic consensus emerged with the triumph of a full Trinitarianism at the Council of Nicea in 325 and the simple but precise language of the Nicene-Constantinopolitan Creed, known commonly as the Nicene Creed. Yet subtle differences continued to exercise considerable debate and, as we will see, have erupted once again through the revival of Trinitarian theology in our own day.

3. East-West Tensions

Differences between the churches of the East and the West are frequently exaggerated in our day, with Augustine often the target of criticism for a more Platonic concentration on the unity of the divine essence that threatened the genuine plurality of the persons.[27] By contrast, the East developed its Trinitarian thinking by starting with the person of the Father rather than the shared essence, with the Spirit as well as the Son finding his origin in him.[28] Consequently, the East has often suspected the West of exhibiting modalistic tendencies, while the West frequently worries that subordinationism (or tritheism) lurks in Eastern formulations.

Like rumors generally, the East's concern contains some truth. Augustine and Jerome were also working on a formulation that would affirm unity and plurality. However, the Cappadocian formulation seems to give more ontological weight to persons, while the tendency of Augustine's thesis is to identify the Father, Son, and Spirit more as *relations* than as *persons* in their own right. Of course, Augustine did not reduce the Father, the Son, and the Spirit to fatherhood, sonship,

---

24. Basil, *St. Basil the Great on the Holy Spirit* (Popular Patristic Series; Crestwood, N.Y.: St. Vladimir's Seminary Press, 1980), 39.

25. Ibid., 41.

26. Gregory of Nazianzus, *Oration 40: The Oration on Holy Baptism*, ch. 41, in *NPNF2*, 7:375.

27. For a sympathetic, well-researched interpretation of Augustine's Trinitarian thinking, see esp. Michel René Barnes, "Rereading Augustine's Theology of the Trinity," in *The Trinity*

(ed. Davis, Kendall, and O'Collins), 145–76.

28. This has long been a standard critique by the Christian East and has been elaborated more recently by John Zizioulas, but among the many contemporary advocates of this position in the West, see especially Colin Gunton, *The Promise of Trinitarian Theology*. For a helpful counterargument, see J. Thompson, *Modern Trinitarian Perspectives* (Oxford: Oxford Univ. Press, 1994).

and love explicitly, but this modalistic move is not inconceivable in view of his argument.[29]

Differences lie more in tendencies of thought than in formal theories, and we may discern these differences in the dominant analogies employed. In the Cappadocian version, the analogy for the Trinity is that of Peter, James, and John sharing a common human essence. Obviously, this could be taken to an extreme (known as tritheism) were it not for the repeated caveats of the Cappadocians that this was merely an analogy and that there were not in fact three Gods but one. However, Augustine offered the analogy of the mind, comparing the divine persons to memory, intellect, and will in the rational soul of an individual. In this analogy, the Father is compared with the mind, the Son with self-knowledge, and the Spirit with the love by which the rational soul loves itself.[30] Understandably, this analogy lends credibility to the suspicion of the Christian East that the West lists toward modalism.

Identifying the three persons of the Trinity as real individuals certainly challenges a modalistic theory, but this term has its own baggage. The Roman statesman and Christian philosopher Boethius (480–524) defined *person* as "an individual substance of a rational nature" (*natures rationalis individua substantia*).[31] At least as John Zizioulas interprets the East's concern, this definition (especially as applied to the persons of the Trinity) set in motion a theologically defective view of persons as autonomous individuals that reaches its fateful climax in modernity.[32] But for the Cappadocians, "true personhood arises not from one's individualistic isolation from others but from love and relationship with others, from communion."[33]

According to Zizioulas, this difference between Western (Augustinian/Boethian) and Eastern (Cappadocian) understandings of divine personhood arises from a more fundamental disagreement about whether its source is *the shared essence* or *the person of the Father*. According to the East, it is not an essence but the Father's (a person's) love that generates the life (including the divine essence) of the Son and the Spirit.[34] (The West has typically responded that this formulation is susceptible to an ontological subordination of the Son that deprives him of full deity.) In addition to these concerns, the East has suspected the West of an implicit "binitarianism," with a weak concept of the full personhood of the Spirit.

There may be some justification for this concern, since Augustine and his heirs

---

29. See Augustine, *The Trinity* (The Fathers of the Church: A New Translation; trans. Stephen McKenna; Washington, D.C.: Catholic Univ. of America Press, 1963), 45.

30. Ibid., 464.

31. Boethius, *De trinitate*, in *Theological Tractates and the Consolation of Philosophy* (trans. S. J. Tester, H. F. Stewart, and E. K. Rand; Loeb Classical Library 74; Cambridge, Mass.: Harvard Univ. Press, 1973). Cf. L. W. Geddes, "Person," in *The Catholic Encyclopedia* (ed. Charles G. Herbermann et al.; New York: Encyclopedic Press, 1913), 11.

32. Zizioulas, "Doctrine of the Holy Trinity," 58.

33. Ibid.

34. Ibid., 59.

(mediated especially through Richard of St. Victor) emphasized that the Spirit was the "bond of love" between the Father and the Son.[35] In his *On the Trinity*, Richard argues that the Father gives without receiving, the Son both gives and receives, but the Spirit is only a recipient of love. But does this not make the Spirit passive both in the intratrinitarian communion and in the economy of creation and redemption? The suspicion of a "binitarian" tendency in Western Trinitarianism had already been exacerbated centuries earlier, at the Third Council of Toledo (589), when the West unilaterally altered the Nicene Creed's statement of the Spirit's procession "from the Father" by adding, "and from the Son" (*ex patre filioque*). Hence, the disagreement about this phrase is called the *filioque* controversy (discussed below).

In connection with so central a doctrine, any nuance is significant, but we should be wary of exaggerated contrasts of East/West formulations. After all, the Western father Tertullian had already pioneered the formula "one in essence and three in persons" in the second century. In addition, he even affirmed the Father as the source of the Godhead and the procession of the Spirit "*from* the Father *through* the Son."[36] Although Augustine, writing a century later, seems to have missed the crucial insight of the Cappadocian distinction between essence (*ousia*) and person (*prosōpon*), Tertullian did not.[37] Furthermore, Athanasius in the East was still using *ousia* to refer to both the essence and the persons seventy years after Tertullian's death. It was not until the Cappadocians brought their crucial insight to bear that the East had the conceptual tools to express Tertullian's formula. Augustine's principal work on the Trinity was written chiefly to refute Arianism, not to provide a thorough treatment of the topic. His primary concern was to challenge the Arian claim that there was a time when the Son was not, by observing that the eternal Father cannot exist without the eternally begotten Son. Understandably, then, the language of relations was prominent.

This being said, it is true that Augustine and Jerome failed to understand the meaning, much less the achievement, of the Cappadocian development.[38] Augus-

---

35. Augustine, *The Trinity* 6.5.7. In the twelfth century, Richard of St. Victor modified Boethius's definition of person in a more emphatically individualistic direction: "something that exists through itself alone, singularly, according to a rational mode of existence." He also concluded that God existed in three persons in order for there to be a third person for the Father and the Son to love and to be the bond of their love (*On the Trinity*, in *A Scholastic Miscellany: Anselm to Ockham* [ed. Eugene R. Fairweather; Philadelphia: Westminster, 1956], 330). Therefore, the more individualistic definition of person and the tendency to treat the Spirit as a bond of love rather than a full partner within the intratrinitarian exchange became more pronounced through Richard of St. Victor. The Father and the Son are givers, but the Spirit is the gift they share in common.

36. Tertullian, *Against Praxeas*, in *ANF*, 4:599: "But as for me, who derive the Son from no other source but from the substance of the Father …"; "I believe the Spirit to *proceed* from no other source than from the Father through the Son."

37. Tertullian was just as able in distinguishing *ousia* and *hypostasis* in Latin (*essentia* and *persona*). Gregory of Nyssa and Augustine of Hippo were united in affirming the plurality of persons as well as the unity of essence, just as Origen in the East and Jerome in the West both had difficulties making these connections.

38. "I do not know what distinction they wish to make," Augustine conceded in *The Trinity* (5.10).

tine expressed confusion at the Cappadocian formulation, in part because of his lack of fluency in reading Greek. The East denied that there were three Gods, and the West rejected the modalistic heresy of one person with three personas. Nevertheless, there are obvious differences in emphasis. Eager to emphasize the consubstantiality of the Son with the Father against Arianism, adoptionism, and subordinationism, Augustine placed his emphasis on the unity of essence. "*Whatever* ... is said of God," he wrote, "is said of the Father, the Son and the Spirit triply, and *equivalently* of the Trinity singly" (emphasis added).[39] This is certainly true with respect to the undivided essence shared by the divine persons, but it cannot be said (and Augustine did not suggest that it could be said) that the Father is begotten and the Son begets. The persons are indeed a triple repetition of the same essence, but they are not triple repetitions of the same person.[40] Though never denied, the distinct characteristics and reality of the persons become marginalized in Augustine's emphasis on the one essence.

This somewhat modalistic tendency in Augustine's thinking becomes more evident in his psychological analogy of the Trinity (in *The Trinity*) as "memory" (the Father), "understanding" (the Son), and "will," which is love (the Spirit). One mind with three faculties expresses a rather different set of assumptions from the East's typical analogy of a family or Peter, James, and John sharing the same essence as human. The language of the divine persons as relations exacerbated the East's suspicions. Clearly, relations do not act, think, speak, or will, as do persons. Furthermore, a single mind with three faculties is rather different from three distinct agents-in-relation. The psychological analogy becomes an explicit proposition in Augustine's treatise: "these three constitute" not only one divine essence but "one mind."[41] Is it any wonder that the most popular analogies employed in Western teaching on the Trinity lean in the modalistic direction, such as the shamrock, a triangle, and water as ice, steam, and liquid?

Although Colin Gunton overstates his case against Augustine, there are weak-

---

39. Augustine, *The Trinity* 5.9 (PL 42, col. 917; subsequent references in this chapter are to this edition): *tantamque vim esse eiusdem substantiae in Patre et Filio et Spiritu sancto, ut quidquid de singulis ad se ipsos dictur, non pluraliter in summar, sed singularieter accipiatur* ("and the effect of the same substance in Father and Son and Holy Spirit is, that whatsoever is said of each in respect to himself, is to be taken of them, not in the plural in sum, but in the singular").

40. Although Augustine did not indulge such speculations, it is his emphasis that may be discerned in extreme formulations such as Cornelius Van Til's that God is both one in person and three in person, which John Frame supports in *The Doctrine of God: A Theology of Lordship* (Phillipsburg, N.J.: P&R, 2002), 228. According to classical Trinitarianism, God is personal but not "a person"; otherwise, there is either a fourth person or one person with three masks or appearances (i.e., modalism). Frame adds, "It is not evident to me why triunity should not be considered an attribute of God" (228). The main reason one might put forward is that it denies God's simplicity and confuses persons with essence. The brilliance of the Cappadocian revolution in Trinitarian formulation was that the Arian objection—namely, plurality in the divine essence (*ousia*)—no longer had any foundation because the plurality referred to the persons (*hypostases*) rather than to the essence. If we adopt Frame's suggestion, the further insight from Reformed treatments of the distinction between essential attributes and personal properties is totally lost.

41. Augustine, *The Trinity* 10.18–20.

nesses that the great theologian bequeathed to Western Trinitarian thinking. There does seem to be a tendency in Augustine's thinking to consider the eternal (*hypostatic*) Word in more abstract terms rather than as "the concrete person of the Son in relation to the Father and the Spirit."[42] Gunton presses, "Is the basis of Augustine's deity personal? What is finally real about him, the community constituted by the relatedness of Father, Son, and Spirit to each other, or something else?"[43]

In the economy we encounter distinct agents engaged in mutual mission yet each in his own way. Augustine's formula that God's external works are undivided (which was also affirmed in the East) can either mean that in every external work the persons act together (mutually), or be taken to imply that their actions are simply the same. I concur with Robert Jenson's judgment on this point that Augustine assumes the latter, wary of attributing "differentiation in God's intrinsic agency." Jenson concludes,

> Either, he thinks, Father, Son, and Spirit must simply do the *same* thing, or simply *different* things; the possibility of a *mutually* single act cannot occur to him. Thus he supposes, for example, that the Son's appearances in Israel could as well be called appearances of the Father or of the Spirit [*The Trinity* 2; 3.3] or that when the voice speaks to Jesus at his baptism—a chief text of original Trinitarianism—the speaker is indifferently specifiable as the Father or the Son or the Spirit or the whole Trinity [1.8].[44]

The tendency to regard the persons simply as triple repetitions of the same substance (without adequate regard for the personal attributes) is evident in Augustine's interpretation of the external works of the Godhead. Although Augustine himself did not argue the point, the logic of his argument is not inimical to the speculation of the medieval theologian Peter Lombard: "As the Son was made man, so the Father or the Holy Spirit could have been and could be now" (*Sentences* 3.1.3). This raises the question as to whether the persons have any personal attributes that distinguish them from each other. In sharp contrast, Jenson notes, Augustine's counterpart in the East, John of Damascus, says, "It was the Son of God who became the son of man, *so that his individuating property might be preserved. As he is Son of God he became a son of man*" (emphasis added).[45] John of Damascus recognized that there were attributes that were shared as the common essence of the persons (essential attributes) and attributes that were unique to each person (personal attributes). Since the latter were incommunicable, the Son alone is the proper subject of incarnation. Lombard's point was never accepted officially by the Western church, it should be noted. Nevertheless, how could it ever have even emerged except as an extreme (though logical) inference from the Augustinian line of thinking?

42. Gunton, *Promise of Trinitarian Theology*, 44.
43. Ibid., 47–48.
44. Robert Jenson, *Systematic Theology*, Vol. 1, *The Triune*

God (New York: Oxford Univ. Press, 2001), 111.
45. John of Damascus, *Expositio fidei* 77.5–8, in Jenson, *The Triune God*, 112.

The fourth-century Western theologian Hilary of Poitiers, after spending time with Eastern bishops, came to understand their suspicions of modalistic tendencies in the West, and he attempted to bring together the Eastern emphasis on distinct persons (*hypostases*) and the Western emphasis on one essence (*ousia*).[46] Manlion Simonetti judges concerning Hilary's principal treatise, "The *De synodis*, a work of rare intelligence and penetration, reveals for the first time in a Western theologian a full awareness of the complex religious reality of the East."[47]

At the Fourth Lateran Council in 1215, the position enunciated in the Athanasian Creed (a sixth-century creed wrongly attributed to Athanasius and used only in the West) became established, with the explicit condemnation of the Trinitarian views of Joachim of Fiore as tritheistic (on Joachim's continuing influence, see comments on Moltmann below, "Privileging the Many," pp. 296–99). This council even cited the insightful comment of Cappadocian father Gregory of Nazianzus to substantiate its argument: "The Father is one (*alius*), the Son another (*alius*), and the Holy Spirit another (*alius*), yet there is not another thing (*aliud*)."[48] This is but another way of saying, "one in essence, three in persons." Thomas Aquinas appropriated and refined the Augustinian interpretation of the Trinity and the Boethian definition of persons.[49] The common Trinitarian faith was affirmed, but with distinct accents and conceptual frameworks, sometimes leading to tension on important points.

KEY DEFENDERS OF THE TRINITY IN THE ANCIENT CHURCH	
Irenaeus (second century)	Bishop of Lyons and student of Polycarp (who was a disciple of John the Apostle). Known especially for his defense of Christianity against Gnosticism (*Against Heresies*).
Tertullian (160–220)	Carthage theologian who pioneered Trinitarian theology in the West; developed the formula "three persons, one essence."
Athanasius (293–373)	Bishop of Alexandria who helped to shape and defend Nicene orthodoxy.
The Cappadocian Fathers (fourth century)	Brothers Basil of Caesarea and Gregory of Nyssa, together with their friend Gregory of Nazianzus, were leaders in Cappadocia (modern Turkey) who played a formative role in developing the Trinitarian theology of the East.
Augustine (354–430)	Bishop of Hippo (in Northern Africa) who contributed important advances to Latin (Western) Trinitarian theology.

---

46. Manlion Simonetti, "Hilary of Poitiers and the Arian Crisis in the West," in *Patrology* (ed. Angelo Di Berardino; Westminster, Md.: Christian Classics, 1988), 4:33–43.

47. Simonetti, "Hilary of Poitiers," 44.

48. Ibid.

49. On his elaboration of Boethius's definition, see Thomas Aquinas, *Summa theologica* 3, q. 16, art. 12, ad 2*um*.

B. REFORMED CONTRIBUTIONS TO TRINITARIAN REFLECTION: ESSENTIAL ATTRIBUTES AND PERSONAL PROPERTIES

The sixteenth century saw a rise of neo-Arianism, especially through the efforts of Michael Servetus and the rising movement known as Socinianism, which came to full flower in modern rationalism and Unitarianism. In his *Institutes* Calvin moves from the polemic against idolatry to the doctrine of the Trinity. Apart from the knowledge of God as Trinity, "only the bare and empty name of God flits about in our brains, to the exclusion of the true God."[50] Calvin was especially attracted to "the Athanasius of the West," Hilary of Poitiers, mentioned above ("East-West Tensions," p. 287). Through his own study of the Eastern writers (especially Basil and Gregory of Nyssa), and his significant appreciation for Hilary, Calvin's Trinitarian thought is more sympathetic to the "Cappadocian revolution."

Although deeply indebted to Augustine on many topics, including the Trinity, Calvin displays his independence, criticizing Augustine's psychological analogy and his failure to understand the significance of the Cappadocian insights: "With what great freedom does Augustine sometimes burst forth?" he asks. "How unlike are the Greeks and the Latins?" Jerome attacked the notion that there are "three substances" in God, but he is "confused" by the word *hypostasis*, Calvin writes, and therefore rashly dismisses unfamiliar terms.[51] After scolding Jerome for his intemperate objections to the Eastern bishops, Calvin explains that Augustine was more moderate both in his tone and in his objections.[52]

Whereas Augustine tended to reduce the divine *persons* (Father, Son, and Spirit) to *relations* (fatherhood, sonship, bond of love), Reformed theologians emphasized that the persons were real and distinct in the fullest sense. Like Hilary, Calvin combined the Western emphasis on God's essential unity—shared consubstantially, with no member ontologically subordinate or inferior to another—with the Eastern emphasis on the distinct reality and mutuality of the persons.

Rather than focus on the essence (almost as if it were its own *hypostasis*—a fourth person of the Trinity), Calvin emphasized that each person is the bearer of the divine essence. In other words, there is no "God" or "divinity" floating somewhere behind or above the persons of the Godhead.

---

50. Calvin, *Institutes* 1.13.2.

51. Calvin writes (ibid., 1.13.5), "For he suspects poison lurking when three hypostases in one God are mentioned!... This would be true even if he spoke sincerely, rather than tried willingly and knowingly to charge the Eastern bishops, whom he hates, with unjust calumnies! Surely he shows little candor in asserting that in all profane schools *ousia* is nothing else but hypostasis, an opinion repeatedly refuted by common and well-worn usage. Augustine is more moderate and courteous, since even though he says that the word hypostasis in this sense is new to Latin ears, yet he leaves to the Greeks their manner of speaking so much that he gently bears with the Latins who had imitated the Greek phrase."

52. Ibid.: "And Augustine's excuse is similar [to that of Hilary]: on account of the poverty of human speech in so great a matter, the word 'hypostasis' had been forced upon us by necessity, not to express what it is, but only not to be silent on how Father, Son, and Spirit are three."

With ancient precedent—for example, Epiphanius (*Refutation of Heresies* 69)—Calvin employs the term *autotheos* (lit., "self-God") for the way in which the Son and the Spirit as well as the Father are "God."[53] Since self-existence is a divine attribute, the Son's *deity* must be as underived as the Father's and the Spirit's. His person, not his divine essence, is begotten of the Father. Much of Calvin's *autotheos* is founded on Augustine's comment that Christ "is called Son, with reference to the Father (*ad patrem*) and God with reference to himself (*ad seipsum*)." Yet he also appealed to Cyril of Alexandria.[54] Without in any way surrendering the ecumenical view of the Father as unbegotten, the Son as begotten, and the Spirit as proceeding, Calvin nevertheless insisted that each person was a subsistence of God *a se* (i.e., from himself). This was, after all, the implication of having life in himself, even if his person is eternally begotten (Jn 5:26).

In making this point, Calvin highlighted the distinction between the shared divine essence and the unique attributes of the persons that distinguish each from the other. The essence is unbegotten, but only the Father is unbegotten in his personhood. Granted, *autotheos* is a bold way of stating this ontological equality of the persons in their distinct subsistence, yet Warfield's verdict seems correct: "By this assertion the *homoousiotes* of the Nicene fathers at last came to its full right and became in its fullest sense the hinge of the doctrine."[55]

Calvin's insistence on each person as *autotheos* in his shared *essence*, yet the Father as the source of the *persons* of the Son and the Spirit, navigated between tendencies toward subordinationism on one side and modalism on the other. Gregory of Nyssa says exactly what Calvin does about there being no greater/lesser in the nature, but only with respect to the persons.[56] In fact, in nearly the same words Calvin's repeated stipulation was already said by Nyssa: "Every operation which extends from God to the creation ... has its origin from the Father, and proceeds through the Son, and is perfected in the Holy Spirit."[57] The persons, not the natures, are caused.[58] Even in the way that Calvin defends the consubstantiality (essential unity) of the Godhead, then, the persons are center stage.

Although this *autotheos* view may at first appear to be even more radical to Eastern theologians than to Western, John Zizioulas makes the same point (without reference to Calvin) in describing the East's position:

> The Father as "cause" is God, or the God in an ultimate sense, *not because he holds the divine essence and transmits it*—this would indeed endanger the fullness of the divine being of the other persons—*but because he is the ultimate ontological principle*

---

53. B. B. Warfield, "Calvin's Doctrine of the Trinity," in *Calvin and Augustine* (ed. Samuel Craig; Philadelphia: P&R, 1956), 187–284, esp. 254.

54. Ibid., 282–84.

55. Ibid., 284. Regarding *homoousios*, see "The Problem of Plurality in God" (p. 280).

56. Gregory of Nyssa, *On the Holy Trinity and of the Godhead of the Holy Spirit: To Eustathius*, in *NPNF2*, 5:338.

57. Gregory of Nyssa, *On "Not Three Gods,"* in *NPNF2*, 5:334.

58. Ibid., 5:336.

of divine personhood. If this is truly understood, apprehension that the causal language of the Cappadocians endangers the fullness of deity of the Son and the Spirit may disappear. For, in fact, the equality of the three persons in terms of substance is not denied by the Father's being the cause of personhood; it is rather ensured by it, since by being cause *only as a person and for the sake of personhood* the Father guards against locating substance primarily in himself.[59]

Unfortunately in my view, not all Reformed theologians countenanced Calvin's concept of the persons as *autotheos* with respect to their essential attributes.[60] Nevertheless, they continued his emphasis on the distinction between the attributes of the one God and the distinct personal properties of the three persons. Essential attributes are shared equally by the three persons. All three persons are infinite, sovereign, loving, and omniscient. However, only the Father begets, only the Son is begotten, and only the Spirit is spirated. The Heidelberg theologian M. F. Wendelin wrote that "the persons of the Son and Spirit have an origin; the essence does not. Person generates and is generated; essence neither generates nor is generated."[61] This had been precisely Calvin's point in referring to the persons as *autotheos*. Even in human generation, it is persons who are begotten, not human nature. In every external work of the Godhead, the Father is the source, the Son is the mediator, and the Spirit is the one who brings about the intended effect. It is one thing to say that each person is mutually engaged in every external work of the Godhead and quite another to say (as Augustine implies) that each person simply does the same work. The latter view reflects a latent tendency toward modalism.

The fuller development of this distinction between essential attributes and personal properties highlighted the unity of the Trinity without subordinationist or modalistic tendencies and highlighted the real differences between persons without tritheistic tendencies. Calvin writes,

> For in each hypostasis the whole divine nature is understood, *with this qualification—that to each belongs his own peculiar quality* [emphasis added].... In this sense the opinions of the ancients are to be harmonized, which otherwise would seem somewhat to clash. Sometimes, indeed, they teach that the Father is the beginning of the Son; sometimes they declare that the Son has both divinity and essence from himself, and thus has one beginning with the Father. Augustine well and clearly expresses the cause of this diversity in another place, when he speaks as follows:

---

59. John Zizioulas, *Communion and Otherness* (London: T&T Clark, 2006), 130, emphasis original. I am grateful to Brian Hecker for providing this reference.

60. Theodore Beza believed that generation equals communication of essence (see Muller, *PRRD*, 4:258–59). In other words, if the Father communicates the person, then he communicates the essence. "The Son," Beza said, "is of the Father by an ineffable communication from eternity of the whole nature" (Theodore Beza, *Axiomat. de trinitate*, Axiom 14, quoted in

PRRD, 274). So too the Lutheran theologian Johann Gerhard wrote, "The Greek doctors call only the Father *autotheos kai autoousios*, not because there is a greater perfection of essence in the Father than in the Son, but because he is *agennētos* [unbegotten] and *a se ipso* [has life in or from himself] and does not have deity through generation or spiration" (Johann Gerhard, as quoted in *PRRD*, 261).

61. M. F. Wendelin, as quoted in Muller, *PRRD*, 4:261.

"Christ with respect to himself [*ousia*: nature] is called God; with respect to the Father [*hypostasis*: person], Son." ... Therefore, when we speak simply of the Son without regard to the Father, we well and properly declare him to be of himself; and for this reason we call him the sole beginning. But when we mark the relation that he has with the Father, we rightly make the Father the beginning of the Son.[62]

This is not to suggest that Calvin is "Augustinian" when talking about the unity and "Cappadocian" when considering the persons. Rather, he understands the essential unity and diversity of persons as interdependent. The persons are God, and apart from the persons there is no divine nature. "And that passage in Gregory of Nazianzus vastly delights me: 'I cannot think on the one without quickly being encircled by the splendor of the three; nor can I discern the three without being straightway carried back to the one.'"[63]

Reformed theologians even spoke of these distinct personal attributes as *incommunicable*. According to Amandus Polanus, "A person of the Deitie is a subsistence in the Deitie, having such properties as cannot be communicated from one to another."[64] Richard Muller notes concerning these writers that "subsistence" gave more ontological weight to persons than *persona* allowed, given its Sabellian (modalistic) associations.[65] Wendelin proposes, "A divine person is usually described as *an incommunicable subsistence* of the divine essence" (emphasis added).[66] Though sharing a common essence, each person has his own "life, understanding, will, and power, by which he is in continual operation," according to Edward Leigh.[67] With such statements we are at a rather far remove from Augustine's conviction that the Godhead consists of one mind and will.

The formula "distinction without division" guides Calvin's understanding of the Trinity. "Indeed, the words 'Father,' 'Son,' and 'Spirit' imply *a real distinction*—let no one think that these titles, whereby God is variously designated from his works, are empty—but a distinction [contra Sabellians], not a division [contra Arians]" (emphasis added).[68] According to Calvin, then, "It is not a mere relation which is called the Son, but *a real somewhat* subsisting in the divine nature" (emphasis added).[69] This, it seems to me, is identical to the Cappadocian construction, even

---

62. Calvin, *Institutes* 1.13.19.

63. Ibid., 1.13.17. While intending no parallels in terms of content, we can see the same tendency in Arius and Jerome that we find in Barth and Rahner, namely, to presuppose as givens certain philosophical definitions (such as nature and person) rather than challenge these time-honored usages by the sheer fact of the Trinity. Why should we either endorse or overreact against certain Trinitarian formulations too closely associated with idealism any more than we endorse or overreact against the Cappadocians in relation to their Platonist inheritance? The point is to find terminology that makes the point—and redefine it if necessary. We should allow the matter itself to burst the wineskins of usage.

64. Amandus Polanus, as quoted in Muller, *PRRD*, 4:177.

65. Muller, *PRRD*, 4:178.

66. Ibid., 4:179. Similarly, John Owen says that the names *Father*, *Son*, and *Spirit* are "not diverse names of the same person, nor distinct attributes or properties of the same nature or being," but real persons with "incommunicable properties." "Thus the Trinity is not the union or unity of three, but it is a trinity in unity" (John Owen, as quoted in Muller, *PRRD*, 4:194).

67. Edward Leigh, as quoted in Muller, *PRRD*, 4:179.

68. Ibid.

69. Calvin, *Institutes* 1.13.6.

as articulated by Zizioulas when he explains that, against the semi-Arians, the Cappadocians argued that the Father's "unbegottenness" identifies his person and not his essence.[70]

Because of this distinction, Reformed theologians could speak without contradiction of the Father as the principium and "the 'origin of all divinity' (*originem totius Deitatis*).' "[71] Each person enjoys the aseity proper to the essence, but for the Father alone it is also an attribute of his person. He is "unbegotten" (*agennētos*), while the Son is begotten and the Spirit proceeds. Yet this in no way means for the Reformed that the Father is first in nature or cause. In fact, Reformed theologians agreed that the category of causality is inappropriate among the persons.[72]

Wary of overstatements concerning East-West disagreements, Gerald Bray nevertheless concludes that Calvin pulled together important threads from both to form a more integrated fabric: "By claiming that the Son and by extension the Holy Spirit also are God in the fullest sense of the word, Calvin not only attacked all forms of Origenism [subordinationism], but also the Sabellianism [modalism] latent in the Western tradition."[73] In Origenism, persons have priority over nature; in Sabellianism, nature has priority over persons, but we affirm the reality of persons and the one nature together.[74] Further, Calvin emphasized that the Father, Son, and Spirit are not just relations but persons while also underscoring that they are persons *in* relation. To know one person is to know something about the others. "It was on this principle that Calvin and the other Reformers rejected the conventional division of labour within the Godhead," writes Bray, "according to which the Father is Creator, the Son is the Redeemer, and the Holy Spirit is the Sanctifier of the people of God." This view, criticized by Calvin, was semi-Sabellian, "because it treated the persons as channels for the threefold activity of God,"[75] more than three persons working in tandem.

Although Colin Gunton goes too far in reading Calvin's formulation as an explicit repudiation of Augustine in favor of the East, he correctly surmises that the Reformer's views represent an advance in Western Trinitarian theology, particularly in his "concern for the particularity of the persons" and their distinct agency in the economy of grace.[76] Gunton is justified in concluding that Calvin

---

70. Zizioulas, "Doctrine of the Holy Trinity," 49–50.

71. See Muller, *PRRD*, 4:253; cf. Calvin, *Institutes* 1.13.18.

72. Muller, *PRRD*, 4:253.

73. Bray, *Doctrine of God*, 201.

74. Ibid., 202.

75. Ibid.

76. Gunton, *Promise of Trinitarian Theology*, 94. On the same page, Gunton adds, "In his discussion of the persons of the Trinity in Book I of the *Institutes*, John Calvin engages in a discussion with the Western tradition, calling in evidence the

theology of Tertullian and Hilary of Poitiers against Jerome, and, indirectly, Augustine." Besides the emphasis on the particularity of the persons, Gunton refers to Calvin's "concern to avoid what we can fairly call individualism in a repeated denial of the loneliness and isolation of God, something Aquinas noted but did not develop." It seems clear from this passage of the *Institutes*, however, that Calvin is actually trying to harmonize Augustine and the Eastern theologians rather than pit one against the other. It is really Jerome whom he targets as uncooperative in this respect.

recognized the revolutionary insight of the Cappadocian treatment of *hypostasis* (person) and wished that this had received greater appreciation and attention in Western theology.[77]

For Calvin, Bray notes, the divine persons work together yet differently in every external work: "Father: beginning; Son: arrangement; Spirit: efficacy."[78] This helps to avoid the pitfalls of both Eastern (subordinationist) and Western (modalistic) leanings. Formulas, such as this one, are replete in these systems of Protestant orthodoxy. Interestingly, Luther's important pupil Martin Chemnitz pointed out that Paul's doxology in Romans 11:36 ("From him and through him and to him are all things") was explicitly Trinitarian, each clause referring to a different person of the Godhead.[79] Calvin writes,

> It is not fitting to suppress the distinction that we observe to be expressed in Scripture. It is this: to the Father is attributed the beginning of activity, and the fountain and wellspring of all things; to the Son, wisdom, counsel, and the ordered disposition of all things; but to the Spirit is assigned the power and efficacy of all that activity. Indeed, although the eternity of the Father is also the eternity of the Son and the Spirit, since God could never exist apart from his wisdom and power, and we must not seek in eternity a *before* or an *after*, nevertheless the observance of an order is not meaningless or superfluous, when the Father is thought of as first, then from him the Son, and finally from both the Spirit.[80]

Essences do not enter into relationships, but the divine persons who share that essence do. We are addressed, judged, redeemed, and raised to everlasting life by the Father, the Son, and the Spirit, who are one God.

In evaluating the common analogies employed in the East and the West, Calvin also reminded his readers to avoid speculations from human analogies projected literally and univocally in an attempt to comprehend the mystery of the Trinity.[81] This is surely relevant in contemporary debates, as we will see. The key in the thinking of all these writers is that Calvin and later Reformed theology expressed dissatisfaction with Augustine's psychological analogy, yet they were also eager to point out that the divine persons are not persons in exactly the same sense as human beings.[82] Our terminology is important only insofar as it preserves us from confusion and error. Nevertheless, let us not speculate beyond the simple formula, "one essence, three persons," Calvin says.[83] "Here, indeed, if anywhere in the secret mysteries of

---

77. Ibid., 94.

78. Bray, *Doctrine of God*, 203.

79. Martin Chemnitz, *Loci theologici* (1591) (trans. Jacob Preus; St. Louis: Concordia, 1989), 1:74–76.

80. Calvin, *Institutes* 1.13.18.

81. Ibid.: While we must not "suppress the distinction that we observe to be expressed in Scripture," Calvin cautions moderation: "I really do not know whether it is expedient to borrow comparisons from human affairs to express the force of this distinction. Men of old were indeed accustomed sometimes to do so, but at the same time they confessed that the analogies they advanced were quite inadequate."

82. On Calvin's criticism of Augustine's psychological analogy, see *Institutes* 1.13.18.

83. Ibid., 1.13.20.

Scripture, we ought to play the philosopher soberly and with great moderation.... Let us then willingly leave to God the knowledge of himself."[84] However "persons" can be appropriately applied to both God and humans, we will never know exactly where the analogy breaks down — but it does.[85]

C. THE TRINITY IN MODERN THEOLOGY

Socinianism (forerunner of Unitarianism) sowed the seeds of Protestant defection, coming to full flower in the Enlightenment. Once religion is reduced to that which may be known by universal reason, morality, or experience, the Trinity can hardly be considered an essential dogma. According to Kant, "The doctrine of the Trinity, taken literally, has *no practical relevance at all*, even if we think we understand it; and it is even more clearly irrelevant if we realize that it transcends all our concepts. Whether we are to worship three or ten persons in the Deity makes no difference."[86] According to Schleiermacher, since theology is reflection on pious experience, and we do not experience the Trinity, "Our faith in Christ and our living fellowship with him would be the same" without it.[87] Alar Laats does not overstate the matter when he judges that "the reduction of the role of Christ to a moral teacher in the liberal theology of the [nineteenth] century happened because of the eclipse of the doctrine of the Trinity."[88]

It was Hegel who first provoked renewed attention to the Trinity with his philosophy of "Spirit" and history, drawing significantly on the combined influences of Joachim of Fiore's Trinitarian historicism and the radical pantheistic mysticism of Meister Eckhart and Jakob Böhme. However, it was not so much the historic doctrine itself that interested him but the use to which it could be put in a speculative ontology of being-as-becoming. Since then, mainline Protestantism, especially in the wake of Karl Barth, has experienced a revival of interest in Trinitarian theology that is as evident in recent Roman Catholic theology. At the same time, this revival has reignited historical debates concerning the unity of essence and plurality of persons. In many respects, contemporary debates in Trinitarian theology reflect the legacy of Barth and Hegel.

---

84. Ibid., 1.13.21.

85. That which seventeenth-century divine Robert South said of the Socinians can easily be a warning to us all — that "all that they urge against a triple subsistence of the divine nature is still from instances taken from created natures, and applied to the divine" (Robert South, as quoted in Richard Muller, *PRRD*, 4:211).

86. Immanuel Kant, *Religion and Rational Theology*, in *The Cambridge Edition of the Works of Immanuel Kant* (ed. Allen W. Wood and George di Giovanni; trans. Allen W. Wood, George di Giovanni, et al.; Cambridge: Cambridge Univ. Press, 1996), 264.

87. Friedrich Schleiermacher, *The Christian Faith* (ed. and trans. H. R. Mackintosh and J. S. Stewart; Edinburgh: T&T Clark, 1928), 741; cf. Gerald O'Collins, "The Holy Trinity: The State of the Questions," in *The Trinity* (ed. Davis, Kendall, and O'Collins), 1–25.

88. Alar Laats, *Doctrines of the Trinity in Eastern and Western Theologies: A Study with Special Reference to K. Barth and V. Lossky* (Frankfurt am Main: Peter Lang, 1999), 160.

89. Jürgen Moltmann, *The Trinity and the Kingdom: The Doctrine of God* (trans. Margaret Kohl; San Francisco: Harper & Row, 1981), 142.

1. PRIVILEGING THE ONE

Karl Barth's radical rethinking of the entire liberal trajectory included a profound recovery of interest in the Trinity, but he has been criticized in the recent revival of Trinitarian reflection for so emphasizing God's absolute subjectivity in self-revelation as to undermine the genuine plurality of persons. By Moltmann and others, the fault for this alleged tendency in Barth is credited to an allegedly modalistic tendency in Augustine and the Western tradition more generally, as well as to a modern concept of *person* inherited from German idealism.[89]

In Barth's section in *Church Dogmatics* where he elucidates what it means to say that God is personal, he insists that the only God with whom we have to do is this triune God.[90] Allegations of modalism on the basis of Barth's preference for *modes of being* over *persons* are historically untenable. Although the terms sound similar, *mode of being* (as a synonym for *person*) has frequently been used in Western theology in *opposition* to modalism.[91] At the same time, Barth does tend to collapse the persons into the essence in his thinking.[92] Barth's adoption of Augustine's definition of the Trinity as "a threefold repetition" or a "threefold way of being" is a marvelous way of indicating the unity of the divine essence, but also like Augustine, Barth marginalizes the distinctness of the personal properties.[93]

Where Barth sounds more explicitly modalistic is in the way he defends his reticence to adopt the term *persons*: in modern thinking, he said, *persons* connotes an individualistic conception that cannot fail to imply tritheism. He seems to suggest that if *person* meant what it did in premodern theology, we could speak of three persons, but given the modern connotations, we cannot.[94] Barth's emphasis on the I-Thou relation that obtains between God and humanity is not as thoroughly developed with respect to the intratrinitarian life. Not only a plurality of Gods, but "a plurality of individuals ... within the one Godhead," is to be denied, according to Barth. "*The name of the Father, Son and Spirit means that God is the one God in threefold repetition....* The truth that we are emphasizing is that of the numerical unity of the essence of the 'persons,' when in the first instance we employ the concept of *repetition to denote the 'persons'*

---

90. Barth, *Church Dogmatics*, vol. 2, pt. 1, 268.

91. According to modalism, there is one mode of being with three personalities, but orthodoxy teaches three modes of being/subsistence sharing one essence.

92. Barth, *Church Dogmatics*, vol. 1, pt. 1, 361. He can even speak of the Trinity as a "threefold way of being," which at least echoes Augustine's tendency to marginalize the distinct personal properties in favor of essential unity. His recurring emphasis on the absolute subjectivity of the one Lord, though not formally inaccurate, often displays a tendency toward investing the essence itself with personhood. "God reveals himself as Lord; in this statement we have summed up our understanding of the form and content of the biblical revelation"—and this

in the section defining the Trinity. See similar expressions on pages 314 and 334.

93. Ibid., 334. This thesis, "reduced to its simplest form," says Barth, is that "the threefold yet single lordship of God as Father, Son and Spirit, is the root of the doctrine of the Trinity."

94. Ibid., 357: "What is called 'personality' in the conceptual vocabulary of the nineteenth century is distinguished from the patristic and medieval *persona* by the addition of the attribute of self-consciousness. This really complicates the whole issue." Karl Rahner has also been singled out on the Catholic side as aiding and abetting the semimodalistic view of the Trinity, and for reasons similar to Barth's. However, we do not have the space to interact with Rahner here.

(emphasis added)."[95] Rather, in the church doctrine "we are speaking not of three divine I's, but thrice of the one divine I," resting on the "identity of substance."[96]

Whereas for the classical Reformed tradition each person derives his deity from himself but his personal existence from the Father, for Barth the latter is again collapsed into the former:

> As God is in himself Father from all eternity, he *begets himself* as the Son from all eternity. As he is the Son from all eternity, he is *begotten of himself* as the Father from all eternity. In this eternal *begetting of himself* and *being begotten of himself*, he *posits himself a third time as the Holy Spirit*, i.e., as the love which unites him in himself.[97]

2. Privileging the Many

Largely in reaction to Barth and Rahner, but sweeping Augustine and Western theology generally into its critique, the theological pendulum has swung toward emphasizing the three persons over the one essence. The most enthusiastic advocate of plurality today is Jürgen Moltmann, who challenges Karl Rahner's claim that tritheism is the greatest danger and holds Barth and Rahner up as evidence for the more perennial Western threat of modalism.[98] Moltmann's critique of classical Trinitarian formulations is part of his more general challenge to classical theism. He has referred to his view as "trinitarian panentheism" or *social trinitarianism*.[99] With this trajectory, a more Hegelian Trinitarian ontology can be detected even among some of Barth's own students.

Strangely (given the Jewish roots of Christian monotheism), Moltmann argues that the problems with classical monotheism begin with Aristotle. From the "one God" to the "one emperor" (Alexander the Great), the "monarchical structure" of the cosmos leads to despotism all the way down the ladder. Monotheism also gave rise to patriarchalism and the subjugation of the body to the soul.[100] Moltmann's aim is to articulate a social doctrine of the Trinity (as divine community) that can become the basis for a democratic socialism that encompasses all of creation. On Moltmann's reading, the East and West had a monarchical conception of God, whether the monarchy of the Father or that of the one essence, respectively, and even in Rahner and Barth the three persons are subordinated to the lordship of the one God through his self-revelation.[101] These approaches have strengthened the

---

95. Ibid., 350. Also on 353 he uses the formula *repetitio aeternitatis in aeternitate*.

96. Ibid., 351. Acknowledging that Protestant liberalism was basically modalistic (Sabellian), Barth nevertheless interpreted this as a reaction to tritheism, although it is difficult to identify anything like a resurgence of tritheism in this period. By appealing to "modes of being," Barth neither rejects the propriety of using the term *person* nor simply by the phrase implies modalism (359–60). Whether he follows through on the claim consistently,

Barth insists that the threeness is essential to the divine being.

97. Ibid., 483.

98. Moltmann, *Trinity and the Kingdom of God*, 150, 174–76.

99. A nice summary of the position more fully developed elsewhere (especially in *The Trinity and the Kingdom of God*) is found in Elisabeth Moltmann-Wendel and Jürgen Moltmann, *Humanity in God* (Cleveland: Pilgrim Press, 1983).

100. Moltmann, *Trinity and the Kingdom of God*, 92–93.

101. Ibid., 94.

basis for domination and passivity. Instead of starting with "the external lordship of God," according to Moltmann, we should start from "the internal community of God."[102]

Although he praises the Cappadocians for creating space for the concept of person, Moltmann also applauds Boethius for his definition of *person*, which—in refusing to reduce *person* to social roles—opened the door to the human rights tradition in Western political thought.[103] Richard St. Victor also receives high marks in Moltmann's account.

Nevertheless, "It was Hegel who carried this line of thought one step further: personal being (*Personsein*) means to dispose of oneself to others and to come in others to oneself. This deepening of the concept of relationships in the Christian doctrine of the Trinity can lead to an understanding of the social character (*Sozialität*) of the human person."[104] The Western individualism that makes Barth and Rahner wary of referring to the divine "persons" could have been avoided had God been understood in Trinitarian rather than theistic terms. So the same history leading to the modern concept of person that made Barth wary of the term in relation to the Trinity makes Moltmann attracted to it.

What then is the unity of the persons? Appealing to John of Damascus, Moltmann posits that the unity consists of the *perichōrēsis* (mutual indwelling) of the persons.[105] However, as with many of his appeals to the Eastern tradition, Moltmann fails to recognize the complete solidarity of East and West regarding the unity of the Godhead in *essence*. Where Moltmann *substitutes perichōrēsis* (mutual intercommunion) for essential unity, he fails to recognize that for the Eastern as well as Western theologians *perichōrēsis presupposed* this unity of essence. In part, he is motivated by a concern to see the Trinity as an open society that draws creatures into its perichoretic fellowship: "The divine Trinity is so inviting and so strong that the divine life reflects itself in true human community and takes human community up into itself, 'that they may be all one; even as thou, Father, art in me, and I in thee, that they also may be in us [John 17:21].' "[106]

Social trinitarianism, especially as advocated by Moltmann and Richard Swinburne, has been widely criticized by patristics scholars for misrepresenting the views of the Christian East (particularly the Cappadocian fathers). For example, Sarah Coakley has offered a thorough rebuttal of social-trinitarian interpretations of these

---

102. Ibid., 95.
103. Ibid., 97.
104. Ibid., 98. It is not exactly clear what Moltmann really thinks of Hegel. While he refers to him here as an important figure in the rise of a social understanding of personhood, he elsewhere writes, "Ever since Hegel in particular, the Christian Trinity has tended to be represented in terms of belonging to the general concept of the absolute subject: *one subject—three modes of being*" (17).

105. Ibid., 98.
106. Ibid. Included at this point is a painting by Giovanni Spague, "Trinity," with its obvious tritheism, followed by several others of the same stripe.

theologians.[107] "In point of fact, Gregory of Nyssa is closer to the Latin tradition than to social trinitarianism."[108] While social trinitarianism offers at crucial points a useful therapy against modalism, its denial of the unity of the Trinity in the substance or essence that they share in common is exegetically and ecumenically untenable. No less forcefully than Augustine, Gregory of Nazianzus declared, "When I say God, I mean Father, Son, and Holy Spirit. For Godhead is neither diffused beyond these, so as to bring in a mob of gods; nor yet is it bounded by a smaller compass than these, so as to condemn us for a poverty stricken conception of deity; either Judaizing to save the monarchia, or falling into heathenism by the multitude of our gods."[109]

According to William Alston, "Moltmann is setting up false dichotomies"—either *perichōrēsis* or a single substance. "This view is based either on a gratuitous insistence on a homogeneity of substance (gratuitous because not required by the category of substance itself), or on taking the unity of divine substance as an 'addition' to the 'fellowship' of the Father, Son, and Spirit."[110] The fact is that Nyssa and the rest did not see things in this way. The two fit together just fine.

More fundamentally, Moltmann's view surrenders the first half of the Trinitarian formula, "one in essence," in his effort to project what he considers to be an ideal society (democratic socialism) onto the Godhead.[111] However, instead of correlating a robust Boethian definition of persons with an equally robust affirmation of essential unity, Moltmann dispenses with the latter. Instead of saying that God is one in essence and three in persons, he says, we should think of "three persons,

---

107. See Sarah Coakley, "'Persons' in the 'Social' Doctrine of the Trinity," in *The Trinity* (ed. Davis, Kendall, and O'Collins), 123–44. Coakley, who specializes in the Cappadocian theologians, notes in comparing Gregory of Nyssa and the social trinitarians (particularly from the analytic school, such as Richard Swinburne), "Freer, and more instrumental, imagery for the divine 'persons' is thus also used evocatively by Gregory in his exegetical work, without any apparent concern for philosophical precision" (136). "Gregory is quite clear about the *difference* between human and divine 'persons' …." He does not start with three; nor is it a "community" of "individuals"—"nor, incidentally, does it—on my reading—prioritize 'person' over 'substance' (a matter that has become polemical in the thought of John Zizioulas)" (137). In any case, Moltmann's relation to the tradition is at best confusing, since he alternates between sweeping criticism and appropriation of the Eastern view. On the one hand, the Eastern view is plagued with monarchical (and patriarchal) analogies to the "one emperor, one king" ideology. On the other hand, throughout *Humanity in God*, he and coauthor Elisabeth Moltmann-Wendel refer to the East's view approvingly as "the social doctrine." Such contemporary writers also misunderstand contemporary defenders of the Cappado-

cian legacy, such as John Zizioulas (see Douglas Knight, *The Theology of John Zizioulas* [London: Ashgate, 2007], 65).

108. Coakley points out that for Gregory of Nyssa, "the language of *prosōpon* used for the divine entities in the Trinity is best seen as analogical (and perhaps even metaphorical in its original coinage)" ("'Persons' in the 'Social' Doctrine of the Trinity," 140).

109. Gregory of Nazianzus, *Orations* 38:8, in *NPNF2*, 7:347.

110. Alston, "Substance and the Trinity," 197. Similarly, Brian Leftow offers a cogent case for his conclusion that in spite of their qualifications, the various versions of social trinitarianism are finally tritheistic ("Anti Social Trinitarianism," in *The Trinity* [ed. Davis, Kendall, and O'Collins], 232).

111. Jürgen Moltmann, "The Reconciling Power of the Trinity in the Life of the Church and the World," in *Triune God: Love, Justice, Peace* (ed. K. M. Tharakan; Mavelikkara, India: Youth Movement of Indian Orthodox Church, 1989), 32: "The social doctrine of the Trinity is in a position to overcome monotheism in the concept of God and individualism in the doctrine of man, and to develop a social personalism and personalist socialism. That is important for the divided world in which we live and think."

one community."[112] The unity of God subsists neither as "homogeneous substance nor as identical subject."[113]

> The unity of the divine tri-unity lies in the *union* of the Father, the Son, and the Spirit, not in their numerical unity. It lies in their *fellowship*, not in the identity of a single subject.... The fellowship of the disciples with one another has to resemble the union of the Son with the Father. *But not only does it have to resemble that trinitarian union; in addition it has to be a union within this union* (emphasis added).[114]

In that last sentence, the specter of univocity is once again raised. As a consequence, "we must dispense with both the concept of the one substance and the concept of the identical subject. All that remains is: the unitedness, the at-oneness of the three Persons with one another, or: the unitedness, the at-oneness of the triune God."[115] "God," thus understood, is a community rather than an essential unity. "If the unity of God is not perceived in the at-oneness of the triune God, and therefore as a *perichoretic* unity, then Arianism and Sabellianism remain inescapable threats to Christian theology." In this definition, Moltmann is clearly motivated by his presupposition that whatever this unity is, it must be the kind of unity that can be shared with creatures univocally. Only this can sustain "the concept of a unity that can be communicated and is open."[116] Understandably, then, the ecumenical doctrine of God's essential unity must be found wanting. The "triune God" is for Moltmann merely the community of three divine beings.[117]

III. ONE *AND* MANY: SYSTEMATIC-THEOLOGICAL DEVELOPMENT

Having offered a biblical-theological interpretation and engaged historical formulations, I will suggest two guidelines for systematic-theological reflection on the Trinity.

A. WE SHOULD RECOGNIZE THAT ALL OF OUR DEFINITIONS OF *PERSON* IN RELATION TO THE GODHEAD ARE ANALOGIES.

At the risk of oversimplifying, the East favors the analogy of a family — of course, a patriarchal family with the Father as its source. If taken univocally, this analogy would lead to tritheism. The same is true of the Cappadocian analogy of

---

112. Moltmann-Wendel and Moltmann, *Humanity in God*, 96.
113. Ibid.
114. Moltmann, *Trinity and the Kingdom*, 95–96.
115. Ibid., 150.
116. Ibid.

117. Parallels with Joachim of Fiore, whose views were condemned as tritheistic by the Fourth Lateran council, are apparent in Moltmann's appeal to analogies of "the oneness of a 'herd' or of a 'populace'" (Muller, *PRRD*, 4:35). Moltmann's frequent appeals to Joachim confirm this impression.

Peter, James, and John as three persons (*hypostases*) who share the same human essence (*ousia*). However, the Cappadocians were very clear about the danger of univocal definitions. Often lacking this kind of reserve, some contemporary Trinitarian theologies treat analogies as univocal definitions. Instead of allowing the reality of the Father, the Son, and the Spirit to transform our concept of persons, Barth rejects the term *person* because of what it means in modern anthropology. Similarly, Moltmann takes the Cappadocian analogy literally while rejecting the Cappadocian affirmation of essential unity.

In adopting an analogical approach to divine and human persons, we must also recall that creatures are analogical of God rather than vice versa. As Athanasius reminds us, God's fatherhood is not an analogy of human relations, but vice versa.[118] Therefore, we cannot begin with our concept of ideal human personhood or society. Augustine's psychological analogy played too great a role in the development of his Trinitarian thinking, but he still held to the ecumenical formula. Moltmann's political analogies, however, lead him to deny it. In *The Trinity and the Kingdom of God*, Moltmann criticizes Barth and Rahner for surrendering the Trinity to the image of "the absolute, identical subject," just as monarchical monotheism in Christian antiquity had been the product of an imperial hierarchicalism with one ruler.[119] Aside from his controversial genealogy of this theory, Moltmann's own projection of an ideal society of democratic socialism onto God is even more explicit.[120]

As in his treatment of God's attributes, Moltmann's discussion of the Trinity exhibits impatience with the incomprehensibility of God. "To talk about 'the mystery of the Trinity' does not mean pointing to some impenetrable obscurity or insoluble riddle," Moltmann insists.[121] Robert Jenson expresses the same impatience with mystery.[122] As God's supposed incomprehensibility and aseity give way to the clear and distinct idea of God, we are at last able to recognize the *kind* of God that Moltmann has identified. Thus, there is little need for analogical provisos.

The most obvious point at which the doctrine of analogy is dissolved in Trinitarian thinking is with respect to the relationship between the *immanent and economic*

118. Athanasius, *Select Works and Letters*, in *NPNF2*, 4:320.

119. Moltmann, *The Trinity and the Kingdom*, 139: "The primordial image of the 'absolute subject' in heaven corresponds to the modern perception of human subjectivity as regards nature and history; and the personal God in eternity corresponds to the bourgeois culture of personality. It is the absolute personality of God that makes man a person."

120. As Ted Peters notes, although Aristotle was Alexander the Great's teacher, it was not the philosopher but Alexander's father Philip of Macedon who bequeathed the goal of a one-world empire with one king (Ted Peters, *God as Trinity: Relationality and Temporality in the Divine Life* [Louisville:

Westminster John Knox, 1993], 40–41). More importantly, Moltmann creates a speculative theology by projecting an ideal human society (*The Trinity and the Kingdom of God*, 100–101). In fact, his survey in *Humanity in God* opens with a reference to the correlation of anthropology and theology proper, citing Calvin's opening to the *Institutes*. Already we see the importance of method: the tendency to see God and humans as mirrors of each other, along the lines of the *imago dei*, without establishing whether this is univocal or analogical.

121. Moltmann, *Trinity and the Kingdom*, 161.

122. Robert Jenson, *Systematic Theology* (New York: Oxford Univ. Press, 1997), 2:67.

trinities, which is basically the same as the distinction between God-in-himself and God-in-relation to us. It is one thing to say that the God who reveals himself in his external relations in the world is the *same God* who exists in the mystery of the internal relations of the Godhead, and quite another to say that this revelation is exhaustive or univocal. Here, as in all of our thinking about the Trinity, there are two dangers to be avoided: (1) the immensely popular move of simply collapsing the immanent into the economic Trinity (encouraged by Barth and many of his students) and (2) the tendency to allow for a contradiction between the hidden and revealed God (sometimes evident in Luther's *Bondage of the Will*). We are on safer ground in saying that the revelation of the Trinity in the economy truly reveals the immanent Trinity (contra equivocity) but is always analogical rather than univocal.[123]

B. OUR FORMULATIONS SHOULD ACKNOWLEDGE THAT THE THREE PERSONS ARE NOT SIMPLY RELATIONS BUT DISTINCT SUBSISTENCES WITH THEIR OWN INCOMMUNICABLE ATTRIBUTES.

The Father, the Son, and the Spirit do not differ in their divine essence and attributes. However, there are also personal attributes that cannot be shared. For example, the Son cannot be eternally spirated (see "Reformed Contributions to Trinitarian Reflection," pp. 288–94); neither the Father nor the Spirit can be begotten. The Son cannot be the origin of the Godhead, and the Spirit cannot be the incarnate Word. The danger of modalistic habits of thinking emerges when we correlate the Father with creation, the Son with redemption, and the Spirit with the new birth. Rather, in *every* external work of the Godhead, the Father is always the source, the Son is always the mediator, and the Spirit is always the perfecting agent.

In my view, John Zizioulas and Colin Gunton overstate the variance between the Cappadocians (East) and Augustine (West) and in the process require a relational concept of person that is susceptible to criticism, at least with regard to human persons.[124] However, their concerns with Augustine's tendency to reduce persons to relations instead of thinking in terms of persons-in-relation seem valid and significant. In the Cappadocian development, as Gunton relates, "The persons are therefore not relations, but concrete particulars in relation to one another."[125]

---

123. I concur with Paul Helm, *John Calvin's Ideas* (Oxford: Oxford Univ. Press, 2004), 49. B. B. Warfield's interpretation of Calvin is exactly right: "This much we know, he says, that God is what his works and acts reveal him to be; though it must be admitted that his works and acts reveal not his metaphysical Being but his personal relations—not what he is *apud se*, but what he is *quoad nos*" (*Calvin and Calvinism* [New York: Oxford Univ. Press, 1931], 154).

124. See Harriet A. Harris, "Should We Say That Personhood Is Relational?" *SJT* 41, no. 2 (1998): 214–34. This is made especially problematic in Zizioulas's construction, according to which the unbaptized are mere "biological individuals" (an ontologically "fallen" condition) and become "persons" (i.e., persons-in-relation) in baptism.

125. Gunton, *Promise of Trinitarian Theology*, 39.

"When we look at Augustine's treatment of the topic, it becomes evident that he has scarcely if at all understood the central point." Like Calvin, Gunton concludes that part of it is conceptual: "It is difficult for [Augustine] to understand the meaning of the Greek *hypostasis*. One reason is that he can make nothing of the distinction so central to Cappadocian ontology between *ousia* and *hypostasis*: 'I do not know what distinction they wish to make' (v.10)." As a consequence, "he had prepared the way for the later, and fateful, *definition* of the person as a *relation*."[126] This is fateful, of course, because it easily reduces the Father to "fatherhood" and the Son to "sonship" and leaves little place for the Holy Spirit — What is *his* relation other than being a "bond of love"?[127]

Admittedly, the term *person* has problems — as all analogies do, particularly when they are predicated on the divine mystery; hence, the frequent preference for *subsistence*, as in Aquinas and, if forced to choose, Calvin.[128] In employing the term *person*, however, in relation to the Father, the Son, and the Spirit, we are in no way bound to a Boethian definition ("an individual nature of a rational essence") any more than we are to the more obscure concept of *persona* ("character" or "mask") taken from the Roman stage.[129] There is also no reason (*pace* Barth) to avoid "person" because of modern assumptions of autonomous individualism.

Again, we must answer that question not by referring to *a priori* concepts of personhood drawn from our own interpretation of human personhood or ideal community but by attending to the actual history in which the divine persons are revealed. Whatever questions may be raised in connection with human personhood, it seems clear enough from Scripture that the persons of the Godhead are persons-*in*-relation, not merely persons-*as*-relations. It is not simply that begetting, being begotten, and being spirated are essential to their identity, but that the Father, the Son, and the Spirit are essential to each other's identity.

Along with their unity in essence and activities, each is an unsubstitutable person who lives and acts differently. This difference never provokes opposition, but love, because each person has something different to bring to the intratrinarian relationship and extratrinitarian works. The Father not only knows his fatherhood from the Son; his person as such is defined by this other who addresses him. Much different from human personhood, the first person's being the Father of the Son is

---

126. Ibid., 40.

127. Ibid., xxvii. At the same time, we must remember that Gunton's laudable concern to give ontological status to the persons is precisely the reason why persons cannot be reduced to relations and why Boethius's definition (correlated later with the term *subsistence*) had so much appeal. Nevertheless, with Zizioulas, Gunton believes that Boethius's definition of *person* as "*naturae rationabilis individua substantia*, an individual sub-

stance of rational nature, is the heart of the troubles" (92).

128. Calvin, *Institutes* 1.13.2, 6.

129. T. F. Torrance points out, rightly I believe, that Boethius's definition of *person* is also evident in Augustine, and together they anticipate the *res cogitans* of Descartes. See Torrance, *Incarnation: The Person and Life of Christ* (ed. Robert T. Walker; Downers Grove, Ill.: InterVarsity Press, 2008), 214.

a necessary rather than contingent aspect of his existence. Precisely because each person is different (i.e., possesses incommunicable properties), each knows himself in and through the other. Not even the Father knows himself as Father apart from the Son through the Spirit.

Furthermore, biblical revelation identifies each of these persons as a thinking, willing, and active agent. Nothing exhibits this fact more than the covenant of redemption (*pactum salutis*) made between the divine persons in eternity, which is presupposed in the way that Jesus speaks (especially in John's gospel) of his having been given a people by the Father who are and will be united to him by the Spirit after his departure. <u>Although all three persons are mutually active in every external work of the Godhead, they are active differently. The Father is the originating agent, the Son is the mediator, and the Spirit brings about the intended effect.</u> In fact, it is precisely this individuation of the persons that Barth mentions as his chief objection to this eternal covenant of redemption formulated in Reformed theology: "Can we really think of the first and second persons of the triune Godhead as two divine subjects and therefore as two legal subjects who can have dealings and enter into obligations one with another? This is mythology, for which there is no place in a right understanding of the doctrine of the Trinity.... God is one God,... the only subject,... the one subject."[130] Even more than in Augustine's formulation, Barth's raises the question as to whether the Trinity is not only one God but one person (i.e., subject).

Renewed attention to the distinction between essential attributes and personal properties, a suspicion of surrendering analogical mystery to univocal projections, and the expectation that the reality of the Trinity in covenant history will provoke revisions of our "unbaptized" philosophical categories remain crucial aids in our Trinitarian reflection.

IV. THE *FILIOQUE* addition of 'and the Son' to the Nicene Creed

With the *filioque* debate (see also "East-West Tensions," p. 284) the subtle differences between the East and the West opened into a formal schism. From *ekporeuomai*, the term *procession* refers to the mode by which the Spirit is related to the Father (the Greek view) or to the Father and the Son together (the Latin view). With the ecumenical consensus of East and West, the First Council of Constantinople (381) added to the creed agreed on at Nicea (325) the following phrase concerning the Holy Spirit (taken from Jn 15:26): "the Lord, the Giver of life,

---

130. Barth, *Church Dogmatics*, vol. 4, pt. 1, 65. He adds, somewhat cryptically, "The thought of a purely inter-trinitarian [*sic*] decision as the eternal basis of the covenant of grace may be found both sublime and uplifting. But it is definitely much too uplifting and sublime to be a Christian thought" (66).

who proceeds from the Father." This is why the Nicene Creed is formally called the Nicene-Constantinopolitan Creed. However, when Visigothic Spain renounced Arianism and embraced catholic Christianity, the Council of Toledo (589) added to the last clause ("who proceeds from the Father") the words "and the Son."[131] Eventually, however, the *filioque* clause ("and the Son") became widely popular in the West, provoking condemnation by Patriarch Photius I of Constantinople in 864. After Benedict VIII included the *filioque* for the first time at Mass in Rome (1014), the Western church adopted the amended text—and this was a major cause of the East-West schism in 1054. In spite of deeply entrenched divisions and mutual condemnations, remarkable gains have been made in ecumenical discussions in the last half century on this question.

Before the acrimonious history following the Council of Toledo, Western theologians (such as Augustine) could say that the Spirit takes his origin from the Father as principle (*principalis*) of the Godhead, even as Cyril of Alexandria could argue (against the Nestorians) that the Spirit proceeds from the Father and the Son.[132] In fact, Greek fathers from Epiphanius to as late as Cyril of Alexandria referred to the Spirit's procession from the Father and the Son.[133] However, the introduction of the *filioque* clause at Toledo brought to a head the deeper divisions between the East and West over the monarchy of the Father that we have already explored. More than Augustine, Thomas Aquinas developed a strict doctrine of the Western *filioque*.[134]

While Calvin's interest in patristic sources has long been recognized, it has become customary in recent decades to recruit him as a witness for the prosecution against Augustine and in defense of the East.[135] With good reason, Calvin believed that a clear distinction between the essence that each person shares from himself and the persons that are generated by the Father helps us to avoid ontological subordination and modalism simultaneously. "In this sense the opinions of the ancients are to be harmonized," he suggests, "which otherwise would seem . . . to clash."[136] Calvin eagerly affirms that "in the Father is the beginning and source," but of the persons rather than of the essence.[137] A little later, Calvin adds, "For even

---

131. Whether this was inserted as a further strike against Arianism or because of the copy available to them, the spread of this version of the Creed in Latin reached Rome. There, Pope Leo III affirmed the doctrinal point but rejected such changes to ecumenical creeds.

132. Augustine, *The Trinity* 15.25, 47: PL 42, 1094–95; on Cyril, see A. Maas, "*Filioque*," in the *Catholic Encyclopedia* (ed. Robert C. Broderick; New York: Robert Appleton, 1909), 6:22.

133. Barth, *Church Dogmatics*, vol. 1, pt. 1, 477, referring to Epiphanius, Ephraim, and Cyril of Alexandria.

134. See Augustine, *The Trinity* 14.27, 50. Also Aquinas, *Summa theologica* 1, q. 27, a. 3–4.

135. Cf. T. F. Torrance, "Calvin's Doctrine of the Trinity,"

CTJ 25, no. 2 (November 1990): 165–93. See, more recently, John Heywood Thomas, "Trinity, Logic, and Ontology," in *Trinitarian Theology Today* (ed. Christoph Schwöbel; Edinburgh: T&T Clark, 1995), 75, appealing to Calvin's *Institutes* 1.13.18, 20, 24, 26. Thomas writes concerning Calvin's formulation of the Trinity, "With his customary honesty and impatience with reductionist clarity he admits that he finds himself perplexed at points; but he nevertheless insists that the Father is the *principium* of the Godhead." However, in the same section Calvin affirms the *filioque*.

136. Calvin, *Institutes* 1.13.19.

137. Ibid., 1.13.20.

though we admit that in respect to order and degree the beginning of divinity is in the Father, yet we say that it is a detestable invention that essence is proper to the Father alone, as if he were the deifier of the Son."[138] So the Father "is the beginning of deity, not in the bestowing of essence ..., but by reason of order."[139] "Thus [the Son's] essence is without beginning; while the beginning of his person is God [the Father] himself."[140] This line of argument was followed by later Reformed theology.

To the extent that the East affirms that the essence does not beget and is not begotten or spirated—that *essence* simply refers to something capable of bearing certain attributes—it avoids ontological subordination. The essence is not a person. Although the Cappadocians insisted on the Father (a person) rather than the essence as the source of the Godhead, they rejected any suggestion that the essence (or substance) is caused.[141] However, while affirming the Father as the source (*principium*) of the persons, Reformed theologians have been wary of causal language applied to either the essence *or* the persons. For example, seventeenth-century theologian Herman Witsius argued that while the East's intentions were sound, "This language of causation ... is 'inaccurate,' not to mention 'harsh, indistinct, and unscriptural.'"[142] Especially given the fact that Scripture identifies the Son as the Word, and the Spirit is associated with engendering the effect of that Word, communicative categories seem more judicious than causal ones in considering the intratrinitarian relations.

On the *filioque* question directly, the Reformed orthodox continued to defend the Western position. Calvin reminded readers of the passages in which the third person is identified in the scriptures as both the Spirit of the Father and the Spirit of Christ.[143] Besides having the original version of the Nicene-Constantinopolitan Creed on their side, the Greeks concentrated on John 15:26, where Jesus says that the Spirit is sent from the Father.[144]

Although Barth was a staunch defender of the *filioque*, it is interesting that some of his leading students have rejected it largely out of consideration of this key verse.[145] Departing from Barth's conclusion, they nevertheless do so in faithfulness to his strict identification of the economic and immanent Trinities. Yet, as John Owen noted in the seventeenth century, these passages in John's gospel reveal the economic rather than the immanent Trinity—the work of the divine persons in redemption rather than their ontological relations.[146] In my view, not much is

---

138. Ibid., 1.13.24.

139. Ibid., 1.13.26.

140. Ibid., 1.13.25.

141. Zizioulas, *Communion and Otherness*, 34–35.

142. Quoted in Muller, *PRRD*, 4:254.

143. John Calvin, *Commentary on Romans* (Ro 8:9), as quoted in Muller, *PRRD*, 4:254.

144. See Theodore Stylianopoulos, "The Filioque: Dogma,

Theologoumenon or Error?" *Greek Orthodox Theological Review* 31, nos. 3–4 (1986): 255–88.

145. Like Moltmann, Pannenberg rejects the *filioque* by appealing to passages that treat the economic subordination of the Son and the Spirit to the Father, for example, in John 15:26 (*Systematic Theology* [Grand Rapids: Eerdmans, 1991], 1:317).

146. John Owen, *Works* (Edinburgh: Banner of Truth, 1966), 3:117.

gained by either side of the controversy from these key biblical passages for just this reason. The same is true of passages in Paul (Ro 8:9; Gal 4:6). At the end of the day, it does not seem that the controversy can be settled by proof texts but by more fundamental and general exegetical assumptions concerning the basis for the divine unity. The complicated issues involved in this debate should not be lightly dismissed. Nevertheless, I share the judgment of Kallistos of Diokleia that the *filioque* question, by itself, does not threaten the ecumenical consensus.[147]

DISCUSSION QUESTIONS

1. Discuss the earliest Christian beliefs and practices that gave rise to the understanding of God as the Trinity.
2. It has often been said that truth has been forged on the anvil of heresy. How did the challenges from Judaism and Hellenism (i.e., Greek thought) generate distinct responses and refinements in the church's faith?
3. Define the following: subordinationism, modalism, and tritheism.
4. Discuss the contribution of the Cappadocian theologians to the development of Trinitarian dogma.
5. Evaluate strengths and weaknesses of Eastern and Western tendencies in Trinitarian formulations.
6. What is the "social Trinity," and how does it compare with the classical Christian consensus?
7. What is the best way of avoiding both modalism and tritheism?
8. What is the *filioque* controversy, and why is it relevant?

---

147. Kallistos of Diokleia's remarks are included in "The Father as the Source of the Whole Trinity," by the Pontifical Council for Promoting Christian Unity, *Catholic International* (January 1996), 36–49.

Part Three

GOD
WHO CREATES

Chapter Nine

THE DECREE: TRINITY AND PREDESTINATION

The doctrines of the Trinity and predestination (or God's decree) converge at the point of the eternal covenant of redemption (*pactum salutis*) between the persons of the Godhead. In that covenant, before the world existed, the Father, the Son, and the Spirit already turn toward us, with a purpose to create, redeem, and gather a church for everlasting fellowship. As in all of God's external operations, both the eternal decree itself and its execution in history are accomplished *from* the Father, *in* the Son, *through* the Spirit.

I. DRAMA TO DOCTRINE TO DOXOLOGY

Predestination is clearly taught in Scripture, but debates over its interpretation and meaning have occupied the greatest minds in church history. The Old Testament refers to the "counsel" or "purpose" (*ʿēṣâ*) of God (see Job 38:2; Isa 14:26; 46:10). Other expressions include the verb "to purpose" (*zāmam*; see Pr 30:32; Jer 4:28; 51:12); "will" (*ḥāpēṣ*; see Isa 53:10); "good pleasure" (*rāṣôn*; see Ps 51:18; Isa 49:8). That nothing comes to pass (including the sinful actions of human beings) apart from God's sovereign governance is attested in many passages, including Genesis 50:20; Daniel 4:34–37; Acts 2:23; and Ephesians 1:11. In fact, an implication of God's omniscience is that the future is determined. God knows the future exhaustively because he has decreed the future exhaustively.

The close connection of foreknowledge and foreordination is further established by the force of the Hebrew word *yādaʿ* (and in the NT the Greek *ginōskō/proginōskō*), which occur frequently in contexts in which more than a bare awareness is in view (see Ge 18:19 ["chosen"]; Am 3:2; Hos 13:5). Adam's "knowing" Eve or Mary's conception of Jesus before she "knew" a man clearly intend an intimate knowledge of the person in question. In Romans 8:29, we are told, "Those *whom* he foreknew he also predestined" rather than *that which* he foreknew (emphasis added). In other words, Paul's point is not that God foreknew human choices but that he knew his elect before they came to exist. Similarly, in 1 Peter 1:20, Jesus Christ is said to have been "foreknown before the foundation of the world." God not only foreknows; he chooses—elects—some for salvation out of a condemned race. The Hebrew word *bāḥar* implies choice, along with the Greek equivalents *eklegomai* and *eklogē*, as the latter appear in connection with divine election explicitly in Romans 9:11; 11:5; Ephesians 1:4; and 1 Thessalonians 1:4. The Greek verb *proorizō* (and its cognates) means to "fore-horizon" (i.e., predetermine), and it appears in close connection also with predestination in passages such as Acts 4:28; Romans 8:29–30; 1 Corinthians 2:7; and Ephesians 1:5, 11.

In addition to being stated explicitly, predestination is demonstrated in the biblical narratives, including sinful actions (Ge 50:20). Nebuchadnezzar eventually learned the lesson of God's sovereignty over all things, including his own kingdom (Da 4:34–37). The times and places of every person's life are included in God's decree (Ac 17:26). Even the falling of a bird and the number of hairs on each person's head are encompassed by God's sovereign wisdom (Mt 10:29–30). Although humans are held responsible for their wicked acts in Jesus' crucifixion, he was "delivered up according to the definite plan [*boulē*] and foreknowledge of God" (Ac 2:23). Using the same term (*boulē*), and adding the phrase *proōrisen genesthai* ("predestined to take place"), the believers later praised God, saying, "for truly in this city there were gathered together against thy holy servant Jesus, whom thou didst anoint, both Herod and Pontius Pilate, with the Gentiles and the peoples of Israel, to do whatever thy hand and thy plan had predestined to take place" (Ac 4:27–28 RSV). Once more, this passage does not tell us *how* God can decree their sin while holding them responsible; it simply states that this is the case.[1]

Therefore, not only the free acts of human beings but sinful actions as well are simultaneously said to be included in God's plan yet freely willed by humans. Hebrews speaks of "the unchangeable character of his purpose" (*boulēs*) (Heb 6:17). Ephesians 1:11 refers to the "counsel" (*boulēn*) of God's "will" (*thelēma*), according to which God "works all things." It is the "good pleasure" (*eudokia*) of God that is

---

1. Charles Hodge, *Systematic Theology* (Grand Rapids: Eerdmans, 1946), 1:547: "It is vain to argue that a holy and benevolent God cannot permit sin and misery, if sin and misery do in fact exist. It is vain to say that his impartiality forbids that there should be any diversity in the endowments, advantages, or happiness of his rational creatures.... So it is utterly irrational to contend that God cannot foreordain sin, if he foreordained (as no Christian doubts) the crucifixion of Christ. The occurrence of sin in the plan adopted by God is a palpable fact; the consistency, therefore, of foreordination with the holiness of God cannot rationally be denied."

the motivating cause of our election in Christ (Eph 1:5, 9 NIV), and *eudokia* is also employed in Matthew 11:26 and Luke 2:14.

According to Paul's argument in Romans 9, God's prerogative to elect whom he will and to leave the rest in their just condemnation has been exercised all along, even within Israel. In this chapter, Paul clearly teaches that election is not based on anything in or foreseen in those who are chosen (vv. 9–13). Yet God is not unfair, since everyone is in a state of condemnation, and God is not bound by any necessity to save anyone (vv. 14–15). "So then it depends not on human will or exertion, but on God, who has mercy" (v. 16). Out of the same mass of fallen humanity God chooses some and rejects others (vv. 17–24). Nor can the scope of this argument be limited to Israel, since Paul concludes, "—even us whom he has called, not from the Jews only but also from the Gentiles" (v. 24).

Predestination is typically understood in theology to refer to God's sovereign determination concerning all events, while election and reprobation refer specifically to God's decree regarding salvation and condemnation. Insofar as God reveals his eternal purpose, it is through the dramatic narrative of history leading from creation to the fall to the promise of the gospel and its fulfillment in Jesus Christ. From this economy (i.e., the external works of the Trinity) we can draw the following brief conclusions.

First, predestination is an exercise of the divine will, which in turn is the free expression of the divine nature. As God is eternal, unchangeable, and simple, so is his decree. God's decree is said to be founded on his wisdom (Pss 33:11; 104:24; Pr 3:19; 19:21; Jer 10:12; 51:15; Eph 3:10–11). Because he is loving, righteous, good, and just, God cannot will any ultimate evil. His purposes are to work even human sin and rebellion together for good (Ro 8:28). That is not to say that everything is good or that sinful actions of human beings are beyond his knowledge or permissive decree. Rather, it is to say that it is inconsistent with God's nature and, in fact, unthinkable that God—who cannot do evil or be tempted by evil (Jas 1:13)—should ever determine that any purpose of his will terminate in evil. Thus, God only permissively decrees evil in such a way that the same decree simultaneously determines the triumph of God's just and gracious purposes in Jesus Christ.

Second, the above line of exegetical argument has led Reformed theology to distinguish between God's permission and his positive determination. God does not cause people to sin. "This means," says Louis Berkhof, "that God does not positively work in man 'both to will and to do' when man goes contrary to his revealed will."[2] The context of Philippians 2:12–13 is the sanctification of believers, not general

---

2. Louis Berkhof, *Systematic Theology* (Grand Rapids: Eerdmans, 1996), 105.

providence. As Berkhof observes, "The decree, in so far as it pertains to these acts, is generally called God's permissive decree. This name does not imply that the futurition of these acts is not certain to God, but simply that he permits them to come to pass by the free agency of his rational creatures."[3] Mere foreknowledge without foreordination makes God a spectator to horrendous evils and leaves us wondering whether God is aloof, like the Stoic sage, or perhaps even malicious. In other words, we can trust God not only in those situations where his goodness is obvious, but when sin and evil seem to be gaining the upper hand. While God never causes sin, he is Lord over it, and it can progress no further than his wisdom and goodness will allow.

Third, we must carefully distinguish the decree in eternity from its execution in history. For example, some hyper-Calvinists held the view that the elect are justified from all eternity. Similar to Barth's view (treated below), this position collapses the execution of the decree (*ordo salutis*)[4] into the decree itself. Scripture teaches that we are justified through faith, yet even this act of faith was graciously determined by the triune God before the creation of the world.

Purposes are different from their fulfillment; determinations are different from their accomplishment. God has determined not only the ends but the means by which he will achieve them. God may have determined our life span and where we would live (Ac 17:26), but these hidden purposes are fulfilled through our planning and investigation, real estate agents, moving companies, employers, and so forth. Even in our salvation, God fulfills his electing decree through myriad means — the prayers of friends and relatives, a neighbor who brings us to church or shares the gospel with us after work, and many other influences and events of which we are not even aware.

As A. A. Hodge points out, human agency is actually included in and therefore made possible by God's decree that "in the case of every free act of a moral agent ... the act shall be perfectly spontaneous and free on the part of the agent."[5] God's decree not only determines that the act will certainly occur (Ps 33:11; Pr 19:21; Isa 46:10), but that it will be freely done by the agent. Like Mary at the annunciation, we may wonder how this is possible, but we too are simply told, "Nothing will be impossible with God" (Lk 1:37).

Finally, God's sovereignty is not only demonstrated in narratives and described in doctrines; it is celebrated in praise. For example, in each of the arguments for God's predestining purposes in Christ, Paul moves from narratively grounded doctrinal arguments to scenic vistas, where he pauses to adore. Immediately after teaching,

---

3. Ibid., 103.

4. The Latin phrase *ordo salutis* means "the order of salvation" and refers to how the Spirit applies the benefits of Christ

to individuals. Cf. ch. 16, "IV. The King and His Kingdom," pp. 535–37.

5. A. A. Hodge, as quoted in Berkhof, *Systematic Theology*, 104.

"Those whom he predestined he also called, and those whom he called he also justified, and those whom he justified he also glorified" (Ro 8:30), he exclaims, "What then shall we say to these things? If God is for us, who can be against us? Who shall bring any charge against God's elect? It is God who justifies" (vv. 31, 33). Then in chapter 11, after treating the same topic in the context of Israel's unfolding narrative, again he is left in wonder at the riches of God's unfathomable knowledge and grace (Ro 11:33–36). Only when we are led to praise have we truly understood that part of the mystery of God's decree that he has revealed.

II. HISTORICAL INTERPRETATIONS OF GOD'S DECREE

Historically, debates over predestination have revealed massive cleavages between theological systems at their heart, encompassing the God-world relation and the doctrine of salvation. *Pelagianism* (named after the British monk Pelagius [354–420], an opponent of Augustine) maintains that election is based on God's foreknowledge of those who would merit their salvation, even apart from gracious assistance. A milder version, known as *Semi-Pelagianism*, held that although the beginning of salvation was due to human free will, growth and final salvation required divine grace. This view was also condemned at the Second Council of Orange (529).

Duns Scotus, Thomas Aquinas, and other seminal theologians of the medieval church (in accord with Augustine) affirmed God's unconditional election and reprobation of people as part of his eternal decree and held that everything that actually happens is included in God's eternal plan, secret to us. Nevertheless, medieval theologians such as Gregory of Rimini and Archbishop Thomas Bradwardine complained that a robust Augustinianism was being threatened by "a new Pelagianism," and this was the concern that precipitated the Reformation.[6]

Arising as a dissenting movement in the Dutch Reformed Church, *Arminianism* holds that grace is necessary not only for the perfecting of faith and obedience but as a precondition for both.[7] Nevertheless, sufficient prevenient grace is given to all people to exercise their free will, and election is based on God's foreknowledge of

---

6. See Thomas Bradwardine, "The Cause of God against the Pelagians," in *Forerunners of the Reformation: The Shape of Late Medieval Thought* (ed. Heiko Oberman; New York: Holt, Rinehart, and Winston, 1966), 151–64. The strong affirmation of original sin and of the necessity of God's prevenient grace at the Council of Trent at first challenges the legitimacy of the Reformed and Lutheran charges of Semi-Pelagianism. Nevertheless, prevenient grace appears by itself (*sola gratia*) only at

the beginning of conversion with the infusion of justifying (i.e., regenerating) grace in baptism. From that point on, the increase of justification and final justification depend on meritorious human cooperation. From an Augustinian perspective, this can only constitute a Semi-Pelagian position.

7. Named after Jacob Arminius (1560–1609), Arminianism contradicted the Reformed confession and was rejected at the Synod of Dort (1618–1619).

those who will in fact cooperate with his grace in faith and good works.[8] *Socinianism* denied not only God's predestination but also God's exhaustive foreknowledge of the free actions of creatures, which Arminians and Calvinists both affirmed.[9]

The Christian East reflects a diversity of views on this subject. First, although some of Pelagius's followers found safe haven in the East, the Pelagian controversy arose in the West. Second, the debate has been typically understood as a "Western" problem because of a Latin emphasis on legal categories. Death and immortality (rather than original sin and justification) are the dominant categories in Eastern theologies. Nevertheless, the East strongly affirms *synergism* (i.e., salvation as a process of grace-assisted cooperation with God).

Lutheranism does not fit into any of the preceding categories. Luther's debate with Erasmus over the freedom of the will and divine election underscored the sovereignty of God's grace. In fact, Luther affirmed both election and reprobation in the strongest terms.[10] The Lutheran confessions, however, affirm God's unconditional election of those on whom he will have mercy but deny his reprobation of the rest as an actual decree. While confessional Lutheran and Reformed theologies differ with respect to the decree of reprobation, the extent of the atonement, and the resistibility of God's grace, they are united in their defense of soteriological *monergism* (i.e., God alone working in salvation), grounded in his unconditional election of sinners in Jesus Christ.[11]

---

8. Richard Watson, *Theological Institutes* (New York: Phillips and Hunt, 1887), 2:392–449; Thomas N. Ralston, *Elements of Divinity* (ed. T. O. Summers; New York: Abingdon-Cokesbury, 1924), 278–327; William B. Pope, *A Compendium of Christian Theology* (New York: Phillips and Hunt, n.d.), 1:317–19; John Lawson, *Introduction to Christian Doctrine* (Grand Rapids: Zondervan, 1967, 1980), 206–35. See also Roger Olson, *Arminian Theology: Myths and Realities* (Downers Grove, Ill.: InterVarsity Press, 2006).

9. Followers of this movement, named after Laelius Socinus (1525–1562) and his nephew Faustus (1539–1604), were radical Protestants who rejected all dogmas that they thought were inconsistent with reason and practical morality. Forerunners of modern Unitarians, Socinians denied the Trinity, the deity of Christ, and the substitutionary character of Christ's atonement. They held that in order to affirm free will, God's foreknowledge must include only necessary truths rather than the contingent decisions and acts of human beings. See the citations from the Racovian Catechism in William Cunningham, *Historical Theology* (Edinburgh: Banner of Truth, 1996), 2:173.

10. Martin Luther, *The Bondage of the Will* (trans. J. I. Packer and O. R. Johnston; Grand Rapids: Revell, 1990).

11. Despite his friendship with Calvin, Philipp Melanchthon eventually came to question reprobation and eventually taught a form of synergism (conditional election) that (in addition to his more Calvinistic understanding of the Supper) led to a strong reaction against him on the part of Luther's orthodox followers. The so-called *gnesio* (original)-Lutherans resolutely defended unconditional election and rejected any form of synergism *but also* the Calvinist view of reprobation (as well as "Philippist" accommodations with Calvinistic eucharistic views). These views were officially adopted in the *Book of Concord*. For a summary of the Lutheran confession on this point (especially the *Formula of Concord*), see Charles Porterfield Krauth, *The Conservative Reformation and Its Theology* (Minneapolis: Augsburg, 1963), 322–24. However, some Lutherans followed Melanchthon's view (conditional election, based on foreseen faith); see, e.g., Heinrich Smid, *Doctrinal Theology of the Evangelical Lutheran Church* (trans. Charles A. Hay and Henry E. Jacobs; Minneapolis: Augsburg, 1889), 272–73. Although often characterized as Arminian by Reformed Christians because it rejects reprobation, particular redemption, and the indefectibility of regeneration, the Lutheran system cannot be pressed into Calvinist-Arminian categories. Confessional Lutheranism simultaneously affirms unconditional election and God's universal grace, monergism and the possibility of losing one's salvation. Krauth summarizes that "on many points in the developed system now known as Arminianism the Lutheran Church has no affinity whatever with it, and on these points would sympathize far more with Calvinism" (Krauth, *The Conservative Reformation*, 127). Lutheranism is its own system with its own integrity and, from a Reformed perspective, peculiar inconsistencies.

The idea that predestination is the central dogma in Reformed theology, from which every other belief is logically deduced, has been refuted by recent historical scholarship.[12] In neither Calvin's writings nor the Reformed confessions does predestination occupy a central place, and especially on this topic warnings abound against speculation (Dt 29:29). Consideration of God's predestination is of inestimable benefit if we find our election in Christ as he is offered to all people in the gospel, but a dangerous labyrinth if we presume to investigate God's secret counsels.[13] Francis Turretin spoke for Reformed scholastics generally when he warned against trying to seek out God and his purposes apart from Christ and the gospel.[14] "Therefore," he adds, "it becomes us to dismiss the curious and useless questions of the [medieval] Scholastics, who by a rash presumption undertake to define the incomprehensible secrets of God's majesty."[15]

III. THE LOGICAL ORDER OF GOD'S DECREE

Given God's simplicity, eternity, and omniscience, there is no before and after in his decision making, but we sometimes speak of his decrees (plural) and a sequential order simply to refer to a *logical* rather than *temporal* succession of decisions. However, did this decree to save come before (at least logically) the decree to create and permit the fall? In other words, does God first of all elect people to be saved and condemned, or does he elect some to be saved from a condemned humanity? The two answers to that question came to be known as *supralapsarianism* and *infralapsarianism*. According to the former, God's decree to save is logically *prior* to his decree to create and permit the fall. According to the latter, the decree to save

---

Arminian (Remonstrant) theology, as it evolved into a system, rejected unconditional election and its kindred doctrines (total depravity, particular redemption, irresistible grace, perseverance of the saints). The Counter-Reformation offered yet another perspective on the divine decree. In between the classic Thomistic-Augustinian position defended by the Dominicans and the more Semi-Pelagian position adopted by the later Franciscans, the so-called Molinists, after Luis de Molina, who with Francisco Suárez defended a position identified as "middle knowledge" (*scientia media*). For a contemporary defense of this view, see William Lane Craig, "The Middle Knowledge View," in *Divine Foreknowledge: Four Views* (Downers Grove, Ill.: InterVarsity Press, 2001).

12. Rooted in the methodological approach of Heiko Oberman, David Steinmetz, and others, Richard Muller is joined by a growing number of historical theologians who have decisively refuted the Torrance school on the relation between Calvin and Calvinism. See, for example, Richard Muller, *After Calvin* (New York: Oxford Univ. Press, 2004), which summarizes much of his research on this relationship; cf. Carl Trueman and R. S.

Clark, eds., *Protestant Scholasticism: Essays in Reassessment* (Carlisle, U.K.: Paternoster, 1998); Paul Helm, *Calvin and the Calvinists* (Edinburgh: Banner of Truth, 1982); W. J. van Asselt and E. Dekker, eds., *Reformation and Scholasticism: An Ecumenical Enterprise* (Grand Rapids: Baker, 2001); Joel Beeke, *Assurance of Faith: Calvin, English Puritanism, and the Dutch Second Reformation* (New York: Peter Lang, 1991); L. D. Bierma, "Federal Theology in the Sixteenth Century: Two Traditions?" *WTJ* 45 (1983): 304–21; "The Role of Covenant Theology in Early Reformed Orthodoxy," *The Sixteenth Century Journal* 21 (1990): 453–62.

13. See Calvin, *Institutes* 3.21.2.

14. Turretin, *Elenctic Theology*, 1:16. Calvin's attitude toward speculation is well known, as is his emphasis on God's condescension and accommodation to us, revealing God not as he is in himself but as he is toward us—not in his being but in his works. "Better to limp along this path," Calvin cautioned, "than to dash with all speed outside it" (*Institutes* 1.6.3).

15. Turretin, *Elenctic Theology*, 1:252.

follows the decision to create and permit the fall. Here especially we should restrain speculation. Nevertheless, since advocates of both positions have appealed to specific biblical passages — and the implications are more important than they might at first appear — some account should be offered here.

A. TRADITIONAL REFORMED INTERPRETATIONS

Although the distinct categories of supralapsarianism and infralapsarianism were coined by Reformed orthodoxy, these positions have a long history in Western theology. Augustine and Aquinas represent a more "infralapsarian" view, while the view of Duns Scotus is closer to "supralapsarianism." Scotus believed that the world was created for the purpose of Christ's incarnation and that the Son would have become flesh even if there had been no fall. The fall, then, is seen as logically dependent on the incarnation rather than vice versa. With the exception of Zwingli, who was consistently supralapsarian, it is difficult to classify the Reformers on this point, since they did not address this as a distinct topic as their predecessors and successors did in their systems.

Reformed orthodoxy tolerated supralapsarianism but favored infralapsarianism. Infralapsarians worried that supralapsarianism risked making God the author of evil and making reprobation (election to judgment) roughly parallel to God's activity in his gracious election to salvation in Christ. As Louis Berkhof observes, both parties generally agreed that the fall was included in God's decree, that this decree in relation to the fall was permissive rather than active, and that reprobation (the rejection of the nonelect) was not capricious or arbitrary but took account of sin.[16] However, infralapsarians typically suspect that supralapsarianism cannot consistently affirm the second and third of these points. In strong terms, the canons of the Synod of Dort (1618–1619) declared, "Reformed Churches ... detest with their whole soul" the view "that in the same manner in which the election is the fountain and cause of faith and good works, reprobation is the cause of unbelief and impiety."[17]

Supralapsarians appeal to Romans 9. Isaac's wife Rebecca was told with regard to her twins that "though they were not yet born and had done nothing either good or bad — in order that God's purpose of election might continue, not because of works but because of him who calls —... 'The older will serve the younger.' As it is written, 'Jacob I loved, but Esau I hated' " (vv. 11–13). Paul's point, supralapsarians argue, is that God's election of one and reprobation of the other were made without reference to their being fallen. Similarly, Paul's example of God's having raised up Pharaoh for his sovereign purposes displays his power to elect and condemn without

---

16. Berkhof, *Systematic Theology*, 119 (cf. p. 120 for an excellent summary of the two views).

17. *Canons of Dort*, ch. 5, "Conclusion," in *Psalter Hym-* *nal: Doctrinal Standards and Liturgy of the Christian Reformed Church* (Grand Rapids: Board of Publications of the Christian Reformed Church, 1976), 115.

either decision being made with respect to sin. "So then he has mercy on whomever he wills, and he hardens whomever he wills" (v. 18). Finally, supralapsarians point to verses 19–24, where Paul says that God as the potter has made "out of the same lump [of clay] one vessel for honorable use and another for dishonorable use" (v. 21).

Infralapsarians also refer to Romans 9 in their defense of unconditional election but do not find there any basis for concluding that the "same lump" is regarded by God as unfallen when he elects and reprobates. In fact, Paul's citation of Exodus 33:19—"I will have *mercy* on whom I have mercy, and I will have *compassion* on whom I have compassion" (emphasis added)—indicates that God's election is of those whom God in his eternal purpose already knows as sinners. God takes no pleasure in the death of the wicked (Eze 18:32) but delights in the salvation of the elect (Eph 1:5–6).

God is not active in hardening hearts in the same way that he is active in softening hearts. Scripture does speak of God hardening hearts, not only in Exodus 7:3 and Romans 9:18 but also in Joshua 11:20; John 12:40; Romans 11:7; 2 Corinthians 3:14. Yet it also speaks of sinners hardening their own hearts (Ex 8:15; Ps 95:8; Isa 63:17; Mt 19:8; Heb 3:8, 13). However, God alone softens and in fact re-creates the hearts of his elect (1Ki 8:58; Ps 51:10; Isa 57:15; Jer 31:31–34; Eze 11:19; 36:26; 2Co 3:3; 4:6; Heb 10:16).

B. BARTH'S REVISED SUPRALAPSARIANISM

Not too long ago, this was widely considered a parochial debate among scholastic Calvinists. However, all of that has changed since Karl Barth's reinvigoration of the supralapsarian position, albeit radically revised.[18] "The election of grace is the sum of the gospel—we must put it as pointedly as that," Barth insists. "But more, the election of grace is the whole of the gospel, the gospel *in nuce*."[19] In fact, Barth complains that predestination was not central enough for the Reformed scholastics.[20] The orthodox were right to place election under the doctrine of God, "but we must do so far more radically than was the case in this very important Reformed tradition."[21] The upshot of Barth's revised supralapsarianism is that "the work of God (the work of all works!) is not creation, but that which precedes creation both

---

18. The best engagement with Barth's views on these matters remains G. C. Berkouwer, *The Triumph of Grace in the Theology of Karl Barth* (trans. Harry R. Boer; Grand Rapids: Eerdmans, 1956).

19. Barth, *Church Dogmatics*, vol. 2, pt. 2, pp. 13–14.

20. Barth rejected the notion that predestination was a central dogma in Reformed orthodoxy, much less that it functioned as "a kind of speculative key—a basic tenet from which they could deduce all other dogmas." "Not even the famous schema

of T. Beza was intended in such a sense," Barth notes (*Church Dogmatics*, vol. 2, pt. 2, pp. 77–78). In fact, "If we read their expositions connectedly, we are more likely to get the impression that from the standpoint of its systematic range and importance they gave to the doctrine too little consideration rather than too much" (78). These comments stand in opposition to the school of Calvin interpretation associated with some of Barth's heirs, especially T. F. Torrance and J. B. Torrance.

21. Barth, *Church Dogmatics*, vol. 2, pt. 2, p. 80.

eternally and in effect temporally, the incarnate Word of God, Christ."[22] "It is for this reason that we understand the election as ordination, as God's self-ordaining of himself."[23] Election, says Barth, is the primal decision on the basis of which the triune God *moves toward humanity*.[24] Nevertheless, there is no point in eternity or time where we encounter God apart from the redeeming grace of Jesus Christ.[25]

Although Barth introduced the novel view that every human being is elect in Christ, he held that God's decree of election was logically prior to all other decrees.[26] In this account, predestination and Christology become "a single event."[27] In this "purified supralapsarianism," election is God's choice, "preceding all his other choices," which is "fulfilled in his eternal willing of the existence of the man Jesus and of the people represented in him."[28] Christ's election and the election of humanity are one and the same event. "In the beginning with God was this One, Jesus Christ. And that is predestination."[29]

Consequently, there is no longer any room for a distinction between elect and reprobate individuals with different ultimate destinies — one under the law and wrath, another under the gospel and grace — or a notion of a covenant of creation that is logically and temporally distinct from the covenant of grace. In fact, there is no "before" or "after" in God's dealings with humanity. In the light of this history of the elect humanity in Jesus Christ, human resistance, rebellion, and unbelief are not ontologically real; it is the history of Jesus Christ (and therefore of God) that is decisive. Sin is the "impossible possibility," the shadow of the light cast by Christ. In truth, Jesus Christ is not the *last Adam* but *precedes* Adam and in fact reduces "Adam" to non-being.[30]

One may continue to object, to refuse to be defined by one's election and reconciliation in Christ, but that rejection is not finally decisive. "God does not permit [the human person] to execute this No of his, this contradiction and opposition."[31] Even God's No is overtaken by God's Yes; hence, law must always be finally subsumed under gospel.[32] "*This* No is really Yes. *This* judgment is grace. *This* condemnation is forgiveness. *This* death is life. *This* hell is heaven."[33] It might be suggested

22. Ibid.

23. Ibid., vol. 2, pt. 2, p. 89.

24. Ibid., vol. 2, pt. 2, pp. 90–92.

25. Ibid., vol. 2, pt. 2, pp. 92–94.

26. Ibid., vol. 2, pt. 1, pp. 319–21; cf. the critique of this position by Berkouwer, *The Triumph of Grace*, 255–58.

27. Barth, *Church Dogmatics*, vol. 4, pt. 2, pp. 105: "In a basic attachment to the Reformed tradition, but without following it in detail, and transcending it at some points, we have given this a sense and position which it did not have in all earlier Christology. We have 'actualised' the doctrine of the incarnation, i.e., we have used the main traditional concepts, *unio*, *communio* and *communicatio* as concentrically related terms to

describe one and the same ongoing process ... a single event."

28. Ibid., vol. 2, pt. 2, p. 25.

29. Ibid., vol. 2, pt. 2, p. 145.

30. See especially Karl Barth, *Man and Humanity in Romans 5* (trans. T. A. Smail; New York: Collier, 1962).

31. Barth, *Church Dogmatics*, vol. 4, pt. 3, pp. 1, 3.

32. Ibid., vol. 2, pt. 2, pp. 13: "The Yes cannot be heard unless the No is also heard. But the No is said for the sake of the Yes and not for its own sake. In substance, therefore, the first and last word is Yes and not No."

33. Karl Barth, *The Word of God and the Word of Man* (trans. Douglas Horton; New York: Harper & Bros., 1957), 120.

that for Barth human existence under the reign of sin, death, unbelief, and condemnation is finally like the existence of the prisoners in Plato's cave. It is not the truth of their reality but a terrible dream from which they need to be awakened.

Placing the decree to create and to permit the fall prior to the decree of election, Barth complains, opens up space between creation and redemption, and the distinction between a covenant of creation and a covenant of grace made matters worse — opening the door to natural theology, historicism, and other ills of modern theology.[34] Representing "an advance on medieval scholasticism," federal (covenant) theology "tried to understand the work and Word of God attested in Holy Scripture dynamically and not statically, as an event and not as a system of objective and self-contained truths.... This theology is concerned with the bold review of a history of God and man which unfolds itself from creation to the day of judgment." It follows Calvin's emphasis on the dynamic history of the covenant in the history of redemption. However, he asks, did it not concern itself "with a whole series of events which are purposefully strung out but which belong together?... Can we historicize the activity and revelation of God? The federal theologians were the first really to try to do this in principle."[35] "They say excellently that the Bible tells us about an event," says Barth, but fail to see that it is "only a *single event*" dependent on "the *single and complete decision* on the part of God.... Because of the difference of the attestation it cannot be broken up into a series of different covenant acts, or acts of redemption, which follow one another step by step, and then reassembled into a single whole" (emphasis added).[36]

A corollary of the monistic tilt in Barth's concept of the Trinity is the tendency to collapse time into eternity. For Barth, the eternal event of Christ's election is the *real* history.[37] This "disperses the last appearance of contingency" with respect to Christ's incarnation. In God's eternal election, heaven is "worldly" and eternity is "this human history."[38] Although philosophical (especially Platonic) categories are evident, Barth is apparently driven by two converging undercurrents that are doctrinal in character — namely, supralapsarianism and universal election (which is to

---

34. Barth, *Church Dogmatics*, vol. 4, pt. 1, pp. 66. Barth is not quite fair in his definition, since these writers believed that there were two historical covenants, not one covenant conceived of in a dualistic fashion.

35. Ibid., vol. 4, pt. 1, p. 55.

36. Ibid., vol. 4, pt. 1, p. 56.

37. Ibid., vol. 4, pt. 2, p. 31: "We have to do with the eternal beginning of all the ways and works of God when we have to do with Jesus Christ — even in his true humanity. This is not a 'contingent fact of history.' It is the historical event in which there took place in time that which was the purpose and resolve and will of God from all eternity and therefore before the being of all creation, before all time and history, that which is, there-

fore, above all time and history, and will be after them, so that the being of all creatures and their whole history in time follow this one resolve and will, and were and are and will be referred and related to them. The true humanity of Jesus Christ, as the humanity of the Son, was and is and will be the primary content of God's eternal election of grace, i.e., of the divine decision and action which are not preceded by any higher apart from the trinitarian happening of the life of God, but which all other divine decisions and actions follow, and to which they are subordinated.... For God's eternal election of grace is concretely the election of Jesus Christ" (cf. 33–34).

38. Ibid., vol. 4, pt. 2, p. 35.

say, the election of Jesus Christ). These undercurrents converge in the thesis that "nothing can precede his grace, whether in eternity or time."[39]

The question that such a thesis provokes, of course, is how the persons of the Trinity—prior to creation, much less the fall—can properly be said to exist in a relationship of fault to which grace and mercy would be an appropriate response. As we have seen, Barth has exactly the right concept of grace. It is more than generosity: "Grace means redemption.... Grace, in fact, presupposes the existence of this opposition [i.e., sin]."[40] Barth is rigorously consistent: If grace is defined as mercy shown to those at fault—in opposition to God's freedom and love—and there is no historical creation in integrity or fall into sin that precedes this redemptive grace in time, then there cannot have been any moment when the creation was not inherently opposed to God. However, for Barth it means that the very notion of "prior to the fall" has to be adjusted. *In himself and as such* man will always do as Adam did in Genesis 3" (emphasis added).[41] "To say man," Barth writes, "is to say creature and sin, and this means limitation and suffering."[42] "Adam" represents a movement from an original relation of divine grace and human obedience to rebellion, whereas Jesus Christ brings about, as Bruce McCormack puts it, "a return to the 'Origin' (reconciliation). These two movements are not to be conceived of as sequential, but rather as parallel and simultaneous."[43]

Besides introducing the error of universal election, Barth presses the supralapsarian logic beyond its traditional limits. In the process, his formulations tend to bring us back, ironically, to something like the "overcoming estrangement" paradigm, where time is absorbed into eternity, the diversity of God's historical acts is assimilated to the eternal decree of election, and human agency is similarly rendered a mere appearance. Berkouwer justifiably concludes that with no real transition from wrath to grace, "Barth's revised supralapsarianism blocks the way to ascribing decisive significance to history."[44] It may be added that this view blocks the way to affirming the integrity of creation and the reality of the fall as a historical event. Berkouwer points out (via H. van Oyen) that Platonism and mythical conceptions of an uncreated darkness and light creep in. "There is no room in Barth's thinking for preservation as a sustaining and keeping work of God apart from the idea of *redemption*. For this reason the distinction between pre-fall and post-fall plays no role in his theology."[45]

The real issue is not whether we think of creation christologically, Berkouwer observes, but whether we reject or accept "the 'step-wise' character of God's

39. Ibid., vol. 2, pt. 2, p. 79.
40. Ibid., vol. 2, pt. 1, p. 355.
41. Ibid., vol. 4, pt. 2, p. 122.
42. Ibid., vol. 4, pt. 1, p. 131.

43. Bruce McCormack, *Karl Barth's Critically Realistic Dialectical Theology* (Oxford: Clarendon, 1997), 147.
44. Berkouwer, *Triumph of Grace*, 256–58.
45. Ibid., 247.

works."[46] Attempts to "construct a *synthesis* of these two elements [decree and history or creation and redemption] which will be perspicuous to our understanding" inevitably cause us to "fall into the abyss of either eternalizing God's works or historicizing them"—either monism or dualism.[47] A "*transition* from wrath to grace *in history* is excluded," and "wrath is no more than 'the form of grace.'"[48] Hence, the "impossible possibility" of sin.[49] Barth's supralapsarianism is motivated by this reaction against the "step-wise" character of God's works.[50]

Like Berkouwer, Emil Brunner concludes that Barth's revised (universalistic) supralapsarianism simply resolves history into eternity.[51] His "objectivism," Brunner judges, is an a priori construct that evades clear exegesis.[52] "Hence the transition from unbelief to faith is not the transition from 'being-lost' to 'being-saved.' This turning-point does not exist, since it is no longer possible to be lost. But if we look at this view more closely, we see also that the turning-point in the historical Event is no real turning-point at all; for Election means that everything has already taken place in sphere of pre-existence."[53]

The Roman Catholic theologian Hans Urs von Balthasar spoke of Barth as evidencing "a dynamic and actualist theopanism, which we define as a monism of beginning and end (protology and eschatology)," drawing on Idealist categories.[54] "Too much in Barth gives the impression that nothing much really happens in his theology of event and history, because everything has already happened in eternity."[55]

My own analysis leads me to the same conclusions. The "step-wise" character of the divine economy gives to the biblical narrative a genuine movement with genuine twists and turns along the way. Jesus scolds his followers not for failing to recognize the simultaneity of his humiliation and exaltation but for failing to realize that he first had to suffer and then enter into his glory (Lk 9:28–45; 24:26; Php 2:6–11; Heb 1:3–4; 2:9–10; 1Pe 1:11). The transition is historical, not merely noetic or logical.

From these criticisms we can discern at least some of the motives for Barth's stress on unity that we have already seen in his Trinitarian thinking. In fact, we have discovered that the dominance of the one Lord over the three persons is the principal reason for his objection to the notion of an intratrinitarian covenant of redemption.[56] One God, one covenant in which law is subsumed under gospel, one

46. Ibid., 252.
47. Ibid., 253.
48. Ibid., 253.
49. Ibid.
50. Ibid., 255.
51. Emil Brunner, *Dogmatics I: The Christian Doctrine of God* (trans. Olive Wyon; Philadelphia: Westminster, 1946), 1:347.
52. Ibid., 1:349–50.
53. Ibid., 1:351.

54. Hans Urs von Balthasar, *The Theology of Karl Barth: Exposition and Interpretation* (trans. Edward T. Oakes, SJ; San Francisco: Ignatius, 1992), 94.
55. Ibid., 371.
56. Barth, *Church Dogmatics*, vol. 4, pt. 1, p. 65. He adds, somewhat cryptically, "The thought of a purely inter-trinitarian [*sic*] decision as the eternal basis of the covenant of grace may be found both sublime and uplifting. But it is definitely much too uplifting and sublime to be a Christian thought" (66).

subject of electing grace, one eternal history of God actualized in one event—unity obtains a controlling status in Barth's dogmatics, which is perhaps one reason why it has been characterized as "Christian monism" and why Barth himself had so little trouble identifying with the "biblical-theocentric monism" of seventeenth-century supralapsarianism.[57]

George Hunsinger reminds us that Berkouwer criticized Barth for a Platonizing "eternalizing" of time (a separation finally leading to monism), while Robert Jenson draws inspiration from Barth in the direction of a Hegelian "historicizing" of eternity.[58] However, I wonder if both moves are entirely possible readings of Barth's own intentions, just as Berkouwer suggested above. As we have seen, Brunner and Berkouwer recognized early on that Barth's all-encompassing reformulation of election entailed a radical revision of theology. Barth speaks of "Jesus the eternally Elect Man," "the pre-existing God-Man, who, as such, is the eternal ground of all election," but Brunner pointedly asserts, "No special proof is required to show that the Bible contains no such doctrine, nor that no theory of this kind has ever been formulated by any theologian."[59]

Finally, although Barth's "revised supralapsarianism" was motivated in part by his concern to eliminate any ontological gap between God's hidden decree and his self-revelation in Christ, he stopped short of embracing the doctrine of universal salvation (*apokatastasis*). Although all of humanity is elect in Christ, it would be an affront to God's sovereign freedom to assert that each and every person will finally be saved.[60] However, this presents a far more ominous threat of a breach between the hidden and revealed God. Barth holds that, despite one's being chosen, redeemed, called, justified, and sanctified, it is at least possible that one may not at last be glorified but will be reprobate after all.

For Calvin and Reformed orthodoxy, there can be no contradiction between the immanent and economic Trinity (or *deus in se est*, "God in himself," and *deus pro nos*, "God for us"). Calvin sharply rejected the nominalist idea of a God of arbitrary will and power behind or above the God revealed in Jesus Christ.[61] The hidden God is not different from the revealed God. All of the elect will be saved, without the possibility of one being lost. At the same time, the well-meant summons of the external Word to repent and believe the gospel is universal. That many do in fact embrace Christ is a miracle of God's electing grace, realized in history. Thus, there is no place for the ontological or epistemological cleavage that worries Barth, although his own reticence to eliminate any question of whether God's electing

---

57. Ibid., vol. 2, pt. 2, p. 135.

58. George Hunsinger, *How To Read Karl Barth: The Shape of His Theology* (New York: Oxford Univ. Press, 1993), 15–16.

59. Brunner, *Dogmatics I*, 1:347.

60. Barth, *Church Dogmatics*, vol. 2, pt. 2, p. 295, 417–18, 475–76.

61. Calvin, *Institutes* 3.23.2.

grace perfectly coincides with the outcome of salvation for everyone elected leaves a question mark over that question.

DISCUSSION QUESTIONS

1. If predestination is an expression of God's nature, can his decrees be considered truly free rather than necessary?
2. What is the difference between God's permission and his positive determination? Is this distinction warranted by Scripture?
3. What is the goal of our knowledge of predestination from Scripture?
4. What is the difference between supralapsarianism and infralapsarianism, and does it matter?
5. Describe and evaluate Barth's revised supralapsarianism.

Chapter Ten

CREATION: GOD'S TIME FOR US

The Hebrew verb (*bārā*, "create") used in Genesis 1:1 is a technical term that is reserved for God's act of creating, occurring nearly fifty times in the Old Testament—and always with God as the subject.[1] This fact already suggests that God's creative acts are qualitatively distinct from creaturely analogies. In Proverbs 8, God's wisdom is personified as that which Yahweh possessed "before the beginning of the earth" (v. 23) and that by which Yahweh created it. God speaks a cosmos into being, and with this statement the chasm separating the biblical understanding of creation from the cosmologies of the nations is measured. Yahweh is Lord of all. "O LORD, how manifold are your works! In wisdom have you made them all; the earth is full of your creatures" (Ps 104:24).

I. CREATION *EX NIHILO* — out of nothing IN BIBLICAL CONTEXT

The context of Genesis is God's assertion of his sovereignty as Israel's suzerain over and against the gods of the nations. Whereas the idols are many, each ruling over its circumscribed domain (the fertility god; the sun god; the storm god; gods of the sea, the air, mountains, and sky), the God of Abraham, Isaac, and Jacob created all that exists. Yahweh, Israel's Lord, is Lord of all.

Israel's faith and practice are exceedingly anomalous and cannot be explained as part of the natural evolution of ancient Mediterranean religions. Even the covenant

---

1. Karl-Heinz Bernhardt, "*bārā*," in *Theological Dictionary of the Old Testament* (ed. G. Johannes Botterweck and Helmer Ringgren; Grand Rapids: Eerdmans, 1975), 2:245–47; cf. Bre- vard S. Childs, *Biblical Theology of the Old and New Testaments* (Minneapolis: Fortress, 1993), 111; Robert Jenson, *Systematic Theology* (New York: Oxford Univ. Press, 1997), 2:5.

theology that organizes and informs every part of this faith and practice is taken from ancient Near Eastern politics rather than religion. For Israel's neighbors, the gods were *witnesses* of these international treaties, but only in Israel is God the nation's *suzerain* (great king). Furthermore, the Gentiles worshiped the rhythms of nature. Time was cyclical—closer to Plato's view of time as a "moving picture" of the eternal realm. However, Israel's God was always forcing his people to break out of this introspective cycle—out to the linear, public horizon of actual history. Hence, Israel's dominant festivals celebrate redemptive-historical events rather than the seasonal cycle of death and rebirth. The biblical creation narrative is just close enough to those of Israel's pagan neighbors (especially the Babylonian "Gilgamesh Epic") to fulfill the polemical function of mocking the idols, yet is radically different in content.

Gerhard von Rad concluded that, far from relying on the ancient Near Eastern mythologies, "Israel's worldview performed a major function in drawing a sharp line of division between God and the world, and by purging the material world of both elements of the divine and the demonic. There were no avenues of direct access to the mystery of the creator emanating from the world, certainly not by means of the image, but Yahweh was present in his living word in acts of history."[2]

According to Paul Tillich's own defense of the "overcoming estrangement" paradigm (see ch. 1), the creation narrative returns to the ahistorical origins of ancient mythology. "The doctrine of creation is not the story of an event which took place 'once upon a time,'" he says. "It is the basic description of the relation between God and the world," answering the question of human finitude.[3] By contrast, Louis Berkhof properly reminds us, "The doctrine of creation is not set forth in Scripture as a philosophical solution of the problem of the world, but in its ethical and religious significance."[4] The creation narrative in Genesis 1 and 2 is not intended as either a scientific description or as a myth conveying ostensibly higher and eternal principles. Rather, it announces God's historical act and claim upon all of reality. It is the preamble and historical prologue for the Law (Torah), with its stipulations and sanctions.

In the ancient myths of the origin of the world, the created world is generally depicted as a piece of reality that arose out of disaster, evil, and chaos, while the divine spark somehow remains, trapped in a material world from which it seeks to be emancipated.[5] In the Babylonian myth, Tiamat is the sea monster who represents

---

2. Gerhard von Rad, quoted in Childs, *Biblical Theology*, 386.

3. Paul Tillich, *Systematic Theology* (Chicago: Univ. of Chicago Press, 1973), 1:60.

4. Louis Berkhof, *Systematic Theology* (Grand Rapids: Eerdmans, 1996), 126.

5. Appealing to these myths, Friedrich Schelling relates that in the Egyptian creation myth, the old and cruel god of the harsh desert, Typhon, kills the younger god of fertility, Osiris, but Typhon's spouse (Isis) raises him from the dead. Similarly

in Vedic (Indian) mythology, the violent Brahma is replaced by Shiva the destroyer-god, yet both surrender to the truly spiritual god of light, Vishnu. A similar story of thesis-antithesis-higher synthesis is told in Greco-Roman mythology (Schelling, *Historical-Critical Instruction to the Philosophy of Mythology* [trans. Mason Richey and Markus Zisselsberger; Albany, N.Y.: SUNY Press, 2007]). The Romantics celebrated this ancient mythology of creation out of violent strife between antithetical powers.

chaos that must be overcome. In Genesis, the darkness and void are called *tᵉhôm* ("the deep"), but unlike its namesake Tiamat, it is not personal and is not a threat to be overcome. It is itself the unformed matter that God had already brought into existence from nothing, the created stuff out of which he fashions the world. "While Greek philosophy sought the explanation of the world in a dualism which involves the eternity of matter, or in a process of emanation, which makes the world the outward manifestation of God," notes Berkhof, "the Christian church from the very beginning taught the doctrine of creation *ex nihilo* and as a *free* act of God."[6]

Exodus 15 records the Song of the Sea, in which the subversive intent of Genesis 1 and 2 is even more evident. Far from the mythological chaos monster that threatens God's sovereignty, the sea in Exodus 15 is simply a natural body of water that God uses for delivering his people and judging Pharaoh and his hosts. God's *ex nihilo* creation is the antithesis of mythological thinking and the worldviews that such thinking generates. Robert Jenson argues, appealing to Basil,

> Genesis' story is not a myth, for it does not in fact tell us anything about what things were like when there were not things. Its "*tohu webohu*" ["without form and void" in Ge 1:2] is not an antecedent nothingness-actuality like the Great Slime dismembered by Babylonian Marduk, nor yet an eternal egg or womb or pure potentiality of primal matter. The fathers [he quotes Basil here] were clear about this: "The heretics say, 'But there was also the darkness...over the deep.' Again new occasions for myth...! 'The deep' is not a fullness of antithetical powers, as some fantasize, nor is the darkness an original and evil force arrayed against the good." Genesis' reference to emptiness and formlessness, and the darkness and "waters" of chaos, is not to a presupposition of creation but to the inconceivable beginning of creation, made inconceivable by the absence of presuppositions. Augustine reads Genesis precisely: "You have made all times; and before all times only you are, nor does time antecede itself."[7]

In the two accounts in Genesis, it is clear that creation comes into being as a history; or, to put it differently, creation and history come into existence together through God's *ex nihilo* speech. The world is not a given, but a gift, and it is there as the theater for the covenantal drama: "He formed it to be inhabited" (Isa 45:18).

Claus Westermann observes that the creation account in Genesis 1 is distinguished from all other creation stories of the ancient Near East by its persistent claim that "there can be only one creator and that all else that is or can be, can never be anything but a creature."[8] God's independent and eternal being is contrasted with the dependent and spatio-temporal becoming of creation: "Before the mountains were brought forth, or ever you had formed the earth and the world,

---

6. Ibid.

7. Jenson, *Systematic Theology*, 2:11.

8. Claus Westermann, *Genesis 1–11: A Commentary* (trans. J. J. Scullion; Minneapolis: Augsburg, 1984), 127.

from everlasting to everlasting you are God" (Ps 90:2). Even "the heavens are the work of your hands" (Ps 102:25). "By faith we understand that the universe was created by the word of God, so that what is seen was not made out of things that are visible" (Heb 11:3). It is this powerful word that is spoken by God into what does not exist in the opening chapter of Genesis, and it is this pattern of *ex nihilo* creation that serves as a constant parallel for the "new creation" language that follows in redemptive history.

As I mentioned in chapter 1, monism (the belief that all of reality is one) is always grounded in a deeper and antithetical dualism. In the dominant Western "demythologization" of the pagan cosmologies, namely Platonism and Neoplatonism, the world is an emanation of divinity—and therefore exists eternally and necessarily. In the biblical worldview, the affirmation of God's absolute independence and therefore the world's existence as a contingent creation freely willed by God also gives to the world its own space, so to speak. Neither divine nor demonic, it is—to borrow Calvin's expression—"the theater of God's glory."[9] It is to be neither worshiped nor abused.

Panentheists, such as Sallie McFague, criticize this biblical doctrine of creation for generating a dualistic outlook. Only if the world is in some sense divine can its exploitation at human hands be overcome. However, this criticism is ironic, since her own view of the world as God's body itself presupposes a Cartesian mind-body dualism (God as the soul, the world as his body).[10] This analogy only highlights the fact that panentheism not only rejects the transcendence, independence, freedom, and sovereignty of God; it does not really acknowledge the world as a theater of creaturely interaction, with creatures given their own "space," as it were. As God's creation, on the other hand, the world has its own peculiar majesty. An absolute distinction between God and creation that is nevertheless positive rather than negative—with a covenantal bond establishing God's lordship over all of created reality (including human beings, who must give account for their stewardship)—affirms the unity of creation as *nature* in its spiritual as well as its material aspects. It is the Creator-creature distinction that overcomes all dualisms and monisms.

Creation does not take place within God's being, as neo-Hegelian theologies assume. Yet it also does not generate itself. Nor is the world a self-sustaining mechanism in the way that deism supposed. It is not only brought into being but sustained in being and becoming and finally brought to its consummated goal by the Father, in the Son, through the Spirit. Creation is rightly described by Christians as one

9. Calvin, *Institutes*, 1.5.8; 1.6.2; 1.14.20; 2.6.1.
10. Sallie McFague, *Models of God* (Minneapolis: Augsburg,

1989), and *The Body of God: An Ecological Theology* (Minneapolis: Augsburg, 1993).

of God's external works (*opera ad extra*) — that is, one of the contingent and freely chosen relations to that which is not God — rather than being one of his internal works (*opera ad intra*), that is, necessary intratrinitarian relations and attributes. "Our material therefore imposes on us a clear choice between a biblical and a Hellenic ontology," writes Colin Gunton. "Either the world creates itself, or it is the product of a personal creator."[11]

The necessary implication of this view is that <u>God created the world for his own glory and not out of any need for self-fulfillment, self-completion, or company</u> (contrary to the opinion of Meister Eckhart and even some of the tendencies in Arminian accounts but especially in Moltmann and process theologies). Appealing to Jonathan Edwards, Jenson rightly insists that we cannot substitute God's love for his glory as the motive and final end of creation. It is a "disastrous" move and "is doubtless one cause of late modernity's degradation of deity into a servant of our self-help."[12]

In sharp contrast, the biblical doctrine of *ex nihilo* ("from nothing") creation maintains that God created finite, temporal, and material-spiritual creatures and pronounced this intrinsic difference "good." Human beings — in the totality of their existence as spiritual and physical — belong in this world of time and space. There is no place for the idea of a divine soul longing to transcend its creaturely finitude in order to return to a primordial condition of eternal preexistence in the unity of being. Neither divine nor demonic, nature was created good but different from God. This doctrine of *ex nihilo* creation is the correlate to the rival paradigm of "meeting a stranger."

II. THE TRINITY AND CREATION

The Greek version of pagan cosmology continued to cast its spell over some early Christian theologians. This is particularly true of the catechetical school in Alexandria led by Origen. Like the Jewish philosopher Philo of Alexandria a century before him, Origen tried to accommodate the Bible to Platonism. Origen held that creation is eternal, in part because of his assumption that if God *became* a creator, he could not be immutable (unchanging).[13] His cosmology was therefore far from historical and linear; it was cyclical, with each soul being reincarnated until all spirits (including Satan and his angelic coconspirators) become purged of their attachment to matter through moral and spiritual education. Furthermore, although Origen's view of the world as eternal comports better with modern science before Einstein,

---

11. Colin Gunton, *The Triune Creator* (Grand Rapids: Eerdmans, 1998), 38.

12. Jenson, *Systematic Theology*, 2:18.

13. Origen was also convinced of this position because of his Platonic assumption that spiritual creatures (namely, angels and souls) were eternal.

the current of scientific consensus has been rushing in the reverse direction over the last half century, emphasizing a temporal beginning as well as evident signs of contingency.

We saw in chapter 1 that the biblical worldview contrasts sharply with the monisms and dualisms of pagan ontologies. The biblical doctrine of creation is at the heart of this contrast. First, since the Creator is personal and is as truly three (in persons) as he is one (in essence), there is no ground for a primordial dualism between the one and many. Second, the biblical doctrine of creation distinguishes reality into creator and creation rather than spirit and matter. Angels and human souls are not eternal; they are as truly a part of God's creation as elephants and human bodies. Therefore, the material creation cannot be conceived in terms of a falling away from divine "being" into corrupt "becoming." In their spiritual as well as their physical aspects, human beings have no history prior to the world's creation. It is this original condition that God pronounced "good." Third, this goodness of original difference is further underscored by the plurality within creation itself, not only in the diversity of living and inanimate nature generally but even in the difference within humanity as male and female.

All of these points underscore the fact that creation is the result of a free decision and activity of intratrinitarian love, the product of an extravagant exchange of gift giving between the Father, the Son, and the Spirit rather than of some event of primordial violence that would cause a tear within the fabric of nature itself.

"In the beginning, God created the heavens and the earth." So, significantly, the Bible begins. After all, it is at this place where God's triune life reaches out ecstatically in openness to that which is other than God. As God's intratrinitarian communion has been dynamic, ecstatic and relational, his creation of the world is just as personal. "The universe," as E. J. Carnell put it, "is ordered by personal interest, not logic."[14] The Logos by whom the worlds were made is not a silent principle or semidivine demiurge, but the second person, who is begotten eternally by the Father in the Spirit. The Spirit (*rûaḥ*) of God who hovered over the watery depths to create dry land for the creature whom he, with the Father, and the Son, would animate as "a living soul" (*nepeš*) is none other than the Holy Spirit who regenerates those who are "dead in the trespasses and sins" (Eph 2:1). "If this phrase ["Spirit of God"] were to be translated 'wind from God,' as some modern versions do," Jenson observes, "again the narrative would be mythic," but such a translation just indicates the translators' prejudice. There is no reason to believe that by *rûaḥ ʾelōhîm* the Spirit of God was not intended.[15]

---

14. E. J. Carnell, *Christian Commitment: An Apologetic* (New York: Macmillan, 1957), 247.

15. Jenson, *Systematic Theology*, 2:11–12.

It is therefore not surprising that Christian theology should begin its discussion of creation, as Berkhof suggests, as "an act of the triune God." "Though the Father is in the foreground in the work of creation (1Co 8:6), it is also clearly recognized as a work of the Son and of the Holy Spirit. The Son's participation in it is indicated in John 1:3; 1 Corinthians 8:6; Colossians 1:15–17, and the activity of the Spirit in it finds expression in Genesis 1:2; Job 26:13; 33:4; Psalm 104:30; Isaiah 40:12, 13."[16] Berkhof adds,

> The second and third persons are not dependent powers or mere intermediaries, but independent authors together with the Father. The work was not divided among the three persons, but the whole work, though from different aspects, is ascribed to each one of the persons. All things are at once *out of* the Father, *through* the Son, and *in* the Holy Spirit. In general it may be said that *being* is out of the Father, *thought* or the *idea* out of the Son, and *life* out of the Holy Spirit. Since the Father takes the initiative in the world of creation, it is often ascribed to him economically.[17]

The importance of the doctrine of the Trinity for this topic is essential, as Berkhof observes when he refers at this point to the first article of the Apostles' Creed: "I believe in God the Father, Almighty, Maker of heaven and earth." "It ascribes to the Father, that is, to the first person in the Trinity, the origination of all things. This is in harmony with the representation of the New Testament that all things are of the Father, through the Son, and in the Holy Spirit."[18]

Colin Gunton has brought to our attention the intimate connection between the Trinity and creation with profound insight.[19] The distinction between the immanent Trinity (the hidden intratrinitarian communion) and economic Trinity (the revealed activity of the Godhead in creation and redemption) remains vital for recognizing that creation is contingent rather than necessary, yet that the divine persons are freely involved in worldly action.[20] Thus, God is free to create a world

---

16. Berkhof, *Systematic Theology*, 129.

17. Ibid.

18. Ibid., 128.

19. Colin Gunton, *The Promise of Trinitarian Theology* (Edinburgh: T&T Clark, 1997), 137–57, 178–92. Gunton points out that both Plato and Kant have a world and timeless ideas, but Kant's is "an inversion of Plato's. The concepts are, indeed, both timeless and, in a sense, objective. But their locus is not reality, 'out there,' so much as the structures of human rationality. The human mind replaces exterior eternity as the location of the concepts by means of which reality is understood. Both proposals ... are idealist, and, indeed, systems of transcendental idealism" (137). They are just different in where they locate the transcendence—one objective, the other subjective (137). Gunton argues for a "trinitarian theology of creation" (141–43). Following Irenaeus, he means by this that because the Father created the world through the Son, "it is real and

good," which the Incarnation reaffirms in its connection of creation and redemption, and the eschatological Spirit guarantees its future consummation (142). God's creation of the world is wholly voluntary. "He does not need to create, because he is already a *taxis*, order, of loving relations" (142). To enter into relationship freely in no way implies some necessity on God's part.

20. Ibid., 142. The Trinitarian approach underscores, in fact, that God is deeply involved in the world. It is in fact "based on the belief that God the Father is related to the world through the creating and redeeming action of Son and Spirit who are, in Irenaeus's expression, his two hands" (142). But in this scheme, God remains God and the world remains world (immanent Trinity), and yet God is involved (economic Trinity) (143–44). Further, in opposition to static conceptions of God, dynamic relation is not merely an external work of God, but an internal aspect of God's very being as triune (145).

that is free to be itself. Contrary to Moltmann's insistence, <u>God would be loving and free even if he had never created the world</u>.[21] And this divine creative action is not static, but dynamic, perichoretic *taxis*—a constant movement of the divine persons from, in, and through each other, not only in the intratrinitarian life but outward in their operations.[22]

In this trinitarian economy, God is simultaneously transcendent and immanent, utterly distinct from creation yet actively involved in every aspect of its existence and preservation. Gunton elaborates: "[God] is clearly 'without' in the sense of being other, transcendent. He is creator and not creation, but he is also, in realization rather than denial of that transcendence, one who in Christ becomes part of that creation, freely involved within its structures, in order that he may, in obedience to God the Father and through the power of his Spirit, redirect the creation to its eschatological destiny."[23] Accordingly, the sharp distinction between God and creation never devolves into an antithesis. The one and the many, unity and difference, God's transcendence and immanence, divinity and humanity are never antitheses to be reconciled or synthesized. All things are from God, through God, and to God not because the Creator is an Unmoved Mover but because he is the Father, the Son, and the Holy Spirit.

III. CREATIVE COMMUNICATION

It is significant that the biblical doctrine represents God's living speech as the means by which the Trinity creates the world. How unlike the analogies of physical force applied to a particular object, a clever watchmaker, or a world that causes itself, is the analogy of the Father speaking in the Son and bringing the effect of that speech to fruition through the agency of the Spirit. As a result of this Trinitarian speech act, the creation itself answers back in its own voice of praise:

> The heavens are telling the glory of God;
>   and the firmament proclaims his handiwork.
> Day to day pours forth speech,
>   and night to night declares knowledge.
> There is no speech, nor are there words;
>   their voice is not heard;
> yet their voice goes out through all the earth,
>   and their words to the end of the world. (Ps 19:1–4 NRSV)

The psalmist moves easily back and forth between the testimony of nature and that of God's historical revelation (vv. 7–14).

---

21. Ibid., 143.
22. Ibid., 145.

23. Gunton, *Triune Creator*, 24.

In this way, we can see that "covenant" is not added to the relationship between God and creation, but is intrinsic to that relationship. The creation of Israel, like the creation of the world itself, is the result of divine speech, evoking a human response. Walter Brueggemann observes, "As Israel believes that its own life is covenantally ordered, so Israel believes that creation is covenantally ordered; that is, formed by continuing interactions of gift and gratitude, of governance and obedience."[24] This expresses the "relentless ethical dimension."[25] "By the word of the LORD the heavens were made, and all their host by the breath of his mouth.... For he spoke, and it came to be; he commanded, and it stood firm" (Ps 33:6, 9, NRSV). The testimony to Yahweh's creation of Israel is expressed in analogous language.[26]

The same Lord who "sent out his word and healed [the Israelites], and delivered them from their destruction" (Ps 107:20), is the one who sent out his Word to create the world and everything in it. Israel's redeemer is the world's creator. The "living and active" Word that brings salvation (Heb 4:12) is the same Word spoken in the beginning. In Christ the whole creation was created and holds together (Jn 1:1–3; cf. Col 1:15–17), and in him a new creation comes into being out of nothing but sin and death (Jn 1:9–14; cf. Col 1:18–20). It is significant that in these references from John's gospel and Colossians both points are made in the same breath. Yahweh is the Alpha and Omega not as a solitary actor but as the Father, the Son, and the Spirit.

The Father who eternally speaks forth his hypostatic Word in the Spirit also spoke the world into existence through the Son and the Spirit. Nevertheless, the two acts of speaking are qualitatively distinct. The word that God speaks in bringing forth creation is an act of his *energies*, while the hypostatic Word is God in his *essence*. God is free to speak or not to speak his words of creation, redemption, and consummation, but the Son is the eternally begotten and eternally necessary Word of the Father. There was no time when the Son was not, but with regard to creation it is different: "For he spoke, and it came to be; he commanded, and it stood firm" (Ps 33:9 NRSV). And the Father sustains creation in his energetic speech by that same Word and Spirit: "The mighty one, God the LORD, speaks and summons the earth from the rising of the sun to its setting" (Ps 50:1).

Notice the covenantal language for these communicative actions: *commanded* and *summons*. Creation is in its very existence and from the very beginning covenantally ordered. Thus, as Brueggemann observes, "Creation has within it the sovereign seriousness of God, who will not tolerate the violation of the terms of creation, which are terms of gift, dependence, and extravagance. For those who

---

24. Walter Brueggemann, *Theology of the Old Testament: Testimony, Dispute, Advocacy* (Minneapolis: Fortress, 1997), 158–59.

25. Ibid., 158.
26. Ibid., 154.

refuse the doxology-evoking sovereignty of Yahweh, creation ends on an ominous warning."[27] It is to this covenant that the natural world gives its testimony (as in Ps 19), and Yahweh even calls on the natural world to testify both for (Ge 15:5 – 6; 8:22; 9:8 – 17; Mt 2:10) and against (Mt 24:28; 27:45; Ac 2:20) his covenant people in history. God's rule in nature and in history, in creation and redemption, is jointly celebrated repeatedly in the Psalter.

"The effect of this understanding of creation was to desacralize the world," notes Brevard Childs, "by removing all demonic and mythical powers from it and by subordinating them to the sole power of the one creator. Similarly in the New Testament Jesus exercised supreme power over the spiritual powers, and in his conquering of the demons demonstrated his control as creator."[28]

Robert Jenson puts his finger on a crucial problem wherever God's mediation of creation through the Logos has been construed in Platonist terms: "Theology ... has often failed to understand the Logos as God's utterance and has substituted the notion that he is God's concept. The Logos is said to proceed from the Father as the Father's act of knowing himself; creation through the Logos is then interpreted as an immanent act of the Father's will, to actualize ideas that belong to what he knows in knowing the Son."[29]

Even in Christian Platonism it becomes all too easy to treat creation as the product of divine ideas rather than of the Father's Word. But this easily supplants Christ: "not the person Christ has the function but Plato's Ideas, relocated in a 'mind of God' that only after the fact is identified with Christ." Jenson adds:

> Of classic theologians, it is perhaps Martin Luther who most straightforwardly corrected the usual interpretation. Commenting on Genesis, he reports the ordinary exegesis and rejects it as at odds with its text. Then he proceeds: "Moses uses the term *amar*, which simply denotes the spoken word.... By a mere word that he speaks, God makes heaven and earth from nothing."[30]

Although creation is an act of God's intellect and will, it "is not enclosed within the subject but takes place as communication" — a command. "Already the Word that is a triune person is God's Utterance in his triune life.... Now we must further insist: therefore the Word by which God creates is not silent within him but is his *address*.... Thus his creating of the world is agency of the same sort as the *torah* by which he creates Israel."[31]

The essence of being creatures in the biblical sense is not simply to contemplate eternal truths, but to be "worded" by God. Creation exists because God has spoken

---

27. Ibid., 156.
28. Childs, *Biblical Theology*, 399.
29. Jenson, *Systematic Theology*, 2:6.

30. Ibid., 2:7.
31. Ibid., 2:7 – 8.

it into existence, sustains it in this existence by his Word (both hypostatic and energetic), and thereby creates a society of speakers as an analogy of the Trinity. Not even God is a self-enclosed individual (like Descartes' *res cogitans* ["a thing that thinks"]; see ch. 1, "The Sovereign Self," pp. 57–59), and human existence is similarly defined by covenantal love and fellowship.

In contrast with pagan cosmologies, the light and darkness in creation are not supernatural forces, but natural effects of God's word, ruled by the sun by day and the moon and stars by night.[32] The word comes before the light.

The second-century church father Irenaeus was the first to challenge gnostic dualism directly and, as a result, to subordinate the metaphor of light to the divine word.[33] The biblical world is filled with living voices, while the Greek world is filled with silent visions in the mind.

God speaks the world into existence, and the world answers back in a symphony of praise, each species chirping, barking, bellowing, or otherwise communicating its delight and dependence on God and each other. Yet it is human beings who are created as communicative partners in covenant. Sight places us in front of things, while sound places us in the middle of things.[34] The world (creation) is therefore not an object to which the human individual (as "a thing that thinks") relates as a sovereign subject, but is the environment to which human beings themselves belong in their spiritual as well as material existence.

The original creation is therefore the correlate for the new-creation imagery of the prophets and apostles. Hans Blumenberg refers to Luther's emphasis in this regard. We were created by a command, not by a thought, and what makes us aware of our responsibility in the world is God's law, not an image or inner light.[35] Oswald Bayer explains concerning Luther's view, "The new creation is a conversion to the world, as a conversion to the Creator, hearing God's voice speaking to us and addressing us through his creatures. Augustine was wrong to say that his voice draws us away from God's creatures into the inner self and then to transcendence."[36] In fact, hearing calls us out of our subjectivity and renders us extrinsic, extroverted, and social creatures. This is as true in the original creation as in the new.

---

32. Hans Blumenberg, "Light as a Metaphor for Truth," in *Modernity and the Hegemony of Vision* (ed. David Michael Levin; Berkeley: Univ. of California Press, 1993), 40–41.

33. Paul Ricoeur, *History and Truth* (trans. Charles A. Kelbley; Evanston, Ill.: Northwestern Univ. Press, 1965), 111: "Let us think about the scope of the revolution in the history of thought that this text [Irenaeus's *Against Heresies*] represents in relation to that Neoplatonism in which reality is a progressive withdrawal, an ineluctable beclouding that increases as we descend from the One, which is formless, to the Mind, which is bodiless, to the World Soul, and to souls which are plunged into matter, which itself is absolute darkness." Ricoeur asks, "Are we sensitive to the distance between this text" and Neoplatonic speculations?

34. Walter Ong, SJ, *The Presence of the Word* (Minneapolis: Univ. of Minnesota Press, 1981), 10, 33–42.

35. Blumenberg, "Light as a Metaphor for Truth," 48.

36. Oswald Bayer, *Living by Faith: Justification and Sanctification* (trans. G. W. Bromiley; Grand Rapids: Eerdmans, 2003), 28.

IV. The Integrity of Creation

Worldviews that conceive nature and history as arising out of primeval violence locate the tragedy of ongoing strife in ontological necessity; it is just the way things are. Nature itself is at war with itself, and history is a conflict in which the fittest survive. As Colin Gunton observes, this pagan cosmology is as evident in modern as in primitive versions:

> The biblical view that the creation has its origins in the covenant love of God is thus a way of understanding the world different in principle from both the myths of the ancient world and much of the Greek philosophy that has its roots in them. Consequently ... it generates a different ethic: a different way of inhabiting the world and treating its inhabitants. The continuing importance of this contrast of worldviews is to be found in the fact that the view of creation as deified conflict is perpetually renewed in human culture, most recently perhaps in Hegel and Marx, as well as in many of their disciples.[37]

Key to the *ex nihilo* doctrine of creation is the conviction that creation has its own space — not that it is independent of God, but that it is different from God. Human beings have their own way of reasoning, experiencing, willing, and acting that is analogical of but not identical with God's. This difference is good; it is when human beings perversely imagine that they can reason, experience, will, and act as gods themselves that they reflect their fall from an original integrity.

Throughout church history, many theologians have affirmed creation *ex nihilo*, on the basis of Scripture, while still presupposing a basically Platonic or Neoplatonic ontology. For example, the influential fifth-century writer Pseudo-Dionysius taught not only that "the supra-essential being of God" is "the underpinning of goodness," but that "by *merely being there* it is the cause of everything" (emphasis added).[38] As the sun necessarily produces its rays, the One necessarily emanates the world in its gradations from spiritual brightness to dark matter. Accordingly, God is understood more as "Cause" than as "Creator." However, this threatens the integrity of God's freedom and transcendence as well as creaturely freedom. Even the Christian Neoplatonism of Pseudo-Dionysius sees reality as "an everlasting circle."[39] However, biblical revelation generates a sense of linear history punctuated by signal events in history. This history and its revelation lead from *promise* to *fulfillment* rather than from *lower* stages of being to *higher*. Not surprisingly, although Pseudo-Dionysius celebrates the Trinity in praise, when it comes to theorizing concerning the divine names, he concludes that the "most enduring of them all" is "Perfect" and "One."[40]

---

37. Gunton, *Triune Creator*, 26.
38. Pseudo-Dionysius, *The Divine Names*, in *Pseudo-Dionysius: The Complete Works* (trans. Colm Luibheid; Mahwah, N.J.: Paulist, 1987), 54.
39. Ibid., 84.
40. Ibid., 127.

Affirming the dependent yet real integrity of creation in all of its difference both from God and within itself, biblical faith does not evidence nostalgia for a lost home beyond creation or long for a "sacred cosmos" from which our soul has been estranged in temporal history and bodily transience. The world need not be *sacred* in order for it to be *good*. It need not be *ultimate* in order for it to be *real*. We do not need to be elevated beyond natural existence but to have our natural existence liberated from the powers of sin and death and brought into the everlasting consummation.

Roman Catholic theology translates the ancient philosophical dualism of matter and spirit into a dualism of nature and grace. Grace is always necessary to elevate nature beyond itself, toward the supernatural. The lower and higher realms of Plato linger throughout the history of Christian theology. However, in Reformation theology, nature is not in trouble, so to speak, until the fall—a historical and willful decision of the covenant partner to transgress God's law. It is not nature and grace, but sin and grace, that define the problematic with which biblical theology is occupied. The context is a historical covenant, not a metaphysics of being and becoming. Not even the human intellect or soul is higher than the body. The dividing line is between the Creator and creation, not between spirit and matter or even "supernatural" and "natural." As we have seen, even heaven is part of God's creation. Neither divine nor demonic, all of creation is good in its intrinsic worldliness. "Creation gives the world a distinct, yet always dependent existence," notes Berkhof.[41] Because we are God's *creatures*, we are not autonomous; our being and becoming are always dependent on God's Word and Spirit. Yet it is precisely in the recognition that we are *God's* creatures that this dependence becomes the source of all true creaturely freedom.

The integrity of creation as natural is also affirmed by the recognition that it was conceived and formed in love, but not grace. Grace presupposes fault. It is true, of course, that God's creation of the world and us in it is in no way conditioned by us, but that does not make it *gracious*. Barth properly notes that grace presupposes sin.[42] However, collapsing the historical fall of humanity into God's eternal decree to permit it, Barth insists that the only relation that God has ever had to humanity is that of *grace* toward *sinners*. "Where grace is manifest and effectual, it is *always a question of the misery of man*" (emphasis added).[43] Grace is "how God loves."[44] But this not only downgrades creation; logically, it makes God's grace necessary rather than free, since God's love is an essential attribute.

Grace is certainly how God loves *sinners*, but God's love for his unfallen world

---

41. Berkhof, *Systematic Theology*, 134.
42. Karl Barth, as cited in Berkhof, *Systematic Theology*, 355.

43. Ibid., 371.
44. Ibid., 357.

was a matter of condescension, goodness, kindness, and wisdom. Furthermore, as the glorious work of God's hands, the world was (and is) in its intrinsic character lovable. Theology needs desperately to recover a sense of God's kindness and generosity that belong properly to the order of *creation* even prior to and distinct from the specific sort of kindness and of generosity that are shown to *sinners*. In spite of Barth's salutary critique of dualism, his view also calls into question the integrity of creation. In both views, there is no moment when creation truly existed in a state of integrity, dependent on God's goodness and care but without any need for redeeming or elevating grace. If grace represents the higher sphere above nature in Roman Catholic theology, for Barth nature is assimilated to grace. In Reformation theology, however, nature has its own essential integrity before the introduction of sin and grace.

V. BEYOND GOD OF THE GAPS: GENESIS AND SCIENTIFIC APOLOGETICS

The remonstrance of Yahweh over against the idols of the nations forms the bookends of the Old Testament. Beginning with Genesis 1–2 (lordship in creation) and Exodus (lordship in deliverance), it continues in the historical books with the intrigue surrounding the contest between Yahweh and the idols that is even waged in the typological Promised Land. David's royal heirs often fight on the wrong side, and idolatry is the chief charge in the case of Yahweh versus Israel in the Prophets. Just as the figure of Jesus loses all significance apart from this story, these narratives themselves find their ultimate unity and significance in Jesus Christ.

Not Adam, Moses, Joshua, or David, but the one whom they so imperfectly foreshadowed drove the serpent from God's holy garden, crushing his head and removing the curse. "Jesus Christ is Lord," conqueror of the gods that are no gods, deliverer from bondage to fear and superstition, and redeemer from God's just judgment. As he led his people through the "darkness and void" of the flood and then through the Red Sea in the exodus, this same Word separates the waters of judgment by baptizing us into himself (Ro 6:1–14; 1Co 10:1–22; 1Pe 3:18–22).

The opening chapters of Genesis, therefore, are not intended as an independent account of origins but as the preamble and historical prologue to the treaty between Yahweh and his covenant people. The appropriate response is doxology:

> Know that the LORD, he is God!
> > It is he who made us, and we are his;
> > we are his people, and the sheep of his pasture.
> Enter his gates with thanksgiving,
> > and his courts with praise! (Ps 100:3–4)

We misunderstand the covenantal context and intent of Genesis if we come to it with questions that it does not address, forcing it to pronounce on matters beyond its scope.

A. THE "GOD OF THE GAPS" APOLOGETIC

Many modern Christians have assumed what has been called the "God of the gaps" apologetic. Typically, science will unravel a natural mystery up to a point and then, running out of data, acknowledge gaps in knowledge. This is where God comes in, according to this apologetic strategy. (Another term for this is *deus ex machina* ["god from the machine"], taken from the dramatic device of literally wheeling or dropping in a god onto the stage in ancient Greek tragedy. Whenever the plot seemed insoluble, the gods would appear out of nowhere to bring easy resolution.) Of course, the problem arises when scientists make further discoveries that close those gaps. Over time, God gets squeezed out of the equation. Already in the late eighteenth century, answering Napoleon's question as to why his work did not include any references to God, the French scientist Pierre-Simon Laplace is said to have answered, "I have no need of that hypothesis" (*Je n'avais pas besoin de cette hypothèse-là*).

The "God of the gaps" apologetic is not simply a weak strategy; it is based on a theological misunderstanding, assuming that God's agency and creaturely agency occupy the same register. Accordingly, to the extent that a certain state of affairs can be attributed to natural (human or nonhuman) causes, God is not involved. Again we meet the troubling univocity of being, which fails to recognize the Creator-creature distinction and the analogical character of creation in its relationship to God.

Although God is always and everywhere at work in creation, he is not one agent among others vying for freedom, power, and control in the same ontological space. Rather, God is mysteriously above, behind, and within the creation and the ordinary relations of cause and effect with which he has endowed it. God is *more* involved in the world—yet less direct, immediate, and therefore evident in his agency—than the "God of the gaps" apologists imagine. When the Word became incarnate, his neighbors—even his own brothers—did not recognize his divinity. Although the Spirit is at work in every atom, his agency even in raising those who are spiritually dead to eternal life remains largely hidden (Jn 3:8; 1Co 2:14).

Science is competent only to study natural causes and effects. Although these effects testify to God's power and wisdom in creation, God's agency itself lies hidden behind the secondary means he employed. Nor can theology discern God's hand in history apart from special revelation. Even in the case of miracles, we can recognize God's extraordinary operations only by their effects; we cannot see God's hidden power. By definition, miracles are anomalies—extraordinary acts—and science investigates ordinary (natural) causes and effects that can be subjected to repeatable tests. Yet the *hiddenness* of God's ordinary agency is no indication of God's *absence*. Scripture reveals God's agency at the points where God considers it relevant to the unfolding plot of creation, redemption, and consummation.

In Calvin's memorable caution, "it must be remembered that Moses does not speak with philosophical acuteness on occult mysteries, but relates those things which are everywhere observed, even by the uncultivated, and which are in common use."[45] Moses was not writing lectures on astronomy.[46] God accommodated his revelation to the conditions and capacities of common people.[47] Accommodation does not entail error but cautions us against treating "discourse adapted to common usage" as if it were intended as a discourse on science.[48] While science and theology often illuminate each other and God is ultimately the source of all truth, their object, sources, methods, and criteria are different. Harvard astrophysicist Owen Gingerich reminds us that Scripture "portrays an orderly, dependable universe. 'The Lord God laid the foundation of the earth that it not be moved forever,' declares Psalm 104. Kepler pointed out in the early seventeenth century that this is not scriptural authority for an immobile Earth in a geocentric cosmology, but rather praise for the stability that makes life possible, 'the fact that after so many ages the Earth has not sunk, cracked, or decayed, even though no one has discovered on what foundation it stands.'"[49] "Philosophical problems aside," adds Gingerich, "the Bible is thoroughly historical in its outlook, a chronicle of particular events of a people who covenanted with God. The scientific picture was not in the first place historical."[50] In fact, Holmes Rolston III argues, "Science does not handle historical explanations very competently, especially where there are emergent novelties; science

---

45. John Calvin, *Commentary on the Book of Genesis* (trans. John King; Grand Rapids: Baker, repr. 1996), 1:84.

46. Ibid. Calvin adds: "By this method (as I have before observed) the dishonesty of those men is sufficiently rebuked who censure Moses for not speaking with greater exactness" (85). Of course, Saturn is a greater light than the moon—but not for us, because of its great distance. "Moses wrote in a popular style things which, without instruction, all ordinary persons endued with common sense are able to understand; but astronomers investigate with great labour whatever the sagacity of the human mind can comprehend. Nevertheless, this study is not to be reprobated, nor this science to be condemned, because some frantic persons are wont boldly to reject whatever is unknown to them. For astronomy is not only pleasant, but also very useful to be known; it cannot be denied that this art unfolds the admirable wisdom of God" (86). "Had he spoken of things generally unknown, the uneducated might have pleaded excuse that such subjects were beyond their capacity" (87).

47. Calvin, *Institutes* 1.14.3. The original Latin reads, "Moses vulgi ruditati se accommodans, non alia Dei opera commemorate in historia creationis, nisi quae oculis nostris occurrunt."

48. Ibid. See also John Calvin, *Commentary on the First Book of Moses, Called Genesis* (trans. J. King; Grand Rapids: Baker, 1984), 87, 256–57. The Reformation played an important role in the rise of modern science, on various counts, but not the least because of its interest in the natural world as the theater of God's creative glory through secondary agency. Thus, science was given its own proper space for investigating matters not clearly addressed in Scripture. In fact, Britain's Royal Society was founded by Puritans. See Amos Funkenstein, *Theology and the Scientific Imagination* (Princeton, N.J.: Princeton Univ. Press, 1986); Keith Thomas, *Religion and the Decline of Magic* (New York: Charles Scribner's Sons, 1971); Peter Harrison, *The Bible, Protestantism, and the Rise of Natural Science* (Cambridge: Cambridge Univ. Press, 1998).

49. Owen Gingerich, "The Universe as Theater for God's Action," *ThTo* 55, no. 3 (1998): 305.

50. Ibid., 307, 309.

prefers law-like explanations. One predicts, and the prediction comes true. If such precision is impossible, science prefers statistical predictions, probabilities."[51]

The natural sciences have their own object, sources, methods, and criteria of investigation. These sciences excel in weighing, measuring, observing, and predicting, but they exceed the bounds of their competence when they reduce all phenomena to natural causes. Similarly, identifying every scientific mystery with a divine explanation—where Scripture does not provide clear evidence—transgresses the scope of religion and theology.

B. DESIGN AND CONTINGENCY

The differences between natural revelation and special revelation and between secondary cause and effect and divine agency do not leave us without any connection between theology and science, however. Colin Gunton judges that ancient Trinitarian thought shares important areas of overlap with recent science, particularly in the emphasis of the former on the concepts of freedom, relation, and energy.[52] The shift from views of God as a solitary monad to a genuinely Trinitarian emphasis on *perichōrēsis* parallels the shift in science from a static to a more dynamic paradigm. Significant overlap also occurs with respect to contingency: "The world does not *have* to be what or as it is."[53] This key underlying assumption of contemporary science is impossible to reconcile with pantheism or other views that make any part of creaturely reality in some sense necessary to God's being.

Nobel Prize–winning physicist Richard P. Feynman observed in the late 1980s that there are some things that cannot be understood by scientific methods that are nevertheless essential assumptions of those methods (especially observation). He writes, "Incidentally, the fact that there are rules at all to be checked is a kind of miracle; that it is possible to find a rule, like the inverse square law of gravitation, is some sort of miracle. It is not understood at all, but it leads to the possibility of prediction—that means it tells you what you would expect to happen in an experiment you have not yet done."[54] Feynman adds, "The rules that describe nature seem to be mathematical. This is not a result of the fact that observation is the judge, and it is not a characteristic necessity of science that it be mathematical. *It just turns out* that you can state mathematical laws, in physics at least, which work to make powerful predictions. Why nature is mathematical is, again, a mystery" (emphasis added).[55]

It is not a "God of the gaps" apologetic to suggest that God's creation of the world

---

51. Holmes Rolston III, "Evolutionary History and Divine Presence," *ThTo* 55, no. 3 (1998): 425.

52. Colin Gunton, "Relation and Relativity," in *Trinitarian Theology Today* (ed. Christoph Schwöbel; Edinburgh: T&T Clark, 1995), 103.

53. Ibid.

54. Richard P. Feynman, *The Meaning of It All: Thoughts of a Citizen-Scientist* (New York: Perseus, 1998), 23.

55. Ibid., 24.

with such intelligent design is the "mystery" to which Feynman refers, because, as Feynman himself notes, science *cannot* make its most necessary presuppositions focal objects of observation and experimentation. God is not a *gap-filler* but the *creator* of all reality and the revealer of all knowledge of that reality. Trinitarian theism claims that we have access to the source of this mathematical order in nature, while naturalism denies such access and, at least in the last century, denies that the world is anything more than the result of random accidents (time plus chance). This cannot help but generate a kind of schizophrenia in science—on the one hand, the world exhibits rule-governed and mathematical characteristics for which there can be no reasonable account; on the other hand, naturalistic presuppositions deny any basis for thinking that the world evidences the design that observation assumes and verifies. Trinitarian theism claims there is a very good reason for the rules and mathematical design of nature, while naturalism's confidence in reason is grounded in irrational and purposeless chance.

In theology and science, Arthur Peacocke observes, there has been a shift from seeing the world as a static mechanism strictly observing laws to a dynamic organism filled with anomalies, unpredictability, and change.[56] Science increasingly recognizes that the universe is "contingent but ordered," Gunton notes. "The world is such that inherent contingencies rule out the possibility of certain prediction. There is chaos but stability, that is to say, contingence but reliability."[57] These observations are confirmed by an emerging consensus across the sciences, as James Gleick expresses the paradox: "Chaos is ubiquitous; it is stable; it is structured."[58]

The older view in modernity, both in theology (deism) and science (Newtonian cosmology), is that individuals are already finished (they are already what they are) and then they enter into relations. But in both fields this is being (and must be) revised. There is a certain interdependence at work between not only personal beings but even between the smallest (microscopic) and largest (macroscopic) entities. Yet this mutual interdependence of created reality should not surprise those who affirm that the archetypal source of this reality is a Trinity engaged in perichoretic relations that turn outward in the external works in which these persons are mutually engaged.

I mentioned above that the idea that our cosmos came into being at a definite point in time—regarded as a vestige of biblical mythology by many liberal theologians—is now affirmed generally by the sciences. More so today than at any point since the Enlightenment, scientists have come to reject the idea of eternal matter infinitely extended "backward" and "forward." "Their repeated insistence

56. Arthur Peacocke, *Creation and the World of Science* (Oxford: Clarendon, 1979), 62.

57. Gunton, "Relation and Relativity," 150–51.

58. James Gleick, *Chaos: Making a New Science* (London: Sphere Books, 1987), 76.

is that science since Einstein has been forced to recognize what Einstein himself resisted, the inherent temporality of the cosmos."[59] Hubble's research in the early twentieth century, Heisenberg's uncertainty principle, and other discoveries have increasingly led science—for perhaps the first time in history—to the consensus that the observable cosmos had an origin at a certain point in time.[60] "Thus, our universe is vast," notes Gingerich, "but not really infinite; it is a universe with an age and a history, albeit an unimaginably long one."[61] Only by recognizing the world as a contingent, finite, and temporal reality rather than as a necessary, infinite, and eternal emanation of divinity can we account for the discoveries of contemporary science.

In addition to temporality, relationality is another place of growing overlap between Christian theology and the sciences. Deism is no longer a tenable alternative to pantheism/panentheism. The universe is not a machine, requiring a divine act in the beginning but running smoothly on its own ever since. Yet a bare theism is also inadequate for dealing with the obvious relationality in the universe. "We may understand the Holy Spirit as the divine energy releasing the energies of the world, enabling the world to realize its dynamic interrelatedness."[62] At the same time, in contrast to the immanent teleologies of Hegel, process thought, and kindred trends, this work of the Spirit in creation cannot be assimilated to the processes of nature or history themselves.

Furthermore, the Spirit's labors are always from the Father and in the Son, so the point at which Scripture especially reveals the Spirit's work is in the application of redemption in Jesus Christ. Sent by the Father and the Son to make all things new, the Spirit brings the perfecting powers of the consummation (the age to come) into this present age that is passing away. Only from God's revelation could we know that which could not be the case if the cosmos were left to itself, namely, that its future is not a mere continuation, surrendering gradually to entropy. There is always a power at work beyond nature that breaks into it, prying it open to a future that it cannot secure for itself.

We live in a world that could not create itself, cannot sustain itself, and surely cannot bring itself into God's everlasting rest. Precisely because the triune God neither is dependent on the world (contra panentheism) nor simply acts upon the world directly (contra deism and nontrinitarian theism) but acts within the world to bring about the effect of divine speech, nature and history can realize a destiny beyond the creation's own immanent possibilities yet without violence to its creaturely integrity.

59. Gunton, "Relation and Relativity," 152–53.

60. I am referring here to the expanding universe resulting from something like an original explosion. See Gingerich, "Uni-

verse as Theater for God's Action," 307.

61. Ibid.

62. Gunton, "Relation and Relativity," 153.

Science does not take into its account the complexities of evil and redemption or the promise of the consummation by direct divine intervention at the end of the age. Limited in its scope to the immanent possibilities of nature itself, it cannot reveal the Trinity or the Trinitarian purposes of creatures in history. Nevertheless, a robust Trinitarian doctrine of *ex nihilo* creation is more consistent than any of its rivals with the kind of cosmos that science recognizes today.

Many Christian philosophers, scientists, and theologians have offered impressive arguments for intelligent design in recent decades.[63] However, we should not react against the emphasis in contemporary science on contingency, flux, and apparent randomness by focusing exclusively on design and order. After all, it is not surprising that a well-designed watch keeps time without constant tinkering. However, if there is design and order even in a cosmos as pregnant with apparent randomness, chaos, change, and unpredictability as ours, then God's constant involvement is necessary in every moment. Atheistic materialism cannot account for the order, and deism cannot account for the radical contingency and apparent randomness of natural reality.

Matter is neither eternal and necessary nor self-consistent and entirely predictable. Gingerich cites the corroborating research from various fields. Fred Hoyle examined the evidence that the carbon necessary for life was (despite the effects of the Big Bang) present in exactly the right resonance level. "Had the resonance level in the carbon been four percent lower, there would be essentially no carbon. Had that level in the oxygen been only half a percent higher, virtually all of the carbon would have been converted to oxygen." In fact, Gingerich relates Hoyle's conclusion that the mathematical possibility of this convergence of factors requires "a superintellect" who guides the process.[64]

Employing Calvin's metaphor of creation as "the theater of God's glory," Gingerich writes, "From a theological perspective, the wonder was not God pushing the mighty 'On!' switch," which deism could affirm, "but the creative planning to make the ensuing universe work."[65] Scientist and theologian John Polkinghorne makes

63. Among the many works worth citing are the following: William A. Dembski and Jonathan Wells, *The Design of Life: Discovering Signs of Intelligence in Biological Systems* (Richardson, Tex.: Foundation for Thought and Ethics, 2008); Fazale Rana, *The Cell's Design: How Chemistry Reveals the Creator's Artistry* (Grand Rapids: Baker, 2008); Michael Behe, *The Edge of Evolution: The Search for the Limits of Darwinism* (New York: Free Press, 2008).

64. Gingerich, "Universe as Theater for God's Action," 310–11: "I am told that Fred Hoyle has said that nothing has shaken his atheism as much as this discovery. Here is what he wrote in the Cal Tech alumni magazine: … 'A commonsense interpretation of the facts suggests that a superintellect has mon-

keyed with physics, as well as with chemistry and biology, and that there are no blind forces worth speaking about in nature. The numbers one calculates from the facts seem to me so overwhelming as to put this conclusion almost beyond question.' … We cannot help but feel intuitively that the stage set has been especially designed in advance for the play that is to follow. While these features cannot prove the intentions of a purposeful Creator, they are certainly coherent with such a view of reality."

65. Ibid., 309. The "anthropic principle"—either "that *we are here because* the universe has been so designed" (soft version) or "*because we are here* the universe must be that way, as otherwise we wouldn't be here and that's that" (hard version) (309–10).

the same point.[66] Although science cannot prove the necessity, much less the actual existence, of the triune God, Trinitarian theology—with the Father constantly speaking in the Son and in the perfecting power of the Spirit—displays striking convergences with science at crucial points.

Theologians with scientific training (and scientists with theological or religious inclinations) have been engaging in a more fruitful dialogue in recent decades.[67] In fact, philosopher of science Ernan McMullin argues that a more traditional doctrine of God and the God-world relation, it turns out, offers the best paradigm for both theology and science, particularly in relation to time and teleology. He argues that the traditional (Augustinian/Boethian) interpretation of God's existence as transcending time (eternity) rather than the Aristotelian view that God merely endures throughout all times (sempiternity or everlastingness) is more consistent with the distinct character of time and finitude encountered by science. To the extent that the Creator and creation become confused, the integrity of both is threatened.[68]

Of course, the processes that conspire to bring about the kind of world that we know may "not *look* like the kind of process human designers would use to accomplish their ends." But if we were able to discern such a process, such action would be necessarily time bound. "If it's not time bound, it's not surprising that we don't read it off the surface of events."[69] Neither univocal nor equivocal construals of the God-world relation will do. Neither hypertranscendent deism nor hyperimmanent pantheism and panentheism can account for the data of Scripture or contemporary science on these points.

VI. "I AM THE ALPHA AND THE OMEGA": ORIGINAL, CONTINUAL, AND NEW CREATION

A further point of possible convergence between contemporary science and classic Christian theology may be found in the doctrine of *continual creation* (*creatio*

---

66. John Polkinghorne, "Natural Science, Temporality, and Divine Action," *ThTo* 55, no. 3 (1998): 329: "In the twentieth century, science has discovered that the universe itself has had a history—that the cosmos was very different in the past from how it is today and that it will be different again in the future; that space is relational and not absolute; that the passage of time and judgments of simultaneity are observer-dependent assessments. The Newtonian picture of the ceaseless rearrangements of the components of an essentially unchanging world, taking place within the fixed container of space and during the steady flow of an absolute time, is no longer on the scientific agenda. Yet absolutes remain, such as the speed of light acting as the limit on the rapidity of information transfer. In relativity theory (in the scientific sense), not all dissolves into a relativistic haze (in the popular sense)."

67. See, for instance, John Polkinghorne, *Quantum Physics and Theology: An Unexpected Kinship* (New Haven, Conn.: Yale Univ. Press, 2008); Robert John Russell, Nancey Murphy, and Arthur Peacocke, eds., *Chaos and Complexity: Scientific Perspectives on Divine Action* (South Bend, Ind.: Univ. of Notre Dame Press, 1996); Keith Ward, *Religion and Creation* (Oxford: Clarendon, 1996); W. H. Vanstone, *Love's Endeavour, Love's Expense* (London: Darton, Longman and Todd, 1977); John Polkinghorne and Michael Welker, *The End of the World and the Ends of God: Science and Theology on Eschatology* (Harrisburg, Pa.: Trinity, 2000). At the same time, many of these conversations reflect a panentheistic tendency.

68. Ernan McMullin, "Cosmic Purpose and the Contingency of Human Evolution," *ThTo* 55, no. 3 (1988): 409.

69. Ibid., 410–11.

continua). With historical precedent, Moltmann encourages us to distinguish three types of creation: original (*creatio originalis*), continual (*creatio continua*), and new (*creatio nova*).[70] Although the world came into existence at a certain point in the past, God is still involved in creating at the level of not only upholding but even altering creatures. Further, the Scriptures represent God's redeeming work as a new creation, with continuities and discontinuities in relation to the existing order.

These first two classic theological categories are receiving renewed attention in part because of their closer resonances with contemporary science—an absolute beginning and changes through time. The notion of continual creation teaches that although the world came into being at a certain time, it is also in the process of becoming, which again is nothing new to traditional (nondeistic) Christian teaching. Nature, no less than history, is dynamic. God is the ultimate author of both original and continual creation, but in different ways—in the first instance, by a fiat declaration (*ex nihilo* creation); in the latter, by the ordinary work of his providence in which natural secondary causes are at work. In that light, it may be better to speak of this ongoing work of God as providence rather than continual creation.

Reacting against naturalistic accounts, it is easy for us to embrace a hypersupernaturalism that attributes this continual creation or providence to immediate divine interventions. However, is this warranted by Scripture? Even in the Genesis account, we encounter two distinct types of divine declarations: the fiats of *ex nihilo* creation—"Let there be ..." (with the report, "And it was so")—and God's command to creation to put forth its own powers with which he has endowed it and within which the Spirit is operative: "Let the waters under the heavens be gathered together into one place, and let the dry land appear" (Ge 1:9); "Let the earth sprout vegetation, plants yielding seed..." (v. 11). In fact, it is reported, "The earth brought forth vegetation..." (v. 12). God adds, "Let the waters swarm with swarms of living creatures, and let birds fly above the earth across the expanse of the heavens" (v. 20), and "Let the earth bring forth living creatures according to their kinds ..." (v. 24). Furthermore, God commands the fish and fowl, as well as humans, "Be fruitful and multiply" (vv. 22, 28). We may put these two types of speech acts in the form of "Let there be ..." and "Let it become what I have 'worded' it to be." Anticipating my argument in part 5 (see ch. 17, "Regeneration as Effectual Calling," p. 572), I would add that this is the same pattern we find in the new creation, in justification and sanctification, respectively.

In panentheistic theologies, where the world is conceived as God's body, or in hypersupernatural creationism, where every divine act in creation must be

---

70. Jürgen Moltmann, *God in Creation* (London: SCM, 1985), 192–93. Distinct from God's original fiat act of *ex nihilo* creation (*creatio originalis*), continual creation (*creatio continua*) refers to God's act not only of preserving and sustaining the works of his hands but of continually bringing about their growth, diversity, and flourishing.

immediate and direct, creation loses the kind of distinct agency that the second type of speech acts ("Let the earth bring forth …") suggests. It is especially in the "becoming" of continual creation that the Spirit's work within the world, bringing about the effect of God's powerful Word, is most evident. Far richer than the deistic picture of divine agency limited to original creation, this recognition of God's constant providential care for creation's flourishing highlights the dependence of creation on the Trinity. Sometimes God intervenes directly, issuing a fiat Word, but in every moment God supervenes upon and within natural processes he has designed in order to bring further diversity and complexity into his world.

Interestingly, a debate erupted in the seventeenth century between scientist-philosophers Gottfried Leibniz and Nicolas Malebranche that in some way anticipated contemporary debates.[71] Descartes taught that motion is the result of dead matter being animated by spiritual substance—and, of course, the highest spiritual substance is God. Building on Descartes, Malebranche argued that every creaturely action or event is directly and immediately caused by God. "By whatever effort of mind I make, I can find force, efficacy, or power only in the will of the infinitely perfect Being," wrote Malebranche.[72] There is therefore only one real agency at work in the world: God's, directly, immediately, and miraculously causing every event. This position is known as occasionalism. Where "continual creation" was thought by traditional theology (Roman Catholic and Protestant) to be an exercise of God's power ordinarily through natural means and processes, occasionalism understood it to mean that every moment is an entirely new, *ex nihilo* act of divine creation.[73]

Leibniz's challenge was also largely theological, drawn from a retrieval of the scholastic doctrine of continual creation. While strongly affirming *ex nihilo* creation, Leibniz also attended to the natural process with which the triune God endowed creation and within which God continues to work.[74]

---

71. On this debate and the respective views regarding creation see Nicholas Rescher, *Leibniz: An Introduction to His Philosophy* (Totowa, N.J.: Rowman & Littlefield, 1979); G. H. R. Parkinson, *Logic and Reality in Leibniz's Metaphysics* (Oxford: Oxford Univ. Press, 1965), 98–110; G. W. Leibniz, *Philosophical Papers and Letters* (ed. and trans. Leroy E. Loemker; Dordrecht, Netherlands: D. Reidel, 1989); Nicolas Malebranche, *Dialogues on Metaphysics and on Religion* (ed. Nicholas Jolley; trans. David Scott; Cambridge: Cambridge Univ. Press, 1997).

72. Nicolas Malebranche, *The Search after Truth: With Elucidations of* The Search after Truth (ed. and trans. T. M. Lennon and P. J. Olscamp; Columbus: Ohio State Univ. Press, 1980), 658.

73. Providence is here understood not only as ultimately dependent on God's preservation of the world through natural causes but as God's direct and immediate creation of everything that exists (including human agency) in every moment. Aris-

ing in Islamic philosophy in ninth-century Iraq, this view was advanced in modern philosophy especially by Malebranche as a critique of deism. On the basis of Descartes' dualism between mind and matter (whose essences were so different that they could not affect each other), Malebranche argued that every event in the world is a new creation. Similar views were held by the British Idealist Bishop George Berkeley (1685–1753) and American theologian Jonathan Edwards (1703–1758).

74. Leibniz, *Philosophical Papers and Letters*, 499. At the end of the day, however, Leibniz seems to have held an almost deistic picture of continual creation as the effect of nothing more than the "mechanism of the world" running as it was created to operate—without any divine involvement along the way. "I consider it sufficient that the mechanism of the world is built with such wisdom that these wonderful things depend on the progression of the machine itself, organic things particularly, as I believe, evolving by a certain predetermined order."

It is significant that the notion of continual creation, distinct from the original act of creation *ex nihilo*, fell into disuse with the rise of a Newtonian cosmology that assumed constancy and, and that that notion is now being reappropriated by some scientists as a way of explaining the obvious evidence that the world is constantly changing.[75] For example, while human beings came into existence at a definite period in time, each human body replaces all of its cells several times during its life. In many respects, the world seems to be constantly emerging, falling apart, and reconstituting itself. And yet, there is still something called "the world," with all of its basic continuities across vast reaches of time. Such continuity in the midst of constant flux is incapable of being explained in terms of either naturalism or hypersupernaturalism. There is no more a contradiction between God's providential activity in continual creation and natural processes than there is in the relationship of divine and human agency. God is as sovereign in the natural processes of the earth "bringing forth" as he is in direct interventions that we usually call miracles.

As great as their differences are, occasionalism and naturalism (or deism) assume a univocity of being that requires every action to be *either* divine *or* creaturely. The classical doctrine of *concurrence*—namely, that God's action supervenes on creaturely agency without violence—is simply lost in both accounts. Something like this standoff is evident in contemporary religion and science debates. However, in the perspective put forward thus far, occasionalism and deism offer a false dilemma that neither theology nor science can accept, for their own reasons.

Because God is not simply a unitary spirit who acts on inert matter but the triune God who speaks from the Father, in the Son, and by the Spirit, there can be a "Let there be!" that directly creates the world out of nothing and a subsequent "letting be" that draws out and guides nature in its praise of God. Precisely because God is qualitatively different from creation (eternal, immutable, immortal, invisible, omnipresent, omnipotent), we have no trouble attributing actions, events, and processes to both God and nature.[76] Because God is qualitatively distinct from creatures, it is wrong to think of ordinary causes and processes in quantitative terms, as if causes could be attributed partially to God and partially to nature.

In our attempts to see points of conversation between theology and science, we cannot be naive. Whether in theology or the natural sciences, presuppositions play a formative role. If one begins with the assumption that nature cannot have any causes external to it, the facts will be interpreted in such a way as to eliminate God's involvement. Contemporary science tends to assume that there is no teleology of hope for creation. It is pointless evolution of an expanding cosmos that will (or may)

---

75. See, for example, the fascinating article by scientist W. H. McCrea, "Continual Creation," *Monthly Notices of the Royal Astronomical Society* 128 (1964): 335.

76. See Ernan McMullin, "Evolutionary Contingency and Cosmic Purpose," in *Finding God in All Things* (ed. Michael J. Himes and Stephen J. Pope; New York: Herder, 1996), 140–61.

eventually lead to implosion or some other purely natural apocalypse.[77] Science is not wrong for its empirical observations and calculations, just incomplete — and therefore to be faulted only when it extrapolates from empirical probabilities to absolute, metaphysical certainties. If our very existence is mathematically improbable apart from a transcendent source, then it would be foolish to draw absolute conclusions about the destiny of our cosmos simply on the basis of the immanent possibilities of the cosmos itself.

The radical contingency and inherent incapacity of creation to bring itself into being, sustain its existence, or realize a future consummation rather than complete dissolution only underscore its radical dependence on God's covenant faithfulness. The hope for a new creation — that is, a miraculous restoration of the cosmos at Christ's return — does not arise from empirical observations and mathematical probabilities but from God's promise in Scripture. Only in the gospel does the world's story become open to a hope that lies beyond observable data — in the new creation:

> For the creation was subjected to futility, not willingly, but because of him who subjected it, in hope that the creation itself will be set free from its bondage to corruption and obtain the freedom of the glory of the children of God. For we know that the whole creation has been groaning together in the pains of childbirth until now. And not only the creation, but we ourselves, who have the firstfruits of the Spirit, groan inwardly as we wait eagerly for adoption as sons, the redemption of our bodies. For in this hope we were saved. Now hope that is seen is not hope. For who hopes for what he sees? But if we hope for what we do not see, we wait for it with patience.
>
> —Romans 8:20–25

DISCUSSION QUESTIONS

1. What do we mean by "creation *ex nihilo*"? How does this differ from rival views?
2. Discuss the significance of a Trinitarian understanding of creation.
3. Discuss the recurring biblical emphasis on God's speech as the medium of creation. Why is this important?
4. Was God's grace the motive for creating the world (including human beings)? What difference does our answer to that question make in our view of the integrity of creation?

---

77. See William R. Stoeger, SJ, "Scientific Accounts of Ultimate Catastrophes in Our Life-Bearing Universe," in *The End of the World and the Ends of God*, 19–28.

5. What is the "God of the gaps" apologetic, and what are its theological and tactical weaknesses? How is God's creative splendor demonstrated in the contingency and apparent chaos, as well as in the order and design of the universe?

6. Evaluate the occasionalist perspective, especially in light of the concept of "continual creation."

Chapter Eleven

PROVIDENCE: GOD'S CARE FOR ALL HE HAS MADE

With the doctrine of providence we meet once more the Trinitarian structure of God's external operations. Scripture tells us, "For by him [the Son] all things were created, in heaven and on earth, visible and invisible, whether thrones or dominions or rulers or authorities — all things were created through him and for him. And he is before all things, *and in him all things hold together*" (Col 1:16 – 17, emphasis added). There is a Logos, but the Logos is a person, not a principle, and that person is Jesus Christ, not an eternal despot. Not only in redemption, but in creation and providence, the Son is "the way and the truth and the Life."

Furthermore, it is the Spirit who is at work within the field spoken into existence by the Father in the Son (Ro 8:26 – 28; Isa 32:15; 2Co 3:17). It is the Spirit who so orchestrates the unfolding plot of redemption around the Son to the glory of the Father that the past becomes a living promise and the future becomes a revivifying reality. Because the Father works not only *upon* but *within* history by his Spirit, and does all things in his Son, God's providence cannot be conceived merely in terms of immediate cause and effect.

There are essentially three classes of providence passages in Scripture: (1) those connected specifically with salvation (soteriological passages), (2) references to God's more general governance (common grace passages), and (3) defenses of God's ways in the world in spite of the reality of evil (theodicy passages). It is important to keep these distinct in our minds. For example, when we are told that "it is God who works in you, both to will and to work for his good pleasure" (Php 2:13), our sanctification is in view. God does not work in us to sin, for example, but he does work all things (including our sin) together for our good (Ro 8:28), because he is Lord even over our failures. Since I treat the soteriological passages in later chapters, I will focus here on the other two groups.

Many Christians who have difficulty accepting divine sovereignty in salvation nevertheless share with the most ardent predestinarian a confidence in the ultimate lordship of God over all natural and historical phenomena. While others speak of good luck and bad luck, the Christian says, "The LORD gave, and the LORD has taken away; blessed be the name of the LORD" (Job 1:21). Rather than Stoic fate, it is the personal lordship of a God who is trustworthy in his purposes that leads the Christian to be content in wealth and poverty (Ro 8:28; Php 4:11–13). Unbelievers are no less beneficiaries of God's general providence than believers. This is what is intended in the doctrine of common grace: "The LORD is good to all, and his mercy is over all that he has made.... The eyes of all look to you, and you give them their food in due season. You open your hand; you satisfy the desire of every living thing" (Ps 145:9, 15–16). Jesus reiterates this general kindness in his Sermon on the Mount: "For [God] makes his sun rise on the evil and on the good, and sends rain on the just and on the unjust" (Mt 5:45). God has appointed the times and dwelling places of all people to the end, so that they will look to him as the source of all good (Ac 17:25–27).

The most seemingly insignificant details are governed by God's providence. With the psalmist, we may wonder, "When I look at your heavens, the work of your fingers, the moon and the stars, which you have set in place, what is man that you are mindful of him, and the son of man that you care for him?" (Ps 8:3–4). Nevertheless, every hair of each person is numbered by God (Lk 12:7), and not a single bird falls to the ground without the Father's will (Mt 10:29). Even the results of every roll of dice in a game of chance are determined by God (Pr 16:33). God's majesty is revealed not only in his sovereignty over rising empires but also in his tender concern for falling sparrows.

Not even this general providence, however, can be abstracted from Christ, as we have noted above from Colossians 1:16–17. Encouraging his disciples to trust in God's providence, this same Jesus Christ reminded his disciples that the Father richly dresses the grass of the field and feeds the birds of the air (Mt 6:25–34). Similarly, Paul calls for contentment, "for we brought nothing into the world, and we cannot take anything out of the world. But if we have food and clothing, with these we will be content" (1Ti 6:7–8). God "gives life to all things" (v. 13) and "richly provides us with everything to enjoy" (v. 17).

Out of the lavishness displayed in the marvelous variety and richness of creation itself, God continues to pour out his common blessings on all people. Therefore, we neither hoard possessions as if God's gifts were scarce nor deny ourselves pleasures as if God were stingy. Believers and unbelievers alike share in the common joys of childbirth and childhood, friendship and romance, marriage and family. Unlike life under the old covenant theocracy, there is no guarantee in this time between Christ's two advents that the lives of Christians will go better than those of non-Christians. The promise, rather, is that even calamities cannot frustrate God's salvation of his elect, but, on the contrary, are turned to our ultimate good.

It is always dangerous to interpret one's temporal circumstances as a sign either of God's favor or of his displeasure. In Psalm 73, Asaph confesses that he "almost stumbled. . . . For I was envious of the arrogant when I saw the prosperity of the wicked. . . . All in vain have I kept my heart clean and washed my hands in innocence" (Ps 73:2 – 3 13). Trying to understand this became "a wearisome task" (v. 16). Our natural reason tells us that good people finish first and cheaters never prosper. However, believers have no right to God's common grace any more than they do to his saving grace. God remains free to show compassion on whomever he will, even to give breath, health, prosperity, and friends to those who breathe threats against him. The psalmist never resolves this paradox philosophically, but eschatologically — that is, by entering God's sanctuary and recognizing that the temporal pleasures of the ungodly conceal their ultimate doom, while the saints' temporal struggles conceal their ultimate glory: "You guide me with your counsel, and afterward you will receive me to glory. . . . My flesh and my heart may fail, but God is the strength of my heart and my portion forever" (vv. 24, 26).

For believers, every common blessing is a mere foretaste of heavenly joys, and "the sufferings of this present time are not worth comparing with the glory that is to be revealed to us" (Ro 8:18). From this assurance the *Heidelberg Catechism* confidently teaches in its first question and answer that "I am not my own, but belong — body and soul, in life and in death — to my faithful Savior Jesus Christ. . . . He also watches over me in such a way that not a hair can fall from my head without the will of my Father in heaven: in fact, all things must work together for my salvation."[1] These passages do not say that God *does* all things or that all things are *good*, but that *he works all things together for our good* — which means, ultimately, for our salvation.

It is especially the third class of providence passages, however, that provokes the strongest reaction in our day — those texts that relate to sin and evil. Job wrestles with God's purposes, and if anything is clear from God's own conclusion to the dialogues, it is that Job's suffering is (1) subject to God's sovereign permission; (2)

---

1. *Heidelberg Catechism*, q. 1, in *Psalter Hymnal* (Grand Rapids: CRC Publications, 1987), 861.

included in God's sovereign plan for Job's life, though that plan is hidden from Job; (3) not the result of any particular sin that Job has committed; and (4) finally resolved not philosophically but historically in the promise of a redeemer and the resurrection of his body. In the examples of Joseph's brothers, Pharaoh, and Nebuchadnezzar—or, in the life of Jesus, Herod, Caiaphas, and the Gentiles who crucified Christ—events unfold as simultaneously the effect of a divine decree and ordinary processes of human desire, planning, and execution. It is this class of passages that is particularly well addressed by the doctrine of *concursus*, which we will explore after addressing some of the challenges involved in defending this doctrine in our day.

I. Cultural Challenges to the Doctrine of Providence

Ironically, providence—at least a general notion—is one of the most universally attested religious assumptions throughout history and yet one of the most challenged doctrines in our day.

First, it is difficult to acknowledge gifts, much less a transcendent Giver, in a world of supposed givens. Luther spoke of the milkmaid and the baker as "masks" God hides behind in order to answer our prayer for daily sustenance.[2] In every gift, God is ultimately the giver; yet tenderly he hides his blinding majesty and otherwise terrifying sovereignty behind the creaturely means that are familiar to us. However, those of us in technologically developed cultures rarely encounter the milkmaids and bakers whose goods we purchase at the supermarket. Rarely are our lives threatened by exposure to the elements. In fact, we have thermostats to control our environment. Our contact with the Giver to whom we pray is not only mediated by fellow creatures, as it has always been, but so obscured by mechanical and highly bureaucratized systems that the world becomes impersonal. Gifts become reduced to givens that can be anticipated, measured, and priced according to the market. The circulation of gifts in personal exchanges becomes marginalized by the flow of capital and debt. Our piety—praying for our daily bread—often seems remote from our actual experience, at least in highly developed modern societies.

It is sometimes difficult, therefore, to identify with the all-encompassing providence in which the psalmist took comfort:

> He who dwells in the shelter of the Most High
> will abide in the shadow of the Almighty.

---

2. Martin Luther, *Day by Day We Magnify Thee* (Philadelphia: Fortress, 1982), 298; see also Gustav Wingren, *Luther on Vocation* (trans. Carl C. Rasmussen; 1957; repr., Evansville, Ind.: Ballast, 1994); G. E. Veith, *God at Work* (Westchester, Ill.: Crossway, 2002).

> I will say to the LORD, "My refuge and my fortress,
>   my God, in whom I trust."
> For he will deliver you from the snare of the fowler
>   and from the deadly pestilence.
> He will cover you with his pinions,
>   and under his wings you will find refuge;
>   his faithfulness is a shield and buckler.
> You will not fear the terror of the night,
>   nor the arrow that flies by day,
> nor the pestilence that stalks in darkness,
>   nor the destruction that wastes at noonday. (Ps 91:1–6)

While placing our destinies in the everlasting arms of God on Sunday, we may find ourselves on Monday morning with the general impression that our lives are really controlled by the Invisible Hand of the Market or the comforting arms of the state, insurance providers, and the companies by which we are employed. While Job confessed, "'The LORD gave, and the LORD has taken away; blessed be the name of the LORD'" (Job 1:21), we are tempted to look to the global economy for ultimate news of deliverance or disaster.

In this context, some long nostalgically for a renewal of the enchanted forests of medieval piety, where the rustling of a leaf is a divine whisper, angels are daily companions, and mythological imagination replaces rationalistic calculation. Others revel in the secularity of the mall, with its theatrical staging, or the movie sets of our suburban dystopias, where surfaces replace depths and the total consummation of immediate gratification replaces natural relationships. Somewhere in between these extremes lies the biblical perspective, which affirms God's active involvement in every moment of history but in indirect, ordinary, and thoroughly mediated ways.

Second, a secularized notion of providence was used as a sentimentalized and cheerful divine sanction for the triumphant progress of particular cultures, nations, and ideologies that left devastation in their wake. This has produced a reaction against a benevolent plan for history. In the Enlightenment era, deists still spoke of God as the Architect. In fact, in many of the writings of America's founders, the impersonal name of "Providence" was usually preceded by the cheerful adjective "benevolent" or "benign," as if God's providence could never be dangerous or judgmental. Empires and nation-states invoked God's providence to underwrite a sense of inevitable conquest and doctrines of "manifest destiny." According to Eusebius, Emperor Constantine was favored by Providence to make Christ's reign visible in the world even by military conquest.[3]

"But in catastrophe, in the trenches, the caves, and the concentration camps of this world, the eternal Philanthropist was exposed as a delusion," notes Berkouwer.

---

3. See Eusebius, *Ecclesiastical History*, book 10, chapter 9.

"This was the beginning of the crisis of faith in our day."[4] Having lived through the Nazi occupation in Holland, Berkouwer asked pointedly, "Does not atheism seem now to be the only logical and permissible conclusion to draw from the reality of our century?" The systems that unleashed triumphalistic terrors left in their wake a passive or nihilistic atheism. "Modern realism is at bottom just as atheistic in its acceptance of reality as was optimism in its avoidance of reality."[5]

Berkouwer also pointed to typical treatments of providence in the nineteenth and twentieth century that discussed the doctrine "in general and timeless terms." The Christian doctrine of providence became secularized as the myth of an immanent and inevitable historical progress, especially since the Enlightenment.

> Providence seemed to be a "truth" which could rely upon universal assent—in distinction from other truths like the virgin birth, the resurrection, and the ascension, which were the *scandalon* of the nineteenth century. Anyone who accepted the existence of God usually believed as well that he sustained and ruled the world. The Providence doctrine was often used as another way of stating man's belief in progressive evolution. God was discernibly leading the world to his own benevolent end....
>
> All this in our century is radically altered. The friendliness of God, which man thought he saw reflected in the stream of history, has become increasingly disputable.[6]

Existentialism was equally one-sided in its preoccupation with dread over comfort, but Psalm 73, Job, and Ecclesiastes all warn the church against too easily dismissing this dread in its confession of God's providential comfort.[7]

For these reasons, and many others, many of our contemporaries hear talk of providence as, at best, a false comfort in the face of the apparent randomness, brutality, and chaos of life—and, at worst, a license to kill. Especially in this context, it is important for Christians to recognize that while God's saving will in Christ, once hidden, is now revealed to everyone through the proclamation of the gospel, God's hand of providence, even in the lives of believers, remains largely hidden.

II. Systematic-Theological Categories for Understanding the Doctrine of Providence

The apparent randomness that we recognize in *nature* (discussed in the previous chapter) also marks *history* on both the personal and global levels. Like any good story, it is only at the end that what seemed like unrelated characters and events are

---

4. G. C. Berkouwer, *Studies In Dogmatics: The Providence of God* (Grand Rapids: Eerdmans, 1952), 28.
5. Ibid., 11.

6. Ibid., 13.
7. See Berkouwer, *The Providence of God*, 14–19.

seen to constitute a narrative plot. And only the divine playwright knows the whole story. Reversals and counterreversals are meaningless apart from some resolution, but a resolution that is easily predicted in advance lacks dramatic depth. Analogous to the more complicated picture of contemporary science, with the paradox of apparent randomness yet general stability and order, a good narrative plot is full of unexpected twists and turns, seemingly unrelated and chaotic elements whose deeper harmony is brought to realization in the climax.

A number of important distinctions bear on this topic and, though not resolving the mystery of human and divine agency, help us to avoid the dangers of both hypersupernaturalistic fatalism and naturalism.

A. DIRECT/INDIRECT CAUSE: THE DOCTRINE OF *CONCURSUS*

From the Latin verb *concurrere*, "to run together," the idea of *concursus*, or concurrence, in theology refers to the simultaneity of divine and human agency in specific actions and events. Aquinas recognized that on one hand Scripture clearly teaches that God has predestined all things that come to pass while on the other hand it attributes decisions and actions to human agents. Sometimes God acts immediately and directly, but ordinarily he works through natural means. Aquinas employed the Aristotelian category of *primary* and *secondary causes* to make this point.

Willing to allow a ministerial rather than magisterial role to philosophy, the Reformers and their theological successors were satisfied in using this category and were even, for the most part, satisfied with the way it had been handled by Aquinas. Calvin calls it a "determinative principle" that "sometimes [God's providence] works through an intermediary, sometimes without an intermediary, sometimes contrary to every intermediary."[8] To affirm *soli Deo gloria* (to God alone be glory) is not to deny that both doctors and God are healers—one as the secondary or instrumental cause and the other as the primary or ultimate cause. In fact, it is only when we recognize God's hand in everyday providence, through means, that we are able to attribute everything ultimately to his glory. We need to recover this balanced understanding of God's work in our lives—and indeed in the lives of all his creatures.

Like nature, history reflects constancy as well as contingency, order as well as freedom, design amid apparent randomness. In fact, writes Calvin, "however all things may be ordained by God's plan, according to a sure dispensation, for us they are fortuitous, ... since the order, reason, end, and necessity of those things which happen for the most part lie hidden in God's purpose, and are not apprehended

---

8. Calvin, *Institutes* 1.17.1.

by human opinion." It is not just that they seem fortuitous; rather, they are fortuitous—but to us rather than to God. "For they bear on the face of them no other appearance, whether they are considered in their own nature or weighed according to our knowledge and judgment."[9]

Similarly, Francis Turretin observes,

Nothing is more contingent than the killing of a man by a woodcutter contrary to his own intention, and yet this is ascribed to God, who is said to deliver him into the hand of the slayer (Ex 21:12–13; Dt 19:4–13). Nothing is more casual and fortuitous than lots [dice], and yet their falling out is referred to God himself: "The lot is cast into the lap; but the whole disposing thereof is of the Lord" (Pr 16:33). Nothing was more contingent than the selling of Joseph and his incarceration and exaltation, yet Joseph himself testifies that these were all ordered in the providence of God: "So now it was not you that sent me hither, but God" (Ge 45:8). "Ye meant it for evil, but God meant it for good, that he might preserve in life a great people as he has done this day" (Ge 50:20). Innumerable similar events, plainly contingent and fortuitous, are expressly ascribed to providence (cf. Ge 22:8, 13; 24:12–61; 27:20; Pr 21:31; Mt 10:29–30).[10]

It was necessary from the perspective of God's decree that Joseph should be sold into slavery. "Yet it was contingent with respect to the brothers of Joseph who might either have killed him or not have sold him."[11] Even Thomas Aquinas says, "When the free will moves itself, this does not exclude its being moved by another, from whom it receives the very power to move itself."[12]

The concurrence that is necessary for a biblical doctrine of providence is not merely a general oversight but a direction of all events to their appointed ends. We can have confidence that God works all things together for our good only because all things are decreed by his wise counsels. "If only a general concourse [concurrence] of God is granted," Turretin observes, "in vain is he prayed to for obtaining anything because he can neither avert evil nor confer good, unless just as it pleases men to determine the motion of God himself."[13] Nor do we have any ground for giving God praise when he confers good things through free human agents and natural means.[14] Prayer is more than a therapeutic catharsis—venting our fears and frustrations or expressing our hopes and dreams to one who cares but is incapable of overruling in the affairs of free creatures. Prayer presupposes that God is sovereign over every contingency of nature and history.

While all Reformed theologians (like Thomists and Dominicans) hold that God has decreed whatever comes to pass, some hold that in concurrence God only

---

9. Ibid., 1.16.9.
10. Turretin, *Elenctic Theology*, 1:499.
11. Ibid., 1:500.
12. Thomas Aquinas, *Summa theologica* (New York: Benz-

inger Brothers, 1947–1948), 1:418, q. 83, art. 1.
13. Turretin, *Elenctic Theology*, 1:503.
14. Ibid.

predetermines the acts and not the will, except with respect to "the good works of grace." Although Turretin notes that there are "weighty reasons on both sides," he refers "previous concourse [*concursus*]," or God's predetermination, to *all* human decisions and actions.[15] Foremost, the Scriptures clearly attribute God's superintendence to all creaturely affairs and not simply to matters pertaining to salvation. Furthermore, it is impossible to neatly separate the former from the latter. God works *all things* together for the salvation of his elect—even their material circumstances. Ordinary daily occurrences—trials, disasters, tragedies, personal encounters, formative events—become occasions for God's saving hand to reach into our lives, whether we recognize it or not.

Turretin asks, "How can the concourse of God be reconciled with the contingency and liberty of second causes—especially the human will?" He replies, "This question is no less difficult than the preceding; nay somewhat more difficult and incapable of being sufficiently explained, unless we follow the light of the divine word and religiously restrain ourselves within the bounds prescribed by it. These two things we derive most clearly from the Scriptures: that the providence of God concurs with all second causes and especially with the human will; yet the contingency and liberty of the will remain unimpaired. But how these two things can consist with each other, no mortal can in this life perfectly understand."[16] We have no warrant to deny a revealed mystery simply because we cannot explain it.[17]

In permitting evil, God does not simply let it happen but determines how far he will let it go and how he will overcome it for good. "The orthodox hold the mean between these extremes, maintaining that the providence of God is so occupied about sin as neither idly to permit it (as the Pelagians think) nor efficiently to produce it (as the Libertines suppose), but efficaciously to order and direct it."[18]

Scripture clearly holds human beings responsible for hardening their hearts against his word and will, and it also teaches that God hardens hearts (Ex 3:19; 6:1; 7:3, 13, 22; 8:15, 19; Ro 9:18). Yet God's sovereign agency is not the same in hardening hearts as it is in softening them. In the latter case, God gives his redeemed a new heart (Jer 31:32–33; Eze 11:19), but in the former case God gives the wicked over to their own desires: "So I gave them over to their stubborn hearts, to follow their own counsels" (Ps 81:12). "Therefore God gave them up in the lusts of their hearts to impurity" (Ro 1:24). God's permission of sin is not a mere acquiescence, but is a determination that ensures its defeat.[19] As Theodore Beza expressed it, "permission" is appropriate if what is meant is that "God does not act in evil, but gives them up to Satan and their own lusts."[20] God does not act in and with evil but over and against

---

15. Ibid., 1:507.
16. Ibid., 1:511.
17. Ibid., 1:512.

18. Ibid., 1:515.
19. Ibid., 1:515–16.
20. Cited in ibid., 1:517.

it. "God therefore properly does not will sin to be done, but only wills to permit it."[21] In the words of Augustine, "God knew that it pertained more to his most almighty goodness, even to bring good out of evil, than not to permit evil to be."[22]

God therefore can be considered neither the author of evil nor the passive spectator of evil. He only actively determines to permit evils that he has already, at great personal cost, determined to overcome for his greater glory and our ultimate good. Even the Counter-Reformation theologian Robert Bellarmine acknowledged that the Calvinists as much as Roman Catholics deny that God is the author of sin.[23] And the Reformed confessions confirm this.[24]

As helpful as Aristotle's categories of primary and secondary causality have been in the history of theology, they may at least be supplemented by a communicative approach. We have seen that God characteristically brings about his purposes through speech. Not only in creation but in providence it is God's lively speech that is at work: "He upholds the universe by the word of his power" (Heb 1:3). So instead of the familiar analogy of the invisible hand, we should think in terms of the audible word. God does not simply operate *on* the world, causing its history and human actions, but *in* the world and *within* its manifold creatures. "The LORD utters his voice before his army, for his camp is exceedingly great; he who executes his word is powerful" (Joel 2:11).

This doctrine of *concursus* was challenged not only by Enlightenment naturalism but also by hypersupernaturalistic interpretations of providence that opposed it. I referred in the previous chapter to the French Catholic philosopher Nicholas Malebranche (see "'I Am the Alpha and the Omega,'" pp. 344–48), especially his debate with Leibniz over the relative independence of natural processes. Founder of the school known as occasionalism, Malebranche argued that every event was an *ex nihilo* creation—a direct and immediate act of God. Like Leibniz, the Protestant orthodox spoke of a continual creation (*creatio continua*) that was nevertheless distinct from the original creation (*creatio originalis*).[25] However, with Jonathan Edwards's adoption of occasionalist ideas, the reality of creaturely agency—even the reality of creaturely existence—became still more questionable. "Therefore the existence of created substances, in each successive moment," he wrote, "must be

---

21. Ibid.

22. Augustine, *Admonition and Grace* 10 [27] in *Fathers of the Church* (Washington, D.C.: Catholic Univ. of America Press), 2:278.

23. See Turretin, *Elenctic Theology*, 1:529.

24. Turretin (ibid.) adds, "The public confessions of the Reformed churches, in express, careful and authoritative words condemn and censure this impiety: as the Augsburg, Art. 19, the French, Art. 8, the Second Helvetic, chap. 8, the Belgic, Art. 13, the Canons of the Synod of Dort, First Head, Art. 1, 5, 15."

Turretin charges Bellarmine with "impiety and blasphemy" for asserting that God actually "twists and turns [the wicked] by his invisible operation," determining their wills to evil (1:530). In his *Bondage of the Will*, Luther speaks of God's activity in hardening the hearts of sinners "in far stronger terms than our divines" (1:531).

25. Charles Hodge provides an excellent summary with numerous citations in his *Systematic Theology* (Grand Rapids: Eerdmans, 1946), 1:577–78.

the effect of the immediate agency, will, and power of God.... It will certainly follow from these things, that God's preserving of created things in being is perfectly equivalent to a continued creation, or to his creating those things out of nothing at each moment in their existence."[26] The falling of a leaf, in this view, is not a natural event in which the triune God was involved in his own distinct agency, but is simply the effect of God's direct fiat.[27]

While Arminians and deists restrict God's involvement in the preservation and government of the world, occasionalists collapse providence into *ex nihilo* creation, Charles Hodge observes.[28] In the occasionalist view, "There is no power, no cause, no real existence but the efficiency and causality of God." Hodge judges, "Between this system and pantheism there is scarcely a dividing line."[29] Although Hodge does not refer to Malebranche, he properly notes that what he calls "the strange doctrine of Edwards" on this point owes much to Platonic realism/idealism, which reduces worldly agency to mere appearances.[30] If Hodge's judgment is too severe, the more recent conclusion of Michael James McClymond seems entirely appropriate: "The concept of God as known, as manifest, as visibly glorious, proved so decisive a factor in Edwards's thinking that it gave birth to idealist metaphysics."[31] Hodge nicely summarizes the Reformed interpretation of the more Thomistic view of providence: "It is best, therefore, to rest satisfied with the simple statement that preservation is that omnipotent energy of God by which all created things, animate and inanimate, are upheld in existence, with all the properties and powers with which he has endowed them."[32] In this perspective, creaturely agency is real, even if (or rather, because) it is dependent ultimately on God's powerful Word.

Platonic realism is also evident throughout Barth's early work, especially his *Römerbrief*, but its logic is persistent to the very last fragment of the *Church Dogmatics*. Barth's ontological assumptions have even been described as "occasionalist."[33] The whole tendency of this realist/idealist trajectory in theology is to render history, and the creaturely action within it, to mere appearances of a single, eternal, and all-

26. Jonathan Edwards, "Original Sin," 4.3, in *Works of Jonathan Edwards* (Edinburgh: Banner of Truth, 1834), 1:223.

27. Jonathan Edwards, *The Philosophy of Jonathan Edwards from His Private Notebooks* (Eugene: Univ. of Oregon, 1955), 185. Edwards even refers to these divine acts as "arbitrary," not in relation to God's own nature, but in relation to natural laws. However, it is difficult to see how there could even be such a thing as natural laws in this system.

28. Hodge, *Systematic Theology*, 1:576–80.

29. Ibid., 1:580.

30. Ibid., 2:220–21. Hodge elaborates his objection to this view here in his treatment of Edwards' view of original sin, which lodges guilt and corruption in the real (numerical) identity of human substance in Adam.

31. Michael James McClymond, *Encounters with God: An Approach to the Theology of Jonathan Edwards* (New York: Oxford Univ. Press, 1998), 34. For a different appraisal see Oliver D. Crisp, "How 'Occasional' Was Edwards's Occasionalism?" in *Jonathan Edwards: Philosophical Theologian* (ed. Paul Helm and Oliver D. Crisp; London: Ashgate, 2003), 61–77.

32. Hodge, *Systematic Theology*, 1:581.

33. As with Edwards, the extent of Barth's "occasionalism" is disputed among specialists. See, for example, Nigel Bigger, *The Hastening That Waits: The Ethics of Karl Barth* (New York: Oxford Univ. Press, 1995), 19–31. For a somewhat different perspective on Barth's alleged occasionalism, see Paul Nimmo, *Being in Action: The Theological Shape of Barth's Ethical Vision* (Edinburgh: T&T Clark, 2007), 19.

encompassing divine existence and agency. In such hypersupernaturalist accounts, the notion of God hiding his majestic glory behind the masks or veils of creaturely mediation, giving to creation its own proper agency and integrity, is surrendered to a direct, majestic, and omnicausal divine sovereignty that threatens to reduce secondary causes in history to unreality.

Ironically, many today who would not affirm a classic Christian notion of divine sovereignty *in salvation* nevertheless often speak as if God does all things *in their daily lives* directly, without any instrumental means or "secondary causes." If one attributes a remarkable recovery from an illness to the skill of the physicians, well-meaning Christians are sometimes inclined to reply, "Yes, but *God* was the one who healed her." In more extreme cases, some believers even excuse their laziness and lack of wisdom or preparation by appealing to God's sovereignty. "Just pray about it"; "If God wants it to happen, it will happen."

To be sure, the truth of God's providence is meant to assure believers that *ultimately* our times are in God's hands, but God does not fulfill all of his purposes *directly*. In fact, it is his ordinary course to employ means, whether human beings or weather patterns, social upheavals, animal migrations, various vocations, and a host of other factors over which he has ultimate control. We are comforted by the truth that God works all things—even adversity—into his plan for our salvation. God provides, but we are commanded to pray for our daily bread and to labor in our callings.

The nearly deistic picture of God's providence evident in open theism, the "omnicausalism" advocated by occasionalism, and the panentheistic outlook of process theology share more with each other than any shares with the classical Thomist and Reformed understanding of *concursus*. Process theologian David Ray Griffin suggests that, ironically, the view of open theism expounded by some evangelicals, such as Clark Pinnock, represents a *weaker* view of God's involvement in the world than does process thought, since process theologians "hold that God exerts variable divine influence in every event (every 'occasion of experience') whatsoever." Whereas free will (open) theists deny God's active involvement in every event, "process theology says that God 'intervenes' in every present event, so that divine influence is a natural part of the world's normal causal sequences," yet "denies that God ever interrupts these normal sequences." "No event in the world, accordingly, is ever brought about unilaterally by God; divinely-creaturely cooperation is always involved. This fact reflects the very nature of the divine-world relation, not simply a voluntary self-limitation."[34]

Therefore, in the process view, God's involvement (even "intervention") in every

---

34. David Ray Griffin, "Process Theology and the Christian Good News," in *Searching for an Adequate God: A Dialogue* *between Process and Free Will Theists* (ed. John B. Cobb Jr. and Clark H. Pinnock; Grand Rapids: Eerdmans, 2000), 13.

event is affirmed at the expense of both the extraordinary freedom of God to intervene miraculously *and* the genuine freedom of creatures. God is inherently limited in his free agency *and* there is no genuine contingency in the creaturely means by which he brings his decrees to pass. Griffin concedes concerning the doctrine of *concursus* or double-agency, "The Bible does indeed express this twofold view. But does this mean that *we* should?" Even the free will theists do not take the Bible at face value on this point, argues Griffin.[35] In process theology, there is no distinction between providence and miracle, since God *never* acts unilaterally.

The principal feature that distinguishes the classical view from these rival accounts is its presupposition that being is analogical rather than univocal. As we have seen from the examples of Pharaoh, Joseph's brothers, and Jesus' crucifixion, God's intention and action are qualitatively distinct from those of human agents — even in the same event. Understood analogically, God's activity in providence never threatens the reality of human agency, nor vice versa. Navigating between these extremes is the classical Augustinian, Thomistic, and Reformed view that God is directing all of history toward his purposes without in any way canceling the ordinary liberty, contingency, and reality of creaturely causes.[36]

B. THE REVEALED/HIDDEN DISTINCTION

Scripture itself distinguishes between hidden and revealed things: "The secret things belong to the LORD our God, but the things that are revealed belong to us and to our children forever, that we may do all the words of this law" (Dt 29:29). Even the fullness of the gospel (particularly the uniting of Jew and Gentile in Christ), as it fulfilled Old Testament prophecy, was "a hidden and secret wisdom of God, which God decreed before the ages for our glory" and has now been "revealed to us through the Spirit" (1Co 2:7, 10). Some of God's decrees are always hidden, never revealed, while others are hidden until God reveals them "in the fullness of time." For example, one may never know the reason for particular tragedies in one's own experience, but the gospel is the revelation of the reason for Christ's death. This distinction between things hidden and things revealed is maintained throughout Scripture.

Calvin emphasized that whatever God has decreed that has not yet been publicly revealed through the prophets and apostles is beyond our capacity to know. God's hidden will is distinguished from his revealed will. God cannot be charged with sin,

---

35. Ibid., 21.

36. The *Westminster Confession* (ch. 3) states: "God, from all eternity, did, by the most wise and holy counsel of his own will, freely, and unchangeably ordain whatsoever comes to pass: yet so, as thereby neither is God the author of sin, nor is violence offered to the will of the creatures; nor is the liberty or contingency of second causes taken away, but rather established" (*Trinity Hymnal*, rev. ed. [Philadelphia: Great Commission Publications, 1990], 850).

but neither does it catch him by surprise.[37] We must not try to figure out God's secret providence, but must attend to the means he has provided for our salvation (through Word and sacrament) and earthly welfare (through vocations, friendship, and other common gifts we share with unbelievers).[38] Where God has not revealed his secret plans in Scripture, we have no way of discerning them. In fact, often God's providence in the world is not apparent to us except by the clear promises in his Word. So we are directed to seek out God's will only in that which he has revealed—"in the law and the gospel."

Though hidden in past ages, God's secret purpose in Christ has been revealed in these last days. This knowledge is sufficient to ground our confidence in God's purpose, even if we cannot discern his hand in our daily circumstances. God's revealed will in his Word is clear. "Yet his wonderful method of governing the universe is rightly called an abyss, because while it is hidden from us, we ought reverently to adore it."[39] Just as we can know God only according to his works, not in his hidden essence, we can know God's will only insofar as he has published it.

We must never forget that the place where the triumph of evil seemed so obvious and God's saving care seemed most hidden was at the cross.[40] God's sovereign rule over nature and history in general cannot be separated from his *saving* purpose. Just as we find God in the "low places" of this world—lying in a dirty feeding trough in Bethlehem, wearily treading the road to Jerusalem, and crying out in dereliction on the cross— we trust that he is most present in our lives precisely where he seems most hidden.

That God has decreed all that comes to pass is not in question, but we lack any promise that we can access this information through proper formulas. In fact, the latter approach is characteristic of superstition rather than of Christian piety. Romans 12:2 promises that "by testing you may discern what is the will of God, what is good and acceptable and perfect." On this basis, some have taught that God has a sovereign plan for our lives, but that we can step in and out of it. Often referred to as God's "perfect will," this notion of God's sovereign plan considers it merely a Plan A—God's best for our lives—rather than God's secret but certain decree. Many believers struggle to discern God's secret will in daily decisions because they confuse it with his "perfect will" in this passage.

However, Romans 12:2 is not speaking of God's eternal counsels, sure to be fulfilled yet hidden to us. Rather, the context (renewing the mind through the Word) indicates that the perfect will that Paul calls us to discern is God's moral and saving will (i.e., the law and the gospel) *insofar as he has revealed it in Scripture*. Therefore, when it comes to our vocations, whom we should marry, where we should live, and so forth, we are responsible to discern God's will only insofar as it is revealed in

---

37. Calvin, *Institutes* 1.18.4.
38. Ibid.

39. Ibid., 1.17.2.
40. Ibid., 3.8.1.

Scripture. For example, we must marry fellow believers (2Co 6:14), but other considerations are left to our wisdom, the counsel of friends, and the desires of our hearts.

Unlike God's good and perfect (revealed) will, God's hidden decree is secret to us. We have no reason to believe that God will reveal to us where we should live, even though he has "determined allotted periods and the boundaries of [our] dwelling place" (Ac 17:26). But we can be confident that he has revealed everything necessary for salvation and godliness. It is liberating to know that we cannot step in and out of God's sovereign will, although it remains hidden to us, even if we discover that a decision was poorly made or circumstances did not work out as we had planned. It is not only unexpected that we should know God's secret purposes; such inquisitiveness is treated in Scripture as an affront to God's majesty (Ro 11:34).

Many Christians assume that, far from a "deep abyss" inaccessible to us, the secrets of God's providence can be discerned by following certain formulas. Calvin rebukes the Stoics for their fatalism: "For he who has set the limits to our life has at the same time entrusted to us its care; he has provided means and helps to preserve it; he has also made us able to foresee dangers; that they may not overwhelm us unaware, he has offered precautions and remedies." We are therefore bound to use them.[41] God has planned our future and is active in bringing it to pass. "Meanwhile, nevertheless, a godly man will not overlook the secondary causes."[42] So confident is Calvin in the sufficiency of that which has been revealed that he can conclude, "And it would not even be useful for us to know what God himself ... willed to be hidden." In fact, recalling a retort reported by Augustine, he added, "When a certain shameless fellow mockingly asked a pious old man what God had done before the creation of the world, the latter aptly countered that he had been building hell for the curious."[43]

C. Common Grace/Special Grace

We have seen that in Roman Catholic theology, nature and grace are related as lower and higher, respectively — or, to change the analogy, dimmer and brighter. Consequently, Rome speaks of a "saving providence" through which non-Christians (even atheists) come to an implicit faith in God apart from the explicit knowledge of the gospel. However, in Scripture God's providence belongs to his common rather than saving grace, although the former ultimately serves the purposes of the latter as he gathers a bride for his Son. Common grace makes human society possible, but saving grace creates a church. In both his general care for all that he has made and his redeeming grace toward the elect, the Father rules in his Son and by his Spirit.

John Murray has justifiably concluded concerning the doctrine of common

---

41. Ibid., 1.17.4.
42. Ibid., 1.17.9.

43. Ibid., 1.14.1.

grace, "On this question Calvin not only opened a new vista but also a new era in theological formulation."[44] What later came to be called common grace was treated by Calvin under the heading of general providence. We naturally think of the Spirit's work in the lives of believers. This, of course, is understandable, given the sheer proportion of biblical passages. And yet we should not overlook the fact that the same Spirit who brooded over the waters in creation upholds all things, along with the Father and the Son, and is just as active in bestowing his gifts of physical life and health, intelligence, love, friendship, passion, vocation, family, culture, government, art, and science on non-Christians as he is in bestowing saving gifts on his people. The Spirit is sent not only to regenerate and indwell the saints but to enlighten and stir up the natural gifts of non-Christian artists, scientists, rulers, and parents to contribute to the common good.

The common grace/saving grace distinction is therefore related closely to those between direct and indirect causes and between God's revealed will and his hidden will. God's revealed will (in Scripture) concentrates on that which we could never have known otherwise, namely, the good news of salvation in Christ. While special revelation certainly provides important wisdom and new spectacles through which every aspect of our lives takes on a different hue, knowledge of God's Word is not necessary in order for one to be an artist, a physician, an autoworker, or even a parent. Yet, even in these instances, unbelievers are not autonomous, but depend on God's common grace, which he sheds on believer and unbeliever alike. From special revelation, however, we learn of God's saving grace—something that does not belong to the general fund of human knowledge, because it is neither innate nor capable of being acquired apart from someone telling us the gospel (Ro 10:14–17). Scripture reveals the mystery of salvation, hidden in past ages (1Co 2:6–10; Eph 3:3–6; Col 1:26).

As Murray points out, common grace is responsible for a variety of benefits to all people indiscriminately. *First, it is a restraint on sin.* Things may be bad because of the human heart and institutions in which sinful habits (including those of believers) become deeply embedded, but they are never as bad as they could be—because of God's common grace. *Second, God's common grace is a restraint on God's own wrath.* God placed his mark even on violent Cain, so that he could build a city (Ge 4:15). Because of his common grace, God was long-suffering in the face of human depravity "in the days of Noah" (1Pe 3:20). Furthermore, after the flood God covenants with humankind and even the nonhuman creation never to destroy the earth by water again. Although this grace overlaps with his concern for the salvation of his people, it was his common grace that led God to overlook the ignorance of humans before Christ (Ac 17:30), and that led him to suspend his judgment on the world for a long

---

44. John Murray, *The Collected Writings* (Edinburgh: Banner of Truth, 1978), 2:94.

period of time (Ro 2:4; 2Pe 3:9). *Third, common grace not only restrains his wrath (i.e., shows mercy) but positively gives (grace).* Murray observes that God motivates unbelievers as well "with interest and purpose to the practice of virtues, the pursuance of worthy tasks, and the cultivation of arts and sciences that occupy the time, activity, and energy of men and that make for the benefit and civilization of the human race. He ordains institutions for the protection and promotion of right, the preservation of liberty, the advance of knowledge, and the improvement of physical and moral conditions."[45] Scripture is replete with examples of God's providential goodness, particularly in the Psalms. "The LORD is good to all, and his mercy is over all that he has made.... You open your hand; you satisfy the desire of every living thing" (Ps 145:9, 16).

In the field of common endeavor ruled by God's creation and providence, there is no difference in principle between believers and unbelievers in terms of gifts and abilities. Jesus calls on his followers to pray for their enemies for precisely this reason: "for he makes his sun rise on the evil and on the good, and sends rain on the just and on the unjust" (Mt 5:45). Christians are called on to imitate this divine disposition. It is clear from the parable of the sower, in fact, that unbelievers may even benefit from the Spirit's work through the Word. It is undoubtedly true that, although much harm has been done in the name of Christendom, innumerable benefits have come to civilization as a result of biblical influences. But even pagan rulers exercise their dominion as a result of God's providence (Ro 13:1–7; 1Pe 2:14). Some non-Christians rescued slaves, while some Christians abused them.

Not only can unbelievers, under God's common grace, sustain their own goods, truths, and beauties, but they actually enrich the lives of believers as well. Against those "fanatics" who would forbid secular influences, Calvin pleads that when we disparage the truth, goodness, and beauty even of unbelievers, we are heaping contempt on the work of the Holy Spirit.[46] Even in its fallenness, the world—including humanity—reflects God's wisdom and goodness, truth and justice, beauty and love.

God secretly governs the nations just as he does his church, although he governs

---

45. Ibid., 2:294.
46. Note the following quote from Calvin, *Institutes* 2.2.15:

Whenever we come upon these matters in secular writers, let that admirable light of truth shining in them teach us that the mind of man, though fallen and perverted from its wholeness, is nevertheless clothed and ornamented with God's excellent gifts. If we regard the Spirit of God as the sole fountain of truth, we shall neither reject the truth itself nor despise it wherever it shall appear, unless we wish to dishonor the Spirit of God. For by holding the gifts of the Spirit in slight esteem, we contemn and reproach the Spirit himself. What then? Shall we deny that the truth shone upon the ancient jurists who established civic order and discipline with such great equity? Shall we say that the philosophers were blind in their fine observation and artful description of nature? Shall we say that those men were devoid of understanding who conceived the art of disputation and taught us to speak reasonably? Shall we say that they are insane who developed medicine, devoting their labor to our benefit? What shall we say of all the mathematical sciences? Shall we consider them the ravings of madmen? No, we cannot read the writings of the ancients on these subjects without great admiration.... But shall we count anything praiseworthy or noble without recognizing at the same time that it comes from God?... Those men whom Scripture calls "natural men" were, indeed, sharp and penetrating in their investigation of inferior things. Let us, accordingly, learn by their example how many gifts the Lord left to human nature even after it was despoiled of its true good.

the former through natural law and common grace and the latter through his Word written and preached. Calvin considers it erroneous to believe, for example, that a government must be framed according to "the political system of Moses"; rather, it is to be "ruled by the common laws of nations."[47] Natural law—the law of God written upon the conscience of every person—allows for a marvelous "diversity" in constitutions, forms of government, and laws.[48] The Mosaic theocracy was limited to the old covenant and is no longer the blueprint for nation-states.[49] The diversity that we recognize in creation is also evident in God's manner of preserving the world and causing it to flourish even in its fallen condition.

To be sure, we must not confuse common grace with God's special or saving grace. Common grace upholds fallen humanity in the sphere of creation but not redemption. Common grace does not save evildoers, nor does it redeem art, culture, the state, or families. The covenant that God pledged to Noah after the flood was made "with every living creature"—animals and human beings alike—to preserve the ordinary succession of seasons. Nevertheless, this covenant included no saving promise. It was a common grace pledge. Unlike saving grace, common grace is limited to this world before the last judgment and will not stay the hand of justice on that dreadful day. But this does not mean that saving grace is at odds with common grace. Murray writes, "Special grace does not annihilate but rather brings its redemptive, regenerative, and sanctifying influence to bear on every natural or common gift; it transforms all activities and departments of life; it brings every good gift into the service of the kingdom of God. Christianity is not a flight from nature; it is the renewal and sanctification of nature." This approach has always challenged ascetic versions of spirituality. "And its practical outlook has been, 'For every creature of God is good, and nothing to be refused, if it be received with thanksgiving: for it is sanctified by the word of God and prayer' (1Ti 4:4–5)."[50]

To affirm common grace as Christians is to take this world seriously not only in all of its sinfulness but in all of its goodness as created and upheld by God. Not only in salvation, but in God's continued upholding of creation and its history, all things hold together in Christ (Col 1:15–17). Christ is therefore the mediator not only in salvation but in creation and providence. Believers are encouraged to participate in secular culture, to wisely enjoy relationships with unbelievers, and to work beside them in common vocations and toward common goals, without always having to justify such cooperation and common life in terms of ministry and outreach.

Even God's common grace ultimately serves the designs of his saving grace. The creation of the church by Christ's redeeming work was not an alternative plan after the original plan for humanity in creation was thwarted by sin. The mystery that

---

47. Ibid., 4.20.14, 16.
48. Ibid., 4.20.16.

49. Ibid.
50. Murray, *Collected Writings*, 2:295.

Paul proclaims as finally revealed but always intended before all ages is that God "created all things, so that through the church the manifold wisdom of God might now be made known to the rulers and authorities in the heavenly places. This was according to the eternal purpose that he has realized in Christ Jesus our Lord, in whom we have boldness and access with confidence through our faith in him" (Eph 3:9–12). God's electing purpose has always been "to bring all things in heaven and on earth together under one head, even Christ" (Eph 1:10 NIV).

D. PROVIDENCE/MIRACLE

Related to all of the preceding is the important distinction between providence and miracle. Unlike God's ordinary providence, his miraculous intervention involves a suspension or alteration of natural laws and processes in particular circumstances. Even in his miraculous activity God usually works through creaturely means, but he sanctifies them for extraordinary service. In reaction against naturalism, it is often asserted by Christians that God is in fact involved regularly in the course of their lives in the form of *miracles*. Starved for some practical sense of God's concern for their daily lives, many Christians flock to groups and individuals promising them a daily encounter with miracles. What is lost in the bargain is a sense of God's ordinary providence in and through creaturely means and natural processes that he has created and sustains.

Probably the most spectacular example of God's ordinary providence is the birth of a child. Yet why must we speak of "the miracle of childbirth" in order to acknowledge God as its ultimate source? The birth of a child is plainly not a miracle. It is an ordinary result of the right use of means, from conception to delivery. Nothing could be more natural. And yet nothing could be a more marvelous testimony to God's providence. Not only in the face of miracles but also in the wonder of God's meticulous design, order, and creativity reflected in the ordinary process of conception, gestation, and birth, we have far more in our lives to be thankful for each day:

> For you formed my inward parts;
> you knitted me together in my mother's womb.
> I praise you, for I am fearfully and wonderfully made.
> Wonderful are your works;
> my soul knows it very well.
> My frame was not hidden from you,
> when I was being made in secret,
> intricately woven in the depths of the earth.
> Your eyes saw my unformed substance;
> in your book were written, every one of them,
> the days that were formed for me,
> when as yet there was none of them.

How precious to me are your thoughts, O God!
   How vast is the sum of them!" (Ps 139:13–17)

Not only when God intervenes extraordinarily, suspending his natural order, but in his design and faithfulness to that order, we have reason to give thanks. Not only when one's cancer mysteriously disappears, but when it is conquered through the countless layers of creaturely mediation, ultimately God is the healer.

It is God who created and preserves the restorative properties in the organic matter and the human beings who harvest them for medical purposes. It is God who endows the medical staff with intelligence, wisdom, and skill. It is God who, according to his wise counsels, ultimately directs the myriad tasks of lab technicians, transporters, manufacturers of medical instruments and products, all the way to the applied labors of doctors and nurses. When a burn heals, it is God who heals it through the natural processes with which he has richly endowed and so carefully attends it.

We frequently distinguish natural and supernatural causes, but this too may reflect the false choice of attributing circumstances either to God or to nature. The Scriptures know nothing of a creation or a history that is at a single moment independent of God's agency. The question is not *whether* God is involved in every aspect of our lives but *how* God is involved. *Therefore, with respect to providence, the question is never whether causes are exclusively natural or supernatural, but whether God's involvement in every moment is providential or miraculous.*

God's ordinary providence, therefore, is not a supernatural intervention, suspending or altering natural processes or human agency. The interventionist picture of providence is not really providence at all, but miracle. It looks like a strong view of God's active involvement in and sovereignty over the world, but it is in fact a much weaker view than the biblical portrait of a God who is active at all times in all things but through ordinary means.

On the interventionist view, God must tinker directly with the DNA of moths to make them more adaptable to a changing environment. It is assumed, according to this view, that to say that *God did something* means that *creatures did not* and that God's sole agency can be discerned by empirical observation, at least in its effects. However, this simply preserves the false choice between deism and occasionalism: either nothing or everything is miraculous. Here once more Calvin's insights are helpful. "Nothing is more natural than for spring to follow winter; summer, spring; and fall, summer—each in turn," he writes. "Yet in this series one sees such great and uneven diversity that it readily appears each year, month, and day is governed by a new, a special, providence of God."[51]

We have seen that God gifted the creation itself with its own propensities in the

---

51. Calvin, *Institutes* 1.16.2.

beginning—issuing the command, "Let the earth sprout ...!" as well as the fiat declaration, "Let there be ...!" "The earth brought forth vegetation," in all of its variety. "And God saw that it was good" (Ge 1:12). Like creation, providence should be understood as involving both extraordinary operations of direct divine action and ordinary direction of history through his secret superintendence.

There are innumerable practical effects of being able to distinguish these related themes without surrendering one or the other. God is Lord, whether in his secret counsel or in his revealed will, whether in his common grace or saving grace, whether in his direct and immediate activity in the world or through his indirect and mediate works, whether in miracle or providence.

It also makes a tremendous difference in our lives when we trust that the same God who wounds also heals. Because he holds all power, and nothing can befall us apart from his will, and he has pledged to us his saving will in Jesus Christ, we can seek relief from him with confidence. Furthermore, as Calvin notes, "The Son of God doth suffer not only with us, but also in us," bearing us up and provoking within us by his Spirit the cry "*Abba*, Father," even in our misery.[52] Following our Savior, we endure the cross in this life in order to reign with Christ in glory. Our ultimate security and prosperity are found only in Christ and will be fully realized only in glory.[53] God's ultimate purposes for our everlasting welfare are greater than "the sufferings of this present time" (Ro 8:18).

Besides offering comfort in affliction, the confession of God's providence also relieves us from standing in final judgment over those who have done us wrong. Joseph was able to show kindness to his brothers because, despite their treacherous motives, God's purpose in his calamity prevailed, turning evil to good. "To sum this up: when we are unjustly wounded by men, let us overlook their wickedness (which would but worsen our pain and sharpen our minds to revenge), remember to mount up to God, and learn to believe for certain that whatever our enemy has wickedly committed against us was permitted and sent by God's just dispensation."[54]

III. PROVIDENCE AND NATURAL REVELATION: THE MEANING OF HISTORY IN CHRIST

Monism, whether naturalistic or pantheistic, cannot account for diversity in history any more than in the natural world, Herman Bavinck observes.[55] "Are the individual men only thoroughfares for the idea, phenomena of the Universal Being,

---

52. John Calvin, *Commentary upon the Acts of the Apostles* (trans. Henry Beveridge; Grand Rapids: Baker, 1974), 2:297.
53. Calvin, *Institutes* 2.15.4.

54. Ibid., 1.17.8.
55. Herman Bavinck, *The Philosophy of Revelation* (Eugene, Ore.: Wipf & Stock, 2003), 121.

expressions of the folk-soul, waves of the ocean; or have they each a significance for eternity?"[56] The unity and triunity of God are the archetype of the unity and diversity that we find not only in nature but in history. In contrast to the Trinitarian theism of Christianity, "The unity of monism is a dead, stark, uniform unity, without life and its fullness."[57] In Christ, history finds its hidden unity even with all of its diversity:

> The special revelation which comes to us in Christ not only gives us the confirmation of certain suppositions, from which history proceeds and must proceed, but *itself gives us history*, the kernel and the true content of all history. Christianity is itself history; it makes history, is one of the principal factors of history, and is itself precisely what lifts history high above nature and natural processes. And that it says and proves by its own act; Christ came to this earth for a crisis; the content of history lies in a mighty struggle. Monism knows nothing about this.... It has only one model—earlier and later, lower and higher, less and more, not yet and already past. It knows no *pro* and *contra*, but thus it does despite to life, to the experience of every man, to the terribly tragic seriousness of history. Revelation is a confirmation and explanation of life when it says the essence of history lies in a mighty conflict between darkness and light, sin and grace, heaven and hell (emphasis added).[58]

Without its vertical (eschatological) dimension, our collective existence loses its meaning; without its horizontal (historical) dimension, it becomes assimilated to a gnostic flight of the soul beyond. However, through the gospel we discover the meaning of history within history itself, as God brings its otherwise indecipherable threads together. Take Christ out of the center, and the world's story "loses itself in a history of races and nations, of nature-and-culture peoples." "It becomes a chaos, without a center, and therefore without a circumference; without distribution and therefore without beginning or end; without principle and goal; a stream rolling down from the mountains, nothing more."[59]

We have seen that in modernity providence was hijacked for secular ambitions, while the postmodern reaction tends to deny any purpose, goal, or meaning for history. However, in a Christian understanding, says Bavinck, "The aim [of history in Christ] is not this or that special idea, not the idea of freedom, or of humanity, or of material well-being. But it is the fullness of the kingdom of God, which embraces heaven and earth, angels and men, mind and matter, cultus and culture, the specific and the generic; in a word, all in all."[60]

Ultimately, then, a Christian defense of providence must always return to Christ and his victory over sin and death. How do we know that God works all things together for our salvation, even in the midst of prevailing circumstances to the

---

56. Ibid., 126.
57. Ibid., 139.
58. Ibid., 140–41.

59. Ibid., 141.
60. Ibid.

contrary? Not because we *see* their resolution here and now or can grasp their resolution in our intellectual vision, but because we have *heard* God's promise. And this promise is already confirmed by the fact that at the moment of the greatest injustice, when God seemed to be most hidden and absent, God was most active and victorious.

Secured by his resurrection from the dead, Christ's promise to us today is that all of the kingdoms of the earth are under the sway of the Lord of life, who is preserving general history in order to bring about his saving purposes within it. When Christ returns, there will be a judgment, leading to the end of sin, death, evil, injustice, and suffering for God's elect. The Father will wipe away every tear of his children. Until that time, the same Spirit who regenerates his covenant people and forms his church is simultaneously at work restraining evil and giving gifts to all flesh for their preservation and flourishing.

> These all look to you,
> to give them their food in due season.
> When you give it to them, they gather it up;
> when you open your hand, they are filled with good things....
> When you send forth your Spirit, they are created,
> and you renew the face of the ground. (Ps 104:27–30)

DISCUSSION QUESTIONS

1. Discuss and evaluate some of the principal challenges in our contemporary culture to the doctrine of providence.
2. What is *concursus*? How does this idea help us to distinguish between direct and indirect causation in God's providential agency? And how does this relate to the occasionalist debate?
3. Discuss the distinction between God's revealed and hidden action in providence.
4. What is common grace and how is it distinguished from special (or saving) grace? What does God's common grace accomplish?
5. What is the difference between providence and miracle? If Christ is the center of creation, is he also the center of providence? How do we know this from Scripture?

Chapter Twelve

BEING HUMAN

Human identity can be discerned only by attending closely to the unfolding covenant drama in which human beings play a supporting role. Just as biblical faith does not speculate on the "whatness" of God's hidden essence but on the "whoness" (i.e., the character, actions, and purposes) revealed in the script, the same may be said of the way in which that faith describes humanity. After framing the discussion in the light of rival accounts, I will offer the outline of a covenantal anthropology.[1]

I. WHAT MAKES US HUMAN? THE STATE OF THE DEBATE

At various points I have contrasted the paradigm of *overcoming estrangement* with *the stranger we never meet*, charting a path toward *meeting a stranger* through the covenant of grace. These different paradigms hold as much for anthropology (our doctrine of humanity) as for theology proper (our doctrine of God). At the present moment, we are witnessing a seismic shift in Western anthropology from a view of the self as a stable, semidivine, spiritual entity that transcends the body, time, and change to the idea of the self as nothing more than a social construction and physical-chemical interactions. In practice, at least, the sovereignty and autonomy of the self govern both the Platonic and materialist accounts: neither is prepared to receive selfhood, humanity, and personhood from another—especially from God—as a gift and as a responsibility.

A. PLATONISM: THE DISTINGUISHING SPARK

The goal of rationalist speculation is to rise from appearances (what things are like) to pure essences (what things are in themselves)—the inner being of divinity

---

1. For greater elaboration, see chapter 4 of my book *Lord and Servant: A Covenant Christology* (Louisville: Westminster John Knox, 2006).

and humanness. In Greek mythology, Prometheus and his brother were given the task of creating the animals. When his brother—leader of the project—ran out of materials by the time they came to the creation of humans, Prometheus tricked Zeus by stealing fire from the sun and giving it to the first human beings. As it turned out, this was the noblest ingredient—an immortal soul—that separated humanity from its fellow creatures. For this theft, Zeus sentenced his junior deity to death. As with other ideas in our Western bloodstream, stories like this one were "demythologized" in the dogma of the immortality of the soul.

The Platonist ontology, summarized in chapter 2, has played a dominant role in philosophical and theological treatments of human personhood. In this perspective, the higher self—indeed, the real self—is the spirit/soul or mind. Even when this is interpreted in Christian categories (e.g., as the image of God rather than an eternal and immortal soul), the locus of our human personhood—that which distinguishes us from the animals—is often restricted to the soul.

Elaborating his own version of Neoplatonism in his *Enneads*, Plotinus (AD 205–270) posits a hierarchy of three divine realms: the One (eternal, absolute, transcendental), the *Nous* (ideas, concepts), and the World Soul (including individual souls, incorporeal and immortal). Below the realm of the Soul is nature, including the terrestrial bodies in which some souls are imprisoned. Individual souls emanate from the World-Soul, turned toward the unchanging, rational One. Thus the human person could be divided into three components in descending order: spirit, soul, and body. The Gnostics tried to blend Greek philosophy with Christianity, dividing humanity into three classes: the *pneumatikoi* ("spirituals"), the *psychikoi* ("soulish"), and the *sarkikoi* ("fleshly").[2] Although a minority view in orthodox circles, this anthropology, known as trichotomy, has been a perennial temptation among various Christian sects.[3]

Trichotomists often appeal to two principal passages—Luke 10:27, where Jesus reiterates the command to love God with all of our heart (*kardia*) and soul (*psychē*) and strength (*ischys*) and mind (*dianoia*), and Hebrews 4:12, where the Word of God is said to divide even "soul and ... spirit." With respect to Luke 10:27, as Robert Reymond points out, Matthew's version (22:37) omits "strength," while Mark includes but reverses Luke's order in Mark 12:30 and in verse 33 mentions loving God with all our heart *and understanding* (*syneseōs*). Reymond responds, "Surely

---

2. See Hans Jonas, *The Gnostic Religion* (Boston: Beacon, 1958); Kurt Rudolph, *Gnosis: The Nature and History of Gnosticism* (San Francisco: Harper & Row, 1983); Dan Merkur, *Gnosis: An Esoteric Tradition of Mystical Visions and Unions* (Albany: SUNY Press, 1993); Edwin M. Yamauchi, "The Descent of Ishtar, the Fall of Sophia, and the Jewish Roots of Gnosticism," *Tyndale Bulletin* 29 (1978): 143–75; Ugo Bianchi, ed., *Selected Essays on Gnosticism, Dualism, and Mysteriosophy* (Leiden: Brill, 1978).

3. In recent times this view has been defended by C. I. Scofield in the *Scofield Reference Bible* (New York: Oxford Univ. Press, 1909), note 1 on 1 Thessalonians 5:23; Watchman Nee, *The Spiritual Man* (3 vols.; New York: Christian Fellowship, 1968); Lewis Sperry Chafer, *He That Is Spiritual* (Grand Rapids: Zondervan, 1967).

no one would insist, on the basis of these series of words connected by 'and,' that each of these words refers to an immaterial, ontologically distinct entity, and that therefore Luke was a quintchotomist, Matthew was a quadchotomist, and Mark was a sexchotomist."[4] In all of these cases, we meet parallelism, that is, a common (especially Hebraic) way of reinforcing a point with different terms.[5] These passages command us to love God with our whole being.

Hebrews 4:12 does not say that the Word divides *between* soul and spirit but that it divides *even* soul and spirit. "Dividing" in this context is examining, judging, "discerning the thoughts and intentions of the heart." It is not a cutting *between* but a cutting *through* that is intended here. The writer's point is that this searching and convicting Word is able to cut into (divide) even the secret recesses of the heart (synonymous with soul/spirit). Reymond notes, "The verse no more intends this [division between soul and spirit] than it intends, when it goes on to say that the Word is the judge of thoughts and of intents of the heart (again, two genitives governed by the noun 'judge'), that thoughts and intents are ontologically distinct things."[6]

I noted in chapter 1 how Descartes transposed Greek dualism's ascent of mind into a distinctly modern key. For him, the true self is a disembodied "thinking thing" (*res cogitans*; see "The Sovereign Self," pp. 57–58). Thus, by turning inward, away from the world of history and other creatures—including his own embodiment—Descartes simultaneously narrows the concept of the self to the mind (or soul) without relations and deepens its pretension to sovereign autonomy. Charles Taylor documents the passage of modernity from a sense of the self (personhood) defined by a complex web of relations to ever-narrower, autonomous, and individualistic concepts—a sense of the self abstracted from the world.[7]

B. A Lucky Animal: Materialist Anthropologies

If all that is real is spiritual for Platonism and idealism, the opposite form of monism is *materialism*. Far from a post-Enlightenment innovation, materialistic monism has a long history in Western thought. In fact, its basic premises were argued by ancient Indian philosophers (around 600 BC) at the same time that Thales, Anaxagoras, Democritus, and Epicurus were defending it in Greece. It was championed in the modern era by Pierre Gassendi, Thomas Hobbes, Karl Marx, and Sigmund Freud and still attracts a committed following in the sciences today.

With respect to human identity (anthropology), materialistic monism assumes that there is no such entity as a soul and therefore no continued existence after

---

4. Robert Reymond, *A New Systematic Theology of the Christian Faith* (Nashville: Nelson, 1988), 420.

5. The same point can be made concerning 1Th 5:23.

6. Reymond, *A New Systematic Theology*, 422.

7. Charles Taylor, *Sources of the Self: The Making of the Modern Identity* (Cambridge, Mass.: Harvard Univ. Press, 1992).

death. There is no supernatural origin or transcendent goal for our lives. The world is not a gift but a given—or a formless void that each person must summon into being by an act of will. Considered biologically, in this view, our own existence is the product of time plus chance. Like the rest of the animals, human beings originated in a string of random (and statistically improbable) accidents; they were born in a cradle of violence that drives the evolutionary process: namely, the survival of the fittest. Michel Foucault captured the sense of this consummation of Nietzsche's materialistic atheism when he observed that the "death of God" necessarily entails the "death of the self." "Man," he wrote, is about to be "erased like a face drawn in the sand at the edge of the sea."[8] Humanness is not a stable quality, according to Nietzsche and his heirs, because it is not a gift of God but is a power of sovereign willing that must be exercised and through which the genius becomes a master.

Philosophical defenses of materialism seem increasingly substantiated by science. Over recent decades of advanced research in neurobiology and related fields, the fact that the mind *is* matter (i.e., the brain) has become firmly established. Many mental pathologies attributed to demons or given spiritual and moral explanations are now diagnosed as chemical imbalances and are treated effectively with medicine. Descartes' thought experiment, imagining that his pure essence was mind floating above his bodily apparatus, is no longer tenable. Impulses and characteristics formerly attributed to a mysterious soul are now seen to be explicable in terms of physical-chemical reactions and interactions in the brain and the human senses. Just as Pierre-Simon Laplace did not need the "God hypothesis" for his scientific explanations, many scientists today conclude that besides a lack of empirical evidence for the soul, there is simply no need for positing a "ghost in a machine."

Many liberal Protestant and Jewish thinkers have argued that the Old Testament is largely silent on the question of a soul and overwhelmingly presupposes that physical death is the end of one's personal existence. Of course, it was sharp disagreement over this question that divided the Pharisees and Sadducees in Jesus' day. However, the heirs of the latter party in the modern era have claimed that the Pharisees invented the idea, probably because of Greek influences. Recent scholarship has challenged this view, demonstrating the antiquity of Jewish belief in the soul's survival of bodily death and the hope of resurrection.[9] Furthermore, if Jewish belief in bodily resurrection is to be attributed to foreign influences, Greek thought is the

---

8. Michel Foucault, *The Order of Things: An Archaeology of the Human Sciences* (New York: Random House, 1970), 387. Contrary to stereotypical descriptions frequently offered by popularizers of postmodernity, modernity was never wholly individualistic (Spinoza, Hegel, Fichte, Schopenhauer, Marx, Freud). Furthermore, postmodernity celebrates atomistic individualism as often as communitarianism. In both modernity and postmodernity are many mansions.

9. See especially Jon Levenson, *Resurrection and the Restoration of Israel: The Ultimate Victory of the God of Life* (New Haven, Conn.: Yale Univ. Press, 2006).

most unlikely candidate. After all, in Greek philosophy the immortal soul longs for its release from the bodily prison-house at death, not its everlasting "incarceration."

Some Christians, especially in reaction against Greek dualism, advocate a *modified monism*, which emphasizes the psychosomatic unity of human beings. Advocates of this view are usually agnostic about whether the soul exists separately from the body at death until the final resurrection.[10]

C. DISTINCTION WITHOUT DUALISM

A biblical anthropology has nothing to lose—in fact, everything to gain—from the dissolution of ancient and modern mind-body dualism. Nowhere in the Bible is the soul identified with the mind. More often, in fact, it is identified with the heart or even the bowels, in a self-consciously figurative manner: the way an English-speaker today might speak of knowing something in his or her "gut."

Nevertheless, Scripture does presuppose and explicitly teaches a distinction between the body and the soul—the view known as dichotomy—especially in its affirmation of the soul's living presence before God at bodily death.[11] However, it will become obvious in the account I offer below that this view in no way entails, much less requires, a radical anthropological dualism. In that light, I would prefer a term such as *psychosomatic holism*, since *dichotomy* implies that the distinction between soul and body is more basic than its unity.[12] The important point is that human nature is not to be identified exclusively or even primarily with the soul; the "real self" is the whole self—body and soul.

The distinction between soul and body is validated not by any speculation concerning essences but on the basis of the economy of grace, in which believers are promised that their souls will not share in their bodily death. Beyond this, we

---

10. This is the view of G. C. Berkouwer. The strong criticism of dualism within the Reformed tradition can sometimes lead to an overreaction in this direction. The same tendency may be seen in Herman Ridderbos, *Paul: An Outline of His Theology* (trans. John R. de Witt (Grand Rapids: Eerdmans, 1975), 497–508, 548–50. More recently, some Christians working at the intersection of science and theology have developed a variation of modified monism known as "non-reductive physicalism," so called because it still acknowledges certain attributes and actions that transcend material substances. See Nancey Murphy, "Non-reductive Physicalism: Philosophical Issues," in *Whatever Happened to the Soul?* (ed. Warren Brown Murphy and H. Newton Maloney; Minneapolis: Fortress, 1998); see also her more recent, revised version of this essay in Richard Lints, Michael Horton, and Mark Talbot, eds., *Human Identity in Theological Perspective* (Grand Rapids: Eerdmans, 2006), 95–117.

11. This is probably the dominant view in evangelical theology today. See, for example, Wayne Grudem, *Systematic Theology* (Grand Rapids: Zondervan, 1994), 472–83, particularly for

his exegetical summary of the dichotomist position and interaction with trichotomy and monism. Affirming the existence of the soul, distinct from the body, traditional Christian theologies have speculated as to whether the soul passed down from our first parents through the entire human race (traducianism) or is immediately created in each instance by God (creationism). *Traducianism* maintains that individual souls are transmitted from the parents to their offspring, in a way similar to the inheritance of physical traits. *Creationism* holds that each soul is a new creation of God. Although creationism is the dominant view at least in the West, traducianism has had notable defenders, including Tertullian, Augustine, and Gregory of Nyssa. These are interesting questions with valuable theological implications but are unlikely to be settled conclusively on exegetical grounds.

12. I find John W. Cooper's position in *Body, Soul, and Life Everlasting: Biblical Anthropology and the Monism-Dualism Debate* (Grand Rapids: Eerdmans, 1989) to be the most satisfying account of biblical anthropology on these points.

should not speculate about the human essence any more than about the divine essence.

Criticism of dualism in general and soul-body dualism in particular is a recurring motif in Reformed theology up to the present day.[13] On this point, the Reformers conflicted sharply with the medieval church, but even more with the Anabaptists. In fact, contemporary Anabaptist theologian Thomas N. Finger acknowledges, "Historic Anabaptists, however, often overplayed Spirit and downgraded matter. I attribute this largely to the (conceptual) ontological barrier that prevented the two from interacting."[14] Early Anabaptists taught that the believer must strive perpetually to rise above the bodily realm and its senses in order for the soul to return to its participation in divinity. "Total personal renewal, where 'all creaturely desires are rooted out and smashed,'" was a significant theme in such preaching, Finger observes.[15] Grace was chiefly seen as a divine substance elevating the believer from creaturely reality to the realm of Spirit. "This grace divinized people so fully that they passed beyond 'the creaturely.'"[16] From a Reformation perspective, these views represented a radical version of medieval mysticism and its dualism more generally, issuing in a theology of glory—the myth of the soul's ascent.

Scripture addresses human beings in their wholeness as persons responsible before him rather than simply as mind, soul, or spirit. Nevertheless, some theologians (like G. C. Berkouwer) have gone so far in affirming the unity of the human person that they place in question the existence of the soul apart from the body in the intermediate state.[17] Earlier Reformed theologians were more judicious in this matter. "As flesh and spirit (taken physically) are *disparates, not contraries,*" explains Francis Turretin, "so also are the appetites, inclinations, and habits of both in themselves. The repugnancy now found in them arises accidentally from sin" (emphasis added).[18]

Platonism sees *embodiment* as a curse, while biblical faith understands *disembodiment* to be a curse. In the biblical understanding, spiritual rebellion, not the body, was responsible for the fall. We are not saved from our bodies, but with them,

---

13. Following Abraham Kuyper and Herman Bavinck, G. C. Berkouwer explicitly defends a relational view of humanity over against abstract consideration of the nature or being of humanity as identified with the soul, heart, mind, or other faculties. See his *Man: The Image of God* (Grand Rapids: Eerdmans, 1962), 194–233. See also Anthony A. Hoekema, *Created in God's Image* (Grand Rapids: Eerdmans, 1986), 203–26.

14. Thomas N. Finger, *A Contemporary Anabaptist Theology: Biblical, Historical, Constructive* (Downers Grove, Ill.: InterVarsity Press, 2004), 563.

15. Ibid., 474. On the same page Finger cites the verdict of recent Anabaptist historian Werner Packull that such views represented a Pelagian or semi-Pelagian assumption.

16. Ibid., 475, referring to Leonhard Scheimer.

17. Berkouwer, *Man: The Image of God*, 194–233.

18. Turretin, *Elenctic Theology*, 1:468. This echoes the Italian Reformer Peter Martyr Vermigli (1500–1562): On the basis of Genesis 9:4, he argues that "the blood is the soul." This represents a metonymy: "Since the blood is a sign of the soul's presence, it may be called the soul itself.... I do not offer this as if I accept it as the reason why God gave that commandment [against eating the blood of animals], but to indicate the communion of man's soul with the body" (*The Peter Martyr Library: Philosophical Works* [ed. Joseph C. McLelland; Kirksville, Mo.: Thomas Jefferson Univ. Press, 1996], 4:42).

in the general resurrection of the dead. Prior to this resurrection, God brings to himself the souls of those who die in Christ, while the body decomposes in the earth, until finally he reconstitutes the psychosomatic unity of the human self in the glory of the resurrection. Jesus promised the believing thief on the cross that he would be present with him in Paradise upon his death (Lk 23:43), and Paul clearly teaches that upon their death believers are present with the Lord in heaven as they await the resurrection of the last day (2Co 5:1–10; Php 1:21–24). While the body and soul *can* be separated, they are not *meant* to be separated, and our salvation is not complete until we are bodily raised as whole persons (Ro 8:23). The intermediate state is not the final state. John Murray summarizes this consensus: "Man is bodily, and, therefore, the scriptural way of expressing this truth is not that man has a body but that man *is* body.... Scripture does not represent the soul or spirit of man as created first and then put into a body ... The bodily is not an appendage."[19]

CONTRASTING ANTHROPOLOGIES	
Trichotomy	Human beings are composed of spirit/mind, soul, and body (in descending rank).
Dichotomy	Human beings are composed of soul (synonymous with spirit or mind) and body.
Monism	Human beings are physical organisms; the characteristics traditionally associated with the soul or mind are attributable to chemical and neurological processes and interactions.

II. THE SELF AS SERVANT: WHAT IS THE "IMAGE OF GOD"?

The origins of creation cannot properly be understood apart from their eschatological aim. If we understand creation (including ourselves) only in terms of an origin (protology) rather than also as a destiny (eschatology), we will miss the crucial point that creation — including humanity — is in an important sense unfinished.[20] Strikingly, Descartes arrived at his concept of the autonomous *res cogitans* (thinking thing) by abstracting himself from the world and his mind from his body in contemplative solitude, while the biblical concept of the self emerged in constant interaction with God and fellow creatures in a particular history of a covenantal relatedness. A. N. Whitehead's famous quip, "Religion is what the individual does

---

19. John Murray, *The Collected Writings of John Murray* (Edinburgh: Banner of Truth, 1977), 2:14.

20. This point, highlighted especially in Reformed biblical theology (Vos, Ridderbos, and others), is a major topic in the theology of the Christian East. See Douglas Knight, *The Theology of John Zizioulas* (London: Ashgate, 2007).

with his own solitariness," is far removed from any view of the self as oriented covenantally.[21]

In contrast to pagan dualism and materialism, the covenantal paradigm ("meeting a stranger") affirms that human persons are intrinsically related to God while denying that there is any divine part or faculty (including the soul or mind). Rather, the meeting place between God and humanity is a *covenant*. This covenantal relationship is not something added to human nature but is essential to it.

Whereas materialism locates human origins in primordial violence in the apparently meaningless lust for survival, and ontological dualism locates human origins in a primordial falling away from being because of embodiment, the Bible locates human origins in peace, love, and justice—with difference as the prerequisite rather than the obstacle to covenantal relationships. To exist as human beings is not to be "thinking things," disembodied and unrelated egos, but is already to be enmeshed in a web of relationships. In spite of its pretensions, modernity does not represent a radical break from the past and its inherited assumptions.[22] The self of modern rationalism is a sovereign knower; for idealism, a sovereign moral legislator and constructor of reality; for empiricism, a sovereign perceiver; for romanticism, a sovereign feeler; for pragmatism, a sovereign chooser. Yet what unites all of these versions of modern personhood is what Charles Taylor calls *disengagement*—the tendency of modern anthropology not only toward individualism but toward a sense of selfhood that is inward and independent not only of God but of the world in which it lives. This trajectory toward the disengaged self surely begins already in the Platonic myth of the divine and immortal soul striving to ascend above its imprisonment in the realm of appearances.

By contrast, the Bible places human beings in a dramatic narrative that defines their existence as inherently covenantal—fully engaged with God, with each other, and with the nonhuman creation. Instead of drawing us deeper within ourselves, a covenantal anthropology draws us outward, where we find ourselves responsible to God and our neighbors. Since we were summoned into being by the powerful Word of the covenant Lord, this covenantal relationality is essential to our being human. There are not first autonomous individuals who then may (or may not) enter into covenantal relations. From the moment of conception, each of us is already a participant in the web of human histories, relationships, genetics, and nurture that condition our personal identity. In the biblical scheme, this network of covenantal relationships extends to the nonhuman creation as well. As God's viceroy, human beings are placed in a position of responsibility within a creation of which they themselves are members in soul as well as body. It was Adam's calling to lead the

---

21. A. N. Whitehead, *Religion in the Making* (New York: Meridian, 1960), 16.

22. Again I refer readers to Charles Taylor's *Sources of the Self* (cited above) for a thorough account.

whole creation into God's everlasting *shalom*, signified and sealed by the Tree of Life. Only with the Bible does there arise a genuine eschatology that orients human existence toward the future—toward a goal to be realized within history yet from the powers that lie beyond it.

Locating the connection with God somewhere *within* the self (i.e., the soul), silently reflecting the upper world, rather than *in between* the whole self and God (i.e., in a covenant), mediated by God's Word, Christian Platonism could never really do justice to the biblical emphasis on the notion of the human person as a psychosomatic unity related ecstatically to God and the rest of creation.[23] Wilhelm Dilthey correctly discerned that in the empiricism and idealism of the Enlightenment period, "no real blood flows in the veins of the knowing subject constructed by Locke, Hume, and Kant."[24]

Having briefly summarized the state of the debate, we turn our attention to the biblical motifs of covenant and eschatology in order to decipher an anthropology that accords with "meeting a stranger." The image of God (*imago dei*) is not something *in* us that is semidivine but something *between* us and God that constitutes a covenantal relationship. To put it differently, it is not because of our soul (or intellect) that we are ranked higher than our fellow creatures, but because we have been created—in the wholeness of our psychosomatic identity—with a special commission, for a special relationship with God.

A. ORIGINS AND ESCHATOLOGY: THE PARADE OF THE CREATURE-KINGS

Instead of allowing Genesis 1 and 2 to tell their own story and perform their own intended operation, many interpreters (both liberal and conservative) have come to the text with modern questions that are alien to the text. The point of these narratives is not to provide a scientific description of natural origins. There are parallels between ancient Babylonian myths and modern nihilism—particularly, the assumption that what the Bible identifies as evil is not an alien intrusion (a corruption of the good by creaturely disobedience), but intrinsic to nature. However, the historical context in which these narratives were written is that of the ancient pagan myths rather than modern naturalism.

It will not surprise those who have read thus far that I take the days of creation to be *analogical*. That is, they are not literal twenty-four-hour periods, but God's accommodation to the ordinary pattern of six days of labor and a seventh day of rest, which he created for humankind. Eschatology is the principal motive: under-

---

23. Augustine should not bear the entire burden, since the identification of the *imago* with the intellect within a basically Platonic scheme was the common inheritance of patristic thought (cf. Gregory of Nyssa, in *NPNF2*, 5:390–442).

24. Wilhelm Dilthey, *Introduction to the Human Sciences* (Princeton, N.J.: Princeton Univ. Press, 1991), xviii.

scoring the fact that human beings were created as God's analogy, imitating his pattern of trial (work-week) and successful completion (Sabbath). Genesis 2:4 recapitulates the creation account in chapter 1, "in the day that the LORD God made the earth and the heavens" — "day" being the same Hebrew word (*yom*) used earlier for the six days. The point of these two chapters is to establish the historical prologue for God's covenant with humanity in Adam, leading through the fall and moral chaos of Cain to the godly line of Seth that leads to the patriarchs.

Drawing on important features of covenant theology, Meredith Kline has written extensively on the remarkable strategy employed in the two creation narratives of Genesis 1 and 2. If these chapters are not intended as a scientific report, it is just as true that they are not mythological. Rather, they are part of a polemic of "Yahweh versus the Idols" that forms the historical prologue for God's covenant with Israel. Kline observes that "these chapters pillage the pagan cosmogonic myth — the slaying of the dragon by the hero-god, followed by celebration of his glory in a royal residence built as a sequel to his victory."[25] As usual, God is not borrowing from but subversively renarrating the pagan myths, exploiting their symbols for his own revelation of actual historical events.

> God sets forth his creative acts within the pictorial framework of a Sabbath-crowned week and by this sabbatical pattern he identifies himself as Omega, the One for whom all things are and were created, the Lord worthy to receive glory and honor and praise (cf. Rev 4:11).
>
> It is the seventh day of the creation week, the climactic Sabbath to which the course of creative events moves, that gives to the pattern of the week of days as a whole its distinctive sabbatical character, and it is then in the unfolding of the significance of the Sabbath day that the disclosure of the Omega name of God will be found.[26]

The creation week itself establishes a point of departure and a destination, already giving birth to the very notion of history that is essential to human identity.

Kline supports his interpretation by appealing to the internal structure of the two narratives, focusing as they do on the appointment of the various vassal-kings to rule the spheres placed under their charge:

> Within the first three day-frames is described the origin of three vast spheres over which rule is to be exercised....
>
> The fourth day-frame depicts the creation of the sun and moon and their royal appointment "to rule over" the day and night, the realms described in the parallel first day-frame. Their rule is expressed in their defining of the boundaries of their realm, as they "separate" the light and darkness (Ge 1:16–18). Then the fish and

25. Meredith G. Kline, *Kingdom Prologue* (South Hamilton, Mass.: Gordon Conwell Theological Seminary, 1989), 1:26–31.

Particularly in view here is the Babylonian Gilgamesh epic.
26. Ibid., 1:26–27.

the birds of day five, the lords of the waters below and the sky above, the realms of the parallel second day-frame, are given the blessing-commission to enter into possession of their domains to their utmost limits. The terms that describe their commission—to be fruitful, to multiply and fill (Ge 1:22)—anticipate the royal mandate that was to be given to man. The sixth day-frame introduces those who are to rule over the dry land of the parallel third day: land animals and man. The lordly beasts are authorized to serve themselves of the natural tributary produce of their land-realm (Ge 1:30), a prerogative they share with man (Ge 1:29).[27]

The account evokes the image of the opening ceremony of the modern Olympics, with each ruler passing the reviewing stand bearing the standard of its creaturely realm before the Great King in joyful approval. The structure of Genesis 1 is explicit on this point, broken down into seven sections with each introduced by the phrase, "And God said..."

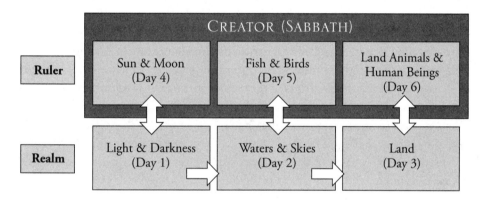

Kline adds,

Even during the pageant of the creature-kings in the narrative of days four through six, their royal splendor is paled by the surpassing glory of the Creator-King who commands them into existence, identifies them in his fiat-naming of them, and invests them with their subordinate dominions. And then when the creation apocalypse has reached the vicegerency of the God-like creature-king of the sixth day, and moves beyond it, we observe the glory of all the creature-kingdoms of all six days being carried along as a tributary offering within the gates of the Sabbath day to be laid at the feet of the Creator-King, now beheld in the brilliance of his epiphany as Sabbath Lord.[28]

So these opening chapters of the Bible do indeed address the question of human origins and history, but with theological interest: "Man is king over creation, but he

---

27. Ibid., 1:26–27. 28. Ibid., 28–29.

is a vassal-king, he reigns as one under the Creator's authority, obligated to devote his kingdom to the Great King."[29]

Kline's interpretation of Genesis 1 can be supported by reference to the covenantal ceremonies instituted during the exodus leading to the typological land of Sabbath-rest, for that exodus and those ceremonies echo this original march through the waters on dry land. The story of Israel's royal march through the sea to Zion on dry land is told in terms that echo the creation narrative explicitly. Throughout the Psalter, especially in Psalms 24; 66; 68; 95–99, the original creation, the exodus conquest, and the new creation converge on Zion and the holy sanctuary where the conquering human vassal enters with his tribute to lay before the Great King.

This interpretation represents a powerful polemic against the idols of the nations that Israel must confront. It is the historical prologue that justifies God's sovereignty not only over Israel but over the whole earth. It also exhibits the unmistakably covenantal character of creation itself even prior to his relationship with Israel. Adam forfeited his destiny of leading creation into the consummated form of its natural existence. Creation is presently filled with strife and sin, not because of an ontological fall from being but because of a historical fall from covenantal obedience. Only with the Last Adam do we see the firstfruits of the consummation. This consummation is not yet fully realized for us. "But we see him who for a little while was made lower than the angels, namely Jesus, crowned with glory and honor because of the suffering of death, so that by the grace of God he might taste death for everyone" (Heb 2:9). We come to a proper understanding of the nature of creation only when we recognize its end as well as its origin, and Jesus Christ as the single person who brings them together.

Therefore, the covenantal relationship is not something added later but is intrinsic to our creation in God's image. A legal command to love God and neighbor and to subdue any ethical threat to this reign of God, this original covenant is indelibly written on the human conscience. All people retain some sense of God as their lawgiver and judge and of the obligation to love. It is not that this religious and moral sense is lost in the fall, but it has been gravely distorted and depraved. Although we invest tremendous industry, creativity, and ingenuity in suppressing our identity as God's image-bearers, the covenantal relationship between God and human beings is ineradicable. We may scratch ourselves raw trying to eliminate the evidence of this relationship and its attendant obligations. We may spend our savings on makeovers and personal programs that promise us self-improvement without having to acknowledge accountability (and therefore guilt) before a transcendent judge.

Soon after the fall itself, the human race was divided between Cain's proud city (Ge 4:17–24) and the City of God represented by Seth. While Cain's descendants are singled out for their cultural accomplishments, we read of Seth and his line, "At

---

29. Ibid., 30.

that time people began to call upon the name of the LORD" (v. 26). It is not, therefore, that unbelievers are no longer related to God. (Recall Cain's own acknowledgment that God's judgment would make him prey for every vigilante and God's commitment to preserve Cain's life for the building of the earthly city.) We are all covenant servants, whether as heirs of promise who call on the LORD's name or as rebels without a cause. God's Word of law brought us into being as covenant servants in creation, and this is why God's universal judgment is just (Romans 1–3). However faint, the sense of belonging to a covenant of creation is natural, a *verbum internum* (internal word) that rings in and yet is not identical to the conscience. It is this status as a commissioned servant of Yahweh, created in his image, which renders every person both dignified and accountable.

The fall could not eradicate the covenantal relationship between God and humanity; but now, after the covenant curses, humanity is divided between Cain's proud city (Ge 4:17–24) and the city of God represented by Seth. Though upheld by God's common grace, those who do not call on the name of Yahweh for salvation remain "in Adam," under the reign of condemnation and death according to the original covenant of works. So every human being is born into this world as an image-bearer of God, installed into an office that, from conception, one holds as a traitor. The stipulations and sanctions of that original covenant (i.e., natural law) ring in the conscience of every human being (Romans 1–3). Thus, the law is a natural and internal voice, distinct from the gospel as a supernatural and externally revealed announcement. Because every person is created in God's image, he or she is a dignified bearer of rights and a responsible moral agent, accountable before God for his or her response to his command. This is why human rights do not derive from the authority of the individual, the majority, or the state, but from God alone.

Ultimately, in a covenantal scheme, responsibilities are more basic than rights, since it is God's claim on us rather than our claims for and against each other that is most basic.[30] It is not simply that my neighbor has a natural right to be left unmolested but that I have a responsibility to do everything in my power to love and respect God's image-bearers. This positive obligation is the real intention of the law, as the Reformed and Lutheran catechisms underscore in treating the second table of the Decalogue.

The apostle Paul explains, "Now we know that whatever the law says," whether written on the conscience or on tablets, "it speaks to those who are under the law, so that every mouth may be stopped, and the whole world may be held accountable to God" (Ro 3:19). The law commands and threatens, but it cannot empower us

---

30. This covenantal view of personhood represents an important area of convergence between Jewish and Christian theologies, as can be seen especially in David Novak, *Covenantal Rights: A Study in Jewish Political Theory* (Princeton, N.J.: Princeton Univ. Press, 2000).

to fulfill its demands or deliver anyone from its sentence (v. 20). By contrast, the gospel is a strange—utterly foreign—announcement of God's saving grace in Jesus Christ. By nature, we understand "law-talk," but "gospel-talk" is a foreign tongue whose basics we must learn and relearn throughout our life. The gospel announces a free decision on God's part in view of the fall and can only be known by a *verbum externum* (external Word), an astounding proclamation that in Christ the righteous Judge of all the earth has redeemed and reconciled us to himself as his own adopted heirs (vv. 21–26). Believers therefore live not only as responsible, accountable, and guilty creatures of God's word of law, but as free, justified, and renewed hearers of God's Good News. As Paul points out in the opening chapters of Romans, this original revelation of our legal accountability before God continues to speak. This fact explains why there are still remnants of human justice in the world and why everyone is accountable for suppressing its ultimate claims when they lead unmistakably to the judgment of a personal God.

The notions of covenant and eschatology are intertwined in biblical theology. Both are oriented toward promise and fulfillment. This promise-fulfillment pattern does not begin after the fall but with creation itself. Human identity was not finished at creation but was to be perfected by fulfilling the trial of the original covenant, winning the right to eat from the tree of everlasting life and blessedness. Hence, human beings are intrinsically future oriented. Though perverted by sin, this eschatological hope—a sense of a destiny to be fulfilled in history—animates human activity and ambition. Thus, even the commission given to Adam to lead creation in triumphant procession into God's Sabbath rest (following God's own pattern of creating and enthronement) is a historical movement from promise to fulfillment rather than an ascent of mind.

This eschatological perspective, in continuity with Irenaeus and the Cappadocians, also extends the logic of Reformed (covenant) theology. As Geerhardus Vos reminds us, the particular covenantal and eschatological orientation found in Scripture is thoroughly concerned with the ethical and personal sphere, not with abstract metaphysics and ontology. "The universe, as created, was only a beginning, the meaning of which was *not perpetuation, but attainment*" (emphasis added).[31] Eschatology is prior to soteriology. Creation began with a greater destiny lying before it. Creation was the stage—the "beautiful theater"—for God's drama, not an end in itself. Life in the garden was not intended to simply go on in perpetuity but was merely the point of departure for the great march of creation behind God's vice-regent into the everlasting life of God's own Sabbath-rest.

---

31. Geerhardus Vos, *The Eschatology of the Old Testament* (ed. James T. Dennison Jr.; Phillipsburg, N.J.: P&R, 2001), 73–74: "Eschatology aims at consummation rather than restoration.... It does not aim at the original state, but at a transcendental state of man."

This has obvious implications for the concept of human immortality. Since death is imposed by God as a judicial sanction against humanity for breaking the covenant, Jürgen Moltmann wrongly suggests that human death is merely "a characteristic of frail, temporal creation."[32] Nevertheless, the possibility of sinning—and therefore of being subject to the curse of death—is to be distinguished from the actual fact. Moltmann is correct when he says that on the basis of God's command to be fruitful and multiply, "human beings were mortal from the beginning."[33] Signified and sealed by the Tree of Life, immortality was promised as the goal of completing the trial. And this was true with respect to the soul as well as the body—created mortal, with the prospect of immortality in the future.

Thus, the emphasis of the Christian East on the attainment of immortality and that of Western theology on legal redemption can be integrated. Prior to the fall, Adam and Eve lived between the two trees: between everlasting confirmation in blessing and everlasting confirmation in death. Eden was a trial. As human beings are by nature covenantal, they are also constitutionally prospective—even utopian, despite the distorted ways in which fallen humanity seeks to win its glorification apart from and even against God. They not only have the law written on their conscience but carry within themselves a sense of some great task of spreading God's kingdom and glory to the ends of the earth. It is both of these senses, that of God's command and that of the promise of glory, that become twisted by human rebellion, but we can discern even in that rebellion the remnants of the original commission.

Already we are drifting rather far from the metaphysics of "overcoming estrangement," with its interest in the inner essence of human identity. Instead, we find ourselves in a deeply personal, relational, covenantal, ethical, historical, and eschatological environment. The contrast becomes even more apparent as we define the image of God in terms of the proper response of human beings to their covenant Lord.

B. THE CONVERGENCE OF HUMAN PERSONHOOD AND THE *IMAGO*: "HERE I AM"

To be created in God's image is to be called persons in communion.[34] There was no moment when a human being was actually a solitary, autonomous, unrelated entity; self-consciousness always included consciousness of one's relation to God, to each other, and to one's place in the wider created environment. And that *koinōnia* (communion) consists originally in the covenant of creation, in which all of humanity participates in Adam as its representative.

---

32. Jürgen Moltmann, *The Coming of God: Christian Eschatology* (trans. Margaret Kohl; Minneapolis: Fortress, 1996), 78.
33. Ibid., 91.
34. See Colin Gunton, "Trinity, Ontology, and Anthropology," in *Persons: Divine and Human* (ed. Christoph Schwöbel

and Colin Gunton; Edinburgh: T&T Clark, 1991), 47–61. At the same time, I find such arguments as those employed by Harriet A. Harris (against a purely relational ontology of person) compelling ("Should We Say That Personhood Is Relational?" *SJT* 51, no. 2 [1998]: 222–23).

Following Luther, Robert Jenson has compared God and humans along the lines of hearing rather than seeing. He correctly reminds us of the contrast between Greek and biblical ways of thinking at this point. Jenson writes

> To be, as a creature, is to be mentioned in the triune moral conversation as something other than those who conduct it. Western intellectual history has for the most part continued the Greek tradition for which "to be" meant to have form and so to appear and be seen, whether with the body's or the mind's eye. But there plainly is another possibility: that to be is to be *heard of*; and it is this interpretation that is demanded by the doctrine of creation.[35]

Augustine certainly believed in *ex nihilo* creation over against Platonism's emanation of the world from the divine One. However, he still had trouble accepting that creation was *spoken* into existence rather than coming into being silently from the forms in the divine mind.

For Thomas Aquinas (and the Protestant scholastics), the language of relation is *archetype* and *ectype* — that is, images. They were correct in affirming an analogical rather than univocal notion of being. In fact, the archetype-ectype analogy may be seen as no more than a way of interpreting the reference in Genesis 1:26 to God creating humanity in his "image" and "after our likeness." Nevertheless, in a more communicative conception, it may make greater sense to think of the relationship in terms of *speaker-answerer*. As we will see more fully below, "image" and "likeness" in this ancient Near Eastern context especially have to do with the relationship of fathers and sons rather than forms and appearances.

Jenson observes that God's creating Word is not, as Augustine believed, "an unspoken mental form actualized by the will; rather, it is an actual utterance."[36] Human "being" is the result of our being *said* by someone else, namely, God. In this case, to be is to be mentioned. The ethical implications of this view are apparent. Even those who are not mentioned by us — the infirm in nursing homes and hospitals, the unborn, those who are deemed "nothing" by society, even the dead — are nevertheless somebody because they have been mentioned by God. God has *called* them into existence, and he will have the last word at the final resurrection. Neither their ability to reason nor to will, but God's covenantal speech, is the source of their personhood. Cornelius Van Til observed,

> Man is not in Plato's cave.... Man had originally not merely a capacity for receiving the truth; he was in actual possession of the truth. The world of truth was not found in some realm far distant from him; it was right before him. That which spoke to his senses no less than that which spoke to his intellect was the voice of God.... Man's

---

35. Robert Jenson, *Systematic Theology* (New York: Oxford Univ. Press, 1997), 2:35–36. He is influenced by Franz K. Mayr, "Philosophie im Wandel der Sprache," *Zeitschrift für*

Theologie und Kirche 61 (1964): 439–91.

36. Ibid., 2:38.

first sense of self-awareness implied the awareness of the presence of God as the one for whom he had a great task to accomplish.[37]

Truth is a covenantal and therefore an ethical concept. It is communicated between persons, within a context of hearing and answering.

If we extend this reflection, we could say that human beings are those who reflect God's image not chiefly in *what they are essentially* but in *how they reply ethically*. Though they are determined *as* human persons by the mere fact of their creation as God's image, their *realization of the purpose* of their personhood depends on whether they correspond to God's intentions. And here we could interject Aristotle for a moment: "Good" is teleologically defined. A good watch is one that tells time well. A broken watch is still a watch, but it is not a good one. Similarly, the creation was pronounced good by God at every stage precisely because it "answered back" appropriately. When God said, "Let there be lights in the expanse of the heavens to separate the day from the night" and to serve "for signs and for seasons" (Ge 1:14), summer was warmer and winter was colder. When God said, "Let the waters swarm with swarms of living creatures, and let birds fly above the earth across the expanse of the heavens" (v. 20), the fish did not despise their lot by trying to become birds, nor did birds covet the sea.

So when humans were created, the superlative benediction was God's evaluation of the "answering back" that he heard. There is an obvious liturgical motif at work here, with the divine melody issuing in the antiphonal reply of the creaturely chorus: " 'Let there be *x*!' And there was *x*." " 'Let the earth sprout *y*.' And the earth brought forth *y*."

Humanity was created as the cantor, to conduct the choir and symphony in celebration of God's creation work:

Ascribe to the LORD, O heavenly beings,
    ascribe to the LORD glory and strength.
Ascribe to the LORD the glory due his name;
    worship the LORD in the splendor of holiness.

The voice of the LORD is over the waters;
    the God of glory thunders,
    the LORD, over many waters.
The voice of the LORD is powerful;
    the voice of the LORD is full of majesty....

The voice of the LORD flashes forth flames of fire.
The voice of the LORD shakes the wilderness;
    the LORD shakes the wilderness of Kadesh.

---

37. Cornelius Van Til, *The Defense of the Faith* (Philadelphia: Presbyterian & Reformed, 1955), 90.

> The voice of the LORD makes the deer give birth
>> and strips the forests bare,
>> and in his temple all cry, "Glory!"
>
> The LORD sits enthroned over the flood;
>> the LORD sits enthroned as king forever.
> May the LORD give strength to his people!
>> May the LORD bless his people with peace! (Ps 29:1–4, 7–11)

Throughout the Psalter, creation imagery blends with God's enthronement in Israel. "Clap your hands, all peoples! Shout to God with loud songs of joy! For the LORD, the Most High, is to be feared, a great king over all the earth." Just as he subdued the watery chaos in the beginning to create space for covenant fellowship with his vice-regent, "He subdued peoples under us, and nations under our feet.... For God is the King of all the earth; sing praises with a psalm!" (Ps 47:1–3, 7). In the history of redemption, Israel interprets its exodus from the waters of destruction, conquest of the defiling serpent, and entrance into the Promised Land for its mission of extending God's glory from Zion as fulfilling the original intention of creation.

Throughout the biblical narrative, the human servant of Yahweh is the one who answers back to the commission of the Great King, "Here I am." This expression (*hinnēh*, "behold," plus *î*, "me") is a common idiom in Hebrew for the response of the covenant partner when God summons, and it is carried forward into the New Testament (*idou*, "behold," plus *egō*, "I"). Whereas Adam and Eve ignore God's call, "Where are you?" (Ge 3:9), the patriarchs, prophets, Mary, and Jesus reply properly as covenant servants. God did not ask Adam, "*Who* are you?" much less "*What* are you?" as if it were a philosophical question. Rather, he asked, "*Where* are you?"—a question of ethical relation, in response to Adam's flight from his presence.

In contrast with Adam's silence, Mary responds to the angel's auspicious announcement that she will conceive the incarnate God with the words, "Here am I, the servant of the Lord; let it be with me according to your word" (Lk 1:38 NRSV). It is noteworthy that Jesus announces his triumphant arrival in heaven with the words, "Here am I [*idou egō*] and the children whom God has given me" (Heb 2:13 NRSV). We were created by God's Word ("Let there be...!"), for the purpose of responding back faithfully as covenant servants ("Let the earth sprout...!").

Thus human existence is *human* regardless, but it is "very good" insofar as humans answer back according to the purpose of their existence. In his first two chapters of Romans, Paul does not claim that the wicked are no longer human persons but that precisely because they are human persons they stand under judgment for having abused their office. "Here I am," as an answer to the other, is diametrically opposed to the autonomous self that is the product of one's own introspective reflection.

We cannot begin to think that we really know ourselves until we know someone other than ourselves. We do not possess ourselves but were spoken into existence by our covenant Lord. Because we were spoken by the Father *in the Son*, our personhood has a definite content, analogous to (but, of course, not identical with) the Father's begetting of the Son. Human beings are the created effect of God's speech, but the Son is the eternally begotten Word. Furthermore, it is only the Spirit who can open us up to the Father's summons in the brilliance of the Son's glory, so that we answer back according to his Word (Ps 143:10; Isa 32:15; 63:14; Eze 3:12; Ac 1:8; 2:17; 4:8; Ro 8:16, 26–27; 1Co 12:3; Gal 4:6).

The covenantal relationality that is integral to human nature opens us up to say, "Here I am," not only to our Creator but also to our creaturely neighbors. At her creation, Eve is greeted by Adam in a way analogous to God's greeting of Adam. Just as God recognized his own reflection in Adam, in spite of vast differences, Adam exclaims concerning Eve, "This at last is bone of my bones and flesh of my flesh" (Ge 2:23). As Stanley Grenz observes, "Adam's cry of elation resembles the traditional kinship formula, 'my bone and my flesh' (cf. Ge 29:14; Jdg 9:2; 2Sa 5:1; 19:12–13), which Walter Brueggemann suggests is actually a covenant formula that speaks of a common, reciprocal loyalty."[38] Hence, the Pauline statement that Eve is Adam's image because she is consubstantial with him in humanity: "In the image of God he created him; *male and female* he created them" (Ge 1:27, emphasis added).

This relational—which is to say, covenantal—pattern is undermined by the identification of human identity in general and the *imago* in particular with something in the individual, such as a mind or soul. The mind-body dualism leads us "into the problems of individualism and ecology," as Colin Gunton warns. "Historically, the roots of this syndrome lie in Irenaeus," who interpreted *ṣelem* ("image") and *dᵉmût* ("likeness") as distinct aspects rather than synonyms. Accordingly, *image* referred to the metaphysical similarity of humans with God in their rational capacity, while *likeness* referred to their moral similarity. "In his famous distinction between image and likeness there began the process of making reason both a chief ontological characteristic and a criterion of difference between human and non-human."[39] This leaves relationality out of the picture.[40] Similarly, John of Damascus locates the closeness of humanity to God on one hand and the rest of creation on the other in the rational soul and the material body, respectively.[41]

The tradition from Augustine to Aquinas deepens this tendency and further draws reflection away from the relational aspect of humanness. When "the inner

---

38. Stanley Grenz, *The Social God and the Relational Self* (Louisville: Westminster John Knox, 2001), 276.

39. Colin Gunton, *The Promise of Trinitarian Theology* (Edinburgh: T&T Clark, 1997), 101.

40. Ibid., 49.

41. John of Damascus, "An Exact Exposition of the Orthodox Faith," *NPNF2*, 9:29–37.

dimensions of the person" are stressed and then the vestiges of the Trinity are identified as within the human soul (especially in Augustine's psychological analogy), "God's relatedness is construed in terms of self-relatedness, with the result that it is as an individual that the human being is in the image of God, and therefore truly human."[42] The biblical emphasis on the image of God as constituted chiefly in the relatedness of persons to God and to each other (and to the nonhuman world) recedes into the background of an anthropology that is basically oriented toward the inmost being of the individual self (i.e., the soul).

Though hardly an intentional innovator, John Calvin broke away from this trajectory at important points. First, he rejected any theological distinction between *image* and *likeness* in Genesis; they are used as synonyms, for emphasis. From there he turns to a discussion of "the faculties of the soul," and here he is apparently more circumspect than the tradition — his suspicion of speculation once more awakened: "For that speculation of Augustine, that the soul is the reflection of the Trinity because in it reside the understanding, will, and memory, is by no means sound. Nor is there any probability in the opinion of those who locate God's likeness in the dominion given to man, as if in this mark alone he resembled God, that he was established as heir and possessor of all things."[43] Calvin has here rather sharply reduced the traditional list — including the rather widespread consensus that the image included humanity's dominion. Nor is the image of God an "emanation," he writes, "as if some portion of immeasurable divinity had flowed into man."[44]

Second, Calvin argues that the proper seat of the image/likeness is the soul, but he goes beyond the earlier tradition in attributing the image's glory to the whole person, encompassing both moral perfections and the "goodly beauty" of the body.[45] This is in contrast to Augustine, who asserted, "Surely not in the body, but in that same mind, was man made after the image of God."[46] According to Calvin, "There was no part of man, not even the body itself, in which some sparks did not glow."[47] For this reason, "it would be foolish to seek a definition of 'soul' from the philosophers," he writes, and to make this definition then the basis for our understanding of the *imago*.[48] At least implicitly, Calvin was criticizing the tradition, represented by Augustine's statement above.

Third, the true nature of this image "can be nowhere better recognized than from the restoration of [man's] corrupted nature."[49] Rather than speculate about essences and faculties, we should be guided in our reflections on what human beings are by a knowledge of what or who they will be as a result of redemption and the

42. Gunton, *Promise of Trinitarian Theology*, 49.
43. Calvin, *Institutes* 1.15.4.
44. Ibid., 1.15.5.
45. Ibid. See also 1.15.3.
46. Augustine, *Commentary on John's Gospel*, in *Lectures or*

Tractates on the Gospel According to John XXIII 10, *NPNF1*, 7:155.
47. Calvin, *Institutes* 1.15.3.
48. Ibid., 1.15.6.
49. Ibid., 1.15.4.

consummation. Eschatology for Calvin does not come later, after the fall, but is already the goal of fulfilled creation. From the redemption of humanity we discern that "God's image was not totally annihilated," but was grossly disfigured. "Consequently, the beginning of our recovery of salvation is in that restoration which we obtain through Christ, who also is called the Second Adam for the reason that he restores us to true and complete integrity."[50] Thus redemption is at least in part understood in terms of "putting on" Christ: "Put on the new self, created after the likeness of God" (Eph 4:24).[51] The understanding of *image* is therefore not to be sought through speculation on the supposedly distinct meanings of *ṣelem* ("image") and *dᵉmût* ("likeness") in Genesis 1:26, but by learning from eschatology the identity of the Second Adam in whom the image is fully expressed: "Now we see how Christ is the most perfect image of God; if we are conformed to it, we are so restored that with true piety, righteousness, purity, and intelligence we bear God's image."[52] Not by an inflowing of divine substance, but by the Spirit's work of conforming us ethically to Christ do we finally become those who bear God's image in grace and, one day, in eschatological glory. "For [Paul] says that by 'beholding Christ's glory, we are being transformed into his very image . . . as through the Spirit of the Lord' [2Co 3:18], who surely works in us without rendering us consubstantial with God."[53]

Stanley Grenz goes so far as to represent Calvin's insights as "the birth of the relational *imago*." He cites Paul Ramsey in this regard: "The image of God, according to this view, consists of man's *position* before God, or, rather, the image of God is reflected in man because of his position before him."[54] We should not overstate Calvin's innovation. Like his contemporaries—and forebears, ancient and medieval—he could still use standard Platonic phrases (such as the body as "the prisonhouse"), but these habits of speech run counter to his principal arguments. Grenz correctly suggests that Calvin, even more than Luther, stands out as the Reformer who gave "greater attention to the *imago dei* 'than any great theologian since Augustine,'" and "Douglas Hall, in turn, cites Calvin as more important than Luther for the emergence of the relational understanding of the *imago dei*."[55] Grenz also points to Calvin's more eschatological (future-anticipatory) approach.[56] Inevitably, this shift from locating the image of God in a part or faculty (i.e., spirit or intellect) to the covenant and commission given to humanity by God marked a significant transition in anthropology from what humans are in their inner essence to their identity before God as responsible creatures in history.

---

50. Ibid.
51. Ibid.
52. Ibid.
53. Ibid., 1.15.5.
54. Grenz, *Social God and the Relational Self*, 162.

55. Ibid., 166.
56. Ibid., 178. However, I disagree with Grenz's suggestion that Calvin, unlike Irenaeus, "believed that the 'end' for which God created humans was completely present in the beginning."

The Reformed scholastics appealed also to the classical (Aristotelian) identification of humanity as a sort of *microkosmos*, displaying in a signal manner God's external works. With rabbinical Judaism, these theologians pointed out the close connection between the temple and human beings as a microcosm of God's holy dwelling. God's likeness in humanity, according to Peter van Mastricht, is "that conformity of man whereby in his own way (i.e., as a creature) he reproduces the highest perfection of God."[57] It is therefore ethical rather than metaphysical — hearing and obeying God's word spoken, not a matter of locating the ontological point of contact between divine and human being. "For the understanding of the Reformed church doctrine of the divine image in man," Heinrich Heppe relates, "it should be noted that it is thoroughly connected with man as such, indeed with the entire man, with his entire spirit-body being."[58]

Peter Martyr Vermigli also emphasized that if we seek to understand the meaning of the original *imago*, we will have to attend to its renewal in Christ and by his Spirit. The fall has not eradicated our sense of God or any of our natural faculties, but it has twisted our whole personality into a parody of its created goodness. For example, we no longer exercise proper dominion in service, but "exercise tyranny over things instead." So we come to understand the fulfillment of the image-commission from the point of view of its restoration in Christ.[59] Furthermore, Christ himself is "the primary and true image" of God.[60]

The *Heidelberg Catechism* identifies the image with the "true righteousness and holiness" in which Adam was created.[61] To this the *Westminster Confession* adds the inscription of God's law on the conscience "and power to fulfill it; and yet, under a possibility of transgressing being left to the liberty of their own will, which was subject unto change." Furthermore, this natural knowledge was not merely an innate idea but was a revealed and spoken command "not to eat of the tree of the knowledge of good and evil" (ch. 4).

Clearly, it is the historical economy of God's covenantal dealings with humanity rather than a speculative soul-body dualism that is determinative in these treatments. Heppe summarizes, "Cocceius (*Sum. theol.* XVII) finds the divine image not in the 'substance of the soul,' nor yet in the 'faculties of the soul,' nor yet in the '*imperium* which man had over the living,' but in the *rectitudo* [justice/righteousness] which he explains (para. 22) as moral reciprocity with God in all a man's parts, in the soul of course as the *hēgemonikos* [ruler] and in the body and limbs as

---

57. Peter van Mastricht, as quoted in Heinrich Heppe, *Reformed Dogmatics* (ed. Ernst Bizer; trans. G. T. Thomson; London: Allen & Unwin, 1950), 232.
58. Ibid.
59. Ibid.
60. Ibid., 44.

61. *Heidelberg Catechism*, q. 6: "God created [people] good and in his own image, that is, in true righteousness and holiness, so that they might truly know God their creator, love him with all their heart, and live with him in eternal happiness for his praise and glory" (*Psalter Hymnal* [Grand Rapids: CRC Publications, 1987], 861).

the *skeuos* [vessel]."[62] Others see the imago in the *dominio*, but even this remains an ethical obligation imposed on humankind rather than a tyrannical lordship. According to Peter Martyr Vermigli, dominion renders man "a kind of representative (vicar) of God."[63] For Ursinus, "the image of God is not to be sought in the sole substance of the soul, but particularly in the virtues and gifts with which it was adorned by God in creation."[64]

From these writers we learn that the image is chiefly rectitude, the law written on the conscience. Whatever may be the eminent marks that distinguish humans from the rest of creation, the image of God that sets them apart is ethical and covenantal—which is to say, relational. Rectitude (righteousness) is both a judicial status and an actual quality that animates human attitudes, thoughts, and actions. It is not because humans possess an immortal soul but because they are created in true righteousness and holiness that they bear God's image and likeness.

The question of the image is not, therefore, a question of some inner faculty or quality in the soul or mind, nor a matter of a supernatural gift added to nature. Even apart from special revelation, human beings possess an inward sense of the law, but only in the gospel do we find liberation from the guilt and tyranny of sin. "Knowledge of natural law did not make them better," says Vermigli, "because even if the law is known it cannot change us nor give us strength to act rightly; therefore, we must run to Christ."[65]

Obviously, the Reformed and Lutheran theologians were drawing on similar resources, though with different conceptual tags. In fact, drawing on Luther and the Lutheran scholastics, Robert Jenson makes a point that God's command upholds human community. Referring to the "first use of the law," Jenson writes, "This 'use' is often identified with natural law 'written in the hearts' of all humans. And for Martin Luther himself, whose drastic use of this concept is a chief incitement of the following, to live in the world and to be 'under the law' are the same thing; God's rule by the gospel in the church and his rule by his law in the world are then God's two 'regimes,' his two ways of establishing his will *ad extra*."[66]

Law and gospel are not inherently antithetical, but they are certainly different "words." Law commands and gospel announces salvation. In the life of the justified, law and gospel are perfectly harmonious: the gospel assures us of God's favor, and the law indicates how we are to walk in the light of our blessings in Christ. However, in a biblical *covenant* of law, commands function as stipulations requiring

---

62. Heppe, *Reformed Dogmatics*, 44.

63. Quoted in ibid., 233. But the view that came to dominate (via Melanchthon) was a distinction between the substance (in the personal nature of man) and the actual endowments (original righteousness). Despite a formal rejection of the semantic

difference between "image" and "likeness," this approximates the patristic distinction.

64. Heppe, *Reformed Dogmatics*, 233.

65. Quoted in ibid., 24.

66. Jenson, *Systematic Theology*, 2:62.

personal and perfect obedience on penalty of death. Therefore, with respect to the question as to how sinners may be justified before God, law and gospel are not only different but totally antithetical principles. In creation, God "worded" us as law-creatures; in the new creation, he "words" us as evangelical creatures. Robert Jenson notes, "Therefore if we humans address one another at all we speak law." Even if our intentions were always pure, our promises cannot secure a future for others. At the end of the day, we shrug and say, " 'Sorry, friend. I did my best. But you know, you really should pull yourself together.' "[67]

Ironically, our neighbor's best interest would be served if only we were faithful to this law that we speak to each other, since God's law is nothing other than the obligation to love. "Thus all our speech to one another finally somehow obligates; 'law' is the necessary discourse of all community," Jenson adds, and it is rooted in God's say-so, his command.[68] Autonomy is thereby excluded. We exist because we are addressed. "If we exist because we are addressed by God and if we have our specific identity as those who respond to God, then we do not possess ourselves."[69] So "it is not only our salvation that is accomplished by God's address, but our being as such."[70]

Not surprisingly, given their own way of making these points, the early Reformed theologians included the covenantal dimension of the *imago*. Heppe quotes Peter van Mastricht:

> Original righteousness was conferred on Adam not as a private but as a public person, or what is the same thing, in Adam on the whole of human nature, whence it would have been transmitted to all his posterity. But this original righteousness is not a substance as Illyricus used to rave, but a quality diffused as it were through all the substance, and so common to body and soul, to the mind, also to the will and the affections.[71]

C. IMAGE AND EMBASSY: THE *IMAGO* AS GIFT AND TASK

To be sure, human beings differ from other creatures in their natural capacities for rational reflection, language, and deliberative action. Their agency is not merely instinctive, but purposeful. They acquire not only experience, but knowledge, wisdom, virtue, and understanding. However, none of these natural capacities by itself distinguishes humanity from other creatures in any sense other than that of being a more complex form of biological life. Both the depth and the range of their intellectual and moral capacities rendered human beings more suitable than other creatures for this covenantal relationship, but it is God's command and promise—the role

---

67. Ibid.
68. Ibid., 2:63.
69. Ibid.

70. Ibid., 2:68.
71. Van Mastricht, as quoted in Heppe, *Reformed Dogmatics*, 240.

that he gives to them in his unfolding drama—that constitute the uniqueness of human beings. The image of God is to be sought in the commission that God gave to humanity in Adam. *In short, the significance of the* imago Dei *is the moral likeness of human beings to their Creator and the covenantal commission with which Adam was entrusted; namely, to enter God's everlasting Sabbath with the whole creation in his train.*

Therefore, a covenantal anthropology focuses our attention on the inherently relational and ecstatic (outward-going) character of human existence rather than on the introspective quest for the inner light. Even in the womb, every human being belongs to a web of covenantal interdependence. Whatever the appropriate prerequisites of human nature as God's covenant partner may be, the image of God, properly speaking, is constituted by the following four characteristics: sonship/royal dominion, representation, glory, and prophetic witness.

1. SONSHIP/ROYAL DOMINION

At least part of the significance of the *imago* as image and likeness (Ge 1:26) is that it is the royal investiture of a servant-son. While the fish, birds, and land mammals are commissioned to rule their respective spheres in Genesis 1, to human beings the mandate is given to fill and rule the whole creation as God's vice-regent (v. 28). In answering the question, "What is man that you are mindful of him, and the son of man that you care for him?" the psalmist answers by recounting the commission that humanity was given to rule over creation as God's vice-regent (Psalm 8:4–8).

In his person and work, Jesus Christ receives in the place of fallen Adam his royal investiture in the seventh day as the image-son of God. The writer to the Hebrews picks up this theme, quoting Psalm 8, noting that God has not subjected "the world to come" to angels but to human beings (Heb 2:5). "Now in putting everything in subjection to him [humanity], he left nothing outside his control. At present, we do not yet see everything in subjection to him" (v. 8). Here we meet the eschatological reserve. The embassy entrusted to humanity has been betrayed. "But we see him who for a little while was made lower than the angels, namely Jesus, crowned with glory and honor because of the suffering of death, so that by the grace of God he might taste death for everyone" (v. 9). Thus, this aspect of the *imago* (as others) must be allowed to emerge as we think of the first and second Adams together.[72]

---

72. By the way, it is worth making explicit the view implied throughout this chapter, namely, that Adam is no more a mythical "symbol" than Jesus Christ, and it is arbitrary to assign the Last Adam a historical status that is radically dissimilar from that of the first Adam. It is not exegesis but philosophical prejudice that renders Adam and Eve nonhistorical. After noting that Hegel, Schleiermacher, Ritschl, Bultmann, Reinhold Niebuhr, and Barth all denied the historicity of Adam, replacing it with the story of Jesus as the paradigm of truly actualized personhood, Brevard Childs correctly perceives that this move can be made only without serious attention to exegesis. The "problem" is modern, not biblical (*Biblical Theology of the Old and New Testaments* [Minneapolis: Fortress, 1993], 593.

The kings of ancient Egypt and Mesopotamia were represented as royal sons of the chief deity. However, in Genesis 1:26–28, the creation of Adam and Eve is not represented as the birth of a divinity or even of a semidivine creature but rather of covenant servants for whom adoption as God's heir was held out as the goal. Furthermore, according to Genesis, this royal investiture includes every human being, "male and female," and not merely the king.[73] In the patriarchal culture of the ancient Near East, *son* was a legal category that we dare not lose in our proper sensitivity to inclusive language. In both creation and redemption, the nearly universal identification of higher (divine) and lower (base) realms with males and females respectively is turned on its head. That is why it is so revolutionary that both genders are comprehended under the term *son*: co-heirs of the image of God and, in redemption, of God's entire estate.

According to Phyllis Bird, while *ṣelem* ("image") by itself tells us nothing, "The *ṣelem ᵓelōhîm* [image of God] in Genesis 1 is, accordingly, a royal designation, the precondition or prerequisite for rule."[74] We already anticipate a theme I will develop more fully under christology: namely, that Jesus Christ fulfills the office of royal son and image-bearer as the Last Adam. This office is distinct from his eternal sonship as the second person of the Trinity. Although he possessed ontological equality with the Father from all eternity, he had to *attain* this sonship-likeness or royal image on behalf of his co-heirs. In other words, he had to succeed precisely where Adam had failed. There is therefore an important sense in which Jesus Christ was adopted by the Father as "son" only after his active and passive obedience: not as eternal Son, but as the faithful covenant servant who fulfilled the commission entrusted to him (Pss 2:7; 89:26 with Heb 1:5). Jesus' fulfillment of this destiny of royal sonship is repeatedly underscored especially in John's gospel (cf. Jn 5:17–21).

At this point we should add that it is not the biblical doctrine of creation that has led to the oppression of nonhuman as well as human creation but the reality of sin that the biblical doctrine of the fall describes. "The LORD God took the man and put him in the garden of Eden to work it and keep it" (Ge 2:15). The phrase *work it and keep it* was commonly used also of the vocation of the Levites in relation to the temple. Thus, the subduing and ruling of creation that is nuclear to the *imago* in Genesis 1 and 2 is not an autonomous exploitation or violent domination but a mandate "to work ... and keep" (2:15) the sanctuary in its holiness, driving

---

73. Phyllis A. Bird, "'Male and Female He Created Them': Gen. 1:27b in the Context of the Priestly Account of Creation," *HTR* 74, no. 2 (1981): 140, 155–58: "The genius of the formulation of Genesis 1:26 may be seen in its use of a common expression and image of Mesopotamian (-Canaanite) royal theology to counter a common image of Mesopotamian (-Canaanite) anthropology, viz., the image of humanity as the servant of the gods, the dominant image of Mesopotamian creation myths. The language that describes the king as the one who stands in a special relationship to the divine world is chosen by the author of Genesis 1 (perhaps under the influence of Egyptian wisdom tradition) to describe humanity as a whole, *adam qua adam*, in its essential nature."

74. Bird, "'Male and Female He Created Them,'" 140.

the serpent from the garden and extending God's reign of righteousness, justice, and peace.

Because the creation is neither divine nor demonic, neither something to be worshiped nor something to be despised or destroyed, violence of the human vice-regent against creation can be understood only as an alliance with Satan.[75] To say that "the earth is the LORD's and the fullness thereof" (Ps 24:1) is to say two things: that the earth is not *God* and that it is not *ours*. It is precisely because "the earth is the LORD's and the fullness thereof" that human beings (1) take their place with the rest of nature as creatures and (2) recognize their commission to be stewards of God's world, not consumers and exploiters of what they take to be their own possession.

We are reminded of Vermigli's comment that it is the fall that transforms human dominion (conceived as stewardship) into tyranny. Only because there is a Creator and Judge who stands outside of human technology can we say that exploitation will not finally go unchecked. Dietrich Bonhoeffer underscores this point:

> This freedom of dominion directly includes our tie to the creatures who are ruled. The soil and the animals whose lord I am are the world in which I live, without which I am not.... It bears me, nourishes me, and upholds me. But my freedom from it consists in the fact that this world, to which I am bound as a lord to his servant, as the peasant to his soil, is subjected to me, that I am to rule over the earth which is and remains my earth. It is by no other commissioned authority except that given by the Word of God to man—which thus uniquely binds and sets him over against the other creatures.[76]

Bonhoeffer reminds us that, far from legitimizing human exploitation, this dominion or rule entrusted to humanity by God from the beginning should keep us from seeking to grasp it for ourselves. "There is no dominion without serving God.... From the very beginning the way of man to the earth has only been possible as God's way to man.... Man's being-free-for God and the other person and his being-free-from the creature in his dominion over it is the image of God in the first man."[77]

We may even go so far as to suggest that the Platonic interpretation of the *imago* easily allows for an irresponsible ecological ethic, however unintentionally, just as materialist views, especially when combined with a radical voluntarism (i.e., emphasis on the will), become coconspirators in tragically distorting the relationship of humans to the rest of creation. If our goal is to transcend the rest of creation, including our own bodies, then our "dominion" will take the form of an antithetical relationship to the material world. If our superiority is determined by our mind, we

---

75. Childs expresses this point well: "If the Bible rejects viewing the world as an object to be possessed and exploited, it also strongly resists all attempts to blur the fundamental distinction between God and the world" (*Biblical Theology*, 400).

76. Dietrich Bonhoeffer, *Creation and Fall: A Theological Interpretation of Genesis 1–3* (trans. John C. Fletcher; London: SCM, 1959), 37–38.

77. Ibid., 38.

master the material world by calculative reason; if by our will, we may bend creation to our decrees and harness its energies, regardless of the ecological cost; if by our physical strength, we may glory in wanton abuse that results from mere self-assertion. If the material world has no transcendent origin or goal but is simply subject to its own immanent laws and random chance, the world becomes little more than the raw material that we can manipulate and exploit in our will to power. Ironically, Platonism and materialism have contributed in their own ways to this alienation of humanity from the environment in which it realizes its own identity and purpose.

To return to the liturgical analogy, human beings are that part of creation that is raised up by God to lead the earth of which they are a part in common praise of the covenant Lord. We have covered this point more fully above (see "Origins and Eschatology," pp. 381–87), appealing to Meredith Kline's treatment of the day-frames in Genesis 1, with the creature-kings parading under the leadership of the human vice-regent before the Great King in his Sabbath enthronement. A covenantal *imago* is desperately needed to challenge rationalistic and dualistic accounts.

The dominion, therefore, rests on God's commission and not on distinguishing faculties or attributes of the human essence. In this truth there is great potential for overcoming some of the theological presuppositions often overlooked in criticism of the alleged Judeo-Christian foundations for ecological violence. Brueggemann reminds us that throughout its employment in the biblical narrative, this dominion is that of a shepherd-king (Eze 34). "Moreover, a Christian understanding of dominion must be discerned in the way of Jesus of Nazareth (cf. Mk 10:43–44). The one who rules is the one who serves. Lordship means servanthood. It is the task of the shepherd not to control but to lay down his life for the sheep (Jn 10:11)."[78] Christ's ministry as the Last Adam, who came to serve rather than to be served (Mt 20:28), transforms all of our inherited notions and experience of sinful dominion (cf. Eph 5:25–33).

As Kline notes, the three principal elements of likeness that appear in all their redolence when the royal son appears are the following: *cultic*, represented by the temple (dominion, kingship, and priesthood); *ethical* (the foundations of the temple are justice, equity, truth, righteousness, holiness, goodness), and *aesthetic* (glory — physical beauty).[79] "To be the image of God is to be the son of God."[80]

2. REPRESENTATION

With its outer court of earth and water basins (representing land and water), its inner court (representing the place of communion with God), and its Most Holy

---

78. Walter Brueggemann, *Genesis: Interpretation* (Atlanta: John Knox, 1982), 33.

79. Meredith G. Kline, *Images of the Spirit* (self-published, 1986), 35.

80. Ibid., 36.

Place, separated by a curtain (representing the observable heavens through which the High Priest passes annually to make atonement), the temple was a microcosm of creation. And at its active nerve center were the priests, whose gem-studded breastplate and multicolored vestments echoed the imagery of the temple itself. It is from this quarry that the New Testament images of the church as temple and each believer as a living stone filled with the glory of the Spirit are mined.

To speak of the image of God as official representation is to place it in the realm of judicial commission (ethical relationship) rather than, as in the more traditional understanding, a mirror of the divine essence (ontology). Humanity represents God analogically, but in the way that the royal heir represents the Great King. To be sure, the image of God includes communicable attributes that humans share analogically with and from God, but its focus is on the vocation entrusted to humanity, an official embassy, for which these characteristics or attributes uniquely prepare this creature among others. This representative (priestly) role will become clearer, especially when we come to Christ as the archetypal Prophet, Priest, and King.

3. GLORY

While royal sonship, representation, and mutuality find ample support in Scripture, perhaps the theme most closely attached to the relevant passages is that of "glory" (*kābôd*).[81] It is this notion that best ties together both Testaments and indicates the closest connection between covenant and eschatology. Furthermore, once we recognize its central importance to the concept of *imago dei*, the latter's significance in even the Old Testament is capable of being recognized as well.

In the ancient myths of Israel's neighbors, the chief deity completes his cosmic house and then builds a temple where he will be served among the other gods. The biblical narrative parodies these cosmogenic myths by recounting the Great King's completion of his cosmic house and filling it with his Glory-Spirit as his own dwelling. In this narrative, God's Glory is simultaneously his Son and his Spirit, whom their creature (humankind) mirrors analogically by reflecting that glory. The Son and the Spirit are the uncreated Glory of God—of the same essence as the Father—while human beings are the created reflectors of divine majesty as those whom the Spirit engenders by the in-breathing of life. As a result human beings are made prophetic witnesses to the glory they reflect. The relationship between creature and Creator is therefore analogical, ethical, and covenantal; at no point is there an ontic or univocal identity between them.

---

81. Paul Ricoeur observes that Paul's development of the *imago dei* theme (e.g., in 2Co 3:18) anchors itself not in the Old Testament notion of creation in the image of God (Ge 1:26) but in the Old Testament motif of *glory* (*Figuring the Sacred* [trans. David Pellauer; Minneapolis: Fortress, 1995], 267–68). There is much exegetical support for such a view, and this underscores how the importance of the *imago dei* concept in Scripture will be determined by corollaries or constituent aspects of the image rather than direct statements concerning the image as such.

Already in Genesis 1:2 the Holy Spirit is at work within the world that is being engendered by the Father's speech in his Son. Adam and Eve were created as the temples of this same Spirit, who breathed life into dust. Analogously, Mary received the glad, if disorienting, news, "The Holy Spirit will come upon you, and the power of the Most High will overshadow you; therefore the child to be born will be called holy — the Son of God" (Lk 1:35). And in inaugurating his new creation, Jesus breathed on the disciples, saying, "Receive the Holy Spirit" (Jn 20:22). Therefore, we can see a pattern throughout creation and redemptive history, with believers and the church corporately as the true Spirit-filled temple, living stones re-created in the image of Christ.

Of course, none of this would make sense if we were restricted to exegesis of Genesis 1 and 2. Rather, we recognize what God was doing in this creative work only as we look back from the fuller vistas of later revelation. Kline notes that "image of God and son of God are thus twin concepts," as the birth of Seth in Adam's image seems to confirm (Ge 5:1 – 3).[82] The eternal Son is the archetypal pattern — the true Son and Image of the Father — according to whom the Spirit creates (and re-creates) human beings as ectypal copies.[83] It is no wonder, then, that the Son — after completing his own work — sends the Spirit to inaugurate a new creation on the pattern of his own glory, both as God and as the glorified new Adam.

In this way, protology ("first things") and eschatology ("last things") are coordinated. Paul demonstrates this especially in 1 Corinthians 15: "Thus it is written, 'The first man Adam became a living being'; the last Adam became a life-giving Spirit.... Just as we have borne the image of the man of dust, we shall also bear the image of the man of heaven" (vv. 45, 49). We receive our original nature (both its glory and its corruption) from the first Adam, but we receive our eschatological identity as part of the new creation from the Last Adam, who has triumphed over sin and death and entered as our head into his Sabbath enthronement. In 1 Corinthians 11:7, as Stanley Grenz notes, "The apostle connects the *imago dei* with the concept of the divine glory (*doxa*). The way was paved by the Old Testament, most directly by the declaration in Psalm 8:5 that God has crowned humankind with 'glory and honor.' "[84] Thus, Christ identifies himself as no less than the Creator and Consummator, "the Alpha and the Omega, the first and the last, the beginning and the end" (Rev 22:13), "the faithful witness" to God's covenant (Rev 1:5). Throughout this marvelous Apocalypse, the church is represented as sharing in this witness.

Therefore, we discern the inextricable link between covenant, eschatology, and the judicial-official character of the divine image.[85] It is not a silent vision of the unity of the human spirit with divinity, but the verbal testimony to God's covenant

---

82. Kline, *Images of the Spirit*, 23.
83. Ibid., 23 – 24.
84. Grenz, *Social God and the Relational Self*, 205.

85. Kline, *Images of the Spirit*, 27: "Nuclear to the divine Glory," writes Kline, "is its official-functional aspect: it is the glory of royal-judicial office" as well as "an ethical dimension."

faithfulness. The whole human person, not merely one faculty (namely, the soul), serves in this official witnessing capacity. "As image of God, man is a royal son with the judicial function appertaining to kingly office. The renewal of the divine image in men is an impartation to them of the likeness of the archetypal glory of Christ."[86]

In Christ, *'ādām* has assumed the throne under God in the Sabbath glory. Everything that Adam should have won for his posterity but lost is restored and fulfilled in Christ, as he enters the heavenly Paradise in triumph, ahead of his co-heirs. In the meantime, the Spirit is re-creating a new humanity to reflect the ethical glory of the Son (see 2Co 3:7–18; 4:4–6—with the investiture figure of "putting on Christ," in Ro 13:14; 1Co 15:53; 2Co 5:2–5; Gal 3:27; Eph 4:25; Col 3:10). It is a re-creation by the Spirit after the archetypal image of the eternal Son of the Father (Ro 8:29–30).

A further indication of this covenantal and eschatological interpretation of the image is the event of *naming*. Adam is given the task of naming the animals, but God names Adam and Eve. Similarly, believers are "named 'sons of God,' just as people customarily are surnamed after the name of their forebears."[87] This naming practice is also a treaty-making practice, as we have seen. "The name *Christian* is a covenantal identification for the servant-son people of the new covenant."[88]

There is no place in this history of creation, redemption, and consummation for an autonomous self. Our covenantal identity is established in creation (in Adam) and in the new creation (in Christ). We do not create our identity by our own decision or effort, but receive it in the process of being named (or "worded") by God. As Anthony Thiselton points out, the biblical text "gives the self an identity and significance as the recipient of loving and transforming address. In this sense, it 'names' the self."[89]

It is significant that in Revelation 22:4 the bearing of God's name on the forehead of the saints is equivalent to their status as his image-bearing witnesses. In baptism, the sign and seal of God's name is placed on the bodies of believers and their children. This official mark serves as a seal not only of God's blessing, but of his commissioning of these servants as witnesses, to declare God's word of command and promise. Hence, the warning to new covenant believers not to follow the folly of the fathers in the wilderness who failed to believe God's promise and to enter his Sabbath rest. "As originally created, man was not yet endowed with this

---

86. Ibid., 28.

87. Ibid., 54. He adds, "The equivalence of the bearing of God's name and the bearing of God's image appears strikingly in Revelation 22:4. Here, in the midst of the description of the glorified covenant community, renewed after the image of the Lord, it is said: 'They will see his face and his name will be in their foreheads.'... To say that the overcomers in the New Jeru-

salem bear the name of Christ on their forehead is to say that they reflect the glory of Christ, which is to say that they bear the image of the glorified Christ."

88. Ibid., 55.

89. Anthony Thiselton, *Interpreting God and the Postmodern Self: On Meaning, Manipulation and Promise* (Edinburgh: T&T Clark, 1995), 63.

[physical] form of Glory-likeness. Physical glorification might only be contemplated in eschatological hope."[90] We too await our full investiture as royal heirs. Adoption is only finally and fully realized for us in our bodily resurrection and glorification (Ro 8:23).

That the image necessarily involves—even centrally—the ethical dimension is evident in the close connection it bears with the repetition of God's work and rest in the seven-day pattern. Yet this is true only in the liminal state of the "already"/"not yet," as believers—together with the whole creation—await their own resurrection from the dead and royal entrance into confirmed righteousness. The glorification (which the Eastern church calls *theosis*), already semirealized in the possession of the Holy Spirit as a down payment, will be the full psychosomatic investiture of each believer as a royal son. This may be why Paul (Ro 8:18–25) puts an eschatological spin on adoption, deferring its full accomplishment until the whole creation is able to participate with redeemed humanity in the Sabbath enthronement of God.

As Francis Watson has pointed out, the centrality of the earth in the universe and of humans on the earth is not a scientific claim but a crucial theological interpretation of reality.[91] Through Israel's vocation, God's glory was to radiate through the gradual extension of his kingdom from Jerusalem to the ends of the earth. This vocation looks back to the original calling of humanity in Adam and forward to the Last Adam as the one who fulfills it, drawing all of creation into his train as he enters as conqueror into the Sabbath rest (Ro 8:18–25).

4. Prophetic Witness

All along I have hinted at the witnessing character of the image-of-God concept, but we see this more clearly in the ministry of the prophets. As Meredith Kline observes,

> The lives of the prophets caught up in the Spirit were prophecies of the eschatological destiny of mankind re-created in God's image.... In the beginning man was created in the image of God by the power of creative fiat after the paradigm of the theophanic Glory-Spirit. In redemptive history the reproduction of the image of God in the new mankind takes place through the mediatorial agency of Jesus Christ, in whom the divine Glory became incarnate. He is the paradigm of the Glory-image, and he is the mediator of the Spirit in the process of replicating the divine likeness.[92]

The descent of the Spirit at Pentecost, then, as a new creation, is nothing less than "a redemptive recapitulation of Genesis 1:2 and 27."[93] "In the command of the

---

90. Ibid., 61.

91. Francis Watson, *Text, Church and World: Biblical Interpretation in Theological Perspective* (Edinburgh: T&T Clark, 1994), 148.

92. Kline, *Images of the Spirit*, 63–64.

93. Ibid., 70.

voice from heaven, 'Hear him,' Peter perceived [Ac 3:22–26] the ultimate application of the Deuteronomic requirement that Israel obey God's prophet (Dt 18:18). That was God's own identification of Jesus as *the* prophet like unto Moses."[94] The preincarnate Son, as "Angel of the Covenant" (Zec 3; Mal 3:1), "was that archetypal prophet behind the human prophet paradigm."[95]

At Pentecost, all of the original creation language, mediated through Israel's cultus, converges in the new creation, as humanity is once again commissioned as God's true and faithful witnesses to the ends of the earth. In Revelation 11, "The figures in whom the likeness of Christ is reproduced are expressly denoted as witnesses (v. 3) and prophets (vv. 10, 18) and their mission is described as one of prophesying (v. 3), prophecy (v. 6), and testimony (v. 7)."[96] Now all believers enter the Most Holy Place (as priests) and are prophets in the Spirit, wearing the garments of the Spirit as a bride adorned for her husband. But for now the church is the bride of Christ, not yet the spouse. The confirmation in righteousness and the consummation of the glory-image that constitutes royal investiture await believers in hope.

Thus, the covenantal self is, to borrow Ricoeur's phrase, "the summoned subject in the school of the narratives of the prophetic vocation."[97] To be human is to be called by God to direct the whole creation to its appointed goal, which is nothing less than sharing in God's Sabbath consummation. These "narratives of vocation" constitute the self-identity of the prophet, and we should bear in mind that this vocation may be understood in the narrower sense (biblical prophets) and the broader sense (the general office of all human beings in creation and of all believers in redemption).

To conclude, we come to know ourselves as human beings—that is, as God's image-bearers—not only by looking within but chiefly by looking outside of ourselves to the divine Other who addresses us. It is only as we take our place in this theater of creation—the liturgy of God's speaking and creaturely response—that we discover a selfhood and personhood that is neither autonomous nor illusory but doxological and real. Who am I? I am one who exists as a result of being spoken by God. Furthermore, I am one of God's covenant children whom he delivered out of Egypt, sin, and death. I am one who has heard his command but not fulfilled it, one in whom faith has been born by the Spirit through the proclamation of the gospel. Because human beings are by nature created in covenant with God, self-identity itself depends on one's relation to God. It is not because I think, feel, experience,

---

94. Ibid., 81–82.

95. Ibid., 83.

96. Ibid., 91.

97. Ricoeur, *Figuring the Sacred*, 262. According to Ricoeur, the narratives of prophetic vocation include three phases: con-

frontation with God, an introductory speech of divine self-identification ("I am the God of your father Abraham"; "I am who I am," etc.), and then finally the "decisive word can be pronounced: 'I send you,' 'go and say to them …'" (265–66).

express, observe, or will, but because in the totality of my existence I hear God's command and promise that I recognize that I am, with my fellow image-bearers, a real self who stands in relation to God and the rest of creation.

No one can escape the reality of God in his or her experience, because there is no human existence that is possible or actual apart from the ineradicable covenant identity that belongs to us all, whether we flee the summons or whether we reply, "Here I am."

III. ANGELS: HEAVENLY MISSIONARIES

Scripture ranks human beings "a little lower than the heavenly beings" (Ps 8:5) and yet treats the angelic hosts as servants of God for the welfare and salvation of humans. Before closing this chapter, then, something should be said concerning the identity of angels.

While angels are considered noncorporeal in Scripture, they are always treated as creatures. Although they inhabit God's heavenly courtroom, they are not eternal but were brought into existence by God. Once again, we see that the decisive distinction in Scripture is between Creator and created, not between the spiritual and the material. Therefore, they are not to be worshiped. In fact, the Colossians are warned against a proto-Gnostic sect drawn toward severe asceticism and "worship of angels, dwelling on visions, puffed up without cause by a human way of thinking" — that is, apart from Christ (Col 2:18 NRSV).

In the Bible, angels are heavenly servants devoted to their Creator in worship day and night (Job 38:7; Pss 103:20; 148:2; Isa 6; Rev 5:11). Ministers of God's saving purposes for the heirs of salvation (Heb 1:14), they rejoice at the conversion of even of one sinner (Lk 15:10). They watch over believers (Pss 34:7; 91:11), learn the truths of God's unfolding mystery in Christ (Eph 3:10; 1Pe 1:12), and are said to bring believers to Abraham's side (Lk 16:22).

In their extraordinary commissions, certain angels are also chosen to bring God's revelation to his people. It is interesting how frequently their work is defined in relation to the Word of God. In fact, an angel is frequently referred to as a messenger (*mal'āk*). They are servants of the Word rather than objects of our gaze and devotion in their own right.

There appear to be different ranks of these heavenly messengers. First, there is the Angel of the Lord, sometimes called the Angel of Presence — often identified in Christian interpretation as a Christophany — that is, an appearance of the preincarnate Son of God. If this is so, then the term *angel* is broader than its commonly recognized sense, including any personal being who is a messenger from God. The defining element is the commission — i.e., one's status as a messenger.

Princes among the angelic hosts are Gabriel (Da 8:16; 9:21; Lk 1:19, 26) and Michael, the latter of whom is identified as an "archangel" (Da 10:13, 21; Jude 9; Rev 12:7). Revelation 8:2 speaks of seven angels that stand before God's throne in worship. Fearful in majesty, Gabriel has the honor of announcing the incarnation to the Virgin Mary (Lk 1:19). The cherubim guard the entrance to Eden (Ge 3:24), gaze on the mercy seat (Ex 25:18; Pss 80:1; 99:1, Isa 37:16; Heb 9:5), and form God's chariot on which he descends to the earth (2Sa 22:11; Ps 18:10; cf. Rev 4), while seraphim guard their faces and feet as they serve in God's presence (Isa 6:2–6).

The New Testament epistles refer to rulers and authorities in heavenly places (Eph 1:21; 3:10; Col 1:16; 2:10; 1Pe 3:22), and this undoubtedly includes fallen angels as well as God's holy servants. The fallen angels are not treated as evil by creation but as followers of Satan in his mutiny (2Pe 2:4; Jude 6). Satan (personal name, Lucifer), at one time the most glorious and powerful angelic agent, was filled with pride and plotted the attempted heavenly coup. He is the personal figure behind every antichrist figure in the biblical narrative who seeks to destroy the seed of the woman, who will crush his head. Satan, "the prince of the power of the air" (Eph 2:2), "the god of this world" who has blinded humanity (2Co 4:4), is the instigator of the human rebellion (Ge 3:1, 4; Mt 25:41; Jn 8:44; 2Co 11:3; 1Jn 3:8; Rev 12:9; 20:2, 10). As Adam and Eve were created to imitate the creation-conquest pattern of their Great King and then be exalted, in their fall they imitate Lucifer's proud rebellion, exalting themselves and in the process being cast down from their lofty position. And just as the heavenly hosts praise God day and night, Satan accuses God's people day and night and seeks their death (Rev 12:10). Nevertheless, even Satan and his demonic hosts are restricted by God's power (Mt 12:29; Rev 20:2) and are destined to be destroyed (Rev 20:10).

DISCUSSION QUESTIONS

1. What makes us human—distinct from the rest of creation?
2. Identify and evaluate the different models of anthropology (i.e., the human constitution).
3. What is the "image of God"? How do the motifs of covenant and eschatology shape our interpretation? Reflect especially on the Hebrew idiom, "Here I am."
4. How is the image of God a commission as well as a gift?
5. What is the role of angels in the history of redemption?

Chapter Thirteen

THE FALL
OF HUMANITY

Solidarity of the human race under Adamic headship is the source both of the grandeur and of the tragedy of our existence. If the world is a theater or a stage, as Calvin and Shakespeare among other notables have told us, then the play is a courtroom drama. Like Hamlet's play-within-a-play, the story of Israel can be read as a condensed version of the original covenant with our race in Adam. We are set before a great trial in which we ourselves are actors and not just audience. This sets the stage for the final recapitulation of all of covenantal history in Jesus Christ, the Last Adam and the true and faithful Israel.

I. THE COSMIC TRIAL

Of course, the courtroom analogy is not the only one that is employed. The parent-child relationship is just as obvious, and therefore we should not play the relational and the legal off of each other but recognize that they are both integral to a covenantal account. The New Testament builds on the Old Testament interpretation of history as the story of a covenant made and a covenant broken.[1] Returning to the categories employed in the last chapter for identifying the image of God, we will see how sin — rather than abolishing these indelible marks of our office — perverts and misuses them for selfish ends.

A. FALSE WITNESS

As we have encountered above, the Holy Spirit is the divine witness who surveys the creation and pronounces his benediction. It is this same Spirit who walked in

---

1. Sigmund Freud's unappointed successor in the field of psychoanalysis, Jacques Lacan, has written, "That tradition alone pursues to the end the task of revealing what is involved in the primitive crime of the primordial law" ("Seminar Lecture," in *The Postmodern God: A Theological Reader* [ed. Graham Ward; trans. D. Porter; Malden, Mass.: Blackwell, 1997], 41).

the garden in judgment, flushing Adam and Eve out of the bushes, and who led the Israelites in pillar and cloud, witnessing to the world that Israel belonged to Yahweh the Liberator (Ex 33:14–16). Taking us under his wing, as it were, this same Spirit makes us witnesses.

But there is also a false witness: the one who would be identified in relation to his persecution of God's people, the one who "accuses them day and night before our God" (Rev 12:10). He is "a liar and the father of lies" (Jn 8:44). Once the chief magistrate under God in heaven, he has become the archetype and ruler of false witnesses on earth. This is seen clearly in the familiar story of the fall in Genesis. Against the Creator's clear instruction, which put the entire garden at the disposal of humanity except for the fruit of one tree, the serpent first misinterprets God's stipulation ("Did God actually say, 'You shall not eat of *any* tree in the garden'?" [3:1]). When this fails, he asserts directly that Eve and Adam will not die but will in fact be like God, autonomous and self-sufficient to determine good and evil for themselves (vv. 4–5). In his deceptive speech, Lucifer makes himself sound like he is more interested in their welfare than God, but his ultimate aim is to make them his image-bearers rather than God's.

"The decisive point," notes Dietrich Bonhoeffer, "is that this question suggests to man that he should go behind the Word of God and establish what it is by himself, out of his understanding of the being of God.... Beyond this given Word of God the serpent pretends somehow to know something about the profundity of the true God who is so badly misrepresented in this human word." The serpent claims a path to the knowledge of the real God behind the Word.[2] It is not atheism that is introduced by the serpent but idolatrous religion, says Bonhoeffer.[3] "The wolf in sheep's clothing, Satan in an angel's form of light: this is the shape appropriate to evil." This will be the doubt that Satan will introduce through false religion through the ages:

> "Did God say?", that plainly is the godless question. "Did God say," that he is love, that he wishes to forgive our sins, that we need only believe him, that we need no works, that Christ has died and has been raised for us, that we shall have eternal life in his kingdom, that we are no longer alone but upheld by God's grace, that one day all sorrow and wailing shall have an end? "Did God say," thou shalt not steal, thou shalt not commit adultery, thou shalt not bear false witness...did he really say it to me? Perhaps it does not apply in my particular case? "Did God say," that he is a God who is wrathful towards those who do not keep his commandments? Did he demand the sacrifice of Christ? I know better that he is the infinitely good, the all-loving father. This is the question that appears innocuous but through it evil

---

2. Dietrich Bonhoeffer, *Creation and Fall: A Theological Exposition of Genesis 1–3* (ed. John W. de Gruchy; trans. Doug-las Stephen Bax; Minneapolis: Augsburg Fortress, 1997), 66.

3. Ibid., 67.

wins power in us, through it we become disobedient to God...Man is expected to be judge of God's word instead of simply hearing and doing it.[4]

Imitating the father of lies, the creature brought into being as God's star witness begins to interpret reality with himself rather than God at the center. "When man proceeds against the concrete Word of God with the weapons of a principle, with an idea of God, he is in the right from the first, he becomes God's master, he has left the path of obedience, he has withdrawn from God's addressing him."[5]

Indeed, the "I" in the "Here I am" that puts the covenant servant at the disposal of the suzerain becomes turned in on itself. Instead of hearing God's Word, the first humans sought to see, control, master, and determine it for themselves (Gen 3:3–6). "Then the eyes of both were opened, and they knew that they were naked. And they sewed fig leaves together and made themselves loincloths" (v. 7). "I heard the sound [*qôl*, voice] of you in the garden," Adam answered God, "and I was afraid, because I was naked, and I hid myself" (vv. 9–10). This will now be the tragic response of the human conscience in the presence of God.

In every subplot of the Bible we discover echoes of this trial of the covenant servant in the cosmic courtroom. The Israelites who gathered at the foot of Sinai, filled with terror by the divine words, entreated Moses, "You speak to us, and we will listen; but do not let God speak to us, lest we die" (Ex 20:19). Moses even replies by calling this a trial (Ex 20:20). Even Isaiah, caught up in a vision of God in holy splendor, could only reply, "Woe is me, for I am lost" (Isa 6:5). It was this same terror that gripped Peter's conscience when after Jesus calmed the storm, he could bring forth only the words, "Depart from me, for I am a sinful man" (Lk 5:8).

Adam's first sin was not in eating the forbidden fruit but in allowing the false witness to become a resident of the garden in the first place. The commission given to Adam and Eve above all else was to "work" and "keep" the sanctuary (Ge 2:15; the same verbs used in the commission given to the priests in the Jerusalem temple). Instead of cleansing God's temple-garden as God's faithful servant and son, Adam entertained Satan himself and failed to protect Eve from his influence. This story will be repeated in many variations, as God's people show themselves unwilling to uproot idolatry and violence (including child sacrifice) entirely from the land and then fall under the spell of foreign beliefs and practices themselves.

The covenantal structure of creation and the probationary trial that ensues underscore the ethical character of this situation. Rather than serving as God's witness, adding verbal testimony to the witness of the whole creation, Adam took the witness stand against God. Against the witness of the Spirit, the testimony of the whole creation, and even the glory, beauty, and integrity of his own high office,

4. Ibid., 68.   5. Ibid.

Adam perjured himself. Evil is not a principle in creation itself, but the willful distortion of good gifts into an arsenal deployed against God's reign.[6] This perversity corrupts that which is noble, suppresses that which is righteous, smears that which is beautiful, and smothers the light of truth.

Adam's role as false witness bears relation not only to God but to the whole creation, since he represents all human beings and humankind collectively as the chief of the rulers over the other creaturely realms. The creation had been placed at the disposal of Adam in a state of integrity, with a commission to be a steward. But now this power, too, is twisted by a perversity of will. Royal stewardship is twisted into tyranny. Every sign of human oppression, violence, idolatry, and immorality in the world can be seen as the perversion of an original good. The commission to be fruitful and to multiply, to work in, guard, protect, and subdue God's garden so that its peace and righteousness extend to the ends of the earth is twisted into empires of oppression in order to secure a consummation without God.

Although pain in childbirth is dreaded in any circumstance, part of God's judgment in the curse is directed to Eve: "'I will surely multiply your pain in childbearing; in pain you shall bring forth children'" (Ge 3:16a). This increased pain undoubtedly included the emotional stress of bringing children into a world that was now fallen and that would be increasingly filled with violence, deprivation, and depravity. Furthermore, God adds, "'Your desire shall be for your husband, and he shall rule over you'" (v. 16b). Enmity with God will draw into its wake enmity between fellow human beings, including husband and wife. As male and female, humanity was the image of God (Ge 1:27), but now they are at enmity not only with God but with each other.

The whole covenantal fabric of human life will become brittle and, in fact, broken. Childbirth and marriage are also joyful, to be sure, because God has not abandoned humanity to its own devices. Creation remains upheld by God's hand. And yet these common gifts are a mixed blessing. They involve pain not only at the beginning, but in the middle and at the end. Similarly, the curse imposed on Adam and the ground is commensurate with the fruitlessness and "vanity" that life now wears for human experience. Every person is now born into the world spiritually "dead in ... trespasses and sins" (Eph 2:1). Adam blamed Eve, Eve blamed the serpent, and the serpent blamed God. At the end of the day, everybody blamed God, and ever since, we follow this course of vanity. In ancient as in modern dualism, the problem of evil is identified with created nature in an effort to externalize sin by attributing it to the "other"—"the woman whom you gave to be with me," the physical environment, our family, society, or other circumstances beyond our

---

6. Augustine, *Confessions* 7.15.22.

control, but ultimately God. We look for scapegoats. Shifting the focus from our own sin to God (ontology and metaphysics) is one of the sources of dualism, ancient and modern. However, the biblical narrative directs us away from ontological fault and back to covenantal transgression. It is this emphasis on unbelief interpreted as covenant-breaking that links soteriology (salvation) and epistemology (knowing), with Romans 1 – 3 as the *locus classicus*. In Adam we have all become false witnesses. As Merold Westphal observes, the "hermeneutics of suspicion" was not invented by Marx and Nietzsche but finds "its true home in the Pauline teaching about the noetic effects of sin, the idea that in wickedness we 'suppress the truth' (Ro 1:18)."[7]

B. False Representative

This courtroom trial presents the accused in the most radical relation to justice—not to abstract justice but to the personal righteousness in which humanity was created and by which it was to enjoy unbroken communion with God in a consummated Sabbath. The accused are discovered fleeing the scene of the crime, covering up the evidence. After this, all human beings will be born into the world "dead in ... trespasses and sins" and "by nature children of wrath" (Eph 2:1, 3). Instead of representing the interests of the Great King in the world, the ambassador has defected to the enemy.

The ambassador driven deeper into the brush, ever more determined to suppress the truth, "'None is righteous, no, not one; no one understands, no one seeks for God.'" In fact, Paul adds in his litany, drawn especially from the Psalms,

> "All have turned aside; together they have become worthless;
>   no one does good,
>   not even one."
> "Their throat is an open grave;
>   they use their tongues to deceive."
> "The venom of asps is under their lips."
> "Their mouth is full of curses and bitterness."
> "Their feet are swift to shed blood;
>   in their paths are ruin and misery,
> and the way of peace they have not known."
>   "There is no fear of God before their eyes." (Ro 3:10 – 18)

Through the law that was once given as the way to everlasting life there is now because of sin only the expectation of death and judgment. The law announces this to everyone who is under it, whether in its written form or as it has been inscribed

---

7. Merold Westphal, *Overcoming Onto-Theology* (New York: Fordham Univ. Press, 2001), 105.

on the conscience, "so that every mouth may be silenced, and the whole world may be held accountable to God" (Rom 3:19 NRSV).

Because of this original covenantal relation and revelation, there is, as in Aldo Gargani's vivid expression, "the nostalgia for God of every living person."[8] And this nostalgia drives us to idolatry and suppression of the truth—a theology of glory that judges by appearances—rather than to the arms of God through the revelation of his Son, a theology of the cross that judges reality by God's promise. Together with this natural nostalgia for God, converted into idolatry, is the nostalgia for leading creation triumphantly into God's everlasting rest, converted now into self-will and tyranny.

The accusation pronounced by God's law, however it is rebuffed, rationalized, therapeutically suppressed or ignored through distraction, rings in the conscience and, as psychologist Robert Jay Lifton observes, drives our sense of guilt for a fault whose source seems forever ambiguous.[9] Thinking that their problem was merely shame rather than guilt, Adam and Eve covered themselves with loincloths, and ever since we have found ourselves incapable—or rather, unwilling—to accept the radical diagnosis of our own depravity. We can talk about evil outside of us—the "others," whoever they may be; evil places, structures, forces, and principles. But, like the religious leaders whom Jesus challenged, we refuse to locate evil within ourselves (Mt 12:33–37; 15:10–20; 23:25–28).

The accused, after offering countersuits, blaming each other for the fault, now face their sentence (Ge 3:15–19). In all of these sanctions, the generous giving and receiving embedded in God's natural order will yield to strife, control, exploitation, and manipulation at every level. And finally, instead of being confirmed in righteousness and everlasting life, Adam and his posterity will return to the dust (v. 19). This is a description of the fall, not, as in the pagan cosmogenic myths, of creation itself.

Guilt, strife, and vanity seem to be the dominant terms in this sentence. Instead of being eschatologically oriented toward Sabbath life with God, each other, and the whole creation, we grow increasingly aware that we are "being toward death" (Heidegger). But this is not *natural*. This play was not intended to be a tragedy. There is no tragedy in God—no "dark side," since only good comes from God, "with whom there is no variation or shadow due to change" (Jas 1:17), but only unmixed blessing and fulfillment that God longed to share with creatures.

Even some of the church fathers, still too much in the grip of Platonism, located

---

8. Aldo Gargani, "Religious Experience," in *Religion* (ed. Jacques Derrida and Gianni Vattimo; Palo Alto, Calif.: Stanford University Press, 1996), 132. See also his great Chekhov quote on 132–33.

9. Robert Jay Lifton, "The Protean Style," in *The Truth about the Truth: De-Confusing and Re-Constructing the Postmodern World* (ed. Walter Truett Anderson; New York: G. P. Putnam's Sons, 1995), 130–40.

guilt, strife, and vanity not in ethical fault but in some ontological aspect of creaturely existence. If it is not "the woman that you gave me," it can be our own bodies and their passions that become the "other" to which we deflect our burden of guilt.[10]

As the interpretation of sin unfolds in redemptive revelation, we encounter again an ethical-covenantal rather than ontological concept: meeting a stranger rather than overcoming estrangement. It is not from the human condition as such—finitude, for example—but from the human condition "under the law," in bondage to sin, death, and condemnation, that we begin to meet the stranger who strikes fear. We hear his approach in the distance, although he is "not far from each one of us" (Ac 17:27). *In short, the human race in Adam is now the false prophet, who misrepresents God's Word in its futile and treasonous demand for autonomy; the false priest, who corrupts God's sanctuary instead of guarding, keeping, and extending it; and the false king, who is no longer the medium of God's loving reign but now exercises a cruel tyranny over the earth and his fellow vice-regents.*

II. VERDICT AND SENTENCE: SOLIDARITY IN ADAM

Trying to avoid our guilt, we focus on the symptoms of sin. We complain of the boredom of life—which the preacher calls "vanity." In Ecclesiastes the preacher concludes, "The end of the matter; all has been heard. Fear God and keep his commandments, for this is the whole duty of man. For God will bring every deed into judgment, with every secret thing, whether good or evil" (12:13–14). There is no note of the gospel struck in his conclusion of the matter, but what is clear is that the "eternity" that God has set in the heart of humanity is his law, the covenant of creation. Transgression of that covenant is the root of all human woe. Every person is now born estranged from the good Father, living in the far country in poverty and degradation. Unwilling to be a faithful son, humanity became a slave of sin and death.

---

10. Typical in this respect is John of Damascus, "An Exact Exposition of the Orthodox Faith," in *NPNF2*, vol. 9. Angelic nature "is not susceptible of repentance because it is incorporeal. For it is owing to the weakness of his body that man comes to have repentance" (19). Paradise: "Free from passion ... free from care and to have but one work to perform, to sing as do the angels, without ceasing or intermission, the praises of the Creator, and to delight in contemplation of Him and to cast all our care on Him" (29). "The tree of life, on the other hand, was a tree having the energy that is the cause of life, or to be eaten only by those who deserve to live and are not subject to death" (ibid.). A similar view may be discerned today—for example, in Jean-Luc Marion's suggestion that vanity and boredom are intrinsic to creation as such. See Jean-Luc Marion, *God without Being* (trans. Thomas A. Carlson; Chicago: Univ. of Chicago Press, 1991), 122–32. However, in Ecclesiastes the Preacher attributes such "vanity" to life on this side of Eden, under the curse of sin and death—all of which he identifies by the phrase "under the sun."

A. VIOLATION OF THE COVENANT OF CREATION

Even in Genesis 1–3 we recognize the features of a covenant that we have delineated: a historical prologue setting the stage (Ge 1–2), stipulations (2:16–17) and the sanctions (2:17b) over which Eve and the serpent argue (3:1–5) and which are finally carried out in the form of judgment (3:8–19). It is only after this fateful decision that an entirely new and unexpected basis is set forth for human destiny (3:21–24). These elements are present, albeit implicitly, in the creation narrative, with the Tree of Life as the prize awaiting the successful outcome of a trial. Just as Yahweh the Great King endured the "trial" of creation and came out at the other end pronouncing victory and entering his Sabbath enthronement, his earthly ectype-vassal was to follow the same course. Genesis 1–3, and their canonical Christian interpretation, have an eschatological rather than simply existential orientation.

As further confirmation, the presence of the Sabbath at the end of the "six-day" work-week-trial holds out the promise of everlasting confirmation in blessedness. This pattern is not the imposition of an arbitrary law, but the image-bearer's reflection of God's own journey from creation to consummation. If Adam should default in this covenantal relationship, he would "surely die," and we learn from the subsequent failure of Adam that this curse brought in its wake not only spiritual but physical, interrelational, and indeed environmental disaster.

Interpreted in the light of the rest of Scripture, Adam's covenantal role entailed that he was the representative for his whole posterity. In fact, every person is judged guilty in Adam, and the effects of this curse extend even to the rest of creation (Ge 3:17–18; Ro 8:20). It is with this simultaneously legal and relational background in mind that Paul makes his well-known statements on the imputation of Adam's guilt and corruption as the corollary of the imputation and impartation of the Second Adam's righteousness (esp. Ro 5) in justification and sanctification.[11]

The theme of covenant solidarity, otherwise regarded as congenial to relational and communal views of the self, is nevertheless put to the test when it involves collective human *guilt*: the tragic aspect of human solidarity and relationality. "The intersubjective matrix which forms individual, related persons," notes Francis Watson, "also simultaneously *de*forms them."[12] Together we stand or fall. The legal and relational basis for this solidarity is the covenant of creation. As John Zizioulas observes,

---

11. This approach also rejects the stance often taken in the last half-century to set the so-called "relational" against the "legal" category of the divine-human relationship. "Covenant" is an inherently legal relationship.

12. Francis Watson, *Text, Church and World: Biblical Interpretation in Theological Perspective* (Edinburgh; T&T Clark,

1994), 110. See also Paul Ricoeur, *Figuring the Sacred: Religion, Narrative, and Imagination* (trans. David Pellauer; Minneapolis: Fortress, 1995), especially ch. 20; idem, *Oneself as Another* (trans. Kathleen Blamey; Chicago: Univ. of Chicago Press, 1992).

> The drive of the human being towards otherness is rooted in the divine call to Adam. The call simultaneously implies three things: relationship, freedom, and otherness, all of them being interdependent.... Through the call, Adam is constituted, therefore, as being other than God and the rest of creation. This otherness is not the result of self-affirmation; it is an otherness granted and is not self-existent, but a particularity which is a gift of the Other.[13]

Human identity therefore originates in being addressed: "the human being is singled out, not merely as a species, but as a particular partner in a relationship, as a respondent to a call."[14] It is precisely this call that humanity, in Adam, refuses, because we wish to be the speaker, not the addressee, in the covenant.

Contrary to the assumptions of Rudolf Bultmann, Ernst Käsemann, and others, Paul's polemic against the law and works of the law is not an abstract opposition. Humanity was created for love, which means for law, since law simply stipulates loving actions. Because of the fall, there is no longer any possibility of being justified by "works of the law." All of humanity, including Israel, is now "in Adam," condemned as a transgressor of the law. Thus, the covenant of creation (also called the covenant of works, law, or nature) is the legal context for God's judgment. This original covenant of creation may be defended by appealing to non-Christian as well as Christian sources.

1. Testimony to the Covenant of Creation from Non-Christian Sources

Along with its creation story (*Enuma Elish*), ancient Babylonian civilization produced the Code of Hammurabi, which bears striking resemblance to the Ten Commandments delivered to Moses centuries later. In fact, it was probably under King Hammurabi (1792–1750 BC) that the Enuma Elish poem was commissioned. The historical prologue to the Code begins,

> When the exalted Anu..., the lord of heaven and earth ... committed the sovereignty over all the people to Marduk ... and in its midst established for him an everlasting kingdom whose foundations are firm as heaven and earth; at that time Anu and Enlil called me, Hammurabi, the reverent prince, the worshipper of the gods, by name, to cause justice to prevail in the land, to destroy the wicked and the evil, to prevent the strong from oppressing the weak, to go forth like the sun over the human race, to enlighten the land and to further the welfare of the people.[15]

Thus, even pagan cultures grounded their laws in a narrative of original creation that was taken to be universally normative.

---

13. John Zizioulas, *Communion and Otherness* (London: T&T Clark, 2006), 41–42.

14. Ibid., 42.

15. Alexander Heidel, ed. and trans., *The Babylonian Genesis* (2nd ed.; Chicago: Univ. of Chicago Press, 1963), 14n9, taken from R. F. Harper, ed. and trans., *The Code of Hammurabi, King of Babylon, about 2250 B.C.* (Chicago: Univ. of Chicago, 1904); see Bruno Meissner, *Babylonien und Assyrien* (Heidelberg, 1925), 2:46.

Judaism grounds human moral solidarity in an original covenant of creation, renewed in the covenant with Noah. In that covenant, David Novak argues, basic precepts of the moral law are made binding on all people, although the specific laws governing Israel's life in the land are not. A covenantal approach to rights, Novak argues, avoids Greek philosophical theories of natural law on one side and modern autonomy on the other. It is, after all, a personal God and not an abstract concept of the Good that ultimately grounds a biblical sense of justice (equity). God establishes by his command the rights and duties that are reciprocally related in all human relationships.[16] Novak remarks, "How fundamentally different all this is from seeing natural law as some sort of translation of a higher nature down to the actual affairs of human beings. In that view, there is no primary voice, but only a vision of a polity that might conform to a higher paradigm in the heavens. It is duty without an originating right/claim, for such a right/claim cannot be imagined, but only heard (emphasis added)."[17] God is the original rights-holder, but he condescends to enter into an asymmetrical yet real relationship in which he accepts claims as well as makes them, which in turn becomes the reciprocal relationship between human beings.[18]

The Mosaic covenant institutes the "clean-unclean" separation, with its specific laws governing the theocracy. Novak continues, "Nevertheless, that separation from the world does not entail a separation from the justice that God requires of the human world, a requirement that is voiced through natural rights, which are the just claims of human persons and communities. The general claims on that world, which the rabbinic tradition sees going back to Noah, even to Adam and Eve, are not overcome by the [Mosaic] covenant; instead, they are subsumed into the covenant intact."[19] Thus, human solidarity is always more basic than national, racial, or cultural solidarity. It is not based on a social contract, but on a divine covenant.[20]

---

16. David Novak, *Covenantal Rights: A Study in Jewish Political Theory* (Princeton: Princeton Univ. Press, 2000), 20.

17. Ibid., 25.

18. Ibid., 85.

19. Ibid., 86.

20. David Novak, *Jewish-Christian Dialogue: A Jewish Justification* (New York: Oxford Univ. Press, 1989), 27. I concur with Novak's assessment that Judaism and Christianity share a theocentric orientation against secularism that grounds human rights not in a social contract but in an original covenant God made with humanity in creation (140). This much-misunderstood "Judeo-Christian ethic" involves the following consensus: (1) humanity is created for covenant with God; (2) it is a practical relationship, "its content being response to commandments from God"; (3) humans are created social beings in covenant with each other, not simply isolated individuals; (4) ultimate human community lies in the future, in a "redemptive act by God, one as yet on the unattainable historical horizon." "If one calls the morality grounded in these affirmations theonomous, then it should be contrasted with the two noncovenantal moral options available in history: autonomy and heteronomy. In making this essential contrast, Judaism and Christianity can discover together the present force of the anthropological border they share" (141–42). "Creation itself is in essence a commandment, a speech-act establishing a reality that is to be" (142). "Speech precedes sight in the divine order of creation," and the human is a hearer first, someone commanded, not an autonomous moral legislator" (143). Vision follows hearing, and Eve got this in reverse (143–44). "Holiness (*qedushah*) is not part of the cosmic order." Those in covenant with God are made holy by his address to them (154).

Novak demonstrates from the Jewish sources that this natural justice is grounded in an original covenant given to humanity in Adam.

Even in Islam, according to Osman bin Bakar, *shari'ah* includes both particular laws governing Muslims and laws that are regarded as universally binding as a result of a common Adamic origin.[21] We find the same consensus in Buddhism and Hinduism, with this universal law identified as *Dharma* (the Right Way) and the *Tao* (Path). Whether it is called the Tao, Dharma, Karma, Torah, the Universal Declaration of Human Rights, or "the little voice within," the most ineradicable report of general revelation is our moral accountability before a holy God for how we treat each other. This is the law above all positive laws of nations and international bodies. No matter how we try to suppress, distort, and deny it, our sense of being personally responsible for our sin is universal and natural. Confucius is reported to have said, "There may be someone who has perfectly followed the way [i.e., the Tao]: but I never heard of one."[22] Even if Scripture did not teach it, experience would require something like the covenant of creation to account for this moral sensibility.

2. TESTIMONY TO THE COVENANT OF CREATION FROM CHRISTIAN SOURCES

One cannot account for this covenantal understanding by reference to a dominance of legal (Western) categories to be contrasted with those of relational (Eastern) theology. The same emphases may be found in Irenaeus, where he not only affirms an Adamic covenant but distinguishes between an "economy of law" or "law of works" (which he associates with Adam in the prelapsarian situation and then again with Israel in the "Mosaic economy" or "legal dispensation") and a "Gospel covenant."[23] John of Damascus adds, "It was necessary, therefore, that man should first be put to the test (for man untried and unproved would be worth nothing), and being made perfect by the trial through the observance of the command should thus receive incorruption as the prize of his virtue."[24] In the West, Augustine also clearly anticipates the covenant of works/covenant of grace scheme, as, for example, in his comment that "the *first covenant* was this, unto Adam: 'Whensoever thou eatest thereof, thou shalt die the death,'" and this is why all

---

21. Osman bin Bakar, "Pluralism and the 'People of the Book,'" in *Religion and Security: The Nexus in International Relations* (ed. Robert A. Seiple and Dennis R. Hoover; Lanham, Md.: Rowman and Littlefield, 2004), 105, 108. Nevertheless, unlike Novak, bin Bakar exploits this universal dimension as a unifying religious factor among the "religions of the book." I would argue that law, whether natural or revealed, is a unifying human factor, but that the gospel is the only unifying religious factor.

22. Confucius, as quoted in C. S. Lewis, *Collected Letters of C. S. Lewis* (San Francisco: HarperSanFrancisco, 2004), 2:561.

23. Irenaeus, *Against Heresies* 4.25, in *ANF*, vol. 1; cf. 5.16.3; 4.13.1; 4.15.1; 4.16.3; cf. Ligon Duncan, "The Covenant Idea in Irenaeus of Lyons," a paper presented at the North American Patristics Society annual meeting, May 29, 1997 (Greenville, S.C.: Reformed Academic Press, 1998); Everett Ferguson, "The Covenant Idea in the Second Century," in *Texts and Testaments: Critical Essays on the Bible and the Early Church Fathers* (ed. W. E. March; San Antonio: Trinity Univ. Press, 1980).

24. John of Damascus, *An Exact Exposition of the Orthodox Faith*, in *NPNF2*, 9:43.

of his children "are breakers of God's covenant made with Adam in paradise" (emphasis added).[25]

Is there then some commonly shared site of revelation not only for Judaism, Christianity, and Islam but for all human beings? Reformation theology emphasizes that while the gospel is revealed only in the proclamation of Christ (*verbum externum*), the law is the native property of all human beings (*verbum internum*), the very law of their being which, though suppressed in unrighteousness, cannot entirely be purged from the conscience. While interreligious agreement on the content of the supernaturally revealed gospel is impossible, we should expect and work toward greater understanding of our common life together in the light of the original creation covenant, whose remnants are kept alive by the continual speaking of the Father in the Son through the Spirit according to common grace.

Although refined by later Reformed theologians, the seeds of the covenantal approach can be easily discerned in the likes of Philipp Melanchthon, Heinrich Bullinger, Martin Bucer, and John Calvin.[26] Parallel to the Jewish view of the Noahide laws summarized by Novak, Calvin writes, "Now that inward law [*lex interior*], which we have ... described as written, even engraved, upon the hearts of all, in a sense asserts the very same things that are to be learned from the two Tables."[27] In contrast to Stoicism (and much of medieval natural law thinking), then, the law of nature is not the product of our participation in Being, but of our being in every moment summoned as covenant creatures. Of Romans 2:14–15, Calvin says, "There is nothing more common than for a man to be sufficiently instructed in a right standard of conduct by natural law (of which the apostle is here speaking)."[28] "If the Gentiles by nature have law righteousness engraved upon their minds, we surely cannot say they are utterly blind as to the conduct of life."[29] In fact, Calvin praises "the sagacity" of the great scientists, philosophers, and jurists "in things earthly," scolding sectarians for insulting the Holy Spirit, who gives such common gifts to humanity.[30]

Once this original covenant is recognized, a host of passages come to mind. The late seventeenth-century theologian Peter van Mastricht, for example, appeals to Hosea 6:7, where it is said of Israel, "Like *Adam*, they have transgressed the covenant" (cf. Job 31:33, where "as *Adam* did" is the most likely translation).[31] Since

---

25. Augustine, *City of God* (ed. David Knowles; trans. Henry Bettenson; New York: Penguin, 1972), 16.28 (pp. 688–89). In fact, Augustine elaborates this point in considerable detail in these two pages, contrasting the creation covenant with the covenant of grace as we find it in the promise to Abraham.

26. For a definitive survey, see J. T. McNeill, "Natural Law in the Teaching of the Reformers," *Journal of Religion* 26 (1946): 168–82. Cf. Philipp Melanchton, *Loci communes* (first pub-

lished in 1521), chapter 7.

27. Calvin, *Institutes* 2.8.1.

28. Ibid., 2.2.22.

29. Ibid.

30. Ibid., 2.2.13, 15.

31. See Byron Curtis, "Hos 6:7 and Covenant-Breaking like/as Adam," in *The Law Is Not of Faith* (ed. B. Estelle, J. Fesko, D. VanDrunen; Phillipsburg, N.J.: P&R, 2009), 170–209.

Israel was a theocracy typological of the eschatological Paradise of God, its *national* existence was a repetition of the covenant of creation—hence, the comparisons drawn by the biblical writers to Adam and the original creation.[32] Israel was called to see itself as a new theocratic garden of God's presence and as a new creation in the sense of representing humanity before God—all of this typological of the true Israel, the faithful *Adam*, who is also the true heavenly temple and everlasting Sabbath of God. As with Adam, the Sinaitic covenant is conditional. If Israel is faithful, the people's days "may be long in the land the LORD your God is giving you" (e.g., Ex 20:12; cf. Dt 11:9). Thus, Israel's tenure in the land, like Adam's, is conditional—although in the earlier case God's *goodness* was presupposed, while in the later, God's *grace* (Dt 7:7–11). Precisely the same terms and sanctions apply: Do this and you will live long in the land and enter into the Sabbath rest. As with his appeal to the two Adams for double imputation, Paul draws on the analogy of two mountains, two mothers, and two cities to contrast the covenant of works (law) and the covenant of grace (promise) (Gal 3 and 4). As Peter van Mastricht pointed out in the seventeenth century, Christ's role as the "fulfiller of all righteousness" is without any legal basis apart from a covenant that demands it as the condition of reward.[33]

More recently, however, some Reformed theologians have questioned or even rejected the idea that this original relationship of humanity to God, in Adam, was a covenant. For example, John Murray insisted that biblical covenants are inherently gracious; the very idea, then, of a covenant founded in love but based on pure law or works he regarded as untenable.[34] However, this fails to appreciate sufficiently the integrity of humanity in the state of rectitude. Adam was not created merely in a state of innocence, but in a state of positive righteousness—with all of the

---

32. While this parallel is drawn by a number of writers, it is given a thorough description and analysis in Herman Witsius (1636–1708), *The Economy of the Covenants* (Escondido, Calif.: The den Dulk Christian Foundation, 1990). For a more contemporary summary, see Charles Hodge, *Systematic Theology* (Grand Rapids: Eerdmans, 1946): "Besides this evangelical character which unquestionably belongs to the Mosaic covenant ["belongs to," not "is equivalent to"], it is presented in two other aspects in the Word of God. First, it was a national covenant with the Hebrew people. In this view the parties were God and the people of Israel; the promise was national security and land prosperity; the condition was the obedience of the people as a nation to the Mosaic law; and the mediator was Moses. In this aspect it was a legal covenant. It said 'Do this and live.' Secondly, it contained, as does also the New Testament, a renewed proclamation of the covenant of works" (117–22).

33. Peter van Mastricht, as quoted in Heinrich Heppe, *Reformed Dogmatics* (ed. Ernst Bizer; London: Allen & Unwin, 1950), 290: "To very many heads of the Christian religion, e.g., the propagation of original corruption, the satisfaction of Christ and his subjection to divine law Rom. 8.3–4 (what the law could not do, in that it was weak through the flesh, God, sending his own Son in the likeness of sinful flesh and for sin, condemned sin in the flesh, that the requirement of the law might be fulfilled in us, who walk not after the flesh, but after the Spirit) Gal. 3:13 (Christ redeemed us from the curse of the law, having become a curse for us...), we can scarcely give suitable satisfaction, if the covenant of works be denied." For further exegetical arguments from Mastricht, see additional citations in Heppe, *Reformed Dogmatics*, 289–90.

34. John Murray denied the covenant of works because he presupposed that a divine covenant must always be gracious. However, he did refer to "the Adamic administration." See John Murray, "The Adamic Administration," in *The Collected Writings of John Murray* (Edinburgh: Banner of Truth, 1977). Nevertheless, Robert Reymond properly replies, "But Murray fails to make clear what the 'Adamic administration' is an administration *of*" (Robert Reymond, *A New Systematic Theology of the Christian Faith* [Nashville: Nelson, 1988], 405).

requisite natural and moral abilities to fulfill the commission entrusted to him. To some, a covenantal relationship based on law seems to exclude love. However, God's law is nothing more than a stipulation of the proper exercise of love toward God and neighbor (Mt 22:37–40). Law and love are typically contrasted in contemporary theology and in popular thought. But the theology of covenant brings these together. Ancient Near Eastern scholar Delbert Hillers points out that in the relationship established by the covenant-treaty, law and love are synonymous. Law prescribes the dictates of love.[35] Love is simultaneously legal and emotional language, and it is the legal that shapes the emotional expression: "To love is to set one's sincere affections on the covenant Lord and to give this affection its expression in loyal service."[36] Who are we, the violators of love, to determine for ourselves its proper exercise when the God who is love has clearly revealed its demands in his law?

It is in the context of a covenant that law is seen as the concrete specification of the duties of love. If Adam obeyed, out of covenant love (*ḥesed*) for his Creator and his fellow creatures, he would win the right to eat from the Tree of Life, confirmed in everlasting peace and righteousness. And as our covenantal head, he would win this right not only for himself but for all of his posterity. In the words of the *Formula Consensus Helvetica*, "the promise annexed to the covenant of works was not just the continuation of earthly life and felicity," but a confirmation in righteousness and everlasting heavenly joy.[37]

A final argument in favor of the covenant of creation is supplied by Cocceius, in terms of *conscience* (Ro 2:15), a point that Calvin had repeatedly emphasized in relation to the law. Created in God's image, humanity was capable of this relationship to which it was bound and in which God had bound himself as well.

3. A COVENANT OF LOVE AND LAW, NOT GRACE

I have already defended the point that creation had its own integrity prior to the fall. The original relationship in which humanity was created is best characterized by "voluntary condescension" (*Westminster Confession* 7.1) rather than by grace.

According to the Roman Catholic view, creation not only possessed the potentiality for corruption (which, of course, we would affirm), but was suspended between higher and lower realms, concentrated in the dualism between the intellectual contemplation of the eternal and unchanging Good and the indulgence of the temporal and fluctuating passions. Adam's sustenance—and therefore that of the created order—depended at every moment not on the integrity of freedom in created righteousness, but on a *donum superadditum*—a gift of grace added to nature, elevating

---

35. Delbert Hillers, *Covenant: The History of a Biblical Idea* (Baltimore: Johns Hopkins Univ. Press, 1969), 153.

36. Hillers, *Covenant*, 153.

37. Heppe, *Reformed Dogmatics*, 295.

it toward the supernatural. Related to this idea is the notion of *concupiscence* (from the Latin, meaning desire for worldly things). According to this teaching, the grace that God added to nature in the beginning gave Adam and Eve an inclination toward transcending their body and its desires by rational ascent.[38] Thus, concupiscence is the inclination toward the ostensibly inferior realm of nature, which was indulged when God withdrew his superadded grace.

In the view of the Reformers, this undermined the integrity of nature as created. If humanity was created in an original justice, as the medieval church affirmed, why did it require a gift of grace to orient it toward God? The Reformers challenged the traditional view also because of its inherent spirit-matter dualism, its liability to making God the cause of Adam's sin, and its identification of the origin of sin in nature itself rather than in a perverse transgression against that natural integrity in which God had created human beings. It is not difficult to conclude that human and, more generally, creaturely integrity was therefore lost when this *donum* was removed, as Augustine himself implies.[39]

By contrast, the Reformers taught that both the integrity of human nature and its depravity after the fall were total, encompassing the mind as well as the body, the soul as well as its passions, the intellect and senses alike. The fall cannot be attributed to humanity's having been "ensnared by the inferior appetites," says Calvin, "but abominable impiety has seized the very citadel of his mind, and pride has penetrated into the inmost recesses of his heart; so that it is weak and foolish to restrict the corruption which has proceeded thence to what are called the sensual appetites." Calvin accuses medieval theologian Peter Lombard of "the grossest ignorance" for identifying "the flesh" in Paul (especially Ro 7:18) with the body and sensual appetites, "as though Paul designated only a part of the soul and not the whole of our nature which is opposed to supernatural grace." In Ephesians 4:17–18, for example, Paul does not merely locate sin in "the inordinate motions of the appetites, but principally insists on the blindness of the mind and the depravity of the heart."[40]

In Roman Catholic theology, concupiscence is not yet the act of sin but a propensity (habitus or disposition) for sin, and this propensity is due to the lower self. However, Reformation theology denied that there was any propensity toward sin or weakness in human nature prior to the fall. In this view, the fall was due to the

---

38. According to the *Catechism of the Catholic Church* (Liguori, Mo.: Liguori Publications, 1994), "The first man was unimpaired and ordered in his whole being because he was free from the triple concupiscence that subjugates him to the pleasures of the senses, covetousness for earthly goods, and self-assertion, contrary to the dictates of reason" (96). In the fall, this original justice "is now destroyed: the control of the soul's spiritual faculties over the body is shattered..." (100). However, "...human nature has not been totally corrupted: it is wounded in the natural powers proper to it; subject to ignorance, suffering, and the dominion of death; and inclined to sin—an inclination to evil that is called 'concupiscence'" (102).

39. *Augustine: Confessions and Enchiridion* (ed. and trans. Albert C. Outler; Philadelphia: Westminster, n.d.), 225–26; cf. Thomas Aquinas, *Of God and His Creatures: An Annotated Translation of Summa Contra Gentiles* (trans. Joseph Rickaby; Westminster, Md.: Carroll Press, 1950), 379.

40. Calvin, *Institutes* 2.1.9.

turning of the whole self away from God and his good gifts in an act of treason. We may summarize this point by saying that it is premature to insert into the creation covenant an element of divine *graciousness*, strictly speaking. Grace is not the same as goodness; mercy is not the same as love. Scripture speaks lavishly of God's goodness, kindness, generosity, and love toward his unfallen creation, but there is not a single verse that refers to God's grace and mercy toward creatures prior to the fall. Grace is synonymous with mercy: not merely unmerited favor, but the kind of loving-kindness that God shows to those who actually deserve the very opposite.

The terms of the covenant of creation cannot be set aside, nor their sanctions simply abandoned. Yet because of his extravagant love, God himself became human and fulfilled in the place of his elect the righteousness required in this original covenant. This is what Reformed theology understands as the active obedience of Christ.[41]

B. THE SANCTIONS OF THE COVENANT: ORIGINAL SIN

"Original sin" is the term that the Western church has employed to refer to our collective human guilt and corruption. No doctrine is more crucial to our anthropology and soteriology, and yet no doctrine has been more relentlessly criticized ever since it was articulated. Protestant liberalism has always had an optimistic view of human morality. Adolf von Harnack called original sin "an impious and foolish dogma."[42] That, however, was before two world wars, to which Harnack's own contribution should not be forgotten.[43]

Not surprisingly, the postwar years allowed a fresh reappraisal of the classical doctrine of original sin. Reinhold Niebuhr correctly surmised, "The Christian doctrine of sin in its classical form offends both rationalists and moralists by maintaining the seemingly absurd position that man sins inevitably and by a fateful necessity but that he is nevertheless to be held responsible for actions which are prompted by an ineluctable fate."[44] As the natural theology par excellence, Pelagianism was the anthropological assumption of Kant's thought.[45] No one has to be taught this

---

41. The fourth gospel once again especially underscores the "fulfilling of all righteousness" that is central to Jesus' mission. Jesus himself uses the language of a victorious second Adam, an obedient and loyal covenant servant, who has "come ... not to do my own will but the will of him who sent me" (Jn 6:38), who always does what his Father says and who can say at the end of his obedient probation, "I ... [have] accomplished the work that you gave me to do" (Jn 17:4). The hauntingly familiar words from the cross, "It is finished," take on fresh significance in its light, as does the rending of the temple curtain, through which humanity is now invited to enter into the Sabbath land and eat from the Tree of Life. In fact, the statement immediately preceding the last cry from the cross is, "After this, Jesus, knowing that all was

now finished, said (to fulfill the Scripture), 'I thirst'" (Jn 19:28).

42. Adolf von Harnack, *History of Dogma* (trans. Neil Buchanan; Boston: Little, Brown, and Company, 1899), 5:217.

43. Harnack helped to create Kaiser Wilhelm's "Deutschland über alles" war policy: one of the reasons for Barth's revulsion toward his liberal mentors.

44. Reinhold Niebuhr, *The Nature and Destiny of Man* (New York: Charles Scribner's Sons, 1964), 241.

45. Immanuel Kant, "Religion within the Boundaries of Mere Reason," in *Religion and Rational Theology* (ed. and trans. Allen W. Wood and George di Giovanni; Cambridge: Cambridge Univ. Press, 1996), 148, 150; Paul Ricoeur, *Figuring the Sacred*, 84–86.

heresy; it is our native tongue. Repeated attempts to dismiss the doctrine of original sin as a peculiarity of Calvin or Luther, Augustine or Paul fail to take seriously the fact that the same assumptions are articulated in the Psalms (Pss 51:5, 10; 143:2), the prophets (Isa 64:6; Jer 17:9) and in the Gospels (Jn 1:13; 3:6; 5:42; 6:44; 8:34; 15:4–5) and catholic epistles (Jas 3:2; 1Jn 1:8, 10; 5:12). The doctrine of original sin may be seen to arise as a result of two principal sources: the covenant itself as the biblical paradigm for relating divine-human relations and the narrative of the fall from an original state of integrity.

Citing examples from Second Temple Judaism, Childs concludes, "Judaism shared the view that human sin derived from Adam (IV Ezra 3.7; Sifre Deut. 323)."[46] In fact, one of the clearest examples of early Jewish belief in original sin is 2 Esdras:

> The same fate befell all of them: just as death came upon Adam, so the flood upon them [of Noah's generation].... For the first Adam, burdened with an evil heart, transgressed and was overcome, as were also all who were descended from him. Thus the disease became permanent; the law was in the hearts of the people along with the evil root; but what was good departed, and the evil remained ... in everything doing just as Adam and all his descendants had done, for they also had the evil heart (2 Esdras 3:10, 21–22, 26 NRSV).

These statements are in the context of explaining God's ways with Israel in her exile: the point is that Israel herself is "in Adam," and the first disobedience is lodged deep within the history of God's own people. The similarities to Paul's treatment, especially in Romans 1–3 and 5, are striking.

The concept of solidarity—human solidarity in Adam and Israel's in Abraham and Moses, is basic to the biblical worldview, however alien to our own. Paul simply elaborates this covenantal outlook when he explains that "sin came into the world through one man," in whom all people became henceforth sinners, condemned by the law and inwardly corrupt (Ro 5:12–21). It follows, then, that if Adam has failed to carry out his commission as the servant-king of Yahweh, all who are "in Adam" are implicated as well, just as the people represented by the vassal in the Hittite treaties would share in the threatened sanctions in the case of a breach.

At this point, everything turns on what kind of credit we give to the historical narrative and whether we are willing to speak, as not only Genesis 3 but subsequent Scripture does, of the human condition *before* and *after* the fall. Whatever one's conclusions concerning the process of human origins, Christian theology stands or falls with a historical Adam and a historical fall. On this point, Roman Catholic

---

46. Brevard Childs, *Biblical Theology of the Old and New Testaments* (Minneapolis: Fortress, 1993), 579.

and Reformation theologies are at one.[47] Against liberal theology, Barth and Brunner affirm that humanity is "in Adam," sharing in original sin, but, denying the historical fall, they can lodge this fact only in God's eternal predestination. In fact, Barth insists, "The guilt and punishment we incur in Adam have no independent reality of their own but are only the dark shadows of the grace and life we find in Christ." For Barth, it appears that "Adam" represents a mere copy, appearance, or shadow of the eternal Form (Christ), the latter swallowing the former.[48] However, if one does not take Adam (i.e., the human *as human*) seriously, two serious problems ensue: first, sin must be attributed to creation itself (and therefore ultimately to the Creator); second, there is no longer any historical basis for Christ's work as the Last Adam, undoing the curse and fulfilling the terms of the covenant of creation.

In Augustine's formulation, the doctrine of original sin concentrates on the metaphysics of nature, the superadded gift of grace, and sin's transmission from the soul of our first parents. Grounding original sin in idealist metaphysics, Jonathan Edwards speculated that we are all sinners because there is no such thing as an individual agent. In his view, the identity between Adam and all human beings is real (in the metaphysical sense): numerical sameness, dependent in every moment on a fresh *ex nihilo* act of God.[49] Hodge provides a suitable rebuttal to this theory.[50] A covenantal account of original sin focuses on the representative, federal, covenantal structure of human existence before God. Like a nation represented by the decrees and actions of its head of state, the human race is one-in-many and many-in-one. As goes the king, so goes the kingdom. To be sure, there are metaphysical and ontological consequences of covenant transgression, such as human death as the judicial sentence, but the essence of sin itself is legal, forensic, and ethical: "The sting of death is sin, and the power of sin is the law" (1Co 15:56).

Obviously, we are once again "meeting a stranger" rather than "overcoming estrangement" in this approach. Just as the image of God consists in a covenantal commission for which God created humanity rather than in a particular substance or faculty, original sin is to be understood within the same context, according to the same principle. Therefore, the emphasis should fall not on a faculty or principle that we all share in common, but on the sheer fact that we *are* in common; that is, we are in covenant.

---

47. *Catechism of the Catholic Church*, 98: "The Church, which has the mind of Christ, knows very well that we cannot tamper with the revelation of original sin without undermining the mystery of Christ. The account of the fall in Genesis 3 uses figurative language, but affirms a primeval event, a deed that took place *at the beginning of the history of man*. Revelation gives us the certainty of faith that the whole of human history is marked by the original fault freely committed by our first parents" (emphasis original).

48. Karl Barth, *Christ and Adam: Man and Humanity in Romans 5* (New York: Harper and Bros., 1957), 36.

49. Jonathan Edwards, *Original Sin*, in *Works of Jonathan Edwards* (2 vols.; Edinburgh: Banner of Truth, 1979), 2:555.

50. Hodge, *Systematic Theology*, 2:216–27.

Although Jenson does not appeal to this covenantal category, he makes essentially the same point:

> Humanity is finally one diachronically extended community, and that community and we in it are idolatrous, lustful, unjust and despairing. Moreover, we just so are compelled to posit a "fall" of humankind, occurring within created time.... The story told in the third chapter of Genesis is not a myth; it does not describe what always and ever happens. It describes the historical first happening of what thereafter always happens; moreover, had it not happened with the first humans it could not have happened at all, since then the first humans would have been omitted from an 'encompassing deed of the human race.'[51]

The fall in which we all participate is "the presence of the past."[52] Our present is the "effective history" (*Wirkungsgeschichte*) of an original transgression that defines our ethical condition and actions. In fact, solidarity in Adam illustrates the fact that covenant is not simply a metaphor for a relationship but *is* the relationship between God and creation. No one is an island. The past is present not only among us but within us. The covenant consciousness that we all share by virtue of our humanity carries with it ever since the fall the ineradicable consciousness of our existence as breach, alienation, and transgression. We are not only guilty *for* Adam's sin; we are guilty *as sinners in Adam*. Although this way of thinking (namely, corporate solidarity) is difficult to understand for those of us reared in liberal democracies, it is basic to Israel's faith. In Joshua 7, Achan steals from the spoils of holy war, and Yahweh commands Joshua, "Get up!... Israel has sinned; they have transgressed my covenant...." Although Achan is stoned, the guilt belongs to the people as a whole (vv. 10–26). In Israel's Passover liturgy, contemporary generations are to regard themselves as having been brought up out of Egypt with their forebears. These, and many more examples, exhibit the covenantal solidarity in the biblical approach to the question of guilt. In Paul's treatment in Romans 5, "sin came into the world through one man, and death through sin, and so death spread to all men because all sinned..." (v. 12). In other words, every human being was present representatively, federally, and covenantally in Adam. Our own personal acts of sin flow from this corrupt nature and add to our original guilt.

Especially in highly developed nations today, an implicitly Pelagian anthropology is often combined with an individualistic theory of the self and a therapeutic understanding of human rights, criminal justice, and social relations that challenges the traditional understanding of sin. In this context, it is inconceivable that one could be held responsible for participation in collective guilt. Furthermore, in the context of changing concepts of jurisprudence there has emerged a sentimental

---

51. Robert Jenson, *Systematic Theology* (New York: Oxford Univ. Press, 1997), 2:150.

52. Ibid., 2:355.

theology in which there is no place for any form of justice that is not exclusively ameliorative and healing. In fact, law professor Jean Bethke Elshtain has argued that the weakening sense of a holy God and human sinfulness even in churches is partially responsible for undermining the very notion of human justice as well.[53]

Moltmann concedes, "The Fathers of the church consistently followed the rabbinic and Pauline doctrine: suffering and death are the divinely appointed *punishment for human sin*. 'The wages of sin is death' (Ro 6:23)." However, he rejects this view: "This reduction of suffering and death to sin means that the beginning of salvation is seen as being the forgiveness of sins. Human redemption then takes place in two steps: sin is overcome through grace, in Christ's sacrificial death on the cross; the consequences of sin—suffering and death—are overcome by power, through the future resurrection of the dead." Moltmann prefers the path taken by Origen; namely, "that death belonged together with the creation of man as finite being." "It is therefore not a consequence of sin, and not a divine punishment either.... Augustine and the Latin Fathers, on the other hand, traced all forms of suffering and death back to sin, reducing the doctrine of redemption to juridical form into the doctrine of grace."[54] Sin brings its own misery, Moltmann concludes; it hardly needs any further punishment.[55] Once again we discern the natural tendency to identify sin merely with its symptoms rather than with its deeper heinousness as a criminal state and stance in relation to a holy God.

The tendency of fundamentalism is to reduce sin to sinful acts and behaviors, while liberalism reduces sin to evil social structures that impede the realization of the ethical kingdom. In contrast to both forms of reductionism, the biblical understanding of sin is far deeper in its analysis. Sin is first of all a *condition* that is simultaneously judicial and moral, legal and relational. Accordingly, we sin because we are sinners rather than vice versa. Standing before God as transgressors in Adam, we exhibit our guilt and corruption in actual thoughts and actions. If we cut off one diseased branch, another one—pregnant with the fruit of unrighteousness—grows in its place.

Furthermore, we are both victims and perpetrators. There is no human being since the fall who is *only* a victim; yet it is also true that every sinner is *also* sinned against. Such is the solidarity of humanity under the curse of the violated covenant of creation. A particular act of sin may be (or include) the fault of someone else, but the sinful condition and the web of sinful actions and relationships that flow from it implicate us as well. It is true that we do not simply choose our vices, but are condi-

---

53. Jean Bethke Elshtain, *Augustine and the Limits of Politics* (Notre Dame: Univ. of Notre Dame Press, 1995); cf. the interview with Elshtain by Ken Myers in *Mars Hill Audio Journal* 64 (September/October 2003).

54. Jürgen Moltmann, *The Trinity and the Kingdom: The Doctrine of God* (trans. Margaret Kohl; San Francisco: Harper & Row, 1981), 50.

55. Ibid.

tioned by the sinful structures to which our particular socio-cultural or familial contexts tend. Yet it is also true that we yield ourselves to these vices and are responsible for our own actions. Simplistic theories of sin easily identify the "righteous" (us) and the "wicked" (them), but as the biblical drama unfolds we recognize with increasing clarity that "all, both Jews and Greeks, are under sin, as it is written: 'None is righteous, no, not one; no one understands; no one seeks for God. All have turned aside; together they have become worthless; no one does good, not even one'" (Ro 3:9–12).

There is no doubt that an *exclusively* juridical concept of the fall cannot account for a host of passages, particularly those that emphasize the reality of systematic and institutional violence. But the covenant—simultaneously legal and relational, individual and collective, ethical and ontological, personal and social-institutional— brings these aspects together.

It is our definition of sin that generates such radically different construals of redemption. As Robert Jenson notes, "The only possible *definition* of sin is that it is what God does not want done. Thus if we do not reckon with God, we will not be able to handle the concept; without acknowledging God, we can—though perhaps not for long—speak meaningfully of fault and even of crime but not of sin."[56] Sin is a crime committed against a person, not just a principle; yet the law that is transgressed is the will of the personal Lord who institutes the relationship. The weight of the law is measured by the character of the one who gives it. Only when we are confronted with God in his holiness do we really understand something of the weight of sin (Isa 6:1–7). When reduced to the horizontal dimension (intrahuman relationships), sin becomes negative behaviors that can be easily managed or a failure to live up to one's potential and expectations. Apart from its vertical reference, sin can produce shame but never guilt. The only judgment that matters in such a scheme is that of society or our own, rather than God's.

The role of God in this perspective is merely to serve the sovereign self in its striving after perfection. Religion can become the chief means by which we suppress our participation in human guilt, as Barth so forcefully argued: "Our self-respect demands, on top of everything else, ... access to a superworld. Our deeds want deeper foundations, transcendent recognition and reward. Our lust for life covets also pious moments and prolongation into eternity."[57] Barth feels the force of Feuerbach's critique of religion, and, contrasting religion with the revelation of Christ, uses that critique to define religion as idolatrous projection:

> We come to our own rescue and build the tower of Babel. In what haste we are to soothe within us the stormy desire for the righteousness of God! And to soothe means, unfortunately, to cover up, to bring to silence.... The longing for a new

---

56. Jenson, *Systematic Theology*, 2:133.

57. Karl Barth, *Der Römerbrief* (2nd ed.; Munich: Chr. Kai-

ser, 1922), 20; quoted in Jenson, *Systematic Theology*, 2:136.

world has lost all its bitterness, sharpness, and restlessness, has become the joy of development, and now blossoms sweetly and surely in orations, donor's tablets, committee meetings, reviews, annual reports, twenty-five-year anniversaries, and countless mutual bows. The righteousness of God itself has slowly changed from being the surest of facts into being the highest among various ideals, and is now at all events our very own affair.... You may act as if you were God, you may with ease take his righteousness under your own management. This is certainly pride.[58]

Religion is one of the chief ways we cover up our shame without actually dealing with the guilt that gives rise to it. And we project a god who will satisfy our suppression of the truth about ourselves. "Idolatry is not an accident," Jenson notes, "as if some of us just happened to hit on wrong candidates for deity."[59] It is the result of a willful suppression of the truth in unrighteousness (Ro 1:18). Not only in our immorality and lying but even in our proud moral striving, self-confident religious devotion, and sincere pretensions, we are storing up God's wrath against us.

With its doctrine of original sin, biblical faith comes to grips with the reality of human tragedy only to enter into the joyful comedy of which pagan revelry is only a pale parody. Deep despair and deep joy belong to those who have encountered God in his law and gospel. By contrast, denial of this doctrine gives to pagan thought a superficial happiness that hides a deeper and final despair.

Writing in the face of the most obvious examples of human sin in the twentieth century, Reinhold Niebuhr reflected deeply on this complexity in *The Nature and Destiny of Man*. Niebuhr's experience especially of two world wars radically challenged his liberal theology and Marxist ideology, and although he never entirely abandoned his earlier convictions, he was increasingly drawn to the realism of a biblical understanding of human nature. One of the important insights of the classical Augustinian and Reformation heritage was its refusal to simplify the problem of sin as something that can be overcome by proper moral instruction and personal or social engineering. Liberalism (including the social gospel) radicalized the medieval tendency to identify sin and grace with the "lower" and "higher" realms of the self. "This remains true even when, as in the thought of men like Schleiermacher and in the theology of the social gospel, this sloth is attributed to the institutions and traditions of history rather than purely to sensual passion or to the finiteness of the mind."[60] According to Walter Rauschenbusch, sin is transmitted primarily through institutions, Niebuhr notes. "The argument by which this is done has not varied from the day of Augustine's critics."[61] Schleiermacher simply repeats the Pelagian reduction of sin to deliberate and conscious malice.[62]

---

58. Karl Barth, *The Word of God and the Word of Man* (trans. Douglas Horton; London: Peter Smith, 1958), 14–16.
59. Jenson, *Systematic Theology*, 2:137.
60. Ibid., 2:246.
61. Ibid., 2:247.
62. Ibid.

However, only in the robust, if tragic, doctrine of original sin is there a recognition that sin is also a condition from which we cannot extricate or exonerate ourselves. One need not have actively sent Jews to gas chambers in order to be guilty of failing to act on their behalf. It is this insight that is expressed in the *Book of Common Prayer*, when worshipers confess their sin as consisting both in "what we have done and what we have left undone," or when the *Westminster Shorter Catechism* (Q. 35) defines sin not only as an explicit violation but as "a lack of conformity to" God's law. "The truth is that, absurd as the classical Pauline doctrine of original sin may seem to be at first blush," says Niebuhr, "its prestige as a part of the Christian truth is preserved, and perennially reestablished, against the attacks of rationalists and simple moralists by its ability to throw light upon complex factors in human behaviour which constantly escape the moralists."[63]

More recently, but also out of deep firsthand experience with human corruption, Miroslav Volf speaks of a "contrived innocence" in affluent modern societies, giving rise to "a glaring incongruity: in a world so manifestly drenched with evil everybody is innocent in their own eyes."[64] Like Niebuhr in his appeal to Calvin's analysis of sin as involving both intentional violation and victimization, Volf says, "In *The Fall to Violence* Marjorie Suchocki argues that there is 'an intertwining of victim and violator through the very nature of violation.'"[65] "The violence ensnares the psyche of the victim, propels its action in the form of defensive reaction, and—robs it of innocence. She writes, 'To break the world cleanly into victims and violators ignores the depths of each person's participation in cultural sin. There simply are no innocents.'"[66] But this is the point that the doctrine of original sin has tried to make, and its demise leaves us trapped within the cycle of blame that perpetuates exclusion and violence.

> In the wake of modernity's belief in progress, the doctrine was progressively dismantled. As Bernhard-Henri Levy rightly argued in *Dangerous Purity...*, the stubborn shadows of modernity, produced in part precisely by modernity's blind optimism, call for a judicious retrieval of the doctrine of original sin.... Solidarity in sin underscores that no salvation can be expected from an approach that rests fundamentally on the moral assignment of blame and innocence. The question cannot be how to locate 'innocence' either on the intellectual or social map and work our way toward it.[67]

This doctrine should undermine our tendency to deflect our own sin to others: "A particular evil not only 'inhabits' us so that we do what we hate (Ro 7:15); it has

---

63. Ibid., 2:249

64. Miroslav Volf, *Exclusion and Embrace: A Theological Exploration of Identity, Otherness, and Reconciliation* (Nashville: Abingdon, 1996), 79.

65. Marjorie Suchocki, *The Fall to Violence*, as quoted in Volf, *Exclusion and Embrace*, 147.

66. Volf, *Exclusion and Embrace*, 80.

67. Ibid., 84.

colonized us to such a thoroughgoing extent that there seems to be no moral space left within the self in which it could occur to us to hate what we want because it is evil. We are ensnared by evil not only with full consent, but without a thought of dissent and without a sigh for deliverance."[68] Volf concludes, "And behind the tumult of 'making' and 'breaking' lies an anthropological constant: human beings are *always already in the covenant* as those who have *always already broken the covenant*."[69]

C. NATURAL AND MORAL ABILITY

All of humanity is guilty together "in Adam," and the sentence is passed onto the entire human race. Yet experience yields many examples of goodness, kindness, and even heroic acts of justice, kindness, and compassion. To address this query, we must retrieve two distinctions that were important especially since the Reformation: (1) between righteousness in *things heavenly* (coram deo, before God) and in *things earthly* (coram hominibus, or before fellow humans) and (2) between *natural* and *moral* ability.

First, human beings—including unbelievers—are credited in Scripture with good actions, just as they are credited with knowledge and wisdom in human affairs. Nevertheless, it is with respect to the righteousness of God's own character, which he has revealed in his law, that God judges all mortals. While we have abundant evidence of knowledge and wisdom in ordinary human affairs, the gospel—identified by the apostle Paul as the heavenly wisdom that confounds us—is a mystery apart from the Spirit's regenerating work.

Second, related to the first, human beings have a *natural* ability to fulfill God's commands, but lack the *moral* ability to love God and neighbor so as to fulfill those commands. Human beings have all of the requisite faculties and abilities with which God endowed them in creation. The fall did not destroy these characteristics of covenantal identity, but twisted and deformed them. Therefore, all human beings are by definition covenantal creatures and image-bearers; being a human person is not dependent on being related to God in rectitude.[70] The problem is that the human will is in moral bondage to sin.

The distinction between natural and moral ability arose especially within the Reformed tradition as a way of guarding against two extremes: on the one end, a *Manichaean* identification of sin with God's creation itself and, on the other end,

---

68. Ibid., 90–91.
69. Ibid., 153.
70. I might add to my earlier citations the following from Jenson: "We are counterparts of God as we believe in the Resurrection, and so in the *homoousia* of Jesus and his Father"

(*Systematic Theology*, 2:72). As with John Zizioulas and similar suggestions along these lines, the logic here leads to restrictive, if not dangerous, anthropological conclusions. We must distinguish between the *goal* of humanity and its *fact*.

the *Pelagian* denial of total depravity. In fact, this distinction that is prominent in the Reformed systems is the very thing that Niebuhr seems to have in mind with his own distinction between the *self-as-subject* (acknowledging right and wrong) and the *self-as-agent* in action (justifying oneself while blaming others).

One of the interesting paradoxes of Calvin's thought is that he simultaneously affirmed the total integrity of humanity as created and the total depravity of humanity as fallen.[71] "For the depravity and malice both of man and of the devil, or the sins that arise therefrom, do not spring from nature, but rather from the corruption of nature."[72] Sin is accidental rather than essential to human nature, he insists. This he distinguishes from the Manichaean error: "For if any defect were proved to inhere in nature, this would bring reproach upon [God]."[73]

Nature *as* nature is in no need of supplemental grace for its perfection but is already oriented toward the perfection that is within Adam's power to attain. Rejecting the medieval doctrine of concupiscence, the Reformers located sin not in the weakness of any faculty (namely, sensuality), but in the total corruption of humanity that proceeds not from nature but from malice.

The remarkable power of the Christian interpretation of creation and the fall to transform our secular presuppositions is evident in the fact that C. S. Lewis, though a Platonist in philosophical tendency, recognized the dissonance between the biblical narrative and this perspective. In an essay, he composed the following dialogue between the body and the soul:

> "You are always dragging me down," said I to my Body. "Dragging *you* down!" replied my Body.... "Who put an end to all those angry and revengeful thoughts last night? Me, of course, by insisting on going to sleep. Who does his best to keep you from talking too much and eating too much by giving you dry throats and headaches and indigestion? Eh?" "And what about sex?" said I. "Yes, what about it?" retorted the Body. "If you and your wretched imagination would leave me alone I'd give you no trouble. That's Soul all over; you give me orders and then blame me for carrying them out."[74]

The biblical view is constantly challenging our attempts to exonerate ourselves by fixing the blame on something outside of ourselves. If we cannot deflect sin to society, we will press charges against our family; if this is inadequate, we will indict our

---

71. He concurs with Aristotle's reference to humankind as a "microcosm" because "he is a rare example of God's power, goodness, and wisdom, and contains within himself enough miracles to occupy our minds, if only we are not irked at paying attention to them" (1.5.3). He praises "the human body" as "ingenious" (1.5.2). Yet in all this, humanity is "struck blind in such a dazzling theater..." (1.5.8). When we catch a glimpse of the "burning lamps" shining for us in God's works, includ-ing ourselves, we smother their light (1.5.14). The dialectic here moves between the exquisite character of nature and the equally unfathomable ruin of that nature to which humans are inclined.

72. Calvin, *Institutes* 1.14.3.

73. Ibid., 1.15.1.

74. C. S. Lewis, *God in the Dock* (Grand Rapids: Eerdmans, 1970), 216–17.

own body as if it were exterior to our real self. The soul flees the approaching footsteps of divine judgment by withdrawing within, protesting its divinity and purity.

Yet God's judgment draws us out, summoning us to account for the fact that "the heart is deceitful above all things, and desperately sick; who can understand it? I the LORD search the heart and test the mind," and the verdict is never encouraging (Jer 17:9–10). Even more pointedly, Jesus excoriated the religious leaders for imagining that there was some innocent citadel of righteousness in the mind or heart, countering that it is from this seat that sin exercises its dominion (Mt 12:34–35; 15:10–11; 23:25). The inner self is not the innocent spark of divinity or island of purity, but is the fountain from which every act of violence, deceit, immorality, and idolatry flows out through the body and into the world.

Total depravity therefore means not that we are incapable of any justice or good before fellow humans (civil righteousness), but that there is no Archimedean point within us that is left unfallen, from which we might begin to bargain or to restore our condition (righteousness before God). As Berkhof points out, total depravity does not mean

> (1) that every man is as thoroughly depraved as he can possibly become; (2) that the sinner has no innate knowledge of the will of God, nor a conscience that discriminates between good and evil; (3) that sinful man does not often admire virtuous character and actions in others, or is incapable of disinterested affections and actions in his relations with his fellow-men; nor (4) that every unregenerate man will, in virtue of his inherent sinfulness, indulge in every form of sin....

What is meant by "total" is that the whole nature of humanity, not only the body and its desires but the soul, mind, heart, and will, is corrupt.[75]

Therefore, when Pelagius, Kant, Charles Finney, and innumerable philosophers, ethicists, and theologians of modernity have insisted that it would be unjust for God to require something of which we are not capable, they confuse natural and moral ability. It is not that we do not freely will that which our mind and heart desire, but that our mind has been darkened and our heart is selfish. Everyone has the *natural* ability to render God faithful obedience, but after the fall, we are "sold [into slavery] under sin" (Ro 7:14), our *moral* ability held captive not to a foreign army but to our own selfishness, idolatry, greed, and deceit. "None is righteous, no, not one; no one understands, no one seeks for God" (Ro 3:10–11). This is not simply hyperbole: even when we pretend to be seeking God, we are in fact running from the God who is actually there. If the self-help sections of the average bookstore are any indication, we are, like Paul's Athenian audience, "in every way ... very religious" (Ac 17:22).

---

75. Louis Berkhof, *Systematic Theology* (Grand Rapids: Eerdmans, 1996), 246–47.

But God is not worshiped; he is used. "Spirituality" no less than atheism suppresses the specificity of the God revealed in Scripture.

The fact that we are still God's image-bearers and consequently possess all of the requisite *natural* ability for relating to God and others in covenant faithfulness—and the fact that this is even realized in our sense of duty to the rule of law—renders us culpable (Ro 1:18–2:16). The fault lies not in that we *cannot* but that we *will not* turn from our sin to the living God (Jn 8:44). Captive to sin, "in Adam," we are nevertheless willing accomplices to our own imprisonment (Ro 5:12). Only when God seizes us and liberates our captivity are we truly free to be the human beings that we are (Jn 8:36).

III. THE PERMANENCE OF THE IMAGE

In both Eastern Orthodoxy and Roman Catholic theology, ecclesiology is the presupposition of anthropology rather than vice versa. There is an important truth in this observation. The community that the triune God takes into his company is *ecclēsia*—the church in embryo, even as Adam and Eve. A court is convened with "two or three witnesses" (1Ti 5:19; cf. Dt 19:15). "'For where two or three are gathered in my name,'" Jesus promised, "'there am I among them'" (Mt 18:20). The image of God is properly functioning when yielding common testimony to God's character, will, works, and ways. Furthermore, it is in the church and as the church that the new humanity is being justified and sanctified, anticipating the day when it will be glorified together with its risen head. It is in the church as the community of the covenant of grace that the powers of the age to come break in on this present evil age, beginning already to make all things new.

Nevertheless, there is a danger of simply collapsing creation into redemption and common grace into saving grace. Not only does this compromise the gospel; it makes the natural status of personhood (based on the image of God) dependent on its moral renewal in Christ. According to John Zizioulas, human beings are born into the world as biological *individuals* (inherently flawed simply as creatures) who only become *persons* at baptism. He does acknowledge the important place for protology as well as eschatology, but finally the latter seems to win out over the former. In fact, "the body tends towards the person but leads finally to the individual."[76] Does this not make fallenness somehow "natural" rather than a corruption of nature? Gunton defends Zizioulas's position, arguing that "we are persons insofar as we are in right relationship to God. Under the conditions of sin, that means, of

---

76. John Zizioulas, *Being as Communion* (New York: St. Vladimir's Seminary Press, 1985), 51.

course, insofar as the image is reshaped, realised, in Christ."[77] "To be in the image of God therefore means to be conformed to the person of Christ."[78]

Traditionally, Lutheran theologians have also argued that the image of God has been lost and is only renewed through regeneration. However, in this case differences rest on definitions. It is noteworthy that there does not seem to have been a major cleavage between traditions over this question at a time when differences between the Reformed and the Lutherans were readily acknowledged and emphasized. Nevertheless, there are differences. Clearly, the Lutheran view turns on the identification of the image of God with "original righteousness," an equation that is further substantiated, for example, in Melanchthon's *Loci communes* (first published in 1521), as also by his apology of the *Augsburg Confession* (art. 2), which is also consistent with the *Formula of Concord* (Solid Declaration art. 1).[79]

If the image is defined as moral rectitude before God, the Reformed agree that this has been lost. Both traditions insist that the law is natural to humankind, while the gospel is a foreign announcement from heaven. Both reject the Roman Catholic view of original righteousness as a supernatural gift or mere neutrality and are equally wary of Eastern Orthodoxy's "ontological realism." "The emphasis here, of course," writes G. C. Berkouwer, "is quite different from that in Lutheran or Reformed theology," which necessarily affects the extent to which one acknowledges the corruption of sin.[80] "Thus the image of God," for Eastern Orthodoxy as opposed to Lutheran and Reformed orthodoxy, "is both ontic and actual, and it is viewed in a manner which relates it closely to a semi-Pelagian view of man's will."[81] Nevertheless, Lutheran theology teaches that the image of God was lost in the fall, while Reformed theology teaches that it remains, albeit marred, disfigured, and corrupted in every way. Or at least this is a common contrast that is drawn, usually on the Reformed side.

However, in this case differences may be more semantic than substantial. For example, the main author of the *Heidelberg Catechism*, Zacharias Ursinus, writes that "after the fall, man lost this glorious image of God."[82] Yet he hastens to add,

77. Colin Gunton, "Trinity, Ontology and Anthropology" in *Persons Divine and Human* (ed. Christoph Schwöbel and Colin Gunton; Edinburgh: T&T Clark, 1991), 58.

78. Ibid., 58–59.

79. Philipp Melanchthon, *Loci communes 1543* (trans. J. A. O. Preus; St. Louis: Concordia, 1992), 48. The Lutheran position is formally embodied in the following statement from the *Formula of Concord*, Solid Declaration article 1: "Furthermore, that original sin is the complete lack or absence of the original concreated righteousness of paradise or of the image of God according to which man was originally created in truth, holiness, and righteousness, together with a disability and ineptitude as far as the things of God are concerned" (*The Book of Concord: The Confes-*

sions of the Evangelical Lutheran Church [ed. and trans. Theodore G. Tappert; Philadelphia: Fortress, 1959], 510). Similarly, the apology of the *Augsburg Confession* (art. 2) declares, "What else is this [image of God] than that a wisdom and righteousness was implanted in man that would grasp God and reflect him, that is, that man received gifts like the knowledge of God, fear of God, and trust in God?" (*Book of Concord*, 102).

80. G. C. Berkouwer, *Man: The Image of God* (Grand Rapids: Eerdmans, 1962), 50.

81. Ibid.

82. Zacharias Ursinus, *The Commentary on the Heidelberg Catechism* (trans. G. W. Williard; Phillipsburg, N.J.: P&R, n.d.; reproduced from second American edition, 1852), 32.

"There were, however, some remains and sparks of the image of God still left in man, after his fall, and which even yet continue in those who are unregenerated," which include the rational soul and will, knowledge of the arts and sciences, "traces and remains" of "civic virtue," "the enjoyment of many temporal blessings," and some measure of stewardship rather than tyranny over other creatures. Yet the gifts that belonged specifically to the image—namely, true knowledge of God, delight in him and his commands, a genuine stewardship over creation and the hope of everlasting life—are lost. In Christ the image is restored. "And the Holy Ghost carries forward and completes what is begun by the Word and the use of the Sacraments."[83]

On the Lutheran side, J. T. Mueller explains, "Therefore we declare on the basis of Scripture that man through the Fall has entirely lost the image of God in its proper sense, that is, his concreate [created] wisdom, righteousness, and holiness, so that his intellect now is veiled in spiritual darkness, 1 Cor. 2:14 and his will is opposed to God, Rom. 8:7."[84]

So what about James 3:9 and Genesis 9:6, where even unbelievers are apparently identified as image bearers?

> Luther and other dogmaticians (Philippi, Hofmann) explain them as describing man as he was originally and as he should again become through faith in Christ Jesus (restoration of the divine image through regeneration). Melanchthon, Baier, Quenstedt, and others regard [these passages] as teaching a divine image in a wider sense, namely, inasmuch as man, even after the Fall, is still an intelligent, self-determining rational being, who even now, though feebly, rules over the creatures of God.[85]

Although Mueller prefers the narrower definition, he acknowledges that the broader is not, properly speaking, contradictory. It seems that this is precisely where the Reformed tradition stands. Berkouwer cites Johann Gerhard's proposal: "If the image could be thought of as man's essence, as will and intellect, then indeed it was not lost; but, he argues, if we think of it supernaturally, as righteousness and holiness, then the image is radically and totally lost: the restoration of the image in Christ presupposes that it has been lost. But Gerhard then unexpectedly adds that there are indeed 'remnants' (*reliquiae*) of the image even in fallen man."[86]

Therefore, the difference in expression turns out to be semantic. Where Lutherans commonly refer to the image in the narrow sense of moral integrity (which the Reformed agree has been lost), Reformed theology commonly refers to the image in the wider sense (which Lutherans agree has not been lost). The important point is the affirmation that all human beings, even after the fall, are God's image-bearers.

---

83. Ibid., 32–33.

84. John Theodore Mueller, *Christian Dogmatics* (St. Louis: Concordia, 1934), 207.

85. Ibid.

86. Berkouwer, *Man*, 46–47.

Coming into the world as relational beings, they are already members of a covenant community: the covenant of creation, "in Adam." Their status apart from being "in Christ" is not that of nonperson or nonbearer of the divine image, but that of false witness and representative. They have lost not the natural image but the moral ability to fulfill its destiny. They remain prophets, priests, and kings, but have abused their office and are born into the world in a state of high treason. It is an indelible status, commission, and office, and, unlike the elected official who is caught with his or her hand in the till, no person is relieved of that office. Instead, this office (image) witnesses against each of us, even as it also demands respect for all human life regardless of one's relation to God in Christ. Only in Christ do we realize the salvation and the goal of our personhood by the gospel, but the law that binds us to our neighbors and cobearers of God's image obliges us to treat them as persons.

IV. STAY OF EXECUTION

So soon after the fall God was ready with the announcement of the merciful salvation that he had already planned in eternity. Instead of confirming Adam, Eve, and the whole human race in everlasting death, God promised the triumph of the seed of the woman who would crush the serpent's head. Although they could not cover their guilt, God "made for Adam and for his wife garments of skins and clothed them" (Ge 3:21). Already we have intimations of the "Lamb of God" who will bear our sins and clothe us in his righteousness (Jn 1:29). I have referred to Vos's point that "eschatology antedates redemption"[87] (see p. 386). Creation was but the origin. The destination was the Tree of Life, with humanity confirmed in everlasting glory, immortality, and righteousness. "That door, however, was never opened," notes Kline.

> It was not the Fall in itself that delayed the consummation. According to the conditions of the covenant of creation the prospective consummation was either/or. It was either eternal glory by covenantal confirmation of original righteousness or eternal perdition by covenant-breaking repudiation of it. The Fall, therefore, might have been followed at once by a consummation of the curse of the covenant. The delay was due rather to the principle and purpose of divine compassion by which a new way of arriving at the consummation was introduced, the way of redemptive covenant with common grace as its historical corollary.[88]

Mercifully, God delayed the consummation, which would have left humanity—indeed, the whole creation—under the everlasting sentence of death and judgment.

---

87. Geerhardus Vos, *The Pauline Eschatology* (Grand Rapids: Eerdmans, 1961), 325.

88. Ibid.

In this delay, God opened up a space for his own saving action of promise and fulfillment. And because of this stay of execution, "the promise of entering his rest still stands" (Heb 4:1).

The scene does not end there, however, nor does the great trial of the covenant. But for now in the story, we pick up with humanity barred from Paradise, tilling the soil "east of Eden." Already in the following chapter we are introduced to Cain's fratricide of Abel over the former's jealousy that his brother's animal sacrifice was accepted by God while "for Cain and his offering he had no regard" (Ge 4:5). As a prelude to this story, Eve announces with Cain's birth, "I have gotten a/the man with the help of the LORD" (v. 1). Without a definite article in the ancient text, we are especially dependent on the context. In light of the unfolding narrative, it makes sense to conclude that Eve is exclaiming that she has brought forth the offspring ("the man") who has been promised to her — the one who will crush the serpent's head and lift the bondage of the curse.

If Eve had assumed that she had given birth to the messiah, she would eventually learn that her firstborn son was instead the first recorded murderer in the Bible. Yet even after the crime, God protects Cain and allows him to build a city and to produce descendants who eventually distinguish themselves as leaders in various cultural endeavors. Just at the point where this genealogy of Cain and the erection of his proud city is recounted (vv. 17–24), we read, by contrast, that another child was born to Adam and Eve. Eve "called his name Seth [*appoint*], for she said, 'God has appointed for me another offspring instead of Abel, for Cain killed him.' To Seth also a son was born, and he called his name Enosh. At that time people began to call upon the name of the LORD" (vv. 25–26). From this point on, two cities rise in history: the one identified by violence, oppression, injustice, sin, and pride — as well as, let it be noted, cultural and technological advance; the other identified by that last sentence announcing Enosh's birth: "At that time people began to call upon the name of the LORD." The obvious covenant language of invoking the name — and not just any name, but *the* name, is striking, even if the specific name Yahweh was not given until much later.

The ensuing biblical narrative does not attempt to produce either a comprehensive chronology or a comprehensive genealogy but rather hits the highlights of redemptive history between Adam and Abraham. Noah is represented as a descendant of Seth, and his family, too, branches out into various nations that will figure prominently in Israel's history. At least one of the points in the narrative is that the promise is always threatened, always hanging by a thread. Disobedience marks the human race at every turn, and just when it seems that there is no one left who will be God's faithful covenant servant, God's grace prevails and a new candidate appears. Intermarriage between the two "cities" threatens to weaken the line of covenant succession to the vanishing point, and the inhabitants of Babel, the successor to Cain's proud city, raise a tower "with its top in the heavens" in order to establish a name for themselves in history by consolidating a centralized empire in the region. By decentralizing the power, wealth, population, and technology through linguistic differentiation, instead of destroying the city, God restrained the devastating potential of evil. All of this is meant to introduce us to the line of Noah, Shem, and Terah, father of Abram.

V. "ISRAEL, MY BELOVED": BETWEEN THE TWO ADAMS

So decisive is the call of Abraham in Genesis 12 that it initiates the history of Israel and renders all that has preceded it a mere prologue to that story. In fact, Bavinck goes so far as to conclude that special revelation begins with the call of Abraham.[89] Redemptive history begins now to move swiftly toward the Messiah, first by type and shadow and then, in the fullness of time, in reality.[90] The prophets, psalmists, Jesus, and the apostles "all teach us unanimously and clearly that the content of the divine revelation does not consist primarily in the unity of God, in the moral law, in circumcision, in the Sabbath, in short, in the law, but appears primarily and principally in the promise, in the covenant of grace, and in the gospel."

> Not law, but gospel, is in the Old and the New Testament alike the core of the divine revelation, the essence of religion, the sum total of the Holy Scriptures. Every other view fails to do justice to special revelation, effaces its difference from general revelation, degrades the Old Testament, rends apart the two economies of the same covenant of grace, and even gradually changes the gospel of the New Covenant into a law, and makes of Christ a second Moses.... The law thus is temporal, transitory, a means in the service of the promise, but the promise is eternal; it had its beginning in paradise, was preserved and developed by revelation in the days of the Old Covenant, received its fulfillment in Christ, and is now extended to the whole human race and all the peoples.[91]

We cannot find this gospel in nature, creation, reason, or conscience: "It is an historical product; the initiative came from God; he so reveals himself as, by the act of revelation, to receive a particular person and people into communion with himself."[92] The law was never confused with the promise nor did it replace it. God's covenant with Abraham was a gracious promise, so that even the moral law that attended it "was not a law of the covenant of works, but a law of the covenant of grace, a law

---

89. Herman Bavinck, *The Philosophy of Revelation* (New York: Longmans, Green, and Co. 1909; repr., Grand Rapids: Baker, 1979), 188.

90. Ibid., 191
91. Ibid., 192–93.
92. Ibid.

of the covenant, a law of gratitude."[93] Jewish scholar Jon Levenson rightly sees the theme of the sacrifice of the firstborn as the heart of the Christian message: "The story of the humiliation and exaltation of the beloved son reverberates throughout the Bible because it is the story of the people about whom and to whom it is told. *It is the story of Israel the beloved son, the first-born of God*" (emphasis added).[94]

Although Israel inherited the land by a gracious promise that God made to Abraham, the covenant that Israel swears at Mount Sinai is the condition for remaining in the land. The Sinai covenant points forward to Christ and his saving work, but the terms of this covenant (e.g., Dt 7:12–14) are far from the unilateral oath that God made to Abraham in Genesis 15. Just as Israel has been brought out of the "darkness and void" of Egyptian bondage, so now she is to occupy the land as a new Adam under probation in anticipation of consummation. Israel's history is a trial within the larger trial of humanity.

Especially in the prophets, creation language is employed for Israel, and the fall of Israel, leading to exile, draws on the imagery of Genesis 3. Streams have become a desert; flourishing fields have become a haven for jackals. The land flowing with milk and honey surrenders to thorns and weeds. Only on the basis of the promised Messiah is there hope of a new creation. Throughout Israel's history, then, the themes of sonship and servant, God's unilateral oath of a Messiah and Israel's oath at Sinai ("We will do all these things!") appear side by side. Even in times of Israel's unfaithfulness to her oath at Sinai, Yahweh suspends judgment for the sake of the promise he made to Abraham, Isaac and Jacob (cf. 2Ki 13:23). Only God's gracious promise keeps Israel's history alive, moving toward its climax in Christ. In the prophets, the Sinai covenant is always the basis for the terrifying judgments, while hope for the new covenant of forgiveness and grace is always held out on the basis of the promise that God made to Abraham.[95]

Eventually, Israel was exiled, and this tragic event is described in terms that echo Adam's fall. In Psalm 78 we are told the whole story in a nutshell: God was loyal, in spite of Israel's repeated acts of treachery, but finally God's representative was evicted. "They did not keep God's covenant, but refused to walk according to his law. They forgot his works and the wonders that he had shown them" (vv. 10–11). Repeatedly in this psalm we read that God put Israel on trial and that she not only failed but even "tested *God*" (vv. 18, 41, 56). Here the language of probation and trial echoes the original covenant with humanity in Adam. "How often they rebelled against him in the wilderness and grieved him in the desert!" (v. 40), and yet God

---

93. Ibid., 197.

94. Jon Levenson, *The Death and Resurrection of the Beloved Son: The Transformation of Child Sacrifice in Judaism and Christianity* (New Haven, Conn.: Yale Univ. Press, 1993), 67; quoted in William C. Placher, "Rethinking Atonement," *Interpretation* 53, no. 1 (January 1999): 11.

95. Walther Eichrodt, *Theology of the Old Testament* (trans. J. A. Baker; Philadelphia: Westminster Press, 1961), 1:26–27.

continued to preserve Israel "because of the covenant with Abraham, Isaac, and Jacob" (2Ki 13:23). In fact, Israel's only hope appears to be the Davidic promise that ends the psalm:

> [God] rejected the tent of Joseph; he did not choose the tribe of Ephraim, but he chose the tribe of Judah, Mount Zion, which he loves. He built his sanctuary like the high heavens, like the earth, which he has founded forever. He chose his servant David and took him from the sheepfolds; from following the nursing ewes he brought him to shepherd Jacob his people, Israel his inheritance. (vv. 67–71)

As Adam had been cast out of the garden, Israel was exiled by none other than Yahweh himself, the suzerain whose treaty had been reduced to shattered tablets by his covenant partner. "Like Adam they transgressed the covenant" (Hos 6:7).

Before and after the exile, the prophets take their place as prosecutors of the covenant lawsuit. Yahweh announces to Jeremiah that he will "[give] this city [Jerusalem] into the hand of the king of Babylon, and he shall burn it with fire" (Jer 34:2). While God had commanded the jubilees — liberating slaves and "proclaiming liberty [to one another]," Judah had come to ignore this stipulation and perpetuated slavery.

> Therefore, thus says the LORD: You have not obeyed me by proclaiming liberty, everyone to his brother and to his neighbor; behold, I proclaim to you liberty to the sword, to pestilence, and to famine, declares the LORD. I will make you a horror to all the kingdoms of the earth. And the men who transgressed my covenant and did not keep the terms of the covenant that they made before me, I will make them like the calf that they cut in two and passed between its parts.... (Jer 34:17–18)

We have seen this "cutting" ritual before, in Abram's vision (Ge 15), but there God alone walks through the pieces, assuming upon his own head the curse sanctions. But now the focus is on the Sinai covenant, according to which Israel's status in the land as God's theocratic nation is determined. Now Israel will have to pass between the pieces, bearing God's judgment.

When King Zedekiah of Judah inquired of Jeremiah whether he had received any word from the Lord, the prophet replied, "You shall be delivered into the hand of the king of Babylon" (Jer 37:17). Further testimony to Israel's own realization that she had become the faithless servant of the covenant may be found, for example, in the Second Temple literature (e.g., Wisdom 6:3–7).

Yet the prophets hold out the hope of a Sabbath rest yet remaining, even for those who have thoroughly violated God's treaty. Delbert Hillers notes,

> The Sinai covenant offered little grounds for optimism, but some hope could be garnered from the promise to Abraham. "When you are in distress and all these things have overtaken you, in the latter time, then you will return to Yahweh your god and hearken to his voice, for Yahweh your god is a merciful god who will not

let you down or destroy you, and who will not forget the covenant with your fathers, that which he swore to them" ([Dt] 4:31).[96]

This is the good news that survives amid the tragic circumstances about to be inflicted, and it is wholly rooted in the Abrahamic-Davidic promise (Jer 33:14–22). It is an unconditional oath, a covenant that cannot be broken, issuing in a kingdom that cannot be shaken. Jeremiah prophesies, "The word of the LORD came to Jeremiah: Thus says the LORD: If you can break my covenant with the day and my covenant with the night, so that day and night will not come at their appointed time, then also my covenant with David my servant may be broken...." Notice especially the echo of the Abrahamic covenant in the last verse: While the Israelites will say that God has rejected his people, Yahweh promises yet again, "If I have not established my covenant with day and night and the fixed order of heaven and earth, then I will reject the offspring of Jacob and David my servant and will not choose one of his offspring to rule over the offspring of Abraham, Isaac, and Jacob. For I will restore their fortunes and will have mercy upon them" (vv. 23–26).

Jeremiah 31 is particularly explicit in founding God's promised future for his people on the Abrahamic-Davidic promise. The "new covenant" will be firm, "not like the covenant that I made with their fathers" at Sinai—"my covenant that they broke, though I was their husband, declares the LORD." Rather, in this covenant *God* will write his law on their hearts; God will be their God, and they will be his people. "For *I will forgive* their iniquity, and I will remember their sin no more" (vv. 31–34, emphasis added). Furthermore, it is not just restoration to a former condition that is promised, but a greater future and a wider hope, with Jerusalem rebuilt and enlarged (vv. 38–40). It will not be Paradise regained, but the consummation that had been forfeited by Adam's and Israel's disobedience.

But how will God be faithful to both covenants, to the law and the gospel? How will he be "just and the justifier" (Ro 3:26)? It will be by causing his own Son, the Last Adam and True Israel, to fulfill all righteousness and yet to pass through the judgment—cut off from the land of the living—for our sins, so that his righteousness becomes definitive for the solidarity of his new creation in and with him. Our focus now turns, therefore, from the dark night of human rebellion to this sunrise of the Messiah: the one who comes as Lord and Servant of the everlasting covenant.

---

96. Hillers, *Covenant*, 154–55. The quoted passage includes Dt 4:30 as well as v. 31.

DISCUSSION QUESTIONS

1. How does the Bible place the fall in the context of a cosmic trial, and how are the positive characteristics of the image of God corrupted by Adam's disobedience?

2. What is the covenantal context of human solidarity in Adam?

3. Define and evaluate the doctrine of original sin. Is it a biblical doctrine, or is it merely an abstract theory imposed on the Scriptures?

4. What do you make of the distinction between natural and moral ability? Does this help us understand the human condition, and if so, how?

5. Has the image of God been entirely lost in the fall?

6. How does Israel recapitulate Adam's trial and its outcome?

Part Four

GOD
WHO RESCUES

Chapter Fourteen

THE PERSON OF CHRIST

Attempting to integrate biblical and systematic approaches, I begin with the titles of Christ. Though cautious of overinterpreting these titles as if they carried all of the freight intended by later formulations, we should also be wary of underinterpreting them as if their original meaning could not have been expanded and enriched by the concrete appearance of the one who bore them.[1]

I. THE MESSIANIC HEIR

All of God's covenantal purposes converge in Jesus Christ. The Son is the eternal Mediator of the *covenant of redemption* which already in eternity rendered him, by anticipation, the one who would become incarnate and give his life for his people (1Pe 1:20–21; Eph 1:4–5, 11). He is also the Last Adam, who undoes the curse of the first Adam and fulfills the *covenant of creation* for his elect, thereby winning the right to be not only the risen head but the resurrection-life-giving Lord. Therefore, the *covenant of grace* of which Christ is the mediatorial head is secured eternally in the covenant of redemption. "For all the promises of God find their Yes in him" (2Co 1:20).

---

1. Although N. T. Wright also warns against christological "proof-texting," this concern is especially evident in Richard A. Horsley, *Hearing the Whole Story: The Politics of Plot in Mark's Gospel* (Louisville: Westminster John Knox, 2001), 231–35. New Testament scholars appropriately caution against reading later church dogma into these titles, losing the context as well as the ironies, twists, and turns in the unfolding Gospel narratives. At the same time, we must remember that Scripture is not simply a collection of historical documents but a canon and that the apostles, following Jesus' own instruction, interpreted the Old Testament and the life of Jesus in the light of his fulfillment of God's promises. Therefore, these texts are meant to be interpreted as Christian Scripture. The Christ of Faith is the Jesus of History. On this point, see the excellent argument of Roman Catholic New Testament scholar Luke Timothy Johnson, *The Real Jesus: The Misguided Quest for the Historical Jesus and the Truth of the Traditional Gospels* (New York: HarperOne, 1997).

A. THE FAITHFUL ADAM AND TRUE ISRAEL

Although Israel, like Adam, failed to drive the serpent out of God's holy garden and instead succumbed to the seduction of God's archenemy, God pledges that he will not utterly destroy Israel but will preserve a remnant from which will emerge the Messiah who will bring an ultimate salvation and an everlasting kingdom of righteousness not only to Jews but to the nations. If the works principle inherent in the Sinai covenant stood alone, neither Israel nor the world would have any hope.

Yet even in its exile, Israel too is given the promise that its coming Shepherd will gather his scattered sheep and bring redemption to the ends of the earth. The enlargement of Jerusalem promised with the new covenant in Jeremiah 31 and 32 is anticipated elsewhere, sometimes in passages that even recast the traditional roles of the oppressor (Egypt and Assyria) as the oppressed who are delivered from bondage and taken as God's own people (Isa 19:18–23). Isaiah 60 sets before us the vision of ships from all over the world entering Israel's harbor, laden this time not with implements of war but with rich treasures. "Nations shall come to your light, and kings to the brightness of your rising" (v. 3). A royal procession of the nations and their kings, into gates that never close (v. 11), echoes the Sabbath enthronement of God in the beginning, with the parade of the creature-kings before the Lord in the day-frames of Genesis 1 and 2. Psalm 2 evokes the courtroom scene, with the creature-kings arrayed before the Sabbath splendor of the Great King and his anointed one (Messiah), but in war rather than tribute, with the Great King laughing at the self-confident posturing of the earth's rulers who reject the Messiah, yet promising salvation from this coming judgment for "all who take refuge in him."

B. MESSIANIC SAVIOR: SON OF DAVID

Like the Abrahamic covenant, the Davidic covenant is an unconditional adoption. It is not David who will build a house for God, but God who will build a house for David. In spite of the unfaithfulness of David and his heirs, God unilaterally pledges to give him an everlasting dynasty (2Sa 7:11–17).

Matthew's Gospel is especially concerned to proclaim Jesus as the fulfillment of Israel's messianic expectations. From the prelude, listing the high points in the genealogical record leading to Jesus, the first point to be made is not the identity of Jesus with God (as in John's prologue), but the identity of Jesus with the people of Israel—and specifically, the Abrahamic promise realized genealogically through the line of David, leading to Joseph and Mary, "of whom Jesus was born, who is called Christ" (Mt 1:16). In spite of so much testimony in the prophets to a new covenant that is qualitatively different from the old covenant, which it renders obsolete (as in Jer 31:32), first-century Judaism was oriented toward a messianic kingdom that would restore the typological theocracy established by the Sinai covenant. It was within this historical context that the angel announced to Mary, "You shall call his name Jesus, for he will save his people from their sins" (Mt 1:21). Although the origin of this name is not certain, the consensus is that it derives from the root *yāšaʿ*, to save. Jesus is an anglicized form of Joshua (Heb. Yeshua). Like Yahweh's own personal name, Jesus' is descriptive of his covenantal relation to his people in faithfulness and mercy. Already his mission is embedded in his personal identity. "Christ," on the other hand, is not a personal name but the title for the office into which he is installed, from *māšah*, to anoint. The *māšîah* is the anointed one. Prophets, priests, and kings in Israel were anointed with oil to their office, and, as we have seen from Psalm 2:2, the Lord's "anointed" is his earthly representative.

Although there were diverse interpretations of the messianic figure in Jesus' day, at least one broad application was that he would be "king of the Jews" — the real one, not one of the Hasmonean or Herodian dynasties who were non-Davidic and therefore pretenders to the throne. The royal son of David would not be a puppet of the Roman Empire. According to the common eschatological expectation of Second Temple Judaism, N. T. Wright explains, "the long night of exile, the 'present evil age,' would give way to the dawn of renewal and restoration, the new exodus, the return from exile, 'the age to come,'" and the messianic king would somehow fulfill this.[2] Examples abound in Zechariah 1–8. "This is precisely the sort of context within which one can understand the crowds' reaction to Jesus as reported in John 6.15: they wanted to seize Jesus and make him king."[3] Wright refers to the examples of various claimants to the messianic title during and after the Maccabean wars, such as Menahem, who "appeared in the Temple in royal robes" to inaugurate the kingdom. "Simon bar Giora appeared, royally appareled, in the spot where the Temple had stood. Bar-Kochba ... gave the rebuilding of the Temple such a high priority that he had it stamped on his coins. Temple and kingship went hand in hand."[4] Further, the royal Messiah would fight Israel's battles.

However, according to the terms of first-century Jewish expectation, Jesus was just another disappointment. To be sure, he rode triumphantly into Jerusalem with great fanfare (claiming fulfillment of Zec 14:21), but in his last week he brought growing confusion and consternation. Arriving in royal state to the shout, "Hosanna to the Son of David! Blessed is he who comes in the name of the Lord! Hosanna in the highest!" (Mt 21:9), he becomes the center of attention. "And when he entered Jerusalem, the whole city was stirred up, saying, 'Who is this?' And the crowds said, 'This is the prophet Jesus, from Nazareth of Galilee'" (vv. 10–11). He then begins to

---

2. N. T. Wright, *Jesus and the Victory of God* (Minneapolis: Fortress, 1996), 482–83.

3. Ibid., 483.

4. Ibid.

assume lordship over the Temple Mount. First, he casts out the traders (vv. 12–13). Second, he receives the blind and the lame into the temple precincts, which according to the tradition of the elders was an act of defilement, and he heals them (v. 14). Indignant at Jesus' toleration of the crowd's acclamation of him as the Son of David as well as at his deeds in the temple precincts, the chief priests and scribes confront him, and Jesus departs for the evening (vv. 16–17). The next day, Jesus returns and pronounces a curse on the fig tree, saying, " 'May no fruit ever come from you again!' And the fig tree withered at once" (vv. 18–19). Explaining the action to his disciples, Jesus said, "Truly, I say to you, if you have faith and do not doubt, you will not only do what has been done to the fig tree, but even if you say to this mountain, 'Be taken up and thrown into the sea,' it will happen" (vv. 20–21).

Everything else that Jesus did on the Temple Mount during this climactic week was scandalous—in fact, blasphemous—from the perspective of those who wished to restore the Sinai theocracy. "In Mark and Matthew," Wright notes, "Jesus' Temple-action is closely linked with the cursing of the fig tree." The "mountain" to be removed and cast into the sea is the Temple Mount, echoing Zechariah 4:6–7, which itself echoes Isaiah 40:4; 42:16.[5] The present temple and its mount are in the way. John the Baptist appeared, clearing a path.[6] So Jesus asks the crowds what they went into the desert to find:

> To see a reed shaken in the wind?... Herod had chosen as his symbol, placed on his coins...a typical Galilean reed.... Jesus' question, uncoded, means more or less: were you looking for another Herodian-style king? Surely not; you wanted something far greater than that, something more than simply yet another pseudo-aristocrat, lording it over you like a pagan tyrant. And you got it. John was a prophet; indeed, the greatest prophet that ever lived, the one of whom Malachi spoke, the last prophet before the final great day dawned. Well, then: if John was the last of the preparatory prophets, where are we now? The one who is least in the kingdom is greater than John. In other words, Jesus himself, the kingdom-bringer, is no mere prophet. He is the one for whom John, and with him the true hopes of Israel, had been waiting. If John is Elijah, this means, without question, that Jesus is the Messiah.[7]

"By what authority are you doing these things?" the leaders demand (v. 23), but they do not press the point for fear of the crowds. Since John, Jesus says, the tax collectors and prostitutes have been coming into the kingdom while the religious leaders refused (vv. 28–32).

Next, in his parable of the tenants, Jesus is the cornerstone rejected by the builders, as he elaborates at this same occasion on the Temple Mount, only this time

---

5. Ibid., 494.
6. Ibid., 495–96.

7. Ibid., 496.

interpreting Psalm 118:22–23 as referring to himself and casting the religious leaders in the role of the Gentile nations who attempt to destroy (Mt 21:33–44; cf. Mk 12:1). Only fear of the crowds keeps the religious leaders from taking him into custody (Mt 21:45–56). Jesus then tells the parable of the wedding feast, with the natural guests refusing the king's invitation while the outsiders are welcomed and clothed with wedding garments. One arrived without a wedding garment and was remanded to the guards " 'into the outer darkness,' " where " 'there will be weeping and gnashing of teeth.' For many are called, but few are chosen" (Mt 22:1–14).

After eluding the theological traps set for him by the religious leaders, Jesus pronounces the covenant's curses ("woes") upon Jerusalem, foretells the temple's destruction and his future return in judgment. Everything else that Jesus says on the Temple Mount, in fact, speaks of his death, resurrection, and return in glory as the Son of Man (chapters 23–25). From the beginning of chapter 26 the plot that Jesus has predicted unfolds in his trial, crucifixion, and resurrection on the third day.

As David's lord as well as son (Mk 12:35–37, from Ps 110), Jesus claimed authority over the temple as a greater king than David and a greater priest than Aaron (both anticipated in Ps 110). He did not come to purify the temple and its worship, but to fulfill it, which renders its service obsolete (Jn 2:19–21). The early title *Christos* (in Paul and before) emphasizes the early Christian belief that Jesus was the Messiah, and those whom he represents as mediator are now seen as "living stones" united to him as God's temple (1Pe 2:5; cf. 1Co 3:16–17; Eph 2:21; Rev 21:22). This time, Jesus says on the Temple Mount itself, the true temple, made without hands (prophesied by Ezekiel), will be utterly destroyed (not merely defiled, as in the wake of Rome's suppression of the Maccabean revolt), but will be raised on the third day (Jn 2:18–22). Yet he also prophesies that the earthly sanctuary will be completely and forever destroyed. As his disciples point out the majesty of the temple buildings, Jesus says, "You see all these, do you not? Truly, I say to you, there will not be left here one stone upon another that will not be thrown down" (Mt 24:1–2). Only the true temple will emerge gloriously from the rubble.

As Moltmann reminds us, the Jewish thinker Martin Buber saw the history of the failure of the kings as the impetus for messianism.[8] When Ahaz proudly refuses a sign, God gives one anyway: "Behold, the virgin shall conceive and bear a son, and shall call his name Immanuel" (Isa 7:10–14).[9] Then a prophecy follows two chapters later that draws upon new creation language, with "a great light" appear-

---

8. Martin Buber, *Das Kommende: Untstehungsgeschichte des messianischen Glauben* (Berlin, 1936), 2:913, cited in Jürgen Moltmann, *The Way of Jesus Christ: Christology in Messianic Dimensions* (Minneapolis: Fortress, 1993), 5.

9. Although "young girl" is lexically possible, parallel pas-

sages suggest that "virgin" brings out the force of the term in those contexts (cf. Ge 24:43; Ex 2:8; Ps 68:25; Pr 30:19). Besides, it is difficult to know why the pregnancy of merely a young woman would constitute a sign of redemption.

ing to "those who dwelt in a land of deep darkness." Israel is "multiplied," its joy increased, as a harvest of the nations is gathered to Zion.

> For to us a child is born,
>   to us a son is given;
> and the government shall be upon his shoulder,
>   and his name shall be called
> Wonderful Counselor, Mighty God,
>   Everlasting Father, Prince of Peace.
> Of the increase of his government and of peace
>   there will be no end,
> on the throne of David and over his kingdom,
>   to establish it and to uphold it
> with justice and with righteousness,
>   from this time forth and forevermore.
> The zeal of the LORD of hosts will do this. (Isa 9:6–7)

Two chapters later, there is the prophecy of the shoot growing from the stump of Jesse, the shoot on whom the Spirit will rest. He will judge righteously and defend the cause of the weak, especially the poor. Again the new creation language is evident, as violence is finally removed from the earth and "the earth shall be full of the knowledge of the LORD as the waters cover the sea" (Isa 11:1–9).

Martin Hengel notes that in Cave 11 the Qumran community speaks of Michael-Melchizedek, who "appears as eschatological victor over all the powers of evil and ushers in the eschatological year of jubilee (according to Lev 25.8), which is identical with the proclamation of liberation in Isa. 61:1 (cf. Luke 4:17ff.)."[10] This theme reappears in Hebrews.[11] Micah 4 envisions the nations streaming to the hill of the Lord, with God's Word going out to the world. Messiah will judge the nations and bring peace to the earth. From Bethlehem will arise Israel's ruler, "whose coming forth is from of old, from ancient days." He will be a tender shepherd to gather his flock and feed them "in the majesty of the name of the LORD his God. And they shall dwell secure, for now he shall be great to the ends of the earth; and he shall be their peace" (Mic 5:2–5a). Zechariah adds his witness to the messianic expectation: "Rejoice greatly, O daughter Zion! Shout aloud, O daughter of Jerusalem! Behold, your king is coming to you; righteous and having salvation is he, humble and mounted on a donkey, on a colt, the foal of a donkey." He will end war, "and he shall speak peace to the nations; his rule shall be from sea to sea, and from the River to the ends of the earth. As for you also, because of the blood of my covenant with you, I will set your prisoners free from the waterless pit." It will be a time of festival, with new wine and grain (Zec 9:9–17).

---

10. Martin Hengel, *The Son of God: The Origin of Christology and the History of Jewish Hellenistic Religion* (trans. John Bowden; Philadelphia: Fortress, 1976), 80.

11. Ibid., 81.

Martin Buber precisely states the expectation of the prophets: "'Immanuel' is 'the king of the remnant, out of whom the nation is to be renewed.'"[12] "The figure of the messiah therefore evolves out of a remembrance of David," writes Moltmann. "But in the prophetic counter-stroke to Assyria's military destruction of the political independence of Israel's monarchy, this messianic figure assumes forms of hope which go far beyond any reminiscence of the historical David." So messianism grows not out of nostalgia, but out of hope in the promise of a greater son of David than David himself.[13]

C. SON OF MAN — SECOND ADAM

The role of humanity, as understood by Israel, was to respond to God's speech, with the reply of the covenant servant, "Here I am." It is the reply of the prophets: those who hear God's word and then declare it and witness to it in the *rib*—the covenant lawsuit that Yahweh brings against his people in the great trial of history under this present age ("in Adam"). Under the rubric of Messiah appear related designations. As the Lord's earthly representative, the Messiah figure is also designated "Son of Man/Adam." While in the canonical texts of Psalm 8:4, Ezekiel, and Daniel, "one like a son of man" appears as a description, by the time of Enoch it appears to become a messianic title (see *1 Enoch* 46 and 62; *2 Esdras* 13).[14]

The lodestar for eschatological interpretation of the Son of Man is to be found in Daniel 7:9–27. The vision begins with the Ancient of Days taking his throne in majesty as he sits in court to judge the nations. There are four beasts, and immediately one is turned into the fire, while the other three are allowed to survive for a time. At this point, "there came one like a son of man, and he came to the Ancient of Days and was presented before him. And to him was given dominion and glory and a kingdom, that all peoples, nations, and languages should serve him; his dominion is an everlasting dominion, which shall not pass away, and his kingdom one that shall not be destroyed" (vv. 9–14). Alarmed by the vision, Daniel asks God to interpret it for him. The four beasts represent earthly kings. "But the saints of the Most High shall receive the kingdom and possess the kingdom forever, forever and ever" (vv. 17–18). The fourth beast will be the most ferocious, devouring the whole earth, but ten kingdoms will arise from it, the last of whom will speak blasphemies against Yahweh "and shall wear out the saints of the Most High..." (v. 25). After God's court does away with this regime, the saints of the Most High will receive

---

12. Buber, as quoted in Moltmann, *The Way of Jesus Christ*, 9.
13. Ibid., 10.
14. This is one place where the inclusive language of the NRSV does not do justice to the original text, translating son of man "human being," while retaining it as a title in the New

Testament. While this may in fact be an appropriate rendering on one level, the fact that Second Temple Judaism raised the description to a title suggests a closer connection between Ezekiel and Daniel and the New Testament.

their everlasting dominion. Daniel has other visions of a similar nature: a ram with two horns, representing "the kings of Media and Persia," and a goat, "the king of Greece" (8:15–21). This mysterious apocalyptic book concludes with the promise of the resurrection of the dead and the last judgment (ch. 12).

Therefore, as Moltmann notes, "The kingdom of the son of man does not evolve out of the succession of world empires. It breaks out of the transcendence into the history of human struggles for power, as something utterly new."[15] Interestingly, the prophecy does not include Israel as a world power. "In the apocalyptic hope, Israel's messianic hope apparently becomes so universal that her special promise and her own history disappear, and the original horizon of creation is reached."[16] Something far greater is envisioned than a renewal of Israel as a geo-political theocracy. Daniel's visions coalesce with the prophets more generally. Israel becomes a world power, to be sure, but not in the way that the other empires have gained ascendancy. Her Messiah will not only destroy the dominion of the worldly kingdoms; he will usher in his kingdom through peace and humility. His empire will be universal in scope, but not in the usual way. His Word will go forth from Zion to the ends of the earth, and righteousness will finally achieve dominion, so that God's glory will fill the earth. The tensions are strong between the Davidic messianism and the "son of man." "It seems to me," says Moltmann, "that the link in eschatology between hope for the messiah and the expectation of the son of man, corresponds to the link between the creation of mankind and Israel's particular history of promise."[17] Biblical history has moved from the widest horizon (i.e., creation) to the narrower (Israel), until it reaches its target: the Son of Man. After the redeeming work of Jesus, the movement is reversed: from the most particular center (Christ) to Jerusalem, and then to the ends of the earth.

It is with this background that the New Testament applies the messianic title and mission to one of Israel's own sons. Although "son of man" was rarely used by others, Jesus' own repeated adoption of the title (over forty occasions) underscores its importance to his "messianic consciousness." These references may be divided roughly into three classes, with distinct emphases: (1) an eschatological advent (Mt 16:27–28; Mk 8:38; 13:26); (2) Jesus' suffering, death, and resurrection (Mt 17:22; 20:18, 19, 28; 12:40; Jn 12:34; Ac 7:56; Rev 1:13; (3) in John's Gospel especially, Jesus' divinity (Jn 1:51; 3:13–14; 6:27, 53, 62; 8:28) and his humanity (Jn 5:27; 6:27, 51, 62; cf. Mk 2:27).[18] The Son of Man comes to *judge*, to *save*, and to *reign*. In all of these passages and classes of passages, he does this as divine and human.

Jesus adopts the Son of Man title with a special emphasis on his *deity*, especially in the fourth Gospel. Thoughtful arguments have been suggested in favor of the traditional

15. Moltmann, *The Way of Jesus Christ*, 14.
16. Ibid., 15.
17. Ibid., 16.

18. See Geerhardus Vos, *The Modern Debate about the Messianic Consciousness* (ed. Johannes G. Vos; Grand Rapids: Eerdmans, 1953). Though dated, its arguments and analysis remain persuasive.

Jewish interpretation of the "Son of Man" as the people of Israel as a whole.[19] However, among others, Craig A. Evans has offered a persuasive argument for interpreting Daniel 7 and its New Testament interpretations as referring to one representative person, as understood even by Second Temple sources.[20] Wright renders a similar judgment.[21] In Daniel 7 especially, "the picture is very sharp: this Messiah-figure will bear the brunt of gentile fury, and will be vindicated."[22] He adds, "The last Adam is the eschatological Israel, who will be raised from the dead as the vindicated people of God."[23]

Very likely appealing to Jacob's vision of the ladder from heaven, with angels ascending and descending in royal procession (Ge 28:11–19), Jesus tells Nathaniel, "Truly, truly, I say to you, you will see heaven opened, and the angels of God ascending and descending on the Son of Man" (Jn 1:51). "No one has ascended into heaven except he who descended from heaven, the Son of Man. And as Moses lifted up the serpent in the wilderness, so must the Son of Man be lifted up, that whoever believes in him may have eternal life" (3:13–15). So even on the heels of claiming oneness with the Father in John 5:17, which the religious leaders recognized as "making himself equal with God" (5:18), having the same power as the Father to raise the dead, give eternal life (v. 21), and exercise judgment so that everyone will honor the Son just as they honor the Father (vv. 21–23), Jesus also claims that he has life in himself just as the Father does (v. 26). Instead of working for the food that perishes, the people are called to receive "the food that endures to eternal life, which the Son of Man will give to you. For on him God the Father has set his seal.... Truly, truly, I say to you, unless you eat the flesh of the Son of Man and drink his blood, you have no life in you.... Do you take offense at this? Then what if you were to see the Son of Man ascending to where he was before?" (6:27, 53, 61–62). Once more assuming an intimate relationship with the Father, Jesus says, "When you have lifted up the Son of Man, then you will know that I am he..." (8:28). Therefore, the title *Son of Man* does not refer simply to Christ's humanity. If the Son of Man were merely human, it is difficult to imagine how a seminal Jewish text such as *1 Enoch* could celebrate the day when all people "shall fall down before him on their faces, and worship and raise their hopes in that Son of Man," even to "beg and plead for mercy at his feet" (*1 Enoch* 62:9).[24]

On one hand, we recognize this title, Son of Man, as the fulfillment of Adamic sonship; on the other hand, it is a reference to his divine identity—his unity with the Father. Therefore, we cannot neatly correlate "Son of Man" and "Son of God" with his

19. See, for example, James D. G. Dunn, *Christology in the Making: A New Testament Inquiry into the Origins of the Doctrine of the Incarnation* (Philadelphia: Westminster Press, 1980), 68–95.

20. Craig A. Evans, "Jesus' Self-Designation 'The Son of Man' and the Recognition of His Divinity," in Gerald O'Collins, *The Trinity: An Interdisciplinary Symposium on the Trinity* (ed. Stephen T. Davis, Daniel Kendall, SJ, and Gerald O'Collins, SJ; New York: Oxford Univ. Press, 1999), 30–39.

21. N. T. Wright, *Jesus and the Victory of God*, 514.

22. Ibid., 515

23. Ibid., 35.

24. Craig A. Evans, "Jesus' Self-Designation 'The Son of Man,'" 39n22.

humanity and deity, respectively. As we will see, "Son of God" is as much a reference to his humanity as "Son of Man" is to his deity. His humiliation is not simply a predicate of his humanity: it was the Word who humbled himself to become flesh, recover what was lost in Adam, and raise it to heaven in glory. And his exaltation is not simply a predicate of his divinity; as the victorious Last Adam, the Son of Man takes his throne in our name. The Son of Man is the Lord who is Servant and the Servant who is Lord.

D. SERVANT OF THE LORD

In the so-called Servant Songs of Isaiah, Israel's corporate office of covenant servant is representatively embodied in the messianic figure to come. In Isaiah 52, Israel is enjoined to rejoice in the "good news" of that salvation, when his people "shall be redeemed without money" (v.3, 7). "The LORD has bared his holy arm before the eyes of the nations; and all the ends of the earth shall see the salvation of our God" (v. 10).

> Behold, my servant shall act wisely;
>> he shall be high and lifted up,
>> and shall be exalted.
> As many as were astonished at you—
>> his appearance was so marred, beyond human semblance,
>> and his form beyond that of the children of mankind—
> so shall he sprinkle many nations;
>> kings shall shut their mouths because of him;
> for that which has not been told them they see,
>> and that which they have not heard they understand (vv.13–15).

The "servant of the LORD" is identified with eschatological judgment and salvation.

The well-known fifty-third chapter continues the prophetic announcement of the servant. Although of no great account in human eyes—in fact, "despised and rejected," he will appear "like a root out of dry ground." Bearing the sins of many, he will be exalted as King (vv. 1–12). Judaism has traditionally interpreted these chapters as personifications of Israel, while Christians read them as clear references to the coming Savior, Jesus Christ. Both interpretations are valid: Jesus Christ is the true Israel, the Living Vine, and every branch that is connected to him receives life and bears fruit.

As a result of the Servant's labors, the covenant of grace will be secured in God's unilateral oath: " 'This is like the days of Noah to me: as I swore that the waters of Noah should no more go over the earth, so I have sworn that I will not be angry with you, and will not rebuke you. For the mountains may depart and the hills be removed, but my steadfast love [ḥesed] shall not depart from you, and my covenant of peace shall not be removed,' says the LORD, who has compassion on you" (Isa 54:9–10). This unconditional note is struck in chapter 55 as well, again referring to "an everlasting covenant"—this time alluding to the Davidic covenant. In that day, "... a nation that did not know you shall run to you, because of the LORD your God, and of the Holy One of Israel, for he has glorified you" (vv. 1, 3–5).

Although "there was no justice" and "no one to intercede" (Isa 59:15, 16) as the Great King looked upon his faithless people, he was moved by compassion to redeem with his own arm.

> "And a Redeemer will come to Zion,
> to those in Jacob who turn from transgression," declares the LORD.

> "And as for me, this is my covenant with them," says the LORD: "My Spirit that is upon you, and my words that I have put in your mouth, shall not depart out of your mouth, or out of the mouth of your offspring, or out of the mouths of your children's offspring," says the LORD, "from this time forth and forevermore." (Isa 59:20–21)

That the Spirit appears at this point is not surprising, given the transition from forgiveness to resurrection and the new creation. Thus, chapter 60 begins with the announcement of life to the dead and a great ingathering that will be more dramatic and extensive than the scattering of Israel and Judah had been. "Nations shall come to your light, and kings to the brightness of your rising" (v. 3). Ships stream into Israel's harbor loaded with gifts, "with their kings led in procession" into the everlasting Sabbath (v. 11). The sun will never set on this empire. "Your people shall all be righteous; they shall possess the land forever" (vv. 19–21).

The relation of the Spirit to the Servant becomes even more pronounced in chapter 61, where the Servant is identified as the one who fulfills the everlasting Year of Jubilee (typologically established in Leviticus 25): "The Spirit of the Lord GOD is upon me, because the LORD has anointed me to bring good news to the poor; he has sent me to bind up the brokenhearted, to proclaim liberty to the captives, and the opening of the prison to those who are bound; to proclaim the year of the LORD's favor, and the day of vengeance of our God; to comfort all who mourn..." (Isa 61:1–2).

The servant people will be righteous in the Servant himself, "for he has clothed me with the garments of salvation; he has covered me with the robe of righteousness, as a bridegroom decks himself like a priest with a beautiful headdress, and as a bride adorns herself with her jewels. For as the earth brings forth its sprouts, and as a garden causes what is sown in it to sprout up, so the Lord GOD will cause righteousness and praise to sprout up before all the nations" (vv. 10–11; cf. 62:10–12). The Servant of Yahweh is the true Israel.

It is with this background that Jesus announces himself as the Servant and is proclaimed as such by the church. Still unwilling at this early hour to unveil his mission publicly, Jesus cured many in the crowds but told them to keep it secret.

This was to fulfill what was spoken by the prophet Isaiah:

> "Behold, my servant whom I have chosen,
> my beloved with whom my soul is well pleased.

> I will put my Spirit upon him,
>> and he will proclaim justice to the Gentiles.
> He will not quarrel or cry aloud,
>> nor will anyone hear his voice in the streets;
> a bruised reed he will not break,
>> and a smoldering wick he will not quench,
> until he brings justice to victory;
>> and in his name the Gentiles will hope." (Mt 12:17–21, appealing to Isa
>> 42:1–4)

In her Magnificat, Mary takes her place in the hall of Israel's "Here I am" servants (cf. Lk 1:38, 48) and realizes from the angel's announcement and Elizabeth's greeting that through her God has now acted in fulfillment of the promise, "as he spoke to our fathers, to Abraham and to his offspring forever" (v. 55).

Jesus came to the Nazareth synagogue on the Sabbath:

> He stood up to read. And the scroll of the prophet Isaiah was given to him. He unrolled the scroll and found the place where it was written,
>
>> "The Spirit of the Lord is upon me,
>> because he has anointed me to proclaim good news to the poor...."
>
> And he rolled up the scroll and gave it back to the attendant and sat down. And the eyes of all in the synagogue were fixed on him. And he began to say to them, "Today this scripture has been fulfilled in your hearing." (Lk 4:16–21)

His auditors knew precisely what Jesus was claiming for himself, as Jesus' words filled the congregation with anger and he narrowly escaped the hostile crowd (vv. 28–30).

As we have seen especially in Isaiah, there is a close bond between the Spirit and the Servant. The Spirit who hovered over the depths in creation, calling a world out of nothing, "will come upon you," the angel tells Mary, "and the power of the Most High will overshadow you; therefore the child to be born will be called holy—the Son of God" (Lk 1:35). It was the Spirit who led the Servant into the wilderness temptation, to endure the probation that Adam and Israel failed to fulfill (Mt 4:1), and who descended in the form of a dove above the waters in Jesus' baptism (Mt 3:16; Mk. 1:9–11; Lk 3:21–22; Jn 1:32–34). As Israel was led through the wilderness by the Spirit in pillar and cloud, which witnessed to God's election of and covenant with his people, so Jesus, in recapitulating Israel's history in his own life, is the new Israel, the new Servant of the LORD—not to replace the Israelites but to fulfill the promises made to Abraham and David on behalf of his covenant people.

The titles I have surveyed are far from exhaustive, but they group together some of the most integral threads of the messianic hope from which the church's Christology emerges.

II. SON OF GOD: THE SON OF THE FATHER IN THE SPIRIT

I have suggested that we cannot assume that "Son of Man" refers to Jesus Christ's humanity while "Son of God" refers to his deity. The Son of Man is God as well as human and the Son of God is a human figure who is also Lord. Jesus Christ is both the one who speaks the divine law and the one who answers the summons with full and perfect obedience as our representative. Similarly, Jesus is not only the eternally begotten Son of the Father, but the true and faithful *human* son. Sonship in this sense is both ontological and official. Jesus is the eternal Son of the Father, but he must fulfill this office that Adam and Israel violated.[25]

A. SONSHIP: ONTOLOGICAL AND OFFICIAL

In the New Testament, as in much of the Second Temple literature, the messianic concept brings together the Adamic and Abrahamic bases of sonship, the former stressing *adoption by obedience*, the latter underscoring his sonship *as unconditional and everlasting*. What is different, however, especially in the case of the New Testament, is that Jesus' sonship in this second sense comes not by adoption but by *eternal generation*. He is the *monogenēs theos* — "the only begotten God," "the only begotten [Son] from the Father" (Jn 1:18, 14; NASB).

As we have seen, the concept of "sonship" is integral to the *imago dei*. Adam and Eve are sons of God in this adoptive sense, as is Israel as God's "firstborn son" (Ex 4:21–23; 12:29–32; Jer 31:9; Hos 11:1–2, 8–11). There is no suggestion, of course, of a natural bond between God and Israelites any more than with Adam. Yahweh has adopted Israel as his firstborn heir. In the covenant that he makes with David, God promises David concerning his offspring, "I will be to him a father, and he shall be to me a son" — punishing but never abandoning (2 Sam 7:14). The author of Psalm 89 sets this narrative to music: "My faithfulness and my steadfast love shall be with him," God promises.

> And in my name shall his horn be exalted....
> He shall cry to me, 'You are my Father,
>   my God, and the Rock of my salvation.'
> And I will make him the firstborn,
>   the highest of the kings of the earth.

---

25. As in anthropology, in Christology *sonship* Christology plays a specific function that subverts the political and social structures that typically reckoned women only slightly higher than slaves. While gender-inclusive language may work more effectively in contexts that do not afford much explanation, at this point it defuses the explosive announcement that not only sons — indeed firstborn sons — inherit the whole estate, but women and slaves become equal title-holders (expressed legally as "sons") in the kingdom of Christ.

My steadfast love I will keep for him forever,
　　and my covenant will stand firm for him.
I will establish his offspring forever,
　　and his throne as the days of the heavens.
If his children forsake my law
　　and do not walk according to my rules,
if they violate my statutes
　　and do not keep my commandments,
then I will punish their transgression with the rod
　　and their iniquity with stripes,
but I will not remove from him my steadfast love
　　or be false to my faithfulness.
I will not violate my covenant
　　or alter the word that went forth from my lips. (Ps 89: 24b, 26–34)

Right where the Sinaitic covenant said, in terms reminiscent of the Adamic covenant, "If you forget the LORD your God and go after other gods and serve them and worship them, I solemnly warn you today that *you shall surely perish*" (Dt 8:19, italics added), this Davidic promise—resting on the Abrahamic covenant—creates an unconditional and irreversible adoption of David and his heirs for an everlasting dynasty.

For Paul the title "Son of God" refers as much to our Lord's fulfillment of his office as to his eternal generation by the Father. The phrase "son of God" (*huios theou*) occurs 124 times in the New Testament, but especially in Paul, and the apostle's preference for this title is surely related to the impact of the Damascus road encounter with the risen and enthroned Christ. In Hebrews, the phrase is used specifically to highlight the uniqueness of Jesus' sonship in contrast to angels and Moses. It occurs also in the Synoptics (Mt 11:27; Mk 12:6; 13:32; Lk 10:22; cf. Mk 14:32–42), and we will consider its frequent occurrence in the gospel of John below. Paul makes a clear distinction between Christ's sonship and ours by adoption.

To summarize this point, then: Jesus Christ is the Son of God in both senses: (1) as the eternally generated Word of the Father and (2) as the true image-bearer, the faithful Adamic "son" and the loyal "firstborn son" that Israel was intended to be. Therefore, to say that Jesus is the Son of God because he is divine is true, but it is also to say that he has fulfilled his office as a human representative, in the place of Adam and Israel. Christ is not only the eternally begotten Son but also "the firstborn among many brothers and sisters" (Ro 8:29 TNIV). Both as Word of God (emphasized in John's preface) and as the seed of Adam, Abraham, and David (emphasized in Matthew's preface), Jesus Christ is our Lord and Savior.

Just as "Son of Man" is pregnant with references to Christ's divinity as well as his humanity, "Son of God" is related as much to his humanity as to his deity. In Psalm 2 the Anointed One (Messiah) reports at his enthronement, "The LORD said to me, 'You are my Son; today I have begotten you'" (v. 7). The writer to the Hebrews (especially in the first two chapters) draws on this and other passages to argue for Christ's superiority to the angels and to Moses. Rather than downplay these passages in favor of those that highlight his ontological sonship, we should recognize his fulfillment of this filial office as the one who is not only the Lord of the covenant who commands, but the Servant of the covenant who answers faithfully, "All that you have spoken I will do," and actually does everything that he hears.

The synoptic Gospels testify to Christ's sonship in both of these senses (i.e., ontological and official). Already in the angelic announcement to Mary we are introduced to the cooperation of the Father and the Spirit in the Son's incarnation and ministry (Lk 1:35). Matthew 2:15 interprets the return of the holy family from its flight into Egypt as the fulfillment of Hosea 11:1: "Out of Egypt I called my Son." In his baptism and call, Jesus' ministry is shaped by his consciousness that God is his Father and he is his Son. "And ... a voice from heaven said, 'This is my beloved Son, with whom I am well pleased" (Mt 3:17). He addresses the Father with an unheard-of intimacy, as "*my* Father." In all of these instances, we must bear in mind both his eternal sonship (which is unique) and the sense in which he is fulfilling the adoptive sonship of Adam and Israel on behalf of his people. In this way, Jesus Christ brings us into his relationship of intimacy with the Father in his humanity as the Spirit-filled covenant servant, even though his ontological unity with the Father remains unique.

Furthermore, besides the myriad references in the fourth Gospel there are many synoptic references to "the Father" and "the Son," with the implication at least that this relationship is eternal and ontological (e.g., Mt 24:36; 11:27). After walking on the sea with dry feet (the event itself is pregnant with creation-exodus imagery), "those in the boat worshiped him, saying, 'Truly you are the Son of God'" (14:28–33). Later, "He said to them, 'But who do you say that I am?' Simon Peter replied, 'You are the Christ, the Son of the living God.' And Jesus answered him, 'Blessed are you, Simon Bar-Jonah! For flesh and blood has not revealed this to you, but my Father who is in heaven'" (16:15–17). In the parable of the wicked tenants, Israel is a tenant of the landowner, while Jesus himself is the owner's son and heir (Mt 21:33–46).

Then there are the passages that relate Jesus' interaction with the officials, where his messianic secret is now unveiled for all to see. "Now while the Pharisees were gathered together, Jesus asked them a question, saying, 'What do you think about the Christ [Messiah]? Whose son is he?' They said to him, 'The son of David.'" Exegeting Psalm 110:1,

> [Jesus] said to them, "How is it then that David, in the Spirit, calls him Lord, saying,
>
>> 'The Lord said to my Lord,
>> Sit at my right hand,

until I put your enemies under your feet'?

If David thus calls him Lord, how is he his son?" And no one was able to answer him a word, nor from that day did anyone dare to ask him any more questions." (Mt 22:41–46)

Standing before the high priest, who said to him, "I adjure you by the living God, tell us if you are the Christ, the Son of God," Jesus replied, " 'You have said so. But I tell you, from now on you will see the Son of Man seated at the right hand of Power and coming on the clouds of heaven.' Then the high priest tore his robes and said, 'He has uttered blasphemy. What further witnesses do we need?' " (Mt 26:63–65). The Pharisees knew better than some modern theologians that Jesus was claiming equality with God and not simply representing himself as a prophet of an ethical kingdom.

In addition to the annunciation and baptism, the transfiguration also provides a narrative account of the relation of the Son to the Father and the Spirit. Just as in the days when the future kingdom erupted in proleptic redemptive-historical situations under the old covenant, the transfiguration was a rare moment in the humiliation of Jesus when his exaltation was semirealized. Nearly a week after reminding his disciples of his impending death and resurrection, Jesus took Peter, James, and John to a mountain. There Jesus "was transfigured before them, and his clothes became radiant, intensely white," as he conversed with Elijah and Moses. "And a cloud overshadowed them, and a voice came out of the cloud, 'This is my beloved Son; listen to him!' And suddenly, looking around, they no longer saw anyone with them but Jesus only" (Mk 9:2–8).

The Shekinah-Spirit, who brooded over the waters in creation, led Israel through the waters to the promised land, and dwelt among the people in the Holy of Holies, now hovered in refulgent splendor to join the Father in pronouncing benediction on the Son. This is both a Trinitarian moment and a coronation of the Son of Man as the one who by his obedience has fulfilled the Father's will. God is pleased with him not simply because he is the eternal Son but because he is the true and faithful son of Adam, Abraham, and David.

The cries of those with demons testify to this sonship that he exercises as divine and human.[26] As Craig Evans points out, "Son of God" was also a familiar appellation of Caesar as a supposed incarnation of Zeus. "There is no reason to think that Jesus' Jewish contemporaries, who were themselves very much part of the Greco-Roman world, would have thought of these expressions in terms significantly

---

26. Craig Evans points out, "The cries of the demonized (Mark 3:11 = Luke 4:41: 'You are the son of God!' Mark 5:7: 'Jesus, son of the Most High God') are all probably rooted in authentic tradition. These epithets remind us of 4Q246, where we find reference to one who will be called 'son of God' and 'son of the Most High.' This Aramaic text, dating from the first century BCE, confirms the expectation of a coming world saviour who would be thought of as 'son of God'; it also confirms that this concept was right at home in Palestine" ("Jesus' Self-Designation 'Son of Man,' " 42).

different from those held by Gentiles."[27] Interestingly, it is not only in the resurrection that Jesus' messianic identity is recognized; it was also recognized by the centurion when Jesus was on the cross: "Truly this was the Son of God!" (Mt 27:54).

It is of course in John's Gospel that the Son of God theme is especially emphasized in terms of the relation of Jesus to the eternal Son of the Father. The fourth Gospel identifies Jesus with the eternal Word who, though distinct from the Father, is nevertheless God. Further, the prologue explicitly echoes that of Genesis: "In the beginning was the Word, and the Word was with God, and the Word was God. He was in the beginning with God. All things were made through him, and without him was not anything made that was made. In him was life, and the life was the light of men. The light shines in the darkness, and the darkness has not overcome it"(Jn 1:1–5). The world that exists by and through him rejected him—but not everyone, by God's gift of new birth (vv. 10–13). "And the Word became flesh and dwelt among us, and we have seen his glory, glory as of the only Son from the Father, full of grace and truth" (v. 14). While the law came through Moses, grace has come through the Son, Jesus Christ, who alone has seen God. "No one has ever seen God; the only God, who is at the Father's side, he has made him known" (vv. 17–18). At the baptism, John announces Jesus as "the Lamb of God, who takes away the sin of the world," and bears witness: "I saw the Spirit descend from heaven like a dove, and it remained on him. I myself did not know him, but he who sent me to baptize with water said to me, 'He on whom you see the Spirit descend and remain, this is he who baptizes with the Holy Spirit.' And I have seen and have borne witness that this is the Son of God" (vv. 29–34).

The sonship of Jesus is developed throughout the Gospel of John with the intra-trinitarian fellowship always in view. The messianic themes are present, as in John 6:69, where Peter declares, "We have believed, and have come to know, that you are the Holy One of God." But the unity with the Father (and later, the Spirit) is dominant. For these passages, readers are referred to the treatment of the Trinity in this volume.

Finally, there is the witness of the epistles. Paul, who, like Stephen—whose stoning Paul (Saul) sanctioned—saw a vision of the ascended Christ at the Father's right hand, provides some of the earliest apostolic witness to Jesus Christ as the Son of God. The former persecutor of the church is now the servant of the gospel "concerning his Son, who was descended from David according to the flesh and was declared to be the Son of God in power according to the Spirit of holiness by his resurrection from the dead, Jesus Christ our Lord, through whom we have received grace and apostleship to bring about the obedience of faith for the sake of his name among all the nations, including you who are called to belong to Jesus Christ" (Ro

---

27. Ibid., 43.

462

1:3–6). According to this gospel, the God who acted in Christ to create the world has now acted in Christ to redeem it in history: "For God has done what the law, weakened by the flesh, could not do. By sending his own Son in the likeness of sinful flesh and for sin, he condemned sin in the flesh, in order that the righteous requirement of the law might be fulfilled in us..." (Ro 8:3–4).

The Adam-Christ typology is underscored in Romans 5, where Israel's plight and solution are placed in the context of the wider human plight and solution laid out in the first four chapters. While the Abrahamic promise runs through the Old Testament and on into the New, the conditional works-covenant that marks both Eden and Sinai is not set aside but fulfilled. In fact, it is on the basis of the fulfillment of the covenant of works in Christ that God's unconditional oath to Adam, Abraham, and David can be realized in a covenant of grace. "But when the fullness of time had come, God sent forth his Son, born of woman, born under the law, to redeem those who were under the law, so that we might receive adoption as sons" (Gal 4:4–5). "[I]n Christ God was reconciling the world to himself..." (2 Cor 5:19a).

Paul attests to the identity of Jesus with God the Son repeatedly, as in the well-known hymn of Philippians 2, where Jesus is identified as "in the form of God" and yet willing to empty himself, "taking the form of a servant, being born in the likeness of men," humbling himself even to the point of going to the cross. "Therefore God has highly exalted him and bestowed on him the name that is above every name, so that at the name of Jesus every knee should bow, in heaven and on earth and under the earth, and every tongue confess that Jesus Christ is Lord, to the glory of God the Father" (vv. 5–11). Here it should be noticed again that the sonship-as-office is as important as his ontological sonship as the eternal Word. It is *because* he has been obedient throughout his life, even to the point of taking upon himself the curse of the cross, that he is exalted above every name. He is the royal son, the faithful Adam, who has led creation in triumphant procession into the everlasting Sabbath. It is for that reason—and not simply because of his deity—that he is worthy to assume such exalted status. Everything that humanity was created to be as God's image-bearer (royal son, glorious representative, and prophetic witness) Jesus Christ actually attained in his humanity. And yet the status of Jesus as God's preexistent Son is just as obvious from this passage.

The beginning of Colossians is similar to John's prologue in declaring that Christ "is the image of the invisible God, the firstborn of all creation; for by him all things were created, in heaven and on earth, visible and invisible, whether thrones or dominions or rulers or authorities—all things were created through him and for him. And he is before all things, and in him all things hold together" (1:15–17). The Creator of the world and the redeemer of the church are one and the same person (vv. 18–23). A closer identification of Jesus with Israel's Yahweh is unimaginable. In fact, Paul's announcement that "every knee should bow and every tongue confess" the name of Christ is itself an allusion to one of the most monotheistic passages in the Bible: Isaiah 45:22–23, which reads, "For I am God, and there is no other.... To me every knee shall bow; every tongue shall swear allegiance." This is precisely the exalted one whom Paul met on the Damascus road. Paul refers to "the glory of our great God and Savior Jesus Christ" (Tit 2:13). The triune benediction (2 Cor 13:14) is also of some significance.

In the Book of Revelation Jesus is the Alpha-Creator and Omega-Consummator (Rev 1:8, 17–18). And the writer to the Hebrews opens his epistle,

> Long ago, at many times and in many ways, God spoke to our fathers by the prophets, but in these last days he has spoken to us by his Son, whom he appointed the heir of all things, through whom also he created the world. He is the radiance of the glory of God and the exact imprint of his nature, and he upholds the universe by the word of his power. After making purification for sins, he sat down at the right hand of the Majesty on high, having become as much superior to angels as the name he has inherited is more excellent than theirs.
>
> For to which of the angels did God ever say,
>
> "You are my Son;
> today I have begotten you"?
>
> Or again,
>
> "I will be to him a father,
> and he shall be to me a Son"? (Heb 1:1–5)

In fact, the contrast is drawn between Moses and Christ along this line:

> For Jesus has been counted worthy of more glory than Moses, as much more glory as the builder of a house has more honor than the house itself. (For every house is built by someone, but the builder of all things is God.) Now Moses was faithful in all God's house as a servant, to testify to the things that were to be spoken later, but Christ is faithful over God's house as a son. And we are his house if we indeed hold fast our confidence and our boasting in our hope. (Heb 3:3–6)

Christ is identified not only as Son but as God, in that he is the "builder" who is himself identified as God.

So far we have affirmed the two sides of the affirmation that Jesus is the Son of God: he fulfills the Adamic sonship as God's royal image, and he addresses God as Father because he is the everlasting Son in the divine Trinity. This leads us briefly to a consideration of his preexistence: the so-called *logos asarkos* (preincarnate Word) or, better, the *logos incarnandus* (the Word who was to become incarnate).

B. PREEXISTENT SON

The liberal trajectory leading from Reimarus's *Fragments* to D. F. Strauss's *Life of Jesus* and Adolf von Harnack's *Essence of Christianity* is essentially *Arian* (or Adoptionist). "The Gospel as Jesus preached it, has to do with the Father only and not with the Son," Harnack claimed.[28] In current scholarship, it is generally acknowledged that there have been three major *quests for the historical Jesus*.[29] From Reimarus to the Jesus Seminar, a key presupposition of such quests (including the "no quest" of Bultmann) is the belief that the earliest "Jesus" was a rabbinical sage who was transformed into the "Christ" of orthodoxy by a Hellenizing process. For Bultmann, it was the Gnostic Redeemer myth that served this transformation of Jesus into a divine figure who existed eternally before he was made flesh.[30]

QUESTS FOR THE HISTORICAL JESUS

Quest	Dates	Characteristics
First Quest	1788–1906	Reimarus to Schweitzer. The Christ of faith (confessed by the church in the creeds) is fundamentally different from the real Jesus of history. In his *Life of Jesus*, David Friedrich Strauss (1808–1874) argued that the high Christology found in the New Testament is mythological. Albert Schweitzer's *The Quest of the Historical Jesus* (1906) ended this initial quest by arguing that Jesus expected an imminent establishment of a kingdom that failed to arrive.
No Quest	1906–1953	Schweitzer to Bultmann. Following Martin Kähler (supplemented by Martin Heidegger's existentialist categories), Bultmann argued that the Jesus of history is of no significance to the Christ of faith.
Second (or New) Quest	1953–present	Especially associated with Ernst Käsemann but also with the Jesus Seminar.
Third Quest	1980s to present	The phrase was coined by an advocate of this quest, N. T. Wright. With the work of G. B. Caird, E. P. Sanders, and others, interest arose in contextualizing Jesus within his Jewish (Second Temple) milieu.

28. Adolf von Harnack, *Essence of Christianity* (New York: Harper and Bros., 1957), 154.

29. For the history of Jesus-questing, see W. Barnes Tatum, *In Quest of Jesus: A Guidebook* (Atlanta: John Knox, 1982); N. T. Wright, *Jesus and the Victory of God* (vol. 2 of *Christian Origins and the Question of God*; Minneapolis: Fortress, 1996), ch. 1; Harvey K. McArthur, *The Quest through the Centuries: The Search for the Historical Jesus* (Philadelphia: Fortress, 1966); Albert Schweitzer, *The Quest of the Historical Jesus: A Critical Study of Its Progress from Reimarus to Wrede* (trans. W. Mont-

gomery; London: A. and C. Black, 1910); Raymond E. Brown, *An Introduction to the New Testament* (Anchor Bible Reference Library; ed. David Noel Freedman; New York: Doubleday, 1997), 819; Colin Brown, "Quest of Historical Jesus," in *Dictionary of Jesus and the Gospels* (ed. Joel B. Green, Scot McKnight, and I. Howard Marshall; Downers Grove, Ill.: InterVarsity Press, 1992), 326.

30. Rudolf Bultmann, *The Theology of the New Testament* (trans. Kendrick Grobel; New York: Charles Scribner's Sons, 1951), 1:174–78.

However, as Brevard Childs has pointed out, critical scholarship has found no basis for the sharp division between Jewish and Hellenistic Christologies in the early church, most Christians being "bilingual from the start."[31] "A basic christological title such as *kyrios* [lord] had both Greek and Aramaic antecedents which quickly fused (cf. Hengel, *Between Jesus and Paul*, 30ff.)."[32] "It is also clear that a similar confession in terms of content could be made by different linguistic conventions. That 'Jesus is Lord' in Paul is not much different in meaning from 'Jesus is the Son of God' in John."[33] "Thus Psalm 110 served as a warrant for Christ's royal rule as Lord, II Samuel 7 for the son of David theology, Psalm 2 for Jesus' claim of sonship, and Psalms 22 and 69 for the passion and resurrection of the redeemer."[34] Only the totality of the actions and teachings of Jesus Christ as reported in the Gospels can explain his trial and crucifixion as something other than religious bigotry. The Jewish leaders of Jesus' day were remarkably tolerant, but not of what they regarded as blasphemy.

As we have already seen, the Synoptics report the charge against Jesus of blasphemy for claiming to be equal with God; Jesus and the evangelists call people to place their faith in Christ and to receive forgiveness of sins through Christ. Jesus himself calls his people to invoke his name in prayer, in baptism, in receiving forgiveness of sins, and in worship throughout the Gospels. Given the covenantal freight of that phrase "in the name of," there is no doubt that Jesus was claiming to be no less than Yahweh incarnate. We have already encountered the conundrum Jesus presents to the religious leaders in Matthew 22:41–45: How can David call "Lord" one who will be his future descendant? At least implicitly, Jesus is claiming to have existed as the Lord prior to David himself.

For Matthew, as Childs notes, "The virgin birth is the sign which identifies him as the Messiah."[35] However, the virginal conception of Christ itself presupposes the existence of the Son prior to his incarnation.[36] It is this dogma especially that liberalism has sought to avoid by dispensing with the unique (miraculous) conception of Christ. In the fourth gospel, Jesus Christ is explicitly identified as the Word who existed with the Father before creation and by whom all things were made (Jn 1), and we have already drawn attention to the many passages in this Gospel where Jesus explicitly claims equality with the Father.

Yet many of the most explicit references to Jesus as the eternally preexistent Son are found in some of the earliest New Testament documents: the Pauline corpus,

---

31. Brevard Childs, *Biblical Theology of the Old and New Testaments* (Minneapolis: Fortress, 1993), 461.

32. Ibid., 462.

33. Ibid.

34. Ibid., 463.

35. Ibid., 470.

36. I refer to "virginal conception" rather than "virgin birth" because, strictly speaking, the miracle of the incarnation refers to his conception rather than to his birth.

where some are even fragments of earlier hymns. If Paul's epistles were written in the mid-50s, and he was incorporating creedal and liturgical fragments that had already been in use, then some of the clearest testimonies to Christ's preexistent deity and sonship are also the earliest. By the late first century, as Raymond Brown demonstrates, the claim that Jesus is God was asserted clearly across wide geographical boundaries, and even the Roman Pliny the Younger, at the turn of the century, criticized Christians in Asia Minor for "singing hymns to Christ as to a god."[37] All of this predates the advent of any recognizable form of Gnosticism, and in any case, the Gnostic Redeemer myth was in substance diametrically opposed to the doctrine of the incarnation.

Martin Hengel shows decisively, against the history-of-religions school, that the title "Son of God" did not emerge as part of a process of alleged Hellenization.[38] He also demonstrates the wide variance between superficially similar dying-and-rising myths and the attribution "Son of God." Bultmann's speculations about the New Testament Christology emerging from the Gnostic Redeemer myth have been refuted.[39] Rather, "Earliest Christology has a quite original stamp, and is ultimately rooted in the contingent event of the activity of Jesus, his death and resurrection appearances."[40] Concerning Paul's reference to Jesus Christ as "[God's] Son, who was descended from David according to the flesh" (Ro 1:3), "The unanimous opinion of scholars is that it contains an early confession," perhaps a creed—and this was written to a church that he did not himself found.[41] Furthermore, "direct pagan influence is extremely improbable if only because of the ethnic composition of these earliest mission communities."[42] "The preexistence of the eschatological redeemer could already be read out of Micah 5.1 or Ps. 110.3: he was begotten by God, older than the dawn of creation." Similar statements about the preexistence of the Son of Man are found in 1 Enoch 48.6; 62.7.[43] So there is no reason to look to Greek paganism for the concept of the eternal existence of the Son prior to his incarnation. Jesus Christ was not just an angel or prophetic messenger. He allowed himself to be worshiped during his earthly mission and was invoked by the earliest Christians as Lord along with the Father, and Old Testament references to Yahweh's actions were routinely interpreted as equally attributable to Jesus Christ. Thomas's confession of Christ's identity is that of the whole church: "My Lord and my God!" (Jn 20:28).

---

37. Raymond Brown, *An Introduction to New Testament Christology* (New York: Paulist, 1994), 194.

38. Hengel, *The Son of God*, 24.

39. Ibid., 33: "There really should be an end to presenting Manichaean texts of the third century like the 'Song of the Pearl' in the *Acts of Thomas* as evidence of supposedly pre-Christian gnosticism and dating it back to the first century BC. In reality there is no Gnostic redeemer myth in the sources which can be demonstrated chronologically to be pre-Christian."

40. Ibid., 58.

41. Ibid., 59.

42. Ibid., 67.

43. Ibid., 69.

III. TWO NATURES IN ONE PERSON: THE INCARNATION

With the preceding lines of development in view, we arrive at the center of Christology: the doctrine of the incarnation. The faith of the church, summarized by the Chalcedonian Creed (451), is directed to "one and the same Christ, Son, Lord, Only-begotten, to be acknowledged in two natures, inconfusedly, unchangeably, indivisibly, inseparably..."

A. EXEGETICAL SUMMARY

"The Word became flesh" (Jn 1:14). The verb "became" [*egeneto*] here does not entail any change in the essence of the Son. His deity was not converted into our humanity. Rather, he *assumed* our human nature. Furthermore, the Logos did not assume an individual person but generic humanity. Through the most inconceivably intimate personal union of the Logos with our humanity, the particular Jewish male, Jesus of Nazareth, was conceived by the Holy Spirit in the virgin's womb. Therefore, the incarnation does not represent a fusion of preexisting natures, much less of preexisting persons, but the eternal Son's assumption of humanity. Strictly speaking, then, his humanity is impersonal; there is a union of the person of the Son with our humanity, not of a divine and a human person. Each nature is entirely preserved in its distinctness yet in and as one person.

This assumption of our complete humanity need not include sin, of course, because sinfulness is accidental rather than essential to our nature. Since Jesus Christ was, in the words of the *Belgic Confession*, "conceived in the womb of the blessed virgin Mary by the power of the Holy Spirit, without male participation,"[44] his humanity was untainted by original sin (Heb 4:15; cf. Is 7:14; Mt 1:18–20; Lk 1:34–35).[45]

The maxim of Gregory of Nazianzus—"What he did not assume he did not redeem"—is already implied in Hebrews 2:10–18. If fallen human beings are to be saved, God must "make the founder of their salvation perfect through suffering" (v. 10).

> Since therefore the children share in flesh and blood, he himself likewise partook of the same things, that through death he might destroy the one who has the power of death, that is, the devil, and deliver all those who through fear of death were subject to lifelong slavery. For surely it is not angels that he helps, but he helps the offspring of Abraham. Therefore he had to be made like his brothers in every respect, so that he might become a merciful and faithful high priest in the service of God, to make a propitiation for the sins of the people. (Heb 2:14–17)

---

44. *Belgic Confession* 18, available at www.crcna.org/pages/belgic_articles17_24.cfm.

45. Perhaps the best book on the virgin birth (or, more prop-erly, virginal conception) of Christ remains that of J. Gresham Machen, *The Virgin Birth of Christ* (New York: Harper, 1930).

The writer speaks of the Son's assumption of our "flesh and blood," but not of our sinful identity. He was born "under the law" to fulfill an obligation, not as one who was subject already to its curses. Like the humanity of Adam before the fall, Christ's humanity was not yet confirmed in righteousness and glory, but it was unfallen.[46]

When we give due attention to Christ's humanity as the servant of the covenant, more space opens up for the person and work of the Spirit. There is no mention in the Gospels of Jesus' divinity overwhelming his humanity. Nor do the Gospels refer his miracles to his divinity and refer his temptation or sorrow to his humanity, as if he switched back and forth from operating according to one nature to operating according to another. Rather, the Gospels routinely refer Christ's miracles to the Father and the Spirit, accomplishing their work in and through Jesus Christ. Jesus was conceived by the Spirit, was filled with the Spirit, grew in wisdom and understanding by the Spirit, was led by the Spirit into the desert for his temptation and was there upheld by the Spirit, and spoke what he heard from the Father and as he was empowered by the Spirit. Jesus is therefore not only God turned toward God, but humanity turned toward God in the power of the Spirit. The Gospels relate the story of one who was not merely a human shell whose inner impulses were determined by the Logos (see Apollinarianism below, "Two Natures in One Person," p. 472). He is at last the Lord who is servant, "the faithful and true witness" (Rev 3:14). As fully human, he fulfilled the covenant of creation.

Jesus' temptations, both religious-ethical and physical, were real (Mt 4:1–11 and parallel passages; Jn 4:6; Heb 2:17–18). In sharp contrast to the fanciful Gnostic gospels, such as Thomas, the canonical Gospels do not narrate the life of a numinous child prodigy whose humanity is incidental if allowed. "The child *grew* and *became* strong, filled with wisdom. And the favor of God was upon him.... And Jesus *increased* in wisdom and in stature and in favor with God and man" (Lk 2:40, 52, emphasis added). His rejection in his hometown underscores that before he began his ministry Jesus was perceived as quite ordinary — "Is not this the carpenter's son? Is not his mother called Mary? And are not his brothers James and Joseph and Simon and Judas? And are not all his sisters with us? Where then did this man get all these things?" (Mt 13:54–56). Even his brothers did not believe in him until late in his ministry (Jn 7:1–9). He himself declared concerning the "day of the Lord," "But concerning that day and hour no one knows, not even the angels of heaven, nor the

---

46. Karl Barth and some of his students teach that the humanity that Christ assumed was fallen, although he did not personally commit any sin. See, for example, T. F. Torrance, *Incarnation: The Person and Life of Christ* (ed. Robert T. Walker; Downers Grove, Ill.: InterVarsity Press, 2008), 61–65, 231–32. At least in Torrance's case, this seems to be due largely to a tendency to run the incarnation and atonement together. Like Barth, Torrance articulates a robust concept of Christ's active obedience, but confuses Christ's sin-bearing with his assumption of our humanity. However, Christ's having been born "under the law" in no way entails having been born under its condemnation.

Son, but only the Father" (Mt 24:36). Without surrendering his divinity (which included omniscience), the eternal Son fully assumed our finite humanity.

There is no reason to be embarrassed by the full humanity of our Lord. In Gethsemane, Jesus agonizes over his destiny: "My soul is very sorrowful, even to death," he tells his disciples (Mt 26:38a). And in his prayer to the Father he petitions, "My Father, if it be possible, let this cup pass from me; nevertheless, not as I will, but as you will" (v. 39). In one sentence we discern both Jesus' intimate unity with the Father ("My Father") and his differentiation ("not as I will, but as you will"). The same paradox occurs in the crucifixion itself. On one hand, Jesus cries out with surprising formality, "My God, my God, why have you forsaken me?" (Mt 27:46) and on the other, his last reported words are in the form of another cry, "*Father*, into your hands I commit my spirit*" (Lk 23:46). The blood that he brings into the heavenly sanctuary to atone for his brothers and sisters is human (Heb 9:11 – 10:18), yet because of the unity of his person it can be called the blood of God (Ac 20:28).

B. Dogmatic Development

It is beyond our scope to evaluate the extent to which the individuals who bear the ignominious burden of being namesakes for specific heresies actually held the views attributed to them. In this summary, we are concerned merely with the positions identified as heretical.

1. The First Controversies: God and Human?

As we have seen above, the first reports from outsiders were that the earliest Christians worshiped Christ as God, on the basis of clear apostolic proclamation. As with the rise of dogmatic formulations regarding the Trinity, a formal Christology arose not in the ivory towers of speculation but in the concrete practices of preaching, sacrament, prayer, and fellowship.

The first reported challenges within the church itself from Jewish influences denied the *deity* of Christ. Emphasizing the continuing significance of the Mosaic law for Gentile converts, the **Ebionite** heresy (*ʾebʿyônîm*, Hebrew for "the poor ones") also regarded Jesus Christ as the Messiah but as an exclusively human person who justified himself by the works of the law and by his example leads his followers to do the same. According to Eusebius, some Ebionites held that he was supernaturally conceived though not preexistent.[47] Similar was the heresy of **adoptionism**,

---

47. For a description of the Ebionites from a Christian perspective, see the early church historian Eusebius, *Ecclesiastical History*, bk. 3 ch. 27: "For they considered him a plain and common man, who was justified only because of his superior virtue, and who was the fruit of the intercourse of a man with Mary." Other Ebionites, according to Eusebius, affirmed the virgin conception but denied the Son's preincarnate existence. However, they all affirmed the continuing validity of the ceremonial law "on the ground that they could not be saved by faith in Christ alone and by a corresponding life," and they rejected Paul and his epistles (*NPNF2*, 1:159–60 [PG 20, col. 273]). See also Hippolytus, *Refutation of All Heresies* 7.22 (*ANF*, vol. 5); Irenaeus, *Against Heresies* 1.26.2 (*ANF*, vol. 1).

which held that although Jesus was essentially nondivine, he was adopted by the Father—perhaps at his baptism or even his birth. As we will see, the effect (perhaps even the motive) of rejecting Christ's divinity is the reduction of his work to that of providing a superior moral example.

If the challenge from a Jewish perspective was attributing full deity to Jesus Christ, the Hellenistic (Greek) problem was with his full *humanity*.[48] How could God become flesh, which in Greek thought was tantamount to saying that the Good became trapped in evil matter? At the very least, how could God's incarnation, obedience, crucifixion, and resurrection in the flesh be construed as the source of redemption and our own bodily resurrection be construed as its goal? If the incarnation sounded too Greek to Jewish ears, it sounded too Jewish to Gentiles. Biblical faith and Greek thought were working with different problems: redemption from the curse of the law (sin's guilt, power, and death) versus redemption from bodily existence.

This typically Greek challenge to Christ's full humanity first gathered as the heresy of **Docetism** (from, *dokeō*, "to appear"), since the Greeks held that Christ's humanity was merely an appearance rather than truly real. Jesus appeared to be human and to die (see the refutation of this view, for example, in 1 John 4:2–3).

A consistent attempt to assimilate Christianity to the pagan worldview was made by the second-century heresy known as **Gnosticism**. Gnostics contrasted *Jesus*, an ordinary man, with *Christ*, the universal principle that is the highest of divine emanations. Well versed in the complex speculations of the various Gnostic sects, Irenaeus, a second-century bishop of Lyons, is best known for his refutation of Gnosticism (*Against Heresies*) and his brilliant exposition of the Christian affirmation of the full incarnation of our Lord. The second century also witnessed the powerful effect of Tertullian (160–222), especially against Marcion, a Gnostic teacher who sharply opposed the Creator God (Old Testament Creator) and the Redeemer God (New Testament Savior). Like Irenaeus, Tertullian stressed the importance of Christ as the fulfillment rather than the antithesis of the Old Testament, along with the point that all that Christ did for us that was of redemptive significance was done in the fullness of our humanity.

Largely dormant after the fourth century, Gnosticism erupted again among the medieval Cathari ("Pure Ones") and Albigensians, and at least a docetic tendency can be discerned among the "spiritualists" of radical Anabaptism. In fact, the Reformed especially emphasized the point that Christ received the substance of his humanity from Mary, against the view expressed by Menno Simons that Jesus had taken his flesh from heaven. Simons called it "celestial flesh," with Mary represented merely as a "channel" through which Jesus was born.[49] It was against this docetic

---

48. This is not a neat and tidy distinction, however. For example, Arianism—influenced by Greek philosophy—was also a denial of Christ's full divinity.

49. See Calvin's critical interaction with Menno Simons on this point in John Calvin, *Institutes* 2.13.3.

view that the ancient creeds insisted that "Christ was born *ex Maria virgine* [from the virgin Mary], which is explained to mean *ex substantia matris suae* [from the substance of his mother]," rather than simply *per* (through) her.[50] To state this point in contemporary terms, the incarnate God had Mary's genes.

All of the heresies thus far mentioned deny that in the incarnation *God* has come *in the flesh*, a denial that John identifies as "the spirit of Antichrist" (1 Jn 4:1–3; cf. 2:22–25). In this connection, one more departure from Christianity should be mentioned. Treated in our discussion of the Trinity, **Arianism** held that the Son is not consubstantial with the Father but is the first created being. Revived by Socinianism, Arian assumptions were carried forward in Protestant liberalism and are explicitly taught today by various groups, including the Jehovah's Witnesses.

2. TWO NATURES IN ONE PERSON

The Council of Nicaea (325) represents the triumph of Trinitarian orthodoxy. However, agreement that Jesus Christ is God incarnate did not settle all christological controversies. Now the question arose as to the *relation* between his deity and his humanity. While claiming to affirm the deity and humanity of Jesus Christ, each of these heresies was drawn toward one or the other.

Based on its view of human beings as composed of three parts — body, soul, and spirit (trichotomy), **Apollinarianism** taught that Jesus' human spirit was replaced with the divine Logos. Charles Hodge explains that Apollinarianism was motivated by "the doctrine then held by many at least of the Platonizing fathers, that reason in man is part of the divine Logos or universal reason."[51] In this way, the soul-body dualism was the conceptual corollary to Christ's deity and humanity. Even some of the orthodox theologians such as Athanasius and Augustine could speak as if the Logos "wielded" a human body, almost the way one might drive a car. A marked discomfort with the idea of the genuine humiliation, suffering, temptation, and anguish of the incarnate Son was often expressed. Nevertheless, Apollinarianism was condemned at the Council of Constantinople in 381. As we have seen above, the New Testament clearly teaches that Jesus was even "in every respect has been tempted as we are, yet without sin" (Heb 4:15). "Since therefore the children share in flesh and blood, he himself likewise partook of the same things" for our salvation (Heb 2:14). "Therefore he had to be made like his brothers in every respect, so that he might become a merciful and faithful high priest in the service of God, to make propitiation for the sins of the people. For because he himself has suffered when tempted, he is able to help those who are being tempted" (vv. 17–18).

50. Charles Hodge, *Systematic Theology* (Grand Rapids: Eerdmans, 1946), 2:400.

51. Hodge, *Systematic Theology*, 2:401. Although it is accu-rate to refer to this influence as "Platonizing," a more direct influence for many (especially Justin Martyr) was Stoicism.

Besides its questionable anthropology, this view was judged by the church as denying the full humanity of Christ. Gregory of Nazianzus wrote, "For that which He has not assumed He has not healed; but that which is united to His Godhead is also saved."[52] Only if Christ was human in every respect except sin is he the Savior of the whole person. Our salvation depends as much on Christ's identity as the son of Adam, Abraham, and David as on his being eternally begotten of the Father. In Christ there are two natures, and each nature retains its distinctive attributes. Even as divine spirit, his soul as well as his body is human. One last time, a revised Apollinarianism arose, insisting that Jesus at least had one divine will (monothelitism), but this too was rejected at the third Council of Constantinople in 681.

ANCIENT CHURCH CHRSTOLOGIES	
The Alexandrian School	Emphasized the unity of Christ's person as divine. This center of early Christian Platonism reflected a *tendency* to assume history into eternity, matter into spirit, historical exegesis into allegorical (spiritualizing) exegesis, and the humanity of Christ into his deity. Its celebrated representatives include Origen, Clement, and Cyril. Though this school was formally orthodox (with the exception of Origen), its excesses led to Apollinarianism and Monophysitism (Eutychianism), which were judged heretical at the Councils of Constantinople (381) and Chalcedon (451).
The Antiochene School	Emphasized the distinction of Christ's person as divine and human, favoring the human. Sharply critical of the allegorizing hermeneutic of the Alexandrians, this school closely followed a historical-literal hermeneutic. Among orthodox theologians this school produced Diodorus of Tarsus (d. 390), Chrysostom (347–407), and Theodore of Mopsuestia (350–428). The excess of the Antiochone emphasis emerged first in Theodore—who refused to acknowledge Mary as "Theotokos" (God-bearer)—but especially in his student, Nestorius. Nestorianism was also condemned by the councils mentioned above.

After the church rejected Apollinarianism, another controversy broke out concerning the relation of Christ's humanity and deity. Broader differences in outlook between Antioch and Alexandria, though often overplayed, cannot be ignored here.

Alexandria had been the seat of Philo, the Jewish philosopher who attempted to

---

52. Gregory of Nazianzus, *Select Letters of Saint Gregory of Nazianzen: Epistle 101 (To Cledonius the Priest Against Apollinarius)*, NPNF2, 5:438 (PG 37, col. 181, 184).

blend Judaism with Platonism. The catechetical school in Alexandria (under Origen and his successors, Clement and Cyril) followed a similar course with Christianity. For them, Christianity is the true gnosis, the higher enlightenment that Greek philosophy anticipated but could not fully know apart from Christ. Presupposing intellectual ascent from the realm of appearances to the contemplation of eternal Truth, Alexandrian theology frequently displays a tendency toward allegorical (spiritualizing) exegesis. Historical, temporal, and sensual reality serves merely as a stepping-stone to ever-higher, eternal, and intellectual realities. The tendency to assimilate history (the realm of appearances) to eternity and matter to spirit prejudiced Alexandrian theology toward assimilating Christ's humanity to his deity. Just as the Platonizing tendency led Apollinarianism to replace Christ's human mind with the Logos, Cyril (early on at least) tended to collapse Christ's humanity into his deity. Before the incarnation, he said, there were two natures, but afterward there is only one; hence the term **Monophysitism**.

More interested in the humanity of Jesus and a literal-historical exegesis, Antioch reflected its milieu: more Middle Eastern and especially Jewish. Whereas the Alexandrian tendency was to absorb the humanity of Christ into his deity, the Antiochene tendency was to separate the two natures. **Nestorianism** (named after the fifth-century Patriarch of Constantinople, a student of the Antiochene theologian Theodore of Mopsuestia) held that the Logos indwelled Jesus morally rather than essentially. Therefore, he differs from us only in degree. Refusing to use the liturgical expression *Theotokos* (God-bearer) for Mary, Nestorius insisted that she was only the mother of Jesus' human nature.

If Mary is not the mother of God, then who was the child she bore? The Marian title was not originally employed in order to praise Mary herself but to affirm that her child was in fact God incarnate. Therefore, Nestorianism represented a division in the natures of Christ that led finally to a denial of his unity as a person. For example, whereas Acts 20:28 (according to the best manuscript traditions) says that the church was purchased by the blood of *God*, the Syriac version used by the Nestorians substitutes *Christ*. So whereas Monophysitism confused the two natures, Nestorianism divided them into two persons. Cyril and Nestorius became bitter opponents and were pushed toward their respective extremes as the controversy wore on. Lacking Cyril's nuance, Eutyches and his followers—identified as *Eutychians*—explicitly championed the view that Christ had only one nature (Monophysitism), assimilating his humanity to his deity.

Finally, with a consensus among Eastern and Western bishops, the **Council of Chalcedon** (451) condemned both views, affirming that Christ is "one person in two natures." Interpreting Scripture, the creed confesses that Jesus Christ is truly God ("consubstantial with the Father according to the Godhead") and also truly human ("of a reasonable soul and body,...consubstantial with us according to the

Manhood; in all things like unto us, without sin"). He is "begotten before all ages of the Father according to the Godhead, and in these latter days, for us and for our salvation, born of the Virgin Mary, the Mother of God, according to the Manhood; one and the same Christ, Son, Lord, Only-begotten, to be acknowledged in two natures, inconfusedly, unchangeably, indivisibly, inseparably." Therefore, "the distinction of natures [is] by no means taken away by the union, but rather the property of each nature [is] preserved, and concurring in one Person and one Subsistence, not parted or divided into two persons, but one and the same Son."[53]

In this confession, Alexandria and Antioch as well as the East and the West reached unanimity and settled the consensus of catholic Christology. The Cappadocian theologians who played such an enormous role in formulating Trinitarian theology were also formative in this consensus. "Each of the three (or four) Cappadocians stood squarely in the tradition of Classical Greek culture," notes Jaroslav Pelikan, "and each was at the same time intensely critical of that tradition."[54] In this crucial consensus the mystery of Christ triumphed over inherited philosophical schemes. The West pushed the East toward an explicit two-natures formulation. "But by this very token it is clear that the doctrine decreed at Chalcedon was nothing new," notes B. B. Warfield, but was implicit even in the theologizing of Alexandrians in the face of explicit challenges.[55] The formula "one person in two natures" was already present in Tertullian's writings and before that, in Clement of Rome (who died in 99) and Melito of Sardis (who died in 180).[56]

CHRISTOLOGICAL HERESIES SPECTRUM:	
Denying Christ's Divinity	Ebionitism Subordinationism Adoptionism Arianism/Semi-Arianism
Denying Christ's Humanity	Docetism/ Gnosticism Apollinarianism Monothelitism
Confusing the Two Natures	Monophysitism/Eutychianism
Dividing the Two Natures	Nestorianism

---

53. "The Chalcedonian Definition," in John Leith, ed., *The Creeds of the Churches: A Reader in Christian Doctrine from the Bible to the Present* (Louisville: Westminster John Knox, 1983), 34–36.

54. Jaroslav Pelikan, *Christianity and Classical Culture: The Metamorphosis of Natural Theology in the Christian Encounter with Hellenism* (New Haven: Yale Univ. Press, 1993), 9.

55. B. B. Warfield, *The Person and Work of Christ* (ed. Samuel G. Craig; Philadelphia: Presbyterian and Reformed, repr., 1950), 213.

56. Ibid., 213, 216.

ECUMENICAL COUNCILS		
Nicaea	325	Formal statement on the Trinity
Constantinople I	381	Rejection of Apollinarianism, Monophysitism (also known as Eutychianism), and Nestorianism
Chalcedon	451	Consolidation of "one person in two natures"
Constantinople III	681	Monothelitism condemned; two intelligences and wills: one human, one divine, united in one person

3. REFORMATION DEBATES

This ecumenical consensus guided Christological reflection in both the Byzantine East and medieval West, although there were always differences in emphasis. In the Reformation, particularly as a result of controversies over Christ's presence in the Lord's Supper, different emphases led to mutual suspicions. Lutherans suspected Reformed theology of tending toward Nestorianism, while Reformed theologians warned of a Monophysite current in Lutheran Christology.

Luther had introduced the novel view (though similar in some respects to Cyril's formulation) that the characteristics (or attributes) of Christ's divine nature are communicated to the *human nature*.[57] Therefore, Christ can be present bodily at every altar because his human nature shares in the omnipresence of his divine nature. "Even as the one who is exalted at the right hand of God, Jesus Christ is still present on earth according to his divine and human natures."[58] Not only is Jesus Christ in his humanity omnipresent; he is also omniscient.[59]

From a Reformed perspective, this view threatened to roll back the ecumenical consensus achieved at Chalcedon. While affirming Christ's presence in the Supper, the Reformed held that he could not be present bodily anywhere on earth until his

---

57. *Formula of Concord*, ch. 8, Solid Declaration 8, par. 78. For a description of the Lutheran position and comparison/contrast with the Reformed view from a Lutheran perspective, see Heinrich Schmid, *Doctrinal Theology of the Evangelical Lutheran Church* (trans. Charles A. Hay and Henry E. Jacobs; 3rd ed.; Minneapolis: Augsburg, 1899), 312–37. Schmid acknowledges that both sides agree that (1) there are two natures in one person; (2) the two natures "have been joined in the closest and most intimate union, which is generally called personal"; (3) the natures are neither mingled (the Eutychian/Monophysite view) nor divided (the Nestorian view); (4) to each nature belongs its own proper attributes; (5) the union of both natures means that "the person of Christ, the God-man, possesses divine properties, uses them, and is named by them"; (6) the hypostatic union imparted "the highest wisdom, though finite" to Christ's humanity; (7) "to the mediatorial acts of Christ each nature contributed

its own part," and his divine nature "conferred upon the acts of the human nature infinite power to redeem and save the human race." "In a word," they agree "that the intimate union of God and man in Christ is so wonderful and sublime that it surpasses, in the highest degree, the comprehension of our mind." However, they differ as to whether the attributes of the divine nature can be ascribed to the human nature—specifically, omnipresence, as this was the heart of differences over the Supper (329–30).

58. Edmund Schlink, *Theology of the Lutheran Confessions* (trans. Paul F. Koehneke and Herbert J. A. Bouman; Philadelphia: Fortress, 1961), 187.

59. *The Book of Concord: The Confessions of the Evangelical Lutheran Church* (ed. and trans. Theodore G. Tappert; Philadelphia: Fortress, 1959), Epitome 8, pp. 16, 30–38; Solid Declaration 8, pp. 73–74.

return in glory. Therefore, in the Supper the Spirit who unites us to Christ feeds us with the whole divine and human Christ, but in a mystical and heavenly manner. To Lutheran ears, talk of Christ being omnipresent as God but not omnipresent according to his humanity sounded like a Nestorian division of natures. Yet Reformed theologians heard in the Lutheran doctrine a Monophysite confusion of natures: allowing the humanity to be absorbed by the divinity.

Like the earlier controversy between Alexandria and Antioch, the meeting between Luther and Zwingli at Marburg was doomed to end in failure, in part because Zwingli defended something close to a Nestorian position. For example, in one place the Zürich Reformer writes, "We must note in passing that Christ is our salvation by virtue of that part of his nature by which he came down from heaven, not of that by which he was born of an immaculate virgin, though he had to suffer and die by this part."[60] Unlike Nestorius, Zwingli tended to divide the natures in favor of Christ's divinity, but the apportioning of salvation to one nature over another was just as apparent and would be as decisively rejected by Calvin and other Reformed leaders. It was their view rather than Zwingli's that defined the Christology articulated in the Reformed confessions, catechisms, and dogmatics. Nevertheless, they just as resolutely opposed Luther's view.

First, the Lutheran-Reformed debate turns on the question of the **communication of attributes** (*communicatio idiomatum*). From the Reformed perspective, this refers to the fact that by virtue of the hypostatic union the attributes of either nature belong to the one person. Hodge explains:

> [Christ] is finite and infinite; ignorant and omniscient; less than God and equal with God; He existed from eternity and He was born in time; He created all things and He was a man of sorrows. It is on this principle, that what is true of either nature is true of the person, that a multitude of passages of Scripture are to be explained.... The forms of expression, therefore, long prevalent in the Church, "the blood of God," "God the mighty maker died," etc., are in accordance with Scriptural usage.... The person born of the Virgin Mary was a divine person. He was the Son of God. It is therefore correct to say that Mary was the mother of God.[61]

Since Reformed theology clearly affirms the unity of Christ's person, along with Mary's title as the "Theotokos" (God-bearer), it cannot be identified as Nestorian.

Second, differences between these traditions can be discerned on the question of whether the deity of Christ can be contained (i.e., circumscribed) by his humanity. Reformed Christology strongly affirms the strictest identification between Jesus and God in the incarnation. There is not a nonincarnate Logos floating above Jesus of

---

60. Ulrich Zwingli, *Commentary on True and False Religion* (ed. Samuel Macauley Jackson and Clarence Nevin Heller; Durham, N.C.: Labyrinth, 1981), 204.

61. Charles Hodge, *Systematic Theology*, 2:392–93. A help-ful treatment of the Reformed position vis-à-vis Lutheranism is also found in T. F. Torrance, *Incarnation: The Person and Life of Christ* (ed. Robert T. Walker; Downers Grove, Ill.: InterVarsity Press, 2008), 213–32.

Nazareth. On the contrary, the Logos *assumed our flesh*. Nevertheless, as God he remains transcendent, omnipotent, omnipresent, omniscient, and eternal, while as human he remains finite, limited in soul and body, and spatio-temporally circumscribed.

This position was expressed in the formula, "The finite cannot comprehend the infinite" (*finitum non capax infiniti*), "comprehend" being understood in the technical sense, as "enclose," "circumscribe," and "fully contain." In other words, the *person* who is divine can become finite, but the *divine nature* of Jesus Christ cannot become finite, nor can the *human nature* become infinite. This gives due weight as much to the humanity as to the deity of Christ, since the Reformed emphasize that his exaltation to the right hand of the Father was as much the prize for his victorious human obedience (passive and active). However, the Lutheran view tends to flatten out this dynamic historical transition from humiliation to exaltation when, in the *Formula of Concord*, it is said that Christ's majesty and exaltation are due to the union of his deity and humanity from conception.[62] During his earthly ministry, he hid this majesty of his human nature, using it only when he chose to.[63] Although the intention of the Lutheran view is to affirm the closest possible union of God and humanity in Christ, the idea that the divine attributes can be predicates not merely of the person but of the human nature of Christ threatens his genuine humanity. It should be noted that there was internal controversy over these views within Lutheran orthodoxy itself.[64]

Like other Reformed pastors, Calvin articulated a more paradoxical formulation: "Here is something marvelous: the Son of God descended from heaven in such a way that, without leaving heaven, he willed to be borne in the virgin's womb, to go about the earth, and to hang upon the cross; yet he continuously filled the world even as he had done from the beginning!"[65] Nicknamed the *extracalvinisticum* (the "Calvinistic extra") by Lutheran critics, the view that even in the incarnation the eternal Son who nursed at Mary's breast continued to fill the heavens is simply the teaching of Chalcedon: ". . . the distinction of natures being by no means taken away by the union, but rather the property of each nature being preserved, and concurring in one Person and one Subsistence, not parted or divided into two persons."[66]

The "non-capax" formula does not say that the infinite cannot become incarnate, but only that the incarnate God cannot be enclosed, circumscribed, and fully contained by the finite. According to his humanity, Jesus Christ was not omniscient,

62. *Book of Concord*, Solid Declaration 8, p. 13.

63. *Book of Concord*, Solid Declaration 8, p. 26.

64. Schlink, *Theology of the Lutheran Confessions*, 191.

65. Calvin, *Institutes* 2.13.4.

66. E. David Willis shows that the so-called *extracalvinisticum* was the common understanding in both the patristic and medieval era, in *Calvin's Catholic Christology* (Leiden: Brill, 1966). See also T. F. Torrance, *Incarnation: The Person and Life of Christ*, 210–26. Not even for Cyril, argues Torrance, did the *communicatio idi-* *omatum* ("communication of attributes"; see above in this section, p. 477) "refer to a mutual interpenetration of the divine and human qualities or properties, as it came to be understood in Lutheran theology" (210). Torrance notes that the Lutheran rejection of the maxim "the finite cannot comprehend the infinite" presupposed a "Greek 'container' conception of space," mediated by William of Ockham, whereas the patristic consensus (shared by Calvin and the Reformed) reflected a relational view of space (218–19).

omnipresent, and omnipotent, as he was according to his deity. This does not entail a division between the natures, much less two persons, since we predicate the attributes of humanity and deity of the one person, Jesus Christ. After all, it is Chalcedon that uses the language of "according to the Godhead" and "according to the Manhood," denying the confusion of the natures and affirming their distinction without division.

In short, the Reformed acknowledge a communication of attributes (both divine and human) to the *person*, while Lutherans teach a communication of attributes of one *nature* to the other. It should be observed that in the Lutheran view (contra Monophysitism) the natures do not become fused into one. However, the specter of confusing the natures is raised by the insistence that whatever is done by the human nature is done by the *divine nature* rather than, as the Reformed would say, by the *one person*.[67] As to whether Christ's humanity can be omnipresent (i.e., the doctrine of ubiquity), there were also serious reservations among early Lutherans, but this view seems to have established itself. These differences continue to mark the most significant cleavage between confessional Lutheran and Reformed traditions, but they have often been exaggerated on both sides. Lutherans do not maintain that there is only one nature in Christ, so they are not Monophysites (or Eutychians), and the Reformed do not separate the natures, so they are not Nestorians. Both claim the Chalcedonian heritage.

4. MODERN CHRISTOLOGIES

With the rise of Socinianism and Protestant liberalism, the Arian heresy returned in full strength. For Schleiermacher, Jesus uniquely possessed a deep personal relationship with God—indeed, union with God—that raised him and all of humanity to a higher level of ideal perfection and mystical influence on the soul. Because of his unparalleled "God-consciousness," Jesus is justly regarded as unique, though as the pioneer of a humanity that now shares in his sense of absolute dependence on God.[68] "And so, if Dogmatics are to be ever more completely purged of scholasti-

---

67. *Book of Concord*, Solid Declaration 8, pp. 62, 66, 72. It is sometimes difficult to determine exactly what is being argued, especially since there have been divergent formulations of this principle ever since Luther. In fact, the *Formula of Concord* (1580) was drafted with the express purpose of uniting various factions on this point. Johannes Brenz argued that in order to become human the Son had to exalt his humanity into his majestic divinity, while the Wittenberg theologians (especially Chemnitz) defended the view that the finite cannot comprehend the infinite and strongly denounced the idea that the attributes of one nature are communicated to the other. Schlink observes that the *Formula of Concord* is a consensus document, reflecting inner tensions, "in which neither Chemnitz nor Brenz had his way" (*Theology of the Lutheran Confessions*, 189). In fact, Schlink says that "it is doubtful whether the Christology of the Formula of Concord follows with theological cogency from the earlier Lutheran Confessions.... Moreover, we must ask whether this Christology is to be considered an interpretation or an abrogation of the christological formulations of Chalcedon to which the church of the

Augsburg Confession always felt obligated. The former assumption was soon denied, and not only by Reformed critics" (192).

68. Friedrich Schleiermacher, *The Christian Faith* (ed. and trans. H. R. Mackintosh and J. S. Stewart from 2nd German edition; Edinburgh: T&T Clark, 1928), 377–429. "The Redeemer, then, is like all men in virtue of the identity of human nature, but distinguished from them all by the constant potency of His God-consciousness, which was a veritable existence of God in Him" (385). Rather than interpret the divinity of Christ in terms of the Son's assumption of humanity, Schleiermacher says that "the being of God in Christ was developed out of the human nature...," as Jesus allowed himself to achieve union with God (400). Schleiermacher considered the doctrine of the virgin birth to be legendary and in any case nonessential to the person of Christ (404). Rather, God exercised such a "higher influence" upon Mary and Joseph that Jesus was preserved sinless (405). With astonishing consistency, Schleiermacher interprets every major triumph in trinitarian and christological formulation over the first five centuries as confusing "scholasticism," a corruption of "Jewish and heathen elements" (389–400).

cism," a revision for which Schleiermacher claims to lay a foundation, "both the expressions, divine nature and the duality of natures in the same Person (which, to say the least, are exceedingly inconvenient) shall be altogether avoided."[69]

If Schleiermacher's Christology is basically adoptionistic and Arian, Hegel's Christology, as Cyril O'Regan demonstrates, is a revival of Monophysitism in a Gnostic key.[70] For Hegel, the incarnation is a symbol of the oneness of divinity and humanity. The imprint of the ontological paradigm of "overcoming estrangement" on Christology becomes readily apparent in this trajectory. Throughout the nineteenth century appeals were made, especially in German theology, to an extreme version of the Lutheran communication of attributes, but this time in the opposite direction: from the humanity to the deity. On the basis of Philippians 2:7 (which speaks of the Son's having "emptied [*ekenōsen*] himself" in the incarnation), *kenotic* Christologies asserted that the Son gave up not only his divine prerogatives but his divine nature. So instead of collapsing the humanity into the divinity, kenotic Christologies dissolved the latter in the former. Reading through the lens of Kantian categories, Ritschl could speak of Jesus as the Christ (i.e., divine as well as human) in terms of his ethical ideal (value) but not in his personal essence (fact).

Whether by a Nestorian route (separating the two natures) or by a Monophysite path (confusing the natures), the arrival point was the same: a denial of Christ's divinity. A basically Gnostic dualism between the Jesus of history and the Christ of faith drove various searches for the former somewhere behind and against the latter (in the higher-critical tradition of liberal theology) and eventually motivated more existentialist theologies (such as Kähler's and Bultmann's) to abandon the historical Jesus altogether in favor of a personal encounter in a nebulous "Christ-Event." In either case, the actual person, Jesus of Nazareth, became irrelevant for the personal faith and piety of the believer and the community. As Berkhof observes, all of these theories reflect a pantheistic tendency.[71] "Modern teaching about Christ is all based on the doctrine of the continuity of God and man."[72]

Against this trajectory Barth recovered a "Christology from above," emphasizing that "in Christ *God* was reconciling the world to himself..." (2Co 5:19). Included with this emphasis was his commitment to Chalcedonian Christology (though not without revisions) and even the virginal conception of Christ. However, we have seen in considering his revised supralapsarianism how easily eternity threatens to reduce history to a mere shadow, and this keeps Barth (like Zwingli) from providing a satisfying treatment of the significance of Christ's humanity and his dependence on the Spirit in winning our redemption.

69. Ibid., 397.

70. Cyril O'Regan, *The Heterodox Hegel* (SUNY Series in Hegelian Studies; Albany: SUNY Press, 1994), 220–30.

71. Louis Berkhof, *Systematic Theology* (Grand Rapids: Eerdmans, 1996), 310.

72. Ibid., 311.

More recently, partly in reaction against Barth, Wolfhart Pannenberg has attempted to revive a "Christology from below," focusing especially on the resurrection as the demonstration of Christ's deity.[73] However, whereas Pannenberg's Christology from below begins with the actual history of Jesus Christ, Karl Rahner starts with a general anthropology rather than theology proper in his Christology and finally embraces an adoptionist Christology.[74] Much of late modern theology (liberal, existential, and liberationist) is, in tendency at least, Socinian. That is, it assumes a Unitarian view of God, a Pelagian view of human moral ability, and therefore an Arian reduction of Christ to a moral example and/or a Gnostic separation between the Jesus of history (who remains dead) and a Christ of faith (who never died and can therefore offer spiritual enlightenment). Similar to Schleiermacher's adoptionism, such approaches merely yield a human being who is quantitatively rather than qualitatively distinct from others. In this perspective, "Jesus" (of history) and "Christ" (of faith) become separated, with the former treated as a paradigmatic revolutionary or moral reformer and the latter as a cosmic principle that Jesus exhibits in a special way.

Reacting against attempts to exploit Christian symbols in order to valorize modern ideologies (especially feminist/womanist and neopagan views), others seek to retrieve elements from patristic sources. Moving beyond the traditional Lutheran affirmation of this consensus, contemporary Lutheran theologian Robert Jenson defends a Monophysite Christology by pitting the East against the West. Cyril of Alexandria's language of "one nature" is defended by Jenson against what he takes to be the Nestorian tendency of Western theology. However, these debates arose in the East (Antioch and Alexandria), and the Christian East and West embraced the formulation that Jenson rejects.[75] In fact, in 433 even Cyril approved the *Formula of Union*, in which both Antiochene and Alexandrian concerns were satisfied: "union of two natures." This became the basis for Chalcedon. To be sure, there are differences between Cyril and Leo (bishop of Rome) in these discussions, but it is far-fetched to suggest with Jenson that Chalcedon represents the victory of the latter over the former.[76] Jenson cannot even claim Luther for his position, given the Reformer's explicit rejection of the death of the divine nature at the cross.[77] Thus, Luther continued to affirm the distinction between Christ's humanity and deity.[78]

73. Wolfhart Pannenberg, *Jesus—God and Man* (trans. Lewis L. Wilkins and Duane A. Priebe; Philadelphia: Westminster, 1968), 33–40.

74. Karl Rahner, "Christology within an Evolutionary View of the World," in *Later Writings* (vol. 5 of *Theological Investigations*; trans. Karl H. Kruger; New York: Seabury Press, 1975), 157–92. Cf. Edward Schillebeeckx, *Jesus: An Experiment in Christology* (London: Collins, 1979).

75. Robert Jenson, *Systematic Theology* (New York: Oxford Univ. Press, 1997), 1:125–33.

76. Ibid., 2:128–32.

77. Although Jenson invokes Luther for his neo-Hegelian concept of the death of God, the Reformer clearly affirmed the Chalcedonian point that "God in his own nature cannot die." Martin Luther, *Von den Konziliis und Kirchen* (Weimar Ausgabe 50; Weimar: Hermann Böhlaus Nachfolger, 1914), 590.

78. With respect to the neo-Hegelian Christologies of the "crucified God," see the helpful essay by Henri A. Blocher, "God and the Cross," in *Engaging the Doctrine of God: Contemporary Protestant Perspectives* (ed. Bruce McCormack; Grand Rapids: Baker Academic, 2008), 125–41.

Only in the distinctiveness of each nature, united in one person, do we find the complete Savior who can bring complete deliverance from sin and death. All Christians share the conclusion expressed by Warfield: "No Two Natures, no Incarnation; no Incarnation, no Christianity in any distinctive sense."[79] As a fact of history it is the heart of the gospel, the basis of any legitimate talk of God's redemption of the world in his Son.

DISCUSSION QUESTIONS

1. Discuss the identity of Jesus Christ within the context of the trial of Adam and Israel.
2. Discuss the biblical significance of New Testament titles attributed to Jesus: Messiah, Son of David, Servant.
3. Can we affirm a doctrine of adoption in biblical Christology without embracing the heresy of adoptionism?
4. Discuss the various quests for the historical Jesus: their shared presuppositions as well as different conclusions.
5. Define the Chalcedonian consensus of "two natures in one person." How did this consensus emerge, and what were the major challenges to it? How do the differences between Alexandria and Antioch play out in christological debates?
6. What is meant by the "communication of attributes," and how is it interpreted differently by various traditions?
7. Identify and evaluate some of the different trajectories in modern christological reflection.

---

79. Warfield, *Person and Work of Christ*, 211.

Chapter Fifteen

THE STATE OF HUMILIATION: CHRIST'S THREEFOLD OFFICE

T his chapter focuses on the intersection between Christ's person and work by referring to Christ's threefold office as prophet, priest, and king, in both his humiliation and exaltation.

I. CHRIST AS PROPHET

Moses and Aaron are both referred to as prophets in the Exodus narrative (Ex 7:1–2) — *nābî'*, the most frequently used term, along with *ḥôzeh*. In that context, Moses is made "like God to Pharaoh" as he, along with Aaron, brings God's word of judgment to the king. In the promise of a new prophet like Moses, this point is especially emphasized in relation to the people of Israel: "The LORD your God will raise up for you a prophet like me from among you, from your brothers," says Moses (Dt 18:15). Thus, in the calling of Moses, Aaron, and especially the later prophets, the books are preceded by a historical prologue providing the account of the prophet's calling. The New Testament comports entirely with this usage (*prophētēs* in Septuagint and NT), reiterating that the biblical prophets did not speak on their own authority but under divine inspiration (Ac 3:22–24; 2Pe 1:21). Unlike pagan soothsayers or fortune-tellers, their vocation is not simply to tell the future of individuals, but to speak God's judgment (curses) and deliverance (blessings) into history. They bring announcements from God that in fact execute God's announced intentions in some instances (e.g., Ge 24:7; 1Ki 13:18).

Prophets are teachers (see, for example, Isaiah 30:18–26), but they are also lawyers and ambassadors carrying out the heavenly policy of which they speak. The coming prophet whom Moses prefigured and prophesied will also bring about a new state of affairs through his words and deeds. There was a common expectation in Jesus' day that Elijah would return to restore Israel, and there are explicit echoes of both Moses' founding and Elijah's renewal in Jesus' ministry.[1] As the narrative unfolds, further parallels with Moses and Elijah appear:

> As Moses engaged in sea crossings and wilderness feedings, so did Jesus. As Elijah healed people and brought a virtually dead child back to life and multiplied food, so did Jesus.... With all these clear parallels to Moses and Elijah, it is no surprise at all when Mark relates that people generally believed Jesus was a prophetic figure—either John the Baptist raised from the dead or Elijah or "a prophet like one of the prophets of old" (6:14–16; 8:27–28)—and that Jesus refers to himself as a prophet (6:4).[2]

The transfiguration, with Jesus attended by Moses and Elijah, confirms all of this. "Indeed, the command to 'listen to him' is a direct allusion to God's promise to raise up a prophet like Moses (Deut. 18:15)."[3]

At the same time, Jesus is not simply another Moses. He not only acts as a mediator on behalf of Israel but offers forgiveness of sins in his person—which aroused the consternation of the religious leaders (Lk 7:48–49). Nor is he simply another Elijah. Although he announces Yahweh's covenant judgment on the faithless nation as Elijah did, this ministry Jesus himself identifies more with John the Baptist (Mt 11:1–19; 17:10–13; cf. 3:1–13). In both his person and his work, Jesus was more than the greatest prophets of the old covenant. "Jesus was announcing a message, a word from Israel's covenant god," N. T. Wright observes. "He was not simply reshuffling the cards already dealt, the words of YHWH delivered in former times."[4]

> In the parable of the wicked tenants, Israel is the vineyard, her rulers the vineyard-keepers; the prophets are the messengers, Jesus is the son; Israel's god, the creator, is himself the owner and father.... Jesus is claiming to be developing a story already used by Isaiah (5.1–7); the present moment is the moment of crisis, the end of exile; behind the covenant stands a god who cannot be blackmailed by its supposed terms; Israel was made for YHWH's will and not vice versa, since he is after all the creator

---

1. Richard A. Horsley, *Hearing the Whole Story: The Politics of Plot in Mark's Gospel* (Louisville: Westminster John Knox, 2001), 238, referring to Malachi 3:1–3; 4:4–6 and Sirach 48:1–10. Clear reminiscences of Moses' founding and of Elijah's renewal recur through the first section on Jesus' inaugural mission in Galilee. Like Moses designating Joshua and Elijah summoning Elisha, Jesus calls those who will assist in his program of renewal. This program becomes unmistakable when he

appoints them as the twelve representative heads of the renewed Israel (cf. Elijah's making an altar of twelve stones, representing the twelve tribes of Israel) (248).

2. Ibid., 238.

3. Ibid., 248–49.

4. N. T. Wright, *Jesus and the Victory of God* (Minneapolis: Fortress, 1996), 171.

who called her into being in the first place; he will return to his vineyard, to judge his wicked tenants.[5]

"The master of the house is coming, and servants who are unready for him will be 'put with the unfaithful' (Lk 12.35–46)." "From now on," observes Wright, "there will be division within Israel (12.49–53), while her citizens, not reading the signs of the times, do not recognize that her hour has come (12.54–6). If they did, they would come to terms with their enemies now, rather than risk total ruin (12.57–9)."[6]

This, after all, was the basic hope of Israel: that the enemies of the chosen people would be destroyed, and the chosen themselves vindicated. True, Jesus says, but it is not what the present regime is expecting. Judgment and vindication will be determined through faith in him (the terms of the Abrahamic covenant), not through a renewal of the Sinai covenant. When Jesus arrives on the Temple Mount after his triumphant procession to begin his passion week, he brings judgment on the current regime and effectively ends the old covenant. Like the Old Testament prophets (especially Isaiah and Jeremiah, in their judgment of the false prophets and priests who lead Yahweh's people astray), Jesus arraigns Israel at the heart of its identity. In the upper room, as he celebrates the Passover and institutes his Supper, Jesus assumes the role of the greater Moses leading his people in the greater exodus. "Like Ezekiel, Jesus predicts that the Temple will be abandoned by the Shekinah, left unprotected to its fate. Like Jeremiah, Jesus constantly runs the risk of being called a traitor to Israel's national aspirations, while claiming all along that he nevertheless is the true spokesman for the covenant god." Thus, he is tried as a false prophet.[7]

Repeatedly Jesus proclaims the same subversive themes as the prophets as well as Paul. Wright remarks,

> Jesus' analysis of the plight of Israel went beyond the specifics of behaviour and belief to what he saw as the root of the problem: the Israel of his day had been duped by the accuser, the "satan." That which was wrong with the rest of the world was wrong with Israel too. "Evil" could not be located conveniently beyond Israel's borders, in the pagan hordes. It had taken up residence within the chosen people.[8]

It is a different analysis of evil and its solution. Again, this was an intra-Jewish, not anti-Jewish, debate, as it had always been between the prophets and the wayward leaders and people.[9]

In the New Testament we learn that Christ's prophetic office was exercised even in the Old Testament (1Pe 1:11), and afterwards, by his Word and Spirit.

---

5. Ibid., 178.
6. Ibid., 331.
7. Ibid., 166.

8. Ibid., 446–47.
9. Ibid., 447.

The prophets themselves share Moses' hope in the greater prophet to come, "one shepherd" who will gather his flock that has been scattered by the false shepherds (Eze 34:11–31). While the false prophets bring their own word of false comfort, God himself will lead his people according to the truth (Jer 23). The difference between true and false prophets is that only the former have "stood in the council of the LORD" (v.18). Yet in this prophetic literature (particularly the texts cited: Eze 34 and Jer 23), the coming shepherd-prophet will be no less than Yahweh himself.[10]

Jesus calls himself a prophet (Lk 13:33), bringing his Father's message (especially in John). He foretells (Mt 24, etc.), speaks with an authority that is unlike that of the scribes (Mt 7:29), authenticates his message with signs, and is thus recognized as a prophet by the people (Mt 21:11, 46; Lk 7:16; 24:19; Jn 3:2; 4:19; 6:14; 7:40; 9:17). And yet, he is more than the prophet who speaks what he hears; he is also the content of what is spoken. Jesus is the fulfillment of the prophetic writings (Mt 1:22; 5:17), and John the Baptist testified about himself that he was not "the prophet," but merely the forerunner (Jn 1:21–23).

Jesus regularly attests, notably in the fourth gospel, that he has not only stood in the council of the LORD, but literally *comes from* the Father. He speaks the Father's Word, in the power of the Spirit, but he is unique in that he is the Word incarnate: not only the prophet who brings the Word, but the one to whom all of the prophets pointed. This messenger is the message (Jn 1:14). The prophets proclaimed the truth, but Jesus is the Truth that they proclaimed (Jn 14:6). Jesus placed his own teaching above that of the religious leaders. In fact, he assumes the authority to announce a "regime change" from the theocratic state mediated by Moses at Sinai when he speaks from his own mountain and delivers his commands for the end-time kingdom (Mt 5). Furthermore, at the conclusion of this sermon, the people recognize that he preaches "as one who [has] authority, and not as their scribes" (Mt 7:29). In proclaiming the Father and his kingdom, Jesus proclaims himself. In doing so, he inaugurates the new world of which he speaks.

II. CHRIST AS PRIEST

Originating in the eternal covenant of redemption between the persons of the Godhead, Christ's priestly ministry is inseparable from his role as mediator of the

---

10. Once again it needs to be said that whether Jesus' contemporaries so understood these passages is of some, but limited, value. They also understood the kingdom as a revival of the Mosaic theocracy, and Christian interpretation has found in the prophetic books themselves a sufficient basis for a different view of the messianic (Davidic) kingdom. Second Temple Judaism casts essential light on the first-century context, but should not be treated as any more infallible in its OT exegesis as Christian interpretation is of Scripture. For theology, it must be the New Testament that normatively interprets the Old, even while we recognize that none of our own interpretations is itself finally normative for any part of Scripture.

elect. Chosen in Christ before time, the elect are redeemed by Christ and called into union with Christ by the Spirit (Eph 1:4–13). Looking forward, the Old Testament saints trusted in Christ through the types and shadows of the sacrificial system. Therefore, it is essential that Christ was "born under the law, to redeem those who were under the law" (Gal 4:4–5). Not only the Sinai covenant but the wider covenant of creation provided the legal context for Christ's entire ministry. "Has not Moses given you the Law?" Jesus asked as he preached in the temple. "Yet none of you keeps the law" (Jn 7:19). This is the root problem that Israel faces. Like Adam, Israel lies under the dominion of sin and the curse of the law.

A. CHRIST'S PRIESTLY LIFE

Jesus' appointment as High Priest is attributed in the New Testament to a higher and older order already prophesied in the Old Testament: the Melchizedek priesthood, after the priest-king whom Abram recognized as his Lord in Ge 14:18–20 (cf. Ps 110:4). Not David, but one of his heirs—heir of the eternal Davidic throne, would be in this order. In Hebrews 5–7, the argument is made that Jesus was installed as high priest "after the order of Melchizedek" (5:6, 10). The writer contrasts the Abrahamic covenant/Melchizedek priesthood and the Mosaic covenant/Levitical priesthood. The one is "an unchangeable oath" sworn by God, while the other depends on the obedience and mediation of sinful human beings:

> Now if perfection had been attainable through the Levitical priesthood (for under it the people received the law), what further need would there have been for another priest to arise after the order of Melchizedek, rather than one named after the order of Aaron? For when there is a change in the priesthood, there is necessarily a change in the law as well. For the one of whom these things are spoken belonged to another tribe, from which no one has ever served at the altar. . . .
>
> This becomes more evident when another priest arises in the likeness of Melchizedek, who has become a priest, not on the basis of a legal requirement concerning bodily descent, but by the power of an indestructible life. (Heb 7:11–13, 15–16)

Therefore, the "former commandment is set aside because of its weakness and uselessness (for the law made nothing perfect)," while Jesus' priesthood is guaranteed by God's oath. "This makes Jesus the guarantor of a better covenant" (vv. 18–22).

The change in *priesthood* therefore requires a change in *covenant*, from a conditional law-covenant based on the types and shadows of the Levitical priesthood to the eternal mediation of Jesus Christ in the covenant of redemption, realized in the covenant of grace.[11] Christ's priesthood has accomplished what the Levitical office

---

11. On this point see Paul Ellingworth, *Commentary on Hebrews* (New International Greek Testament Commentary series; Grand Rapids: Eerdmans, 1993), 372–73.

could never do and so has annulled it altogether (alteration in the covenant annuls it, as a divorce annuls a marriage: Heb 7:18). Not only a prophet greater than Moses (Heb 3:1–6), he is the mediator of a better covenant (7:22); his priesthood is eternal, because (unlike the Levitical priests) he never dies (vv. 23–25), and is sinless, so that he does not offer a sacrifice for himself but only for his people (vv. 26–28). Furthermore, while the high priests served in the earthly sanctuary, standing to offer sacrifices year after year, Jesus has entered the heavenly sanctuary, ascended to the right hand of the Father's throne, interceding for us as one seated after completing his work (8:1–10:18, esp. 10:11–14). Finally, he has entered with his own saving blood rather than the typological blood of animals, which could never itself remove guilt (9:23–10:23).

Thus, the Levitical priesthood is already seen as limited to a particular time and place, while the Melchizedek priesthood, like the Davidic covenant, is eternal and unchangeable. Like the new covenant itself, this priesthood is tied to the Abrahamic covenant and not specifically to the conditional and temporary shadows of the law (see Gal 3–4). In fact, the Levitical priests were not faithful in their office, and eventually the line came to an end in Israel's history.

Although Jesus himself made no explicit declaration of his being a high priest, his actions demonstrate this self-understanding. Especially toward the end of his ministry, he raises the ire of the religious leaders precisely by circumventing the temple, directly forgiving sins (Mt 12; cf. Jn 2:13–22). He placed himself at the center of the feasts (Jn 7–8). He saw his own death as a substitutionary sacrifice and gave a priestly benediction to his disciples (Lk 24:51; Jn 20:19). As with the prophetic office, Jesus' own self-understanding is that he not only fulfills the priestly office but transcends it. He is not just another high priest who serves in the Holy of Holies, but is one greater than the temple itself.

The New Testament proclaims Jesus as sinless (2Co 5:21; 1Pe 2:21–25; 3:18; 1Jn 3:5, 7), the sacrificial Lamb (Mt 20:28; 26:28; Jn 1:29, 36; 1Co 5:7; Eph 5:2; 1Pe 1:19; 3:18; Rev 5:6–6:5; 12:11; 14:1–5; 19:6–10; 21:9–14; 22:1–5), exalted to the Father's right hand where he intercedes for us (Ro 8:34; 1Jn 2:1), the one mediator (1Ti 2:5) who provides access to God (Ro 5:2; Eph 2:18; 3:12; and throughout Hebrews).

However, even in Hebrews this high priestly ministry of Jesus Christ already begins in the assumption of our humanity: "For it was fitting that he, for whom and by whom all things exist, in bringing many sons to glory, should make the founder of their salvation perfect through suffering. For he who sanctifies and those who are sanctified all have one source. That is why he is not ashamed to call them brothers..." (Heb 2:10–11). In fact, we are here introduced again to that faithful response of the covenant-servant in biblical history, this time on the lips of Jesus:

"Behold, I" — or better, *"Here am I, and the children God has given me"* (v. 13, quoting Isa 8:18).

> Since therefore the children share in flesh and blood, he himself likewise partook of the same things, that through death he might destroy the one who has the power of death, that is, the devil, and deliver all those who through fear of death were subject to lifelong slavery.... Therefore he had to be made like his brothers in every respect, so that he might become a merciful and faithful high priest in the service of God, to make propitiation for the sins of the people. (Heb 2:14–15, 17)

In the words of the *Heidelberg Catechism*,[12] "During his whole life on earth, but especially at the end, Christ sustained in body and soul the anger of God against the sin of the whole human race." As one "born under the law" (Gal 4:4), he lived a life of suffering not as a private individual but as a public representative, winning our redemption as much by his incarnation and daily obedience as by his death and resurrection.

Israel's sacrifices may be grouped into two main types: *thank offerings* and *guilt (or sin) offerings*. God created human beings in his image to live in gratitude before him all their days; in fact, the source of sin according to Paul in Romans 1 is the transition from no longer giving thanks to foolishness and futility (Ro 1:21). The writer to the Hebrews points out that sin offerings bring full delight neither to the worshipers nor to God, since "in these sacrifices there is a *reminder* of sins every year" (Heb 10:3, emphasis added).

> For it is impossible for the blood of bulls and goats to take away sins.
>   Consequently, when Christ came into the world, he said,
>
> "Sacrifices and offerings you have not desired,
>   but a body have you prepared for me;
> in burnt offerings and sin offerings
>   you have taken no pleasure.
> Then I said, 'Behold, I have come to do your will, O God,
>   as it is written of me in the scroll of the book.'" (Heb 10:4–7, citing Ps 40:6–8)

A genuine thank offering — that is, a human life of grateful obedience — is greater than all of the bulls and goats on Israel's altars.

> When he said above, "You have neither desired nor taken pleasure in sacrifices and offerings and burnt offerings and sin offerings" (these are offered according to the law), then he added, "Behold, I have come to do your will." He does away with the first [the old covenant sacrificial system] in order to establish the second [his own

---

12. *Heidelberg Catechism*, q. 37, in *Psalter Hymnal* (Grand Rapids: CRC Publications, 1987), 876.

obedience]. And by that will we have been sanctified through the offering of the body of Jesus Christ once for all. (Heb 10:8–10)

In contrast to Adam and Israel in the wilderness, Jesus said, "My food is to do the will of him who sent me and to accomplish his work" (Jn 4:34). God prepared a body for the eternal Son to be given not only for atonement but for that living obedience for which humanity was created. Even more than his sacrifice of atonement, the positive sacrifice of thanksgiving is God's delight (Heb 10:5–10). As our priestly representative, Jesus fulfills Psalm 40:6–8, which the writer to the Hebrews puts on the lips of Jesus: "Then I said, '*Here I am*—it is written about me in the scroll—I have come *to do your will*, O God'" (Heb 10:7, my translation, emphasis added).

Jesus' priesthood does not, therefore, begin at Golgotha, but from eternity to his incarnation, life, and death, all the way to his present intercession in glory. His priestly life is referred to as his *active obedience* (i.e., actively obeying the entire law), distinguished from his *passive obedience* (i.e., his suffering at the cross). In short, Christ is our priestly Savior by offering both the lifelong "living sacrifice" of praise and thanksgiving and by offering himself as the guilt sacrifice for our sins. He was not only *sinless* but *righteous*, not only a *nontransgressor* of the law but the joyful *fulfiller* of all righteousness. His commission was to bring not only forgiveness of sins but also that positive righteousness that God wills for us and his world—and beyond even this, the confirmation in that righteousness, peace, and blessedness of which the Tree of Life was the sacramental sign and seal.

Thus we cannot sufficiently appreciate the servant theme apart from what has come to be called the active obedience of Christ. He is baptized by John "to fulfill all righteousness" (Mt 3:15). In contrast to Adam and Israel, the messianic Servant refused autonomy. While Adam and Israel "[demanded] the food they craved" (Ps 78:18), in Jesus' forty-day temptation by the serpent he responds by appealing to "every word that comes from the mouth of God" (Mt 4:4).

As the serpent repeats his strategy of abusing God's Word in order to lure Jesus into apostasy, this time the covenant servant refuses to be seduced. That this forty-day trial is intended to recapitulate Israel's forty years in the wilderness is explicitly correlated with Deuteronomy 9, where Moses reminds Israel that it was only his intercession that stayed God's execution of wrath in the wilderness. When Moses ascended the mountain, he remained there "forty days and forty nights; I neither ate bread nor drank water" (Dt 9:9). Moses' intercession stayed God's execution of judgment for a time, but only on the basis of God's promise to Abraham and therefore in view of the messianic seed (vv. 17–18, 25–27). Only the Servant of the LORD could fulfill the obedience to God's law that was requisite for obtaining the everlasting rest.

Jesus' entire life, however, was an extension of this trial of Adam in the garden and Israel in the wilderness. Peter's attempt to distract Jesus from bearing his cross obediently was met with the sharpest rebuke: "Get behind me, Satan! You are a hindrance to me; for you are not setting your mind on the things of God, but on the things of man" (Mt 16:23). Like Adam (and Israel), the disciples of Jesus have their thoughts set on earthly glory—their own kingdom of power—while the Suffering Servant sets his face toward the cross.

> "And what shall I say—'Father, save me from this hour'? But for this purpose I have come to this hour. Father, glorify your name." Then a voice came from heaven: "I have glorified it, and I will glorify it again." The crowd that stood there and heard it said that it had thundered. Others said, "An angel has spoken to him." Jesus answered, "This voice has come for your sake, not mine. Now is the judgment of this world; now will the ruler of this world be cast out. And I, when I am lifted up from the earth, will draw all people to myself. (Jn 12:27–32)

For the first time, the world has an Adam and Israel has a king who will do only what he hears the Father say (Jn 5:19–20, 30, 43–44; 6:38; 8:26, 28, 50, 54; 10:37; 12:49–50). "I always do the things that are pleasing to him," Jesus could singularly say without arrogance or hypocrisy (Jn 8:29). Yet it is important to remind ourselves that these references to Jesus' victory over temptation and despair are not simply proof texts for his divinity. As a public representative and covenant head, the Last Adam fulfills all righteousness on behalf of his people. Adam and Israel failed to drive the serpent out of God's garden, but a servant has arrived now who not only will cleanse the temple but is in his own person the true temple to which the earthly sanctuary merely pointed (Jn 1:14; 2:19–22). None but this faithful high priest could be bold enough to declare, in complete honesty and truth, "Father, the hour has come; glorify your Son that the Son may glorify you, since you have given him authority over all flesh, to give eternal life to all whom you have given him.... And for their sake I consecrate myself, that they also may be sanctified in truth" (Jn 17:1–2, 19).

In the obedience of this servant, Yahweh in fact becomes his people's righteousness and sanctification in the power of the Spirit (Jer 23:6; 1Co 1:30; Ro 5:18; 2Co 5:21). In this way, believers are not only forgiven their sins but justified—that is, declared righteous by God's imputation of Christ's obedience to their account—and not only justified but renewed, and one day they will be glorified in union with their already-glorified head. In his High Priestly Prayer, Jesus says to the Father, "I glorified you on earth, having accomplished the work that you gave me to do" (Jn 17:4). As he prepares for the cross, his heart carries the thought of "all whom you have given [me].... Yours they were, and you gave them to me, and they have kept your word.... I have guarded them, and not one of them has been lost except the son of destruction, that the Scripture might be fulfilled." (vv. 2, 6, 12).

Not just the absence of sin, but the total positive obedience in thought, word, deed, and motivation rendered Jesus Christ both a perfect offering for sin (guilt offering) and a fragrant "living sacrifice" of praise (thank offering). He not only died for us; he lived for us, obedient even unto death but not only in his death, obedient throughout his life of service to his Father's Word and will. On this basis he will lead his people into the consummation. But before he ascends, he must descend to the depths.

Not only does the majestic Son descend to earth and suffer humiliation at human hands; he descends even deeper in his humiliation, to the grave itself. Not only viewed by his people as cursed by God for being crucified, but actually suffering the Father's curse, he goes deeper in his humiliation, sharing the common lot of humanity under the curse. Christians confess with the Apostles' Creed that Christ "was crucified, died, and was buried; he descended into hell."[13] Whatever interpretation we adopt, it seems clear enough that Christ's descent into hell represented his deepest humiliation—even if also it can be seen (like the cross, as I argue below) as the signal of victory as well.

B. CHRIST'S PRIESTLY DEATH: THE MEANING OF THE CROSS

For good reason it has been suggested that the Gospels are passion narratives with long introductions. When we abstract Christ's vicarious sacrifice from the long introduction, we lose our proper focus on that event. At the same time, none of the other important aspects of Christ's saving work—his active obedience, conquest over the powers, vindication of his just government, and moral example—can be established unless his death is understood as a vicarious substitution of himself in the place of sinners.

---

13. *Apostles' Creed*, in *Psalter Hymnal* (Grand Rapids: CRC Publications, 1987), 813. First used in a version of the creed in 390, the phrase *descended into hell* (in Latin, *descendit in inferna*) eventually became part of the common text of most churches. Interpretations of the descent have varied. The most relevant (albeit sparse) passages are Ephesians 4:9 (quoting Ps 68:18) and 1 Peter 3:18–19. Roman Catholic theology has interpreted these passages (especially the one from 1 Peter) as teaching the doctrine of the *Limbus Patrum*: the place referred to as the bosom of Abraham, where Old Testament saints awaited Christ's victory. Berkhof notes, "The common Protestant interpretation of this passage is that in the Spirit Christ preached through Noah to the disobedient who lived before the flood, who were spirits in prison when Peter wrote, and could therefore be designated as such" (Louis Berkhof, *Systematic Theology* [Grand Rapids: Eerdmans, 1996], 341). Lutherans understood the descent not as the culmination of Christ's humiliation but as the beginning of his exaltation, announcing his conquest. Calvin understood the clause as referring to Christ's suffering on the cross, which could hardly be less severe than hell itself (*Institutes* 2.16.8–10). For a helpful discussion of the history and the issues involved in Christ's descent into hell, see Herman Bavinck, *Reformed Dogmatics* (ed. John Bolt; Grand Rapids: Baker, 2006), 3:410–17.

1. AN EXEGETICAL (BIBLICAL-THEOLOGICAL) ACCOUNT OF CHRIST'S CROSS

At Mount Sinai, Moses delivered the covenant to the people, with its commands and sanctions: long life in the land for obedience, and the threat of being cut off, exiled from the land of the living, for disobedience. "All the words that the LORD has spoken we will do," the people replied (Ex 24:3, 7). To seal the covenant, "Moses took the blood and threw it on the people and said, 'Behold the blood of the covenant that the LORD has made with you in accordance with all these words'" (Ex 24:1–8). Israel did not fulfill its commission and was exiled from the temporal and typological garden of God. "For thus says the LORD: Your hurt is incurable, and your wound is grievous. There is none to uphold your cause, no medicine for your wound, no healing for you" (Jer 30:12–13). There is nothing that the covenant people can do to reconcile themselves to God.

And yet once again God promises a new covenant that will "not [be] like the covenant that I made with their fathers" at Sinai. It will be dependent on his performance rather than theirs. In this new covenant God will renew their hearts and join them to himself; "for I will forgive their iniquity, and I will remember their sin no more" (Jer 31:31–34). After finishing the Passover meal in the upper room in Jerusalem, Jesus took bread and said, "'Take, eat; this is my body.' And he took a cup, and when he had given thanks he gave it to them, saying, 'Drink of it, all of you, for this is my blood of the covenant, which is poured out for many for the forgiveness of sins'" (Mt 26:26–28). Christ will offer himself up to death in order to put into effect the "last will and testament" that makes his brothers and sisters co-heirs of his estate. In the upper room, Jesus in effect splashes the blood upon himself, bearing the curse that lies upon his people, drinking the cup of wrath so that they may drink the cup of salvation.

a. Lamb of God: Sacrifice and Satisfaction

Blood atonement lies at the heart of both the wonder and the offense of the Christian proclamation. "Indeed, under the law almost everything is purified with blood, and without the shedding of blood there is no forgiveness of sins" (Heb 9:22). This is not an abstract principle, much less the arbitrary command of a bloodthirsty deity. Rather, it belongs to the covenantal context of God's law. God's wrath is an expression of his righteous judgment, and blood is a synecdoche for the whole life of the person that God requires of transgressors.

The Old Testament background of substitutionary sacrifice is seen in the role of the animal victim to whose head sins are transferred from the offender (Lev 1:4; 4:20, 26, 31; 6:7). Not only does the Old Testament foreshadow Christ's sacrifice by its Levitical system, but the prophets point to the Suffering Servant. Most famously, in Isaiah 53 the Servant is the bearer of the iniquities of those whom he represents, and then he is exalted in glory. From the very beginning of his ministry, Jesus' mission was marked, as John the Baptist announced, "Behold, the Lamb of God, who takes away the sin of the world!" (Jn 1:29).

Appealing to Gerhard von Rad, Robert Jenson observes, "Throughout Scripture, the central moral and historical category is 'righteousness.'"[14] Once more the priesthood emerges in the context of a covenant, and we have seen that in the secular treaties of the ancient Near East tribute offerings were brought annually in a renewal ceremony that reaffirmed the vassal state's loyalty (*hesed*) to the suzerain. The offerings the priest brought included thank offerings and tithes. This fits with the tribute offerings (usually firstfruits of the flock or harvest) brought by a vassal to a suzerain to renew the vassal's pledge.

We have no explicit mention of any sacrifices offered by Adam and Eve, but it would have been consistent with the covenantal economy if they had brought the thank offering. Obviously, there could not have been a guilt offering prior to the fall. Just after the fall, God replaced the loincloths covering Adam and Eve with the skins of an animal, and Abel brought a bloody sacrifice (Ge 4:4). Already in Genesis 4, Abel brings the "the firstborn of his flock" (the proper guilt offering), but Cain, "a worker of the ground," brought a portion of his produce (the proper thank offering). The judicial language is unmistakable: The one who offers the proper sacrifice will be *accepted*. God "*had regard for* Abel and his offering" — by which Abel acknowledged his guilt and God's provision of a substitute — but "*for* Cain and his offering he *had no regard*." "So Cain was very angry, and his face fell" (Ge 4:4 – 5, emphasis added). Therefore, it is not an overstatement to suggest that the first religious war is provoked by Cain's denial of the need for a substitutionary sacrifice for his sin and by his jealousy toward Abel for having been justified ("accepted"/"regarded") by God's grace. In fact, Jesus refers to Abel as the church's first martyr and identifies the religious leaders who are plotting his own death as unwitting pawns in the serpent's long war against the gospel (Mt 23:33 – 36).

The guilt offering was simply a type of the Lamb of God to come, and the thank offering was merely a tribute that demonstrated publicly the servant's whole life of gratitude to the Great King. The essence of sin can be summarized by ingratitude. It is not too speculative to extrapolate from this that the covenantal structure was already in place with Adam and Eve, involving their regularly bringing tithe or thank offerings to their Great King in tribute as a token of their dependence and gratitude: "For although they knew God, they did not honor him as God *or give thanks to him*, but they became futile in their thinking, and their foolish hearts

---

14. Robert Jenson, *Systematic Theology* (New York: Oxford Univ. Press, 1997), 1:71.

were darkened" (Ro 1:21, emphasis added). Together, the thank offering (owed by humanity apart from sin) and the guilt offering (necessary after the fall) constitute the positive righteousness that God requires and the forgiveness of transgressions that must be obtained in order to be accepted by God.

It is especially in Leviticus that we see the sacrificial system inaugurated in Israel. The clearly expiatory nature of the sacrifices in Israel is seen in Lev 1:4; 4:29–35; 5:10; 16:7; 17:11, including transfer of guilt (Lev 1:4; 16:21–22). The burnt offering—singled out for atonement—was to be either from the flock or the herd, but in either case "a male without blemish" (Lev 1:3). Guilt would be transferred from the worshiper to the sacrifice by a laying on of hands, "and it shall be accepted for him to make atonement for him" (v. 4). Further, on the Day of Atonement the priest would sprinkle the blood of the sin offering on the altar and mercy-seat, which contained the treaty-tablets in the ark of the covenant. "Thus the priest shall make atonement for him, and he shall be forgiven" (4:30–31; cf. 16:21–27).

The Hebrew and Greek terms for priest (*kôhēn*/*hiereus*) could designate a sacred official, perhaps also a secular official (1Ki 4:5; 2Sa 8:18; 20:26). Unlike our own legal traditions, those of ancient Israel did not have a division of labor between a prosecution and defense in the courtroom: the prophet plays both roles. And yet, as in Isaiah 59, God looks for someone "to intercede" for the accused who have just confessed their individual and collective covenant breaking and can find none— and so his own arm saves and his own righteousness sustains him. The two roles that we know in our courtrooms, prosecution and defense, are somewhat divided between the prophet and priest, although, as we have said, the prophet's negotiating went in both directions.

I have already pointed out that especially in the series of actions that Jesus performs on the Temple Mount that will lead to his crucifixion he assumes the role of the temple itself: forgiving sins directly, bypassing the temple, to the outrage of the religious leaders. Proclaiming himself the true Temple, cursing the fig tree, and casting the religious leaders in the role of antagonists who will deliver him up to death even as they did the prophets since Abel (Mt 21–22), Jesus pronounces his curses upon the scribes and Pharisees (ch. 23), laments over Jerusalem (23:37–39), and predicts the destruction of the temple and the coming of the Son of Man in glory to judge the nations (chs. 24–25). Jesus' roles of prophet, priest, and king converge in these words and deeds on the Temple Mount after his triumphal entry.

Instead of reviving Israel's national hopes for a reinstitution of the theocracy, centering on the temple, Jesus brings about the end of the old age and the beginning of the new. N. T. Wright observes at this point,

> What then does the parallelism between the Temple-action and the Supper say about Jesus' understanding of his death? It says, apparently, that Jesus intended his

death to accomplish that which would normally be accomplished in and through the Temple itself. In other words, Jesus intended that his death should in some sense function sacrificially. This should not surprise us unduly, or be regarded as necessarily meaning that the texts that suggest this viewpoint must be a later Christian retrojection.[15]

After all, even in his ministry, Jesus "regularly acted as if he were able to bypass the Temple system in offering forgiveness to all and sundry right where they were."[16] "When you make his life an offering for sin," in Isaiah 53, this passage "by the first century was certainly taken to refer to a sacrifice."[17] But he also saw his death as a battle and the victory of God.[18] All of these themes are brought together at least in a fully orbed atonement doctrine, as we will see. In Christ's flesh, both his life and his death, we have a thank offering that restores what we owed to God's law—a fragrant life well pleasing to the Lord—and a guilt offering that propitiates God's wrath.

The New Testament sees these Old Testament sacrifices as prefiguring Christ's work—not only his death and resurrection but his faithful life, as shadow is related to the substance or type to fulfillment (Col 2:17; Heb 9:23–24; 10:1; 13:11–12; 2Co 5:21; Gal 3:13; 1Jn 1:7). The Christian claim is that Jesus is "the Lamb of God, who takes away the sin of the world," the scapegoat caught in the thicket (Jn 1:29), "our Passover" (1Co 5:7; 1Pe 1:19).

The whole human race stands condemned under the law, but "now the righteousness of God has been manifested apart from law, although the Law and the Prophets bear witness to it—the righteousness of God through faith in Jesus Christ for all who believe" (Ro 3:20–22a). Although we are by nature God's enemies, Christ's death secured peace with God (5:1, 6–10). Together with the resurrection, of first importance in the gospel is "that Christ died for our sins in accordance with the scriptures..." (1Co 15:3). He "loved us and gave himself up for us, a fragrant offering and sacrifice to God" (Eph 5:2), "and he is the propitiation for our sins..." (1Jn 2:2; cf. 4:10). The sacrificial motif is at the heart of Jesus' own self-identity: "The Son of Man came not to be served but to serve, and to give his life as a ransom for many" (Mk 10:45). "I am the good shepherd [of Ezekiel 34]. The good shepherd lays down his life for the sheep" (Jn 10:11) and does so voluntarily (v. 18), and whenever Jesus speaks of his impending death, he describes it by saying that "for this purpose I have come to this hour" (Jn 12:27). In his priesthood, Christ is both the Sovereign Lord of the covenant and the Mediator who fulfills its stipulations and bears its sanctions on behalf of his people whom he has loved from all of eternity.

---

15. Wright, *Jesus and the Victory of God*, 604.
16. Ibid., 605.

17. Ibid.
18. Ibid., 606–10.

This vicarious mediation is so nuclear to Jesus' self-consciousness that it lies at the heart of his intercession as he is about to go to his cross.

Peter adds his testimony to the expiatory nature of Christ's death: "He himself bore our sins in his body on the tree, that we might die to sin and live to righteousness. By his wounds you have been healed.... For Christ also suffered once for sins, the righteous for the unrighteous, that he might bring us to God" (1Pe 2:24; 3:18). Just as all who looked to the brass serpent in the wilderness were healed from the bites of venomous snakes, all who look to Jesus Christ are saved (Mk 10:45; 1Pe 2:24).

Throughout the Gospels and Epistles we discover references to redemption through "the blood of Christ" (Mt 26:27–28 and parallels; Ac 20:28; 1Co 11:25; 1Pe 1:2, 19). As the only atoning sacrifice that truly avails in the heavenly courtroom, it is not only sufficient but final. *Hapax* or *ephapax* (once and for all) appears repeatedly throughout Hebrews (Heb 9:12, 26, 28; 10:10). It is successful because of the superiority of the one who offers and is offered (Heb 1:1–2:18; 3:1–6; 4:14–5:10). "Where there is forgiveness of these [sins], there is no longer any offering for sin" (Heb 10:18). While Christ's sacrifice provides an example of self-giving love, it is a unique and unrepeatable event, bringing to an end all scapegoats, all bloody sacrifices, all substitutions, and all attempts to reconcile ourselves to God by our own efforts.

All three persons of the Trinity are involved in this sacrifice: the Father gives his only Son out of his love (Jn 3:16); the Spirit sustains the Son in his grief and vindicates him in his resurrection. The Son himself is not an unwilling victim of divine or human violence. Rather, Jesus, "for the joy that was set before him endured the cross, despising the shame, and is seated at the right hand of the throne of God" (Heb 12:2). He is a willing sacrifice (Jn 10:11, 18; cf. Mt 16:23; Lk 9:51; Jn 4:34; Heb 10:5–10), knowing that his suffering will lead to glory not only for him but for his people. And yet it is an agonizing struggle (Lk 12:50; Mk 10:38). Jesus sees it as a baptism (Lk 12:50). "He learned obedience through what he suffered," even with "loud cries and tears" (Heb 5:7–10). Yet in spite of his grief, he determines, "Shall I not drink the cup that the Father has given me?" (Jn 18:11). His obedience undoes Adam's disobedience (Rom 5).

Israel's sacrificial system of guilt offerings, the prophetic anticipation of the suffering servant, and the main narrative and doctrinal themes of the New Testament converge in the concept of *penal substitution* (i.e., Christ's death in the place of sinners, bearing their judicial sentence). In affirming the doctrine of penal substitution (whose name comes from the Latin word for penalty, *poena*), the church properly recognized that Christ's sacrifice was the payment of a debt to divine justice. In Jesus Christ, the damning verdict that believers had every right to expect at the last judgment is now poured out instead on Christ. It is impossible to understand the New Testament terms *anti* and *hyper* (in place of) as intending anything other than a substitution: Christ in the place of sinners; the guiltless for the guilty; the righteous for the unrighteous. "For our sake [God] made him to be sin who knew no sin" (2Co 5:21). The penal aspect is evident in the phrase "made sin" (*harmartian epoiēsen*), and its substitutionary aspect in the words "for us" (*hyper hēmōn*). He "suffered once for sins, the righteous for the unrighteous" (1Pe 3:18), suffered "for you" (*hyper hymōn*, 2:21), "bore ... sins in his body on the tree" (2:24). He was made a "curse for us" (Gal 3:13) and was "offered once to bear the sins of many" (Heb 9:28).

Christ's sacrificial death was at the heart of his self-consciousness. In his anticipation of arrival at Jerusalem, he repeatedly refers to his impending death and resurrection (Mk 8:31–33; 9:30–32; 10:32–34), although in each instance the disciples do not understand and grow impatient with Jesus' talk of crucifixion. After his triumphal entry into Jerusalem, which buoyed the disciples' anticipation of imminent glory, Jesus said, "Now is my soul troubled. And what shall I say 'Father, save me from this hour'? But *for this purpose I have come to this hour*. Father, glorify your name." Not for his sake but for theirs, the voice from heaven declared, "I have glorified it, and I will glorify it again." "Now is the judgment of this world; now will the ruler of this world be cast out," Jesus explained. " 'And I, when I am lifted up from the earth, will draw all people to myself.' He said this to show by what kind of death he was going to die" (Jn 12:27–33). In instituting the Last Supper, he gives central place to his role as the substitutionary sacrifice who will save his people by his blood (1Co 11:25; Lk 22:19–20). He gives his flesh for the life of the world (Jn 6:51). He "laid down his life for us" (1Jn 3:16), was delivered for us (Ro 8:32; Eph 5:2), died for us (Ro 5:8), for our sins (1Co 15:3), as "a ransom for all" (1Ti 2:6), delivered himself up for the church (Eph 5:25), to "give himself as a ransom for many" (Mt 20:28; Mk 10:45). The goal of the substitution is that "in him we might become the righteousness of God" (2Co 5:21) and be brought to God (1Pe 3:18). He carried away our sins into the wilderness.

To the sacrificial imagery is added the economic analogy: we were slaves whom God bought back (redeem/ransom: *agorazō, exagorazō, lytroō*; redemption: *apolytrōsis, antilytron*) in order to liberate us and reconcile us to himself. Where such terms appear, they are in the context of redemption from sin: its curse and tyranny. The price is paid in the marketplace (Mt 20:28; Mk 10:45; Ro 3:24; Eph 1:7; Col 1:13–14; Tit 2:14; Heb 9:12; 1Pe 1:18–19). Because this price is paid to God's justice, it frees us from the evil powers that hold us in bondage—especially Satan. However, the price is paid to God's justice rather than to Satan. Christ is the *lytron* (redeemer) who buys back his people by paying their debt at the highest personal price (Mt 20:28; 1Co 6:20; 7:23).

Closely related to penal substitution is *propitiation*. From the Greek verb *hilaskesthai* and its cognate noun *hilastērion*, *propitiation* refers to the necessity that God's justice be satisfied (cf. also *hilasmos* in 1Jn 2:2; 4:10). Because God is holy and righteous, he cannot overlook transgression (Ex 34:7; Num 14:18; Ps 5:4–6; Nah 1:2–3). "For the wrath of God is revealed from heaven against all ungodliness and unrighteousness of men, who by their unrighteousness suppress the truth" (Ro 1:18). Propitiation, therefore, focuses on God's relationship to the sinner. God must be just in his justification of sinners (Ro 3:25–26).

Albrecht Ritschl and other liberal theologians articulated the sentiment that is held by many (including some evangelical theologians) today when he eliminated the concept of divine wrath upon which the doctrine of propitiation rests.[19] Propitiation was increasingly eliminated even from more conservative vocabularies in the wake of the New Testament scholar C. H. Dodd, who argued in 1931 that *hilastērion* should be translated "expiation" rather than "propitiation."[20] Even the New International Version (NIV) translates *hilastērion* as "sacrifice of atonement" ("covering-over"; cf. Ro 3:25), which loses the force of the announcement that God's anger has been fully assuaged—i.e., propitiated.

However, the bias against propitiation reflects a number of misunderstandings, beginning with the doctrine of God. God's simplicity resists our temptation to identify a single attribute, including love, as more definitive of God than others. God cannot exercise love and mercy at the expense of his righteousness and justice. But this works in the other direction as well: God's wrath is not arbitrary or capricious but is the necessary response to the violation of his justice, righteousness, holiness, and goodness. God is not essentially full of wrath, but is only stirred to anger in the presence of sin. God is not "bloodthirsty," like the violent deities of ancient paganism. Rather, he is righteous, and his law requires that "the wages of sin is death. . ." (Ro 6:23). "But now the righteousness of God has been manifested apart from the law, although the Law and the Prophets bear witness to it—the righteousness of God through faith in Jesus Christ." Although "all have sinned and fall short of the glory of God," Paul adds, they are now "justified by his grace as a gift, through the redemption that is in Christ Jesus, whom God put forward as a propitiation [*hilastērion*] by his blood, to be received by faith" (Ro 3:21–25).[21]

God's holy wrath is clearly displayed by God against sin throughout Scripture.

---

19. This is the whole thrust of Ritschl's classic, *The Christian Doctrine of Justification and Reconciliation: The Positive Development of the Doctrine* (trans. H. R. Mackintosh and A. B. Macaulay, 1900; Eugene, Ore.: Wipf & Stock, repr. 2004). For an important orthodox analysis of Ritschl's treatment (especially his rationalistic presuppositions), see B. B. Warfield, "Albrecht Ritschl on Justification and Reconciliation: Article I," *Princeton Theological Review* 17 (1919): 533–84.

20. C. H. Dodd, *The Bible and the Greeks* (London: Hodder and Stoughton, 1935), 82–95. For refutations of Dodd's interpretation, see Leon Morris, *The Apostolic Preaching of the Cross* (Grand Rapids: Eerdmans, 1984), 136–56; Roger Nicole, "C. H. Dodd and the Doctrine of Propitiation," *WTJ* 17 (1954–1955): 117–57; and D. A. Carson, "Atonement in Romans 3:21–26," in *The Glory of The Atonement: Biblical, Historical, and Practical Perspectives* (ed. C. E. Hill and F. A. James III; Downers Grove, Ill.: InterVarsity Press, 2004), 129.

21. The NRSV and NIV translate *hilastērion* here as "sacrifice of atonement," but "propitiation" is closer to the meaning of the Greek noun (cf. ESV, used here).

Throughout both testaments, it is clear not only that in our fallenness we are at enmity with God, but that God is also at enmity with us (Ro 5:10 and 11:28, for example, refer to us as having been the subjects of God's enmity). As long as there is the reality of divine wrath, the reality of divine propitiation will be warmly received as its antidote. It is God's love that moves him to provide his own satisfaction of justice. Rather than being set in opposition, God's love and propitiatory sacrifice of his Son are mentioned in the same breath, for example, in Romans 3:25 and 1 John 4:10. Jesus suffered "outside the gate," as the covenant-breaker, cursed by God.

The result of God's just wrath being satisfied is *reconciliation* (*katallassō, katallagē*). Just as we are first of all passive subjects of God's wrath when God propitiates, we are passive subjects of God's reconciliation at the cross. We do not reconcile ourselves to God; God reconciles himself to us and us to him. Paul especially emphasizes this point in Romans 5. Perhaps on rare occasions someone might die for a righteous person. "But God shows his love for us in that while we were still sinners, Christ died for us. Since, therefore, we have now been justified by his blood, much more shall we be saved by him from the wrath of God. For if while we were enemies we were reconciled to God by the death of his Son, much more, now that we are reconciled, shall we be saved by his life." We boast in Christ, "through whom we have now received reconciliation" (Ro 5:7–11). Central to the gospel's announcement, then, is the fact that "in Christ God was reconciling the world to himself, not counting their trespasses against them, and entrusting to us the message of reconciliation.... For our sake he made him to be sin who knew no sin, so that in him we might become the righteousness of God" (2Co 5:19, 21). The Old Testament background here is the transition from a state of war to a state of peace (*šālôm*), a kingdom where only righteousness dwells. It is not only the lifting of the covenant's curses but the positive harmony between erstwhile foes (Ro 5:10–11; Col 1:19–20; Eph 2:11–22, especially v. 14; 2Co 5:18–21).

b. Conquering Liberator: Victory over the Powers

Sacrificial, judicial, and economic images of Christ's atoning work combine with those of the battlefield. Christ's cross is a *military conquest*. Christ is King not only in his resurrection and ascension but already at the cross—precisely at the place where Satan and his principalities and powers of death thought that they had triumphed. The event that in the eyes of the world appears to display God's weakness and the failure of Jesus to establish his kingdom is actually God's mightiest deed in all of history.

Throughout redemptive revelation, from the promise of the serpent-defeating seed of the woman in Genesis 3, the plot turns on the war between Satan with his human followers and Yahweh with his covenant people, as attempts are made all along the way to extinguish the ancestral line leading to the Messiah. It begins with Cain's murder of Abel (Gen 4), continues with the intermarriage between God's covenant people and the ungodly, culminating in God's judgment through the flood (Ge 6–7), and through various Satanic conspiracies to kill the "seed of the woman" through Pharaoh and even through the wicked kings of Israel and Judah, all the way to Herod's slaughter of the children in order to eliminate his rival claimant—the Son of David himself. All of this is recapitulated in Satan's persecution of the church, driven by rage that his time is short and his kingdom is being looted by the one over whom he thought he triumphed at the cross (Rev 12).

This war between the serpent and the seed of the woman looms large across Jesus' whole life and ministry, as he casts out demons, heals the sick, reconciles outcasts to himself, and announces the arrival of his kingdom. The real conquest is underway. What Adam and Israel failed to do—namely, drive the serpent from God's holy garden and extend his reign to the ends of the earth—the Last Adam and True Israel will accomplish once and for all. The serpent's head is crushed and the powers of evil are disarmed (Ro 16:20; Col 2:14–15). Death and hell no longer have the last word. Oppressors and those who perpetrate violence, injustice, and suffering throughout the earth have been delivered their own death warrant. In the meantime, it is a time of grace—when enemies are reconciled and even Satan's coconspirators can be forgiven, justified, and renewed as part of God's new creation.[22]

2. SYSTEMATIC THEOLOGY: THEORIES OF THE ATONEMENT

In the light of the preceding summary, then, Christ's passion is a multifaceted work that cannot be reduced to a single theme, although these other aspects are suspended in midair apart from the theme of propitiatory sacrifice. The account I have offered thus far would have been regarded as noncontroversial by the pastors and theologians of the Christian church with few exceptions. In the light of this narrative, the following theories have received attention in church history.

One view, called the "classical" or **ransom theory**—formulated by Origen—regarded the atonement as a ransom paid to Satan. Assuming that the devil was the rightful owner of sinners, Origen taught that Christ was a trap: his humanity was the necessary bait for luring Satan into thinking that he had at last won out over Yahweh, and then he conquered the devil by his deity. Although attracted to aspects of the theory, Gregory of Nanzianzus challenged the idea of God conquering through deception, but the more basic question is whether it can be said in any sense that Satan was the rightful owner of human beings. Theologians throughout the centuries have pointed out the speculative character of this idea. Furthermore, it contradicts several lines of biblical teaching on this subject. The curse of sin and death was a sentence imposed by God for the violation of his law; Satan's role in the drama is that of seducer and prosecutor rather than judge or claimant in the dispute.

---

22. On this important aspect of Christ's reconciliation in this time between the times, see especially Miroslav Volf, *Exclu-* *sion and Embrace: A Theological Exploration of Identity, Otherness, and Reconciliation* (Nashville: Abingdon, 1996).

The truth in this conception is that God outwitted Satan and the rulers of this age by triumphing over them precisely where they celebrated God's defeat.

Whereas the Gnostics sought to draw attention away from the descent, life, death, and resurrection of God in the flesh, Irenaeus emphasized from Scripture that it is precisely by becoming the Last Adam that Christ saves. His teaching (especially in Book 5 of *Against Heresies*) became known as **recapitulation**—literally, "re-headshiping." As we have seen, the Reformed view underscores the importance of Christ's whole life as part of his saving work. Not only his death, but his incarnation and active obedience are essential in order for Christ to save his people as their federal head. We will develop this important aspect especially in treating union with Christ.

A more general way of speaking about Christ's death as a conquest over Satan is identified as the **Christus Victor** (Christ the Victor) model. Once again, in the light of my summary above, there is a lot of truth in the military analogy. Christ indeed "disarmed the rulers and authorities and put them to open shame, triumphing over them in [the cross]" (Col 2:15). This aspect of Christ's work received special emphasis in the writings of Martin Luther, who regarded the cross not only as the climax of Christ's humiliation for us but as the beginning of his exaltation. Giving due attention to Christ's saving life (active obedience) also affords a link between the sacrificial model and *Christus Victor*. We have seen above how the category of active obedience especially answers the "obedience rather than sacrifice" position of the prophets (and Jesus). Strictly speaking, it is not simply the forgiveness of transgressions and satisfaction of divine justice or dignity that is envisioned, but the beauty before God of a life that truly conforms to his covenantal will revealed in creation and in Israel (Ps 24; 51:6–7). Christ brings not only forgiveness, but fulfillment of God's design for an obedient humanity. He crushes the serpent's head—as was foreshadowed in his victory over the demons, sickness, and death—during his earthly ministry. Neither Satan nor Caesar is Lord.

Ever since Gustaf Aulen's *Christus Victor*, the West has enjoyed a renewed appreciation for the often-neglected model of conquest over the powers, and the model is especially preferred by many today over against the emphasis on vicarious substitution.[23]

It is clear from my earlier summary that there is a crucial political theme in the New Testament atonement doctrine. Human "principalities and powers" on earth are often witting or unwitting emissaries of the evil powers in heavenly places that

23. Gustaf Aulen, *Christus Victor* (trans. A. G. Herbert; London: SPCK, 1975). See Walter Wink's works, especially *The Powers That Be: Theology for a New Millennium* (New York: Doubleday, 1999); N. T. Wright, *Evil and the Justice of God* (Downers Grove, Ill.: InterVarsity Press, 2006), and Brian McLaren, *Everything Must Change: Jesus, Global Crisis, and a Revolution of Hope* (Nashville: Nelson, 2007). *Christus Victor* is also the favored interpretation of liberation theologies and in recent Anabaptist defenses of a nonviolent atonement. See, for example, J. Denny Weaver, *The Nonviolent Atonement* (Grand Rapids: Eerdmans, 2001).

seek to thwart God's redemptive plan. The "rulers of this age" who are "doomed to perish" do not understand God's unfolding redemptive mystery "which God decreed before the ages for our glory." "For if they had, they would not have crucified the Lord of glory" (1Co 2:6–8). The powers here are not limited to spiritual beings (Satan and demons), but are visible to us in the regimes of oppression and violence.

Although the kingdom Christ inaugurates is not like the unjust kingdoms of this age, it is for that very reason scorned by all. It is not a passive or apolitical kingdom, but its activity and politics are Christ's, exercised in the power of the Spirit, through preaching and sacrament. The defeat of Pilate, Caiaphas, even the abandonment of the disciples and denial of Peter (as well as our own), *was* the defeat of Satan and the demonic "principalities and powers" that conspire to keep the world under sin, death, and judgment. The so-called givens of the kingdom of power, whatever regime of it we happen to be living under, are exposed as the "elemental spirits of the world" (Col 2:8), a sham, childish playacting gone terribly wrong, something no longer in any way determining the obligations, loyalties, and destinies of those who are in Christ. However, Christ's victory does not inaugurate a kingdom of glory here and now. It is not a power alongside other powers, vying for control through sociopolitical action. The danger of contemporary theories of *Christus Victor* that push out the propitiatory character of Christ's death in the place of sinners is a superficial view of sin, identifying its symptoms with its root cause, and treating Christ's cross more as a model for the church's redeeming work in the world than as the unique and unrepeatable act of reconciliation.

Reflection on Christ's death as a vicarious sacrifice for sinners is not only evident but prominent in patristic sources, in the East as well as the West. However, with Anselm of Canterbury (1033–1109) a specific formulation emerged that emphasized Christ's death as the satisfaction paid to God's offended dignity.[24] This view has come to be identified as the **satisfaction theory**. Like a monarch slighted by a subject, God must have a suitable tribute to outweigh the affront to his honor. However, God's majesty is infinite and therefore a sin against it demands an infinite penalty. Yet how can a finite creature offer an infinite compensation? Only human beings owe it, but only God can pay it. Therefore, the Savior must be both God and human. As with the others, there is important truth in this formulation. Criticism of this theory as owing more to the feudal system of medieval chivalry than to Scripture easily overlooks its similarities with the ancient Near Eastern background of the biblical world (especially its understanding of covenant). Anselm's

---

24. *Cur Deus Homo*, in *Anselm: Basic Writings* (trans. S. N. Deane; 2nd ed.; London: Open Court, 1998).

formulation properly directs our attention to the objective character of the atonement: *God's* problem with sin. The problem is that God has been offended, not simply that lives and human relationships have been broken.

Nevertheless, the Anselmian interpretation has certain exegetical and doctrinal weaknesses. Contrary to the widespread insistence of critics of vicarious satisfaction more generally, this particular formulation has never been accepted without reservation by Protestants, much less made the sole interpretation of Christ's death. Berkhof explains, "The theory of Anselm is sometimes identified with that of the Reformers, which is also known as the satisfaction theory, but the two are not identical."[25] While Anselm grounds the atonement in the need to satisfy God's offended *dignity*, Reformation theology recognized that it was God's *justice* that was at stake. There is no room in Anselm's theory for Christ meriting life for us by his active obedience or for his suffering the penalty for our sin, only for the offer of a tribute that more than compensated for human offense—"and this is really the Roman Catholic doctrine of penance applied to the work of Christ."[26] Furthermore, Reformed theology has faulted the theory for reducing the atonement to a commercial transaction between God and Jesus Christ without any treatment of its communication to sinners.[27]

Already in the twelfth century, Abelard (1079–1142) challenged the interpretation of his contemporary, Anselm, by offering his own view, which has come to be called the **moral influence theory**. According to this theory, the purpose of Christ's death was to provide a moving example of God's love for sinners that would provoke repentance. The image of Christ's death on the cross demonstrates God's love in such a powerful way that only the coldest hearts could resist its lure and remain enemies of God. In fairness it must be observed that Abelard also included other elements (particularly in his *Exposition of the Epistle to the Romans*). However, the Pelagian tendency of modern theology adopted this model as the proper interpretation of Christ's death. Already in the late sixteenth and early seventeenth centuries the Socinian movement embraced this subjective view—and, not surprisingly, rejected the divinity of Christ's person. A moral example or influence need hardly be God incarnate. Eventually, this view appealed to the leaders of the Enlightenment. Especially in Kant, Christ's death can offer only a motive to repentance, but it is our own repentance that finally effects absolution.[28]

Formulated by the great Arminian legal scholar, Hugo Grotius (1583–1645), the **governmental theory** attempted to mediate between a Socinian (moral influence) view and the Reformation understanding of Christ's work.[29] Like the moral influ-

---

25. Berkhof, *Systematic Theology*, 385.
26. Ibid., 386.
27. Ibid.
28. Kant, *Religion and Rational Theology*, in *The Cambridge Edition of the Works of Immanuel Kant* (ed. and trans. Allen W. Wood, George di Giovanni, et al.; Cambridge: Cambridge Univ. Press, 1996), 76–97, 104–45.

ence theory, this view presupposes a strong version of *voluntarism*: that is, the priority of God's will over God's nature. Therefore, the principal rationale for Christ's work is not that it is the only way in which God can be true to both his love and his justice, but that it provides the general ground on which God can offer terms of salvation to sinners. Thus, Christ's death need not be regarded as a real payment of a debt, but merely as the basis upon which God's just rule is exhibited.[30] In this view, God saves sinners not on the basis of Christ's perfect life, death, and resurrection, but on the basis of their own imperfect obedience to a relaxed divine law.[31] Schleiermacher and Ritschl broke entirely from any juridical understanding of the atonement. "With them and with modern liberal theology in general atonement becomes merely at-one-ment or reconciliation effected by changing the moral condition of the sinner. Some speak of a moral necessity, but refuse to recognize any legal necessity."[32]

Closer to home, the nineteenth-century American revivalist Charles G. Finney made the same arguments regarding Christ's work, although (unlike Schleiermacher and Ritschl) he did not deny Christ's divinity. Denying original sin, Finney asserted that we are guilty and corrupt only when we choose to sin.[33] In fact, Finney's *Systematic Theology* is almost entirely dedicated to expounding the moral government theory of the atonement in all of its aspects. Christ's work on the cross could not have paid our debt, but could only serve as a moral example and influence to persuade us to repent. "If he had obeyed the law as our substitute, then why should our own return to personal obedience be insisted upon as a sine qua non of our salvation?"[34] The atonement is simply "an incentive to virtue."[35] Rejecting the view that "the atonement was a literal payment of a debt," Finney can only concede, "It is true, that the atonement, of itself, does not secure the salvation of any one."[36] By itself, this theory assumes that God neither requires satisfaction of his justice nor receives it from Christ's work. The real significance of Christ's cross lies in the moral change

---

29. H. Orton Wiley, *Christian Theology* (Kansas City, Mo.: Beacon Hill Press, 1952), 2:241.

30. Referring to the penal substitution theory as "the Calvinistic theory" (ibid., 2:241), Wiley asserts, "It is in this attempt to impute our sin to Christ as His own that the weakness of this type of substitution appears" (245). "Our final objection to the satisfaction theory is based upon the fact that it leads logically to antinomianism," for the following reasons: "(1) It holds that Christ's active obedience is imputed to believers in such a manner that it is esteemed by God as done by them. They are, therefore, righteous by proxy. (2) This imputation in reality makes Christ's suffering superfluous; for if He has done for us all that the law requires, why should we be under the necessity of being delivered from penalty by His death? (3) If Christ's active obedience is to be substituted for that of believers, it shuts out the necessity of personal obedience to the law of God.... Man is therefore left in the position of being tempted to license of

every kind, instead of being held strictly accountable for a life of righteousness" (249). Wiley points out that John Miley "is the outstanding representative of the governmental theory in modern times" (255). Wiley denied that Christ's death involved "a substitution in penalty as the merited punishment of sin" (257).

31. Berkhof, *Systematic Theology*, 368.

32. Ibid., 369.

33. Charles G. Finney, *Systematic Theology* (Oberlin, Ohio: J. M. Fitch, 1846; repr., Minneapolis: Bethany, 1976), 31, 179–80, 236. Arminian theologian Roger Olson points out that Finney's theology is much closer to Pelagianism than to Arminianism (*Arminian Theology* [Downers Grove, Ill.: InterVarsity Press, 2005], 28, including footnote 20).

34. Finney, *Systematic Theology*, 206.

35. Ibid., 209.

36. Ibid.

that it provokes in us rather than in any change in legal standing of the sinner before a holy God. Christ's death produces an incentive, but the believer's own obedience is the ground of acceptance before God.

With the exception of Finney (who held that the believer's perfect obedience to the law is a sine qua non of redemption and justification), the moral example/influence and governmental theories assume that God can relax his law and remain just, as if this law were merely the arbitrary dictates of his moral will rather than a necessary expression of his moral character. A judge who transgresses his own law can hardly be said to demonstrate his moral government in the cosmic courtroom of history. Death is not an arbitrary punishment that God deems suitable for making a point, but the legal sanction that God incorporated into the covenant of creation. God clearly announced this penalty in the beginning, and his nature requires that it be executed (Eze 18:4; Ro 6:23). Objective injustice entails objective guilt and requires objective satisfaction. A purely subjective atonement leaves the sinner under the wrath of God, regardless of whatever moral lessons it may exhibit or changes in behavior it may induce. Furthermore, the theories that represent atonement in this way are subjective theories of human repentance more than of an objective divine atonement. Christ's death provides the possibility for redemption, but does it actually redeem sinners?

Yale theologian George Lindbeck says that at least in practice, Abelard's view of salvation by following Christ's example (and the cross as the demonstration of God's love that motivates our repentance) now seems to have edged out any notion of an objective, substitutionary atonement. "The atonement is not high on the contemporary agendas of either Catholics or Protestants," Lindbeck surmises. "More specifically, the penal-substitutionary versions ... that have been dominant on the popular level for hundreds of years are disappearing."[37] This situation is true for evangelicals as for liberal Protestants, he observes. This is because justification through faith alone (*sola fide*) makes little sense in a system that makes central our subjective conversion (understood in synergistic terms as cooperation with grace) rather than the objective work of Christ.[38] "Our increasingly feel-good therapeutic culture is antithetical to talk of the cross," and our "consumerist society" has made the doc-

---

37. George Lindbeck, "Justification and Atonement: An Ecumenical Trajectory," in *By Faith Alone: Essays on Justification in Honor of Gerhard O. Forde* (ed. Joseph A. Burgess and Marc Kolden; Grand Rapids: Eerdmans, 2004), 205.

38. Ibid., 205–6. He adds, "Those who continued to use the *sola fide* language assumed that they agreed with the reformers no matter how much, under the influence of conversionist pietism and revivalism, they turned the faith that saves into a meritorious good work of the free will, a voluntaristic decision to believe that Christ bore the punishment of sins on the cross *pro me*, for each person individually. Improbable as it might

seem given the metaphor (and the Johannine passage from which it comes), everyone is thus capable of being 'born again' if only he or she tries hard enough. Thus with the loss of the Reformation understanding of the faith that justifies as itself God's gift, Anselmic atonement theory became culturally associated with a self-righteousness that was both moral and religious and therefore rather nastier, its critics thought, than the primarily moral self-righteousness of the liberal Abelardians. In time, to move on in our story, the liberals increasingly ceased to be even Abelardian" (207).

trine a pariah.[39] Similarly, Princeton Seminary's George Hunsinger notes, "The blood of Christ is repugnant to the Gentile mind, whether ancient or modern. This mind would prevail were it not continually disrupted by grace." If it isn't disruptive, it isn't grace.[40] In contemporary discourse on the atonement and justification, Hunsinger judges, "The social or horizontal aspect of reconciliation ... eclipses its vertical aspect."[41] Gustaf Aulen observed,

> The subjective type has connections with Abelard, and with a few other movements here and there, such as Socinianism; but its rise to power came during the period of the Enlightenment,...with the disintegration of the 'objective' doctrine.... In the Middle Ages it was gradually ousted from its place in the theological teaching of the church, but it survived still in her devotional language and in her art.... The theologians of the Enlightenment were the declared enemies of orthodoxy; and a chief object of their assault was just the satisfaction-theory of the Atonement, which they described as a relic of Judaism surviving in Christianity.[42]

At the center of such criticism stood the doctrines of vicarious atonement and justification, which Kant regarded as morally debilitating.[43]

Protestant liberalism repeated the Socinian arguments against any judicial concept of the cross. "And so it came about," notes Colin Gunton, "that various forms of exemplarism took the field, under the impulses provided by the rational criticism of traditional theologies by Kant, Schleiermacher, and Hegel. In place of an act of God centered in a historic life and death, towards the otherwise helpless, the emphasis came to be upon those who by appropriate action could help themselves."[44]

When theology dispenses with propitiation as a theme, it must eventually surrender forgiveness as well. In his essay "Sin and Atonement in Judaism," Jewish theologian Michael Wyschogrod contrasts the modern (especially Kantian) notion of ethics with the biblical concept of law.[45] Like an error in arithmetic, a violation of a principle may be a mistake but is hardly something that demands forgiveness from an offended party. In other words, it is a mistake against a principle rather than an offense against a person. Yet the Hebrew texts speak of sin as an offense "with a high hand," equivalent to certain familiar gestures in popular culture. It is

---

39. Ibid., 207.

40. George Hunsinger, *Disruptive Grace: Studies in the Theology of Karl Barth* (Grand Rapids: Eerdmans, 2000), 16–17.

41. Ibid., 21.

42. Aulen, *Christus Victor*, 3, 6, 7.

43. See, for instance, Kant, *Religion within the Limits of Reason Alone* (trans. Theodore M. Greene and H. H. Hudson; New York: Harper & Row, 1960), 65–66, 134. However, for his own part, Kant was not motivated by a suspicion of the concept of divine judgment; on the contrary, the fear of final judgment

was meant to motivate moral effort, which the substitutionary satisfaction by Christ was thought to subvert.

44. Colin Gunton, "The Sacrifice and the Sacrifices: From Metaphor to Transcendental?" in *Trinity, Incarnation, and Atonement: Philosophical and Theological Essays* (ed. Ronald J. Feenstra and Cornelius Plantinga Jr.; Notre Dame, Ind.: Univ. of Notre Dame Press, 1989), 211.

45. Michael Wyschogrod, *Abraham's Promise: Judaism and Jewish-Christian Relations* (ed. R. Kendall Soulen; Grand Rapids: Eerdmans, 2004), 53–74.

not a mistake but a personal offense. "But precisely because this is so, forgiveness is possible," as it cannot be from principles and problems.[46]

Through the influence of Hegel and Romanticism, several contemporary theologies treat the cross as an illustration (or actualization) of the eternal suffering within God rather than as the solution to our offenses against God. Combining, at least implicitly, various subjective theories already mentioned, this trajectory is especially represented in the work of Jürgen Moltmann and liberation theology but also in much of the popular preaching and teaching in contemporary evangelicalism.[47] Especially in some contemporary Anabaptist and feminist theologies, the theme of God's wrath against sinners is regarded as a form of violence that legitimizes human revenge. Rather than see Christ's work as *bearing a sentence* that we deserved, according to these theories, we should see it as *moral empowerment* for our just praxis (good works) in transforming the world.[48] Like some Arminian theologians in the past, Clark Pinnock dismisses the doctrine of propitiation as if it were simply a curious and dangerous holdover from Calvinism.[49] However, as Roman Catholic scholar John Knox observes, "The concept of the cross as sacrifice belongs to the very warp and woof of the New Testament, while there is no evidence whatever that the early Church entertained the view that the purpose of Christ's death was to disclose the love of God."[50] Of course, Christ's death does disclose God's love and is motivated by it, but its purpose is to *save* those whom he loves.

---

46. Ibid., 70.

47. See, for example, Clark Pinnock, *A Wideness in God's Mercy: The Finality of Jesus Christ in a World of Religions* (Grand Rapids: Zondervan, 1992), esp. 49–80; Clark Pinnock and Robert Brow, *Unbounded Love: A Good News Theology for the 21st Century* (Downers Grove, Ill.: InterVarsity Press, 1994), esp. 100–105.

48. I interact at length with these views in *Lord and Servant: A Covenant Christology* (Louisville: Westminster John Knox, 2006), 178–207. On feminist critiques, see Rosemary Radford Ruether, *Introducing Redemption in Christian Feminism* (Sheffield, U.K.: Sheffield Academic, 1998); Joanne Carlson Brown and Rebecca Parker, "For God So Loved the World?" in *Christianity, Patriarchy, and Abuse: A Feminist Critique* (ed. Joanne Carlson Brown and Carole R. Bohn; New York: Pilgrim Press, 1989). Incorporating these critiques, along with the pacifist perspective of Anabaptism and the cultural theory of René Girard, see Anthony W. Bartlett, *Cross Purposes: The Violent Grammar of Christian Atonement* (Harrisburg, Pa.: Trinity Press International, 2001); Robert Hamerton-Kelly, *Sacred Violence: Paul's Hermeneutic of the Cross* (Philadelphia: Fortress, 1992); Denny Weaver, *The Nonviolent Atonement* (Grand Rapids: Eerdmans, 2001).

49. For example, John Wiley refers to "The Penal Satisfaction Theory, generally known as the Calvinistic theory..." (*System-atic Theology* [New York: Hunt and Eaton, 1892], 241). Pinnock observes that his adoption of Arminianism led him to reject the classical doctrine of the substitutionary atonement: "Obviously it caused me to reduce the precision in which I understood the substitution to take place.... It caused me to look first at the theory of Anselm and later of Hugo Grotius, both of whom encourage us to view the atonement as an act of judicial demonstration rather than a strict or quantitative substitution as such.... It is my strong impression that Augustinian thinking is losing its hold on present-day Christians. It is hard to find a Calvinist theologian willing to defend Reformed theology, including the views of Calvin and Luther, in all its rigorous particulars now that Gordon Clark is no longer with us and John Gerstner is retired." Pinnock concedes that his changes are part of a growing accommodation to the secular mind: "We are finally making peace with the culture of modernity" ("From Augustine to Arminius: A Pilgrimage in Theology," in *The Grace of God, The Will of Man: A Case for Arminianism* [ed. Clark H. Pinnock; Grand Rapids: Zondervan, 1989], 23, 26, 27).

50. John Knox, *The Death of Christ: The Cross in the New Testament History and Faith* (New York: Abingdon, 1958), 145. Knox also points out that the conception "of a victory won ... [also] belongs to the very warp and woof of the New Testament" (146).

ATONEMENT THEORIES	
Theory	**Description**
Recapitulation	Associated especially with Irenaeus and Eastern theology, this view underscores Christ's life as well as death as undoing humanity's collective transgression, replacing Adam's headship over the human race with his own. This view also emphasizes immortality as the supreme gift of Christ's saving work.
Ransom	Also known as the "classic" theory (because of its association with Origen and other early Alexandrian theologians), this view held that Christ's death was a ransom paid to Satan for the ownership of humanity.
Christus Victor	A key aspect of atonement theology especially in the East (as well as in Lutheran and Reformed teaching), this theory emphasizes Christ's victory over the powers of death and hell at the cross.
Satisfaction	Associated especially with the eleventh-century theologian Anselm, this view understands Christ's atonement primarily as an appeasement of God's offended *dignity*. Reformation theologies focus on the satisfaction of divine *justice*.
Moral Influence	This view interprets the atonement as a demonstration of God's love rather than as a satisfaction either of God's dignity or his justice. The effect of the atonement is to provide a moving example of God's love that will induce sinners to repentance. This view is associated with Abelard (1079–1142), has been held by Socinians and some Arminians, and has been the central idea in Protestant liberalism.
Moral Government	According to this view, Christ's atonement exhibits God's just government of the world and thereby establishes repentance as the basis on which human beings approach God. It was formulated in Arminian theology, especially by Hugo Grotius (1583–1645).

3. RESPONDING TO CONTEMPORARY CRITICISM
OF SUBSTITUTIONARY ATONEMENT

The doctrine of substitution has encountered repeated objections throughout history. According to the Socinians, moral debts cannot be paid by one party on behalf of another.[51] The same argument may be found in the New Haven divinity school and Charles Finney, to which I referred above. The Arminians held that Christ's death made it possible for him to forgive sins on a more relaxed basis than perfect conformity to his law and strict justice.[52] More recently, the argument has been pressed by liberation, feminist, and Anabaptist theologies that representing

---

51. Bavinck, *Reformed Dogmatics*, 3:399.
52. Ibid., 3:400.

53. I interact with these views at length in *Lord and Servant*, 178–205.

Christ's death as a vicarious sacrifice valorizes domestic violence and social scape-goating.[53] All of these objections share at least three assumptions that have been challenged above, namely, (1) a denial of God's wrath and the necessity of his justice being fully satisfied by Christ's death, (2) a rejection of the principle of substitution in this relationship between God and sinners, and (3) an emphasis on the exemplary character of Christ's death as inciting human love and obedience rather than on its expiatory character as providing the sole basis for our acceptance before God.

However, according to Scripture, that which makes sin *sinful* is the fact that it is first of all an offense against God (Ps 51:3–5). For a variety of reasons, the notion of justice has been replaced in our culture by a therapeutic vocabulary. This is not altogether wrong from a Christian perspective: there is much in the gospel about the healing that Christ's work brings in its wake. Restored relationships, renewal, and empowerment have their important place in a Christian doctrine of sanctification. However, in a therapeutic worldview, the whole purpose of religion is to improve our sense of well-being rather than to address the situation of sinners before the judgment of a holy God. As we have seen from Jeremiah 30, confirmed by many other passages in Old and New Testaments, the condition in which Israel finds itself is precisely that of the world in Adam: hopeless and helpless, beyond cure, unable to recover from either the guilt and condemnation or the corruption of sin. Whatever truth there may be in Christ's cross securing restored relationships, renewal and moral empower-ment can be justified only on the deeper basis of Christ's fulfilling the law in his life, bearing the curse in his death, and rising victoriously from the dead.

If therapeutic categories dominate, however, every article of the Christian faith is tested by whether it will help us to feel better about ourselves, have a more fulfill-ing life, and contribute to human flourishing. When humans rather than God are at the center, the cross can be understood as a moving example of loving self-sacrifice, an illustration of how much God loves us, and a demonstration that God has rees-tablished his sovereignty over the kingdoms of darkness. But the one thing that it *cannot* be is the means by which "we have been justified by his blood [and] ... saved by him from the wrath of God" (Ro 5:9). In defending the doctrine of substitution-ary atonement, we should bear the following points in mind.

First, we can conclude on the basis of the texts we have considered that the cause of the atonement lies in God's own pleasure (Isa 53:10) and love (Jn 3:16). Yet God takes pleasure not only in one attribute abstracted from his total character. God is love regardless of whether he chose to save the guilty. His decision to save sinners is not based on an arbitrary will, but reflects God's essential character (including justice as well as love), and the persons of the Godhead mutually committed themselves to Golgotha from all of eternity in the covenant of redemption. Yet God's love toward sinners even from all eternity is an act of *mercy*, which by definition he is not bound to show toward any transgressor (Ex 33:19; Ro 9:11–18). God is not only "love," but "just and justifier" (Ro 3:26). He delights in righteousness as much as in love. In fact, in the cross God acts both as gracious and as righteous simultaneously (vv. 24–25).

Second, sin is not represented simply as a weakness that could be reformed, but as guilt incurred, invoking sanctions (1Jn 3:4; Ro 2:25–27). Human beings "are storing up wrath for [themselves] on the day of wrath when God's righteous judgment will be revealed" (Ro 2:5). God's law, whether written on the conscience in creation (for Gentiles) or written on tablets (for Jews), is the basis for God's judgment (Ro 2:1–29) and since "no one is righteous" (3:9–18), the law cannot reform or restore; it can only announce the guilty verdict over all humankind (vv. 19–20). "The law brings wrath…" (4:15). Therefore, the cross as a means of expiation is not simply one way of handling the plight of humanity in general and Israel in particular; it is the *only* way that God can uphold his justice and his love in the salvation of covenant breakers. By definition, mercy need not be shown, but once God has decided to exercise mercy, he can do so only in a way that does not leave his righteousness, holiness, and justice behind.

Third, the atonement is grounded not only in God's moral character and freedom but in the united determination of the persons of the Trinity. The covenant of redemption emphasizes this point, as we have seen. Therefore, the impression sometimes conveyed by representations of vicarious satisfaction, with a vengeful Father acting out his rage upon a passive Son, is a serious distortion. The Father is not only the one who receives the satisfaction of his justice from the Son; he is also the one who "so loved the world, that he gave his only Son" (Jn 3:16). "In Christ *God* was reconciling the world to himself" (2Co 5:19). From the day of his baptism, when Jesus first heard the benediction of the Father and the Son on his new creation ministry, he knew that he was executing the plan of redemption together with the Father and the Spirit. God did not demand first satisfaction and then love, but was moved by his love to send his Son to make satisfaction.

Thus, reconciliation is not first of all subjective but objective. Because God can now legally forgive and justify the ungodly, he can simultaneously reconcile the world to himself (Ro 5:10; 2Co 5:19–20). Other terms employed for this sacrifice (*lytron* and *antilytron*), as well as the prepositions *peri*, *hyper* and *anti* (in the place of), underscore the substitutionary, vicarious nature of this sacrifice. Martin Hengel observes that "dying for" is a Pauline formula rooted in the earliest Jerusalem community. The Jewish council accused Jesus, Stephen, and Paul of attacking the temple (cf. Ac 6:13), which suggests (according to Hengel) that the heart of the church's earliest proclamation was "the death of the crucified Messiah, who had vicariously taken upon himself the curse of the Law, [and] had made the Temple obsolete as a place of everlasting atonement for the sins of Israel.... Therefore the ritual Law had lost its significance as a necessary institution for salvation."[54] Apart from the notion of appeasement of God's wrath, the joyful announcement, "Behold, the Lamb of God, who takes away the sin of the world" (Jn 1:29) is inconceivable. It is the sinless substitute for the sinful people that is of central importance in the biblical doctrine of atonement (Mt 26:28; 2Co 5:21; Gal 3:13; Heb 9:28; 1Pe 2:24, 3:18; etc.).

Interestingly, it is this view of the atonement that guards most resolutely against anti-Semitic construals of the cross. In Isaiah 53, Yahweh is the one who offers up the Servant on behalf of the people. And the Good Shepherd himself says that *he* lays down his life for the sheep, even adding, "No one takes it from me, but I lay it down of my own accord. I have authority to lay it down, and I have authority to take it up again" (Jn 10:18). While those involved in carrying out the execution, both Jews and Gentiles, can be blamed in one sense, ultimately they did "whatever [God's] hand and [God's] plan had predestined to take place" (Ac 4:28). As "a lamb without defect or blemish," Peter declares, "He was foreknown before the foundation of the world but was made manifest in the last times for the sake of you" (1Pe 1:20–21). That God's wrath required punishment underscores his justice, but the fact that he himself gave what was required in the place of our punishment underscores his merciful love. And in both cases it is God who gives up his Son to the cross and the Son who gives himself up in the Spirit.

Fourth, because his active obedience is just as essential to his redeeming work as his passive obedience, Christ's sacrifice is not only a guilt offering but a thank offering, a whole life of representative service. As we have already seen, the apostolic announcement is that God has done in Christ what Israel and the world could never achieve by the law. Jesus' vicarious ministry does not begin at the cross but at his birth and throughout his life, especially in his ministry—from the baptism and temptation all the way to Gethsemane and the cross. "In short," noted Calvin, "from the time when he took on the form of a servant, he began to pay the price of liberation in order to redeem us."[55] Atonement cancels debts, but justification raises us upright in God's presence, with Christ's righteousness credited to our account. Atonement bears away our guilt, but justification gives us that positive standing in God's court so that we are not only forgiven but wholly acceptable, righteous, holy, and pleasing to God for Christ's sake. Therefore, rather than accept a false choice between a substitutionary death and a saving life, the Irenaean theory of recapitulation has much that belongs to the warp and woof of vicarious substitution itself. Christ's

54. Martin Hengel, *The Atonement in New Testament Teaching* (Philadelphia: Fortress, 1981), 36–38, 49.

55. Calvin, *Institutes* 2.16.5.

512

penal substitution is not the whole of Christ's work, but without it nothing else matters.

In covenant theology, the legal and relational aspects are never set at odds, as they typically are in modern theology. No more than in adoption or in marriage can legal status be set over against a relationship. On the basis of the full satisfaction of legal demands, the organic union of believers with Christ is given its due. It is just this organic union that is emphasized in Irenaeus's model of recapitulation, with Jesus as the "leaven" that makes the whole lump holy, first by being incarnated and then by filling up the years of human disobedience with his own obedience. As we have observed, Reformed theologians have often taken exception to Anselm's theory as too exclusively "commercial"—excluding this wider covenantal horizon of Christ's active obedience in fulfilling all righteousness and our mystical union with him through faith.[56] Aquinas improves on the theory, though with insufficient attention to the cosmic horizon.[57]

At various points in the history of evangelical theology, distorted treatments of penal substitution have provoked reactions (overreactions) within evangelical circles. Rejection of the objective satisfaction of God's justice in Christ's cross drives a wedge between the Old and New Testaments, failing to recognize the promise of Christ's atonement foreshadowed in the substitutionary sacrifices and fulfilled in Christ's death. Second, we have seen that the New Testament itself speaks of the atonement not only as God's reconciliation of the world to himself but as God's *propitiation* of his wrath, his satisfaction of his justice, and the ground of his acceptance of sinners. It speaks of a great exchange: Christ's righteousness for the sinner's unrighteousness, his obedience for our disobedience, his vindication for our condemnation, his life for our death. All of his riches are given to us, and all of our debts are borne by him. The sacrificial, commercial, and legal metaphors are so replete in the New Testament that it is impossible to deny the good news that Christ's merits are put to our account.

At the same time, the penal aspect is often abused when expressed in terms of an angry Father who takes out his frustrations on a loving and passive Son. This is why it is so important to emphasize the three points above: (1) the cross is rooted in God's character (love and justice), (2) it was the love of God that moved him to send Christ, and (3) he did not begin to love us after the cross, but from all eternity (Eph 1:4). Yet his love had to comply with his justice. The punishment that Christ bore was not an arbitrary act of revenge, but a fulfillment of the standard that God had

---

56. Berkhof, *Systematic Theology*, 386.

57. Even Aquinas maintains that God *could* have (*de potentia absoluta*) saved humankind in some other way than the incarnation and cross, but it was the most suitable route (*de potentia ordinata*). Condemnation befalls unbelievers not because original or personal sins are too serious (contra Anselm) but because they are without grace—i.e., remission of sins. The focus is on justice, not honor (*Summa theologica* 3, q. 1, art. 2).

established in creation: namely, life for obedience, death for disobedience. The cross was a satisfaction of the claim of justice, not of dignity or irrational anger. Further, it was an action in which all three persons of the Trinity were involved.

Thus, the Son was not a passive victim but freely gave himself, even as the Father gave the Son: "I lay down my life for the sheep.... No one takes it from me, but I lay it down of my own accord. I have authority to lay it down, and I have authority to take it up again. This charge I have received from my Father" (Jn 10:15b, 18). In this light, John Stott's warning is salutary: "Any notion of penal substitution in which three independent actors play a role—the guilty party, the punitive judge, and the innocent victim—is to be repudiated with the utmost vehemence."[58] At the cross, the Father was fulfilling his loving purpose toward sinners through the one whom he loved most dearly. Yet he could not satisfy his love at the expense of his justice. The Son did not endure the Father's rage, but the sentence that he agreed from all eternity must be carried out for the sake of his loved ones.

Just as his love was the motive, the satisfaction of God's justice, pouring out his wrath at the cross, was not the end but the means to the greater end of justifying, renewing, and glorifying a people for himself, restoring his fallen creation. It was not a cathartic release of anger, but a just satisfaction of God's covenantal righteousness, that provided the basis for both our forgiveness and our rectitude: legal rectitude in justification, moral rectitude in sanctification, and consummate rectitude of body and soul in glorification. In this way, Christ is victor even as he is the sacrificial victim. The picture in Revelation 5 expresses this paradoxical unity of *Christus Victor* and vicarious substitution, with the slaughtered Lamb seated victoriously on a throne, surrounded by thronging worshipers from every nation.

At their best, every tradition of Christianity—the East as well as the West—has affirmed the cross as Christ's triumph as well as his vicarious substitution. Not only Calvin, but Chrysostom; Irenaeus as well as Augustine; Luther and Athanasius, lend their voices to this choir. Only in its covenantal context—that is, under certain stipulations and certain sanctions—can we understand what it means to say that "Christ redeemed us from the curse of the law by becoming a curse for us...." (Gal 3:13). "And just as it is appointed for man to die once and after that comes judgment," says the writer to the Hebrews, "so Christ, having been offered once to bear the sins of many" (Heb 9:27–28 ESV). "He himself bore our sins in his body on the tree..." (1Pe 2:24). Even in the context of the justly beloved verse, John 3:16, we cannot avoid the legal, "courtroom" language, language that says, "This is the

---

58. John Stott, *The Cross of Christ* (Downers Grove, Ill.: InterVarsity Press, 1986), 158.

verdict" (v. 19 NIV). "Whoever does not believe *is condemned* already, because he has not believed in the name of the only Son of God" (v. 18). Jesus spoke of the forgiveness of sins in terms of paying debts (Lk 7:42).

Far from indicating incoherence or contradiction, the diversity of biblical representations is due to the massive scale and implications of Christ's work. If there is a danger in reducing Christ's accomplishment to penal substitution, the opposite danger is to see other aspects as *alternatives* to it.

What is the moral lesson that Jesus' crucifixion teaches? It cannot teach the importance of laying down one's life for one's friends (Jn 15:13) apart from some account as to how Jesus died *in our place*, for us, as our substitute. Furthermore, what is the point of such a moral example? Is it that we should affirm the value of "scapegoats" in general? The good news of Christ's cross is that it brought all expiatory and propitiatory sacrifices to an end. Precisely because of this fact, his death can only be a moral example in a restricted sense; we can give ourselves in service to others, but we cannot give ourselves in the place of others before God's tribunal. Therefore, we can be exhorted to have the same attitude of humility and self-giving affection that Jesus exhibited (Php 2:5–11) and recognize in Christ's cross the unsurpassable love of the Triune God (Jn 3:16).

Further, the cross not only *demonstrates* God's justice (as if it took the cruel death of the Son of God to offer us merely an object lesson) but *fulfills* God's justice. "God put [him] forward as a propitiation by his blood, to be received by faith. This was to show God's righteousness ... at the present time, so that he might be just and the justifier of the one who has faith in Jesus" (Ro 3:25–26).

Finally, in Colossians 2—a primary text for the *Christus Victor* model—Christ's death certainly "disarmed the rulers and authorities," "[putting] them to open shame," "... triumphing over them in him" (v. 15). However, this victory itself is based on his having made judicial satisfaction, as becomes apparent when we read verses 12–15 together. Within a span of a mere three verses, we may recognize clear signs of (1) recapitulation, (2) legal substitution, and (3) *Christus Victor*: (1) "And you, who were dead in your trespasses and the uncircumcision of your flesh, God made alive together with him, (2) having forgiven us all our trespasses, by canceling the record of debt that stood against us with its legal demands. This he set aside, nailing it to the cross. (3) He disarmed the rulers and authorities and put them to open shame, by triumphing over them in him."

As Paul indicates in 1 Corinthians 15:56, "the sting of death is sin, and the power of sin is the law." Apart from the lifting of the curse justly imposed by God because of sin, there can be no final victory from death's grip. Sin does not lie on the surface of human existence. Its symptoms are evident in the powers of evil that work against justice, righteousness, peace, and life in the world; in the diseases, poverty, violence, and oppression that mangle the lives of individuals and societies. If the problem of sin were merely negative actions, behaviors, or social systems, a moral example or a demonstration of God's opposition to such actions would perhaps suffice. If the problem were simply disease, disappointment, and suffering, it might make some difference to know that God cares and heals, and even that he has made eternal life possible. However, the condition of sin and its penalties is first of all judicial. Christ's death saves because it resolves the serious crisis between God and human beings in the cosmic courtroom. Myriad other effects follow in the wake of the announcement that Christ has presented his blood in the heavenly sanctuary. The divine solution is as deep as the human problem.

4. THE EXTENT OF CHRIST'S ATONEMENT

For whom did Christ die? This is not a speculative question but one that receives considerable exegetical attention and has significant theological and practical implications. In fact, Arminian theologians properly recognize that if Christ's death actually accomplishes the redemption of sinners (rather than simply making their redemption possible), then all of those for whom Christ died are objectively redeemed and will be brought to eternal life. According to John Miley, "The penal substitutionary theory leads of necessity either to universalism on the one hand, or unconditional election on the other." Miley makes the charge that "such an atonement, by its very nature, and by immediate result forever frees them from all guilt as a liability to the penalty of sin."[59] Thus, the nature of the atonement is bound up with the question of its extent. In broad terms, three main answers have been given in church history.

One answer is that Christ's death objectively redeemed every person. The Scriptures unmistakably teach that God loves the world and that Christ died for the world (Jn 1:29; 3:16; 6:33, 51; Ro 11:12, 15; 2Co 5:19; 1Jn 2:2). Therefore, advocates of this first view conclude that it was Christ's purpose to save each and every person who has ever lived or will ever live. Officially condemned in the sixth century, Origen's theory of universal restoration (*apokatastasis*) held that all spirits (though not bodies), including Lucifer, would be reunited in heavenly bliss.[60] Refusing to bind God's freedom, Barth stopped short of a formal doctrine of universal salvation, although his doctrine of election and reconciliation suggests it.[61] Confessional Lutheranism also teaches a universal and objective atonement, although it also holds to a limited and unconditional election. Only the elect will

59. John Miley, *Systematic Theology* (New York: Hunt and Eaton, 1889; repr. Peabody, Mass.: Hendrickson, 1989), 2:246.

60. See *The Seven Ecumenical Councils,* in *NPNF2,* vol. 14.

61. Barth, *Church Dogmatics,* vol. 1, pt. 2, pp. 417–23; vol. 3, pt. 2, pp. 136; vol. 4, pt. 1, pp. 91, 140, 410. For responsible evaluations, see especially G. C. Berkouwer, *The Triumph*

of Grace in the Theology of Karl Barth (trans. Harry R. Boer; London: Paternoster, 1956), 215–34; Garry J. Williams, "Karl Barth and the Doctrine of the Atonement," in *Engaging with Barth: Contemporary Evangelical Critiques* (ed. David Gibson and Daniel Strange; Nottingham, U.K.: Apollos, 2008), 232–72.

be finally saved, but some receive the saving benefits of Christ's work only for a time and then lose these benefits through mortal sin or unbelief. In this view, then, not all of those for whom Christ died will be saved, in spite of the universal intention of his death. Yet the point of agreement among these proposals is that Christ's death actually redeemed (objectively) every human being.

A second option is that Christ died to make salvation of every person possible. The intent of Christ's death, according to the Dutch Remonstrants (Arminians), was to make it possible for God to offer salvation to believers by their grace-enabled cooperation: namely, their faith and evangelical obedience. A mediating position between the orthodox Calvinism defined by the Synod of Dort in 1618–1619 and Arminianism became known as "hypothetical universalism" (also "Amyraldian-ism," after its architect, Moises Amyraut). Christ bore the sins of every person without exception, but since God knew that no one would embrace Christ apart from the gift of faith, he elected some to receive the benefits of Christ's work. Many evangelical Protestants hold to either an Arminian or an Amyraldian view, in either case agreeing with the position expressed by Lewis Sperry Chafer: "Christ's death does not save either actually or potentially; rather it makes all men savable."[62]

A third view is that Christ died for all of the sins of the elect, thereby redeeming them at the cross. According to this view, expressed by the *Canons of Dort*,[63] Christ's death is "of infinite worth and value, abundantly sufficient to expiate the sins of the whole world," although he objectively and effectively bore the sins of the elect alone. Dort was repeating a common formula, "sufficient for the whole world but efficient for the elect alone." This formula is found in various medieval systems, including the writings of Aquinas, Gregory of Rimini, and Luther's mentor, Johann von Staupitz. As the formula indicates, this view does not limit the sufficiency or availability of Christ's saving work. Rather, it holds that the specific intention of Christ as he went to the cross was to save his elect. Sometimes identified as "limited atonement," this view is better described as "particular redemption." As the seventeenth-century Puritan John Owen observed, every position that recognizes that some will finally be lost places a limit on the atonement at some point: it is limited either in its *extent* or in its *effect*. Owen summarizes the options: Christ died for (1) all the sins of all people, (2) some of the sins of all people, or (3) all of the sins of some people.[64] If unbelief is a sin, and some people are finally condemned, then there is at least one sin for which Christ did not make adequate satisfaction.

---

62. Lewis Sperry Chafer, "For Whom Did Christ Die?" *BSac* 137 (October–December 1980): 325.

63. *Canons of Dort*, ch. 2, art. 3, in *Psalter Hymnal: Doctrinal Standards and Liturgy of the Christian Reformed Church* (Grand Rapids: Board of Publications of the Christian Reformed Church, 1976), 99.

64. John Owen, "The Death of Death in the Death of Christ," in *Works of John Owen* (London: Johnstone and Hunter, 1850–1854; repr. Carlisyle, Pa.: Banner of Truth Trust, 1965–1968), 10:233.

Extent of the Atonement		
Thesis	**Extent and Nature**	**Position**
Christ saved every person	Unlimited in extent and effect	Universal salvation
Christ made possible the salvation of every person	Unlimited in extent, but limited in effect	Hypothetical universalism
Christ saved all the elect	Sufficient for all, efficient for the elect	Definite atonement

Among the arguments in favor of particular redemption are the following. *First, this view emphasizes the relationship between the Trinity and redemption.* In the eternal councils of the Trinity (the covenant of redemption), the Father elected a certain number of the human race and gave them to his Son as their guardian and mediator, with the Spirit pledging to bring them to Christ to receive all the benefits of his mediation. Not only are there explicit passages on this eternal pact (Eph 1:4–13; 2Th 2:13, 14; Tit 3:4–8), but Jesus referred repeatedly to his intention to redeem his elect (Ro 8:32–35), his sheep (Jn 10:11, 15), his church (Ac 20:28; Eph 5:25–27), and his people (Mt 1:21).

Jesus said that he came not to make salvation possible but to actually save everyone "that the Father gives me." He adds, "And this is the will of him who sent me, that I should lose nothing of all that he has given me, but raise them up at the last day.... This is why I told you that no one can come to me unless the Father has enabled him" (Jn 6:37–39, 65 NIV). In John 10, Jesus said, "The good shepherd lays down his life for the sheep.... I am the good shepherd. I know my own and my own know me, just as the Father knows me and I know the Father; and I lay down my life for the sheep" (Jn 10:11, 14–15), which includes Gentiles as well as Jews (v. 16). With Golgotha heavy on his heart, Jesus prays to the Father, "Father, the hour has come; glorify your Son that the Son may glorify you, since you have given him authority over all flesh, to give eternal life to all whom you have given him.... Yours they were, and you gave them to me, and they have kept your word.... I am praying for them. I am not praying for the world but for those whom you have given me, for they are yours" (Jn 17:1–2, 6, 9). And once more Jesus includes all "who will believe in me through their word, that they may all be one" (v. 20–21a).

In the Epistles as well, there is the correspondence between the will and work of the Father, that of the Son, and that of the Spirit in election, redemption, and calling, which creates an unshakable ground of comfort (Ro 8:30–34; Eph 1:4–13).[65]

---

65. See Stephen M. Baugh, "Galatians 3:20 and the Covenant of Redemption," *WTJ* 66, no. 1 (2004): 49–70.

The Savior entered paradise as conqueror with the triumphant announcement, "Behold, I and the children God has given me" (Heb 2:13). All of this shows "the heirs of the promise the unchangeable character of his purpose," which was "guaranteed ... with an oath, so that by two unchangeable things, in which it is impossible for God to lie, we who have fled for refuge might have strong encouragement to hold fast to the hope set before us" (Heb 6:17–18).

Second, this view emphasizes the efficacy and objectivity of Christ's saving work. How do I know if I am one for whom Christ died? The only answer given in Scripture is that we look to Christ, in whom we were chosen, and whose death is sufficient for a thousand worlds. The alternative views, however, though not affirming universal salvation, hold that in spite of Christ's objective work, many for whom he died will be finally lost, bearing their own judgment. But what then of Christ's promise above that he will not lose any of those whom the Father has given him? This possibility of Christ's redeeming work falling short of its intention is not eliminated even in Barth's conception, since he allows for the possibility of final condemnation of some.

Because it is not hypothetical but actual, we can proclaim to everyone with confidence, "God so loved the world, that he gave his only Son, that whoever believes in him should not perish but have eternal life" (Jn 3:16). Again, as we have seen, particular redemption does not limit the *sufficiency* of Christ's death. With the New Testament, advocates of particular redemption can cheerfully proclaim, "Christ died for sinners," "Christ died for the world," and "Christ's death is sufficient for you," acknowledging also with the Scriptures that the assurance "Christ died for you" is to be given only to believers. If Christ's sin-bearing does not actually bear away God's wrath for every person for whom he died, then, as Bavinck concludes, "The center of gravity has been shifted from Christ and located in the Christian." Instead of Christ's objective work, "Faith is the true reconciliation with God."[66]

Far from being thwarted, the clear invitations of Scripture for all to come to Christ (Mt 11:28; Jn 6:35; 7:37) are even more fully justified by the fact that the Spirit will use this universal good news to draw his elect to Christ. The Sinai covenant focused Israel's hopes on the Messiah through types and shadows, but the Abrahamic covenant promising salvation for the nations is now announced to the world. It is in this sense that we understand the verses that refer to Christ's death on behalf of "all" and "the world." Since Christ's blood "ransomed people for God from every tribe and language and people and nation" (Rev 5:9), there is no distinction any longer between Jew and Gentile, male and female, slave and free (Gal 3:28). Through the flood, God simultaneously judged and saved the world—even

---

66. Bavinck, *Reformed Dogmatics*, 3:469.

though only eight persons were rescued. How much greater then is the salvation that is assured by the Triune God through his promise that there will be a remnant from every nation entering into the heavenly sanctuary as his new humanity.

DISCUSSION QUESTIONS

1. How does Christ fulfill the office of prophet, especially in terms of his relationship to Moses and Elijah in the Gospels?

2. Discuss Christ's office of priest in redemptive-historical perspective. How does he fulfill this office in his life, even prior to his crucifixion?

3. What is the difference between Christ's "active" and "passive" obedience?

4. Is Christ's death properly interpreted as a penal substitution? Does this idea arise naturally from the history of redemption, or is it an abstract theory? What about "propitiation"? Is this a biblical concept, or is it unworthy of a God of love?

5. Integrate the various biblical motifs of Christ's cross, and evaluate the various theories of the atonement in that light. Is there more to Christ's death than his vicarious substitution? If so, how is this sacrificial aspect of his work essential for the other motifs and theories to carry any validity?

6. What is the extent of Christ's atonement, and how does this relate to its nature?

Chapter Sixteen

THE STATE OF EXALTATION: THE SERVANT WHO IS LORD

With Christ's resurrection and ascension all the things we have discussed so far—God's character and purposes, creation, humanity as the covenant servant, and Christ as Lord and Servant—converge. And from this exaltation everything that we will say in future chapters concerning the application of redemption, the inauguration of Christ's kingdom of grace through the ministry of the church, and that kingdom's future manifestation as a kingdom of glory will be unfurled. There can be a church in history only because in this same history the Lord who became the servant was the servant who became Lord. Of course, Jesus Christ was always Lord in his consubstantiality with the Father, but he "was declared to be the Son of God in power according to the Spirit of holiness by his resurrection from the dead..." (Ro 1:4). There is a church because there is one who stood in his resurrected flesh and declared, "All authority in heaven and on earth has been given to me. Go therefore and make disciples of all nations..." (Mt 28:18–19).

I. RESURRECTION AND ROYALTY

We have already encountered the first half of Paul's appeal to Christ's priestly service in the state of humiliation: a lifelong obedience "to the point of death, even death on a cross" (Php 2:5–8). With the second half we meet Christ's exaltation: "Therefore God has highly exalted him and bestowed on him the name that is above every name, so that at the name of Jesus every knee should bow, in heaven and on earth and under the earth, and every tongue confess that Jesus Christ is Lord, to the glory of God the Father" (vv. 9–11). Steeped in the Hebrew scriptures, Paul knew well what he was claiming when he appropriated Isaiah 45:23 to Jesus. The only true God had a personal name—Yahweh—and no other name could be invoked for salvation or worship. The Father gave Jesus this name, not only because of his identity as the divine Son from all eternity, but because of the work that he had fulfilled in the unity of his person.

Throughout his ministry, Christ was God's "No" to the powers of sin and death. Healing the sick, casting out demons, and even raising the dead, Jesus provided morsels of that victory that would be consummated on the basis of his resurrection, his ascension, the sending of the Spirit at Pentecost, and Christ's triumphant return in glory. Even at the cross, as we have seen, Christ's royal office is publicly displayed as he triumphs over the powers of this present age. Right where those powers can see him only as rejected, helpless, foolish, and weak, he is in fact accomplishing his most decisive victory over his enemies and ours.

Since he is the eternal Word of the Father, Christ's kingship does not begin at Golgotha but in creation (Jn 1:1–4, 10; Col 1:15–20; Heb 1:2–3). The Son reflects the Father's glory in eternity as well as in time (Heb 1:3). As we have seen, in every external work of the Godhead, the Father speaks in the Son and by the Spirit. If there were any other Word than he, creation would immediately collapse into chaos. Yet does it not seem on many hands that this is precisely what has happened to God's world? How can we say that God is Lord when we see injustice, oppression, violence, suffering, and disaster all around us? In the pattern of Christ's resurrection, ascension, and return in glory, we begin to recognize the answer to that question.

In his redemptive work, Christ is exhibited as the mediator of the church as well. This is not another creation, but a new creation. In other words, there are not two realms: creation and redemption. Rather, the church is that part of the creation that has been redeemed and is being called into fellowship with the Son in anticipation of the renewal of the whole earth (Ro 8:18-25). Christ is "the firstborn of all creation" because he is "the image of the invisible God," "by him all things were created, in heaven and on earth ..." and "he is before all things" (Col 1:15–17). "Firstborn" must therefore be taken to imply not that the Son was the first created being, but that he was the source of creation itself. In precisely the same manner, says the apostle, Christ is the firstborn of the new creation. "He is the head of the body, the church; he is the beginning, the firstborn from the dead, that in everything he might be preeminent. For in him all the fullness of God was pleased to dwell, and through him to reconcile to himself all things, whether on earth or in heaven, making peace by the blood of his cross" (vv. 18–20). Just as "in him all things hold together" in creation, so also in the church. As goes the king, so goes the kingdom. The same idea is conveyed when Paul refers to Jesus Christ as the "first-fruits" of the whole harvest (1Co 15:23). As goes the head, so goes his body. This, as we have seen, is the covenantal way of thinking, drawing on organic analogies.

Everything that Jesus performs by his speaking and priestly mediation he accomplishes for the good of his co-heirs, and when he rose and ascended in glory as King, he took up his scepter for the same purpose. Christ rules history and nature in the service of redeeming, creating, and ruling his church. Death, the last enemy, lost its legal foothold in creation by the cross (Heb 2:14; 2Ti 1:10), although it awaits its final abolition at Christ's return (1Co 15:23–26). In Christ's ascension, the age to come has already dawned. He is the forerunner who is already glorified as the church's head but will not rest until his body shares in his consummated life.

God did not abandon his messiah to the grave (Ps 16:10). In his Pentecost sermon, Peter cited Psalm 16:8–11 as the proof text for his announcement of God's saving work in Christ: "But God raised him up, loosing the pangs of death, because it was not possible for him to be held by it" (Acts 2:24–28). Since David's tomb is not empty, David could only have been referring to "the resurrection of the Messiah." "This Jesus God raised up, and of that we all are witnesses. Being therefore exalted at the right hand of God, and having received from the Father the promise of the Holy Spirit, he has poured out this that you yourselves are seeing and hearing.... Let all the house of Israel therefore know for certain that God has made him both Lord and Christ, this Jesus whom you crucified" (vv. 29–36; cf. 3:15–26).

This pattern, "whom you crucified, [but] God raised from the dead," appealing to Old Testament prophecies, and announcing salvation in no other name, marks all of the sermons in Acts (4:10–12, 24–30; 5:30–32, 42; 7:1–53; 10:39–43; 13:16–39; 17:30–32; 26; 25:19; 26:4–8; 26:22–23; 28:20, 23–24). In fact, before the Jewish council Paul noted with some irony, since the Pharisees were distinguished by their belief in the resurrection of the dead, "Brothers, I am a Pharisee, a son of Pharisees. It is with respect to the hope and the resurrection of the dead that I am on trial" (23:6).

Although there is a certain priority of each of Christ's three offices in successive phases of his ministry, at no moment was Jesus a prophet without being a priest or a priest without being a king. Even in his "state" of humiliation, he was a king building his empire of grace, and even in his "state" of exaltation, he served the will of the Father and the good of his people. Even in the depths of his humiliation, the cross itself was also a kind of exaltation. Jesus said, "And I, when I am lifted up from the earth, will draw all people to myself" (Jn 12:32). Although this may sound at first like the ascension, the next verse explains, "He said this to show by what kind of *death* he was going to die" (v. 33). He is the "brass serpent" raised in the wilderness, so that all who look upon him will be saved (Jn 3:14 with Nu 21:8–9). So while there is a general progression from the state of humiliation to exaltation and from prophet to priest to king, they are all present simultaneously in the unity of Christ's person and work. Even as he was hanging on the cross in dereliction as the enemy of God and humanity, Christ was winning our redemption as our conquering King. "There is no tribunal so magnificent," Calvin wrote, "no throne so stately, no show of triumph so distinguished, no chariot so elevated, as is the gibbet on which Christ has subdued death and the devil."[1]

Reformed as well as Lutheran theology has typically followed the eschatological distinction of Christ's kingship between his reign in grace (*regnum gratiae*) and his reign in glory or power (*regnum gloriae potentiae*). God has installed his king on his holy mountain and now demands universal homage (Ps 2:6; 45:6–7 [with Heb 1:8–9]; 132:11; Isa 9:6–7; Jer 23:5–6; Mic 5:2; Zec 6:13; Lk 1:33; 19:27, 38; 22:29; Jn 18:36–37; Ac 2:30–36). But this kingdom is not simply an extension or reinvigoration of the kingship in Israel, as many of Jesus' admirers had expected—even the disciples after the resurrection (Ac 1:6). During the trial Pilate asked Jesus, "Are you the King of the Jews?" and Jesus replied, "Do you say this of your own accord, or did others say it to you about me?"

> Pilate answered, "Am I a Jew? Your own nation and the chief priests have delivered you over to me. What have you done?" Jesus answered, "My kingdom is not of this world. If my kingdom were of this world, my servants would have been fighting, that I might not be delivered over to the Jews. But my kingdom is not from the world." Then Pilate said to him, "So you are a king?" Jesus answered, "You say that I am a king. For this purpose I was born and for this purpose I came into the world—to bear witness to the truth. Everyone who is of the truth listens to my voice." Pilate said to him, "What is truth?" (Jn 18:33–38)

What a paradox: The King of kings and Lord of lords standing bound and silent before an officer of Caesar and the rulers of his own people, reigning even as he submits voluntarily to the cruelest human injustice.

In its present phase, the kingdom is like its King before he was raised from the dead and exalted to the right hand of the Father. It can only appear weak and foolish to the world, even though this kingdom is more extensive in its global reach and more intensive in its redemptive power than any earthly empire in history. In the old covenant the kingdom was typologically concentrated in the outward glory of Israel's cultic and civil structures, but during "this present age" its glory is hidden

---

1. John Calvin, *Commentary on Philippians–Colossians* (Grand Rapids: Baker, repr. 1979), 191.

under the cross. It claims hearts, not geopolitical lands. It brings new birth (Jn 3:3–7) from the future reign of the Spirit and as a prolepsis of the consummation that the "Lord and giver of life" will bring in "the resurrection of the body and the life everlasting."[2]

Christ's kingship, like the other roles we have explored, involves both a human and a divine aspect. Again, the messianic king is greater even than David not simply because he is divine, but also because he fulfills the human commission that Adam, Israel, and even David fell short of achieving. As God and human, he establishes righteousness in all the earth. This can be especially seen in Hebrews 2, where the "dominion" entrusted to God's image-bearers is finally realized in Jesus Christ:

> Now in putting everything in subjection to him [humanity], he left nothing outside his control. At present, we do not yet see everything in subjection to him. But we see him who for a little while was made lower than the angels, namely Jesus, crowned with glory and honor because of the suffering of death, so that by the grace of God he might taste death for everyone.
>
> For it was fitting that he, for whom and by whom all things exist, in bringing many sons to glory, should make the founder of their salvation perfect through suffering. For he who sanctifies and those who are sanctified all have one source. That is why he is not ashamed to call them brothers, saying, . . . "Behold, I, and the children God has given me." (Heb 2:8–13)

Only on the basis of the resurrection can we say that the righteous and peaceful dominion of humanity has been restored. It certainly cannot be discerned from the daily headlines or from the state of the church throughout the world. Yet it has been recovered and fulfilled in Christ as our Living Head. By his sanctification we are sanctified, and by his reign the world is assured its participation in the cosmic glory that he has already inherited in his investiture as "King of kings and Lord of lords" (1Ti 6:15). His investiture at the right hand of God is a reward for his meritorious obedience (Ps 2:8–9; Mt 28:18; Eph 1:20–22; Php 2:9–11).

Christ is already a king with his kingdom, but for now this realm is visible chiefly in the public ministry of Word, sacrament, and discipline, and also in the fellowship of the saints as they share their spiritual and material gifts in the body of Christ. Thus, in all times and places since Pentecost, the Spirit is opening up worldly reality to the new creation that has dawned with Christ's resurrection from the dead. Through the waters of baptism, the breaking of bread, the hearing of the Word, the guidance of pastors and elders, the priestly service of deacons, and the witness of all believers to Christ in the world, the powers of the age to come begin

---

2. *The Nicene Creed* and *The Apostles' Creed*, *Trinity Hymnal* (rev. ed.; Philadelphia: Great Commission Publications, 1990), 846, 845.

to penetrate this fading evil age. The church is not yet identical with the kingdom that Christ will consummate at his return, but it is the down payment on "the time for restoring all the things about which God spoke by the mouth of his holy prophets long ago" (Ac 3:21). As Paul confirms, the resurrection of Christ is not distinct from the resurrection of believers, but the "firstfruits" of the whole harvest (1Co 15:21–26, 45, 49).

We should not be surprised, then, by all of these organic metaphors for the relationship of Christ to his church: vine and branches, tree and its fruit, living stones being built into a Spirit-indwelled temple, and the head and its body.

> [God] worked in Christ when he raised him from the dead and seated him at his right hand in the heavenly places, far above all rule and authority and power and dominion, and above every name that is named, not only in this age but also in the one to come. And he put all things under his feet and gave him as head over all things to the church, which is his body, the fullness of him who fills all in all. (Eph 1:20–23)

None of these analogies reflects a model of sheer domination of one person over another, but an intimate union. Christ rules *over* by ruling *within* those who are identified as part and parcel of his own body. And he does so for their salvation. Even now Christ reigns secretly and invisibly over all empires and nations for the ultimate purpose of building his church (Eph 1:20–22; 4:15; 5:23; 1Co 11:3). The writer to the Hebrews assures us that even now, since his resurrection, all things are under Christ's personal dominion, even though "at present, we do not yet see everything in subjection to him" (Heb 2:8). At present, it is only in the church where Christ's universal reign becomes partially visible.

The Spirit justified Jesus Christ by raising him from the dead, and so too he "was delivered up for our trespasses and raised for our justification" (Ro 4:25). As one who was "declared to be Son of God in power according to the Spirit of holiness by his resurrection from the dead" (Ro 1:4), Jesus traded places with the Holy Spirit in the economy of redemption. In fact, the Spirit justified Christ on his way to Pentecost, to justify the Jews and Gentiles he would make into one body with him.

Therefore, as Berkhof summarizes, the kingdom of grace is founded upon Christ's redemption, not creation.[3] The creation mandate to rule and subdue was given to all image-bearers in the beginning, but the Great Commission is entrusted to the saints and is fulfilled by their testimony to the gospel, by baptism, and by teaching the nations everything that he has declared. It is not a geopolitical kingdom, as in the theocracy (Mt 8:11–12; 21:43; Lk 17:21; Jn 18:36–37), much less one like the Gentile empires (Mk 10:42–43), although it will one day be revealed in

---

3. Louis Berkhof, *Systematic Theology* (Grand Rapids: Eerdmans, 1996), 407.

power and glory. In fact, it is interesting that after each of the three Markan episodes in which Jesus foretells his death and resurrection, the disciples erupt in jealousy and controversy about who will be greatest in the kingdom (implied in 8:34–38, explicit in 9:33–37 and 10:35–45). Just as the empirical reality that we see all around us, epitomized by the decay of our bodies, speaks against the claim that a "new creation" has truly dawned, the weakness of a church aptly described in the hymn as being "by schisms rent asunder, by heresies distressed"[4] witnesses against the participation of the earthly body, the church, in its heavenly head. Yet the resurrection of Christ makes it so, not only because it sets the rest of the redemptive economy in motion but because it is the first installment on the full consummation.

The principle that Paul applies to the physical body, "What is sown is perishable; what is raised is imperishable. It is sown in dishonor; it is raised in glory. It is sown in weakness; it is raised in power" (1Co 15:42–43), is illustrative of the already–not yet scheme involved in the manifestation of the kingdom in history. Entered by the new birth (Jn 3:3–5), this kingdom nevertheless cannot remain a merely spiritual reality. It must one day become as tangible and complete as the resurrection itself will be for the human person. But for now, it is a mustard seed (Mk 4:30–32), leaven being worked into the dough of humanity generally (Mt 13:33). The kingdom is present (Mt 12:28; Lk 17:21; Col 1:13), yet not consummated (Mt 7:21–22; 19:23; 22:2–14; 25:1–13, 34; Lk 22:29–30; 1Co 6:9; 15:50; Gal 5:21; Eph 5:5; 1Th 2:12; 2Ti 4:18; Heb 12:28; 2Pe 1:11). The decisive victory has been accomplished, but we have yet to hear that the cities of oppression and violence have been destroyed and "the kingdom of the world has become the kingdom of our Lord and of his Christ, and he shall reign forever and ever" (Rev 11:15). Jesus' resurrection not only confirms but effects his status as the Israel of God, the eschatological temple in whom each member, Jew or Gentile, fits as a "chosen" and "living [stone]" (1Pe 2:4–5).

The claim "Jesus is Lord" is not simply a confession of his deity. It is that and more. The important eschatological point that this claim makes is that in Jesus Christ the threats to God's promises being fulfilled have been conquered objectively and will be realized fully in the age to come. There are no powers, authorities, thrones, or dominions that can thwart his purposes, although they may present fierce opposition until they are finally destroyed. Moltmann reminds us,

> Anyone who sees the risen Christ is looking in advance into the coming glory of God. He perceives something which is not otherwise perceptible, but which will one day be perceived by everyone.... In talking about a resurrection of Jesus *from the*

---

4. "The Church's One Foundation," in, e.g., *Trinity Hymnal* (rev. ed.; Philadelphia: Great Commission Publications, 1990), #347.

dead, the Christians have altered the old apocalyptic hope in quite a decisive way. In making this alteration, what they are saying is this: in this one person, ahead of all others, the End-time process of the raising of the dead has already begun. With Jesus' resurrection from the dead, history's last day is beginning: "The night is far gone and the day is at hand" (Rom. 13.12). That is why they proclaim him as "the first fruits of those who have fallen asleep" (I Cor. 15.20), "the first-born from the dead" (Co. 1.18), "the pioneer of salvation."[5]

As Jesus was raised from the dead, we too shall be raised. Salvation is neither simply a resuscitated existence, picking up where we left off, nor a liberation of the soul from the body at death. It is the bodily entrance of the dead into a condition and place that creation has never yet known: life everlasting. "Jesus is risen into the coming kingdom of God."[6] Accordingly, adds Moltmann, "Wherever people confess that Jesus is the Christ of God, there is living faith. Where this is doubted or denied or rejected, there is no faith."[7]

> Anyone who pares the theme of christology down to "the Jesus of history," anyone who reduces the eschatological person of Christ to the private person of Jesus, and anyone who historicizes his presence to the time of his life on earth, must not be surprised to discover that christology is no longer a subject that has any relevance at all. For who could still get up any interest after 2,000 years in a historical Jesus of Nazareth who lived a private life and then died?[8]

To say, "Jesus is Lord," one must try to hear it with Jewish as well as Gentile ears. It means that the God of Israel—the one who won the duel with Egypt's gods and led his people through the sea and wilderness into the promised land—is the one who raised Jesus from the dead and, in turn, gave the human person thus raised the name above every name. It is to say that he is the one who will restore Israel's fortunes, not by simply reinvigorating a typological theocracy, but by bringing about the universal judgment of sin and vindication for his people that the Mosaic economy could only foreshadow. To hear "Jesus is Lord" as a slogan for nothing more than "my personal relationship with Jesus" is not to hear it as it is meant to be heard. It is to truncate the message that Jesus both *is* and *proclaims*.

Against the temptation to reduce salvation to an inner, personal experience, Moltmann rightly suggests, "It is therefore more appropriate to present the salvation which Christ brings in ever-widening circles, beginning with the personal experience of reconciliation and ending with the reconciliation of the cosmos, heaven and earth."[9]

---

5. Jürgen Moltmann, *The Trinity and the Kingdom: The Doctrine of God* (trans. Margaret Kohl; San Francisco: Harper & Row, 1981), 85.

6. Ibid., 88.

7. Jürgen Moltmann, *The Way of Jesus Christ: Christology in Messianic Dimensions* (Minneapolis: Fortress, 1993), 39.

8. Ibid., 40–41.

9. Ibid., 45.

Therefore, the announcement of Christ's lordship is as much a part of the gospel as the announcement of his prophetic and priestly ministry are. Christ's reign topples all rivals who hold us in bondage, so that even death has lost its legal authority to keep us in the grave: "The sting of death is sin, and the power of sin is the law. But thanks be to God, who gives us the victory through our Lord Jesus Christ" (1Co 15:56–57). Yet once again we see that Christ's cosmic victory and lordship is good news only because it first deals with the root problem. Death is a sanction invoked by transgressing the law, so that the solution to the latter brings salvation from the former. Jesus "was delivered up for our trespasses and raised for our justification" (Ro 4:25).

Although this truth brings innumerable blessings in its wake that can justly be called "good news" in the broader sense, *the* good news—the specific announcement that creates faith—is the forgiveness of sins and justification in Christ. While God's commands in Scripture are to be presented, explained, and obeyed, the *gospel* does not exhort us to do certain things, but announces what God has done in his Son.

II. CHRIST AS KING: THE ASCENSION

To Christ's unique fulfillment of the prophetic and priestly offices is added his triumph as King. For illustration of this role, we may turn to Psalm 24, one of the psalms of ascent. These were appointed to be sung during annual feasts, when pilgrims would make their way together up the hill leading to the temple. Psalm 24 is especially poignant, with its antiphonal (responsive) pattern:

> The earth is the LORD's and the fullness thereof
>   the world and those who dwell therein,
> for he has founded it upon the seas
>   and established it upon the rivers.
> Who shall ascend the hill of the LORD?
>   And who shall stand in his holy place?
> He who has clean hands and a pure heart,
>   who does not lift up his soul to what is false
>   and does not swear deceitfully.
> He will receive blessing from the LORD
>   and righteousness from the God of his salvation.
> Such is the generation of those who seek him
>   who seek the face of the God of Jacob. (Ps 24:1–6)

So far there the popular use of these words as chiefly an exhortation to believers might seem plausible. However, the verses that follow direct our attention elsewhere:

> Lift up your heads, O gates!
>   And be lifted up, O ancient doors,
>   that the King of glory may come in.

Who is this King of glory?
    The LORD, strong and mighty,
    the LORD, mighty in battle!
Lift up your heads, O gates!
    And lift them up, O ancient doors,
    that the King of glory may come in.
Who is this King of glory?
    The LORD of hosts,
    he is the King of glory! (Ps 24:7–10)

Jewish as well as Christian commentators have pointed out that this psalm encapsulates Israel's military march from the desert of Sinai to Jerusalem—God's earthly Zion (see also Psalm 68, with the reference to Yahweh's solemn "processions" from wilderness to Zion). Only Jesus Christ perfectly fulfills this commission and is qualified to demand that the ancient doors of the heavenly throne room open to his triumphal entry with his liberated hosts behind him. He claims his victory, announcing, "Behold, I and the children whom God has given me" (Heb 2:13).

The most direct ascension account comes from Luke (24:13–51). Meeting two of his disillusioned disciples on the road, the recently risen (though as yet unrecognized) Jesus pushes them regarding their knowledge of the Scriptures: "Was it not necessary that the Christ should *suffer these things* and *enter into his glory?*' And beginning with Moses and all the Prophets, he interpreted to them in all the scriptures the things concerning himself" (Lk 24:26–27). Having commanded them to remain in Jerusalem until the promised Spirit is given, so that they might be "clothed with power from on high," he then, we read, "led them out as far as Bethany, and lifting up his hands he blessed them. While he blessed them, he parted from them and was carried up into heaven. And they worshiped him and returned to Jerusalem with great joy, and were continually in the temple blessing God" (vv. 49–53).

This episode is retold in Acts 1, as Jesus commands his disciples to remain in Jerusalem until the promised Spirit comes:

> And when he had said these things, as they were looking on, he was lifted up, and a cloud took him out of their sight. And while they were gazing into heaven as he went, behold, two men stood by them in white robes, and said, "Men of Galilee, why do you stand looking into heaven? This Jesus, who was taken up from you into heaven, will come in the same way as you saw him go into heaven." (Ac 1:9–11)

At this point, Christ's ascension (and return in glory) becomes part of the gospel itself. Crucified for our sins and raised for our justification, this one will come again, "that is, Jesus, who must *remain* in heaven *until the time of universal restora-*

tion that God announced long ago through his holy prophets" (Ac 3:20–21 NRSV, emphasis added).

In the forty days between his resurrection and ascension, Jesus taught the disciples about the nature of the kingdom. He reminded them about the coming of the Holy Spirit, about which he had spoken in the Olivet and Upper Room discourses (Matthew 24–25 and John 14–16, respectively). Although the disciples did not seem to understand these things during Jesus' ministry—even at the ascension itself, when they still asked, "Lord, will you at this time restore the kingdom to Israel?" (Ac 1:6)—they did when the Spirit descended at Pentecost. All of the preaching in the book of Acts reveals that the apostles were now aware of the plot and the history of their Lord leading from descent to ascent to return. His departure is as real and decisive as his incarnation, and he "will come [again] in the same way as you saw him go into heaven" (Ac 1:11)—that is, in the flesh. For now, he is absent on earth in the flesh, but he reigns in heaven while his Spirit creates for him an ever-expanding kingdom on earth. The church is born in this precarious tension between the ascension and second coming of Christ, sustained by the Spirit. The same pattern is evident in the epistles, where Christ's ascension in glory is the basis for his present intercession on our behalf at the Father's right hand (Ro 8:33–34; Eph 4; 1Jn 2:1). He reigns in power, even though for now his body suffers below. Jesus Christ is the firstfruits of the harvest (1Co 15), who will return from heaven (1Th 4:13–5:11) in judgment and salvation to fulfill the "Day of the LORD" (Ro 2:5; 1Th 5:2; cf. Heb 10:25; Jas 5:3; 2Pe 3:10).

Additional testimonies to Christ's ascension are found in Stephen's vision at his martyrdom as well as Paul's vision on his way to Damascus. United to Christ, believers have been seated with him in the heavenly places (Eph 2:6–7), and there is explicit mention of the ascension (interpreting Psalm 68:18) as the source of the gifts being poured out on the church (Eph 4:7–10). The writer to the Hebrews appeals to the ascension as part of the contrast between old and new covenant worship (Heb 7:23–26; 9:25). Whereas the Levitical priests were always standing in their liturgical service before the altar, because their work was never finished, "when Christ had offered for all time a single sacrifice for sins, he *sat down* at the right hand of God, waiting from that time until his enemies should be made a footstool for his feet" (Heb 10:11–13, emphasis added).

In his heavenly exaltation, Jesus Christ exercises all three offices. As prophet, he continues to declare both his law and his gospel, judging and absolving sinners through the frail ministry of human beings. We have been given rest in a greater land through the gospel, led by a greater prophet than Moses (Heb 3:1–19) or Joshua (4:1–12) and with a greater priest than Aaron or his descendants. "Since then we have a great high priest who has passed through the heavens, Jesus, the Son of God, let us hold fast our confession" (4:14). Chapters 8–10 argue that not only does our High Priest minister in the true sanctuary rather than in its earthly copy; he has entered with his own blood, ending the sacrificial system, and cannot have his service interrupted by his death. "He holds his priesthood permanently, because he continues forever. Consequently, he is able to save to the uttermost those who draw near to God through him, since he always lives to make intercession for them" (7:24–25). "But when Christ had offered for all time a single sacrifice for sins, he sat down at the right hand of God, waiting from that time until his enemies should be made a footstool for his feet" (10:12–13).

Therefore, Christ's priesthood does not end at the cross but continues in heaven. Believers are not only saved by Christ's work in the past; God has "raised us up with him and seated us with him in the heavenly places in Christ Jesus, so that in the coming ages he might show the immeasurable riches of his grace in kindness toward us in Christ Jesus" (Eph 2:6–7). Christ's ongoing priestly work is connected to his ascension again in chapter 4, interpreting Psalm 68:18 ("You ascended on high, leading a host of captives in your train and receiving gifts among men"):

> He who descended is the same one who ascended far above all the heavens that he might fill all things. The gifts he gave were apostles, prophets, evangelists, pastors, and teachers, to complete the saints through the work of [their] ministry, for building up the body of Christ, until all of us come to the unity of the faith and of the knowledge of the Son of God, to maturity, to the measure of the full stature of Christ. We must no longer be children, tossed to and fro and blown about by every wind of doctrine, by people's trickery, by their craftiness in deceitful scheming. But speaking the truth in love, we must grow up in every way into him who is the head, into Christ, from whom the whole body, joined and knit together by every ligament with which it is equipped, as each part is working properly, promotes the body's growth in building itself up in love. (Eph 4:10–16, author's trans.)[10]

Similarly, John assures, "But if anyone does sin, we have an advocate with the Father, Jesus Christ the righteous" (1Jn 2:1). "Who is to condemn?" Paul asks. Not only has Christ died and been raised; he "is at the right hand of God, who indeed is interceding for us," so that even in our suffering we can say that "we are more than conquerors through him who loved us" (Ro 8:34, 37). In the vision in Zechariah 3, Satan accuses and the Angel of the LORD stands in the heavenly courtroom, defending Joshua the high priest and exchanging his filthy clothes with royal garments. Now this vision is fulfilled, although with all of the saints clothed with Christ and Satan barred from access to the heavenly chamber. Through his heavenly reign, with the Spirit leading the ground war, Jesus Christ loots Satan's kingdom and sets the prisoners free.

---

10. For the rationale in the translation I have offered here (basically the same as the Authorized Version), see Andrew Lin- coln, *Ephesians* (Word Biblical Commentary 42; Dallas: Word, 1990), 253.

Jesus prepared his followers for his absence by promising "another *paraklētos*" — a defense attorney whom he will send when he ascends to the Father (Jn 14:16; cf. 1Jn 2:1). The Son has accomplished everything necessary for securing salvation, and now the Spirit is sent to apply it to his people. The exaltation of Jesus is inextricable from the descent of the Spirit: "Being therefore exalted at the right hand of God, and having received from the Father the promise of the Holy Spirit, he has poured out this that you yourselves are seeing and hearing" (Ac 2:33). Unique among all the rulers of the earth, this king reigns in order to intercede as priest. We see this again in Revelation 12:10, as the heavenly hosts sing of the defeat of the dragon: "And I heard a loud voice in heaven, saying, 'Now the salvation and the power and the kingdom of our God and the authority of his Christ have come, for the accuser of our brothers has been thrown down, who accuses them day and night before our God." It is in this intercession that believers take their assurance of never being "cut off" by God (Ro 8:31–35).

From his incarnation to his reign at the Father's right hand, Jesus is not only the Lord who became the servant, but the servant who is Lord and continues even in this exalted state to serve his Father's will and his people's good. From eternity to eternity, he offers his "Here I am" to the Father on behalf of those who have gone their own way. For now, Christ reigns in grace; when he returns in judgment and vindication, his kingdom will be consummated in everlasting glory.

III. THE SIGNIFICANCE OF THE ASCENSION

Given the place of the ascension in the New Testament (especially the Epistles), it is surprising that it plays a comparatively minor role in the faith and practice of the church. Though affirmed, it does not seem to occupy the same status as Christ's incarnation, death, and resurrection.

Douglas Farrow has sought to remedy this marginalization of the ascension in theology, seeing it as "the point of intersection in Christology, eschatology, and ecclesiology."[11] Much of twentieth-century theology has pressed a false choice between history and eschatology, but this is to misunderstand both. New Testament eschatology does not escape history, but redefines it. Farrow follows Eric Franklin's suggestion "that the ascension is used by Luke not to *abandon* eschatology for history, as the 'delay of the parousia' scholars would have it, but to bring history into the *service* of eschatology."[12] The ascension is not merely an exclamation point

---

11. R. Maddox, *The Purpose of Luke-Acts* (Edinburgh: T&T Clark, 1982), 10, quoted in Douglas Farrow, *Ascension and Ecclesia* (Edinburgh: T&T Clark, 1999), 16. I draw significantly on Farrow for my own interpretation of the ascension in *People and Place: A Covenant Ecclesiology* (Louisville: Westminster John Knox, 2008), ch. 1.

12. Ibid., 17.

to the resurrection, but a distinct event within the history of redemption. Farrow rightly contends that the conflation of resurrection and ascension "puts in jeopardy the continuity between our present world and the higher places of the new order established by God in Christ."[13]

When eschatology is treated as an alternative to history, the ascension is given a "docetic" (i.e., spiritualized) interpretation that not only separates this event from Old Testament expectations, but "eventually rebounds on the doctrine of the resurrection itself—if indeed it is not already the sign of a docetic version of that doctrine—and binds it closely to an otherworldly eschatology that has little in common with that of scripture." "Resurrection comes to mean 'going to heaven,' which in some theologies makes it rather hard to distinguish from dying!" The promise of the angels that "this [same] Jesus" will return in the flesh simultaneously affirms the *continuity* between our resurrection and Christ's and the *dis*continuity between Jesus-history and the common history of this passing age. Apart from this discontinuity, we substitute "our own story (the story of man's self-elevation) as the real kernel of salvation history in the present age."[14] In contrast to the ascent of mind, the gospel keeps us focused on the historical economy of grace: Christ's pattern of coming, going, and returning in the flesh. Nevertheless, Farrow writes,

> From Origen onwards ... much of what Irenaeus had fought for, though upheld in official doctrine, was increasingly undermined. Logos christologies of a strictly speculative kind, together with a tendency towards what may be called eschatological docetism, were prevalent even in orthodox circles. And this situation was further aggravated by the failure of the greatest post-Nicene theologian, St Augustine, to free himself from the limitations of neoplatonism and from certain features of the Origenist heritage passed on to him by Ambrose.[15]

Farrow traces this Origenist tendency all the way to the present day. Downplaying the significance of Christ's absence in the flesh, the church has sought various means of substitution: the emperor, the pope, Mary (with the infant Jesus in her lap), and an elaborate system of ecclesiastical equipment for making Christ bodily present at the ringing of a bell.

Jesus did not downplay his ascension, but comforted his disciples with the promise of the Spirit and his Word. The same point is made by Paul in Romans 10, when he says that we do not have to ascend to the heavens to bring Christ down or into the depths as if to bring him up from the dead—since he comes near to us through his Word. Only when we take seriously Christ's real absence in the flesh are we able to appreciate the significance of eschatology (our being seated with him yet not yet

---

13. Ibid., 29.
14. Ibid.

15. Ibid., 88.

seeing him face to face), pneumatology (the Spirit as the one who now mediates Christ's presence through preaching and sacrament), and ecclesiology (the church as a pilgrim community lodged precariously between the two ages). An overrealized eschatology, an underdeveloped pneumatology, and an inflated ecclesiology can easily result. When Christ's real absence in the flesh is faced, the Spirit's work of uniting us to Christ and causing us to long for his return qualifies the church's tendency to substitute itself for the glorified Lord who was born of Mary. Otherwise, the confident claim in the eucharistic liturgy, "Christ will come again," becomes easily allegorized, spiritualized, or moralized as something that happens again and again even now (whether through the Mass or through more private and nonsacramental practices). However Christ is truly present here and now through Word and Sacrament, the doctrine of the ascension keeps us longing for his return in the flesh at the end of history.

Because of the ascension, there are now two "histories": the history of this passing evil age, subject to sin and death; and that of the age to come, subject to righteousness and life. Because Jesus Christ is Lord, we are made alive by the Spirit, drawn away from our alliance with death, and made cosufferers as well as co-heirs with Jesus Christ. It is the ascension that both grounds the struggle of the church militant and guarantees that one day it will share fully in the triumph of its King.

IV. THE KING AND HIS KINGDOM

One could justifiably treat the doctrine of the church and the means of grace at this point. However, the application of redemption to believers in the *ordo salutis* ("the order of salvation," i.e., how the Spirit applies the benefits of Christ to individuals) by the Spirit creates the church. According to the *Heidelberg Catechism*, the Spirit "produces [faith] in our hearts by the preaching of the holy gospel, and confirms it through our use of the holy sacraments."[16]

A great deal happens in Acts 2. From the throne of the ascended Christ the Spirit is sent, creating and indwelling a body that will witness to Christ from Jerusalem to the ends of the earth (vv. 1–13). Its first sign is Peter's sermon, which announces that the Old Testament promises have been fulfilled in Jesus Christ's life, death, resurrection, and ascension, and in the sending of the Spirit (vv. 14–36). From this announcement a new covenant community is born. "Repent and be baptized every one of you in the name of Jesus Christ for the forgiveness of your sins, and you will receive the gift of the Holy Spirit. For the promise is for you and for

---

16. *Heidelberg Catechism*, q. 65, in *Psalter Hymnal* (Grand Rapids: CRC Publications, 1987), 889.

your children and for all who are far off, everyone whom the Lord our God calls to himself" (vv. 38–39). While individuals—"about three thousand souls"—were "cut to the heart" by this message, repented, believed, and were baptized, they were organized by the Spirit into a human community. "And they devoted themselves to the apostles' teaching and the fellowship, to the breaking of bread and the prayers" (v. 42). From this shared union with Christ, these pilgrims from faraway regions were so united with each other that the worshiping community itself was a witness to the world. "And the Lord added to their number day by day those who were being saved" (v. 47).

Though converts entered as individuals, they were added to the church. Henceforth they would be "catholic" persons: no longer mere individuals but living parts of Christ's ecclesial body. This new creation was never as fully realized even in Christ's earthly ministry as it was at Pentecost and has been ever since. The Spirit has come to apply the benefits of Christ, making all things new. Furthermore, the promise is for believers and for their children. As in its Old Testament administration, the covenant of grace includes the children of believers. Yet it also reaches outside of this community, to bring the gospel to those who are far off.

Therefore, the *ordo salutis* is inseparable from the *historia salutis* (the historical events of Christ's life, death, resurrection, and ascension, and the coming of the Spirit), and soteriology (the doctrine of salvation) is inseparable from ecclesiology (the doctrine of the church). The means by which the church became identifiably visible in this age were (and are) the same means by which the kingdom of grace conquers the hearts and lives of its heirs. As we see in Acts 2, the preaching of the gospel and the administration of the sacraments (baptism and the breaking of bread or Communion) are the means by which the ascended King creates and extends his kingdom.

The eschatological tension that we have observed in relation to personal salvation is as evident in ecclesiology. As a "mixed body," the visible church as we now know it is neither hidden under the types and shadows of the old covenant theocracy nor fully revealed as the elect spouse of Christ in glory. The kingdom of God is present in a semirealized way even now in and through the church, yet it is a more encompassing reality than the church and will be fully realized only when Christ returns.

Theologians have sought to identify this difference between the present and future states of the kingdom and the church in various ways. Familiar ever since the medieval era is the distinction between *the church militant* and *the church triumphant*. Echoing Christ's states of humiliation and exaltation, this distinction is useful up to a point; however, it refers to the generations of the church who are now alive (the church below) and those who have died in the Lord (the church above). Although it expresses an important truth, this distinction does not contribute to an eschatological understanding of the church and kingdom.

More useful in that regard is the distinction between *the kingdom of grace* and the *kingdom of glory*. Like the previous one, this distinction does not imply two different churches or kingdoms, but the two different states of Christ's realm. The status and character of Christ's kingdom are always determined by the status and character of its King. Like its Lord during his earthly ministry, at present this kingdom has a glory that lies hidden under the cross, even though its power is at work as the Spirit makes the rays of the age to come penetrate into the darkness of this present evil age. Like its gospel, the kingdom's form, means, government, and effect seem weak in the eyes of the world. It is often persecuted or simply ignored by the powers and principalities of this present age, and yet it grows precisely in and through the apparent weakness of its message and ministry. Yet one day the announcement will ring out, "'The kingdom of the world has become the kingdom of our Lord and of his Christ, and he shall reign forever and ever'" (Rev 11:15). The old covenant theocracy was merely typological of the union of cult and culture, worship and geopolitics, church and state, that will occur when Jesus Christ returns in judgment and vindication, setting all things right in the earth forever.

A. COVENANT AND KINGDOM

The kingdom of God is not a generic concept that can simply be applied in any epoch; its character is determined in every era of history by the covenant according to which it is administered. As we have seen, some of the biblical covenants are of the suzerainty type: on the basis of the victory of the suzerain (great king), the lesser king pledges entire loyalty, and if he fails to keep the stipulations imposed by the suzerain, he will fall under the sanctions of the treaty. It is a "do or die" type of covenant. We have seen that other covenants are more along the lines of a royal grant: on the basis of a previous victory, the heirs are simply beneficiaries of an inheritance. The covenant with Abraham as "the father of many nations" is clearly such a grant (Ge 15), especially as interpreted in the New Testament (cf. Ro 9:6–8; Gal 3:1–29). In contrast, the Mosaic covenant is dependent on Israel's obedience (Dt 1:34–45; 4:1–24, 26–27; 5:25–33; 6:1–3, 10–25; 7:12–26; 9:1–11:32; 26:16–19; 27:11–26; 28:1–30:20; Jos 8:30–35; chs. 23–24; Jdg 1–2; Jer 4–11; 13:15–27; 15:1–9; chs. 25–28; Ezek 10; 12–22; etc.; Jn 1:17; Ro 2:27; 4:15; 7:12; Ro 10:4; Gal 3:23–24; ch. 4; Heb 7:19).

Even when God relents in judgment or pledges to restore Israel after judgment, it is not on the basis of the Sinai covenant but because he "will not ... forget the covenant with your forefathers, which he confirmed to them by oath" (Dt 4:31 NIV)—a point that is frequently made throughout the prophets. Like the covenant servant in Eden, Israel must resist the temptation of autonomy and serve only the living God. But the prophets are sent as attorneys for the prosecution, with such ominous courtroom announcements as, "Hear the word of the LORD, O children of Israel; for the LORD has a controversy with the inhabitants of the land" (Hos 4:1). This is a *rîb*: covenant lawsuit. They bring this word of judgment, sometimes reluctantly, when the covenant is being violated or when Yahweh insists on extending the ethnic boundaries (as in the case of the prophet Jonah). Jesus also appropriates this prophetic stance, invoking covenant curses (Mt 21:18–22; Lk 11:37–54; Rev 2–3) and blessings (Mt 5:1–12; Jn 20:29; Rev 2–3).

Unlike the covenant that Israel swore at Sinai, the covenant (royal grant) that God swore to "the fathers" (Abraham, Isaac, and Jacob) is inviolable, and this unwavering faithfulness of Yahweh to his promise in spite of the faithlessness of his human partner is also expressed in the covenant with David (2Sa 7) and in the new covenant (Jer 31:31–34). In the day that God fulfills his promise, he will act unilaterally in salvation: forgiving and renewing them, to the end that "I will be their God, and they shall be my people" (Jer 31:31–33).

The Abrahamic covenant is fulfilled because Jesus (who also fulfills the conditions of the Mosaic covenant by his obedience) is the "seed" in whom all the nations are blessed. Jesus is the promised son of Abraham. The Mosaic covenant is not altered in any way; rather, it too is fulfilled by Jesus so that in Jesus the children of God may receive the inheritance on the basis of the Abrahamic covenant:

> To give a human example, brothers: even with a man-made covenant, no one annuls it or adds to it once it has been ratified. Now the promises were made to Abraham and to his offspring. It does not say, "And to offsprings," referring to many, but referring to one, "And to your offspring," who is Christ. This is what I mean: the law, which came 430 years afterward, does not annul a covenant previously ratified by God, so as to make the promise void. For if the inheritance comes by the law, it no longer comes by promise; but God gave it to Abraham by a promise. (Gal 3:15–18)

The kingdom issues chiefly in remission of sins, the new creation, and a new relation to God (fatherhood-sons), and these are all thoroughly eschatological, not abstract and static, concepts.

That he came to seek and save the lost is exactly the opposite of what the Pharisees have told the people to expect, since "the lost" are those who refuse to follow the Pharisaical regulations. Further, Jesus clearly reconstitutes "Israel" (twelve tribes/twelve apostles, etc.)—not with a replacement, but with an announcement that the one proclaimed beforehand by the law and the prophets is now here and is in his own person the Seed in whom alone we are blessed.

We have already seen how Jesus, in his Sermon on the Mount, assumes the seat of Moses and announces a regime change. Not because the old covenant was wrong but because it has fulfilled its role of leading by type and shadow to Christ, the theocratic polity is no longer in force. Deuteronomy—the constitution of the law-covenant—is no longer canonically binding for the people of God. Instead of calling down God's judgment and driving out the Gentile nations, Jesus commands us to pray for our enemies. God no longer sends plagues among the godless, but "makes his sun rise on the evil and on the good, and sends rain on the just and on the unjust," and expects us to imitate his kindness (Mt 5:43–48). This is not the time to judge our neighbors, but to take the log out of our own eye (7:1–5), to diligently seek God's good gifts (vv. 7–11), to enter through the narrow gate (vv. 13–14), and bear good fruit (vv. 15–27). In fact, when Jesus went to a Samaritan village preaching the good news, and was rejected, James and John wanted to call for fire to fall from heaven in judgment upon them. "But he turned and rebuked them. And they went on to another village" (Lk 9:51–56). Nicknamed "sons of thunder," James and John, it should be remembered, were clearly looking for a kingdom of glory all the way to the very end (Mk 10:35–45).

In covenantal terms, Jesus was announcing the arrival of the new covenant, which he would inaugurate in his own blood (Mt 26:28). The Sinai law-covenant was no longer in effect. Christ's kingdom would be, in this phase, a reign of grace. Confusing Christ's kingdom of grace with the Sinai theocracy was precisely the error that Paul addressed, especially in Galatians.

Although the expression "kingdom of heaven" is not found in the Hebrew scriptures (occurring first in the Second Temple period), the roots are clearly in the Old Testament, without which neither Jewish nor Christian messianism could have emerged. Yahweh is clearly the Great King over all the earth, and Israel is "a kingdom of priests and a holy nation" (Ex 19:6), with the Sinaitic theocracy determining all aspects of cultic and cultural life in minute detail. Only with Israel's failure to preserve its typological function in the land does the occasion arise for a theology of hope-after-exile.

This more eschatological concept of the kingdom—the expectation of a messianic ruler—emerges in the prophets (Isa 40–55; Ob 21; Mic 4:3; Zep 3:15; Zec 14:16–17). "The coming kingdom of God will be inaugurated by the great day of the Lord," Herman Ridderbos summarizes, "the day of judgment for the apostate part of Israel, as well as for the nations in general, and at the same time, however … the day of deliverance and salvation for the oppressed people of the Lord."[17] We find the expectation of a last judgment, for example, in Hosea 4:3, Isaiah 2:10–22, Amos 4:12; 5:18–20, and elsewhere. The coming day of salvation, when Yahweh himself acts in judgment and deliverance, is also mentioned throughout the prophetic writings (Hos 2:17; Mic 4:1–13; Isa 9:1–6; 11:1–10).

---

17. Herman Ridderbos, *The Coming of the Kingdom* (St. Catharines, Ont.: Paideia, 1979), 5.

The coming salvation is imperishable (Is 51:6); a supramundane reality will begin (Is 60:1ff.); a new heaven and a new earth will come into existence (Is 60:19; 65:17; 66:22); death will be annihilated (Is 25:7ff.); the dead will be raised (Is 26:19). In opposition to the eternal woe of the wicked there will come to be the eternal bliss of the redeemed (Is 66:24). Even the heathen will share the blessing with Israel (Is 25:6; 45:22; 51:4–6), with YHWH as the world's king in that day (Micah 4:1ff.).[18]

The messianic kingdom of peace is anticipated in Isaiah 9:6–7; 11:9–10; 32, and Micah 5:1. The redeemer-king will come from David's house, enthroned in majesty (2Sa 7:12–16; Ps 89:19–29; Lk 1:32–33). Jesus himself appealed to Daniel 7 for his title as Son of Man. God *is* king in status, but will one day *be* king eschatologically in all the earth.

Especially given the parody of kingship in Roman-occupied Israel, with the Second Temple period there is an intensification of messianic longing, with explicit references to the *malkût šāmayim* (*basileia tōn ouranōn*, kingdom of heavens). It entailed (a) God's sovereignty; (b) coming deliverance/vindication. A prayer in the Jewish prayer book (the Kaddish) reads,

> Glorified and sanctified be his great name in the world he has created according to his own pleasure. May he establish his royal dominion and start his deliverance of his people, and may he bring his Messiah and redeem his people in the time of your life, and in your days, and in the time of the life of the whole House of Israel, with haste and in a short time; and thou shalt say Amen.[19]

At the same time, there were diverse eschatologies on offer from various groups: some emphasize restoration of Israel (namely, *Psalms of Solomon, Testaments of the Twelve Patriarchs, Assumption of Moses*), while others are more apocalyptic and focus on supernatural-transcendent irruptions (*Apocalypse of Baruch, 4 Ezra*). According to the latter especially, "this age" is marked by disaster and oppression, while "the age to come" is marked by the appearance of Messiah and the resurrection of the dead. Among other Jewish scholars, Jon Levenson has documented the widespread association of the messianic kingdom with the resurrection of the dead and the last judgment.[20]

The New Testament announces the arrival of the kingdom of God/heaven generally: "the time is fulfilled," a "great turning-point of history."[21] The two Second Temple eschatologies are clearly in view: nationalistic-messianic and prophetic-apocalyptic; yet this schema is too tidy for the New Testament. We must not begin with any eschatological a priori but allow the New Testament itself to give us the

---

18. Ibid.

19. See ibid., 10.

20. Jon Levenson, *Resurrection and the Restoration of Israel: The Ultimate Victory of the God of Life* (New Haven: Yale Univ. Press, 2008); cf. Kevin J. Madigan and Jon Levenson, *Resurrection: The Power of God for Christians and Jews* (New Haven: Yale Univ. Press, 2008).

21. Ridderbos, *Coming of the Kingdom*, 13.

proper horizon.[22] "The coming of the kingdom is first of all the display of the divine glory, the re-assertion and maintenance of God's rights on earth in their full sense," theocentric and cosmic, not (contra Ritschl and Harnack) anthropocentric, individualistic, and limited to the moral/spiritual sphere—the "infinite value of the individual soul."[23]

Nor can the kingdom be reduced to the covenant or justification by faith, but encompasses both, as God's self-assertion over "*all*" his works."[24] This should not be surprising, since all of the covenants find their fulfillment in Jesus Christ and his kingdom. The covenant of creation provides the wider cosmic horizon, while the Sinai covenant is specific to Israel. Yet both require the successful completion of the probation by the covenant servant. The postfall promise to Adam and Eve and the Abrahamic, Davidic, and new covenants are all fulfilled in Jesus Christ's kingdom as well, inasmuch as they all represent God's immutable commitment to deliver his people through the faithful seed of the woman.

Ridderbos points out that according to the New Testament, "The kingdom of God is not a state or condition, not a society created and promoted by men (the doctrine of the 'social gospel'). It will not come through an immanent earthly evolution, nor through human moral action; it is not men who prepare it for God." Rather, it is something that humans pray and wait for, "nothing less than the great divine-break-through, the 'rending of the heavens' (Is 64:1), the commencement of the operation of the divine *dunamis* (Mk 9:1)," the revelation of God's glory (Mt 16:27; 24:30; Mk 8:38; 13:26, etc.).[25] It is a *dynamic* concept ("at hand," "comes," "is coming," "has come," etc.).[26] Yet it is a space of peace and a state of peace (Mt 8:11; Lk 14:15; Mt 26:29; 22:1–14), "an order of things in which there will be 'superiors and inferiors' (Mt 5:19; 11:11; 18:1, 4)."[27]

John the Baptist's view of the kingdom transcends the political ideal. "John calls it 'the wrath to come' (Mt 3:7), which indicates the last judgment."[28] Baptizing the outcasts—tax-collectors and prostitutes—John warns that the axe is laid at the root of the trees, and no longer can anyone claim Abraham as his or her father simply on the basis of ethnic descent (Lk 3:7–9). A great separation within Israel is coming. "Every tree therefore that does not bear good fruit is cut down and thrown into the fire" (v. 9). "I baptize you with water," said John, "but he who is mightier than I is coming, the strap of whose sandals I am not worthy to untie. He will baptize you with the Holy Spirit and with fire. His winnowing fork is in his hand, to clear his threshing floor and to gather the wheat into his barn, but the chaff he will

---

22. Ibid., 14–15.
23. Ibid., 20–21.
24. Ibid., 22–23.
25. Ibid., 24.

26. Ibid., 25.
27. Ibid., 26.
28. Ibid., 29.

burn with unquenchable fire" (vv. 16–17). Israel's remnant saved, the will be rest judged along with the world. "Salvation and perdition are the two stages into which the tremendous future will diverge according to the prophecies: first the descent of the Holy Spirit, and then the day of judgment (cf. Joel 2:28–32; Ezek. 36:26–31; Zec 12:9–10)."[29]

Identifying the kingdom of God with his own role as the Son of Man, Jesus' own view, then, was in line with the prophetic-apocalyptic concept rather than the nationalistic. In the Beatitudes, notes Ridderbos, "Jesus describes the bliss of the kingdom of heaven as the inheritance of the [new] earth, as being filled with the divine righteousness, as the seeing of God, as the manifestation of the children of God, all of these expressions pointing beyond the order of this world to the state of bliss and perfection that shall be revealed in the future."[30] Right now, it exists in heaven, but we pray even now for it to come to earth (Mt 6:10). "The coming of the kingdom is the consummation of history, not in the sense of the end of the natural development, but in that of the fulfillment of the time appointed for it by God (Mk 1:15); and of what must happen before it." Thus it is not only a vertical intrusion (*übergeschichtliche*) but an event in time (*endgeschichtliche*). "This is why the practical-existential meaning of the preaching of the coming kingdom is not only expressed by the categories of 'conversion,' 'decision' [*Entscheidung*], but no less also those of 'patience,' 'perseverance,' 'vigilance' and 'faithfulness.' "[31] In Oscar Cullmann's words (contra Bultmann), "It is not *a new time* that has been created with Christ, but *a new division of time*."[32]

B. THE KINGDOM AND ESCHATOLOGY

In his study of the covenant theology in the Epistle to the Hebrews, Geerhardus Vos explains that the new covenant is to the writer of Hebrews as limitless as the old was provisional: "It is the ocean into which all the rivers of history roll their waters from the beginning of the world."[33] It is not merely something on the horizontal line of history: either linear progress or "futurity," but an exchatological irruption from above. Heaven (the age to come) breaks into history (this present age). "The New Covenant, then, coincides with the age to come; it brings the good things to come; it is incorporated into the eschatological scheme of thought."[34] While for Paul, "this age" represents sin and death (flesh) and "age to come" represents righteousness and life (Spirit), for Hebrews these two ages represent two covenants: the old and the new.[35]

29. Ibid., 30.
30. Ibid., 44.
31. Ibid., 44.
32. Oscar Cullman, as quoted in ibid., 45.

33. Geerhardus Vos, *The Teaching of the Epistle to the Hebrews* (repr., Eugene, Ore.: Wipf & Stock, 1998), 194.
34. Ibid., 195.
35. Ibid., 196.

> From thinking of the eschatological state as future, the Christian mind is led to conceive of it as actually present but situated in a higher sphere [semieschatological]. The horizontal, dramatic way of thinking gives place in part to a process of thought moving in a perpendicular direction and distinguishing not so much between before and after, but rather between higher and lower.[36]

Therefore, the kingdom is "from above," created by the powers of the age to come; it is an eschatological in-breaking rather than an immanent historical progress drawn from the resources of this present age. It is not a kingdom that we are building but a kingdom that we are receiving; therefore, unlike all other kingdoms (including Israel), it cannot be shaken (Heb 12:25–29).

Conditioned as it was on Israel's faithfulness, the theocratic kingdom was shakable, as the exile—and the destruction of the temple—testified. However, the kingdom that has been inaugurated in Christ's death and resurrection is inviolable. It has come, is coming, and will one day come in all of its fullness. The contrast between "shadows" and "substance" in Paul (Col 2:17) and between "earthly" and "heavenly" in Hebrews (see especially Heb 8:5; 9:1–14; 10:1) is not one of falsehood (the realm of appearances) and eternal truth, but of promise and fulfillment, types and antitype.[37] In Hebrews 7:3, it is said not that Christ was made like unto Melchizedek, "but, on the contrary, Melchizedek was made like unto the Son of God." The same is said of the Sabbath.[38] Vos coins the suggestive term "prelibations" for the semieschatological existence of Israel in the theocratic land.[39] The future itself has no more possibilities for a new creation than the past or the present; the kingdom must come down from heaven—it must be the work of the triune God—in order to secure everlasting peace.

The challenge for us in this age is to avoid both *underrealized* and *overrealized* eschatologies of the kingdom. According to dispensationalism, covenantal history is marked by failure. Even when the Messiah came and offered the kingdom to Israel, they rejected it—and, since it was offered only to the Jewish nation, this meant that God had to postpone its arrival. Right now, the kingdom is not present; it will appear at Christ's second coming. "The kingdom, however, will also be a period of failure."[40] Thus, even in this future millennial kingdom the purpose is not only to dispense Christ's gifts, which he has already won by his own trial, but "is the final form of moral testing."[41] At the other extreme are various views that tend to see Christ's present reign as encompassing the blessings that he has promised to bring only at his return. Such views fail to distinguish between the kingdom in its present

---

36. Ibid., 198.
37. Ibid., 201.
38. Ibid., 202.
39. Ibid., 203.

40. Lewis Sperry Chafer, *Major Bible Doctrines* (rev. by John Walvoord; Grand Rapids: Zondervan, 1974), 136.
41. Ibid.

manifestation as a reign of grace and in its future manifestation in power and glory at Christ's return. (I treat these millennial views more fully in the final section of this volume.)

The New Testament proclamation of the kingdom shares with liberation theology a holistic conception of redemption. Not only souls but bodies, not only individuals but the whole creation, will be liberated from its bondage. As Joyce Murray points out, for liberation theologian Gustavo Gutiérrez, "liberation that truly saves the individual and society is 'integral'; it involves all dimensions of human experience. It is a society that makes all people one family."[42] However, in Scripture this final liberation is credited to the resurrection of the body at the end of the age when Christ returns in glory (Ro 8:18–25). This also means that, for now, the society that Christ's reign is creating is completely distinct from the secular societies, nations, and ethnic groups to which we also belong in our temporal citizenship. Unlike the old covenant society, with its civil laws, a godly commonwealth has no divine blueprint except for the instructions Christ and his apostles gave to the church for its faith and practice.

As difficult as it is to hold both simultaneously, the New Testament eschatology indicates that the kingdom of Christ is present now but not yet in its consummated form. We just spoke of the kingdom as a present ("already") reality (Mk 1:15; Mt 11:5–6; 12:28; 13:1–46; Lk 11:5–6, 20; 17:20–23; 15:4–32), but also as something "not yet," belonging to the future (Mt 6:10; 16:28; Mk 9:1; Lk 6:20–26; 9:27; 11:2; 13:28–29). The kingdom is coming, but also has come (Mt 12:28–29; Lk 11:20). The strong man is bound. "At the same time," Ridderbos observes, "it appears that the victory over Satan to be gained by the kingdom of God is not only a matter of *power*, but first and foremost one of *obedience* on the part of the Messiah."[43] The manner in which the demons respond to Jesus shows his authority over them, but not just a raw power: it is his coming in his kingdom that they fear most. Now is the time, the end of their kingdom. The kingdom comes with words and deeds. In the miracles, it is said that Satan has bound these people (Lk 13:11, 16). Christ is breaking into Satan's territory, setting history toward a different goal, bound to his own rather than to demonic powers.

In Luke 16:16, redemptive history is divided between the time of the law and the prophets and the time of the kingdom. Ridderbos writes,

> Here the dispensation of the law and the prophets is opposed to the preaching of the gospel of the kingdom of God. In other words, in the preaching of the gospel has been realized that which was only an expectation in the law and the prophets.

---

42. Joyce Murray, "Liberation for Communion in the Soteriology of Gustavo Gutiérrez," *Theological Studies* 59, no. 1 (March 1998): 53.

43. Ridderbos, *Coming of the Kingdom*, 62.

This is why Jesus can call the disciples blessed not only for what they see, but also for what they hear. In this respect they were favored above the OT believers even in their most important representatives (Mt 13:16–17; Lk 10:23–24). The preaching of the gospel is no less a proof than the miracles that the kingdom of heaven has come.[44]

Jesus is not just preaching a promise, but in his preaching inaugurates its fulfillment: "His word is not only a sign, it is charged with power.... For the new and unprecedented thing here is not that forgiveness is being *announced*, but that it is being *accomplished on earth*."[45] His Word brings the kingdom with it, and that kingdom is founded in his blood. Thus, only as prophet and priest is Jesus Christ also the king.

Throughout Jesus' preaching there is the recurring "must." Jesus is driven along by the Spirit. "The whole of the gospel of the kingdom must also be qualified as the gospel of the cross," since this is the whole mode of his messianic consciousness.[46] "The whole structure of the gospel preached by Jesus is determined by the idea of the covenant." In fact, his words of institution ("the blood of the new covenant") show that his whole life and death are to be seen in this light.[47]

There are clear signs of his kingdom in the healing of the sick (even the dead), the blind, the deaf, and the demon-possessed, and in the ingathering of the outcasts for the wedding feast, redrawing the true Israel around himself. Yet the greatest sign of the kingdom was his forgiveness of sins, which he offered in his own person rather than through the temple. The signs in the prophetic era were not only of salvation (Isa 35:5–10; 61:1–2) but of judgment (Isa 61:2; Mal 3:1–4), and the same was true of Jesus.

According to some biblical scholars, the kingdom theme disappears in the rest of the New Testament because Jesus failed to actually bring in the kingdom that he promised and the church had to transform his expectation of an imminent, apocalyptic arrival of the kingdom into a spiritualized notion of life after death. For example, Adolf von Harnack suggested that Paul distorted the message of the kingdom, shifting the focus from God to Jesus. However, we should note that the term "kingdom" is not necessary for the concept to be present. Paul's message is the description of that kingdom reality: Peter's confession (Mt 16:16–23) and the mission that leads to Jerusalem (cross and resurrection). It was this gospel of the kingdom that Peter and the other apostles proclaimed immediately after Jesus' ascension (Ac 2:14–36; 3:12–16; 17:2–3). And this is also the heart of Paul's message (1Co 15:3–4).

44. Ibid., 71.
45. Ibid., 73–74.
46. Ibid., 164.
47. Ibid., 200.

Whether one views Jesus' mission as a success or failure and therefore the preaching of the apostles (including Paul) as consistent with that of Jesus depends in large measure on the kind of kingdom that one assumes as essential to Jesus' own expectations. If his own conception of the kingdom was simply that held by many of his contemporaries (including his disciples), he would not have gone to Jerusalem to suffer, die, and be raised. He would not have rebuked Peter repeatedly for misinterpreting their road to Jerusalem as leading to something other than the cross, and he would not have told James and John (assisted by their mother's pleas) that their enthronement on his right and left hands would mean their own crucifixion rather than glory, or have rebuked them for wanting to execute heavenly judgment on the Samaritan village that rejected their preaching. Rather, his march to Jerusalem with his disciples would have been for the purpose of cleansing the land of Gentile profanation, driving out the Romans and the outcasts, and restoring the temple worship.

To the very end, there is no indication that his kingdom, at least in its present manifestation, will take the form that his contemporaries are expecting. Jesus warns his followers not to seek the kingdom in its present phase as a renewal of the old covenant theocracy. In fact, he lifts the "eye for an eye" principle of judgment on Israel's enemies and announces that in this epoch God's common grace restrains his judgment, sending rain upon the just and the unjust alike (Mt 5:44–45). In the present era, it is a kingdom of grace rather than of power and glory. It is the reprieve for repentance and faith in Israel and throughout all nations before the coming Day of the LORD. "Being asked by the Pharisees when the kingdom of God would come, [Jesus] answered them, 'The kingdom of God is not coming with signs to be observed, nor will they say, 'Look, here it is!' or 'There!' for behold, the kingdom of God is in the midst of you" (Lk 17:20–21). It is a new creation at work in the world, a new covenant yielding new relationships with God and with each other based on forgiveness and fellowship rather than on judgment and exclusion.

In Matthew 24 Jesus prepares his followers for persecution after his death and resurrection and predicts the destruction of the temple, as well as nations rising up against each other. Yet "all these are but the beginning of the birth pains" (Mt 24:8). In fact, "this gospel of the kingdom will be proclaimed throughout the whole world as a testimony to all nations, and then the end will come" (v. 14). After these trials, "Then will appear in heaven the sign of the Son of Man, and then all the tribes of the earth will mourn, and they will see 'the Son of Man coming on the clouds of heaven' [Da 7:13] with power and great glory. And he will send out his angels with a loud trumpet call, and they will gather his elect from the four winds, from one end of heaven to the other" (vv. 30–31). Only then will the Son of Man gather the nations for the last courtroom trial that ends in a final separation—not of Jew from Gentile in Palestine but of believers and unbelievers, for "eternal punishment" and "eternal life" (Mt 25:31–46).

Jesus inaugurated the kingdom that Paul and the other apostles proclaimed. It is not a kingdom that arises from any place or program on earth, but descends from heaven. Wherever the King is present, his kingdom is present also. Yet he was present in weakness and humility, for us and for our salvation. When he comes in glory, his kingdom will be glorious in power and might. Paul, too, teaches that the new creation/kingdom has been inaugurated in Christ's conquest: the righteousness of God has been revealed from heaven (Ro 1:16–17), including justification of sinners and new birth, the Spirit and his gifts poured out (Ro 5:5). In Matthew 28:18, the climax is that all kingdom authority is in Christ's hands, which Paul also emphasizes (Ro 1:3–4; Eph 1:18–22; Php 2:9–11; Col 1:15–20). Jesus Christ is already now "heir of all things" (Heb 1:1–4). We turn now to the spoils of Christ's triumph that are poured out by his Spirit upon people "from every tribe and language and people and nation," being made into "a kingdom and priests to our God" (Rev 5:9–10).

DISCUSSION QUESTIONS

1. In what sense was Christ exalted even at the cross?
2. What is the relationship between the resurrection and Christ's royal office?
3. Discuss the significance of the ascension in the New Testament and in the history of theology. Is this an important doctrine—and if so, why?
4. What is the connection between the ascension and the new creation, whose consummation we are awaiting?
5. What is the character of Christ's present reign, especially in relation to the past (old covenant theocracy) and the future (consummation)?

Part Five

GOD
WHO REIGNS
IN GRACE

Chapter Seventeen

CALLED TO BE SAINTS: CHRIST'S PRESENCE IN THE SPIRIT

Christ's threefold office, we have seen, continues in the present even though he has ascended. In fact, it is Christ's ascension that both secures our salvation before the throne of God and dispenses it on earth in the power of the Spirit working through the proclamation of Christ. After summarizing the person and work of the Holy Spirit and his descent at Pentecost, this chapter begins the treatment of the Spirit's application of redemption.

I. THE SPIRIT OF PROMISE

As expressed in a traditional formula, the external works of the Trinity are undivided (*opera trinitatis ad extra sunt indivisa*), yet each person contributes distinctively to every work. We have already seen that the Spirit is the effectual agent behind every word spoken by the Father in the Son.

A. THE HOLY SPIRIT IN CREATION AND HISTORY

The opening sentences of the Bible report, "In the beginning, God created the heavens and the earth. The earth was without form and void, and darkness was over the face of the deep. *And the Spirit of God was hovering over the face of the waters*" (Ge 1:1–2, emphasis added). In the flood narrative in chapter 8, we encounter the first instance of the Spirit appearing as a dove, announcing the appearance of dry land (Ge 8:8–12), but earlier in this chapter it is said, "And God made a wind [*rûaḥ*] blow over the earth, and the waters subsided" (v. 1b). Given the parallelism with the creation account (of waters being divided for human habitation), there is no good reason not to translate *rûaḥ* "Spirit" rather than "wind" in 8:1b. The exodus narrative (Ex 14) also invokes this creation imagery with the Spirit descending, hovering over the waters, and separating them in order for dry land to appear, then leading the redeemed host by pillar and cloud to the Sabbath rest.[1] The Spirit also descends over, upon, and within the tabernacle and then the temple, as well as resting upon the prophets for their unique mission.

As we have seen, Jesus' self-consciousness as the Servant of the LORD prophesied by Isaiah was inseparable from the endowment of the Spirit. After quoting Isaiah 61:1–2 ("The Spirit of the Lord GOD is upon me, because the LORD has anointed me to bring good news to the poor"), Jesus announces, "Today this Scripture has been fulfilled in your hearing" (Lk 4:18–21). His conception was attributed to the Spirit as well. When Mary asked, "How will this be, since I am a virgin?" the angel answered, "The Holy Spirit will come upon you, and the power of the Most High will overshadow you; therefore the child to be born will be called holy—the Son of God" (Lk 1:34–35). In Matthew's Gospel, before the engagement and conjugal union of Mary and Joseph, Mary "was found to be with child from the Holy Spirit" (Mt 1:18).

After his baptism by John, Jesus, "full of the Holy Spirit,... was led by the Spirit in the wilderness for forty days, being tempted by the devil" (Lk 4:1–2a; cf. Mt 4:1), recapitulating Adam's temptation and Israel's forty years in the wilderness. Jesus performs his miracles by the Spirit—in fact, to attribute them to Satan is to "[blaspheme] against the Holy Spirit" (Mk 3:28–30; Lk 12:10). Jesus also bestows the Spirit on his disciples (Jn 20:22). In Ezekiel 1, the momentous event of the Spirit's descent is represented by the sound of winged creatures in a moving cloud, a scene that is repeated throughout Ezekiel and will return at Pentecost with the erection of the end-time sanctuary "made without hands" that Ezekiel prophesied (see also 2Co 5:1; Heb 13; Rev 21:2).

To the Spirit particularly is attributed the dignity of transforming created space into covenantal place: a home for communion between Creator and creatures, extending to the ends of the earth in waves of kingdom labor. In the prophets, the Spirit is associated with a glory-cloud (Isa 63:11–14; Hag 2:5) and divine wind or breath—*rûaḥ*, the same Hebrew word for spirit/the Spirit (Ps 104:1–3). It is, in

---

1. M. G. Kline, *Images of the Spirit* (S. Hamilton, Mass.: self-published, 1986), 14–15.

fact, by this Spirit that all things are created and renewed (v. 30). The presence of the Spirit always signals the arrival of God's kingdom in judgment and salvation.

The Spirit, like the Son, is the archetypal image of God, as we have seen. As such, the Spirit shares the glory of the Father and the Son, which human beings reflect analogically. Yet there is one more parallel between the Spirit and human image-bearers: namely, the role of *witness*.[2] The Spirit's witness involves judgment as well as salvation (Ge 3:8).[3] It is by the Spirit that the incarnate Son was conceived, clothed in our flesh, and upheld during his earthly ministry. And it is this same Spirit who clothed Jesus Christ with eschatological glory in the resurrection and both witnesses to Christ and clothes us with Christ, empowering us as his witnesses.[4]

The Creator Spirit is, even in the very beginning, a divine witness to the goal of creation: namely, the consummation.[5] Thwarted by Adam in the first creation, this goal is finally achieved by the Last Adam in the new creation, but he accomplishes this as our representative by constant dependence on the Spirit. *The age to come is Christ's to win; it is the Father's to give and it is the Spirit's to actually bring into the present, even in the midst of this present evil age.* No wonder, then, that the outpouring of the Spirit is identified with the "last days" and the age to come. The Spirit comes from the consummated future of Sabbath glory, like the dove that brought Noah a leafy twig in its beak as a harbinger of new life beyond the waters of judgment. Already in creation, therefore, we meet the Spirit of promise: the one who propels creation toward its goal, which is nothing less than the consummation at the end of the trial. This interpretation of the relationship between the Spirit of Glory and judgment is especially supported by 2 Corinthians 3 and 4. In Christ, the veil that prevents us from seeing the glory of God in the face of Christ (2Co 4:6) is now removed (2Co 3–6).

The Spirit who clothed Christ in our flesh and in consummated glory now clothes us with Christ. In all of these various ways, the appeal is to the old covenant history of royal investiture that begins in Eden, with the Spirit's in-breathing, followed by all of the priestly imagery of glorious temple vestments and the event of Christ breathing on his disciples. "When the investiture figure is used," writes Meredith Kline, "what is 'put on' is the new man created in the image of God (Eph 4:24; Col 3:10), or Christ the Lord (Ro 13:14; Gal 3:27; cf. Eph 2:15; 4:13), or the resurrection glory of immortality (1Co 15:53; 2Co 5:2ff.).... In the vocabulary of

---

2. See M. G. Kline, "The Holy Spirit as Covenant Witness" (ThM diss., Westminster Theological Seminary, 1972).

3. God came "in the cool of the day" is a less likely rendering than "in the Spirit of the day." Although *rûah* can be variously translated as "wind" or "spirit," the sense (especially in the obvious context of judgment) seems to favor the Spirit coming in the day of judgment. See M. G. Kline, *Images of the Spirit*, ch. 4; cf. Kline, *Kingdom Prologue: Genesis Foundations for a Covenantal Worldview* (Overland Park, Kans.: Two Age Press, 2000), 128–29.

4. Kline, *Images of the Spirit*, 16.

5. Ibid., 20.

Peter, 'partakers of the divine nature' expresses renewal in the image of God (2Pe 1:4)."[6] Believers are now, in Christ, "the image and glory of God" (1Co 11:7).

The Spirit evacuated the earthly temple, exiling Judah to Babylon, and now the Spirit returns to fill his temple. However, this time, it is the eschatological end-time temple: Christ and his "living stones." Throughout the history of revelation, it is the Spirit who turns a house into a home. In Genesis 2:7, the creation of humankind climaxes with the in-breathing of the Spirit, causing Adam to become "a living creature." This is echoed again in the revitalization of the Spirit in Ezekiel 37, as well as in Mary's annunciation (Lk 1:35). Jesus breathed on the disciples, issuing the performative utterance, "Receive the Holy Spirit" (Jn 20:22), and now at Pentecost the Spirit takes up residence in his end-time sanctuary: the people of God. The external witness of the Father and the Spirit to the Son were sufficient authority. Echoing the original creation, the Father and the Spirit issue their heavenly benediction on Jesus in his baptism (Mk 1:11), repeated by the Father at the Transfiguration (Mk 9:7), testifying from heaven. Nevertheless, since the hearers are "dead in the trespasses and sins" (Eph 2:1), there must be an inner work of the Spirit to bring about conviction and trust in Jesus Christ. Even after spending three years at Jesus' side, the disciples' understanding of, much less testimony to, Christ's person and work depended on the descent of another witness from heaven: the Holy Spirit. In the last recorded words before the ascension in Luke's Gospel Jesus tells them, "You are witnesses of these things. And behold, I am sending the promise of my Father upon you. But stay in the city until you are clothed with power from on high" (Lk 24:48–49). The Spirit brings about within us the "Amen!" of faith to all that Christ has accomplished. In the cosmic courtroom, the Spirit is the archetypal Cloud of Witnesses whose animating agency creates an ectypal cloud of witnesses.

We recognize this close connection between the Spirit and judgment in Peter's Pentecost sermon, where he announces the fulfillment of Joel's prophecy, which itself is unmistakably judicial in character (and dependent on Nu 11:1–12:8, in which a weary Moses longs for the day when all the people are filled with the Spirit [Nu 11:29]). As Raymond Dillard comments,

> Both contexts also reflect a judicial function in the possession of the Spirit. The seventy elders are to be Moses' surrogates and to serve as judges (Num 11:17; cf. Exod 18:13–27); in Joel, the eschatological outpouring of prophetic enduement is conjoined with the Lord's coming in judgment on the nations [Joel 2:31: 3:12]. Multitudes come not to *make* a decision, but to *hear* the decision of God [3:14; emphasis added].[7]

---

6. Ibid., 29.

7. Raymond B. Dillard, "Intrabiblical Exegesis and the Effusion of the Spirit in Joel," in *Creator Redeemer, Consummator*: *A Festschrift for Meredith G. Kline* (ed. Howard Griffith and John R. Muether; Greenville, S.C.: Reformed Academic Press, 2000), 90.

Pentecost inaugurates the day of reckoning—not the final day of judgment, but its prolepsis, as Israel and the nations are gathered to be judged and justified in these last days before the last day in which only judgment will prevail.

B. THE SPIRIT AT PENTECOST

Acts 1 marks the transition from the ascension to Pentecost. Jesus ordered the disciples to remain in Jerusalem "for the promise of the Father": the baptism with the Holy Spirit "not many days from now" (Ac 1:1–5). About 120 people were gathered in the upper room, near the temple, where pilgrims had gathered for the feast from far-flung regions.

> When the day of Pentecost arrived, they were all together in one place. And suddenly there came from heaven a sound like a mighty rushing wind, and it filled the entire house where they were sitting. And divided tongues as of fire appeared to them and rested on each one of them. And they were all filled with the Holy Spirit and began to speak in other tongues as the Spirit gave them utterance. (Ac 2:1–4)

Astonished that uneducated Galileans were proclaiming the gospel in their own languages, the visitors were provoked to reactions ranging from "amazed and perplexed" to outright incredulity: "They are filled with new wine" (vv. 12–13).

Just as the Spirit's presence in Christ's ministry was identified with his proclamation of the gospel (Isa 61:1–2; Lk 4:18–21), the consequence of the Spirit's descent at Pentecost was not unrestrained pandemonium but the public proclamation of the gospel by Peter, with the other apostles standing at his side (Ac 2:14–36). The one who had cowardly denied Christ three times was now risking his life for the message that the one who had been crucified a short distance from there had been raised, was at God's right hand, and would return to judge the earth. Stringing together a series of citations from the prophets and the Psalter, Peter proclaimed Christ and this remarkable descent of the Spirit as the fulfillment of everything the Scriptures had foretold. "Cut to the heart," three thousand people embraced Peter's message and were baptized (vv. 37–41). The Spirit was accomplishing inwardly the perlocutionary effect of the illocutionary speech publicly proclaimed by Peter [see ch. 1, "Revelation Is a Speech Act," pp. 117–22]. The disciples having been united to the true and faithful witness in heaven and empowered by the indwelling Spirit as witnesses, the rest of Acts can be summarized by the theme, "The word of God spread."

When we refuse to collapse the resurrection, ascension, and parousia into one event, a pneumatological space appears for the time between the times. The Spirit is the mediator of, not the surrogate for, Christ's person and work. The redeeming work of Christ lies behind us, but the perlocutionary effect of that Word is at work in "these last days." With the Father, the Spirit gave the Son to sinners in the incarnation (cf. "conceived by the Holy Spirit" in the Apostles' Creed), and in the Upper Room Discourse (Jn 14–16) Jesus promised that when he ascended he would give the Spirit. We are the beneficiaries of this intratrinitarian exchange of gifts.

C. THE SPIRIT'S ONGOING MINISTRY: FULFILLING CHRIST'S PLEDGE IN THE UPPER ROOM DISCOURSE (JOHN 14—16)

The Father spoke in the Son to create the world, and yet it was the Spirit who brought about within the unformed cosmos and thus created that ordered realm of which they spoke. Even in common grace, as Calvin noted, wherever goodness, truth, and beauty flourish in this fallen world, it is because the Spirit grants wisdom, health, and other benefits that we do not deserve.[8] Thus, even in the old creation the Spirit is at work, holding up the columns of the earthly city while bringing the heavenly Jerusalem into this age.

In the new creation, the Spirit inwardly convicts us of God's judgment and convinces us of God's mercies in Christ. Jesus' discourse in the upper room recorded in John 14–16 highlights the way in which the Spirit will mediate (and now mediates) Christ's prophetic, priestly, and kingly reign. Christ now reigns over us in exalted grace and glory, and by his Spirit he also reigns within us, bringing us from death to life, answering the triune Creator, "Here I am."

First of all, the Spirit's ongoing ministry is judicial. The Spirit is sent not only to announce the coming judgment, but to "convict the world concerning sin and righteousness and judgment," with unbelief in Christ as the focus of that conviction (Jn 16:8). We see the empirical effects of this promise in Peter's Pentecost sermon — which characterizes the spread of the gospel throughout Acts — when the apostle's hearers were "cut to the heart, and said to Peter and the rest of the apostles, 'Brothers, what shall we do?'" (Ac 2:37). The Spirit will not speak another word, but will inwardly renew, convicting and persuading us of our guilt and Christ's righteousness.

Second, as the Son is the sole embodiment of all truth, the Spirit will be sent "to guide you into all the truth" (Jn 16:13). The Father speaks and the Son is the content (Word) that he speaks, both hypostatically (eternal begetting) and energetically (the gospel). It is always the Spirit's role, we have seen, to bring about the perlocutionary effect of that speech within creatures. The Spirit is not the content, but the regenerating source of faith in Christ. The Son did not speak on his own authority

---

8. Calvin, *Institutes* 2.2.15.

during his earthly ministry, but delivered the word of his Father. In the same way, Jesus explained to his disciples that the Spirit "will not speak on his own authority, but whatever he hears he will speak, and he will declare to you the things that are to come" (Jn 16:13). The Spirit does not replace Jesus, but unites us to our heavenly head. Disrupting our ordinary history, the Spirit inserts us into the new creation.[9]

Thus, the Spirit is not a resource that we can use, but is no less than the sovereign God who claims us for himself along with the Father and the Son. In the upper room, Jesus teaches that the Spirit will come not to confirm our pious experience or to help us to realize the ethical kingdom, but to convict the world of guilt and righteousness and judgment. Of course, the Spirit's coming has its profound effects in our experience and ethical action, but the focus of his work is to convince us of our guilt and of Christ's imputed righteousness and to lead us into all truth as it is in Christ. Although the Spirit preaches Christ rather than himself, Jesus Christ's personal history must be for us a distant and fading memory, except for the Spirit's work of ushering us into the courtroom where even now Christ pleads on behalf of his witnesses on earth and prepares a place for them.

Yet this means conflict, not conquest. "Witness" in the New Testament is a translation of the Greek word *martys*, from which we get "martyr." The church militant is that part of the world that has been seized by the Spirit, freely answering its "amen" to Christ that contradicts the "No!" of the powers of this present age. Neither defeated nor quite yet triumphant, the church militant is a suffering witness to the truth as it is in Christ.[10] This "in-between" space is a precarious place for the church, which is why it often prefers to imagine itself as reigning in glory like its ascended Head. In fact, when, just before ascending, the resurrected Jesus told his disciples to go to the upper room and wait for the Spirit's baptism, they replied, "Will you at this time restore the kingdom to Israel?" (Ac 1:4–6).

Yet for now the church must be content to be assembled like the disciples in the upper room, recognizing Jesus in the Word and the breaking of bread, and filled with the Spirit to proclaim the gospel to the ends of the earth. In between Pentecost and parousia, the Spirit brings inward conviction of guilt and forgiveness, by making sinners hearers of the Word. Indeed, the Spirit himself is a hearer of the Word. As the missionary of the Trinity, the Spirit will speak "whatever he hears" (Jn 16:13). Indwelled and empowered by the Spirit, the church has not only the external Word of the prophets and the apostles, but the inward confirmation of that testimony by

---

9. Douglas Farrow, *Ascension and Ecclesia* (Edinburgh: T&T Clark, 1999), 257.

10. It is customary to invoke the distinction between the *church militant* and the *church triumphant* as referring to the saints living on earth now and those in heaven. However, in Rev 6:10, the souls of the martyrs cry out, "How long before you will judge and avenge our blood on those who dwell on the earth?" Even though these souls are in the presence of God, they too are part of the church militant. Only when Christ returns with his saints to the earth at the final resurrection and judgment will the *whole* church be finally and forever triumphant with its head.

the one who is of the same essence as the Father and the Son. The one by whom the Word was conceived in the flesh is the source and the interpreter of the word concerning him. And he will tell the truth not only about the past (what God *has* done in Christ), but about the future (what God *will do* in Christ): "and he will declare to you the things that are to come" (Jn 16:13). Although the Spirit works within us, it is with the intention of drawing us outside of ourselves to focus on this economy of grace. The Spirit is an extrovert, always going forth on missions with his Word, creating an extroverted community who can at last look up to God in faith and out to the world in love, witness, and service. And, as Jesus teaches in John 16, the same Spirit who led Christ to his destiny—through the cross to the resurrection—also leads us in Christ's train.

It is significant that the first evidence of the Spirit's descent at Pentecost is Peter's proclamation of Christ as the fulfillment of God's promises through the prophets. In this discourse, Reinhard Hütter wisely reminds us, the Spirit's leading "into all the truth" is not a vague sentiment about a supposedly direct and immediate "inspiration of Spirit into individual religious consciousnesses, but in the form of concrete church practices which as such are to be understood as the gifts of the Spirit in the service of God's economy of salvation."[11] The Spirit causes us to recognize Jesus Christ as the Savior and Lord in proclamation and in the breaking of bread, as he did the disciples in Luke 24. And he leads the church into all truth through these creaturely means of baptism, teaching, Communion, and the spiritual and material care of elders and deacons. Most directly, Christ's promise was made to the apostles, who would be guided by the Spirit to communicate inspired truth to the new covenant community.

Third, Jesus says concerning the Spirit, "He will glorify me" (Jn 16:14). This surely denotes the point of the Spirit's testimony, just as vv. 14b and 15 underscore this mutuality (*perichōrēsis*) between the Son and the Spirit in the covenant of redemption: the Spirit and the Son share a common treasure, a treasure that they together with the Father intend to share also in common with us. This comes to fullest expression perhaps in Jesus' prayer in chapter 17. Jesus has glorified the Father, and now the Father and the Spirit glorify the Son. The Son is the content (the illocutionary act), but the Spirit brings all of God's words to pass and makes them fruitful (perlocutionary effect).

So Jesus comforts his disciples, assuring them that his real absence from them (and us) on earth is not a deficit but a continuation of his threefold ministry: only now in heaven itself. "In my Father's house there are many rooms. If it were not so, would I have told you that I go to prepare a place for you? And if I go and prepare

---

11. Reinhard Hütter, *Suffering Divine Things: Theology as Church Practice* (Grand Rapids: Eerdmans, 2000), 127.

a place for you, I will come again and will take you to myself, that where I am you may be also" (Jn 14:2–3). However, Jesus' departure opens up a fissure in history, into which the Spirit enters in order to create a covenantal body for Christ. "I will not leave you as orphans," says Jesus, but "I will ask the Father, and he will give you another Helper, to be with you forever"—"the Spirit of truth" (Jn 14:16–18). Jesus Christ indwells believers and the church, but by his Spirit, not immediately in the flesh (2Co 1:22; cf. Ro 8:17, 26; 1Co 3:16; Gal 4:6; Eph 5:18). For this immediate presence nothing short of Christ's bodily return is required. Because of the ascension, the church on earth is not triumphant and must wait for the bodily return of its head in the future for the renewal of all things.

The disciples may have seen Jesus Christ in the flesh, but we see him in the Spirit through the proclamation that they were authorized by Christ and endowed by his Spirit to deliver to us. Although they walked and ate with him, the disciples did not recognize him as their redeemer until the Spirit opened their eyes (Mt 16:17). From the perspective of this present age, the career of their Master ended in defeat. Yet after Pentecost, the disciples came to recognize him as the firstfruits of the age to come. It is the Spirit who causes us to recognize the Jesus of history as the Christ of faith (2Co 5:16–17). The ecclesial body is inseparably united to Christ, but for now it exists at a different place in redemptive history than its glorified head. It is Jesus Christ who has secured our ultimate glorification together with him, and it is the Spirit who keeps drawing our personal history into Christ's. So we are even now seated "with [Christ] in the heavenly places" (Eph 2:6). The Father speaks the liturgy of grace, while the Son is himself its embodiment, and the Spirit then works in "the sons of disobedience" to create a choir of antiphonal response that answers with its appropriate "Amen" behind its glorified forerunner (2Co 1:19–22). "He who has prepared us for this very thing"—immortality—"is God, who has given us the Spirit as a guarantee" (2Co 5:5).

With the descent of the Spirit, we are now in the last days. The clock is running down on this present evil age. The gates of hell will not be able to prevail against the church. The outpouring of the Spirit will guarantee a believing community in "these last days," one that not only remembers Christ's completed work, but is actually inserted into the covenantal history (and eschatology) of its glorified head. In fact, as Paul teaches, the Spirit is not only sent *among* believers but *into* them, to indwell them, as a deposit (*arrabōn*) of their final redemption. It is precisely because we "have the firstfruits of the Spirit" that "we ourselves groan ... inwardly as we wait for adoption as sons, the redemption of our bodies" (Ro 8:23; cf. Gal 4:6). As the *arrabōn* (down payment) of our final redemption, the Spirit gives us the "already" of our participation in Christ as the new creation, and it is the Spirit within us who gives us the aching hope for the "not yet" that awaits us in our union with Christ (Ro 8:18–28; cf. 2Co 1:22; 5:5; Eph 1:14). Although it keeps us from despair, the presence of the Spirit does not lead to triumphalism. In fact, the paradox is that the *more we receive* from the Spirit of the realities of the age to come, the *more restless we become.* Yet it is a restlessness born not of fear but of having already received a foretaste of the future.

From John 14–16 we also see that the Spirit brings about the perlocutionary effect of the threefold office of Christ in these last days. The Spirit mediates Christ's *prophetic* ministry by prosecuting God's case against the world, convicting us of guilt, and giving us faith in Christ. Thus, the Triune God is not only the speaker and the Word spoken, but in the ministry of the Spirit is also the one who enables us to hear and receive that Word. As Barth famously put it, "The Lord of speech is also the Lord of our hearing."[12]

The Spirit also mediates Christ's *priestly* ministry, as "another Paraclete" (attorney), not by replacing Christ but by inwardly convicting us of sin, giving us faith in Christ, and assuring us of forgiveness. In this discourse, Jesus emphasizes that he is the content of the Spirit's teaching ministry (Jn 15:26b). The Spirit does not bring another Word, but brings about within us the "amen" to Christ.

The Spirit mediates Christ's *royal* ministry by subduing unbelief and the tyranny of sin, giving sinners the faith that unites them to Christ so that they can receive all of his heavenly gifts. The ascended Christ gives, and the Spirit equips ministers and elders as his undershepherds (Eph 4:11–16). Through this ministry of the Spirit, Moses' request in Numbers 11:29 ("Would that all the LORD's people were prophets, that the LORD would put his Spirit on them!") will be fulfilled beyond his wildest dreams. Not only the seventy elders, but the whole camp of Israel is made a Spirit-filled community of witnesses. The Spirit gives and orchestrates the many gifts bestowed on the whole body through the ministry of the ordained office-bearers, who differ only in the *graces* (vocation), not in the *grace* (ontic status) of the Spirit. Thus, the mission of the twelve in Luke 9:1–6 widens to the seventy in chapter 10. Yet this was but a prelude to the commissioning ceremony of Pentecost. Through the Spirit's ministry, we too are remade in Christ's likeness as prophets, priests, and kings: true and faithful witnesses in the cosmic courtroom, a choir answering antiphonally in praise to our Redeemer.

1. ELECTION AND EFFECTUAL CALLING

Despite its brevity, the preceding account reminds us that the focus of the Spirit's work is not simply individual hearts. Cosmic in scope, salvation in both Old and New Testaments encompasses nothing short of a renewal of the whole earth. Nevertheless, Scripture does not present us with a choice between the per-

---

12. Barth, *Church Dogmatics*, vol. 1, pt. 1, p. 182.

sonal and cosmic dimensions of the new creation. Anticipating the transition now to the *ordo salutis* (logical order of the application of redemption to individuals), the same point may be made by saying that the question as to how individuals are saved is not inimical but integral to the question as to what God is doing in the world in these last days. The new creation is not first of all the new birth of individuals, but the dawn of the age to come in this present age. Individuals are swept into it by the Spirit. Nevertheless, the renewal of all things begins with the Spirit's regeneration of sinners, effectually calling them into union with the Son, through the faith that the Spirit gives through the preaching of the gospel. The first sign of the renewal of these latter days is the Spirit's act of raising those who are spiritually dead to life in Christ. Only when Christ returns to consummate his kingdom will this renewal characterize the whole earth and human community to the fullest extent.

Paul himself can define the gospel in terms of the history of salvation (*historia salutis*), as in Romans 1:1–6, and in terms of the logical chain of individual participation in that history (*ordo salutis*), as in Romans 8:29–30. Following well-established precedent, I will use the latter as the basic outline for treating the order of salvation: "Those whom he predestined he also called, and those whom he called he also justified, and those whom he justified he also glorified." In the remainder of this chapter I will take up election and calling.

2. THE STATE OF THE CONTROVERSY

According to Pelagius and his disciples, every human being is born in the same state as Adam before the fall, free to choose good and gain eternal life or sin and eternal death.[13] Led especially by Augustine, the church condemned Pelagianism in no uncertain terms. From a common Augustinian heritage, many Roman Catholic as well as Protestant theologians have affirmed that God's grace precedes all human decision and effort. In fact, the fifth-century Second Council of Orange in 529 condemned the Semi-Pelagian view that God gives his grace in response to human decision and effort.[14] However, especially in its subtler (Semi-Pelagian) form, this type of teaching remained intractable throughout church history, proving the adage that Pelagianism is the natural religion of humanity. According to Semi-Pelagianism, human beings are affected by sin but can still choose the good and, in the common formulation of the late medieval period, "God will not deny his grace to those who do what lies within them" (repeated substantially in Benjamin Franklin's famous adage, "God helps those who help themselves"). Nevertheless, a

---

13. See B. R. Rees, *Pelagius: Life and Letters* (London: Boydell Press, 2004); *Pelagius's Commentary on St. Paul's Epistle to the Romans* (trans. Theodore De Bruyn; Oxford Early Christian Studies; Oxford: Oxford Univ. Press, 1998).

14. See *Creeds of the Churches* (ed. John H. Leith; 3rd ed.; Louisville: Westminster John Knox, 1982), 37–44.

strain of Augustinian teaching persisted throughout this era and formed much of the positive influence on Martin Luther and the other Reformers.[15]

Within Protestantism, however, consistent Augustinianism was challenged by various groups, most notably, the Arminians. Arising from within the Dutch Reformed Church, the followers of Jacob Arminius issued their *Five Points of the Remonstrants* in 1610: (1) God's election of sinners is conditional (based on foreseen faith); (2) Christ died to make salvation possible for every person; (3) all human beings are born in sin and therefore incapable of being saved apart from grace; (4) this grace is offered to all and may be resisted; (5) it is possible for regenerate believers to lose their salvation. Arminianism soon divided into two trajectories: a more liberal version that became increasingly drawn toward Pelagian/Socinian convictions, and an evangelical Arminianism represented by Arminius himself and by later figures such as Richard Baxter and John Wesley.

At the Synod of Dort (1618–1619), with the representation of various Reformed bodies throughout the Continent as well as the Church of England and the Church of Scotland, Arminianism was carefully analyzed and refuted. The *Canons of Dort*, to which we will return, locate unbelief in the total inability of sinners to effect their own liberation from the bondage of the will, and they locate faith in the unconditional election, redemption, and effectual calling of the triune God alone. God gives not only *sufficient grace* (that is, enough grace to enable sinners to respond positively to God if they choose to do so), but *efficient grace* (that is, regeneration as well as faith and repentance as gifts).

Eastern Orthodoxy and Roman Catholicism identify effectual calling (or regeneration) with baptism — though with different formulations. Largely removed from the Western controversy between Augustine and Pelagius, the East nevertheless teaches an *ordo salutis* that is similar to that of Arminianism, with "preparatory grace and means sufficient for the attainment of happiness" given to all.[16] "In the exposition of the faith by the Eastern Patriarchs, it is said, 'As [God] foresaw that some would use well their free will, but others ill, he accordingly predestined the former to glory, while the latter he condemned.'"[17]

For Rome, baptism infuses a new habit or disposition into the soul, negatively, washing away original sin and (in the case of adults) actual sins up to that point, and

---

15. Gregory of Rimini (1300–1358) and Archbishop Thomas Bradwardine (1290–1344) are especially notable in this regard. See also a tract by Luther's mentor and the head of the Augustinian Order in Germany, Johann von Staupitz, "On the Eternal Predestination of God," in *Forerunners of the Reformation: The Shape of Late Medieval Thought* (by Heiko A. Oberman; London: James Clarke, 2003). Staupitz affirms all of the points (known popularly as the "five points of Calvinism") that would be defended at the Synod of Dort, including

the maxim that Christ's death is sufficient for the world, efficient for the elect only. Luther included all of these emphases in his *Commentary on Romans* (Grand Rapids: Kregel, 1982), esp. 126–30, 141–42.

16. *The Longer Catechism of the Orthodox, Catholic, Eastern Church*, Q. 123, in *The Greek and Latin Creeds* (ed. Philip Schaff; vol. 2 of *The Creeds of Christendom*; New York: Harper and Brothers, 1905, 1919).

17. Ibid., Q. 125.

positively, strengthening the soul to cooperate with grace. This baptismal regeneration is called the "first justification" and is said to be followed by an increase in inherent holiness through cooperation with grace, with the ultimate hope of attaining to final justification through grace and merit.[18] At any stage along the way, this justification (as an infused habit) may be lost, but there is in most cases the possibility of renewing one's beginning in justification through the sacrament of penance.[19]

Confessional Lutheranism also ties regeneration closely to the moment of baptism, but clearly distinguishes justification (a declaration of righteousness) from sanctification (an actual transformation in the moral life of the baptized). Imputation, not infusion, is the Lutheran (as well as Reformed) understanding of justification. In the Lutheran view, new life (*regeneratio prima*) is begun in baptism but is constantly renewed throughout the Christian life (*regeneratio secunda* or *renovatio*). Although the principle of new life is given in baptism, the flowering of this new birth occurs through the preaching of the gospel. Since Lutherans do not distinguish (as the Reformed do) between external calling and inward or effectual calling, they regard this ministry of the Spirit as effectual except in the case of those who willfully resist it. Confessional Lutheranism teaches total depravity and unconditional election while also holding to God's universal grace (*gratis universalis*). Accordingly, all of the elect will believe and persevere, but others who have been regenerated and justified may lose their salvation.[20] Free will "does nothing" in preparing for, cooperating with, or completing God's gracious work of calling sinners to himself; in fact, the Lutheran confessions regard this as the essence of works righteousness.[21]

With Lutheranism, the confessions of the Reformed and Presbyterian churches teach that human beings are conceived in sin, spiritually dead in relation to God, unable to prepare themselves for grace because their will is in bondage to sin. These traditions are agreed also in their confessional affirmation of unconditional election. However, the Reformed are distinguished by their belief that all of those for whom Christ died will be effectually called by the Spirit and preserved in faith until the end. The following summary explicates this view.

---

18. *Catechism of the Catholic Church* (Liguori, Mo.: Liguori Publications, 1994), 321–25.

19. Ibid., 363–69.

20. Edmund Schlink, *Theology of the Lutheran Confessions* (trans. Paul F. Koehneke and Herbert J. A. Bouman; Philadelphia: Fortress, 1961): "Embraced by God's election and act at the beginning and at the end, the believer is completely secure.... According to A. C. [Augsburg Confession] V, the Holy Spirit works faith 'when and where he pleases' ('ubi et quando visum est Deo')," which is "to be understood in a predestinarian sense even though it speaks only of God's volition and not of his non-

volition" (289). The *Formula of Concord* (art. 11) rejects conditional election (i.e., based on foreseen faith) but also rejects reprobation (election to judgment). Luther taught reprobation as well as election in *The Bondage of the Will* (as did the earlier Melanchthon) but related it to the hidden God (*deus absconditus*) rather than to the God who is revealed in Christ (*deus revelatus*). Lutheran theology typically reconciles the apparent contradiction of unconditional election and universal grace by appealing to this distinction.

21. Schlink, *Theology of the Lutheran Confessions*, 90.

3. EFFECTUAL CALLING AND THE BONDAGE OF THE WILL

Our will can choose only that in which our nature delights. If our nature is in bondage to unbelief, then our will is not free with respect to God. Jesus knew why some did not believe: "No one can come to me unless the Father who sent me draws him. And I will raise him up on the last day.... This is why I told you that no one can come to me unless it is granted him by the Father" (Jn 6:44, 65). This is why Jesus told Nicodemus that one cannot even "see the kingdom of God" without being "born again [*or* from above]" (Jn 3:3). As the conversation unfolds, it becomes clear that Jesus is not telling Nicodemus how he can bring about his new birth but how the Spirit accomplishes it. Jesus explains, "The wind blows where it wishes, and you hear its sound, but you do not know where it comes from or where it goes. So it is with everyone who is born of the Spirit" (v. 8). The new birth is a mysterious work of the Spirit in his sovereign freedom, not an event that we ourselves can bring about, any more than our natural birth.[22] Two chapters earlier, we read, "But to all who did receive him, who believed in his name, he gave the right to become children of God, who were born, not of blood nor of the will of the flesh nor of the will of man, but of God" (Jn 1:12–13).

By nature, we "by [our] unrighteousness suppress the truth" (Ro 1:18). It is not that we are ignorant, but that we willfully reject, distort, and deny even that which we know about God from creation (vv. 20–32). Paul asks his fellow Jews, "Are we Jews any better off? No, not at all. For we have already charged that all, both Jews and Greeks, are under sin, as it is written: 'None is righteous, no, not one; no one understands; no one seeks for God ...'" (3:9–11). The fallen mind is darkened to the gospel apart from the Spirit's gift of faith (1Co 2:14). Believers "were dead in the trespasses and sins in which [they] once walked.... But God, being rich in mercy, because of the great love with which he loved us, *even when we were dead* in our trespasses, *made us alive* together with Christ ..." (Eph 2:1–2, 4–5, emphasis added). Even faith belongs to the gift that is freely given to us by God's grace (vv. 5–9). We are saved *for* works, not *by* works (v. 10). Therefore, salvation "depends not on human will or exertion, but on God, who has mercy" (Ro 9:16).

In our fallen condition, we try to justify ourselves by assuming that while we

---

22. Reflecting Arminian presuppositions, much of contemporary evangelicalism understands the new birth as something that is in our power (at least partially) to effect. Especially in its American expression, this form of synergism (cooperative regeneration) is combined with a pragmatic and almost technical apparatus of formulas for being born again. For example, this can be seen even in the title of a best-selling book by Billy Graham from the 1970s, *How to Be Born Again* (Nashville: Nelson, 1977, 1989); cf. Billy Graham, *The Holy Spirit: Activat-* *ing God's Power in Your Life* (Nashville: Nelson, 1978, 1988, 2000). Shaped by the Keswick "Higher Life" movement, this broad stream of contemporary evangelical piety tends to treat the Spirit's person and work as a resource that we can access, activate, and manage through various steps and techniques. For a critique of this view see especially B. B. Warfield, *Studies in Perfectionism* (Phillipsburg, N.J.: P&R, 1958); J. I. Packer, *Keep in Step with the Spirit* (Old Tappan, N.J.: Revell, 1987), 146–63.

may commit sins from time to time, we are basically good "deep down." At least our hearts are right. However, Scripture challenges this perspective. Jeremiah lamented, "The heart is deceitful above all things, and desperately sick; who can understand it?" (Jer 17:9). The Sinai covenant required Israel to circumcise its own heart (Dt 10:16), but the command could not effect any change. Even in this constitution of the Sinai covenant itself, God looks ahead to Israel's disobedience and the new covenant in which he will circumcise their heart and the heart of their children (Dt 30:1 – 10). This is more clearly prophesied in Jeremiah 31, where God's circumcision of the hearts of his people will be based on his forgiveness and grace alone. God's commands — even the command to repent and believe — cannot change hearts so that they can obey them. Through the law the Spirit inwardly convicts, but only the gospel — the announcement of Christ's saving person and work — can absolve us and give us a new heart. Jesus, too, emphasized that wickedness is not first of all perverse actions, but a fountainhead of perversity in the heart, from which these acts spring (Mt 12:34). We cannot change our own heart by an act of will or by changing our behavior.

Most Arminians will agree that we cannot make the slightest move toward God apart from his grace. It is a caricature to suggest that Arminianism (at least the evangelical variety) denies original sin and the fallenness of human beings in heart, mind, and will.[23] Nevertheless, Arminians generally hold that God provides sufficient grace to all unbelievers so that they may be regenerated if they fulfill certain conditions. According to H. Orton Wiley, "The Holy Spirit exerts His regenerating power only on certain conditions, that is, on the conditions of repentance and faith."[24] To Calvinist ears, this sounds like demanding that a blind person see before he or she has been healed of blindness. The glory of the new covenant is that God gives in the gospel what he demands in his law: both justification and the renewal of heart and life. Only because of God's one-sided act of regeneration does anyone repent and believe.

4. EFFECTUAL CALLING AND ELECTION

Jesus said, "You did not choose me, but I chose you and appointed you that you should go and bear fruit and that your fruit should abide ..." (Jn 15:16). In the New Testament, the new birth and the presence of the Spirit in our hearts are harbingers

---

23. Roger Olson offers a helpful distinction between evangelical and rationalistic Arminianism ("Arminianism of the heart" and "Arminianism of the head," respectively) in *Arminian Theology: Myths and Reality* (Downers Grove, Ill.: InterVarsity Press, 2006). He quotes John Mark Hicks's comparison and contrast of Arminius and Philip Limborch in this respect: "For Arminius man is deprived of the actual ability to will the good, but for Limborch man is only deprived of the knowledge which

informs the intellect, but the will is fully capable within itself, if it is informed by the intellect, to will and perform anything good" (quoted on p. 57). Olson comments that at least indirectly, "Limborch's interpretation of the effects of original sin is very similar to Charles Finney's..." (57).

24. H. Orton Wiley, *Christian Theology* (Kansas City, Mo.: Beacon Hill, 1941), 2:419.

of the age to come. In some remarkable sense, the future consummation has already penetrated this evil age, so that even now it is beginning to make all things new from the inside out. This is God's work.

Chosen in Christ before the creation of the world, redeemed by Christ in history, receiving an inheritance in Christ, and being sealed in Christ by the gospel, we are being saved from start to finish by the work of the Father, in the Son, through the Spirit (Eph 1:3–14). In fact, in Romans 8 it is this realization of God's gracious election, calling, justification, and glorification (vv. 29–30) that leads Paul to the summit of doxology, first in verses 31–39, and then again finally in 11:33–36. All of this means that the gospel is not an experience that we have, much less one that we can bring about. It is an announcement that creates faith in the Redeemer who makes it. It comes to us from the outside. It *creates* new experiences and inner transformation that yields good works, but the gospel itself—and the Spirit's effectual calling through that gospel—remains the source of everything that is done by us or within us. The gospel is God's life-giving word, creating a new world out of nothing (Ro 4:16–17; 1Pe 1:23, 25).

Those whom God chose before the creation of the world, he also calls in due time by his Spirit (Eph 1:4–15). The connection between election and calling is well attested, both within the Pauline corpus (Ro 9:6–24; Eph 1:4–13; 2Th 2:13–15; 2Ti 1:9) and elsewhere (Jn 6:29, 37, 44, 63–64; 15:16, 19; Ac 13:48; 1Pe 1:2; 2Pe 1:10), and both election and calling proceed as the execution of an eternal covenant of redemption within the context of a historical covenant of grace. In effectual calling, the Spirit unites us here and now to the Christ who redeemed us in the past.

We see Jeremiah's prophecy fulfilled throughout the book of Acts: as Christ is proclaimed, people respond in repentance and faith. As the businesswoman Lydia heard Paul's message, "the Lord opened her heart to pay attention to what was said by Paul," and she and her household were baptized (Ac 16:14–15). The accused become the justified and then witnesses in the courtroom. When the Gentiles in Antioch heard the gospel, "they began rejoicing and glorifying the word of the Lord; and as many as were appointed to eternal life believed" (Ac 13:48). Far from inhibiting evangelism, God's electing and regenerating grace ensured that "the word of the Lord was spreading throughout the whole region" (v. 49). Left to ourselves, none of us would receive this Word. God's sovereign grace guarantees the success of evangelism and missions.

5. EFFECTUAL CALLING AND THE QUESTION OF COERCION

Reformed theology understands the divine call in terms of an *outward call*, by which God summons the whole world to Christ through the preaching of the gospel, and an inward or *effectual call*, as the Spirit illumines our hearts and gives us faith through the gospel. Yet it is crucial to recognize that, according to this view, the internal (effectual) calling of the elect occurs through the external call of the same gospel that is announced externally to everyone.[25] The Father preaches, the Son is preached, and the Spirit is the "inner preacher" who illumines the understanding and inclines the will to receive him.

Although the relationship between union with Christ and the means of grace (preaching and sacrament) will be explored later, it is important to add here that the Spirit delivers the gift of faith through the preaching of the gospel and confirms and strengthens it through the sacraments.[26] Yet some are attracted to the light, others repelled by it. Those who do come to trust in Christ are represented as having been "dead in … sins" (Eph 2:1–5), unable to respond until God graciously grants them the gift of faith to freely embrace what they would otherwise reject (Jn 1:13; 3:7; 6:44; Ac 13:48; 16:14; 18:10; Ro 9:15–16; 1Co 2:14; Eph 2:1–5; 2Ti 1:9–10; 2:10, 19). The gospel is proclaimed to everyone as a universal invitation, but the Spirit supervenes upon this external call by drawing sinners inwardly to Christ. Traditionally, Reformed theology has referred to the latter, then, as effectual calling rather than irresistible grace. However, the latter term became more widespread as the "I" in popular presentations, with the advent of the famous "TULIP" acronym. "Irresistible" suggests coercion, the sort of causal impact that is exercised when force is applied to someone or something. As we will see, this idea of coercion is excluded from the classic Reformed formulations.

We encounter again that useful distinction between *natural* and *moral* ability from our discussion of original sin (see ch. 13, "Natural and Moral Ability," pp. 431–34). In Adam, we freely choose our alliance with sin and death. The fall has not destroyed our natural ability to reason, observe, experience, and judge, but our moral ability to reason, observe, experience, and judge our way to God as our Lord and Redeemer. It is our moral blindness to God's Word that keeps us from raising our eyes to heaven to say, "God, be merciful to me, a sinner!" (Lk 18:13). The problem is not the *power* to will and to do, but the *moral* determination of that willing and doing by slavery to sinful autonomy. The will is moved by the mind and affections; it cannot act in isolation. "For the word of the cross is folly to those who are perishing, but to us who are being saved it is the power of God" (1Co 1:18).

---

25. The Reformed theologian Johann Heinrich Heidegger (1633–1698), for example, writes, "The word is the same which man preaches and which the Spirit writes on the heart. There is strictly one calling, but its cause and medium is twofold: instrumental, man preaching the word outwardly; principal, the Holy Spirit writing it inwardly in the heart." Quoted in Heinrich Heppe, *Reformed Dogmatics* (ed. Ernst Bizer; trans. G. T. Thomson; London: Allen & Unwin, 1950), 518. Heidegger adds, "The first effect of calling is regeneration" (518).

26. See, for instance, *Heidelberg Catechism*, q. 65: "It is by faith alone that we share in Christ and all his blessings: where then does that faith come from? A. The Holy Spirit produces it in our hearts by the preaching of the holy gospel, and confirms it through our use of the holy sacraments" (*Ecumenical Creeds and Reformed Confessions* [Grand Rapids: CRC Publications, 1988], 41).

The *Second Helvetic Confession* teaches, "Therefore, in regard to evil or sin, man is not forced by God or by the devil but does evil by his own free will, and in this respect he has a most free will." In "heavenly things," he is bound in sin. "Yet in regard to earthly things, fallen man is not entirely lacking in understanding." While passive in this initial regeneration, those who are regenerated work actively in good works. "For they are moved by God that they may do themselves what they do.... The Manichaeans robbed man of all activity and made him like a stone or a block of wood.... Moreover, no one denies that in external things both the regenerate and the unregenerate enjoy free will," as in deciding whether to leave the house or remain at home. However, with respect to salvation, their will is bound by sin until God graciously acts.[27]

More precisely, the *Westminster Confession* states, "God hath endued the will of man with that natural liberty that it is neither forced, nor by any absolute necessity of nature determined to good or evil." Before the fall, the will was entirely free to choose good or evil, but after the fall, humanity "has wholly lost all ability of will to any spiritual good accompanying salvation," rendering every person "dead in sin ... not able, by his own strength, to convert himself, or to prepare himself thereunto."

When God converts a sinner and translates him into the state of grace, he frees him from his natural bondage under sin and, by his grace alone, enables him freely to will and to do that which is spiritually good, yet in such a way that, by reason of his remaining corruption, he does not perfectly or only will that which is good, but does also that which is evil. The will of man is made perfectly and immutably free to good alone in the state of glory only.[28]

Such statements reflect a basic Augustinian consensus, filtered through the Reformation. The Westminster divines add that God is pleased "in his appointed and accepted time, effectually to call, by his Word and Spirit," all of the elect "out of that state of sin and death in which they are by nature, to grace and salvation by Jesus Christ." He accomplishes this by "enlightening their minds, ... taking away their heart of stone, ... renewing their wills, ... and effectually drawing them to Jesus Christ; *yet so as they come most freely, being made willing by his grace*" (emphasis added).[29]

The Synod of Dort affirmed that God's inward calling always meets with success. However, just as the fall "did not abolish the nature of the human race" but "distorted" it and led to spiritual death, "so also this divine grace of regeneration does not act in people as if they were blocks and stones; nor does it abolish the will and its properties or coerce a reluctant will by force, but spiritually revives,

27. *Second Helvetic Confession*, ch. 9 ("Free Will"), in *The Book of Confessions* (Louisville: PCUSA General Assembly, 1991).

28. *Westminster Confession of Faith*, ch. 9.
29. Ibid., ch. 10 ("Effectual Calling").

heals, reforms, and—*in a manner at once pleasing and powerful*—bends it back" (emphasis added).[30] The will is liberated, not violated. "If it be compelled," says John Owen, "it is destroyed."[31] The classic terminology of effectual calling (rather than the more recent term, "irresistible grace") already indicates a more communicative model of divine action than causal grammars imply.[32]

Employing the traditional Aristotelian categories, Reformed theologians affirmed that the Holy Spirit is the *efficient cause* of regeneration. While I agree with this point, I share Kevin Vanhoozer's appreciation for speech act theory as a conceptual resource that is actually more congenial to the position that Calvinists wish to defend.[33] Throughout this volume we have seen that every external operation of the Godhead is done by the Father in the Son and through the Spirit. This way of thinking, as I have already indicated, is hardly innovative: for example, as Calvin expressed it (echoing the Cappadocians), "To the Father is attributed the beginning of activity, and the fountain and wellspring of all things; to the Son, wisdom, counsel, and the ordered disposition of all things; but to the Spirit is assigned the power and efficacy of that activity."[34]

When Jesus commands, "Lazarus, come out" (Jn 11:43), Vanhoozer observes, his speech "literally wakes the dead":

> Only God, of course, has the right to say certain things, such as "I declare you righteous."... Is the grace that changes one's heart a matter of energy or information? I believe it is both, and speech act theory lets us see how. God's call is effectual precisely in bringing about a certain kind of understanding in and through the Word. The Word that summons has both propositional content (matter) and illocutionary force (energy).[35]

In this scheme, the parallels between creation and redemption to which Scripture makes frequent allusion are more apparent. "The effectual call thus provides the vital clue as to how God interacts with the human world. In my opinion, the Reformers were right to stress the connection between God's Word and God's work of grace.... Perhaps the most adequate way to view the God-world relation is in terms of *advent*."[36] The Spirit's work is not a matter of overcoming estrangement (confusing the Holy Spirit with our inner self), but of meeting a stranger who comes to us from outside of ourselves. The very term, *effectual calling*, highlights that this is a *communicative* event.

30. *Canons of Dort* (1618–1619), in *Ecumenical Creeds and Reformed Confessions*, 135–36.

31. John Owen, *The Works of John Owen* (ed. William H. Gould; Edinburgh: Banner of Truth Trust, 1965), 3:319.

32. For further elaboration of the following argument see Michael Horton, *Covenant and Salvation: Union with Christ* (Louisville: Westminster John Knox, 2007), 216–42.

33. Kevin J. Vanhoozer, "Effectual Call or Causal Effect? Summons, Sovereignty and Supervenient Grace," in Vanhoozer, *First Theology: God, Scripture and Hermeneutics* (Downers Grove, Ill.: InterVarsity Press, 2002), 96–124.

34. Calvin, *Institutes* 1.13.18.

35. Vanhoozer, "Effectual Call or Causal Effect?" 118.

36. Ibid., 119.

Vanhoozer refers to the case of the conversion of Lydia, for example, in Acts 16:14 ("The Lord opened her heart to pay attention to what was said by Paul"): a communicative act changes her heart.[37]

> Yes, God "bends and determines" the will, but even the seventeenth-century theologians knew that God "moves the will to attend to the proof, truth and goodness of the word announced" [*Canons of Dort*]. Divine communicative action is thus of a wholly different sort from instrumental action, the kind of action appropriate if one were working on wood or stone. God's work of grace is congruous with human nature. Jesus immediately qualifies his statement "No one can come to me unless the Father ... draws him" with a quote from Isaiah 54:13: "And they shall all be taught by God." On this he provides the following gloss: "Every one who has heard and learned from the Father comes to me" (Jn 6:44–45). The Father's drawing, in other words, is not causal but communicative. The Word itself has a kind of force. One might say, then, with regard to grace, that the *message* is the medium.[38]

God's Word is not, therefore, only the speech of the Father concerning the Son, which we then make effective by our own decision, but the action through which the Spirit brings about within us the corresponding response. It is a *performative* Word. In effectual calling, the Spirit draws us into the world that the Word not only *describes* but *brings into existence*. Through this Word, the Spirit not only works to propose, lure, invite, and attract, but actually kills and makes alive, sweeping sinners from their identity "in Adam" to the riches of their inheritance in Christ. Spectators become participants in the unfolding drama.

It is particularly when *God* is the dramatist, in command of both the plot (redemption) and the casting (effectual calling), that we can conclude that in this case at least, the "new creation" is simultaneously effective and uncoerced.[39] Ezekiel's vision of the valley of dry bones (Eze 37) provides a striking example. So indeed does God's original fiat in creation and the resurrection of Christ, to which both Scripture and the Reformed confessions appeal in describing this remarkable work of grace.

"Persuasion" is too weak a term to express this analogical connection. God did not *persuade* creation into being or lure Christ from the dead, but summoned and it was so, despite all the odds. At the same time, one can hardly think of these acts of creation and resurrection as *coerced*. As the "minister of the Word" par excellence, the Spirit applies "both the propositional content and the illocutionary force of the gospel in such a way as to bring about perlocutionary effects: effects that in this case include regeneration, understanding and union with Christ," says Vanhoozer. "Not for noth-

---

37. Ibid.

38. Heinrich Heppe, *Reformed Dogmatics*, 520, quoted in Vanhoozer, "Effectual Call or Causal Effect?" 120.

39. For this reason, anthropomorphic theologies (such as Moltmann's) actually end up deepening the causal scheme, as

if God (or each divine person) is a humanlike subject acting on or in relation to another. God's omniscience, omnipresence, wisdom, eternity, immutability, and aseity, as well as trinity, ensure that his omnipotence is *not* like the overpowering of one person by another.

ing, then, does Paul describe the Word of God as the 'sword of the Spirit' (Eph 6:17). It is not simply the impartation of information nor the transfer of mechanical energy but the impact of a total speech act (the message together with its communicative power) that is required for the summons to be efficacious."[40] Rather than say that the Spirit *supervenes* on the preached gospel (since regeneration is not always given with it), Vanhoozer prefers to say that the Spirit *advenes* on it, "when and where God wills," to make it effective.[41] God is not merely trying to talk us into believing in Christ. Despite its glorious content, the gospel would still be foolishness unless the Spirit replaced our heart of stone with a heart of flesh. *Yet it is by talking that the Spirit changes our hearts.*

Communication does not work like brute causes, but it also is not mere information or exhortation. Scripture already assumes a communicative approach. "The Word of God is living and active ..." (Heb 4:12). We are reminded in Isaiah 55:10–11,

> For as the rain and the snow come down from heaven
>   and do not return there but water the earth,
> making it bring forth and sprout,
>   giving seed to the sower and bread to the eater,
> so shall my word be that goes out from my mouth;
>   it shall not return to me empty,
> but it shall accomplish that which I purpose,
>   and shall succeed in the thing for which I sent it.

God's speech not only reaches its addressee, but because the Spirit is always already present in creation to bring that speech to fruition, its illocutionary stances, which are always deployed in a covenantal context (commands, promises, curses, blessings, etc.), actually bring about the reality they announce.

Christ is not only promised; he *is* the promise. "For all the promises of God find their Yes in him. That is why it is through him that we utter our Amen to God for his glory" (2Co 1:20). Christ as the Father's illocutionary act restores the liturgical exchange that the fall has turned into a disordered Babel of confusion and discord. The natural creation still manages to utter its liturgical lines even under the curse (Ps 19:1–2), but the divine image-bearer sings Walt Whitman's "Song of Myself." Yet once the ones who "by their unrighteousness suppress the truth" (Ro 1:18) are swept into the story that God is telling the world, they find themselves "born again, not of perishable seed but of imperishable, through the living and abiding word of God.... This word is the good news that was preached to you" (1Pe 1:23, 25b). And, "According to his great mercy, he has caused us to be born again to a living hope through the resurrection of Jesus Christ from the dead, to an inheritance that is imperishable, undefiled, and unfading, kept in heaven for you, who by God's power are being guarded through faith for a salvation ready to be revealed in the last time" (1Pe1:3–5).

---

40. Vanhoozer, "Effectual Call or Causal Effect?" 121.   41. Ibid., 122.

More like being overwhelmed by beauty than by force, the call is effectual because of its *content*, not because of an exercise of absolute power independent of it. And yet the appropriate "amen" cannot be attributed to the recipient, since it is the Father's communication of the Son and the Spirit's effective agency within the natural processes of even truth-suppressing consciousness that bring it about.

6. REGENERATION AS EFFECTUAL CALLING

The gospel is not simply the good news concerning Christ, but Christ's own declaration to sinners of that reality of which the gospel speaks. Christ himself declares his absolution to the ungodly through the lips of his messengers (Ro 10:8–17). Election makes salvation certain, and Christ's redeeming work secures it. Nevertheless, when the Spirit grants the gift of faith in Christ through the proclamation of the gospel, all of Christ's riches are actually bestowed. Whether or not one is conscious of this moment, it is the effectual calling of God the Spirit, and it brings justification and renewal of the whole person in its wake. After explaining that believers have been chosen in Christ before the creation of the world and redeemed by Christ, Paul adds, "In him you also, when you heard the word of truth, the gospel of your salvation, and believed in him, were sealed with the promised Holy Spirit, who is the guarantee of our inheritance until we acquire possession of it, to the praise of his glory" (Eph 1:13–14). Faith is not something that we must contribute in order to make the gospel effective; it is itself given to us through the gospel that is proclaimed. God does not ordinarily work directly, but uses means. Although the gospel is proclaimed to every person (an external call), the Spirit draws the elect to Christ inwardly (the effectual call). The gospel is freely announced to all people and to every person indiscriminately, although only the elect embrace it through the Spirit's effectual call.

The question at least among the Reformed is whether the effectual call is synonymous with regeneration or whether regeneration is a distinct and logically antecedent work of the Spirit. Earlier in the tradition the terms *regeneration* and *effectual calling* were used interchangeably. Regeneration (or effectual calling) is the Spirit's sovereign work of raising those who are spiritually dead to life in Christ through the announcement of the gospel.[42] Later, especially after extensive interaction with Arminianism, many Reformed theologians argued for regeneration as God's act

---

42. A standard way of putting this earlier view is stated by Herman Witsius: "Regeneration is that supernatural act of God whereby a new and divine life is infused into the elect person, spiritually dead, and that *from incorruptible seed of the word of God, made fruitful by the infinite power of the Spirit*" (emphasis added) (Herman Witsius, *The Economy of the Covenants* [trans. William Crookshank; 2 vols.; London: Edwards Dilly, 1763; lithographed from 1822 ed., Phillipsburg, N.J.: The den Dulk Christian Foundation/P&R Publishing, 1990]), 357. In this,

Witsius is simply following the *Canons of Dort* (chs. 3–4), which is consistent with the assumption of the *Westminster Confession* (10.2) that regeneration and effectual calling are one and the same event. Similarly, q. 65 of the *Heidelberg Catechism* teaches that the Spirit creates faith "in our hearts by the preaching of the holy gospel, and confirms it by the use of the holy sacraments." Here, as in the *Canons of Dort*, even the language of "new and divine life infused" is employed, but this is said to occur *through* the ministry of the gospel.

of infusing the habit or principle of life in those who are dead so that they will embrace the gospel when they are effectually called by the Spirit. Regeneration, then, became understood as a direct act of God, without any creaturely means, while effectual calling was seen as mediated through the preaching of the gospel. The special concern of those who embraced this distinction between regeneration and effectual calling was to guard the important point that regeneration (the new birth) is not dependent on human decision or activity but is a sovereign work of God's grace. Even after acknowledging the impressive exegetical and confessional credentials of the older view, Louis Berkhof follows Charles Hodge in regarding the distinction between immediate regeneration and effectual calling through the Word as a useful one.[43]

I adopt the earlier view on exegetical grounds. *Although we must distinguish regeneration from conversion, I do not see the basis for a further distinction between regeneration and effectual calling.* Scripture indicates that we "have been born again ... through the living and abiding word of God" (1Pe 1:23). "Of his own will he brought us forth by the word of truth, that we should be a kind of firstfruits of his creatures" (Jas 1:18). In John 6 Jesus says, "No one can come to me unless the Father who sent me draws him" (v. 44). Humans do not effect this new birth. "It is the Spirit who gives life; the flesh is no help at all," yet he immediately adds, "The *words* that I have spoken to you are spirit and life" (v. 63, emphasis added).

If this is the case, why do we need an immediately infused *habitus* to intervene between these mediated events? Does such an adaptation of this medieval category save us from synergism only to open the door again to a dualism between God's person and Word? According to the above-cited passages, the Spirit implants the seed of his Word, not a principle or habit distinct from that Word. At no point in the *ordo salutis*, then, is there an infusion of a silent principle rather than a vocal, lively, and active speech. In attributing all efficacy to the Spirit's power, Scripture nevertheless represents this as occurring through the Word of God that is "at work" in its recipients (1Th 2:13; cf. 1Co 2:4–5; 2Co 4:13; Eph 1:17; Gal 3:2; 1Th 1:4; Tit 3:4) — specifically, that message of the gospel, which is "the power of God for salvation" (Ro 1:16; 10:17; 1Th 1:5).

Therefore, the external call *includes the locutionary act of the Father's speaking and the Son as the illocutionary content. The* internal call *(effectual calling), synonymous with regeneration, occurs through the Spirit's perlocutionary effect.* As in all of God's

---

43. Witsius, *Economy of the Covenants*, 476. In addition to explicit passages that speak of the new birth occurring through the Word (e.g., Jas 1:18; 1Pe 1:23; and the parable of the sower), Berkhof acknowledges that the Reformed confessions (*Belgic Confession*, arts. 24–25; *Heidelberg Catechism*, q. 54; *Canons of* *Dort* 3–4, arts. 11, 12, 17) "speak of regeneration in a broad sense, as including both the origin of the new life and its manifestation in conversion." Nevertheless, in his view, "They fail to discriminate carefully between the various elements which we distinguish in regeneration."

works, the Spirit brings to fruition the goal of divine communication. The Father objectively reveals the Son, and the Spirit inwardly illumines the understanding to behold the glory of God in the face of Christ (2Co 4:6; cf. Jn 1:5; 3:5; 17:3; 1Co 2:14), liberating the will not only to assent to the truth but to trust in Christ (Eze 36:26; Jer 32:39–40; Heb 8:10; Eph 2:1–9). Regeneration or effectual calling is something that happens to those who do not have the moral capacity to convert themselves, yet it not only happens *to* them; it happens *within* them, winning their consent. The God who says, "Let there be.... And there was ..." also says, "Let the earth bring forth..." (see ch. 10, "I Am the Alpha and the Omega," pp. 344–48). Because the Word of God is not mere information or exhortation but the "living and active" energies of the triune God, it is far more than a wooing, luring, persuasive influence that might fail to achieve the mission on which it was sent. In both instances, it is the work of the Father, in the Son, by the Spirit.

Here we once again call upon the essence-energies distinction advocated by the East (see ch. 10, "Creative Communication," pp. 331–34), but with a specific focus on the Word. There is always a distinction between the incarnate Word (consubstantial with the Father and the Spirit) and the spoken and written Word. Yet the Word in its spoken and written form is not only a creaturely witness that may or may not correspond to God's Word at specific moments; it is the *working* (energy) of God. Combining this distinction with speech act theory, we may say that in this respect God's *working* is God's *wording*. In fact, the gospel "is the power [*dynamis*, energy] of God for salvation ..." (Ro 1:16).

Nor is regeneration something done at a distance, but is already the presence of Christ mediating the voice of the Father in the power of the Spirit who not only works upon us but within us. Calvin comments, "We must also observe that form of expression, *to believe through the word*, which means that faith springs from hearing, because the outward preaching of men is the instrument by which God draws us to faith. It follows that God is, strictly speaking, the Author of faith, and men are *the ministers by whom we believe*, as Paul teaches (1Co 3:5)" (emphasis added).[44] Commenting on Romans 10:17 ("So faith comes from hearing, and hearing through the word of Christ"), Calvin writes,

> And this is a remarkable passage with regard to the efficacy of preaching; for he testifies that by it faith is produced. He had indeed before declared that of itself it is of no avail; but that when it pleases the Lord to work, it becomes the instrument of his power. And indeed the voice of man can by no means penetrate into the soul; and mortal man would be too much exalted were he said to have the power to regen-

44. John Calvin, *Commentary on the Gospel According to John* (trans. William Pringle; Grand Rapids: Baker, repr., 1996), commenting on Jn 17:20.

erate us; the light also of faith is something sublimer than what can be conveyed by man: but all these things are no hindrances, that God should not work effectually through the voice of man, so as to create faith in us through his ministry.[45]

Against both the medieval doctrine of justification according to infused habits and the Anabaptist emphasis on a direct and immediate work of the Spirit within us, the Reformers insisted upon the mediation of the Word—specifically, the gospel. "For faith and the Word belong together," Wilhelm Kolfhaus notes concerning Calvin's view. "The foundation of both expressions is always the faith produced by the Spirit through the Gospel."[46] Dennis Tamburello nicely summarizes Calvin's view of the *ordo*: "The Holy Spirit brings the elect, through the hearing of the gospel, to faith; in so doing, the Spirit engrafts them into Christ."[47]

In the account I have offered thus far, believers are seen to be "worded" all the way down: through the covenant of redemption, the covenant of creation, and now in the covenant of grace. The Spirit has voluntarily bound himself in his activity to the Word spoken by the Father in the Son. There is simply no place for infused habits in this kind of covenantal ontology. Not by silent thoughts and infused dispositions apart from the Word but by living speech God creates and recreates his world. A covenantal paradigm, rather than distinguishing between a forensic event (justification) and infused habits (regeneration), renders the entire *ordo* forensically charged, without confusing justification with sanctification or denying that union with Christ includes organic and transformative as well as forensic aspects.

Furthermore, even regeneration and sanctification are effects of God's performative utterance: a declaration on the level of *ex nihilo* creation: "Let there be ..." It was only on the basis of having first created the world by this fiat declaration that there were now creatures who could "bring forth" the proper response. While union with Christ and the sanctification that results from that union are more than forensic, they are the consequences of God's forensic declaration. Both justification ("Let there be ...!") and inner renewal ("Let the earth bring forth ...!") are speech acts of the Triune God. These arguments in favor of seeing the entire *ordo salutis* in communicative, covenantal, and energetic terms will be especially important in our discussion of justification and sanctification.

7. Conversion

If there is no reason to distinguish regeneration and effectual calling, there is nevertheless every reason to distinguish this event from conversion. In regenera-

---

45. John Calvin on Ro 10:17, in *Commentary on the Epistle of Paul the Apostle to the Romans* (ed. and trans. John Owen; vol. 19 of *Calvin's Commentaries*; Edinburgh: Calvin Translation Society, 1843–1855; repr., Grand Rapids: Baker Books, 1993), 401.

46. Wilhelm Kolfhaus, as quoted in Dennis Tamburello, *Union with Christ: John Calvin and the Mysticism of St. Bernard* (Louisville: Westminster John Knox, 1994), 86.

47. Tamburello, *Union with Christ*, 86.

tion we are passive. We hear the gospel, and the Spirit creates faith in our hearts to embrace it. However, in conversion we are active. "In the covenant of grace, that is, in the gospel ...," notes Bavinck,

> there are actually no demands and no conditions. For God supplies what he demands. Christ has accomplished everything, and though he did not accomplish rebirth, faith, and repentance in our place, he did acquire them for us, and the Holy Spirit therefore applies them. Still, in its administration by Christ, the covenant of grace does assume this demanding, conditional form.[48]

There are commands to repent and believe, yet even these human responses are gifts of grace:

> The covenant of grace, accordingly, is indeed unilateral: it proceeds from God; he has designed and defined it. He maintains and implements it. It is a work of the triune God and is totally completed among the three Persons themselves. *But it is destined to become bilateral*, to be consciously and voluntarily accepted and kept by humans in the power of God.[49]

In conversion (unlike regeneration), we are told, "Work out your own salvation with fear and trembling, for it is God who works in you, both to will and to work for his good pleasure" (Php 2:12–13). This does not mean that in conversion our salvation shifts from God's sovereign grace in Christ to our activity and cooperation, but that the salvation that has been given is worked out by that same Spirit, through the same gospel, in a genuine relationship in which we become covenant partners who are now alive to God in Christ. Apart from our repentance and faith, there is no justification or union with Christ. Yet even this human response is a gift of the Spirit through the gospel.

The ministry of John the Baptist is compared and contrasted with that of Jesus at various points in the Gospels. Later in his ministry Jesus said, "I tell you, among those born of women none is greater than John. Yet the one who is least in the kingdom of God is greater than he" (Lk 7:28)—because of the superior phase of redemptive history Jesus was inaugurating. Those who refused to be baptized by John "rejected the purpose of God for themselves" (Lk 7:30). Jesus then compares the present generation to children playing the funeral game and the wedding game, "and calling to one another, 'We played the flute for you, and you did not dance; we sang a dirge, and you did not weep'" (v. 32). John played the funeral dirge, but most of the people and religious leaders did not feel the sting of their guilt, but claimed that he had a demon; Jesus brings the good news of the gospel to sinners, and he is

---

48. Herman Bavinck, *Reformed Dogmatics: God and Creation* (ed. John Bolt; trans. John Vriend; Grand Rapids: Baker, 2004), 3:230.

49. Ibid. (emphasis added).

rejected as "a glutton and a drunkard, a friend of tax collectors and sinners!" (v. 34). "Now after John was arrested, Jesus came into Galilee, proclaiming the good news of God, and saying, 'The time is fulfilled, and the kingdom of God is at hand; repent and believe in the gospel'" (Mk 1:14–15).

As in Jesus' day, the children of this age know neither how to mourn nor how to dance properly. G. K. Chesterton observed that Christianity's outer ring is dark enough, with its grave view of original sin, judgment, and hell, but in its inner ring "you will find the old human life dancing like children, and drinking wine like men; for Christianity is the only frame for pagan freedom." "But in the modern philosophy the case is opposite; it is its outer ring that is obviously artistic and emancipated; its despair is within."[50] For the unbelieving world a kind of superficial happiness and general well-being full of entertainments but lacking any real plot hides the fear of death. Apart from God's grace, we can neither come to terms sufficiently with our mortal wound nor enter into the genuine revelry and mirth of God's kingdom. Denying our sin (not just *sins*, but our sinful condition), we're too silly for a funeral; finding the gospel foolish, we are too timid for a real celebration. "Repent, and believe in the gospel": this command forms the two aspects of conversion: repentance toward sin and faith toward God. After the funeral there is dancing. In repentance, we say no to the idols, powers, rulers, and lies of this present evil age, and in faith we say yes to Christ, in whom "all the promises of God find their Yes.... That is why it is through him that we utter our Amen to God for his glory" (2Co 1:20).

8. REPENTANCE

Christ does not come to improve our lives—the "old self," to use Paul's vocabulary—but to crucify it and bury it with him so that we may be raised with him in newness of life (Ro 6:1–5). Repentance (*metanoia*) means "change of mind." It is treated in Scripture as first of all the knowledge of sin produced by the law (Ro 3:20). As we have seen above from Jesus' Upper Room Discourse, the Spirit is an attorney sent to convict us inwardly of God's righteousness and our unrighteousness. This knowledge, however, is not merely intellectual but emotional—it involves the whole person.

We see the features of repentance finely exhibited in David's prayer of confession:

Have mercy on me, O God,
  according to your steadfast love;
according to your abundant mercy
  blot out my transgressions.

---

50. G. K. Chesterton, *Orthodoxy: The Romance of Faith*
(New York: Doubleday, 1959, 1990), 157.

> Wash me thoroughly from my iniquity,
>   and cleanse me from my sin!
> For I know my transgressions,
>   and my sin is ever before me.
> Against you, you alone, have I sinned,
>   and done what is evil in your sight,
> so that you may be justified in your words
>   and blameless in your judgment.
> Behold, I was brought forth in iniquity,
>   and in sin did my mother conceive me.
> Behold, you delight in truth in the inward being,
>   and you teach me wisdom in the secret heart.
> Purge me with hyssop, and I shall be clean;
>   wash me, and I shall be whiter than snow.
> Let me hear joy and gladness;
>   let the bones that you have broken rejoice.
> Hide your face from my sins,
>   and blot out all my iniquities. (Ps 51:1–9)

First, we recognize that David is not simply ashamed of his behavior but guilty. Second, although he has sinned cruelly against Bathsheba and plotted the death of her husband, he recognizes that his sin is first and foremost against God. Repentance is not only remorse for having wronged our neighbor, but is a recognition that God is the most offended party. Third, David does not try to atone for his sins or pacify God's just anger by his remorse. David confesses that before God's throne he is condemned, and he does not try to justify himself. Fourth, David acknowledges not only his sinful *actions* but his sinful *condition* from the hour of conception. Repentance pertains not simply to certain sins; pagans can be remorseful for their immoderate behavior. Rather, it is the revulsion of the whole soul toward its alliance with sin and death.

Although such godly sorrow leads David to despair of his own righteousness, it does not lead him to the final despair that often leads the ungodly to either self-destruction or a searing of their conscience. As Paul observes, "For godly grief produces a repentance that leads to salvation without regret, whereas worldly grief produces death" (2Co 7:10). After all, "God's kindness is meant to lead you to repentance" (Ro 2:4). While the law produces a *legal repentance* (fear of judgment), the gospel engenders an *evangelical repentance* that bears the fruit of real change. David turns outside of himself to his merciful God. Here we see the closest possible link between repentance and faith. By itself repentance is merely the experience of damnation—until one looks by faith to Jesus Christ.

Often repentance is more broadly defined to include actual change in character and behavior, but Scripture describes this as the "fruit in keeping with repentance"

(Mt 3:8) or "deeds in keeping with their repentance" (Ac 26:20; cf. Mt 7:16; Lk 3:9; 8:15; Jn 12:24; Ro 7:4; Gal 5:22; Col 1:10). In this sense, of course, repentance is always partial, weak, and incomplete in this life. Nor is it a one-time act. As the first of Luther's Ninety-five Theses states, "Our Lord and Master Jesus Christ, in saying 'Repent ye,' etc., intended that the whole life of believers should be penitence." The Spirit brings us to repentance by convicting us of sin by the law, the gospel leads us to faith in Christ, and this faith produces within us a hatred of our sin and a craving for righteousness. Since our tendency even as believers is still to turn back toward ourselves and trust in our repentance, we must be driven again to despair of our righteousness or of any possibility of ridding ourselves of our sins by the law and cling to Christ. Therefore, this is not a once-and-for-all transition from legal repentance to faith in Christ to evangelical repentance, but a perpetual cycle that defines the Christian life.

In Roman Catholic theology and practice, this call to repentance is replaced with a system of penance. As the Renaissance scholar Erasmus discovered, the Latin Vulgate had erroneously translated the Greek imperative "Repent!" (*metanoēsate*) in Acts 2:38 as "Do penance!" (*poenitentiam agite*). Rome defines such penance as involving four elements: contrition, confession, satisfaction, and absolution.[51] Since few are able to rise to the level of true contrition (genuine sorrow for sin), attrition (fear of punishment) is deemed suitable for this first stage. For forgiveness, each sin must be recalled and orally confessed to a priest, who then determines a suitable action or series of actions to perform in order to make satisfaction for the sin. Only then can the penitent receive the absolution.[52]

However, powerful currents within Protestantism (especially in more Arminian versions) have taught that God's forgiveness and justification are conditioned on the degree of earnestness of their repentance and on new obedience.[53] Even in broader evangelical circles, some Christians struggle to the point of despair over whether the quality and degree of their repentance is adequate to be forgiven, as if repentance were the ground of forgiveness and the former could be measured by the intensity of emotion and resolve.

However, according to Scripture it is not our tears but Christ's blood that satisfies God's judgment and establishes peace with God (Ro 5:1, 8–11). In the words

---

51. *Catechism of the Catholic Church*, 364–67. "Christ instituted the sacrament of Penance for all sinful members of the Church: above all for those who, since Baptism, have fallen into grave sin, and have thus lost their baptismal grace and wounded ecclesial communion. It is to them that the sacrament of Penance offers a new possibility to convert and to recover the grace of justification. The Fathers of the Church present this sacrament as 'the second plank [of salvation] after the shipwreck which is the loss of grace'" (363).

52. Ibid., 364–67.

53. William Law's *A Serious Call to a Devout and Holy Life*, which had a formative impact on John Wesley, is especially representative of this tendency. See the thorough analysis of C. FitzSimons Allison, *The Rise of Moralism: The Proclamation of the Gospel from Hooker to Baxter* (Atlanta: Morehouse Publishing, 1984). Allison especially illuminates the role of Jeremy Taylor in this trajectory.

of "Rock of Ages," "Could my zeal no languor know, / Could my tears forever flow ... All for sin could not atone; Thou must save, and Thou alone."[54] God heals the bones that he crushes and raises up those whom he has cast down. "But he gives more grace. Therefore it says, 'God opposes the proud, but gives grace to the humble' " (Jas 4:6). The law begins repentance, by convicting us of sin, but only the gospel can lead us to boldly claim God's promise with David: "Let me hear joy and gladness; let the bones that you have broken rejoice. Hide your face from my sins, and blot out all my iniquities" (Ps 51:8 – 9).

Whenever repentance is marginalized in conversion, it is usually because of an inadequate sense of God's holiness and the just demands of his righteous law. The consequence is that conversion is represented merely as moral improvement: the *addition* of certain distinctives of Christian piety. Biblical repentance, however, involves a fundamental *renunciation* of the world, the flesh, and the devil: including the spirituality, experiences, and moral efforts in which one has trusted. The whole self must be turned away both from self-trust and from the autonomy that demands final say as to what one will believe, whom one will trust, and how one will live.

9. FAITH

Arrested, arraigned, and indicted, in repentance we turn away *from* ourselves — our untruths, our sins, and our fraudulent claim to righteousness — and in faith we look *to* Christ for salvation and for every spiritual gift. To put it differently, in repentance we confess (with David) that God is justified in his verdict against us, and in faith we receive God's justification. Dead to sin and alive to Christ once and for all in regeneration (Ro 6:1 – 11), we are called to die daily to our old self and live daily by "the free gift of God," which "is eternal life in Christ Jesus our Lord" (vv. 12 – 23).

In the Hebrew scriptures to believe (*he'mîn*, in the hiphil form of *'âman*) means to acknowledge as an established fact. However, this is not merely intellectual assent. It is, literally, to say "amen" to what God has performed as pertaining to oneself. Other words (*ḥāsâ*, "to take refuge"; *bāṭaḥ*, "to trust or lean upon") also convey the idea of faith as involving trust as well as knowledge and assent. In the New Testament, the noun *pistis* (and its cognate verb *pisteuein*) has various connotations. The Greeks believed in the existence of their gods, but the New Testament carries over from the Old Testament this understanding of faith as trust in and reliance upon the saving action of a personal God.

The passive form (faithfulness) occurs only in a few places (Ro 3:3; Gal 5:22;

---

54. Augustus Toplady, "Rock of Ages" (1776), in *Psalter Hymnal* (Grand Rapids: Publication Committee of the CRC, 1959), #388.

Tit 2:10). More often, faith is understood as trust or belief in what is said on the testimony of another (Php 1:27; 2Co 4:13; 2Th 2:13 and especially in John). More often still, it is specifically exhibited as faith in Jesus and his declarative Word (Jn 4:50; 5:47; Ro 3:22, 25; 5:1–2; 9:30–32; Gal 2:16; Eph 2:8; 3:12), a trustful reliance in Jesus Christ (*en* for "in": Mk 1:15; Jn 3:15; Eph 1:13; *epi* plus dative for "in": Isa 28:16, quoted in Ro 9:33; Ro 10:11; 1Pe 2:6; Lk 24:25; 1Ti 1:16; cf. Ac 16:34; Ro 4:3; 2Ti 1:5, 12). The use of *epi* with the accusative or of *eis* ("into") emphasizes the transfer of trust from ourselves to God in Christ (Jn 2:11; 3:16, 18, 36; 14:1; Ro 10:14; Gal 2:16; Php 1:29, etc.). Such faith is described as looking to Christ (Jn 3:14–15, with Nu 21:9), hungering, thirsting, and drinking (Mt 5:6; Jn 6:50–58; 4:14), coming and receiving (Jn 1:12; 5:40; 7:37–38; 6:44, 65). These instances (besides many others) underscore the role of faith *in the act of justification* as a passive receiving and resting in Christ. However, the faith of the justified is also active in good works (Jas 2:26).

In other cases we find references to "*the* faith" (Ac 6:7; Eph 4:5; 1Ti 1:19; 3:9; 5:8; 6:12; Jude 3). Therefore the distinction often made in theology between *the* faith (i.e., the content) that is believed (*fides quae creditur*) and faith as the personal act of believing (*fides qua creditur*) seems well-founded (see also ch. 4, "Inerrancy after Barth," p. 184). This means that the personal act of faith has an object (Christ as he is clothed in the gospel), a content (the doctrine concerning Christ and his gospel), and a subject (the believing sinner).

Faith is the same in both testaments, both in its act and in its object. In fact, Abel, Noah, David, and other Old Testament figures are treated in the New Testament as examples of those who had faith in Christ (esp. Heb 11). Abraham is especially paradigmatic as the one who was justified by faith and is the father of all who have faith in Christ (Ro 4; Gal 3; Heb 11; Jas 2). Throughout the New Testament this continuity is assumed (Jn 5:46; 12:38–39; Hab 2:4; Ro 1:17; 10:16; Gal 3:11; Heb 10:38). As Berkhof reminds us, "The giving of the law did not effect a fundamental change in the religion of Israel, but merely introduced a change in its external form. The law was not substituted for the promise; neither was faith supplanted by works."[55]

Paul's legalists had misunderstood the true nature of the law: to lead us to Christ, not to lead us to self-salvation. The demand for faith does not turn faith into a work. On the contrary, it is a command to cease our labors and enter God's rest (Heb 4). We are commanded to repent not only of our immoral life that we once approved but of self-trust, which is the greatest sin of all — the chief offense of

---

55. Louis Berkhof, *Systematic Theology* (Grand Rapids: Eerdmans, 1996), 498.

idolatry. Again, the history of salvation (*historia salutis*) and the order of salvation (*ordo salutis*) converge (see ch. 16, "The King and His Kingdom," p. 535): Just as "the grace of God has appeared" (Tit 2:11), so Paul also speaks of faith as arriving: "Now before faith came, we were held captive under the law, imprisoned until the coming faith would be revealed." Because "Christ came," "faith has come ..." (Gal 3:23–25). Again, this cannot mean that the Old Testament saints were not justified through faith—especially since this same chapter underscores continuity on this point. Rather, the contrast for Paul lies in the fact that the old covenant (Sinai) was an external form of government for the nation that established cultic and legal practices that clearly pointed to Jesus Christ (hence, the contrast between the "two covenants" in 4:21–31). Yet this Sinai covenant did not—and could not—replace the Abrahamic covenant of grace (Gal 3:15–18).

While upholding the continuity of faith in Christ from Abraham (indeed, from Adam and Eve after the fall) to the present, the New Testament also announces that something new has dawned. The law itself could not create faith, hope, or love, but because of sin could only place the world in prison awaiting the redeemer (Gal 3:22–23) or under a guardian awaiting its maturity in order to receive the inheritance (v. 24). Throughout Acts, Christ is proclaimed and the appropriate response is repentance and faith. In Hebrews, the great fathers and mothers of Israel are commended for having faith in the promise even though they did not yet see its fulfillment (Heb 11:1–12:2). Moses and his liberated followers, according to Paul, "drank from the spiritual rock that followed them, and the rock was Christ" (1Co 10:4). In fact, the wilderness generation is said to have "put Christ to the test" when they rebelled (v. 9).

10. Differing Conceptions of Faith

In the ancient church, faith seems to be identified primarily with *the* faith (orthodox doctrine) and with personal assent to that doctrine, though not in antithesis to personal faith. According to medieval scholasticism, faith was understood as assent to church teaching (*fides informis*), which became justifying faith only when it was formed or completed by love (*fides formata*). Therefore, justifying faith became a virtue along with hope and love: an act of doing and giving rather than receiving. In Roman Catholic theology, faith is not only assent to all church teaching but is, properly speaking, an act of the church rather than of the individual.[56]

The Reformation challenged this understanding of faith in the light of the passages cited above, among others. Faith cannot simply be assent to *whatever the church teaches*, since this would make the church rather than Christ the object of faith. One must know the content to which one yields assent. Furthermore, faith

---

56. *Catechism of the Catholic Church*, 46. At the same time, the element of personal trust is not entirely absent in these more recent definitions of faith (see especially pages 40–41).

cannot be sufficiently defined as mere assent even to true doctrines.[57] Faith is not only the belief that Christ is God incarnate, crucified, and raised on the third day, but is, in Calvin's words, "a firm and certain knowledge of *God's benevolence toward us*, founded upon the truth of the freely given promise in Christ, both revealed to our minds and sealed upon our hearts through the Holy Spirit."[58] Faith is simply "confidence in divine benevolence and salvation."[59]

Faith therefore involves the intellect, the will, and the affections. It is knowledge (*notitia*), assent (*assensus*), and trust (*fiducia*). Given definition by doctrine, faith is nevertheless directed to a person: the triune God as he has revealed himself in Christ as our redeemer. It would be mere assent to say even that Christ died for sinners generally, without recognizing that he died *for me*. According to the Lutheran confession, "The faith here spoken of 'is not that possessed by the devil and the ungodly, who also believe the history of Christ's suffering and resurrection from the dead, but we mean such true faith as believes that we receive grace and forgiveness of sin through Christ.'" It is not merely acknowledging the truth of Christ's person and work, but receiving and clinging to Christ himself.[60] The same view is expressed on the Reformed side in the *Heidelberg Catechism*: "True faith is not only a sure knowledge, whereby I hold for truth all that God has revealed to us in His Word, but also a firm confidence which the Holy Spirit works in my heart by the gospel, that *not only to others, but to me also*, remission of sins, everlasting righteousness and salvation are freely given by God, merely of grace, only for the sake of Christ's merits" (emphasis added).[61]

Nor is faith's justifying power located in any inherent quality or virtue of faith itself. Faith is only the instrument rather than the basis for justification: it simply lays hold of Christ and his merits. Hence, the common Reformation formulation of justification: *per fidem propter Christum* (through faith because of or on the basis of Christ). Strictly speaking, one is not justified *by* faith but by Christ's righteousness which is received *through* faith. Therefore, faith is always extrospective: looking outside of itself. Faith does not arise within the self, but comes to us from the outside, through the preaching of the gospel (Ro 10:17). This means that in the act of justification faith is itself completely passive, *receiving* a gift, not offering one. The faith that justifies is immediately active in love, honoring God and serving neighbor, but this active love is faith's fruit, not the act of justifying faith itself. Given our native instincts, we can always turn gospel back into law—in this case, by making faith into faithfulness, the act of receiving into an act of working.

---

57. This is in opposition to the view of Gordon H. Clark, *What Is Saving Faith?* (Union, Tenn.: Trinity Foundation, 2004), 9–10, 55–63.

58. Calvin, *Institutes* 3.2.7, emphasis added.

59. Ibid., 3.2.15.

60. Edmund Schlink, *Theology of the Lutheran Confessions*, 96.

61. *Heidelberg Catechism*, q. 21, in *Psalter Hymnal* (Grand Rapids: Publication Committee of the CRC, 1959), "Doctrinal Standards," p. 25.

As already noted in connection with the atonement, Arminianism held that the work of Christ, though not itself the satisfaction of justice, made it possible for God to offer salvation on lower terms than perfect obedience. For some Arminians (for example, Richard Baxter), faith and repentance became the "new law," serving as the ground of God's pardon and justification.[62] Berkhof observes, "The Arminians revealed a Romanizing tendency when they conceived of faith as a meritorious work of man, on the basis of which he is accepted in favor by God."[63]

In modern theology, Schleiermacher reduced faith to an inner experience of union with God. Though "supported by the historical representation of [Christ's] life and character," faith comes through "testimony as to one's experience, which shall arouse in others the desire to have the same experience."[64] Ever since, in Protestant liberalism the Romantic celebration of inner emotion and universal religious experience turned faith into a general openness to and dependence upon the divine. Ritschl saw Christ as the object of faith but chiefly as lawgiver and example, and defined the nature of faith as beginning the work of building his kingdom.[65] In this theology, Berkhof notes, faith is made "a human achievement; not the mere receiving of a gift, but a meritorious action; not the acceptance of a doctrine, but a 'making Christ Master' in an attempt to pattern one's life after the example of Christ."[66]

Barth, Brunner, and especially Bultmann saw faith as an obedient response to God's command and downplayed (or denied) that it involved knowledge of and assent to particular doctrines. Bultmann radically reinterpreted both justification and faith in existentialist terms. The perennial danger of turning faith into a work is exhibited in Bultmann's view of faith as "venture."[67] "Faith is a 'leap in the dark'.... For man is not asked whether he will accept a theory about God that may possibly be false, but whether he is willing to obey God's will." For us, the meaning of Christ's cross is found in our "crucifying the affections and lusts ..., overcoming our natural dread of suffering,... and the perfection of our detachment from the world." This constitutes "the judgment ... and deliverance of man."[68] But here Bultmann not only confuses justification with sanctification, but with a view

---

62. Richard Baxter, *Aphorismes of Justification, with their Explication Annexed, Etc.* (London: Francis Tyton, 1649). See also Hans Boersma, *A Hot Pepper Corn: Richard Baxter's Doctrine of Justification in Its Seventeenth-Century Context of Controversy* (Zoetermeer, Netherlands: Boekencentrum, 1993).

63. Berkhof, *Systematic Theology*, 497.

64. Friedrich Schleiermacher, *The Christian Faith* (ed. and trans. H. R. Mackintosh and J. S. Stewart; Edinburgh: T&T Clark, 1928), 69.

65. Albrecht Ritschl, *The Christian Doctrine of Justification and Reconciliation: The Positive Development of the Doctrine* (trans. H. R. Mackintosh and A. B. Macaulay; Edinburgh: T&T Clark, 1900 [German original, Volume III, 1874]; repr.,

Clifton, N.J.: Reference Book Publishers, 1966), 12.

66. Berkhof, *Systematic Theology*, 498. Similarly, J. Gresham Machen writes, "According to modern liberalism, faith is essentially the same as 'making Christ Master' in one's life," *Christianity and Liberalism* (New York: Macmillan, 1923; repr., Grand Rapids: Eerdmans, 2002), 143.

67. Rudolf Bultmann, "Faith as Venture," in *Existence and Faith: Shorter Writings of Rudolf Bultmann* (London: Hodder and Stoughton, 1960), 57.

68. Rudolf Bultmann, "New Testament and Mythology," in *Kerygma and Myth: A Theological Debate* (ed. Hans Werner Bartsch; trans. Reginald H. Fuller; rev. ed.; New York: Harper and Row, 1961), 64–65.

of sanctification that can be reckoned only as Gnostic. The gospel comes not to detach us from the world or to overcome "our natural dread of suffering," but to save us—and the world—from the reign of sin and death. As Julius Schniewind pointed out, for Bultmann, "The 'crucifixion of our passions' is then no more than a striking euphemism for self-mastery, which is the quest of all the higher religions and philosophies."[69] In all of these ways, faith loses its specific object (Christ and all his benefits) and therefore its proper character as an act of receiving that which has already been achieved for us. *In the act of justification, we must insist, faith merely receives, embraces, and clings to Christ; it does not do anything but receives everything.*

Faith is not a probable opinion or conjecture, nor mere assent to an external authority—even the Bible or the church. Nor is faith an immediate certainty, like the knowledge of logical, geometrical, or mathematical axioms or of sense experience. It is not a general attitude, characteristic, or virtue—such as an optimistic outlook or positive thinking. Faith is not a genus of which faith in Christ is a species, as is often assumed especially in our day when we speak of "faith communities" or the importance of "faith." Faith is not even a general trust in God and his promises. Evangelical faith—that is, faith as defined by the gospel—is the specific conviction of the heart, mind, and will that God is gracious to us in Jesus Christ on the basis of God's Word. Faith is clinging to Christ.

11. FAITH AND ASSURANCE

Although Hebrews 11:1 defines faith as "the assurance of things hoped for," Roman Catholic teaching denies the inextricable relationship of faith and assurance. Faith is mere assent to the church's teachings, as we have seen. Even when faith is "completed" by becoming loving action, believers are never certain of final salvation. There may be a reasonable confidence that one is presently in a state of grace. "Moved by the Holy Spirit, we can merit for ourselves and for others all the graces needed to attain eternal life, as well as necessary temporal goods."[70] However, assurance of one's election and final justification is regarded as presumptuous.

By contrast, the Reformers insisted that faith *is* assurance because Christ's meritorious work is already completed. Since faith and repentance remain weak and imperfect, the *experience* of assurance may encounter highs and lows, but believers remain *objectively* assured of their salvation in Christ alone. This view of assurance as belonging to the essence of faith is found in the Lutheran and Continental Reformed confessions and catechisms. Although the Puritans distinguished faith from assurance, they did so in part to focus trembling consciences on Christ—the object of faith—even if their experience of assurance was lacking (see *Westminster*

---

69. Julius Schniewind, "A Reply to Bultmann," in *Kerygma and Myth*, 65–66.

70. *Catechism of the Catholic Church*, 486, 490.

Confession, ch. 18).[71] Often, this was wise pastoral counsel, reckoning with the fact that doubt is frequently mingled with faith in the Christian life. Yet it could also become a source of anxiety, encouraging excessive introspection.

In later Puritanism and Lutheran Pietism, this separation of faith from assurance often led to a tendency to build assurance on the foundation of the quality of faith rather than the object of faith. The proper balance does not lie in the recognition that assurance is of the essence of faith itself, even though the experience of assurance may be encouraged by the signs of faith and its fruit. In this way we are always directed outside of ourselves to Jesus Christ alone. The gifts received through this faith are the focus of the next several chapters.

DISCUSSION QUESTIONS

1. Trace the person and work of the Spirit from creation to consummation. Do we tend to identify the Spirit's work too narrowly with the individual experience of conversion and sanctification?

2. What is the significance of Pentecost in the history of redemption, especially in relation to the ascension of Christ? How does the Spirit communicate Christ's heavenly ministry to us here and now?

3. Explore the connection between election and effectual calling. Does God force people to come to Christ? How does Scripture describe this work of the Spirit?

4. Are we regenerated (born again) because we believe or do we believe because we have been regenerated?

5. What is conversion in the New Testament and how does it differ from regeneration (or effectual calling)? Also, how would you distinguish the nature of conversion itself from its fruit?

---

71. Joel Beeke helpfully explores the continuities between Calvin (and the Continental Reformed view) and Puritanism on faith and assurance in *Assurance of Faith: Calvin, English Puritanism, and the Dutch Second Reformation* (American University Studies Series 7; New York: Peter Lang, 1994).

Chapter Eighteen

UNION WITH CHRIST

What a wondrous thing it is that even though Jesus Christ has been exalted to the throne of God, absent from us in the flesh, we may nevertheless only now be united to him in a manner far more intimate than the fellowship enjoyed by the disciples with Jesus during his earthly ministry. Having united himself to us in our flesh, in our sins, in our suffering and death, he now unites us to himself in his new-creation life by his Spirit.

Union with Christ is not to be understood as a "moment" in the application of salvation to believers. Rather, it is a way of speaking about the way in which believers share in Christ in eternity (by election), in past history (by redemption), in the present (by effectual calling, justification, and sanctification), and in the future (by glorification). Nevertheless, our subjective inclusion in Christ occurs when the Spirit calls us effectually to Christ and gives us the faith to cling to him for all of his riches. We will first treat union and then its effects in the following chapters.

The intratrinitarian covenant of redemption made in eternity realizes itself through the mutual working of the Father, the Son, and the Spirit, in that *ordo salutis* of Paul in Romans 8:30–31, which William Perkins aptly called "the golden chain": "Those whom he predestined he also called, and those whom he called he also justified, and those whom he justified he also glorified." Behind all of the covenants in history lies the eternal "purpose of election" to which Paul repeatedly refers (Ro 8:28; 9:11; Eph 1:4–5, 11; 3:11; 2Ti 1:9). First Peter is addressed to those who have been chosen "according to the foreknowledge of God the Father, in the sanctification of the Spirit, for obedience to Jesus Christ and for sprinkling with his blood," which explains the sense in which he can say, "He was foreknown before the foundation of the world but was made manifest in the last times for the sake of you who through him are believers in God, who raised him from the dead and gave him glory, so that your faith and hope are in God" (1Pe 1:2, 20–21). "Here the basis of all covenants was found in the eternal counsel of God," writes Bavinck, "in a covenant between the very persons of the Trinity, the *pactum salutis* (counsel of salvation)."[1]

I. THE NATURE OF THE UNION

The motif of mystical union has often been presented as an alternative to the forensic (legal) motifs of redemption, especially vicarious substitution and justification. Since Albert Schweitzer, the thesis has repeatedly been advanced, refuted, and then advanced again that justification is a "subsidiary crater" in Paul, while the real central dogma is mystical union. Reginald Fuller notes, "Attempts have been made to pinpoint some other center or focus for Pauline theology, such as 'being in Christ' (Schweitzer) or salvation history (Johannes Munck)." However, "Romans, the most systematic exposition of Paul's thought, clearly makes justification the center." Not only in Paul but in the pre-Pauline creedal hymns we find this affirmation (2Ti 1:9 and Tit 3:4–5).[2]

Like Schweitzer, a variety of contemporary trends in Pauline studies as well as Reformation scholarship are driven by the presupposition that mystical participation in Christ stands over against a forensic emphasis on Christ's alien righteousness imputed to believers.[3] Through the interpretive lens of union with Christ we can move beyond the false choice of a legal, judicial, and passive salvation on one hand and a relational, mystical, and transformative participation in Christ on the other. Nevertheless, as I argued in relation to Christ's atoning work, the integral unity of these motifs is possible only because the latter is grounded in the former. As Geerhardus Vos expressed it,

> In our opinion Paul consciously and consistently subordinated the mystical aspect of the relation to Christ to the forensic one. Paul's mind was to such an extent forensically oriented that he regarded the entire complex of subjective spiritual changes that take place in the believer and of subjective spiritual blessings enjoyed by the

1. Herman Bavinck, *Reformed Dogmatics* (ed. John Bolt; trans. John Vriend; Grand Rapids: Baker Academic, 2006), 3:194. On the structural significance of the *pactum salutis*, see, e.g., Heinrich Heppe, *Reformed Dogmatics* (ed. Ernst Bizer; trans. G. T. Thomson; London: Allen & Unwin, 1950), 373–83.

2. Reginald Fuller, "Here We Stand," in *By Faith Alone: Essays on Justification in Honor of Gerhard O. Forde* (ed. Joseph A. Burgess and Marc Kolden; Grand Rapids: Eerdmans, 2004), 91. Especially in light of my earlier criticism of the "central dogma" thesis, it is important to point out that to discern a central emphasis on the basis of Paul's explicit arguments is different from starting with an abstract proposition or thesis and

requiring the data to be subsumed under it or deduced from it. I have argued that the New Perspective on Paul is actually closer to modern dogmatics at this point than are pre-Enlightenment systems.

3. Pauline scholars associated with the New Perspective on Paul pursue this line, at least implicitly, by forcing a contrast between Paul and the Reformation interpretation of Paul, while the New Finnish Perspective on Luther tries to reconcile Luther with Eastern Orthodox *theōsis* over against the Lutheran confessions. A similar tack is taken with respect to Calvin by T. F. Torrance, "Karl Barth and the Latin Heresy," *SJT* 39 (1986): 461–82.

believer as the direct outcome of the forensic work of Christ applied in justification. The mystical is based on the forensic, not the forensic on the mystical.[4]

However, before we consider justification as the judicial ground of our union with Christ, we must examine the broader theme of union.

A. EXEGETICAL DEVELOPMENT

The doctrine of union with Christ may be gathered from various biblical sources. First, there is the covenantal theme that underlies the entire biblical narrative from creation to consummation. From the very beginning, the goal is to bring creatures into fellowship (*koinōnia*) with God and each other that is as close as humanly possible to that communion between the Father, the Son, and the Spirit.

From creation to the flood to the exodus all the way to the new creation, there is a close connection between the covenant and union with the covenant mediator, effected by the Spirit, through a separation of the waters of judgment so that his people may cross through to the other side on dry land (Ge 1:1–2, 9–10; 8:1, 13; 9:17; Ex 33:12–23; Ps 18:1–19, 27–50). This same motif is recognized and extended by the apostles in relation to Christ and the Spirit: "I want you to know, brothers, that our fathers were all under the cloud, and all passed through the sea, and all were baptized into Moses in the cloud and in the sea, and all ate the same spiritual food, and all drank the same spiritual drink. For they all drank from the spiritual Rock that followed them, and the Rock was Christ" (1Co 10:1–4). After referring to the deliverance of the world through Noah, Peter adds, "Baptism, which corresponds to this, now saves you, not as a removal of dirt from the body but as an appeal to God for a good conscience, through the resurrection of Jesus Christ, who has gone into heaven and is at the right hand of God, with angels, authorities, and powers having been subjected to him" (1Pe 3:21–22). As the old creation was "formed out of water and through water by the word of God," and by that same means was deluged in the flood of judgment, the same Word dams up God's judgment until the last day (2Pe 3:5–7).

As in Eden, the curse for covenant breaking is that the land flowing with milk and honey returns to "darkness" and "void" (cf. Ge 1:2), a waterless wasteland, "so desolate that none will pass through" (Eze 33:23–29). However, the restoration of Israel will be like a new creation and a new exodus, when Yahweh delivers and gathers his people from the nations. "I will sprinkle clean water on you, and you

---

4. Geerhardus Vos, "The Alleged Legalism in Paul's Doctrine of Justification," in *Redemptive History and Biblical Interpretation: The Shorter Writings of Geerhardus Vos* (ed. Richard B. Gaffin Jr.; Phillipsburg, N.J.: P&R, 1980), 384. The same point is made by Louis Berkhof, *Systematic Theology* (Grand Rapids: Eerdmans, 1996), 452, against those who would make the imputation of Christ's righteousness depend on mystical union rather than vice versa. See also John V. Fesko, *Justification: Understanding the Classic Reformed Doctrine* (Phillipsburg, N.J.: P&R, 2008), ch. 10.

shall be clean from all your uncleanness, and from all your idols I will cleanse you. And I will give you a new heart, and a new spirit I will put within you. And I will remove the heart of stone from your flesh and give you a heart of flesh.... I will make the fruit of the tree and the increase of the field abundant" (Eze 36:22–30). Then follows the prophet's vision of the valley of dry bones, as a new Israel is raised in the last days from death to life (37:1–14).

In Romans 5, the covenantal union of humanity in Adam is contrasted with Christ's covenantal headship, and then in chapter 6 we encounter his most explicit description of union with Christ in his death and resurrection (Ro 6:1–23; cf. 1:3–4; 4:25; 1Co 15:35–58). Though they have been "in Christ" in God's electing grace from all eternity (Eph 1:4, 11; 2Ti 1:9), their actual union with Christ occurs in time through the work of the Spirit. Throughout the Pauline corpus we encounter this emphasis on union with Christ.

However, the crucial elements of the Pauline understanding of union are also evident in the Gospels, though of course in a more narrative form, as Jesus—in his words and deeds—redraws the boundaries of Israel around himself. He takes the seat of Moses in delivering his own Sermon on the Mount, and when he is transfigured on the mountain, with a face reflecting a greater glory than that of Moses when he descended Sinai, again he is the center of attention as Moses and Elijah testify about him (Mt 17:1–8 and parallels).

Yet it is in John where Jesus is depicted as the locus of true worship and of the ingathering of Israel (4:1–26), the one who "gives life to whom he will" (5:21), who gives the true manna from heaven for eternal life (ch. 6), who is the source of living water (7:37–39), the Good Shepherd (ch. 10), the Resurrection and the Life (ch. 11), and the Way to the Father (14:1–14), who will send the Spirit to unite them to him as branches to the Vine (14:15–15:17). As we have seen in considering the atonement, Christ speaks in John 6, 10, and 17 of the Father's gift of a people to the Son, "that they may all be one, just as you, Father, are in me, and I in you, that they also may be in us, so that the world may believe that you have sent me" (Jn 17:21–22).

From such sources we may draw the following conclusions about the nature of this union: First, it is a *mystical* union. It is designated "mystical," as A. A. Hodge notes, "because it so far transcends all the analogies of earthly relationships, in the intimacy of its communion, in the transforming power of its influence, and in the excellence of its consequences."[5] However, it is also designated mystical in order properly to distinguish between Christ's natural body—the flesh that he assumed from the Virgin Mary and that is now glorified in heaven—and his mystical or covenantal body, the church.

---

5. A. A. Hodge, *Outlines of Theology* (Edinburgh: Banner of Truth, 1972), 483.

Second, it is a *legal* union. Christ's action in the upper room when he instituted the Supper was the public and official issuance of his last will and testament, offering the cup as "my blood of the [new] covenant, which is poured out for many for the forgiveness of sins" (Mt 26:28). Paul also compares the covenant to a person's will that has been ratified, so that nothing can be added or annulled (Gal 3:15).

The writer to the Hebrews adds,

> Therefore he is the mediator of a new covenant, so that those who are called may receive the promised eternal inheritance, since a death has occurred that redeems them from the transgressions committed under the first covenant. For where a will is involved, the death of the one who made it must be established. For a will takes effect only at death, since it is not in force as long as the one who made it is alive. Therefore not even the first covenant was inaugurated without blood. For when every commandment of the law had been declared by Moses to all the people, he took the blood of calves and goats, with water and scarlet wool and hyssop, and sprinkled both the book itself and all the people, saying, "This is the blood of the covenant that God commanded for you." (Heb 9:15–20)

Therefore, when a person trusts in Christ, to him or her is granted the entire inheritance that Christ won for us in history. The last will and testament goes into effect, which declares even the ungodly to be justified and even strangers and aliens to be the adopted children of God and co-heirs with Christ (Gal 3:15–4:7). This legal aspect of the union is the basis for God's righteous and just dispensing of all other gifts of this union, from sanctification to glorification.

Third, it is an *organic* union. On the basis of the union's legal aspect (justification and adoption), the Spirit begins to "deliver the goods," as it were. Objectively declared to be righteous heirs of the kingdom, believers immediately receive the subjective benefits of their vital engrafting to their life-giving Vine. Passively receiving Christ and his benefits in justification, the believer now actively and immediately begins to bear the fruit of righteousness. "And *because you are sons*, God has sent the Spirit of his Son into our hearts, crying, 'Abba! Father!' So you are no longer a slave, but a son, and if a son, then an heir through God" (Gal 4:6–7, emphasis added). Thus, the Spirit not only takes what is Christ's and gives it to us (Jn 16:14), but works within us to bear the fruit of the Spirit (Jn 15:1–11; cf. Gal 5:22–26).

This organic union with Christ is far richer than any notion of the Christian life as an imitation of Christ (*imitatio Christi*). Although it certainly entails our *following Christ*, the New Testament emphasis is upon our *living in Christ*. Hence, before Jesus explains the practical effects of this union in the fruit-bearing of sanctification, he declares, "Already you are clean because of the word that I have spoken to you" (Jn 15:3). Legally pronounced just and claimed by God, engrafted into his Son, believers bear fruit that is not the result of their imitation of Christ's life but of their being incorporated into Christ and his eschatological resurrection-life in the Spirit.

Although we are justified by Christ's external righteousness imputed to us, our Savior does not remain outside of us, simply leading the way to a better life; rather, we live in him and therefore in and for each other. "I am the vine; you are the branches," says Jesus. "Whoever abides in me and I in him, he it is that bears much fruit, for apart from me you can do nothing" (v. 5). This "abiding" is not something that believers can move in and out of: one moment abiding and another moment not abiding. In fact, those who do not abide in Christ (and therefore do not produce fruit) are cut off (v. 2). Abiding is simply a synonym for faith: cleaving to Christ for all of our life. He is not simply a distant example in history, but our living head in heaven.

B. Historical Development

1. Ancient Church to the Reformation

Although the ancient and medieval church's teaching concerning justification is ambiguous, the best accounts of pre-Reformation teaching concerning the marvelous exchange between the believer's sin and Christ's righteousness are to be found in the writings, hymns, and liturgies that treat union with Christ. Nevertheless, even here one discerns two trajectories: the more Platonic/Neoplatonic ascent of mind associated with Origen and the more biblical concentration on our identification with Christ in the economy of grace: the historical pattern of his descent, ascent, and return in the flesh, associated with Irenaeus. Wherever mystical union was allowed to be unduly determined by the categories of Platonism, the economy of dying-and-rising with Christ became allegorized into the soul's ascent from the body and history to intellectual-mystical contemplation in which the soul finally became one with God. The two-age eschatology of the New Testament (with its tension between the "already" and the "not yet") was assimilated to the two-world cosmology of Plato. "Union with God" became another way of introducing Creator-creature confusion, as though God's essence could be communicated to creatures. It was the essence-energies distinction developed especially in Byzantine theology that sought to block this path while still upholding the realism of union with Christ.

In medieval circles influenced by Origen and Pseudo-Dionysius, a covenantal concept of union with Christ (namely, head-and-body, vine-and-branches, mediating testator-and-beneficiaries, husband-and-wife, etc.) was replaced with a metaphysical conception that simultaneously downplayed our union with Jesus in the flesh in the power of the Spirit and fused the human spirit with Christ's divinity. All things considered, this trajectory can be traced all the way to Hegel, Schleiermacher, and the mediating theologians of the nineteenth century, and to contemporary theologies for which union with Christ becomes yet another pathway to fusing the essence of the believer (or the church) with divinity.

2. REFORMATION VIEWS OF THE MYSTICAL UNION

Luther's "evangelical breakthrough" was in some ways a reaction against medieval mysticism as a theology of glory. However, it was also from some of these mystics that he learned crucial dimensions of the theology of the cross. Medieval treatments of union with Christ were often more about a union (even fusion) of human essence with God, either intellectually or volitionally, through the self's ascending efforts. However, some (especially more Augustinian) writers concentrated on union with God *in Christ* by appealing to the biblical analogy of marriage. This emphasis can be seen especially in the reforming French abbot Bernard of Clairvaux (1090–1153). His influence is clearly evident in the view of union as "the marvelous exchange," found in Luther and Calvin.[6] Everything that can be considered good in us is so because Christ lives in the believer and the believer in Christ. As we have seen, both Reformers held that human striving to behold "the naked God" in his blinding majesty leads to death, while receiving God in Christ our Mediator, as he has clothed himself in the humility of our humanity, leads to salvation and life. In God's incarnational descent, the Son first unites himself to us and then, also by his Spirit, he unites us to himself.

However, Luther's advance turned upon his recognition that this marriage is first judicial—the imputation of our sin to Christ and of his righteousness to sinners, and then (as a consequence) a growing relationship of trust, love, and good works in which the union is realized subjectively more and more. Far from rejecting the believer's actual righteousness (sanctification), Luther says that Christ's imputed righteousness "is the basis, the cause, the source of all our own actual righteousness."[7] Far from separating these distinct works of God, justification is made the ground and animating principle of sanctification.

> We conclude, therefore, that a Christian lives not in himself, but in Christ and his neighbor. Otherwise he is not a Christian. He lives in Christ through faith, in his neighbor through love. By faith he is caught up beyond himself into God. By love he descends beneath himself into his neighbor. Yet he always remains in God and in his love.[8]

Faith not only suffices for justification, but is the constant source of the believer's renewal and service toward others. Faith not only justifies; it "unites the soul with Christ as a bride is united with her bridegroom," says Luther.[9]

---

6. See, for example, Dennis E. Tamburello, *Union with Christ: John Calvin and the Mysticism of St. Bernard* (Louisville: Westminster John Knox, 1994).

7. Martin Luther, "Two Kinds of Righteousness," in *Luther's Works* (ed. Helmut T. Lehmann; Philadelphia: Fortress, 1957; repr., 1971), 31:298.

8. Martin Luther, "The Freedom of a Christian", in *Luther's Works*, 31:371; cf. Cornelis P. Venema, "Heinrich Bullinger's Correspondence on Calvin's Doctrine of Predestination," *Sixteenth Century Journal* 17 (1986): 435–50.

9. Luther, *The Freedom of a Christian*, in *Luther's Works*, 31:351.

In fact, the mystical union of Christ and the believer was so prominent in Luther's thinking that he sometimes tended to blur the distinction between Christ and the believer. This occasional tendency became an explicit position in an important associate of Luther's, Andreas Osiander (1498–1552), who lodged justification in Christ's indwelling presence rather than in the forensic imputation of Christ's righteousness. Luther rejected this position, but it was especially Calvin and the Lutheran theologian Flacius (1520–1575) who offered detailed rebuttals.

Though certainly a follower of Luther, Calvin was also indebted to Irenaeus and the Cappadocians, Cyril of Alexandria, Augustine, Hilary of Poitiers, and Bernard, among others. Referring to Bernard at least twenty-one times in the *Institutes*, Calvin writes,

> For in Christ [God] offers all happiness in place of our misery, all wealth in place of our neediness; in him he opens to us the heavenly treasures that our whole faith may contemplate his beloved Son, our whole expectation depend upon him, and our whole hope cleave to and rest in him. This, indeed, is that secret and hidden philosophy which cannot be wrested from syllogisms. But they whose eyes God has opened surely learn it by heart, that in his light they may see light [Ps 36:9].[10]

Interestingly, Calvin begins his treatment of the Holy Spirit's work (the application of redemption) in the *Institutes* by returning to the mystical union. The Spirit grants sinners the gift of faith through the gospel, and this same faith receives Christ for both justification and sanctification.[11] Christ's work *for* us must be distinguished but never separated from his union *with* us and work *within* us, both of which are

---

10. Calvin, *Institutes* 3.20.1. On the number of references to Bernard, see François Wendel, *Calvin: Origins and Development of His Religious Thought* (trans. Philip Mairet; New York and London: Harper & Row, 1963), 127n43.

11. The importance of union with Christ in Calvin's theology has been recognized for some time. However, a number of recent studies have shown in great detail the extent to which Calvin returns to this motif at numerous points in his thinking. Among noteworthy examples is Mark Garcia's *Life in Christ: Union with Christ and Twofold Grace in Calvin's Theology* (Milton Keynes, U.K.: Paternoster, 2008). However, while illuminating Calvin's crucial and distinctive interpretations, Garcia (in my view) overstates Calvin's discontinuity with his contemporaries (especially Melanchthon), particularly by eliminating any dependence of sanctification on justification. He labors the point that for Calvin sanctification "does not flow from the imputation of Christ's righteousness but from Christ himself with whom the Spirit has united believers. In other words, for Calvin, sanctification does not flow from justification.... Rather, together they are 'effects,' or, better, aspects of union with Christ" (146). This seems to me to present a false dilemma. Without any contradiction, one could also say that all of our spiritual blessings are given to us because of Christ's redemp-

tive work for us in history while also affirming that glorification follows sanctification in logical (and temporal) sequence. Garcia seems to assume that if justification and sanctification are both gifts of union with Christ, then there can be no dependent relationship between these gifts themselves. Calvin does maintain that Spirit-given faith unites us to Christ for justification and sanctification, but he also sees justification as the basis for sanctification. In his opening argument of his commentary on Romans, Calvin calls justification "the main subject of the whole Epistle." He treats union with Christ only (as Paul does) when the question of justification's relation to sanctification is raised (Ro 6). While Garcia is certainly correct that Calvin explains this relation in terms of the double-grace given through union with Christ, the Reformer also sees (with Melanchthon) that justification is the judicial ground of the union, and this same declaration (i.e., the gospel) is the instrumental means of sanctification as well. For example, Calvin says that "since we are clothed with the righteousness of the Son" in justification, "we are reconciled to God and renewed by the power of the Spirit to holiness" (*Commentary on the Epistle to the Romans*, in *Calvin's New Testament Commentaries* [ed. David W. Torrance and Thomas F. Torrance; Grand Rapids: Eerdmans, 1964], 138).

accomplished by the Spirit.[12] Following Paul in Romans 6, Calvin relates justification to sanctification by extrapolating our union with Christ. "First, we must understand that as long as Christ remains outside of us, and we are separated from him, all that he has suffered and done for the salvation of the human race remains useless and of no value for us. Therefore, to share with us what he has received from the Father, he had to become ours and to dwell within us." It is by "the secret energy of the Spirit" that "we come to enjoy Christ and all his benefits.... To sum up, the Holy Spirit is the bond by which Christ effectually unites us to himself."[13] The grace that justifies and renews is not a principle that is infused by the sacraments. Rather, it is nothing less than *Christ himself*, delivered to us *by the Spirit* who unites us to Christ *through faith*.

Even more than other Reformers, Calvin emphasized union with Christ as the link between justification and sanctification. Calvin was not satisfied simply to say that all of those who are justified are also necessarily sanctified, much less that justification was a free gift and sanctification was now a goal to attain by human striving. Rather, he recognized that faith grasps Christ for everything in salvation: not only for absolution and right-standing before God, but for adoption, holiness, triumph over sin, and final glorification. Baptism into Christ is the heart of Calvin's doctrine of the Christian life.

In the light of these reflections, the charge that the Reformers substituted a personal and relational conception of salvation for an impersonal transaction is wholly unfounded. In fact, the opposite is the case. Where medieval scholasticism concentrated on the infusion of supernatural habits (something done within the believer but at a distance), and some Protestants like Andreas Osiander simply collapsed faith into regeneration (as sanctification), the believer into Christ, Christ's humanity into his deity, and everything into God, Calvin focuses on the role of the Holy Spirit as the bond of our union with Christ. Difference and affinity are always simultaneously affirmed, and pneumatology provides the crucial link. All supernatural gifts are found in Christ alone by the Spirit alone, though working through means. Because all of God's external works are done by the Father, in the Son, through the Spirit, there is no gift of salvation that can be considered impersonal. That we are in Christ *and* that Christ is in us are both due to the mediation of the Spirit. "But faith is the principal work of the Holy Spirit."[14] Here we recall again the recurring motif that every external work of the Trinity is done by the Father in the Son through the effective power of the Holy Spirit. It is the Spirit who brings us into union with

---

12. A helpful recent summary of Calvin's understanding of union with Christ in relation to justification and sanctification may be found in Richard B. Gaffin Jr., "Justification and Union with Christ," in *Theological Guide to Calvin's Institutes: Essays*

and Analysis (ed. David Hall and Peter Lillback; Phillipsburg, N.J.: P&R, 2009), 248–69.

13. Calvin, *Institutes* 3.1.1.

14. Ibid., 3.1.4.

Christ even as this same Spirit brought the Son into union with us through the incarnation.

Drawing, like Luther, on the wide range of biblical analogies for this union, Calvin complemented his judicial emphasis concerning *justification* with the organic imagery of union and engrafting in relation to the *inner renewal* and communion with Christ, including his holiness. Thus, commenting on John 17, Calvin explains, "Having been engrafted into the body of Christ, we are made partakers of the Divine adoption, and heirs of heaven."[15] "This is the purpose of the gospel," he says, "that Christ should become ours, and that we should be engrafted into his body."[16] Though justified by an alien righteousness imputed, we cannot grasp Christ without receiving all of his benefits.[17] All of those who are justified are united to Christ and become fruit-bearing branches. We might put it in the following way:

- "We in Christ"—sharing in his election, flesh, life of obedience, atoning death, resurrection, justification, holiness, and glorification. We are in the family (*inheritance*).
- "Christ in us"—regeneration and sanctification, "the hope of glory." The family is in us (*resemblance*).

Calvin's pneumatological emphasis, which we will meet again in his formulation of the way in which Christ is communicated to us in the Supper, is already apparent in his treatment of the mystical union. The Spirit's mediation of Christ's person and work, not an immediate participation in the divine essence, is a critical aspect of his account. We are "one with the Son of God; not because he conveys his substance to us, but because, by the power of the Spirit, he imparts to us his life and all the blessings which he has received from the Father."[18] Commenting on John 17:23 ("I in them and you in me . . ."), he draws the image of a vast ocean with innumerable tributaries and channels, which "water the fields on all sides."[19] The foundation of our assurance that we are loved by God is "that we are loved because the Father hath loved his Son."[20] "With such a love did the Father love him before the creation of the world, that he might be the person in whom the Father would love his elect."[21] The clause in verse 26, "and I in them," "deserves our attention," he says, "for it teaches us that the only way in which we are included in that love

---

15. John Calvin, *Commentary on the Gospel according to John* (trans. William Pringle; Grand Rapids: Baker, repr., 1996), 166, commenting on Jn 17:3.

16. Calvin, *Commentary on Romans*, 1:9.

17. Two superb treatments of Calvin's emphasis on the "two-fold grace" of justification and sanctification should be noted here: Cornelis P. Venema, "The Twofold Nature of the Gospel in Calvin's Theology: The 'Duplex Gratia Dei' and the Interpre-

tation of Calvin's Theology" (PhD diss., Princeton Theological Seminary, 1985), and, more recently, J. Todd Billings, *Calvin, Participation, and the Gift: The Activity of Believers in Union with Christ* (New York: Oxford Univ. Press, 2008).

18. Calvin, *Commentary on John*, 183–84.

19. Ibid., 185.

20. Ibid., 186.

21. Ibid., 187.

which he mentions is that Christ dwells in us; for, as the Father cannot look upon his Son without having likewise before his eyes the whole body of Christ, so, if we wish to be beheld in him, we must be actually his members."[22] On the "vine and branches" in John 15:1 he notes that this union is not natural or universal, but is a gift of electing grace. It is not an abstract participation in being, "as if it had been implanted in them by nature," but a personal union with the mediator of the covenant: "But Christ dwells principally on this, that the vital sap — that is, all life and strength — proceeds from himself alone."[23]

The mystical union of believers with Christ (and therefore with his body) is the wider field within which the Reformers recognize the integral connection of justification and sanctification, the imputation of righteousness and the impartation of Christ's holy love in the lives of those united to him through faith. Faith looks to Christ for justification and "puts on" Christ for renewal and life. In this way, not only justification but sanctification and glorification are assured in Christ alone, through faith alone. Establishing the legal basis of this new relationship, union with Christ is first of all forensic. Yet because it is spoken by the Father, in the Son, through the effective power of the Spirit, God's Word always creates the world of which it speaks. The role of believers in this matter is to "reckon" themselves righteous according to God's reckoning as well as dead to sin and alive to God (Ro 6:3–11). Only on the basis of this reckoning or crediting of God's declaration as the truth of the matter can they then actually begin their new obedience, "since you are not under law but under grace" (vv. 12–14).

Taking root in the forensic soil of justification, from which it derives its effective power as well as its legal basis, union with Christ produces the life of Christ within believers, which bears the fruit of righteousness. This life is not simply *like* Christ's life (*imitatio Christi*); it *is* Christ's life into which we are baptized. He is the first-fruits, we are the harvest; he is the head, we are his members; he is the achiever, we are the beneficiaries; he is the vine, we are the branches. Christ is always therefore unique, but his co-heirs share fully in the new humanity that he has attained in his exaltation at the Father's right hand.

Christ is not simply a moral example to imitate, says Calvin. "As if we ought to think of Christ, standing afar off and not rather dwelling in us!"[24] We are not merely admirers or even followers of Christ, but members of his body. By virtue of this mystical union, we can be assured that we are already accepted in Christ and that everything that belongs properly to him is given freely to us. Warning that "if you contemplate yourself, that is sure damnation," Calvin adds,

---

22. Ibid., 189.
23. Ibid., 107, commenting on John 15:1.

24. Calvin, *Institutes* 3.2.24.

But since Christ has been so imparted to you with all his benefits that all his things are made yours, that you are made a member of him, indeed one with him, his righteousness overwhelms your sins; his salvation wipes out your condemnation; with his worthiness he intercedes that your unworthiness may not come before God's sight. Surely this is so: We ought not to separate Christ from ourselves or ourselves from him. Rather we ought to hold fast bravely with both hands to that fellowship by which he has bound himself to us. So the apostle teaches us: "Now your body is dead because of sin; but the Spirit of Christ which dwells in you is life because of righteousness" [Ro 8:10].[25]

If we are united to Christ, how can we ever fail to be assured "that that condemnation which we of ourselves deserve has been swallowed up by the salvation that is in Christ"? "Not only does he cleave to us by an indivisible bond of fellowship, but with a wonderful communion, day by day, he grows more and more into one body with us, until he becomes completely one with us." Justified once and for all through faith by a righteousness that is external (alien) to us, we are united to Christ by an inseparable communion so that, in spite of our weaknesses, we will always seek our salvation in him.[26] Although Christ's example remains instructive, sanctification is not a life of striving to imitate Christ, but of seeking all of our blessings—including our conformity to his image—in Christ and not in ourselves.

With Paul, Calvin links union with Christ to baptism as its sign and seal, writing that "our faith receives from baptism the advantage of its sure testimony to us that we are not only engrafted into the death and life of Christ, but so united to Christ himself that we become sharers in all his blessings." He adds,

> For he dedicated and sanctified baptism in his own body [Matt. 3:13] in order that he might have it in common with us as the firmest bond of the union and fellowship which he has deigned to form with us. Hence, Paul proves that we are children of God from the fact that we put on Christ in baptism [Gal. 3:26–27].... *For this reason we obtain and, so to speak, clearly discern in the Father the cause, in the Son the matter, and in the Spirit the effect, of our purgation and our regeneration* (emphasis added).[27]

The last sentence points up again the Trinitarian thinking that shapes his theology generally and no less in consideration of this topic.

Union with Christ became the chief image for the whole sweep of salvation in Reformed theology. Chosen, redeemed, and justified in Christ alone, believers are also sanctified, adopted, and finally glorified in him as their living head. There are no gifts that we receive from God apart from Christ, and his work is inseparable from

---

25. Ibid.
26. Ibid.

27. Ibid., 4.15.6.

his person. It is impossible to receive the benefits of Christ apart from Christ himself. Therefore, the believer receives Christ simultaneously for a perfect (though "alien") righteousness before God and for sanctification and the hope of glory (1Co 1:30).

It is not the Reformers, but their opponents, who force a false choice between a legal verdict of justification and the inner renewal of sanctification, Calvin argued. "Surely those things which are connected do not destroy one another!"[28] So when we consider ourselves, there is nothing but despair; when we consider ourselves *in Christ*, there is faith, which brings hope and love in its train. In the gospel, God calls forth a new world of which Christ is the sun, into whose orbit we are drawn. Again Calvin quotes Bernard: "Surely if we think, 'If he has decreed to save us, we shall be immediately freed' [cf. Jer 17:14]; in this, then, we may take heart." We are therefore raised from the status of transgressors to that of dignified heirs, "but by his dignifying us, not by our own dignity."[29] We do not prepare our hearts for grace; the sovereign guest accomplishes all things simply by taking up his residence.[30] A strange guest this is indeed.

Where medieval theology, codified at Trent, developed its *ordo salutis* by appealing to various infusions of a gracious substance into the soul, enabling meritorious cooperation on our part, Calvin insists that all of our blessings—justification and sanctification—are found only in Christ, through the Spirit.[31] Calvin recognizes here that justification need not be *confused* with sanctification by means of an all-encompassing ontology of union in order to recognize the *inseparability* of the legal (forensic) and organic (effective) aspects of that union.

When discussing justification, Calvin cautions emphatically that "the question is not how we may become righteous but how, being unrighteous and unworthy, we may be reckoned righteous. If consciences wish to attain any certainty in this matter, they ought to give no place to the law."[32] However, the same act of faith that constantly looks to Christ alone for justification looks to Christ alone for sanctification and glorification. There are not two sources of the Christian life: one forensic and found in Christ alone, while the other is moral and found within us. United to Christ by Spirit-given faith, we receive Christ for justification and discover that with this forensic verdict we receive also every spiritual blessing for the renewal of our lives.[33] Everything that Christ does within us by his Spirit in this union is the result of his work for us in the past and his imputation of righteousness in the present.

---

28. Ibid., 3.2.25.

29. Ibid.

30. Ibid., 3.3.2. This is one of many examples in Calvin's *Institutes* where he argues against the medieval notion of "preparatory fear" as the engine that gets the Christian life going. Instead, Calvin insists, one can never bring about the fruit of repentance until one first trusts in God as a merciful Father, and this can be derived

only from the confidence that we are fully accepted in Christ.

31. Ibid., 3.16.1.

32. Ibid., 3.19.2.

33. For more on this topic (especially in relation to Calvin's debate with Osiander), see Michael Horton, *Covenant and Salvation: Union with Christ* (Louisville: Westminster John Knox, 2007), 143–44.

In Calvin's view, it made little difference whether one said that one was justified by cooperation with an infused righteousness or that, as Osiander argued, one was saved by the "essential righteousness" of Christ indwelling the believer. In either case the ground of justification would be an internal act of making righteous, rather than the imputation of an alien righteousness. Nevertheless, Calvin could just as heartily celebrate the participatory, effective, and transformative aspects of mystical union. In fact, he complained that Erasmus's rendering of *koinōnia* as *societas* and *consortium* fell far short of the mystical union, so he chose *communio*.[34] "But Osiander has introduced some strange monster of 'essential' righteousness by which, although not intending to abolish freely given righteousness, he has still enveloped it in such a fog as to darken pious minds and deprive them of a lively experience of Christ's grace."[35] Besides indulging in "speculation" and "feeble curiosity," Osiander is faulted for "something bordering on Manichaeism, in his desire to transfuse the essence of God into men."[36] In Calvin's understanding, however, "it comes about through the power of the Holy Spirit that we grow together with Christ, and he becomes our Head and we his members...." The upshot of Osiander's teaching is that justification is confused with regeneration and the believer is confused with the divine essence. Yet we can still affirm a communion with Christ's person, Calvin counters, without surrendering the doctrine of forensic justification.[37] In Osiander's treatment, "to be justified is not only to be reconciled to God through free pardon but also to be made righteous, and righteousness is not a free imputation but the holiness and uprightness that the essence of God, dwelling in us, inspires."[38]

In conclusion, Calvin observes, "that mystical union" is "accorded by us the highest degree of importance, so that Christ, having been made ours, makes us sharers with him in the gifts with which he has been endowed." Only because justification is constituted by an imputed rather than an inherent righteousness are believers able "not to tremble at the judgment they deserve, and while they rightly condemn themselves, they should be accounted righteous outside themselves."[39] So we discern complementary emphases in Calvin's account: the righteousness of Christ that justifies us is "outside of us," although, by virtue of the mystical union, Christ himself—including his righteousness—*cannot* remain outside of us. There is a balance, therefore, between a strict realism ("overcoming estrangement") on one side and an arbitrary nominalism ("the stranger we never meet") on the other. This is precisely the logic of Romans 6, where instead of threatening believers with

---

34. B. A. Gerrish, *Guilt and Grace: The Eucharistic Theology of John Calvin* (Minneapolis: Augsburg Fortress, 1993), 83. See Calvin's commentary on 1 Cor. 1:9 (CO 49:313).

35. Calvin, *Institutes* 3.11.5, in refutation of Andreas Osiander's *Disputation on Justification* (1550). Osiander was a Lutheran theo-logian whose views were finally rejected in the *Book of Concord*.

36. Calvin, *Institutes* 3.11.5.

37. Ibid.

38. Ibid., 3.11.6.

39. Ibid.

the loss of salvation or rewards the apostle simply declares that union with Christ ensures both justification and moral renewal (vv. 2–6).

In some ways like medieval piety, Protestant pietism richly and beautifully emphasized the "marvelous exchange": Christ's riches for our poverty. However, in its mystical tendency there has always been the danger that "Christ *in* us" pushes "Christ *for* us" to the periphery. Strictly speaking, it is not Christ who personally indwells believers, but the Spirit. Because the Spirit unites us to Christ, his indwelling presence delivers Christ's person and work to us here and now, but our glorified head remains in heaven until he returns to raise our bodies in his glorious likeness. Thus, Christ does not dwell in our hearts immediately, but through the indwelling of the Spirit. Furthermore, the Spirit's ministry is always to point us outside of ourselves to Christ's person and work. The righteousness that alone will withstand God's judgment *always* remains Christ's rather than the believer's. Therefore, even in our sanctification we must look outside of ourselves and cling to Christ alone, realizing more and more each day the effects of the fact that we have been declared righteous in Christ and that we have been baptized by the Spirit into his death and raised with him in life. Similar to Osiander's treatment in pietism, the believer and Christ seem to merge, losing their respective identity. "Jesus in my heart" replaces Jesus in the flesh, winning our redemption and ruling at the Father's right hand. On the other hand, the New Testament represents the work of the Spirit within our hearts as the very source both of the confidence in redemption already won and of the effects of that redemption still awaiting us, so that we groan inwardly, longing for Christ's bodily return (Ro 8:18–27).

As a decadent form of later pietism, shaped also by the Enlightenment and Romanticism, Protestant liberalism developed a pantheistic conception of mystical union with God over against a substitutionary atonement and forensic justification. Charles Hodge summarizes this trend, which had reached its climax in his day:

> The incarnation of God is continued in the Church; and this new principle of "divine-human life" descends from Christ to the members of his Church, as naturally and as much by a process of organic development, as humanity, derived from Adam, unfolded itself in his descendants. Christ, therefore, saves us not so much by what He did, as by what He is. He made no satisfaction to the divine justice; no expiation for sin; no fulfillment of the law. There is, therefore, really no justification, no real pardon even, in the ordinary sense of the word. There is a healing of the soul, and with that healing the removal of the evils incident to disease. Those who become partakers of this new principle of life, which is truly human and truly divine, become one with Christil.... What the Scriptures and the Church attribute to the Spirit working with the freedom of a personal agent, when and where he sees fit, this system attributes to the "theanthropic-life" of Christ, working as a new force according to the natural laws of development.... This system may be adopted

as a matter of opinion, but it cannot be an object of faith. And therefore it cannot support the hopes of a soul conscious of guilt.[40]

Again similar to Osiander (not to mention Meister Eckhart and other extreme mystics of the medieval period), these theologians transformed the genuine humanity of Christ into a "spiritualized" and cosmic Christ who replaces (or is indistinguishable from) the Holy Spirit. "The Christ within (as some of the Friends [Quakers] also teach), is, according to this system, all the Christ we have. Ebrard, therefore, in one view, identifies regeneration and justification": we are pronounced just on the basis of this new life infused.[41] All crucial distinctions between God and humanity, the Son and the Spirit, and justification and regeneration are dissolved. As we will see in our consideration of ecclesiology, this neo-Hegelian fusion of Christ and believers (or the community) is evident in diverse quarters today, from Radical Orthodoxy to the emergent church movement.

Clearly, there is a divergence between these trajectories: the one, more Irenaean, emphasizing union with Christ in his economic and redemptive-historical position as the head of a new humanity, and the other, more Origenist (Platonic), striving for an essential union with divinity through spiritual ascent. Once again we encounter the contrast between "meeting a stranger" and "overcoming estrangement."

II. UNION VERSUS FUSION: CONTRASTING PARADIGMS

Reflecting the contrasting ontologies of "overcoming estrangement" and "meeting a stranger" is the contrast between a Neoplatonic concept of ontological participation (*methexis*) and a covenantal concept of union (*koinōnia*). From Origen to John Milbank, there has been a pronounced tendency to identify union with Christ with a Platonic or Neoplatonic scheme of an ontic union of the soul with divinity on an ever-ascending ladder of being. Through various monastic movements, the teaching of Clement of Alexandria, more extreme mystics in the middle ages such as Nicholas of Cusa, Meister Eckhart, and Jacob Böhme, as well as modern speculative philosophers such as Fichte and Hegel, this version of participation has found renewed interest in our day especially through Radical Orthodoxy and the New Finnish Interpretation of Luther, which in many respects repeats Osiander's errors.[42]

As we have seen in considering God's attributes, the world depends on God;

---

40. Charles Hodge, *Systematic Theology* (Grand Rapids: Eerdmans, 1946), 3:21–32.

41. Ibid., 24. It is worth noting that this identification of justification and regeneration is also maintained by N. T. Wright in *What Saint Paul Really Said: Was Paul of Tarsus the Real Founder of Christianity?* (Grand Rapids: Eerdmans, 1997), 113–29.

42. I interact at length with these positions in part 2 of *Covenant and Salvation: Union with Christ*.

God does not depend on the world. The world participates in God analogically as the created effect of his Word and Spirit, though God remains transcendent. God's essence is never communicated to creatures. Nevertheless, God relates human beings to himself, first, as his creation, and second, as the creaturely partner-in-covenant. It is significant that the New Testament writers selected *koinōnia* (communion) rather than *metochē* (the Platonic term for participation) as their dominant term for union with Christ.[43] Thus, union with God-in-Christ is not the goal to which the soul aspires in its striving ascent, but the freely-given communion that every believer enjoys from the very beginning. Believers live *from* this union, not *toward* it, and it is a forensic and relational reality: a communion of persons and their gifts rather than an exchange (much less fusion) of essences.

There is a close connection in the New Testament between faith, baptism, the Spirit, and union with Christ (Ro 6:1–2; 1Co 10:1–4; 12:13; Col 2:11–13). Thus, Christ's obedience is ours: a legal, corporate solidarity (Ro 5:12–21). But it is also a dynamic effect (divine power or energy) in us: the same power by which Christ was raised from the dead is *at work in us* (Ro 6:1–9; Eph 1:18–22). *Koinōnia* involves, therefore, a mutual indwelling of believers in each other in that place that is called Christ's body, an analogy of the mutual indwelling of the persons of the Trinity (Jn 14:20–23; 17:20–23). Christ indwells us not immediately or essentially, as if our natures were somehow transfused or mingled, but by his Spirit (Eph 2:18, 22). This is the sense in which, through God's "precious and very great promises," we have now become "partakers of the divine nature" (2Pe 1:4). The Lord's Supper is a communion/participation (*koinōnia*) in his incarnate body and blood, and in each other as his covenantal body (1Co 10:16–17).

As a result, the New Testament writers refer not to a general participation in being as the locus of our redemption, but to union with Christ. The New Testament, even when it contrasts visible and invisible, earthly and heavenly, temporal and eternal, changing shadows and unchanging realities, interprets them in terms of *eschatology* rather than *ontology*. In other words, it is the Jewish apocalyptic of two ages rather than Platonism's two worlds that dominates the biblical horizon. Where Platonism divides reality into upper and lower realms, the two-age eschatology of Scripture interprets reality in its condition under the reign of sin and death (this present age) and under the reign of righteousness and life (the age to come). We rest our hope on things that are invisible not because they are intrinsically (ontologically) invisible to physical sight, but because their fulfillment still lies in the future. Heavenly realities are contrasted with earthly realities not in any abstract antithesis but as a way of referring to the impotence of earthly powers to bring about redemption

---

43. For a fuller treatment of this terminology, see ibid., 153–215. See also John Zizioulas, *Being as Communion* (Crest-wood, N.Y.: St. Vladimir's Seminary Press, 1985), 94.

from the curse. However, the goal of redemption is a renewal of creation rather than its destruction. And the changing shadows are not the realm of material things, but the whole of created reality that depends on the precarious conditionality of human obedience rather than on the absolute security of God's immutable grace.

This means that union with Christ is a *soteriological* category. However true it may be that all creatures exist in analogical dependence on God's being, the Spirit communicates Christ's eschatological righteousness and life, not the divine essence, to believers. Paul explains in Romans 5 that we enter the world united to Adam as our covenant head, with his guilt imputed and corruption imparted. From the womb, we are declared ungodly, and we live out that status in daily unbelief and sinful actions. Baptized into Christ, we are transferred to another covenant head, who is the source of righteousness imputed and holiness imparted. Hence, Calvin encourages us to find our purity in Christ's virginal conception, our anointing with the Spirit in his baptism, our mortification in his tomb, our life in his resurrection, and the gifts of the Spirit in his sending of the Spirit at Pentecost, which is echoed also in the Great Litany of the *Book of Common Prayer*.[44]

Therefore, union with Christ is to be understood in covenantal terms. The Messiah not only saves; he is the corporate head of the people whom he represents and makes to share in the spoils of his victory. As goes the King, so goes the kingdom. As the firstfruits of the whole harvest, Jesus Christ is not merely an example to be imitated by his followers, but the head of a covenantal body to be incorporated into by the Spirit. Whatever is true concerning the King must also be true in principle concerning his people.[45] This is what it means to be baptized into Christ.[46] There is therefore no question of any fusion of persons. As in marriage, the two become "one flesh," not one person. They are united persons, not a single person. N. T. Wright observes that Daniel 7, Psalm 8, Genesis 1, and Isaiah 45 (esp. v. 23) "all point towards the nexus of thought which we have seen . . .: the obedience of Israel, the obedience of Adam, the exaltation of the human figure and/or the Israel-figure to a position of pre-eminence in virtue of that obedience."[47] Paul is basically working out the theme of the "servant songs" of Isaiah.[48]

Consistent with the story I have offered so far, Morna D. Hooker concludes, "Israel should have been obedient to God; this obedience has now been fulfilled, so Paul argues, in the person of Jesus Christ."[49] Thus, union with Christ through faith is the only way of obtaining the status that Israel was, according to Paul, still seeking through the law. This covenantal understanding of union with Christ is

---

44. Calvin, *Institutes* 2.16.19.

45. N. T. Wright, *The Climax of the Covenant: Christ and the Law in Pauline Theology* (Edinburgh: T&T Clark, 1991), 46.

46. Wright, *The Climax of the Covenant*, 47–49.

47. Ibid., 58.

48. Ibid., 60.

49. Morna D. Hooker, *Pauline Pieces* (London: Epworth, 1979), 66, cited in Wright, *The Climax of the Covenant*, 61.

consistent also with the interpretation of Passover in the Jewish literature. In *m. Pesaḥ* 10:5, we read a well-known guideline for celebration of Passover: "In every generation a person is duty-bound to regard himself as if he has personally gone forth from Egypt."[50] Our modern democratic sensibilities bristle at such a strong identification of representative solidarity as Israel's collective guilt for Achan's theft or humanity's collective guilt "in Adam." (Of course, premodern thinkers like Pelagius bristled at such federal concepts as well.) Nevertheless, the welcome correlate of such solidarity is the collective participation of the wicked in the obedience and victory of the Last Adam that forms the heart of the gospel.

Particularly in Paul's interpretation, union with Christ corresponds to the new world of grace, faith, promise, justification, and life, in contrast to the old world of sin, unbelief, law, condemnation, and death. In spite of appearances, everything outside of Christ is dead, and everything in Christ is alive. As we have seen, the Old Testament believers share with us in the reality for which they hoped in type and shadow. In fact, this *koinōnia* between the old and new covenant saints is so strong that the writer to the Hebrews can say of the Old Testament heroes, "And all these, though commended through their faith, did not receive what was promised, since God had provided something better for us, that apart from us they should not be made perfect" (Heb 11:29–40).

III. NATURE AND GRACE

The relationship of nature and grace has been treated at various points in this volume, under different topics. In relation to union with Christ, the contrast between Platonic/Neoplatonic and biblical/covenantal paradigms becomes even more obvious. In the former paradigm, the soul strives to ascend away from the flesh toward a fusion with the divine One. In the latter, the Son is sent by the Father, in the power of the Spirit, to unite our flesh to himself and transform that human existence by his own history as our covenantal representative.

A. UNION WITH GOD THROUGH THE SOUL'S ASCENT VERSUS UNION WITH CHRIST THROUGH THE SON'S DESCENT

Following especially Romans 10 and 1 Corinthians 1, Luther contrasted these paradigms in terms of a theology of glory and the theology of the cross. Gerhard Forde explains,

---

50. *m. Pesaḥ* 10:5, in *The Mishnah* (trans. Jacob Neusner; New Haven, Conn.: Yale University Press, 1988), quoted in Mark Seifrid, *Christ, Our Righteousness: Paul's Theology of Justification* (Downers Grove, Ill.: InterVarsity Press, 2000), 24.

> The most common overarching story we tell about ourselves is what we will call the glory story. We came from glory and are bound for glory. Of course, in between we seem somehow to have gotten derailed—whether by design or accident we don't quite know—but that is only a temporary inconvenience to be fixed by proper religious effort. What we need is to get back on "the glory road." The story is told in countless variations. Usually the subject of the story is "the soul." ... The basic scheme is what Paul Ricoeur has called "the myth of the exiled soul."[51]

It was this myth of the exiled soul that fascinated Plato, Plotinus, and the Gnostics, as well as some of the most sensitive intellects of the Middle Ages and the Renaissance, and it is still very much with us today. Thrown off of our course by the fall (through following our bodily instincts rather than our higher self), we can be saved by the infusion of grace that heals the soul and sets it back on its upward journey. For Thomas Aquinas, grace is primarily a healing medicine for the soul.[52]

The notion of infused grace is part of a wider ontology that is applied to the original created state. Augustine had maintained that Adam was upheld in righteousness by an enabling grace that was added to an ontologically unstable nature. The fall occurred with the withdrawal of this *donum superadditum* ("infused gift of grace") and the consequent shift of vision from the invisible and intellectual to the visible and corporeal. Following Augustine, the early medieval scholastics distinguished between an operative grace (liberating the will from its bondage) that always precedes human effort and a cooperative grace that assists human effort.[53] Following Aquinas, the Council of Trent decreed that through prevenient grace God prepares the soul, while it is "through his stimulating and assisting grace [that individuals] are disposed to convert themselves to their own justification."[54] It is worth noting Wilhelm Pauck's observation that the verb *ekkechytai* in Romans 5:5 ("God's love *has been poured into* our hearts through the Holy Spirit") was rendered *infusa est* ("was infused") by the Vulgate, and this became a key basis for the doctrine of infused habits.[55] In baptism (the first justification), grace is infused into the soul so that the guilt of original sin is obliterated and the soul is made just (or righteous). Yet this infused grace merely *disposes* one toward faith and good works; it does not *confer* these gifts. Only when one actively cooperates with this grace by his or her free will does one increase in justification.

51. Gerhard Forde, *On Being a Theologian of the Cross: Reflections on Luther's Heidelberg Disputation, 1518* (Grand Rapids: Eerdmans, 1997), 5.

52. Ibid., 85; cf. Thomas Aquinas, *Summa theologica* 1a2ae, q. 3, art. 2; 1a2ae, q. 3, art. 3. Joseph P. Wawrykow offers a careful analysis and defense of Aquinas on this point in *God's Grace and Human Action: "Merit" in the Theology of Thomas Aquinas* (South Bend, Ind.: University of Notre Dame Press, 1995).

53. Peter Lombard, *Sentences* 2, dist. 26, 1, cited in Herman Bavinck, *Reformed Dogmatics* (ed. John Bolt; trans. John Vriend;

Grand Rapids: Baker Academic, 2006), 3:512.

54. Council of Trent, session 6, canon 5, quoted in Heinrich Denzinger, *The Sources of Catholic Dogma* (trans. Roy J. Deferrari; London: Herder, 1955), 250. This view is developed in Thomas Aquinas, *Summa theologica* 1a2ae 1121.

55. Wilhelm Pauck, introduction to *Christ and Adam: Man and Humanity in Romans 5*, by Karl Barth (trans. T. A. Smail; New York: Harper and Bros., 1956; originally published as *Christus und Adam nach Römer 5* [Zollikon-Zürich, Switzerland: Evangelischer Verlag, 1952]), 5.

Bavinck points out that the differences here go to the very heart of ontology, particularly in the understanding of grace.

Concerning this grace, there is an important difference between Rome and the Reformation, particularly in its Reformed development. In Catholic theology, the grace referred to here is called *gratia gratum faciens*, the grace that makes humans pleasing to God, and it is further differentiated into actual and habitual grace. The former is granted humans to enable them to engage in saving activities. For the natural human, the human without the superadded gift, though still capable of performing many naturally and morally good works, cannot perform the works that belong to a higher order and are linked with supernatural, heavenly blessedness.[56]

The categories are clearly those of nature and grace (the lower and higher realms) rather than sin and grace (the totality of creation in bondage to sin and liberated by Christ):

By actual grace, Catholic theology means not merely the external call of the gospel with its moral influence on the human intellect and will, but thinks in this connection of an illumination of the intellect and inspiration of the will that communicates to humans not only moral but even natural (physical) powers. At this point already we need to note that Rome bases the absolute necessity of habitual grace not so much on the sinful state of humankind as on the thesis that humans, having lost the superadded gift, are now purely natural beings who in the nature of the case cannot perform supernatural good works or saving acts, for "it is fitting that acts leading to an end should be proportioned to that end." [Aquinas] ... Of habitual (infused) grace it is stated even more sharply that it is a gift of God by which humanity "is elevated to the supernatural order and in some manner made a participant of the divine nature." It is a "divine quality inhering in the soul; like a kind of brightness and light it removes all stains from our souls and renders these same souls more beautiful and more bright."[57]

Thus, grace "divinizes" individuals and "elevates them 'into the divine order.' " The assumption is that grace makes us something *more* than human instead of liberating us *for* the full humanity for which we were created.

It "lifts us not merely above human nature but above every nature, above the highest choirs of heavenly spirits ... not merely above the whole existing creation but also above all possible beings, the most perfect beings conceivable not excepted." And since only God stands above all possible beings, "this grace-filled elevation must transpose us into a divine sphere."[58]

This grace "seeks to elevate and to make well."[59] Bavinck judges, "The forgiveness of sins is secondary here. Faith has only preparatory value. The primary thing is the

---

56. Bavinck, *Reformed Dogmatics*, 3:574.

57. Thomas Aquinas, *Summa theologica* 2, 1, q. 109, a. 5, quoted in Bavinck, *Reformed Dogmatics*, 575; C. Pesch, *Praelectiones dogmaticae* (Freiberg: Herder, 1989–1900), 5, 19, 21 and *Roman Catechism*, 2, 2, qu. 38, quoted in Bavinck, *Reformed Dogmatics*, 576.

58. J. Henrich and C. Gutberlet, *Dogmatische Theologie* (Mainz: Franz Kirchheim, 1873–1901), 8:588ff., quoted in Bavinck, *Reformed Dogmatics*, 576.

59. Bavinck, *Reformed Dogmatics*, 576.

elevation of human beings above their nature: divinization, 'both becoming like God and union with him' [Pesch]."[60]

In contrast, says Bavinck, "The Reformation rejected this Neoplatonic mysticism, returned to the simplicity of Holy Scripture, and consequently gained a very different concept of grace." "Grace serves, not to take up humans into a supernatural order, but to free them from sin. Grace is opposed not to nature, only to sin. In its real sense, it was not necessary in the case of Adam before the fall but has only become necessary as a result of sin." In the biblical conception, "The 'physical' opposition between the natural and the supernatural yields to the ethical opposition between sin and grace."[61]

For Rome, grace "is an aid to humans in their pursuit of deification." "In the Reformation, however, grace is the beginning, the middle, and the end of the entire work of salvation; it is totally devoid of human merit. Like creation and redemption, so also sanctification is a work of God."[62] Healing has an important place within a covenantal account of participation in Christ, but in reducing the *ordo salutis* to this motif, the Roman Catholic paradigm does not accommodate the forensic element. Furthermore, "healing," in a covenantal ontology, is effected by the Spirit through the gospel, not by the infusion of a gracious substance.

B. INFUSED HABITS

A habit (*habitus*) is a disposition. One may be disposed toward certain characteristics, for example, by one's genetic inheritance, without having yet exercised that inclination through explicit choices and actions. According to Augustine, human beings were composed of mind, soul, and body, and even in their created state were susceptible to being pulled down from contemplating eternal verities by their bodily passions. Therefore, God added to human nature an infused gift of grace (*donum superadditum*) to elevate nature beyond itself. Already one discerns a marked contrast with a covenantal understanding of this situation. According to Reformation theologians, Adam and Eve were never in a state of grace before the fall.[63] Endowed in their creation with all of the requisite gifts necessary for fulfilling God's eschatological purposes, they lacked nothing and therefore required no gracious supplement. In body as well as mind, Adam and Eve were already oriented covenantally to God, in whose image they were created. Therefore, Reformed theology does not

---

60. Ibid., 577.
61. Ibid.
62. Ibid., 579.
63. For example, Peter van Mastricht says that God's grace is "nothing but grace towards the wretched" (cited by Heppe, *Reformed Dogmatics*, 96), and the same view of grace as synonymous with mercy (i.e., God's favor shown to those at fault and not simply without merit) can be found in Rollock, Ussher, Perkins, Ursinus, Olevianus, Zanchi, Owen, and others. The *Westminster Confession* deliberately uses the term "voluntary condescension" rather than "grace" to describe God's original relation to humankind. Grace is always shown not only to those who do not deserve favor, but to those who "have deserved otherwise" (Amandus Polanus, cited in Heppe, *Reformed Dogmatics*, 96).

speak in terms of nature and grace, as if these were contrasting substances, but in terms of the covenant of creation (or works), before the fall, and the covenant of grace, after the fall. Bavinck writes,

> The covenant of grace differs from the covenant of works in method, not in its ultimate goal. It is the same treasure that was promised in the covenant of works and is granted in the covenant of grace. Grace restores nature and takes it to its highest pinnacle, but it does not add to it any new and heterogeneous constituents. From this it follows that in Reformation theology, grace cannot in any respect bear the character of a substance.[64]

If grace is a spiritual substance infused into a person in order to perfect nature, rather than divine favor shown to those who are at fault, we have a perfect example of the contrast between ontological-metaphysical and ethical-covenantal construals of the problem.[65]

Reformed writers noted a further problem with the Augustinian interpretation at this point: namely, that locating the fall in (a) an inherent weakness in the constitution of humanity as such (i.e., the lower appetites) and (b) God's withdrawal of a *donum superadditum* made God responsible for the fall.[66] To this extent at least, Augustine, for all of his great accomplishments as a theologian of grace, introduced the legacy of an ontology significantly determined by neoplatonist sensibilities, a legacy that was refined by Thomas Aquinas. Anthony Kenny explains Thomas's position. Unlike animals, human beings have certain capacities — for instance, to learn languages or to be generous.

> These capacities are realized in action when particular human beings speak particular languages or perform generous actions. But between capacity and action there is an intermediate state possible. When we say that a man can speak French, we mean neither that he is actually speaking French, nor that his speaking French is mere logical possibility.... States such as knowing French ... are dispositions. A disposition ... is halfway between a capacity and an action, between pure potentiality and full actuality.[67]

---

64. Bavinck, *Reformed Dogmatics*, 580.

65. After affirming the goodness of the original creation, specifically, of the creature made in God's image, the *Heidelberg Catechism* teaches that God is not unjust in requiring perfect performance of his law, "for God so made man capable of performing it; but man, through the instigation of the devil, by his own willful disobedience, deprived himself and all his posterity of these gifts" (Answer 9, in *Ecumenical Creeds and Reformed Confessions* [Grand Rapids: CRC Publications, 1988]; cf. Q. & A. 6). Similarly, the *Belgic Confession* (art. 14) states, "We believe that God created man out of the dust of the earth, and made and formed him after His own image and likeness, good, righteous, and holy, capable in all things to will agreeably to the will of God. *But being in honor, he understood it not* [Ps 49:20], neither knew his excellency, but willfully subjected himself to sin and consequently to death and the curse, giving ear to the words of the devil. For the commandment of life [another term for the covenant of works], which he had received, he transgressed ..." (*Ecumenical Creeds and Reformed Confessions*).

66. On this point, see for example William Ames, *The Marrow of Theology* (1623; trans. John Dykstra Eusden; repr., Grand Rapids: Baker, 1968), 1, 11, 8.

67. Anthony Kenny, ed., introduction to Thomas Aquinas, *Summa Theologica*, "Dispositions for Human Acts" (Blackfriars ed.; New York: McGraw-Hill, 1964), XXII:xxi.

Thus, for Aquinas, regeneration is an infused habit or disposition that is somewhere between a mere logical possibility and a realized action: prevenient, but not actual, grace. The fall has thrown the proper ordering of the appetites out of whack, with the lower (bodily) appetites reigning over the higher (intellectual/moral) ones. The grace infused into the soul through the sacraments restores the right ordering of appetites, and this is the first justification. By cooperating with this grace, we actually become just.

As Bruce McCormack points out, the case of infants in baptism was paradigmatic for this process from infused justification to forgiveness of sins.[68] Regeneration replaces imputation: God's work *in* us is the basis of forgiveness.[69] For Calvin, by contrast, "we say that [justification] consists in the remission of sins and the imputation of Christ's righteousness."[70] However, McCormack goes too far in the other direction, marginalizing the regenerating work of the Spirit within believers. The wisdom in Calvin's approach is that he refuses to choose between the forensic (justification) and the mystical-transformative (regeneration and sanctification). While clearly distinguishing them, he sees both as gifts of our faith union with Christ. Within this union, sanctification is the inevitable effect of the justifying verdict: by speaking, the Triune God creates the world of which he speaks.

The question is whether we can articulate an *ordo* (i.e., the application of redemption) without *any* appeal to infused habits. In other words, does God's Word, rendered effectual by the Spirit, have the illocutionary and perlocutionary force to bring about the world of which it speaks? Yes. The gospel creates faith to trust in Christ for justification *and* sanctification. Unlike the declarations of a human judge, who can only call them as he sees them, God's declaration, as McCormack concludes, "creates the reality it declares." "God's declaration, in other words, is itself constitutive of that which is declared."[71] However, the reality that it declares extends beyond a new status; it brings a new creation.

Once more we see the superiority of communicative and covenantal over purely causal and metaphysical grammars. In the latter case, a discussion of justification becomes a debate over the mechanics of the inner life, while in the former, justification has to do with a Covenant Lord pronouncing upon the servant a courtroom verdict that issues in a completely new ontological, ethical, and eschatological orientation — including the inner life in its sweep. No less than God pronounced "Let there be ..." when there was nothing, Abram "the father of many" while he was childless, Sarah fruitful while she was barren, and a young woman pregnant while

---

68. Bruce McCormack, "What's at Stake in the Current Debates over Justification?" in *Justification: What's at Stake in the Current Debates* (ed. Mark Husbands and Daniel J. Treier; Downers Grove, Ill.: InterVarsity Press, 2004), 89.

69. Ibid., 90.
70. Calvin, *Institutes* 3.2.2.
71. McCormack, "What's at Stake," 107.

she was a virgin, God pronounces believers righteous while they are unrighteous. In fact, Paul compares justification to God's *ex nihilo* fiat in creation in Romans 4:17. Elsewhere Paul adds concerning the gospel, "For God, who said, 'Let light shine out of darkness,' has shone in our hearts to give the light of the knowledge of the glory of God in the face of Jesus Christ" (2Co 4:6). Thus, the entire reality of the new creation — not only justification, but renewal, and not only the renewal of the individual but of the cosmos — is constituted by the covenantal speech of the Trinity.

In this light, justification is an exclusively legal declaration based on the imputation of Christ's righteousness to the believer through faith alone, and yet this declarative Word also begins then and there to recreate the believer's entire existence "in Christ." Righteousness is not a substance, however, as the metaphor of infusion implies. Rather, Christ's righteousness that is imputed to believers is the record of his perfect fulfillment of the law and his sin-bearing. On the basis of this imputed righteousness, the believer is simultaneously made the beneficiary of Christ's personal existence as the source of the new creation. Believers are united to Christ: not only to his benefits, but to his person; yet this does not involve a fusion of persons or essences. Rather, it is a covenantal and eschatological participation in *the kind of humanity* that Christ brought into existence by his own incarnation, obedience, death, and resurrection.

There is a further benefit of the Reformation's conception of union. There is a tendency in evangelical theology to treat justification as one doctrine among others to which the effective and transformative aspect must be added in order to have a "balanced" soteriology. Implicitly, justification is treated as necessary for one problem (the condemnation of guilt), while regeneration and sanctification are treated as the solution to a different (and often, it seems, more important) problem: how we are transformed morally. The New Testament does not attribute justification to a judicial verdict and sanctification to infused habits that elevate nature beyond itself; rather, sanctification is the effect of justification, just as the command, "Let the earth bring forth …" is the effect of the fiat, "Let there be …" That judicious language of the *Westminster Confession* (ch. 13) reminds us that believers are justified "not for anything wrought in them or done by them, but for Christ's sake alone." Not even Christ's indwelling of the believer can be the basis for justification, but merely his active and passive obedience on our behalf. Conversion and sanctification can therefore be seen as the Spirit's work of bringing about the perlocutionary effect of the illocutionary speech act (Christ in the gospel), originating in the locutionary act of the Father.

Christ is not only the *last* Adam. That is, he not only undoes Adam's disobedience and bears our guilt. He is the *eschatological* Adam. By fulfilling the Adamic trial, he enters into the Sabbath consummation in our flesh, as our representative.

He is the "Adam" that Adam himself never was, and he therefore inaugurates a new kind of humanity. It is precisely in the covenant of grace that we come to participate in this kind of humanity that he mediates, not by mere imitation nor by an onto-logical participation that would make the believer or the church an extension of the incarnation, but by sharing an inheritance that belongs to Christ by right and to us by gift. It is an inheritance communicated not directly (by imitation or fusion), but by the Spirit through the means of grace.

From the covenantal perspective, the divine Stranger comes to us not as an essence to be participated in but as a Father, a Son, and a Spirit, who, each in his own unique and unrepeatable way, initiate us into "the mystery hidden for ages in God who cre-ated all things, so that through the church the manifold wisdom of God might now be made known to the rulers and authorities in the heavenly places. This was accord-ing to the eternal purpose that he has realized in Christ Jesus our Lord, in whom we have boldness and access with confidence through our faith in him" (Eph 3:9–12).

Although the ontological boundary will never be breached, it is precisely by overcoming the ethical enmity that results from being law breakers that a new relationship of intimate and organic union can emerge. In other words, *justifica-tion establishes the legal basis without which our relationship with God would have to remain merely ethically and legally defined, as under the curse of the law.*

C. Essence and Energies

Many of the attempts have been made in modern theology to assimilate the radical insights of the Reformers to a Platonic/Neoplatonic ontology as a way of reconciling not only Protestant and Roman Catholic traditions but those of the East and West as well. Ironically, however, such proposals typically ignore or reject one of the most important qualifications to a Creator-creature confusion that the East developed. Consequently, Western mysticism has been more prone to pantheism and panentheism. We certainly do not find in the East a forensic doctrine of justification, much less a forensic ontology as the source for the *ordo salutis*. Nevertheless, this tradition does offer a critical distinction that may be transplanted within the latter.

I have referred several times to the distinction in Eastern Orthodoxy between God's essence and energies (see, e.g., ch. 1, "God's Incomprehensible Majesty," p. 52; ch. 6, "A. Simplicity (Unity)," p. 228; "Immutibility" p. 237; ch. 17, "Essence and Energies," p. 574). Since this distinction is especially applicable to the present discussion, I will elaborate it here. We cannot know God in his essence but only in his works. Yet God's works are nothing less than God's working. Where the West typically works only with the categories of divine essence (source) and creaturely essence (effect), the East's distinction recognizes that God's working is divine while not being an emanation or extension of his essence. This view is also richly integrated within a Trinitarian theology of the Father working in the Son and by his Spirit.

Vladimir Lossky argues that the priority that western Trinitarianism places on the divine essence over the divine persons gives rise to a somewhat different mystical theology of union:

> If one speaks of God it is always, for the Eastern Church, in the concrete: "The God of Abraham, of Isaac and of Jacob; the God of Jesus Christ." It is always the Trinity: Father, Son, and Holy Ghost. When, on the contrary, the common nature assumes the first place in our conception of Trinitarian dogma the religious reality of God in Trinity is inevitably obscured in some measure and gives place to a certain philosophy of essence. Likewise, the idea of beatitude has acquired in the West a slightly intellectual emphasis, presenting itself in the guise of a vision of the essence of God.... Indeed, in the doctrinal conditions peculiar to the West all properly theocentric speculation runs the risk of considering the nature before the persons and becoming a mysticism of "the divine abyss," as in the *Gottheit* of Meister Eckhart; of becoming an impersonal apophaticism of the divine-nothingness prior to the Trinity. Thus by a paradoxical circuit we return through Christianity to the mysticism of the neo-platonists.[72]

By contrast, says Lossky,

> In the tradition of the Eastern Church there is no place for a theology, and even less for a mysticism, of the divine essence. The goal of Orthodox spirituality, the blessedness of the Kingdom of Heaven, is not the vision of the essence, but, above all, a participation in the divine life of the Holy Trinity; the deified state of the co-heirs of the divine nature, gods created after the uncreated God, possessing by grace all that the Holy Trinity possesses by nature.[73]

Whatever remaining differences between Eastern Orthodox and Reformed theologies—and they are not insignificant—the distinction between essence and energies itself may reflect a point of convergence.

Just as the rays are not the sun itself, yet are not mere effects of the sun, the energies of God are neither God's essence nor simply creaturely realities. "Thus, according to St. Gregory Palamas, 'to say that the divine nature is communicable not in itself but through its energy, is to remain within the bounds of right devotion.' "[74] "In the same way, St. Basil talks of the role of the energies in manifesting, opposing them to the unknowable essence: 'It is by His energies'—he says—'that we say we know our God; we do not assert that we can come near to the essence itself, for His energies descend to us, but His essence remains unapproachable.' "[75] "St. Maximus

---

72. Vladimir Lossky, *The Mystical Theology of the Eastern Church* (Crestwood, N.Y.: St. Vladimir's Seminary Press, 1976), 65. See also his *In the Image and Likeness of God* (London: Mowbrays, 1967), especially 97–101.

73. Lossky, *The Mystical Theology of the Eastern Church*, 70.
74. Ibid.
75. Ibid., 71–72.

the Confessor expresses the same idea when he says: 'God is communicable in what He imparts to us; but He is not communicable in the incommunicability of His essence.'"[76]

Lossky points out that whereas the medieval West eschewed the essence-energies distinction, focusing on the essence, it introduces its own distinctions between nature and supernature, "the infused virtues, and habitual and actual grace." Rome speaks about "created grace," as if there is some supernatural realm somewhere between the Creator and creation.

Eastern tradition knows no such supernatural order between God and the created world, adding, as it were, to the latter a new creation. It recognizes no distinction, or rather division, save that between the created and the uncreated. For Eastern tradition the created supernatural has no existence. That which Western theology calls by the name of the *supernatural* signifies for the East the *uncreated*—the divine energies ineffably distinct from the essence of God.[77]

On the basis of these moves, the West, according to Lossky, adopted a causal paradigm in its doctrine of grace:

> The difference consists in the fact that the western conception of grace implies the idea of causality, grace being represented as an effect of the divine Cause, exactly as in the act of creation; while for eastern theology there is a natural procession, the energies, shining forth eternally from the divine essence. It is in creation alone that God acts as cause, in producing a new subject called to participate in the divine fullness; preserving it, saving it, granting grace to it, and guiding it towards its final goal. In the energies *He is, He exists*, He eternally manifests Himself. Here we are faced with a mode of divine being to which we accede in receiving grace; which, moreover, in the created and perishable world, is the presence of the uncreated and eternal light, the real omnipresence of God in all things, which is something more than His causal presence—"the light shineth in the darkness, and the darkness comprehendeth it not." (John i, 5)[78]

According to this paradigm, the divine-human relationship is not conceived in terms of cause and effect, but in a more pneumatologically oriented gift of "interior light." Instead of seeing God as a sole agent acting upon the world, then, we should recognize the Spirit as the one at work within creation to bring about the perlocutionary effect of the Word spoken by the Father in the Son. Similarly, Lossky argues,

> The energies, bestowed upon Christians by the Holy Spirit, no longer appear as exterior causes, but as grace, an interior light, which transforms nature in deifying it. "God is called Light," says St. Gregory Palamas, "not with reference

---

76. Ibid., 72–73.
77. Ibid., 88.

78. Ibid., 88–89.

to His essence, but to His energy." ... Perfect vision of the deity, perceptible in its uncreated light, is "the mystery of the eighth day"; it belongs to the age to come. But those who are worthy attain to the vision of "the Kingdom of God come with power" even in this life, a vision such as the three apostles saw on Mount Tabor.[79]

The Eastern view of union with Christ remains deeply synergistic and lacks an adequate forensic grounding in the doctrine of justification. In fact, this tradition, too, forces the false choice between mystical union and forensic justification. Nevertheless, its essence-energies distinction, especially in relation to union with Christ, helps us to avoid the tendency in the West either to undervalue the realism of this union or to collapse into pantheism.

IV. COVENANT AND CONDITIONALITY

Union with Christ also yields a dynamic effect in us: the same power by which Christ was raised from the dead is at work in us (Ro 6:1–9; Eph 1:18–22). Christ indwells us by his Spirit (Col 1:27). Not only are we formed in him; Christ is said "to be formed" in us (Gal 4:19). Having "put on" Christ, believers now "grow up ... into him who is the head" (Eph 4:15). At last we begin to see more clearly the magnanimous designs of the Trinity in the covenant of redemption. Not only did the divine persons form a pact concerning our salvation; they also included as part of that salvation our own creaturely participation in the fellowship of the Trinity itself (Jn 14:20–23; 17:20–23). This is the sense in which, through God's "precious and very great promises" we now "become partakers of the divine nature" (2Pe 1:4). The effects of our union with Christ are justification, sanctification, and glorification. Beyond the fellowship of the individual believer with Christ, this union establishes a heavenly (i.e., eschatological) *koinōnia* between believers, their mutual indwelling (Jn 14:20; 17:23), which will be explored under ecclesiology.

The question naturally arises at this point whether there are any conditions, especially since this union rests ultimately in the covenant of redemption—an intratrinitarian pact to which we were not even a party. Critics insist that the Reformation teaching so emphasizes salvation as the unilateral act of God in grace that there is no real place for human responsiveness and activity. However, at least in the Reformed system of covenant theology, the unilateral basis of the covenant of grace—grounded in God's electing, redeeming, regenerating, and justifying action alone—actually *creates* genuine human freedom for righteousness.[80]

---

79. Ibid., 220.
80. For a contemporary defense of this interpretation, see J.

Todd Billings, *Calvin, Participation, and the Gift* (New York: Oxford Univ. Press, 2008).

While the eternal covenant of redemption (*pactum salutis*) establishes the unconditional ground of our saving union with Christ, it is administered in a covenant of grace. The absolute and unconditional basis of the covenant of grace in God's eternal counsels is evident in the inclusion of the children of believers in baptism. Nevertheless, it is just as true in the new covenant as in the old that not all physical descendants of the covenant community are living branches of the Vine (Ro 9:6; 11:6–24). In this covenant there are some who belong outwardly to Christ's visible body but do not actually trust in Christ. They may imitate Christ, follow the example of eminent believers who have influenced them, restrain their attitudes and behaviors, and even assume that they are believers because of their formal relation to the church. However, branches that do not bear fruit are broken off by Christ (Jn 15:2; Ro 11:1–30). In the covenant of grace, there are two parties: the Triune God and believers together with their children. Yet only through faith in the gospel that is heard do members of the covenant enter God's rest and receive the eternal inheritance of the saints in Christ (Heb 4).

Resting as it does on the covenant of redemption, the covenant of grace is in its basis unconditional, inviolable, and irrevocable. Even repentance and faith are gifts of this royal grant, not conditions that human beings fulfill in order to receive grace. Nowhere in Scripture is our salvation attributed even partially to our choice or activity; we are recipients of God's election, redemption, justification, and glorification. However, as we were reminded earlier by Bavinck, the covenant of grace, which is unilateral in its basis, is determined to become bilateral in its administration.[81] The ungodly are declared righteous and are therefore called to walk in righteousness; the dead are made alive in Christ and are therefore to die to sin and live to God. Passive recipients of grace, the elect are made active by that same grace, so that they are able to respond as faithful covenant creatures for the first time. God's covenantal faithfulness is not based on anything in us, but creates us for good works (Eph 2:8–10).

From the "amen" of faith—itself a gift—the fruit of righteousness blossoms. Bavinck elaborates,

> When in Genesis 15:8f. God makes a covenant with Abraham, it is not really a compact but a pledge. God gives his promise; he obligates himself to fulfill it and passes between the pieces of the sacrificial animal.... This unilateral character had to come out with ever-increasing clarity in the course of history. True, the covenant of God imposed obligations also on those with whom it was made—obligations, not as conditions for entering into the covenant (for the covenant was made and based only on God's compassion), but as the way the people who had by grace been incorporated into the covenant henceforth had to conduct themselves.[82]

---

81. Bavinck, *Reformed Dogmatics*, 3:225.   82. Ibid., 3:203, 204.

Bavinck concludes, "In distinction from and contrast to the covenant of works, God therefore established another, a better, covenant, not a legalistic but an evangelical covenant."[83]

God did, of course, impose obligations on Abraham, but they were the consequence rather than the conditions of his promise. In some sense, faith may be considered a condition of receiving Christ and all of his benefits, but even in this instance it is contrasted with works. The works that believers are called to "walk in" are the way *of* life, not the way *to* life. Despite its imperfection, this grateful response can be offered by us precisely because the stability of the covenant depends on Christ's life of thanksgiving and his guilt offering cancels the sin clinging even to our best works. While the moral commands continue to indicate the course that our sanctification is to take, it is from the gospel alone that we draw our strength. Union with Christ is not a goal, but the presupposition, of our new obedience: "If we died with him, we will also live with him; if we endure, we will also reign with him; if we deny him, he will also deny us; if we are faithless, he remains faithful—for he cannot deny himself" (2Ti 2:11–13).

To be autonomous is really to be "in Adam," but to be "in Christ" is to be free indeed (Jn 8:36). This side of the fall, bondage to the law and bondage to sin amount to the same thing. "Apart from the law sin lies dead," Paul explained. But "sin, seizing an opportunity through the commandment, deceived me and through it killed me.... Did that which is good, then, bring death to me? By no means! It was sin, producing death in me through what is good, in order that sin might be shown to be sin, and through the commandment might become sinful beyond measure" (Ro 7:8, 11, 13). "Under the law" and therefore "under sin," the self is, as Augustine observed, curved in on itself. Whether by seeking to justify our morality or immorality, we are evading the judgment that would force us to look outside of ourselves for security. By itself, "law" merely deepens that incurvation, guilt, death, and a troubled conscience that provokes us to self-deception and conceit, alternating between self-righteousness and self-condemnation, and leading to the "works of the flesh" in interpersonal relationships that Paul lists in Galatians 5:19–21. The Spirit-grace-promise-gospel-faith matrix introduces us to a new Word (gospel), and with it a new world (the new creation), turning our eyes upward in faith toward God and outward in love toward our neighbors.

It is precisely this contrast that energizes so much of Pauline theology especially. In Galatians 2:19–20 there is a close connection here between being dead to the law, being alive to God, and being identified with Christ in such a way that the identity of the self who lives by faith is defined by Christ's circumcision-death and

---

83. Ibid., 3:225.

resurrection. Similarly, in Romans, Paul meets the objection that forensic justification offers no ethics by appealing to our union with Christ (Ro 6). The gains of being in Christ are so great that even Paul's suffering is not, properly speaking, his own — in which he might either glory or because of which he might despair — but is a matter of suffering *with Christ*. "For to me to live is Christ and to die is gain. . . . For it has been granted to you that for the sake of Christ you should not only believe in him but also suffer for his sake . . ." (Php 1:21, 29). There is no autonomous Paul any longer, not because he has lost his selfhood in mystical ascent, or has had his finite ego absorbed into an infinite Ego, or surrendered it to ecclesial identity, or attained mastery over his "lower" appetites. These would simply be different (Greek) ways of pursuing the goal by works.

In Paul's understanding, "boasting" in one's own righteousness, far from unseating the reign of sinful autonomy, is the throne from which the autonomous self spreads its dominion. However, when its real intentions and demands are announced, the law begins to break up this autonomy at its heart by exposing our delusions of grandeur and stability, allowing the gospel to do its work of taking us entirely outside of ourselves and locating our existence in Christ alone. In this sense, the law in its wrath even serves as a merciful accomplice to the gospel:

> For through the law I died to the law, so that I might live to God. I have been crucified with Christ. It is no longer I who live, but Christ who lives in me. And the life I now live in the flesh I live by faith in the Son of God, who loved me and gave himself for me. I do not nullify the grace of God, for if righteousness were through the law, then Christ died for no purpose. (Gal 2:19–21)

Christ, therefore, is the new creation; to be in Christ is to be exiled from this age and to be relocated in the age to come.

The following litany of the benefits of our union with Christ indicated by Calvin offers a fitting summary of this chapter:

> We see that our whole salvation and all its parts are comprehended in Christ. We should therefore take care not to derive the least portion of it anywhere else. If we seek salvation, we are taught by the very name of Jesus that it is "of him." If we seek any other gifts of the Spirit, they will be found in his anointing. If we seek strength, it lies in his dominion; if purity, in his conception; if gentleness, it appears in his birth. For by his birth he was made like us in all respects that he might learn to feel our pain. If we seek redemption, it lies in his passion; if acquittal, in his condemnation; if remission of the curse, in his cross; if satisfaction, in his sacrifice; if purification, in his blood; if reconciliation, in his descent into hell; if mortification of the flesh, in his tomb; if newness of life, in his resurrection; . . . if inheritance of the heavenly kingdom, in his entrance into heaven; if protection, if security, if abundant supply of all blessings, in his kingdom; if untroubled expectation of judg-

ment, in the power given him to judge. In short, since rich store of every kind of good abounds in him, let us drink our fill from this fountain, and from no other.[84]

DISCUSSION QUESTIONS

1. What is meant by "mystical union"?
2. If we are saved by Christ's person and work outside of us (*extra nos*), what is the saving significance of being *united* to Christ?
3. How do we enter into and remain in this union?
4. What is the difference between a more Platonic understanding of "union with God" and the New Testament teaching of union with Christ in terms of *koinōnia*?
5. Compare and contrast Roman Catholic and Reformation interpretations of the relationship between nature and grace.
6. What are the effects of this union with Christ?
7. Are there any conditions in the covenant of grace, especially in its New Testament administration, and if so, what are they? How do conditions function differently in a covenant of works than in a covenant of grace?

---

84. Calvin, *Institutes* 2.16.19.

Chapter Nineteen

FORENSIC ASPECTS OF UNION WITH CHRIST: JUSTIFICATION AND ADOPTION

With the wider analogy of union with Christ we may now move through the *ordo salutis*, noting the connection between the forensic basis and the transformative effects of our salvation in Christ.

I. JUSTIFICATION OF THE UNGODLY

"God justifies the wicked." As counterintuitive as it is simple, that claim which lies at the heart of the good news has brought immeasurable blessing — and trouble — to the church and the world. It is not the Pharisee, confident in his own righteousness, who went home justified, said Jesus, but the tax collector, who could not even raise his eyes to heaven but cried out, "God, be merciful to me, a sinner!" (Lk 18:9 – 14). It was precisely these outcasts who would be seated at the wedding feast clothed in the wedding garment, said Jesus, while those who entered in their own attire would be cast out (Mt 22:1 – 14).

It was this simple claim that caused the apostle Paul to look back on all of his zealous obedience to the law as that of "a Pharisee" and to call it "rubbish," "in order that I may gain Christ and be found in him, not having a righteousness of my own that comes from the law, but that which comes through faith in Christ, the righteousness from God that depends on faith" (Php 3:8 – 9). As the revelation of the righteousness *of* God, the law condemns and leaves no one standing. Yet the gospel is the revelation of the righteousness *from* God, the good news that sinners "are justified by his grace as a gift, through the redemption that is in Christ Jesus, whom God put forward as a propitiation by his blood, to be received by faith" (Ro 3:24–25). "Therefore, since we have been justified by faith, we have peace with God through our Lord Jesus Christ" (Ro 5:1). Paul considered this doctrine to be so central that he regarded its explicit denial as "anathema"—that is, an act of heresy that the Galatian church was on the verge of committing (Gal 1:8–9). For Paul, a denial of justification was tantamount to a denial of grace and even to a denial of Christ, "for if righteousness were through the law, then Christ died for no purpose" (Gal 2:21).

God justifies *the wicked*—not those who have done their best yet have fallen short, those who might at least be judged acceptable because of their sincerity, but those who at the very moment of being pronounced righteous are in themselves unrighteous. "And to the one who does not work but believes him who justifies the ungodly, his faith is counted as righteousness, just as David also speaks of the blessing of the one to whom God counts righteousness apart from works . . ." (Ro 4:5–6).

Numerous passages testify to the imputation or crediting of our sins to Christ (on the basis of his substitutionary atonement) and his righteousness to us (on the basis of his active obedience). Following Paul's banking, clothing, and courtroom analogies from our everyday experience, the Reformers called this the "marvelous exchange." Jesus Christ, sinless in himself, becomes the greatest sinner who ever lived, while we become "the righteousness of God [in him]" (2Co 5:21). In Romans 4:17, God's work in justification is compared to his work in creating the world out of nothing. Justification is the fiat declaration, "Let there be righteousness!" even where, at present, there is nothing but guilt and unrighteousness in the sinner, because Christ's righteousness is imputed through Spirit-given and gospel-created faith. As in creation, only after God's declarative Word of justification ("Let there be . . . And there was . . .") can there be an appropriate creaturely response ("Let the earth bring forth . . .").

A. The State of the Controversy

This claim that God justifies the wicked brought enormous controversy to the apostolic church and has continued to do so throughout the history of the church.[1] And in spite of the heroic efforts of representatives on both sides during

---

1. The teaching of the ancient church is ambiguous with respect to justification. On one hand, there are marvelous testimonies to God's justification of sinners, as Thomas Oden observes in *The Justification Reader* (Grand Rapids: Eerdmans, 2002). On the other hand, there are many threads of synergism that later Eastern Orthodoxy developed in Byzantine theology in a manner that parallels Western (medieval) developments.

the sixteenth-century, the Council of Trent (1545–1563) in no uncertain terms condemned the Reformation's understanding of justification.

1. THE REFORMATION DEBATE

Rome teaches that "'justification is not only the remission of sins, but also the sanctification and renewal of the interior man.'"[2] Justification is therefore regarded as a process of becoming actually and intrinsically righteous. The first justification occurs at baptism, which eradicates both the guilt and corruption of original sin.[3] Entirely by God's grace, this initial justification infuses the habit (or principle) of grace into the recipient. By cooperating with this inherent grace, one merits an increase of grace and, one hopes, final justification.[4] So while initial justification is by grace alone, final justification depends also on the works of the believer, which God graciously accepts as meritorious.[5] Since the believer's progress in holiness is never adequate to cancel the guilt of actual sins, he or she must be refined in purgatory before being welcomed into heaven.

By contrast, the Reformers taught, and evangelicals teach, that justification is distinct from sanctification. Although all of Christ's gifts are given in our union with him through faith, justification is a verdict that declares sinners to be righteous even while they are inherently unrighteous, simply on the basis of Christ's righteousness imputed to them. Whereas Rome teaches that one is finally justified by being sanctified, the evangelical conviction is that one is being sanctified because one has already been justified. Rather than working toward the verdict of divine vindication, the believer leaves the court justified in the joy that bears the fruit of faith: namely, good works.

In Scripture, especially in Paul, Luther discovered that the righteousness that God is, which condemns us, is the same righteousness that God gives, freely, as a gift, through faith in Jesus Christ (Ro 3:19–31). As have seen, this "marvelous exchange" of Christ's righteousness for the sinner's guilt was beautifully articulated by some medieval theologians. True, the Reformers, especially Luther and Calvin, were influenced by some more Augustinian writers like the Cistercian monk Bernard of Clairvaux (1090–1153). However, the understanding of justification as an exclusively forensic (legal) declaration, based on the imputation of Christ's righteousness through faith alone, was the chief insight of the Reformation.

The inextricable connection between doctrine and experience is acutely evident in Luther's spiritual wrestling that led to his fresh interpretation of Scripture. Though to some extent motivated by his own confusion and anxiety as to

---

2. *Catechism of the Catholic Church*, 492, quoting the Council of Trent (1574).

3. Ibid., 482.

4. Ibid., 483.

5. Ibid., 486–87.

whether he was the object of God's grace or wrath, Luther did not arrive at his conclusions simply out of his own experience of "tortured subjectivity," as some modern interpreters suggest,[6] but rather from doctrinal reflection, for which others had already laid a foundation. Jacques Lefèvre d'Étaples (1455–1536), an eminent French humanist and biblical scholar (who made the first French translation of the Bible from the Latin Vulgate) arrived at some of Luther's principal insights a decade earlier. Erasmus also had made important textual contributions that paved the way for the Reformers. Luther's own mentor, and the head of Germany's Augustinian Order, Johann von Staupitz, also set the Reformer on his course. Then, appointed by Staupitz as a professor of Bible, Luther undertook his own close exegesis of Scripture and was gradually led to further insights with radical implications.

Like Luther, Calvin and the other magisterial Reformers were humanists, steeped in the original languages and guided by the Renaissance cry, *Ad fontes*, "Back to the sources!" In the process, they recaptured the clear biblical teaching that God "justifies the ungodly" (Ro 4:5). According to the fourth article of the apology of the *Augsburg Confession*, God justifies the wicked on the basis of Christ (*propter Christum*), apart from our inherent righteousness. This is the *solo Christo* (by Christ alone). And he credits this righteousness through faith alone (*sola fide*), apart from works. Believers are just before God not to the extent that they are inherently righteous; rather, they are "simultaneously just and sinner" (*simul iustus et peccator*).

All of the Reformers were at one on this point, over against both Roman Catholic and Anabaptist interpretations. Calvin regarded justification as "the primary article of the Christian religion," "the main hinge on which religion turns," "the principal article of the whole doctrine of salvation and the foundation of all religion."[7] In fact, Melanchthon and Calvin influenced each other in working out the refinements of this common evangelical position.[8] This righteousness "consists in the remission of sins, and in this: that the righteousness of Jesus Christ is imputed to us."[9]

According to this evangelical interpretation, justification is not a process of transformation from a condition of sinfulness to a state of justice. Believers are *simultaneously* justified and sinful.[10] Sin's dominion has been toppled, but sin still indwells believers.[11] Consequently, whatever works believers perform will always

---

6. Krister Stendahl's *Paul: Among Jews and Gentiles* (Minneapolis: Augsburg Fortress, 1976) pioneered this psychological thesis, which has become a largely unexamined assumption among advocates of the New Perspective(s) on Paul (especially James D. G. Dunn and N. T. Wright). Bizarre attempts to psychoanalyze Luther to explain his "evangelical breakthrough" began with Erik H. Erikson's *Young Man Luther: A Study in Psychoanalysis and History* (New York: Norton, 1962).

7. Calvin, *Institutes* 3.2.1, 3.11.1; also sermon on Luke 1:5–10 in *Corpus Reformatorum* (ed. W. Baum; Berlin: C. A.

Schwetschke, 1863–1900), 46:23.

8. See, for example, Richard Muller, *The Unaccommodated Calvin: Studies in the Foundation of a Theological Tradition* (New York: Oxford University Press, 2000), 126–27. Calvin, however, sharply criticized Melanchthon's later synergistic turn, which the orthodox (Gnesio) Lutherans also rejected.

9. Calvin, *Institutes* 3.11.2.

10. Ibid., 3.3.10.

11. Ibid., 3.3.11.

fall short of that righteousness that God's law requires; nevertheless, believers are accepted as fully righteous already through faith in Christ.

This orientation stood in sharp contrast not only with Rome, but with the radical sects. "Certain Anabaptists of our day conjure some sort of frenzied excess instead of spiritual regeneration," Calvin relates, thinking that they can attain perfection in this life.[12] Rome teaches that Christ's sacrifice remits the guilt but not the punishment of sins.[13] In either case, justification is understood as a process of inner transformation, rather than as God's free acquittal of sinners for the sake of Christ and his imputation of Christ's righteousness to their account. Of course, a diversity of moral character is evident to us as human beings, but Calvin reminds us (repeating Luther's contrast) that righteousness before humanity (*coram hominibus*) is not the same as righteousness before God (*coram deo*).[14] "Therefore," Calvin responds, "we explain justification simply as the acceptance with which God receives us into his favor as righteous. And we say that it consists in the remission of sins and the imputation of Christ's righteousness."[15]

The logic of Calvin's argument in the *Institutes* (book 3, chapters 11–19) may be summarized as follows:

- To save us from judgment, the Son became flesh and merited our salvation (2.15–17);
- Thus, the righteousness by which we are saved is alien to us (3.11.2, etc.);
- Yet Christ must not only be given *for* us; he must be given *to* us (3.1.1);
- We are not only recipients of Christ's gifts but of Christ himself with his gifts (3.1.1.; 3.1.4; 3.2.24; 4.17.11)

Faith unites us to Christ (3.1.1), but it is the Holy Spirit who gives faith and it is Christ, rather than faith itself, who always remains the sole ground of salvation. In other words, faith is nothing in itself; it receives *Christ* and with him all treasures (3.11.7; 3.18.8). After all, "if faith in itself justified one by its own virtue, then, seeing that it is always weak and imperfect, it would be only partly effectual and give us only a part of salvation" (3.11.7).

One of the clearest summaries of the evangelical doctrine of justification is found in chapter 13 of the *Westminster Confession*:

> Those whom God effectually calls, he also freely justifies: not by infusing righteousness into them, but by pardoning their sins and by accounting and accepting their persons as righteous; not for anything wrought in them or done by them, but for Christ's sake alone; not by imputing faith itself, the act of believing, or any

12. Ibid., 3.3.14.
13. Ibid., 3.4.30.

14. Ibid., 3.12.2.
15. Ibid., 3.11.2.

other evangelical obedience to them as their righteousness; but by imputing the obedience and satisfaction of Christ unto them, they receiving and resting on him and his righteousness by faith; which faith they have not of themselves, it is the gift of God. Faith, thus receiving and resting on Christ and his righteousness, is the sole instrument of justification; yet is it not alone in the person justified, but is ever accompanied with all other saving graces, and is no dead faith, but works by love.

The justified may fall into grave sin and "fall under God's Fatherly displeasure," but they "can never fall from the state of justification."[16]

The *Heidelberg Catechism* also emphasizes that this divine verdict has Christ's righteousness, not ours, as its basis, so that through faith alone we who "have grievously sinned against all the commandments of God and have not kept any one of them" are nevertheless regarded as though we had never sinned and had perfectly kept the commands. Not even the gift of faith itself can be considered the ground of justification, but simply the empty hand that receives it. This teaching cannot be used to justify moral carelessness, however, "for it is impossible for those who are engrafted into Christ by true faith not to bring forth the fruit of gratitude."[17] Similar summaries can be found, of course, in the Lutheran *Book of Concord*, the Anglican *Thirty-nine Articles*, and the *1689 Baptist Confession of Faith*.[18]

It was this understanding that Rome officially anathemized at the Council of Trent in its longest decree, which included the following:

> Canon 9. If anyone says that the sinner is justified by faith alone ... let him be anathema.
> Canon 11. If anyone says that men are justified either by the sole imputation of the righteousness of Christ or by the sole remission of sins ... let him be anathema.
> Canon 12. If anyone says that justifying faith is nothing else than confidence in divine mercy, which remits sins for Christ's sake, or that it is this confidence alone that justifies us, let him be anathema.
> Canon 24. If anyone says that the justice [righteousness] received is not preserved and also not increased before God through good works, but that those works are merely the fruits and signs of justification obtained, but not the cause of the increase, let him be anathema.
> Canon 30. If anyone says that after the reception of the grace of justification the guilt is so remitted and the debt of eternal punishment so blotted out to every repentant sinner that no debt of temporal punishment remains to be discharged

---

16. *The Westminster Confession of Faith*, in *Book of Confessions* (Louisville: PCUSA General Assembly, 1991), ch. 11.

17. *Heidelberg Catechism*, questions 60–64 (quote is A. 64), in *Book of Confessions*.

18. The Confession was adopted in London by Calvinist Baptists and eventually affirmed in Philadelphia (see www .reformedreader.org/ccc/1689lbc/english/1689econtents.htm).

either in this world or in purgatory before the gates of heaven can be opened, let him be anathema.

Canon 32. If anyone says that the good works of the one justified are in such manner the gifts of God that they are not also the good merits of him justified; or that the one justified by the good works that he performs by the grace of God and the merit of Jesus Christ, whose living member he is, does not truly merit an increase of grace, eternal life, and in case he dies in grace the attainment of eternal life itself and also an increase of glory, let him be anathema.[19]

Much has happened since the Council of Trent, to be sure, especially in the fruitful ecumenical discussions since the Second Vatican Council. Nevertheless, Trent remains binding dogma, and even if it could be amended, the official statements of the magisterium to the present day continue to deny the evangelical view. Not even in the *Joint Declaration on the Doctrine of Justification* between the Lutheran World Federation and the Vatican (whose status is not confirmed, much less binding, on the Roman Catholic side) is the Reformation's formulation of justification affirmed.[20] Furthermore, the Vatican's Pontifical Council for the Promotion of Christian Unity issued a caution when the *Joint Declaration* was released. While applauding the consensus reached by the two sides, the statement added, "The Catholic Church is, however, of the opinion that we cannot yet speak of a consensus such as would eliminate every difference between Catholics and Lutherans in the understanding of justification."[21] Citing the Council of Trent, the official statement reminded Roman Catholics that they must hold as dogma that "eternal life is, at one and the same time, grace and the reward given by God for good works and merits."[22]

The Roman Catholic Church has never denied the necessity of grace — indeed, its priority. The Council of Trent expressly repeated the condemnations of Pelagianism, in fact. However, the addition of works to faith as the instrument of justification is as strongly affirmed today as it was in the sixteenth century. From the evangelical perspective, the strongest affirmation of the importance of God's grace

19. *Canons and Decrees of the Council of Trent: Original Text with English Translation* (trans. H. J. Schroeder, OP; St. Louis: B. Herder Book Company, 1960), 43, 45–46.

20. *Joint Declaration on the Doctrine of Justification: The Lutheran World Federation and the Roman Catholic Church* (Grand Rapids: Eerdmans, 2000). Among other problems, the *Joint Declaration* teaches, "The justification of sinners is forgiveness *and being made righteous* ..." (4.3.27, emphasis added), and particular acts of sin require the sacrament of penance (4.3.30). Thus, the Roman Catholic position is not altered on this fundamental point; it is the evangelical view that is surrendered. Only on that basis can both partners conclude that

the condemnations of the sixteenth century no longer apply to each other's respective communions. It should be noted that the Lutheran World Federation, like the World Alliance of Reformed Churches, represents the more liberal wing of its tradition. Their confessional rivals (including the Lutheran Church Missouri Synod) rejected the *Joint Declaration*, because they do still hold the views condemned by the Council of Trent and all subsequent reaffirmations by the magisterium.

21. Reprinted in the official Vatican newspaper, *L'Osservatore Romano*, weekly edition in English, 8 July 1998, p. 2.

22. Ibid.

does not mitigate the corruption of the gospel by including our own merits. "But if it is by grace, it is no longer on the basis of works; otherwise grace would no longer be grace" (Ro 11:6).

Differences over justification are motivated by different understandings of grace. In Roman Catholic theology grace is understood as a medicinal substance infused into a person at baptism, elevating nature to supernatural appetites. In Reformation theology grace is understood as God's favor to those who are dead in sins and ungodly, on account of Christ's merit alone. Through faith, God gives believers nothing less than Christ and all of his benefits. Among these gifts is rebirth and sanctification, but this renewal is the consequence of justification rather than part of its definition.

2. DIVERGENCES AMONG PROTESTANTS

Though in some respects more radical in distancing itself from the medieval church than were the Reformers, *Anabaptists* were closer to Rome on justification. Contemporary Anabaptist theologian Thomas Finger observes, "Robert Friedmann found 'A forensic view of grace, in which the sinner is ... undeservedly justified ... simply unacceptable' to Anabaptists. A more nuanced scholar like Arnold Snyder can assert that historic Anabaptists 'never talked about being "justified by faith." ' "[23]

Rejecting any conception of a forensic (substitutionary) atonement, *Socinians* (forerunners of modern Unitarianism) rejected a forensic justification in favor of a basically Pelagian soteriology, and this became the presupposition of Enlightenment rationalism. Kant rejected a forensic doctrine of justification as counterproductive to moral striving, and the same arguments may be found in the writings of American revivalist Charles Finney, as noted below (p. 628).

Although the classical *Arminianism* of the original Remonstrants (led by Arminius) affirmed justification through faith alone, the atonement came to be understood along the lines of Grotius's governmental theory. Rather than a satisfaction of God's justice in the place of sinners, Christ's atonement was seen as the basis for the propriety of God's offering salvation on the basis of the sinner's repentance and new obedience. Some Arminians, like Philip van Limborch, moved in a Pelagian (Socinian) direction. Evangelical Arminians, such as John Wesley, taught God's free

---

23. Thomas A. Finger, *A Contemporary Anabaptist Theology: Biblical, Historical, Constructive* (Downers Grove, Ill.: InterVarsity Press, 2004), 109. Finger believes that Anabaptist soteriological emphases (especially on divinization) can bring greater unity especially between the soteriologies of marginalized Protestant groups (Pentecostals and Quakers) and those of the Orthodox and Roman Catholic churches (110). Finger observes that recent Anabaptist reflection is no more marked in its interest in this topic than its antecedents, with discipleship ("following Jesus") and the inner transformation of the believer as central (132–33).

justification of sinners, but sometimes confused it with sanctification and in general subordinated it to the inner renewal and perfection of personal holiness.[24]

From the New Haven divinity of Nathaniel Taylor, some Arminians (especially in the United States) also moved in a more Pelagian direction. Justification by the imputation of Christ's righteousness not only is "absurd," said evangelist Charles Finney, but undermines all motivation for personal holiness. Christians can perfectly obey God in this life if they choose, and only in this way are they justified. In fact, "full present obedience is a condition of justification." No one can be justified "while sin, any degree of sin, remains in him."[25] Finney declared concerning the Reformation formula, "simultaneously justified and sinful," "This error has slain more souls, I fear, than all the universalism that ever cursed the world." For, "Whenever a Christian sins, he comes under condemnation and must repent and do his first works, or be lost."[26] The basis of justification is perfect obedience, but that of the believer rather than Christ:

> As has already been said, there can be no justification in a legal or forensic sense, but upon the ground of universal, perfect, and uninterrupted obedience to law.... The doctrine of an imputed righteousness, or that Christ's obedience to the law was accounted as our obedience, is founded on a most false and nonsensical assumption, for Christ's righteousness could do no more than justify himself. It can never be

---

24. As ardent a defender of Arminian theology as Roger Olson recognizes Wesley's somewhat confusing position concerning justification (*Arminian Theology: Myths and Realities* [Downers Grove, Ill.: InterVarsity Press, 2006], 213). Olson also points up differences in later Arminianism. For example, Richard Watson states unambiguously, "This whole doctrine of the imputed righteousness of Christ's personal and moral obedience, as their own personal moral obedience, involves a fiction and impossibility inconsistent with the Divine attributes" (Richard Watson, *Theological Institutes* [New York: Lane & Scott, 1851], 2:216, quoted in Olson, *Arminian Theology*, 215). Olson argues that this view does not characterize all Arminian representatives, but even some of his contrary examples seem to suggest a closer proximity to Watson's position, although Olson does not cite these passages. William B. Pope (*A Compendium of Christian Theology* [New York: Hunt and Eaton, 1880]) states that "to justify" in the New Testament means both "a declaratory and imputed righteousness, and at the same time the power of a righteousness internal and inherent" (2:404). At the same time, Pope properly insists that we are justified through faith (*dia pisteōs* or *ek pisteōs*), not on account of faith (*dia pistin*) (2:414). Nevertheless, "Faith, with works, justifies instrumentally the person believing: inasmuch as its works give evidence of its genuineness as a permanent living principle. It retains the soul in a state of justification, and is the power of a Divine life by which the righteousness of the law is fulfilled" (2:415). Pope states that "Arminianism was in its doctrine of the Atonement a mediation between Socinianism and the Anselmic teaching as revived at the Reformation ...," "although

... Arminianism gradually declined from its first integrity" and "does not now represent any fixed standard of confession" (2:442). He points out that original Arminianism (including the belief of Arminius himself), which he affirms, denied the active obedience of Christ as well as the imputation of Christ's righteousness (2:443). However, Pope says, Limborch went further than this, toward "the Romanist error" and Socinianism (2:443). According to Pope the English Arminians (Methodists) never denied the Reformation doctrine of justification, although they taught the doctrine of entire sanctification (perfection) and stressed forgiveness rather than the imputation of Christ's righteousness (2:444–48). Watson explicitly denies that justification includes the imputation of Christ's righteousness (Watson, *Institutes*, 2:215). After warning that the Reformation view tends to treat justification merely as a change in legal status, John Lawson writes in his *Introduction to Christian Doctrine* (Grand Rapids: Francis Asbury, 1967, 1986), "To be justified, therefore, is the first and all-important stage in a renewed manner of life, actually changed for the better in mind and heart, in will and action" (226). In fact, "regeneration" is "an alternative word for 'the initial step ...'" (227). At least these statements of the Methodist position reflect a basic affinity with the Roman Catholic view. On the other hand, Methodist theologian Thomas Oden has labored to defend the Reformation doctrine of justification, especially in *The Justification Reader* (Grand Rapids: Eerdmans, 2002).

25. Charles G. Finney, *Systematic Theology* (Oberlin, Ohio: J. M. Fitch, 1846; repr., Minneapolis: Bethany, 1976), 46.

26. Ibid., 57.

imputed to us.... It was naturally impossible, then, for him to obey in our behalf. Representing the atonement as the ground of the sinner's justification has been a sad occasion of stumbling to many.[27]

3. Justification in Modern and Contemporary Theology

In *Protestant liberalism* (especially Schleiermacher and Ritschl), justification loses its objective and forensic character as a verdict before God in favor of a consciousness of the realization that God never really was at enmity with the believer in the first place. We have already observed this in relation to the atonement. In this conception, justification is not an objective change in status from wrath to grace (as Paul states explicitly, for example, in Romans 5:8–11); rather, the believer merely overcomes estrangement—the *feeling* that one is alienated from God.

While affirming, against liberalism, the necessity and fact of God's wrath being turned away by Christ's death, Karl Barth refused to see the various elements of the *ordo salutis* as occurring successively in time. Rather, they are simultaneous, belonging to a single event in God's eternal history of election: objectively true of every person yet ever-new in every moment of faith and obedience.[28] God's justification of the ungodly is a major theme in Barth. He saw himself as recovering the insights of the Reformation over against a Protestantism that was at least as guilty as Roman Catholicism for exchanging a complete, perfect, and finished justification by God alone in Christ alone received through faith alone for a progressive, incomplete, and unfinished justification by the believer's cooperation with grace.[29] Nevertheless, if the usual temptation is to collapse justification into sanctification, for Barth the tendency is to collapse justification into election (conceived in universal terms) and the law into the gospel. As a consequence, he denies the necessity of faith for receiving this justification. Faith simply acknowledges the status that pertains objectively to every person.

More recently, criticism of the evangelical doctrine of justification has been growing within Protestant circles. First, trends in New Testament scholarship (especially identified with the "New Perspective on Paul") sharply criticize the Reformation interpretation both of Judaism and of Paul. Although there is some diversity among proponents

---

27. Ibid., 321–22. Referring to the framers of the *Westminster Confession* and their view of an imputed righteousness, Finney wondered, "If this is not antinomianism, I know not what is" (322).

28. See Michael Horton, "A Stony Jar: The Legacy of Karl Barth for Evangelical Theology," in *Engaging with Barth: Contemporary Evangelical Critiques* (ed. David Gibson and Daniel Strange; New York: T&T Clark, 2008), 346–81.

29. This concern was already evident in Karl Barth, *The Epistle to the Romans* (trans. Edwyn C. Hoskyns from the 6th German ed.; London: Oxford Univ. Press, 1933), 366: "The

Church must therefore know that nothing is gained by replacing an objective by a subjective religion, by transforming the service of God into 'pious practices' and righteousness into *a law of righteousness*, because even so it does not find what it is seeking. The Church can, of course, pursue religion and busy itself in the human work of the law. It can cultivate religious experience aesthetically, ethically, and logically. But it cannot do more than this: for religious experience is not the same thing as faith or righteousness; it is not the presence and reality of God, nor is it the divine 'Answer.' Religious experience is our human and, consequently, our very questionable, relation to God."

of this perspective, they agree that justification does not mean for Paul the imputation of Christ's righteousness to the believing sinner.[30] Second, trends in historical and ecumenical theology criticize the confessional Lutheran and Reformed interpretations of Luther and Calvin and try to draw the Reformers closer to Eastern Orthodox and/or Roman Catholic positions that they contend were lost to later orthodoxy.[31] An impressive movement in theology known as Radical Orthodoxy (led by John Milbank) has attracted many Protestants, including evangelicals, to its renewal of Christian Neoplatonism over against the "extrincisism" and "forensicism" of Reformation theology.[32] Third, Anabaptist and Arminian theologies and various types of liberation theology have combined to renew their challenge of the emphasis on justification and in many cases the doctrine itself, as inhibiting personal and social transformation.[33]

For the remainder of this chapter I will summarize the exegetical basis for the classic evangelical doctrine of justification, interacting along the way with contemporary criticisms.

B. Defining Justification Exegetically

"And those whom he called he also justified" (Ro 8:30). Understanding what Paul meant by justification depends on whether we can come to terms with his anthropology (universal human depravity)[34] and therefore his compelling interest in, as Peter Stuhlmacher puts it, "whether Jews and Gentiles will or will not survive before God's throne of judgment."[35] The gospel is not simply that Jesus was crucified and raised, or that these events demonstrate his lordship, but that he "was delivered up *for our trespasses* and raised *for our justification*" (Ro 4:25, emphasis added).

1. Declarative (Judicial) Meaning

"In the *qal*," notes E. P. Sanders, "the verb [*ṣādaq*] usually means 'to be cleared in court' and is not really distinguishable from the use of the *zakah* root to mean

---

30. I interact at length with these views in the first half of my *Covenant and Salvation: Union with Christ* (Louisville: Westminster John Knox, 2007).

31. One prominent example is the "evangelical catholic" circle associated with Robert Jenson and Carl Braaten and the New Finnish interpretation of Luther led by Tuomo Mannermaa and others. See Tuomo Mannermaa, *Christ Present in Faith: Luther's View of Justification* (ed. Kirsi Stjerna; Minneapolis: Augsburg Fortress, 2005). I interact with these views in *Covenant and Salvation*, 127–260.

32. John Milbank et al., *Radical Orthodoxy: A New Theology* (London: Routledge, 1999).

33. Stanley Grenz challenged the older evangelical preoccupation with "Christ alone" as the material principle and "Scripture alone" as the formal principle of the Christian faith (Stanley Grenz, *Revisioning Evangelical Theology* [Down-

ers Grove, Ill.: InterVarsity Press, 1993], 62). Similarly, Brian McLaren, in *A Generous Orthodoxy* (Grand Rapids: Zondervan, 2004), faults Reformation theology for its commitment to the solae: Christ alone, Scripture alone, grace alone, through faith alone, and to God alone be glory (221). For both writers, as for the generation of evangelicals that preceded them, the heart of Christianity is our imitation of Christ's example, which—at least for McLaren—does not even require one to become a Christian, but only to be a better Buddhist, Moslem, or Jewish followers of Jesus (221).

34. See Timo Laato, *Paul and Judaism: An Anthropological Approach* (Atlanta: Scholars Press, 1995).

35. Peter Stuhlmacher, *Revisiting Paul's Doctrine of Justification: A Challenge to the New Perspective* (Downers Grove, Ill.: InterVarsity Press, 2001), 43.

'innocent.'"[36] "It may also mean to make something correct, as in the phrase 'make the scales just.' The hif'il, 'to justify,' also has a forensic connotation. When the passage in Ex. 23.7 says 'I will not justify the wicked,' it is clearly understood to mean 'hold innocent.'"[37] Berkhof correctly notes that the Hebrew word *hiṣdîq* means, in most cases, "to declare judicially that one's state is in harmony with the demands of the law" (Ex 23:7; Dt 25:1; Pr 17:15; Isa 5:23), as does the piel form *ṣiddēq* (Jer 3:11; Eze 16:51–52).[38] *Dikaioō*, "to declare just," is unmistakably judicial in character. Just as the medieval system of penance was founded exegetically on a mistranslation in the Latin Vulgate of *metanoeō* (to change one's mind, repent) as *poenitentium agite* (do penance), *dikaioō* (to declare just) was erroneously rendered *iustificare* (to make righteous).[39]

Though hardly motivated by doctrinal concerns, Erasmus had pointed out these lexical inconsistencies even before Luther. Obviously, being *made* righteous is quite a different thing from being *declared* righteous. By itself, the latter term does not require the evangelical doctrine of justification, but it does render erroneous the Vulgate's translation and therefore the interpretation of justification as moral transformation. A number of Roman Catholic New Testament scholars have pointed out in recent years that *dikaioō* has to do with a legal vindication.[40] The lexical definition of *to be justified* is "to be cleared in court,"[41] which, as Sanders has said above, is true even in relation to the Old Testament (*ṣādaq* and cognates), and can be amply attested. That significant consensus can be reached on this point even among those who stand in some critical relation to the Reformation interpretation demonstrates that we are quite far from witnessing the destruction of a forensic definition of justification.

While the verb is judicial or forensic (that is, it expresses a declaration rather than a process), the use of it does not by itself indicate the basis on which or the means by which one is justified before God. It simply indicates that the demands of the law have been fully met (Ac 13:39; Ro 5:1, 9; 8:30–33; 1Co 6:11; Gal 2:16; 3:11). Its opposite is condemnation, which is quite evidently a judicial concept as well (Jn 3:17–18; Ro 4:6–7; 8:1, 33–34; 2Co 5:19).

2. The Righteousness of God

So far, even some vigorous proponents of the New Perspective such as N. T. Wright will agree: justification is a declarative, judicial verdict. It cannot be under-

---

36. E. P. Sanders, *Paul and Palestinian Judaism* (Philadelphia: Fortress, 1977), 198.

37. Ibid., 199.

38. Louis Berkhof, *Systematic Theology* (Grand Rapids: Eerdmans, 1996), 510.

39. Alister E. McGrath, *Iustitia Dei: A History of the Christian Doctrine of Justification* (Cambridge: Cambridge Univ. Press, 1986), 11–14.

40. See for instance Joseph Fitzmeyer, "The Letter to the Romans," and "The Letter to the Galatians," in *The Jerome Biblical Commentary* (ed. Raymond S. Brown, Joseph A. Fitzmyer, and Roland E. Murphy; Englewood Cliffs, N.J.: Prentice-Hall, 1968), esp. 241–44 and 303–15, respectively.

41. See BDAG, 246–50.

stood as a process, at least on lexical-semantic grounds. The further question concerns the nature of the phrase "the righteousness of God" and whether it can be credited or imputed to believers. According to Wright, the term *God's righteousness* can refer only to his own faithfulness to the covenant.[42] Though certainly "a forensic term, that is, taken from the law court," *righteousness* does not refer to something that can be transferred from God to us. Nor can it refer to a righteous condition inherent in the defendant, making him or her deserving of acquittal. Rather, "for the plaintiff or defendant to be 'righteous' in the biblical sense *within the law-court setting* is for them to have that status *as a result of the decision of the court*."[43] However, this courtroom verdict cannot involve an imputation of righteousness. It makes no sense to say that the judge somehow gives his own righteousness to the defendant.[44] God's people will be "justified." "*But the righteousness they have will not be God's own righteousness*. That makes no sense at all. God's own righteousness is his covenant faithfulness" (emphasis original).[45]

However, it is crucial to point out that it has never been the Reformation position that *God's righteousness* is imputed. First, this assumes that righteousness is a substance or a commodity that is transferred from one person to another, rather than a legal status. Second, missing from Wright's courtroom setting is the third party: the mediator who, as representative head, fulfills the law and merits for himself and his covenant heirs the verdict of "righteous" or "just" before God. Although the one who fulfilled the terms of the law covenant as the human servant is also the divine Lord, it is his active obedience rather than the essential divine attribute of righteousness that is credited to believers.

In fact, the mature Reformation doctrine of justification was articulated against both Rome's understanding of justification as an infused quality of righteousness and Andreas Osiander's notion of the believer's participation in the essential righteousness of Christ's deity. The Reformers and their heirs labored the point that it is Christ's successful fulfillment of the trial of the covenantal representative that is imputed or credited to all who believe. This is what keeps justification from being abstract or a legal fiction, since the justified do in fact possess "in Christ" the status of those who have perfectly fulfilled all righteousness. This is the covenantal language that is everywhere presupposed but so clearly comes to expression in Romans 5, where Adam's federal headship imputes guilt and condemnation as well as imparting inherent corruption, while Christ's federal headship imputes righteousness and imparts his inherent new life. The forensic language of the courtroom and the organic language of head and body, tree and fruit, vine and branches converge

42. N. T. Wright, *What Saint Paul Really Said: Was Paul of Tarsus the Real Founder of Christianity?* (Grand Rapids: Eerdmans, 1997), 96.

43. Ibid., 97–98.
44. Ibid., 98.
45. Ibid., 99.

without being confused. In Christ we have both justification and new life, an alien righteousness imputed and Christ's own resurrection life imparted.

To build on Paul's banking analogy, for one to have not only one's debts cancelled but one's account filled by a transfer of funds from someone else renders that wealth no more a fiction than if it were the fruit of one's own labors. As Paul looks over his ledger in Philippians 3, he places all of his own righteousness in the liabilities column and all of Christ's righteousness in his assets column. Wright's account so far does not seem to allow for an inheritance actually to be given to anyone in particular. Justification may be forensic (that is, judicial), but there can be no transfer of assets, if you will, from a faithful representative to the ungodly. If guilt can be imputed from one person to another (which Wright affirms), why not righteousness? The sin of Adam was imputed to the human race as a covenantal entity in solidarity because it was imputed to each member (Ro 5:12). This notion of imputing the sin of one person to each Israelite—and thus to the nation generally—is found elsewhere, as in Achan's theft (Jos 7:10–26).

Interpreting "the righteousness of God" (*dikaiosynē tou theou*) as a subjective genitive, Wright paraphrases Romans 1:17: "The gospel, [Paul] says, reveals or unveils God's own righteousness, his covenant faithfulness, which operates through the faithfulness of Jesus Christ for the benefit of all those who in turn are faithful ('from faith to faith')."[46] However, does this make adequate sense of the rest of the verse: "as it is written, 'The righteous shall live by faith'"? Paul's citation of Habakkuk 2:4 refers to the human partner in the covenant rather than to God. It seems more consistent with Paul's wider argument in Romans 1–3 to say, in agreement with Luther, that the law reveals God's essential righteousness (his justice that condemns us), while the gospel reveals God's gift of righteousness that saves us. After establishing the point that everyone, Jew and Gentile, is condemned by the law and will never be justified by it because of their sin, Paul adds, "But now the righteousness of God has been manifested apart from the law, although the Law and the Prophets bear witness to it—the righteousness of God through faith in Jesus Christ for all who believe." They are now "justified by his grace as a gift, through the redemption that is in Christ Jesus, whom God put forward as a propitiation

---

46. Ibid., 109. Related to this debate over the righteousness of God is the question as to whether "faith in Christ" should also be given the subjective genitive construction (as "the faith of Christ"). This does not seem to make sense of the ordinary way Paul describes the relation of faith and justification, however. For example, Paul speaks of "the righteousness of God through faith in Jesus Christ for all who believe" (Ro 3:22), the last clause repeating the same idea as the middle (*dia pisteōs Iēsou Christou*), and in verse 25 adds that Christ's propitiatory death is "to be received by faith." This debate is beyond our scope here, but for a defense of the subjective genitive construction, see Bruce W. Longenecker, "Contours of Covenant Theology in the Post-Conversion Paul," in *The Road from Damascus: The Impact of Paul's Conversion on His Life, Thought, and Ministry* (ed. Richard N. Longenecker; Grand Rapids: Eerdmans, 1997), 133; cf. Richard Hays, *The Faith of Jesus Christ: An Investigation of the Narrative Substructure of Galatians 3:1–4:11* (Chico, Calif.: Scholars Press, 1983); Richard B. Hays, "Justification," *The Anchor Bible Dictionary* (ed. D. N. Freedman et al.; New York: Doubleday, 1992), 4:1129–33.

by his blood, to be received by faith" (Ro 3:21–25). According to this view, God indeed reveals his covenant faithfulness, but by itself this is not good news—unless God reveals that the righteousness that he is and that his law requires has been given to us as a gift in Jesus Christ.

Whereas the Reformation interpretation recognizes that Paul speaks of the righteousness of God as his essential justice and faithfulness to the covenant *and* as the gift of righteousness, Wright reduces all references to the former. Yet the dialectical play between these two seems to lie at the heart of Paul's argument especially in Romans 1–3: the righteousness that God *is* (as revealed in the law) condemns everyone, Jew and Gentile alike. It makes little sense, especially in the sweep of Paul's argument, to say that *God's* covenant faithfulness is disclosed through *our faith* in Christ. Rather, Paul argues that the righteousness that God is (i.e., his essential righteousness) actually *condemns* everyone—Jew and Gentile alike, because no one has fulfilled it; the gospel, however, discloses the gift of righteousness which is received through faith. The revelation of God's righteousness that is revealed by the law, "so that every mouth may be stopped, and the whole world may be held accountable to God" (3:19), is different from the revelation of God's righteousness that is revealed in the gospel "apart from law," through faith in Christ (v. 21). The law reveals that God is just (and therefore must condemn all transgressors), but the gospel reveals that God is just and justifier (v. 26).

There is no place for a transfer of righteousness to the believer in Wright's interpretation, but for Paul, in this passage, "the righteousness of God through faith in Jesus Christ" is a "justification" that is "a gift" given to "all who believe." The closest that Wright comes to allowing for justification as a gift of right-standing given to individuals is in the statement that believers "are declared, in the present, to be what they will be seen to be in the future, namely the true people of God. Present justification declares, on the basis of faith, what future justification will affirm publicly (according to 2:14–16 and 8:9–11) *on the basis of the entire life*" (emphasis added).[47] Not only do we meet the distinction in Roman Catholic theology between present and future justification; the basis of the latter is one's own covenant faithfulness. Where for Paul the verdict of the last day has already been rendered in favor of those who have faith in Christ—through faith alone—according to Wright this future verdict is merely anticipated in faith.

According to Wright, faith is not how one is "saved," but "is the badge of the sin-forgiven family."[48] "The emphasis of the chapter [Ro 4] is therefore that covenant membership is defined, not by circumcision (4:9–12), nor by race, but by faith."[49]

---

47. Wright, *What Saint Paul Really Said*, 129.

48. For a good critique of Wright's argument on this point, see Mark A. Seifrid, *Christ, Our Righteousness: Paul's Theology*

of Justification (Downers Grove, Ill.: InterVarsity Press, 2000), 176n13.

49. Wright, *What Saint Paul Really Said*, 129.

However, this faith is now also redefined as faithfulness—our own covenantal obedience, which is the basis for the final justification. Crucially absent from his list is Paul's clause, "nor by works," or the apostle's statement that this justification comes to the one (notice the individual-personal reference) "who does not work but believes in him who justifies the ungodly" (v. 5). Paul's contrast is between working and trusting, not between circumcision and our Spirit-led obedience. Basically, Wright's claim is tantamount to saying that we are justified by some works (our covenant faithfulness), but not by others (ethnic purity).

As we have already seen in relation to the substitutionary atonement, a legal satisfaction of God's justice on the part of sinners is only part of the story. It is so central that without it the other theories are left hanging in midair. Nevertheless, it provides the basis for a cosmic and eschatological victory of Yahweh over the powers that hold us in bondage. Similarly, far from excluding personal and cosmic renewal, the justification of the ungodly is the source of the abundant and varied fruit of Christ's conquest.[50]

3. Imputed Righteousness?

The Reformation view of justification rests on the declarative character of the verb and the twofold meaning of the righteousness of God as that justice that God *is*, which condemns us, and the justice that God *gives*, which saves us. Yet it requires a further point: namely, *imputation* as the way in which God gives this righteousness or justice to the ungodly through faith.

The verb "to impute" (*logizomai*) is used explicitly in Romans, especially in chapter 4, where Paul refers to Abraham, quoting Genesis 15:6: "Abraham believed God, and it was counted to him as righteousness" (Ro 4:3). Notice how imputation fits in Paul's argument: "Now to the one who works, his wages are not counted [imputed] as a gift but as his due. And to the one who does not work but believes in him who justifies the ungodly, his faith is counted as righteousness" (vv. 4–5). Clearly something is being transferred or given from one person (employer) to another (employee): namely, wages. But in this case it is different: God does not justify those who work for it but only imputes righteousness to those who trust in the justifier of the ungodly. David is another example of one "against whom the Lord will not count his sin" (v. 8). Abraham could not even count his circumcision as the instrument of his justification before God (vv. 9–12). "But the words 'it was counted to him' were not written for his sake alone, but for ours also. It will be counted to us who believe in him who raised from the dead Jesus our Lord, who was delivered up for our trespasses and raised for our justification" (vv. 23–25).

---

50. I develop this cosmic-eschatological aspect in my *Covenant and Salvation*, 289–302.

In Galatians 3, with the contrast between "the works of the law" and "hearing with faith," Paul repeats the quotation from Genesis 15:6. "Counting as" or "being counted as," *logizomai eis*, is also found in Romans 2:26; 9:8 and 2 Corinthians 12:6, as well as Acts 19:27 and James 2:23. Although the term does not appear in Romans 5, the idea is evident throughout Paul's comparison and contrast between Adam and Christ. Under Adam's headship, the whole race is guilty and corrupt; under Christ's headship, many are justified and made alive. These passages unmistakably teach that the righteousness by which the believer stands worthy before God's judgment is *alien*: that is, belonging properly to someone else. It is Christ's righteousness imputed, not the believer's inherent righteousness — even if produced by the gracious work of the Spirit.

As we have seen, N. T. Wright holds that God's final justification is a declaration that believers are righteous based on their whole life lived. While generally eschewing talk of the *ordo salutis* ("how individuals 'get saved'"), he does make regeneration the basis for the verdict that one is at present a member of this community that will be justified on the last day. Therefore, whatever other differences there might be on other points, he shares Rome's view of justification as an analytic verdict. In the quotation from the *Westminster Confession* above, the clause is added that not only works "done by us" but even works "wrought in us" — by the Holy Spirit — are excluded from justification. Far from denying the Spirit's work within us, the *Confession* is simply saying that this is not justification.

The notion of one person's righteousness being imputed to another is already present in Second Temple Judaism (the "merit of the fathers").[51] Furthermore, we have already seen that Wright strongly affirms that our sins were transferred or credited to Christ, so his rejection of an imputation of righteousness from Christ to the believer seems arbitrary. Criticisms of imputation are not restricted to representatives of the New Perspective(s) on Paul. For example, Mark Seifrid remains unconvinced that the language of "imputation" is necessary. Justification grants forgiveness of sins; what need is there for an imputation of righteousness on the basis of Christ's active obedience, which Seifrid considers "unnecessary and misleading"?[52] "In reducing 'justification' to a present possession of 'Christ's imputed righteousness,' Protestant divines inadvertently bruised the nerve which runs between justification and obedience. It is not so much *wrong* to use the expression 'the imputed righteousness of Christ' as it is *deficient*."[53]

---

51. Hermann Lichtenberger, "The Understanding of the Torah in the Judaism of Paul's Day," in *Paul and the Mosaic Law: The Third Durham-Tübingen Research Symposium on Earliest Christianity and Judaism* (ed. James D. G. Dunn; Grand Rapids: Eerdmans, 2001), 16. He refers to rabbinical sources that God will keep petitioners from sin "so that you may find joy at the end of the age …, this being *counted to you for righteousness* if you do what is true and good before God for the salvation of yourself and of Israel."

52. Seifrid, *Christ, Our Righteousness*, 175.

53. Ibid.

However, the Reformed interpretation cannot be reductive or deficient if it actually says *more* than Seifrid allows.[54] More critically, the question arises, how does forgiveness by itself establish rectitude? It is not mere *forgiveness* (negation of guilt) that withstands the last judgment, but *righteousness* (positive standing). Without the latter, both the goal of the covenant and its conditions are unfulfilled. Seifrid concludes, "Justification" cannot be "reduced to an event which takes place for the individual at the beginning of the Christian life" within "an 'order of salvation' (*ordo salutis*)."[55] Yet does not Paul place it in an *ordo salutis* in Romans 8:30? Apart from the positive imputation of righteousness, based on Christ's active obedience (fulfilling the law in our place), justification truly is a "legal fiction," as its critics allege. On the other hand, because the obedience of Christ is actually imputed or credited to us, we are legally just before God.

Robert Gundry also objects to the doctrine of imputation. First, he highlights the texts that refer to imputation of righteousness explicitly. "But none of these texts says that Christ's righteousness was counted," writes Gundry, "so that righteousness comes into view not as what is counted but as what God counts faith to be."[56] What God counts or imputes is faith, not Christ's righteousness, Gundry argues.[57] To be sure, "Paul rejects the Jewish tradition that God counted Abraham's faith as righteousness because it was a work (a good one, of course)."[58] Yet if faith is the ground of justification rather than the instrument, one wonders how that Jewish interpretation could be faulted. Gundry clearly states that "the righteousness that comes 'from' (*ek*) faith (Ro 9:30: 10:6) and from God 'through' (*dia*) faith and 'on the basis of' (*epi*) faith (Php 3:9) is the faith that God counts as righteousness. Paul's language is supple: faith is the *origin*, the means, and the *basis* of righteousness in that God counts it as righteousness" (emphasis added).[59]

However, *epi* has a much broader lexical range than Gundry allows.[60] While in technical theological jargon the basis (or formal cause) of something is distinguished from the means (or instrumental cause), *epi* and *dia* both are used with greater range and flexibility in Scripture, as their English equivalents are in common use. In fact, *epi* appears as a basis ("on account of," "because of"), a marker of basis for a state of being, an action, or a result, in numerous places.[61] In other words, *epi* ("on account

54. In an intriguing remark, Herman Bavinck judges, "The rationalistic school is rooted basically in Piscator's teaching, according to which the righteousness we need is accomplished not by the active but solely by the passive obedience of Christ!" (*Reformed Dogmatics* [ed. John Bold; trans. John Vriend; Grand Rapids: Baker Academic, 2006], 3:531).

55. Seifrid, *Christ, Our Righteousness*, 176.

56. Robert Gundry, "The Nonimputation of Christ's Righteousness" in *Justification: What's at Stake in the Current Debates* (ed. Mark Husbands and Daniel J. Treier; Downers Grove, Ill.: InterVarsity Press, 2004), 18.

57. Ibid., 22.

58. Ibid. Gundry notes the following survey of the Jewish literature: J. A. Ziesler, *The Meaning of Righteousness in Paul: A Linguistic and Theological Inquiry* (SNTSM 20; Cambridge: Cambridge Univ. Press, 1972), 43, 103–4, 109, 123, 125–26, 175, 182–83.

59. Gundry, "Nonimputation," 25.

60. According to Danker (BDAG, 363–67), there are no fewer than eighteen possible renderings.

61. Ibid., especially 366.

of") is interchangeable with *dia* ("through"). In the light of various challenges to the Reformation understanding of justification from Protestant as well as Roman Catholic quarters, the terminology became more refined: justification by grace, through faith, because of Christ. However, it would be anachronistic to impose the more refined distinctions of scholasticism on the New Testament. Even Luther can say, in his exegesis of Galatians, that we are justified "for the sake of our faith in Christ or for the sake of Christ," as if the two phrases are interchangeable.[62] It all depends on what one is contrasting: is it between faith and works or between faith as an inherently worthy basis and faith as a passive instrument? In Gundry's formulation, however, one would say that we are justified by faith, through faith, on the basis of faith. This view makes our faith the meritorious ground of our justification.

Rejecting the imputation of Adam's sin, since the people's sinning (before the law) "was not like the transgression of Adam," Gundry denies imputation in relation to justification.[63] Yet this verse (Ro 5:14) seems to make the opposite point: namely, that even though they did not commit the *same* sin, they were still sinners in Adam. Further, Gundry speaks of "the failure of Paul, despite his extensive discussion of law and writing that Christ was 'born under the law' (Gal 4:4), ever to make a point of Christ's keeping the law perfectly on our behalf (not even his sinlessness in 2Co 5:21 being put in relation to law-keeping)."[64]

Yet what other import might the phrase "born under the law" have served? And how else would a Jew have understood sinlessness other than "in relation to law-keeping"? And why does Paul contrast Adam's one act of disobedience and Christ's one act of obedience? Does this not suggest that Christ's obedience, rather than our faith, is imputed? Gundry argues,

> To be sure, *dikaiōma*, translated "act of righteousness" in Romans 5:18 and "righteous requirement" in Romans 8:4 (also in Ro 1:32), may be collective in Romans 8:4 for all the requirements of the law. But that collective meaning is unsure, even unlikely, for Paul writes in Galatians 5:14 that "the whole law is fulfilled in one command, 'You shall love your neighbor as yourself.' "[65]

Yet even such an interpretation of Galatians 5:14 seems strained. Paul was merely summarizing "the whole law" (i.e., all the requirements of the law collectively comprehended). Surely loving one's neighbor does not consist in one act. And in the context of his running polemic in Galatians, would it not be legitimate to assume here that Paul is simply repeating the claim in 3:10 that to offend at one point (failing to love God and neighbor perfectly) is to be "under the curse" of the law? Although he has argued that faith is not a work, Gundry says, "The righteousness

---

62. Martin Luther's, *Commentary on Galatians*, in *Luther's Works* (ed. Jaroslav Pelikan; St. Louis: Concordia, 1963), 26:233.

63. Gundry, "Nonimputation," 28.
64. Ibid., 32.
65. Ibid., 34.

of faith is *the moral accomplishment* that God counts faith to be even though it is not *intrinsically* such an accomplishment" (emphasis added).[66] Christ's "obediently righteous act of propitiation made it right for God to count faith as righteousness."[67]

It is worth noting in passing that this view has a theological history. Although Arminius held simultaneously that the meritorious ground of justification was Christ's imputed righteousness, his followers (Simon Episcopius and Hugo Grotius) taught that faith itself (and repentance) becomes the ground of justification. The Puritan Richard Baxter made a similar argument, treating faith and evangelical obedience as the "new law" that replaces the "old law" as the basis for justification. Chapter 11 of the *Westminster Confession* targets this error of neo-nomianism when it states that God justifies believers "[not] by imputing faith itself, the act of believing, or any other evangelical obedience to them, as their righteousness; but by imputing the obedience and satisfaction of Christ unto them, they receiving and resting on him and his righteousness, by faith; which faith they have not of themselves, it is the gift of God."[68] In fact, there are obvious similarities between neo-nomianism and the covenant (or better, contractual) theology of late medieval nominalism, according to which justification is granted on the basis of one's imperfect obedience. In this view, no one merits final justification according to strict merit (*de condigno*), but only according to God's gracious decision to accept it as if it were meritorious (*de congruo*).

Aside from historical parallels, is Gundry's position exegetically plausible? D. A. Carson responds, first, by offering a salutary reminder that systematic and biblical (or exegetical) theology represent different fields of discourse that should serve each other's ends, but often speak past each other, failing to take each other's fields and research into account.[69] "In Jewish exegesis," Carson points out, "Genesis 15:6 was quoted not to prove that Abraham was justified by faith and not by works," but rather to prove his meritorious obedience (Rabbi Shemaiah, 50 BC; *Mekilta* on Ex 14:15 [35b]; 40b). "What this means, for our purposes, is that Paul, who certainly knew of these traditions, was explicitly interpreting Genesis 15:6 in a way quite different from that found in his own tradition, and he was convinced that this new way was the correct way to understand the text."[70]

More specifically, Carson draws our attention to the parallelism in Romans 4:5–6:

- 4:5 God justifies the ungodly
- 4:6 God credits righteousness apart from works

---

66. Ibid., 36.

67. Ibid., 39.

68. *The Westminster Confession of Faith*, ch. 13, in *Book of Confessions* (Louisville: PCUSA General Assembly, 1991).

69. D. A. Carson, "The Vindication of Imputation," in *Justification: What's at Stake*, 49.

70. Ibid., 56.

"In other words, 'justifies' is parallel to 'credits righteousness'; or, to put the matter in nominal terms, justification is parallel to the imputation of righteousness."[71] And it has to be an "alien" righteousness, since "God justifies *the ungodly* (Ro 4:5); he credits righteousness *apart from works* (Ro 4:6)."[72]

In response to Gundry's argument, Carson reasons, "If God has counted or imputed our faith to us as righteousness, then, once he has so counted or imputed it, does he then count or impute the righteousness to us, a kind of second imputation?"[73] In Philippians 3, it is clearly not an inherent righteousness.[74] "In 2 Corinthians 5:19–21, we are told that God made Christ who had no sin to be sin for us, so that *in him* we might become the *righteousness* of God. It is because of God that we are in Christ Jesus, who has become for us *righteousness* (and other things: 1Co 1:30). Passage after passage in Paul runs down the same track."[75] Having faith—even if it is faith in Christ—is not the same as having a righteousness that is "not of my own." If we think the two are the same, then faith, not Christ, becomes the basis for the transfer from unrighteous to righteous.[76]

4. THEOLOGICAL PRESUPPOSITIONS AND EXEGESIS REGARDING JUSTIFICATION

I have referred to the sibling rivalry between biblical and systematic theology, but the arguments we have encountered thus far in opposition to the traditional Protestant account of justification reveal that theological convictions and exegetical conclusions are inextricably connected. Schweitzer judged, "But those who subsequently made [Paul's] doctrine of justification by faith the centre of Christian belief, have had the tragic experience of finding that they were dealing with a conception of redemption, from which no ethic could logically be derived."[77]

Yet this conclusion completely misses the quite natural transition in Paul's logic even in Galatians, where, as in his other epistles, ethical imperatives are extrapolated from gospel indicatives. The gospel of free justification liberates us to embrace the very law that once condemned us. This new life Paul calls "life in the Spirit," yielding "the fruit of the Spirit" (Gal 5:16–26). When we were "in Adam," that law yielded death and condemnation; "in Christ," the law approves us—hence, Calvin's view that the so-called third use (guiding believers in the way of gratitude) is, for the Christian, "the primary use" of the law.[78] Only when it no longer can condemn us is the law a friend rather than an enemy.

Reformation theology, as we will see, has certainly derived an ethic from justification—as well as from the rest of the *ordo*, as evidenced by the division of the *Heidelberg Catechism* into guilt, grace, and *gratitude*. Every Lutheran and Reformed

---

71. Ibid., 61.
72. Ibid.
73. Ibid., 64.
74. Ibid., 69.
75. Ibid., 72.

76. Ibid.
77. Albert Schweitzer, *The Mysticism of the Apostle Paul* (New York: Seabury, 1968), 225.
78. Calvin, *Institutes* 2.7.12.

catechism includes an application of the Ten Commandments to the Christian life. In fact, the first question-and-answer of the *Heidelberg Catechism* underscores the point that because Christ paid the price for our redemption and sent the Spirit, "[My] only comfort in life and in death [is] that I am not my own, but belong—in body and soul, in life and in death—to my faithful Savior Jesus Christ."[79] Justification is not only a promise; it is a claim upon one's total life.

Proponents of covenantal nomism (synergism) have regularly insisted that a gospel of free grace—*sola gratia, solo Christo, sola fide*—can lead logically only to license. E. P. Sanders, who pioneered the New Perspective, assumes that an unconditional election is arbitrary: there must be *something* in the chosen that explains the gift.[80] To be sure, "getting in" depends on obedience, but this does not constitute "works-righteousness," since there are things that we can do to make up for our mistakes. Apparently such provisions for re-balancing the scales by our own efforts constitute grace on God's part. These theological presuppositions guide Sanders's verdicts on Second Temple Judaism and Paul. James D. G. Dunn concedes that his interpretation of Paul is consistent with his Arminian theological commitments.[81] N. T. Wright pleads, "If Christians could only get this [doctrine of justification] right, they would find that not only would they be believing the gospel, they would be practicing it; and that is the best basis for proclaiming it."[82] Thus, the gospel is something to be done by us, not simply an astonishing and disruptive announcement of what has already been achieved once and for all on our behalf.[83] Faith and holiness belong together, Wright properly insists, but the only way to keep them together, he seems to suggest, is to conflate them. "Indeed, very often the word 'faith' itself could properly be translated as 'faithfulness,' which makes the point just as well," although he reminds us that "faith" is not the way one gets in but is the badge indicating who is in.[84] Gundry appeals to Mark Seifrid's far-from-novel charge that "in reducing 'justification' to a present possession of 'Christ's imputed righteousness,' Protestant divines inadvertently bruised the nerve which runs between justification and obedience." He appeals also to Wesley's criticism on the same ground: it leads to antinomianism.[85]

In this, the well-worn path of criticism, illustrated in Albert Schweitzer's charge that "there is no road from it [forensic justification] to ethics" is followed.[86] Gundry sees his own treatment as going "a long way toward satisfying the legitimate

---

79. *Heidelberg Catechism*, q. 1, in *Psalter Hymnal* (Grand Rapids: CRC Publications, 1987), 861.

80. Sanders, *Paul and Palestinian Judaism*, 101–6.

81. "An Evening Conversation on Jesus and Paul with James D. G. Dunn and N. T. Wright," (NTWrightpage.com/Dunn_Wright_Conversation.pdf, 2007), p. 20.

82. Wright, *What St. Paul Really Said*, 159.

83. Even where Paul speaks of "obeying" the gospel, what he has in mind is believing: "But they have not all obeyed the gospel. For Isaiah says, 'Lord, who has *believed* what he has heard from us?' So faith comes from hearing, and hearing through the word of Christ" (Ro 10:16–17).

84. Wright, *What Saint Paul Really Said*, 160.

85. Seifrid, *Christ, Our Righteousness*, 175, quoted in Gundry, "Nonimputation," 44.

86. Schweitzer, *Mysticism of the Apostle Paul*, 225.

concerns not only of Roman Catholics but also of pietists in the Lutheran tradition, in the Anabaptist and Baptist tradition, in the Keswick movement, in the Holiness movement and in Pentecostalism."[87] No less than the Reformers and their heirs, therefore, are such criticisms of the evangelical doctrine of justification shaped by systematic-theological categories and assumptions.

II. ADOPTION: A NEW STATUS THAT CREATES A NEW RELATIONSHIP

Adapting the ancient Near Eastern treaties to God's covenantal purposes, Scripture indicates that to be adopted by the Great King, the vassal "puts on" the identity of the suzerain, including its regal glory. It is this lost glory that is recovered—and, because it is no less than the glory of the God-Man, it is greater than the original glory of "the first man ... from the earth, a man of dust" (1Co 15:47). "Just as we have borne the image of the man of dust, we shall also bear the image of the man of heaven" (v. 49).[88] "To be the image of God is to be the son of God."[89] To "put on Christ" is to derive all of one's righteousness from him, both for justification and for sanctification. That is not only because he is the eternal Son, but because he is the justified covenant head of his people, "and was declared to be Son of God in power according to the Spirit of holiness by his resurrection from the dead ..." (Ro 1:4). In Christ, our rags are exchanged for robes of regal splendor, and we are seated at the same table with Abraham, Isaac, and Jacob.

The clothing analogy is not original to Pauline theology. It occurs first with God's clothing of Adam and Eve after the fall, the vision of Joshua the high priest having his filthy clothes exchanged for a robe of righteousness in Zechariah 3, and a host of other passages. In Isaiah 61:10, we read, "I will greatly rejoice in the LORD; my soul shall exult in my God, for he has clothed me with the garments of salvation; he has covered me with the robe of righteousness, as a bridegroom decks himself like a priest with a beautiful headdress, and as a bride adorns herself with her jewels" (cf. Rev 21:2, which paraphrases this verse). The guests at the wedding feast in Jesus' parable are adorned in festive garments (Mt 22:1–14), and the prodigal son is decked out by the father in the best clothes upon his return (Lk 15:11–32). So when Paul says that Christ is "our righteousness and sanctification and redemption" (1Co 1:30) and refers repeatedly to our being "clothed with Christ" and "having put on

87. Gundry, "Nonimputation," 44–45.

88. Appealing to the research of Phyllis Bird, I pointed out in *Lord and Servant* (ch. 4) that Genesis 1–2 exploits Egyptian mythology for polemical purposes. While the Pharaoh was thought to be the son of the gods, in Genesis this royal sonship

extends beyond the king, and not only to all sons but to all human beings: "male and female" created in God's *image*, the language of sonship.

89. M. G. Kline, *Images of the Spirit* (Eugene, Ore.: Wipf & Stock, 1999), 35

Jesus Christ," and calls us on that basis to "put on Christ" in our daily conduct, this same connection between justification and sanctification is being drawn.

We could make the same point by drawing on the analogy of drama. In effectual calling, God has "rescripted" us and recasts us in his story. No longer trying to fit "God" or the gods into our own life story, we become characters in his unfolding drama: seated at the table with Abraham, Isaac, and Jacob. From God's perspective, our own script was all wrong. Regardless of the role we thought we had, our inherited character was that of "strangers to the covenants of promise" who were "having no hope ... in the world" (Eph 2:12). But God calls us, as he did Abram and the disciples, away from our dead-end character. In God's story, our old character dies and a new character emerges who is now given a supporting role in a plot that centers on Christ. As the casting director, the Spirit gives us not only a new identity with new clothes but a new script, with new lines.

In common with the practices of its neighbors, Israel's law made the firstborn son heir of the estate, which was also the inheritance law of the Greco-Roman world. Yet in the new covenant (fulfilling the promise to Adam and Eve as well as the covenant with Abraham and Sarah), with Christ as the head, "There is neither Jew nor Greek, there is neither slave nor free, there is no male and female, for you are all one in Christ Jesus. And if you are Christ's, then you are Abraham's offspring, heirs according to promise" (Gal 3:28–29). Everyone who is in Christ is a "firstborn son," co-heir of the entire estate.

A lodestar for justification, Galatians 3 and 4 are also crucial for our understanding of adoption. After all, the same logic that announces freedom from the bondage of the law for righteousness also pertains to the right of inheritance, which is a question of "sonship." Paul unfolds his argument redemptive-historically, with the law (here intending the whole old covenant administration) as the "guardian until Christ came, in order that we might be justified by faith" (3:24).

> I mean that the heir, as long as he is a child, is no different from a slave, though he is the owner of everything, but he is under guardians and managers until the date set by his father. In the same way we also, when we were children, were enslaved to the elementary principles of the world. But when the fullness of time had come, God sent forth his Son, born of woman, born under the law, to redeem those who were under the law, so that we might receive adoption as sons. And because you are sons, God has sent the Spirit of his Son into our hearts, crying, "Abba! Father!" So you are no longer a slave, but a son, and if a son, then an heir through God. (Gal 4:1–7)

These "sons" who are legally entitled to the inheritance include females as well as males, Gentiles as well as Jews, slaves as well as free citizens, without distinction (Gal 3:28–29).

Furthermore, these brothers and sisters are not only heirs of whatever is left over from the spoils of the firstborn son's inheritance. In fact, the very passage we are using for the structure of the *ordo salutis* (Ro 8:30) begins first with the statement, "For those whom he foreknew he also predestined to be conformed to the image of his Son, in order that he might be the firstborn among many brothers" (v. 29). Jews and Gentiles alike are "fellow heirs, members of the same body, and partakers of the promise in Christ Jesus through the gospel" (Eph 3:6). Properly speaking, it is Christ who is the "heir of all things" (Heb 1:2; cf. Lk 20:14), but precisely because he possesses all things not only as a private but as a public person, his inheritance is a public trust. Believers hold all things in common with Christ and therefore with each other.

In the economy of the Sinai covenant, Moses is a servant in God's house, while Jesus Christ is the firstborn son (Heb 3:1–6). So even Moses' adoption is dependent not only on the condition of his personal fulfillment of the law covenant made at Sinai but on Christ's personal fulfillment of that covenant by which he has won the inheritance for his brothers and sisters in the covenant of grace: "For the one who sanctifies and those who are sanctified all have one Father. For this reason Jesus is not ashamed to call them brothers and sisters, saying, 'I will proclaim your name to my brothers and sisters, in the midst of the congregation I will praise you.' And again, 'I will put my trust in him.' And again, 'Here am I and the children whom God has given me'" (Heb 2:11–13, NRSV). As with justification, this adoption is not a legal fiction, since the law is fulfilled: the firstborn Son has won the entire estate by his victorious service to the crown, but, as established in the mutuality of the covenant of redemption (i.e., election), every adopted child has an equal share.

At this point, the character of the covenant of grace as founded on a royal grant becomes especially obvious. Having merited his estate by his loyal service to the Great King, the Son passes on the inheritance in perpetuity to all of those co-heirs included in his last will and testament. Jesus' High Priestly Prayer in John 17 is pregnant with this covenantal grant, even to the point of linking his own fulfillment of his earthly mission to the intratrinitarian covenant of redemption, referring to "those whom you gave me," who are now to be included in the *koinōnia* (fellowship) of the Trinity itself.

The children need not worry about their future or jockey for their Father's favor (as Jacob and Esau). After all, "He who did not spare his own Son but gave him up for us all, how will he not also with him graciously give us all things?" (Ro 8:32). As Calvin comments on Ephesians 1:23,

> This is the highest honour of the Church, that, until He is united to us, the Son of God reckons himself in some measure imperfect. What consolation is it for us to

learn, that, not until we are along with him, does he possess all his parts, or wish to be regarded as complete! Hence, in the First Epistle to the Corinthians, when the apostle discusses largely the metaphor of a human body, he includes under the single name of Christ the whole Church.[90]

If union with Christ in the covenant of grace is the matrix for Paul's *ordo*, justification remains its basis, even for adoption. We do not move from the topic of justification to other (more interesting) ones, but are always relating the riches of our inheritance to this decisive gift. In William Ames's words, "Adoption of its own nature requires and presupposes the reconciliation found in justification.... The first fruit of adoption is that Christian liberty by which all believers are freed from the bondage of the law, sin, and the world."[91]

Adoption, like justification, is simultaneously legal and relational, as is the obverse: alienation and condemnation. Adoption is not a goal held out to children who successfully imitate their parents; nor is it the result of an infusion of familial characteristics or genes. Rather, it is a change in legal status that issues in a relationship that is gradually reflected in the child's identity, characteristics, and actions. From the courtroom, with the legal status and inheritance unalterably established, the child moves into the security of a growing and thriving future.

Just as there is no opposition between forensic and relational categories in the earthly process of adoption, we are not forced to choose between forensic and effective categories in describing spiritual adoption either. God's Word declares us to be righteous heirs of the kingdom, and this same Word immediately begins to conform us existentially, morally, and socially to this new-creation reality, with the firstborn Son as its archetype. As Oswald Bayer expresses this point, "What God says, God does ... God's work is God's speech. God's speech is no fleeting breath. It is a most effective breath that creates life, that summons into life."[92] Justification is not an inert but a living Word, on a par with creation *ex nihilo*, according to Paul (Ro 4:17, with Ps 33:6) — not only the Word *about* God, but *of* God, that creates the reality that it announces.[93]

---

90. John Calvin, *Commentaries on the Epistles of Paul to the Galatians and Ephesians* (trans. William Pringle; Grand Rapids: Eerdmans, 1957), 218.

91. William Ames, *The Marrow of Theology* (1623; trans. John Dykstra Eusden; Grand Rapids: Baker, repr. 1997), 165.

92. Oswald Bayer, *Living by Grace: Justification and Sanctification* (trans. Geoffrey W. Bromiley; Grand Rapids: Eerdmans, 2003), 43.

93. The second Anglican–Roman Catholic International Commission, appealing to 1Co 6:11, stated that "justification and sanctification are two aspects of the same divine act: God's grace effects what he declares: his creative word imparts what it imputes. By pronouncing us righteous, God also makes us righteous. He imparts a righteousness which is his and becomes ours" (*Growth in Agreement II: Reports and Agreed Statements of Ecumenical Conversations on a World Level, 1982–1998* [ed. Jeffrey Gros, Harding Meyer, and William G. Rusch; Geneva: WCC Publications; Grand Rapids: Eerdmans, 2000], par. 15). In my estimation at least, ARCIC II, though still insufficiently attentive to the purely forensic character of justification, is more consistent with the Reformation perspective than is the *Joint Declaration on Justification* between the Lutheran World Federation and the Vatican.

CONCLUSION

Paul appeals to the examples of Abraham and David (especially in Romans 4 and Galatians 2–4). In fact, the familiar prophecy of Isaiah 53 describes this imputation or exchange. The suffering Servant bears our sins, suffers in our place, and by his righteous act "shall ... make many to be accounted righteous, and he shall bear their iniquities" (v. 11). Our sins are put on his account, and his righteousness is credited to us. In Zechariah 3, there is the prophecy of Joshua the high priest in the heavenly courtroom, with Satan as the prosecuting attorney and the Angel of the LORD as his defender. Although condemned in himself, Joshua has his filthy clothes removed and is arrayed instead in a spotless robe. All of these passages flood the New Testament's testimony to Jesus Christ as "the LORD ... our righteousness" (cf. Jer 23:5–6; 33:16, with 1Co 1:30–31; 2Co 5:21). "There is therefore now no condemnation for those who are in Christ Jesus" (Ro 8:1). Nothing remains to be done; all has been accomplished for us by Christ, and in him we are already holy and blameless before the Father.

Far from denying the subjective transformation of the new birth and sanctification, the classic evangelical view points to its only possible source. As with all sound teaching in the Scriptures, the goal of the doctrine is to bring us to doxology, giving all praise to God with nothing left for ourselves. "What then shall we say to these things? If God is for us, who can be against us? ... Who shall bring any charge against God's elect? It is God who justifies. Who is to condemn? ... Who shall separate us from the love of Christ?" (Ro 8:31–35).

However, perhaps the best image in the New Testament for justification comes from Jesus' parable of the tax collector and the Pharisee. "The Pharisee, standing by himself, prayed thus: 'God, I thank you that I am not like other men, extortioners, unjust, adulterers, or even like this tax collector. I fast twice a week; I give tithes of all that I get.' But the tax collector, standing far off, would not even lift up his eyes to heaven, but beat his breast, saying, 'God, be merciful to me, a sinner!'" (Lk 18:10–13). Luke introduces this parable as intended by Jesus for "some who trusted in themselves that they were righteous, and treated others with contempt" (v. 9). Clearly, Jesus saw the problem of the religious leaders as self-righteousness, which bore fruit of course in exclusionary practices. Furthermore, the Pharisee and tax collector both "went up into the temple to pray" (v. 10), so the contrast was not between some works (circumcision and dietary laws) and others. Finally, the Pharisee even thanked God for his righteousness, tipping his hat to grace (v. 11). Nevertheless, the tax collector asked for mercy rather than for an approval of his righteousness. "I tell you," Jesus concluded, "this man went down to his house justified, rather than the other" (v. 14).

DISCUSSION QUESTIONS

1. Discuss the main differences between Roman Catholic and Reformation interpretations of Paul's statement that God "justifies the ungodly" (Ro 4:5).

2. Do the Scriptures treat justification as a legal declaration or as a process of growth in grace? Identify the *basis* of justification and the *instrument* of justification.

3. How would you respond to the charge that the evangelical doctrine of justification amounts to a "legal fiction"?

4. What does "imputation" mean, and how does it relate to justification?

5. Why is this doctrine of justification a perennially difficult one to confess, preach, and believe — even for Christians? Conversely, why is it so important and relevant? Is it just one doctrine among many, or is it central to our faith and life?

6. How does the doctrine of adoption relate to union with Christ and justification? How does it reflect especially the simultaneously legal and relational aspects of this union?

Chapter Twenty

THE WAY FORWARD IN GRACE: SANCTIFICATION AND PERSEVERANCE

We have seen that one reason for the ongoing criticism of the evangelical doctrine of justification is that it is thought to undermine sanctification.[1] However, this assumption (even among many Protestants) presupposes a false choice that the Reformers did not make between the imputation of Christ's righteousness and the renewal of believers according to Christ's image. While Rome simply assimilated justification to sanctification, the Reformation position affirmed both as distinct yet inseparable gifts. G. C. Berkouwer replies to those who deny Luther's interest in God's gracious renovation of believers: "To anyone who has had a whiff of Luther's writings this conception is incredible. Even a scanty initiation is enough to be convinced that justification for Luther meant much more than an external event with no importance for the inner man."[2] Like the relation of the doctrine of substitution in relation to other aspects of the atonement, forensic justification not only allows room for other benefits of Christ; it is their source and security.

The Reformers saw "Christ for us" and "Christ in us," the alien righteousness imputed and the sanctifying righteousness imparted, as not only compatible but necessarily and inextricably related. Those who are justified through faith are new

---

1. According to an uncharacteristically ill-informed assertion of the great Roman Catholic historian of philosophy, Étienne Gilson, "For the first time, with the Reformation, there appeared this conception of a grace that saves a man without changing him, of a justice that redeems corrupted nature without restoring it, of a Christ who pardons the sinner for self-inflicted wounds but does not heal them" (*The Spirit of Medieval Philosophy* [London: Sheed and Ward, 1936], 421).

2. G. C. Berkouwer, *Studies in Dogmatics: Faith and Sanctification* (Grand Rapids: Eerdmans, 1952), 29.

creatures and begin then and there to love God and their neighbor, yielding the fruit of good works. Reformed churches agree with the Lutheran confession that if sin has free sway over one's life, "the Holy Spirit and faith are not present."[3] However, it is not simply that justification and sanctification always go together in the application of redemption, as if they were parallel tracks; rather, justification is the judicial ground of a union with Christ that also yields renewal and sanctification. For Rome, we are justified because we are sanctified; for evangelicals, we are being sanctified because we have been justified.[4] In this chapter, we turn our attention to sanctification as the perlocutionary effect of the evangelical Word pronounced upon us by the Father in grace.

In the Greek language we must differentiate between the *indicative* mood, which is declarative (simply describing a certain state of affairs), and the *imperative* mood, which sets forth commands). For example, in Romans Paul first explains who believers were in Adam and their new status in Christ (justification) and then reasons from this indicative to the imperatives as a logical conclusion: "Do not present your members to sin as instruments for unrighteousness, but present yourselves to God as those who have been brought from death to life ..." (Ro 6:13). He concludes with another imperative (command), but this time it is really an indicative: "For sin will have no dominion over you, since you are not under law but under grace" (v. 14). This seems just as contradictory to our moral reason as his earlier statement that "[God] justifies the ungodly" (Ro 4:5). What judge declares the unjust to be just? And how can the apostle tell us that sin no longer has dominion over us because we are not under law but under grace? Isn't it the role of religion to give people moral instruction so that they will no longer be dominated by their sinful habits?

As counterintuitive as this may seem to our natural way of thinking, Paul says that the gospel is the answer not only to our guilt and condemnation but to our corruption and slavery to sin. In his hymn "Rock of Ages," Augustus Toplady spoke of the gospel as "the double cure,"[5] saving us from both sin's guilt and its power. In the act of justification, works and grace are totally opposed. However, once our persons are justified, so too our works can be "saved" in spite of their imperfections. *The faith that receives Christ apart from works for justification also receives Christ for works in sanctification.* Only as the fruit of grace-wrought faith are good works even

---

3. *Smalcald Articles* 3, 3, 44, quoted in Edmund Schlink, *Theology of the Lutheran Confessions* (trans. Paul F. Koehneke and Herbert J. A. Bouman; Philadelphia: Fortress, 1961), 160.

4. A point from the previous chapter bears repeating. There is no reason to have to choose between justification and union with Christ as the source of sanctification. Both are given through faith in Christ. The "marvelous exchange" involves both imputation (our sins to Christ and his righteousness to us) and the communication of Christ's new-creation life by the Spirit. Nevertheless, within this covenantal union, sanctification follows logically from justification.

5. Augustus Toplady, "Rock of Ages" (1776), in *Psalter Hymnal* (Grand Rapids: Publication Committee of the CRC, 1959), #388. See the superb study by Cornelis P. Venema, *Accepted and Renewed in Christ: The "Twofold Grace of God" in the Interpretation of Calvin's Theology* (Göttingen: Vandenhoeck & Ruprecht, 2007).

possible. The tyranny of sin over your life has been toppled; therefore, do not live as though this has not happened: this is the order of Pauline logic. In fact, presenting our bodies as a living sacrifice, according to Paul, is our "spiritual [*logikēn*; "reasonable," KJV] worship" in the light of "God's mercies" that have been explored to that point (Ro 12:1 NRSV). It is the good news that yields good works.

I. HOLY TO THE LORD: DEFINITIVE AND PROGRESSIVE SANCTIFICATION

Sanctification is grounded in election, the incarnation, and redemption, but most immediately in effectual calling, justification and adoption. Called into union with Christ by the Spirit through the gospel, the elect are adopted into God's family as joint-heirs with Christ, renewed according to the image of their elder brother.

A. DEFINITIVELY SANCTIFIED

In both the Hebrew and the Greek, the root of the verb translate "to sanctify" is "to separate." God's sanctification separates people, places, and things *away* from their ordinary association *for* his own use. Although we will come to the sense in which sanctification is more commonly understood as moral renewal, it is important to recognize at the outset that it is *God's* action of electing, separating or cutting, claiming a people for himself. It is not the gold that makes the sanctuary sacred, nor the gift on the altar that sanctifies the altar, but the sanctuary that sanctifies the gold and the altar that sanctifies the gift, Jesus reminded the religious leaders (Mt 23:16–19). Jesus even refers to himself as one whom "the Father has sanctified [set apart] and sent into the world" (Jn 10:36 NRSV). Paul reminds Timothy that approved ministers in God's house are vessels set apart from ordinary use for special use (2Ti 2:21).

As John Murray helpfully explains, *progressive sanctification* depends not only on justification but on God's once-and-for-all act of claiming us as saints.[6] For many Christians, the change in subject from justification to sanctification roughly corresponds to God's work for us and our work for God, respectively. The result of this assumption, however, is that for a brief moment at the beginning of the Christian life the focus was on Christ and his blessing of justification that was received through faith alone—itself, in fact, a gift of God. But then the rest of our life is a matter of striving for moral improvement. "Having begun by the Spirit," Paul

---

6. See especially John Murray, *Collected Writings of John Murray* (Edinburgh: Banner of Truth Trust, 1977), 2:277–93. Unlike Murray, however, I would treat definitive and progressive sanctification as two aspects of the same reality rather than two distinct points in the *ordo salutis*.

asked the Galatians, "are you now being perfected by the flesh?" Sanctification, like justification, has its source not in the "works of the law" but in "hearing with faith" (Gal 3:3–5).

We are confident that we are holy and are being made holy in Jesus Christ simply on the basis of his promise, not because of what we see visibly in ourselves or each other. In sanctification as well as justification God the Father is the giver, the Son is the gift, and the Spirit is the one who creates faith within us through the gospel. In both, Christ is the object, the gospel is the means of its communication from God, and faith is the means of our receiving it from him. Nor does sanctification require a different act of faith than that exercised in justification. The faith through which we are united to Christ simultaneously lavishes us with every spiritual blessing in heavenly places.

Before we can speak of our being put to holy use and growing in grace, then, we must see that sanctification is first of all God's act of setting us apart from the world for himself. This looks back retrospectively to our election in Christ, which is frequently mentioned as the ultimate source of our sanctification (Jn 15:16; Eph 1:4; Col 3:12; 1Th 1:2–7; 2Th 2:13–16; 2Ti 1:9–10; 1Pe 1:2). John Webster draws our attention to this point nicely:

> The sanctifying Spirit is *Lord*; that is, sanctification is not in any straightforward sense a process of cooperation or coordination between God and the creature, a drawing out or building upon some inherent holiness of the creature's own. Sanctification is *making* holy. Holiness is properly an incommunicable divine attribute; if creaturely realities become holy, it is by virtue of election, that is, by a sovereign act of segregation or separation by the Spirit as Lord.... From the vertical of "lordship" there flows the horizontal of life which is truly *given*. Segregation, election to holiness, is not the abolition of creatureliness but its creation and preservation.[7]

To Israel God says that as long as the people obey his law, they will be "my treasured possession among all peoples, for all the earth is mine; and you shall be to me a kingdom of priests and a holy nation" (Ex 19:5–6). It is this same description that Peter applies to the church because of Christ's faithfulness, even to those who "were not a people" and "had not received mercy" (1Pe 2:9–10). In his baptism, their baptism is sanctified. In his active obedience, they are holy. "And for their sakes I sanctify myself," says Jesus, "so that they also may be sanctified in truth" (Jn 17:19 NRSV). In his death, burial, and resurrection they die and are raised to new life. They have been saved out of the world. Therefore, even before Jesus tells the disciples about their own fruit-bearing life as part of the Vine, he declares, "Already you are clean because of the word that I have spoken to you" (Jn 15:3).

---

7. John Webster, *Holy Scripture: A Dogmatic Sketch* (Cambridge: Cambridge Univ. Press, 2003), 27.

In his message to the Ephesian elders, Paul said, "And now I commend you to God and to the word of his grace, which is able to build you up and to give you the inheritance among all those who are sanctified" (Ac 20:32). He addresses his letters to the churches as those "who are ... called to be saints [*hagiois*]" (Ro 1:7), "to those sanctified [*hēgiasmenois*] in Christ Jesus" (1Co 1:2; cf. 2Co 1:1; Eph 1:1; Php 1:1; Col 1:2). Similarly, Peter addresses his first letter to Christians of the Jewish diaspora as those "elect ... according to the foreknowledge of God the Father in the sanctification [*hagiasmos*] of the Spirit, for obedience to Jesus Christ and for sprinkling with his blood" (1Pe 1:1–2), and his second letter "to those who have obtained a faith of equal standing with ours by the righteousness of our God and Savior Jesus Christ" (2Pe 1:1).

All that is found in Christ is holy, because it is in Christ. He is our sanctification — "the LORD is our righteousness" (1Co 1:30 with Jer 23:6), our Holy Place. The sprinkling of Christ's blood is vastly superior to that of the blood of goats and bulls in sanctifying, since it purifies "our conscience from dead works to serve the living God!" (Heb 9:13–14). "And by [God's] will we have been sanctified through the offering of the body of Jesus Christ once for all" (Heb 10:10). It is this "blood of the covenant by which he [the covenant member] was sanctified" (v. 29). Jesus suffered outside the camp "in order to sanctify the people through his own blood" (Heb 13:12). God "saved us and called us to a holy calling, not because of our works but because of his own purpose and grace, which he gave us in Christ Jesus before the ages began, and which now has been manifested through the appearing of our Savior Christ Jesus, who abolished death and brought life and immortality to light through the gospel" (2Ti 1:9–10).

In spite of the fact that the Corinthian church had become filled with immorality, strife, division, and immaturity, Paul begins both letters to this body by addressing them as "saints" (holy ones) and reintroduces the wonder of the gospel. Precisely because their status was defined by the gospel's indicatives, the apostle could recall them to repentance as the only legitimate response. *Where most people think that the goal of religion is to get people to become something that they are not, the Scriptures call believers to become more and more what they already are in Christ.* Because they were definitively sanctified or set apart as holy to the Lord, the Corinthians must reestablish proper relationships, order, and behavior in the church. Their practice must be brought in line with their identity.

The same point can be discerned in John 15:3, where Jesus says, "You are clean [*katharos*, 'clean, pure'] because of the word that I have spoken to you," and only then calls them to bear fruit that is consistent with this forensic declaration. Before warring nations can enter into an era of peaceful relations, they must formally and legally conclude a peace, and before orphans can enjoy the love and care of a new family, they must be legally adopted. The weaker have full security in relation to the stronger because they know that the legal obstacles that might withdraw their status have been finally and forever resolved. The status being settled once and for all, our new relationship to God and the promised inheritance is a *terminus a quo* (starting point) of divine accomplishment and not a *terminus ad quem* (goal) of our striving. To insist upon the logical priority of legal justification is simply to recognize that God's love is consistent with God's justice, righteousness, holiness, and beauty.

Just as the metaphor of adoption, in the *covenantal* context, stresses the legal and relational together, the organic metaphors associated with regeneration and sanctification underscore the power of that justifying Word to actually insert the believer into the world that it announces. Here we encounter the familiar vocabulary of vine and branches, tree and fruit, head and body, firstfruits and full harvest, living stones being built into a temple. Thus, the reference point for sanctification remains Christ's person and work, mediated by the Spirit through Word and sacrament, received through faith alone — but not by a faith that is alone. Furthermore, sanctification is treated in the New Testament in terms of the "already"/"not yet," justifying, to my mind at least, a distinction between definitive and progressive sanctification. Just as the temple vessels were not intrinsically holy before they were set aside for holy purposes, there is no preparation on our part that can make us holy.[8]

B. PROGRESSIVELY SANCTIFIED

However, the New Testament also speaks of this setting apart as an ongoing work within believers that renews them inwardly and conforms them gradually to the image of God in Christ. We *are* holy (definitive sanctification); therefore, we are *to be* holy (progressive sanctification). Although we are not saved *by* works, we are saved *for* works (Eph 2:10). The power of God is not only at work in Christ for us but is also "the power at work within us" (Eph 3:20), so that, despite our own weakness, Christ's energies are at work within us by his Spirit (2Co 12:9–10). Believers are called to pursue purity, to dwell on excellent things, so that "what you have learned and received and heard and seen in me — practice these things, and the God of peace will be with you" (Php 4:9). Such holiness distinguishes itself by producing the fruit of wisdom, purity, peace, gentleness, without partiality or hypocrisy (Jas 3:13–18). Already holy in Christ, we are to offer ourselves as "a living sacrifice, holy and acceptable" (Ro 12:1), as stones in a holy temple and those who offer a spiritual sacrifice of holy living (1Co 3:17; 1Pe 2:4–5).

---

8. For an excellent treatment of this topic, see John Webster, *Holiness* (Grand Rapids: Eerdmans, 2003), esp. ch. 4.

This growth in holiness has its source in God alone, but God works through means. We are called to regularly attend to God's Word in public worship as well as in family and personal meditation on the law and the promises. Claiming God's promise to us in our baptism, we die daily to sin and rise anew in faith and repentance. The indicative (definitive sanctification) leads to the imperatives (progressive sanctification): "Put on then, as God's chosen ones, holy and beloved, compassionate hearts, kindness, humility, meekness, and patience, bearing with one another and, if one has a complaint against another, forgiving each other; as the Lord has forgiven you, so you also must forgive. And above all these put on love, which binds everything together in perfect harmony" (Col 3:12–14).

However, we should beware of turning the distinction into a separation, where our status as holy in Christ is one thing and our own progress in holiness is another. In our pilgrimage, we are not simply growing in *our* holiness, but bearing the fruit of our union with Christ and *his* holiness. The flesh (*sarx*) is not given a new lease on life, improved, elevated, and revived. Rather, the Adamic self is put to death, and the person thus raised is now a participant in the Spirit, sharing with Christ in the powers of the age to come. Thus, our justification and union with Christ cannot be seen merely as the starting point for a life of personal transformation, but as the only source of any fecundity throughout the Christian life. Our mortification and vivification in sanctification are not our own contribution alongside justification and union with Christ, but are the effect of that new relationship. Nevertheless, it is not Christ who dies and rises daily, putting to death indwelling sins, but believers. Faith is given in regeneration and passively receives justification, but in sanctification it is active in love.

Calvin offers helpful insights on this point in his comments on Jesus' High Priestly Prayer in John 17. Believers are "sanctified by the truth," which is God's Word (v. 17), "for the word here denotes the doctrine of the Gospel": here Calvin challenges the "fanatics," who imagine a sanctification that comes from an "inner word" apart from the external Word.[9] "And for their sakes I sanctify myself," Jesus prays (v. 19 NRSV).

> By these words he explains more clearly from what source that sanctification flows, which is completed in us by the doctrine of the Gospel. It is because he consecrated himself to the Father that his holiness might come to us; for as the blessing on the firstfruits is spread over the whole harvest, so the Spirit of God cleanses us by the holiness of Christ, and makes us partakers of it. Nor is this done by imputation only, for in that respect he is said to have been made to us righteousness; but he is likewise said to have been made to us sanctification (1Co 1:30) because he has, so

---

9. John Calvin, *Commentary on the Gospel According to John* (trans. William Pringle; Edinburgh: T&T Clark, 1840; repr., Grand Rapids: Baker, 1996), 179–80.

to speak, presented us to his Father in his own person, that we may be renewed to true holiness by his Spirit. Besides, though this sanctification belongs to the whole life of Christ, yet the highest illustration of it was given in the sacrifice of his death; for then he showed himself to be the true High Priest, by consecrating the temple, the altar, all the vessels, and the people, by the power of his Spirit.[10]

The goal is "that they may all be one" (v. 21).[11] Calvin is as much on home ground in discussing the richness of the organic-horticultural metaphors as in discussing the legal. While they are distinct, the organic and the legal are two sides of the same covenantal coin.

The same harmony can be found in the confessional treatments, as in the *Second Helvetic Confession*, chapter 15: "Wherefore, in this matter we are not speaking of a fictitious, empty, lazy and dead faith, but of a living, quickening faith. *It is and is called a living faith because it apprehends Christ who is life and makes alive, and shows that it is alive by living works*" (emphasis added). It is not the quality of faith itself, but of the person it apprehends, that makes it the sufficient means of receiving both our justification and sanctification. Not because of what faith is, but because of who Christ is, faith in Christ cannot fail to bring forth good works. In fact, precisely because believers do not trust at all in their own piety, the works that spring from faith are truly pious.[12]

Paradoxically, it is this very liberation that issues in constant inner struggle, since on the one hand we belong definitively to the new creation—"the age to come"—with Christ as our firstfruits and the Spirit as the pledge, yet on the other we still live in "this present evil age" and continue to pretend that we are not those whom God has worded us to be in Christ. By contrast, the struggle of the unregenerate, according to William Ames, is "not the striving of the Spirit against the flesh but that of the flesh fearing flesh inordinately desiring."[13] Ames's statement points up the fact that however useful Aristotelian or Kantian conceptions of "ethics," "virtue," and "duty" may be, the definitive categories for theology are covenantal and eschatological: the tyranny of sin (flesh) and the reign of life in righteousness (the Spirit). Natural ethics and the enabling power of the Spirit in common grace may check immoderate habits, but the Spirit creates a new world through the gospel.

Just as Paul's treatment of justification led logically to the question, "Are we to continue in sin that grace may abound?" (Ro 6:1), the Reformation unleashed radical elements that went well beyond the views of the Reformers. Lutheran theologian

---

10. Ibid., 180–81.

11. Ibid., 183.

12. *Second Helvetic Confession*, ch. 15, in *Book of Confessions* (Louisville: PCUSA General Assembly, 1991): "This all the pious do, but they trust in Christ alone and not in their own works. For again the apostle said: 'It is no longer I who live, but

Christ who lives in me; and the life I now live in the flesh I live by faith in the Son of God, who loved me and gave himself for me. I do not reject the grace of God; for if justification were through the law, then Christ died to no purpose' (Gal 2:20)."

13. William Ames, *The Marrow of Theology* (1623; trans. John Dykstra Eusden; Grand Rapids: Baker, repr., 1968), 171.

Gerhard Forde reminds us, "Luther had hardly begun to proclaim the freedom of the Christian before he had to fight against abuse of the term. He did not do this in such a way as to speak about the good works that must be added to faith. Instead, he did so by calling people back to that faith that occurs 'where the Holy Spirit gives people faith in Christ and thus sanctifies them.' "[14] Luther's response at this juncture was precisely Paul's: To infer from justification that we are free to remain in sin is to ignore the vast scope of what justification actually accomplishes. Though we are justified through faith alone, this faith "is never alone, but is always accompanied by love and hope."[15]

Although it is not itself a renovation, justification issues, as an effective Word, in a completely new reality. The God who declares the wicked righteous simultaneously (though distinctly) makes the dead alive. Acquittal and acceptance lead inevitably to new life and new obedience, not vice versa. While our first impulse is to return to the law and self-effort in order to stem the tide of antinomianism, Paul and the Reformers call us back to the gospel, whose power in the face of continuing sin we have not sufficiently weighed. Apart from the imputation of righteousness, sanctification is simply another religious self-improvement program determined by the powers of this age (the flesh) rather than of the age to come (the Spirit).

This gospel announces not only our justification, but our participation in the power of Christ's crucifixion and resurrection. Therefore, we cannot look to Christ at the beginning, for our justification, and then, when it comes to the Christian life (sanctification), look away from Christ to our own progress and countless manuals that offer formulas for spiritual and moral ascent. Again Forde is insightful:

> In our modern age, influenced by Pietism and the Enlightenment, our thinking is shaped by what is subjective, by the life of faith, by our inner disposition and motivation, by our inward impulses and the way they are shaped. When we think and live along these lines, sanctification is a matter of personal and individual development and orientation. It is true that we also find this approach in Luther. No one emphasized more sharply than he did our personal responsibility and irreplaceability. But this approach is secondary. "The Word of God always comes first. After it follows faith; after faith, love; then love does every good work, for ... it is the fulfilling of the law."[16]

Even in sanctification,

> the focus is not upon the saints but upon sanctification, upon the Word of God in all its sacramental forms, and also upon secular institutions that correspond to the

14. Gerhard Forde, *On Being a Theologian of the Cross: Reflections on Luther's Heidelberg Disputation, 1518* (Grand Rapids: Eerdmans, 1997), 56–57.

15. See *Formula of Concord* (Epitome 3, art. 11; cf. solid declaration 3, arts. 23, 26, 36, 41).

16. Forde, *On Being a Theologian of the Cross*, 58; Forde quotes Luther from *Luther's Works* (ed. Helmut T. Lehmann; Philadelphia: Fortress, 1957; repr., 1971), 36:39.

second table of the law ... Only God is holy, and what he says and speaks and does is holy. This is how God's holiness works, which he does not keep to himself, but communicates by sharing it.[17]

What this means is that we who once were curved in on ourselves (Augustine; see ch. 18, "Covenant and Conditionality," pp. 615–19), seeing the world but not really seeing it rightly, must be called out of ourselves to be judged as ungodly and then dressed in Christ's righteousness. This is necessary not only for our justification but for our sanctification as well. Our identity is no longer something that we fabricate in our bondage that we mistake for freedom. "To become new men means losing what we now call 'ourselves,'" C. S. Lewis observes. "Out of our selves, into Christ, we must go."[18] "Your real, new self (which is Christ's and also yours, and yours just because it is His) will not come as long as you are looking for it," he adds. "It will come when you are looking for Him." To be in Christ is to be "very much more themselves than they were before."[19] "He invented — as an author invents characters in a novel — all the different people that you and I were intended to be. In that sense our real selves are all waiting for us in Him. It is no good trying to 'be myself' without Him."[20] "To enter heaven," he says, "is to become more human than you ever succeeded in being on earth."[21]

Far from creating a morbid subjectivity and individualism, as is often charged, this view frees us from being curved in on ourselves, fretting over our own souls. In a moving and friendly letter to Cardinal Sadoleto, Calvin made much the same point, when he argued that only by being freed of having to love our neighbor in the service of our own salvation are we able to really love them for their own sake.[22] Sanctification is a life not of acquiring but of receiving from the excess of divine joy, which then continues to overflow in excess to our neighbor and from our neighbor to us.

II. Eschatology: Simultaneously Justified and Sinful

With Luther, the Reformed have always emphasized that the believer remains just and sinner simultaneously: perfectly righteous before God's judgment, yet full of corruption and actual sins. As the sign and seal of our incorporation into Christ, baptism is a one-time event, completed in the past, yet with continuing effects as

---

17. Ibid., 59
18. C. S. Lewis, *Mere Christianity* (San Francisco: HarperSanFrancisco, 2001), 224.
19. Ibid., 161.
20. Ibid., 225.

21. C. S. Lewis, *The Problem of Pain* (San Francisco: HarperSanFrancisco, 2001), 127–28.
22. John Calvin, *A Reformation Debate: Sadoleto's Letter to the Genevans and Calvin's Reply* (ed. John C. Olin; Grand Rapids: Baker, 1966), 56.

well as obligations throughout our life. We believe the indicative promise that we are dead to sin and alive to God in Christ even though our experience and actions do not always match that reality. Nevertheless, Reformed teaching is more pronounced in emphasizing that the radical announcement of the "already" is assigned to our ethical as well as legal relation to God.

A. AVOIDING AN UNDERREALIZED ESCHATOLOGY OF SANCTIFICATION

Especially against the antinomians, Luther highlighted the inseparability of faith and good works, but in other places the absolute newness of the believer's identity in Christ is downplayed by what sometimes verges on an underrealized eschatology, as in his statement, "I have heard of it but as yet have seen *nothing* of it. '*Not in essence,* but by promise, I have eternal life.' I have it in obscurity. I *do not see it*, but I believe it and will *hereafter surely feel it*" (emphasis added).[23] While we do indeed live by faith rather than by sight, believing what we hear even when we do not see it, is it really the case that we have seen *nothing* of the age to come and have felt no impact of the new creation? Or is it that the age to come is even now breaking in on this present age, already beginning to transform everything from the inside out?

While our failures should send us back to Christ rather than to the law for safety, Reformed theology seems less reticent to encourage believers to be cheered by the newness that they actually experience. An underrealized eschatology loses the agonizing paradox of the *simul iustus et peccator* just as surely as an overrealized perfectionism.[24] We are *iustus* (just) as well as *peccator* (sinner). Exactly because Paul is the figure described in Romans 6 — not only justified but also truly "alive in Christ" and definitively liberated from the tyranny of sin — he is disturbed by the discrepancy between this fact and indwelling sin that he discovers in himself in Romans 7.[25]

According to Jane E. Strohl, Luther has an "eschatological reserve." "For Calvin the transformation of the believer is measurably advanced and manifest, whereas for Luther the reality of redemption remains deeply hidden until the

---

23. Martin Luther, *Luther's Works*, 16:52, 19–21, quoted in Gerhard Forde, *On Being a Theologian of the Cross*, 35.

24. As Tuomo Mannermaa points out, Luther speaks of the *simul* in two senses: the believer is totally sinner in herself and totally righteous in Christ (*totus-totus*), yet also partially sinful and partially righteous in terms of sanctification (*partim-partim*) (*Christ Present in Faith: Luther's View of Justification* [ed. Kirsi Stjerna; Minneapolis: Augsburg Fortress, 2005], 58–60). It is that second sense that I am stressing here, although it must always keep the first in view.

25. Serious exegetical objections have been raised against the traditional Reformed and Lutheran interpretation of the "I" in

Romans 7, beyond those raised by Arminian theology. Werner G. Kümmel, *Römer 7 und die Bekehrung des Paulus* (Leipzig: Hinrichs, 1928), regarded the "I" in Romans 7 as a stylistic device that is not to be read as autobiographical. Herman Ridderbos (*Paul: An Outline of His Theology* [trans. John R. De Witt; Grand Rapids: Eerdmans, 1975]) also develops an intriguing line of exegesis. Nevertheless, I remain persuaded that there are good exegetical reasons to retain the autobiographical "I" while recognizing that it is illustrative also of a wider redemptive-historical reality — i.e., the transition from the era of "this age" (law, sin, condemnation, death) to "the age to come."

Last Day."[26] "Finally for Luther what matters most is not what the believer does in or for the world, but how he or she survives it."[27] I think that this exaggerates the differences between Luther and Calvin, but even so it does point up different emphases. If taken to an extreme, the "not yet" emphasis can lead to a kind of quietism in which this world remains untouched in its depths by the forensic Word and its transforming effects, while an overemphasis on the "already" and "more and more" of sanctification can yield a moralistic impulse that mistakes activism for holiness. At their best, both the Lutheran and Reformed nuances on this point reflect the inner tension of Pauline eschatology, and the challenge is to hold them together. God speaks judgment, and creation withers; he speaks grace, and a desert springs to life with myriad streams, blooming flowers, and lush pastures.

We can avoid moralism and passivity at least in part by recognizing that the divine grace of sanctification does not render the subject immobile or passive but definitively and progressively transforms the character of that agency. In fact, it was prior to our regeneration that we were immobile and passive, at least in relation to God and his righteousness. God's work frees us for the first time for the pursuit of the very source of truth, goodness, and beauty. Simultaneously justified and sinful, we are also simultaneously renewed and sinful. Though less complete than justification, the renewal is no less definitive.

B. Avoiding an Overrealized Eschatology of Sanctification

In some ways like medieval Christians, some evangelicals assume that there are two classes of Christians: those who are common (perhaps even carnal) Christians and those who are "victorious" and truly sanctified. However, this view reflects an eschatology that is simultaneously underrealized (for some) and overrealized (for others). According to the New Testament, *every* believer is buried and raised with Christ and at the same time struggling with indwelling sin. Some evangelicals teach that believers can become "carnal Christians" — devoid of good works and even of faith itself.[28] In this view, the call is constantly to enter the "higher" or "victorious life" of spiritual Christians.

However, Paul does not imagine the possibility of a believer being at one period defined by Christ's resurrection-life, with the tyranny of sin definitively toppled (Ro 6), and then in another period "carnal" (Ro 7) and then still another "victorious"

---

26. Jane E. Strohl, "God's Self-Revelation in the Sacrament of the Altar," in *By Faith Alone: Essays on Justification in Honor of Gerhard O. Forde* (ed. Joseph A. Burgess and Marc Kolden; Grand Rapids: Eerdmans, 2004), 107.

27. Ibid., 109.

28. Zane Hodges, *Absolutely Free* (Dallas: Redención Viva, 1989), 75, 125, 131, esp. p. 111, where he says a believer can cease believing and remain a Christian. See also Charles Ryrie, *So Great Salvation* (Wheaton, Ill.: Victor Books, 1989), 74, 141–42, 151.

(Ro 8). *The believer described in Romans 6 as delivered completely from the dominion of sin through baptism into Christ is the same person in Romans 7 who is consistently frustrated by his or her failures to follow the script. And this same person is simultaneously identified in Romans 8 as not condemned and as alive in the Spirit, awaiting the final act: the resurrection of the body and the renewal of creation.* It is the very presence of the "already" (including the Spirit's indwelling presence) that creates a heartfelt yearning for the "not yet" of freedom from the struggle with sin. This is the flow of Paul's argument in Romans 6–8. Once the Spirit subdues us, uniting us to Christ, we become active agents of God's love and service to our neighbors. Still, we can concur with Barth's pastoral wisdom: "If justification is a happening which we experience in ourselves, if we can find ourselves in it, so that there is no puzzle, but it can be readily conceived, then we must have made a mistake."[29]

As with all of God's redemptive actions, sanctification is both historical and eschatological. Because it is historical, there is personal continuity. The person who dies and is buried with Christ is the same person who is raised with Christ, even though he or she is no longer the same. This personal continuity is also connected with the history of the covenant and with the communion of the whole body with its living head. God works through ordinary means, over a long period of time. Conversion is a lifelong process that cannot be necessarily identified with a radical experience in the past. We are never isolated individuals in our union with Christ, but share this union and grow up into it more and more together with the whole church through its ordinary means.

Some believers, like John Wesley, may be able to identify their initial conversion with precision (a quarter to nine in the evening on the twenty-fourth of May, 1738), but this experience cannot be made into a rule. Those who struggled with drug addiction or sexual immorality before conversion will ordinarily struggle with it afterward. Nevertheless, sanctification is an eschatological judgment that breaks up, separates, disrupts, and reorganizes life according to the Spirit's recreating work. Sanctification is the radical in-breaking of the powers of the age to come into this present evil age. The Spirit's transcendent grace can never be domesticated to the ordinary powers of nature, however well programmed and effectively managed. If we focus on our experience rather than on Christ, on what we see rather than what we hear, then instead of drawing us out of ourselves in faith our experience will drive us deeper into ourselves in alternating moods of self-trust and despair. With some justification, Bavinck argued that pietism and Methodism both reflected and contributed to the "turn to the subject" in modernity. "For all their differences, all the religious movements listed have this feature in common: they allow the objec-

---

29. Barth, *Church Dogmatics*, vol. 4, pt. 1, p. 546.

tive factors of salvation (Christ, church, word, sacrament) to recede and place the religious subject in the center."[30]

Like initial conversion, sanctification is a process of growth and maturation that requires a diligent use of the public means of grace as well as the ecclesial, familial, and private disciplines of prayer, meditative reading of Scripture, witness, fellowship, service to those in need, and the discerning care of faithful elders. In progressive sanctification, our focus should not be the visibility of our experience and growth but Christ as he is given to us in the gospel.

III. MORTIFICATION AND VIVIFICATION

Progressive sanctification has two parts: *mortification* and *vivification*, "both of which happen to us by participation in Christ," as Calvin notes.[31] These occur simultaneously and continuously throughout the Christian life, rather than in stages. Christ's death alone is atoning, and cannot be repeated. He died *for* our sins, but we die *to* our sins. Christ took up his cross once and for all as a sacrifice for sin, but he calls his disciples to "take up [their] cross daily," facing persecution from within and without (Lk 9:23). Although we have died definitively to the law and to sin (Paul uses the analogy of remarriage after a death in Romans 7:1–6; cf. Gal 2:19), we continue to struggle inwardly with our new identity (Ro 7:7–24). Subjectively experiencing this definitive reality signified and sealed to us in our baptism requires a daily dying and rising.

This is what the Reformers meant by sanctification as a living out of our baptism. We were circumcised by the Spirit, "having been buried with him in baptism, in which [we] were also raised with him through faith in the powerful working of God, who raised him from the dead" (Col 2:11–12; cf. Ro 6:4–5, 11). Therefore, Paul says, we are not only freed *from* the rigor and condemnation of the law, much less the legalistic regulations of ascetic sects (Col 2:16–23), but freed *for* our heavenly calling which the moral law defines: "If then you have been raised with Christ, seek the things that are above, where Christ is, seated at the right hand of God.... Put to death therefore what is earthly in you: sexual immorality, impurity, passion, evil desire, and covetousness, which is idolatry" (Col 3:1, 5). God's moral law, then, continues to show us the right path, but only the gospel can give us arms and legs.

Question 86 of the *Heidelberg Catechism* poses the practical question that Paul raises in Romans 6 after his treatment of justification: "We have been delivered

---

30. Herman Bavinck, *Reformed Dogmatics* (ed. John Bolt; trans. John Vriend; Grand Rapids: Baker, 2004), 3:540.

31. Calvin, *Institutes* 3.3.2, 9. The "mortification/vivifica- tion" distinction was first formulated by Melanchthon in his *Commentary on Romans* (*Corpus Reformatorum* [ed. W. Baum; Berlin: C. A. Schwetschke, 1863–1900]), 15:636.

from our misery by God's grace alone through Christ and not because we have earned it: why then must we still do good?" The Catechism answers that the tree cannot fail to bear its fruit.[32] In fact, Question and Answer 87 denies that any can be saved "who do not turn to God from their ungrateful and impenitent ways."[33] "In this life even the holiest have only a small beginning of this obedience. Nevertheless, with all seriousness of purpose, they do begin to live according to all, not only some, of God's commandments."[34] Therefore, the law must still be proclaimed: first, to continue to convict us of sin and our need for Christ and, second, as the directives for our new obedience.[35] Definitive and progressive, "already" and "not yet," mortification and vivification, sanctification also claims the body as well as the soul (1Th 5:23; 2Co 5:17; Ro 6:12; 1Co 6:15, 20). More will be said on this point under the doctrine of glorification.

IV. DIVINE GRACE AND HUMAN ACTIVITY

Sanctification includes our own activity as enabled by God's grace (Jn 15:2, 8, 16; Ro 8:12–13; 12:9, 16–17; 1Co 6:9–10; 2Co 7:1; Gal 5:16–23; 6:7–8, 15; Col 3:5–14; 1Pe 1:22). It is not Christ but believers who die daily, take up their cross, and follow in the way of righteousness. As those who were spiritually dead and incapable of pleasing God, we were completely unable to cooperate with grace for our regeneration and justification. We were not active but acted upon by the Spirit through the gospel. However, as those who are now alive in Christ, we are exhorted, "[W]ork out your own salvation with fear and trembling; for it is God who works in you, both to will and to work for his good pleasure" (Php 2:12–13). Although we cannot work *for* our own salvation, we can and must work *out* that salvation in all areas of our daily practice, realizing more and more the amazing truth of our identity in Jesus Christ. When God calls, "Adam, where are you?" the Spirit leads us to answer, "In Christ," to the glory and pleasure of the Father. "If we live by the Spirit, let us also walk by the Spirit. Let us not become conceited, provoking one another, envying one another," Paul exhorts (Gal 5:25–26).

We believe that we are new creatures because God has told us so, and he is in the business of *ex nihilo* re-creation. We therefore joyfully say "amen" to this truth because he is also in the business of *continual* re-creation, bringing about by his Spirit the effects of the Word that he has spoken in his Son. Just as the fiat declaration, "Let there be ..." was complemented by the imperative, "Let the earth sprout

---

32. *Heidelberg Catechism*, q. 86, in *Psalter Hymnal* (Grand Rapids: CRC Publications, 1987), 901.

33. Ibid., q. 87, p. 901.

34. Ibid., q. 114, p. 915.

35. Ibid.

...," God's justifying verdict creates a state of affairs in which it is now possible for fallen creatures to bear the fruit of righteousness. Now that we *have been turned* toward the Word by the Word and Spirit, our conversion (faith and repentance) is a decisive, once-and-for-all *human turning* that marks our awareness of God's calling, and this conversion yields lifelong mortification and vivification, "again and again." Yet it is crucial to remind ourselves that in this daily human act of turning, we are always turning not only from sin but toward Christ rather than toward our own experience or piety.

Berkhof correctly observes that the moralism evident in the ancient church not only confused justification and sanctification but tended to separate sanctification from the work of Christ. Christ's life, death, and resurrection were necessary for getting us back on the road to paradise, but after baptism, it was thought, one's standing before God is always dependent on the cooperation of grace and good works.[36] Therefore, the tendency, at least among ancient as well as medieval Christian writers, was to treat sanctification as if, instead of flowing evidently out of Christ's redeeming work and justification, it was the process of moral effort through which one hoped to attain union with God.

Along with the mystical (Platonist) theory of the soul's ascent from the world of sense, this moralistic view of sanctification is no doubt a major reason for the rise of asceticism and monasticism in the ancient church. Berkhof notes that even Augustine, who emphasized the graciousness of God's saving work,

> manifested a tendency to take a metaphysical view of the grace of God in sanctification—to regard it as a deposit of God in man. He did not sufficiently stress the necessity of a constant preoccupation of faith with the redeeming Christ, as the most important factor in the transformation of the Christian's life.... In a great deal of modern liberal theology sanctification consists only in the ever-increasing redemption of man's lower self by the domination of his higher self. Redemption by character is one of the slogans of the present day, and the term 'sanctification' has come to stand for mere moral improvement.[37]

Yet in both Old and New Testaments, even in the ethical sense "holiness is not mere moral rectitude, and sanctification is never mere moral improvement," as the contemporary connotations might suggest.[38] Scripture "describes it as a work of God, I Thess. 5:23; Heb 13:20, 21, as a fruit of the union of life with Jesus Christ, John 15:4; Gal. 2:20; 4:19, as a work that is wrought in man from within and which for that very reason cannot be a work of man, Eph. 3:16; Col. 1:11, and speaks of its manifestation in Christian virtues as the work of the Spirit, Gal. 5:22."[39]

---

36. Louis Berkhof, *Systematic Theology* (Grand Rapids: Eerdmans, 1996), 529.

37. Ibid.

38. Ibid., 532.

39. Ibid., 533.

The two most obvious dangers to be avoided with respect to sanctification are legalism and antinomianism. Both are errors especially concerning the relationship of believers to the moral law.

A. LEGALISM

Legalism (or neonomianism) errs by either (1) requiring complete and perfect obedience to the commands of Scripture or (2) lowering the demands by substituting either imperfect obedience or more accessible rules for Christian behavior. Affirming the first, Pelagianism introduced the principle that became a hallmark especially of Kant's ethics, known popularly as "ought implies can." This principle was also invoked by the nineteenth-century revivalist Charles G. Finney, who insisted that because God cannot command something that we cannot fulfill, "As has already been said, there can be no justification in a legal or forensic sense, but upon the ground of universal, perfect, and uninterrupted obedience to law."[40] As we have already seen, this principle confuses *natural* and *moral* ability (see ch. 13, "Natural and Moral Ability," pp. 431–34). Created in God's image, humanity is naturally capable of fulfilling God's law perfectly, but its whole nature is morally bound by sin. With Paul, we must reject the Pelagian heresy: "I do not nullify the grace of God, for if righteousness were through the law, then Christ died for no purpose" (Gal 2:21). "For by works of the law no human being will be justified in his sight, since through the law comes knowledge of sin" (Ro 3:20).

A more common error (associated with Semi-Pelagianism) relaxes the law's demands and, consequently, lowers also its conception of grace. According to the late medieval nominalists, "God will not deny his grace to those who do what lies within them" (*facientibus quod in se est deus non denegat gratiam*).[41] No one will be saved by strict justice (*condign* merit), but one can be saved by God's decision to accept our good effort as adequate (*congruent* merit). This view lowers the demands of God's righteousness expressed in his law while falsely assuming that doing "what lies within" us can merit salvation even congruently. It was this error that the Apology of the *Augsburg Confession* targets: "But when a conscience is properly aware of its sin and misery, all joking, all playful thoughts vanish and the situation becomes one of utmost gravity.... But such terrified consciences surely feel that nothing can be merited either by condignity or of congruity, and so they quickly sink into fear and despair."[42]

---

40. Charles G. Finney, *Systematic Theology* (Oberlin, Ohio: J. M. Fitch, 1846; repr., Minneapolis: Bethany, 1976), 320–22.

41. Heiko Oberman, "Facientibus quod in se est deus non denigat gratiam: Robert Holcot O.P. and the Beginnings of Luther's Theology," in *The Dawn of the Reformation: Essays in Late Medieval and Early Reformation Thought* (Edinburgh: T&T Clark, 1992), 84–103.

42. *Augsburg Confession*, apology 4, art. 20, as found in *The Book of Concord: The Confessions of the Evangelical Lutheran Church* (ed. and trans. Theodore G. Tappert; Philadelphia: Fortress, 1959).

In the history of Protestantism as well as in Roman Catholic and Eastern Orthodox circles, there have been many who treat the gospel as a new law. Hence, the term "neonomianism," coined by English Puritanism to identify this error. In fact, the *Catechism of the Catholic Church* (1994) calls the gospel "the new law." "It works through charity; it uses the Sermon on the Mount to teach us what must be done and makes use of the sacraments to give us the grace to do it."[43] "The Law of the Gospel fulfills the commandments of the Law."[44] Similarly among Anabaptists, Socinians, Arminians, and liberals (though to differing degrees), it is often assumed that the Old Testament requires strict observance to a multitude of laws while the New Testament replaces law with love.

However, as Jesus pointed out, love of God and neighbor is actually the summary of the whole law (Mt 22:36–40). In fact, Moses had already given this exact summary in Deuteronomy 6:5 and Leviticus 19:18, as Paul did after Jesus in Galatians 5:14 (referring only to the Lev. 19:18 passage; cf. also Ro 13:9). In fact, Paul directly applies this to the daily life of Galatian believers, as he goes on to extrapolate it in terms of the fruit of the Spirit versus the fruit of the flesh (vv. 5:15–6:10). The commandments simply stipulate what true love of God and neighbor entails. Therefore, we cannot contrast New Testament commands (such as exhortations to bear the fruit of the Spirit or obey the law of Christ) with the moral law of the Old Testament. Every command in Scripture is a form of law, telling us what we must do. The gospel is not a new law, a relaxation of moral rigor, but the free announcement of forgiveness and justification in Christ alone. Furthermore, the relegation of the law to mere external observance (such as that of the religious leaders whom Jesus judged) is actually easier than the inward love of God and neighbor that God's law demands. An external holiness that masks inward depravity is attainable, while we cannot give ourselves a new heart (Mt 23:25–28).

Easier still was obedience to the humanly devised rules that the religious leaders had accumulated. Although burdensome, they were all regulations that a dedicated person could actually fulfill: the cessation of all labor, including works of necessity or mercy, on the Sabbath; tithing; refusing all contact with those judged morally, ethnically, physically, or ritually unclean; and so forth. But in fulfilling them, Jesus says, the religious leaders "have neglected the weightier matters of the law: justice and mercy and faithfulness" (Mt 23:23). Familiar to many reared in evangelical circles are taboos that are nowhere condemned in Scripture, while true worship of God and tangible acts of loving service to our neighbors often seem less important as evidence of our discipleship. Like the lawyer in Jesus' parable of the good

---

43. *Catechism of the Catholic Church* (Liguori, Mo.: Liguori Publications, 1994), 477.   44. Ibid., 478.

Samaritan who was "desiring to justify himself," we look for loopholes in the law (Lk 10:25–37). The tendency to hide real sins under a cloak of piety, abstaining from things that are never prohibited in Scripture, and following practices that are never commanded, is as evident in the history of Protestantism as elsewhere.

One form of legalism is the theory of *perfectionism*, which holds that believers can live above sin.[45] Advocates often appeal to 1 John 3:3–4, 9: "And everyone who thus hopes in [Christ] purifies himself as he is pure. Everyone who makes a practice of sinning also practices lawlessness; sin is lawlessness.... No one born of God makes a practice of sinning, for God's seed abides in him, and he cannot keep on sinning because he has been born of God."

While the Pelagian view assumes that believers can (indeed, must) attain absolute perfection of holiness in order to be acceptable to God, the Arminian version of perfectionism taught by John Wesley holds that it is possible for believers to live above all *known* sin. While they may still make *mistakes*, such believers have been made perfect in love.[46] Wesley's view is distinguished by the fact that he seems to have held to the doctrine of justification through faith alone but to have believed that sanctification was given through a subsequent act of faith, ordinarily a crisis experience, in which one receives "entire sanctification."[47] Charles G. Finney moved beyond the Wesleyan view, rejecting original sin, the substitutionary atonement, justification through faith alone, and an understanding of the new birth as a supernatural gift of grace.[48]

It is from this tradition that the "Higher Life" movement emerged, especially through the Keswick conferences.[49] This movement introduced a mystical piety that distinguished sharply between "carnal" and "victorious" Christians. Accord-

---

45. Louis Berkhof, *Systematic Theology*, 538: "It is taught in various forms by Pelagians, Roman Catholics or Semi-Pelagians, Arminians, Wesleyans, such mystical sects as the Labadists, the Quietists, the Quakers, and others, some of the Oberlin theologians, such as Mahan and Finney, and Ritschl. These all agree in maintaining that it is possible for believers in this life to attain to a state in which they comply with the requirements of the law *under which they now live*, or *under that law as it is adjusted to their present ability and needs*, and, consequently, to be free from sin."

46. John Wesley, "A Plain Account of Christian Perfection," in vol. 1 of *The Works of John Wesley* (ed. Thomas Jackson; Pub. City: Pub., 1872), 11, 366–446; cf. H. Orton Wiley, *Christian Theology* (Kansas City: Beacon Hill, 1958), vol. 2, ch. 29. For Reformed critiques, see especially B. B. Warfield, *Studies in Perfectionism* (New York: Oxford Univ. Press, 1931–1932), vols. 1–2; Charles Hodge, *Systematic Theology* (Grand Rapids: Eerdmans, 1946), 3:245–58.

47. Wesley wrote of a woman whom he thought to have singularly attained this condition: "I believe that she received the

great promise of God, entire sanctification, fifteen or sixteen years ago and that she never lost it" (*Journal and Diaries VI* [vol. 23 of *The Works of John Wesley*; ed. Ward W. Reginald and Richard P. Heitzenrater; Nashville: Abingdon, 1995], 109).

48. The logic that runs throughout Finney's rejection of these doctrines is clear: "If he obeyed the law as our substitute, then why should our own return to personal obedience be insisted upon as sine qua non of our salvation?" (*Systematic Theology*, 206).

49. With roots in the American (Wesleyan) Holiness Movement, the Higher Life movement received its name from William Boardman's book, *The Higher Christian Life* (1858). New York evangelists Walter and Phoebe Palmer promoted these views in England, as did Robert Pearsall Smith and Hannah Whitall Smith. With support from D. L. Moody, the first major Keswick Convention was held in Keswick, England (1875), continuing to the present day. A full-scale analysis and critique was written by B. B. Warfield, *Perfectionism*, available in *The Works of Benjamin Warfield* (New York: Oxford Univ. Press, 1927), vols. 7–8.

ing to its leading proponents, believers can attain a higher level of sanctification (sometimes described as "full surrender") through a second act of faith (usually a crisis experience) subsequent to their initial conversion. This distinctive teaching of the "second blessing" unites Wesleyans (Methodists), followers of the Keswick movement, and Pentecostals, although there are often significant differences over the necessary evidences of this experience.

Besides the separation of justification and sanctification (and therefore the justified and the fully sanctified), this type of perfectionism exhibits a tendency toward an eschatology that is underrealized with respect to some believers (i.e., those described as carnal) and overrealized with respect to others (i.e., victorious Christians). Most significantly, the question has been raised as to whether this tradition focuses attention on the inner life, experience, and morality of the believer rather than on Christ's objective work.

It is true that Scripture calls for complete obedience (1Pe 1:16; Mt 5:48; Jas 1:4). Nevertheless, the question again is whether *ought* implies *can.* It is one thing to say that the regenerate commit themselves to holiness and are able, by God's grace, to yield their body to righteousness, and quite another to say that we are so sanctified in this life that we can do this perfectly and consistently. Scripture teaches that the dominion of sin has been broken, and on that basis it commands us not to let sin exercise dominion over us (Ro 6:12). However, it also speaks of the believer's constant "struggle against sin" (Heb 12:4) and calls us to "confess [our] sins to one another" (Jas 5:16).

The clearest challenge to a perfectionistic reading of 1 John 3 comes from the same epistle. John writes in chapter 1,

> If we say we have no sin, we deceive ourselves, and the truth is not in us. If we confess our sins, he is faithful and just to forgive us our sins and cleanse us from all unrighteousness. If we say we have not sinned, we make him a liar, and his word is not in us. My little children, I am writing these things to you so that you may not sin. But if anyone does sin, we have an advocate with the Father, Jesus Christ the righteous. He is the propitiation for our sins, and not for ours only but also for the sins of the whole world. (1Jn 1:8 – 2:2)

Furthermore, 1 John 3:9 does not refer to a special class of those who have received a second blessing but to everyone who is "born of God."

In view of the fact that in the preceding verses John especially targets a proto-Gnostic teaching concerning Christ (i.e., the docetic view that he only appeared to be human but did not really assume our flesh), it is possible that this teaching was attended by the antinomian view discerned in the more explicit Gnosticism of the next century, that sins committed in the body are also mere appearances. Just as what Jesus Christ did in the flesh is a mere appearance, sins that we commit in the flesh are of no consequence. If this is John's target, the most likely interpretation is that those whose lives are given over to *bodily license* are not *inwardly regenerated*. In any case, the teaching of the first chapter explicitly refutes the view that "we have no sin" and therefore do not need to "confess our sins" in full assurance that he will "forgive us our sins and ... cleanse us from all unrighteousness."

Whether justification is collapsed into sanctification or separated from it, the results are the same: a moralism that can neither embrace the promise nor bring about any genuine transformation at the deepest level—namely, the struggle between the two ages. G. C. Berkouwer's observation is still relevant in our own day when he writes that "the problem of the renewal of life is attracting the attention of moralists."

> Amid numberless chaotic and demoralizing forces is sounded, as if for the last time, the cry for help and healing, for the re-organization of a dislocated world. The therapy prescribed perhaps varies, the call for moral and spiritual re-armament is uniformly insistent.... These are the questions we must answer. For implicit in them is the intent to destroy the connection between justification and sanctification, as well as the bond between faith and sanctification.[50]

Paul relates everything, including sanctification, the problems of ethics, and ecclesial harmony, to Christ's cross and resurrection.

So when we move from justification to discussion of sanctification, "we are not withdrawing from the sphere of faith." "We are not here concerned with a transition from theory to practice. It is not as if we should proceed from a faith in justification to the realities of sanctification; for we might as truly speak of the reality of justification and our faith in sanctification." *Separating* justification from sanctification is as serious as *confusing* them, because it means that the latter is "cut loose or abstracted from justification."[51] When that happens, says Berkouwer, "The distinction between justification and sanctification could then be traced to the subject of each act: God or man. Such an obvious division would have taken place; man—this would be our conclusion—is not called upon to justify but to purify himself. It is not hard to see that the Scriptures are intolerant of this division."[52] Paul teaches that believers are "sanctified in Christ Jesus" (1Co 1:2, 30; 6:11; 1Th 5:23; cf. Ac 20:32; 26:18). As Bavinck puts it, "Many indeed acknowledge that we are justified by the righteousness of Christ, but seem to think that—at least they act as if—they must be sanctified by a holiness they themselves have acquired."[53] Something close to this error seems to have been held by Paul's opponents in Galatia (Gal 3:1–9).

---

50. Berkouwer, *Studies in Dogmatics: Faith and Sanctification*, 11–12.

51. Ibid., 20.

52. Ibid., 21.

53. Herman Bavinck, *Reformed Dogmatics*, as quoted in Berkouwer, *Studies in Dogmatics: Faith and Sanctification*, 22.

Of particular interest in the light of our last chapter's discussion is Berkouwer's suggestion that this problem goes back to "the Roman Catholic doctrine which teaches that justification must be understood as the infusion of supernatural grace."

> On this basis, sanctification can have meaning only as the successive development, with the cooperation of a free will, of the grace implanted.... Sanctification, on these terms, takes place in an atmosphere of forces and counter-forces, among which faith may then perform its now very modest function of preparing for justification; and justification itself becomes almost indistinguishable from sanctification. Once the sanctifying grace takes root, many forces throw in their weight.[54]

Instead we must see that faith always feeds "on the forgiveness of sins"; it does not just begin there. It is a life constantly grounded in promise, always received through faith.[55]

At no point in the *ordo salutis*, in sanctification any more than in justification, is there a place for introducing the notion of an infused principle into the soul that elevates nature to supernatural capacities. Grace is not a medicine injected into us so that we may recover from the weakness of being drawn down by the lower self and get back on the path of holiness. Rather, grace is God's favor and gift that liberates nature to become truly natural again—in other words, to be what it was created to be by God's Word.[56] Even more, God's grace liberates nature to share in the eschatological life of Jesus Christ. Reformed theology "has always protested vigorously against the Catholic 'donum superadditum' as a new dimension in this sinful world."[57] Reformed theology shares the Lutheran concern to defend "a 'theologia crucis' rather than a 'theologia gloriae'" in sanctification as well as justification.[58]

> The renewal is not a mere supplement, an appendage, to the salvation given in justification. The heart of sanctification is the life which feeds on this justification. There is no contrast between justification as act of God and sanctification as act of man. The fact that Christ is our sanctification is not exclusive of, but inclusive of, a faith which clings to him alone in all of life. Faith is the pivot on which everything revolves. Faith, though not itself creative, preserves us from autonomous self-sanctification and moralism.[59]

Not even at the point of sanctification, then, do we need to introduce the concept

---

54. Berkouwer, *Studies in Dogmatics: Faith and Sanctification*, 27.

55. Ibid., 28.

56. Ibid., 83.

57. Ibid., 85. For a summary and defense of this Roman Catholic view see Johann Adam Möhler, *Symbolism: Exposition of the Doctrinal Differences between Catholics and Protestants as Evidenced by Their Symbolical Writings* (trans. James Burton Robertson; New York: Crossroad, 1997): "This relation of Adam to God, as it exalted him above human nature, and made him participate in that of God, is hence termed ... a super-natural gift of divine grace, superadded to the endowments of nature." The fall, therefore, arises in the strife between "higher" (intellectual) and "lower" (sensual) powers of nature (27). Luther regarded this original acceptability of Adam before God as natural rather than supernatural (30). Calvin followed suit, although he distinguished between free will in the prelapsarian and postlapsarian states (33–36). On justification, see ch. 3.

58. Berkouwer, *Studies in Dogmatics: Faith and Sanctification*, 87.

59. Ibid., 93.

of infused habits. It is the gospel that creates faith (as our confessional statements maintain, following especially Mt 13:1–9; Jn 6:63; Ro 10:8–17; Jas 1:18; 1 Pe 1:23), and this faith, engendered by the effectual call, lays claim to justification, sanctification, and all other blessings in Christ. The Spirit, working through the gospel, gives it all: faith, yielding repentance, love, and the fruit of the Spirit. There is inward regeneration and progressive renewal only because the Spirit continually gives us faith in Christ through the gospel. The source of our new life is never an infused principle, but a living person.

"The sola-fide is at the heart of justification but no less at that of sanctification," says Berkouwer.[60] In Wesley's doctrine, "Sola-fide becomes a point of departure and breaks its connections with sanctification. Here lies the cause of Wesley's tendency toward synergism, in spite of his adherence to Sola-fide."[61] The church is called not to "work for a second blessing," but to "feed on the first blessing, the forgiveness of sins."[62]

Paul stresses that his goal is simply to "press on to make [resurrection and perfection] my own, because Christ Jesus has made me his own" (Php 3:12). The struggle of the church militant is not to envelop Christ in our faithfulness, but to be enveloped by Christ's. In fact, Berkouwer goes so far as to say,

> Perfectionism is a premature seizure of the glory that will be: an anticipation leading irrevocably to nomism [legalism]. The "second blessing" constitutes the link.... When Peter, stupefied by the wonderful catch of fish, confronts the goodness of his Master, he cries out: "Depart from me; for I am a sinful man, O Lord!" (Luke 5:8). Surrounded by the radiance of the Master, Peter can only bow his head. Later those other words were to cut through the night: "If all shall be offended in thee, I will never be offended" (Matt. 26:33). By these words Peter meant to envelop Christ with *his* fidelity and love. Christ must here bathe in Peter's glory, not Peter in Christ's. We know the outcome. Not these words, but rather those spoken over the bonanza of fish, belong to the Militia Christiana.[63]

The real question, says Berkouwer, is whether justification is sufficient to ground *all* of the blessings communicated in the mystical union. "The same Catechism [Heidelberg, Lord's Day 24] which denies us even a partial righteousness of our own mentions the earnest purpose with which believers begin to live" according to all the commandments.

> It is this beginning which has its basis solely in justification by faith.... It is not true that sanctification simply succeeds justification. Lord's Day 31, which discusses the keys of the kingdom, teaches that the kingdom is opened and shut by proclaiming "to believers, one and all, that, whenever they receive the promise of the gospel

---

60. Ibid., 33.
61. Ibid., 52.

62. Ibid., 64.
63. Ibid., 67.

by a true faith, all their sins are really forgiven them." This "whenever" illustrates the continuing relevancy of the correlation between faith and justification.... The purpose of preaching the ten commandments, too, is that believers may "become the more earnest in seeking remission of sins and righteousness in Christ." [HC Q 115] ... Hence there is never a stretch along the way of salvation where justification drops out of sight.[64]

"Genuine sanctification—let it be repeated—stands or falls with this continued orientation toward justification and the remission of sins." Therefore, "The victim of this view" of sanctification as a human work subsequent to the divine work of justification "can arrive only at a sanctification that is a causal process, and he is bound, in the end, to speak as Rome of an infused grace and of a quantitative sanctification."[65] The alternative to a sanctification flowing from justification—and therefore, to recognizing that all of our blessings flowing from Christ through faith—is a moralistic activism that identifies growth in Christlikeness with the *imitation* of Christ more than with the *union* with Christ.[66]

"Disciple" in the New Testament, however, includes but is hardly reducible to imitation. Even the imitation to which we are called in the New Testament is related to the sufferings of Christ; our sufferings in imitation of his are not atoning but nevertheless contribute to the progress of the gospel in the world (1Pe 2:21, 24). As Berkouwer recognizes, "Hence those who follow do not have to repeat anything: they are healed." Imitation, in this scheme, "is to live conformably to, and on the basis of, the Atonement.... And they [the sheep] are to walk not on paths that will at length lead them to communion with Christ but on the path that lies open because of the communion with Christ which they enjoy right alone."[67]

At the same time, we should note that discipleship includes imitation. Once we recognize that Christ is first and foremost the one who heard and obeyed in our place, we too, in organic and mystical as well as legal union with him, no longer "live by bread alone, but by every word that comes from the mouth of God" (Mt 4:4). There is a difference between an admirer imitating a hero and a child imitating an older sibling. And the bond between believers and Christ is far more intimate, as it is created and sustained by the Spirit, who makes our elder brother the forerunner of our own glorification.

George Lindbeck reminds us that the proper category for discipleship and *imitatio Christi* is the third use of the law, not the atonement or justification.[68] Otherwise, the Christian life is reduced to a moralistic attempt to live up to Christ's

---

64. Ibid., 77.
65. Ibid., 78.
66. Ibid., 138.
67. Ibid., 142–43.

68. George Lindbeck, "Justification and Atonement: An Ecumenical Trajectory," in *By Faith Alone: Essays on Justification in Honor of Gerhard O. Forde*, 208.

example rather than our living out of the realities of Christ's saving work. In such theologies, writes Lindbeck, "not only does revelation subsume soteriology but, so the reformers would say, law absorbs gospel." "This is what happens when the crucified God is first of all the prototype of authentic human existence so that it is by being prototype that Jesus Christ is Savior. From a traditional perspective, the error here is in the reversal of the order: Jesus is not first Example and then Savior, but the other way around."[69] Once we put the theme of imitation in its place, so to speak, we can speak again of the law, precisely because it returns this time (in its third use) after having pronounced its verdict on us as those who *in Christ* have already fully met its requirements. "Hence Paul can say without a qualm that he is 'under law to Christ' (1 Cor. 9:21)," notes Berkouwer.

"In numerous ways, throughout the history of the church, the true relationship between Gospel and Law has been obscured," in sanctification as well as in justification, Berkouwer reminds us. "Two opposite tendencies are apparent: the tendency to make the Gospel into a new law and the tendency to sever the Gospel from the law."[70] Yet this can result only in a confused mixture of legalism and antinomianism, both of which are opposed to God's grace.[71] "Some, among them Barth, have spoken of the law as the form of the gospel whose content is grace." However, says Berkouwer, "We protest against the reduction of the law to this status; by it the law is practically dissolved in the gospel."[72]

In true faith the inner and outer aspects of life are harmoniously developed. The law directs the believer out into the world — to his neighbor, to his poor brother and sister (Jas 2:15), to his enemy, to his brother in prison, to the hungry and thirsty ones — and thrusts him into contact, for good or for ill, with earthly gods, marriage, and civil authority.[73]

"The apostle Paul," Berkouwer writes, "preaches holiness with repetitive fervor, but in no way does he compromise his unequivocal declaration: 'For I determined not to know anything among you, save Jesus Christ, and him crucified' (1 Cor. 2:2)."

> Not for a moment would he do violence to the implications of that confession. Hence in every exhortation he must be relating his teaching to the cross of Christ. From this center all lines radiate outward — into the life of cities and villages, of men and women, of Jews and Gentiles, into families, youth, and old age, into conflict and disaffection, into immorality and drunkenness. If we would keep this center, as well as the softer and harder lines flowing from it, in true perspective, we must be thoroughly aware that in shifting from justification to sanctification we are not withdrawing from the sphere of faith. We are not here concerned with

---

69. Berkouwer, *Studies in Dogmatics: Faith and Sanctification*, 209.
70. Ibid., 188.
71. Ibid.
72. Ibid., 190.
73. Ibid., 192.

a transition from theory to practice. It is not as if we should proceed from a faith in justification to the realities of sanctification; for we might as truly speak of the reality of justification and our faith in sanctification.[74]

B. ANTINOMIANISM

At the other end of the spectrum from legalism or perfectionism is *antinomianism*. Literally, "anti-law-ism," this perspective holds that the law—not only its penalty and rigor but its normative status—is completely abolished for the believer. Many of the same arguments offered above in response to legalism are also relevant here. We have seen the complete consistency between the appeal to the moral law as the rule of life from Deuteronomy to Matthew to Galatians. The difference does not lie between the Old and New Testaments but between our relation to the law in Adam and our relationship to it in Christ. In Adam, we are condemned by the law. In fact, circumcision more explicitly obligates Jews to keep the whole law (Gal 5:3). Yet Paul goes on to say that we have been set free from the law in this sense (as a condition of life) not to be *anomos* (without law), but to use our freedom to serve each other in love (v. 13). It is in verse 14 where Paul invokes the summary of the law as love, going on to extrapolate its exhibition as the fruit of the Spirit. Therefore, Paul clearly applies the moral law according to what Lutheran and Reformed theologians call its "third use"—that of directing Christian conduct.[75]

In many respects, antinomianism and legalism share the same misunderstandings of the law. Like human laws, God's laws are not abstract principles for living but are *stipulations* in a *covenant*. God's law functions differently depending on the type of covenant. In a covenant of law, the principle is "Do this and you shall live; break it and you shall die." The basis of blessings and curses is personal fulfillment of the covenant's terms. However, in the covenant of grace, the basis is the personal fulfillment of the law by our representative head and his bearing of the covenant curses on the cross. In this exchange—our sins imputed to Christ and his righteousness imputed to us—we are pronounced just according to the fullest letter and spirit of God's law. No longer capable of condemning us in God's courtroom, the law directs our steps in the way of faith-filled gratitude. Antinomianism and legalism seem to assume that the only function of the law—even in relation to believers—is that of condemning those who fail to keep it. Neither recognizes sufficiently the completely new relationship that the believer has to God's law.

Further, like legalism, antinomianism typically reintroduces some concept of law

---

74. Ibid., 20.

75. The "third use of the law" (i.e., for directing Christian conduct) was first formulated by Melanchthon in 1534 and was taken up by Calvin in his 1536 edition of the *Institutes*. See Timothy Wengert, *Law and Gospel: Philip Melanchthon's Debate with John Agricola of Eisleben over 'Poenitentia'* (Grand Rapids: Baker, 1997), 195.

(such as "the law of Christ," "the law of the Spirit," "the law of love," or various rules never mentioned in Scripture), which it easily confuses with gospel—as if these commands were somehow less demanding than the Ten Commandments. Ironically, antinomianism can lead to a new kind of legalism by replacing God's law with an almost Gnostic preoccupation with the inner spirit as opposed to "external observance." Forgetting that the interpretation of the law given in the Old Testament and most deeply extrapolated by Jesus encompasses inner motives and attitudes as well as outward behavior, antinomians often give the impression that sanctification is after all a human work, even if it is expressed in exhortations to "let go and let God," "abide," and to abolish all consciousness of self. As we have seen, not even the rule of love is anything different from the moral law. *Every* exhortation in Scripture is a form of law.

The law remains the standard of measurement both for justification and for sanctification. By it the sinner is condemned and even the best works of believers are found wanting. Yet it remains the revelation of God's will for our lives. While the first use of the law drives us to Christ as the only hope for deliverance, so that we are freed from its condemnation, the third use ensures that we are freed from the burdensome rules, techniques, and formulas for sanctification often imposed by those who dispense with God's moral law.

Now written on our heart and not merely on our conscience, the law is cherished by believers. They long to keep it, not as a way of attaining life but as way of living the life that they have been given by grace alone. No less than in justification, the law cannot sanctify. It can only reveal God's moral will to which our sanctification corresponds. God's people are never at a loss for knowing God's will for their life. "He has told you, O mortal, what is good; and what does the LORD require of you but to do justice, and to love kindness, and to walk humbly with your God?" (Micah 6:8 NRSV). Jesus summarized the law as the love of God and neighbor. The fruit of the Spirit mentioned by Paul in Galatians 5 fits that summary: love, patience, kindness, self-control, and gentleness. As the expression of God's essential character, his moral will never changes.

Also like legalism, antinomianism has an unrealistic view of the serious requirement of God's law and the Christian's ongoing struggle with sin. The gospel is not an imperative for us to effect anything, even if transformed into the minimal requirement of "letting go and letting God." In actual practice, this exhortation can become the severest law. How does one really know that one has really let go of everything and surrendered all to Jesus? In such mystical quietism the legalistic and antinomian streams of perfectionism converge. Antinomianism never leads to genuine freedom, but returns to legalism by a different route.

However, when Paul addresses sanctification in Romans 6, he begins with the triumphant indicative: the announcement that God has baptized us into Christ's death and raised us in newness of life. "So you also must consider yourselves dead to sin and alive to God in Christ Jesus" (Ro 6:11). This is not a second blessing attained by a special class of Christians who have fully surrendered themselves or have let God have his way, but the blessing of all who are in Christ. It is his experience of death and resurrection, into which we are baptized, not a crisis experience that we must achieve. On the basis of Christ's work, we "present [ourselves] to God as those who have been brought from death to life, and [our] members to God as instruments for righteousness" (Ro 6:13). Regardless of how far we fall short of acting on it, the fact of our indicative condition is that sin cannot dominate us; it has lost its claim, precisely because we are "not under law but under grace" (v. 14). Our ongoing struggle with sin of which Paul speaks in Romans 7 does not cancel this fact; on the contrary, it most clearly evidences the reality of our new birth and sanctification.

In the Roman Catholic view, there is no *relating* of justification and sanctification because they are really one and the same. However, the Christian life should not be seen as a struggle between nature and grace or cooperation between God's grace and human striving, but as God's justifying verdict that radiates outward into every nook and cranny of our existence, bearing the fruit of love.[76] Thus Berkouwer finds it "incomprehensible" that the Reformation view could have ever been criticized as having no bearing on sanctification or the life of holiness. It has everything to do with it, because it brings everything back to faith in Christ.[77] Faith is hardly an "external" thing with no subjective impact; rather, it links us to Christ along with all of his benefits. *The covenant that is unilaterally given and always remains unconditional in its basis as pure gift gives rise to a genuinely bilateral relationship of hearing and answering, of passive receiving and an active return of thanksgiving to God and service to neighbor.* In justification, faith and works are entirely opposed; in sanctification, they are related as seed and flower.

According to the account thus far, justification is not the first stage of the Christian life, but the constant wellspring of sanctification and good works. Luther summarizes, " 'Because you believe in me,' God says, 'and your faith takes hold of Christ, whom I have freely given to you as your Justifier and Savior, therefore be righteous.' Thus God accepts you or accounts you righteous only on account of Christ, in whom you believe."[78] Whatever other piece of good news (concerning the new birth, Christ's conquest of sin's tyranny and promise to renew us throughout our life, the resurrection of our body and freedom from the presence of sin), much less the useful exhortations that we may offer, the announcement that Luther here summarizes alone creates and sustains the faith that not only justifies but sanctifies as well, not because of any virtue in faith, but because it clings to Christ.

---

76. Berkouwer, *Studies in Dogmatics: Faith and Sanctification*, 28.

77. Ibid.

78. Martin Luther, *Commentary on Galatians*, comment on Gal 2:16, in *Luther's Works*, vol. 26, 132.

Good works now may be freely performed for God and neighbors without any fear of punishment or agony over the mixed motives of each act. Because of justification in Christ, even our good works can be "saved," not in order to improve either God's lot or our own, but our neighbor's. As Calvin explains,

> But if, freed from this severe requirement of the law, or rather from the entire rigor of the law, they hear themselves called with fatherly gentleness by God, they will cheerfully and with great eagerness answer, and follow his leading. To sum up: Those bound by the yoke of the law are like servants assigned certain tasks for each day by their masters. These servants think they have accomplished nothing and dare not appear before their masters unless they have fulfilled the exact measure of their tasks. But sons, who are more generously and candidly treated by their fathers, do not hesitate to offer them incomplete and half-done and even defective works, trusting that their obedience and readiness of mind will be accepted by their fathers, even though they have not quite achieved what their fathers intended. Such children ought we to be, firmly trusting that our services will be approved by our most merciful Father, however small, rude, and imperfect these may be.... And we need this assurance in no slight degree, for without it we attempt everything in vain.[79]

"Because of justification," adds Ames, "the defilement of good works does not prevent their being accepted and rewarded by God."[80]

Not only does such a view properly ground works in faith; it also frees believers to love and serve their neighbors apart from the motive of gaining or fear of losing divine favor. It liberates us for a world-embracing activism that is deeply conscious that although our love and service contribute nothing to God and his evaluation of our persons, they are, however feebly, halfheartedly, and imperfectly performed, means through which God cares for creation.

The evangelical doctrine of justification honors and upholds the law of God. It does so first by announcing that the perfect righteousness that it requires has been completely fulfilled in Christ, our covenant head, and second, by giving sinners this righteousness as a gift by imputation (justification) and by union with Christ (sanctification). Only the condemnation of the law is abolished; the two tables of the law remain firmly established in heaven and on earth forever.

Far from providing an account of salvation as imputation without sanctification and ethics, the *Scots Confession* (1560) declares, "[I]t is blasphemy to say that Christ abides in the hearts of those in whom there is no spirit of sanctification." "For as soon as the Spirit of the Lord Jesus, whom God's chosen children receive by true faith, takes possession of the heart of anyone, so soon does he regenerate and renew him, so that he begins to hate what before he loved, and to love what he hated before. Thence comes that continual battle which is between the flesh and the Spirit

---

79. Calvin, *Institutes* 3.19.5.

80. William Ames, *Marrow of Theology*, 171.

in God's children...."[81] The *Second Helvetic Confession* reiterates the unanimous consensus of the Reformation concerning the nature of the faith that justifies:

> The same apostle calls faith efficacious and active through love (Gal 5:6). It also quiets the conscience and opens a free access to God, so that we may draw near to him with confidence and may obtain from him what is useful and necessary. The same [faith] keeps us in the service we owe to God and our neighbor, strengthens our patience in adversity, fashions and makes a true confession, and in a word, brings forth good fruit of all kinds, and good works.

Such good works are done not for any desire for personal gain or merit, but merely "to show gratitude to God and for the profit of the neighbor."[82]

Therefore, sanctification is not a human project supplementing the divine project of justification, nor a process of negotiating the causal relations between free will and infused grace, but the impact of God's justifying Word on every aspect of human life. *The Westminster Confession* states, "They who are effectually called and regenerated, having a new heart and a new spirit created in them, are further sanctified, really and personally, through the virtue of Christ's death and resurrection, by his Word and Spirit dwelling in them...."[83] All of this is "in Christ," not in ourselves.[84] Instead of a double *source* (synergism), redemption is concerned with a double *effect*: justification and inner renewal. In Lesslie Newbigin's words,

> The idea of a righteousness of one's own is the quintessence of sin. Against this, therefore, against every trace of a holiness or righteousness which does not depend simply upon God's mercy to the sinner, we have to set our faces as relentlessly as Paul did. But equally with Paul we have to recognize that if any man be in Christ there is a new creation, not a fiction but a real supernatural new birth, the life of the risen Christ in the soul.[85]

V. THE LAW AND THE CHRISTIAN LIFE

The difference between the law in the old and new covenants is primarily *eschatological*. The ceremonies and civil codes governing the old covenant theocracy were merely temporary appendices to the Ten Commandments, summarized as love of God and neighbor. Thus, their fulfillment in Christ and subsequent obsolescence in no way threatens the eternal validity of these two tables. The apostle John enjoins believers to love one another, which is the summary of the second table of the law: "Beloved, I am writing you no new commandment, but an old commandment that you had from the beginning.... At the same time, it is a new commandment that I am writing to you,

---

81. *The Scots Confession*, ch. 13, in *Book of Confessions*.

82. *Second Helvetic Confession*, ch. 16, in *Book of Confessions*.

83. *The Westminster Confession of Faith*, ch. 13, in *Book of Confessions*.

84. For a fine elaboration of this point, see again Webster, *Holiness*, 81.

85. Lesslie Newbigin, *The Household of Faith* (London: SCM Press, 1953), 128–29.

which is true in him [Christ] and in you, because the darkness is passing away and the true light is already shining" (1Jn 2:7–8). In terms of its content, this command is God's eternal, unchanging moral will from the beginning. Yet like everything of God's kingdom that cannot be shaken, nothing is preserved without being taken with Christ into the grave and brought out into his new-creation life. The command to love is a threat to us as fallen creatures, because we do not love. Yet that which is impossible in the old creation, lying under the power of sin and death, is possible in the new creation, on this side of Christ's resurrection. The commandment to love is "true in Christ" and therefore "in you," because the night is passing away and the day is already dawning. It is not the bright noon of Christ's return in glory, but it is daybreak.

This is why Calvin called the third use of the law (i.e., guiding believers) "the principal use."[86] Believers always need to hear the law's condemnation of all righteousness apart from Christ's, but he regarded it as a gross miscarriage of the preachers' office when they used the law to terrify the conscience of believers. This is to put them back under the law as a ministry of death, as if the light had not yet dawned in Christ. When discussing the "fatherly indulgence of God," Calvin explains Paul's reference to "the spirit of bondage" versus "the spirit of adoption," in Romans 8:15:

> One he calls the spirit of bondage, which we are able to derive from the Law; and the other, the spirit of adoption, which proceeds from the Gospel. The first, he states, was formerly given to produce fear; the other is given now to afford assurance. The certainty of our salvation, which he wishes to confirm, appears, as we see, with greater clarity from such a comparison of opposites.... From the adverb again we learn that Paul is here comparing the Law with the Gospel.... He assigns to the Law its own quality, by which it differs from the Gospel.[87]

Therefore, there is no graciousness in the law itself. It commands, but does not have any power to move us to obedience. In many places Calvin appears to treat the first use of the law (i.e., driving sinners to despair of their own works) as the primary use.[88] He basically echoes Luther's maxim, "The law always accuses":

> The Law only begets death; it increases our condemnation and inflames the wrath of God.... The Law of God speaks, but it does not reform our hearts. God may show us: "This is what I demand of you," but if all our desires, our dispositions and thoughts are contrary to what he commands, not only are we condemned, but, as I have said, the Law makes us more culpable before God.... For in the Gospel God does not say, "You must do this or that," but "believe that my only Son is your

---

86. John Calvin, *Commentary on the Epistle of Paul to the Romans* (trans. and ed. John Owen; Edinburgh: Calvin Translation Society, 1843–1855; repr. Grand Rapids: Baker, 1996), 296.

87. Ibid.

88. "The specific office of the Law [is] to summon consciences to the judgment-seat of God" (Calvin, *Commentary on*

John, 2:140). In fact, "Moses had no other intention than to invite all men to go straight to Christ" (ibid., 1:217). "The special function of the Law was not to incline people's hearts to the obedience of righteousness. The office of the Law, rather, was to lead people step by step to Christ that they might seek pardon from him and the Spirit of regeneration" (on Ex 24:5: I think).

Redeemer; embrace his death and passion as the remedy for your ills; plunge yourself beneath his blood and it will be your cleansing."[89]

Like a mirror, the law can only expose our dirty faces; it cannot cleanse.[90] "Paul often means by the term 'law' the rule of righteous living by which God requires of us what is his own, giving us no hope of life unless we completely obey him, and adding on the other hand a curse if we deviate even in the slightest decree."[91] In short, "the life of the Law is man's death."[92] "The gospel promises are free and dependent solely on God's mercy, while the promises of the law depend solely upon the condition of works."[93]

Therefore, the believer no less than the unbeliever must have the Gospel "daily repeated in the Church."[94] No less in sanctification than in justification, Calvin writes, "The contrast between the Law and the Gospel is to be understood, and from this distinction we deduce that, just as the Law demands work, the Gospel requires only that men should bring faith in order to receive the grace of God."[95]

So how can Calvin then say that the third use is the main function of the law for believers? Here again Calvin recognizes the new eschatological situation of saints under the new covenant. First and foremost in Calvin's mind, the Law has no jurisdiction over the believer in the point of condemnation: "For the law is not now acting toward us as a rigorous enforcement officer who is not satisfied unless the requirements are met," but is rather pointing out "the goal toward which throughout life we are to strive." Before, the law only accused, but now it has a different purpose: "Now, the law has power to exhort believers. This is not a power to bind their consciences with a curse," but to point the way toward divinely-approved service.[96] The believer gives ear to the law's directives, but not to its threats. In fact, Warfield cites a Lutheran theologian who argues that while Calvin shared Luther's belief that "fear and love" of God are to be held together, Calvin emphasized the "fatherly benevolence" over "fear" even more than Luther. Thus, Warfield himself concludes, "In a word, with all his emphasis on the sovereignty of God, Calvin throws an even stronger emphasis on His love," so that even zeal was inspired not by fear of punishment, but by the sense of a son defending the honor of his father.[97]

---

89. The Isaiah 53:11 reference is cited by I. John Hesselink, *Calvin's Concept of the Law* (Allison Park, Pa.: Pickwick, 1992), 212 n188 and is found in Calvin, *Institutes*, 2.7.7.

90. Calvin, *Institutes*, 2.7.7.

91. Ibid., 2.9.4.

92. John Calvin, *Four Last Books of Moses* (Grand Rapids: Baker, repr. 2005), 1:316. Similarly, on Galatians 3:10: "From the Law, therefore, it is useless to seek a blessing. He calls them of the works of the law who put their trust for salvation in those works. Such modes of expression must always be interpreted by the state of the question. Now we know that the controversy here relates to the cause of righteousness.... The Law justifies him who fulfills all its commands, whereas faith justifies those

who are destitute of the merit of works and rely on Christ alone. To be justified by our own merit and by the grace of another are irreconcilable; the one is overthrown by the other."

93. Calvin, *Institutes* 3.11.17.

94. Calvin, *Commentary on Roman*, 136.

95. Ibid., 391.

96. Calvin, *Institutes* 2.7.12–13.

97. B. B. Warfield, *Calvin and Augustine* (Philadelphia: Presbyterian & Reformed, 1980), 175–76. B. A. Gerrish also writes, "It is particularly striking how often Calvin simply identifies believing in God with recognizing God's fatherhood" (*Grace & Gratitude: The Eucharistic Theology of John Calvin*; Edinburgh: T&T Clark, 1993), 66.

In a further irony, Calvin emphasized more than Luther at times the weakness of the believer's faith and therefore the *simul iustus et peccator*. Luther declared, "Therefore, [faith] is also a very mighty, active, restless, busy thing, which at once renews a man, gives him a second birth, and introduces him to a new manner and way of life, so that it is impossible for him not to do good without ceasing. For as naturally as a tree bears fruit good works follow upon faith."[98] Calvin certainly would not have disagreed concerning the necessary link between faith and works, but he was somewhat less confident about the spontaneous obedience of the new creature. Calvin often emphasizes the abiding doubt and laziness of the believer, and this condition is true even for the genuine believer in his or her regenerated state. Obedience flows from faith, but there is not always an automatic answer of mind, heart, and body to the master's command. Faith must generate the gratitude necessary for good works, but the law disturbs our believer's laziness by reminding him of his duty. When we are seeking righteousness, duty is a legal preoccupation, but once the law's thunder is silenced, God often uses the law to discipline his children and to recall them to their former course.

Nevertheless, the law cannot do anything more than remind us of our duty. Only the gospel promises can move us to grateful obedience:

> He lays hold not only of the precepts, but the accompanying promise of grace, which alone sweetens what is bitter. For what would be less lovable than the Law if, with importuning and threatening alone, it troubled souls through fear, and distressed them through fright? David especially shows that in the Law he apprehended the Mediator, without whom there is no delight or sweetness.[99]

VI. Perseverance of the Saints

From all of the other elements of the *ordo salutis* it should be obvious that not just some but all of those who are chosen in Christ, redeemed by Christ, and called into union with Christ receive every blessing, including glorification (Ro 8:30). In the words of Augustine, "This grace [God] placed 'in Christ in whom we have obtained a lot, being predestined according to the purpose of Him who worketh all things.' And thus as he worketh that we come to Him, so He worketh that we do not depart."[100]

A. Exegetical Overview

Jesus taught, "All that the Father gives me will come to me, and whoever comes to me I will never cast out. For I have come down from heaven, not to do my own

---

98. Martin Luther, "Preface to Romans," in *Luther's Works*, 35:370.

99. Calvin, *Institutes* 2.7.12.

100. Augustine, *On the Gift of Perseverance*, ch. 16 in vol. 5, *NPNF1*.

will but the will of him who sent me. And this is the will of him who sent me, that I should lose nothing of all that he has given me, but raise it up on the last day" (Jn 6:37–39). "My sheep hear my voice, and I know them, and they follow me. I give them eternal life, and they will never perish, and no one will snatch them out of my hand. My Father, who has given them to me, is greater than all, and no one is able to snatch them out of the Father's hand. I and the Father are one" (Jn 10:27–30). Only if the eternal pact between the persons of the Godhead can be broken can one of the elect be lost.

If there is "now no condemnation for those who are in Christ Jesus" (Ro 8:1), on the sole basis of Christ's righteousness imputed, then a reversal of the court's verdict is impossible. That verdict has already set into motion the process of inward renewal, as the believer has been inserted by the Spirit into the powers of the age to come. "Therefore, if anyone is in Christ, he is a new creation. The old has passed away; behold, the new has come. All this is from God, who through Christ reconciled us to himself ..." (2Co 5:17–18). Even our sanctification is the result of "the power [of God] at work within us" (Eph 3:20), and not only our justification but our walking in good works is predestined by God (Eph 2:10). Not only some but all of those *and only those* whom God chose before time began in Christ are effectually called, justified, and glorified (Ro 8:30). "As many as were appointed to eternal life believed" (Ac 13:48). God calls those whom he has chosen (2Th 2:13; Eph 1:11–13; Jn 15:16, etc.). There is no indication in Scripture that God effectually calls (i.e., regenerates) those whom he has not chosen or that he draws into vital union with his Son those whom he allows finally to perish. The believer's perseverance is guaranteed by God's perseverance, so that Paul can say, "And I am sure of this, that he who began a good work in you will bring it to completion at the day of Jesus Christ" (Php 1:6). And to Timothy he writes, "But I am not ashamed, for I know whom I have believed, and I am convinced that he is able to guard until that Day what has been entrusted to me" (2Ti 1:12).

God *does* what he *declares*. When he pronounces someone righteous in Christ, he immediately begins also to conform that person to Christ.

> What then shall we say to these things? If God is for us, who can be against us? He who did not spare his own Son but gave him up for us all, how will he not also with him graciously give us all things? Who shall bring any charge against God's elect? It is God who justifies. Who is to condemn? Christ Jesus is the one who died—more than that, who was raised—who is at the right hand of God, who indeed is interceding for us. Who shall separate us from the love of Christ? Shall tribulation, or distress, or persecution, or famine, or nakedness, or danger, or sword? ... For I am sure that neither death nor life, nor angels nor rulers, nor things present nor things to come, nor powers, nor height nor depth, nor anything else in all creation, will be able to separate us from the love of God in Christ Jesus our Lord. (Ro 8:31–35, 38–39)

If our regeneration is the consequence of God's election, redemption, and effectual calling (Jn 1:12–13; 3:3, 5; 15:16; Ro 9:11–18; Eph 1:4–13; 2Th 2:12–13; 2Ti 1:9, etc.) rather than our decision and effort, then he will enable us to persevere to the end: "But the Lord is faithful; he will establish you and guard you against the evil one" (2Th 3:3). "Therefore I endure everything for the sake of the elect, that they also may obtain the salvation that is in Christ Jesus with eternal glory. The saying is trustworthy, for: If we have died with him, we will also live with him; if we endure, we will also reign with him; if we deny him, he also will deny us; if we are faithless, he remains faithful—for he cannot deny himself" (2Ti 2:10–13). First Peter adds,

> Blessed be the God and Father of our Lord Jesus Christ! According to his great mercy, he has caused us to be born again to a living hope through the resurrection of Jesus Christ from the dead, to an inheritance that is imperishable, undefiled, and unfading, kept in heaven for you, who by God's power are being guarded through faith for a salvation ready to be revealed in the last time." (1Pe 1:3–5).

For this reason, "your faith and hope are in God" (v. 21). "You have been born again, not of perishable seed but of imperishable, through the living and abiding word of God" (v. 23). Of course, left to ourselves, we not only could but would fall from grace, but God "is able to keep you from stumbling" (Jude 24).

Crucial to the biblical analogies for the organic character of this covenantal relationship are the botanical and biological images. As Israel is God's vine, Christ is the Vine and we are his branches (Jn 15:1–11; cf. Mt 13:24–30; 17:20; 20:1–6, 17:20). Thus, the New Testament member of the covenant of grace is in the same position as a covenant member in the Old Testament: outwardly received by Christ as belonging to his people, each member must inwardly receive Christ as his Savior. And just as John the Baptist and Jesus warned of the breaking off of unproductive branches, and as Pentecost initiated the fulfillment of the annual Jewish feast of harvest or ingathering, Paul can speak of Gentiles as wild branches grafted onto the living vine of Israel, branches that may also be broken off if they do not yield the fruit of faith (Ro 11:16–24). Thus, there are dead and living branches: those who are related merely outwardly and visibly and those who are united to Christ inwardly and invisibly in the communion of the elect.

So apostasy is not only hypothetical; it actually happens. Even if we are unfaithful, "he remains faithful—for he cannot deny himself." Yet in the same breath Paul warns that "if we deny him, he also will deny us" (2Ti 2:10–13). Jesus warned that "every branch in me that does not bear fruit [the Father] takes away" (Jn 15:2), yet he tells his disciples, "Already you are clean because of the word that I have spoken to you.... You did not choose me, but I chose you and appointed you that you should go and bear fruit, *and that your fruit should abide...*" (15:3, 16). The gospel is proclaimed publicly to all people, but only the elect receive it, Jesus says (Mt 22:14). Similarly, in Romans 9 Paul addresses the question provoked by the unbelief of the majority of Jews by explaining, "It is not as though the word of God has failed, for not all who are descended from Israel belong to Israel, and not all are children of Abraham because they are his offspring..." (v. 6). God has always exercised his sovereign mercy, electing Isaac rather than Ishmael, and Jacob rather than Esau, "though they were not yet born and had done nothing either good or bad — in order that God's purpose of election might continue, not because of works but because of him who calls ..." (v. 11). Therefore, our perseverance in faith is guaranteed by God's electing, redeeming, and calling grace. "So then it depends not on human will or exertion, but on God, who has mercy" (v. 16).

Although Peter denied Christ three times, Christ did not put out the smoldering wick or break off the bruised reed, but brought him back to faith by his Spirit after the resurrection. Yet those who deny Christ to the very end, even though they may perhaps have been outward members of the visible church, are lost because they were never living members through faith. "They went out from us," says John concerning those who deny Christ, "but they were not of us; for if they had been of us, they would have continued with us. But they went out, that it might become plain that they all are not of us. But you have been anointed by the Holy One, and you all have knowledge" (1Jn 2:19–20).

This is why the writer to the Hebrews, in warning Jewish Christians during tremendous persecution not to return to Judaism, appeals to the example of the wilderness generation under Moses: "For good news came to us just as to them; but the message they heard did not benefit them, because they were not united by faith with those who listened. For we who have believed enter that rest.... So then, there remains a Sabbath rest for the people of God, for whoever has entered God's rest has also rested from his works as God did from his." Entering that rest means not only hearing but believing the gospel (Heb 4:1–11).

In this light we are better able to understand the dire warnings against falling away in Hebrews 6. The writer describes those who belong only outwardly to the covenant community as "those who have once been enlightened, who have tasted the heavenly gift, and have shared in the Holy Spirit, and have tasted the goodness of the word of God and the powers of the age to come, and then have fallen away ..." (vv. 4–6). Those who apostatize have been beneficiaries of the Spirit's ministry through the means of grace even as merely formal or external members of the covenant community. Having been baptized ("enlightened"), they have also *tasted the heavenly gift* in the Supper and *"tasted the goodness of the word of God and the powers of the age to come,"* but they have not actually received or *fed upon* Christ for eternal life, which Jesus linked to faith (Jn 6:27–58, 62–65).

According to Hebrews 6, then, those who apostatize by returning to the shadows of the law after Christ has come are basically "crucifying once again the Son of God ... and holding him up to contempt" (v. 6). Belonging to the visible church places one in the very heart of the Spirit's activity of uniting sinners to Christ through the means of grace. It is therefore a tremendous benefit; yet it is also a greater threat for those who do not actually trust in Christ. "For land that has drunk the rain that often falls on it, and produces a crop useful to those for whose sake it is cultivated, receives a blessing from God. But if it bears thorns and thistles, it is worthless and near to being cursed, and its end is to be burned" (vv. 7–8). The blessings of the covenant ordinarily lead to salvation, but when instead one hardens his or her heart to these blessings and does not receive the Christ who gives them, they become curses. Happily, this severe warning is followed by the encouragement of verse 9: "Though we speak in this way, yet in your case, beloved, we feel sure of better things—*things that belong to salvation.*" This salvation is exhibited in the case of these who are actually saved by the fruit that it yields (vv. 10–12). The writer then goes on to assure them of the unchangeable character of God's promise in Jesus Christ, so that "we who have fled for refuge might have strong encouragement to hold fast to the hope set before us" (v. 18). So these warning passages themselves target those who are visible members of the covenant community, in some sense benefiting from the Spirit's ministry, who have nevertheless failed to embrace the gift of salvation.

Identified as the "P" in the Calvinistic TULIP, the doctrine I have summarized was defended by Augustine in his treatise *On the Perseverance of the Saints*. It is the view that is taught not only in the Reformed and Presbyterian confessions but in the *Thirty-nine Articles* (Anglican), the *Savoy Declaration* (Congregationalist), and the *1689 Baptist Confession of Faith* (Calvinistic Baptists).[101]

B. ALTERNATIVE INTERPRETATIONS

Challenges to this doctrine usually appear in two broad forms. The first form is *synergism*, meaning "working together": the view that salvation is attained through a cooperative process between God and human beings. Representatives of this perspective are, therefore, neither fully Pelagian nor Augustinian but range somewhere between these positions. Though with their own distinct emphases, Eastern Orthodoxy, Roman Catholicism, and Arminianism are synergistic, teaching that the believer's security depends at least to some extent on his or her own cooperation with God's grace and that this grace may be finally lost.[102] For them, the warning

---

101. For a fine recent defense of this doctrine, see Thomas R. Schreiner and Ardel B. Caneday, *The Race Set before Us: A Biblical Theology of Perseverance and Assurance* (Downers Grove, Ill.: InterVarsity Press, 2001).

102. William B. Pope, *A Compendium of Christian Theology*

[New York: Hunt and Eaton, 1880), 3:137–47. A contemporary defense of the dominant Arminian position may be found in Robert Shank, *Life in the Son: A Study of the Doctrine of Perseverance* (2nd ed.; Minneapolis: Bethany, 1989).

passages refer to those who were regenerated, justified, and even in the process of being sanctified but at some point lose their salvation through unbelief and serious (mortal) sin. According to the *Catechism of the Catholic Church*, "the children of our holy mother the Church rightly hope for the grace of final perseverance and the recompense of God their Father for the good works accomplished with his grace in communion with Jesus."[103]

The fifth point of the Remonstrant (Arminian) articles reads as follows:

> That they who are united to Christ by faith are thereby furnished with abundant strength and succor sufficient to enable them to triumph over the seductions of Satan, and the allurements of sin; nevertheless they may, by the neglect of these succors, fall from grace, and, dying in such a state, may finally perish. This point was started at first doubtfully, but afterward positively as a settled doctrine.[104]

Neither the Roman Catholic and Orthodox nor the Arminian view is Pelagian. Both insist on the necessity of grace, but this grace is regarded as making final salvation merely possible; it becomes effectual only to the extent that the believer cooperates with its infused powers.

Another important view is what we might refer to as an *inconsistent synergism*. Generally known as *eternal security*, this view seems in some respects indistinguishable from the perseverance of the saints. However, at least as it is articulated by many of its leading proponents, this view locates security in the believer's decision to accept Christ.[105] According to this view, although genuine Christians may fail to grow in their sanctification and persevere in their faith — in fact, may never even begin to bear the fruit of righteousness — they are assured of eternal life. Such "carnal Christians" may leave the church, even deny Christ, and thereby lose the blessings of living as "victorious Christians" as well as the rewards in the next life for faithful service, but they will be saved, though "as through fire" (1Co 3:15).[106] Although advocates often represent this position as *moderate Calvinism*, it is more appropriately identified as *moderate Arminianism*, since it implies that human beings are capable of responding to God in faith apart from a prior regeneration, bases election on

---

103. *Catechism of the Catholic Church*, 489.

104. As quoted in H. Orton Wiley, *Christian Theology* (Kansas City: Beacon Hill, 1941), 3:351.

105. Lewis Sperry Chafer, *Major Bible Doctrines* (ed. John Walvoord; rev. ed.; Grand Rapids: Zondervan, 1974), 214, 220, 222, 230–35. Though representing what he calls the "moderate Calvinist" position (in defense of eternal security), Norman L. Geisler presupposes a basically Arminian scheme: "God's grace works synergistically on free will.... Put in other terms, God's justifying grace works cooperatively, not operatively" (*Chosen but Free* [Minneapolis: Bethany, 1999], 233). Elsewhere he writes, "Indeed, God would save all men if He could.... God

will achieve the greatest number in heaven that He possibly can" ("God, Evil, and Dispensations," in *Walvoord: A Tribute* [ed. Donald K. Campbell; Chicago: Moody Press, 1982], 102, 108). I interact with Geisler on this issue in J. Matthew Pinson, ed., *Four Views on Eternal Security* (Grand Rapids: Zondervan, 2002).

106. Lewis Sperry Chafer, *Major Bible Doctrines*, 283–86. Charles Stanley argues that Jesus' description of the "outer darkness" of "weeping and wailing and gnashing of teeth" refers not to hell but to a region of heaven occupied by carnal Christians (*Eternal Security: Can You Be Sure?* [Nashville: Nelson, 1990], 121–29).

foreseen faith, rejects the particular scope of the atonement, and maintains that the Spirit's sovereign call may be resisted. Even its teaching of eternal security is based on the believer's decision to accept Christ, which renders this view actually closer to Arminianism than to a Calvinist interpretation of perseverance of the saints.

Over every form of synergism, confessional Lutheranism strongly affirms a monergistic soteriology: God alone saves; it is not a process of human cooperation with God's grace. Nevertheless, from a Reformed perspective the Lutheran system represents an *inconsistent monergism*. Confessional Lutheranism affirms total depravity and unconditional election while nevertheless holding with equal rigor to a universal atonement and the possibility of resisting the Spirit's inward calling through the outward gospel. Lutheranism affirms with Reformed theology that the elect will persevere and that "those who still take pleasure in their sins and continue in a sinful life do not believe,"[107] yet also holds that it is possible that (a) the elect may lose their salvation for a time (e.g., David, Peter), but will not finally; (b) others might once have truly believed and been regenerated and justified, but then lose all of these gifts through apostasy.[108] According to some Lutherans, salvation can be lost only through unbelief, while according to others it may also be lost because of mortal sin.[109] How can one say that God alone saves, from beginning to end, while also affirming the possibility of losing one's salvation? It seems undeniable that in this view the gift of salvation depends in some sense on the sinner's nonresisting, although this conclusion is rejected by confessional Lutherans.

The doctrine of the perseverance of the saints reflects a *consistently monergistic* view of salvation as entirely due to God's grace alone from beginning to end. Although some professing members may be devoid of saving faith, those who receive the reality that is promised to them in Word and sacrament are assured that they will continue to trust in Christ. In spite of the weakness of our faith and repentance, we are "more than conquerors through him who loved us," so that nothing "will be able to separate us from the love of God in Christ Jesus our Lord" (Ro 8:37, 39).

DISCUSSION QUESTIONS

1. Explain and evaluate the difference between definitive and progressive sanctification. Is this distinction scriptural—and is it valuable?

---

107. *Augsburg Confession*, art. 20, as found in *The Book of Concord: The Confessions of the Evangelical Lutheran Church* (ed. and trans. Theodore G. Tappert; Philadelphia: Fortress, 1959).

108. "Final Perseverance," in *Christian Cyclopedia* (ed. Erwin L. Lueker, Luther Poellot, and Paul Jackson; St. Louis: Concordia, 1954). The article points out that while Lutherans stress the assurance of all who trust in Christ, the severe warnings of the law should be borne in mind, to guard against "carnal security."

109. A regenerate believer may apostatize, "[b]ut the cause is not as though God were unwilling to grant grace for perseverance to those in whom He has begun the good work ... [but that these persons] wilfully turn away ..." (*Formula of Concord*, solid declaration, art. 11, par. 42; see *Book of Concord*).

2. What should Christians expect in terms of their progressive conformity to Christ's image? Relate your discussion especially to eschatology.

3. What are mortification and vivification, and are these done mainly by imitating Christ?

4. What does Paul mean when he exhorts us to "work out your own salvation, with fear and trembling ..." (Php 2:12)?

5. What are some of the dangers to avoid with respect to this doctrine?

6. If sanctification is not to be confused with justification, is there nevertheless a necessary connection? Why or why not?

7. What is the role (if any) of God's law in the Christian life?

8. What is meant by the perseverance of the saints? Compare and contrast this with the concept of eternal security.

Chapter Twenty-One

THE HOPE OF GLORY: "THOSE WHOM HE JUSTIFIED HE ALSO GLORIFIED" (RO 8:30)

As we have seen, creation was only the beginning of God's purposes for the world. As God's image-bearer and covenantal head of his posterity, Adam was commissioned to fulfill the work that God had given him to do, winning the right to eat from the Tree of Life. As the Last Adam and True Israel, Jesus Christ joyfully embraced his calling, fulfilled his trial, bore our debts, and entered the glory of the everlasting Sabbath day in triumphal procession as our representative head. Because of his achievement, we have been delivered from a bondage greater than Egypt's and from being swallowed by more foreboding waters than the Red Sea. The writer to the Hebrews casts new covenant believers in the role of the new wilderness generation, exhorting us, "Therefore, while the promise of entering his rest still stands, let us fear lest any of you should seem to have failed to reach it. For good news came to us just as to them, but the message they heard did not benefit them, because they were not united by faith with those who listened" (Heb 4:1–2). Christ's conquest purchased for us a new creation far greater than an earthly paradise: "For if Joshua had given them rest, God would not have spoken of another day later on. So then, there remains a Sabbath rest for the people of God, for whoever has entered God's rest has also rested from his works as God did from his" (vv. 8–10). Not only regenerated, forgiven, justified, adopted, and sanctified, God's elect will one day be raised bodily to inherit the everlasting kingdom won for them by their head. As Jesus is now, we will be also together with him: head and members joined in unending joy. This future hope is what theology identifies as *glorification*.

I. GLORIFICATION: THE "NOT YET" ASPECT OF OUR REDEMPTION

On this point we again meet the New Testament eschatology of "already" and "not yet." Already we share in Christ's election and redemption. We have already been raised from spiritual death by the gospel and been given faith to receive Christ with all his gifts. Our election, new birth, and justification are objective, perfect, and complete. Yet our progressive sanctification continues and even at death remains unfinished, but nevertheless real, as the *Heidelberg Catechism* summarizes: "In this life even the holiest have only a small beginning of this obedience. Nevertheless, with all seriousness of purpose, they do begin to live according to all, not only some, of God's commandments."[1]

In glorification, the apparent contradiction between God's verdict and our actual lives is finally and forever resolved. The "already" and the "not yet" converge, completing immediately and perfectly that which the Spirit began when he called us into fellowship with Christ by the gospel (Php 1:6–11). Even here, at the very end of the *ordo*, we see the inextricable connection of the forensic verdict of God's Word that inaugurates the new creation with our progressive re-creation according to Christ's image. These inseparable aspects actually converge in our glorification, when there will no longer be a "not yet" to our salvation; no longer a *simil iustus et peccator*. Rather, God's declaration that we are righteous in Christ will correspond to the actual reality of our moral condition.

II. DIFFERING VIEWS OF GLORIFICATION

If important differences exist between theologies of East and West with respect to this question, Protestant interpretations of glorification add to the complexity of views. However great these differences, there are also some surprising areas of potential understanding and agreement regarding the doctrine that the East identifies as *theōsis*, the West as divinization/beatific vision, and the churches of the Reformation as glorification.

A. EASTERN ORTHODOXY: THEŌSIS (DEIFICATION)

"For Orthodoxy our salvation and redemption mean our deification," writes Bishop Kallistos Ware.[2] This deification is referred to as *theōsis*, which is the central theme of Eastern Orthodox soteriology.[3] Taking its coordinates from 2 Peter 1:4,

---

1. *Heidelberg Catechism*, q. 114, in *Psalter Hymnal* (Grand Rapids: CRC Publications, 1987), 915.

2. Timothy (Kallistos) Ware, *The Orthodox Church: New Edition* (New York: Penguin, 1997), 231.

3. See Jaroslav Pelikan, *The Christian Tradition: A History of the Development of Doctrine*, vol. 2, *The Spirit of Eastern Christendom (600–1700)* (Chicago: Univ. of Chicago Press, 1977), 125.

where God's promises to believers include their becoming "partakers of the divine nature," this prominent patristic theme attained systematic formulation especially by the Byzantine theologian Gregory Palamas (1296–1359).

It is important to point out that deification has never meant for Orthodoxy that the soul becomes one with God in essence. We have seen that the ancient theologians of the Eastern church were at great pains to emphasize the Creator-creature distinction. God so transcends creation in his incomprehensible majesty that we cannot even know God's being in itself but only according to God's works. Following this Creator-creature distinction, the East carefully distinguished between God's *essence* and *energies*. I have referred to this distinction several times under different topics, but its prominence is especially evident in Orthodox treatments of *theōsis*.

Typically, the West works with only two categories of existing beings: Creator and created. Therefore, something either belongs to God's essence or is a created effect—a created person or thing. For example, where the East speaks of the divinizing energy of God as "uncreated," Aquinas regarded it as "created light."[4] With *energies*, the East introduced a third category. God's energies, we have seen, are his "workings." They are radiations of divine glory, but no more the divine essence than the sun's rays are the sun itself. God's uncreated glory emanates, but the essence does not. Therefore, union with God—also known as *theōsis* (divinization)—is brought about not by a confusion of the creature with God's essence but by the "effulgence" or radiance of the light from "the energies or grace in which God makes Himself known."[5] When our only categories are the divine essence and created essences, the danger of pantheism becomes apparent.[6] "Divinization" must mean that either creatures merge with God's essence or that grace is not God's favor and gift (energy), but a created substance infused into the soul.[7] It was against this view that the Reformation insisted that in salvation the gift is Christ—the God-Man himself. As I pointed out in considering the mystical union, we cannot receive Christ's gifts, Calvin argued (with Luther) without receiving Christ himself. Yet, against Osiander, Calvin argued that this never makes us sharers in God's essence.

---

4. Thomas Aquinas, *Summa theologica* (trans. English Dominican Fathers; New York: Benziger Brothers, 1947), 1a.12.5.

5. Vladimir Lossky, *The Mystical Theology of the Eastern Church* (Crestwood, N.Y.: St. Vladimir's Seminary Press, 1976), 221.

6. Ibid.

7. This is the ontology that supports the dogma of transubstantiation, according to which bread and wine no longer retain their creaturely essence but become the divine body and blood, worthy of adoration. However, with the middle category of energies, God's gracious working ("the powers [*dynameis*] of the age to come," Heb 6:5) may be seen as divine action without being collapsed into the divine essence; the rays, but not the sun. We do not worship the Bible, baptism of water, or the bread and wine in the Lord's Supper, but we also do not regard them simply as created things. United to God's energetic speech, they are means of grace. Similarly, believers are never sharers in the divine essence, but they are made beneficiaries of God's gracious energies, glorified to the degree that creatures can ever be like God.

Reflecting this emerging distinction, Athanasius affirmed, "[God] is outside all things according to his essence, but he is in all things through his acts of power."[8] Similarly, Basil writes, "We know the essence through the energy. No one has ever seen the essence of God, but we believe in the essence because we experience the energy."[9] So there is deification without pantheism, union without fusion. Furthermore, the deifying energies come to us from the Father, in the Son, by the Spirit. To be deified is to be *transfigured*, so that the rays of God's energies (again, not the divine essence) permeate (rather than obliterate) the creature. The Old Testament theophanies, as well as the transfiguration, and the experience of Paul on the Damascus road, represent such events.[10] In the transfiguration, Christ himself underwent no change, but the apostles were able to see during that time the glory (energies) that was always present yet hidden from their view previously. In this light, they saw light. "The apostles were taken out of history and given a glimpse of eternal realities."[11]

Alongside the unfortunate allegorical ascent (including the flight from matter) exhibited by Gregory's autobiographical account, there is also an eschatological and matter-affirming dimension. "Our ultimate destiny," says Lossky, "is not merely an intellectual contemplation of God; if it were, the resurrection of the dead would be unnecessary. The blessed will see God face to face, in the fullness of their created being."[12] As the eleventh-century theologian Symeon of Constantinople summarized, there are two judgments: a judgment in this life that leads to salvation (despair leading to repentance and forgiveness), where the depths of our sin are made known only to us, and a future judgment to condemnation, where sin is made public.[13]

Lossky explains,

> Those who in this life undergo such a judgment [to salvation] will have nothing to fear from another tribunal. But for those who will not, in this life, enter into the light, that they may be accused and judged, for those who hate the light, the second coming of Christ will disclose the light which at present remains hidden, and will make manifest everything which has been concealed.[14]

The second coming will be a manifestation of sin " 'outside grace,' as St. Maximus has it."[15]

> What man ought to have attained by raising himself up to God, God achieved by descending to man.... Nicholas Cabasilas, a Byzantine theologian of the four-

---

8. St. Athanasius, *On the Incarnation* 17, in *Athanasius: Contra gentes and De incarnatione* (Oxford: Clarendon, 1971), 174, quoted in Bishop Timothy (Kallistos) Ware, *The Orthodox Way* (Crestwood, N.Y.: St. Vladimir's Seminary Press, 1979), 22.

9. Basil, *Doctrina patrum de incarnatione verbi* (ed. Franz Kiekamp; 2nd ed.; Münster: Aschendorff, 1981), 88–89.

10. Lossky, *The Mystical Theology of the Eastern Church*, 223.
11. Ibid.
12. Ibid., 224.
13. Ibid., 233–34.
14. Ibid., 234.
15. Ibid.

teenth century, said on this subject: "The Lord allowed men, separated from God by the triple barrier of nature, sin and death, to be fully possessed of Him and to be directly united to Him by the fact that he has set aside each barrier in turn: that of nature by His incarnation, of sin by His death, and of death by His resurrection."[16]

Whatever one's evaluation of the Eastern formulation, it is not as susceptible as the Western view to allowing the absorption of the creature into the Creator and plurality into unity (panentheism or even pantheism). The "overcoming estrangement" paradigm witnesses to the East's suspicion that Western mysticism always tends toward this very confusion. The doctrines of creation *ex nihilo* and the Trinity become more legible, I suggest, in the Eastern account. Further, precisely because creatures participate in the energies rather than in the essence of God, there is no need to talk about kenotic theories that imply a more emanationist scheme of diminishing "being" as one descends the ontological ladder.

B. The Doctrine of Glorification in Reformed Theology

Theōsis or deification does not occupy a locus in Reformed theology, much less serve as a central dogma of its soteriology. In fact, in at least some of its representative expressions, the doctrine seems to Reformed ears susceptible to a theology of glory. From a Reformed perspective, the problem is not that human beings have simply lost their way from the path of the soul's upward ascent, but that they are guilty of breaking the covenant of creation, lie under the penalty of the law, and are therefore in bondage to sin and death. Consequently, salvation is a forensic or judicial matter that brings about a new condition of actual existence. Furthermore, Reformed theology stands in a critical relation to the synergism that dominates Eastern and Western ideas of *theōsis*/divinization. With that said, there are nevertheless surprising parallels between the Reformed understanding of glorification and *theōsis* that were recognized by older orthodox writers and should be rediscovered for the enrichment of our Christian hope.

Closer to Irenaeus than to Athanasius on this point, Reformed theology maintains that God became flesh not to make us God but to make us fully human — not only God's image-bearers but sharers in his Sabbath glory. The Platonist scheme of spiritual and moral ascent touches the ancient churches of the East as well as the West. Like helium in a balloon, grace raises or elevates nature beyond itself, toward the divine. We have already shown the criticism that Reformed theologians have often offered of this paradigm. Instead of making us something *more than* human, grace saves and liberates humans to become *more human*: finally to glorify and to

---

16. Ibid., 136.

enjoy God forever. The total person is the subject of glorification; there is no elevation of a privileged aspect of humanity (i.e., the soul) above its own created nature. However, the East more consistently affirms these points, over against Platonism, than Roman Catholic theology. Not surprisingly, then, Irenaeus occupies a leading role as a patristic source, although other ancient Greek theologians also occupy a privileged place in Calvin's reading, especially John Chrysostom and Cyril of Alexandria.[17] Exploring these connections should be of great importance, for greater mutual enrichment of both traditions.[18]

Therefore, the key difference between the East's doctrine of *theōsis* and the Reformed doctrine of glorification lies in that the former leaves out or at least downplays the forensic element. That emphasis in Calvin and the Reformed tradition generally is the basis for rather than the alternative to the actual transformation of creaturely reality in anticipation of its glorification. Calvin can even say, "Let us mark that the end of the gospel is to render us eventually conformable to God, and, if we may so speak, to deify us." Nevertheless, explicitly invoking the East's essence-energies distinction, he adds the following qualification:

> But the word nature is *not here essence but quality*. The Manicheans formerly dreamt that we are a part of God, and that after having run the race of life we shall at length revert to our original. There are also at this day fanatics who imagine that we thus pass over into the nature of God, so that his swallows up our nature. Thus they explain what Paul says, that God will be all in all (1Co 15.28) and in the same sense they take this passage. But such a delirium as this never entered the minds of the holy Apostles; they only intended to say that when divested of all the vices of the flesh, we shall be *partakers of divine and blessed immortality and glory*, so as to be as it were *one with God as far as our capacities will allow*. This doctrine was not altogether unknown to Plato, who everywhere defines the chief good of man to be an entire conformity to God; but as he was involved in the mists of errors, he afterwards glided off to his own inventions. But we, disregarding empty speculations, ought to be satisfied with this one thing—that the *image of God in holiness and righteousness*

---

17. See Irena Backus, "Calvin and the Greek Fathers," in *Continuity and Change: The Harvest of Later Medieval and Reformation History* (ed. Robert J. Bast and Andrew C. Gow; Leiden: Brill, 2000), 253–76; cf. Johannes van Oort, "John Calvin and the Church Fathers," in *The Reception of the Church Fathers in the West: From the Carolingians to the Maurists* (ed. Irena Backus; Leiden: Brill, 1997).

18. Further, as J. Todd Billings cautions, a certain account of deification (the Byzantine version of *theōsis* articulated by Palamas) is often read back into the earlier tradition as the definitive Eastern position. Whatever convergences might obtain between this position and Reformed theology, Billings wisely suggests that they should be related to the concept of *divinization* more broadly rather than to the doctrine of *theōsis* with

its distinct Palamite refinements. See J. Todd Billings, "United to God through Christ: Assessing Calvin on the Question of Deification," *Harvard Theological Journal* 98, no. 3 (2005): 315–34. While pointing out potential parallels, Billings carefully distinguishes Calvin's references to "deification" (which are sparse to begin with) from the distinctively Palamite notion of *theōsis*. This relationship has been fruitfully explored in the Orthodox-Reformed discussions, especially (on the Reformed side) by Thomas F. Torrance. However, Billings is, in my view, a more reliable guide for interpreting Calvin's relationship to the topic of divinization. See especially his recent book, *Calvin, Participation, and the Gift: The Activity of Believers in Union with Christ* (New York: Oxford Univ. Press, 2008).

is restored to us for this end, that we may at length be partakers of eternal life and glory *as far as it will be necessary for our complete felicity* (emphasis added).[19]

This is a gloss on 2 Peter 1:4, the only biblical passage that speaks directly of our sharing in the divine nature. Nevertheless, while cautioning us against "empty speculations," Calvin here seems to affirm a sharing in the energy ("quality") rather than in the essence of God and even includes under this many of the attributes that the East has identified (divine immortality and glory through the restoration of the image of God in holiness and righteousness).

Calvin's interpretation bears affinities to the thought of the great Syrian theologian John of Damascus (676–749), who gave systematic expression to Eastern Orthodox teaching, when the latter expresses the goal of salvation: "becoming deified, in the way of participating in the divine *glory* and not in that of a change into the divine *being*" (emphasis added).[20] Through the essence-energies distinction, the East was able to avoid the temptation of Western mysticism toward the more nearly Neoplatonist absorption of the ostensibly "higher self" (the soul or mind) into the divine essence.

Focusing on the economy of grace as it is revealed in Scripture, rather than on the essence as an object of speculation, Calvin stipulated, "The essence of God is rather to be adored than inquired into."[21] In fact, "They are mad who seek to discover what God is."[22] Rather, we come to know God through his works in creation (Ro 1:20) but especially through his Word. "Thereupon his powers are mentioned, by which he is shown to us *not as he is in himself,* but *as he is toward us*: so that this recognition of him consists more in living experience than in vain and high-flown speculation" (emphasis added).[23]

Far from distorting Calvin in the direction of rationalism, Reformed scholasticism insisted that, in the words of Francis Turretin, "theology treats God not like metaphysics as a being or as he can be known from the light of nature, but as the Creator and Redeemer made known by revelation."[24] Rather than being motivated by nominalism, these Reformed scholastics were actually reacting to the univocity of being as introduced by Franciscus Suárez, among others.[25] In particular, they stressed the Thomistic analogy of being over against the univocal understanding of Suárez.[26] However, they went further than Thomas by emphasizing that even in our glorified state, we can know God only in his works, not in his essence.

---

19. Calvin on 2Pe 1:4 in *Commentaries on the Catholic Epistles* (ed. and trans. John Owen; Edinburgh: Calvin Translation Society, 1855; repr., Grand Rapids: Baker, 1996), 371.

20. John of Damascus, *An Exact Exposition of the Orthodox Faith*, in *NPNF2*, 9:31.

21. Calvin, *Institutes* 1.2.2.

22. Calvin on Ro 1:19 in his *Commentary on Paul's Epistle*

to the Romans (ed. and trans. John Owen; Grand Rapids: Eerdmans, 1948), 69.

23. Calvin, *Institutes* 1.10.2.

24. Turretin, *Elenctic Theology*, 1:16–17.

25. Muller, *PRRD*, 3:109.

26. Ibid., 3:113.

For both Eastern and Western theologies, soteriology (as other loci) is tethered to the doctrine of the Trinity and vice versa.[27] In fact, Calvin directly appeals to the Cappadocians, particularly Gregory of Nazianzus. "And that passage in Gregory of Nazianzus vastly delights me: 'I cannot think on the one without quickly being encircled by the splendor of the three; nor can I discern the three without being straightaway carried back to the one.' Let us not, then, be led to imagine a trinity of persons which includes an idea of separation, and does not at once lead us back to that unity."[28]

This is especially so, I would argue, in more Irenaean and Reformed theologies, where the focus is on the identity of the three persons in their economic operations rather than on the inner essence. If we are guided by Scripture rather than by "high-flown speculations," we will discover this pattern: "to the Father is attributed the beginning of activity, and the fountain and wellspring of all things; to the Son, wisdom, counsel, and the ordered disposition of all things; but to the Spirit is assigned the power and efficacy of that activity."[29]

Calvin can use realistic language to speak of the believer's incorporation into the very life of the Trinity, without (as is often done in contemporary theologies) simply identifying this communion with the unique *perichōrēsis* of the divine persons. Peter van Mastricht is representative of the Reformed scholastics when he adds that in believers' union with Christ "there is a certain shadowing forth" of the unity of the divine persons in the Trinity.[30] That qualification, "a certain shadowing forth," preserves the Creator-creature distinction, maintaining an analogical rather than univocal connection. To repeat a line from Calvin cited above, "we shall be partakers of divine and blessed immortality and glory, so as to be as it were one with God *as far as our capacities will allow.*" At no point does the Reformer countenance a communication of the divine essence.

Reformed theology is even willing to speak of glorification in terms of the beatific vision, but here again it is closer to an Eastern (Irenaean) emphasis on the resurrection of the body than it is to the preoccupation of much of Western reflection on beholding and ascending into the divine essence. Although revised in some significant ways, the mystical piety of Augustine, the Cappadocians, Hilary, and Bernard is freely appropriated in an ad hoc manner. Calvin writes,

> The ancient philosophers anxiously discussed the sovereign good, and even contended among themselves over it. Yet none but Plato recognized man's highest good

27. For recent consensus on the Trinity and Christology between mainline Reformed and Orthodox bodies, see *Growth in Agreement II: Reports and Agreed Statements of Ecumenical Conversations on a World Level, 1982–1998* (ed. Jeffrey Gros, Harding Meyer, and William G. Rusch; Geneva: WCC Publications; Grand Rapids: Eerdmans, 2000), 275–90.

28. Calvin, *Institutes* 1.13.17.
29. Ibid., 1.13.18.
30. Peter van Mastricht, as quoted in Heinrich Heppe, *Reformed Dogmatics* (ed. Ernst Bizer; trans. G. T. Thomson; London: Allen & Unwin, 1950), 512.

as union with God, and he could not even dimly sense its nature. And no wonder, for he had learned nothing of the sacred bond of that union. Even on this earthly pilgrimage we know the sole and perfect happiness; but this happiness kindles our hearts more and more each day to desire it, until the full fruition of it shall satisfy us. *Accordingly, I said that they alone receive the fruit of Christ's benefits who raise their minds to the resurrection* (emphasis added).[31]

We notice in that last sentence the raising of the mind not in Plato's contemplative ascent beyond material things (as emphasized in both Eastern and Western mysticism), but in consideration of Jesus' bodily resurrection, in which we share. That "beatific vision" extolled by the ancient philosophers is "not even dimly sensed" apart from Christ and the resurrection. Why the resurrection particularly? The reason will become clearer as we elaborate Calvin's treatment.

However, before we arrive at his connection between vision (divinization-glorification) and the resurrection, we should recognize that restoration of the *imago* is also crucial in Calvin's understanding of the Spirit's work of making us participate in Christ and all of his benefits. In fact, as Philip Butin recalls, "Calvin's most complete definition of the *imago dei* in the *Institutes* is based on the assumption that 'the true nature of the image of God is to be derived from what scripture says of its renewal through Christ.'"[32] The Son is God's image, Calvin writes, not only according to his deity but according to his humanity—the true image of the Adamic representative.[33] In fact, the whole purpose of the gospel is to restore this image.[34]

This correlation of deification or glorification with restoration of the *imago* reflects an important convergence with patristic teaching. However—and this is a critical point that reflects a more Eastern emphasis—human participation in this image is mediated by the Son in the Spirit; it is not an immediate participation in God's deity. Particularly in his debates with Servetus and Osiander, Calvin emphasized that the Spirit, rather than any infusion of divinity flowing into human beings, is the source of this restoration.[35] To be sure, justification and inner renewal are completely distinct. "Yet you could not grasp this [imputed righteousness] without at the same time grasping sanctification also," Calvin insists. "For he 'is given unto us for righteousness, wisdom, sanctification, and redemption' [1 Cor. 1:30]."[36]

31. Calvin, *Institutes* 3.25.2.

32. Philip Walker Butin, *Revelation, Redemption, and Response* (New York: Oxford Univ. Press, 1995), 68.

33. John Calvin, *Commentary on the Gospel According to John* (trans. William Pringle; Grand Rapids: Baker, repr., 1996), commenting on 17:21.

34. John Calvin, *Commentary on 2 Corinthians* (trans. John Pringle; repr. Grand Rapids: Baker, 2003), comment on 2Co 3:18.

35. John Calvin's comment on Luke 17:20 in *Harmony of the Evangelists*, as quoted in Butin, *Revelation, Redemption, and Response*, 69. Butin writes, "He inferred from II Corinthians 3:18 that a human being 'is made to conform to God, not by an inflowing of substance, but by the grace and power of the Spirit'.... Eschatological categories ultimately shape the way in which Calvin understands the progressive and gradual nature of this trinitarian restoration ...: 'we now begin to be reformed to the image of God by His Spirit so that the complete renewal of ourselves and the whole world may follow in its own time.'"

36. Calvin, *Institutes* 3.16.1.

So far, then, we may see that for Calvin (and the Reformed tradition generally), the notion of participation in God—with its ancillary concepts of the *visio dei* and deification—is eschatologically oriented, with vertical descents of the Son and the Spirit. Rather than sending the human soul upward, away from history and embodiment, this view sees redemptive history moving forward to the consummation. Because of this emphasis on the historical economy of grace, Calvin and the wider tradition emphasized the future resurrection of the dead as the place where the consummation occurs. It is the cosmic, eschatological, and redemptive-historical event of the parousia, not the allegorical, contemplative, striving ascent of the lone soul, that characterizes the Reformed expectation of the beatific vision.

Reformed theology comes closest to the classic category of divinization when it takes up the topic of *glorification* as both final vindication and restoration of the image. Yet even here, Reformed theology insists on looking forward by looking back at justification. There is no final vindication or justification that is anything other than the verdict that has already been rendered in this present age. Thus, William Ames can say that redemption in general and glorification in particular refer to "a real deliverance from the evils of punishment, *which is actually nothing but the carrying out of the sentence of justification.* For in justification we are pronounced just and awarded the judgment of life. In glorification the life that results from the pronouncement and award is given to us: We have it in actual possession" (emphasis added).[37] In glorification of the saints, the effective Word that pronounces the ungodly just finally reaches to the last vestiges of sin and death. *It is not a different Word that renews and glorifies, but the same Word in its different operations and effects.* At last, salvation will have been worked out for us and within us, from the inside out, until the new age has fully transformed every part of creation (as in Ro 8:18–25).

Echoing the East's emphasis on the whole person as the subject of this vision, Turretin criticizes Thomists and Scotists for forcing a choice between the intellect and the will as the seat of human agency, with its corollary choice between vision and love, respectively.[38] "Sight, joy, and love" are the essential features of the eternal state, yet at no point are uncreated and created essences fused, any more than rays become the sun itself. Nevertheless, it is not a created glory that causes the blessed to shine forever, but the "efflorescences" (energies) of God, says Turretin. In glorification, faith yields to sight; hope is fulfilled in joy, and love consummated "will

---

37. William Ames, *The Marrow of Theology* (1623; trans. John Dykstra Eusden; repr., Grand Rapids: Baker, 1968), 172.

38. Turretin, *Elenctic Theology*, 3:209: "Both are at fault in this—they divide things that ought to be joined together and hold that happiness is placed separately, either in vision or in love, since it consists conjointly in the vision and the love of God.... This the Scripture teaches, describing it now by 'sight' (1 Cor. 13:12; 2 Cor. 5:7; 1 Jn. 3:2), then by 'love' and perfect holiness (1 Jn. 4:16; 1 Cor. 13:13)."

answer to love begun" in our sanctification. "God cannot be seen without being loved; love draws joy after it because he cannot be possessed without filling with joy."[39]

Interpreting 1 Corinthians 13:12, Turretin surmises that while the beatific vision involves a clearer, intuitive apprehension of God, "the distinction between the Creator and the creature is preserved, so that only a similarity, not an equality is denoted."[40] In a direct nod to the East, Turretin adds,

> God cannot be seen by the creature with an adequate and comprehensive vision, but only with an inadequate and apprehensive because the finite is not capacious of the infinite. In this sense John of Damascus truly said, "The deity is incomprehensible" (*akatalēpton to theion*). And if anywhere the saints are said to be apprehenders, this is not to be understood in relation to vision as if they could apprehend God, but in relation to the course and the goal. For the race having been finished, they are said to have apprehended (i.e., to have reached the goal, Phil. 3:13, 14).[41]

Notice again the eschatological orientation. Rather than an upward, contemplative ascent, the direction is turned toward the future: finishing the race, reaching the promised goal. A clearer and perfect analogical knowledge of God will be given in glory, yet never a sight or knowledge of God's essence.[42]

Turretin reflects the balance of the Reformed scholastics generally in affirming a genuine participation in God that is nevertheless distinct from a participation in God's essence. His view can be sharply contrasted with that of Aquinas when the latter writes, "When ... a created intellect sees God in his essence, the divine essence becomes the intelligible form of that intellect."[43] In such expressions, not only the epistemological distinction between archetypal and ectypal knowledge, but the ontological distinction between created and creaturely being, is rendered questionable.

Yet even in the present, as a foretaste of the future, God personally indwells believers by the Spirit, who also joins us to the Father and the Son. Not only the gifts but the giver is the possession of all the saints. This does not violate the axiom that for God uniquely essence and existence are identical, since the question is not about God's essence "in itself," but about God's communication of life, salvation, and glory (i.e., his energies) to creatures. Turretin cites an intriguing verse from Psalm 17: "As for me, I shall behold your face in righteousness; when I awake, I shall be satisfied with your likeness" (v. 15).

From [love] will afterwards flow a perfect likeness of the saints to God, the fulfill-

---

39. Ibid., 3:609.
40. Ibid., 3:610.
41. John of Damascus, *Orthodox Faith* 3, as quoted in

Turretin, *Elenctic Theology*, 3:610.
42. Turretin, *Elenctic Theology*, 3:610.
43. Aquinas, *Summa theologica*, i.12.5.

ment of their desires and of their perfect happiness, to which tends, and in which is consummated, the covenant of God. There is nothing else than a certain effusion and emanation (*aporroē*) of the deity upon the souls of the saints, communicating to them the image of all his perfections, *as much as they can belong unto a creature* (emphasis added).[44]

Notice again the assumption of an essence-energies distinction: what is shared with the creature is "the image of all his perfections," not his essence itself. Thus, redemption does not make humans something more than human, nor does it simply restore them to the original status of being innocent image-bearers; rather, it transforms them into the state of glorified image-bearers that was never attained by the first covenant head. The eschatological emphasis of Irenaeus, with the consummation as something beyond a mere return to an original state, is also a crucial working assumption of covenant theology. The difference between this age and the age to come is not that God communicates himself only in the latter, but that only then "God will be seen without end, loved without cloying, praised without weariness."

> "And he will be all in all" (1 Cor. 15:28) inasmuch as he will pour immediately upon the saints his light, love, holiness, joy, glory, life and a fullness of all blessings and will dwell in them forever (Rev. 21:3). Here God in grace communicates himself to his people mediately by the word and sacraments and imparts his gifts not fully, but in part. But then he will communicate himself immediately to the saints, nor only in part but fully and wholly (*holōs*). He will be "all things" as to the universality of good things which can be required for absolute happiness and "in all" as to the universality of the subjects because he will bestow all these blessings undividedly upon all the blessed. Here belongs what is said in Rev. 21:22, 23: "I saw no temple in the city: for the Lord God Almighty and the Lamb are the temple of it. And the city had no need of the sun, neither of the moon, to shine in it: for the glory of God did lighten it, and the Lamb is the light thereof."[45]

"For since 'God dwells in inaccessible light' (1 Tim. 6:16)," Calvin reasons, "Christ must become our intermediary."[46] Even in the kingdom of glory, Christ remains the mediator and covenant head of the church, Turretin argues.[47]

In summary, Lutheran and Reformed theologies restricted the beatific vision to the consummation and distinguished even this from any *visio oculi*, "a vision of the eye, except with reference to the perception of the glorified Christ."[48] In contrast to the self's ascending, the emphasis of this version of the beatific vision falls on the Shepherd's gathering of scattered sheep in a communion of love that has been

---

44. Turretin, *Elenctic Theology*, 3:612.
45. Ibid.
46. Calvin, *Institutes* 3.2.1.
47. Turretin, *Elenctic Theology*, 2:490–94.

48. Richard Muller, *Dictionary of Latin and Greek Theological Terms Drawn Principally from Protestant Scholastic Theology* (Grand Rapids: Baker, 1985), 325.

the triune purpose from eternity. It envisions a whole creation not only restored but consummated.

There is a movement from cross to glory, from the promise heard with the ear to the vision beheld with the eye, from justification to sanctification to consummation in glorification and the renewal of the whole creation. Commenting on Ephesians 1:10, Calvin writes,

> As for this word "gather" [ESV "unite"], St. Paul meant to show us thereby how we are all of us in a state of dreadful dissipation, till such time as our Lord Jesus Christ restores us. And this has reference not only to us, but also to all other creatures. In brief, it is as though he had said that the whole order of nature is as good as defaced, and all things decayed and disordered by the sin of Adam till we are restored in the person of our Lord Jesus Christ.[49]

Even the angels are included, since all possibility for falling from their created integrity is excluded by this restoration as well. Although Jacob's vision in Genesis 28 of the ladder from heaven to earth was for mystics an allegory for the soul's ascent, Reformed interpreters recognized it as referring to Jesus Christ and his pattern of descent, ascent, and return in the flesh (Jn 1:51). "Now our Lord Jesus Christ is the true living and eternal God who touches both heaven and earth, because in his person he has joined his own divine essence and human nature together," Turretin explains.[50] Where the ascent of mind transforms Jesus-history into the soul's vision of God, the relationship between the general resurrection and glorification is left unclear.[51]

Reformed systems retained the topic of *theologia unionis* (theology of union): that is, the face-to-face knowledge of God that belongs not to a few special pilgrims on the way but to all of the glorified saints. One discerns in Calvin a strong Irenaean emphasis that is at once forensic and ontological. "Christ aggregated to his body," says the Reformer, "that which was alienated from the hope of life: the world which was lost and history itself."[52] It is not the essence of the historical person of Christ, either his deity or humanity, that is communicated to us, but his energies: life, glory, righteousness, power, light—and the communion that he has with the Father and the Spirit. Similarly, Turretin writes that this glory will be bestowed "both as to the soul as to the body," to be "enjoyed by the whole person in communion with God forever, which on this account Paul calls 'a far more exceeding and eternal weight of glory' (2Co 4:17) under which the mind is so overwhelmed that it is better expressed

---

49. John Calvin, *Sermons on the Epistle to the Ephesians* (trans. Arthur Golding; rev. ed.; Edinburgh: Banner of Truth Trust, 1973), 63.

50. Ibid., 64.

51. For fuller development of this theme, see Douglas Far-

row, *Ascension and Ecclesia* (Edinburgh: T&T Clark, 1998), from which I will draw a great deal of inspiration for the opening chapter of the next section.

52. John Calvin, *Corpus Reformatorum* (ed. W. Baum; Berlin: C. A. Schwetschke, 1863–1900), 55:219.

by silence and wonder than by eloquence."[53] It is described as light, a nuptial feast, treasures of richest gems, an estate, a garden full of fruit-bearing trees and a land flowing with milk and honey, a royal priesthood and a kingdom, an eternal Sabbath free of oppression.[54]

Therefore, this deification or glorification is not a deliverance from our body; rather, we are "'delivered from the bondage of corruption and from vanity' (Rom. 8:21)...."[55] Christ's transfiguration was a foretaste of this "weight of glory," and his resurrection its beginning.[56] Although God alone possesses immortality (1Ti 6:16), "the saints are immortal by grace from the beatific vision of God."[57] No contrast is drawn between an ostensibly immortal soul and a mortal body: both are mortal, but are raised in immortality by grace. "Now as dishonor denotes the meanness of human nature liable to various defects, so this glory will consist of a splendor and beauty of the body by which they will shine and glitter like the stars and the sun, hardly capable of being looked at by mortal eyes." Foreshadowed by Moses' face (Ex 34:29), and even more in Christ's transfiguration (Mt 17:2), "that splendor will flow both from the blessed vision of God, whom we shall see face to face, and from the glorious view of Christ exalted in his kingdom; and it will be nothing else than the irradiation of God's glory, from which the bodies will be made to shine."[58] They will be agile bodies: "vigorous, firm and strong, able to perform their duties rightly."[59] As to spirituality, "this spiritual does not refer to the very substance of the soul, as if it [the spiritual body] was to be changed into a spirit, for thus it could no longer be called a body, but a spirit." Their bodies will be "spiritual" — that is, "purged from all impurity and defilement" — not "spirit."[60] Here the Irenaean emphasis prevails over the Athanasian: just as Jesus' humanity was not swallowed by his deity, the consummation will not render us something more than human but perfectly human.

Language will even continue to characterize the society of the age to come, since "God is to be worshipped by the whole person, no less with the body than with the soul as he has commanded should be done now.... If the body no less than the soul was created and redeemed by God and is to be glorified by the same, what is more just than that this body glorified by him should glorify him both in works and in word?" Turretin also cites "the vocal language" of the doxologies in the Apocalypse and the conversation in the transfiguration.[61] With a common tongue, glorified and glorifying "in body and soul, we may in unison sing an eternal Hallelujah to him."[62]

This emphasis on the participation of the body in the new age is characteristic of

---

53. Turretin, *Elenctic Theology*, 3:612.

54. Ibid., 3:614–15.

55. Ibid., 3:618.

56. Ibid.

57. Ibid.

58. Ibid., 3:619.

59. Ibid., 3:620.

60. Ibid.

61. Ibid., 3:635.

62. Ibid., 3:637.

these Reformed writers. Similarly, the seventeenth-century divine Thomas Watson first quotes the answer to Question 38 of the *Westminster Shorter Catechism*: "At the resurrection, believers being raised up in glory, shall be openly acknowledged and acquitted in the day of judgment, and made perfectly blessed in the full enjoyment of God to all eternity." He then interprets, "Some hold that we shall be clothed with a new body; but then it were improper to call it a resurrection, it would be rather a creation. 'Though worms destroy this body, yet in my flesh shall I see God.' Job xix 26. Not in another flesh, but my flesh. 'This corruptible must put on incorruption.' I Cor xv 53."[63]

This bodily resurrection is required by the fact that believers are mystically united to Christ's flesh, which has been raised. Further,

> If the body did not rise again, a believer would not be completely happy; for, though the soul can subsist without the body, yet it has *appetitus unionis*; "a desire of reunion" with the body; and it is not fully happy till it be clothed with the body. Therefore, undoubtedly, the body shall rise again. If the soul should go to heaven, and not the body, then a believer would be only half saved.[64]

Anticipating the resurrection, then, Watson opines, "What a welcome will the soul give to the body! Oh, blessed body! When I prayed, thou didst attend my prayers with hands lifted up, and knees bowed down; thou wert willing to suffer with me, and now thou shalt reign with me; thou wert sown in dishonour, but now art raised in glory. Oh, my dear body! I will enter into thee again, and be eternally married to thee."[65] In fact, he goes so far as to conclude, "The *dust* of a believer is part of Christ's mystic body" (emphasis added).[66]

In sum, wherever the Reformed typically addressed glorification and the beatific vision, it was ordinarily in connection with the resurrection of the body, as it is throughout the New Testament epistles. Paul encourages the Philippians with these words:

> But our citizenship is in heaven, and from it we await a Savior, the Lord Jesus Christ, who will transform our lowly body to be like his glorious body, by the power that enables him even to subject all things to himself. Therefore, my brothers, whom I love and long for, my joy and crown, stand firm thus in the Lord, my beloved. (Php 3:20–4:1)

Although the soul departs the body at death, there can be no glorification of the soul apart from its reunion with the body at the end of the age.[67] Not the mere intel-

---

63. Thomas Watson, *A Body of Divinity Contained in Sermons upon the Westminster Assembly's Catechism* (repr. Edinburgh: Banner of Truth Trust, 1986), 305–6.

64. Ibid., 306.

65. Ibid., 308.

66. Ibid., 309.

67. See the quotations in Heinrich Heppe, *Reformed Dogmatics*, 695–712.

lectual vision of God (which can supposedly in some measure be attained at least by some saints now), but the bodily presence of the whole church with its glorified head in the everlasting presence of the triune God on the last day, is the emphasis that one finds in Reformed theology under consideration of this topic.

III. DEIFICATION AND THE BEATIFIC VISION AS RESURRECTION AND SABBATH

We have seen that eschatology draws together the forensic and the effective, individual and corporate, spiritual and bodily, human and cosmic aspects of salvation. This is no less true with respect to glorification.

As the firstfruits, the resurrection-justification of Jesus and his triumphal entry into the heavenly sanctuary (glorification) both ground and anticipate our justification in the present, which will be empirically verified in our own resurrection to life everlasting. Thus, the "heavenly man" (Jesus) is the eschatological person who was raised from the dead and ascended to heaven to reign at the Father's right hand. The comparison of "the man of dust" (*anthrōpos ek gēs choïkos*) and the "man of heaven" (*anthrōpos ex ouranou*) in 1 Corinthians 15 has nothing to do with the Gnostic redeemer myth, but is thoroughly eschatological. Nor is there a contrast here between Adam as a mere human being and Christ as divine. As in Romans 1:3–4, Christ's "sonship" and glory are referred not simply to his eternal deity, but in these contexts, to his Adamic role. Had Adam, in imitation of the Creator, fulfilled the "six days" of labor successfully as our covenant head, he—and all of us in Adam—would have entered triumphantly into the "seventh day" of everlasting Sabbath. In other words, glorification (at once individual and cosmic, spiritual and bodily) would immediately have followed as the judicial verdict of the last day.

The fall, however, interrupted this protological goal, so Adam—and all of us in solidarity—remained "the man of earth," except that now he was not only capable of mortality, but in actual fact sentenced to decay and death. There is no life in this covenant head, but only a poisoned stream. The second Adam, however, crossed over from death to life, from this age to the age to come, fulfilling the "six days'" probation in order to enter the "seventh-day" rest with liberated hosts in his train.[68] "Man of heaven" here is therefore the resurrected-vindicated, and therefore glorified, representative of his covenant people. Not only because he is the Son of God by eternal right, but because he is the eschatological image-son by his completion

---

68. I develop this theme more fully in chapters 4 and 5 of my *Lord and Servant: A Covenant Christology* (Louisville: Westminster John Knox, 2006).

of his commission, does his resurrection achieve a public-representative rather than simply personal character.

Jesus' resurrection was not only the divine imprimatur on the judicial work of the cross, but was itself a forensic act in its own right. Paul summarizes the Christian message as "the gospel of God, which he promised beforehand through his prophets in the holy Scriptures, concerning his Son, who was descended from David according to the flesh and was declared to be the Son of God in power according to the Spirit of holiness by his resurrection from the dead, Jesus Christ our Lord ..." (Ro 1:1–4). As Geerhardus Vos points out, Paul is not referring here to Christ's two natures but to "two successive stages in His life." His life "according to the flesh" originated from David, while his life "according to the Spirit" had its source in his resurrection from the dead.[69] Eschatology, not ontology, is the point of this particular statement of the gospel. While Jesus is the Son from all of eternity, his resurrection gives rise to "a new status of sonship" that is distinct from his essential deity.[70] As John Murray adds, Paul's point is that our conformity to Christ, which begins in sanctification, is consummated when we are actually made like him, not in his eternal deity but in the resurrection and glorification of his flesh; "the conformity embraces the transformation of the body of our humiliation to the likeness of the body of Christ's glory (Phil. 3:21) and must therefore be conceived of as conformity to the image of the incarnate Son as glorified by his exaltation."[71]

It is not surprising, therefore, that Paul later says that our adoption, by which we even now "cry, 'Abba! Father!,'" is publicly confirmed in "the redemption of our bodies" on the last day (Ro 8:15–16, 23–25). And just as our new birth, justification, and sanctification are first of all eschatological realities of cosmic significance that we are then as individuals brought into by the Spirit, the personal glorification of individuals will be a part of a wider event in which the triune God consummates the renewal of all things (vv. 19–21).

The Spirit is not waiting in the wings as the Son fulfills his mission, so that he can then work exclusively within individual believers. Paul of course speaks often about this aspect of the Spirit's work: calling believers, giving them faith, uniting them to Christ, sanctifying them, assuring them, interceding for them, and so forth. However, the work of the Spirit is seen here as being just as comprehensive in its cosmic and eschatological scope as that of the Son, and from this wider horizon everything else that accrues to individual believers is surveyed.[72]

The Spirit gives birth to the new age called into being by the Father in the Son.

69. Geerhardus Vos, "Paul's Eschatological Concept of the Spirit," in *Redemptive History and Biblical Interpretation: The Shorter Writings of Geerhardus Vos* (ed. Richard B. Gaffin Jr.; Phillipsburg, N.J.: P&R, 1980), 104.

70. Ibid.

71. John Murray, *The Epistle to the Romans* (Grand Rapids: Eerdmans, 1965), 319.

72. Geerhardus Vos, "Our Lord's Doctrine of the Resurrection," in *Redemptive History and Biblical Interpretation*, 322.

It is the Glory-Spirit by whom humanity was created as an image of the archetypal Image-Son, who declares to the entire cosmos that those whom he now clothes with bodily glory are heavenly (glorified) rather than merely earthly (created and fallen) beings. *In other words, the day of judgment is the day of resurrection: they are one and the same event.*[73] The judgment that would have been pronounced upon humanity in Adam after successful completion of the trial is pronounced upon Christ and all of those in union with him.

Nor is this found only in the Pauline corpus. Although even among the Pharisees there were various expectations concerning the nature of the resurrection and its relation to the last judgment, Jesus authorizes the expectation of rewards not at some event subsequent to the resurrection, but "at the resurrection of the just" (Lk 14:14; cf. 20:35). Those in their graves "will hear his voice and come out—those who have done good to the resurrection of life, and those who have done evil to the resurrection of judgment" (Jn 5:28–29).[74]

Offering an interpretation similar to that of Reformed exegetes, N. T. Wright and others have pointed up the judicial aspect of the resurrection as the last judgment. However, he sees this as justification itself rather than its end result, namely, glorification: "Resurrection is therefore, as in much contemporary Jewish thought, the ultimate 'justification': those whom God raises from death, as in [Rom.] 8.11, are thereby declared to be his covenant people."[75] He correctly identifies the resurrection with the judicial atmosphere of the last judgment, yet fails to recognize that justification is the "already" verdict that corresponds to the "not yet" verdict of glorification. There is no future aspect to justification itself. In justification, the believer has already heard the verdict of the last judgment. Glorification is the final realization not of our justification itself but of its effects.

Furthermore, this future event both *discloses* the true identity of the covenant people as an act of the cosmic revelation of the justified children of God (ecclesiology) and *actually transforms* the whole justified person into a condition of immortality and perfect holiness (soteriology). The great assize awaiting the world at the end of the age is therefore not with respect to justification but to glorification. All who have been justified are inwardly renewed and are being conformed to Christ's image, but their cosmic vindication *as* the justified people of God will be revealed in the resurrection of the dead. "And just as it is appointed for man to die once, and after that comes judgment, so Christ, having been offered once to bear the

---

73. See John Fesko, *The Doctrine of Justification: Understanding the Classic Reformed Doctrine* (Phillipsburg, N.J.: P&R, 2008), 299–331.

74. Only if this refers to justification is it susceptible of being interpreted as resurrection on the basis of works. However, such

passages (as well as the Olivet Discourse) merely identify the just(ified) as those who have been renewed and thus have begun even in this age to produce the fruit of the Spirit.

75. N. T. Wright, *Climax of the Covenant: Christ and the Law in Pauline Theology* (Edinburgh: T&T Clark, 1991), 203.

sins of many, will appear a second time, not to deal with sin but to save those who are eagerly waiting for him" (Heb 9:27 – 28). Through faith in Christ, the *verdict* of the last judgment itself has already been rendered in our favor, but, as our meager growth in holiness and the unabated decay of our bodies attests, the full *consequences* of this verdict await a decisive future completion. We receive our justification through believing what we have heard; we will receive our glorification by seeing the one we have heard face to face. And in that face-to-face encounter, we will be fully and finally changed, sharing in his glory.

To the very last, therefore, the forensic Word of justification reverberates throughout the entire *ordo*. "The resurrection of the dead in general, therefore, is primarily a judicial act of God," Bavinck notes.[76] The "inner person," on the basis of justification and through the organic union with Christ, is being invisibly renewed through faith day by day according to the glorious image of the exalted Son even while the "outer self" is visibly wasting away (2Co 4:16 – 5:5). On the last day, how-ever, the whole person — and the whole church — will be radiant with the light that fills the whole earth with the glory of God, and this new humanity will be joined by the whole creation as it is led by the Servant-Lord of the covenant into the day whose sun never sets. In this view, both justification and glorification are judicial verdicts resulting in transformative effects. Justification is the rendering of that verdict in the present, on the basis of which the inner renewal begins, while the resurrection of the body is the judicial investiture and enthronement of the children of God with their Son-King in glory, completing both the inward and outward renewal of all things. "Thus it is written, 'The first man Adam became a living being'; the last Adam became a life-giving spirit" (1Co 15:45).

If this is so, then the highest union that believers will ever attain with God is a gift of the resurrection on the last day, when they are raised to immortality. This *is* the last judgment, the final separation: a resurrection to death for unbelievers and a resurrection to life for those who are in Christ, clothed outwardly and inwardly with his beauty. That which has been possessed in faith will at last yield to public vision, with no more discrepancy between a perfect justification and an imperfectly realized sanctification, or between inward renewal and outward decay.

This argument that we find especially in 2 Corinthians 4:16 – 18 is elaborated in terms of the metaphor of clothing, which is a simultaneously judicial and royal image signifying both the imputation of Christ's righteousness and the imparta-tion of Christ's resurrection-immortality (5:1 – 5). "For in this tent we groan, long-ing to put on our heavenly dwelling, if indeed by putting it on we may not be

---

76. Herman Bavinck, *The Last Things* (ed. John Bolt; trans. John Vriend; Grand Rapids: Baker, 1996), 133.

found naked" (vv. 2–3). While the very distinction between inner and outer will be regarded as a Platonizing dualism by proponents of anthropological monism (i.e., physicalism), the divergence from Platonism is obvious.

No self-respecting Platonist would puzzle over the problem of being "found naked" by taking leave of the decaying body, since the flight of the soul from its fleshly prison-house *is* salvation. Yet in Paul's thinking, for the soul to be found naked is tantamount to condemnation. There is a judicial aspect to disembodied existence: it is a sign of sin and death, not of justification and immortality. If the outward renewal does not occur, then the judicial verdict has failed. It is no wonder, then, that we find the souls of the martyrs crying out from the heavenly throne, "Sovereign Lord, holy and true, how long before you judge …?" (Rev 6:10). By faith, those who have already been inwardly renewed await with confidence this clothing of the "earthly tent" with immortality. "For while we are still in this tent, we groan, being burdened—*not that we would be unclothed*, but that we would be *further clothed*, so that what is *mortal* may be swallowed up by *life*. He who has prepared us for this very thing is God, who has given us the Spirit as a guarantee" (2Co 5:4–5). Not disembodiment versus embodiment, but this body in its mortality versus this body in its immortality, is the contrast that we find here.

It is now the hour to "put off the old self" (Col 3:9) and to "put on Christ" (Gal 3:27). Like the clothing of the priests (Ex 40:14), which is already interpreted in terms of forgiveness and justification in the prophets (cf. Isa 59:6, 16; Eze 16:10; but especially Zec 3) and in the gospels (Lk 24:4; Mt 22:1–14), Christ is the garment that allows believers to appear in God's presence (Eph 6:13–17).

This connection between the judicial aspect (the last judgment) and the transformative (the last resurrection) is explicitly drawn in the passage above (2Co 5): "For we must all appear before the judgment seat of Christ, so that each one may receive what is due for what he has done in the body, whether good or evil" (v. 10). The judicial emphasis appears once more, with explicit appeal to the conscience, justification, and the forgiveness of sins through "the ministry of reconciliation" in the verses that follow (vv. 11–21). The link between justification in the present and glorification-resurrection in the future, of course, is the Spirit, who is the pledge or down payment on this final reality. By possessing the Spirit in the present, believers are assured of their final clothing (investiture) in glorification and resurrection, since it has already appeared in their justification and rebirth.

No wonder, then, that we can "consider that the sufferings of this present time are not worth comparing with the glory that is to be revealed to us" (Ro 8:18). The last judgment is a settled affair for those who are in Christ, for whom there "is therefore now no condemnation" (Ro 8:1), while even now "the wrath of God remains on" those who do not believe in Christ (Jn 3:18–21, 36). There is, therefore, an

707

already–not yet aspect to this total restoration, but not to justification and rebirth. The latter are the "already," which correspond to the "not yet" of bodily resurrection and glorification.

In this way, the believer's hope is directed not to a timeless allegory of the soul's ascent, but once again to the economy of grace—in this case, to the parousia. To reign with Christ in the future, however, we must suffer with Christ in the present. Our union with Christ is an exodus *through* the cross to a glory that is as yet dimly perceived.

By focusing on the economy of grace, the redemptive-historical events of Christ's descent-ascent-return in the flesh, as well as the descent of the Spirit to raise us with Christ, orient the beatific vision toward a corporate and corporeal future rather than to a timeless individual and intellectual encounter with the "naked God." For Jew and Gentile alike, only in Christ is Moses' veil removed (2Co 3:7–4:6). From such passages, Reformation theology has maintained that the divinization of human beings, or their participation in the glory of God, is never something to be attained by human ascent, but is a divine Word (energy) that has been spoken into our hearts and will be definitively pronounced over our bodies. It is not something that we have to go get, but something that comes to us through the Word of Christ (Ro 10:6–17). It is that light, always mediated through the incarnate Son, which has already dawned, that will be reflected in its effulgence in the consummation. We have *been justified*; we have *been given* new birth and have *been seated* with Christ; even now we are "*being transformed* into the same image [as Christ] from one degree of glory to another" (2Co 3:18). Although they give rise to human action, these are all passive verbs.

IV. The Golden Chain

I am suggesting that we view all the items in the Pauline *ordo* as constituting one train, running on the same track, with justification as the engine that pulls adoption, new birth, sanctification, and glorification in tow. "Those whom he justified he also glorified" (Ro 8:30). This means that we never leave the forensic domain even when we are addressing other topics in the *ordo* besides justification proper. Although there is more to the new birth, sanctification, and glorification than the forensic, all of it is forensically charged. Grace is never a supernatural substance infused into the soul, but the favor of God that justifies and the gift of God that renews (both *favor* and *donum*, as Luther expressed it). In addition to this grace that is equally shared by every believer, God gives varying graces (charisms) for the upbuilding of the church (Eph 4), but even these are energies or actions—most notably, speech acts—of God rather than a communication of divine essence. Instead of saying that our judicial acceptance is rooted in justification while our sanctification is grounded in an infused *habitus* of grace, the New Testament repeatedly returns to the forensic domain even in treating the new birth and sanctification. The indwelling Spirit, not an impersonal substance infused, is the source of our inward renewal and the pledge of our resurrection-glorification (Ro 8:15–25).

Yet beyond this, even the resurrection of the dead is interpreted as the consequence of a judicial verdict. Christ was raised *because death no longer has a legal claim on him* (Ro 6:9). Therefore, "the life he lives he lives to God" (v. 10). Precisely the same is true of all those who are in Christ, says Paul. In other words, he is not thinking in terms of two sources of Christ's resurrection life: one derived from his judicial vindication and another from his resurrection from the dead. Rather, the latter is simply the final, outward, and fully visible consequence of the former. This means that "the life he [now] lives … to God" is the result of his justification. His resurrection was the public unveiling in the cosmic courtroom of the forensic verdict: the last judgment begun with respect to our covenantal head, and announced to us now, even on this side of our own resurrection glory. Righteousness is "counted to us who believe in him who raised from the dead Jesus our Lord, who was delivered up for our trespasses and raised for our justification" (Ro 4:24–25). That is why Paul can refer even to glorification in his *ordo* (Ro 8:30) in the aorist tense: it is an already certain event because it is already true of its head and is therefore in principle already assured for the rest of his body.

Consistent with the broader covenantal assumptions of death as an effective power at work precisely because it is the judicial sanction for covenant breaking, Paul says that "the sting of death is sin, and the power of sin is the law" (1Co 15:56). While exercising mysterious forces well beyond the judicial sphere, into every nook and cranny of creaturely reality, death is fundamentally recognized by Paul as "the wages of sin" (Ro 6:23). Death came to everyone in Adam because of sin (Ro 5). On the other hand, the second Adam was raised from the dead because there was no legal claim that death could secure on the basis of the law. Christ's victory over the powers is predicated on the cancellation of the legal debt (Col 2:12–15). Christ *for* us is the basis of Christ *in* us, and this is the "mystery, which is Christ in you, the hope of glory" (Col 1:27).

The same Spirit who made the Word fruitful in creation and pronounced his approval, who led his people safely through the Red Sea and whose presence in pillar and cloud provided a clear judicial witness to their status, who raised Jesus from the dead and made him participate fully in the age to come as our representative head—this same testifying Spirit is now a present possession of believers as they await the last installment of the inheritance. Glorification, then, is the consummation of our union with Christ, writes Elizabethan divine William Perkins:

> In this union not our soul alone is united with Christ's soul, or our flesh with his flesh, but the whole person of every faithful person is verily conjoined with the whole person of our saviour Christ, God and man. The manner of this union is this. [A believer] first of all and immediately is united to the flesh or human nature of Christ and afterward by reason of the humanity to the Word itself, or divine nature. For salvation and life dependeth on the fullness of the Godhead which is in Christ, yet it is not communicated unto us but in the flesh and by the flesh of Christ.

It is a "spiritual union" because it is the Holy Spirit who effects it, but it is a union of the whole believer with the whole Christ.[77] As "head of the faithful," Christ "is to be considered as a public man sustaining the person of all the elect."[78] Therefore, "Glorification is the perfect transforming of the saints into the image of the Son of God."[79]

To be united to God in Christ is to be *where* Christ is (in the everlasting Sabbath) and *what* Christ is (glorified, beyond the reach of sin and death). As goes the King, so go the people; as goes the head, so go the members. This is what Reformed theology understands by glorification—and why it is so closely tied to justification in the past, sanctification in the present, and the resurrection in the future.

As we conclude this unit on soteriology, I will summarize one of the main lines of argument throughout our consideration of the *ordo salutis*. It is by situating our soteriology within a forensic ontology of the Word spoken by the Father in the Son by the Spirit—at once individual and cosmic in its result—that we get the effective and cosmic renewal in the bargain. If we reverse this relation, even the latter are left suspended in midair. To put it more succinctly, what happens *for* us is the basis for what happens *to* us and *in* us—and to reverse that order is to eventually surrender soteriology to ecclesiology or ethics without remainder.

DISCUSSION QUESTIONS

1. What is the relationship between justification, sanctification, and glorification?
2. Compare and contrast Reformed treatments of glorification with the Eastern Orthodox teaching of *theōsis* or divinization.
3. What is the connection between glorification and the resurrection of the dead at the end of the age?
4. Compare and contrast this understanding of glorification with the concept of the beatific vision.

---

77. William Perkins, "The Golden Chaine," in *The Work of William Perkins* (ed. and introd. Ian Breward; Abingdon, U.K.: Sutton Courtenay, 1970), 226–27.

78. Ibid., 227.
79. Ibid., 246.

Chapter Twenty-Two

THE KINGDOM OF GRACE AND THE NEW COVENANT CHURCH

Often, especially in evangelical circles, thinking about salvation is unrelated to thinking about the church, but this is a serious distortion of the biblical understanding of both topics. On the other hand, there is a danger at the opposite extreme of confusing the church with God as the agent of redemption. As with so many other topics, "distinction without division" is the watchword: refusing to confuse or to separate the doctrines of salvation and the church.

The same is true concerning the relationship of the kingdom of God to the church. Some Christians so stress the "kingdom living" of individual believers in the world that the church and its partial manifestation of the kingdom of God through the means of grace become subordinate. Others confuse the church with that kingdom in its fully realized form. Alfred Loisy, a modernist Roman Catholic, quipped, "Jesus foretold the kingdom, and it was the Church that came."[1] At first, the apocalyptic concept of a kingdom—especially the type of kingdom that Jesus announced—seems quite different from a historical institution extending through all times and places. Admittedly, Jesus does not often employ the noun "church" (*ekklēsia*) but refers repeatedly to the kingdom (*basileia*). Nevertheless, he

---

1. Alfred Loisy, *The Gospel and the Church* (ed. Bernard B. Scott; trans. Christopher Home; Philadelphia: Fortress, 1976), 166. Loisy continues: "She [the church] came, enlarging the form of the gospel, which it was impossible to preserve as it was, as soon as the Passion closed the ministry of Jesus." Echoing the "consistent eschatology" of Albert Schweitzer, this statement reflects the assumption that Christ was not raised, did not ascend to the seat of all rule, did not send the Spirit, and will not return in glory.

promised, "I will build my church, and the gates of hell shall not prevail against it" (Mt 16:15–18). The important question is not how many times the word *ekklēsia* is used, but whether Jesus Christ, by his words and deeds, was in fact building his church. It is clear enough from the narrative plot of the Gospels that Jesus is redefining the *qāhāl* (assembly) of Israel. Insiders become outsiders and outsiders become insiders. Not only does Jesus *describe* this; by his teaching and signs he is actually *bringing this reversal about* in his ministry. He gathers the nucleus of the new Israel (the prophesied remnant) and promises to gather other sheep from another fold into one flock under himself as one Shepherd (Jn 10 as the fulfillment of Eze 34).

To understand the distinctiveness of the kingdom in its present phase and its relation to the church, we should first recognize the differences between the *cultural mandate* and the *Great Commission*.

I. THE CULTURAL MANDATE AND THE GREAT COMMISSION

All human beings, even as fallen, remain God's image-bearers—with the original commission to rule, guard, and keep, and to "be fruitful and multiply and fill the earth and subdue it," extending God's reign with Eden as the capital (Ge 1:26–28; cf. 2:15). Often referred to as the *cultural mandate*, this original vocation given to humanity remains the source of that indefatigable impulse to build cities and civilizations, farms and vineyards, houses and empires. Every person, believer and unbeliever alike, receives a distinct vocation for his or her calling in the world, and the Spirit equips each person for these distinct callings in common grace. However, God's Word in the cultural mandate is "law": the command to subdue, rule, fill, and expand.

Only after the fall in the garden is the gospel announced, creating a new community within the human race that will be given an additional mandate: the *Great Commission*. They will subdue, rule, fill, and expand, but not by creating just governments and empires of cultural advancement—for this is now common rather than holy labor—but by Word and sacrament. Instead of dominating and subduing by sword, this community will fill the earth with God's glory by announcing the fulfillment of God's promise and his gathering of the remnant from all the nations to Zion.

With the Sinai covenant, however, God establishes a new theocratic kingdom, reuniting the cultural and cultic mandates. As God's new Adam, Israel is to drive the serpent from the garden, rule and subdue the nations occupying God's land, and establish righteousness in all the earth. Nevertheless, "like Adam they transgressed the covenant" (Hos 6:7). And yet Yahweh reissues the promise after Israel's fall: he will descend to judge and deliver. The theocracy will be dismantled (signaled by the

Spirit's evacuation from the temple, rendering it common rather than holy), and the land will be ruled by foreign oppressors, but Yahweh will again hear and answer the cries of his exiled people and send his Messiah.

In this phase of the kingdom, with the King himself present in the flesh on the earth in humiliation and forgiveness rather than power and glory, the cult and culture once again become distinct activities. The kingdoms of this age, like Rome, pursue their common vocations, and now believers are commanded by Jesus, "Therefore render to Caesar the things that are Caesar's, and to God the things that are God's" (Mt 22:21). Even oppressive rulers are "God's ministers" in the cultural sphere of our common curse and common grace as we live alongside unbelievers; we must honor and submit to these governors (Ro 13:1–7; 1Pe 2:13–17). Believers pursue their common vocations alongside unbelievers in the world with distinction in service and godliness.

At the same time, believers also pursue the aims of the Great Commission that Jesus gave to his disciples rather than to the world at large. Like Joseph and Daniel, who held positions of secular leadership during periods of exile, some believers may become rulers of state and leaders in many other cultural labors. Nevertheless, like Joseph and Daniel, they are not to confuse their cultural mandate (which they share with unbelievers) and their evangelical mandate to spread God's kingdom. While refusing to accommodate their faith and practice to the idolatry of the nations they serve, such leaders also do not seek to advance and expand God's kingdom by means of the powers that they are given as secular rulers. Christ's followers will not imitate the Gentile rulers, who "lord it over" their people, but will instead imitate the Son of Man, who "came not to be served but to serve, and to give his life a ransom for many" (Mt 20:25–28). Unlike the theocracy in Eden before the fall and in Canaan, instituted at Sinai, cult (worship) and culture (common vocations in the world) are sharply distinguished, though not intrinsically opposed. Nowhere in the New Testament is the Great Commission fused with the cultural mandate. Rather than offer a blueprint for establishing Christ's kingdom through cultural, political, or social power, Paul's instructions for daily conduct of believers in civil society seem rather modest: "to aspire to live quietly, and to mind your own affairs, and to work with your hands, as we instructed you, so that you may walk properly before outsiders and be dependent on no one" (1Th 4:11–12). *Believers and unbelievers continue to share equally in cultural vocations, by God's common grace. However, Christ's kingdom of grace is advanced in the Great Commission, by God's saving grace.*

Like the prophets (and in contrast to the false shepherds accused in Jeremiah 23 of leading the people astray by their own words from the Lord), the twelve apostles are identified as those who were "standing ... in the presence of the LORD" (cf. Dt. 29:10 NIV) and are therefore sent to proclaim his Word. Initially sent "to the lost sheep of the house of Israel," they are commissioned to "proclaim the good news, 'The kingdom of heaven has come near,'" with attending signs of Christ's victory over the powers of darkness (cf. Mt 10:5–8 NRSV). So we see already the divine authority and commission being given to Peter (representative of the disciples), the Twelve (representative of Israel), and the Seventy (representative of the whole earth, echoing the seventy included in the table of nations in Ge 10).

The similarities of the cultural mandate and the Great Commission exhibit the crucial point that grace renews rather than destroys nature. Nevertheless, it must never be forgotten that for now the new creation is planted in the midst of the old creation, and while it grows and bears fruit in this present age, it can never be identified with the kingdoms of this age until Christ decisively judges and restores at his return. In Matthew 16, Jesus tells Peter upon the latter's confession, "I will give you the keys of the kingdom of heaven, and whatever you bind on earth will be bound in heaven, and whatever you loose on earth will be loosed in heaven" (vv. 17–19). Then two chapters later we read of Jesus telling the Twelve more generally, "Truly, I say to you, whatever you bind on earth shall be bound in heaven, and whatever you loose on earth shall be loosed in heaven. Again I say to you, if two of you agree on earth about anything they ask, it will be done for them by my Father in heaven. For where two or three are gathered in my name, there am I among them" (Mt 18:18–20).

Just as Ezekiel prophesied, this will involve a judgment not simply between sheep and goats (the last judgment), but the house of Israel itself will be divided and judged as the Twelve, and then also the Seventy, fulfill their commission from village to village (Lk 10:1–20). Jesus sent the Seventy (representative of the nations) in pairs (the legal rule for witnesses). "The one who hears you," Jesus tells them, "hears me, and the one who rejects you rejects me, and the one who rejects me rejects him who sent me" (v. 16). They do not themselves exercise this judgment, but on the contrary, "the dust ... that clings to [their] feet [they] wipe off" if they are not welcomed, warning those who reject them: "'Nevertheless know this: that the kingdom of God has come near.' I tell you, it will be more tolerable on that day for Sodom than for that town" (vv. 11–12). The Seventy return to announce to Jesus with jubilation, "Even the demons are subject to us in your name!" (vv. 17), and Jesus responds, "I saw Satan fall like lightning from heaven. Behold, I have given you authority to tread on serpents and scorpions, and over all the power of the enemy; and nothing shall hurt you. Nevertheless, do not rejoice in this, that the spirits are subject to you, but rejoice that your names are written in heaven" (vv. 18–20).

In their commission, the Twelve become the undershepherds of the Great Shepherd, bearing their Suzerain's own authority. They are his ambassadors. Again, this is in contrast to the "false shepherds" of Israel — the "teachers of the law" — and this contrast with respect to the authority of their respective teachings was not lost on the people (Lk 11:52; Mt 23:1–2; Jn 8:33; Mt 11:25–26). In the heavenly worship of Revelation 7, the church militant becomes the church triumphant, sheltered by the one seated on the throne in their midst. "They shall hunger no more, neither thirst anymore; the sun shall not strike them, nor any scorching heat. For the Lamb in the midst of the throne will be their shepherd, and he will guide them to springs of living water, and God will wipe away every tear from their eyes" (Rev 7:16–17).

II. Biblical-Theological Development: Metaphors of the Church

First, I will explore the redemptive-historical development of the church by means of the rich variety of imagery employed in Scripture. Second, I will summarize various historical interpretations of the concept. Finally, I will offer some systematic-theological conclusions that will serve as road markers throughout this treatment of ecclesiology.

A. Suzerain (Lord) and Vassal (Servant)

Covenant theology has been a recurring motif throughout this volume, as I believe it to be in Scripture itself. The church (in both testaments) is the covenant assembly. Even the image of the shepherd and the sheep was already a familiar analogy for the suzerain's rule over and care for the sheep of his pasture—in other words, the various peoples under his patronage. The "rod and staff" that comfort the Psalmist (Ps 23) are like the scepter and mace ceremonially held in coronations of European royalty.

It is in this light that we recognize the prophetic announcement in Ezekiel 34, where Yahweh promises to search for his sheep himself, rescuing them "from all the places to which they have been scattered ...," bringing them out of the nations into the lush pasture of Israel's mountain heights.

> I will set up over them one shepherd, my servant David, and he shall feed them: he shall feed them and be their shepherd. And I, the LORD, will be their God, and my servant David shall be prince among them. I am the LORD; I have spoken.
> I will make with them a covenant of peace and banish wild beasts from the land, so that they may dwell securely in the wilderness and sleep in the woods. And I will make them and all the places around my hill a blessing, and I will send down the showers in their season; they shall be showers of blessing.... They shall no more be a prey to the nations, nor shall the beasts of the land devour them; they shall dwell securely, and none shall make them afraid.... And they shall know that I am the LORD their God with them, and that they, the house of Israel, are my people,

declares the Lord GOD. And you are my sheep, human sheep of my pasture, and I am your God, declares the Lord GOD. (Eze 34:23–26, 28–31)

Notice that this new security will arise entirely from the faithfulness of the Great King, who promises to bring about blessing, safety, and lavish fruitfulness after the curse has taken its toll. The imagery of wild beasts, clearly present also in the secular treaties, refers to the status of the land: safety or threat from marauders. Here Yahweh promises to drive out the wild beasts that threaten his people, although he has used these very "beasts" to scourge his people in the recent past. Finally, the goal of this arrangement—a "covenant of peace," is to restore the immediate presence of Yahweh in the midst of his people: "I will be your God, and you will be my people."

This passage no doubt forms the background for Jesus' announcement in John 10: "I am the good shepherd," where he is the fulfillment of the promise. In contrast to the false prophets, priests, and kings, "I am the good shepherd. I know my own and my own know me, just as the Father knows me and I know the Father; and I lay down my life for the sheep. And I have other sheep are not of this fold. I must bring them also, and they will listen to my voice. So there will be one flock, one shepherd" (vv. 14–16). Again, the royal overtones in this pastoral image are prominent, especially toward the end: the Good Shepherd, Yahweh's Servant David, will not only reunite the scattered sheep that previously belonged to his empire, but also gather the "other sheep" outside the fold who will also hear his summoning voice and be united together under his reign.

The human race is divided no longer between Jew and Gentile, but between those who are "in Adam" (under the covenant of law) and those who are "in Christ" (in the covenant of grace). We see this representative theme, for example, in Paul's salutation in 1 Corinthians: "To the church of God that is in Corinth, to those sanctified in Christ Jesus, called to be saints [holy] together with all those who in every place call upon the name of our Lord Jesus Christ, both their Lord and ours" [catholic and apostolic] (1Co 1:2). Believers are individually and corporately united to Christ. Thus, in 2 Corinthians 6:16–7:1, for example, "cleanness" is transferred from the ethnic to the ecclesial domain. To be "in Adam" is to belong to the covenant of works, the transgression of which means that all those represented by Adam are under bondage to sin and death. On the other hand, to be "in Christ" is to be justified, sanctified, and glorified. Romans 5, of course, draws this contrast most sharply in the New Testament (cf. 1Co 1:30).

It is within this context of covenant and its representative headship, then, that we encounter references to the church as an embassy and its ministers as ambassadors. No other foundation can be laid than the one already established by the apostles, which the ministers as their successors then build upon (1Co 3:10–11). An ambassador cannot negotiate the terms, but only convey them. The treaty is fixed—not like the law of gravity, but like the constitution of a state. It is *apostolic*. We believe, teach, and confess what we, like they, have received: this is what is meant in the confession of the "one holy catholic and *apostolic* church." Even Jesus did not bring his own word, but that of his Father (Jn 7:16; 8:26, 38), and the Spirit does not bring another Word but brings about in us the effect of that Word spoken in and by Christ (Jn 16:12–15).

With good reason, then, Edmund Clowney warns against appealing to "invisible" unity as an excuse for ignoring the visible unity (and disunity) of the church.[2] Precisely because it is already given as a gift—because, in other words, Christ himself "is our peace" (Eph 2:14), in whom "the covenant of peace" (Eze 34:25) is realized, we are called "to maintain . . . the bond of peace" (Eph 4:3). The indicative always generates, and is not generated by, the imperative. In its essence, then, catholic unity is not a human task but a divine gift. The church *is* one, holy, catholic, and apostolic: this is already an established fact, appearances to the contrary notwithstanding. The elect *are* one in Christ by virtue of the covenant of redemption, worked out by the triune God in the covenant of grace.

Even the visible church, with all of its weeds sown among the wheat, can be regarded as a unity generated by the Word and Spirit, although its eschatological unity is only as yet provisional and largely hidden. In this way, the invisible-visible distinction remains useful, but is given a more eschatological emphasis. The church triumphant is simply the church militant that has ceased from its warfare, entering God's sanctuary in worship together with the cloud of witnesses (Heb 12:1–2). Similarly, the invisible church is not a different church, but is the final form of the visible church that is known only to God and will be revealed at the last day.

B. A Missionary People

This covenantal motif is the context for the church's prophetic-missional identity as well: officers of the new covenant as covenant attorneys, bearing the authority of the Covenant Lord himself. Fortifying this shepherd analogy for this relationship is the designation of Israel as the people of God (Ex 19:4–6). The goal is covenantal presence in blessing, with God taking up his residence in their midst. "And I will walk among you and will be your God, and you shall be my people. I am the LORD your God, who brought you out of the land of Egypt, that you should not be their slaves. And I have broken the bars of your yoke and made you walk erect" (Lev 26:11–13). Yet, just as in Exodus 19, this status as the "chosen nation" is condi-

---

2. Edmund P. Clowney, *The Church: Contours of Christian Theology* (Downers Grove, Ill.: InterVarsity Press, 1995), 78.

tional, the passage just cited from Leviticus 26 is placed between a delineation of the rewards for obedience and the sanctions for disobedience.

In the prophets, even when the conditional, national covenant is broken and its sanctions invoked, the new covenant assures a different basis for security and hope, grounded as it is in God's eternal covenant of redemption and the covenants of promise with Adam and Eve after the fall and then with Abraham, Isaac, and Jacob:

> I am the LORD, your Holy One,
>   the Creator of Israel, your King....
> Remember not the former things,
>   nor consider the things of old.
> Behold, I am doing a new thing;
>   now it springs forth, do you not perceive it?
> I will make a way in the wilderness
>   and rivers in the desert.
> The wild beasts will honor me,
>   the jackals and the ostriches,
> for I give water in the wilderness,
>   rivers in the desert,
> to give drink to my chosen people,
>   the people whom I formed for myself
> that they might declare my praise. (Isa 43:15, 18–21)

Allusions to "wild beasts" becoming part of God's flock indicate the peace between Jews and Gentiles through faith in Christ.

God chose, delivered, and called Israel. "Yet you did not call upon me, O Jacob; but you have been weary of me, O Israel" (v. 22). Instead of bringing sacrifices and tributes to their Great King, "You have burdened me with your sins," God tells Israel; "you have wearied me with your iniquities" (v. 24). Nevertheless, "I, I am he who blots out your transgressions for my own sake, and I will not remember your sins" (v. 25). Yahweh declares,

> "For I will pour water on the thirsty land,
>   and streams on the dry ground;
> I will pour my Spirit upon your offspring,
>   and my blessing on your descendants.
> They shall spring up among the grass,
>   like willows by flowing streams.
> This one will say, 'I am the LORD's,'
>   another will call on the name of Jacob,
> and another will write on his hand, 'The LORD's,'
>   and name himself by the name of Israel."
> Thus says the LORD, the King of Israel
>   and his Redeemer, the LORD of hosts:

"I am the first and I am the last;
   besides me there is no god." (Isa 44:3–6)

Similarly, Hosea's prophecies begin with the covenant curses, according to which Israel as a nation is renamed *Lo-ruhama* ("she has not received mercy") and *Lo-ammi* ("not my people"; cf. ESV notes). "Yet the number of the children of Israel shall be like the sand of the sea, which cannot be measured or numbered; and in the place where it was said to them, 'You are not my people,' it shall be said to them, 'Children of the living God' " (Hos 1:6–10).

This promise echoes the oath God made to Abraham in Genesis 15. It is just such passages that the apostles had in mind when we read, for example, "But you are a chosen race, a royal priesthood, a holy nation, a people for his own possession, that you may proclaim the excellencies of him who called you out of darkness into his marvelous light. Once you were not a people, but now you are God's people; once you had not received mercy, but now you have received mercy" (1Pe 2:9–10). The elect people of God, says Paul, is called out "not from the Jews only but also from the Gentiles" (Ro 9:24), quoting our passage above from Hosea 1.

Thus it becomes clearer that we are dealing not with two peoples but with one (cf. Eph 2:11–22), and not with a displacement of Israel but with its enlargement. While the national covenant (i.e., the theocracy) has come to an end, the Abrahamic covenant, according to which all nations will be blessed in Abraham and his seed, has reached its appointed goal. Jew and Gentile in Christ form one flock with one shepherd (Gal 3:13–18, 27–29), not a replacement for the ancient people of God, but "the Israel of God" indeed (Gal 6:16). The inclusion of believing Gentiles is simply the realization of the promise made to the patriarchs and prophets: a promise to the Jews that is realized as blessing for the whole world.

As we have seen, the cultural mandate and the Great Commission are distinct. In this era of redemptive history, cultural activity is common, not holy; affirmed, preserved, and furthered through God's common grace, but not redemptive. The church, on the other hand, is the embassy of the kingdom of heaven, sent to the nations with good news.

The New Testament typically substitutes *ekklēsia* (from the Hebrew *qāhāl*, "assembly" or "gathering") for "people of God." Yet this reflects the new thing that God is doing in these last days. In Old Testament usage, Edmund Clowney notes, "The exodus redemption culminates at Sinai 'in the day of the assembly' (Dt 4:10 LXX [Septuagint]; 9:10; 10:4; 18:16).... The prophets described the future blessing of God's presence when they announced a great festival assembly that would include the Gentiles (Isa 2:2–4; 56:6–8; Joel 2:15–17; cf. Ps 87)."[3] This is anticipated

---

3. Clowney, *The Church*, 30.

in the report of Moses' final blessing on Israel before his death (Dt 33:2–3), and especially in Psalm 68:17–18, where the royal procession from Sinai to Zion is celebrated. The transition from Sinai to Zion is the procession from shadow to reality, from the promise that is heard to the fulfillment that is fully seen and possessed as a living experience, and from a national blessing dependent on Israel's obedience to universal blessing dependent on the obedience of the faithful Israel, Jesus Christ, on behalf of his people. In ecclesiological terms, it is a progression from "people of God" (as promise) to *ekklēsia* (as fulfillment). The church is the end-times gathering of the scattered sheep of Israel and the nations under the sovereign care of Yahweh the Good Shepherd.

Joseph Cardinal Ratzinger (the current pope) offers a helpful summary of this transition. Jesus proclaimed first a kingdom, not a church, he says, noting that the New Testament mentions the kingdom 122 times (99 in the Synoptics alone). At the same time, these should not be set in opposition.[4] Eschatology and ecclesiology are closely entwined: Jesus sees his own mission in terms of gathering the scattered people of God.[5] At the same time it is also crucial to remind ourselves that the same passage (John 10) in which Jesus proclaims himself the Good Shepherd of the end-times gathering of the scattered sheep underscores that the basis for this gathering is his own self-sacrifice. Not only are eschatology and ecclesiology closely entwined, therefore; both are inseparable from the atonement. Jesus did not simply come to gather a people, but to die for them. What a strange king is this, who says that, unlike the Gentile rulers, who "lord it over" their subjects, "the Son of Man came not to be served but to serve, and to give his life a ransom for many" (Mt 20:28).

"In Jesus' mouth," Ratzinger recognizes, "'Kingdom of God' does not mean some thing or place but the present action of God. One may therefore translate the programmatic declaration of Mark 1:15, 'the Kingdom of God is near at hand,' as 'God is near.' We perceive once more the connection with Jesus, with his person; he himself is God's nearness. Wherever he is, is the Kingdom."[6] The constitution of the Twelve is patterned on the twelve tribes, as the seventy "was, according to Jewish tradition (Ge 10; Ex 1:5; Dt 32:8), the number of the non-Jewish peoples of the world."[7]

> The words of the institution of the Eucharist, whether read in the Markan or in the Pauline tradition, always have to do with the covenant event; they refer backward to Sinai and forward to the New Covenant announced by Jeremiah. Moreover, both the Synoptics and John's Gospel, though each in a different way, make the connection with the events of Passover. Finally, there is also an echo of Isaiah's

---

4. Joseph Cardinal Ratzinger, *Called to Communion: Understanding the Church Today* (trans. Adrian Walker; San Francisco: Ignatius Press, 1996), 21.

5. Ibid., 22.
6. Ibid., 22–23.
7. Ibid., 25.

words regarding the suffering servant of God. With Passover and the Sinaitic covenant ritual, the two founding acts whereby Israel became and ever anew becomes a people are taken up and integrated into the Eucharist.

Christ is now the temple, the locus of this common cultic life.[8] "The institution of the most holy Eucharist on the evening before the Passion cannot be regarded as some more or less isolated cultic transaction. It is the making of a covenant and, as such, is the concrete foundation of a new people: the people comes into being through its covenant relation to God."[9]

Therefore, the transition from "people of God" to "church" is due largely to the fact that the former is eschatological, especially after the exile, with Israel anticipating a future regathering of the people of God. Ratzinger adds,

> The supplication for this gathering—for the appearance of the *ecclesia*—is a fixed component of late Jewish prayer. It is thus clear what it means for the nascent Church to call herself *ecclesia*. By doing so, she says in effect: This petition is granted us. Christ, who died and rose again, is the living Sinai; those who approach him are the chosen final gathering of God's people (cf., for example, Heb 12:18–24).[10]

The church is the place where this final, eschatological gathering of the scattered people of God occurs. Remarkably, the church is what Jews are praying for in that ancient supplication.

The covenantal ecclesiology is furthered by the emphasis on corporate solidarity in a representative head. Just as the suzerain and vassal-people are united as shepherd and sheep, king and kingdom, the people are represented to the Great King through the mediation of one of their own. It is at least in part what we should think of when we confess our faith in "one holy catholic and apostolic church"—a formula whose marvelous depths we will be exploring throughout this topic. It is not "one" or "catholic" because it is a single institution hierarchically filling the earth: that would hardly distinguish the church from a multinational corporation. The unity and catholicity of the church is derived from the person and work of Jesus Christ himself. He draws the many to and into himself by his Spirit, so that they remain (like the Trinity itself) many and yet one.

C. REMNANT

Another analogy for the church is that of remnant, which is closely related to the eschatological aspect just addressed. In the New Testament as well as the Old, the church cannot take its identity for granted but must always receive it anew in faith. Throughout biblical history, the people of God surrender their missionary

---

identity either by failing to bring God's Word to the nations or by accommodating their faith and practice to the nations to such an extent that they become virtually indistinguishable from the world. Yet God always reserves a remnant, called out of the world, to belong to him. The Word creates the church, and where this Word is received, proclaimed, taught, and applied in baptism and Eucharist, the church continues to exist and grow in this world. The remnant idea keeps us from an immanentistic and self-confident ecclesiology, with the church seen merely as a historical institution. The church's status as church is always questionable, because it is simultaneously a historical institution and the result of an eschatological irruption from heaven, by the Spirit working through the Word.

The notion of Israel being saved through a remnant is hardly a New Testament innovation. God's prerogative in election has always been upheld in redemptive history, separating not only Cain from Seth, but Ishmael from Isaac and Esau from Jacob. Therefore, it is important not to confuse the national election of Israel (conditional) with the personal election of Israelites (unconditional). This, it seems to me, is the backbone of Paul's argument in Romans 9–11. Thus, the designation "people of God" refers to a visible community identified by baptism, the proclamation of the gospel, and the Supper. It has formal offices for the administration of God's covenantal blessings. And yet, "not all who are descended from Israel belong to Israel" (Ro 9:6), and not all who belong outwardly to the people of God actually belong to God. "The Lord knows those who are his" (2Ti 2:19).

The "day of the LORD" means judgment as well as deliverance for Israel (Am 3:1, 11–15; 5:18–24), with the nation itself indistinguishable from "the Ethiopians" as far as Yahweh is concerned:

> "Behold, the eyes of the Lord GOD are upon the sinful kingdom,
>   and I will destroy it from the surface of the ground,
> except that I will not utterly destroy the house of Jacob,"
>
>   declares the LORD....
>
> "In that day I will raise up
>   the booth of David that is fallen,
> and repair its breaches,
>   and raise up its ruins
>   and rebuild it as in the days of old,
> that they may possess *the remnant* of Edom
>   and all the nations who are called by my name,"
>   declares the LORD who does this. (Am 9:8, 11–12, emphasis added)

Paradoxically, this remnant ecclesiology is simultaneously a "sifting," "pruning," or narrowing of Israel *and* an unprecedented expansion of its precincts.

On this day, Zion's sanctuary will be elevated above all other mountains, and "all the nations shall flow to it." As the "word of the LORD" goes forth "from Jerusalem," the "many peoples" will be gathered into Zion, and after the judgment of the nations there will finally be the end of war (Isa 2:1 – 4).

> On this mountain the LORD of hosts will make for all peoples
> > a feast of rich food, a feast of well-aged wine,
> > of rich food full of marrow, of aged wine well refined.
> And he will swallow up on this mountain
> > the covering that is cast over all peoples,
> > the veil that is spread over all nations.
> He will swallow up death forever;
> and the Lord GOD will wipe away tears from all faces,
> > and the reproach of his people he will take away from all the earth,
> > for the LORD has spoken.
> It will be said on that day,
> > "Behold, this is our God; we have waited for him, that he might save us.
> This is the LORD; we have waited for him;
> > let us be glad and rejoice in his salvation."
> For the hand of the LORD will rest on this mountain.... (Isa 25:6 – 10)

When this comes to pass, "Let not the foreigner who has joined himself to the LORD say, 'The LORD will surely separate me from his people'; and let not the eunuch say, 'Behold, I am a dry tree.'.... The Lord GOD, who gathers the outcasts of Israel, declares, 'I will gather yet others to him besides those already gathered'" (Isa 56:3, 8).

A remnant of the nations will be united with the remnant of Israel (Isa 60). There will be a highway connecting Egypt, Assyria, and Israel. "In that day Israel will be the third with Egypt and Assyria, a blessing in the midst of the earth, whom the LORD of hosts has blessed, saying, 'Blessed be Egypt my people, and Assyria the work of my hands, and Israel my inheritance'" (Isa 19:18 – 25). When that day comes, the people will be given true shepherds. No one will ask, "Where is the ark of the covenant?" "It shall not come to mind or be remembered or be missed; it shall not be made again. At that time Jerusalem shall be called the throne of the LORD, and all nations shall gather to it, to the presence of the LORD in Jerusalem, and they shall no more stubbornly follow their own evil heart" (Jer 3:15 – 17). Children of Israel's erstwhile enemies, even Egyptians and Babylonians, will be told that they were born in Zion and of Zion (Ps 87:1-7).

With this remnant ecclesiology in mind, John reports the "new song" in heaven addressed to the Lamb: "Worthy are you to take the scroll and to open its seals, for you were slain, and by your blood you ransomed people for God from every tribe and language and people and nation, and you have made them a kingdom and priests to our God, and they shall reign on the earth" (Rev 5:9 – 10). Jesus Christ alone is worthy to open the seals of history — the mystery of the ages — because it is in him alone that the "two peoples" have been made one.

D. FAMILY

To these analogies for a covenant ecclesiology is added the familial. Once again we encounter a familiar metaphor in ancient Near Eastern politics for the imperial lord's relationship to his people. The federation is a family, with the suzerain as the father and the vassal-people as his son—and therefore brothers and sisters to each other.

In establishing his "everlasting covenant" with David, Yahweh promises, "I will be to him a father, and he shall be to me a son." However, whereas the suzerainty treaties made this relationship conditional upon the vassal's obedience to all of the stipulations, in this covenant God pledges concerning David and his heirs, "When he commits iniquity, I will discipline him with the rod of men, with the stripes of the sons of men, but my steadfast love will not depart from him, as I took it from Saul, whom I put away from before you. And your house and your kingdom shall be made sure forever before me. Your throne shall be established forever" (2Sa 7:14–16).

In this light, Paul refers to the church as "the household of God" (1Ti 3:15), as does Peter (1Pe 4:17). There is one Father over the house, and a Son who is represented as our elder brother, legal heir of the whole estate, which he nevertheless enjoys as a public (representative) person only to dispense to his co-heirs (Ro 8:17). Once again, the traditional political and legal practices undergo modification as analogies in this new covenant relationship, since it is after all Christ who in this case is the "Son" and "heir of all things" (Heb 1:2). As he has made us his joint heirs, he has made Jews and Gentiles fellow heirs of the promises made to Abraham (Gal 3:29; 1Pe 3:7). All of those united to Christ, who is the very "image of the invisible God" (Col 1:15), are adopted as God's children (Ro 8:23; Gal 4:5), and therefore are being transformed into the likeness of Christ's image: "For those whom he foreknew he also predestined to be conformed to the image of his Son, in order that he might be the firstborn among many brothers" (Ro 8:29).

E. BRIDE

This covenantal relationship can also be expressed in terms of the marriage analogy, rooted first of all in the union of male and female, becoming "one flesh," a point that will be developed more fully in our consideration of the body of Christ. It is especially in the prophets that the marital analogy is appealed to, particularly as a way of highlighting the gravity of Israel's infidelity to the covenant. One classic example is Ezekiel 16, where God pronounces a judgment on his faithless bride. Whatever superior airs she puts on at present, Israel is reminded of her ignoble origins when Yahweh found her: "Your origin and your birth are of the land of the

Canaanites; your father was an Amorite and your mother a Hittite" (Eze 16:3). Passing by, Yahweh found her, "cast out on the open field" and "wallowing in your blood" (vv. 5–6).

> And when I passed by you and saw you wallowing in your blood, I said to you in your blood, "Live!" ... I made you flourish like a plant in the field. And you grew up and became tall and arrived at full adornment. Your breasts were formed, and your hair had grown; yet you were naked and bare. When I passed by you again and saw you, behold, you were at the age for love. I spread the corner of my garment over you and covered your nakedness: I made my vow to you and entered into a covenant with you, declares the Lord GOD, and you became mine. (vv. 6–8)

Then God bathed his bride and clothed her in the finest garments, and adorned her with the finest jewelry. God spared no expense for his bride (vv. 10–13). "And your renown went forth among the nations because of your beauty, for it was perfect through the splendor that I had bestowed on you, declares the Lord GOD. But you trusted in your beauty and played the whore because of your renown and lavished your whorings on any passerby" (vv. 14–15).

From her splendid clothes she made tents for pagan shrines, decking out her idols with the bridal jewels, showering the gifts she had been given by her husband on the gods of the nations that have no breath—even sacrificing the sons and daughters she bore in this marriage to the cruel pagan deities. "And in all your abominations and your whorings you did not remember the days of your youth, when you were naked and bare, wallowing in your blood" (vv. 16–22).

Israel differed from an ordinary prostitute only in one respect, says God: "No one solicited you to play the whore, and you gave payment, while no payment was given to you; therefore you were different" (v. 34). Samaria and Sodom have not committed half the sins that Judah did (vv. 46–51), but Yahweh will give his bride to her lovers—the Egyptians, Assyrians, Philistines, and Chaldeans, as their lust turns to violence against her. Just when it seems hopeless, the announcement comes:

> For thus says the Lord GOD: I will deal with you as you have done, you who have despised the oath in breaking the covenant, yet I will remember my covenant with you in the days of your youth, and I will establish for you an everlasting covenant.... I will establish my covenant with you, and you shall know that I am the LORD, that you may remember and be confounded, and never open your mouth again because of your shame, when I atone for you for all that you have done, declares the Lord GOD. (vv. 59–63)

Notice the distinction he makes here between "the covenant" (Sinai), which *they* made at Sinai, whose transgression is the source of their judgment, and his promise to "remember *my* covenant with you *in the days of your youth*." In other words, the Sinai covenant is the basis for their judgment; the prior covenant made with Abraham is the basis for their forgiveness. As such, it will be an "everlasting covenant"—the unbreakable, immutable, unconditional oath sworn by Yahweh.

More poignant still is the Book of Hosea, where the prophet is commanded by the LORD to marry a prostitute as a parable of the LORD's covenant relationship with Israel. Nevertheless, there is the promise: "Afterward the children of Israel shall return and seek the LORD their God, and David their king, and they shall come in fear to the LORD and to his goodness in the latter days" (Hos 3:1–5). The covenant lawsuit is prosecuted in chapter 4, listing the violations in concrete detail, with the sentence pronounced in chapter 5. Yet, as with the prophets generally, gospel follows law; hope in the everlasting covenant overcomes the despair over having transgressed the national covenant, as the one-sided, unconditional note is once again struck:

> I will heal their apostasy;
> > I will love them freely,
> > for my anger has turned from them.
> I will be like the dew to Israel;
> > he shall blossom like the lily;
> > he shall take root like the trees of Lebanon;
> his shoots shall spread out;
> > his beauty shall be like the olive,
> > and his fragrance like Lebanon.
> They shall return and dwell beneath my shadow;
> > They shall flourish like the grain;
> They shall blossom like the vine
> > their fame shall be like the wine of Lebanon. (14:4–7)

The only hope of the faithless Bride is her faithful Husband: "It is I who answer and look after you" (v. 8).

The bridal imagery is carried forward into the New Testament. The New Jerusalem is represented in John's Apocalypse as "coming down out of heaven from God, prepared as a bride adorned for her husband" (Rev 21:2), and there is the invitation to take at last the fruit from the Tree of Life and the water of life: "The Spirit and the Bride say, 'Come.' And let the one who hears say, 'Come.' And let the one who is thirsty come; let the one who desires take the water of life without price" (22:17).

Ephesians, with its rich ecclesiology, provides a corollary witness: "Husbands, love your wives, as Christ loved the church and gave himself up for her, that he might sanctify her, having cleansed her by the washing of water with the word, so that he might present the church to himself in splendor, without spot or wrinkle or any such thing, that she might be holy and without blemish" (Eph 5:25–27). In fact, the act of two people becoming "one flesh" is itself a "profound [mystery], and I am saying that it refers to Christ and the church" (vv. 31–32). Once more, the eschatological aspect must be recognized: the visible church is the *bride* of Christ;

the invisible church is his *wife*, the church as it exists on the other side of the marriage supper of the Lamb. The "already" of union with Christ must always confess the "not yet" of the nuptial wonders that yet await Christ's bride, arrayed in the precious garments and jewels he gives her.

F. CITY

The federal (i.e., covenantal-representative) imagery is supported also by reference to the analogy of a city. As the paradigmatic City of God, Eden was to expand outward from the garden itself until the glory of God filled the whole earth. This was humanity's commission in Adam. The goal of the mandate given to humanity in creation was, as Kline reminds us, "to develop his original paradise home into a universal city."[11] "In carrying out the duty of Sabbath observance, man was culturally structuring time."[12] For God, there is no time to be so structured. No more than separating space (light from darkness or the watery tempests from habitable land) does God need to separate time: all of it is filled with his glory and all of it is holy. This was also true ectypally for us in creation. After the fall, however, it became necessary to distinguish holy from common. No longer sacred, neither is the profane (or common) a territory abandoned by God. Despite its negative connotations in ordinary usage, the English word *profane* derives from the Latin compound *profano* (lit., beyond or outside the holy sanctuary).

Eden, like Adam and Eve themselves, was an earthly image of the heavenly reality, an analogue of God's home and of God's own triune communion. The Garden of Eden was a "space-sign" of the consummation; the Sabbath a "time-sign." "To be like God was not just man's duty; it was his very beatitude."[13] The fall shattered this unity of cult and culture: humanity now lived *east of Eden*, as the cherubim guarded the tree of life, barring reentry from all directions with a flaming sword (Ge 3:24). Living under a common curse, creation also shares in God's common grace, which preserves all that God has made, even those who will not finally be preserved from God's wrath on the last day. The pseudotemple of apostate civilization symbolized by Babel from Genesis 11 to Revelation 18 and 19 would be overthrown by the typological temple in Jerusalem but ultimately only by the true temple who came down from heaven to create the focus-city in himself, a true gathering that renders all such attempts of the City of Man as nothing more than crude parodies.

The goal of all biblical eschatology is that God's dwelling would be with humanity. After the fall, the cultural and cultic activities diverge into two distinct cities,

---

11. M. G. Kline, *Kingdom Prologue: Genesis Foundations for a Covenantal Worldview* (Overland Park, Kans.: Two Age Press, 2000), 70.

12. Ibid., 80.

13. Ibid., 80–81.

with Cain's line and Seth's line, respectively. Cain builds a city recognized for its cultural achievements (Ge 4:17–24), while of Seth's line we read, "At that time people began to call on the name of the LORD" (v. 26). The interaction between these two cities becomes the theater for the repeated showdowns between Yahweh and his covenant people ("the seed of the woman") on the one hand and Lucifer and his allies ("the seed of the serpent") on the other. However, Israel, too, becomes like the nations, seeking other lords than Yahweh. When the Spirit evacuates the Jerusalem temple because of the broken covenant, Judah too will be exiled east of God's city, in Babylon. The significance of the east gate in the prophets, especially Ezekiel, is its intentional parallel with Genesis 3.

The proud cities of this evil age are not irreligious, but idolatrous. Babylon's Nebuchadnezzar forced his subjects to bow down to his golden statue on penalty of death. Yet even in Judah's exile, God preserved his remnant and raised up Daniel as well as Shadrach, Meshach, and Abednego. When the latter three were thrown into the fiery furnace for refusing the Babylonian cult, a fourth person appeared with them, "and the appearance of the fourth is like a son of the gods," Nebuchadnezzar said in astonishment as he beheld a figure of the pre-incarnate Savior (Da 3:25).

Given the fact that cultural activity was part of the holy work of the cultural mandate in creation, building cities and civilizations is not inherently evil. Rather, it is the corruption of the fallen heart that erects violent, oppressive, unrighteous, and idolatrous cities that are not only properly distinct from but rivals to the City of God. Incapable of creating, Satan can only distort that which God makes, imitating God's city-building while also using his antichurch as a means of destroying the true church. We see this contest at the Tower of Babel with its sacred skyscraper attempting to conquer heaven as well as in the rivalry between Yahweh and Satan represented by Moses and Pharaoh, and in the conquest of Canaan with its holy wars in anticipation of the last judgment. Of course, this trial reaches its apogee on Good Friday, and its outcome is secured on Easter morning, yet skirmishes continue to the end of the age. Only on the last day will the cities of this world be made the City of God. Paul spoke of the church—in a way that would suggest an analogy with the cities in which his readers lived—as a "colony of heaven," especially in relation to the "body of Christ," as a confederated (covenantal) body constituted by the Spirit in the Son through Word and sacrament.

The writer to the Hebrews explains that believers have not come to Mount Sinai, but

> to Mount Zion and to the city of the living God, the heavenly Jerusalem, and to innumerable angels in festal gathering, and to the assembly of the firstborn who are enrolled in heaven, and to God, the judge of all, and to the spirits of the righteous

made perfect, and to Jesus, the mediator of a new covenant, and to the sprinkled blood that speaks a better word than the blood of Abel. (Heb 12:18–24).

Unlike the earthly cities, including Jerusalem, the heavenly city cannot be shaken. It is not a kingdom that we are *building*, but one that we are *receiving* (vv. 26–28). "For here we have no lasting city, but we seek the city that is to come" (13:14). In fact, this was true even in the case of Abraham:

> For he was looking forward to the city that has foundations, whose designer and builder is God ... These [patriarchs] all died in faith, not having received the things promised, but having seen and greeted them from afar, and having acknowledged that they were strangers and exiles on the earth. For people who speak thus make it clear that they are seeking a homeland. If they had been thinking of that land from which they had gone out, they would have had opportunity to return. But as it is, they desire a better country, that is, a heavenly one. Therefore God is not ashamed to be called their God, for he has prepared a city for them. (Heb 11:10, 13–16)

Believers are already citizens of this heavenly city, "seated ... with [Christ] in heavenly places" (Eph 2:6; see also 1Co 1:2; Gal 4:25–26; Eph 1:3; 2:5–6; Php 3:20–21; Col 1:12–18; 3:1–4).

G. THE ISRAEL OF GOD

Even with this analogy we are still in the ambit of the political metaphor of the city or commonwealth. Gentiles are told,

> Remember that you were at that time separated from Christ, alienated from the commonwealth of Israel and strangers to the covenants of promise, having no hope and without God in the world. But now in Christ Jesus you who once were far off have been brought near by the blood of Christ. For he himself is our peace, who has made us both one and has broken down in his flesh the dividing wall of hostility by abolishing the law of commandments expressed in ordinances, that he might create in himself one new man in place of the two, so making peace, and might reconcile us both to God in one body through the cross, thereby killing the hostility.... So then you are no longer strangers and aliens, but you are fellow citizens with the saints and members of the household of God, built on the foundation of the apostles and prophets, Christ Jesus himself being the cornerstone.... (Eph 2:12–16, 19–21)

"Commonwealth" and "covenants of promise" are mutually interpreting. In this holy city and nation, the people of the covenant form a commonwealth, co-heirs of everything together. Each citizen's welfare is bound up with that of the others: no one is ever left behind to fend for himself or herself. When one member suffers, the whole body politic suffers; when one rejoices, the whole commonwealth rejoices (1Co 12:26). Thus once more the federal character is emphasized: Christ as the public representative, acting on behalf of his people entrusted to his surety. As we will see, this notion of "commonwealth" is closely related to the "body of Christ" analogy and keeps the latter from slipping away from its covenantal moorings into metaphysical abstraction.

Not merely *like* Israel, as if it were a parallel to the old covenant people, this new commonwealth is the true Israel, which now includes Gentiles as well as Jews and, as Hebrews expresses the point, is no longer a mere architectural drawing or shadow (*skia*), but the city itself. This is counterintuitive, of course, since we are prone to think of the Jewish theocracy in all of its geopolitical, legal, cultic, and military visibility as real and the "heavenly Jerusalem" as shadowy. No doubt, this is why many were returning to Judaism in the face of persecution, but the writer to the Hebrews emphasizes that it is the old covenant that is a passing shadow, while the new covenant is its fulfillment.

In fact, in the spirit of the covenant lawsuit, Jesus announces that the day is coming when his hearers will claim their privileged access to his house. Nevertheless, the owner of the house will say,

> "I do not know where you come from. Depart from me, all you workers of evil!"
> In that place there will be weeping and gnashing of teeth, when you see Abraham and Isaac and Jacob and all the prophets in the kingdom of God but you yourselves cast out. And people will come from east and west, and from north and south, and recline at table in the kingdom of God. And behold, some are last who will be first, and some are first who will be last. (Lk 13:27–30)

This is why the heavenly temple has twelve gates, upon which the names of the twelve tribes are inscribed. "And the wall of the city had twelve foundations, and on them were the twelve names of the twelve apostles of the Lamb" (Rev 21:12, 14).

Just as the New Testament church is complete only as it grows out of the Old Testament church, the Israel of God attains its eschatological form only with the inclusion of the nations: "And all these [OT saints], though commended through their faith, did not receive what was promised, since God had provided something better for us, that apart from us they should not be made perfect" (Heb 11:29–40). Paul adds, "For I tell you that Christ became a servant to the circumcised to show God's truthfulness, in order to confirm the promises given to the patriarchs, and in order that the Gentiles might glorify God for his mercy" (Ro 15:8–9). "And if you are Christ's, then you are Abraham's offspring, heirs according to the promise" (Gal 3:29). The whole *ekklēsia*, then, is "the Israel of God" (Gal 6:16).

In view of these points, then, the church does not replace Israel; it fulfills the promise God made to Abraham that in him and his seed all the nations would be blessed. Of course, concerning the covenants and promises, Israel is especially blessed (Ro 3:1–2; 9:4). The unbelief of some—even many—cannot "nullify the faithfulness of God" (Ro 3:3). Yet it is precisely because of these privileges that Israel is especially judged now that the reality to which they pointed has arrived. So on the one hand, we must avoid a *supercessionism* that identifies the church as "the *new* people of God" (Vatican II), while, on the other hand, we must resist the largely Gentile growing temptation since the Holocaust to downplay the affirmation that Christ has always been the gate for his sheep in the old covenant and the new. Israel is not replaced by the church, but is the church *in nuce*, just as the church is the anticipation of the kingdom of God.

"I ask, then, has God rejected his people?" asks Paul. "By no means!" (Ro 11:1). First of all, "at the present time there is a remnant, chosen by grace," just as when, under Elijah, God reserved for himself seven thousand who did not bow to Baal (vv. 4–5). "But if it is by grace, it is no longer on the basis of works; otherwise grace would no longer be grace" (v. 6). Earlier Paul had defended the conclusion that no sinner—Jew or Gentile—will ever be justified by the works of the law (Ro 3:19–20). There are not two programs, covenants, or peoples, but one, and this one people is saved by grace alone, in Christ alone, through faith alone. Jews who try to justify themselves by observance of the law are "cut off," to make room for wild branches (Gentiles) grafted in by faith. But Gentiles are reminded that "you stand fast through faith.... So do not become proud, but fear. For if God did not spare the natural branches, neither will he spare you" (vv. 17–21). Gentile believers and churches that do not "continue in his kindness" (v. 22), forgetting that they are saved by grace, will be broken off so that some of the natural branches that had been broken off can be regrafted into the tree of Israel (vv. 23–24). In fact, Paul seems to teach that after "the fullness of the Gentiles has come in," there will be a wide-scale regrafting of ethnic Jews into Christ's body (vv. 25–32).

For the prophets, the messianic kingdom will not be a non-Jewish reality, or a way of working with Gentiles on a parallel but nonintersecting track with Jews, but precisely the fulfillment of God's promises to Israel. The only way a Gentile can belong to the elect and redeemed people of God is to be grafted onto the vine that is Israel. On the other hand, "Israel" undergoes redefinition already in the prophets. There is still enough continuity to recognize that we are talking about the concrete people of Israel, whose tents are enlarged, not replaced. Nevertheless, there is no way back to a geopolitical, theocratic Zion for Jews any more than humanity at large can return to Eden. The only way forward through the rubble of Adamic sin and death, to which Israel too has succumbed, is through Christ as the "narrow gate." Israel will be saved through an elect remnant, and although this remnant seems slight, it will be augmented by a remnant from the nations that acknowledges Israel's Yahweh as the only true God.

"In a sense," writes Jewish theologian Michael Wyschogrod, "the Christian doctrine of election is a demythologizing of the Jewish doctrine of election, which Christianity interprets as the concrete symbol of a possibility open to all people."[14] He is correct in observing that the rejection of supercessionism by Vatican II is difficult to reconcile with the Council's continuing belief that the church is "the new people of God."[15] From Wyschogrod's perspective, no consensus can ever be reached over the definition of the people of God that treats non-Jews as belonging to God's elect people, even if it is possible to conceive of them as "associate members" in some way.[16]

I think that Wyschogrod correctly perceives at this point what many Christians today refuse to confess — namely, that Jewish and Christian "ecclesiologies" are diametrically opposed. The demolition of the "dividing wall of hostility" is not accidental but essential to the mystery that the church is, according to Paul (Eph 2:11 – 3:13). In the new covenant, Gentiles are not "associate members" of Israel, as Wyschogrod argues, any more than Jews who do not believe in Christ are "associate members" of the church. In Christ, there is only one category for the true Israel: full membership in his body. At one time, Paul tells the Ephesians, Gentiles were "alienated," "strangers," "having no hope," and "without God in the world." In Christ, however, Jews and Gentiles are co-heirs through faith (Eph 2:12 – 15). Just as Jews cannot give up their exclusionary view of election and remain faithful to Judaism, Christians cannot give up their exclusionary view of election — which is also inclusionary from an ethnic perspective — and remain faithful to their canonical understanding of redemptive history centering in Christ.

Not only Paul, but the Jerusalem Council, settled this ecclesiological trajectory. Peter declares that God has given the Gentile believers the same Spirit, "having cleansed their hearts by faith," and hence "he made no distinction between us and them." "Now, therefore, why are you putting God to the test by placing a yoke on the neck of the disciples that neither our fathers nor we have been able to bear? But we believe that we will be saved through the grace of the Lord Jesus, just as they will" (Ac 15:8 – 11). Peter (and later James) appeals to the words of the prophets on this score (especially Isa 54:1 – 5; Hos 3:5; Am 9:11 – 12; Mic 5:2). Lesslie Newbigin summarizes,

> The same absolute dichotomy — either law or faith — is further pressed home in the next chapter [Gal 3]. First, like Peter at the Jerusalem conference, [Paul] appeals to the acknowledged fact that it was by "the hearing of faith" that the Spirit and all His works were made theirs (3.1 – 5). Then, he goes back behind the Mosaic law, behind even the institution of circumcision, to the verse which tells us that Abraham was accepted as righteous on the ground of his faith in the divine promise. Therefore the true son of Abraham is he who founds upon faith, and he who founds upon the law is under the curse which God pronounced upon all who do not keep the whole law.

---

14. Michael Wyschogrod, *Abraham's Promise: Judaism and Jewish-Christian Relations* (Grand Rapids: Eerdmans, 2004), 186.

15. Ibid., 184.

16. Ibid.

Law and faith are incompatibles. But Christ has accepted for us the curse of the law that we might inherit the blessing of Abraham and receive—through faith—the promise of the Spirit. (6–14)[17]

Thus circumcision (when treated as a necessary rite for covenant membership) places one within the sphere of law, which because of sin leads only to the curse, while faith in Christ places one within the sphere of the covenant of grace that God made with Abraham.[18] Circumcision counts for nothing: everything turns on faith in Christ, announced by the gospel (Ro 2:17–29).

The church that inhabits the covenant of grace can also be described by architectural metaphors. Closely related to the image of the city, the church is a building (1Co 3:11; Eph 2:20) and a temple (Jn 1:14 [lit., "the Word ... tabernacled among us"]; 2:19; 4:21–24; 1Co 3:16; 6:19–20; 2Co 6:16–7:1; Eph 2:21; 1Pe 2:4–6). A temple is where *people* and *place* come together. As Shakespeare opined, "What is the city but the people? True, the people are the city."[19] In the New Testament eschatology (as in the Old), metaphors of people and place get jumbled together.

H. BODY

Perhaps the most central metaphor in contemporary ecclesiology is the *body of Christ*. While it is indeed an illuminating image of the covenantal bond between Christ and his people, it occurs explicitly in only two passages: Ephesians 5:23 and Colossians 1:18. Our own bodies are temples of the Holy Spirit (1Co 6:19; 3:16–17), but beyond this "Christ is the head of the church, his body, and is himself its Savior" (Eph 5:23), and "he is the head of the body, the church" (Col 1:18). To be sure, this analogy is assumed in other places where the church is called the body of Christ (1Co 12:12; Eph 1:23; 3:6; 4:4, 12; Col 3:15), but they occur only in the Pauline corpus.

This is not to diminish the significance of this image, but to caution against treating it as the all-encompassing and all-controlling ecclesiological analogy. Even this important image is itself subservient to the covenantal context that animates and grounds all of the other analogies. In his *Models of the Church*, Avery Cardinal Dulles rightly notes that Scripture provides images of the church more than straightforward definitions.[20] In fact, Paul Minear's *Images of the Church in the New Testament* lists ninety-six images.[21] What we have, then, are models—analogies.[22] It is important to allow all of the analogies to interpret each other, like a kaleidoscope, rather than reduce them to a single image. For example, notes Dulles,

17. Lesslie Newbigin, *The Household of God: Lectures on the Nature of the Church* (London: SCM Press, 1953), 40.

18. Ibid., 42.

19. William Shakespeare, *Coriolanus* (ed. G. Blakemore Evans; Boston: Houghton Mifflin, 1974), 3.1.198–99.

20. Avery Dulles, SJ, *Models of the Church* (Garden City, N.Y.: Doubleday, 1974), 17.

21. Paul Minear, *Images of the Church in the New Testament* (Philadelphia: Westminster, 1960).

22. Dulles, *Models of the Church*, 21–30.

organic models are richly illuminating, but "fail to account for the distinctively interpersonal and historical phenomena characteristic of the Church as a human community that perdures through the generations. Thus societal models, such as that of God's People on pilgrimage, are used to supplement the organic meta-phors."[23] Rather than derive our entire ecclesiology from one image, Dulles advises, we should follow the New Testament itself in the vitality of its multiple analogies.[24] Even the analogy of the body of Christ, if taken exclusively and literally, leads "to an unhealthy divinization of the Church," as if the union "is therefore a biological and hypostatic one" and all actions of the church are *ipso facto* actions of Christ and the Spirit.[25] In fact, Dulles observes, like other analogies (such as "people of God"), "The root of the metaphor is the kind of treaty relationship into which a suzerain state entered with a vassal state in the ancient Near East. That kind of military and political treaty afforded the raw material out of which the concept of 'People of God' was fashioned."[26] Therefore, instead of assimilating the covenantal metaphors to an exaggerated notion of the body of Christ, this image itself must be interpreted in relation to the more basic paradigm of covenant.

The meaning of the "body of Christ" metaphor is to be found not in meta-physics but in the concrete historical context in which it was given, and since it is found explicitly only in the Pauline corpus, we must begin with his own assump-tions, which were derived chiefly from his Jewish background, but also from the Gentile world. Paul no doubt also had some familiarity with Greco-Roman law, and we should not be embarrassed by the similarities between his argument in 1 Corinthians 12 and Stoic political philosophy. Challenging the divisiveness in the Corinthian church, Paul insists that the church is one body with one head but many members or parts. To be sure, this unity is not (as in any secular *polis*) merely a voluntary association or hereditary fate, but a living unity brought about by baptism into one body by the Spirit (vv. 12–13). The foot cannot prefer to be the hand; the ear should not think that because it is not an eye it does not belong to the body, and so forth. "As it is, there are many parts, yet one body" (vv. 17–20). Just as a Greek or Roman philosopher would have said concerning the *polis*, Paul insists, "If one member suffers, all suffer together; if one member is honored, all rejoice together. Now you are the body of Christ and individually members of it" (vv. 26–27). In this *polis*, God has appointed various offices with differing ministries (vv. 27–31). For precisely this reason, those who abuse the Lord's Supper as an occasion for dis-sension and division along socio-political, economic, ethnic, or sectarian lines are eating and drinking unworthily, "without discerning the body," and therefore are incurring judgment (1Co 11:17–22, 27–34). Once we see this Supper as a covenant

23. Ibid., 22–23.
24. Ibid., 29–30.

25. Ibid., 51.
26. Ibid., 50.

renewal meal, the body of Christ analogy comes increasingly to be recognized in this covenantal light, as an organic metaphor that is itself allied to a political one.

If the church is not simply another republic, like Athens or Rome, it is not because the "body" analogy is metaphysical rather than political; rather, it is because the head of this body is Christ and the Spirit has baptized each member into him. Thus, this holy commonwealth exceeds common communities by virtue of the fact that it alone is elected by the Father in the Son through the work of the Spirit. It is held together by the sinews of covenantal love (Heb. *ḥesed*/Grk. *agapē*), not simply of friendship (*philia*); it is the fellowship of brothers and sisters (a family) and not simply of neighbors who share the same racial, ethnic, national, socio-economic, or cultural affinities.

So the body of Christ analogy should be restricted to its own proper bounds. The body that Jesus offered in the upper room and on the cross is a literal rather than metaphorical body. The church is Christ's body in an analogical yet no less real manner. In addition to 1 Corinthians 11, this analogy appears in the following passages: (1) Believers "are one body in Christ" (Ro 12:5); (2) Each believer's body is "a temple of the Spirit" and a "[member] of Christ" (1Co 6:15, 19); (3) All believers are "baptized into one body" (1Co 12:13); (4) The church "is his body" (Eph 1:23); (5) "There is one body and one Spirit — just as you were called to the one hope that belongs to your call — one Lord, one faith, one baptism, one God and Father of all, who is over all and through all and in all.... Rather, speaking the truth in love, we are to grow up in every way into him who is the head, into Christ, from whom the whole body, joined and held together by every joint with which it is equipped, when each part is working properly, makes the body grow so that it builds itself up in love" (Eph 4:4–6, 15–16); (6) Christ is "the head of the body, the church" (Col 1:18; cf. Eph 5:32).

Although the letter to the Ephesians is hardly a systematic ecclesiology, the mystery of the church lies at its heart. Union with Christ (soteriology) and communion with his body (ecclesiology) form an integral pattern throughout this epistle. Chosen in Christ, redeemed in Christ, sealed in Christ by the Spirit, the church is the one place where worldly divisions no longer take place. A new division to end all rival divisions has occurred: being on the inside of God's kingdom, with free access to the tree of life, is determined by participation in Christ's body, regardless of whether one is a Jew or a Gentile. Then in chapter 4, Paul links this ecclesiology to the ascension of Christ, as the source of the gifts that he now pours out lavishly by his Spirit to his saints through the ministry of Word and sacrament. It is this ministry alone that creates, sustains, unites, and brings maturity to the body of Christ. In chapter 5, Paul says that Christ is one with his body (the church) in a way that is similar to the union of husband and wife as "one flesh."

From this we may surmise that the unity of head and members is not a *fusion of essences*, assimilating the diversity of persons to the unity of a corporate entity, but a *communion of persons* who in all of their differences from each other form one body. This underscores the fact that this relationship is willed "from above," as Ratzinger observed:

> The origin of the Church is not the decision of men; she is not the product of human willing but a creature of the Spirit of God. This Spirit overcomes the Babylonian world spirit. Man's will to power, symbolized in Babel, aims at the goal of uniformity, because its interest is domination and subjection; it is precisely in this way that it brings forth hatred and division. God's Spirit, on the other hand, is love; for this reason he brings about recognition and creates unity in the acceptance of the otherness of the other: the many languages are mutually comprehensible.... The spirit of the world subjugates, the Holy Spirit opens.[27]

Thus far we can see that there is no sharp line to be drawn between federal/legal and organic/relational imagery in a covenantal ecclesiology. One simply cannot pit the former against the latter in the doctrine of the church any more than in soteriology. While they should be distinguished, they cannot be separated.

To be "in Christ" is to be justified and sanctified; to enjoy a new status and a new life; to receive a unilateral divine gift and to produce the fruit of thanksgiving and joy in worship to God and service to neighbor. It is to enjoy everything together with Christ as his co-heirs and to suffer everything together as well. Thus the body of Christ analogy serves to amplify the same covenantal ecclesiology as the other images: Vine and branches, tree and fruit, a temple made up of living stones, a city, a bride adorned in wedding garments for her husband, the pilgrim people of God, the Israel of God, and the colony of heaven in this passing evil age.

Ratzinger has devoted much of his life to this subject. He properly challenged the evaporation of ecclesiology in existentialist theologies, especially via Bultmann. "Such a Jesus, who repudiates cultic worship, transforms religion into morality and then defines it as the business of the individual, obviously cannot found a church. He is the foe of all institutions and, therefore, cannot turn around and establish one himself."[28] Yet it is increasingly recognized that Jesus of Nazareth cannot be understood apart from the church he founded.[29] In the wake of liberation theology and its "dialectical model, the 'popular Church' is pitted against the institutional or 'official Church.'"[30]

However, the body of Christ is not patterned on liberal democracy but on the covenantal monarchy of the triune God. The people of God thus gathered form the church. "In all places it is the gathering of this one."[31] It is the body of Christ.

27. Ratzinger, *Called to Communion*, 43.
28. Ibid., 15.
29. Ibid., 16, referring to F. M. Braun, *Neues Licht auf die Kirche. Die protestantische Kirchendogmatik in ihrer neuesten*

Entfaltung (Einseideln: Verlagsanstalt Benziger, 1946).
30. Ibid., 19.
31. Ibid., 32.

To be sure, there are echoes of Stoic conceptions of the body politic (especially 1Co 12:17–26), notes Ratzinger.

> However, Saint Paul's conception of the Body of Christ does not exhaust itself in considerations of sociology or moral philosophy such as these.... The Platonic idea that the entire world is *one* body, one living being, was developed in Stoic philosophy, where it was associated with the belief that the world was divine.... But the real roots of the Pauline idea of the Body of Christ are entirely inner-biblical.... In the first place, the Semitic conception of the "corporate personality" stands in the background; this conception is expressed, for example, in the idea that we are all in Adam, a single man writ large. In the modern era, with its apotheosis of the subject [individual], this notion became entirely incomprehensible. The "I" was now a fortified stronghold with impassable walls. Descartes' *"cogito"* — because only the "I" still appeared accessible in any way — is typical in this regard. Today the concept of the subject is gradually unraveling; it is becoming evident that the "I" locked securely in itself does not exist but that various influences pass in and out of us.[32]

So far, a covenantal ecclesiology is in wholehearted agreement. Yet precisely because the roots of Paul's "body of Christ" understanding are "entirely inner-biblical," they are no more susceptible to an Idealist notion of "corporate personality" than to Stoic political philosophy.

In contrast to the federal (or covenantal) view of a corporate body, Ratzinger's adoption of the idea of a "corporate personality" (especially from Fichte, Hegel, and Schelling) dissolves the many into a metaphysical unicity. It was this philosophy that spoke of individuals sacrificing themselves for the whole, contributing to disastrous consequences in German culture in the early twentieth-century. In Ratzinger's explanation of this mystery, the union that the Eucharist creates "means the fusion of existences, just as in the taking of nourishment the body assimilates the foreign matter to itself...." In precisely the same way, "my 'I' is 'assimilated' to that of Jesus...." Consequently, all who partake of Communion are "assimilated to this 'bread'...."[33] However, Paul's use of the body of Christ analogy nowhere compares communicants with foreign matter assimilated into the body; rather, they are regarded as parts of the body: hands, legs, eyes, noses, mouths, and ears. There is no fusion or assimilation, but a unity that preserves difference.

III. Ecclesiologies in Historical Perspective

Meeting at first in the temple, synagogues, and private homes (Ac 2:46), each local expression of the church was constituted as "church" both by the people who

---

32. Ibid., 35.

33. Ibid., 37.

were gathered (i.e., the saints) and by the actions that occurred in that place: "They devoted themselves to the apostles' teaching and the fellowship, to the breaking of bread and the prayers" (Ac 2:42). While the apostles were living, they could be appealed to by ordinary pastors and elders to settle the various divisions that erupted over doctrine and practice. As a result of the rise of various heresies, the church increasingly stressed the importance of the visible institution and the outward discipline of the church in the form of bishops who now ruled over groups (presbyteries) of local churches rather than over particular congregations.

A. Ecclesiology in the Ancient Church

In reaction to the growing worldliness of the church, especially alliance with imperial power, various sects in the second through the fourth centuries (Montanism, Novatianism, and Donatism) identified the true church not with its visible order but with the holiness of its members.[34] Cyprian, a North African bishop and martyr during a revived Roman persecution in the mid-third century, responded sharply to sectarians, heretics, and members who offered the required sacrifice to Caesar and the gods to preserve their life. In his *De unitate ecclesiae* (*On the Unity of the Church*), he famously wrote, "He can no longer have God for his Father who has not the Church for his mother; ... he who gathereth elsewhere than in the Church scatters the Church of Christ"; "nor is there any other home to believers but the one Church."[35] Like Rome, Eastern Orthodoxy claims to be the one true church and locates its authenticity in the succession of bishops, although the latter denies the primacy of any bishop over the others.

Augustine developed the concept of the church as the company of the elect, known fully only by God, though in its present form it is a "mixed body," with goats among the sheep. Augustine therefore distinguished between the invisible church (the communion of the elect) and the visible church (identified by apostolic succession). In his debate with the Pelagians, he emphasized the invisible church, while his confrontation with Donatism led him to stress that the visible church is identified by its historic succession of bishops from the apostles. Perhaps the most important legacy of Augustine with respect to ecclesiology is his concept of the *totus Christus*: the whole Christ, which refers not only to the one person, Jesus Christ, but to the union of Christ with his church.[36] As we will see, this idea is affirmed across widely varying ecclesiologies, with quite different interpretations.

---

34. Especially the last two groups denied readmission of members who had "lapsed" (i.e., recanted their faith) during persecution. After Augustine's thorough rebuttal, Donatism has been charged with making the validity of the church's ministry to depend on the holiness of the officers who perform it.

35. Cyprian, *On the Unity of the Church* 6 and 9 (vol. 5, *ANF*).

36. *The Anti-Donatist Works of St. Augustine*, NPNF1, vol. 4.

B. THE SHAPING OF MEDIEVAL ECCLESIOLOGY

Whereas the East has always regarded the church as the whole communion of saints (clergy and laity), gifted by the diverse graces (charisms) of the Spirit, the West increasingly adopted a more centralized hierarchy that reflected the organization of secular institutions (especially feudal-imperial politics). The elevation of one bishop over others, which had been opposed in the West as well as the East, became repeatedly asserted by the Roman bishops already in the early medieval era. In the fifth century, Innocent I defended papal supremacy over the whole church, and later in that century the dispute between Gelasius I and the Byzantine emperor anticipated the further claim that Roman bishops would make to supremacy over the state as well as the church.

An allegorical interpretation of the Old Testament narratives identified Christendom with Israel. Emperors, kings, and knights revived the image of David and his noble warriors, driving the Canaanites from the Holy Land. The *totus Christus* ("whole Christ") now encompassed European civilization, which together with the church was called the body of Christ (*corpus Christianum*). At the same time, the hierarchical ranking of a feudal society was mirrored in the orders in the church. In the fifth century Pseudo-Dionysius, an anonymous theologian writing under the name of a convert of Paul's at his famous speech in Athens named in Acts 17, brought Christian Neoplatonism to its zenith with his speculations concerning the celestial and ecclesiastical hierarchy.[37] Few had as great a hand in shaping medieval thought (including Thomas Aquinas) as Dionysius. Increasingly, the church was conceived as a ladder from heaven to earth, the visible replacement for its absent Lord, whom the church could *make present* in the Mass and whose presence the church could control. The ecclesial hierarchy was an image of Neoplatonism's ontological hierarchy.

Reflecting the superiority of the soul over the body and of grace over nature, the church was identified especially with the clergy: from its head (the pope) down to the magisterium, bishops, and the rest of the clergy (priests and monks). Nature's inferior sphere was occupied by the laity, most of whom could not understand the words of the Latin Mass and none of whom could receive Communion except for the bread. The higher life (supernatural) was attained by keeping the "evangelical counsels" — requiring celibacy, contemplation, and monastic vows — while the ordinary (natural) life of lay Christians involved marriage, family, and secular vocations. The distinct grace infused through the sacrament of ordination was believed to communicate a

---

37. He is also known as Dionysius the Pseudo-Areopagite as well as St. Denis. See Paul Rorem, *Pseudo-Dionysius: A Commentary on the Texts and an Introduction to Their Influence* (New York: Oxford Univ. Press, 1993); Eric D. Perl, *Theophany: The Neoplatonic Philosophy of Dionysius the Areopagite* (Albany, N.Y.: SUNY Press, 2007).

new ontological identity and status to priests, distinguishing them from the laity not only in office and function but in their elevated essence.[38] Strictly speaking, "the Church" refers to the pope and magisterium (and to the lower clergy who represent them)—what Rome calls the *ecclesia docens* (the church that teaches).

As the soul is higher than the body, and grace is above nature, it was argued (for example, by Hugh of St. Victor), the church—with the pope as its earthly head—is above the state.[39] Papal supremacy, even over the whole church, much less the state, was contested at various points throughout the Middle Ages, but ultimately protests ended in failure.[40] Along with other long-standing differences, the assertion of papal supremacy led to the Great Schism between Eastern and Western Christendom in 1054.

In the ancient and early medieval era the church was understood as the mystical bride and body of Christ, but there was a clearer distinction between the *natural* body of the ascended Christ, the *eucharistic* body (the bread in the Supper) and the *ecclesial* body (the visible church): the so-called *corpus triforme* (threefold body). Robert A. Krieg observes,

> It was only in the late Middle Ages that the notion of the church as an institution gained prominence. In his bull Una Sanctam (1302) Pope Boniface VIII took it for granted that the church is an organization with binding legal powers over both individuals and civil states. Later, in response to the Reformation, the Council of Trent (1545–63) conveyed an institutional ecclesiology in the juridical language of its doctrinal and disciplinary decrees.[41]

Thus the church became a legal institution invested with authority over the "treasury of merits," to dispense salvation and exercise authority over all souls and bodies. Robert Bellarmine, a staunch defender of Trent, declared, "The one and true Church is the community of men brought together by the profession of the same Christian faith and conjoined in the communion of the same sacraments, under the government of the legitimate pastors and especially the one vicar of Christ on earth, the Roman pontiff."[42]

Though tempered by other images, this view of the church as a universal legal institution, with power over the souls and bodies of all people, has never been withdrawn.

---

38. See the *Catechism of the Catholic Church* (Liguori, Mo.: Liguori Publications, 1994), 395–99.

39. One notable test of papal supremacy over Christendom came when Emperor Henry IV was excommunicated and deposed by Pope Gregory VII. The pope eventually lifted the excommunication but left the deposition in place.

40. "Gallicanism" sought to lodge authority in the bishops and the king of France, anticipating the more radical "Anglicanism" of Henry VIII. In defiance of Pope Innocent XI, Louis XIV and the French bishops asserted that church councils

supersede papal decrees and that monarchs are independent of papal authority.

41. Robert A. Krieg, in his introduction to Karl Adam, *The Spirit of Catholicism* (trans. Dom Justin McCann; New York: Crossroad, 1924; repr., 1977), ix.

42. Ibid., ix–x, quoting Robert Bellarmine, "De definitione ecclesiae," cap. 2 in *De ecclesia militante* (tom. 2, liber 3 of *De controversiis christianae fidei adversus haereticos*; Roma: Typographia Bonarum Artium, 1832-1840), 75.

C. ROMAN CATHOLIC ECCLESIOLOGIES IN THE MODERN ERA

In the early nineteenth century, Johann Adam Möhler (1796–1838) advocated a more organic ecclesiology. His disciple, Karl Adam (1876–1966), led a more wide-scale transformation from a view of the church as a legal organization, in accordance with the Council of Trent, to a more organic (church-as-community) and pneumatological perspective.[43] This trajectory became known as "reform Catholicism." Möhler wrote, "Thus, the visible Church ... is the Son of God, everlastingly manifesting himself among men in a human form, perpetually renovated, and eternally young—the permanent incarnation of the same."[44] Like Hegel and Schleiermacher, Möhler and Adam saw the relation of the kingdom of God and the church in terms of an oak and acorn—not a mechanical but an organic relation.[45] The chief goal of the church, Adam argued, was for all professing believers to return to the Church of Rome in order "to create a new spiritual unity, a religious centre, and so to prepare *the only possible foundation for a rebuilding and rebirth of Western civilization.*"[46] Not only the kingdom, but Christ's personal existence, became identical with the Roman Catholic Church.

Far from challenging the displacement of Christ by the church and of the Spirit by an *ex opere operato* notion of the sacraments, the organic analogy only deepened the conviction that the Roman Catholic Church is simply "the realisation on earth of the Kingdom of God."[47] "Christ the Lord is the real self of the Church." The church and Christ: "one and the same person, one Christ, the whole Christ."[48] With Karl Adam we discover the roots of a Hegelian version of Augustine's notion of *totus Christus* that has come to dominate not only Roman Catholic but many Protestant ecclesiologies of late. The church is "the incarnation of Christ in the faithful," he said.[49]

The less one-sidedly one is focused on the church as a legal institution, the reforming ecclesiology does not fundamentally alter the principles of traditional dogma but even heightens the priority of unity over plurality, the whole over its different parts. Thus Augustine's *totus Christus* became not only the unity of Christ as head *with* his body but Christ *as* his body. Even the distinct personal identity of Jesus Christ is submerged in the visible church with the pope as its visible head.

John Paul II reiterated these commitments during his own pontificate, especially

---

43. Johann Adam Möhler, *Symbolism, or, Exposition of the doctrinal differences between Catholics and Protestants* (trans. J. R. Robertson; New York: Edward Dinigan, 1944), on the church: chs. 5–6.

44. Ibid., ch. 5, par. 46–48.

45. Karl Adam, *The Spirit of Catholicism* (trans. Dom Justin McCann; New York: Crossroad, 1924; repr., 1977), 2.

46. Ibid., 6, emphasis added.

47. Ibid., 14.

48. Ibid., 15.

49. Ibid.

in *Dominus Iesus*: "The Catholic faithful *are required to profess* that there is an histori-cal continuity — rooted in the apostolic succession — between the Church founded by Christ and the Catholic Church.... 'This Church, constituted and organized as a society in the present world, subsists in [*subsistit in*] the Catholic Church, governed by the Successor of Peter and by the Bishops in Communion with him' [*Lumen gentium*, 8]." With respect to those bodies outside of this jurisdiction, "'they derive their efficacy from the very fullness of grace and truth entrusted to the Catholic Church' (*Unitatis redintegratio*, 3)." While churches retaining "the valid Episcopate" and "a valid Eucharist" (i.e., Eastern Orthodox bodies) "are true particular churches" that do not yet exist "in perfect communion with the Catholic Church," others "are not Churches in the proper sense," although their baptism qualifies them for "a certain communion, albeit imperfect, with the Church."[50] Echoing the language of Möhler and Adam, the encyclical adds that the church is "called to announce and to establish the kingdom," church and kingdom being related as a seed to a fully mature tree.[51]

While affirming that the fullest realization of the kingdom of God lies up ahead, *Dominus Iesus* is critical of recent theologies that regard the church merely as its sign. "These theses are contrary to Catholic faith because they deny the unicity of the relationship which Christ and the Church have with the kingdom of God."[52] Members of other religions may truly receive saving grace, but do not have "the fullness of the means of salvation."[53] Therefore, we see that in this perspective the church is really the totality of humanity, in varying degrees of communion with the one, true Catholic Church.

At the First Vatican Council (1869–1870) the dogma of papal infallibility was officially promulgated. With the Second Vatican Council (1959–1965) a less reactionary spirit prevailed, and the consequence was a much fuller and more biblically informed doctrine of the church. Not only conceived as a hierarchically determined juridical organization, the church was also to be seen as the people of God. Nevertheless, these elements are refinements and elaborations of the traditional self-understanding of Roman Catholicism as the one true visible body of Christ with the pope as its earthly head. Rome continues to assert papal supremacy over the entire church. According to the recent *Catechism of the Catholic Church*, "the Roman Pontiff, by reason of his office as Vicar of Christ, and as pastor of the entire Church has full, supreme, and universal power over the whole Church, a power which he can always exercise unhindered."[54] Christ's flock is one only "in so far as it is assembled under one head" who "enjoys this infallibility in virtue of his office...."[55]

50. John Paul II, *Dominus Iesus* (Boston: Pauline Books and Media, 2000), 11 of 21, citing *Mysterium Ecclesiae*, 1.

51. Ibid., 12 of 21.

52. John Paul II, *Dominus Iesus*, 13 of 21.

53. Ibid., 14 of 21.

54. *Catechism of the Catholic Church*, 234.

55. Ibid., 234–35.

Another important contribution to contemporary Roman Catholic ecclesiology has come from Hans Urs von Balthasar, especially in his *Church and World* (1967). Emphasizing that individual Christians are part of one body because they are "*his* members, and not actually members of the Church," von Balthasar advanced an ecclesiology that was christocentric.[56] In fact, he added, "There can be no ecclesiology which is not, at its core, Christology."[57] Nevertheless, the Hegelian version of the *totus Christus* is dominant, allowing Christology to be assimilated to ecclesiology. Particular persons — including Jesus Christ — are surrendered to the whole:

> In fact, this violent, this often "crucifying" sacrifice of the pious subject to the ecclesial object (that is what Schleiermacher and Hegel call "community-consciousness") is, ultimately, one of the conditions for the presence of the Eucharistic Lord: "Where two or three are gathered together …" — that is, where individuals, in profound faith and obedience, desire to be and to realize the Church — "there I am in the midst of you."[58]

The acorn-and-oak analogy is not far from von Balthasar's mind when he writes,

> The Church is, at one and the same time, the redeemed world in course of becoming and Christ's instrument for the full redemption of the world. Consequently, the individual member of the Church in time is not, actually, functional as regards the Church, as if it were the executive bearer of this function. He is, rather, functional in and with the Church as a whole … for charity fills all functions, not as if they were something disparate to it, but as its own living organs, distinct one from the other.[59]

These contributions give us a taste of contemporary Roman Catholic ecclesiology at first hand.

As Cardinal Dulles shows, a variety of metaphors and models have been employed over the last century. Shifting from the societal model to the Mystical Body and, after Vatican II, to the People of God and the Sacrament of Christ, each reflects the emphasis of a different era.[60] The World Council of Churches at its Uppsala Assembly in 1968 echoed Vatican II: the church is "the sign of the coming unity of mankind."[61] Today, there is also much discussion in Roman Catholic theology of the church as Servant and Healer. "People of God" seemed more relevant in a democratic age, just as "the Servant Model has become popular because it satisfies a certain hunger for involvement in the making of a better world — a hunger that, although specifically Christian in motivation, establishes solidarity between the Church and the whole human family."[62]

---

56. Hans Urs von Balthasar, *Church and World* (trans. A. V. Littledale with Alexander Dru; Montreal: Palm Publishers, 1967), 20.

57. Ibid., 23.

58. Ibid., 32.

59. Ibid., 107–8.

60. Dulles, *Models of the Church*, 15, 27, 59, 66.

61. Cited in ibid., 70.

62. Ibid., 27–28.

In spite of their diversity, each of these models continues to advance the thesis that the visible church (identified fully with the Church of Rome), in the words of Henri de Lubac, "really makes [Christ] present," and that she "not only carries on his work" but "is his very continuation...."[63]

D. REFORMATION ECCLESIOLOGIES

For Lutheran and Reformed ecclesiologies Cardinal Dulles selects "The Church as Herald" as the most appropriate identification.[64] Through its official and public ministry of preaching, teaching, administering the sacraments, all of the saints become witnesses to Christ. In fact, all of the church's activity is oriented to this mission of heralding Christ. The church has its own origin and daily existence solely through the power of this Word, but this means that the church must live for others and not only for herself. It is in heralding Christ to all people, including the church's own children, that the church itself continues to live. Luther's ecclesiology was also marked by his emphasis on the priesthood of all believers, the church as a mixed assembly whose visibility resides exclusively in Christ's presence in preaching and sacrament, and the right of the civil government to determine the ecclesiastical confession and worship in its jurisdiction.

Lutheran and Reformed ecclesiologies share many common themes and emphases, but Veli-Matti Kärkkäinen aptly labels the latter "The Church as Covenant."[65] Rome locates the unity, catholicity, and apostolicity of the church in the historical institution that is led by the bishops in obedience to the pope. Eastern Orthodoxy finds it in the Eucharist, which presupposes apostolic succession of bishops (without the additional commitment to a primal see). Free churches identify it with the heart of the individual believer. However, the churches of the Reformation lodge this unity, catholicity, and apostolicity in the preaching of the gospel and the administration of the sacraments. In this way, they refuse to locate the essence of the church in a sheer objectivity of an ostensibly infallible and indefectible institution or in the subjectivity of individual response.

This means that, for the Reformed, the church is not merely the sum total of the children but is also the mother of her children, as Calvin says, endorsing Cyprian's dictum above. "Our weakness does not allow us to be dismissed from her school until we have been pupils all our lives. Furthermore, away from her bosom, one cannot hope for any forgiveness of sins or any salvation."[66] Calvin opposed the "pure church" ideal of the Anabaptists as firmly as he did Rome's absolutism.[67] "Now

---

63. Henri de Lubac, *Catholicism* (London: Burns, Oates, and Washbourne, 1950), 29.

64. Dulles, *Models of the Church*, 68–80.

65. Veli-Matti Kärkkäinen, *An Introduction to Ecclesiology: Ecumenical, Historical, and Global Perspectives* (Downers Grove,

Ill.: InterVarsity Press, 2002), 50–58.

66. Calvin, *Institutes* 4.1.4.

67. Ibid., 4.1.12. Calvin also refers here to the Anabaptist model as a revival of Donatism.

this society is catholic, that is, universal, because there could not be two or three churches. But all God's elect are so united and conjoined in Christ that, as they are dependent upon one Head, they also grow together into one body...." It is this church that cannot be overthrown.[68]

Philip Walker Butin observes of Calvin's view,

If believers' sense of membership in Christ and the church were based primarily on the faithfulness of their own Christian commitment (or visible holiness, works, or even faith, subjectively understood), it would always be subject to doubt in the face of their human sin and failures. Calvin was well aware of how debilitating this subjectivistic understanding of church membership could be to the church's stability. On the other hand, when the "invisible" conception of the church was properly understood to aim at establishing the Trinitarian basis and stability of the church's necessarily corporeal, contextualized existence, the two perspectives could be seen as inseparably aspects of a single reality.[69]

Calvin says that Scripture speaks of the church sometimes as "that which is actually in God's presence," but also as "the whole multitude of people spread over the earth who profess to worship God and Christ.... Just as we must believe, therefore, that the former church, invisible to us, is visible to the eyes of God alone, so we are commanded to revere and keep communion with the latter, which is called 'church' in respect to human beings."[70] "The saints are gathered into the society of Christ on the principle that whatever benefits God confers upon them, they should in turn share with one another. This does not, however, rule out diversity of graces, inasmuch as we know the gifts of the Spirit are variously distributed."[71] The communion of saints, in Calvin's thinking, has its source in union with Christ.

Agreeing with Luther on the principal points mentioned above, the Reformed also gave more place to the visibility of the church in the communion and fellowship between believers. As we observed in chapter 19, despite agreement on the doctrines of justification and sanctification (as well as the uses of the law), there were different nuances between Luther and Calvin (as well as other Reformed leaders) with respect to the visibility of sanctification in this life. While Luther sometimes seems to suggest that our sanctification is entirely hidden, Reformed theology encourages believers to expect signs of growth and to be prepared for successes as well as failures in the Christian life.

These different emphases regarding sanctification carry over into ecclesiology. Reformed leaders, including Calvin, emphasized the duty that Christians owe to their brothers and sisters because none of us is united to Christ apart from our

---

68. Ibid., 4.1.2–3.

69. Philip Walker Butin, *Revelation, Redemption, and Response: Calvin's Trinitarian Understanding of the Divine-*

Human Relationship (New York: Oxford Univ. Press, 1995), 100.

70. Calvin, *Institutes* 4.1.7.

71. Ibid., 4.1.3.

communion with each other. Where Luther expresses relative indifference to the outward form of the church (where it does not touch directly on preaching and sacrament), Calvin sought—even more than some of his Reformed colleagues— to subject every aspect of the church to Scripture. Nothing beyond Christ's Word should be imposed upon Christians—even by the pastors, much less the secular authorities—and nothing required can be omitted. Christ is the only head of the church; the authority he gives to his pastors, elders, and deacons is ministerial rather than magisterial. The outward form of the church (its worship, discipline, government, and order) was so important that it was eventually made a third mark of the church. It is true that Calvin acknowledged only two marks,[72] but he clearly insisted upon the authority of God's Word alone over all matters of faith and practice— which is the intent of the "third mark" (discipline).

Discipline in this connection refers not only to the doctrinal and practical care (and, as needed, correction) of members (including officers), but more generally to the regulating of the church's order and offices, the liturgy, and diaconal care so as to accord as closely as possible to God's Word. Zwingli and Bullinger (even Bucer, Calvin's mentor) were actually closer to Luther in regarding these issues as largely *adiaphora* (things indifferent), which could be regulated by the prince. Especially with the fragmentation of "Christendom" (the Holy Roman Empire) by the Reformation and the power of rising nation-states, many Lutheran and Reformed churches transferred their obedience from the pope to the prince or the city council. Although Calvin spent enormous energy on behalf of the independence of the church from Geneva's city council, many Reformed churches either acquiesced to the status quo or defended it, as did Thomas Erastus (1524–1583), who lent his name to this view: *Erastianism*.[73] In fact, the influential guidance of Bullinger and Bucer largely shaped the views of the English Reformers and bishops under Elizabeth, with whom the more Genevan "presbyterians" collided.[74]

Calvin had considered presbyterian government most conformable to Scripture (and therefore not indifferent), and yet was willing for the sake of unity to allow an

---

72. Ibid., 4.1.9.

73. Thomas Erastus (1524–1583), a Swiss theologian, vigorously defended Zwingli's views not only on the Supper but on the subordination of the church to the state. In his view, the church could not discipline members (i.e., by withholding Communion in extreme cases); this was the role of the civil magistrate. Opposing Caspar Olevianus (coauthor of the *Heidelberg Catechism*) on both grounds (eucharistic theology and church discipline) at a symposium at the University of Heidelberg in 1570, Erastus sought in vain to keep the "Genevan" approach from acceptance in that city.

74. During the violent reign of Mary in England, many lead-

ing Reformed pastors fled to Zürich, and a few to Geneva, still fewer to other cities. Those who returned from Zürich became bishops under Elizabeth, and many who returned from Geneva became the leading agitators for presbyterian government and independence of church courts from the state. See *The Zürich Letters* (Cambridge: Cambridge Univ. Press, 1842), Parker Society edition. Later, when for a brief time presbyterians gained the ascendancy, the English parliament that called the Westminster Assembly adopted all but one of the chapters of the *Westminster Confession*: "Of Church Censures." However, Erastianism could be held by Presbyterians as well as Episcopalians, both of whom expected the civil government to establish the church's polity.

episcopal government for Reformed churches. However, his successor, Theodore Beza, and some English presbyterians (like Thomas Cartwright and Walter Travers) viewed presbyterian polity as essential. Following the counsel of Zürich (particularly Bullinger), England's bishops defended episcopacy as part of the prerogative of the monarch to determine the church's outward discipline, and in the struggle for a united Church of England, politics played a decisive role.

Although a tragedy from the perspective of ecumenism, such a concern for the visible government of the church points up the fact that, far from spiritualizing the church, the Reformed tradition has been critical of dualistic ecclesiologies. Not only the soul of doctrine but the body of practice is the sphere of God's redeeming and sanctifying work, under the lordship of the ascended Christ and regulated by his Word. The great difference between Roman Catholic and Reformed ecclesiologies at this point, then, is not over the importance of the church's outward form but over its actual shape. The Reformed believed that they were going back to the apostolic and ancient church practice of shared governance by ministers and elders together at local and broader assemblies.

While eager to affirm the public order of the church as a visible mark of the church, Reformed and Lutheran confessions agree that the church is not identified primarily with a historical organization (in contemporary terms, denominations), but with the communion that all professing believers enjoy with each other by virtue first and foremost of their union with Christ, which is made visible by the faithful preaching of the Word and the administration of the sacraments according to Christ's institution. Only God's promise attached to preaching and sacrament validates ecclesiastical ministry. Where in Roman Catholic teaching cultural labors of Christians are subservient to the church, Reformed ecclesiology distinguishes these common vocations from the official ministry of the visible church. Even Christian voluntary organizations such as schools, publishing houses, charities, and hospitals, therefore, cannot be regarded as part of the ministry of the visible church and, consequently, as subservient to the church and its officers.[75]

E. Anabaptist, Free Church, and Pentecostal Ecclesiologies

Emerging from the traditions of Anabaptism and Puritan Independency, Free Church ecclesiologies emphasize the pure or *gathered church* model. Affirming Augustine's understanding of the visible church as a mixed body, Luther, Calvin, and their colleagues were reformers rather than separatists, and this impulse was

---

75. Louis Berkhof, *Systematic Theology* (Grand Rapids: Eerdmans, 1969), 571.

evident among the Puritans as well. However, Anabaptism arose as a movement of radical separation, viewing the established churches (whether Roman Catholic, Lutheran, or Reformed) as invalid.

For the Reformers, the priesthood of all believers simply denied any ontological divide between clergy and laity before Christ, the only mediator. However, this in no way eliminated the necessity of public offices in the church, as if everyone were ordained by baptism to preach, teach, and administer the sacraments. Anabaptist movements frequently took this further step, which became especially pronounced in the Society of Friends (Quakers). Most Anabaptists were pacifists rather than political revolutionaries; few were as radical in their denunciation of all human learning and even Scripture (in favor of direct revelations) as Thomas Müntzer or Luther's one-time associate, Andreas Carlstadt. Nevertheless, there was a general tendency among the various groups (exhibited in the Schleitheim Confession) to (1) identify the true church exclusively with regenerate believers, (2) emphasize personal holiness (understood as complete separation from the world) rather than preaching and sacrament, as the mark of the church, and (3) display a marked spirit-matter dualism applied to the outward forms and ministry of the church as well as the state.[76]

Consequently, the magisterial Reformers shared the Roman Catholic concern that the Anabaptist movements reflected a Donatist ecclesiology of the "pure church" (consisting only of the truly regenerate) rather than a "mixed body." The denial of the baptism of believers' children represented the culmination of this ideal, and Lutheran and Reformed churches shared Rome's theological opposition to this denial, some (notably, Zwingli) even sharing its enforcement of the ancient Justinian Code, which made rebaptism a capital offense. In the context of Christendom, the concept of the church as a mixed body became a parody in Protestant as well as Roman Catholic and Orthodox realms. Not only believers and their children, but all citizens, were regarded as belonging at least outwardly to the body of Christ. Surely this vision of Christendom itself contributed as much to the secularization of the church as the Enlightenment. By contrast, Free Church ecclesiologies have highlighted the importance of the individual and especially of the decision of the individual to separate from the world, including the visible churches that they judge to belong to this corrupt order.

Some, like the Anabaptists and English Separatists, rejected all connection with official churches then in existence, regarding their movements as a restoration of original Christianity, while others, like some of the later pietist and revivalist

---

76. *The Schleitheim Confession*, in *Confessions and Catechisms of the Reformation* (ed. Mark Noll; Grand Rapids: Baker, 1991), 50–58.

groups, considered themselves to be renewal movements within larger bodies—the "true church" witnessing to the wider communion. The Dutch Arminians, as Berkhof observed, "made the Church primarily a visible society...."[77] "The Pietists, on the other hand, manifested a tendency to disregard the visible Church, seeking a Church of believers only, showing themselves indifferent to the institutional Church with its mixture of good and evil, and seeking edification in conventicles."[78] This is not quite fair. After all, most pietists did not separate from the established churches, but created a church-within-a-church (*ecclesiola in ecclesia*). Nevertheless, by treating the inner ring of the conventicle as the place where genuine discipleship occurs, in contrast to the official ministry of the church, pietism tended to marginalize the importance of that official ministry. Neither reforming the church nor separating from it, pietism endured the outward forms while locating genuine Christian fellowship and nurture elsewhere. By identifying the true church with the nucleus within the church that could be recognized as truly regenerate, pietism tended toward an overrealized eschatology, as if the invisible church could become fully visible before the consummation.

Kant's pietistic heritage may be discerned in his contrast between "pure religion" (i.e., practical morality) and "ecclesiastical faith" (the formal ministry, creeds, and rituals)—a contrast that remains evident whenever surveys of Westerners (especially Americans) reveal a high degree of commitment to "spirituality" but not "religion" or formal church membership. In the wake of the Enlightenment, with redemption reduced to moral enlightenment, the church was increasingly regarded as one human institution among others. Reacting against rationalism, the Romantic movement sought to recover the mystical aspect of life, and under the influence of Romanticism the concept of the church (especially under Schleiermacher) became identified with the spirit of the community. The church is visible almost exclusively for Schleiermacher in its mystical fellowship. All along the way, pietism, Methodism, the Quakers, and similar movements tended to downplay the significance of the public ministry and its offices in favor of informal fellowship and individual practices.

This concept of a church-within-the-church was reflected in the creation of small groups, which German pietists referred to as "colleges of piety" (*collegia pietatis*) and early Methodists called "holy clubs." Although they usually accepted the creeds and confession of their church, these groups drew up their own standards for membership with a more rigorous discipline and examination of the inner life, which became their central concern. Eventually, many of these *ecclesiolae* either separated or were expelled and formed their own separate denominations. To a large

---

77. Berkhof, *Systematic Theology*, 561.   78. Ibid.

extent, the vast parachurch network of global evangelicalism represents the triumph of the *ecclesiola* over the *ecclesia*, infusing the movement with remarkable vitality and creativity as well as a somewhat marginal ecclesiology.

Among free churches, Pentecostalism especially emphasizes "the church in the power of the Spirit."[79] While the evangelical movement is shaped by various streams, it is perhaps more decisively shaped by the Free Church and Wesleyan-Pentecostal traditions than any other. Its emphasis on the church as regenerate believers rather than on formal marks has made evangelicalism remarkably open to cooperation between members of disparate denominations. At the same time, it has also made the movement somewhat rootless and susceptible to secular patterns of organization and growth. A growing number of evangelicals recognize a dangerous trend toward viewing the church less as a communion of saints than as a niche market of consumers. Engaging all of these different ecclesiological paradigms will be the goal of the following chapters.

DISCUSSION QUESTIONS

1. What is the difference between the cultural mandate and the Great Commission?
2. Discuss some of the biblical images for the church, especially considering the ways in which they seem to indicate a covenantal framework.
3. Has the church replaced Israel? Discuss that question in the light of the remnant theology in the prophets and its New Testament (especially Pauline) application.
4. How should we interpret the "Bride of Christ" image?
5. Summarize some of the main principles of Roman Catholic, Orthodox, Lutheran, Reformed, and Free Church ecclesiologies. What do they share in common, and what distinguishes each from the others?
6. How significant is eschatology to ecclesiology? Relate your discussion to the following problems in church history: Donatism, "Christendom" (including Erastianism), and ecclesiastical absolutism.

---

79. So Kärkkäinen, *An Introduction to Ecclesiology*, 68–78, labels this model.

Chapter Twenty-Three

WORD AND SACRAMENT: THE MEANS OF GRACE

The ministry entrusted to the church is also the source of the church's own existence and identity. Therefore, we begin with the means of grace as the intersection between soteriology (our previous section) and ecclesiology.

I. THE SACRAMENTAL WORD: PREACHING AS A MEANS OF GRACE

In chapter 3, I examined two of the three forms of the Word of God: (1) first and foremost as Jesus Christ, the hypostatic Word, who is one with the Father in essence, and (2) the canonical Word, which is neither God's essence nor merely a created effect, but the living and active energies of the triune God in the form of communication. Now we come to (3) the Word of God as preaching. In the words of the *Second Helvetic Confession*, "The preached Word is the Word of God."[1] In Scripture we find the canon of saving speech; in preaching, the ongoing means by which this saving speech generates a new creation, so that even in this present evil age we "[taste] the goodness of the word of God and the powers of the age to come" (Heb 6:5). This is *how* the kingdom comes.

A. THE CHURCH AS THE "CREATION OF THE WORD"

From this line of thinking it has been rightly claimed that the church is the creation of the Word (*creatura verbi*). The new birth, as part of the new creation, is

---

1. *Second Helvetic Confession* 1.4, "The Preaching of the Word of God Is the Word of God," in *Creeds and Confessions of the Reformation Era* (ed. Jaroslav Pelikan and Valerie Hotch-kiss; vol. 2, part 4 of *Creeds and Confessions of Faith in Christian Tradition*; New Haven, Conn.: Yale Univ. Press, 2003), 460.

effected *in* the church (i.e., through its ministry of the Word), but not *by* the church. The individual does not give birth to him- or herself, nor does the community give birth to itself; both are born from above (Jn 3:3 – 5). The origin and source of the church's existence is neither the autonomous self nor the autonomous church: "So then it depends not on human will or exertion, but on God, who has mercy" (Ro 9:16). Where there is God's Word and Spirit, there is faith, and where there is faith there is a church. In the Reformed – Roman Catholic dialogue, the former partner summarized this view well:

> The church existing as a community in history has been understood and described in the Reformed tradition as a *creatura verbi*, as "the creation of the word." ... The church, like faith itself, is brought into being by the hearing of God's word in the power of the Spirit; it lives *ex auditu*, by hearing. This emphasis upon hearing the word of God has been of central importance in Reformed theology since the sixteenth century. This is why the Reformed have stressed "the true preaching of the word" together with "the right dispensing of the sacraments according to the institution of Jesus Christ" as a decisive "mark of the true church."[2]

The dialogue adds, again from the Reformed side,

> Against the appeal to continuity, custom and institution, the Reformed appealed to the living voice of the living God as the essential and decisive factor by which the church must live, if it will live at all: the church, as *creatura verbi*. ... The church is the creation of the word because the word itself is God's creative word of grace by which we are justified and renewed. ... The community of faith is thus not merely the community in which the gospel is preached; by its hearing and responding to the word of grace, the community itself becomes a medium of confession, its faith a "sign" or "token" to the world; it is itself part of the world transformed by being addressed and renewed by the word of God.[3]

As an external Word, God's speech breaks up the presuppositions, attitudes, longings, felt needs, pious impulses, speculations, and ideals of individuals and even of the church itself. Yet as public communication, it is inherently social and reorganizes the creation that it disrupts into the new creation of which it speaks. Conceived in the event of hearing, the church always remains on the receiving end of its redemption and identity.

B. God's Creative and Redemptive Speech

Across the entire field of God's external works we have seen that the Father

---

2. "Reformed – Roman Catholic Dialogue," *Growth in Agreement II: Reports and Agreed Statements of Ecumenical Conversations on a World Level, 1982 – 1998* (ed. Jeffrey Gros, Harding Meyer, and William G. Rusch; Geneva: World Council of Churches; Grand Rapids: Eerdmans, 2000), 802. For the Lutheran – Roman Catholic Dialogue on this point, see 495 – 98.

3. Ibid., 803.

accomplishes all things by his Word and in the power of the Spirit. Not only are all things created and upheld through the mediation of his hypostatic Word, Jesus Christ; they are brought forth through the energetic Word that God speaks into creation (Ps 33:6). Even when God speaks through human representatives, human words do not simply coincide at certain points with God's Word, but are in fact God's "breath" (2Ti 3:16). Although the divine essence does not emanate, God's words do in fact "go forth" and are "sent" on their missions. The Word is that living and active energy that creates and recreates. It may harden hearts or melt them, but it is never inert, since it is the Word of the Father, spoken in the Son, made effectual by the Spirit. God's speech never returns to him empty-handed (Isa 55:11).

Although the phrase *word of God* has various meanings in Scripture, notes Bavinck, "it is always a word of *God*, that is, never just a sound, but a power, not mere information but also an accomplishment of his will, Isa. 55:11, Rom. 4:17, 2 Cor. 4:6, Heb. 1:3, 11:3. By this word Jesus quiets the sea, Mk. 4:38, heals the sick, Mt. 8:16, casts out demons, 9:6, raised the dead, Luke 7:14, 8:54, John 5:25, 28; 11:43, etc."[4] Wherever God speaks the Son in the Spirit, a mass of individuals become the covenant people and anonymous space becomes "a broad place" of lavish abundance and freedom where the Lord dwells in the midst of Zion (Ps 18:19).

Just as creation begins with a command, "Let there be.... And there was ...," so too does the new creation originate in the womb of the Word. The church is "a chosen race" and a "holy nation," "that you may proclaim the excellencies of him who called you out of darkness into his marvelous light" (1Pe 2:9). Although "[the] gospel is veiled, it is veiled only to those who are perishing ... For God, who said, 'Let light shine out of darkness,' has shone in our hearts to give the light of the knowledge of the glory of God in the face of Jesus Christ" (2Co 4:3, 6). It is not surprising that Paul also thinks of justification as analogous to *ex nihilo* creation (Ro 4:17–18). By speaking righteousness into a condition of unrighteousness, God brings into existence a new creation, which is not only a class of justified and renewed individuals but a living community: his church.

No contrast is drawn here between divine and human action: the human signs are sanctified as divine signs that communicate the reality signified. Within the appropriate covenantal context, the words of commissioned representatives actually bear God's Word, accomplishing that of which it speaks. Analogous to a wedding, the public ratification of an international treaty, or similar ceremonies, the *illocutionary* speech act (such as promising) is given through the *locutionary* act of uttering certain words in a certain context, which then have the *perlocutionary*

---

4. Herman Bavinck, *Reformed Dogmatics*, vol. 4, *Holy Spirit, Church, and New Creation* (ed. John Bolt; trans. John Vriend; Grand Rapids: Baker Academic, 2008), 449.

effect of creating a new state of affairs, such as a union between husband and wife or between nations. Although the personal characteristics of the human agent are never overwhelmed or circumvented, they are sanctified so that the prophetic word has its source neither in the prophet's person nor in the community's judgment, but in God (2Pe 1:20–21).

God's words are event-generating discourse; they are not only enlightening or informative, but *fulfilled* (Eze 12:28; cf. Isa 55:10–11). In fact, the scene of the prophet preaching to the valley of dry bones in Ezekiel 37 vividly portrays this living and active Word that creates the reality of which it speaks. We have already recognized the way in which God speaks creation into existence and brings about its fruitfulness by his Word. It is this same Word that draws us out of our self-enclosed prison of sin and death, effectually calling, justifying, and renewing us from the inside out. By this Word the Spirit builds a temple-house for the Father in the Son.[5]

Only the written canon occupies constitutional status in the church, but the subsequent preaching of ministers after the apostles communicates exactly the same Word (i.e., Christ and all of his benefits) in the power of the same Spirit. We see this in the event of Pentecost itself, where the first public evidence is Peter's proclamation of the gospel (Ac 2:14–36). Repeatedly in Acts, the growth of the church is attributed to the fact that "the word of God spread" and "prevailed" (Ac 6:7; 13:49; 19:20), and "proclaiming the good news" is the central activity described this history of the early church. In fact, the spreading of the Word is treated as synonymous with the spreading of the kingdom of God. By the Word we are legally adopted, and by the Spirit we receive the inner witness that we are the children of God (Ro 8:12–17). Through the Word *of* Christ the Spirit creates faith *in* Christ, and where this is present, there is the church. The difference between Peter's Pentecost sermon and that of an ordinary minister today is that the former is part of the canon that norms our preaching. However, when preaching today is faithful to that canon, it conveys exactly the same content and therefore is the same Word as that spoken by the prophets and apostles.

Preaching involves teaching, but it is much more than that. The sacramental aspect of the Word—that is, its role as a means of grace—underlies Reformation teaching. The preaching of the gospel not only calls people to faith in Christ; it is the means by which the Spirit creates faith in their hearts (as expressed in Q 65 of the *Heidelberg Catechism*).[6] In evangelical theologies, this sacramental aspect of God's Word is often marginalized by a purely pedagogical (instructional) concept. It is therefore not surprising that when the Word is reduced to its didactic function

---

5. As I have noted elsewhere, M. G. Kline's treatment of this theme is richly suggestive in *The Structure of Biblical Authority* (Grand Rapids: Eerdmans, 1989), ch. 3.

6. *Heidelberg Catechism*, q. 65, in *Ecumenical Creeds and Reformed Confessions* (Grand Rapids: CRC Publications, 1988), 41.

there arises a longing of the people to encounter God here and now through other means. However, by affirming its sacramental as well as the regulative (canonical) character, we can recognize the Word as God's working *and* ruling, saving *and* teaching.

B. A. Gerrish observes, "Calvin felt no antagonism between what we may call the 'pedagogical' [teaching] and the 'sacramental' functions of the word."[7] "God's word, for Calvin, is not simply a dogmatic norm; it has in it a vital efficacy, and it is the appointed instrument by which the Spirit imparts illumination, faith, awakening, regeneration, purification, and so on.... Calvin himself describes the word as *verbum sacramentale*, the 'sacramental word,'" that gives even to the sacraments themselves their efficacy.[8] "It therefore makes good sense to us when we discover that in Theodore Beza's (1519–1605) edition of the Geneva Catechism the fourth part, on the sacraments, actually begins with the heading 'On the *Word* of God.'"[9] As with baptism and the Supper, the Spirit creates a bond between the sign (proclamation of the gospel) and the reality signified (Christ and all his benefits). The word is a ladder, to be sure, but, like the incarnation, one that *God* always *descends* to us (Ro 10:6–17). This view integrates the truth in the models of revelation as doctrine, history, and personal encounter.

It is important to recognize that while God's Word is living and active, its "two words" of *law* and *gospel* do different things.[10] The law kills by revealing our guilt, while the Spirit makes alive by the gospel (2Co 3:6–18). By speaking law, God silences and convicts us; by speaking the gospel, God justifies and renews us. God's energies, mediated by human language, not only inform us of judgment and grace but judge and save.

Specifically, the *gospel* is that part of God's word that gives life. While everything that God says is true, useful, and full of impact, not everything that God says is *saving*. First Peter 1:23–24 adds, "You have been born again, not of perishable seed but of imperishable, through the living and abiding word of God." Furthermore, it is not the word in general but the gospel in particular that is credited with this vivifying effect: "This word is the good news that was preached to you" (v. 25). Similarly, Paul says that "faith comes from hearing ... the word of Christ," and more specifically, "the gospel of peace," (Ro 10:15, 17). Salvation is not something

---

7. Life is found only in God, located in Christ, mediated by his Word. "It is crucial to Calvin's interpretation that the gospel is not a mere invitation to fellowship with Christ, but the effective means by which the communion with Christ comes about" (B. A. Gerrish, *Grace and Gratitude: The Eucharistic Theology of John Calvin* [Minneapolis: Augsburg Fortress, 1993], 84–85, referring especially to Calvin's *Petit tracté de la sancta Cene* (1541), OS 1:504–5, and Calvin's *Institutes* 4.14.4; cf. 3.2.6–7; 3.2.28–30, and many other places).

8. Ibid., 85, referring to Calvin, *Institutes* 4.14.4.

9. Ibid., 84, referring to Calvin, *Institutes* 3.5.5.

10. The identification of the Word of God as consisting of law and gospel is familiar not only in Lutheran but also in Reformed systems, from Ursinus (coauthor of the *Heidelberg Catechism*) to Louis Berkhof, who distinguishes law and gospel as the "two parts of the Word of God as a means of grace" (*Systematic Theology* [Grand Rapids: Eerdmans, 1996], 612).

that one has to actively pursue, attain, and ascend to grasp, as if it were far away, but is as near as "the word of faith that we proclaim" (v. 8). We do not have to bring Christ up from the dead or ascend into heaven to bring him down, since he addresses us directly in his word (vv. 6–9). The gospel is "the power of God for salvation" (Ro 1:16).

Calvin observes that some parts of God's Word engender fear and judgment.[11] "For although faith believes every word of God, it rests solely on the word of grace or mercy, the promise of God's fatherly goodwill," which is realized only in and through Christ.[12] "For in God faith seeks life," says Calvin, "a life that is not found in commandments or declarations of penalties, but in the promise of mercy, and only in a freely given promise."[13] The only safe route, therefore, is to receive the Father through the incarnate Son. Christ is the saving content of Scripture, the substance of its canonical unity.[14] "This, then, is the true knowledge of Christ, if we receive him as he is offered by the Father: namely, clothed with his gospel. For just as he has been appointed as the goal of our faith, so we cannot take the right road to him unless the gospel goes before us."[15]

C. THE WORD CREATES COMMUNITY

Private prayer is enjoined and exemplified by Jesus as crucial to the Christian life (Ps 6:9; 54:2; Mt 6:5–13; 26:36; 1Th 5:17; Eph 6:18). It is not without reason that the *Heidelberg Catechism* calls prayer "the most important part of the thankfulness God requires of us" (q. 116).[16] We may meditate on Scripture in private, especially as we have it in our own language. Many of our acts of discipleship and fellowship can be done by us rather than to us, without having to be gathered as a public assembly. However, if genuine community is to emerge, not simply an aggregate of souls deciding to create community (along the lines of a voluntary association), God's saving action must be public and social at the outset. As Bonhoeffer explains,

> If there were an unmediated work of the Spirit, then the idea of the church would be individualistically dissolved from the outset. But in the word the most profound social nexus is established from the beginning. *The word is social in character, not only in its origin but also in its aim.* Tying the Spirit to the word means that the Spirit aims at *a plurality of hearers* and establishes a visible sign by which the actualization is to take place. The word, however, is qualified by being the very word of Christ; it is effectively brought to the heart of the hearers by the Spirit (emphasis added).[17]

11. Calvin, *Institutes* 3.2.7; 3.2.29.
12. Ibid., 3.2.28–30.
13. Ibid., 3.2.29.
14. Ibid., 1.13.7.
15. Ibid., 3.2.6.
16. *Heidelberg Catechism*, q. 116, in *Psalter Hymnal* (Grand

Rapids: CRC Publications, 1987), 916.

17. Dietrich Bonhoeffer, *Dietrich Bonhoeffer Works*, vol. 1, *Sanctorum Communio: A Theological Study of the Sociology of the Church* (ed. Joachim von Soosten; English edition, ed. Clifford J. Green; trans. Reinhard Krauss and Nancy Lukens; Minneapolis: Fortress, 1998), 158.

As important as it is to read the Scriptures regularly, God has appointed public preaching because "it is another who speaks, and this becomes an incomparable assurance for me."

> Total strangers proclaim God's grace and forgiveness to me, not as their own experience, but as God's will. It is in the others that I can grasp in concrete form the church-community and its Lord as the guarantors of my confidence in God's grace. The fact that others assure me of God's grace makes the church-community real for me; it rules out any danger or hope that I might have fallen prey to an illusion. The confidence of faith arises not only out of solitude, but also out of the assembly.[18]

Not only entrusted with the gospel, therefore, the church is itself created and constantly renewed and corrected by this living and active Word.

Even baptism and the Supper are effective means of grace because of the Word. Bonhoeffer adds,

> To summarize, the word is the sociological principle by which the entire church is built up ... both in numbers and in its faith. Christ is the foundation upon which, and according to which, the building of the church is raised (1 Corinthians 3; Eph. 2:20). And thus it grows into a "holy temple of God" (Eph. 2:21), and "with a growth that is from God" (Col. 2:19), "until all of us come to maturity, to the measure of the full stature of Christ" (Eph. 4:13), and in all this growing "into him who is the head, into Christ." The entire building begins and ends with Christ, and its unifying center is the word.[19]

The preaching creates the community, while the Supper, by evoking personal acceptance through faith, makes that community in some sense visible—or better still, audible.[20] "We hear the word of God through the word of the church, and this is what constitutes the authority of the church."[21] Only because of this does one owe obedience to the church, submitting private opinions to her tutelage, yet never contrary to the Word itself.[22] Insofar as the church speaks God's Word, its authority is not illusory or an exercise in arbitrary power.

Rome and the radical Protestant "enthusiasts" regarded the external Word as important, but subordinated it to an allegedly ongoing work of the Spirit in bringing new revelations.[23] Though highly esteemed as divine revelation, Scripture was regarded by both groups as a dead letter that had to be supplemented by ongoing revelation: the living voice of the Spirit through the living church or a prophet. Enthusiasts have always appealed to John 6:63 to support their sharp antithesis between outer and inner, visible and invisible, divine and human, contrasting the Spirit's

---

18. Ibid., 230.
19. Ibid., 247.
20. Ibid.
21. Ibid., 250.

22. Ibid., 251.
23. See Willem Balke, *Calvin and the Anabaptist Radicals* (trans. William J. Heynen; Grand Rapids: Eerdmans, 1981).

inner witness with the allegedly "dead letter" of Scripture and preaching. In that verse, Jesus says, "It is the Spirit who gives life; the flesh is no help at all." And yet, Jesus immediately adds, "The *words* that I have spoken to you are Spirit and life." The Spirit's role is to make the external Word an inwardly experienced and embraced reality, not to offer a gnosis superior or supplemental to the Word itself.

It is crucial to realize that for the Reformers the proclamation of the Word is not simply teaching concerning Christ, but the personal address of Christ himself through which the Spirit delivers Christ to us and unites us to him.[24] This is Paul's point in Romans 10, when he says that we do not have to ascend to heaven to pull God down to us or descend into the depths to raise Christ from the dead. Rather, " 'The word is near you, in your mouth and in your heart' (that is, the word of faith that we proclaim)" (v. 8). Paul's logic is clear: "But how shall they believe him of whom they have never heard? And how are they to hear without someone preaching? And how are they to preach unless they are sent?" (vv. 14–15). Ambassadors do not send themselves (this was the mark of the false prophets in Jeremiah 23, who proclaimed their own word as the Word of God); they are sent by the King to herald the message. When they speak, in Christ's name, it is Christ's voice that they hear (v. 17).

Far from a dead letter awaiting animation, "The gospel *is* the kingdom. It does not simply proclaim it or point to it; it brings and causes all the hearers, including myself, to enter it." The gospel is God's own utterance. "As Jesus Christ, as God himself, the gospel, when preached by word of mouth, does more than simply offer us the possibility that I can actualize and make it real by my own decision of faith. The Word itself is the power of God, God's kingdom."[25] Luther famously declared that one is made a "Christian" by "the hearing of the Word of God, that is, faith." "Therefore, the ears alone are the organs of a Christian man, for he is justified and declared to be a Christian, not because of the works of any member but because of faith."[26] The preached Word is neither God's essence nor merely a human witness but God's energetic activity of judging and justifying.

The choice of preaching as a medium is not incidental. It puts us on the *receiving* end of things, because not only does justification come through faith alone, but faith itself comes through hearing.[27]

---

24. Oswald Bayer, *Living by Faith: Justification and Sanctification* (trans. Geoffrey W. Bromiley; Grand Rapids: Eerdmans, 2003), 49.

25. Bayer, *Living by Faith*, 50; see Ro 1:16–17 with 1Co 4:20.

26. Martin Luther, *Luther's Works*, vol. 29, *Lectures on Titus, Philemon, and Hebrews* (ed. Jaroslav Pelikan; St. Louis: Concordia, 1968), 224.

27. This comparison between hearing and seeing is not meant to suggest that there is some magical quality to hear-ing or that God is bound by this medium. Rather, it is to say that God has bound himself to the spoken word as the *ordinary* method of self-communication. Like Augustine, many Christians would refer to their reading of Scripture as a moment of conversion. Furthermore, physical disabilities such as deafness are no obstacle to God's grace. Stephen H. Webb offers a well-informed treatment of this issue in *The Divine Voice: Christian Proclamation and the Theology of Sound* (Grand Rapids: Brazos, 2004), 51–55.

The same emphasis is found in the Reformed confessions. "For Calvin as for Luther," as John H. Leith observes, " 'The ears alone are the organ of the Christian.' "[28] Calvin summarized, "When the Gospel is preached in the name of God, it is as if God himself spoke in person."[29] Leith elaborates, "The justification for preaching is not in its effectiveness for education or reform.... The preacher, Calvin dared to say, was the mouth of God." It was God's intention and action that made it effective. Just as the ordinary elements of water, bread, and wine—consecrated by God's Word and Spirit—are united to the reality of Christ and his benefits, so too in the ordinary human language of fallen ambassadors, Christ himself is present in judgment and mercy. The Word not only describes salvation, but conveys it. "Calvin's sacramental doctrine of preaching enabled him both to understand preaching as a very human work and to understand it as the work of God."[30] Calvin follows Paul's logic in Romans 10, refusing to set the external Word against the Spirit's internal witness. "We hear his ministers speaking just as if he himself spoke.... God breathes faith into us only by the instrument of his gospel, as Paul points out that 'faith comes by hearing.' "[31] In fact, Paul "not only makes himself a co-worker with God, but also assigns himself the function of imparting salvation."[32] Without the work of the Spirit, the word would fall on deaf ears, but the Spirit opens deaf ears *through* the external word.[33]

Similarly, the *Heidelberg Catechism*, after treating justification, asks, "It is by faith alone that we share in Christ and all his blessings: where then does that faith come from?" and answers, "The Holy Spirit produces it in our hearts by the preaching of the holy gospel [Ro 10:17; 1Pe 1:23–25], and confirms it through our use of the holy sacraments [Mt 28:19–20; 1Co 10:16]."[34]

According to the *Second Helvetic Confession*,

> The preaching of the Word of God is the Word of God. Wherefore when this Word of God is now preached in the church by preachers lawfully called, we believe that the very Word of God is proclaimed, and received by the faithful; and that neither any other Word of God is to be invented nor is to be expected from heaven: and that now the Word itself which is preached is to be regarded, not the minister that preaches; for even if he be evil and a sinner, nevertheless the Word of God remains still true and good.[35]

---

28. John H. Leith, "Doctrine of the Proclamation of the Word," in *John Calvin & the Church: A Prism of Reform* (ed. Timothy George; Louisville: Westminster John Knox, 1990), 212.

29. John Calvin, as quoted in Leith, "Doctrine of the Proclamation of the Word," 211.

30. Ibid., 210–11.

31. Calvin, *Institutes* 4.1.5–6.

32. Ibid., 4.1.6.

33. John Calvin, *Commentary on the Gospel According to John* (trans. William Pringle; Grand Rapids: Baker, repr., 1996), comment on 15:27.

34. *Heidelberg Catechism*, q. 65, in *Psalter Hymnal* (Grand Rapids: CRC Publications, 1987), 889.

35. *Second Helvetic Confession*, ch. 1, in *The Book of Confessions* (PCUSA: General Assembly, 1991).

The concluding sentence underscores the objectivity of the Word: its effectiveness regardless of the subjective condition of the minister. It is not the minister, but the ministry, that the Spirit makes effective as a means of grace. The medium is consistent with the message of the cross. The fact that some of the most significant witnesses in the history of redemption are characterized as inferior speakers—Moses (Ex 4:10), Isaiah (Isa 6:5–8), and Paul (1Co 2:4–5; 2Co 11:6), among others—is surely of some consequence. Yet all of this is "that your faith might not rest in the wisdom of men but in the power of God" (1Co 2:5). "The supreme judge of all controversies," according to the *Westminster Confession*, "is the Holy Spirit speaking in the Scripture."[36]

Only this particular canon can create this particular community, called the church. After all, only these texts have been "exhaled" (*theopneustos*) by the Spirit (2Ti 3:16; 2Pe 1:21). And God still speaks today in power through the ministry that is normed by this canon.

Challenging the radical sects for their contrast between the Word that "merely beats the air" and the "inner Word" resident within the individual, the *Second Helvetic Confession* continues, "Neither do we think that therefore the outward preaching is to be thought as fruitless because the instruction in true religion depends on the inward illumination of the Spirit, or because it is written, 'And no longer shall each one teach his neighbor ..., for they shall all know me' (Jer 31:34)."[37] That God *can* illumine inwardly apart from the external preaching is not denied, but this work of the Spirit within is in Scripture connected to the outward preaching of mere mortals (the confession cites Mark 16:15; Acts 16:14; and Romans 10:17).

The *Westminster Larger Catechism* adds,

> The Spirit of God maketh the reading, *but especially the preaching* of the Word, an effectual means of enlightening, convincing, and humbling sinners, of *driving them out of themselves*, and drawing them unto Christ, of conforming them to his image, and subduing them to his will; of strengthening them against temptations and corruptions; of building them up in grace, and establishing their hearts in holiness and comfort through faith unto salvation (emphasis added).[38]

It is not only the message but the method that *drives us out of ourselves*, which of course an "inner word" cannot do. We have ingenious ways of evading the law and the gospel, judgment and deliverance. We justify ourselves until the Lord brings us the external Word of his verdict, and we busy ourselves with good advice until the Lord brings us the Good News that contradicts our inner light.

G. K. Chesterton observed how different Christianity is from the doctrine of the "inner light" that unites rationalists and mystics alike:

---

36. *Westminster Confession of Faith*, ch. 1, in *The Book of Confessions*.

37. *Second Helvetic Confession*, ch. 1.

38. *Westminster Larger Catechism*, q. 155, in *The Book of Confessions* (Louisville: PCUSA General Assembly, 1991).

Christianity came into the world firstly in order to assert with violence that a man had not only to look inwards, but to look outwards, to behold with astonishment and enthusiasm a divine company and a divine captain. The only fun of being a Christian was that a man was not left alone with the Inner Light, but definitely recognized an outer light, fair as the sun, clear as the moon, terrible as an army with banners.[39]

An inner light creates an inner savior and an inner church: the self alone with the divine. However, the Word calls us out of ourselves to be judged and justified by a proclamation that is heard by fellow sinners to whom we are joined by the faith that the Spirit gives through that proclaimed word.

Because the Spirit works through creaturely means, rather than directly and immediately, a creaturely community arises. The church does not first of all exist and then create a canon; rather, it is spoken into existence by the same Word that rules it.[40] In the flight from time and space to a naked encounter with God face to face, the mystical soul strives to secure salvation by its striving ascent. However, this encounter is never saving but always dangerous, because God is "a consuming fire" (Heb 12:29). The only safe route is to stop striving to ascend and receive God as he has descended in his Son, clothed in the gospel. *Though seemingly powerless and ineffective, the creaturely mediation of his Word through faltering human lips is the most powerful thing on earth.*

D. CHALLENGES TO PREACHING AS MEANS OF GRACE

In the modern era, Karl Barth recovered the Reformers' emphasis on proclamation; in fact, he insisted that the whole apparatus of theological education and biblical studies is designed to serve the ministry of preaching. Barth pictures the modern view in terms of a volcano that "throws out lava or the sea mussels" in exuberant expression and pious feeling.[41] By contrast, sound dogmaticians and pastors "are working on something given when they reflect on God's Word. What is given is the wonderful song of praise of the Christian church as we may hear it each dear Sunday or even each weekday."[42] Rationalists base their belief in God on the idea of God that exists within us, while romantic liberals speak of "an achieved experience of God," but this is a theology of glory (human ascent in works righteousness) rather than a theology of the cross (divine descent in grace).[43] Preaching normed by

---

39. G. K. Chesterton, *Orthodoxy: The Romance of Faith* (New York: Doubleday, 1959, 1990), 76.

40. Of course, something of a Luther renaissance on this score has occurred within the so-called New Hermeneutic in the 1970s (Fuchs and Ebeling), with its theology of the "word-event." However, the tendency was to domesticate this eschatological radicalism by relegating it to the field of the individual's

existential encounter rather than locating it in the sweep of redemptive history. To that extent, it is significantly different from Luther's concept.

41. Barth, *Church Dogmatics*, vol. 1, pt. 1, p. 26.

42. Ibid.

43. Ibid., vol. 1, pt. 1, p. 48.

Scripture, however, is the speech of "a king through the mouth of his herald" and is meant to be received as God's own address. While we dare not confuse our own proclamation with grace itself, it is a means of grace by God's appointment.[44] At the same time, "Church proclamation itself, in fact, regards itself only as service of the Word of God, as a means of grace in God's free hand. Hence it cannot be master of the Word, nor try to regard the Word as confined within its own borders."[45]

Through preaching God himself is present among us in Christ by his Spirit, Barth points out. As a divine announcement proclaimed through a herald, preaching "cannot be arbitrary religious discourse." "It must be homily, i.e., discourse which as the exposition of Scripture is controlled and guided. Calling, promise, exposition of Scripture, actuality—these are the decisive definitions of the concept of preaching."[46] Preaching is not free speech, but holy speech—a message not only about God but from God.

The liberal Protestant and Roman Catholic tendencies that concerned Barth—the tendency to reduce preaching to an "expression of the personal piety of the speaker" or to a "higher level of instruction in religion and morals"—seem just as evident today in evangelical churches.[47] But in truth, preaching can be a means of grace only inasmuch as it repeats the announcement that it has heard from God himself.[48] "We may ignore at this point the fact that it is specifically Evangelical [Lutheran]-Reformed dogmatics which has done this in detail."[49] "Modernist dogmatics," Barth adds, "is finally unaware of the fact that in relation to God man has constantly *to let something be said to him*, has constantly to *listen* to something, which he constantly *does not know and which in no circumstances and in no sense can he say to himself. Modernist dogmatics hears man answer when no one has called him. It hears him speak with himself*" (emphasis added).[50] Refusing the external Word that comes to us from outside of our own familiar thoughts and experience, we turn to idols that cannot speak.

The law and the gospel continue also to teach us God's moral and saving will, guiding and norming our speech and action in relation to God and our neighbors. Nevertheless, apart from the Word of God as a means of grace, all instruction would be mere moralism and dogmatism. To the extent that in more conservative circles preaching has been reduced to its didactic function or to inspiration and moral uplift, it is not surprising that younger believers look for alternative means of grace. Typically, we prefer what we can see to what we hear: "A picture tells a thousand words." Our new images may not be statues that we venerate, but there is a real

44. Ibid., vol. 1, pt. 1, p. 52.
45. Ibid., vol. 1, pt. 1, p. 54.
46. Ibid., vol. 1, pt. 1, p. 59.
47. Ibid., vol. 1, pt. 1, p. 60.

48. Ibid.
49. Ibid., vol. 1, pt. 1, p. 61.
50. Ibid., vol. 1, pt. 1, p. 63.

danger in Protestant churches of once again silencing God's living and active speech (i.e., the exposition of Scripture) in a sea of our own insights, visual drama, and the blue luminosity of our computer screens. Yet our Lord chose not only the content but the medium. We do not find God; he finds us. Faith comes not by feeling, thinking, seeing, or striving, but by *hearing*.

Proclamation does involve doctrinal and ethical instruction, of course. The law and the gospel not only kill and make alive; they direct our life and doctrine. However, we must come to church expecting nothing less than God's gracious assault on the citadels of our autonomy, our supposing that we could ascend to God by our theological acumen any more than by our actions. This confrontation occurs not only in the sermon, but in the entire liturgy, including the singing, whose purpose is to "let the word of Christ dwell in you richly, teaching and admonishing one another in all wisdom, singing psalms and hymns and spiritual songs, with thankfulness in your hearts to God" (Col 3:16). While carefully distinguishing the Spirit's illumination of the preached Word from the Spirit's inspiration of the canonical Word, we can affirm that the content—Christ and all of his benefits—is exactly the same. This should create a sense of urgency and expectancy in our public assembly, as God addresses us here and now.[51]

II. THE SACRAMENTS

So great is God's love and care for his people that he not only calls them into fellowship with his Son by his Word; he assures them of his goodwill, binding himself to them, them to himself, and them to each other through sacraments that he has personally instituted. Together with the Word, these sacraments are means of grace and are therefore essential marks of the true church.

---

51. For example, Wayne Grudem discusses the different forms of God's word as speech: personal address, mediated discourse through human lips, and the written canon. However, he does not mention any sense in which God speaks through preaching today. "God's words as spoken through human lips ceased to be given when the New Testament canon was completed" (*Systematic Theology: An Introduction to Bible Doctrine* [Grand Rapids: Zondervan], 1994), 50–51). In fact, in treating the "means of grace" (numbering 11), all of which are interpreted chiefly as *our* service, he begins with "Teaching the Word," and throughout this discussion the reference is to the written text rather than preaching as such, as it is based on Scripture. While the Word of God as a means of grace certainly involves teaching, preaching (proclamation) is more than this. Traditionally, the Reformers and the Puritans regarded preaching as "prophesying," although it no longer occurs under divine inspiration. However, Grudem suggests, "Although several definitions have been given for the gift of prophecy, a fresh examination of the New Testament teaching on this gift will show that it should be defined not as 'predicting the future,' nor as 'proclaiming a word from the Lord,' nor as 'powerful preaching'—but rather as 'telling something that God has spontaneously brought to mind'" (1050). Interestingly, Grudem devotes considerable space to the role of spiritual gifts, including words of prophecy (1016–87). In this way, the concept of the Word of God is limited to the written text as teaching, while God in some sense still speaks to individuals apart from either Scripture or its proclamation. For an exegetical critique of Grudem's view, see Edmund P. CLowney, *The Church: Contours of Christian Theology* (Downers Grove, Ill.: InterVarsity Press, 1995), 255–68.

A. HISTORICAL-THEOLOGICAL EXAMINATION OF THE SACRAMENTS

From the Latin *sacramentum*, the term *sacrament* derives originally from the Roman courts, where litigants were required to give a prescribed monetary pledge that the winner of the case would receive back. It also came to be used in a military context, as an oath sworn by soldiers. Early Christian writers used the term more as the equivalent of the Greek term *mystērion* ("mystery"), which (following Pauline precedent) included the great doctrines of the faith once hidden under types and shadows but now fully revealed (Ro 11:25; 16:25; 1Co 15:51; Eph 1:9; 3:3–4, 9; 5:32; 6:19; Col 1:26–27; 4:3; 1Ti 3:9, 16). "This is how one should regard us [apostles]," writes Paul: "as servants of Christ and stewards of the mysteries of God" (1Co 4:1).

1. ANCIENT AND MEDIEVAL VIEWS

Taking the New Testament at face value in regarding baptism and the Supper as God's means of communicating saving grace, the ancient church reflects a fairly broad range of views as to the relation between the *sign* (baptizing with water and the Word; eating the bread and drinking the wine) and *the thing signified* (regeneration; Christ and all of his benefits).[52] Distinguishing without separating the sacramental sign from the reality signified, Augustine taught that the efficient cause of all grace is God rather than the sacraments themselves. Therefore, he did not believe that recipients truly received the reality signified in baptism and the Supper apart from faith.[53]

With the increasing dominance of Neoplatonism and the concept of grace as a habit or disposition infused into the soul to elevate it from natural to supernatural ends, the sacraments were seen as conduits for this process. Because grace was understood as a physical substance infused into the soul, the sacraments themselves came to be regarded as causing regeneration (in the case of baptism) and perpetual union with Christ (in the case of the Supper). The medieval formulation of this idea is expressed in the phrase *ex opere operato*, which means literally, "from the work having been worked"; this phrase expresses the Roman Catholic view that simply by virtue of a priest's administering the sacraments the reality signified is accomplished, as long as one did not place an obstacle in its way.

Throughout the medieval period debates erupted over this understanding of the sacraments (especially the Supper), as illustrated in the ninth-century controversy

---

52. Even the *Catholic Encyclopedia* (New York: J.Appleton, 1908) entry by J. Pohle, "The Real Presence of Christ in the Eucharist," acknowledges a confluence of sign terminology and realism among the ancient fathers. On Athanasius and Augustine, see especially J. N. D. Kelly, *Early Christian Doctrines* (New York: Harper Bros., 1958, 1960), 446–48. Among other references, Kelly cites Athanasius (*Letters to Serapion* 4, 19) and Augustine (*Narrations on the Psalms* 3, 1; 98, 9; *Sermons* 131, 1; *Tractates on the Gospel of John* 27, 5; 25, 12; 26,1).

53. See Calvin's citations and interpretation of Augustine on this point in the *Institutes* 4.17.34.

between Radbertus and Ratramnus.[54] Increasingly, the church substituted itself for Christ's physical body as the ladder of grace. Claiming authority to institute new sacraments that are not explicitly appointed in Scripture, the medieval church added confirmation, penance, ordination, marriage, and extreme unction and gave a quasisacramental status to relics, pilgrimages, and shrines, as well as to pictures, icons, and statues. To each additional sacrament further acts bearing sacramental efficacy could be added. For example, the sale of indulgences (which continues to this day), which could purchase time off in purgatory for oneself as well as for friends and relatives, was an extension of the sacrament of penance.

Beginning especially with the Fourth Lateran Council (1214), official Roman Catholic teaching on the sacraments received its most elaborate formulation by Thomas Aquinas and attained its clearest dogmatic status at the sixteenth-century Council of Trent. According to Aquinas, unlike just any sign of a sacred thing, a sacrament "makes people holy."[55] Thus, "only those are called sacraments which signify the perfection of holiness in man."[56] The sacraments accomplish this by causing grace to be infused into the recipient, and this is where the different understandings of grace underlying the sacraments emerge.[57]

2. ANABAPTIST VIEWS

Although Anabaptism was a diverse movement that arose more out of late medieval spirituality than out of the Reformation, it was united by a mystical tendency to sharply contrast the inner work of the Spirit with the outer work of the church in its official ministry.[58] With its strong emphasis on personal decision and complete obedience to Christ's commands, baptism and the Supper became chiefly means of discipline. The Supper is often treated merely as a memorial with social (horizontal) implications rather than as a means of grace.[59] While the social dimension

---

54. Both Benedictine monks at the same French abbey, Radbertus defended transubstantiation, while Ratramnus rejected this view.

55. Thomas Aquinas, *Summa theologica*, q. 60, art. 2, part 3 (trans. Fathers of the English Dominican Province; New York: Benziger Bros., 1947–1948; Westminster, Md.: Christian Classics, 1948), 4:2340.

56. Ibid., q. 60, art. 2, pt. 3, 4:2340.

57. Ibid., q. 69, art. 9, pt. 3, 4:2409: "While infants, all being equal in capacity, receive the same effect in baptism, adults, who approach Baptism in their own faith, are not equally disposed to Baptism; for some approach thereto with greater, some with less, devotion. And therefore some receive a greater, some a smaller share of the grace of newness," just as those who come closer to the fire receive more of its heat. Grace is obviously a power (*potentia*) and a substance (*substantia*) with which one must cooperate in order to receive its fullest effect: "Consequently in

order that a man be justified by Baptism, his will must needs embrace both Baptism and the baptismal effect.... Wherefore it is manifest that insincerity hinders the effect of baptism."

58. Thomas N. Finger offers helpful nuances in interpreting various strands of Anabaptist teaching on this subject in *A Contemporary Anabaptist Theology* (Downers Grove, Ill.: InterVarsity Press, 2004), ch. 6.

59. For a contemporary statement, see John Howard Yoder, *Body Politics* (Nashville: Discipleship Resources, 1992), 16; Thomas Finger recognizes, "[Balthasar] Hubmaier stressed the Supper's communal dimension and its expression through concrete, outward ethical activity." He quotes Hubmaier: "For the Supper has to do 'completely and exclusively with fraternal love'" (see *Contemporary Anabaptist Theology*, 187). Like Zwingli, many of the Anabaptists presupposed that "an ontological barrier separated spirit and matter" (190).

is important for a biblical conception, as I will argue, Berkhof's judgment seems substantially correct:

> The Anabaptists, and other mystical sects of the age of the Reformation and later times, virtually deny that God avails Himself of means in the distributing of His grace. They stress the fact that God is absolutely free in communicating His grace, and therefore can hardly be conceived of as bound to such external means. Such means after all belong to the natural world, and have nothing in common with the spiritual world. God, or Christ, or the Holy Spirit, or the inner light, works directly in the heart, and both the Word and the sacraments can only serve to indicate or to symbolize this internal grace. The whole conception is determined by a dualistic view of nature and grace.[60]

The Anabaptist contrast of the outer means and the inner working of the Spirit did not, however, lead to the abandonment of these ordained rites, as was the case among the Society of Friends (Quakers).

3. REFORMATION VIEWS

The Reformation introduced a view of the sacraments that differed substantially from both medieval Rome and Anabaptism. The church is not itself a means of grace, Martin Luther insisted, but the servant of the Word that created the church in the first place. Therefore, the sacraments have efficacy only in connection with the Word. Together with the Word, the sacraments promise God's favor on account of Christ. They are a "visible Word," "a seal and confirmation of the Word and promise."[61] Yet because God gives his promise—indeed, Christ himself—through these signs, they are not separated from the reality that they signify.[62]

Because the Word embraces the baptismal water, it becomes "a gracious water of life and a washing of regeneration in the Holy Spirit."[63] Baptism removes the guilt of original sin and brings "God's grace, the entire Christ, and the Holy Spirit with his gifts."[64] Because Christ is objectively present and is given bodily in baptism and Communion, every recipient of these sacraments receives Christ, although unbelievers receive them to their judgment. Faith, therefore, contributes nothing to the nature and efficacy of the sacraments; they are what they are and do what they do, regardless. However, there can be no saving profit if one refuses the gift that Christ gives through these means.

Crucial to this view is the belief that Christ is *bodily* present, not only at the altar but in the words of proclamation and the waters of baptism. This is predicated on

---

60. Berkhof, *Systematic Theology*, 607.

61. *The Book of Concord: The Confessions of the Evangelical Lutheran Church* (ed. and trans. Theodore G. Tappert; Philadelphia: Fortress, 1959), see *Apology of the Augsburg Confession*, 13.5; 24.70.

62. Ibid., see *Apology of the Augsburg Confession*, 24.70; *Larger Catechism*, 5.30.

63. Ibid., see *Smalcald Articles*, 4.10.

64. Ibid., see *Apology of the Augsburg Confession*, 2.35; *Larger Catechism*, 4.41.

the belief that in the unity of Christ's person as God incarnate the characteristics (or attributes) of divinity are communicated to his humanity (in this case, omnipresence). Consequently, Christ can be present in the flesh wherever he wills. Not only according to his divinity but according to his humanity, he is present at every altar with the bread and wine (which remain unchanged).[65]

The Zürich Reformer Ulrich Zwingli (1484–1531) differed from Luther's view of sacraments on several points. Assuming a sharp dualism between spiritual and material things as well as between the divine and human natures of Christ, Zwingli came to regard the sacraments more as a human than as a divine pledge. Consequently, he viewed the sacraments as teaching and motivating ordinances rather than means of grace. Charles Hodge summarizes Zwingli's sacramental theology well:

> According to the doctrine of Zwingli afterwards adopted by the Remonstrants [Arminians], the sacraments are not properly "means of grace." They were not ordained to signify, seal, and apply to believers the benefits of Christ's redemption. They were indeed intended to be significant emblems of the great truths of the Gospel. Baptism was intended to teach the necessity of the soul's being cleansed from guilt by the blood of Christ and purified from the pollution of sin by the renewing of the Holy Ghost. They were further designed to be perpetual memorials of the work of redemption, and especially to be the means by which men should, in the sight of the Church and of the world, profess themselves to be Christians.[66]

As "badges of Christian men's profession," they offer "an objective presentation of the truth which they signify to the mind."[67] For Zwingli the sacraments are "no more means of grace than the rainbow or the heaps of stone on the banks of the Jordan."[68]

Meeting at Marburg in 1529, Luther and Zwingli (attended by various other representatives) agreed on fourteen out of fifteen points. The disagreement, however, concerned Christ's real presence in the Supper. Reformed leaders (including Martin Bucer, who was present at Marburg, and Zwingli's successor in Zürich, Heinrich Bullinger) rejected Zwingli's view, but in spite of important concords, this breach was never healed. It was in this context that John Calvin gained prominence, giving refinement to the view found in the Reformed and Presbyterian confessions (i.e., the *Belgic* and *Westminster* confessions, the *Thirty-nine Articles* of the Church of England, and minor confessions of the Scottish and French churches). Philip Walker Butin observes, "Calvin's concern for 'the visibility of grace' was also expressed in his particular understanding of the sacraments.…'" The Word creates faith, Calvin

---

65. Ibid., see *Formula of Concord*, Solid Declaration 7, arts. 36–38 (pp. 575–76).
66. Charles Hodge, *Systematic Theology* (Grand Rapids:

Eerdmans, 1946), 3:498.
67. Ibid.
68. Ibid., 3:499.

insists. " 'But the sacraments bring the clearest promises. . . .' "[69] In asking, "Where does faith come from?" the answer of the *Heidelberg Catechism* works just as well for the origins of the church: "The Spirit creates faith in our hearts by the preaching of the holy gospel and confirms it by the use of the holy sacraments."[70]

Affirming with Zwingli the significance of Christ's bodily ascension (convinced that the idea of an omnipresent human body emptied Christ's glorified flesh of its reality), Calvin nevertheless agreed with Luther on the principal definition: namely, that God does in fact bring about spiritual effects through physical means and that sacraments are primarily God's action rather than that of the recipients. As we will observe more closely in relation to the Supper, Calvin was especially influenced in his understanding not only by Augustine but also by Cyril of Alexandria, Chrysostom, and other theologians in the East. In the *sacramental union* of sign and thing signified, Calvin emphasized, God truly offers and gives his saving grace *through* earthly means. Just as the preaching of the Word is valid in and of itself, apart from human response, baptism and the Supper remain objective sacraments even apart from one's faith. Faith does not *make* a sacrament, but it does *receive* the reality of the sacrament; otherwise one receives only the sign without the thing signified.

Especially in debates with Anabaptists, Lutheran and Reformed theologians stressed the continuity of the one covenant of grace in both testaments and therefore the relationship of circumcision (type) and baptism (antitype), but Zwingli placed his emphasis on the human side of the covenant. Chiefly, baptism was regarded as an obligation (placed upon parents and the children); the divine promise was made secondary. In contrast, although Calvin and the other Reformed leaders did not deny the appropriate obligations of recipients, they regarded God's promise as the primary purpose of the sacraments. It was this emphasis that shaped the particular features of the covenant theology exhibited in the Reformed interpretation of the sacraments. "The first point clearly taught on this subject in the Symbols of the Reformed Church is that the sacraments are real means of grace," Hodge notes, "that is, means appointed and employed by Christ for conveying the benefits of his redemption to his people. . . . The word grace, when we speak of the means of grace, includes three things. 1st. An unmerited gift, such as the remission of sin. 2nd. The supernatural influence of the Holy Spirit. 3rd. The subjective effects of that influence on the soul."[71] Though they have no inherent power, Hodge emphasizes, through them the Spirit truly *confers* saving grace.[72]

It is *God* alone who saves. Nevertheless, God ordinarily works *through means*, especially through those that he has explicitly instituted and to which he has

---

69. Philip Walker Butin, *Revelation, Redemption, and Response: Calvin's Trinitarian Understanding of the Divine-Human Relationship* (New York: Oxford Univ. Press, 1995), 103.

70. *Heidelberg Catechism*, q. 65, in *Ecumenical Creeds and Reformed Confessions*, 41.

71. Hodge, *Systematic Theology*, 3:499.

72. Ibid., 3:500.

attached his promise. As Berkhof explains this view, God "is not absolutely bound to them but ordinarily binds himself to them."

> God has appointed them as the ordinary means through which He works His grace in the hearts of sinners, and their willful neglect can only result in spiritual loss.... The special grace of God operates only in the sphere in which the means of grace function. This truth must be maintained over against the Mystics, who deny the necessity of the means of grace. God is a God of order, who in the operation of His grace ordinarily employs the means which He has Himself ordained.[73]

A sacrament consists of a visible sign (signs and seals: Ge 9:12–13; 17:11; Ro 4:11) and spiritual grace: "the covenant of grace, Gen. 9:12, 13; 17:11; the righteousness of faith, Rom. 4:11; the forgiveness of sins, Mark 1:4; Matt. 26:28; faith and conversion, Mark 1:4; 16:16; communion with Christ in His death and resurrection, Rom. 6:3, and so on."[74] According to Reformed interpretation, then, the sacramental union is not a fusion of substances, but a relative action of God in the covenantal economy, that is, a giving of gifts from one person (God) to others (believers). "The close connection between the sign and the thing signified explains the use of what is generally called 'sacramental language,' in which the sign is put for the thing signified or vice versa, Gen. 17:10; Ac 22:16; 1 Cor. 5:7."[75]

While the more mystical view associated with Anabaptism identifies the work of the Spirit exclusively with a direct and immediate operation within the soul, *Socinianism* (named after Laelius Socinus and his nephew Faustus) arose in the sixteenth century as an early form of Unitarianism and rationalism. Given the emphasis on the inner over the outer and of individual decision over God's electing grace, Anabaptists, Socinians, Arminians, neonomians, mystics, and rationalists were united in their opposition to the conviction that the sacraments are means of grace.[76]

4. CONTEMPORARY EVANGELICAL VIEWS

Fed by the streams of the Reformation and confessional Protestantism as well as by Arminianism, revivalism, and Pentecostalism, the oceanic breadth of the evangelical movement defies simple definition. This is especially true regarding the sacraments. Even among many Lutheran, Presbyterian, and Reformed evangelicals the views summarized in their official confessions and catechisms are often (at least implicitly) modified by the Anabaptist currents of the broader movement.

---

73. Berkhof, *Systematic Theology*, 608.

74. Ibid., 618; cf. *Belgic Confession*, art. 33, and *Heidelberg Catechism*, q. 66, in *Ecumenical Creeds and Reformed Confessions*; see also *Westminster Confession*, ch. 27.

75. Berkhof, *Systematic Theology*, 618.

76. Ibid., 607–8. Although Laelius Socinus expected baptism to become an obsolete superstition, his followers retained the outward form of both rites. However, they allowed them only a "moral efficacy," denying any "mystical operation of the Holy Spirit" through them. "In fact, they placed the emphasis more on what man did in the means of grace than on what God accomplished through them, when they spoke of them as mere external badges of profession and (of the sacraments) as memorials. The Arminians of the seventeenth century and the Rationalists of the eighteenth century shared this view."

Karl Barth rejected all forms of synergism with great vigor. However, he came to regard baptism as nothing more than a human act of response. Logically, he eventually rejected the baptism of covenant children. Baptism witnesses to grace, says Barth. "It is not itself, however, the bearer, means, or instrument of grace. Baptism *responds to* a mystery, the sacrament of the history of Jesus Christ, of His resurrection, of the outpouring of the Holy Spirit. *It is not itself, however, a mystery or sacrament*" (emphasis added).[77] What is lost in Barth's treatment is the Reformed understanding of baptism as, first and foremost, *God's* act and pledge. Taking a step even beyond Zwingli, he wrote, "The Reformed Church and Reformed theology (even in Zürich) could not continue to hold" to Zwingli's teaching, and took a "backward step" toward Calvin's "sacramentalism." "We for our part cannot deny that both negatively and positively Zwingli was basically right."[78]

However, in most of its expressions evangelicalism is less indebted to Zwingli or Barth than to the more explicitly Anabaptist heritage as well as the traditions of pietism and revivalism. Therefore, personal practices or spiritual disciplines are often regarded as more central than the sacraments of the church in the ordinary nurture and sustenance of faith. Introducing baptism and the Supper as "Community Acts of Commitment," Stanley Grenz holds that "the ordinances symbolize the gospel."[79] Grenz explains that from the perspective of the Radical Reformers and their Baptist heirs, baptism and the Supper "are basically human, and not divine acts." "At the heart of this theology was a focus on obedience. Believers participate in the ordinances out of a desire to be obedient to the one who ordained these acts for the church. The ordinances, therefore, are signs of obedience."[80]

Millard Erickson recognizes that the Reformed view, which "is tied closely to the concept of the covenant," emphasizes "the objective aspect of the sacrament."[81] In opposition to this view Erickson argues, "The act of baptism conveys no direct spiritual benefit or blessing." "It is, then, a testimony that one has already been regenerated," and is only performed after candidates "have exhibited credible evidence of regeneration" and have therefore "met the conditions for salvation (i.e., repentance and active faith)."[82] "It is a public indication of one's commitment to Christ."[83] Concerning the Supper, Erickson notes that in the Reformed view, "There is, then, a genuine objective benefit of the sacrament. It is not generated by the participant;

---

77. Barth, *Church Dogmatics*, vol. 4, pt. 4, pp. 73, 102.

78. Ibid., vol. 4, pt. 4, p. 130. I concur with John Webster's evaluation of Barth's concluding fragment: "The exegesis is sometimes surprisingly shoddy, dominated by special pleading, as well as by what seems at times an almost Platonic distinction between water baptism (an exclusively human act) and baptism with the Spirit (an exclusively divine act).... Clearly the Reformed tradition on sacraments had lost its appeal for him, though what replaced it lacked the nuance and weightiness of

earlier discussion" (*Barth* [New York: Continuum, 2000], 157).

79. Stanley Grenz, *Theology for the Community of God* (Nashville: Broadman & Holman, 1997), 644.

80. Ibid., 670.

81. Millard Erickson, *Christian Theology* (Grand Rapids: Baker, 1985), 1093–94.

82. Ibid., 1096.

83. Ibid., 1101.

rather, it is brought to the sacrament by Christ himself," but according to Erickson the Supper is "basically commemorative."[84] "The Lord's Supper has the effect of bringing preconscious beliefs into consciousness."[85]

It should be noted that in terms of historical theology, the Reformation views concerning the sacraments are at no less variance with these views than with the Roman Catholic position. From a Reformed (as well as Lutheran) perspective, once the sacraments are understood exclusively as human acts of obedience rather than as God's means of grace, disagreements over symbolic and realistic theories are comparatively insignificant. Although every covenant involves two parties, the covenant of grace rests not on the basis of our personal performance of the law's stipulations but on Christ's fulfillment of all righteousness. It is God's pledge that has priority and in fact brings about our corresponding response.

B. IDENTIFYING THE SACRAMENTS: HOW MANY?

Lutheran and Reformed theologians have traditionally affirmed that in order for a practice to be considered a sacrament it must be *instituted by Christ* and *evangelical* (i.e., a means of grace) in substance. With respect to the latter, Berkhof offers a precise definition:

> They are in themselves, and not in virtue of their connection with things not included in them, means of grace. Striking experiences may, and undoubtedly sometimes do, serve to strengthen the work of God in the heart of believers, but this does not constitute them means of grace in the technical sense, since they accomplish this only in so far as these experiences are interpreted in the light of God's Word, through which the Holy Spirit operates. The Word and the sacraments are in themselves means of grace; their spiritual efficacy is dependent only on the operation of the Holy Spirit.[86]

Furthermore, "They are continuous instruments of God's grace, and not in any sense of the word exceptional." They are not merely "occasional" or "accidental" to the working of grace — that is, providing an opportunity for God to work immediately in one's heart apart from these means, "but are the regularly ordained means for the communication of the saving grace of God and are as such of perpetual value." Finally, "they are the official means of the Church of Jesus Christ ... by which the Holy Spirit works and confirms faith in the hearts of men."[87]

We can see the validity of this specific definition by examining the undisputed sacraments of the Old and New Testament.

---

84. Ibid., 1120, 1122.
85. Ibid., 1126.

86. Berkhof, *Systematic Theology*, 605.
87. Ibid.

1. OLD TESTAMENT SACRAMENTS

(a) Circumcision was *instituted directly by God* as a sign and seal of the *covenant of grace* (Ge 15; 17). The gracious character of this covenant is evident in the form and content in which we find it in Genesis 15, where God issues unilateral promises and confirms them in a vision in which he passes alone through the severed animal pieces. It is evident also from the New Testament interpretation, as I have already argued. Hence, the covenant that was pledged to Abraham is the covenant of grace to which new covenant believers and their children belong (Gal 3:7–9, 24–29, etc.).

(b) Similarly, the Passover was *instituted by God* as a perpetual sign and seal of *the Lord's "passing over"* the homes of the righteous when he saw the blood on the door on his day of judgment in Egypt (Ex 12:11–27). Again, the *substance* of this sacrament was God's promise, even though (like circumcision) it also *created* the obligations of the covenant partners as their reasonable response of worship.

2. NEW TESTAMENT SACRAMENTS

(a) *Baptism* replaces circumcision (Col 2:11–12; cf. Ro 4:11; Gal 3:27). To be sure, the New Testament is just as clear that there are *discontinuities*, not in the substance but in the administration, with the Old Testament history of the covenant of grace. It is no longer those who are circumcised (Ro 4), but those who are baptized, who are now identified with Christ in his death and resurrection (Ro 6). While John's baptism was a sign of repentance, preparing the way for the kingdom of God, Jesus brought the reality of the kingdom itself through his ministry; thus there is no longer a baptism of repentance in preparation for Christ, but the Spirit's baptism into Christ that brings new birth (Jn 1:19–34; 3:3, 5). Jesus submits to John's baptism, endures the baptism of judgment in our place, and then commands his disciples to bring the gospel to the nations, "baptizing them in the name of the Father and of the Son and of the Holy Spirit…" (Mt 28:19). A further discontinuity appears with respect to the subjects of circumcision and baptism: only males in the Old Testament, but now males and females in the New. Yet not even this matter is decided by the church itself, but is anticipated by the prophets (Joel 2:28–29) and fulfilled in the ministry of the apostles (see, for example, Ac 16:15). The New Testament is greater than the Old, as fulfillment is to promise, yet all along the substance of faith—Christ and all of his benefits—remains the same.

In spite of discontinuities in administration, the substance of the covenant of grace remains the same in both Old and New Testaments. Even on the day of Pentecost itself, those who believed the gospel that Peter proclaimed asked, "Brothers, what shall we do?" "And Peter said to them, 'Repent and be baptized every one of you in the name of Jesus Christ for the forgiveness of your sins, and you will receive the gift of the Holy Spirit. For the promise is for you and for your children and for all who are far off, everyone whom the Lord our God calls to himself" (Ac 2:37–39).

(b) The *Lord's Supper* replaces Passover. At Passover—on the evening on which he would be handed over rather than passed over in judgment—Jesus instituted the Supper as "my *blood of the covenant*, which is poured out for many *for the forgiveness of sins*" (Mt 26:26–29; cf. Mk 14:22–25; Lk 22:18–20; 1Co 11:23–26). Baptism and the Lord's Supper are therefore explicitly instituted by Christ, and their substance is the same: the promise of forgiveness of sins and the gift of the Spirit because of Jesus Christ's person and work.

Many things are prescribed for New Testament saints as means of encouragement, growth, discipleship, and service in the body of Christ and in the world. However, these are means of gratitude rather than means of grace.

3. EVALUATING THE CLAIMS FOR ADDITIONAL SACRAMENTS

With these two criteria in mind (instituted by Christ and means of grace), confirmation, penance, ordination, matrimony, and extreme unction cannot be said to constitute sacraments of the church, as Roman Catholic teaching requires.[88]

(a) *Confirmation*. According to the Roman Catholic practice of *confirmation*, the bishop lays his hands on those who are about to receive their first Communion so that they will receive the Holy Spirit. While the practice has been retained in many Lutheran and Reformed bodies, it is not regarded as a sacrament because the promise of receiving the Holy Spirit was related by the apostles to baptism alone (Ac 2:38). If confirmation is to be retained without calling into question the validity of baptism, it cannot be a sacrament. Rather than a means of grace, it is the profession of faith on the part of adult converts and those brought up in the visible covenant who publicly confess Christ before their brothers and sisters and become full communicant members. Confirmation or profession of faith is the believer's act, a response to the promise made in baptism. Therefore, while public profession is certainly commanded (Ro 10:9–10) and is the prerequisite for adult converts (as witnessed throughout Acts), believers also brought their children for baptism, and the children's profession of faith is their means of accepting the promise ratified in their baptism rather than a means of grace in its own right.

(b) *Penance* offers absolution (forgiveness) as a result of verbal confession of each sin to a priest, attrition (fear of penalty), and satisfaction (fulfilling certain compensatory works assigned by the priest). However, this rite is nowhere prescribed in Scripture. Furthermore, as an explicit form of works righteousness, penance not only fails consideration as a means of grace; it emphatically contradicts the gospel.

---

88. For a summary description of these additional sacraments see the *Catechism of the Catholic Church* (Liguori, Mo.: Liguori Publications, 1994), 325–420.

Church discipline and pastoral care certainly involve moral instruction and guidance, often requiring members to reconcile differences and repair offenses. They may even be kept from the Lord's Table for refusing the teaching, correction, and admonition of the elders. However, these are the appropriate duties of Christians toward their neighbors in response to God's grace and forgiveness, not means of making satisfaction for sin.

Certainly, confession of sins and absolution have biblical precedent, and in Lutheran and Reformed churches these elements of penance were part of the public service rather than a private sacrament, and the sole basis was Christ's satisfaction rather than the believer's. In the regular liturgy, ministers declare to the people in Christ's name that their sins have been forgiven for Christ's sake. This public practice was also retained in the form for excommunication and absolution in Reformed and Presbyterian churches. In fact, Calvin argued that tender consciences that are anxious over particular sins should be encouraged to confess them to a minister and receive private absolution.[89] Therefore, the elements that have biblical support can be retained without corrupting the gospel and multiplying sacraments. From the Reformed perspective, absolution (both in public and in private) is simply the application of the Word of God.

(c) *Ordination*—that is, the laying on of hands by the presbytery (*presbyterion*)—is clearly an ordinance of Christ according to the New Testament (1Ti 4:14; 5:22; Tit 1:5; Ac 6:6). Although spiritual gifts for ministry are given through this ordinance (1Ti 4:14), the phrase "means of grace" refers to *saving* grace, which all believers share in common. All believers are ordained to the *general* office of prophets, priests, and kings in their baptism; some believers are ordained to the *special* office of pastor, elder, and deacon. Once again we should recall that according to Roman Catholic teaching grace is a substance infused into the soul in order to elevate it from natural to supernatural status. Consequently, ordination is understood to infuse an additional "character" or "imprint" on the soul that renders the priest qualitatively different from the rest of the baptized.[90] By contrast, Paul says that he gave ministers as gifts *to his church*, for the edification and building up of the whole body into its head, not for the private elevation of particular members (Eph 4:11–16). "For in one Spirit we were all baptized into one body ... and all were made to drink of one Spirit. For the body does not consist of one member but of many. If the foot should say, 'Because I am not a hand, I do not belong to the body,' that would not make it any less a part of the body" (1Co 12:13–15).

(d) *Marriage.* Although most spouses would attest to the fact that marriage affords opportunities for recognizing shortcomings and maturing in life and faith,

---

89. Calvin, *Institutes* 3.4.14.

90. *Catechism of the Catholic Church*, 395–99.

it is not identified in Scripture as a means of grace. In fact, marriage was instituted as a creation ordinance and is shared with non-Christians, though covenant families, even with one believing spouse, are holy (1Co 7:14). However, it is the ministry of Word and sacrament in which the family shares rather than the common grace institution of marriage itself that constitutes a means of grace.

(e) *Extreme unction* (often called last rites) claims James 5:14 – 16 for support, but this passage mentions only calling "for the elders of the church" to pray over the one who is ill, "anointing him with oil in the name of the Lord," hearing his confession of sins and pronouncing forgiveness. From this passage has evolved an elaborate ritual in which the priest administers oil (specially blessed by the bishop) to the eyes, ears, nostrils, lips, hands, feet, and (for men only) the loins. With each application, the priest absolves sins committed by each organ. The purpose of extreme unction is to bring miraculous restoration of health and, short of this, to prepare the recipient for death. The Council of Trent anathematized all who deny that this rite was "instituted by Christ our Lord" but was merely instituted "by a human invention."[91]

However, several things may be noted. First, in the immediately preceding verse, James says, "Is anyone among you suffering? Let him pray. Is anyone cheerful? Let him sing praise." Prayer and singing are of course central Christian practices, but they are not regarded in Roman Catholic teaching as sacraments, or even as ingredients of this alleged sacrament. Second, if penance made satisfaction for sins, why would there be a need for a further sacrament of absolution in order to die in a state of grace? Third, especially when compared to baptism and the Supper (which become marginalized or diluted), extreme unction seems to hang by a slender thread, and the various actions regarded as essential to it are nowhere mentioned in this passage or anywhere else in the Scriptures. It seems unlikely that Christ would have instituted a new sacrament for the church through the pastoral advice of a single apostle, with no evidence of its sacramental status in the apostolic church more generally.

From the Reformation perspective, then, the means of grace have a very specific reference. Not everything that is useful, or even commanded in Scripture, as an aid to the Christian life is to be regarded as a sacrament (i.e., means of grace). The church itself is not a means of grace, but administers the means of grace, and has no canonical authority to create new sacraments. Berkhof observes,

> Moreover, faith, conversion, and prayer, are first of all fruits of the grace of God, though they may in turn become instrumental in strengthening the spiritual life. They are not objective ordinances, but subjective conditions for the possession and

---

91. *Canons and Decrees of the Council of Trent: Original Text with English Translation* (trans. H. J. Schroeder; St. Louis: Herder, 1960), session 14, art. 1.

enjoyment of the blessings of the covenant.... Strictly speaking, only the Word and the sacraments can be regarded as means of grace, that is, as objective channels which Christ has instituted in the Church, and to which He ordinarily binds Himself in the communication of His grace.[92]

The addition of sacraments in the medieval church does not reflect an *exaggerated* view of sacraments but a *weakened* view of the efficacy of baptism and the Supper.

Ironically, we may observe a similar tendency in contemporary Protestantism, including evangelicalism. As the nature of sacraments is understood largely as the work of the believer, it is no wonder that the list of sacraments or ordinances can be open ended so as to include virtually anything that testifies to God's existence. However, this is to confuse general with special revelation, common grace with saving grace.[93]

Inadequate views of the purpose and efficacy of the sacraments allow virtually any helpful aid to spiritual growth to qualify as a means of grace. Charles Ryrie says that unlike a sacrament, an ordinance "does not incorporate the idea of conveying grace but only the idea of a symbol."[94] Do we need "actual baptism" in order to symbolize "leaving the old life and entering into the new"? Ryrie suggests, "Why not erect a little closet on the church platform, have the candidate enter it in old clothes, change his clothes inside the closet, and then emerge in new clothes? Would that not illustrate the same truth as baptism does? And is it not a scriptural illustration? (Col. 3:9–12)." Therefore, he concludes, we should have "more flexibility" in our practices.[95]

Contemporary evangelical theologian Wayne Grudem criticizes Louis Berkhof's restriction of the sacraments to baptism and the Supper, administered by ordained ministers, as carrying "overtones of 'sacerdotalism.' ..."[96] "But is it wise to make such a short list of 'means of grace'? If we wish to list and discuss all the means of receiving the Holy Spirit's blessing that come to believers specifically through the fellowship of the church, then it does not seem wise to limit the 'means of grace' to three activities whose administration is restricted to the ordained clergy or officers of the church." He recognizes, of course, that "such a list may become quite long ..."[97] However, the consequence is that "baptism is not a 'major' doctrine" that should remain church-dividing, although it is "a matter of importance for ordinary church life...."[98]

---

92. Berkhof, *Systematic Theology*, 604–5.

93. It may not be surprising that Brian McLaren praises Roman Catholicism's seven sacraments, suggesting that once there are seven, eventually anything—for example, the playfulness of a puppy, dinner with friends, or the smile of a child with Down's Syndrome—can be considered sacramental (*Generous Orthodoxy* [Grand Rapids: Zondervan, 2004], 254).

94. Charles Ryrie, *Basic Theology: A Popular Systematic Guide to Understanding Biblical Truth* (Chicago: Moody Press, 1986, 1999), 487.

95. Ibid., 467.

96. Grudem, *Systematic Theology*, 950.

97. Ibid., 951.

98. Ibid., 976–77.

C. BIBLICAL-THEOLOGICAL EXAMINATION OF THE SACRAMENTS: COVENANTAL RATIFICATION

While debates over the sacraments traditionally become mired in metaphysical speculations, the proper point of departure is once again the covenant as the context within which the sacraments emerge in the first place. In Exodus 24:3–8, for example, the people swear, in response to the law given at Sinai, "All the words that the LORD has spoken we will do" (v. 3). Moses then sprinkles blood on the people because they are assuming responsibility for the oath's fulfillment. The ritual is consistent with the words that it confirms. "Behold the blood of the covenant that the LORD has made with you in accordance with all these words" (v. 8). Not only in the Bible but in the secular politics of ancient Near Eastern treaties, the words and the signs were inextricably bound in the making (i.e., "cutting") of a covenant. The purpose of this section is to treat the sacraments as the means of grace alongside the Word. As the argument unfolds, it should become clearer that a covenantal account of the sacraments will deepen the cleavage between the rival ontologies of "meeting a stranger" and "overcoming estrangement."

As in secular treaties, biblical rites are means of binding strangers to the Other who summons them to his fellowship: "I will be your God and you will be my people." Particularly in the case of a royal grant, the ratification ceremony is the handing over of a gift. Neither, on one hand, is it the testator's transformation of the physical instruments (i.e., the parchment and the wax seal) into his personal body nor, on the other hand, is it a merely symbolic event. Rather, it is an official, public, and legally binding rite according to which the inheritance is delivered to the beneficiary. It is not the transfer of substances, but the transfer of title to an inheritance that the covenantal context presupposes. Especially when God is the author of this covenant, this action has sweeping ontological presuppositions (i.e., the Creator-creation relationship) as well as effects (i.e., lifting of the sanctions, including death, conquest of evil powers, bodily resurrection, and a redeemed creation). However, the action of "cutting a covenant" is itself neither a magical annihilation of natural substances by supernatural substances nor a merely symbolic gesture. Rather, God consecrates nonmysterious, ordinary, and natural substances as means by which he performs his mysterious, marvelous, and miraculous work.

Whatever important metaphysical questions may be asked in any treatment of divine presence, particularly in relation to the sacraments, the categories of presence and absence, "near" and "far away," are spatial metaphors for a covenantal relationship. Roughly speaking, these terms correspond to blessing and curse, respectively. So, for example, Gentile believers are described as those who were in the past "*separated* from Christ, *alienated* from the commonwealth of Israel and *strangers to the covenants of promise*, having *no hope* and *without God* in the world. But now in Jesus

Christ you who once were *far off* have been *brought near* by the blood of Christ. For he himself is our peace," making one family in Christ (Eph 2:12–14).

In addition to its covenantal context, the concept of presence—particularly in relation to creaturely mediation—is always eschatologically conditioned. The same Spirit who brings about in us the filial cry "Abba! Father!" (Ro 8:15) also provokes a longing cry for the parousia that Jesus has promised. "He who testifies to these things says, 'Surely I am coming soon.' Amen. Come, Lord Jesus!" (Rev 22:20–21). Those who are within the covenant even as no more than visible members are within the sphere of the Spirit's activity of separating the waters of this age so that through the penetrating energies of the age to come a dry place may be prepared for communion (Heb 6:4–9).

It is crucial, therefore, to place the sacraments in their covenantal context rather than seek to explain them according to philosophical categories that are alien to this scriptural habitat. In a covenant, signs do not function either merely to represent something absent (as if to bring it to mind) or to actually become the reality signified. Rather, words and signs together constitute an act of covenant making, analogous to political unions or personal unions, as in marriage or adoption. *In this context, the question is not what the signs themselves do (or don't do), but what the agent executes through these words and signs.* Biblical covenants are typically ratified with a rite involving the pouring or sprinkling of blood or passing through severed animal carcasses. However, this was already a familiar practice in ancient Near Eastern diplomacy, with the emperor (suzerain) adopting a dependent ruler and realm (vassal) on the condition that the stipulations that the suzerain was laying down would be strictly kept. "Passing through the halves" meant publicly, officially, and legally accepting the terms of the treaty, including the threat of winding up like the severed carcasses through which the vassal ceremonially walked. This suzerainty treaty therefore required perfect, perpetual, and personal fulfillment of the stipulations, promising tenure in the land for obedience and death for disobedience.

There is no need to repeat the arguments for recognizing the form and content of such a treaty in the covenant that God made with Adam before the fall and with Israel at Sinai, except to add that each had its sign and seal. The Adamic covenant was signified and sealed by the Tree of Life, through which God would grant everlasting life and confirmation in righteousness upon Adam's completion of his task, and the Sinai covenant was ratified by the sprinkling of blood on the people after they had said "'All the words that the LORD has spoken we will do'" (Ex 24:3, 6–8). The sacrament always corresponds to the words of the covenant itself, and in this case the oath of the people to personally perform the law's stipulations corresponds to their being splashed with blood. As we will see, this contrasts sharply with the words and actions of Jesus Christ in the Last Supper.

Unlike the law covenant (i.e., suzerainty treaty), the covenant of grace is a royal grant: a bequest or inheritance that God pledges. It is the covenant of promise that God made immediately after the fall to Adam and Eve and in the Abrahamic and Davidic covenants, which came to their fullest expression in the New Covenant. The promise to Adam and Eve was signified and sealed by God's covering of their nakedness, to Abraham by the vision of Yahweh passing through the pieces (and after this, circumcision), and to David by reference to God's "covenant with the day ... and night" (Jer 33:20; cf. 2Sa 7:16; 1 Ki 2:4; Ps 89:3–4).

Both the law covenant of Sinai and the prior covenant of promise are in play when Jeremiah is called by Israel's suzerain to prosecute his case against his people and promise ultimate redemption. Only curses can be pronounced on the basis of the Sinai treaty. "They did nothing of all you commanded them to do," the prophet acknowledges with tears before Yahweh. "Therefore you have made all this disaster come upon them" (Jer 32:23). Yet from the national covenant, a suzerainty treaty based on Israel's own obedience, only disaster can come because of its complete desecration. Yahweh announces the defeat and exile of Jerusalem by Nebuchadnezzar, lists the commands of the Sinai covenant that have been consistently violated, reminds them that they (through their representative ancestors) swore allegiance to this covenant, and then pronounces the curses: "And the men who transgressed my covenant and did not keep the terms of the covenant that they made before me, I will make them like the calf that they cut in two and passed between its parts ..." (Jer 34:1–22). Nevertheless, on the basis of the covenant of grace, renewed in the New Covenant (see Jer 31), God promises a new creation and a new exodus. God renews his oath: "And they shall be my people, and I will be their God" (Jer 32:38). From all of this we can see that sacraments function as ratification rites. This is why circumcision, for example, was called a "sign" and "seal" of the righteousness that we have through faith (Ge 17:10–11; Ro 4:11–12).

As signs and seals of the covenant (and every covenant involves two parties), sacraments oblige the human partner to faith and obedience. However, baptism and the Supper are first and foremost means of grace because they are the sacraments of the covenant of grace. In fact, in instituting circumcision, Yahweh pledges, "And *I will establish my covenant* between me and you and your offspring after you throughout their generations for an everlasting covenant, to be God to you and to your offspring after you" (Ge 17:7). Circumcision will not only symbolize this promise but also ratify the entitlement of each recipient to it: "So shall my covenant be in your flesh an everlasting covenant" (v. 13). As Paul pointed out, this in no way meant that Abraham and his heirs were justified by circumcision itself, since it was "a seal of the righteousness that he had by faith while he was still uncircumcised" (v. 11).

Similarly, an adult convert is justified the moment he or she trusts in Christ, but this justification is sealed or ratified by baptism. The choice, then, is not between salvation by grace through faith and salvation by sacraments; the latter signify and seal the former. Precisely for that reason, they must not be withheld from entitled recipients. In fact, withholding the visible sign and seal excommunicates one from the visible covenant community: "Any uncircumcised male who is not circumcised in the flesh of his foreskin shall be cut off from his people; he has broken my covenant" (Ge 17:14). Furthermore, just as the old covenant sacraments promised grace and threatened judgment for those who did not receive the reality signified, the New Testament provides the same dire warnings (1Co 10:1–22; 11:27–32; Heb 4:1–13; 6:1–12).

In the covenantal economy, the function of signs is not primarily to express an inner experience or wish. Nor is it primarily to refer symbolically to a state of affairs that transcends it. Rather, it is a judicial act: an obligation-assuming event in the present, entailing obligations that can obtain only in a relationship of persons. A classic example of this function can be found in the covenant with Noah, although there Yahweh assumes the role of the oath taker, which turns the tables on the usual relationship between suzerains and vassals. "I have set my bow in the cloud, and it shall be a sign of the covenant between me and the earth" (Ge 9:12–13). The bow of judgment—once drawn toward human beings, and the arrow released in the deluge—is now drawn and pointing toward God himself in a self-maledictory oath similar to that taken by God before Abraham in Genesis 15. In Revelation 4:3 (cf. 10:1), the bow of judgment hangs behind the throne as a gesture of peace.

The sign does not stand for something else. It is not a question of something that is present representing something that is absent or of somehow making the beloved present in one's mind (like looking at a picture). It is not an object lesson or illustration. On the other hand, it does not overwhelm or replace ordinary natural phenomena, but sanctifies them for an extraordinary communicative event. Not because it undergoes ontological metamorphosis, therefore, but because of God's practical use of it, the rainbow can be called "the covenant." A common meteorological phenomenon becomes holy. If the meaning of language is its use, then the meaning of water, bread, and wine in the context of a covenantal ceremony between God and human beings must be determined in terms of their relation to covenant treaty that they ratify. God consecrates the natural sign of a rainbow, taking upon himself the curses of violating this pledge. It is an assurance to us because it is first of all *God's* act of remembering *his* oath: "When I bring clouds over the earth," Yahweh adds, "and the bow is seen in the clouds, I will remember my covenant that is between me and you and every living creature of all flesh.... When the bow is in the clouds, I will see it and remember the everlasting covenant..." (vv. 14–17).

Similarly, God's promise to Abraham is ratified by the vision of God (symbolized by the smoking firepot) passing through the severed halves—and then also by circumcision (Ge 15–17). Although Abram "believed the LORD, and he counted it to him as righteousness" (Ge 15:6), Abram asks only two verses later, "O Lord God, how am I to know that I shall possess it?" (v. 8), and God accedes to the request by ratifying the spoken promise in the vision of Yahweh passing through the halves (vv. 9–21). As a sign and seal of God's promise, then, a sacrament serves not only to assure the believer of God's favor in Christ but to "remind" *God* of his commitment, even when our sins provoke his anger. It brings subjective assurance because it is an objective pledge.

Unlike the pagan feasts that celebrated natural cycles, Israel's feasts solemnized a perpetual, present participation in the redemptive events of the past and their fulfillment in the future. The Israelites who left Egypt "were baptized into Moses in the cloud and in the sea," and drank of the rock in the wilderness, "and the Rock was Christ" (1Co 10:1–4). Significantly, Paul's comments here begin an extended discussion of public worship, focusing especially on the Supper, as a way of challenging the immaturity, divisiveness, and chaos of the Corinthian church. Through the sacraments, with the Word, the Spirit relocates us from whatever niche demographic we inhabit in this present age and makes us citizens of the age to come. Clearly, the apostles taught that the signs participate in the reality that they signify and seal. But what does that mean? How does this "participation" occur? I have argued that we come to know *who* God is from the covenantal drama rather than *what* God is in his inner essence from philosophical speculation. I have argued the same point with respect to the question of human identity, as well as the nature of sin and grace. The tendency of much of Roman Catholic theology on all of these points is to develop elaborate metaphysics of "whatness," focusing on the inner essence of things. However, in a covenantal context, God and human beings are actors whose character we discern in the unfolding plot. Sin is not due to a natural propensity toward the lower realm but to a transgression of the covenant. Grace is not a commodity, but God's *ḥesed* (Heb.: covenant mercy and faithfulness)—his favor toward sinners on account of Christ's having fulfilled the covenant of law and handing over his inheritance to us in a covenant of grace.

The same must be said concerning the sacraments. Scholastic terminology may help us say certain things, but philosophy cannot tell us what a sacrament is or what it means for a sign to participate in the reality signified. For secular backgrounds to the biblical concept, we have to return to the world of ancient Near Eastern treaty making, as in the Hittite example, where "This is the head of Mati'ilu and his son" is explained by the suzerain as the assumption of the treaty's obligations and curses for violation. In the ceremony it is announced that the severed head of the goat is no longer a mere goat's head but the head of Mati'ilu and his sons.[99] Witnesses to such

---

99. This example is cited in Dennis J. McCarthy, *Treaty and Covenant: A Study in the Ancient Oriental Documents and in the*   *Old Testament* (Rome: Biblical Institute Press, 1963), 195.

a ceremony knew what was intended. They did not imagine that the goat's head was magically transformed into the head of Mati'ilu and his sons, nor that it was merely symbolic. Rather, they recognized that in swearing the oath along with the ritual they were sealing their own doom if they failed to keep its terms.

Like the secular examples of treaty making above, the biblical covenants bind the sign so closely to the reality that circumcision was called simply "the covenant," just as Jesus designated the cup he raised in the upper room as "the blood of the new covenant" (Mt 26:25–28). Clearly, these covenantal actions are not merely illustrations. Yet they are also not a magical transformation of earthly substances into divine substances. Rather, they are performative actions that do what they say. In and through the act of consecrating bread and wine as his body and blood, Jesus hands himself over to death as the sacrifice for the sins of those who eat and drink in faith. He offers them the "cup of salvation" because he will drink the "cup of wrath" to its dregs, a cup that he will dread in Gethsemane but will accept for us. It is no wonder, then, that Paul called the cross "the circumcision of Christ" (Col 2:11).[100] It was he of whom Isaiah prophesied that "he was *cut off* out of the land of the living, *stricken* for the transgression of my people.... [H]e bore the sin of many, and makes intercession for the transgressors" (Isa 53:8–12).

United to Christ in his circumcision-death, the baptized, too, come under God's sword of judgment. "It is a judicial death as the penalty for sin," says Kline. "Yet to be united with Christ in his death is also to be raised with him whom death could not hold in his resurrection unto justification."[101] And as Peter affirms, baptism, foreshadowed by the salvation of Noah and his family in the flood ordeal, "now saves" not by cleansing the body but "as an appeal to God for a good conscience, through the resurrection of Jesus Christ, who has gone into heaven and is at the right hand of God ..." (1Pe 3:21–22). "Now conscience has to do with accusing and excusing; it is forensic," Kline emphasizes. "Baptism, then, is concerned with man in the presence of God's judgment throne."[102] Here, as in the exodus, we are reminded of the eschatological nature of both the water and the fire ordeals: Now when the people pass through the waters, they will not be drowned, because God is with them as he was in the exodus (Isa 43:1–3).

Just as circumcision could be called "the covenant" because of the close union of the sign and the thing signified, the Passover ritual was itself called "the LORD's

---

100. M. G. Kline reminds us that like Isaac, Jesus was circumcised as an infant, "that partial and symbolic cutting off"—the "moment, prophetically chosen, to name him 'Jesus.' But it was the circumcision of Christ in crucifixion that answered to the burnt-offering of Genesis 22 as a perfecting of circumcision, a 'putting off' not merely of a token part but 'of the [whole] body of the flesh' (Col. 2:11, ARV), not simply a symbolic oath-

cursing but a cutting off of 'the body of his flesh through death' (Col. 1:22) in accursed darkness and dereliction" (*By Oath Consigned : A Reinterpretation of the Covenant Signs of Circumcision and Baptism* [Grand Rapids: Eerdmans, 1968], 45).

101. Ibid., 47.

102. Ibid., 66–67.

passing over," with successive generations called upon to regard themselves as representatively (i.e., covenantally) present with the founding generation, dressed for the road in anticipation of their redemption (Ex 13:14–16). So too, in the Supper's words of institution, Jesus simply calls the cup and the bread "the new covenant in my blood." "This is my body.... This is my blood of the new covenant shed for many for the remission of sins."

As we have seen (in ch. 2), the invocation of Yahweh parallels the invocation of the suzerain (great king) by the vassal (lesser king) in times of threat. This language is closely bound to the sacraments in the New Testament. It is in this context of treaty invocation that Israel took up its Passover cup: "I will lift up the cup of salvation and call on the name of the LORD" (Ps 116:13). The same cup that was filled with judgment for the messiah (Mt 26:39) is now drunk by those who, united to his death and resurrection, receive from it only forgiveness and life. The sacraments correspond to the word (law and gospel) as the ratification of covenantal sanctions: "The cup of blessing that we bless, is it not a participation [*koinōnia*] in the blood of Christ? The bread that we break, is it not a participation in the body of Christ? Because there is one bread, we who are many are one body, for we all partake of the one bread" (1Co 10:16–17). Thus the union is covenantal and centers on legal and relational mediation between erstwhile enemies.

Therefore, the focus is not on substances and accidents or the way in which Christ is (or is not) present either as or with the elements. The issue is what God is doing with and through these signs. Through the Word and the sacraments, we are dislocated from this present age of sin and death "in Adam" and are relocated "in Christ," as citizens of the age to come. No longer under the dominion of the flesh (i.e., the possibilities inherent in this present age), we are under the reign of the Spirit (i.e., the powers of the age to come). Of course, the recipient must *receive* the gift; otherwise, the sacrament becomes a sign and seal of the judgment that he or she will have to bear personally, apart from the substitutionary judgment borne by the Covenant Mediator.

Once strangers and enemies of the Great King, we are now brought near by the blood of Christ. We know this because God has sworn his covenant mercies in the gospel and ratified them in our baptism and in the Supper. Yet just as with the preaching of the gospel, Christ must be personally embraced through faith. The gospel was preached to the wilderness generation long ago, we are reminded in Hebrews, but they did not respond to it in faith. Though they had been circumcised in the flesh, their hearts remained uncircumcised. Nevertheless, "we who have believed enter that rest" (Heb 4:2–3). Through Word and sacrament, God gives us the title deed to the estate, but we must beware of forfeiting our inheritance like Esau. We must embrace the reality that is promised in and through the signs. "So then, there remains a Sabbath rest for the people of God, for whoever has entered God's rest has also rested from his works as God did from his" (vv. 9–10).

Differences between Roman Catholic and Reformation approaches to the sacraments, then, are not far from the wider contrasts between the paradigm of "overcoming estrangement" and "meeting a stranger." Aquinas spends eight articles in his *Summa theologica* providing a series of philosophical arguments for "the way in which Christ is in this sacrament."[103] Yet again, this is consistent with his treatment of grace as a metaphysical substance whose infusion is caused by baptism and subsequent sacraments. However, in a covenantal understanding, sacraments involve a giving of gifts from one person to another, not an exchange of substances. Its interest is not in what happens *to the signs* but in what happens *between persons through them*, not *how* Christ is present in the sacraments, but *that he is present in saving action toward us*. Grace is God's favor, and the sacraments ratify God's favor toward us. Their purpose is to reconcile enemies, not to elevate nature beyond itself.

Consequently, the Reformation's understanding of sacraments as means of grace is striving to overcome an ontological concept of grace and a causal understanding of sacraments in favor of a covenantal, relational, promissory, and proclamatory function that is thoroughly eschatological and therefore pneumatological. This personal work of the Spirit can be identified with grace because it is a gift: the gift of participation in the realities of the age to come. This close connection of the Spirit with eschatology is crucial in the Reformed understanding.[104] God condescends in an astonishing display of love to deliver *Christ* and all of his benefits to us here and now by the Word and Spirit. Nevertheless, Jesus told his disciples, "I tell you I will not drink again of this fruit of the vine *until that day* when I drink it new with you in my Father's kingdom" (Mt 26:29). "For as often as you eat this bread and drink the cup, you proclaim the Lord's death *until he comes*" (1Co 11:26).

It is neither the action of the *signs* themselves nor of the *people* but the action of *God* that makes the sacraments; they are, in the words of the *Westminster Shorter Catechism*, "the outward and ordinary means whereby Christ communicates to us

---

103. Thomas Aquinas, *Summa theologica*, q. 76, pt. 3. Thomas does not deny the reality of the ascension, and he carefully distinguishes his understanding of presence from natural and local concepts (involving movement from one place to another, for example). Yet for all that, "the whole substance of the bread is changed into the whole substance of Christ's body, and the whole substance of the wine into the whole substance of Christ's blood. Hence this is not a formal, but a substantial conversion; nor is it a kind of natural movement: but, with a name of its own, it can be called *transubstantiation*" (q. 75, art. 5, pt. 3, 2444). I am inclined to believe that such an account (and rival accounts that remain in this circle) could evolve only within

the onto-theological discourse. Even when Thomas engages in proof texts from scripture, Aristotle is everywhere in the treatment of the sacraments the dominant voice.

104. Geerhardus Vos, "Paul's Eschatological Concept of the Spirit," in *Redemptive History and Biblical Interpretation: The Shorter Writings of Geerhardus Vos* (ed. Richard B. Gaffin Jr.; Phillipsburg, N.J.: P&R, 1980), 125: "For Paul," writes Vos, "the Spirit was regularly associated with the world to come, and from the Spirit thus conceived in all His supernatural and redemptive potency the Christian life receives throughout its specific character."

the benefits of redemption...."[105] Each time the Word is preached and the sacraments are attached as signs and seals, we receive our own answer to Abram's query, "How can I know that this will happen?" Since God's presence is not always felicitous (since he also frequently comes in judgment), we need the assurance that he comes to us now in peace. The focus is not on what the water, bread, and wine really are or whether Christ is substantially present in them but whether through these particular actions Christ is really giving himself to us.

The *Heidelberg Catechism* relates the efficacy of the sacraments in their covenantal setting along the lines that I have argued thus far: "First, as surely as I see with my eyes the bread of the Lord broken for me and the cup given to me, so surely his body was offered and broken for me and his blood poured out for me on the cross." But this is not only past-tense: "Second, as surely as I receive from the hand of the one who serves, and taste with my mouth the bread and cup of the Lord, given me as sure signs of Christ's body and blood, so surely he nourishes and refreshes my soul for eternal life with his crucified body and poured-out blood."[106] The *Belgic Confession* adds, "the sacrament of Christ's body and blood" was instituted "to testify to us that just as truly as we take and hold the sacraments in our hands and eat and drink it with our mouths, by which our life is then sustained, so truly we receive into our souls, for our spiritual life, the true body and true blood of Christ, our only Savior."[107] Calvin writes, "Nor does he feed our eyes with only a bare show but leads us to the reality (*rem praesentem*), and what he depicts (*figurat*) he effectively accomplishes at the same time.... God works through external means."[108] God's fatherly goodness in Christ is uppermost in Calvin's interpretation of the sacraments: through baptism God adopts us into his family, and through the Supper he continually feeds us.[109] Therefore, as I have argued at length elsewhere, infusion is the wrong category for God's gracious action.[110]

III. Prayer: The Chief Part of Gratitude

Prayer is indispensable to our fellowship with God. As such, it is not, strictly speaking, God's means of grace but our means of communication with him. As the *Heidelberg Catechism* expresses it, prayer is "the most important part of that thankfulness God requires of us."[111] Every relationship, especially a covenantal one,

---

105. *Westminster Shorter Catechism*, q. 88, in *Trinity Hymnal* (Philadelphia: Great Commission Publications, 1990), 867.

106. *Heidelberg Catechism*, q. 75, in *Ecumenical Creeds and Reformed Confessions* (Grand Rapids: CRC Publications, 1988), 45.

107. *Belgic Confession*, art. 35, in *Ecumenical Creeds and Reformed Confessions*, 115.

108. Calvin, *Institutes* 4.15.14–15.

109. Gerrish, *Grace and Gratitude*, 122–23, citing Calvin, *Institutes* 4.15.1 and 4.17.1.

110. I develop this point at some length throughout part 2 of my book *Covenant and Salvation* (Louisville: Westminster John Knox, 2007).

111. *Heidelberg Catechism*, q. 116, in *Ecumenical Creeds and Reformed Confessions* (Grand Rapids: CRC Publications, 1988), 57.

involves two parties. God communicates his grace through Word and sacrament, and we communicate with God in prayer. Preaching and sacrament communicate the gifts that we need *from God* for our spiritual survival, and prayer is our Spirit-provoked reply. It encompasses the whole range of human response to God's gift: the "amen" of faith and joyful thanksgiving for his grace as well as the groaning for Christ's return and the consummation of the new creation. Just as the first expression of an infant's filial dependence on his or her mother is a cry, prayer is the first expression of faith on the part of God's adopted heirs.

I argued in the beginning of this volume that our Christian life consists of a perpetual cycle of dramatic narrative, doctrine, doxology, and discipleship. Especially in prayer, the Spirit reshapes the human response, internalizing that which we have heard and received through the means of grace, so that we are no longer ungrateful strangers to his promises, but joyful heirs. Therefore, far from drawing us away from the world, prayer is the link between the means of grace and our active love and service to our neighbor.

Like preaching and the sacraments, prayer and praise—especially public worship—occupy a covenantal context. In my remarks so far, I have mentioned only thanksgiving. There are also prayers of lament in the Psalms, where the covenant partner complains about a certain state of affairs in the hope that God will be moved to compassion and answer the cry of desperation. Such laments not only invoke God or celebrate his faithfulness, but sometimes wrestle with God on the public stage of covenant history. It is not the accusations of a false witness but the persistent plea of a friend that provokes the cry, "Why, O Lord, do you stand far away? Why do you hide yourself in times of trouble?... Arise, O Lord; O God, lift up your hand; forget not the afflicted" (Ps 10:1, 12). "How long, O Lord? Will you forget me forever? How long will you hide your face from me?" (Ps 13:1). After praising God for his covenant faithfulness and salvation in the past, the Psalmist pleads his case: "Awake! Why are you sleeping, O Lord? Rouse yourself! Do not reject us forever! Why do you hide your face? Why do you forget our affliction and oppression?... Rise up; come to our help! Redeem us for the sake of your steadfast love!" (Ps 44:23–26). There are also laments in which the psalmist pours out his heart to the Lord in confusion, wondering why he no longer experiences the joy of his salvation or joins the procession to the sanctuary with the godly in devout awe and love. For those of us raised on worship songs that focused only on praise, singing these Psalms in corporate worship can seem inappropriate. However, God heard and answered these prayers—and he still does today.

In his condescending love, God allows himself to be treated as a covenant partner. Even in our laments, we make God the only object of our hope for relief. God's covenant promises in Christ are the basis for our welcome into his presence and for our petitions for God to act in accordance with that promise, as well as the basis for our praise. Prayer takes on a richer meaning when we realize that it is covenantal speech in the cosmic courtroom of history, in which we take the witness stand for God, even as we wrestle with his ways as well as praise him for his saving mercy.

Theology itself, I argued, is a form of prayer: meditation on God's Word that is simultaneously study and invocation. Calling on the name of the LORD, we saw, is the invocation of the rescue clause of the treaty, claiming the promise of the Great King to save us and rule over us for our good and his glory. If the whole purpose of theology is the proper invocation of the one true God in Jesus Christ, on the basis of the gospel, then prayer is the most original form of true faith. It is the goal of the Word and the sacraments to create and strengthen this faith so that we come *boldly* to the throne of grace, without fear, because our mediator is also our brother and the Spirit intercedes for us and within us, provoking that filial cry, "Abba! Father!" (Heb 4:16; 10:19–25; Ro 8:15).

DISCUSSION QUESTIONS

1. What is meant by the term "sacramental Word"? How does this help to supplement the teaching function of the Scriptures?
2. Does the conception of the church as "creation of the Word" have a decisive impact on one's ecclesiology? If so, how? What is the relationship, in this conception, between the gospel and the church?
3. What is a "sacrament"? Discuss the different definitions in Roman Catholic, Lutheran and Reformed, and Anabaptist traditions. Where would you place your own church's view on this spectrum?
4. What constitutes a sacrament? How many are there? Include in your discussion old covenant as well as new covenant ordinances.
5. What role do sacraments play in Scripture with respect to the making of a covenant? Discuss specific examples.
6. Is prayer a means of grace or the chief exercise of Christian thankfulness? Evaluate the strengths and weaknesses of different answers in the light of specific passages.

Chapter Twenty-Four

BAPTISM AND THE LORD'S SUPPER

The Hebrew idiom for making a covenant is actually *cutting* a covenant (*kārat bᵉrît*) — so closely is the ratification rite (circumcision) associated with the treaty itself. With the last chapter having provided the wider covenantal horizon for a theology of the sacraments, this chapter focuses specifically on baptism and the Lord's Supper.

I. BAPTISM

After treating baptism first of all in its connection with circumcision, I will discuss its efficacy, proper subjects, and administration.

A. CIRCUMCISION AND BAPTISM

The connection between the work of Christ and its application is nowhere more obvious than in considering circumcision and baptism. Circumcision demonstrates the substitutionary principle of the atonement in the most vivid terms. Although indeed a blood-shedding rite, circumcision was only a partial "cutting off" that spared the recipient of being cut off entirely from life. Like the Passover blood on the doorposts, circumcision identified the recipient with the Mediator of the covenant of grace. In an intriguing episode recorded in Exodus 4, Moses is intercepted along his path from Midian back to Egypt along with his Midianite wife Zipporah and two sons, one of whom Moses had not yet circumcised. "At a lodging place on the way the LORD met him and sought to put him to death. Then Zipporah took a flint and cut off her son's foreskin and touched Moses' feet with it and said, 'Surely you are a bridegroom of blood to me!' ... because of the circumcision" (Ex 4:24–26). In spite of her revulsion at the rite, Zipporah saves her husband's life by performing the circumcision herself, "touching Moses' feet with it," as a visible identification that turned away God's wrath.

The role of circumcision varies according to the covenant that it is supposed to ratify. If it is the sign and seal of justification—the cutting away of sin rather than the cutting off of the sinner—then it functions as God's gracious promise to provide a substitute. This is how it functioned in the covenant of grace that God made with Abraham, Isaac, and Jacob. However, in terms of the *national* covenant (Sinaitic), circumcision obligated the one circumcised to personal fulfillment of all stipulations. Paul was simply reiterating this teaching when he wrote, "I testify again to every man who accepts circumcision that he is obligated to keep the whole law" (Gal 5:3). However, he warns the Galatians that if his opponents trust in their circumcision for their eternal inheritance (which was never God's intention), they are, ironically, "severed [cut off] from Christ." Attempting to be "justified by the law," he warns, "you have fallen away from grace" (v. 4). This is the absolute contrast between being "under the law" as a covenant of works and being "in Christ" in the covenant of grace.

Circumcision was a partial "cutting off" that kept one from being wholly cut off (excommunicated) from the people of God. So one was devoted either to the blessings of the covenant (through circumcision) or to its curses (without circumcision). It was this sort of thorough "cutting off" that was symbolized in the offering of Isaac, but prevented by the Lord's provision of a substitute, a ram caught in the thicket (Ge 22).

At his own circumcision on the eighth day, Abraham's greater heir was prophetically named "Jesus," identifying him in the history of redemption with the ram caught in the thicket, John's "Lamb of God" (Jn 1:29). "But it was the circumcision of Christ in crucifixion that answered to the burnt-offering of Genesis 22 as a perfecting of circumcision," Kline notes, "a 'putting off' not merely of a token part but 'of the [whole] body of the flesh' (Col 2:11, ASV), not simply a symbolic oath-cursing but a cutting off of 'the body of his flesh through death' (Col 1:22) in accursed darkness and dereliction."[1] Just as circumcision was a knife drawn in judgment yet "passed over" the recipient by cutting away merely the foreskin, in baptism, too, we come under the sword of divine judgment. In this event, however, we are entirely dedicated to judgment in order to be entirely raised in newness of life (Ro 6:1–11).

In connection with justification Paul calls circumcision a "sign" and "a seal of the righteousness that he had by faith while he was still uncircumcised" (Ro 4:11).

---

1. M. G. Kline, *By Oath Consigned: A Reinterpretation of the Covenant Signs of Circumcision and Baptism* (Grand Rapids: Eerdmans, 1968), 45.

What is signified and sealed in baptism is nothing less than the eschatological judgment of the last day: our curse in Adam swallowed by our blessing in Christ. In Colossians 2:9–12, as Vos reminds us,

> The "circumcision" of the Christian is not to be understood as following his baptism. Instead, the two actions are to be regarded as simultaneous. The rite of cleansing found in the old covenant finds its fulfillment in the rite of cleansing ordered in the new.... The meaning of the passage would be communicated best by a rendering such as "when you were buried with him in baptism, you were circumcised"; or "by being buried with him in baptism you were circumcised." ... In the fullest possible sense, baptism under the new covenant accomplishes all that was represented in circumcision under the old. By being baptized, the Christian believer has experienced the equivalent of the cleansing rite of circumcision.[2]

The "baptism" of the Israelites into Moses prefigures the union of believers with Christ (1Co 10:2), and Peter appeals to the rescue of Noah and his family through the waters of judgment as a precursor of baptism (1Pe 3:20–21). Jesus emphasized over against the theologians of glory at his own side that none but he could bear the "baptism" of the cross (Lk 12:50; cf. Mk 10:38), yet we now are included in the benefits of his circumcision-death and resurrection-life. As the promises are greater in the new covenant, so also are the curses for refusing to receive the substance that it promises (Mt 8:12; Jn 15:1–8; Ro 11:17–21; Heb 4:2; 6:4–8; 12:25). The exile of Israel from the land was typological of the ultimate "cutting off" from the heavenly rest.

The sign and thing signified are treated in the New Testament, as in the Old, as intimately connected. Christ has "cleansed [the church] by *the washing of water with the word*" (*katharisas tō loutrō tou hydatos en rhēmati* [Eph 5:26]) and "saved us, not because of works done by us in righteousness, but according to his own mercy, by the washing of regeneration and renewal of the Holy Spirit" (Tit 3:5).[3] Believers have been "buried with [Christ] in baptism" and raised with him in newness of life. Baptism, in fact, is now the true circumcision (Col 2:11–12). The contrast between baptism and works righteousness points up that the sacraments cannot be treated as human works, much less as attempts to attain righteousness before God.

The earliest apostolic preaching enjoins hearers to "'be baptized ... for the forgiveness of your sins, and you will receive the gift of the Holy Spirit. For the promise is for you and for your children and for all who are far off, everyone whom the Lord our God calls to himself.' ... So those who received his word were baptized, and there were added that day about three thousand souls" (Ac 2:38–41). Although

---

2. Geerhardus Vos, *Redemptive History and Biblical Interpretation: The Shorter Writings of Geerhardus Vos* (ed. Richard B. Gaffin Jr.; Phillipsburg, N.J.: P&R, 1980), 165–66.

3. So, for example, Karl Barth, *Church Dogmatics*, 4, pt. 4, pp. 113–14. Despite considerable technical skill and knowledge of a wide variety of classical and contemporary interpretations of each passage (acknowledging in the preface the debt to his son, Markus Barth, in this regard), Barth's exegesis presupposes from the outset that these passages cannot be interpreted in a sacramental manner.

the effects of baptism cannot be tied to the moment of administration, there is no indication of two baptisms—one with water and one by the Spirit. No less than the ritual baptisms of Second Temple Judaism, including John's, were the postascension baptisms performed with water (for example, Ac 8:36).

Nevertheless, the reality that baptism communicates must be embraced by faith. Otherwise, it is not that there is no effect; on the contrary, the effect is a total cutting off from Christ and his blessings, the assuming in one's own person of the curses of the covenant of works without a mediator. We know from covenantal history that while circumcision in the flesh was the *sign and seal* of the circumcision in the heart, the former did not *cause* the latter. The two are distinguished in the old covenant (Dt 10:16; 30:6; Jer 4:4; 31:32–34), even before we reach the Pauline contrast between outward and inward circumcision (Ro 2:28–29; 3:30; 4:10; 1Co 7:19; Gal 5:2–6; Php 3:3; Col 2:11). Apart from faith, outward circumcision (and baptism in the new covenant) is the sign and seal of judgment leading to death: a final cutting off of the whole person (excommunication). Hence, the severe warnings about falling away, especially in Hebrews 4, 6, and 10.

Similarly, Paul reminds the Roman Christians that if God has broken off unfruitful branches of the natural tree to engraft wild branches, how much less will he tolerate wild branches that are only connected externally to the tree rather than united vitally to Christ through faith (Ro 11:19–24)? "If the dough offered as firstfruits is holy, so is the whole lump, and if the root is holy, so are the branches" (v. 16). Nevertheless, it is one thing to be related to the covenant externally and another to be actually united to Christ through faith. One believing parent sanctifies the covenant children (1Co 7:14), and as Hebrews 6 confirms, the covenant is the sphere in which the Spirit is at work visibly even among those who are not (yet) believers, but as the visible means of bringing about a life-giving participation in the Vine.

As Paul reminds us, not all physical Israelites are true descendants of Abraham (Ro 9:6–18). There is one covenant of grace running through both testaments, with a "mixed assembly" of elect and nonelect members in the visible society of the church. In baptism, God pledges to be a God to us and to our children, but the threat of being cut off remains for all who fail to embrace for themselves the reality that God promises and certifies. As Paul affirms, the sacraments are signs and seals of the righteousness that we have by faith (Ro 4:11).

B. THE EFFECT OF BAPTISM

According to this view, then, preaching and sacrament are neither mere *witnesses* to grace nor *causes* of grace, but *means* of grace inasmuch as they ratify the promise and thereby strengthen our faith in the one who promises. Taken up by Word and

Spirit, baptism itself as "visible word" is not merely representative or symbolic, but "living and active." Like preaching, it is the lively action of God's energies.

In the administration of a sacrament, the Father ratifies his pledge toward us in the Son by the Spirit. As a sign, it objectively witnesses to our inclusion in the covenant of grace; as a seal, it is the means by which the Spirit brings about within us the "amen" to God's promise and command, not only once but throughout our pilgrimage.[4] Baptism itself does not effect this in an *ex opere operato* fashion, but achieves its perlocutionary effect when and where the Spirit chooses. "The efficacy of baptism is not tied to that moment wherein it is administered," according to the *Westminster Confession* (28.7), "yet, notwithstanding, by the right use of this ordinance, the grace promised is not only offered, but really exhibited and conferred, by the Holy Ghost, to such (whether of age or infants) as that grace belongeth unto, according to the counsel of God's own will in His appointed time."[5]

Therefore, a covenantal view of the sacraments serves rather than undermines the crucial point that this is a covenant of *grace*. The Reformers and their heirs emphasized that baptism was, first of all, an action of the whole Trinity. Calvin writes,

> For he [Christ] dedicated and sanctified baptism in his own body in order that he might have it in common with us as the firmest possible bond of the union and fellowship which he has deigned to form with us.... All the gifts of God displayed in baptism are found in Christ alone. Yet this cannot take place unless he who baptizes in Christ invokes also the names of the Father and the Spirit.... For this reason we obtain and, so to speak, clearly discern in the Father the cause [*causa*], in the Son the matter [*materia*], and in the Spirit the effect [*effectio*] of our purgation and our regeneration.[6]

C. THE MODE AND ADMINISTRATORS OF BAPTISM

Although proponents of immersion and sprinkling (or pouring) have often argued that a prescribed mode is explicitly evident from the meaning of *baptō/ baptizō* in ordinary usage, the range of use eludes a definitive conclusion. Baptism was already in use among Second Temple groups as a purification rite when John began his ministry. Like the vessels in the sanctuary, such purification washings of people were administered by sprinkling or pouring (Nu 8:7; 19:13, 18–20; Ps 51:7; Eze 36:25; Jn 3:25–26; Mk 7:3–4 with Ac 2:38; 22:16; Lk 11:38; Rom 6:4–5; 1Co 6:11; Tit 3:5; Heb 9:10; 10:22; 1Pe 3:21; Rev 5:1).

Immersion does seem more suggestive of being buried and raised with Christ and of being drawn out of God's waters of judgment alive. At the same time, those who "passed through the sea and ... were baptized into Moses in the cloud and in

4. *Belgic Confession*, art. 34, in *Ecumenical Creeds and Reformed Confessions* (Grand Rapids: CRC Publications, 1988).
5. *Westminster Confession of Faith*, Art. 28.7, in *The Book of* *Confessions* (Louisville: PCUSA General Assembly, 1991).
6. Calvin, *Institutes* 4.15.6.

the sea" in the exodus from Egypt (1Co 10:1–2) actually escaped immersion in the waters. In view of the varied examples and precedents for ritual purification, the church's historical acceptance of immersion, sprinkling, and pouring as valid modes of baptism seems entirely justified. Partisans on all sides should beware of rejecting the validity of one's baptism on the basis of the amount of water administered.

The proper *administrators* of baptism and the Supper are ministers of the Word. As a public-covenantal rite, baptism (like the Supper) cannot be considered merely a personal, private matter. Christ himself baptizes, through his ambassadors who are called and set apart by ordination for this task.[7] Further exhibiting its covenantal role, baptism must be administered in an ordinary, public service of the Word rather than in private or with the family alone.[8] Reformed churches also reject the practice of allowing parents, midwives, or nurses in extreme cases to administer baptism, which arose in connection with the doctrine of baptismal regeneration. As Turretin explains, it is not the lack of baptism that excludes one from the covenant but its refusal.[9] The thief on the cross was saved without baptism (Lk 23:43), Abraham received circumcision as a "seal of the righteousness that he had by faith while he was still uncircumcised" (Ro 4:11), and adult converts are justified through faith before they are baptized. Christian parents should not doubt that their children who die in infancy before they can receive baptism in the public assembly are elect in the Lord (2Sa 12:23; 1Co 7:14). Consequently, there is no need to suspend the ordinary and proper administration of baptism out of a superstitious attachment to the sacrament as absolutely necessary for salvation.

The question of proper administration also arose in the church with the question of the *lapsed*—that is, those who apostatized during the persecutions. The Donatist sect declared invalid all baptisms that had been performed by bishops and pastors who had apostatized, but Augustine rightly argued that the validity of the ministry of Word and sacraments in no way depends on the piety or sincerity of the administrator. Baptism is a sacrament of Christ and his church, not of individual ministers. Lutheran and Reformed churches adopted this position, acknowledging even the baptism of heretics, as long as it was administered with water and the triune formula of Matthew 28:19. As a public and covenantal rite rather than a private religious experience, a valid baptism is never to be repeated. There is "one Lord, one faith, one baptism" (Eph 4:5).[10]

---

7. Louis Berkhof, *Systematic Theology* (Grand Rapids: Eerdmans, 1996), 631: "The Reformed Churches always acted on the principle that the administration of the Word and of the sacraments belong together, and that therefore the teaching elder or the minister is the only lawful administrator of baptism."

8. Ibid.

9. Turretin, *Elenctic Theology*, 3:386–93.

10. From the Anabaptist perspective, the name given to them (Anabaptist = "re-baptizers") is a misnomer, since they believed that they were baptizing Christians for the first time. With regard to the validity of Roman Catholic baptism, Robert L. Dabney and James Thornwell, both Southern Presbyterian theologians in the nineteenth century, argued that since the Church of Rome did not bear the marks of the true church, its baptisms were to be regarded as invalid. However, as Hodge points out, this view is an exception to the general consensus of Reformed and Presbyterian practice.

D. The Proper Subjects: The Question of Infant Baptism

It is as ironic as it is tragic that although baptism is the sacrament of union with Christ and the communion of saints, the question concerning the proper subjects of baptism is one of the most divisive issues in Christianity today. All Christians affirm that adult converts should be baptized only after they have made a profession of faith. However, disagreement arises over whether children of believers ought to be baptized as well. "Under the influence of Socinians, Arminians, Anabaptists, and Rationalists," Berkhof notes, "it has become quite customary in many circles to deny that baptism is a seal of divine grace, and to regard it as a mere act of profession on the part of man."[11] Missing from Berkhof's list, however, is the important heritage of Calvinistic Baptists. Affirming the priority and sovereignty of God's grace, these brothers and sisters hold that God alone saves but that baptism is a visible sign of one's profession of God-given faith and may therefore be administered only to adults. Like Anabaptists, however, contemporary Baptists generally hold that they are not rebaptizing Christians as adults but administering baptism to them for the first time.

Anabaptists and Baptists argue that in the New Testament baptism is a symbol of the believer's profession to be a follower of Jesus Christ (therefore excluding infants) and that nowhere does it teach that children are to be baptized. In defense of the first point, appeals are made to the examples of baptism in the book of Acts, where the rite clearly follows the profession of faith. For the second point, the lack of any command to baptize children places the burden of proof on paedobaptists (i.e., those who do baptize children).

At least from the Reformed perspective, both objections are best addressed by attending to the continuity of the covenant of grace.[12] New covenant believers are children of Abraham, belonging to the same covenant that was pledged to him (Mt 19:14; Mk 10:13–16; Ac 2:39; 4:12; 10:43; 15:10–11; Rom 3:27–4:25; 1Co 7:14; Gal 3:16; 1Ti 2:5–6; 1Pe 1:9–12). Abraham was justified *before* he was circumcised, and this is the pattern also for baptism of adult converts; but the patriarch obeyed the command to circumcise his sons *unto* repentance and faith. Only males were circumcised, but now females are baptized as well—as they were in John's baptism (Jesus mentions even "prostitutes" in Mt 21:32), in fulfillment of the prophecy that the Spirit would be poured out on all flesh, males and females alike.

Yet the principle of covenant succession—that is, the inclusion of believers'

---

11. Berkhof, *Systematic Theology*, 627.

12. Among several helpful (and nontechnical) books in defense of a Reformed understanding of baptism, I recommend

Daniel R. Hyde, *Jesus Loves the Little Children: Why We Baptize Infants* (Grand Rapids: Reformed Fellowship, 2006).

children — is constant. It is still true, as Peter announced, that "the promise is for you and for your children . . ." — and this is said in the context of baptism (Ac 2:39). As the *Belgic Confession* argues, children in the new covenant, as in the old, should be baptized, since "Christ has shed his blood no less for washing the little children of believers than he did for adults. . . . Furthermore, baptism does for our children what circumcision did for the Jewish people. That is why Paul calls baptism the 'circumcision of Christ' [Col 2:11]."[13]

From a covenantal perspective, it is impossible to separate the claim that the children of believers are holy (1Co 7:14) from the sign and seal of the covenant. According to the traditional Anabaptist/Baptist view, the children are not regarded as holy until they personally repent and believe. However, the New Testament preserves the clean/unclean distinction, only now it pertains not to Jew and Gentile, circumcised and uncircumcised, but to believing and unbelieving families, with baptism as the covenant's ratification. In fact, Paul especially labors the point that all, Jew and Gentile, circumcised and uncircumcised, are Abraham's children and heirs of the Abrahamic covenant through faith alone, just like Abraham (Ro 4:3 with Ge 15:6; cf. Gal 3–4). The church, in its unity of Jew and Gentile in Christ, is understood as the fulfillment of Israel's existence (Mt 21:43; Rom 9:25–26; 2Co 6:16; Tit 2:14; 1Pe 2:9; Gal 6:16; Rev 5:9). Everything turns on whether we assume continuity or discontinuity as most fundamental to interpreting the relationship between the Old and New Testaments. Given the way that the New Testament itself interprets the Old, we should privilege continuity.

If this is the case, then the burden of proof shifts from paedobaptists (i.e., infant baptizers) to Baptists. Given the Jewish background of the first Christians, it would not be the command to *administer* the sign and seal of the covenant to their children that would have been surprising but the command to *cease administering* it to them. However, we are not left to an argument from silence. This promise for believers and their children is exhibited in the conversion and baptism of Lydia. After she believed the gospel, "she was baptized, and her household as well" (Ac 16:15). Later in the same chapter, we read of the conversion of the Philippian jailer. He too is told, "Believe in the Lord Jesus, and you will be saved, you and your household . . . and he was baptized at once, he and all his family" (vv. 31, 33). Paul recalls having baptized the household of Stephanas (1Co 1:16). If children are included in the covenant of grace under its Old Testament administration, surely they are not excluded in the new covenant administration, which the writer to the Hebrews calls "better" than the old (Heb 7:22).

According to Baptist theologians, however, such arguments ignore the discontinuity between old and new covenants. Wayne Grudem argues that the old covenant

---

13. *Belgic Confession*, art. 34, in *Ecumenical Creeds and Reformed Confessions* (Grand Rapids: CRC Publications, 1988).

"had a physical, external means of entrance into the 'covenant community,'" while "[t]he means of entrance into the church is voluntary, spiritual, and internal."[14] Reflecting a more Greek (indeed, modern) dichotomy, this interpretation would seem to count against recognizing even the baptism of adults as their entrance into the church. According to this argument, the church might be regarded as entirely invisible and as constituted not by Christ's promise through Word and sacrament, made effectual by the Spirit in the communion of saints, but by the decision and commitment of individuals apart from any necessary connection to the visible church. As we will see, this view of baptism has enormous implications for ecclesiology more generally.

The New Testament certainly distinguishes the new covenant (promise) from the old covenant (law), but when it does so the new covenant is the *realization* of the Abrahamic covenant, a realization to which the now-obsolete old covenant (Sinaitic law) pointed. Just as the former cannot be abrogated by the latter (Gal 3:15–18), the obsolescence of the types and shadows of the Mosaic economy cannot include the covenant to which circumcision was originally attached. If the Abrahamic covenant remains in effect, then so too does its promise to include our children among the people of God. Paul explicitly refers to the Abrahamic covenant and the Sinai covenant as "two covenants" that must be distinguished (Gal 4:21–31). It is not the Old and New Testaments, then, but the Abrahamic and Sinai covenants that Paul contrasts.

Therefore, one would be on solid exegetical ground (with Paul and the writer to the Hebrews) in contrasting a *merely* external circumcision, national/ethnic identity, outward observance, and earthly form of the temple worship belonging to the old covenant theocracy, on the one hand, with the *true* circumcision of the heart, renewal, and forgiveness of sins fulfilled in the new covenant, on the other. However, Grudem's contrast with the New Testament not only encompasses the Abrahamic covenant but evidences a philosophical dualism between visible and invisible, material and spiritual, external and internal, covenantal nurture and voluntary decision.

A final point in relation to the exegetical argument should be made. The Anabaptist/Baptist traditions have in general defended the notion of an age of accountability, when individuals are old enough to decide for themselves whether they will become Christians.[15] In addition, many of these bodies practice infant dedication. Nevertheless, there is no reference to an age of accountability or to the practice of

---

14. Wayne Grudem, *Systematic Theology: An Introduction to Bible Doctrine* (Grand Rapids: Zondervan, 1994), 976–77.

15. See, for example, Millard Erickson, *Christian Theology* (Grand Rapids: Baker, 1985), 639. However, Wayne Grudem sees no exegetical basis for the view and offers a sound rebuttal on the basis of the participation of all people from conception in original sin (*Systematic Theology*, 499–500).

infant dedication in the New Testament, while there are references to household baptism.

With respect to the historical argument, Baptists point out the paucity of evidence for infant baptism in the earliest postapostolic communities. This has been a matter of considerable debate among church historians for some time, but there is considerable evidence in favor of infant baptism in the early church.[16] Regardless, the same response can be made here as is offered in relation to the lack of New Testament commands to baptize infants. We have no evidence of any commands to *forbid* infant baptism, and by the second century the literature is replete with references to the practice.

Just as the exclusion of believers' children would have provoked controversy among early Jewish Christians, surely such a radical change from apostolic to postapostolic practice on such an important matter would have sparked considerable debate. On the contrary, Tertullian in the second century, largely because of his involvement in the Montanist movement, questioned the propriety of infant baptism, though he did not question that it was a generally accepted practice in his day (*On Baptism*, ch. 18). His contemporary, Origen, testified to the practice: "The Church has received the tradition from the apostles to give baptism even to little children."[17] Taking infant baptism for granted, the Council of Carthage (253) debated whether it should be performed on the eighth day (like circumcision).[18]

Given these and similar arguments, it follows that children of believers are baptized because they are visible members of the covenant of grace. Some Reformed theologians held to presumptive regeneration as the ground of infant baptism.[19] However, more widely held is the view that the ground of baptizing the children of believers is that they are the heritage of the Lord and therefore are included in his visible company, receiving his sure pledge that he will be their God and they will be his people. In the words of *the Canons of Dort*, "Since we are to judge of the will of God from His Word, which testifies that the children of believers are holy, not by nature, but in virtue of the covenant of grace, in which they together with their parents are comprehended, godly parents ought not to doubt the election and salvation of their children whom it pleases God to call out of this life in their infancy."[20] Far from making parents lax, the baptism of covenant children obligates them to

---

16. Origen (AD 185–254) testifies to the practice as "from the apostles" (Maxwell E. Johnson, *The Rites of Christian Initiation* [Collegeville, Minn.: Liturgical, 2007], 74. Around the year 215, Hippolytus refers to the standard practice of infant baptism (*Apostolic Tradition* 21:15, in *ANF*, vol. 5). For support of infant baptism as the practice of the early church, see especially Joachim Jeremias, *Infant Baptism in the First Four Centuries* (trans. David Cairns; Philadelphia: Westminster, 1962).

17. Origen, *Commentary on the Epistle to the Romans: Books 1–5* (Fathers of the Church 103; trans. Thomas P. Scheck; Washington, D.C.: Catholic Univ. of America Press, 2001), 367 (bk. 5, ch. 9.11).

18. Ibid.

19. Berkhof, *Systematic Theology*, 639.

20. *Canons of Dort*, ch. 1, art. 17, in *Ecumenical Creeds and Reformed Confessions*.

raise their children in the Lord, leading them (as far as it is up to them) to public profession of their faith.[21]

Nevertheless, the priority of baptism is placed on God's gracious action. Although baptism may certainly be considered a testimony to the world and an answer of a clear conscience before God's throne (1Pe 3:21), the New Testament elsewhere associates baptism with the forgiveness of sins and the gift of the Spirit, which are divine acts. Therefore, even apart from the question of the proper subjects, the very nature of baptism is understood in radically different ways by those who believe that sacraments are God's means of grace and those who treat them exclusively as the believer's act of commitment.

II. THE SUPPER

Although the priority lies with God's gracious action, baptism also involves the responsive pledge of the whole church, the family, and eventually the children who will profess faith later in life. If baptism is the bath for the beginning of this journey, the Supper is the table that God spreads in the wilderness along the way. I have already indicated that covenant meals were part and parcel of the treaty-making events in the ancient Near East, and in Israel particularly. As with baptism, then, I will begin with the covenantal context.

A. THE CUP OF SALVATION: THE SUPPER IN ITS COVENANTAL CONTEXT

Covenant meals both celebrated and ratified the treaty, as when the mysterious king of Salem, "priest of God Most High," "brought out bread and wine" and then pronounced Yahweh's blessing on Abraham (Ge 14:17–20). The Passover meal is the participation of the generations to come in their night of safely passing under God's sword because of the blood on the doorpost (Ex 12). Analogous to the secular treaty sworn by Mati'ilu cited in the previous chapter (ch. 23, "Biblical-Theological Examination of the Sacraments," pp. 781–82), the blood oath is a communicative, judicial, and covenantal event. The head of the ram becomes the head of Mati'ilu and his sons representatively, not substantially. Of course, something more is involved when Christ makes himself the food and drink of his people, uniting them to himself by his Spirit. However, the covenantal action itself must be defined by the covenantal context. The

---

21. Berkhof explains that baptism of adults and infants not only is a sign and seal of "the truth of the promise," but also "assures the recipients that they are the appointed heirs of the promised blessings." "This does not necessarily mean that they are already in principle in possession of the promised good, though it is possible and may even be probable, but certainly means that they are appointed heirs and will receive the heritage, unless they show themselves unworthy of it and refuse it" (*Systematic Theology*, 641).

prophets also spoke of God's judgment as a "cup of wrath." Are we not to assume the same covenantal background in Jesus' announcement, "This is my body" and "This is the blood of the new covenant," especially when he speaks of his own crucifixion as the drinking of the "cup of wrath" to its dregs in the place of those he represents (Mk 10:38; Lk 22:42)? In fact, that night he sealed his fate as the one upon whose head the covenant curses would fall. For those who receive the reality—namely, Christ and all of his benefits—the sacraments signify and seal the passing from death to life, judgment to justification, bondage to liberty. However, those who do not discern the Lord's body and receive the Supper in faith "eat and drink judgment to themselves" (1Co 11:29). This suggests that even those who receive Communion unworthily do in fact receive Christ, but as judge rather than as justifier, although in the immediate context temporal rather than eternal punishment is in view.

In the making of international treaties today, state dinners usually follow the signing ceremony. However, in the ancient Near East, the dinner *was* the signing ceremony. In this light, we are better able to understand the scene with Moses, Aaron, and the elders atop Mount Sinai, eating and drinking with Yahweh their Great King (Ex 24:9–11). The theme of "eating and drinking in the presence of the LORD" is apparent not only in the patriarchal narratives and the prophets; it is carried forward into the New Testament, especially in Luke's Gospel.[22] In a climactic meal, the two disciples along the Emmaus road heard the resurrected Christ proclaim himself from all the Scriptures, and "their eyes were opened" to recognize him when he broke the bread. As Douglas Farrow points out, there are obvious comparisons and contrasts with the covenant-*breaking* meal that Adam and Eve decided to have *without* God, by themselves. Their eyes were "opened," to be sure, but now only to see their guilt.[23]

In our Western (Greek) intellectual heritage, "remembering" means "recollecting": recalling to mind something that is no longer a present reality. Nothing could be further from a Jewish conception. For example, in the Jewish Passover liturgy, "remembering" means participating here and now in certain defining events in the past and also in the future. Together with their forebears, those who share in the Passover meal invoke the name of the suzerain for rescue: "I will lift up the cup of salvation and call on the name of the LORD" (Ps 116:13). And also, like the rainbow in the Noahic covenant, the Supper involves *God's* remembering the oath that he made. The close bond between sign and signified in Passover is carried over into the New Testament celebration of the Lord's Supper.[24]

22. For the significance of meal fellowship, see especially David P. Mossner, *The Lord of the Banquet: The Literary and Theological Significance of the Lukan Travel Narrative* (Minneapolis: Fortress, 1989).

23. Douglas Farrow, *Ascension and Ecclesia: On the Significance of the Doctrine of the Ascension for Ecclesiology and Christian Cosmology* (Edinburgh: T&T Clark, 1999), 7n23, drawing on the insights of Earl Ellis.

24. On the significance of the phrase "in remembrance of me" in the light of Old Testament "memorials," see especially Joachim Jeremias, *The Eucharistic Words of Jesus* (trans. Norman Perrin; Philadelphia: Fortress, 1964), 237–54.

To be sure, the use of philosophical terms in order to convey theological formulations more clearly is proper within bounds. However, we will miss the nature and purpose of sacraments if we allow philosophical questions and formulations a determinative role. The sacraments are instituted in the active life of making covenants, not in the contemplative life of abstract speculation.

Furthermore, the Supper (like baptism) is defined eschatologically by the successive events in Jesus' history. Our baptism is not exactly like John's, which Jesus underwent, and the Lord's Supper, in its benefits after our Lord's resurrection, ascension, and the sending of the Spirit, is qualitatively different than when he instituted it in the Upper Room. And it will be different again when Christ returns. In Luke's account (22:14–23; cf. Mt 26:26–30; Mk 14:22–25), Jesus emphasizes twice that he will not share this meal with his disciples "until the kingdom of God comes" in all of its fullness (vv.16 and 18). Even in the physical presence of Jesus at this unique table, there is the expectation of absence, "till he come again." Through this celebration, the Spirit will bind saints together not only to the past (the fulfillment of Passover) and the present (Christ's sacrifice), but also the future (Christ's return), as Paul observes in 1 Corinthians 11:26. However, because the Spirit runs interference, as it were, between these tenses, they are not impenetrable compartments.

Herman Ridderbos is especially helpful in exploring this relationship between Christ's expiatory death and the eschatological feast in the celebration of the Supper. Some scholars, like Markus Barth, Ridderbos notes, reflect an overrealized eschatology, according to which the concentration in the Supper is on Christ's present reign as king rather than on his cross and sacrifice.[25] However, Ridderbos points out that this overlooks the already–not yet tension that is highlighted in the text.[26] "The relation between the Eucharist and eating and drinking in the coming kingdom of God is *not merely that between symbol and reality, but that between commencement and fulfillment....* In a word, it is the meal in which 'the powers of the world to come' have been released in Christ's coming, and in which the 'heavenly gift' and the Holy Spirit have been given and tasted' [Heb 6:4ff.]" (emphasis added).[27]

An overrealized eschatology misses the connection *and temporal gap* between the expiatory death (to which the Supper refers) and the fullness of the kingdom (which it anticipates in the marriage feast still future). In telling his disciples that he will no longer eat and drink with them until he returns, Jesus issues what amount to "parting words," says Ridderbos, "a farewell pointing to the future."[28] "When he

---

25. Markus Barth, cited in Herman Ridderbos, *The Coming of the Kingdom* (ed. Raymond O. Zorn; trans. H. de Jongste; Philadelphia: P&R, 1962), 405–6.

26. See Ridderbos, *Coming of the Kingdom*, 406–11, for a text-critical argument in favor of the authenticity of Luke

22:19b–20, which emphasizes the expiatory death along with the synoptic parallels and 1 Corinthians 11.

27. Ibid., 412–13.

28. Ibid., 414.

speaks of the "fulfillment of the Passover" and of "the new wine" in the kingdom of God, "he has in view the great future to be inaugurated by the *parousia* of the Son of Man," not simply a kingdom that is realized in the present in all of its fullness.[29]

Our Lord's discourse in John 14–16 also seems to support this line of interpretation. Over and beyond all of the postresurrection meals that Jesus shared with his disciples, the meal that we now share occurs on this side of the ascension and Pentecost. In the power of the Spirit, we not only recognize Jesus as the Christ; we receive a foretaste of the eschatological feast (the marriage supper of the Lamb). Yet it is still not the fully consummated reality. If "Zwinglian" views tend to eclipse our present participation (proleptically) in the eschatological feast, Roman Catholic and Lutheran views exhibit an overrealized eschatology of the Eucharist, resolving the productive tension between the "already" and "not yet" that this covenant meal not only reveals but intensifies. In our contemporary celebration of the Supper, we are participating in a foretaste of that greater meal, to be sure, but the primary reference for us now is to a present participation in the past sacrifice.[30] (Hence, the significance of Paul's instruction in 1 Corinthians 11:26: "For as often as you eat this bread and drink the cup, you proclaim the Lord's death until he comes.") As a profanation of the sacrament of Christ's sacrifice, which put into effect his last will and testament, the Corinthian abuse of the Supper provoked God's temporal judgments, including sickness and even death (1Co 11:30), just as he sought to kill Moses until Zipporah circumcised her son and threw the skin at his feet (Ex 4:24–26). The sacraments are not playthings, but are signs and seals of the covenant.

For now, the disciples must regularly eat the bread and drink the wine that Jesus allows to pass by his lips precisely because he will drink the cup of wrath instead. "Only, they must do so realizing that what they in this way will henceforth eat and drink is *the body and the blood of the Lord*."[31] In other words, for now Christ is the sacrificial meal, but when he returns he will join us as a fellow diner.[32] The Supper, then, is more than the Passover meal: Jesus instituted the Supper after that old covenant feast was concluded. Yet it is not yet the Lamb's wedding feast.[33] The Lord's Supper occurs between the old age and the new age, locating the church in this precarious intersection of the two ages.

In this sense, notes Ridderbos, "that which is received in bread and cup is the sacrificial food and drink of the new covenant, the fruits of the New Testament sacrificial blood.... In one supreme concentration as it were, in one turn of the hand, the Lord's Supper focuses the whole preaching of the gospel upon Christ's sacrifice and sets the table with it."[34] Therefore, we are invited to a table, and not an altar.

---

29. Ibid., 415.
30. Ibid., 416.
31. Ibid.

32. Ibid., 417.
33. Ibid., 431.
34. Ibid., 427.

Like the paschal meal, the Supper is not a *sacrifice*, but it is a *sacrificial meal*: receiving Christ's body that was crucified and his blood that was shed on our behalf.[35] Wherever "Christ's body and blood are eaten and drunk at the Communion table, the cross becomes an actual and living reality in the midst of the congregation" and a witness to the world.[36] Thus, it is not the action of the individual or the church, but God's action through these creaturely means, that traverses the temporal gap between the "then and there" of Golgotha, the "here and now" of our existence, and the future feast. For now, Christ is not a fellow guest with whom we eat and drink, but rather the one who gives himself as the meal. "The connection between bread and body, wine and blood, rests in Christ's words, in his command, in the fact that he is the dispenser and the host. So everything here depends on the reliability of his promise, on the efficacy and the authority of his words."[37]

Instead of the blood dashed on the people at Sinai, confirming their oath to do everything prescribed in the law, Jesus inaugurates the new covenant by saying, "This is my body, which is *given for you*.... This cup that is *poured out for you* is the new covenant in my blood" (Lk 22:19–20). In fulfilling his promise to Abraham, which he had confirmed by the vision of the smoking torch (Ge 15), our Lord's words and deeds in the upper room seal the new covenant, giving it binding legal authority as his last will and testament. Jesus, God and human, bears our sanctions. As the writer to the Hebrews explains, even appealing to the role of sprinkling blood in old covenant worship, Christ's death is both a sacrifice for sin and an inauguration of a new covenant in the sense of a last will and testament, which is rather different from a conditional arrangement. In the new covenant, believers are simply beneficiaries of an estate. The death of the testator puts the will into effect (Heb 9:17–22). The writer then goes on to declare the superiority, finality and unrepeatable character of Christ's sacrifice.

Similarly, in 1 Corinthians 10 and 11 Paul teaches that his readers were baptized into Christ just as their old covenant predecessors were "baptized into Moses in the cloud and in the sea" (1Co 10:2). However, the exodus generation enters the true promised land only together with us, their entry having been foreshadowed when they "all ate the same spiritual food, and all drank the same spiritual drink." "For they drank from the spiritual Rock that followed them, and the Rock was Christ" (vv. 3–4).

It is not Greek metaphysics or Roman mystery cults, but biblical covenantalism, that provided Paul with his conceptual fund for this view of participation. Then when we come to his treatment of the Supper, Paul represents the sign and

---

35. Ibid., 428.
36. Ibid., 432.

37. Ibid., 438.

signified as distinct yet united (1Co 10:16). As a covenantal meal, the Supper binds us vertically to the crucified, risen, and ascended Christ and horizontally to our brothers and sisters. It is not a common meal, much less a private spiritual experience. In fact, Paul's discussion of the Supper in 1 Corinthians is occasioned by the divisiveness of the community. Christ's existence as the head of his body makes us co-heirs of his last will and testament. Therefore, the horizontal vector is immediately linked to the vertical: "Because there is one bread, we who are many are one body, for we all partake of the one bread" (v. 17). By contrast, those who share in idol feasts are "participants in the altar" of false gods (v. 18). In fact, this is part of an argument already begun in chapter 6 in relation to participation in the common civic practice of cultic prostitution (1Co 6:15 – 17). To put it somewhat crudely, the church *is* what it *eats*. As we participate in the Lord's Supper, we are identified covenantally with the triune God, in whose name we have also been baptized. We become more and more what we are, namely, the covenantal body of Christ. From its life-giving head, the church receives its existence and strength here and now. Therefore, together with the Word, baptism and the Supper are the means through which the Spirit creates, shapes, sustains, and expands his ecclesial body.

B. HISTORICAL VIEWS OF THE LORD'S SUPPER

All of the ancient church writers held to the view that Christ was truly offered and given in the Supper and received through faith.[38] Beyond this, one may find support for any number of later theories as to the mode of Christ's presence and its relation to the elements. To this day, Eastern Orthodoxy affirms Christ's real presence in the Eucharist, even employing terms like "transelementation," "transformation," and "change," but refuses to develop a scholastic argument about how this is so. The bread and wine are truly the body and blood of Christ. Nevertheless, wrote John of Damascus, "if you enquire how this happens, it is enough for you to learn that it is through the Holy Spirit. We know nothing more than this, that the Word of God is true, active, and omnipotent, but in its manner of operation unsearch-

---

38. Writing against the Gnostics about AD 106, the church father Ignatius of Antioch (possibly a disciple of John) warned believers to avoid "such heretics" as "abstain from the Eucharist and from prayer, because they confess not the Eucharist to be the flesh of our Saviour Jesus Christ, which suffered for our sins, and which the Father, of His goodness, raised up again" (*Epistle to the Smyrneans*, 7; in *The Apostolic Fathers* [trans. J.B. Lightfoot, J.R. Harmer , and Michael W. Holmes; Grand Rapids: Baker, 1989]). See also Athanasius, *On the Incarnation* 17, in *Athanasius: Contra Gentes and De Incarnatione* (trans. R. W. Thomson; Oxford: Clarendon Press, 1971), 174 (PG 25, col. 125).

39. John of Damascus, *On the Orthodox Faith* 4.13, quoted by Timothy Ware in *The Orthodox Church: New Edition* (New York: Penguin, 1993), 285. While the churches of the East affirmed a mystical change in the elements, they resisted attempts to resolve the mystery by philosophical arguments. In 1672, the Eastern Orthodox Synod of Jerusalem produced a statement (also known as the *Confession of Dositheus*), which singled out the Zwinglian and Lutheran views for rejection, but did not refer to the Reformed position (Decree 17). Available at www.crivoice.org/creeddositheus.html.

able."[39] Even with respect to Western theologians like Augustine, it is anachronistic to read later theories into earlier writers. Augustine clearly distinguished the sign from the reality and denied that unbelievers receive the latter. However, throughout the Middle Ages the dogma of transubstantiation began to take shape.

1. THE RISE OF THE DOGMA OF TRANSUBSTANTIATION

In the ninth century, Radbertus especially developed the belief that the earthly elements are actually converted into the body and blood of Christ, although he was challenged by Ratramnus.[40] Other controversies erupted, until transubstantiation was defined as binding dogma at the Fourth Lateran Council (1215). Yet still there remained wide divergences as to the formulation of this dogma among scholastic theologians. The term itself comes from a compound word meaning "a change in the substance of" (Greek, *metaousiōsis*; Latin, *transubstantiatio*). Apparently, the term was first employed by a French archbishop, Hildebert de Lavardin, in the twelfth century.[41] In this view, at the moment of priestly consecration the elements continue to have the sensual (accidental) appearance of bread and wine, but they are actually (essentially) Christ's body and blood.[42]

Eventually, the elaborate (Aristotelian) interpretation of transubstantiation received its refined shape at the hands of Thomas Aquinas, and this explanation was officially adopted at the Council of Trent (Session 13). The Supper is a memorial, an atoning sacrifice, and a thanksgiving (eucharist), all of which are offered by the church.[43] "As often as the sacrifice of the Cross by which 'Christ our Pasch has been sacrificed' is celebrated on the altar, the work of our redemption is carried out."[44] In fact, "The sacrifice of Christ and the sacrifice of the Eucharist are one single sacrifice," with Christ as the victim and the priest (on behalf of the worshipers) as the one who offers it to the Father.[45] In the consecration, the bread and the wine are converted into the body and blood of Christ, so that it is not only proper but required that believers offer adoration of the Host (i.e., the consecrated bread and wine).[46] At the Eucharistic altar, "all laws of nature are suspended," wrote Pope Leo XIII, and "the whole substance of the bread and wine are changed into the Body and Blood of Christ," including his physical organs.[47]

---

40. Commissioned by Charlemagne to refute Radbertus, Ratramnus defended Christ's true presence, but not a transubstantiation of the natural elements into Christ's body and blood. However, Ratramnus's view was condemned by the Fourth Lateran Council in the thirteenth century, though the treatise reappeared and received support among some during the Reformation.

41. "Eucharist," in *Oxford Dictionary of the Christian Church* (Oxford: Oxford Univ. Press, 2005), 475–77.

42. *Catechism of the Catholic Church* (Liguori, Mo.: Liguori Publications, 1994), 1376.

43. Ibid., 335, 342.

44. Ibid., 343, quoting "Lumen gentium," 3 (November 21, 1964), from the Second Vatican Council.

45. Ibid., 344, referring to the Council of Trent (1562): DS 1743.

46. Ibid., 346–47.

47. Pope Leo XIII, *Mirae caritalis*, in *The Great Encyclical Letters of Pope Leo XIII* (Rockford, Ill.: TAN Books, 1995), 524.

2. THE LUTHERAN VIEW

Just as the water of baptism cleaves to the Word, and as Christ is present according to both natures, the bread and wine, consecrated by the words of institution, communicate the whole Christ to believers and unbelievers alike (though, in the latter case, in judgment). God's Word alone makes these ordinary elements bearers of Christ.[48] The Word brings forgiveness through the sacrament.[49] As such, the bread and wine are only secondarily "signs by which people might be identified outwardly as Christians"; they are primarily "signs and testimonies of God's will toward us."[50]

Luther strongly rejected the Roman Catholic doctrine of transubstantiation (i.e., that the bread and wine become the body and blood of Christ), declaring, "[W]e do not make Christ's body out of the bread.... Nor do we say that his body comes into existence out of the bread [i.e., impanation]. We say that his body, which long ago was made and came into existence, is present when we say, 'This is my body.' For Christ commands us to say not, 'Let this become my body,' or, 'Make my body there,' but, 'This is my body.' "[51] Instead of saying that the bread and wine *become* the body and blood of Christ, Christ comes *to* the bread and wine *with* his body and blood. The sign and the signified become "coupled."[52]

George Hunsinger points out that whereas Aquinas appealed to the analogy of *ex nihilo* creation, Luther used the incarnational analogy.[53] There is no need for the human nature of Jesus Christ to be transubstantiated into the divine nature, Luther argued in *The Babylonian Captivity of the Church*.

> Both natures are simply there in their entirety, and it is truly said: "This man is God; this God is man." Even though philosophy cannot grasp this, faith grasps it nonetheless. And the authority of God's Word is greater than the capacity of our intellect to grasp it. In like manner, it is not necessary in the sacrament that the bread and wine be transubstantiated and that Christ be contained under their accidents in order that the real body and real blood may be present. But both remain there at the same time, and it is truly said, "This bread is my body; this wine is my blood," and vice versa.[54]

However, Luther defended his position by positing that by virtue of the hypostatic union the attributes of the divine nature could be communicated to the human

---

48. *Larger Catechism*, 5, 9, 14, in *The Book of Concord: The Confessions of the Evangelical Lutheran Church* (ed. and trans. Theodore G. Tappert; Philadelphia: Fortress, 1959).

49. Ibid., 5, 32–33, 35.

50. *Augsburg Confession* 13, 1; *Formula of Concord*, epitome 7, 27; Solid Declaration 7, 115), both in *The Book of Concord*.

51. Martin Luther, *Luther's Works* (ed. Jaroslav Pelikan and Helmut Lehmann; St. Louis: Concordia, 1955–1986), 37:187;

cf. *Formula of Concord*, Solid Declaration 7.59.

52. Luther, *Larger Catechism*, 5, 18.

53. George Hunsinger, *The Eucharist and Ecumenism* (Cambridge: Cambridge Univ. Press, 2008), 28.

54. Martin Luther, *The Babylonian Captivity of the Church*, in *Luther's Works* (American Ed.) (Philadelphia: Fortress, 1959), 36:35.

nature. According to the *genus maiestaticum* (genus of majesty), the whole Christ may be present in many places, a view to which we will return.

Luther's view is sometimes identified as "consubstantiation" because of the belief that Christ's body is present "in," "with," and "under" the consecrated bread and wine. However, Lutherans generally eschew this term because it suggests a local (circumscribed) presence of Christ's body and therefore a physical (cannibalistic) eating, which the *Formula of Concord* rejects as "gross, carnal, and Capernaitic."[55] Nevertheless, with the bread and the wine Christ's body and blood are received by all who partake, with the mouth, and not simply through faith. This feeding is just as true for the unworthy (*manducatio indignorum*).

Martin Chemnitz states that the feeding on Christ is neither merely physical nor spiritual but sacramental, "a threefold eating in the Lord's Supper" that Christ's words of institution imply:

> First, there is the eating of the bread, which is rightly and properly called a physical eating. Second, there is the eating of the body of Christ, which although it does not take place in a physical or gross way, yet (according to the words of Christ) takes place orally, for He says: "Take, eat; this is My body." This is called a sacramental eating in the old method of designation. Third, there is the spiritual eating of the body of Christ.[56]

How can Christ's body and blood be eaten and drunk "orally" yet not "physically" (since this would reduce to the "Capernaitic" heresy condemned by the ancient church)? Chemnitz and Lutherans generally respond to this objection in the same way that they respond to the objection that Christ cannot be present everywhere in the flesh without injury to his true humanity: namely, by invoking God's omnipotent will and the words of institution, "This is my body."[57]

The Lutheran view emphasizes that these words of institution are not figurative (Solid Declaration 7, 59) and also stresses the importance of the words "given for you" and "shed for you" (*Small Catechism* 6, 6). Edmund Schlink explains, "When the Sacrament of the Altar is defined as 'the true body and blood of our Lord Jesus Christ, under the bread and wine' (*Small Catechism* 6, 2)," "the true body" is to be understood as the body crucified and now glorified.[58] Believers have life from Christ and in Christ not merely according to his divinity or spirituality but in his flesh (Apology 10, 3). Therefore, in the Supper Christ's body and blood are present "in, with, and under the bread and wine," and thereby Christ himself is "offered and

---

55. *Formula of Concord*, epitome 7, 42; solid declaration 7, 127; *Triglot Concordia* 817, 1015.

56. Martin Chemnitz, *The Lord's Supper* [*De coena Domini*, 1590] (trans. J. A. O. Preus; St. Louis: Concordia, 1979), 58–59. This work remains the most significant statement and

defense of the Lutheran view of the Supper.

57. Ibid., 59–64, 198–209.

58. Edmund Schlink, *Theology of the Lutheran Confessions* (trans. Paul F. Koehneke and Herbert J. A. Bouman; Philadelphia: Fortress, 1961), 161–62.

orally received."[59] Or, in the words of the *Formula of Concord* (Solid Declaration 7, 35, 37), the body of Christ is given "under the bread, with the bread, in the bread."

Therefore, everyone who communicates receives Christ's body and blood, but "the promise is useless unless faith accepts it" (Apology 13). According to the *Formula of Concord* (7, 7), even "the unworthy and unbelieving receive the true body and blood of Christ," but their "receiving turns to their judgment and condemnation, unless they be converted and repent (1Co 11:27, 29)." The Supper communicates the benefits not only of justification but of sanctification as well, "for the strengthening and encouragement of the sinner in the battle against sin."[60] In this view, the Supper is emphatically not a sacrifice that we offer to God (which would vitiate its character as a means of grace), but is God's gift of his Son for us and to us.

How can Christ be present bodily at every eucharistic celebration, in, with, and under the bread and the wine? In other words, is his bodily presence affirmed at the expense of his having a real body? At this point, arguments broke out among Lutherans themselves, and, according to Schlink, they were not fully resolved even in the *Formula of Concord*.[61] Ultimately, this is a christological issue, treated in chapter 13. To avoid a Nestorian separation of Christ's natures, for Lutherans (and the Reformed agree with this point) the real presence of Christ can mean only the *whole* presence Christ. Yet to affirm the presence of the whole Christ at every eucharistic celebration, Lutherans offered the novel argument that Christ is omnipresent in the flesh because his divine attributes penetrate his humanity. Christ's exaltation to the right hand of the Father refers not to a place but to a position (Solid Declaration 8, 28). This view came to be known as *ubiquity* (ability to be omnipresent). Chemnitz repeated Luther's warning that "we must not debate about the ubiquity of the body of Christ or make this matter the point of controversy."[62] However, it did in fact become "the point of the controversy," not only because of objections raised against the view but from staunch Lutheran theologians in the Reformation era.

3. THE REFORMED VIEW

It has been observed frequently that Calvin's entire theology is "eucharistic" in orientation.[63] B. A. Gerrish suggests, "The holy banquet is simply the liturgical

---

59. Ibid., 169.

60. Ibid., 163.

61. Ibid., 189–93.

62. Chemnitz, *Lord's Supper*, 203. With Luther, Chemnitz repeats at this point the words of institution and the appeal to divine omnipotence, "that Christ with His body can do what He wills and be wherever He wills" (203). Chemnitz argues for poly-spatiality rather than ubiquity (Chemitz, *The Two Natures of Christ* [trans. and ed. J. A. O. Preus and Nicholas Selnecker; St. Louis: Concordia, 1971], 43–37). While ubiquity implies an ontological omnipresence, poly-spatiality simply means that

Christ may be present (in both natures) wherever he chooses. This view is defended in Francis Pieper, *Christian Dogmatics* (St. Louis: Concordia, 1953), 325. See also Warren A Qunbeck, "'Sacramental Sign' in the Lutheran Confession," in *The Eucharist as Sacrifice: Lutherans and Catholics in Dialogue III* (Minneapolis: Augsburg, 1974), 85–86.

63. Owen F. Cummings, "The Reformers and Eucharistic Ecclesiology," in *One in Christ* 33, no. 1 (1997): 47–54; B. A. Gerrish, *Grace and Gratitude: The Eucharistic Theology of John Calvin* (Minneapolis: Augsburg Fortress, 1993), 52.

enactment of the theme of grace and gratitude that lies at the heart of Calvin's entire theology, whether one chooses to call it a system or not.... It is this focal image of the banquet that made Calvin's doctrine (in his own estimate) simple, edifying, and irenic."[64] However, it was not Calvin but the Zürich pastor Ulrich Zwingli with whom Luther met in Marburg in 1529. For nearly a week the two Reformers engaged in frank conversation with their assistants, agreeing on all but one point: the nature of the Supper.

Among others, Geoffrey W. Bromiley points out that not even Zwingli was a "Zwinglian," as this position has come to be identified with a "real absence" position. Nevertheless, on the basis of Zwingli's own writing it is clear that Christ was present in the Supper only according to his divinity and power. Like Augustine, Zwingli did not see the ascension as a "problem" for us here and now, since Jesus Christ is omnipresent according to his divinity and this is of greater importance for our salvation.

At the heart of Zwingli's thinking was a spirit-matter dualism. "For faith springs not from things accessible to sense nor are they objects of faith," he insists.[65] Of course, one wonders how, if such a view were to be followed consistently (which, happily, he did not do), faith could come by *hearing* (Ro 10:17). The suggestion that in the sacrament one fed on the true body of Christ but in a spiritual manner (which became the confessional Reformed position) Zwingli considered as ludicrous as saying that Christ was chewed with the teeth.[66] In fact, Zwingli concludes, faith "draws us to the invisible and fixes all our hopes on that. For it dwelleth not amidst the sensible and bodily, and hath nothing in common therewith."[67] In fact, this dualistic ontology underwrites a not so subtle Nestorianizing Christology, as in Zwingli's remark, "We must note in passing that Christ is our salvation by virtue of that part of his nature by which he came down from heaven, not of that by which he was born of an immaculate virgin, though he had to suffer and die by this part."[68] Luther and Zwingli realized that they were working with different conceptions not only of the Supper, but of Christology and even cosmology.

In 1536, Luther and his associates reached agreement on the Supper with Martin

---

64. Gerrish, *Grace and Gratitude*, 20, 13.

65. Zwingli, *Commentary on True and False Religion* (ed. Samuel Macauley Jackson and Clarence Nevin Heller; trans. Samuel Macauley Jackson; Durham, N.C.: Labyrinth Press, 1981), 214.

66. Ibid.

67. Ibid.

68. Ibid., 204. Besides Gerrish's work, a growing number of helpful studies have appeared, including Ronald S. Wallace, *Calvin's Doctrine of Word and Sacrament* (Grand Rapids: Baker, 1988); Jill Rait, *The Eucharistic Theology of Theodore*

Beza: Development of the Reformed Doctrine (AAR Studies in Religion; Chambersburg, Pa.: American Academy of Religion, 1972); Keith Mathison, *Given for You: Reclaiming Calvin's Doctrine of the Lord's Supper* (Phillipsburg, N.J.: P&R, 2002); and Leonard J. Vander Zee, *Christ, Baptism and the Lord's Supper: Recovering the Sacraments for Evangelical Worship* (Downers Grove, Ill.: InterVarsity Press, 2004). Where Reformed theology has attracted a growing following among evangelicals, the Reformed understanding of the church and sacraments has been often treated as nonessential to the system or a Zwinglian interpretation is regarded as an adequate Reformed option.

Bucer and other Reformed leaders. Known as the *Wittenberg Concord*, this agreement was accepted also by John Calvin. However, Calvin—influenced by Bucer and perhaps even more so on this point by Peter Martyr Vermigli—developed a fuller treatment that became standard in the Reformed confessions. Appealing especially to the eleventh-century Orthodox archbishop of Bulgaria, Theophylact, Vermigli defended the notion of "transelementation," according to which the signs of bread and wine were transformed by their union with the reality signified.[69] Like an iron rod placed in a fire, the bread is transformed while remaining bread. Vermigli's interpretation influenced other Reformed theologians, like Bucer and Cranmer.[70] "Calvin went so far as to state of him that 'the whole [doctrine of the Eucharist] was crowned by Peter Martyr, who left nothing more to be done.'"[71] Like these other Reformed leaders (and unlike Zwingli), Calvin affirmed with Luther the "sacramental union" of sign and reality. This view is defined in the *Westminster Confession* (art. 27): "There is, in every sacrament, a spiritual relation, or sacramental union, between the sign and the thing signified: whence it comes to pass, that the names and effects of the one are attributed to the other." Calvin applied the common formula of Chalcedonian Christology—"distinction without separation"—to this sign-reality relationship. Indeed, the incarnation was as much Calvin's dominant analogy as Luther's. However, he agreed with Zwingli that the idea of Christ's ubiquitous (omnipresent) flesh represented a "monstrous phantasm" rather than an actual human being, even if he is God incarnate.

Farrow points out that Calvin faced more resolutely the reality of Christ's bodily ascension and return without surrendering the reality of Christ's presence in the sacrament. Calvin realized that the question "*Where* is Christ?" is decisive for the question "*Who* is Christ?"[72] If Christ can be present bodily on earth prior to his return, then the reality of his humanity after the resurrection is called into question. Hunsinger is justified in concluding, "The Lutheran idea that Christ's human body is 'ubiquitous' and the Zwinglian idea of Christ's 'disembodied' spiritual presence, though extreme polar opposites, are in some ways reverse mirror images of one another."[73] One might add the same concerning the Roman Catholic view. According to Aquinas, Christ's presence in the sacrament is "a spiritual, non-visible presence," though real and bodily.[74] What is the point of feeding on one whose flesh

---

69. See George Hunsinger's intriguing discussion in *The Eucharist and Ecumenism*, esp. the description of this view in 34–46. See also Peter Martyr Vermigli, *The Oxford Treatise and Disputation on the Eucharist, 1549* (ed. Joseph C. McLelland; Kirksville, Mo.: Truman State Univ. Press, 2000), 93.

70. Hunsinger, *The Eucharist and Ecumenism*, 42–43.

71. Ibid., 39.

72. Douglas Farrow, *Ascension and Ecclesia*, 204, points out

that Calvin—especially in the eucharistic debate—picked up on the historical economy and reckoned with the real absence and real presence of Christ in ways that had been blocked by the medieval "ascent of mind."

73. Hunsinger, *The Eucharist and Ecumenism*, 48.

74. Thomas Aquinas, *Summa theologiae* 3.75.1 (New York: McGraw-Hill Co., 1964).

and blood are spiritual and invisible? How far is Aquinas, really, from Zwingli after all? The danger in all of these views is that Christ's presence in the flesh at the altar is announced at the price of having to redefine Christ's humanity.

So where Rome, Luther, and Zwingli concentrated on how Christ was or was not present *in the bread and the wine*, Calvin directed his attention to how Christ is present *in action* in the sacrament even though he is absent from earth in the flesh until his return. This required a robustly pneumatological understanding of the sacrament that had been more fully developed in the East but was lacking in Western debates. Reckoning more resolutely with the bodily ascension of Jesus Christ in the flesh than Rome or Luther, Calvin nevertheless affirmed, against Zwingli, a true feeding on the very body and blood of Christ in the sacrament. As strongly as Calvin rejected the Lutheran doctrine of ubiquity, he and his Reformed colleagues (other than those in Zürich) were convinced that they did not disagree with Wittenberg over the question of *what* was received in the Supper.[75]

All of the Reformed confessions affirmed these main lines of treatment that we find in Calvin among others. Although we also bind ourselves to God, the principal purpose of the Supper is God's ratification of his promise. Although Christ is raised to the right hand of the Father, we feed on his body and blood through the mysterious agency of the Spirit. The whole Christ (his person and not merely his work) is given in the Supper and received through faith. Even Heinrich Bullinger, Zwingli's successor, moved toward this view, rejecting (in the *Second Helvetic Confession*) "the doctrine of those who speak of the sacraments just as common signs, not sanctified and effectual. Nor do we approve of those who despise the visible aspect of the sacraments because of the invisible, and so believe the signs to be superfluous because they think they already enjoy the things themselves, as the Messalians are said to have held."[76] It is difficult to imagine that Bullinger did not know that he was rejecting a prominent line of his predecessor's argument.

"From the very first," notes Gerrish, Calvin "was convinced that Zwingli was wrong about the principal agent in both Baptism and the Lord's Supper. A sacrament is first and foremost an act of God or Christ rather than of the candidate, the communicant, or the church."[77] Where Zwingli can only force a choice

---

75. Gerrish, *Grace and Gratitude*, 8. "Later, after Marburg," as B. A. Gerrish points out, "it was repeatedly argued that the point at issue between the Lutherans and the Reformed was no longer whether, but only how, the body and blood of Christ were present in the Sacrament. Calvin himself so argued." Since even Bullinger (Zwingli's successor) came to embrace the sacramental union of sign and signified, the focus was on *what* is received (Christ and all of his benefits) in the Supper, rather than on the *manner* of eating—in other words, presence as such.

76. *Second Helvetic Confession*, ch. 19, in *The Book of Confes-*

sions (Louisville: PCUSA General Assembly, 1991), 180–81. See also the agreement between Calvin and Bullinger, known as the *Consensus Tigurinus*; English translation found in John Calvin, *Tracts and Treatises* (trans. Henry Beveridge; Grand Rapids: Eerdmans, 1958), 2:212–20. See Timothy George, "John Calvin and the Agreement of Zürich (1549)," in *John Calvin and the Church: A Prism of Reform* (ed. Timothy George; Louisville: Westminster John Knox, 1990), 42–58.

77. Gerrish, *Grace and Gratitude*, 204.

between God's action and creaturely action, Calvin says, "Whatever implements God employs, they detract nothing from his primary operation."[78]

So far we have surveyed some of the representative arguments. I will now summarize the main substance of the Reformed position as it has come to expression in our confessions and catechisms.

We begin with the most basic question:

(a) *What is the nature of the Supper?* Gerrish offers a faithful summary in answer to this question. *First, the Supper is God's gift.* This emphasis Calvin shared with Luther, against the Roman Catholic idea of the Eucharist as the church's offering of a sacrifice for sin and the Zwinglian tendency to treat it primarily as the believer's act of remembering, testifying, and recommitment.

Especially in the *Institutes* 4.17.6, Calvin underscores this point that "the Supper is a gift; it does not merely remind us of a gift." As with receiving the gospel through the preached Word, in the sacrament we are receivers: it is "an *actio mere passiva* (a 'purely passive action')."[79] The human response to a gift is thanksgiving, says Calvin, which is why it is called the Eucharist, in opposition to the Mass, which instead is an atoning sacrifice that the people pay. "The sacrifice differs from the Sacrament of the Supper as widely as giving differs from receiving."[80]

Second, "The gift is Jesus Christ himself," not only his divinity but the whole Christ.[81] Third, *The gift is given with the signs.* Once again a criticism of both Zwingli and Rome is implied."[82] Fourth, *"The gift is given by the Holy Spirit,"* which Calvin goes on to detail in 4.14.9 and 12.[83] Fifth, *"The gift is given to all who communicate, pious and impious, believers and unbelievers."*[84] One may refuse the gift, but this does not negate the sacrament any more than the preaching of the gospel is invalidated by unbelief. "The integrity of the Sacrament, which the whole world cannot violate," says Calvin, "lies in this: that the flesh and blood of Christ are no less truly given to the unworthy than to God's elect believers."[85] At the same time, the reality is embraced only through faith. "The sacramental word is not an incantation," Gerrish summarizes, "but a promise." "The eucharistic gift therefore benefits those only who respond with the faith that the proclamation itself generates."[86] Thus, for Calvin, the Supper seals God's promise toward us and in this way confirms our faith, just as the Spirit creates faith through the preaching of the gospel. For Zwingli, however, the sacrament is a sealing of or testimony to the believer's faith rather than of God's promise.

---

78. Calvin, *Institutes* 4.14.17.

79. Gerrish, *Grace and Gratitude*, 150, from *Institutes* 4.14.26.

80. Calvin, *Institutes* 4.18.7.

81. Gerrish, *Grace and Gratitude*, 136, citing Calvin, *De la cène, OS* 1:508; *TT* 2:170; cf. *Confessio fidei de eucharistia* (1537), *OS* 1:435–36 (LCC 22:168–69; 4.17.7, 9).

82. Gerrish, *Grace and Gratitude*, 137.

83. Ibid.

84. Ibid., 138.

85. Calvin, *Institutes* 4.17.33.

86. Gerrish, *Grace and Gratitude*, 139; see Calvin, *Institutes* 4.14.4; 4.17.15.

Furthermore, God's promise is inextricably bound to Christ's person. When we receive the bread and the wine, says Calvin, "let us no less surely trust that the body itself is also given to us."[87] Rather than transform the sign into the signified (Rome), confuse the sign and the signified (Luther), or separate the sign and the signified (Zwingli), Calvin affirmed that signs were "guarantees of a present reality: the believer's feeding on the body and blood of Christ."[88] In explicit contrast with Zwingli, Calvin held that the reality—Christ and his benefits—could be truly communicated to believers through earthly means. Otherwise, he says (appealing to Chrysostom), faith becomes a "mere imagining" of Christ's presence.[89] Although he was not alone in its formulation, Calvin's interpretation of the Supper is the view that is confessed in the symbols of the Reformed churches, including the Church of England's *Thirty-nine Articles*, of which article 28 rejected transubstantiation as "repugnant to the plain words of Scripture."

Therefore, with respect to *what* is received in the sacrament, the Reformed unanimously answered, in the words of the *Belgic Confession*, that it is nothing less than "the proper and natural body and the proper blood of Christ."[90] Reflecting Calvin's contention that there is no communication of Christ's benefits apart from his person, the confession adds that "Christ communicates *himself* to us *with all his benefits. At that table he makes us enjoy himself as much as the merits of his suffering and death,* as he nourishes, strengthens, and comforts our poor, desolate souls by the eating of his flesh, and relieves and renews them by the drinking of his blood."[91]

(b) *How is Christ given in the Supper?* Where rival views turned to the mechanics of substantial presence, Calvin turned to the Spirit's mediation. Calvin firmly rejected any rationalizing of the Eucharist, insisting that Christ is not received "only by understanding and imagination."[92] The Supper, according to Calvin, is

---

87. Calvin, *Institutes* 4.17.10.

88. Gerrish, *Grace and Gratitude*, 165.

89. Calvin, *Institutes* 4.17.5–6.

90. For the Reformed, Berkhof summarizes in his *Systematic Theology*, 651–64, the Supper gives the believing sinner the assurance "that he personally was the object of that incomparable love" in Christ's sacrifice, "the personal assurance that all the promises of the covenant and all the riches of the gospel offer are his by a divine donation, so that he has a personal claim on them," and "assures him that the blessings of salvation are his in actual possession." Secondarily, and as a consequence, the Supper is a profession of allegiance to Christ as King (651). For Zwingli, although it is not entirely clear what he believed about the Supper consistently throughout his life, "for him the emphasis falls on what the believer, rather than on what God, pledges in the sacrament.... He denied the bodily presence of Christ in the Lord's Supper, but did not deny that Christ is present there in a spiritual manner to the faith of the believer. Christ is present only in His divine nature and in the *apprehension* of the believing communicant" (653). The Reformed view

followed Calvin, who rejected Zwingli's view on several counts, including "(a) that it allows the idea of what the believer does in the sacrament to eclipse the gift of God in it; and (b) that it sees in the eating of the body of Christ nothing more nor higher than faith in His name and reliance on His death." For Calvin, the Supper has to do not only with Christ's work in the past, but his work in the present. Though not present locally in the bread and wine, Christ nevertheless gives "His entire person, both body and blood," through the meal (653). The efficient agent of this sacramental union is the author of the mystical union itself: namely, the Holy Spirit. "This view of Calvin is that found in our confessional standards" (654, citing *Belgic Confession*, art. 35; *Heidelberg Catechism*, questions 75–76; and the communion form used at that time in his denomination [CRC]).

91. *Belgic Confession of Faith*, art. 35, *Psalter Hymnal: Doctrinal Standards and Liturgy of the Christian Reformed Church* (Grand Rapids: Board of Publications of the CRC, 1976), 87–88.

92. Calvin, *Institutes* 4.17.9.

the assurance of our own participation in what Luther described as the *mirifica commutatio* ("marvelous exchange").[93] If, unlike Zwingli, we affirm that the substance of the sacrament is Christ's true and natural body, Calvin wondered, "What could be more ridiculous than to split the churches and stir up frightful commotions" over *how* this happens?[94] The only pious conclusion, he says, is "to break forth in wonder at this mystery, which plainly neither the mind is able to conceive nor the tongue to express."[95] Calvin writes, "Inquisitive persons have wanted to define how the body of Christ is present in the bread." After summarizing the rival theories, he urges, "But the primary question to be put was how the body of Christ, as it was given for us, became ours; and how the blood, as it was shed for us, became ours. What matters is how we possess the whole Christ crucified, to become partakers of all his blessings."[96] The point is to assure trembling consciences that the Supper is "not a bare figure, but is joined with the reality and substance."[97]

Typical of Reformed confessions, the *Westminster Larger Catechism* points out that the *mode*, not the *substance*, is spiritual.[98] Furthermore, it is crucial to bear in mind that "spiritual" here refers to a person—the Holy Spirit—and not to a merely intellectual or imaginary mode of feeding. As A. A. Hodge notes, the phrase "spiritual presence" is ambiguous. It is not that in the sacrament Christ is only spiritually present, for this would be to receive a phantom rather than a real person. Nor is Christ merely subjectively present to the mind, as a photograph might remind us of a loved one, since Paul teaches that eating and drinking the bread and wine is a participation in Christ's body and blood. Nor can it mean that the Holy Spirit replaces Christ as the substance of the meal. It also "does not do to say that the divinity of Christ is present while his humanity is absent, because it is the entire indivisible divine-human Person of Christ which is present."[99] "But what do we mean by 'presence'?" asks Hodge. "It is a great mistake to confuse the idea of 'presence' with that of nearness in space.... 'Presence,' therefore, is not a question of space; it is a relation" (emphasis added).[100]

While Christ is not present on earth in the flesh until his return in glory, he is active in grace from his heavenly throne through the agency of his Spirit. Therefore, he can make himself the substance of the sacrament without bodily descending to the bread and the wine. Because of the agency of the Spirit, who unites us to the

93. Ibid., 4.17.2.

94. John Calvin, *Defensio doctrinae de sacramentis* [*Doctrinal Defense of the Sacraments*], *OS* 2:287.

95. Ibid.

96. Calvin, 1536 edition of *Institutes*, in *OS* 1:139.

97. Ibid., in *OS* 1:508–9.

98. See, for example, the *Westminster Larger Catechism*, Q. 170, in *The Book of Confessions* (Louisville: PCUSA General Assembly, 1991), 7.280. The catechism underscores this point

by confessing that believers truly "feed upon the body and blood of Christ" (the substance of the sacrament), "not after a corporeal but in a spiritual manner; yet truly and really, while by faith they receive and apply to themselves Christ crucified and all the benefits of his death."

99. A. A. Hodge, *Evangelical Theology: Lectures on Doctrine* (Edinburgh: Banner of Truth Trust, 1976), 355.

100. Ibid., 356.

whole Christ in the first place, there can be a real communication of Christ's person and work to the church. It is not simply Christ's divinity but the Spirit who makes Christ's reign universally present, so that even Christ's true and natural body and blood can be communicated to believers.

"When this perichoretically trinitarian framework is recognized," Philip Butin observes, "Christ's ascension is no longer a 'problem' for Calvin."

> To the contrary, it contributes a distinctively positive and "upward" emphasis to his entire theology of the eucharist. Calvin's approach at this point thus complements and completes the "downward" Lutheran emphasis on incarnation with an equal "upward" emphasis on resurrection and ascension. There is "a manner of descent by which he lifts us up to himself." Not only does Christ (in the Spirit) condescend to manifest himself to believers by means of visible, tangible, created elements; at the same time by the Spirit, the worshiping church is drawn into the heavenly worship of the Father though the mediation of the ascended Christ, who is seated with the Father in the heavenlies. For Calvin, this accentuates, rather than diminishes, the true humanity of Christ.

Hence, the emphasis in the eucharistic liturgy on the *sursum corda* ("We lift up our hearts to the Lord") and *epiclesis* (calling upon the Spirit).[101]

By the effective working of the Spirit, says Calvin, "the flesh of Christ is like a rich and inexhaustible fountain that pours into us the life springing forth from the Godhead into itself."[102] We are not only related to Christ generically as fellow humans, but eschatologically, pneumatologically, mystically, and soteriologically.[103] Thus, "the Spirit makes things which are widely separated by space to be united with each other, and accordingly causes life from the flesh of Christ to reach us from heaven."[104]

Similarly the *Belgic Confession* declares that while the mode "cannot be comprehended by us, as the operations of the Holy Spirit are hidden and incomprehensible, . . . we nevertheless do not err when we say that what is eaten and drunk by us is the proper and natural body and the proper blood of Christ."[105] The Spirit, in this view, is not a substitute for Christ, but is the agent who unites us to Christ and therefore communicates Christ and his benefits to believers.

(c) *Where is Christ received in the Supper?* Reformed theologians were unfairly criticized by their Lutheran interlocutors as holding a crude literalism with respect to

---

101. Philip Walker Butin, *Revelation, Redemption and Response: Calvin's Trinitarian Understanding of the Divine-Human Relationship* (New York: Oxford Univ. Press, 1995), 118.

102. Calvin, *Institutes* 4.17.8.

103. John Calvin, *Commentary on Paul's Epistle to the Ephesians* (Grand Rapids: Baker, repr. 1979), commenting on Eph 5:30–31.

104. John Calvin, "The Best Method of Obtaining Concord," in *Selected Works of John Calvin: Tracts and Letters* (ed. Henry Beveridge and Jules Bonnet; trans. Henry Beveridge; Grand Rapids: Baker, repr. 1983), 578.

105. *Belgic Confession of Faith*, in *Psalter Hymnal: Doctrinal Standards and Liturgy of the Christian Reformed Church*, 87–88.

Christ's whereabouts, as if he were confined to an actual chair in heaven. However, the Reformed concern was simply to point out the apparent contradiction between Jesus' own promise that he would depart in the flesh and not return until the last day—and his promise that he would be with them by his Word and Spirit. This follows the coming-and-going pattern of the Son and Spirit in Jesus' Upper Room Discourse (Jn 14–16). Even Lutheran theologian Robert Jenson remarks, "But if there is no place for Jesus' risen body, how is it a body at all? For John Calvin was surely right: ' … this is the eternal truth of any body, that it is contained in its place.' "[106]

A sacrament is not only the signs, but the reality signified that is joined to them. Therefore, the Reformed argued, the whole Christ may be said to be present and to offer himself in the sacrament without being enclosed in the elements. "It is one thing to say that Christ is present in the bread, another to assert the presence in the Holy Supper," says the Reformed scholastic Johannes Wollebius.[107] Zwingli's argument seemed to stop at the ascension, whereas Calvin's equally emphatic affirmation of a true feeding on Christ drew his attention to the activity of the Spirit in this time between the two advents.

Reformed theologians were only extrapolating from the doctrine of union with Christ in their view of the Supper. Although Christ has not yet returned bodily to earth, we are "seated with Christ in heavenly places" (Col 3:1–4; Eph 1:20; 2:6). Christ is not seated with us on earth, but we are seated with him in the heavenlies—in a semirealized manner now, but one day face to face. Even now, the Spirit takes that which is Christ's and makes both him and his gifts our own. Calvin found ample evidence for this eschatological, heavenly feeding also in the church fathers. In fact, his positive statement of his view of this true feeding (*Institutes* 4.17.8–39) is basically a gloss on a host of passages drawn from Scripture and the church fathers. Integrating comments from Cyril, Chrysostom, and Augustine, Calvin concludes that although Christ has been bodily raised to the right hand of God, "this Kingdom is neither bounded by location in space nor circumscribed by any limits. Thus Christ is not prevented from exerting his power wherever he pleases, in heaven and on earth." But right where one might have expected him to correlate this unbounded extension of Christ's reign with his omnipresent *deity* (as in Augustine and Zwingli), Calvin says, "In short, he feeds his people with his own body, the communion of which he bestows upon them *by the power of his Spirit*" (emphasis added).[108] We need not transform Christ's natural substance into a divine substance in order to affirm that his personal agency is omnipresent.

---

106. Robert W. Jenson, *Systematic Theology* (New York: Oxford Univ. Press, 1997), 1:202, citing 1536 edition of *Institutes* 4.122. See his excellent treatment on 202ff.

107. Johannes Wollebius, as quoted in Heinrich Heppe,

Reformed Dogmatics (rev. and ed. Ernst Bizer; trans. G. T. Thomson; London: Allen & Unwin, 1950), 642.

108. Calvin, *Institutes* 4.17.18.

Calvin complains that his critics seem to think that "Christ does not seem present unless he comes down to us." But how is Christ less present "if he should lift us to himself"? Why must he be present in the bread and the wine in order to be present in the sacrament? Is this not the point of the Holy Spirit's work of uniting us to Christ in heaven?[109] "Shall we therefore, someone will say, assign to Christ a definite region of heaven?" Again Calvin eschews speculation: "But I reply with Augustine that this is a very prying and superfluous question; for us it is enough to believe that he is in heaven."[110]

As Calvin and the Reformed tradition emphasized, the prospective aspect, "until he comes again," is meaningless if in fact Christ returns bodily to earth in order to be present at every altar or table. Calvin thus interprets the copula ("is") in the words of institution ("This *is* my body") in the light of Paul's elaboration. Paul says neither that the bread and cup are mere *symbols* nor that they *are* Christ's body and blood, much less that Christ's body and blood are *in, with, and under* the bread and cup. Rather, he says that the bread and wine are "*a participation in*" the body and blood of Christ (1Co 10:16).[111] Instead of saying that because Christ is Lord over time and space, he does not conform to the rules of ordinary bodies, we should say that because Christ is Lord over time and space *in the power of his Spirit*, the past of his work in the flesh for our salvation and the future consummation converge in a semirealized manner at the Lord's Table.

If Christ's bodily return occurs at every Eucharist, what is the significance of his return at the end of the age? It is significant that the angel comforts the disciples at Jesus' ascension by saying, "This Jesus, who was taken up from you into heaven, will come in the same way as you saw him go into heaven" (Ac 1:11). This eschatological tension is *accentuated* rather than *resolved* by the Supper, which is why the memory of his redeeming work (anamnesis) and the invocation of the Spirit for its effects in the present (epiklesis) necessarily engender a longing for his appearing in the future (epektasis). It is significant that the prayer for the Spirit's work in the Eucharist (the epiklesis), crucial in Eastern liturgies but gradually omitted in the West, became an important part of Reformed liturgies. The eucharistic event occurs here—and places us here—in this nexus where the powers of the age to come penetrate this present age. A qualitatively different presence will occur in the parousia: "When Christ who is our life appears, then you also will appear with him in glory" (Col 3:4). Nevertheless, even now, he "is our life." The Spirit communicates the energies of Christ's life-giving flesh. "If the sun sheds its beams upon the earth and casts its substance in some measure upon it in order to beget, nourish, and give growth to its offspring—why should the radiance of Christ's Spirit be less in order to impart to us the communion of his flesh and blood?"[112]

---

109. Ibid., 4.17.31.
110. Ibid., 4.17.26.

111. Ibid., 4.17.22.
112. Ibid., 4.17.1.

Here, I suggest, we detect the East's essence-energies distinction, including the usual analogy of the sun and rays. Such statements have sometimes been regarded (especially in American Presbyterian circles) as an odd inconsistency in Calvin's sacramental teaching.[113] However, this presumed inconsistency is largely due to the fact that Calvin appropriates the critical Eastern distinction between essence and energies. Athanasius affirmed, "[God] is outside all things according to his essence, but he is in all things through his acts of power."[114] This distinction provides the context for Calvin's (and broader Reformed) reflection on everything from how we know God to union with Christ to sacramental theology. Regardless of one's conclusions concerning this perspective, it is not an odd inconsistency but is deeply embedded in Calvin's doctrine of union with Christ.[115] His eucharistic view at this point did not run counter to his forensic understanding of justification, as Bruce McCormack suggests, because he saw justification as the basis but not the sole aspect of the mystical union.[116] Furthermore, if we interpret the "energies" as "the powers [*dynameis*] of the age to come" (Heb 6:5), which Christ fully possesses as the firstfruits of the whole harvest, then the same pneumatological mediation that is the hallmark of a Reformed doctrine of mystical union is at work in its sacramental theology. Recent scholarship has confirmed that Calvin's formulations at this point reflect his reading of patristic sources, especially Irenaeus and Chrysostom, but also Cyril of Alexandria.[117] Yet Calvin was hardly alone, his theological contemporaries

---

113. Charles Hodge, "Doctrine of the Reformed Church on the Lord's Supper," selected from *The Princeton Review* in Charles Hodge, *Essays and Reviews* (New York: Robert Carter & Brothers, 1957). With John Williamson Nevin in his sights, Hodge characterizes even Calvin's understanding of Christ's whole vivifying person being communicated in the Supper (which he acknowledges to be taught in some of the Reformed confessions) as "an uncongenial foreign element" drawn from patristic sources, a too literal reading of John 6, and a desire to placate the Lutherans (363–66). Even sharper views were expressed by James Henley Thornwell, R. L. Dabney, and William G. T. Shedd, the last of whom attempted to assimilate Calvin's view to his own Zwinglian conception (*Dogmatic Theology* [ed. Alan W. Gomes; 3rd ed.; Phillpsburg, N.J.: P&R, 2003], 814–15). Otto Ritschl expresses the same frustration with Calvin's Cyrillian interpretation of the sacrament in *Die reformierte Theologie* (1926).

114. Athanasius, *On the Incarnation* 17, in *Athanasius: Contra Gentes and De Incarnatione*, 174.

115. Calvin explicitly connects his view of union with Christ to the Supper (Calvin, *Institutes* 4.17.9). In a letter to Peter Martyr Vermigli (8 August 1555), Calvin writes,

> What I say is that the moment we receive Christ by faith as he offers himself in the gospel, we become truly members of his body, and life flows into us from him as from the head…. That is how I interpret the pas-

sage in which Paul says that believers are called into the *koinōnia* of Christ (1 Cor. 1:9). The words "company" or "fellowship" do not seem adequate to convey his thought: it suggests to me the sacred unity by which the Son of God engrafts us into his body, so as to communicate to us all that is his. Thus we draw life from his flesh and blood, so that they are not undeservedly called our "food." How it happens, I confess, is far above the measure of my intelligence. Hence I adore the mystery rather than labor to understand it (*CO* 15:722–23).

116. Bruce McCormack, "What's at Stake in Current Debates over Justification?", in *Justification: What's at Stake in the Current Debates?* (ed. Mark Husbands and Daniel J. Treier; Downers Grove, Ill.: InterVarsity Press, 2004), 104–5.

117. See Irena Backus, "Calvin and the Greek Fathers," in *Continuity and Change: The Harvest of Later Medieval and Reformation History* (ed. Robert J. Bast and Andrew C. Gow; Leiden: Brill, 2000), 253–76; cf. Johannes van Oort, "John Calvin and the Church Fathers," in *The Reception of the Church Fathers in the West: From the Carolingians to the Maurists* (ed. Irena Backus; Leiden: Brill, 1997), 680–90. See also Anthony Lane, *John Calvin: Student of the Church Fathers* (Grand Rapids: Baker, 1999), 41–42. Especially in van Oort, Calvin is cited as estimating that Cyril is next to Chrysostom in depth of insight (693).

and heirs reflecting similar views, including the essence (sun) and energies (rays) analogy.[118]

Calvin's view of the Supper as communicating Christ's flesh for our immortality is not a slip of the pen, and he was hardly alone in this line of thinking among the Reformed. Only with the Eastern category of God's energies, distinct from his essence and from created things, was Calvin able to affirm that Christ is an inexhaustible life-giving fountain communicated in the Supper (4.17.9), without suggesting any more than Cyril that the essence of Christ—either divinity or humanity—was poured into creatures. After all, he added a section to the 1559 *Institutes* in refutation of Osiander's formulation of that view. Interpreted eschatologically, this does not mean a fusion of essences, as if our personal identity is assimilated to Jesus' or vice versa. Nevertheless, it does mean that the efficacy (energy) of the sun (Christ) is communicated to us, so that even now both Christ's exalted flesh and his divine power reach us and renew us with their vigor. The branches share in the life, not simply the effects, of the vine; the relation of Christ to his body is that of the firstfruits to the harvest.

(d) *To whom is it administered?* Since the children of believers are baptized on the basis of their visible membership in the covenant of grace, why should they not be admitted to the Table as well? Because the worthy reception of Communion requires repentance and faith, necessarily involving some understanding of the sacrament, it is properly administered to those who have made a public profession of faith.[119] Our children are not excluded from any promises of the covenant of grace by waiting to receive Communion. The Word, baptism, and the Supper do not convey different realities but are the threefold manner in which God delivers Christ and all of his benefits to us by his Spirit. Faith comes from hearing the gospel; baptism is the sign and seal of our inclusion in the covenant of grace with all of its blessings, and the Supper strengthens and confirms that faith that we have professed. In Paul's teaching, admission to the Supper requires discernment, so as not to eat and drink unworthily (1Co 10:21–22; 11:17–32).

---

118. Heinrich Heppe, *Reformed Dogmatics*, 641, offers a number of citations that are pertinent. Like many early Reformed theologians, Wollebius explicitly appeals to the category of energies in discussing the Supper, including the usual analogy of the sun and its rays, so that "what is remote spatially is present in efficacy." He adds, "The presence is opposed not to distance but to absence." The eating and drinking of Christ's body and blood in John 6:51 cannot be reduced to believing or "simple cognition," adds Guillaume Bucanus; rather, it teaches that "by true participation in himself we should be quickened." Christ's whole life becomes the food that quenches our starvation, according to Olevianus, one of the authors of the *Heidelberg Catechism*. "Is our soul merely without the body, united to Christ's soul only, or our flesh also with Christ's flesh?" asks Bucanus. "Indeed the

whole person of each believer, in soul and body, is truly joined to the whole person of Christ." As he assumed our mortal flesh, so we participate in his immortal flesh. How else, asks Bucanus, could we be assured of our own glorification and resurrection? Martin Bucer, Peter Martyr Vermigli, Wolfgang Musculus, and other prominent Reformed leaders (seniors and contemporaries of Calvin) occupied essentially the same eucharistic terrain. The fact that Reformed and Presbyterian confessions (as Charles Hodge concedes) reflect these views further challenges the notion that Calvin introduced an "uncongenial foreign element" into the tradition's eucharistic teaching.

119. See Cornelis Venema, *Children at the Lord's Table?* (Grand Rapids: Reformation Heritage Books, 2009).

Some have taken these instructions beyond their intended scope, keeping from the Table those who have a right to it. Paul's warnings address a specific crisis in the church at Corinth, which involved gross immorality, drunkenness, gluttony, and the division of the church into sections according to economic status and attachment to persons. How could such a schismatic and immature church come appropriately to the Lord's Table to be nourished by Christ and be built into one body by it while in actual practice subverting its intended use? There is nothing in the passage that would suggest that those who repent and believe, having made a public profession of faith before the elders, should either be in effect excommunicated or excommunicate themselves for lack of a sense of "worthiness" defined by excessive rigor and introspection.

On one hand, the church may err in laxity, admitting to Communion those whose profession is unknown to the elders who are charged with guarding the Table. The writer to the Hebrews instructs, "Obey your leaders and submit to them, for they are keeping watch over your souls, as those who will have to give an account" (Heb 13:17). Christ has entrusted to his officers the power of the keys, to open and shut the kingdom of heaven (Mt 16:19; 18:15 – 20). On the other hand, the church may err in severity, keeping Christ's sheep from their pasture. The Supper is a means of grace for the weak, not a reward for the strong. In any case, none of us has the right to excommunicate others or ourselves; this solemn responsibility is given to the elders. If we are living in unbelief and open rebellion against God's commands, we should come under the discipline of the church and allow its admonitions and censures to lead us to repentance. However, all members in good standing must be admitted to the Table, and none may excuse himself or herself from this feast.

Obviously, this matter has a lot to do with the question of church membership, which presupposes public profession of faith, submission to the elders, and various other responsibilities required by Scripture. On this point, too, there are extremes to be avoided. On one hand, in many churches members are kept on rolls who have not formally professed faith or are lapsed and have never been visited by a pastor or elder. In the case of European state-churches especially, church membership simply coincided with citizenship.

At the other extreme is the ideal of a regenerate membership, with none admitted who do not offer persuasive evidence of being truly converted. "According to this theory," notes Hodge, "the Church consists of those who are 'judged' to be regenerate.... They alone are entitled to the sacraments either for themselves or for their children.... It may be remarked on this theory, that it is a novelty.... It has no warrant from Scripture either by precept or example."[120] In fact, Hodge goes so far as to conclude,

---

120. Hodge, *Systematic Theology*, 3:571.

The attempt to make the visible Church consist exclusively of true believers must not only inevitably fail of success, but it must also be productive of evil.... Experience proves that it is a great evil to make the Church consist only of communicants and to cast out into the world, without any of that watch and care which God intended for them, all those together with their children, who do not see their way clear to come to the Lord's table.[121]

Hodge adds that this undue rigor may well have contributed to the exodus of many from the church who might otherwise have been gradually affected by its ministry.[122]

(e) *What is the effect of the Supper?* Consistent with their view as to the nature of the Supper, the Reformed confessions affirm unanimously that it is a means of grace. Zwingli's way of speaking about the divinity of Christ as the true source of our salvation could be understood either as a sort of Apollinarian reduction of his humanity to a merely instrumental role or a nearly Nestorian division of natures. However, Calvin emphasized the union of the natures in one person without falling into a Monophysite[123] confusion. We cannot receive the gifts of Christ apart from his person, and we cannot be united to his person without being united to the whole Christ.[124] Calvin writes,

The situation would surely have been hopeless had the very majesty of God not descended to us, since it was not in our power to ascend to him. Hence, it was necessary for the Son of God to become for us "Immanuel, that is, God with us," and in such a way that his divinity and human nature might by mutual conjunction coalesce with each other [*ut mutual coniunctione eius divinitatas et hominum natura inter se coalescerent*]. Otherwise, the nearness would not have been enough, nor

---

121. Ibid., 3:572.

122. Ibid. Berkhof similarly observes, "Naturally, she [the church] cannot look into the heart and can only base her judgment respecting an applicant for admission on his confession of faith in Jesus Christ. It is possible that she occasionally admits hypocrites to the privileges of full communion, but such persons in partaking of the Lord's Supper will only eat and drink judgment to themselves." If such a lack of credibility of public profession becomes evident, the church disciplines. "It should be stated explicitly, however, that lack of the assurance of salvation need not deter anyone from coming to the table of the Lord, since the Lord's Supper was instituted for the very purpose of strengthening faith" (*Systematic Theology*, 657).

123. Regarding these three heresies, see pp. 472–74.

124. In the light of this retrieval of Eastern patristic emphases, it is interesting to compare Calvin with contemporary Orthodox theologian Alexander Schmemann: "Like the entire eucharist, the remembrance is not a repetition. It is the manifestation, gift and experience, in 'this world' and therefore again and again, of the eucharist offered by Christ once and for all, and of our ascension to it." The Supper does not complete or extend Christ's redemptive work, adds Schmemann. "No—in

Christ all is already accomplished, all is real, all is granted. In him we have obtained access to the Father and communion in the Holy Spirit and anticipation of the new life in his kingdom." He adds,

The purpose of the eucharist lies not in the change of the bread and wine, but in our partaking of Christ, who has become our food, our life, the manifestation of the Church as the body of Christ. This is why the holy gifts themselves never became in the Orthodox East an object of special reverence, contemplation and adoration, and likewise an object of special theological "problematics": how, when, in what manner their change is accomplished.... Nothing is explained, nothing is defined, nothing has changed in "this world." But then whence comes this light, this joy that overflows the heart, this feeling of fullness and of touching the "other world"? We find the answer to these questions in the epiclesis. But the answer is not "rational," built upon the laws of our "one-storied" logic; it is disclosed to us by the Holy Spirit. (Alexander Schmemann, *The Eucharist: Sacraments of the Kingdom* [Crestwood, N.Y.: St. Vladimir's Seminary Press, 1988], 224–27).

the affinity sufficiently firm, for us to hope that God might dwell with us [*Deum nobiscum habitare*].[125]

Therefore, for all who receive the reality that is given through the sacrament, Christ is as surely present in self-giving through Communion as he is in the preached Word. In both, the effect is assurance of God's saving favor toward us in Jesus Christ.

(f) *The frequency of Communion.* One's view of the efficacy of Communion largely determines one's views concerning frequency. It has often been noted that the confessional theology of Reformed and Presbyterian churches often differs from their practice. Reformed and Presbyterian church directories call for a frequent celebration of Communion, in sharp contrast with the infrequent practice of Orthodox and Roman Catholic churches (and then only according to one element: the bread). Against the traditional medieval practice of infrequent communion, Calvin offered a sustained plea that the Supper should be celebrated whenever the Word is preached, "or at least once a week."[126] "The Eucharist is the communion of the body and blood of the Lord," so infrequent communion is in effect, says Calvin, a withholding of Christ and his benefits from the covenant assembly.[127] In fact, only a year after the city of Geneva officially embraced the Reformation, Calvin's "Articles concerning the Organization of the Church and of Worship at Geneva" (1537) stated, "It is certain that a Church cannot be said to be well ordered and regulated unless in it the Holy Supper of our Lord is always being celebrated and frequented."[128]

From the beginning Reformed and Presbyterian church orders and directories called for "frequent" observance. Lee Palmer Wandel goes so far as to suggest that "Calvin articulated a new conceptualization of 'liturgy' itself." "For him, certainly, the Supper was a drama, but the source of that drama was God. No human movement could add to that meaning in any way, no crafted object could draw greater attention to those earthly elements." She adds, "Perhaps most important of all, however, was Calvin's insistence on frequency. Most evangelicals condemned the medieval requirement of annual communion as nonscriptural.... But no other evangelical so explicitly situated the Eucharist within a dialogic process not simply of deepening faith, but of the increasing capacity to read the signs of the Supper itself, and by extension, of God, in the world."[129] In both Roman Catholic and Zwinglian conceptions, the Eucharist was chiefly a human work, either of offering Christ again for sacrifice, or of remembering and pledging. However, says Wandel, "The Supper, for

125. Calvin, *Institutes* 2.12.1.

126. Ibid., 4.17.44–46.

127. Mary Beaty and Benjamin W. Farley, eds., *Calvin's Ecclesiastical Advice* (Louisville: Westminster John Knox, 1991), 165.

128. John Calvin, "Articles concerning the Organization of the Church and of Worship at Geneva proposed by the Minis-

ters at the Council, January 16, 1537," in *Calvin: Theological Treatises* (ed. and trans. J. K. L. Reid; Library of Christian Classics 22; Philadelphia: Westminster, 1954), 48.

129. Lee Palmer Wandel, *The Eucharist in the Reformation: Incarnation and Liturgy* (Cambridge: Cambridge Univ. Press, 2006), 171.

Calvin, was not 'external' —a ceremony ... nor even 'worship' in the sense that other evangelicals, such as Zwingli and Luther, used: a mode of honoring God." Rather, it is a means of binding us together more and more with Christ in an ongoing relationship in which "Christ 'is made completely one with us and we with him.' "[130]

Although Reformed theology emphasizes the priority of God's action in the Supper, it also recognizes a broader efficacy, which underscores the importance of its frequent celebration. The forensic yields the effective; justification, sanctification; the vertical, disrupting, objective work of God *extra nos* (outside of us) issues in a new system of horizontal, ordered, and subjective relationships between human beings. Like the Word, the sacraments draw us out of our private rooms into the public dining room. Here we are co-heirs at the family table, not consumers of exotic or meaningful religious experiences. Christ gives his body, and we thereby become "one body by such participation."[131]

Injury to one member affects the whole body, and the Supper not only illustrates this unity but confirms and strengthens it. "Accordingly," Calvin writes, "Augustine with good reason frequently calls this Sacrament 'the bond of love.' "[132] In this sacrament, Christ makes himself the common property of all believers, Calvin insists, no believer possessing any greater or lesser participation in Christ or any of his benefits than the others.[133] Besides the apostle Paul, Calvin echoes his mentor Martin Bucer on this point.[134] One cannot share in Jesus Christ without being a co-sharer with the rest of his body.

"Here we have the very root of diaconal work," notes Karl Deddens. "The festive spirit in which we celebrate the Lord's Supper is also an occasion for us, in accordance with Lord's Day 38 of the *Heidelberg Catechism*, to show compassion for the poor.... And this ideal would become reality if the festive character of the Lord's Supper came to full expression in our services."[135] As we have seen, the Supper is not the church's offering of a sacrifice for guilt, but rather (a) God's gift of his Son as our only sacrifice for sin and (b) our response of joy, a sacrifice of thanksgiving (Eucharist), that draws us out of ourselves to care for our brothers and sisters.

Some mention may be made of secondary matters. According to the regulative principle affirmed by Reformed churches, only that which has clear divine warrant may be done in the public service. However, historically those churches have distinguished between elements (instituted in Scripture) and circumstances (the order of service, liturgical forms, time of meeting, ministerial dress, etc.). Among the latter

130. Ibid.
131. Calvin, *Institutes* 4.17.38.
132. Ibid.
133. Ibid.
134. See Martin Bucer, "The Reign of Christ," in *Melanch-*

thon and Bucer (ed. Wilhelm Pauck; Library of Christian Classics; Philadelphia: Westminster, 1969), 182, 236–59.

135. Karl Deddens, *Where Everything Points to Him* (trans. Theodore Plantinga; Neerlandia, Alberta: Inheritance Publications, 1993), 93.

was the mode of receiving the Supper. Although the elements were received at the table by kneeling, standing, or walking, the dominant practice in early Reformed and Presbyterian churches was to sit at a large table (or tables) in the front, highlighting the character of the Supper as a festive meal. The practice of receiving the elements while sitting in pews, introduced by the Independents, was met with considerable opposition as "irreverent" (especially by the Dutch and the Scots).[136] In addition, the Independents introduced the practice of receiving the wine from individual cups rather than a common cup. Nowhere in the New Testament is a particular posture or method of reception commanded; therefore, as with baptism, differences on these questions do not vitiate the efficacy of the sacrament.[137]

EUCHARISTIC VIEWS		
Eastern Orthodox	A meal in which believers feed on Christ's true body and blood for everlasting life through the work of the Spirit *Primary Actor: the Triune God*	Transelementation
Roman Catholic	A sacrifice offered by the church to the Father. The bread and wine are transformed (in their essence) by priestly action into the body and blood of Christ *Primary Actor: the church/priest*	Transubstantiation
Lutheran	A meal in which all participants feed on Christ's true body and blood for salvation in the bread and the wine *Primary Actor: the Triune God*	True Presence in the elements
Reformed	A meal in which God ratifies his covenant of grace by feeding believers with Christ's true body and blood in heaven through the power of the Spirit *Primary Actor: the Triune God*	True Presence in the sacrament
Zwinglian	A meal in which believers pledge their continuing faith, love, and obedience to Jesus Christ and each other *Primary Actor: the church/believer*	Memorial/symbolic

136. B. B. Warfield provides a helpful survey of these variations in his essay, "The Posture of the Recipients at the Lord's Supper: A Footnote to the History of Reformed Usages," in *Selected Shorter Writings of Benjamin B. Warfield* (ed. John H. Meeter; Phillipsburg, N.J.: P&R, 1973), 351–69.

137. I would argue, however, that the use of wine in the Supper is essential to the proper administration of the sacrament. Although arguments could be adduced on the basis of the significance of wine in scriptural celebration, the only valid question is whether it is the element chosen by Christ for this meal along with the bread. Valid baptism requires water and the Supper requires bread and wine.

C. EUCHARIST AND ECCLESIA

Although important differences remain with respect to the Eucharist, recent ecumenical conversations have yielded impressive areas of consensus.[138] However, I will conclude this chapter by indicating the significance of our sacramental theology for ecclesiology more generally.

1. SEPARATING THE SIGN FROM THE SIGNIFIED

As we saw in the previous chapter, Karl Barth lamented the "sacramentalism" of the confessional Reformed position.[139] The sacraments are merely human acts of obedience rather than God's means of grace, he insisted. For Zwingli, spiritual blessings do not come through material means. The Spirit does not need "a channel or vehicle."[140] Where the Reformed view holds that God works through creaturely means, Barth shared Zwingli's tendency to see divine and creaturely agency as running on parallel tracks that never intersect. Throughout the last fragment of the *Church Dogmatics* that he was able to complete, Barth repeats his sharp distinction between God's work of salvation and the purely human work of liturgical obedience done in water baptism and the Supper.[141] "He is He, and His work is His work, *standing over against all Christian action*, including Christian faith and Christian baptism" (emphasis added).[142] "The *verbum visibile*, the objectively clarified preaching of the Word, is the only sacrament left to us."[143] Barth's overreaction was motivated by the tendency of both Roman Catholicism and Protestant liberalism to "contain" Christ and his saving work, conflating divine and human action.[144] The Supper, for Barth, is concerned with "the action of *the community*, and indeed with the action by which *it* establishes fellowship" (emphasis added).[145]

---

138. On the Lutheran-Reformed consensus, see Keith F. Nickle and Timothy F. Lull, *A Common Calling: The Witness of Our Reformation Churches in North America Today; The Report of the Lutheran-Reformed Committee for Theological Conversations, 1988–1992* (Minneapolis: Augsburg Fortress, 1993), 37–49. See also "XI. Lutheran-Reformed Dialogue," in *Growth in Agreement II: Reports and Agreed Statements of Ecumenical Conversations on a World Level, 1982–1998*, edited by Jeffrey Gros, Harding Meyer, and William G. Rusch (Geneva: World Council of Churches; Grand Rapids: Eerdmans, 2000), 230–47, esp. 242. However, significant branches of Lutheran and Reformed families have not participated in these discussions and would not endorse their conclusions or consensus. On the Reformed-Roman Catholic discussions, see *Growth in Agreement II*, 815. For a general consensus among member bodies of the World Council of Churches, see *Baptism, Eucharist & Ministry, 1982–1990: Report on the Process and Responses*, Faith and Order Paper No. 149 (Geneva: WCC Publications, 1990), 115–16.

139. Barth, *Church Dogmatics*, vol. 4, pt. 4, pp. 128–30. Under a discussion of how the Spirit works in the life of the believer and the community to direct them to Christ (vol. 4, pt.

2, pp. 360–77), baptism and the Supper do not even receive mention.

140. W. P. Stephens, "An Account of the Faith," quoted in *The Theology of Huldrych Zwingli* (Oxford: Clarendon, 1986), 186. Cf. Ulrich Zwingli, *Commentary on True and False Religion* (ed. Samuel Macauley Jackson and Clarence Nevin Heller; Durham, N.C.: Labyrinth Press, 1981), 204–5, 214–15, 239.

141. Barth, *Church Dogmatics*, vol. 4, pt. 4. Titled *The Christian Life*, this volume is a fragment that Barth developed and published as part of his unfinished dogmatics. Cf. *Church Dogmatics*, vol. 4, pt. 3, pp. 2, 756, 783, 790, 843–901.

142. Ibid., vol. 4, pt. 4, p. 88.

143. Karl Barth, *The Word of God and the Word of Man* (trans. Douglas Horton; New York: Harper Torchbooks, 1957), 114. He adds cheerfully though erroneously from a historical perspective, "The Reformers sternly took from us everything but the Bible."

144. See David Allen, "A Tale of Two Roads: Homiletics and Biblical Authority," *JETS* 43, no. 3 (September 2000), esp. 492. Cf. Barth, *Church Dogmatics*, vol. 1, pt. 1, p. 127.

145. Barth, *Church Dogmatics*, vol. 4, pt. 3, pp. 2, 901.

The separation of the sign and thing signified opens a fissure in ecclesiology from top to bottom between, on one side, the visible church as a historical institution with its structure, offices, order, and sacraments, and, on the other side, the invisible church as a relatively unknown and unknowable community of believers. As has frequently been observed, a weak pneumatology is one reason for (and perhaps result of) this divide.[146] As that which Barth calls "the subjective side in the event of revelation," the Spirit's work consists entirely of awakening people to that which has already happened rather than contributing in his own distinct manner to our salvation.[147]

The dominant view of the Supper in contemporary evangelical theology, as observed in the previous chapter, may even go beyond a Zwinglian conception, with the efficacy of the sacraments lodged entirely in their symbolic role of testifying to the believer's "act of commitment."[148] Sacramental theology shapes ecclesiology, regardless of the perspective. Where the main goal of preaching is to motivate our decision and action and the main goal of baptism and the Supper is to testify to our decision and action, the church will be most likely conceived as a voluntary association of like-minded individuals but hardly "the mother of the faithful." A personal relationship with Jesus Christ may then easily be set over against church membership and covenantal nurture.

2. CONFUSING SIGN AND SIGNIFIED

With the doctrine of transubstantiation the sign is absorbed (hence, lost) in the reality signified. Rather than natural creatures penetrated by the *energies* of God (while remaining what they are), the bread and wine are simply obliterated and converted into a supernatural *essence*. But in this case, neither remains what it is. The natural body of Jesus Christ becomes identified as the church as his ongoing incarnation and the natural signs are no longer consecrated creatures but elevated to become something else. This tendency is evident in a variety of contemporary theologies.[149]

It is evident, for instance, in Graham Ward's appraisal of Calvin's eucharistic

146. Among the many criticisms of Barth in this connection, see especially Robert Jenson, "You Wonder Where the Spirit Went," in *Pro Ecclesia* 2 (1993): 296–304; Wolfhart Pannenberg, *Systematic Theology* (trans. G. W. Bromiley; Grand Rapids: Eerdmans, 1998), 3:1–27.

147. Barth, *Church Dogmatics*, vol. 1, pt. 1, p. 449.

148. Interestingly, something close to this interpretation is also articulated as "transsignification" by some Roman Catholic theologians today. For the most thorough development and defense of transsignification, see Edward Schillebeeckx, *The Eucharist* (London: Sheed & Ward, 1968), 108–19.

149. One indicator of this trend is the movement known as Radical Orthodoxy, led by John Milbank, Graham Ward, and Catherine Pickstock. On this point especially, see John Milbank, "Alternative Protestantism," in *Radical Orthodoxy and the Reformed Tradition: Creation, Covenant, and Participation* (ed. J. K. A. Smith and James H. Olthuis; Grand Rapids:

Baker Academic, 2005), 31. For lengthy interaction with some of these trends, see Michael Horton, *People and Place: A Covenant Ecclesiology* (Louisville: Westminster John Knox, 2008), 153–89. Milbank writes that "Calvin's sacramental theology is not really coherent. In relation to the Eucharist he is indeed to be thoroughly commended for his strong pneumatological emphasis—reminiscent of Greek views and perhaps superior to some Catholic treatments.... But the idea of the spiritual participation in a body that is in heaven makes very little sense." Better is the doctrine of transubstantiation, which avoids a local presence of Christ's body and blood either in heaven or in the bread and the wine by suggesting instead "that participation in a physical—albeit mysteriously physical—reality is itself mysteriously physical" ("Alternative Protestantism," 35). The other essays in this volume (*Radical Orthodoxy and the Reformed Tradition*) offer tremendous insights and responses.

theology. According to Ward, Calvin seems fixated on the body of the "gendered Jew," but Ward's own solution is to regard this body as infinitely expanded — "transcorporeal" — so that Christ "returns" in and as the church.[150] He argues that this spiritual body is *more real than any physical body* (emphasis added).[151] Matter is at last transcended. The body and blood of Christ are the sign (*sacramentum*); the church is the reality (*res*) — "*only this ecclesiastical Body should be called purely* res" (emphasis added).[152] Like myriad attempts to substitute the church for Jesus Christ in the flesh, from Origen to Schleiermacher and on into the present day, Ward's proposal leaves nothing for the Spirit to mediate and nothing to anticipate by way of Christ's return in glory. The church simply *is* the expanded Christ. Ironically, what gets lost in the process is the one who has died, is risen, and will come again just as the disciples saw him leave. The one who has died, is risen, and will come again just as the disciples saw him leave is no longer the object of Christian faith and proclamation. Given the correlation of head and members, is it any wonder that in the displacement-as-expansion of Jesus' natural body, the eschatological hope according to Milbank and Pickstock is not the resurrection of the body but a transcorporeal existence?[153] Since Christ is the firstfruits, if his natural body has vanished, so too has our resurrection hope. If he is "transcorporeal," so will we be but so many drops in an ocean of spirit. As goes the head, so go the members. A docetic Eucharist means a docetic consummation. Avoiding the reality of the ascension, which keeps us praying, "Amen. Come, Lord Jesus!" the church substitutes itself as the real and only true body of its absent Lord.

3. Sign and Signified: Union without Confusion

Only the communication of Christ himself with all his benefits is sufficient to generate an ecclesial body. However, the church is not Jesus Christ. It does not extend his incarnation or complete his saving work, but receives the benefits of this work and shares it with others.

It is properly said that the Eucharist gives the church. There is not first of all a church and then certain practices, like preaching, baptism, and the Supper. Together with the first two, the Supper identifies the true church because it is through these means of grace that the Spirit is at work creating a communion for the Father in the Son. Paul asks, "The cup of blessing that we bless, is it not a participation in the blood of Christ? The bread that we break, is it not a participation in the body of Christ? *Because there is one bread*, we who are many are one body,

---

150. Graham Ward, *Cities of God* (New York: Routledge, 2000), 154–72.

151. Ibid.

152. Ibid., 180.

153. John Milbank and Catherine Pickstock, *Truth in Aqui-* nas (London: Routledge, 2001), 37. I am grateful to James K. A. Smith for pointing to this reference in his carefully nuanced interpretation in "Will the Real Plato Please Stand Up?" in *Radical Orthodoxy and the Reformed Tradition*, 70.

for we all partake of the one bread" (1Co 10:16–17, emphasis added). But unless the matter of the Eucharist remains the *natural* body of Jesus Christ, the *ecclesial* body will also be a docetic illusion.

A eucharistic theology that confuses the sign and the signified and collapses the eschatological "not yet" into an overrealized "already" makes the church a substitute for Jesus Christ and the Holy Spirit. And a eucharistic theology that separates the sign and the signified as well as this age from the penetrating powers of the age to come already breaking in on us will likely yield an association of choosers rather than a communion of saints. The first error leads to a triumphalistic ecclesiology, while the latter leads to a weak one. Whatever our view of the Supper, it must be one that places the church in the precarious collision of the powers of death and life, in complete dependence on the Spirit. Taking our coordinates from the redemptive economy of Christ's descent, ascent, and parousia — concretely manifested and in fact constituted by the Spirit through Word and sacrament, this covenantal ecclesiology locates the church's identity at this unsettling, strange, even dangerous yet wonderful intersection between the two ages.

DISCUSSION QUESTIONS

1. Discuss the relationship between circumcision and baptism.
2. How does our view of the continuity and discontinuity of the covenant of grace affect our understanding of the baptism of the children of believers?
3. What is accomplished through baptism?
4. How is the Lord's Supper a ratification of the new covenant? Discuss some relevant passages, comparing and contrasting the Sinai covenant and the new covenant administration of the Abrahamic promise.
5. Compare and contrast Roman Catholic, Lutheran, Reformed, Zwinglian, and Anabaptist interpretations of the Lord's Supper. Relate your own interpretation to Christ's ascension, Pentecost, and the return of Christ.
6. In the light of specific passages in Scripture, how would you understand the relationship between the sign and the reality signified in the sacraments?

Chapter Twenty-Five

THE ATTRIBUTES OF THE CHURCH: UNITY, CATHOLICITY, AND HOLINESS

The church is most typically referred to as the called-out assembly (Heb., *qāhāl*; Gk., *ekklēsia/synagōgē*).[1] The passive concept of "called out" underscores the fact that this community is formed by the Word. It does not come together as an aggregate of individuals who have determined to form such a society, but is summoned, gathered, and called out by God's electing, redeeming, justifying, and renewing grace. Ecclesiology is not a topic that exists alongside the gospel, which needs to be related somehow to it. Rather, the gospel itself, as God's saving speech act (energies), generates a community called the church. The attributes, marks, and mission of the church therefore form the threads of a single bolt of fabric that is woven by the Spirit through the gospel as it is delivered through Christ's appointed means.

We cannot help but think within certain frameworks or paradigms. In the last chapter I noted that one's view of the sign-signified relationship with regard to the sacraments will show up also in one's ecclesiology. In fact, different ecclesiological paradigms reflect different ontologies. Especially when we take up the attributes of the church identified in the Nicene Creed, there is a danger of two extremes between which we need to navigate.

---

1. As Louis Berkhof points out, the English noun *church* (similar to Kirk, Kerk, Kirche) is derived not from *ekklēsia* but from *kyriakē*, "belonging to the Lord" (*Systematic Theology* [Grand Rapids: Eerdmans, 1996], 557).

I. THE MANY AS ONE: CONFLATING CHRIST AND THE CHURCH

At one extreme end there is the tendency simply to collapse Christology (and soteriology) into ecclesiology. The concept of the church and Christ together comprising "the whole Christ" (*totus Christus*) was developed by Augustine.[2] However, over time it grew into a cosmic ecclesiology (and Christology) that fused the head with his members in one corporate personality. As the creatures of bread and wine are transubstantiated into Christ's body and blood, the members of Christ's body become fused into a single essence: the *totus Christus*. According to the broader ontological paradigm of Platonism/Neoplatonism, "the real" is one rather than plural, sameness rather than diversity. Everything that is real emanates from the One in ever-diminishing grades of being, from the bright glory of the soul to the dark prison house of the body. Even in its Christian forms, this ontology made it difficult to break with the idea that grace was a spiritual substance infused into nature (including persons) in order to elevate them to a supernatural plane of existence. (Monasticism became an institutionalized version of this paradigm.)

We have already challenged this outlook by observing that in Scripture the proper dualism is not between nature and grace but between sin and grace. The problem is not one of transforming natural creatures into something else, but of forgiving sinners and liberating creation from sin's guilt and power so that everything that has breath may glorify and enjoy God forever. To the extent that an ecclesiology emerges from Platonic/Neoplatonic and Hegelian presuppositions, the tendency will be toward the one over the many, sameness over difference, and a hierarchy of being with grace flowing from the top of the ladder to its lower rungs. There is nothing questionable, ambiguous, or precarious about the church's location or identity in this age, according to this perspective. The church is simply the kingdom of God—the historical replacement for the natural body of Jesus Christ. Therefore, "the whole constitution of the Church is completely aristocratic, and not democratic, her authority coming from above, from Christ, and not from below, from the community."[3]

In Roman Catholic ecclesiologies. Platonism's ladder of being is transformed into a hierarchical ladder of grace, flowing in diminishing grades from Christ and

---

2. For example, he wrote, "Let us rejoice and give thanks that we are made not only Christians but Christ," in *Homilies on the Gospel of John*, NPNF1, vol. 7, comment on Jn 21:8. Cf. Augustine's "On the Epistle of John," translated by H. Browne and Joseph Myers, in the same volume, 462: "The Word was made flesh and dwelled among us; to that flesh is joined the church,

and there is the whole Christ, head and body."

3. Karl Adam, *The Spirit of Catholicism* (trans. Dom Justin McCann, OSB; New York: Crossroad, 1924; repr., 1977), 21. See also the important work of Michael J. Himes, *The Ongoing Incarnation: Johann Adam Möhler and the Beginnings of Modern Ecclesiology* (London: Herder and Herder, 1997).

Mary to the pope and magisterium all the way down to all who do what lies within them. Through this hierarchy, writes Karl Adam, "*the divine is objectivised, is incarnated in the community*, and precisely and only in so far as it is a community.... So the Church possesses the Spirit of Christ, not as a many of single individuals, nor as a sum of spiritual personalities, but as the compact unity of the faithful, as a community that transcends the individual personalities ..., *the many as one*." Christ's mission is "to reunite to God mankind as a unity, as a whole, *and not this or that individual man*" (emphasis added).[4] Not only *unity* (common fellowship in Christ) but *unicity* (numerical oneness in a hierarchy with a papal head) is Adam's understanding of the church.[5]

In a somewhat chilling illustration of his time and place, Adam passionately asserts, "One God, one faith, one love, one single man: that is the stirring thought which inspires the Church's pageantry and gives it artistic form."[6] Echoing Hegel even more explicitly, he declares, "For only in the whole can the divine realise itself, only in the totality of men and not in the individual."[7] As a consequence, "The structural organs of the Body of Christ, as that is realised in space and time, are pope and bishops."[8] This empirical polity—the observable structure of the ecclesiastical hierarchy—*constitutes* the visibility of the church in the world. Where is the true church? The answer is obvious and unambiguous: the historical institution that possesses the apostolic succession of bishops under the primacy of the bishop of Rome.

For all of these reasons, says Adam, "The Catholic Church as the Body of Christ, as the realisation in the world of the Kingdom of God, is the Church of Humanity." So the church is simultaneously exclusive (there is no other ladder of grace) and inclusive (since God's grace flows through her down to the lowest rungs).[9] This grace operates "not only in the Christian communions, but also in the non-Christian world, in Jews and in Turks and in Japanese"—at least to "all those who hold themselves ready for it, *who do what in them lies*, who perform what their conscience bids them" (emphasis added).[10]

Although this ecclesiology was refined and balanced with other images, it has remained the dominant interpretation and has been reasserted by the current pope. Prior to becoming Pope Benedict XVI, Joseph Cardinal Ratzinger, in his book *Called to Communion: Understanding the Church Today* (1996), wrote, "The tem-

---

4. Adam, *The Spirit of Catholicism*, 31–32.

5. Ibid., 38.

6. Ibid., 41. Like many Catholic and Protestant theologians of his generation, Adam at first welcomed Hitler's ascendancy, but later he criticized the regime.

7. Ibid., 53.

8. Ibid., 97.

9. Ibid., 159–65.

10. Ibid., 168. The italicized clause is from the nominalist maxim, "To those who do what lies within them, God will not deny his grace" (*facientibus quod in se est deus non denigat gratiam*), which the Reformation especially targeted in its criticisms.

poral and ontological priority lies with the universal Church; a Church that was not catholic would not even have ecclesial reality."[11] Apart from papal primacy, not even a valid succession of bishops is adequate.[12]

> If Orthodoxy starts from the bishop and from the Eucharistic community over which he presides, the point on which the Reformed position is built is the Word: the Word of God gathers men and creates "community." The proclamation of the Gospel produces—so they say—congregation, and this congregation is the "Church." In other words, the Church as institution has in this view no properly theological status; only the community has theological significance, because what matters is the Word alone.[13]

Of course, this statement caricatures the Reformed position, but it does highlight the difference between a communion of saints generated by the Word and a hierarchical oneness generated by a single pastor.

The transubstantiation of the eucharistic body into the natural body of Jesus Christ is the basis for the transubstantiation of the ecclesial body into the *totus Christus* (in effect, replacing Jesus Christ and those united to him as persons). The marriage analogy often employed in Scripture suggests that the two become "one flesh," yet in such a way that they remain two people. Yet for Rome, universal and numerical oneness is ontologically supreme.[14] Accordingly, says Ratzinger, this leads to a "fusion of existences."[15]

The sacrifice of the individual to the "corporate personality" in Ratzinger's account is especially evident in his reiteration of the traditional Roman Catholic view that faith itself is "a gift of the church." The belief of the individual subject (i.e., the personal act of faith) is entirely subsumed under the belief of the church as a whole.[16] Noting the obvious influence of German idealism, Miroslav Volf comments, "Ratzinger even elucidates this notion of cobelief with the church with the expression 'surrender one's act [of faith] to it [the church].'"[17] In the previous chapter we encountered similar language from Hans Urs von Balthasar, in his appeals to Schleiermacher and Hegel.

The *eschatological* dualism (or better, paradox) between the already and the not yet is replaced in this trajectory by the *ontological* dualism between visible and invisible. Plato rather than Paul dominates this ecclesiological horizon. As Volf judges,

> Ratzinger has a tendency to search for something more profound or real behind the historical, and to view concrete reality merely as a sign for spiritual, transcendent

11. Joseph Cardinal Ratzinger, *Called to Communion: Understanding the Church Today* (trans. Adrian Walker; San Francisco: Ignatius Press, 1996), 44.

12. Ibid., 79–80.

13. Ibid., 80–81.

14. Ibid., 82.

15. Ibid., 37.

16. Joseph Ratzinger, *Principles of Christian Morality* (trans. Graham Harrison; San Francisco: Ignatius Press, 1968), 38.

17. Miroslav Volf, *After Our Likeness: The Church as the Image of the Trinity* (Grand Rapids: Eerdmans, 1998), 35, 37.

content. Hence the earthly Jesus is portrayed less as a concrete human being than as "merely an *exemplum* of human beings".... This is the result of Ratzinger's Platonizing "commitment to the primacy of the invisible as that which is genuinely real (Ratzinger, *Einführungin das Christentum*, 48)."[18]

It is the pope who makes this invisible reality visible, as he is "placed in direct responsibility to the Lord ... to embody and secure the unity of Christ's word and work."[19] "Loss of this element of unity with the successors of Peter wounds the church 'in the essence of its being as church.'"[20]

We have already encountered Graham Ward's thesis that the "displacement" of Jesus-in-the-flesh is not a loss, but a transubstantiation of his personal existence in and as the church. So once again we return to the basic substance of the "ascent of mind" that can be traced from Origen to Schleiermacher: the disappearance of Jesus is not a problem because he did not really disappear after all, but is just as present—or rather, more fully present—today in and as the church. Despite his disclaimer that his "interpretation of the ascension is not in accord with Origen's 'ascension of the mind rather than of the body ...,'"[21] Ward's arguments do little to allay the contrary judgment. According to this rather extreme version of the notion of Christ's ubiquity, "We have no access to the body of the gendered Jew.... *It is pointless because the Church is now the body of Christ, so to understand the body of Jesus we can only examine what the Church is and what it has to say* concerning the nature of that body as scripture attests it" (emphasis added).[22] Ward adds, "As Gregory of Nyssa points out, in his thirteenth sermon on Song of Songs, 'he who sees the Church looks directly at Christ.'"[23]

Eastern Orthodoxy reflects a more eschatological ("already"/"not yet") and pneumatological ecclesiology.[24] Eschatology keeps ecclesiology from becoming a mere affirmation of a historical institution.[25] Christ *in-stitutes* the church; the Spirit *con-stitutes* it.[26] This leads to an emphasis on the common participation of all believers in the gifts of the Spirit and on the authority of the plurality of bishops in assembly rather than on papal supremacy.

18. Ibid., 49.

19. Ratzinger, *Das neue Volk*, 169, quoted in Volf, *After Our Likeness*, 58.

20. Ratzinger, *Gemeinschaft*, 88, quoted in Volf, *After Our Likeness*, 59. On the same page, quoting Ratzinger's "Kirche," 178–79, Volf notes Ratzinger's claim, albeit before Vatican II, "The *sedes apostolica* as such is Rome, so that one can say that *communio catholica = communio Romana*; only those who commune with Rome are standing in the true, that is, catholic *communio*; whoever Rome excommunicates is no longer in the *communio catholica*, that is, in the unity of the church."

21. Ward, *Cities of God*, 115.

22. Ibid.

23. Ibid., 116.

24. John Zizioulas, *Being as Communion* (Crestwood, N.Y.: St. Vladimir's Seminary Press, 1985), 132–33.

25. Ibid., 140.

26. Ibid.: "The fact that Orthodoxy has not experienced situations similar to those of the Western Churches, such as the problem of clericalism, anti-institutionalism, Pentecostalism, etc. may be taken as an indication that *for the most part* Pneumatology has saved the life of Orthodoxy up to now."

Vladimir Lossky points out that catholicity and apostolicity are both dependent on the Truth.[27] Thus, catholicity cannot simply mean universality: that which is widely held in many places. After all, Islam and Buddhism claim worldwide adherents.[28] "A layman is even bound to resist a bishop who betrays the Truth and is not faithful to the Christian tradition," Lossky insists.[29] "At the same time, we must not fall into the contrary error which occurs when, in giving catholicity a charismatic character, we confuse it with holiness, seeing it in the personal inspiration of the saints, the sole witness of the Truth, the only true catholics. This would be to profess an error similar to Montanism and to transform the Church into a mystical sect."[30] Lossky adds,

> To desire to base ecclesiology solely on the Incarnation, to see in the Church solely "an extension of the Incarnation," a continuation of the work of Christ, as is so often stated, is to forget Pentecost and to reduce the work of the Holy Spirit to a subordinate role.... The Pneumatological element of the Church must not be underestimated, but fully accepted on an equal footing with the Christological, if the true foundation of the catholicity of the Church is to be found.[31]

The church is made "in the image of the Trinity," and every ecclesiological error is ultimately an error concerning the Trinity and vice versa.[32] The emphasis on the one essence over the person in Western trinitarian formulations carries over to ecclesiology. Lossky observes:

> When, as often happens in the treatment of catholicity, the emphasis is placed on unity, when catholicity is above all other considerations based upon the dogma of the Body of Christ, the result is Christocentrism in ecclesiology.... On the other hand, when the emphasis is placed on diversity at the expense of unity, there is a tendency to base catholicity exclusively on Pentecost, forgetting that the Holy Spirit was communicated in the unity of the Body of Christ. The result is a disaggregation of the Church: the truth that is attributed to individual inspirations becomes multiple and therefore relative; catholicity is replaced by "ecumenism."[33]

Lossky responds to both dangers once again by referring to the Trinity: "As in God each one of the three persons, Father, Son, and Holy Spirit, is not a part of the Trinity but is fully God in virtue of His ineffable identity with the one nature, so the Church is not a federation of parts: she is catholic in each one of her parts, since each part in her is identified with the whole, expresses the whole, has the value which the whole has, does not exist outside the whole." And this is expressed not only locally, but in wider

---

27. Vladimir Lossky, *In the Image and Likeness of God* (Oxford: Mowbray, 1967), 175. He refers to the expression of Maximus the Confessor, who replied to those who insisted that he accept communion with the Monothelites, "Even if the whole world should be in communion with you, I alone should not be." In doing so, says Lossky, "he was opposing his catholicity to an ecumenicity which he regarded as heretical."

28. Ibid.
29. Ibid., 176.
30. Ibid.
31. Ibid., 177.
32. Ibid., 179.
33. Ibid.

assemblies and synods.[34] Yet even such synods, in order to have validity, must conform to the catholicity of the Truth that makes the church catholic. Their authority cannot be determined simply by the power of a hierarchy any more than by the democratic consensus of the majority. Both would be parodies of catholicity. "There is no other criterion of truth than the Truth itself."[35] As is evident enough in Jesus' High Priestly Prayer in John 17, the unity of Christ's people is found in their union with him, which is also, through him, a fellowship with the Trinity. And this is a unity in the *truth*. The church is catholic when it is united in the truth of God's Word in the Spirit.

There is a great deal of wisdom in Orthodox teaching concerning the nature of the church. Nevertheless, this tradition also reflects a tendency toward an overrealized eschatology of the *totus Christus*, identified this time not with a historical institution led by a single bishop, but with every celebration of the Eucharist, which can be valid only when officiated in communion with the Orthodox bishops. "The one Christ event takes the form of *events* (plural), which *are as primary ontologically as the one Christ event itself*." On one hand, this is an improvement on Roman Catholic ecclesiologies: "The local Churches are as primary in ecclesiology as the universal Church."[36] No priority of the universal over the local Church is conceivable in such an ecclesiology. On the other hand, the *totus Christus* motif is still articulated in terms that can easily undermine the difference between Christ and the church. This is because the Eucharist is understood not as the meal that places us in the precarious intersection of this age and the age to come, but as the fully realized Wedding Supper of the Lamb.

Nowhere in Scripture do we read that the church together with Jesus of Nazareth constitutes "the whole Christ" (*totus Christus*). Rather, the historical Christ is the representative head of his ecclesial body. Even in the few passages that directly invoke the body of Christ analogy (Eph 4, Rom 12, 1Co 12), we are reminded that each member has its role *in* the body, not that each member *is* the whole body or that each member is *assimilated* to the whole.

This first paradigm (the one over the many) carries forward its assumptions consistently with respect not only to the unity and catholicity of the church, but also to its holiness. Augustine left a complex legacy to future generations for ecclesiological reflection. On one hand, he strove valiantly against Pelagianism and Donatism, underscoring the fact that the church's existence is due to God's grace alone. Yet he also tended to identify the church with the kingdom of God in a relatively noneschatological manner, preparing the way unintentionally for an inflated ecclesial ego.[37] However, the medieval developments that we have already considered added to this church-kingdom identity a notion that Augustine would never have accepted: namely, the sinlessness of the church as Christ's bride. After all, Augustine's argu-

34. Ibid., 180.
35. Ibid., 181.

36. Ibid.
37. Berkhof, *Systematic Theology*, 559.

ment against the Donatists was that the church was the kingdom even though it is a "mixed body" of elect and reprobate, and even the elect remain sinners.

Concerned that Augustine's interpretation of predestination opened the door to an invisible-visible church distinction exploited by Protestantism, von Balthasar in the twentieth century reaffirmed the traditional Roman Catholic concept of the sinless body of Christ by appealing to Dionysian mysticism with its descending and ascending ladders.[38] Like saving revelation, ecclesial identity is actually universal, with diminishing grades, and "sees in the Church all gradations of holiness from the highest, most unsullied sanctity of Mary to the very brink of damnation, in fact even beyond it, in the case of the gravely sinful who are not yet, in some way, members of the Church...."[39] In this conception, grace merely elevates nature. According to Vatican I, "the Church itself, with its marvelous extension, its eminent holiness, and its inexhaustible fruitfulness in every good thing, with its Catholic unity and its invincible stability, is a great and perpetual motive of credibility and an irrefutable witness of its own divine mission."[40] Thus, holiness and catholicity flow from the unicity of the *totus Christus*: the single subject that is Christ and his church. The church, in this view, is less a *communion of persons* with *Christ* as its head than a *single person* represented by a *human head* (the Pope)

II. THE ONE AS MANY: CONTRASTING CHRIST AND THE CHURCH

At the other extreme is the view of the church as a purely spiritual reality brought into being by the will and effort of many individuals, with no definite relationship between the sign and reality signified. In this paradigm, Christ's presence is located in the heart of individual believers. Like the first paradigm, this approach easily surrenders Christ's transcendence over the whole church as its ascended head, only this time to the immanence of individual experience.

However different it is from the first paradigm, this approach can just as easily lose sight of the paradox of the real absence of Christ in the flesh and his real presence mediated by the Spirit through the means of grace. The Roman Catholic concept of the church as the ongoing incarnation of Jesus Christ, completing his saving work, has become a major emphasis in Protestant ecclesiologies (especially missiologies).[41] In

38. Hans Urs von Balthasar, *Church and World* (trans. A. V. Littledale with Alexander Dru; Montreal: Palm Publishers, 1967), 145–46.

39. Ibid., 152.

40. See Avery Dulles, SJ, *Models of the Church* (Garden City, N.Y.: Doubleday, 1974), 123.

41. Pioneers of a more explicitly "incarnational missiology" include Sherwood G. Lingenfelter and Marvin K. Mayer, *Ministering Cross-Culturally: An Incarnational Model for Personal Relationships* (Grand Rapids: Baker, 1986), and Charles van Engen and Jude Tiersma, *God So Loves the City: Seeking a Theology for Urban Mission* (Monrovia, Calif.: MARC, 1994). Latin American theologies of liberation have also shaped this emphasis, especially Orlando Costas, *Christ Beyond the Gate* (Maryknoll, N.Y.: Orbis, 1982). For a balanced theological analysis of the concept, see J. Todd Billings, "'Incarnational Ministry': A Christological Evaluation and Proposal," *Missiology: An International Review* 32, no. 2 (April 2004): 187–201.

this case, the incarnation is said to be extended not by the church as an institution or by its official ministry of preaching, sacrament, and discipline, but by the church as a movement of disciples—and not principally by proclamation and sacrament, but by "living the gospel" among their neighbors. Especially in the Emergent Church movement, the notion of the church as the ongoing incarnation merges with an essentially Anabaptist ecclesiology. God "creates the church as a missional community to join him in his mission of saving the world."[42] One often encounters the counsel attributed to Francis of Assisi: "Always preach the gospel, and when necessary use words."

Although "living the gospel" has long been a familiar refrain in evangelical piety, this approach is increasingly radicalized, by relocating the church's identity and mission to its work in the world more than the means of grace in local churches.[43] Often, "incarnational ministry" is simply a call to greater sensitivity to our ministry context. In more extreme versions, it is more literal in its understanding of the church (or community of disciples) as the extension of the incarnation.[44]

As in Roman Catholic versions, the principal problem with this approach is that it undermines the uniqueness of Christ's person and work. "Christ" becomes a pattern or principle for our work rather than a unique person who redeemed us once and for all by his work. The gospel becomes an exhibition of our good works rather than the announcement of God's work in Christ. The tendency of this way of thinking is to confuse the Creator and the creature, Christ and his body, his incarnation and completed work of redemption with our own, and the gospel with the law. Where the uniqueness of Christ's historical incarnation is elided, Christology cannot help but capitulate to docetism with respect to his ascension (real absence) and return in the flesh. In the process, the work of the Spirit in mediating Christ's presence here and now through preaching and sacrament is sacrificed to the work of the church as Christ's presence here and now already.

The major difference between this radical Protestant paradigm and Roman Catholic versions of the idea of the church as an ongoing incarnation lies in the Anabaptist presuppositions of the former. Preaching and the sacraments are seen merely as human

---

42. Brian McLaren, *A Generous Orthodoxy* (Grand Rapids: Zondervan, 2004), 108. Drawing eclectically from ancient and medieval Christian mysticism, Anabaptism, Zen Buddhism, and liberation theology, McLaren even speaks of "The Great Chain of Being" (279–80). This is one of many instances that could be cited to indicate that the "overcoming estrangement" paradigm of Plato, Neoplatonism, Hegel, and New Age thought can find popular expression in evangelical "low church" traditions as well as in others.

43. See, for example, I. Mobsby, *Emerging and Fresh Expressions of Church* (London: Moot Community Publishing, 2007), 54–55; *The Becoming of G-d* (Oxford: YTC Press, 2008).

44. Controversial writers in the Pentecostal movement have argued that "the Church is Christ." "The Second Coming of

Christ, therefore, is through the Church, not Jesus returning in the flesh; we should not wait for Him to return in order to set the world in order, but we are to take His authority over the world and the spiritual realm now" (Earl Paulk, quoted in A. Dager, *Vengeance Is Ours: The Church in Dominion* [Redmond, Wash.: Sword, 1990], 148). Paulk writes, "Jesus Christ is the firstfruit, but without the ongoing harvest, the incarnation will never be complete" (*Held in the Heavens Until* [Atlanta: K Dimension Publishing, 1985], 60–61). "We are on the earth as extensions of God to finish the work He began. We are the essence of God, His ongoing incarnation in the world" (*Thrust in the Sickle and Reap* [Atlanta: K Dimension Publishing, 1986], 132). This "theology of dominion" may be traced from the Latter Rain Movement to successive movements (Vineyard and New Apostolic Reformation).

testimonies to God's grace and the individual's personal commitment, rather than chiefly as means through which God actually communicates his grace. From this it follows logically that the visible church and its public ministry bears no essential relationship to the invisible church and the relationship with God that each regenerate person enjoys. In philosophical terms, this view represents a radically voluntarist/nominalist ontology, while the first ("overcoming estrangement") reflects a realist/idealist ontology.

The first paradigm has difficulty accounting for genuine *plurality* (the church as "many") and the *distinction* between sign and reality. However, the second paradigm has difficulty accounting for genuine *unity* (the church as "one") and the *union* of sign and reality. Consequently, the latter tends to exchange a covenantal interpretation of the church for a contractual view. To the extent that the relationship of the believer to Christ may be conceived as a contract in which God offers certain benefits in exchange for our making him Savior and Lord, our relationship to the church is simply a matter of personal decision based on the services we think it can provide for us.

If, according to Roman Catholic ecclesiology, the faith of the believer tends to be absorbed into the faith of the church, the obverse is evident in Free Church ecclesiologies. The personal decision of each person to believe in Christ and to join a church actually constitutes ecclesial existence. In evangelical contexts, the church is often regarded chiefly as a resource for fellowship and a platform for individuals to serve the body and the world in various ministries.[45] Especially when wedded to an Arminian soteriology, such an ecclesiology gives rise to a voluntaristic emphasis, with human decision as the contractual basis for both conversion and ecclesial existence.[46] From this perspective, the church has come increasingly to be regarded primarily as a service provider for a personal (unique and individual) relationship with Christ. Actual membership in the visible church can be left to private judgment, and in some cases formal membership does not even exist. Taken to a radical extreme, this perspective leads the argument now being made that the visible church and its public ministry are even impediments to personal growth and Christian mission.[47]

---

45. At least in the history of pietism, the individual or circle of believers who were thought to be more truly earnest about the Christian life remained members of the wider church. In many forms of nondenominational evangelicalism, especially since the "Jesus movement" of the 1970s, church membership is optional or even eliminated. Seeking to replicate the worship of the first Christians (with dubious historical interpretations), the house-church movement is one of many examples of the "triumph of the laity," as it is sometimes called. In fact, as George Barna observes (and celebrates), the coming generation that he identifies as the "Revolutionaries" insists on finding forms of spiritual edification and community outside the organized church (*Revolution* [Carol Stream, Ill.: Tyndale, 2005]). Just how revolution-

ary this is may be open to debate, since pietism and revivalism have a long history of such experimentation.

46. See, for example, Stanley Grenz, *Theology for the Community of God* (Nashville: Broadman & Holman 1997), 611.

47. The Willow Creek Association (led by Bill Hybels) concluded that as Christians mature their dependence on the church diminishes and they need to become "self-feeders" (Greg Hawkins and Cally Parkinson, *Reveal: Where Are You?* [South Barrington, Ill.: Willow Creek Association, 2007]). George Barna (in *Revolution*, cited above) argues that most believers will increasingly abandon local churches and receive their spiritual resources from the Internet.

Not all tendencies to set Christ in sharp contrast with the church fit neatly in the preceding description. Especially in Bultmann and Brunner priority is given to an existential "I-Thou" encounter that often marginalizes the "We-Thou" emphasis of covenantal faith and practice.[48] Yet we have also seen this tendency in Barth, treating the outward ministry of the church as providing not means of grace but rather means of testifying to grace. The sources of Barth's ecclesiological reflections are far from contractual, individualistic, and synergistic.[49] In fact, his sometimes sharp criticism of pietism is well known in this regard.[50] However, his attraction to an independent ecclesiology, his rejection of the sacraments as means of grace, and his explicit rejection of infant baptism,[51] point up what seems to me to be the dominant tendency of his thought that is already discernable in his first edition of his commentary on Romans.

Going beyond Zwingli (though, ironically, more closely echoing Luther), Barth says that the true church belongs to the "submarine island of the 'Now' of divine revelation" that lies beneath observable reality.[52] In *Romans*, he speaks explicitly of "the *contrast* between the Gospel and the Church" (emphasis added).[53] Christ is the only sacrament. In fact, not only is there a difference between the sign and its eschatological fullness; the "invisible church" is taken to extreme limits when Barth writes, "In the heavenly Jerusalem of Revelation nothing is more finally significant than *the church's complete absence*: 'And I saw no temple therein'" (emphasis added).[54] Totalizing ecclesiologies may be faulted for an overrealized eschatology. However, Barth's dualistic ecclesiology is not underrealized; he simply does not have any place for the church even in the consummation. Therefore, "the activity of the community is related to the Gospel only in so far as it is no more than a crater formed by the explosion of a shell and seeks to be no more than a void in which the Gospel reveals itself."[55]

One of Barth's great achievements was to turn attention back to Jesus. He is properly concerned to see that Christ's reconciling work is in need of no further supplementation, no historical development, thus countering liberal historicism and synergism. The church is not an extension of Christ's person and work.[56] There is

---

48. Dulles observes, "Rudolph Sohm, for instance, taught that the essential nature of the Church stands in antithesis to all law. Emil Brunner, in *The Misunderstanding of the Church*, argued that the Church in the biblical sense (the *Ecclesia*) is not an institution but a brotherhood (Bruderschaft); it is 'a pure communion of persons (*Personengemeinschaft*).' On this ground Brunner rejected all law, sacrament, and priestly office as incompatible with the true being of the Church" (*Models of the Church*, 44).

49. Barth, *Church Dogmatics*, vol. 4, pt. 1, p. 150.

50. These differences are recounted and interpreted in fascinating detail in Eberhard Busch, *Karl Barth and the Pietists* (trans. Daniel W. Bloesch; Downers Grove, Ill.: InterVarsity Press, 2004).

51. Barth, *Church Dogmatics*, vol. 4, pt. 4.

52. Karl Barth, *The Epistle to the Romans* (trans. Edwyn C. Hoskyns from the 6th ed.; London: Oxford Univ. Press, 1933), 304; cf. 396 for the same analogy.

53. Ibid., 340.

54. Ibid. That this is the expression of 1920 should perhaps be taken into account here.

55. Ibid., 36.

56. Barth, *Church Dogmatics*, vol. 4, pt. 3, pp. 7, 327; vol. 4, pt. 2, p. 132.

hardly a better statement of a covenantal ecclesiology than the following: "What constitutes the being of man in this [covenantal] sphere is not a *oneness* of being but a genuine *togetherness* of being with God" (emphasis added).[57] However, the same logic (actualism) that keeps Barth from identifying God's action directly with human words and deeds in his doctrine of revelation is also decisive for his ecclesiology.[58] Barth offers important warnings about collapsing Jesus Christ into the church.[59] However, in my view, it represents an overcorrection of the neo-Hegelian trajectory.

Superior to the contractual and existentialist-actualist versions we have considered is the revised Free Church ecclesiology proposed by Miroslav Volf in his remarkable work *After Our Likeness*. He affirms the Reformers' view of the church as "mother" and distances himself from the counsel of Separatist leader John Smyth that those who are "born again . . . should no longer need means of grace," since the persons of the Godhead "are better than all scriptures, or creatures whatsoever."[60] Furthermore, Volf emphasizes the priority of God's gracious activity over human response in *salvation*. Interacting extensively with Ratzinger and Zizioulas, he recognizes their common debt to idealist metaphysics and critiques their reduction of the many to the totalizing unicity of a "corporate personality." Constructively, he wrestles deeply with the tendency of Free Church ecclesiologies to become captive to modern individualism and consumerism and brings a richer eschatological and pneumatological perspective to bear.[61]

Nevertheless, Volf's own ecclesiology remains rather subjective. A church exists, he says, wherever there is a faithful confession of Christ (1Co 15:11; 2Co 11:4; Ac 2:42).[62] The "being of the church" is "constituted by the assembled people confessing Christ."[63] "That which the church *is*, namely, believing and confessing human beings, is precisely that which (as a rule) also constitutes it."[64] Not only the

---

57. Ibid., vol. 3, pt. 2, p. 141.

58. It is interesting that while Calvin rejects Erasmus's translations of *koinōnia* as *societas* and *communio*, in favor of stronger participationist language, Barth prefers *Gemeinde* (community, society, fellowship) to *Kirche* (church). To be sure, Barth affirms the New Testament motif of *koinōnia*, founded on Trinitarian presuppositions: the persons (modes of being) in communion with each other; the communion between God and human beings; the communion of believers with each other, and indeed with all creatures. Each communion is a different kind of *koinōnia*, but is ultimately grounded in this Trinitarian perichoresis (*Church Dogmatics*, vol. 3, pt. 2, pp. 256–60). There are more recent historical reasons, of course, for preferring *Gemeinde* to *Kirche*, such as the way these are distinguished in German Protestantism.

59. Even better than Barth, in my estimation, is John Webster's treatment in *Word and Church: Essays in Christian Dogmatics* (Edinburgh: T&T Clark, 2001), 227–32.

60. Volf, *After Our Likeness*, 161–62.

61. Volf (ibid., 16–17) points out that the privatization of faith that warps Free Church ecclesiologies threatens "the transmission of faith." Yet he also judges that this adaptability to a culture of personal choice renders such ecclesiologies especially effective in our day (17). "Whether they want to or not, Free Churches often function as 'homogeneous units' specializing in the specific needs of specific social classes and cultural circles, and then in mutual competition try to sell their commodity at dumping prices to the religious consumer in the supermarket of life projects; the customer is king and the one best suited to evaluate his or her own religious needs and from whom nothing more is required than a bit of loyalty and as much money as possible. If the Free Churches want to contribute to the salvation of Christendom, they themselves must first be healed" (ibid., 18).

62. Ibid., 147–49.

63. Ibid., 150n93.

64. Ibid., 151.

particular form of church government, but the very notion of ordained office is represented as belonging to the *bene esse* (well-being) rather than the *esse* (existence) of the church.[65] Not even the sacraments are ultimately constitutive, but "are a public representation of such confession."[66] Therefore, the unity of the visible church is identified not with its organic unity, exhibited in a connectional government, but with "the openness of every church toward all other churches...."[67] While offering the most trenchant critique of the dominance of the one over the many, especially in the ecclesiologies of Ratzinger and Zizioulas, the Social Trinitarian model on which he draws is as unlikely to generate an adequate account of the church's essential unity as of that of the Trinity itself.[68]

Baptist theologian Stanley Grenz observes, "The post-Reformation discussion of the *vera ecclesia* [true church] formed the historical context for the emergence of the covenant idea as the focal understanding of the nature of the church."[69] With their insistence on the marks of the church, "the Reformers shifted the focus to Word and Sacrament," but the Anabaptists and Baptists "took yet a further step," advocating a congregational ecclesiology. "This view asserts that the true church is essentially people standing in voluntary covenant with God."[70] The decision concerning baptism is decisive for this conception of the church.

Free Church traditions remind us that the church is not a department of religious affairs under an empire, nation-state, or city council and that belonging to a church formally cannot be a substitute for personal faith in Christ. Grenz properly reminds us that the church is "a spiritual people gathered out from the wider society," even when that society is nominally "Christian."[71] The Reformers often spoke in similar terms, insisting that the Word alone and not secular power should be allowed to persuade people of the gospel. Nevertheless, in actual practice, the magisterial Reformation remained too attached to the patterns of "Christendom."

However, the Lutheran and Reformed view that the visible church consists of believers *together with their children* violates the rule that is basic to an independent church polity: namely, a *voluntary* covenant, which entails not only the independence of local churches but the independence of individuals within them until they mutually agree on the terms of that relationship. "No longer did the corporate whole take precedence over the individual as in the medieval model," notes Grenz. Rather, individuals formed the church rather than vice versa. "As a result, in the order of salvation the believer—and not the church—stands first in priority."[72] "Because

65. Ibid., 152.
66. Ibid., 153.
67. Ibid., 156–58.
68. Ibid., 78–79, emphasis in original.

69. Grenz, *Theology for the Community of God*, 609.
70. Ibid., 610–611.
71. Ibid., 611.
72. Ibid.

the coming together of believers in mutual covenant constitutes the church, it is the covenant community of individuals," although it has a history as well.[73]

Separating the visible sign from its consummated reality, radical Protestant ecclesiologies also tend to identify ecclesial holiness with the inherent sanctity of individual members. Whereas Rome teaches that the true church is to be found in communion with the papacy, this approach identifies the holy church exclusively with the sum total of regenerate believers. At least for Bultmann, Brunner, and Barth, the unambiguous identification of God's saving presence with the institutional history of the visible church represented the domestication of God's transcendence, placing revelation and reconciliation under human control. In this respect, especially Barth discerned similarities between Roman Catholicism and Protestant liberalism, in which "culture Protestantism" smothered any conception of God's disrupting encounter in judgment and grace. For Roman Catholicism and Protestant liberalism, eschatology (God's action) and history (human action) were not united but conflated. In reaction, these theologians argued that the event of personal encounter makes us contemporaneous with Christ. As a consequence, the Spirit's mediation of ecclesial holiness *within* history and *across* the generations through the visible covenant community and its ordinary ministry is at the very least marginalized.

Free Church and Pentecostal traditions reflect a similar dualism, as we have seen, and therefore an underrealized eschatology when it comes to the relation between the sign (the visible church) and the reality signified (the invisible or consummated church). However, at least with respect to the individual believer and perhaps even the local assembly, they also often reflect an overrealized eschatology, with the notion of the church as a pure gathered church of the regenerate. Consequently, the church's holiness lies not so much in the promise of Christ, which is proclaimed and ratified through its public ministry, but in the inherent experience and piety of each believer. In Pentecostal traditions especially, this holiness is identified with visible evidence of a "second blessing" of sanctification.[74] Similar to the Roman Catholic

---

73. Ibid., 614. For all of their differences, some of the modern versions of *totus Christus* we have encountered share with Protestant individualism a contractual rather than covenantal outlook. Reflecting his heritage in pietism, Schleiermacher wrote, "The Christian Church is formed through regenerate individuals coming together for mutual interaction and cooperation in an orderly way" (Friedrich Schleiermacher, *The Christian Faith* [ed. and trans. H. R. Mackintosh and J. S. Stewart; Edinburgh: T&T Clark, 1928], 532). So, ironically, he could simultaneously view the church as a voluntary society among others (though of *regenerate* individuals) and speak of the sacrificing of the individual to the community. Ratzinger and Zizioulas also speak of the "sacrificing" of the individual to the community, while much of radical Protestantism today seems to assume a more autonomous individualism. However, the equal danger in contemporary mainline and evangelical Protestantism is to overreact against this individualism (marked especially in North America) by embracing a romantic notion of community.

74. Amos Yong, *The Spirit Poured Out on All Flesh* (Grand Rapids: Baker Academic, 2005), 84. Yong provides a helpful survey of the differences that emerged within the Wesleyan-Holiness/Pentecostal traditions, including debates over "whether there are one, two, or even three 'works of grace'" (98–120). Throughout this discussion, Yong defends the importance of successive "crisis experiences" throughout the Christian life. This contrasts with a covenantal orientation, in which such experiences may or may not occur, yet life in the Spirit is seen as the common property of all believers.

conception of the church's holiness as inherent and complete, this view nevertheless identifies holiness with individuals rather than the institution.

Negotiating our way between these two extremes is the goal of this chapter.[75] Neither a *conflation* of Christ and his church (along with a fusion of believers) nor a *contract*, the church is founded on a *covenant* that originates in the counsels of the eternal Trinity.

III. FINDING OUR BEARINGS, LOCATING COORDINATES

As we embark on this journey through the attributes of the church, it is worth bearing in mind our coordinates thus far.

A. THE ESCHATOLOGICAL COORDINATE

As Douglas Farrow has observed, the ascension of Jesus Christ in the flesh most radically challenges the Platonist/Neoplatonist ontology.[76] Origen, the church father most enthralled by Greek philosophy, said that this event was "more an ascension of mind than of body."[77] Rather than an *eschatology* ("already"/"not yet") wedded to history (past, present, and future), the Origenist trajectory prefers the *allegory* of the soul's ascent from temporal appearances to eternal realities. Even Augustine said that the ascension was a benefit because it finally afforded the disciples (and us) the opportunity to concentrate on Christ's deity rather than his humanity.[78]

This is in stark contrast to the reason Jesus gave for the benefit of his departure: namely, that he would send the Spirit to lead them to himself by his Word. Looking away from the concrete person, Jesus of Nazareth, and a departure that was as real as his incarnation and resurrection, thinkers such as Origen and Augustine made the church the surrogate for its absent Lord.[79] A docetic ascension opened up the space for the church's apotheosis in and as Christ, who keeps his deity for himself but surrenders his humanity (i.e., his visibility in the world) to his ecclesial body. The *totus Christus* (whole Christ) now referred primarily not to the historical Jesus as a whole and undivided person in two natures, but to the church as site of Christ's body. His natural body was increasingly forgotten—and with it, the sense of dependence on the Spirit for mediating his presence here and now as well as a longing for Christ's

---

75. I explore these issues more extensively in *People and Place: A Covenant Ecclesiology* (Louisville: Westminster John Knox, 2008).

76. Douglas Farrow, *Ascension and Ecclesia: On the Significance of the Doctrine of the Ascension for Ecclesiology and Christian Cosmology* (Edinburgh: T&T Clark, 1999), chap. 4, pp. 87–164.

77. Ibid., 97, citing Origen's *First Principles* 23.2.

78. Ibid., 119–20, citing Augustine's *Sermons* 264; cf. *The Trinity* 1.18.

79. Ibid., esp. 150–60.

return. At the hands of Hegel and Schleiermacher, this notion became radicalized to the point that any distinction between Christ and the believer (or the believing community) vanishes. In fact, as we have seen from recent theologians such as John Milbank and Graham Ward, the particular person of Jesus Christ ("the gendered Jew") vanishes as well.

In contrast to an ascension of mind, the ascension of Christ in the flesh does not allow us to entertain an overrealized eschatology or an overidentification of Christ (the head, in the unity of his person) with the church (his ecclesial body). There is no substitute for Jesus Christ in the flesh. His absence from us in the flesh is as real as will be his return in the flesh. Nevertheless, he reigns in heaven and on earth by the Spirit, whom he has sent to begin the renovation of all things. Christ is absent from us in time and space, but we are not absent from him in the Spirit. That is to say, Christ is present among us here and now, but not in the same way that he will be when he returns—as the host of the unending feast rather than the sacrificial meal. Through the Spirit's work, there is a real union with Christ and, consequently, a real sacramental union of sign and signified with respect to the creaturely form of the church and its ministry on one hand and the consummated kingdom and its glory on the other.

Therefore, the signs and their reality are neither confused nor separated; the former participate in the latter through the energies of the triune God. Lodged by the Spirit between "this age" and "the age to come," the church has an existence and visibility that are at present ambiguous: "already" and "not yet." Christ has ascended and he will return, but he has poured out his Spirit in the meantime to gather a living community out of death and judgment. The church is different from Christ not only in terms of who he is but in terms of where he is in the economy of redemption. He has already experienced the exaltation and glorification that is our hope together in him, while we are still subject to decay, death, and sin. Yet because he is our head and we are his body, in Calvin's words, Christ "reckons himself in a measure imperfect" until we all, with him, are glorified in the everlasting Sabbath.[80] Until then, he breaks into this present age by his Spirit, sowing seeds of the new creation through Word and sacrament.

The same demand for immediacy that we have encountered in problematic views of revelation and redemption is evident in both "high church" and "low church" ecclesiologies. No formal ecclesiology will save a church from triumphalism (indeed, idolatry) when it embraces an overrealized eschatology. The oldest denominations and the newest sects often evidence this tendency to identify the full presence of Christ and his Spirit with their own organizations, movements, and

---

80. John Calvin, *Commentaries on the Epistles of Paul to the Galatians and Ephesians* (trans. William Pringle; Grand Rapids: Eerdmans, repr. 1957), 218 (on Eph 1:23).

uniquely gifted leader. Lording it over other churches, these bodies often claim even to be either a continuation or a restoration of Christ's kingdom in its absolute form.

Whether it is the full identification of the kingdom of God with the church and its actions or with believers and their actions, jumping the eschatological gun always opens the door to dangerous parodies rather than signs of the age to come. Unwilling to wait for Moses to return with God's Word—a Word that Israel did not want because it filled them with fear—the Israelites (led by Aaron) fashioned a golden calf through which they could attain a visible, immediate, and meaningful religious experience without having to wait for Christ, "the image [*eikōn*, icon] of the invisible God" (Col 1:15). Similarly, when the church is weary—or perhaps bored—waiting for Christ to return in the flesh and is unsatisfied with its fragile, fallible, ambiguous, and precarious location between the two ages in dependence on the Word and the Spirit, it conjures substitutes for a direct and immediate encounter here and now.

This demand for immediacy is found in the claim that the visible church (even a particular denomination) *is* Jesus Christ. Although it would seem that there is mediation all the way down, through the sacraments, orders, images, and other creaturely forms, there is actually nothing to be mediated when the visible church is simply Jesus Christ in his visible form. In more "low-church" ecclesiologies such immediacy is sought in a personal relationship with Jesus that is direct, private, and unique. This view is expressed in a once-popular evangelical hymn by C. Austin Miles, "In the Garden": "I come to the garden alone.... And he walks with me and he talks with me and he tells me I am his own. And the joy we share as we tarry there, none other has ever known." In both versions, the eschatological tension of the already and not yet is resolved before its time, as if Jesus Christ were just as present on earth today as he was in Jerusalem and will be when he returns in glory. If Eastern Orthodox and Roman Catholic ecclesiologies over emphasize the "already" of the eucharistic gathering, radical Protestants tend to under appreciate the reality (viz., the in-breaking of the age to come) here and now that the Spirit gives *through* the signs.

B. THE COVENANTAL COORDINATE

Originating in God's choice and redeeming work, the church does not gather itself in this time between the times but is gathered by the triune God. Therefore, it is not defined by the personal faith and piety of its members or by the intrinsic holiness of its hierarchical graces but by the Word that creates and rules it. Accordingly, the church is not first of all the place where believing sinners are active. Nor is it the people who are active in works of service. All of this follows, but it is not the formative source and principle of ecclesial existence. Only hearers of God's judging and saving speech can become doers of the Word. Before it is active in the world, the church is that part of the world that has been acted upon by the Father, in the Son, through the powerful agency of the Spirit. This priority of divine agency has already been defended in treating the doctrine of salvation and the means of grace (Word and sacrament).

Therefore, the visible church is not composed only of the regenerate; it is the covenant community where the Spirit brings to repentance and faith "those who are near" (i.e., "you and your children") and "all who are far off, everyone whom the Lord our God calls to himself" (Ac 2:39). We expect the baptized to grow up into Christ, coming to faith and maturing gradually in that faith, in the communion of saints.

In terms of polity, a covenantal ecclesiology also means that the church is constituted in neither a hierarchical-aristocratic nor egalitarian-democratic fashion, but as a representative body governed by a plurality of elders under Christ as its only head. Regardless of the church's polity, the catholicity of the church depends on its being worded as "in Christ" rather than "in Adam." There are legitimate voluntary associations and societies to which believers might belong together with non-Christians. However, the church is not this kind of a society. The world creates rival catholicities around gender, ethnicity, generational profiles, political persuasion, socio-economic class, and consumer preferences, but the unity, holiness, catholicity, and apostolicity of the church derive from our being in Christ, who is the head of the body.

This means that the church cannot be reduced to a historical organization. After all, it is the result of a vertical disruption of the powers of this age by the powers of the age to come. It is an *eschatological event*: a kingdom that we are receiving rather than building (and that therefore cannot be shaken) (Heb 12:28), "the holy city, new Jerusalem, coming down out of heaven from God, prepared as a bride adorned for her husband ..." (Rev 21:2–3). However, as a covenant community, it is not merely a crater left by the impact of God's eschatological event of revelation (see quotation from Barth above, under "The One as Many," p. 838) but a partially realized form of the kingdom of God *within history*. The church does not therefore merely "happen" through vertical events that can never be recognized along a horizontal time line; it endures "from generation to generation." In a covenantal perspective, the personal, corporate, and missional aspects of ecclesial identity converge: "From you comes *my* praise in the great congregation.... *All the ends of the earth* shall remember and turn to the LORD, and all the *families* of the nations shall worship before you.... *Posterity* shall serve him; it shall be told of the Lord to the coming generation; they shall come and proclaim his righteousness to a people yet unborn, that he has done it" (Ps 22:26, 27, 30–31, emphasis added). This conviction, if not this hymn itself, echoes in Peter's Pentecost sermon: "For the promise is for you and for your children and for all who are far off, everyone whom the Lord our God calls to himself" (Ac 2:39).

C. THE PNEUMATOLOGICAL COORDINATE

Eastern Orthodox theologians are correct to point out that Western ecclesiologies tend to be either Christ-centered or Spirit-centered rather than Trinitarian. As a result (as Lossky observed; see above, pp. 833–34), the church easily mistakes itself for the ongoing incarnation of Christ or falls apart into private experiences and spiritual fanaticism.

To be sure, the church is a historical institution that has developed over time and in many different places, bearing all of the marks of any public institution. In a realist/idealist paradigm, the kingdom of Christ (the eschatological reality) is simply identified with the sign (the visible church). The Spirit's intrusive work of disrupting and reorganizing human history and community is brought under the control of the ecclesiastical institution. In a voluntarist/nominalist paradigm, the kingdom is separated from the institutional church and the Spirit's work becomes sharply distinguished from the visible church and its official ministry. A proper pneumatology, however, affirms simultaneously the sovereign freedom of the Spirit over and within the church as well as the orderly way in which the Spirit works through the church's public offices and ministry. If the Roman Catholic view tends to make the Spirit's work identical with the church and its ministry, radical Protestantism tends to separate the Spirit's eschatological ministry from creaturely-historical means.

Christ is present and active in and through his visible church today because it is that part of the world that is being penetrated by the rays of the new age as the Spirit unites us to Christ, disturbing and reorganizing our fellowship around his person and work. The church is not merely an invisible entity based merely on a spiritual unity or experience, but it also cannot guarantee its existence simply by pointing to its history. The church is a covenant community extended through all times and places, but any particular church remains in communion with this true church only by constant dependence on the free mercies of the Spirit, who has bound himself to his Word.

IV. UNITY AND CATHOLICITY

Catholic means *universal*, but in its actual use it has a richer meaning, especially as a summary term for the communion of the redeemed as one body. Every racial barrier (beginning with the Jew/Gentile distinction), every socio-economic wall, every demographic profile and generational niche, and every political-ideological partition that defines this present age disintegrates as the rays of the age to come penetrate. Wherever the Word and Spirit—"one Lord, one faith, one baptism" (Eph 4:5)—break up the givens of this age and reconstitute a new people, there is a piece of the catholic church. The unity and catholicity of the church are interdependent themes.

A. NEW TESTAMENT PRESUPPOSITIONS FOR UNITY AND CATHOLICITY

Although the Word and sacraments are the Spirit's means of constituting the church, this catholicity is reflected in the reorganized sociality of the visible church. One striking example in the New Testament is the collection for the saints in Jerusalem initiated and executed under the leadership of the apostle Paul. After reiterating that his ministry is to present the Gentiles as an acceptable offering to God through the gospel (Ro 15:7–21), the Apostle exhorts the Roman Christians to contribute to the offering for the saints in Jerusalem who are suffering extreme hardship (vv. 22–33). Even the poverty-stricken Gentile believers in Macedonia and Achaia have given generously out of the recognition that God has given them every spiritual blessing in Christ. They realized that this was not an act of charity: "For if the Gentiles have come to share in their spiritual blessings, they ought also to be of service to them in material blessings" (v. 27). Their gift was a tangible response to the gospel that they have been given and to the heritage of the Jews to which they have been made co-heirs in Christ.

The same appeal is made to the Corinthians: each Lord's Day an offering is to be taken for the general collection (1Co 16:1–4). Nevertheless, Paul, though an apostle, respects the integrity and authority of each local church to appoint and send its own deacons with Paul to Jerusalem (v. 4). A year later, the Corinthians—though citizens of a wealthier port city—had made only slight progress in contributing to the great collection (2Co 8–9). They needed to be reminded that Christ became poor so that we might become rich (2Co 8:9). The body of Christ is most visibly expressed locally, but each local church reaches out to the wider assembly of churches in catholic unity, love, and fellowship. In Christ's body, the local church needs the other churches; Jews need Gentiles and Gentiles need Jews; the poor need the rich and the rich need the poor, so there will be no lack of spiritual and material benefits (2Co 8:13–15).

It was a turning point when the church officially, at the Jerusalem Council, embraced Gentile believers without requiring their acceptance of Jewish distinctives (Ac 15). It must have been an equally remarkable day when Paul, the Apostle to the Gentiles, arrived in Jerusalem attended by Gentile deacons to present a large treasury to their suffering Jewish brothers and sisters. Where the dividing wall of hostility had been broken down through the preaching of the gospel, one baptism, and one eucharistic meal, catholicity was also expressed in such concrete ways for the upbuilding of the church and a witness to the world.

I have defended the Reformation claim that the church is the creation of the Word. What constitutes the unity and catholicity of the church? As Paul Avis has observed, "Reformation theology is largely dominated by two questions: 'How can I obtain a gracious God?' and 'Where can I find the true Church?' The two questions are inseparably related...."[81] The Lutheran and Reformed confessions offer the same response to both questions: wherever God's Word is truly preached and the sacraments are administered according to Christ's command.[82] The unity of the church arises from its origin, and since the canon (even prior to its formal inscripturation) created and still creates the church, this unity cannot be lodged either in a historical office or in personal experience.

First, the catholicity and unity of the church is found only in fellowship with the triune God. These attributes of the church do not arise from the individuals or a religious society, but from the Father, in the Son, by the Spirit. In Roman Catholic ecclesiology, Christology and ecclesiology become virtually indistinguishable. It is easy in such an approach to identify the catholicity and apostolicity of the church simply with the institution in its historical form. To be catholic is to belong to the Roman Catholic Church; to be apostolic is to be in communion with Peter's successor. However, in some Free Church ecclesiologies (especially charismatic and Pentecostal), a one-sided focus on the Spirit often unhinges the vital connection between apostolicity and the visible means of grace.

Second, the catholicity and unity of the church is evident wherever God is at work through his ordained means of grace. The church cannot give birth to itself; it is born from above (Jn 3:3 – 5). As Jesus acknowledged in his prayer in John 17, the catholic church is united by orthodox faith in the triune God, with whom it enjoys fellowship in the Spirit and truth. And, as this great prayer teaches, this is the source also of its holiness and apostolicity. A church is present even where there is egregious disorder (as in Corinth) and even where there is a lack of spiritual earnestness and vitality (as in Laodicea), but if the Word really is being faithfully proclaimed and taught and baptism and Communion are living, formative, dynamic realities in the community, these weaknesses will be addressed.

For the alternative perspectives we have encountered, human action comes first: either in terms of a hierarchical order or in terms of personal experience and obedience. From a Reformation perspective, however, God speaks and ratifies this speech so that a community emerges as a platform for *God's* ministry of bringing an evan-

---

81. Paul D. L. Avis, *The Church in the Theology of the Reformers* (Atlanta: John Knox, 1981), 1.

82. The Reformed confessions added discipline, which I discuss below (pp. 896 – 97).

gelical order, experience, and obedience into being. Neither a particular government nor personal conversion, but the Word and the sacraments, identify the true church. We know that the Spirit is active wherever these marks are evident.

Nowhere in Scripture do we read of salvation coming by surrendering oneself to the church or even to Christ. In Christ, our personal identity is no more lost than his; rather, our personhood is redescribed, rescripted, redeemed, and renewed. Preaching, water, bread and wine remain ordinary creaturely elements, even when they are united by the Word and Spirit to their heavenly reality. Similarly, in the church the many remain, in all of their ethnic, social, and generational distinctiveness, yet now in a communion of life rather than in a state of perpetual war. In Christ, there is no scarcity to be overcome by an ecclesiastical rationing of grace; it is an economy of sheer abundance: the grace that exceeds the guilt and power of sin (Ro 5:20), "the riches of his grace, which he lavished upon us" (Eph 1:7), and "the grace of our Lord [that] overflowed for me with the faith and love that are in Christ Jesus" (1Ti 1:14). We are one because we have all received the same Gift and have been made sharers in "one Lord, one faith, [and] one baptism" (Eph 4:5). There is no mention in this seminal passage (or any others) of "one pastor" as essential to this unity; in fact, the following verses speak of Christ's gifts being delivered to us through a variety of pastors and teachers.

Third, the reality of the ascension should keep us from substituting a pyramidal church for Jesus Christ. The ascension directs us to the work of the Spirit in uniting us to Christ so that there is real affinity despite real difference. We are one *with* Christ (and therefore with each other), but not *one Christ*. With such qualifications, we can affirm the truth in the *totus Christus* motif, as we find it, for example, in the following statement of Calvin's:

> This is the highest honour of the Church, that, until He is united to us, the Son of God reckons himself in some measure imperfect. What consolation is it for us to learn, that, not until we are along with him, does he possess all his parts, or wish to be regarded as complete! Hence, in the First Epistle to the Corinthians, when the apostle discusses largely the metaphor of a human body, he includes under the single name of Christ the whole Church.[83]

Nevertheless, for Calvin and his heirs, this version of *totus Christus* is eschatologically oriented: "the Son of God reckons himself in some measure imperfect" or incomplete only because he is the firstfruits of the harvest, the head of a body. What he possesses perfectly and completely in himself is at present only imperfectly and

---

83. John Calvin on Eph 1:23, in *Commentaries on the Epistles of Paul to the Galatians and Ephesians* (trans. William Pringle; Grand Rapids: Eerdmans, 1957), 218.

incompletely realized in his body. Even more than we, Christ longs for the day when we share in his glory, and he is not sitting idly by but working toward that final end.

Taken univocally, the theory of the church "as 'the extension of the Incarnation,'" as Lesslie Newbigin observes, "springs from a confusion of *sarx* with *soma*." "Christ's risen body" — that is, his ecclesial as distinguished from his natural body — "is not fleshly but spiritual." "He did not come to incorporate us in His body according to the flesh but according to the Spirit." Hence, his promise that when he ascends he will send the Spirit.[84] Newbigin's point reminds us of the importance of both the ascension of Christ in the flesh and the descent of the Spirit. Our union with Christ does not occur at the level of fused natures, but as a common participation of different members in the same realities of the age to come by the same Spirit. Similarly, Volf argues, "A *theological interpretation* going beyond Paul himself is needed to transform the Pauline 'one *in* Christ' into Ratzinger's 'a single subject *with* Christ,' or certainly into 'a single ... Jesus Christ.'"[85] To be sure, Ratzinger says that "through the Holy Spirit, the Lord who 'departed' on the cross has 'returned' and is now engaged in affectionate dialogue with his 'bride,' the church." "Yet even recourse to the representational work of the Holy Spirit," says Volf, "cannot free the idea of dialogue within the *one, single* subject of the suspicion of being mere conversation with oneself. It does not seem possible to conceive the juxtaposition of church and Christ without giving up the notion of the one subject that includes both bridegroom and bride."[86]

Furthermore, it is worth noting that in the few places where the church is identified as the body of Christ, the Pauline phrase is deployed to affirm plurality as much as unity, as in 1 Corinthians 12:12: "For just as the body is one and has many members, and all the members of the body, though many, are one body, so it is with Christ." Not only are the many and the one treated with the same ontological weight, but the formula itself expresses a simile: "just as ... so it is with Christ." Analogies are not rhetorical flourishes, but the communication of truth in a way that accommodates to our capacities. The counsel that we have heard from Dulles is wise: the various metaphors must be allowed to mutually interpret our ecclesiology, without selecting one (like "body of Christ") and turning it into a literal concept.[87]

In a covenantal context, there is both affinity and difference. The vassal is so identified with the suzerain that a threat or injury to the one is a threat or injury to the other. As we have seen, the treaty-making ceremony in these secular treaties takes the form of a cutting of an animal that not only symbolizes but ratifies the

---

84. Lesslie Newbigin, *The Household of God: Lectures on the Nature of the Church* (London: SCM, 1953), 80.

85. Volf, *After Our Likeness*, 34. Since Volf's references are to Cardinal Ratzinger before he became Pope, I will use this reference throughout this chapter.

86. Ibid.

87. Dulles, *Models of the Church*, 17, 21–30. In fact, Paul Minear's *Images of the Church in the New Testament* (Philadelphia: Westminster Press, 1960) lists 96 images.

participation of the whole community in its representative head. In the covenant of grace, Christ is both that representative head and mediator, on the one hand, and the divine suzerain who stands over against the covenant people, imposing the terms of the treaty, on the other. There is union without fusion, communion without absorption, with the covenant people (ecclesia) always in the position of receiving rather than of extending the personal existence and gracious reign of its ascended Lord. Because this covenant is constituted by the work of the Father, the Son, and the Holy Spirit, it is qualitatively different from all other forms of society and international politics. Yet, as Cardinal Dulles points out, the body-of-Christ metaphor is a subset of this covenantal analogy of suzerain and vassal.[88]

Fourth, the ultimate source of the church's unity and catholicity is to be found in God's electing grace. Hence, this unity is a *gift*, whose visible expression we are called to defend and preserve in peace and purity. Behind, above, and underneath all evidences of visible unity in the body of Christ lies the original, inviolable, and largely hidden unity of that body in God's eternal election. According to the *Heidelberg Catechism*, to affirm "one holy catholic church" means, "I believe that the Son of God, through his Spirit and Word, out of the entire human race, from the beginning of the world to its end, gathers, protects, and preserves for himself a community chosen for eternal life and united in true faith. And of this community I am and always will be a living member."[89]

Taking the catholicity of the church entirely out of our hands, election proscribes all overrealized eschatologies, whether they identify the pure church with a universal institution or with the sum total of the regenerate. Although proleptically we anticipate the catholic church, only in the eschaton will the visible church be *identical* with the catholic church. The union of Christ and his body — i.e., the one, holy, catholic, and apostolic church — is the eschatological communion of the elect, chosen "in [Christ] before the foundation of the world, that we should be holy and blameless before him" (Eph 1:4).

With the Augustinian tradition more generally, Reformation theology lodges the church's catholicity (i.e., unity and universality) in God's electing grace. "Now this society is catholic, that is, universal, because there could not be two or three churches. But all God's elect are so united and conjoined in Christ that, as they are dependent upon one Head, they also grow together into one body ...," Calvin argues. It is *this* church that is indefectible. It must always have its visible expression in every era, but this visibility is always ambiguous, both because the church is a mixed assembly and because even the elect are simultaneously justified and sinful.[90]

---

88. Dulles, *Models of the Church*, 46–47.

89. *Heidelberg Catechism*, q. 54, in *The Psalter Hymnal: Doctrinal Standards and Liturgy of the Christian Reformed Church* (Grand Rapids: Board of Publications of the CRC, 1976), 27.

90. Calvin, *Institutes* 4.1.2–3.

B. VISIBLE AND INVISIBLE

Thus, "invisible" and "visible" refer not to two different churches (much less do they correspond to true and false), but to the body of Christ as known to God in eternity and as known to us now as a mixed assembly. So, for example, the *Westminster Confession* first defines the catholic church as "*invisible*," which "consists of the whole number of the elect, that have been, are, or shall be gathered into one, under Christ the Head thereof; and is the spouse, the body, the fullness of him that filleth all in all" (emphasis added). Yet in the next article, "The *visible* church, which is *also catholic* or universal under the gospel (not confined to one nation, as before, under the law), consists of all those throughout the world that profess the true religion; and of their children: and is the kingdom of the Lord Jesus Christ, the house and family of God, out of which there is no ordinary possibility of salvation" (emphasis added).[91] As such, it truly participates in the signified, but is not yet identical with it as one day it will be. "For the creation waits with eager longing for the revealing of the sons of God" (Ro 8:19), and despite the confusion, error, and dissension that have always plagued the church, "God's firm foundation stands, bearing this seal: 'The Lord knows those who are his ...'" (2Ti 2:19).

Analogous to the sacraments, this visible church is neither identical with nor separate from the invisible church. Rather than see the relation in Platonic terms as spiritual and physical, we should see it in eschatological terms as "already" and "not yet." The Spirit, working through the Word, ensures that Christ is present in the world as the Good Shepherd gathering his elect, but only when Christ returns in the flesh will the one, holy, and catholic church be revealed. Only then will the invisible church be fully visible.

In contrast both to totalizing models of the *totus Christus* and to social models of plurality that downplay an essential unity, a covenantal model affirms both unity and difference as essential to the being of the church, because it is rooted in election. We are not *one Christ* (*methexis*), but one *in* Christ (*koinōnia*), and this is the result ultimately of God's choice rather than our own. Just as my belonging to this church is ultimately grounded in God's gracious choice rather than my own decision, these other people with whom I am gathered were given to me—chosen for me—as my brothers and sisters. Jesus reminds us, "You did not choose me, but I chose you and appointed you that you should go and bear fruit and that your fruit should abide" (Jn 15:16). Consequently, we are commanded to "love one another" (v. 17). A local church (or wider body of churches) is not free to develop its identity in continuity simply with the givens of racial, ethnic, socio-economic, or consumer affinities.

---

91. *Westminster Confession*, ch. 25, in *Trinity Hymnal* (rev. ed.; Philadelphia: Great Commission Publications, 1990), 863.

Each particular expression of the church must seek to exhibit the catholicity that is grounded in God's electing choice rather than in our own.

It is not only the *church* that has been elected, Bonhoeffer reminds us, but *each member*.[92] "God therefore really sees the individual, and God's election really applies to the individual." Nevertheless, it is only part of the story. The communion that Christ creates by his Spirit is unique not because it overcomes ontological barriers in a miraculous fusion of persons, but because it justifies the ungodly and, consequently, liberates them for each other in Christ.

Far from legitimizing a spiritual elitism, the doctrine of election is meant to ensure that in spite of the failures of the visible church, God will preserve a remnant, and not only from one nation, but "from every tribe and language and people and nation" (Rev 5:9). And yet, this ransomed plurality constitutes a single "kingdom" (v. 10). Like its unity and holiness, the church's catholicity is affirmed in faith, not by sight. Its security lies in God's election, not in determinations that can be made by empirical inspection of its historical continuity and structure or of the piety and enthusiasm of its membership.

Also, in both Ephesians 4 and 1 Corinthians 8–14, the Supper (along with baptism and preaching) plays a critical role in the visibility of the church. It is not just common doctrine ("one faith") that creates ecclesial unity, but "one baptism," sharing "one loaf," and drinking one cup. Notice again from these examples that in its most visible moments, the church is caught in the act of *receiving* Christ and his gifts. The church's activity in the world is always ambiguous, riddled with inconsistency, hypocrisy, and pride. As we are shaped by the gospel through the means of grace and directed by the commands of the law, the church's public activity will be transformed. Nevertheless, it is God's action that creates and sustains the reality of his church in the world.

Nothing in these seminal passages suggests that this unity and catholicity is generated by a particular church order (much less a papal office) *or* the decision of individuals to belong to it. Neither the church nor the individual is creating this new reality in the world; it is the work of God. In Ephesians, the communion that each of the elect enjoys with Christ (chapter 1) simultaneously creates on the horizontal register (to which Christ also belongs as head) a communion of saints that defies the divisions of both Rome and Jerusalem. In the work of the Spirit through the event of Word and sacrament, the church is not simply reminded or brought to a new awareness of its unity, but becomes more and more the catholic church in truth (1Co 10:17).

---

92. Dietrich Bonhoeffer, *Dietrich Bonhoeffer Works*, vol. 1, *Sanctorum Communio: A Theological Study of the Sociology of the Church* (ed. Joachim von Soosten; English edition ed. Clifford J. Green; trans. Reinhard Krauss and Nancy Lukens; Minneapolis: Fortress, 1998), 162.

C. COVENANT AND CONNECTIONALISM

A covenantal ecclesiology favors a connectional polity or form of government. If Orthodox and Roman Catholic ecclesiologies exaggerate the identity between the eschatological ("invisible") church and the visible church in its present form, Free Church ecclesiologies fail sufficiently to appreciate the connection between the heavenly reality and its earthly-visible sign. If the heavenly Jerusalem coming down to earth as a bride adorned for her husband is one universal city, then this reality should come to some visible expression, however imperfect, in this age. The church is not simply a collection of individuals or even a collection of local churches. Rather, each local church is a particular expression of the catholic church.

The covenant of grace has its origin in the eternal covenant of redemption, which makes it unconditional in its gracious basis, yet it is administered in history, with elect and nonelect members related visibly to it. Churches are collectively addressed as "saints," even though there are weeds among the wheat. Consequently, the covenant of grace is the site where the invisible church becomes partly visible even in this present evil age. Since we cannot identify the elect in this age, the church has no authority to separate the sheep from the goats. The visible church of professing believers and their children, not the invisible church of the elect, is available to us now.

The covenantal motif has tremendous potential to orient ecclesiology toward an integration of the one and many, local and broader assemblies, the invisibility of the church in election and the visibility of the church in the covenant community. To the extent that more recent Roman Catholic ecclesiologies have appealed to this motif, for example, there has been a deeper understanding of plurality in *koinōnia*.[93] On the Free Church side, Stanley Grenz notes that a covenantal perspective challenges the individualism to which congregationalism may be prone.[94]

If Reformed ecclesiology is designated "Church as Covenant," it is not surprising that the form of its outward organization is *connectional*. This is to say that "the church" refers not only to particular (local) churches, nor to the clerical hierarchy, but to local congregations, broader assemblies (regional and ecumenical), and to the whole communion of professing believers and their children in all times and places. The New Testament refers to the church as wider than a local congregation (Ac 9:31; 1Co 12:28; Eph 4:4–16), and the churches addressed in the epistles (though in the singular) consisted of more than one local congregation (Ac 20:20; Ro 16:5; Phm 2). It is important to say at the outset that although I am discussing church

---

93. See, for example, Kilian McDonnell, SJ, "Vatican II (1962–1964), Puebla (1979), Synod (1985): Koinonia/Communio as an Integral Ecclesiology," *Journal of Ecumenical Stud-* *ies* 25, no. 3 (Summer 1988): 414.

94. Grenz, *Theology for the Community of God*, 614.

government under the broader rubric of the essential attributes of the church, it is only because it is an implication of what I regard as a New Testament view of church unity, not because I regard a particular polity (presbyterian) as essential to the being of the church.

A covenantal ecclesiology suggests a concrete praxis, which is neither hierarchical nor democratic. "Presbyterian" comes from the word *presbyteros* (elder), with *presbyterion* (presbytery) being the New Testament term for a broader assembly of elders. We will examine specific passages, but first the main outlines of a presbyterian polity can be seen in the Council of Jerusalem in Acts 15, where a local church dispute was taken to the broader assembly of the church. It is striking that several times the report refers to "the apostles and the elders" as the decision-making body. Commissioners (including Paul and Barnabas) were sent from the local church in Antioch to the wider assembly, convened at Jerusalem. In fact, it was James rather than Peter who said, for his part, "Therefore my judgment is that we should not trouble those of the Gentiles who turn to God ..." (v. 19). Still, the final verdict awaited the assent of the full assembly. "Then it seemed good to the apostles and the elders, with the whole church, to choose men from among them and send them to Antioch with Paul and Barnabas," to relate the written decision to that local church (vv. 22–29).

At the Jerusalem Council, the unity that the Spirit had established at Pentecost was preserved visibly not by the sacrifice of the one to the many or the many to the one, but by the consent of the many as one. The covenant community *functioned covenantally* in its outward and interpersonal government, in mutual submission rather than hierarchical unity or independent plurality. Already in the following chapter we see the salutary practical effects of this Council in the mission to the Gentiles, when Timothy joined Paul and Silas. "As they went on their way through the cities, they delivered to them for their observance the decisions [*dogmata*] that had been reached by the apostles and elders who were in Jerusalem. So the churches were strengthened in the faith, and they increased in numbers daily" (Ac 16:4–5). These emissaries were delivering not merely godly advice that churches could either accept or reject, but decisions to be observed by the whole body. At the same time, the decisions were not imposed hierarchically, but arrived at ecumenically by representatives of the broader church. The catholic church was present federally (covenantally) at the Jerusalem Council, whose decisions remain in effect for us.

A covenantal conception of apostolicity—seems to me at least to imply a connectional yet non-hierarchical polity (i.e., presbyterial government). Elders are to be "worthy of double honor," although for this reason, "Do not ordain anyone hastily ..." (1Ti 5:17, 22). Qualifications for ministers and elders are clearly laid out in 1 Timothy 3:1–7, distinct from the office of deacon (vv.8–13). It is not because of his charisma, personality, communicative skills, or any other characteristics of his person, but in virtue of his office that Timothy is told by Paul, "Command and teach these things," in spite of his youth. "Until I come, devote yourself to the public reading of Scripture, to exhortation, to teaching. Do not neglect the gift you have, which was given you by prophecy when the council of elders [*presbyterion*] laid their hands on you" (1Ti 4:11, 13–14). So Paul can also remind Titus, "This is why I left you in Crete, so that you might put what remained into order, and appoint elders in every town as I directed you," again listing the qualifications (Tit 1:5–9). It is significant that the most successful (and busiest) missionary in history did not consider a church to be planted adequately until elders were appointed in every local assembly.

Those who hold a special office in the church have greater responsibility to serve the saints, not greater standing before God. Even Peter can identify himself as an apostle in his salutation and yet immediately add, "To those who have obtained a faith of equal standing with ours by the righteousness of our God and Savior Jesus Christ" (2Pe 1:1). In his first letter, Peter says,

> So I exhort the elders among you, as a fellow elder and a witness of the sufferings of Christ, as well as a partaker in the glory that is going to be revealed: shepherd the flock of God that is among you, exercising oversight, not under compulsion, but willingly, as God would have you; not for shameful gain, but eagerly; not domineering over those in your charge, but being examples to the flock. And when the chief Shepherd appears, you will receive the unfading crown of glory. (1Pe 5:1–4)

Because the majority of the elders are not ministers of Word and sacrament, the distinction between those who exercise spiritual oversight and those who are served is not the same as that between clergy and laity in the usual sense. Just as the Jerusalem Council consisted of "the apostles and the elders," broader and local assemblies are composed of ministers (teaching elders) and ruling elders together.[95]

As is evident in Peter's example, all ministers are elders but not all elders are ministers. Together, they are "overseers" (*episkopois*), which is often translated "bishops." This is evident from Acts 20, where the Ephesian elders are called *episkopous* (v. 28), as also in Philippians 1:1. In calling Titus to "appoint elders in every town," Paul uses *presbyterous* and *episkopous* interchangeably (Tit 1:5–7). Significantly, it is Peter who says that Christ is "the Shepherd and Overseer of your souls" (1Pe 2:25). Together with other elders, the apostles oversaw the flock under Christ, its only Chief Shepherd, but they gradually widened this pastoral ministry to the ordinary

---

95. Differing largely in nothing more than terminology, Presbyterian churches refer to the local session, a regional presbytery, and a national General Assembly, while for Reformed churches these bodies are referred to as consistory, classis, and synod, respectively.

ministers who were trained and ordained for the specific office of preaching, prayer, and teaching (Eph 4:7–16).

Whereas a hierarchical model directs the focus of unity and catholicity upward and inward from the lower rungs of the ecclesiastical ladder to a single earthly head or to a college of bishops, a presbyterian model directs the focus downward from the ascended Christ and outward in the power of his Spirit to the church and the ends of the earth. At the same time, individual believers and local churches are not left to themselves, nor merely open informally to other churches, but are gathered together as one flock under one shepherd. The responsibility for mutual encouragement, fellowship, and correction is not only local; instead, the churches are called to care for each other and to bring all of their resources to bear in common confession, discipline, evangelism, mission, and service.

The interchangeability of the terms *episkopos* (bishop) and *presbyteros* (elder) is also evidence in Clement of Rome's *Letter to the Corinthians* (AD 95).[96] Likewise, *The Didache* (AD 98) acknowledges "bishops [overseers] and deacons."[97] Even as late as the fourth century, theologians of such stature as Jerome could assume the presbyterian government of the early church and trace the gradual migration toward episcopacy. After adducing various passages in which the apostles "clearly teach that presbyters are the same as bishops," Jerome observed that presbyters selected one of their number to moderate their meetings. Yet presbyters were "all alike of equal rank" in the apostolic era. In a letter, he repeated the point that "with the ancients, these names [bishops and presbyters] were synonymous," and only grew into separate orders or offices by later custom rather than from "an arrangement by the Lord."[98] Writing in AD 376, Ambrose noted:

> After churches were planted in all places, and officers ordained, matters were settled otherwise than they were in the beginning. And hence it was that the Apostles' writing do not, in all things, agree with the present constitution of the Church; because they were written under the first rise of the Church; for he calls Timothy, who was created a Presbyter by him, a Bishop, for so, at first, the Presbyters were called.[99]

It is significant that ancient church leaders who themselves held the episcopal office recognized the gradual shift from presbyterian government. More recently, in his commentary on Philippians, the Anglican scholar J. B. Lightfoot observed the agreement of Chrysostom, Theodore of Mopsuestia, Theodoret, and others. "Thus in every one of the extant commentaries on the epistles containing the crucial pas-

---

96. Clement of Rome, *1 Corinthians*, in *The Apostolic Fathers: Greek Texts and English Translation* (2nd ed.; ed. Michael W. Holmes; Grand Rapids: Baker, 1989), 22–100.

97. *The Didache*, in ibid., 246–69.

98. Jerome, "Letter CXLVI to Evangelus" and "Letter LXIV to Oceanus," in "Earliest Textual Documentaton," *Paradigms in Polity* (ed. David W. Hall and Joseph H. Hall; Grand Rapids: Eerdmans, 1994), 57–58.

99. Quoted by Samuel Miller in "Presbyterianism: The Apostolic Constitution," in *Paradigms in Polity*, 81.

sages, whether Greek or Latin, before the close of the fifth century, this identity [of bishops and presbyters] is affirmed."[100]

The *Second Helvetic Confession* repeats some of the patristic quotes often appealed to by the Reformers. Besides Cyprian, Jerome is cited: "Before attachment to persons in religion was begun at the instigation of the devil, the churches were governed by the common consultation of the elders."[101] The significance of Peter in the apostolic college was never denied by the evangelical confessions, yet it was pointed out that Christ gave the keys of the kingdom to all of the apostles equally, and it pertained to the confession of Christ as the Son of God (Mt 16:19 with 18:18–20). Especially given the recognition by Ratzinger and Zizioulas that it was the earliest working constitution of the apostolic community, I suggest that presbyterian polity (though often overlooked in recent evangelical and Pentecostal ecclesiologies) holds greater potential for transcending the choice between hierarchy and egalitarianism.[102]

Free churches properly remind us that "We are the church!"[103] There is "one body" because the one Spirit has called us — Jew and Gentile — into one body: "one Lord, one faith, one baptism" (Eph 4:4–5). Nevertheless, this same passage includes pastors and teachers as the gifts dispensed by the ascended Christ to bring his body to maturity in him. Although constituted by its total membership, the church is instructed, governed, and served by different offices with different gifts (1Co 12:27–31; Ro 12:4–8).[104]

The manifold gifts that the ascended King has poured out on his church by his Spirit include not only offices pertaining to the sound instruction in the one faith and spiritual government but the ministry to the temporal needs of the saints. In order to give due diligence to this important work without distracting the apostles from their work of preaching and prayer, the *diaconate* was created (Ac 6; cf. Php 1:1; 1Ti 3:8–12). Just as the particular offices of minister and elder equip all of the saints as witnesses in their general office as prophets, priests, and kings, "works of service" are done officially in the name of the whole church by the deacons even though all believers are given gifts of hospitality, generosity, and mutual service in the body. The Spirit mediates Christ's threefold office as prophet, priest, and king in this age through these three offices of pastor-teacher, deacon, and elder.[105] Just

100. J. B. Lightfoot, *St. Paul's Epistle to the Philippians* (London: Macmillan, 1868; repr. Grand Rapids: Zondervan, 1974), 98–99.

101. *Second Helvetic Confession*, in *The Book of Confessions* (Louisville: PCUSA General Assembly, 1991), ch. 18, 5.160–62.

102. Interestingly, both Cardinal Ratzinger (*Called to Communion*, 122–23) and John Zizioulas (*Being as Communion*, 195) acknowledge that *presbyteros* and *episcopos* are used interchangeably in the New Testament and were synonymous offices

in the earliest Christian communities.

103. Volf, *After Our Likeness*, 135.

104. For a helpful defense of office from a Free Church perspective, see Mark Dever, "The Priesthood of All Believers: Reconsidering Every-Member Ministry," in *The Compromised Church: The Present Evangelical Crisis* (ed. John Armstrong; Westchester, Ill.: Crossway, 1998), 85–116.

105. Derke Bergsma, "Prophets, Priest, Kings: Biblical Offices," in *The Compromised Church*, 117–32.

as no believer is an island, no local church or denomination is the one catholic church; they are only one and catholic as they exist together in Christ through faithful preaching and sacrament. In this communion—expressed locally and universally—Christ cares for the temporal as well as eternal welfare of his commonwealth (see discussion of Paul's collection, p. 847).

Pastors preach and teach, elders rule, and deacons serve. At the Jerusalem Council, not even the apostles acted without consulting the elders. Since elders are ordained members who are not called to the full-time ministry of prayer and preaching, the church—in both its local and its broader assemblies—resists the temptation of our fallen hearts toward domination. "You know that the rulers of the Gentiles lord it over them, and their great ones exercise authority over them," Jesus told his disciples as they jockeyed for positions in his kingdom. "It shall not be so among you" (Mt 20:25–26). Knowing our frame, Jesus instituted checks and balances. Although this outward organization cannot save a church from apostasy and tyranny, such general declensions often coincide with a gradual loss of checks and balances.

At the same time, we are the church only with Christ as our head, from whom alone the church receives its unity and catholicity. The source of ecclesiastical authority is no more the members of the local congregation than it is the bishops or the pope. Rather, it is possessed *magisterially* by Christ alone (Mt 28:18; Jn 15:1–8; Eph 1:10–23; 2:20–22; 4:15; 5:30; Col 1:18; 2:19; 3:11; Phil 2:10–11; Rev 17:14; 19:16) and *ministerially* by delegated representatives (Mt 10:1, 40; 16:18–19; 28:19–20; Mk 16:15–16; Lk 22:17–20; Jn 20:21–23; 1Co 11:23–29; 2Co 13:3; Eph 4:11–12; 1Ti 3:1–7, 6–15; 2:14–4:3). Although the elders function representatively in the covenant community, they represent the Lord rather than the people.

In practical terms, a covenantal ecclesiology challenges the widespread tendency today to allow rival catholicities to determine ecclesial character. Of course, all of us see things from our location, but for Christians the most decisive location is "in Christ." To be sure, we interpret reality within particular communities (ethnic, national, socio-economic, generational, etc.), but for Christians, again, the most decisive community is the church—and not only the local church, but the visible catholic church in all times and places. In our day, it is not so much confessional and denominational fragmentation that threatens our visible catholicity, but the worldly divisions of race, class, politics, and the consumer preferences that have been molded by the words and sacraments of a culture of demographic niche-marketing.

The Scriptures locate believers "in Christ," which means in his church: "As many of you as were baptized into Christ have put on Christ. There is neither Jew nor Greek, there is neither slave nor free, there is no male and female, for you are all one in Christ Jesus" (Gal 3:27–28). In 1970, Donald McGavran formalized a missiological theory: "People like to become Christians without crossing racial, linguistic, or class barriers. This principle states an undeniable fact.... The world's population is a mosaic, and each piece has a separate life of its own that seems strange and often unlovely to men and women of other pieces."[106] McGavran anticipates the objection that this simply capitulates to cultural narcissism: "It is better, they think, to have a slow growing or nongrowing church that is really brotherly, integrated, and hence 'really Christian,' than a rapidly growing one-people church."[107]

Though clearly rejecting forced segregation on the basis of race, McGavran argues that before people can embrace true "brotherhood" they must become Christians and since people become Christians more rapidly in culturally homogeneous units, we should do whatever it takes to serve that missional end.[108] South African theologians Allen Boesak and John de Gruchy argue that it was pietist missionaries who assumed this very principle when they planted "homogeneous" churches that inadvertently helped to bring apartheid into existence.[109] I cannot see how we can reconcile the dissolution of Christ-centered catholicity with a proper concern for mission.

Yet this is not all that different from the situation that Paul faced in writing to the Corinthians. Where the problem in Galatia was especially the catholicity of Jew and Gentile in Christ, the problem in Corinth was that the Communion service and its following fellowship feast were divided by class, with the wealthiest enjoying the best food and wine in the central dining hall, free citizens in the outer hall, and slaves outside where they received whatever was left. So Paul writes,

> When you come together, it is not the Lord's supper that you eat. For in eating, each one goes ahead with his own meal. One goes hungry, another gets drunk. What! Do you not have houses to eat and drink in? Or do you despise the church of God and humiliate those who have nothing? What shall I say to you? Shall I commend you in this? No, I will not. (1Co 11:20–22)

Today Paul might say, "Don't you have your own homes, cars, workplaces, and circle of friends with whom you can listen to your favorite music, display your dis-

---

106. Donald McGavran, *Understanding Church Growth* (3rd ed.; rev. C. Peter Wagner; Grand Rapids: Eerdmans, 1990), 163.

107. Ibid., 174.

108. Ibid., 174–75. C. Peter Wagner defends McGavran's approach in *Our Kind of People: The Ethical Dimensions of Church Growth in America* (Atlanta: John Knox, 1979).

109. Allan Boesak responds, "Manipulation of the word of God to suit culture, prejudices, or ideology is alien to the Reformed tradition" (*Black and Reformed: Apartheid, Liberation and the Calvinist Tradition* [ed. Leonard Sweetman; Maryknoll, N.Y.: Orbis, 1984], 87). According to John de Gruchy, Reformed churches were not segregated until the "revivals in the mid-nineteenth century" by holiness preacher Andrew Murray and pietist missionaries. "It was under the dominance of

such evangelicalism," says de Gruchy, "rather than the strict Calvinism of Dort, that the Dutch Reformed Church agreed at its Synod of 1857 that congregations could be divided along racial lines." He adds, "Despite the fact that this development went against earlier synodical decisions that segregation in the church was contrary to the Word of God, it was rationalized on grounds of missiology and practical necessity. Missiologically it was argued that people were best evangelized and best worshipped God in their own language and cultural setting, a position reinforced by German Lutheran missiology and somewhat akin to the church-growth philosophy of our own time" (*Liberating Reformed Theology: A South African Contribution to an Ecumenical Debate* [Grand Rapids: Eerdmans, 1991], 23–24).

tinctive styles, and enjoy the peculiarities of your own niche demographic?" However, the church of God is the place where the young, the old, and middle-aged, men and women of all races, the sick and the healthy, those with disabilities and without, the unemployed and the wealthy gather to become one in Christ. Our churches should exhibit the kind of community that is formed by God's choice rather than our own. Christ is our most decisive location.

V. ECCLESIAL HOLINESS IN CHRIST: THE CHURCH SANCTIFIED "OUTSIDE OF ITSELF"

In addition to being "one" and "catholic," the church is "holy." Two important questions with respect to the church's holiness present themselves: (1) What is its source? Is the church distinguished from the world by its own pious willing and activity or as that part of the world that is claimed by God as the field of his saving activity and mission to the world? (2) Is this holiness merely an eschatological event from above, a merely historical institution from below, or both?

As with the attributes of unity and catholicity, the crucial question with respect to the church's holiness is not whether it arises from the community or the individual, although that is also an important question. The principal question is whether the church's holiness arises from *Christ* or from *us* (whether considered corporately or individually). It is appropriate to bring our soteriological convictions to our consideration of ecclesiology. Both individually and corporately, we are holy *in Christ*; by God's election, redemption, and calling, the church is holy.

The church is distinguished from the world by God's act of claiming it for himself, and it is this indicative announcement of the gospel that both assures us of the church's holiness in spite of its empirical condition and perpetually grounds the imperatives to realize this visible holiness more and more. After reviewing the moral and theological disarray of the Corinthian church, we might conclude that it was not even a church—and yet Paul addresses it as such and on that basis recalls it to its identity.

Nevertheless, that which God declares holy in Christ is also made holy in Christ. Sanctification is a gift that already belongs to the church, but it is also an ongoing process in which the church is being constantly provoked, challenged, renewed, and reformed by the Spirit, conformed to the image of Christ through God's Word. Because the reality of the age to come is united to the sign of the visible church in this present age, the church is called to radical obedience, realizing more and more the implications of God's holy claim on its existence and actions in the world. Yet it is always God's sanctifying action that keeps the church from becoming assimilated again into the world out of which it has been called.

A. NATURE AND GRACE: HISTORICAL INSTITUTION OR ESCHATOLOGICAL EVENT?

Are creaturely signs elevated ontologically and transubstantiated into the reality signified? Are they mere symbols or illustrations of that reality but not really conveyors of it? Or are creaturely signs means of grace, participating in the reality signified, while remaining in every respect natural? Defending this third view, I have argued that in sanctifying persons, places, and things, God claims creaturely reality in all of its essential goodness and historical fallenness and liberates it to serve his purposes.

It is God's promise that makes ordinary water, bread, and wine holy elements. They do not lose the slightest degree of their created nature. God's Word consecrates them for his saving service. Analogously, Jesus prays concerning his followers, not that they be taken out of the world, but that they may be sanctified in it: "Sanctify them in the truth; your word is truth" (Jn 17:17). Before sanctification is a process of inner renewal, it is a definitive claim made by the triune God: a declarative word that, like justification, initiates reverberations through every nook and cranny of personal and ecclesial existence. No longer *lô²ʿammî*, "Not My People" (Hos 1:9–10), we are proclaimed to be the very people of God (1Pe 2:9–10, alluding to Hos 1:6, 9–10). Even while the church remains sullied both internally and externally, it calls on the name of the Lord in assurance, knowing that Christ "became to us wisdom from God, righteousness and sanctification and redemption, so that, as it is written, 'Let the one who boasts, boast in the Lord'" (1Co 1:30).

Anticipated by the prophets, the day finally arrived when the "clean"/"unclean" distinction between Jews and Gentiles was rendered obsolete. The revelation of this promise's fulfillment staggered and scandalized Peter, yet it resulted in the mission to the Gentiles (Ac 10:1–11:18). In Christ, even the "unclean" are holy; strangers to the covenants and promises can become children of Abraham (Lk 3:8; Jn 1:12; Gal 3:13–18; 4:21–5:1; Eph 2:11–19; 1Pe 2:10) and their children can be holy to the Lord (1Co 7:14). The church's holiness is attributed not only to the invisible church (i.e., those who are elect and regenerated), but to the visible church as a mixed company. Just as the visible catholicity of the church is threatened when we allow other lords to locate us under their dominion, the church's visible holiness is threatened when its words and ways become assimilated to cultural traditions and fashions.

The tendency to conflate Christ and the church locates the church's holiness in the visible form of the church itself. In the era of Christendom, the secular empire itself can become the body of Christ: the *Holy* Roman Empire, contrasted with the heathen nations under God's judgment. Eschatology and history become one, with the church identified fully with the kingdom of God in its progressive unfolding. In this conception, eschatology loses its force in breaking up the givens of history. To be a Christian is simply to be a part of *this* history.

On the other hand, the rediscovery of eschatology, especially since Barth, can reduce history to a shadow, with the vertical irruptions of divine acts barely related to God's faithfulness "from generation to generation." Taken to an extreme, this view can lead us to think the work of the Spirit in the lives of individual believers bears no necessary connection to formal membership in the church. Even preaching and the sacraments can become optional resources for an entirely personal spiritual quest. The historical institution and its public ministry may even be treated as a humanly devised impediment to genuine spiritual growth.

In a covenantal conception, there is a history of redemption, but it unfolds not from its own immanent possibilities, either located in an institution or in the piety of individual believers. In fact, this history continues precisely because of God's eschatological interruptions of its ordinary flow, judging, justifying, killing and making alive. The Spirit is always with his people, leading them from exodus to their homeland, but as a gift — never as a given. Israel and Judah learned this hard lesson when they witnessed the Spirit's evacuation of the temple and were sent into exile.

It is into "this present age" (Tit 2:12; cf. Gal 1:4; Eph 1:21) that is "passing away" (1Jn 2:17; cf. 1Cor 7:31) that "the powers of the age to come" are penetrating by the work of the Spirit through Word and sacrament (Heb 6:5). The prophets refer to the arrival of the Messiah in "the latter days" (Jer 49:39), and the apostles indicate that the period in which we are now living between Christ's two advents is "the last hour" (1Jn 2:18) and "these last days" (Heb 1:2). Familiar already in the eschatologies of Second Temple Judaism, the categories of "this age" and "the age to come" are directly invoked by Jesus (Mk 10:30; Lk 20:34). In the Pauline corpus, these categories are equivalent to "flesh" and "Spirit," with the former representing the immanent powers and resources available to us under the conditions of sin and death and the latter indicating the new creation inaugurated by Christ's resurrection and the indwelling of the Spirit, both of which he calls "the firstfruits" or down payment on our final glorification in the age to come (see esp. Ro 8:7–27).

Therefore, *history* itself has been claimed by God as the theater of his *eschatological* victory from heaven. In this history, Adam broke the covenant and brought death, and Christ fulfilled the covenant, bore its judgment, and inaugurated the new creation. This history is not transcended or elevated. Nor is it a secular history alongside God's eternal history. Just as grace liberates rather than overwhelms nature, eschatology does not abolish history or turn it into something nonhistorical. Rather, God's radical judgment and radical grace redefine the meaning of history as the nexus of these two ages where the church is born. The church is an institution in history, but it is a history that history could never have generated.

We have already seen that Roman Catholic ecclesiology sees the church's holiness cascading down the one ladder of being, unified by its visible head, the pope. As a consequence, the church cannot be considered simultaneously justified and sinful. The holiness of the church is in no way compromised by the sins of its members, not because of an *alien* righteousness but because of an *inherent* righteousness that is infused into the church and flows from her. Rahner summarizes, "As the great theologians of the Middle Ages used to say (St. Thomas, *Summa Theologica*, I, IIae, q. 106, a.1), what principally constitutes the Church is the Holy Spirit in men's hearts, all the rest (hierarchy, papacy, Eucharist, sacraments) are in the service of this inner transformation."[110]

Dulles correctly perceives that from the viewpoint of Lutheran and Reformed ecclesiology, the Roman Catholic perspective can be seen only as a "theology of glory."[111] In spite of his salutary summons toward a more eschatologically sensitive ecclesiology, Dulles concludes, "The final coming of the Kingdom, I believe, will be the work of God, dependent on his initiative. But it seems likely that, as Rahner suggests, "the parousia will not occur until human effort 'has gone to its very limits and so is burst open by salvation from above by developing its own powers.'"[112] As a failure to appreciate the full impact of the ascension has contributed to the confusion of the church with an ongoing incarnation of Jesus Christ, so also it is unlikely that such a confusion could have developed apart from a synergistic soteriology. From a Reformation perspective, it is this synergistic view of the church's holiness that unites Roman Catholic, Wesleyan, and Pentecostal traditions.[113] However, from a covenantal perspective, all ways of locating holiness in someone or something other than Jesus Christ overlook the inseparable connection between Christology and pneumatology already highlighted.

A biblical view of the church's holiness stands in sharp contrast with this conception. First, there is a distinction between Christ, who is our holiness (Jer 23:5–6; 33:16; 1Co 1:30; 2Co 5:21; Phil 3:9; Eph 1:7; Col 1:14), and the church, which is definitively and progressively holy only in him. The church is not the source of the holiness of its members, but the body that receives its holiness from outside of itself, in Christ. Second, this definitive holiness does not radiate in diminishing degrees, from the brightness of Mary and the saints to the clergy to the laity. Rather, all believers are saints, holy (*hagios*) in Christ.

From the perspective of Reformation theology, grace neither *absorbs* nature nor arrives *independently of it*; it is given *through* it. The claim of the triune God that

---

110. Karl Rahner, "The Church," in *Sacramentum Mundi: An Encyclopedia of Theology* (ed. K. Rahner SJ et al.; New York: Herder and Herder, 1968), 1:319.

111. Dulles, *Models of the Church*, 72–73.

112. Karl Rahner, "Christianity and the 'New Man,'" in *Later Writings* (Theological Investigations 5; trans. Karl-H. Kruger; (Baltimore: Helicon., 1966), 5:149, quoted in Dulles, *Models of the Church*, 114.

113. See, for example, Yong, *The Spirit Poured Out on All Flesh*, 130. Drawing on the doctrine of dispensations developed by John Fletcher (Wesley's successor), Yong, a Pentecostal theologian, reaches the same goal, but by way of the immediacy of the Spirit apart from any necessary connection to the word of Christ or the church. This allows him also to affirm that "the mystical and universal body of Christ would include the entire spectrum from all those who explicitly confess his name to all who may not be knowledgeable about Jesus but are spiritually united with him by the power of the Holy Spirit."

makes the church holy in no way transubstantiates it into something divine. Yet the Spirit works through the ordinary means of grace in the church to bring about a communion of saints across all generations and ethnicities.

The church is holy — that is, the sphere of God's saving, covenantal action — when it is "in Christ," and it is the gospel that determines and audibly identifies this location. If a professing church no longer defines itself and its ministry — that is, its methods as well as its message — by that promise and command, it no longer has a valid ministry. It is no longer authorized to speak and act in Christ's name to his people and to the world. Deprived of its holiness (which is given to it from outside of itself), it becomes just another secular institution.

We have seen that the idea of the church as the ongoing incarnation of Christ is increasingly prominent in Protestant (including evangelical) as well as Roman Catholic circles. There is, to be sure, an incarnational *analogy* in the New Testament, where we are called to have the same "mind" as Christ by imitating his humility (Php 2:5 – 8). However, to the extent that this is turned into a *univocal* concept, "incarnational ministry" can actually undermine the church's holiness. Often, in an effort to incarnate itself in the world and redeem the culture, the church builds a Holy Roman Empire, Christendom, and, in our own day, produces a panoply of "Christian" things (music, exercise programs, politics, economics, entertainment, businesses, art, fiction, science, etc.) that are often poor imitations of their "secular" alternatives. Ironically, many voices in the churches today recognize that the church has capitulated to culture with respect to Christendom, empire, and Western (especially American) consumerism, militarism, and civil religion, while cheerfully accommodating the church's message, identity, and mission to "our postmodern context."

Christians are not distinguished from non-Christians — which is to say, are not holy — because they show love and kindness to their neighbors, defend justice, and care for the environment. These are obligations of the law of creation that Christians recognize in their conscience together with non-Christians. It is only the gospel that marks believers as holy, and it is only the preaching of that gospel and its ratification in baptism and Communion that generate a city of light in a dark world. Our holiness, then, will be expressed more and more in the world as a witness to our neighbors, but it will be the reverberating impact of the definitive holiness that makes the church something other than another charitable organization, spiritual community, political action committee or circle of like-minded friends.

In its holiness as well as its catholicity, the body is constituted "from above" by the always surprising and disruptive announcement of the gospel, and the covenant community receives its catholicity along with its entire being *extra nos*, outside of itself, in spite of its own history of unfaithfulness. As extended "from below" in history ("to a thousand generations"), catholicity and holiness are mediated through the faithful ministry of Word and sacrament, yielding a succession of faith from one generation to another across all times and places. The Spirit constantly disrupts the church, pulling it back from its tendency to become assimilated again to this passing age, but the same Spirit also constantly reorganizes the church so that it can maintain its historical continuity with past and future generations of the one covenant of grace.

Taking its bearings from both of these coordinates — the eschatological and the historical — a covenantal ecclesiology affirms that just as each believer must be joined to the visible body and each generation must be connected to those which precede and follow it, particular (local) churches must be "eager to maintain the unity of the Spirit in the bond of peace" (Eph 4:3) by ever wider and deeper solidarity that expresses itself in concrete, visible, and enduring structures.

Of course, God may meet strangers wherever he chooses, but he has *promised* to meet us in the covenant of grace, through the invocation of Christ's name (Ac 4:12; Php 2:9 – 11). Persons, places, and things are holy because God has claimed these natural creatures for himself. The covenant of grace is the sphere of God's sanctifying activity, where he has promised to unite believers and their children to Christ and his benefits. Lesslie Newbigin nicely expresses a perennial Reformed objection to the notion of the "anonymous Christian":

> Nor can we attempt to preserve some remnants of consistency by the use of the conception of uncovenanted mercies, by suggesting that we can acknowledge fully the works of grace outside the visible Church and yet retain intact our conviction that the Church only exists where visible continuity has been preserved. This attempt lands us into an impossible situation. If God can and does bestow His redeeming grace with indiscriminate bounty within and without the confines of His Church, then the Church is no essential part of the whole scheme of salvation, and its order and sacraments, its preaching and ministering have no inherent and essential relation to God's saving work in Christ, but are merely arbitrary constructions which God Himself ignores.[114]

While the visible church is indeed a "mixed assembly," according to Reformation theologies, it is the exclusive site of God's covenanted blessings in Christ. It is in fact this affirmation that fuels the missionary spirit that is intrinsic to Christian identity.

While Rome identifies this inherent holiness with the historical institution as such, independent ecclesiologies tend to identify it with the piety and actions of the individual, ranging from identifiable conversion experiences to speaking in tongues. To the extent that free churches treat as central the inner experience of conversion and renewal, there is substantial agreement with Rahner's description of the Roman Catholic position cited above, namely, that "what principally constitutes the Church

---

114. Newbigin, *Household of God*, 79.

is the Holy Spirit in men's hearts, all the rest ... are in the service of this inner transformation." Roman Catholic theology emphasizes the Mass as "the work of the people."[115] Protestant evangelicals typically regard the church primarily as the platform for their service to God and neighbor more than as the place where God serves them.

Reflecting a broad evangelical consensus in our day, Miroslav Volf suggests that "authentic Christian worship takes place in a rhythm of adoration and action."[116] However, adoration *is* action — and both are *our* actions. Of course, worship is the activity of worshipers, but this is precisely why it is important to see the weekly gathering of Christ's people as broader than worship. Volf adds, "As Christians worship God in adoration and action they anticipate the conditions of this world as God's new creation."[117] Lost in this exclusive emphasis on imperatives (adoration, action, and anticipation) are the grand indicatives of God's actions in Christ by his Word and Spirit. We can only adore and act in anticipation of God's new creation if in fact the powers of that new creation are already at work, penetrating this present evil age, uniting sinners to Jesus Christ. As we are gathered, the Spirit makes us share in the new creation. Only because *God* is at work is there any reason, much less any ability, for fallen creatures to participate in faith, hope, and love.

Covenant theology has taken a different route from either of these paradigms. Regardless of the personal holiness of its members, the church (understood in terms not only of its local but also of its broader assemblies) is holy simply because it is the field of divine activity in which the wheat is growing up into the likeness of its firstfruits, even though weeds are sown among the wheat. In this conception, the church admits people into her fellowship not because they are inherently holy but because the Lord has consecrated this space as the place of his holy action. Even if only one parent is a believer, the children are holy (1Co 7:14). This is due not to any inner transformation or infused grace, but simply to God's promise. In covenantal thinking, the tree is holy even if some of its branches will finally fail to yield fruit and be broken off to make room for others (Ro 11:16–24). The tree is holy neither because it is collectively identical to Christ, nor because it is the sum total of the regenerate, but because of the eschatological connection of the covenant people to their living root (v. 16, 18–20). At any given moment, in any local expression, the church will be a "mixed assembly" and yet the field of God's action where faith is

---

115. From *leitourgia*, the term "liturgy" can refer to the service of the people or the service to the people, rendered by the state. It was appropriated by the early church as the Divine service. Churches of the Reformation have interpreted the weekly gathering of the church as God's service to his people, provoking their response of faith in Christ and love for neighbor.

116. Miroslav Volf, "Worship as Adoration and Action: Reflections on a Christian Way of Being-in-the-World," in *Worship: Adoration and Action* (ed. D. A. Carson; Carlisle, UK: Paternoster, 1993), 207.

117. Ibid., 208.

created and sustained. The whole field is holy in this ecclesial sense even though there are weeds sown among the wheat.

The very people whom Paul "could not address ... as spiritual people, but as people of the flesh, as infants in Christ," are nevertheless infants *in Christ* (1Co 3:1). The letter is even addressed, "To the *church* of God that is Corinth, to those *sanctified* in Christ Jesus, *called to be saints* together with all those who in every place *call upon the name of our Lord Jesus Christ*, both their Lord and ours: Grace to you and peace from God our Father and the Lord Jesus Christ" (1Co 1:2–3, emphasis added). The *Westminster Confession* reminds us, "The purest churches under heaven are subject both to mixture and error; and some have so degenerated, so as to become no churches of Christ, but synagogues of Satan. Nevertheless, there shall be always a church on earth, to worship God according to his will."[118]

Like its individual members, the church remains simultaneously justified and sinful in this age. The calling of the church is not to witness to its own piety or to transform the world into Christ's holy kingdom. In the words of Dietrich Bonhoeffer, "The intention of the preacher is not to improve the world, but to summon it to belief in Jesus Christ and to bear witness to the reconciliation which has been accomplished through Him and His dominion."[119] It is the Word that "breaks up" the church into "the community-of-the cross," to be "built up" into "the Easter community."[120] Although Christ works through the ministry of his church, the church can never regard its actions as identical with his.[121] It is not the church but the Spirit who makes Christ present in the world for salvation and life. As we see in Paul's address to the Corinthians, the church is holy because it consists of those who are "called to be saints," chosen, redeemed, justified, and in the process of being sanctified by his Spirit. However imperfectly the church manifests this holiness in empirical terms, it is nevertheless called to become what it already is according to God's recreating Word. Oswald Bayer reminds us, "Even the institutions sanctified by God can therefore never be the path to salvation, and even though they are and remain holy, in them we may either be lost or we may find deliverance — by faith alone."[122]

Berkhof points out that whereas Rome locates the holiness of the church in its intrinsic character as the bearer of salvation, Lutheran and Reformed confessions "maintain that the Church is absolutely holy in an objective sense, that is, as she is considered in Jesus Christ. In virtue of the mediatorial righteousness of Christ, the Church is accounted holy before God."[123]

118. *Westminster Confession*, ch. 25.5, in *Trinity Hymnal* (rev. ed.; Philadelphia: Great Commission Publications, 1990), 863.

119. Dietrich Bonhoeffer, *Ethics* (New York: Macmillan, 1965), 350.

120. Ibid., 212–13.

121. Ibid., 214.

122. Oswald Bayer, *Living by Grace: Justification and Sanctification* (trans. Geoffrey W. Bromiley; Eerdmans, 2003), 62; cf. Martin Luther, *Luther's Works* (ed. Helmut T. Lehmann; Philadelphia: Fortress, 1957; repr., 1971), 37:365.

123. Berkhof, *Systematic Theology*, 575.

Similarly, Lesslie Newbigin argues on the basis of Romans 9,

There is a covenant and a covenant people, and God is faithful to His covenant. But the substance of that covenant is all pure mercy and grace. If men presume to claim for themselves upon the basis of the covenant some relationship with God other than that of the sinner needing God's grace, the covenant has been perverted. And where that has happened God, in the sovereign freedom of His grace, destroys these pretensions, calls "No people" to be the people, breaks off natural branches and grafts in wild slips, filling them with the life which is His own life imparted to men.... She who is essentially one is divided; she who is essentially holy is unclean; she who is essentially apostolic forgets her missionary task.[124]

The grace of God does not flow down a cosmic ladder by gradations and degrees; rather, every believer is a co-heir with Christ and each other. Everything that is in Christ is as holy as he is, because he *is* its sanctification (1Co 1:30–31). This being the case, the objective holiness of the whole body in its head is also *at work* throughout the body, so that each member will realize more and more the fruit of that definitive identity which can be neither improved nor diminished.

Even the church's unregenerate members are in some sense beneficiaries of the Spirit's activity in the covenant community, which, according to Hebrews (esp. chs. 4, 6, 10), makes them all the more responsible for embracing the promises signified and sealed to them in baptism. The church is never the effectual agent, but the recipient and field of God's sanctifying work in the world: the theater in which the Spirit is casting and staging dress rehearsals of the age to come.

B. HOLY SERVICE

While the church (like each believer) is simultaneously justified and sinful, holy in Christ yet often unholy in its ambitions, affections, and actions, it is called to greater maturity in faith and practice. Just as the "invisible church" cannot be an excuse for neglecting the visible unity and catholicity of Christ's bride, the empirical failures of the church keep us from triumphalism but should not keep us from responding faithfully to the imperative to reflect the righteousness as well as truth of our Living Head.

We need not—indeed, must not—choose between a view of the church as a purely passive recipient of grace and a view of it as an active bearer of grace. We are always passive recipients of grace from God and active agents of love to our neighbor. Grace activates works; love flows from faith. A forensic economy yields effective transformation: the word does what it declares; the believer and the church become what they already are in Christ. *In this light, the church is always a recipient of grace in relation to God yet also active in witness, love, and service toward the neighbor.*

---

124. Newbigin, *The Household of God*, 84.

The main point to be drawn from these arguments is that these attributes do not belong to the church as a result of its decision and activity, but God's. The church's unity and catholicity do not arise immanently within individual believers or a historical institution; they are gifts from the Father, in the Son, and by the Spirit. They are given because the triune God has elected, redeemed, and called us in Christ to belong to him and to each other. The church was chosen in Christ to be holy (Eph 1:4) and was sanctified by Christ's life, death, and resurrection—applied by the Holy Spirit. The church's apostolicity is grounded not in its orthodoxy or orthopraxy, but in the external Word, made fruitful in us by the Spirit. As long as the church hears, receives, and proclaims this Word that it has been given, it is something other than a club, neighborhood association, theological school, or political action committee.

A church that, weary of its ambiguous location between the two ages, preaches another gospel or corrupts the sacraments is no longer holy, but is assimilated into the world—the age that is passing away—despite its outward forms (Gal 1:6–9; 1Co 3:10–17). We cannot deny that there will be those finally who hear these chilling words of Jesus Christ: "I never knew you; depart from me," although they protest that they performed wonders in his name (Mt 7:22–23). The candlestick of any particular church or group of churches can be removed when it ceases to bear illuminating witness to Christ in the world (Rev 2:5). This tragic end may come upon a church not only for abandoning the doctrine of the gospel itself, but for failing to bear witness to it. To deny that this eschatological judgment of one's professing church is impossible by virtue of its inherent holiness and eminent history is itself a harbinger of apostasy, and it is a tendency to which all of our churches can easily succumb.

Yet we have Christ's promise that he will build his church. Despite the church's compromised, ambiguous, schismatic and sinful character, the covenant of redemption ensures that our unfaithfulness will not have the last word.

DISCUSSION QUESTIONS

1. Discuss the importance of eschatology, covenant, and pneumatology for our ecclesiology.
2. Evaluate the idea of the *totus Christus*. Where did it originate, and how did it come to be interpreted by different theologians and traditions? What is the impact of this concept on the unity and catholicity of the church?
3. As with the sacraments, different ecclesiologies are engendered by different views of the relationship between sign and reality signified. Evaluate these different approaches across the ecclesial spectrum, especially in relation to the question of the "one" (unity) and the "many" (plurality).

4. What is the source of unity and catholicity according to the Scriptures?
5. What is the difference between the invisible and visible church? How are they related?
6. How do the churches relate to the one church in New Testament teaching?
7. In light of the holiness of the church, how do we understand the relationship between the church as a historical institution and the church as an eschatological event? What are some of the practical implications of our answer for church life?

Chapter Twenty-Six

APOSTOLICITY: A FELLOWSHIP OF RECEIVERS AND DELIVERERS

Like the other attributes of the church, apostolicity is a gift rather than a given and is determined by the gospel. So far we have seen the danger of two extremes: either to confuse Christ and his saving work with the church or to separate them. The same is true of the relation between the church as a historical institution (a place) and the church as an eschatological event that is always constituted de novo by the gathering itself (people).

These extremes are evident also in considering the *apostolicity* of the church. On one hand, there is the danger of identifying this attribute with a historical office, turning the gift of Christ into a given of the church itself. In this view, the church need not ask whether it is in touch with the faith of the apostles; it is apostolic—and will always be apostolic—simply because it is in historical continuity with the apostles themselves. On the other hand, there is the danger of dismissing the importance of the church as an official institution (its ministry and offices) as merely human rather than divine in origin.

I. THE MESSAGE AND THE MEDIA

Once more, Romans 10 provides a clue for navigating these twin dangers. God alone saves, but he does so through creaturely means. The outward ministry of the church is not simply a witness to God's grace, much less an obstacle. Rather, it is the means through which the Father delivers his Son to us by the Spirit. We do not "make Christ present," relevant, real, and a living agent in people's lives. He makes himself relevant whenever he addresses us in judgment and grace.

The apostle is not naive about the need for methods of delivery. He does not believe that the Spirit will simply draw the elect apart from any outward ministry. That is why he immediately adds,

> How then will they call on him in whom they have not believed? And how are they to believe in him of whom they have never heard? And how are they to hear without someone preaching? And how are they to preach unless they are sent? As it is written, "How beautiful are the feet of those who preach the good news!" (vv. 14–15)

Paul's argument follows an inexorable logic: Salvation comes down to us from God; it is not something that we can attain by our own striving. Therefore, this application of redemption comes to us in the form a gospel that is proclaimed to us rather than by a goal that is attained by us. Consequently, God uses authorized ambassadors who are sent. Just as we do not find God ourselves, we do not send ourselves. The message, the methods, and the ministry yield the church's mission. In conforming itself to this evangelical logic, the church is apostolic.

A sound *eschatology* ("already"/"not yet") keeps us from taking the apostolicity of the church for granted, as if we did not have to receive it again as a gift through the Word that is preached, in dependence on the Spirit. It reminds us that the church is caught in the cross fire of this present evil age as it is confronted with the powers of the age to come. The church that Christ promised to build is not a denomination or a succession of apostolic ministers, but a visible herald and succession of apostolic ministry. The sovereign Word can always challenge and even invalidate an ecclesiastical institution's claim to catholicity, holiness, and apostolicity.

Nevertheless, our *covenantal* coordinate also reminds us that the covenant of grace is a historical promise with a canon, rites, and offices that were instituted by Christ and continue into the future. Like its other attributes, the church's apostolicity is always a gift from heaven, but it is visibly transferred "from generation to generation."

On one hand, as Newbigin observes, Reformed ecclesiology affirms the visibility of the church through its public ministry and affirms the historical continuity of this covenant community from generation to generation.

> When, on the other hand, the Church is identified simply with whatever society has continued in unbroken succession from the time of the apostles, then the flesh, not the Spirit, has been made determinative. There is in truth no "extension of the Incarnation," for His incarnation was in order to make an offering of Himself in the flesh "once for all." The fruit of that offering, of that casting of a corn of wheat into the earth, is the extension of His risen life to all who are made members of His Body

in the one Spirit—until He comes again.... The fundamental error into which Catholic doctrines of the Church are prone to fall is ... the error of *subordinating the eschatological to the historical* (emphasis added).[1]

This is precisely what is at stake in recognizing that the church is the creation of the Word. Thus, a professing church community cannot be identified as apostolic apart from its doctrine. It is the relation of our churches to the apostles' teaching, not to their persons or genealogy of ordination, which determines apostolicity.

If not an angel or apostle (Gal 1:8), then certainly not any earthly pastor can become the criterion for apostolicity. Neither continuity with a historical succession of pastors nor connection to an allegedly Spirit-filled apostle today guarantees that a church is apostolic. Not one pastor or one denomination, but "one faith"—*the fides quae creditur* (the faith that is believed)—is the criterion of one holy, catholic, and apostolic church. It is "the faith that was once for all delivered to the saints" (Jude 3) that establishes the unbroken thread running from Genesis 3:16 to the present moment.

II. APOSTOLICITY AND APOSTLESHIP

In very different ways, Orthodoxy and Roman Catholicism as well as many Pentecostal groups identify the apostolicity of the church with the office of apostle. Accordingly, the Spirit's presence and activity is identified visibly with those holding this position, and those who maintain this view are often unwilling in varying degrees to test such claims and those who make them by God's Word. By contrast, churches of the Reformation identify the presence of the Spirit and the mark of apostolicity, once again, with the Word properly preached and the sacraments rightly administered. Secondarily, as I will argue below, Lutheran and Reformed traditions hold that the apostolic office ceased with the end of the New Testament era, and therefore these traditions distinguish between the extraordinary ministry of the apostles and the ordinary ministry of pastors.

A. DIFFERING INTERPRETATIONS

Closely following the two tendencies that we have already encountered, we may discern two distinct approaches that are prominent in historical and contemporary treatments of this subject.

1. BINDING APOSTOLICITY TO AN OFFICIAL OFFICE

Irenaeus, especially in his conflict with Gnostic sects in the second century (who developed a parallel canon, ordinances, and bishops), emphasized that the autho-

---

1. Ibid., 82.

rized form of Christian faith and practice was defined by the apostolic writings and the ministers (bishops) who could trace their ordination to the apostles. Given the confusion of competing claims, his apologetic is understandable. However, this argument from *historical succession* evolved into a formal doctrine of *apostolic succession*. Today, the Orthodox East still holds that it is the "one holy, catholic, and apostolic Church," corporately preserved from error by unbroken succession of its bishops from the apostles, and Rome identifies this apostolicity with the pope as Peter's successor. (For the transition from a presbyterian to an episcopal government, see p. 858, esp. fn. 102.)

Ancient Christian leaders of the East never accepted the supremacy of the Roman bishop, however, and Cyprian, among others, warned that any assertion of episcopal primacy would constitute schism. Gregory the Great, a sixth-century bishop of Rome, added his testimony, expressing offense at being addressed by a bishop as "universal pope": "a word of proud address that I have forbidden.... None of my predecessors ever wished to use this profane word ['universal'].... But I say it confidently, because whoever calls himself 'universal bishop' or wishes to be so called, is in his self-exaltation Antichrist's precursor, for in his swaggering he sets himself before the rest."[2] Many other examples could be adduced to make the point that not only the Reformers but the ancient fathers testify against the pretense of Rome that it is the supreme guarantor of apostolicity.

Nevertheless, something more deeply theological is at stake in this question: namely, whether the church is saved by law or gospel. Lesslie Newbigin, who was a bishop in the Church of South India, contended, "The fundamental flaw" in making a valid episcopate essential to apostolicity "is that it forgets that the substance of the covenant is pure mercy, and that God retains His sovereign freedom to have mercy upon whom He will, and to call 'No People' His people when they that are called His people deny their calling by unbelief and sin."[3] Although a valid ministry of Word and sacrament is essential, Newbigin rightly argues that this does not entail a particular form of government as essential to the very being of the church.

The same must be said also of presbyterian government. A theory that makes the essence of the church consist in its polity *assimilates* the gospel to law, although it should be added that a theory that regards the church's outward form as indifferent *separates* the gospel from law. Although the church is saved and sustained and expands by grace alone, the Great Commission obliges the church to "teach them to observe everything I have commanded" (Mt 28:20). I believe that the New Testament teaches a particular form of government, to which presbyterian polity

---

2. Gregory the Great, *Letters* (Books 1 and 2) in *NPNF2*, 12:75–76, 170, 171, 179, 166, 169, 222, 225.

3. Lesslie Newbigin, *Household of God*, 82.

conforms most closely. If this can be demonstrated, then it would be insubordinate for us to ignore such expectations. Nevertheless, as much as a biblical form of government supports the faithful ministry of Word, sacrament, and discipline, it does not ensure it. Nor does disagreement concerning polity invalidate an authentic ministry. To make the form of government a sine qua non of ecclesial identity is in effect to substitute the church — perhaps even a single denomination — for the gospel itself, a move that, as Yves Congar laments, is actually made in Roman Catholic theology.[4] According to Cardinal Hosius, a theologian of Trent, "the living gospel is the Church itself."[5] Ironically, as I will note more fully below, a similar view is increasingly expressed in evangelical circles, with the assumption that the witness of the church (or at least believers) to its own moral transformation is more effective than the proclamation of the gospel concerning Christ.

2. Separating Apostolicity from the Official Ministry

It was against the anthropocentric trend in modern Roman Catholicism and Neo-Protestantism that Barth launched his epochal program. Redemption is concerned with God's action, not ours — whether individual or corporate — and consequently the church exists simply as a witness to divine action. Fearful of making God's grace a human possession, Barth seems hesitant to affirm that God ordinarily works through creaturely agency, although he may *commandeer, overwhelm, disrupt,* and otherwise use human words and actions as *witnesses* to revelation. Barth's actualist ontology underwrites this emphasis: "The Church is when it takes place...."[6] In part, Barth was reacting against the neo-Hegelian ecclesiologies of Rome and liberal Protestantism. "To speak of a continuation or extension of the incarnation in the Church is not only out of place but even blasphemous," he boldly and properly insists.[7] The strength of Barth's position (similar at this point with Free Church evangelicalism) is that it recognizes the primary role of the church as *witnessing* to Christ and identifies apostolicity with the apostolic preaching of Christ.

However, where the rival paradigm virtually eliminates any difference between Christ and the church, Barth virtually eliminates affinity. As we have already seen, distinctions often become dichotomies between God and humanity, the divine Word and human words, baptism with the Spirit and baptism with water. These dichotomies belong to the map of eternity and time, respectively. Especially in his commentary on Romans, the "kingdom of God" (apocalyptic and eschatological) is not only distinguished from but set over against the visible church (historical and transient). The church's activity "is related to the Gospel only in so far as it is no

---

4. Yves Congar, *I Believe in the Holy Spirit* (New York: Crossroad, 1999), 154.

5. Ibid., 153.

6. Barth, *Church Dogmatics*, vol. 4, pt. 1, p. 652.

7. Ibid., vol. 4, pt. 3.2, p. 729.

more than a crater formed by the explosion of a shell and seeks to be no more than a void in which the Gospel reveals itself."[8] The church's words and actions "by their negation are sign-posts to the Holy One," never sacred themselves.[9]

In this view, the connection between the sign (the visible church) and the reality signified (God's reign) is negligible. We are part of, cling to, and preserve the unity of the Esau-like church, Barth insists. However, "the work of the Church is the work of men. It can never be God's work."[10] "The Church is the Church of Jacob — only when the miracle occurs. Otherwise it is nothing more than the Church of Esau."[11] This would seem to question the very possibility of an actual church extending "from generation to generation" rather than simply moment by moment. The invisible church is thoroughly identified with Christ. In fact, he calls it Christ's "heavenly-historical form of existence ... at the right hand of the Father...."[12] However, the visible church (which he calls "the community" as "the earthly-historical form" of Christ's existence) is *purely secular in its empirical form* and spiritual only in those momentary flashes when its witness to Christ coincides with revelation.[13]

Assuming that "secularity" is neutral, Barth allows himself by this dualism to treat the outward form of the church as relatively unimportant. Real history (the eschatological history of Jesus Christ) is in fact opposed to "history so-called," just as the creaturely ministry of the church and the gracious action of God stand in contrast. Since he believed that the sacraments are not God's means of grace, but are merely the responsive activity of believers, it is not surprising that he held that the work of God and the work of the church always occupy parallel tracks that never intersect. However, how can we reduce the visibility of the church to its secularity, since the institutions of preaching, sacraments, offices, and order are directly established by Christ as the means by which the kingdom irrupts in this age, not only as a momentary event but as a historical community? It is this second point that I want to challenge here, especially because it reflects assumptions commonly held at least implicitly by evangelicals, Pentecostals, and others in Free Church or independent ecclesial traditions.

Barth clearly articulates an assumption that seems to be held more widely by evangelicals in the Free Church heritage: namely, that the content of the church's teaching is essential, while the church's forms and methods are left to each generation's creativity and pragmatic judgments. However, to regard the outward and visible form of the church — its public worship, ministry of preaching and sacrament, and offices of discipline and diaconal care — as indifferent reflects a somewhat

---

8. Karl Barth, *The Epistle to the Romans* (trans. Edwyn C. Hoskyns from the 6th ed.; London: Oxford Univ. Press, 1933), 36.

9. Ibid.

10. Ibid., 353.

11. Ibid., 366.

12. Ibid., 661.

13. Barth, *Church Dogmatics*, vol. 4, pt. 1, p. 652.

Gnostic disregard of the body over against the soul. Against both legalism and antinomianism, Reformed and Presbyterian churches maintain that everything that Christ commands, but only that which he commands, is obligatory on churches and individual believers. This view is known as the *regulative principle.*

Based on the sole lordship of Christ over the church and the freedom of the believer's conscience from bondage to the religious laws imposed on merely human authority, this rule (especially articulated in Reformed faith and practice) stipulates that nothing can be required that is not expressly commanded by Christ or can be deduced by good and necessary consequence from Scripture. There can be no arbitrary division between the regulation of the inner life of individual believers by Scripture and the regulation of the outer life of the corporate body according to human whim.

This principle involves a distinction between *elements* and *circumstances*: the former required for public worship and the government of the church, while the latter may be established according to the wisdom of the church so long as they are not made binding on the conscience. For example, *elements* of worship include preaching, the administration of the sacraments, the prayers, offerings, singing, confession of sin and declaration of pardon, and the benediction. The order of these elements, the wearing of a gown, the frequency of Communion, the specific details concerning the election of officers, and the hours set for public worship are *circumstances*.

As Lesslie Newbigin points out, Barth's interpretation goes beyond the Reformers (even Luther) when he sets the event of proclamation against the history of a covenant community. Although he has noted that Roman Catholic ecclesiology assimilates eschatology to history, Newbigin properly complains that in Barth's view, "the eschatological has completely pushed out the historical."[14] While it is true that Word and sacrament create and sustain the church, Newbigin rightly insists that "they do not create the Church *de novo*, or *ex nihilo*." After all, "Every setting forth of the word and sacraments of the Gospel is an event in the life of an actually existing Christian church...."[15]

The semirealized eschatological event occurs each Lord's Day. It is through this event that the church receives anew each week the gift of Christ and his benefits, through which the Spirit creates and sustains the faith by which the church exists. To the extent that this heavenly banquet is corrupted or diminished, the community gathered in Christ's name withers and eventually dies. Even if it continues to exist as a historical organization, it is no longer apostolic, and its candlestick is removed. Nevertheless, wherever the Word is preached and the sacraments are administered, a desert blossoms into a lush garden with the streams of living water.

---

14. Newbigin, *The Household of God*, 50.   15. Ibid., 50–51.

Based on Christ's inviolable pledge, there has always been and will always be a visible church that is fed by apostolic truth, but there is no guarantee that a particular congregation or denomination will always belong to this apostolic church apart from that ministry. The Spirit who sometimes disorders the settled life of the church when it does not conform to his Word also reorders it, so that the church is always being built up. This upbuilding takes place across generations through a public, ordered, and disciplined ministry. Chaotic use of spiritual gifts in the church may edify the individuals who employ them, but it does not build up the church, Paul warns (1Co 14:15–17). "Let all things be done for building up," he exhorts. "For God is not a God of confusion but of peace" (vv. 26, 33).

Reflecting the Separatist more than the Puritan Congregationalist legacy, the traditions of independent Protestantism today often seem reticent to identify even the well-being of the church with any outward order or form. In fact, the work of the Spirit is often not only separated from but contrasted with ecclesial forms and public rites. Even preaching is increasingly regarded in evangelical circles as an indifferent form of communication. If other media teach, edify, or persuade more relevantly, then why should we feel constrained by this traditional form? In fact, the extraordinary work of the Spirit is often identified with the degree to which an event or experience is direct and immediate, circumventing creaturely agency. As Baptist theologian Dale Moody concludes, "The priority of the spiritual organism over the institutional organization is obvious in all this great theological stream."[16] In this heritage, the church may be regarded as necessary chiefly for fellowship, but it is not typically understood as the mother of the faithful. Often, in fact, the church's official ministry is subordinated to (or even contrasted with) a spontaneous, unmediated, and private experience of conversion. Becoming a Christian is frequently contrasted with joining a church.

For Lutheran and Reformed traditions, apostolicity is identified with the apostolic preaching of Christ by which the church's speech and action are normed. A church is not apostolic because its office bearers trace their ordination to the apostles nor because it enjoys an ongoing charismatic ministry of revelation and prophecy, but because it passes on what it has heard from this qualitatively unique circle of ambassadors appointed by Christ in his earthly ministry. As an *eschatological* and *pneumatological* community, the church is always put in question as to its apostolicity and must receive it ever anew from the Word and Spirit. As a *covenantal* community, it is historically continuous from generation to generation. A biblical view of apostolicity refuses to set the formal against the informal, the external and

---

16. Dale Moody, *The Word of Truth* (Grand Rapids: Eerdmans, 1981), 441.

visible against the internal and invisible. The Trinity works within creation and history while never becoming assimilated.

B. Apostolicity in Covenantal Perspective

I have argued that Reformed ecclesiology refuses the false choice between the church as a historical organization and as an eschatological event, between the church as a formal ministry employing divinely ordained means and offices and the church as an informal ministry of believers in dependence upon the Spirit. This perspective also refuses to identify apostolicity with an ongoing office of apostleship, with regard to the papal claims of Rome or the charismatic ministry of self-proclaimed prophets.

1. Apostolicity Identified with the Apostolic Gospel: The End of an Era

Even when the apostles were living, the saints were gathered weekly for the ministry of Word and sacrament. "They devoted themselves to the apostles' teaching and the fellowship, to the breaking of bread and the prayers" (Ac 2:42). Through this ministry, "the Lord added to their number day by day those who were being saved" (v. 47). The centrality of the Word is incontestable from the apostolic mission in Acts. Wherever growth occurs, it is attributed to the Word (Ac 6:7; 12:24; 19:20). It is the Word that prevails against unbelief. So Paul adds that Christ in his ascension distributed gifts: apostles, prophets, evangelists, pastors, and teachers. Through their ministry the saints will be built up into the body of Christ, "until we all attain to the unity of the faith and of the knowledge of the Son of God, to mature manhood, to the measure of the stature of the fullness of Christ," no longer tossed back and forth "with every wind of doctrine" (Eph 4:11 – 14).

As breathed out by the Spirit of God, the apostolic preaching of the Word created the church just as the original creation was the gift of the Father, speaking his Word, in the power of the Spirit. Against carnal sectarianism, the apostle insists that the Corinthian church "may learn by us not to go beyond what is written, that none of you may be puffed up in favor of one against another" (1Co 4:6). It is not simply the preaching of the Word, but specifically the preaching of the gospel, that is "the power of God for salvation" (Ro 1:16). It is not in "lofty speech or wisdom" that the kingdom advances, but through the preaching of Christ. "For I decided to know nothing among you except Jesus Christ and him crucified" (1Co 2:1 – 2). "So faith comes from hearing, and hearing through the word of Christ" (Ro 10:17).

At a bare minimum, then, a true visible church is recognized by this continuity with the apostolic proclamation. "Where the gospel is preached," there is a church; where a professing body fails to proclaim this message, or distorts and contradicts it, it cannot be considered a valid visible church. If it is possible even for a church that is in fellowship with the living apostles to become a false church (Gal 1:6–9; 3:1–10; 4:11, 20; Rev 2–3), then it is surely possible for churches in fellowship with their ministerial successors to have their lampstand removed. The church receives its identity, like its salvation, from outside of itself, in the gospel that gives it birth and constantly defines, nourishes, and establishes its unity, catholicity, holiness, and apostolicity.

We have seen that the Reformers identified Rome and Anabaptism as evidencing "enthusiasm" by insisting that the apostolic office remains open, and with it, fresh revelations. The New Testament draws a clear line between the extraordinary ministry of the apostles and the ordinary ministry of pastors and elders (1Ti 6:20; 2Ti 1:13–14). Although the apostles were eyewitnesses of Christ, and Paul himself asserts his apostleship on the basis of having received it directly and immediately from Christ rather than from the church (Gal 1:11–23), ordinary ministers, assisted by elders, must diligently teach and to refute anything that "is contrary to sound doctrine, in accordance with the gospel of the glory of the blessed God with which I have been entrusted" (1Ti 1:10–11). The distinction is qualitative, not quantitative. The apostles heard Christ directly, and their proclamation and writings were "breathed out" by the Spirit (2Ti 3:16), whereas we now, illumined by the Spirit, hear Christ through the word of the prophets and apostles, through the mouth of pastors and teachers.

While there were certainly traditions in the apostolic era that were unwritten but nevertheless binding on those who received them, all of those traditions that are normative for the whole church in all times and places have been committed to the canon. Furthermore, the offices for which Paul provides instruction to Timothy, in transition from the extraordinary apostolic ministry to the ordinary ministry that Timothy signals, are those of pastor/overseer (*poimēn/episkopos*), elder (*presbyteros*), and deacon (*diakonos*). While God "*gave . . . apostles [and] prophets*" (Eph 4:11) and the gifts of healing, languages, and prophecy were exhibited in the extraordinary ministry of the apostolic era, there are no instructions in these epistles for the ordination of the apostles' successors to their office.

Through the extraordinary ministry of the prophets and apostles, the Spirit delivered Christ's canon by inspiration, constituting the new covenant community; through the ordinary ministry of pastors, the Spirit guides the church by illumination as it is being shaped and normed by that constitution. Just as the event to which the apostles bore witness is unique, unrepeatable, and completed, their office is extraordinary and unique in the church's history.[17] Paul describes himself as part

---

17. See esp. Richard B. Gaffin Jr., *Perspectives on Pentecost: Studies in New Testament Teaching on the Gifts of the Holy Spirit* (Phillipsburg, N.J.: P&R, 1979).

of the foundation-laying episode in the church's history, adding, "For no one can lay a foundation other than that which is laid, which is Jesus Christ" (1Co 3:11). I take this to be a reference not only to the content but to the historical-eschatological uniqueness of the apostolic ministry. He is not issuing an imperative not to lay another foundation but is simply stating an indicative: another foundation *cannot* be laid.

2. THE DIVERSITY OF SPIRITUAL GIFTS: APOSTOLICITY AND THE GENERAL OFFICE

Apostolicity is especially connected to the special offices of pastors and teachers. Nevertheless, from this ministry of Word and sacrament the Spirit clothes Christ's body in a diversity of rich attire. Although some believers are given the responsibility of special office, all receive the general office of prophet, priest, and king. Although there are other references to spiritual gifts in the New Testament, the three primary passages are found in Paul's epistles: Romans 12, 1 Corinthians 12, and Ephesians 4. Significantly, these are also the primary passages in which Paul employs the metaphor of the head and body for the relationship of Christ and his church. "To each is given the manifestation of the Spirit for the common good" (1Co 12:7).

As we have seen, the Spirit's role in every external work of the Godhead is to bring to completion the effect of that word spoken by the Father in the Son. In creation, the Spirit is found brooding over the waters that are separated in order to create the dry land for God's dwelling place with humanity. This separation of the waters recurs in the exodus and is drawn upon by the apostles for baptism into Christ. The Spirit is also described as the breath of God, through whom he breathes life into Adam, and Jesus also breathes upon the disciples so that they may receive the Holy Spirit (Jn 20:22). In Exodus 31:1, God tells Moses that he has called Bezalel, "and I have filled him with the Spirit of God" in order to supervise the artists and craftsmen in the building of the tabernacle.

The more the Israelites complained against Moses, the more Moses complained to God:

> Why have you dealt ill with your servant? And why have I not found favor in your sight, that you lay the burden of all this people on me? Did I conceive all this people? Did I give them birth, that you should say to me, "Carry them in your bosom, as a nurse carries a nursing child," to the land that you swore to give their fathers? Where am I to get meat to give to all this people?... If you will treat me like this, kill me at once, if I find favor in your sight, that I may not see my wretchedness." (Nu 11:11–15)

Acceding to Moses' complaint, the Lord commanded him to appoint elders to assist him in his ministry. "And as soon as the Spirit rested on them, they prophesied.

But they did not continue doing it" (v. 25). Moses' prophetic ministry was continual, but the elders prophesied only in this unique instance—just long enough for their "deputy-assistant" office to be validated before the people. When Joshua complained to Moses that two elders were prophesying in the camp rather than around the tent with the other seventy, the prophet responded, "Are you jealous for my sake? Would that all the LORD's people were prophets, that the LORD would put his Spirit on them!" (v. 29). Obviously, that would make the people less of a burden.

Centuries later, Joel prophesied concerning the messianic age, "And it shall come to pass afterward, that I will pour out my Spirit on all flesh; your sons and your daughters shall prophesy, your old men shall dream dreams, and your young men shall see visions. Even on the male and female servants in those days I will pour out my Spirit" (Joel 2:28–29). In his Pentecost sermon in Acts 2, Peter announced to his hearers that this prophecy was fulfilled in their presence, as the crowd of visitors from many nations heard the gospel in their own language.

In his ascension, Christ poured out upon his people the same Spirit who had rested upon him during his earthly ministry. Unlike Moses, Christ was sufficient for the task of bearing God's people alone on his shoulders, even in the face of steeper opposition. Unlike Moses, he never complained of his burden. And unlike Moses, he not only interceded for transgressors, but fulfilled the law and bore their judgment in their place. He was not barred from entering Canaan, but was welcomed triumphantly into the true Promised Land, raised and exalted above every name in heaven and on earth. Now at last, the typological offices of prophet, priest, and king that had been reserved for special office bearers in the old covenant were realized in Christ as the head and in his whole body as his members. In the new creation, the office of prophet, priest, and king that was part and parcel of being created in God's image was restored. "But you are a chosen race, a royal priesthood, a holy nation," Peter tells believers in Christ (1Pe 2:9).

In Ephesians 4:7–16, the apostle says that the offices of prophets and apostles as well as pastors, teachers, and evangelists are gifts of Christ's heavenly ascension. Through this ministry, Christ builds up his body in sound doctrine. All believers are prophets, priests, and kings in their general office. Together they walk in godliness and spur each other on in the apostolic doctrine, faith, and good works. They are "filled with the Spirit, addressing one another in psalms and hymns and spiritual songs ..., submitting to one another out of reverence for Christ" (Eph 5:15–21).

Romans 12 and 1 Corinthians 12 expand the list. In addition to the gifts pertaining to the ministry of the Word (prophecy, teaching, and exhortation), there are the gifts of service and hospitality, healing, helping, administrating, tongues and their interpretation, giving, and mercy. Some of these gifts are exercised in the special offices of elders and deacons, but all of them are exercised in a general way by the whole body. Therefore, Christ exercises his public ministry of Prophet, Priest, and King through the special office of pastors, deacons, and elders, respectively, but these gifts are also distributed in varying degrees beyond the officers to the wider body.

The controversial question arises as to whether any of these gifts has ceased in the church. Particularly in the wake of the Pentecostal and charismatic movements, this question has divided Christians into two camps: cessationists (believing that the gifts of healing, prophecy, and tongues have ceased) and noncessationists. Noncessationists find no exegetical reason to distinguish some of these gifts and offices from others in terms of their perpetuity. However, cessationists hold that the New Testament itself makes a distinction between the foundation-laying era of the apostles and the era of building the church on their completed foundation (1Co 3:10–11). Although the New Testament establishes the offices of pastors/teachers, elders, and deacons, it does not establish perpetual prophetic or apostolic offices with their attendant sign-gifts. With this in mind, we must examine each gift in question.

Paul treats prophecy (*prophēteia*) as preaching, which although illumined by the Spirit is (unlike the Scriptures) noninspired and therefore must be tested (1Co 12:29; 14:29–32; 1Th 5:19–21). At Pentecost, the gift of tongues was a Spirit-given ability to proclaim the gospel in languages that one had not been taught. The diverse crowd of visitors to Jerusalem for the feast asked, "And how is it that we hear, each of us in his own native language?" (Ac 2:8). We should therefore understand "tongues" as synonymous with natural languages, which some were miraculously gifted to speak and others to interpret. This served not only as a sign that Christ's universal kingdom has dawned but as a practical way of disseminating the gospel from Jerusalem to the ends of the earth. None of these gifts was given for the personal edification of believers alone, but for the spread of the gospel and the maturity of the saints in that Word.

Similarly, the gift of healing was a sign that Christ's kingdom had arrived, bringing a preview of the consummation in all of its fullness at the end of the age. Yet signs always cluster in the Bible around significant turning points in redemptive history. Like the temporary prophesying of the elders in Moses' day, the extraordinary gifts of signs and wonders are given to validate the sacred ministry of human ambassadors. Once that ministry is validated, it no longer requires further confirmation.[18] It would seem, then, that the gift of prophets and apostles (along with the gifts of miracles, prophecy, and tongues) was given but fulfilled its foundation-laying function. Just as Paul's understudy Timothy was an ordinary minister, we find no evidence that his ministry was attended by extraordinary signs and wonders.

---

18. For an excellent treatment of this topic, see Gaffin, *Perspectives on Pentecost*, esp. 94–95, in relation to Grudem's contention that "prophets and apostles" in 1 Corinthians 12:28 and Ephesians 4:11 refer to the same group.

Some theologians, such as Wayne Grudem, recognize that the office of apostle has ceased, but are "unsure if this question" of the cessation of spiritual gifts "can be decided from Scripture."[19] With Grudem I agree that 1 Corinthians 13:8–13, which speaks of prophecies and tongues passing away "when the perfect comes," is inconclusive.[20] Paul is most likely referring to the consummation, when there will be no need for faith and hope and all that will endure into eternity is love (v. 13).

However, I do not find Grudem's case for continuing prophecy persuasive. He clearly distinguishes prophecy today from the prophecy that delivered the sacred oracles of Holy Scripture. This is both the strength and the weakness of his position. Grudem believes that the kind of prophecy that is ongoing in the church is distinguished from preaching and teaching by being "a spontaneous 'revelation' from God...."[21] "So the distinction is quite clear: if a message is the result of conscious reflection on the text of Scripture, containing interpretation of the text and application to life, then it is (in New Testament terms) a teaching. But if a message is the report of something God brings suddenly to mind, then it is a prophecy."[22]

In my view, this interpretation introduces a definition of prophecy that is not consistent with its practice in the apostolic church. Nowhere is prophecy distinguished by its spontaneous quality. Furthermore, in spite of his salutary caution against raising such prophecies to the level of Scripture, this interpretation still raises the question as to whether the Spirit issues new revelations that are not already communicated in Scripture. If prophecy is defined simply as proclaiming a Spirit-given insight into Scripture, then is this not synonymous with preaching?

Today, the Spirit validates this ordinary ministry of the gospel through preaching and sacrament: the signs and wonders that Christ instituted to confirm his Word. If it is true that the apostles understood their work to be an extraordinary ministry of foundation laying and their miraculous signs as its validation, then "no one can lay a foundation other than that which *is* laid, which is Jesus Christ.... If the work that anyone has built on the foundation survives, he will receive a reward" (1Co 3:11, 14, emphasis added).

While living stones are continually being added to the temple, the edifice itself is "built on the foundation of the apostles and prophets, Christ Jesus himself being the cornerstone" (Eph 2:20). As the person and work of the head is distinct from that of its members, the foundation-laying ministry of the apostles is different from the "upbuilding" ministry of their successors.

---

19. Wayne Grudem, *Systematic Theology: An Introduction to Bible Doctrine* (Grand Rapids: Zondervan, 1994), 906–12, 1031; cf. Wayne Grudem, *The Gift of Prophecy in the New Testament Today* (Westchester, Ill.: Crossway, 1988), 226–52.

20. For a good defense of the opposite view, see Robert Reymond, *What about Continuing Revelations and Miracles in the Presbyterian Church Today?* (Phillipsburg, N.J.: P&R, 1977), 32–35. See also Edmund P. Clowney, *The Church* (Downers Grove, Ill.: InterVarsity Press, 1995), 237–68.

21. Grudem, *Systematic Theology*, 1058.

22. Ibid.

Whereas apostolic preaching became Scripture, our proclamation, faith, and practice stand in continuity with the apostles to the extent that they conform to that rule. To understand Scripture as canon, within its ancient Near Eastern background, is to recognize that, like the redemptive work to which it testifies, it cannot be revised by addition or subtraction (Dt 4:2; Rev 22:18–19). While interpretations are always subject to change, the constitution has been given once and for all.

Similarly, the canon that witnesses to Jesus is the covenant that he ratified in his self-sacrifice. In its appeal to this canon and its practice of its stipulated rites, the church participates in the heavenly reality as servant rather than Lord of the covenant. Just as Jesus-history is qualitatively distinct from our own, the apostolic canon is qualitatively distinct from the subsequent tradition that interprets it. One is magisterial, the other ministerial. Just as the church does not extend or complete the work of redemption but receives, interprets, and proclaims it, so also the church does not extend or complete revelation. The interim between Christ's advents is not an era of writing new chapters in the history of redemption.[23] Rather, it is a period in which the Spirit equips us for the mission between Acts and the Apocalypse—right in the middle of the era of the ordinary ministry with its new covenant canon. Just as the church cannot extend the incarnation or complete Christ's atoning work, it cannot repeat Pentecost or prolong the extraordinary ministry of the apostles, but must instead receive this same word and Spirit for its ordinary ministry in this time between the times.

3. THE IMPORTANCE OF CHURCH OFFICE IN THE ORDINARY MINISTRY

Rejecting the view that the apostolic office itself is still in effect, I have argued that the church today is apostolic when it continues the apostolic faith and practice. However, this in no way diminishes the importance of the nonapostolic offices that Christ instituted in his church. Similar to the false separation of Christ from his church, the eschatological from the historical, and the unity of the church from its plurality is the division often made today, especially in evangelical circles, between the church as building and the church as people. In fact, it is through the ministry of Word and sacrament (addressed in Eph 4) that the Spirit gifts all of the saints for their role in the body.

Darrell Guder suggests that the Reformation's emphasis on "the marks of the church" tended to weaken its missional vocation by focusing on the church as place ("a place where certain things happen") rather than as the people ("a people who do certain things").[24] However, this undermines the very source of mission, namely, the priority of God's work over our work. In other words, if the church is not "a place where certain things happen" (i.e., preaching and sacrament), but is merely "a people

23. For this argument, see N. T. Wright, "How Can the Bible Be Authoritative?" *Vox Evangelica* 21 (1991): 7–32.

24. Darrell Guder, *The Missional Church: A Vision for the Sending of the Church in North America* (Grand Rapids: Eerdmans, 1998), 79–81.

who do certain things," then our works take precedence over God's works in salvation. The church becomes simply another group of moral, social, and political activists. However, precisely because the church is first of all the place where God does certain things, it becomes a people who belong to the new society that is being formed in this present evil age. By their acts of witness and deeds, they share the gifts they have been given with their neighbors. However, before they can serve they must be served. Before they can act, they must receive.

All of the people are priests, living stones being built into a holy sanctuary. Yet not all of the covenant people are ministers. All are sheep, but not all are shepherds under the Great Shepherd (as Paul especially argues in 1 Corinthians 11 and 12). There are different gifts and different callings within the one body. Christ is the sole mediator between God and humanity (1Ti 2:5), but he has given "the apostles, the prophets, the evangelists, the shepherds and teachers" to his body "building [it] up" (Eph 4:5–16). These differing gifts generate special offices of ministry and oversight. However, such graces are not qualities (or, as in Roman Catholic terminology, an indelible "character") sacramentally infused into ministers so that they might be elevated ontologically above the laity. They are simply gifts for particular offices, given in order to serve the rest of the body. As Christ has promised, he has not left us orphans, but is present by the Spirit through the ministry of the Word.

Admittedly, this is a difficult interpretation to affirm, especially since most of our modern translations (in contrast to older ones) render Ephesians 4:11–12 as follows: "The gifts he gave were that some would be apostles, some prophets, some evangelists, some pastors and teachers, to equip the saints for the work of ministry …" (NRSV, but also essentially the same construction in other modern translations, including the ESV). However, there are good reasons for preferring the older translations (for example, the King James Version), which render the verses, "And he gave some, apostles; and some, prophets; and some, evangelists; and some, pastors and teachers; for the perfecting of the saints, for the work of the ministry, for the edifying of the body of Christ."

Reflecting the actual construction of the Greek, the older translation draws three lines of purpose clauses from the offices given that newer translations obscure. The same officers who are given for the completion (not equipping) of the saints are also given for the work of ministry and edification of the body.[25] On this reading,

---

25. Our interpretation depends largely on whether we render *katartismon* in verse 12a "equip" and *eis* "for" or render them "complete" and "in." It is possible lexically to render *katartismon* either "equip" or "complete" (also train). However, "completion" fits better with the logic of the argument, where the analogy is that of a body growing up into maturity. This occurs through Christ's gift of evangelists, pastors, and teachers. Furthermore, this gift is given for the express purpose of "building up the body of Christ, until we all attain to the *unity of the faith* and of the *knowledge of the Son of God*, to mature manhood … so that we may no longer be children, tossed to and fro by the waves and carried about by every wind of *doctrine* …," but instead be engaged in "speaking the truth in love …" (vv. 12–15).

Christ has given apostles, prophets, evangelists, and pastors and teachers for the ministry of the Word that brings the whole body to unity, maturity and completion in the truth. This is not to say that the body is *complete* in and through these offices alone, for there are other gifts mentioned elsewhere (esp. Ro 12 and 1Co 12). However, the focus here is restricted to that work of bringing unity and maturity to the body through sound doctrine.

Favoring this interpretation of Ephesians 4, Andrew Lincoln comments, "An active role for all believers is safeguarded by vv. 7, 16, but the primary context here in v. 12 is the function and role of Christ's specific gifts, the ministers, not that of all the saints. Rendering *katartismon* 'completion' has a straightforward meaning which does not require supplementing by a further phrase, and *diakonia*, 'service,' is more likely to refer to the *ministry* of the *ministers* just named." Thus, it is "hard to avoid the suspicion that opting for the other view is too often motivated by a zeal to avoid clericalism and to support a 'democratic' model of the Church."[26]

It is significant that the gifts mentioned in Romans 12:3–8 and 1 Corinthians 12:4–28 include hospitality, giving, administration, and other acts of service, but Ephesians 4 only mentions Christ's gift of officers to his church for the maturity of the whole body in sound doctrine. So the point is that in his ascension Christ has given the ministry of the Word to his people as a gift. This does not mean that those who are not ministers are not gifted and called to love and serve each other, but that comes later in verses 17 through the whole of chapter 5. Before they serve, they are served. This underscores again the remarkable generosity of the church's victorious head, that he would make his people receivers first and active givers as a result.

While every member and every gift is needed in order for the body to be fully operative, the very life of the body depends on the faithful maintenance of the ministry of Word and sacrament. Not all members of the body can devote themselves exclusively to the Word and prayer, as Peter observed (Ac 6:2–7), but if some do not (especially out of a misguided assumption that every member is a minister), the sheep will not be fed and the body will not be built up into Christ. In fact, when the apostles were freed for this work by the appointment of deacons, we read, "So the word of God continued to increase" (Ac 6:7). If Peter needed to be freed up for this work, then certainly ordinary ministers must be preserved as much as possible from secular affairs and even the necessary and important details of church administration.

26. Andrew T. Lincoln, *Ephesians* (WBC; Dallas: Word, 1990), 253; cf. T. David Gordon, "'Equipping' Ministry in Ephesians 4," *JETS* 37, no. 1 (March 1994): 69–78. It is also interesting to read Calvin's commentary on this passage (*Commentaries on the Epistles of Paul to the Galatians and Ephesians* [trans. William Pringle; Grand Rapids: Baker, 1996], 277–86), especially since the more recent translation does not even occur to him. For this very reason, he seems to capture the flow of the passage's argument more smoothly than many commentators who follow the newer translation.

Through this ministry, we are all recipients of the unity of the faith, the knowledge of the Son of God, and maturity in Christ. Therefore, that which we all possess jointly already in Christ (one God and Father, one Spirit, one Lord, one faith, one baptism) is preserved by Christ from generation to generation. On the basis of this gift of ambassadors, the other members of the body receive what they need so that they may "no longer walk as the Gentiles do, in the futility of their minds" (Eph 4:17), but live out their calling in the world (vv. 18–24). They even participate in the service, not only as recipients but as actors, "addressing one another in psalms and hymns and spiritual songs, singing and making melody to the Lord with [their] heart, giving thanks always and for everything to God the Father in the name of our Lord Jesus Christ, submitting to one another out of reverence for Christ" (5:15–21). For all of this, a formal ministry of the Word is essential.

Not only as a community but as a church, the body is connected to its head in audible and visible bonds. For example, the *Westminster Confession* declares,

> The Lord Jesus, as king and head of his Church, hath therein appointed a government in the hand of Church officers, distinct from the civil magistrate. To these officers the keys of the Kingdom of Heaven are committed, by virtue whereof they have power respectively to retain and remit sins, to shut that kingdom against the impenitent, both by the word and censures; and to open it unto penitent sinners, by the ministry of the gospel, and by absolution from censures, as occasion shall require.[27]

In addition to the local church, there are broader assemblies of the church, whose conclusions "are to be received with reverence and submission, not only for their agreement with the Word, but also for the power whereby they are made, as being an ordinance of God, appointed thereunto in his Word."[28]

The confession acknowledges that such bodies "have erred and do err" and adds, "Synods and councils are to handle or conclude nothing but that which is ecclesiastical and are not to meddle with civil affairs which concern the commonwealth unless by way of humble petition in cases extraordinary...."[29] The Word and the Spirit create a historical community, but precisely because they are Word and Spirit, they always put that community in question, breaking up its presumptuous autonomy, so that the event of Christ's action among us will not be assimilated to the history of this passing age.

Paul claimed a direct commission from Christ (Gal 1:1–2:14), and Peter referred to Paul's letters as "Scriptures" (2Pe 3:16). Yet both submitted themselves to the broader assembly. As branches can be broken off and candlesticks can be removed, particular churches can lose their living connection to the visible body of Christ

---

27. *Westminster Confession of Faith*, in *The Book of Confessions* (Louisville: PCUSA General Assembly, 1991), 32.1–2.

28. Ibid., 33.2.

29. Ibid., 33.4.

(implied in Rev 2 and 3). Paul threatened as much in his stern remarks to the Galatians. The book of Acts reveals the gradual consensus reached by the apostles and elders through a process of mutual correction and admonition—sometimes even stern rebukes—concerning the mission to the Gentiles. Everything was defined by the gospel, which was beyond their command or control, and the Spirit used the collegial process of new covenant government to bring about this consensus. Christ is the sole Head, who creates his body by his Word and Spirit, regulating it by his sovereign decrees. This reign of Christ is mediated by the Word and Spirit through a plurality of pastors and elders in assembly. Ordinary ministers today can hardly be exempt from this mutual correction and admonition that the apostles were bound to uphold. In fact, as Calvin points out in commenting on Ephesians 4, it is significant that no mention is made in this passage of the papal office as essential to the unity of the church in faith and doctrine. "If he knew a primacy which had a fixed residence, was it not his duty, for the benefit of the whole church, to exhibit one ministerial head placed over all the members, under whose government we are collected into one body?"[30]

Ambassadors are not just witnesses, but they are also restricted in their authority by the commission that they have received. As with the catholicity of the church, apostolicity is constituted by the ministry of the apostolic faith and is maintained by the assembly of ministers and elders together, over which Christ himself presides. Drawing on the Antiochene emphasis on "ambassadorship," Orthodox theologian John Zizioulas points out that ministers receive grace *to serve others*. "This does not imply that the minister himself is not in need of that grace. The point is that he needs it precisely because he does not 'possess' it but gets it himself as a member of the community."[31] For this reason, Zizioulas suggests, we should be cautious about such terms as "vicar," as if it were "a representation of someone who is absent."[32]

> The fundamental implication of this is that there is no priesthood as a general and vague term, as it was to become later on in theology under the name of *sacerdotium.*... The true and historically original meaning of the term [priest] is this: as Christ (the only priest) becomes in the Holy Spirit a community (His body, the Church), His priesthood is realized and portrayed in historical existence here and now as a Eucharistic community in which His "image" is the head of this community offering with and on behalf of the community the Eucharistic gifts.[33]

In this way, "the community itself becomes priestly in the sense of 1 Peter 2:5, 9," not by flowing from the priest, but resulting from the eucharistic gathering (*synaxis*) of the whole body.[34]

---

30. Calvin, *Commentaries on Galatians and Ephesians*, 280.
31. John Zizioulas, *Being as Communion* (Crestwood, N.Y.: St. Vladimir's Seminary Press, 1985), 227–28.
32. Ibid., 230.
33. Ibid.
34. Ibid., 231.

As I argued in the previous chapter (appealing especially to Acts 15), even in the era of the apostles themselves, ecclesiastical power was not concentrated in one apostle or even in the apostolate collectively, but in the consensus of the "apostles and elders" in solemn assembly. Distributed across the wider framework of pastors and elders from local assemblies who formed a broader assembly, this power reflected the diversity as much as the unity of Pentecost.

Apostolic succession, like all other attributes of the church, is therefore determined by the *content* of the church's ministry rather than by the historical succession of *persons* ordained to office. At the same time, those who minister in Christ's name must be called to that office by Christ through the agency of the church: they cannot send themselves on the basis of an inward call alone, but must be sent, which again emphasizes the mission as concerned chiefly with heralding good news (Ro 10:14–15).

Analogous to the Father's sending of the Son and the sending of the Spirit by the Father and the Son, and their joint-commission of the apostles, is the wider church's calling and sending of pastors and elders to their local post and the local church's sending of its representatives to its wider assemblies. Because these officers do not send themselves (any more than the Son or the Spirit sent himself), and because their commission from God is tested and validated by the church that bears the marks, their hearers can be assured that they are not speaking on their own authority when they bring God's Word. The ordinary ministers do not receive their gift and commission directly from God alone, but through "the laying on of the hands of the eldership [*presbyterion*]" (1Ti 4:14).

The church's order, government, liturgy, and discipline do not create the church; the Spirit does this, working through the Word. Nevertheless, God's Word creates a real, concrete, visible society over which Christ reigns as Savior and Lord. Under Christ, each believer has been gifted for a particular function in the one body. "If the whole body were an eye, where would be the sense of hearing?" (1Co 12:12–26). The church is not, properly speaking, the magisterium or the ministerium, but the whole body. Nevertheless, this does not mean that every part does the same thing. As the pastoral epistles elaborate, the transferable aspects of the extraordinary apostolic vocation have been entrusted to the ordinary offices of pastors and elders. So we must avoid a legalism that subverts the unique authority of Christ and his Word by addition as well as an antinomian spirit of subtraction. The authority that Christ delegates to ministers, elders, and deacons is real, but it is unlike the domination exercised by Gentile rulers. Although all believers are prophets, priests, and kings in Christ, they receive and grow up together in this identity through the ministry of some believers who are specially called to particular offices as servants of the Word, deacons, and elders. The officers fulfill their ministry in the official administration of the church, while the rest fulfill their broader calling as believers in the world through their secular callings as parents, teachers, businesspeople, nurses, and neighbors.

The forensic word generates an effective, transformative, and regulated existence in history. Christ is both Savior and Lord. The gospel, in other words, leads to obedience. Between the extremes of *divinizing* and *secularizing*, there is the *sanctification* of creaturely reality by the Spirit for the work of bringing about the perlocutionary effect of the gospel.[35] Drawing on Jesus' petition in John 17:17, we recognize that sanctification in the word of truth draws together not only the themes of holiness and catholicity but apostolicity as well.

Apostolicity is guaranteed neither by immanent history nor by inner immediacy, but is a gift *from* above *in* time and *across* time. On this point, as on the others that we have considered, only the ministry of the Spirit working through the Word and the sacraments, maintaining discipline across the generations, is able to sustain this kind of integrated praxis.

C. KEYS OF THE KINGDOM: THE MINISTRY OF RECONCILIATION

A minister is not a master. Yet it is also true that a minister is not a facilitator, coach, or team leader. Ministers do not serve at the pleasure of the people, but at the pleasure of the King. It is not their church or their ministry, but Christ's; and it is in their office, not in their person, that they represent his heavenly authority. Not only in the sermon, but throughout the service, they are God's covenant attorneys. Many Christian liturgies include at some point the Aaronic blessing: "The LORD bless and keep you.... The LORD lift up his countenance upon you and give you peace" (Nu 6:24–26). These words are not mere well-wishing, but are God's act of blessing his people. Ministering as diplomats of Yahweh, the priests actually placed God's benediction on the people. It was a legal, covenantal action, a performative utterance that placed the people under the blessings rather than the curses of the covenant: "So shall they *put my name upon* the people of Israel, *and I will bless them*" (v. 27, emphasis added). And in the mouths of ministers of the Word today, it has the same performative nature.

We could cite many other examples (such as Ps 4:6; 34:16, 18, repeated in 1Pe 3:10–12) showing this close connection between God's *face* and God's *nearness* in *ḥesed*, covenant faithfulness. Christ himself placed God's covenantal blessing on his people, as in the beatitudes (Mt 5:1–11) and in his postresurrection meal in the upper room with the disciples, declaring, "Peace to you!" (Lk 24:36). These are

---

35. In two recent books, *Holy Scripture: A Dogmatic Sketch* (Cambridge: Cambridge Univ. Press, 2003), 5–41, and *Holiness* (Grand Rapids: Eerdmans, 2003), John Webster has richly developed this theme.

performative utterances: indicatives, rather than imperatives. In the beatitudes, the disciples are blessed not because they are poor in spirit, mourn, or are meek, hungry, merciful, pure in heart, peacemakers, or persecuted. Rather, these who *are* blessed by Christ are for that reason reviled by the world yet persevere in showing good to their enemies (vv. 11 – 12). They bless because they are already blessed.

As we have seen in the repeated assurances God gave to Moses, God's handing over of his personal name to invoke as Israel's suzerain is his covenantal pledge. "Everyone who calls on the name of the Lord shall be saved" (Ro 10:13, quoting Joel 2:32; cf. Ac 2:21). "I will lift up the cup of salvation and call on the name of the Lord, I will pay my vows to the Lord in the presence of all his people" (Ps 116:13 – 14). At the same time, God's covenant attorneys (the prophets) were given the unpleasant task of prosecuting God's judgment — of declaring their hearers *lōʾ-ʿammî*, "Not My People" (Hos 1:9), though they were also charged with making "ready a people prepared for the Lord" (Lk 1:17) and even with announcing to those who "once were not a people" that they are now "the people of God" (Hos 1:10; Ro 9:25; 2Co 6:16; Tit 2:14; 1Pe 2:10; Rev 21:3).

In this in-between time, the business of the church is receiving and delivering the gift of salvation, not contributing to the gift, negotiating its terms, or determining either its content or methods of delivery. The authority of ambassadors is always representative and delegated, not autonomous and absolute. Since it is the era of gathering guests from the highways and byways to be seated at the heavenly banquet, the mission that the marks serve is that of opening and shutting doors. Jesus faulted the religious leaders of his day on this very point: "For you shut the kingdom of heaven in people's faces. For you neither enter yourselves nor allow those who would enter to go in" (Mt 23:13). Jesus is not only the shepherd; he is the "gate" of his sheep (Jn 10:7). This gate is flung wide now but is about to be closed by "the owner of the house." The insiders who think that they have a right to sit at the table of the kingdom will be outsiders, while those "from east and west, and from north and south" gather at the feast with "Abraham and Isaac and Jacob and all the prophets in the kingdom of God." "And behold, some are last who will be first, and some are first who will be last" (Lk 13:22 – 30).

The question of the marks is therefore bound up with the subject of the keys, with its Old Testament backdrop. In Isaiah 22, Jerusalem's destruction is prophesied and the self-seeking officials are denounced. They are a "shame of [their] master's house" (v. 18). Therefore, God declares, "I will thrust you from your office, and you will be pulled down from your station." Instead, another will be installed. "I will place on his shoulder the key of the house of David; he shall open, and none shall shut; he shall shut, and none shall open. And I will fasten him like a peg in a secure place, and he will become a throne of honor to his father's house" (vv. 19 – 23).

In that light, we overhear Jesus' announcement to Peter: "And I tell you, you are Peter, and on this rock I will build my church, and the gates of hell will not prevail against it. I will give you the keys of the kingdom of heaven, and whatever you bind on earth shall be bound in heaven, and whatever you loose on earth shall be loosed in heaven" (Mt 16:18–19). This office is extended to the whole apostolate in chapter 18, when Jesus establishes the ecclesiastical court for the settling of disputes, where "whatever you loose on earth shall be loosed in heaven" (vv. 15–20).

In the Gospels we see the disciples slowly coming to understand Christ's identity and mission, especially as he opened the Scriptures (Lk 24:6–8, 13–27) and made himself known in the breaking of bread (vv. 28–35), concluding with the benediction, "Peace to you!" (v. 36). Furthermore, a direct link to Isaiah 22 is made in Revelation 3:7: "And to the angel of the church in Philadelphia write: 'The words of the holy one, the true one, who has the key of David, who opens and no one will shut, who shuts and no one opens.'" Similarly, in John 20, the resurrected Jesus breathes on his disciples, saying, "Receive the Holy Spirit. If you forgive the sins of any, they are forgiven them; if you withhold forgiveness from any, it is withheld" (vv. 22–23). Anyone who receives the apostles receives Christ himself (Mt 10:40; cf. John 13:20).

Jesus' commissionings of his disciples in Matthew 16, 18, and climactically in 28:16–20 all make the point that the act of opening and shutting heaven's gates is identical with the ministry of Word, sacrament, and discipline. *In other words, the mission of the church is identical with the marks of the church.* Even now, Christ exercises his threefold office through his ambassadors. Herman Ridderbos points out the origins of the concept of apostle (*šālîaḥ*) in the power of attorney stipulated in the Jewish legal system. This heralding of the direct words of Christ himself "designates the content of the gospel in its original, historically visible and audible form."[36]

The apostles were called directly and immediately, by Christ himself. After that era, ordinary ministers are called through the voice of the church. Every time the Word is preached and the sacraments are administered (or not administered to particular individuals), this magisterial ministry of Christ is exercised ministerially by his officers. In fact, the context of "binding and loosing" in Matthew 18 is church discipline: again we must remember both the difference between and the union of sign and reality, and remember both the "already" and the "not yet." The church's decisions and actions have real authority, though not final authority. The determinations of the servant may not always coincide with those of the Master; nevertheless, as we see in the Great Commission, the basis for the commission to go into all the world and preach the gospel through the ministry of Word, sacrament,

---

36. Herman Ridderbos, *Redemptive History and the New Testament Scriptures* (trans. H. De Jongste; rev. Richard B. Gaffin Jr.; Phillipsburg, N.J.: P&R, 1963; 2nd rev. ed., 1988), 14.

and discipline is Christ's completed work: "All authority in heaven and on earth has been given to me. Go therefore and make disciples of all nations, baptizing...[and] teaching..." (Mt 28:18–20). The apostles were ambassadors (2Co 5:12; 5:18–6:2); they did not create the kingdom or its policies, but communicated them. In Romans 10, Paul summarizes the logic that links the message of the gospel to the mission of the church. Salvation comes from heaven: by grace alone in Christ alone. This salvation is applied to us here and now through hearing the proclamation of Christ through an earthly emissary. All of this stands in contrast with the logic of works righteousness, by which one attempts to ascend to heaven to acquire salvation. So the minister (*doulos, didaskalos*) is also a "herald" or "ambassador" to whom God has given "the ministry of reconciliation," and all for one purpose: "so that in him [Christ] we might become the righteousness of God" (2Co 5:18–21). Seyoon Kim relates that even this language is borrowed from the world of ancient treaty making. The Greeks never used it "in a religious context for the relationship between God and human beings," but in the process of political or military peace-treaties. It is in this light that we recognize the import of Paul's invocation of such terminology as "'ambassadors' (*presbeuō*) sent to 'petition' (*deomai*) or 'appeal' (*parakaleō*) to warring parties for reconciliation."[37] John Webster wisely reminds us that this ministry of reconciliation spoken of in 2 Corinthians 5 "is that which God *gave.*" "That is to say, it is a matter of election or appointment. It does not spring into being as an activity of a busy imagined community with a lively sense of the need for alternatives to oppression and marginalization." "Reconciliation" is not a general work of improving the world for which the church has volunteered, but is "strictly derivable from the content of the church's proclamation of salvation."[38] This ministry of reconciliation is described as primarily speech, "the message of reconciliation" (v. 19), of which we are "ambassadors."[39] It is announcing the policy of Christ's regime, not using the name of Christ for whatever "reconciling" activities the church might find useful or important in the world.

An apostle is Christ's own representative, even if perhaps "an ambassador in chains" (Eph 6:20). Even Timothy, who is a minister in the ordinary office rather than an apostle, is said to be "our brother and *God's co-worker* [*synergon tou theou*] in proclaiming the gospel of Christ ..." (1Th 3:2, author's trans.). Ministers in their office do in fact serve Christ's own saving reign by his Word and Spirit—"God making his appeal through us" (2Co 5:20a). Therefore, the call to be reconciled to

---

37. Seyoon Kim, "The Origin of Paul's Concept of Reconciliation," in *The Road from Damascus: The Impact of Paul's Conversion on His Life, Thought, and Ministry* (ed. Richard N. Longenecker; Grand Rapids: Eerdmans, 1997), 104. Cf. C. Breytenbach, *Versöhnung: Eine Studie zur paulinischen Soteri-*

ologie (Neukirchen-Vluyn: Neukirchener Verlag, 1989).

38. John Webster, "Christ, Church and Reconciliation," in *Word and Church* (Edinburgh: T&T Clark, 2001), 222.

39. Ibid.

God is made "on behalf of Christ" himself (v. 20b).[40] "As we work together with him [Christ], we urge you also not to accept the grace of God in vain ... Behold, now is the favorable time; behold, now is the day of salvation!" (2Co 6:1–2).

Besides preaching and sacrament, the ministry of the keys includes church discipline. The word "discipline" has a negative connotation today, but it is a cognate of the word for "teaching." The Word corrects by public and private instruction. Every time the Word is faithfully taught and applied (in public and in private), Christ disciplines—that is, makes disciples. Reformed churches therefore recognized discipline as a third mark of the church.[41]

Ironically, many Protestant bodies today (on the left and right) want to impose a discipline on the world, making pronouncements on a wide variety of political, moral, social, and economic issues, while often neglecting proper oversight of their own churches. Paul points out explicitly in 1 Corinthians 5:9–13 that this is exactly backwards. The church has no authority to direct secular affairs, but it does have the responsibility to preserve the peace and prosperity of Christ's sheep, in both doctrine and life.

The point of a presbyterian polity is to spread the ministerial authority and accountability in the church out to the many, at the local level and with recourse to broader assemblies, rather than to place it in the hands of one pastor or oligarchy of power. Therefore, Christ's earthly government is neither monarchical nor democratic, but representative (federal). The elders and deacons do not represent the people, but the Covenant Lord, and are chosen for their godly wisdom in faith and practice. And yet, because this ministerial authority is spread out rather than

---

40. Mark Gignilliat, "2 Corinthians 6:2: Paul's Eschatological 'Now' and Hermeneutical Invitation," *WTJ* 67 (2005): 147–61: "Paul's quotation of Isa 49:8 in 2 Cor 6:2 is an eschatological reading of the text in its plain sense that is faithful to its final canonical form and an invitation into the eschatological world of Isa 40–55 (66), a text that for Paul has abiding theological/eschatological significance for our understanding of Christ's person and mission" (160).

41. Although some Reformed theologians (Calvin, Bullinger, Zanchius, Junius, Gomarus, van Mastricht, à Marck) identified only the preaching of the gospel and the administration of the sacraments as the marks of the church, others added discipline (Hyperius, Vermigli, Ursinus, de Brès), and the latter came to expression in the *Belgic* as well as the *Westminster Confession*. Ironically, for those who are fond of setting Luther and Calvin in opposition on the third use of the law (i.e., guiding believers), Calvin acknowledged only the two marks in his writings, while Luther had included church discipline as a mark in "On the Councils and the Church": "Now where you see sins forgiven or reproved in some persons, be it publicly or privately, you may know that God's people are there. If God's people are not there, the keys are not there either; and if the keys are not present

for Christ, God's people are not present. Christ bequeathed them as a public sign and a holy possession, whereby the Holy Spirit again sanctifies the fallen sinners redeemed by Christ's death, and whereby the Christians confess that they are a holy people in this world under Christ. And those who refuse to be converted or sanctified again shall be cast out from this holy people, that is bound and excluded by means of the keys, as happened to the unrepentant Antinomians." Martin Luther, "On the Councils and the Church," in *Church and Ministry III* (ed. E. W. Gritsch; vol. 41 of *Luther's Works*; Philadelphia: Fortress, 1966), 153; cf. David Yeago, "The Office of the Keys: On the Disappearance of Discipline in Protestant Modernity," in *Marks of the Body of Christ* (ed. Carl Braaten and Robert Jenson; Grand Rapids: Eerdmans, 1999), 95–123. Questions in the Reformed churches have arisen as to whether discipline was necessary to the being (*esse*) or to the well-being (*bene esse*) of the church. As Berkhof observes, Abraham Kuyper concluded that only the preaching of the Word and administration of the sacraments distinguish the church from all other institutions, are the objective means of grace, and constitute the church in its very existence (Louis Berkhof, *Systematic Theology* [Grand Rapids: Eerdmans, 577).

consolidated in one place (locally, nationally, or internationally), both members and officers have access to due process in church courts.

In commissioning his disciples with the keys that are properly his own, Jesus explicitly announced a union of the sign (ministerial binding and loosing "on earth") and the signified (magisterial binding and loosing "in heaven"). God's sanctification of ordinary, creaturely action for divine, heavenly purposes means, on one hand, that the church's juridical authority is *ministerial rather than magisterial* and, on the other hand, that it is *more than witness.*

To be sure, ministerial authority is often abused. However, at least in a connectional form of government, there are checks against arbitrary acts of power. The threat of magisterial authority is greater when power is lodged, explicitly or implicitly, in the personal charisma, skills, or success of leaders rather than in their office. Besides the tragic cases of abuse, our nervousness about acknowledging the New Testament commands to submit to office bearers owes much to our highly egalitarian culture, which celebrates individualism, narcissism, and disregard for external norms.

The distinct gifts and offices that Christ has given to his church for its existence and maturity are intended to build up the whole body precisely for its varied acts of mutual service and mission. The ministry of binding and loosing, when placed in the context of gospel proclamation, is not ancillary to mission; it *is* the mission of the church in the world. It is the *authorization* to go, given by the one to whom all authority has been given, and to know that "whoever receives the one I send receives me, and whoever receives me receives the one who sent me" (Jn 13:20). This ministry is now entrusted publicly to officers, but all believers share in the general office of prophets, priests, and kings under Christ.

A church may be lacking in hospitality, administration, giving, or service. While these wounds may certainly be serious, they are not deadly. However, the absence or corruption of God's Word and sacraments blocks the delivery of heavenly gifts to the world. Therefore, discipline is essential for upholding these two marks. Christ does not gather his scattered sheep only to leave them susceptible to external and internal threats. Therefore, although the Word and the sacraments are the means of the church's existence and sustenance in a way that cannot be said of any other characteristic, discipline may be properly called a mark of the church.[42] Pastors feed, elders rule, and deacons service the saints in their temporal welfare.

D. THE MARKS AND THE MISSION

Contemporary church life is often impoverished by a false choice between the church as a place where certain things happen (the public ministry outlined in Acts

---

42. Berkhof, *Systematic Theology*, 578.

2:42) and as a people who do certain things. Churches judged to be of the former stripe are reckoned ingrown, while the latter embrace a "missional" perspective.[43] To be missional, in this view, is not the same as being missions minded. Rather than thinking of the church as a place where the people are served and then sending missionaries to plant churches in other parts of the world, a missional approach sees the church as a people who are sent to serve their neighbors in their community. Concomitant with this view is the idea that our "living the gospel," especially in our postmodern environment, will be more effective than its proclamation.

This emphasis on the church as God's mission into the world (*missio Dei*) offers many bracing criticisms and constructive proposals that we would be unwise to ignore.[44] It is certainly true that the church is not simply a place where certain things happen but is also a people who do certain things. In fact, this point was emphasized in the Reformation. However, the Reformers drew a crucial distinction between the church in its public ministry of preaching, sacrament, catechesis, discipline, diaconal service, and missions on one hand and the church as the people scattered in their worldly vocations during the week. In the former sense, the body of Christ is served, enjoying its Sabbath rest from secular callings and commitments, to be fed at Christ's banquet and filled with his Spirit. In the latter sense, the same body loves and serves its neighbors in the world. However, if the church is not first of all the place where Christians are made, then it cannot be a community of witnesses and servants. Resting comes before working. Justification comes before sanctification. God's decision and activity come before ours. Christians are not the gospel, because they are not the ongoing incarnation of Christ. The gospel is Christ's life, death, and resurrection. It is not a message about the love, virtues, and good works of the church, but of God's love, mercy, and work in Jesus Christ. Therefore, the gospel-shaped lives of believers are the "aroma" of Christ, but the gospel's content is Christ himself. As we have seen, faith comes through hearing the gospel, brought to us by heralds sent from God. Our faithful living, in love and service to our neighbors, prepares the way for this hearing of the gospel, but we must never forget that it is this hearing that brings the justification and new life that create, sustain, build up, and expand the church. Thus, the church must be missions minded, treating both its members and the unchurched, at home and abroad, as sinners who need to hear and receive the gospel. And it also needs to be missional in the sense of living out its faith through its activity in the many callings that belong to every believer as employee, employer, parent, child, volunteer, citizen, and neighbor.

---

43. The term *missional* (at least as a label) seems to have originated with Darrell L. Guder and Lois Barrett, eds., *The Missional Church: A Vision for the Sending of the Church in North America* (Grand Rapids: Eerdmans, 1998).

44. In my view, this emphasis is given a more balanced articulation in Lesslie Newbigin, *The Open Secret: An Introduction to the Theology of Mission* (Grand Rapids: Eerdmans, 1995).

Two other dangers in this polarization between the church as place where certain things are done and as a people who do certain things are a deadening formalism and clerical elitism on one hand and a moral activism that keeps the sheep from being served the Bread of Life on the other. In Acts, the mission of the church and its actual growth are always attributed to the means of grace, which the so-called marks of the church (preaching, sacrament, and discipline) identify.

The preaching of the Word and the administration of the sacraments have (or at least should have) such preeminence in the church not because of the desire for clerical dominance over the laity; on the contrary, it is because of the unique and essential service that this ministry provides for the health of the whole body and its mission in the world. So instead of treating the formal ministry and marks of the church as one thing and the mission of the church as another, we should regard the former not only as the source but as in fact the same thing as the latter. Throughout the book of Acts, the growth of the church—its mission—is identified by the phrase, "And the word of God spread." The regular gathering of the saints for "the apostles' teaching and the fellowship," "the breaking of bread," and "the prayers" (Ac 2:42) is not treated in Acts merely as an exercise in spiritual togetherness but as itself the sign that the kingdom had arrived in the Spirit.

Furthermore, it issued in a community that brought wonder and awe to its neighbors. Being built up into Christ, the members of this community realized a communion with each other that crossed the lines established by this present age. Richly fed with Christ and his gifts, they shared their gifts—spiritual and temporal—with each other and with outsiders, so that the Word of Christ continued to reverberate in ever-expanding rings from pulpit, font, and table to pew and then out into office buildings, homes, and restaurants as believers lived out their existence in the world.

The mission of the church is to execute the marks of the church, which are the same as the keys of the kingdom. Where the gospel is being preached, the sacraments are being administered, and the officers are caring for the flock, we may be confident that the mission is being executed, the keys are being exercised, and the attributes of "one holy, catholic, and apostolic church" are being exhibited. Preaching, sacrament, and discipline are singled out in the Great Commission and, as we have seen, in Acts 2:42. If these are missing, marginalized, or obscured, there is no office, no charismatic ministry, and no innovative program that can build and expand Christ's kingdom. God may use many means, but he has ordained these and has promised to work the greatest signs and wonders through them.

At least in American Protestantism, the tendency to pit the formal ministry of the church against the mission of its members (principally, in terms of personal and societal transformation) owes much to revivalist Charles Finney. Concerning the complex of doctrines that he associated with Calvinism (including original sin, vicarious atonement, justification, and the supernatural character of the new birth), Finney concluded, "No doctrine is more dangerous than this to the prosperity of the Church, and nothing more absurd."[45] Not only was he willing to set aside the ordinary means of grace for extraordinary "seasons of revival"; he insisted, "A revival is not a miracle." In fact, "there is nothing in religion beyond the ordinary powers of nature. It consists in the right exercise of the powers of nature. It is just that, and nothing else.... It is a purely philosophical result of the right use of the constituted means—as much so as any other effect produced by the application of means."[46] Find the most useful methods, "excitements sufficient to induce conversion," and there will be conversion. "God Has Established No Particular Measures" is the subheading of one of his chapters in his *Systematic Theology*. "A revival will decline and cease," he warned, "unless Christians are frequently re-converted."[47]

Toward the end of his ministry, as he considered the condition of many who had experienced his revivals, Finney wondered if this endless craving for ever-greater experiences might lead to spiritual exhaustion.[48] In fact, his worries were justified. The area where Finney's revivals were especially dominant is now referred to by historians as the "burned-over district," a seedbed of both disillusionment and the proliferation of esoteric sects.[49] If, as Bonhoeffer said, American religion has been decisively shaped by "Protestantism without the Reformation," then Finney is its clearest spokesperson.

Citing numerous contemporary heirs, Michael Pasquarello goes so far as to suggest that Finney's approach itself represents a "practical atheism" according to which the success of Christian mission depends on human technique, style, planning, and charisma, "without having to surrender ourselves and our words to the presence and work of the Word and Spirit."[50] The Great Commission just said, "Go," says Finney. "*It did not prescribe any forms.* It did not admit any.... And [the disciples'] object was to make known the gospel in the *most effectual way* ... so as to obtain attention and secure obedience of the greatest number possible. No person can find any *form* of doing this laid down in the Bible."[51] This is an odd conclusion, however, especially since the Great Commission explicitly mandates preaching, teaching, and baptizing.

The Second Great Awakening changed the landscape of American Protestantism, and its effects are with us on all sides today. Even if believers still gather

---

45. Charles G. Finney, *Revivals of Religion* (orig. 1835; Old Tappan, N.J.: Revell, n.d.), 4.

46. Ibid., 4–5.

47. Ibid., 321.

48. See Keith J. Hardman, *Charles Grandison Finney: Revivalist and Reformer* (Grand Rapids: Baker, 1990), 380–94.

49. See, for example, Whitney R. Cross, *The Burned-over District: The Social and Intellectual History of Enthusiastic Religion in Western New York, 1800–1850* (Ithaca, N.Y.: Cornell Univ. Press, 1982).

50. Michael Pasquarello III, *Christian Preaching: A Trinitarian Theology of Proclamation* (Grand Rapids: Baker Academic, 2007), 24.

51. Charles G. Finney, as quoted in ibid.

for sermons and songs, in many cases the real source of spiritual life — means of grace — is located in private disciplines or public acts of political, moral, social, or cultural transformation. If more traditional ecclesiologies can marginalize the notion of the church as people in their emphasis on the church as place, movement-driven approaches risk making the opposite mistake.[52] From this is drawn the familiar contrast between evangelism (mission) and the marks of the church (means of grace). However, there is a gathering — an *ekklēsia* — because there is a work of God through preaching and sacrament called the gospel that does its work before we can get around to ours. We cannot create the church by our acts of service, missionary zeal, church orders and liturgies, pragmatic programs, authenticity, or romanticizing efforts at generating community. Rather, it is God who creates his own unique community in the world by speaking it into existence and sustaining it in its pilgrimage.

We must therefore resist the false choice between looking after the sheep already gathered through preaching, sacrament, and discipline (the marks) and reaching out to the lost sheep who have yet to hear and believe (the mission). The church is created and sustained by the Spirit through preaching and sacrament, and the church grows numerically — expanding in its mission — by these same means. The New Testament knows of no contrast between being saved and joining the church.

The proper balance is found in Peter's Pentecost sermon: "The promise is for you and for your children and for all who are far off, everyone whom the Lord our God calls to himself" (Ac 2:39). Peter draws no contrast between ministering the gospel to covenant members (believers and their children) and mission to the world. Instead, there is an ever-widening circumference, as the ecclesial body expands through the apostolic teaching, the Supper, the fellowship, and the prayers (vv. 40–47). *This means that the same ministry that creates the church sustains the church and expands the church throughout the world until Christ returns.*

This means that a genuinely missional church should provoke a disrupting encounter with a holy and gracious God not only in its preaching and teaching, but in the regular celebration of the Supper. Why should the Supper be celebrated so infrequently and, in many cases, at an evening service where visitors are less likely to attend (and therefore, to be offended, perplexed, convicted, or intrigued)? Decades ago, Scottish minister William M. Cant argued, "Of course what our Lord has to say is not simply commands for another week, though worship will include these.... Yet before the imperatives ... there must come the indicatives. He who is the risen One tells of what He has done for us."[53] Where in the service is this forgiveness and

---

52. See, for example, Dan Kimball, *The Emerging Church: Vintage Christianity for New Generations* (Grand Rapids: Zondervan, 2003), 91. A thoughtful representative of the emerging church movement, Kimball tells us that "it is actually impossible to 'go to church.'" Not only is the church not to be identified with the building (a salutary point); "nor is it the meeting" (a not-so-salutary point). Rather, "the church is the people of God who gather together with a sense of mission (Acts 14:27). We can't *go* to church because *we are* the church."

reconciliation given — even to lifelong believers? First of all, in preaching. Yet today, many ministers are suggesting that there are more meaningful ways of communicating the gospel, such as more "conversational" methods. But is this listening to the risen Lord or to the preacher and each other?[54] Do we come to church expecting Christ to raise the dead and the weak and feeble?[55]

> It is surely right, then, that the worshipers should come away from this worship, not only with a Gospel message for the individual, but with a strong sense of having been made a member again of the one Holy Catholic and Apostolic Church, with a new awareness of being joined once more to the joyful believing and committed company of the whole church in heaven and upon earth in whose fellowship they happily unite in the Lord's Prayer. If the transformation of life is a reality within the service of the Word through the presence of the risen Lord, how much more in the service of the Word *and* sacrament.[56]

Remembering Christ's death is a key part of the sacrament. "Yet it has to be said that it is very easy along this memorialist road to become a Pelagian — we remember what Christ has done for us in the past, we recall the wonder of His dying love for our sins, and then we seek to make our human progress. We very easily forget that the ability to make the response of dying and rising again comes from the ascended Christ through the Spirit."[57] Merely imitating Christ's example is quite different from being united to him like a branch to a living vine.[58] Cant reminds us, "This paschal mystery has two sides to it: a descending and ascending movement, both *katabasis* and *anabasis*.... As we partake of the Table, we are lifted up into sharing in the glorified humanity of Christ, into sharing in the life of heaven."[59]

The Word that is preached, taught, sung, and prayed, along with baptism and the Eucharist, not only prepare us for mission; it is itself *the* missionary event, as visitors are able to hear and see the gospel that it communicates and the communion that it generates. To the extent that the marks define the mission and the mission justifies the marks, the church fulfills its apostolic identity.

Discussion Questions

1. Looking at Romans 10, discuss the connection that Paul makes between the message of the gospel and the method of its delivery. Does this teach us something about the relationship between the marks of the church and its mission?

---

53. William M. Cant, "The Most Urgent Call to the Kirk: The Celebration of Christ in the Liturgy of Word and Sacrament," *SJT* 40 (1987): 110.

54. Ibid., 113.

55. Ibid., 114.

56. Ibid., 115.

57. Ibid., 117.

58. Ibid., 119.

59. Ibid., 120–21.

2. What constitutes the church's identity as "apostolic"? Identify and evaluate the principal answers to that question in various traditions.

3. What is the "regulative principle"? Is the distinction between elements and circumstances biblical? Is it useful, especially in debates over the church's life in its ministry, worship, and outreach?

4. Is the visible organization of the church—particularly its offices—indifferent (i.e., left up to the judgment of each body in its own time and place), or is it established in the New Testament? Which passages would you appeal to in order to defend a particular kind of government? Is a particular form of government essential to the very existence of the church?

5. In light of Christ's gift of the keys of the kingdom to his officers, how does the New Testament relate the official ministry of the church to its mission to reach the lost? Imagine two different church scenarios. In the first, there is faithful preaching of the Word, administration of the sacraments, and church discipline, but a lack of hospitality, giving, and service as well as outreach to unbelievers. In the second, there is zeal for mission and service, but a general weakness—perhaps even serious errors—in doctrine, worship, and discipline. If you had the leaders of both churches together in a room, what would you say to them, drawing especially on concrete examples from the book of Acts?

Part Six

GOD
WHO REIGNS
IN GLORY

Chapter Twenty-Seven

A DWELLING PLACE

Etymologically, *eschatology* means "study of the last things." By now, however, readers will have discerned that eschatology is not simply a concluding topic but an indispensable lens through which we come to understand the whole system of Christian faith and practice. We have seen that eschatology comes even before soteriology, since the consummation (the Sabbath rest) was the goal of Adam's trial. Graciously, God kept Adam from eating the fruit of the Tree of Life, which would have confirmed him and his posterity in everlasting death (Ge 3:22–24). Instead, God opened up a history of promise leading to the Last Adam, who won the right for all who are in him to eat the fruit of everlasting life (Rev 22:2).

In this section, then, we focus on eschatology more narrowly conceived: *For what do we hope?* What happens when we die, and what do we mean when we confess our faith in "the resurrection of the body and the life everlasting"? In spite of the failures of Adam and Israel, "there remains a Sabbath rest for the people of God, for whoever has entered God's rest has also rested from his works as God did from his" (Heb 4:9).

I. DEATH AND THE INTERMEDIATE STATE

It is the gospel itself that organizes our meditations concerning life, death, and the everlasting hope. From this perspective, the promise of being welcomed into God's gracious presence immediately upon death is joyful news. And yet it is only the intermediate state. Going to heaven when we die is the way station, not the final hope announced in the gospel.

A. CREATION-CONSUMMATION VERSUS THE IMMORTALITY OF THE SOUL

Eschatology and creation are interdependent themes. Are all things, visible and invisible, the good creation of a good God, as reported in Genesis 1:10, 18, 21, 25, 31 and throughout Scripture? Do we expect salvation *of* nature or *from* nature?

For centuries, Christians have borrowed the language of the immortality of the soul. However, as with many terms borrowed from ancient philosophy, the ancient writers of the church did not borrow uncritically.

1. DUALISM AND THE MYTH OF THE EXILED SOUL

There are two extreme positions in debates over the immortality of the soul. At one end is the Platonist view, most obviously expressed in Plato's own *Phaedo* (esp. 64a–67b). According to this view, the soul or spirit is that higher (even divine) self that transcends bodily existence. Existing eternally in the invisible realm of the forms, the soul knows the Good, the True, and the Beautiful. However, its "fall" consists in its bodily incarceration. Cast mercilessly into time and space, the soul must strive to ascend beyond material, spatial, and temporal embodiment in order to remember the things that it has always known in the eternal realm. In this conception, "salvation" is the liberation of the soul from the body at death and final reunion with the One after a series of educative reincarnations. Philo of Alexandria translated the Old Testament into this Platonist scheme, while Origen of Alexandria accomplished the same distortion of Christianity a century-and-a-half after Philo's death. Remarkably similar views are found in Eastern religions (especially in the doctrines of karma, samsara, and reincarnation) and in the popular mysticism of the West, from Gnosticism to the New Age movement.

We encounter this idea also today in process theology, and in various expressions of radical feminism and neopaganism. At death, according to Protestant theologian John Hick (drawing on the Tibetan Book of the Dead for support), the soul survives, and in the final state all self-identity merges into the One.[1] He writes, "We cannot know how many worlds or series of worlds there are; and indeed the number and nature of the individual's successive embodiments will presumably depend upon what is needed for him to reach the point at which he transcends ego-hood and attains the ultimate unitive state, or nirvana."[2] Grenz observes,

> Feminist theologian Rosemary Radford Ruether articulated an even more obviously monistic vision. She saw death as "the final relinquishment of individuated ego into the great matrix of being." For her, the Absolute is a "great collective personhood ... in which our achievements and failures are gathered up, assimilated into the fabric of being, and carried forward into new possibilities."[3]

Ontological monism destroys personal existence, but as Grenz notes, "In losing personhood, monism also destroys community."[4] When, as Eastern religions commonly teach, the self finally achieves its unity with all being, there is no personal

---

1. John Hick, *Death and Eternal Life* (New York: Harper & Row, 1976): 399–424.

2. Ibid., 417.

3. Stanley Grenz, *Theology for the Community of God* (Nash-

ville: Broadman and Holman, 1994), 760, from Rosemary Radford Ruether, *Sexism and God-Talk* (Boston: Beacon, 1983), 258.

4. Grenz, *Theology for the Community of God*, 760.

consciousness of this ostensible benefit. The raindrop dissolves into an ocean of being. Lost in this paradigm of "overcoming estrangement" are both the reality of persons and community.

Even in the Christian West the lingering thrall of native paganism has kept alive the immortality of the soul. In pagan religious and philosophical worldviews, sin, evil, and death are considered part of the cycle of nature. They are simply "the way things are" because of finite embodiment. One is born, lives, and dies: each stage is as natural as the other. Mary Baker Eddy, the founder of Christian Science, introduced the phrase "pass on" (and "pass away") into the popular vocabulary, and argued that illness and death are illusions (what Eastern religions call *maya*).[5] In this basically Gnostic worldview, the material world (including our bodies), evil, and suffering are erroneous beliefs that can be overcome by proper enlightenment in the eternal principles of universal harmony. The fall is not to be explained in historical terms—as the result of a representative act of covenant breaking in which we were included—but as essential to material creation as such. However, such ontic wounds, inasmuch as they pertain to the realm of matter, belong to mere appearances. We must transcend them, and death is the most decisive point at which this happy goal is finally attained.

However, in Scripture there is no assumption that the soul is immortal. Rather, like the body, it is a created substance with a beginning and an end. Immortality was the goal held out to Adam and Eve in the Tree of Life, and not merely for the soul but for the whole person. It is this immortality that was forfeited by Adam but has been promised to those who trust in Jesus Christ. Nor is human existence cyclical, through the endless rebirths of the soul. Rather, the soul comes into existence with the body and is oriented to a fulfillment in time and history that is identified in Christian eschatology as the consummation.

The pagan idea of the immortality of the soul and the Christian doctrine of the gift of everlasting life issue in radically different worldviews. It is interesting that whereas Jesus, when he was raised, immediately set about to find his companions for a meal, Descartes locked himself in a room by himself and contemplated his own existence, pretending that he was shorn of arms and legs, eyes and ears, left as a naked soul. It is no wonder that he concluded that the most indubitable reality in the universe was consciousness of his real self as pure mind.

2. Physicalism/Materialism

If the real world is exclusively spiritual for the first view, the second reduces

---

5. Mary Baker Eddy, *Science and Health with a Key to the Scriptures* (Boston: Trustees Under the Will of Mary Baker Eddy, 1934), 186 (ll. 11–15).

reality to matter; hence, it is typically called *materialism*. As old as pre-Socratic philosophy, atheistic materialism became especially popular in the wake of Friedrich Nietzsche. There is no "beyond" and therefore no transcendent telos marked by a significant origin or destiny. Although Nietzsche adopted a cyclical view of temporal reality, he argued that we create our own meaning for ourselves, striving for "immortality" in the form of a heroic legacy. That thread of thinking that leads from Nietzsche to Derrida is, more than anything else, a sharp reaction against Platonism—which for these writers included Christianity.[6] Right through to the end of our theology, then, we discern the outline of the contrasting worldviews: *overcoming estrangement*, *the stranger we never meet*, and the biblical paradigm of *meeting a stranger*.

Not all denials of the existence of the soul and its life after bodily death are atheistic. Often drawing on nineteenth- and twentieth-century Jewish scholarship, some biblical scholars and theologians have argued, with G. B. Caird, that "during most of the long period covered by the Old Testament the Hebrew people had no belief in an after-life."[7] Only when Jewish apocalypticism became tainted with Greek philosophy was the idea of a life after death introduced into Judaism, we are told. Accordingly, it is suggested that preexilic Jews hoped for a long life, not for survival beyond death in either a disembodied or an embodied form. Nevertheless, this thesis has been unraveling in recent Jewish interpretation. Among others, Jon Levenson has shown that the notion of a soul and its survival beyond death, prior to a final resurrection, has been essential to the Jewish hope well before the Second Temple period.[8]

Valiantly defending the reality of Christ's resurrection and of the believer's hope in bodily resurrection, some Christian theologians (such as Wolfhart Pannenberg and G. C. Berkouwer) nevertheless overreact against the Platonist heritage by questioning an intermediate state of disembodied existence.[9] Some defenders refer to this position as "nonreductive physicalism," because although it denies the existence of the soul distinct from the body, it does acknowledge a spiritual aspect of bodily existence.[10]

---

6. Michael Horton, "Eschatology after Nietzsche," in *Covenant and Eschatology: The Divine Drama* (Louisville: Westminster John Knox, 2004), 20–45.

7. G. B. Caird, *The Language and Imagery of the Bible* (Philadelphia: Westminster Press, 1980), 244.

8. Jon D. Levenson, *Resurrection and the Restoration of Israel: The Ultimate Victory of the God of Life* (New Haven: Yale Univ. Press, 2006); cf. Kevin J. Madigan and Jon D. Levenson, *Resurrection: The Power of God for Christians and Jews* (New Haven: Yale Univ. Press, 2008).

9. Wolfhart Pannenberg, *What Is Man?* (trans. Duane A.

Priebe; Philadelphia: Fortress, 1972), 46–47; *Jesus—God and Man* (Philadelphia: Westminster Press, 87). I pointed out in chapter 12 the reticence of G. C. Berkouwer to affirm an intermediate state (see page 377, esp. fn. 10). It is not surprising that among more conservative and confessional Protestants, Reformed theologians are especially drawn to this view out of an understandable suspicion of a nature-grace (and correlatively, body-soul) dualism.

10. See especially Nancey Murphy, *Bodies and Souls or Spirited Bodies?* (Cambridge: Cambridge Univ. Press, 2006).

A biblical anthropology navigates between these extremes, affirming the distinction between body and soul while understanding their separation at death as a curse rather than a blessing.[11] In spite of this curse, believers enjoy God's gracious presence upon their death, awaiting the day when they will be raised as a psychosomatic unity in his everlasting kingdom.

As I argued in considering human personhood in chapter 12, Christianity denies any confusion of the Creator and creature. No more than our bodies are our souls in any sense divine or intrinsically immortal. If the soul survives physical death, it is only because God grants this life as a gift in Christ. In its Christology, Christianity displays its clearest opposition to the Platonist/Gnostic scheme by its announcement that God himself became flesh to win our redemption by his incarnation, life, death, and resurrection. Furthermore, by focusing all attention on Christ's historical descent, ascent, and return in the flesh, the gospel is diametrically opposed to the myth of the exiled soul and its ostensible liberation from its bodily "prison house." The gospel concentrates on the good news not that our soul survives death but that Christ welcomes us into the fellowship of the Trinity when we die, in which fellowship we await final salvation of our whole person in the bodily resurrection at the end of the age.[12] In its ecclesiology, it speaks not of a fusion of essences, where personal identity is submerged in a cosmic unity, but of a communion of persons, gathered at the lavish feast to enjoy each other's company forever with its gracious host.

B. THE FALL VERSUS THE NATURALNESS OF DEATH

Biblical eschatology moves forward, from promise to fulfillment, not in cycles. Already in Paradise creation is merely the anteroom for a fuller human purpose and destiny for creation. In this intervening time between the fall and the consummation, there have been various periods of God's direct intervention in history and nature, as we have seen. However, during most of this history (including our own), nature is governed by God's providence. Believers share in the common curse and in God's common grace.

Furthermore, death is not "passing away," and it is certainly not an illusion. For believers, it is "the last enemy" that must be destroyed (1Co 15:26). We share in Christ's death and therefore also in his life (Ro 6:1–12; Php 3:10). Therefore, by looking to our head, we already know the outcome of this struggle, and so there is no reason for believers to fear death's ultimate triumph (Ps 23:4; Heb 2:15; Ro

---

11. For an excellent treatment of this topic, which encompasses "last things," see the excellent book by John W. Cooper, *Body, Soul, and Life Everlasting: Biblical Anthropology and the Monism-Dualism Debate* (Grand Rapids: Eerdmans, 1989).

12. Although there are reasons to be wary of certain aspects of his construction, the contrast I am drawing here can be seen also in the title of Oscar Cullman's *Immortality of the Soul or Resurrection of the Dead* (London: Epworth, 1958).

8:38–39; 1Co 15:55–57; Php 1:21–23; 2Co 5:8; Rev 14:13). For unbelievers, this death is merely the harbinger of "the second death": everlasting judgment (Rev 20:14).

Part of the curse is the separation of soul from body (Ge 2:17; 3:19, 22; 5:5; Ro 5:12; 8:10; 1Co 15:21). Death is an enemy, not a friend (1Co 15:26) and a terror (Heb 2:15), so horrible that even the one who would triumph over it was overcome with grief, fear, and anger at the tomb of his friend Lazarus (Jn 11:33–36). Jesus did not see death as a benign deliverer, the sunset that is as beautiful as the sunrise, or as a portal to "a better life." Looking death in the eye, he saw it for what it was, and his disciples followed his example. After the deacon's martyrdom, we read, "Devout men buried Stephen and made great lamentation over him" (Ac 8:2). The reason that believers do not mourn as those who have no hope (1Th 4:13) is not that they know that death is good, but that they know that God's love and life are more powerful than the jaws of death. Although believers, too, feel its bite, Christ has removed the sting of death (Jn 14:2–3; Php 1:21; 1Co 15:54–57; 2Co 5:8). That is because "the sting of death is sin, and the power of sin is the law. But thanks be to God, who gives us the victory through our Lord Jesus Christ" (1Co 15:56–57). Downplaying the seriousness of the foe only trivializes the debt that was paid and the conquest that was achieved at the cross and the empty tomb.

1. Immediate, Conscious Existence in the Presence of the Lord

In the intermediate state, believers are not simply in contemplative repose. Nor are they lost souls wandering throughout the realm of shadows or crossing back and forth over the river Styx ferried by Charon. Rather, they are made part of the company assembled at the true Zion, with "innumerable angels in festal gathering" and "the assembly of the firstborn who are enrolled in heaven, and to God, the judge of all, and to the spirits of the righteous made perfect, and to Jesus, the mediator of a new covenant, and to the sprinkled blood that speaks a better word than the blood of Abel" (Heb 12:22–24). Admittedly, we know very little from Scripture about the intermediate state. Nearly all of the passages cited concerning heaven refer to the everlasting rather than the intermediate state.

2. Opposition to Immediate, Conscious Existence in the Presence of the Lord

Several views have been put forward against the immediate, conscious existence of believers in the intermediate state.

(a) *Soul sleep.* Advocates of soul sleep, also known as *psychopannychism*, hold that upon one's death the soul enjoys neither heaven nor hell during the intermediate state, but unconsciousness until the final judgment. A similar belief is *thnetopsychism*, which teaches that the soul also dies along with the body and both are raised together. Some who hold this position adopt an anthropological monism, denying the existence of a soul distinct from the body.

Although these views found few champions in church history, soul sleep of the first type seems to have enjoyed a revival at the time of the Reformation. In fact, Calvin wrote his first theological treatise against this view, defending the position most closely associated with early Jewish and Christian teaching: namely, that at "Abraham's side," the soul does survive the body at death, which is neither the new heavens and new earth of the consummation nor a place of suffering, but a place of intermediate joy in the presence of the Lord with his people. The Scriptures speak of the intermediate state as conscious existence, not soul sleep (Ps 16:10; 49:14–15; Ecc 12:7; Lk 16:22; 23:43; Php 1:23; 2Co 5:8; Rev 6:9–11; 14:13).

A variation of thnetopsychism is defended by Wolfhart Pannenberg as the *restorationist* theory.[13] A similar perspective was suggested by G. C. Berkouwer.[14] According to this view, Jesus' parable of the rich man and Lazarus cannot be considered historical even if one adopts the traditional view, since the existence of the one in hell and the other in heaven presupposes that the final judgment has already taken place. Accordingly, as George Eldon Ladd concluded, the scope of this parable is not the intermediate state but "the hardness and obduracy" of the Pharisees who "refuse to accept the witness of Scripture to the person of Jesus."[15]

In my judgment, Ladd's exegesis is entirely sound. Jesus' parables are never historical narratives or doctrinal descriptions, and they all concentrate on the kingdom as it is dawning in Christ's person and work. Yet the fact still remains that even in Sheol, believers are "gathered to [their] fathers" and are conscious of being in the presence of God and the saints, even when their body lies in the grave. The contrast between the wicked and believers is that the latter will be brought out of the pit of death (Sheol) and see the light of life (Ps 49:7–15), "for you will not abandon my soul to Sheol, or let your holy one see corruption. You make known to me the path of life; in your presence there is fullness of joy; at your right hand are pleasures forevermore" (Ps 16:10–11). Jesus told the believing criminal, "Today you will be with me in Paradise" (Lk 23:43), even though Jesus himself would not be raised until the third day, and when he died he called out, "Father, into your hands I commit my spirit" (v. 46).

The body, apart from the soul, is dead (Jas 2:26), yet for believers, to be absent from the body is to be present with the Lord (2Co 5:8). Neither the everlasting consummation nor unconsciousness, this intermediate state is God's preservation of

13. Wolfhart Pannenberg, "Constructive and Critical Functions of Christian Eschatology," *HTR* 77 (1984): 130–31.

14. G. C. Berkouwer, *Studies in Dogmatics: The Return of Christ* (ed. Marlin J. Van Elderen; trans. James Van Oosterom;

Grand Rapids: Eerdmans, 1972), 38–40, 59.

15. G. E. Ladd, *The Last Things* (Grand Rapids: Eerdmans, 1978), 34.

the personal consciousness of believers in his presence awaiting the resurrection of the dead. In the book of Revelation, "the souls of those who had been slain for the word of God and for the witness they had borne" cry out from before God's throne, "O Sovereign Lord, holy and true, how long before you will judge and avenge our blood on those who dwell on the earth?'" (Rev 6:9–10). Conscious of their blessedness, the souls of the martyrs are also conscious that their complete salvation has not yet been fully realized.

At the same time, it should not be surprising that the resurrection of the body was especially pushed to the forefront with "the appearing of our Savior Christ Jesus, who abolished death and brought life and immortality to light through the gospel" (2Ti 1:10). Christianity therefore does not build on the pagan ruins of the immortality of the soul, but brings "immortality to light through the gospel." It is an immortality that is bestowed as a gift in the resurrection, not a given of our nature as such. In other words, immortality finds its definition in eschatology and soteriology rather than anthropology.

(b) *Postmortem salvation*. Another challenge to immediate, conscious existence in the Lord's presence is the concept of postmortem salvation. Since the ancient church there have been those who have argued that the intermediate state offers the opportunity for condemned souls to repent and be saved. This view is increasingly attractive especially among Christians who want to affirm both the possibility of salvation for non-Christians and the necessity of hearing and responding to the gospel.[16] However, this position is also contradicted by passages that teach explicitly the decisiveness of repentance and faith in this life, followed by judgment (Lk 16:26; Heb 9:27; Gal 6:7–8).

(c) *Purgatory*. Also at odds with immediate, conscious presence of the soul with God is the Roman Catholic dogma of purgatory. According to this teaching, even if the guilt of sin is forgiven, the punishment for particular sins must be suffered before entrance into paradise. Purgatory is but an extension of the doctrine of penance, which denies the sufficiency of Christ's active and passive obedience. If the guilt of our sins has been fully remitted, then punishment would be capricious and unjust. Besides contradicting central doctrines of the gospel, the idea that after people die they enter a state of purgation has no biblical support. Rather, the idea can be traced through Origen to the speculations of Plato and the Greco-Roman belief in three levels of existence in Hades: the lower region Tartarus (hell), a middle region for those who were neither good nor evil, and the Elysian Fields, often identified with the Isles of the Blessed.

---

16. See for example Gabriel Fackre, "Divine Perseverance," in G. Fackre, R. Nash, and J. Sanders, *What about Those Who Have Never Heard? Three Views on the Destiny of the Unevan-* *gelized* (ed. J. Sanders; Downers Grove, Ill.: InterVarsity Press, 1995), 71–95.

The wide evidence of belief in a period of probation—of testing—before attaining everlasting glory in many religions may be considered a relic of the original covenant given to humanity in Adam. However, the Bible identifies this probation with the representative headship of Adam, recapitulated and fulfilled by the Last Adam. Non-Christian religions, however, place this trial in the hands of every person, to be fulfilled personally by works, if not in this life then in the next.[17]

By contrast, some in early Judaism taught that the soul at death goes to Gehenna, a holding place for final resurrection and judgment, and, as we have already seen above, Jesus taught that while unbelievers go to Gehenna at death, believers are with him in paradise. Roman Catholic theology bases the idea of purgatory on 2 Maccabees 12:42–45, which speaks of Judas Maccabeus having "made atonement for the dead, that they might be delivered from their sin." However, this act of Judas Maccabeus was a large sum of money that he sent to the temple "for a sin offering." This is precisely the background of the temple worship that the writer to the Hebrews (among others, including Jesus) says has come to an end with Christ's sacrifice of himself. By using this apocryphal (i.e., noncanonical) verse as a proof text for purgatory, Roman Catholic interpretation returns to the shadows of the law after the reality has come. Those who die in mortal sin go directly to hell, but with few exceptions all believers die with some venial sins that must be atoned for.

According to the *Catechism of the Catholic Church*,

> All who die in God's grace and friendship, but still imperfectly purified, are indeed assured of their eternal salvation; but after death they undergo purification, so as to achieve the holiness necessary to enter the joy of heaven. The Church gives the name Purgatory to this final purification of the elect, which is entirely different from the punishment of the damned. The Church formulated her doctrine of faith on Purgatory especially at the Councils of Florence and Trent.... The Church also commends almsgiving, indulgences, and works of penance undertaken on behalf of the dead.[18]

As for those who die in mortal sin, "the teaching of the Church affirms the existence of hell and its eternity. Immediately after death the souls of those who die in a state of mortal sin descend into hell, where they suffer the punishments of hell, 'eternal fire.'"[19]

The clear teaching of Scripture, however, is that every believer goes to be with the Lord upon death. Therefore, there is no point in praying for the dead, much

---

17. Interestingly, for example, Mary Baker Eddy even calls this "afterlife" a period of "probation." There is no heaven or hell—no place for the soul to "go" at death—but only a higher state of consciousness for those who have done well. Those who have failed to do well encounter God's "suffering love" until they are purified (*Miscellaneous Writings, 1883–1896* [Boston:

A. V. Stewart, 1896], 160). This is nearly identical to the views of Plato and Origen, with clear parallels in Eastern religions.

18. *Catechism of the Catholic Church* (Liguori, Mo.: Liguori Publications, 1994), 268–69.

19. Ibid., 270.

less *for* purchasing indulgences, or otherwise expending effort on behalf of securing an earlier release of the departed from their punishments in purgatory. "Just as it is appointed for men to die once, and after that comes the judgment ..." (Heb 9:27). Furthermore, it is just as clearly and centrally taught in Scripture that believers do not "achieve the holiness necessary to enter the joy of heaven,"[20] but are clothed in the righteousness and holiness of Christ's sufficient merit.

II. THE RESURRECTION OF THE BODY

The concept of the essential immortality of the soul is not a subset of the Christian doctrine of the resurrection of the body but its antithesis. Especially in contrast to contemporary assumptions—even among many Christians—it is significant that Christianity does not teach salvation by death. It is striking that the Apostles' Creed insists upon our ultimate hope as "the resurrection of the body and the life everlasting," not "going to heaven when I die." This is not to say that we do not go to heaven when we die, nor that this is not an obvious gain, especially since the Scriptures expressly teach otherwise.[21] However, it is important to remind ourselves that as wonderful as it is to be in God's presence, even separated from our flesh, it is the intermediate rather than the final state.

Our baptism presupposes the resurrection of the body, which is why it is a bodily sacrament and not merely a spiritual exercise of the mind. Every time we eat of the bread and drink of the wine in the Lord's Supper we proclaim not only Christ's death but his return in the flesh and even now feed on his body and blood for our salvation. Through these sacraments, our decaying bodies receive God's pledge that they will be raised and receive immortality from his own risen and glorified flesh.

In the consummation, not only the earth but heaven itself will become new. As human bodies will be reunited in everlasting joy and integrity with their souls, so too earth and heaven will become one cosmic sanctuary of everlasting joy. Jesus spoke of it as a *palingenesis* (re-creation) in Matthew 19:28. For believers, at the resurrection the whole person—embodied soul and ensouled body—will be granted the *gift* of everlasting life (immortality). It is remarkable that Job longed to be in God's presence even in the same flesh that was wasting with pain and disease: "For I know that my Redeemer lives, and at the last he will stand upon the earth. And after my skin has been thus destroyed, yet in my flesh I shall see God, whom I shall see for myself, and my eyes shall behold, and not another. My heart faints within me!" (Job 19:25–27). Similarly, Paul observes that although we groan in body and

---

20. Ibid.
21. See Robert Strimple, "Hyper-Preterism and the Resurrection of the Body," in *When Shall These Things Be?* (ed. Keith Mathison; Phillipsburg, N.J.: P&R, 2004), 287–352.

spirit now, "we wait eagerly for adoption as sons, the redemption of our bodies. For in this hope we were saved" (Ro 8:23–24).

A lodestar for the Christian hope is 1 Corinthians 15, where Paul not only treats the resurrection of believers as belonging to the same event (though in two stages) as that of their forerunner, Jesus Christ,[22] but also considers the way in which the renewal of all things takes place. Even now, the resurrection of the dead in the age to come is being partly realized in the present by the renewal of the inner person (regeneration). Those who were "dead in the trespasses and sins" are already raised spiritually and are seated with Christ (cf. Eph 2:1–6; Ro 6). In 1 Corinthians 15:26, 51–55, Paul makes it clear that there is an order to this renewal: first spiritual resurrection, and then bodily resurrection, completing the total renewal of believers. As is also taught in 2 Corinthians 4:16–18, the "outer self" is wasting away while the "inner self" is being renewed day by day in the image of Christ (cf. Ro 8:9–30; 2Ti 1:10; Col 3:1–17). In 1 Corinthians 15:50 Paul says, "Flesh and blood cannot inherit the kingdom of God, nor does the perishable inherit the imperishable." Yet notice the comparison: "As was the man of dust, so also are those who are of the dust. . . . Just as we have borne the image of the man of dust, we shall also bear the image of the man of heaven" (v.v. 48–49).

Is Jesus raised bodily? Not only is that answered affirmatively in the Gospels, where Jesus eats with his disciples and even invites Thomas to inspect his wounds; it is answered affirmatively in this same chapter. In fact, Paul's whole point in 1 Corinthians 15 is to challenge a sect that is teaching that the resurrection has already happened as a "spiritual" event. If Christ is not raised bodily, then we will not be raised bodily either. If this is Paul's argument, it would not make any sense that he should turn the resurrection into a nonbodily event after all.

As with his flesh/Spirit contrast more generally, Paul is not thinking in terms of an ontological dualism (bodies/spirits) but an eschatological dualism (this age/the age to come). The powers and potentialities of this present age (such as modern medicine) may keep us from dying as soon as we might, but they cannot raise us to immortal glory. In its present condition, this body cannot withstand the glory of the heavenly city; it must be glorified, as Christ's body was, in order to participate in the age (such as modern medicine) to come. Flesh and blood in its present, fallen condition cannot endure the joys of Zion. Nevertheless, our bodies will be *changed* (1Co 15:51), not *replaced*. "For . . . the *dead* will be raised imperishable, and we shall be changed. For *this* perishable body must put on the imperishable, and *this* mortal body must put on immortality" (v.v. 52–53, emphasis added). We cannot imagine the glory of our future existence, but we can look to Christ as our forerunner: "He

22. This is the thrust of Richard Gaffin's richly insightful argument in *Resurrection and Redemption: A Study in Paul's Sote-* *riology* (Phillipsburg, N.J.: P&R, 1987).

who raised Christ Jesus from the dead will also give life to your mortal bodies ...” (Ro 8:11), and Christ “will transform our lowly body to be like his glorious body” (Php 3:21). So the contrast is not between this body and another body but between this body *in its lowly condition* and this body *changed* into the glorious condition of Christ's own body.

There is something to be noted about Paul's analogy in 1 Corinthians 15:42–44 of the seed that is planted in the earth and rises as a plant. Whatever the apparent discontinuities between an apple seed and an apple tree, it is the same substance. Paul does not contrast embodiment with disembodiment; rather, he contrasts being with not being in the presence of Jesus Christ. The Platonist longs to be stripped not only of sin and death but of the body itself, while Paul longs to be “further clothed” (2Co 5:4). As Robert Reymond observes, “What Paul would most prefer would be that he might be alive at the return of the Lord and be clothed with the resurrection body without laying the mortal body down in death (vv. 2–4). But even the intermediate state is better by far than this present existence, beset as the present is with sin in which we have less direct communion with the Lord (v. 6).”[23]

Just as Jesus ate and drank after his resurrection, there will be eating and drinking in the new creation, although this time at the consummated marriage supper of the Lamb (Rev 19:9), with Jesus drinking wine with us (Lk 22:18), it is his eager expectation to feast with us when he returns (Mt 26:29–30). The prominent theme of eating and drinking in the presence of the Lord that one finds in the Old Testament historical books, recapitulated in the ministry of Jesus, is consummated in the new order. In the closing chapter of John's Apocalypse, there is a river flowing (Rev 22:1), with the Tree of Life “yielding its fruit each month” (Rev 22:2). Although the consummation is expressed in this powerful apocalyptic imagery, the purchase of such imagery is lost if there is no physical creation. We are creatures of time and space, and we will not transcend our humanity but the bondage of our humanity to the conditions of sin and death. Wayne Grudem is exactly right when he argues, “Although a popular hymn speaks of the time ‘when the trumpet of the Lord shall sound and time shall be no more,’ Scripture does not give support to that idea.”[24] Rather, all of our times will be gathered together in the fullness of God's Sabbath rest: everlasting joy.

DISCUSSION QUESTIONS

1. How does the historical economy of Christ's descent, ascent, and return in

---

23. Robert Reymond, *A New Systematic Theology of the Christian Faith* (Nashville: Nelson, 1998), 1018.

24. Wayne Grudem, *Systematic Theology: An Introduction to Bible Doctrine* (Grand Rapids: Zondervan, 1994), 1162.

the flesh reorient our hope, away from the pagan idea of the eternal state as disembodied existence?

2. On the question of the intermediate state (i.e., between death and the final resurrection), we may err in two directions. What are those extremes, and where would we go in Scripture to find the proper balance?

3. Is the Roman Catholic concept of purgatory capable of being harmonized with the gospel? Why or why not?

4. Is death "natural"?

5. What is the Christian's ultimate hope for the future?

Chapter Twenty-Eight

THE RETURN OF CHRIST AND THE LAST JUDGMENT

Christians confess that Jesus Christ "will come again in glory to judge the living and the dead; whose kingdom shall have no end"(Nicene Creed). This hope includes "the resurrection of the body and the life everlasting" (Apostles' Creed). Given our propensity for disagreement over end-times scenarios, this represents a remarkable Christian consensus. We cling to the angel's promise at Christ's ascension: "This Jesus, who was taken up from you into heaven, will come in the same way as you saw him go into heaven" (Ac 1:11). He came first in humility and grace, but will return in glory and power.

Where paths diverge among Christians today is on the question of a literal millennium—that is, a thousand-year reign of Christ. The only biblical passage that speaks directly of such an era is Revelation 20. In a vision John beholds an angel descending from heaven to bind the dragon "so that he might not deceive the nations any longer, until the thousand years were ended. After that he must be released for a little while" (20:3).

> Then I saw thrones, and seated on them were those to whom the authority to judge was committed. Also I saw the souls of those who had been beheaded for the testimony of Jesus and for the word of God.... They came to life and reigned with Christ for a thousand years. The rest of the dead did not come to life until the thousand years were ended. This is the first resurrection. Blessed and holy is the one who shares in the first resurrection! Over such the second death has no power, but they will be priests of God and of Christ, and they will reign with him for a thousand years. (Rev 20:4–6)

After the thousand years, Satan is released for a final time (the "little while" mentioned in v. 3), before the last battle, which concludes with the final banishment of Satan and the false prophet to the flames where "they will be tormented day and night forever and ever" (vv. 7–10). These events are followed by the last judgment, with Death and Hades thrown into the lake of fire along with "[anyone whose] name was not found written in the book of life" (vv. 11–15), and then by the arrival of the new heavens and earth (chs. 21–22).

Belief in a literal one-thousand-year reign of Christ is called *millenarianism*, from the Latin *mille* (thousand), which translates the Greek word for thousand, *chilia*, in Revelation 20. Hence, for much of church history belief in a literal millennium was referred to as "chiliasm." I will point out distinct schools below, but it is useful first to highlight the three main approaches to the end times.

Christ will return prior to the millennium according to *premillennialists* and after this golden era according to traditional *postmillennialists. Amillennialism*, however, understands the reference to a one-thousand-year period as figurative for the era between Christ's two advents.[1] Premillennialism anticipates increasing decadence in the condition of the world (including the visible church) until Christ returns at the end of history to establish his kingdom. Postmillennialism expects things to improve gradually through God's gracious blessing on the church's missionary endeavors until the nations officially recognize Christ as Messiah and wars, famine, disease, and other global disasters gradually cease. It is then expected that Christ will return to receive his kingdom, to judge the living and the dead, and to commence the everlasting state. Amillennialism expects simultaneous growth and decline, suffering and success, witness and apostasy throughout this era between Christ's two advents.[2]

I. THE HISTORY OF THE FUTURE: MILLENNIAL DEBATES

These categories (a-/pre-/postmillennialism) originated in the nineteenth century, so we should be wary of imagining that there was such refinement in end-time

---

1. Among the best recent defenses of amillennialism are Kim Riddelbarger, *A Case for Amillennialism* (Grand Rapids: Baker, 2003); Cornelis Venema, *The Promise of the Future* (Edinburgh: Banner of Truth, 2000); G. K. Beale, *The Book of Revelation: A Commentary on the Greek Text* (New International Commentary on the Greek Text; Grand Rapids: Eerdmans, 1998), especially his excursus on the kingdom. Recent defenses of postmillennialism include Keith Mathison, *An Eschatology of Hope* (Phillipsburg, N.J.: P&R, 1999) and John Jefferson Davis, *The Victory of Christ's Kingdom: An Introduction to Postmillennialism* (Moscow, Ida.: Canon Press, 1996). More than traditional postmillennialists, Mathison's interpretations display greater overlap with amillennialism. George Eldon Ladd's works remain standard as an interpretation of historic premillennialism, but an outstanding recent defense of this view is found in Craig Blomberg and Sung Wook Chung, eds., *The Case for Historic Premillennialism: An Alternative to "Left Behind" Eschatology* (Grand Rapids: Baker Academic, 2009). A statement of classic dispensational premillennialism is Charles Ryrie's *Dispensationalism* (rev. and exp. ed. (Chicago: Moody Press, 2007), and the view known as progressive dispensationalism (considered below) is defended in Craig A. Blaising and Darrell L. Bock, *Progressive Dispensationalism* (Grand Rapids: BridgePoint, 2000).

2. This point is also affirmed by Keith Mathison in *From Age to Age* (Phillipsburg, N.J.: P&R, 2009), 374.

thinking throughout church history. The principal division on this subject historically was simply between millenarians (those who affirmed a literal thousand-year kingdom on earth) and amillennialists (those who interpreted Revelation 20 as referring symbolically to the present era).

A. EARLY JEWISH AND CHRISTIAN ESCHATOLOGIES

Already in Second Temple Judaism apocalyptic fervor was evident on every hand. At least among those who took seriously the resurrection of the dead, world history was divided between "this age" and "the age to come." Not by steady development but by the personal arrival of the Messiah, David's true heir, there would be a golden age on the earth in which the Mosaic theocracy would be fully and perfectly revived. This would entail the reconsecration of Palestine as holy, with the Gentile oppressors driven from the land. From the earthly city of Jerusalem, the Messiah would extend his kingdom to the ends of the earth, culminating in the resurrection of the dead.

More than a century before Christ, the vision of a literal golden age at the end of history was anticipated in 1 Enoch. A similar eschatology may be found in the much later apocryphal text of 4 Ezra, although there the whole creation is destroyed—including the Messiah himself—after a four-hundred-year reign. Only then (seven days after the apocalypse) will the resurrection and judgment take place, ushering in a new heaven and a new earth. Although differing in the details, this vision of a messianic age that is geopolitical and temporary was kept alive during the era of Jesus Christ and afterward in the rabbinical writings even after the destruction of the temple in AD 70.

In the days of Jesus' earthly ministry, eschatological views ranged as broadly as they do among professing Christians today. The Sadducees were syncretistic, borrowing heavily from Greco-Roman (especially Stoic and Epicurean) philosophy and were sharply critical of rabbinical tradition. Consequently, they were largely compliant with their Roman overlords and supportive of the status quo under their titular king. According to Josephus, the Sadducees doubted God's sovereignty and placed everything in the power of humans, denied the survival of the soul at death "and the punishments and rewards in Hades."[3] In Matthew 22:23–33 there is the account of the Sadducees, "who say that there is no resurrection" (v. 23), trying to trap Jesus on this point. Jesus left no doubt as to where he stood on this central question of eschatology: " 'You are wrong, because you know neither the Scriptures nor the power of God.... And as for the resurrection of the dead, have you not read

---

3. Flavius Josephus, *The Wars of the Jews, or History of the Destruction of Jerusalem*, trans. William Whiston; available at Project Gutenberg, Etext #2850, 105 (www.gutenberg.org/etext/2850); cf. F. F. Bruce, *New Testament History* (Garden City, N.Y.: Doubleday, 1969), 74–80.

what was said to you by God: 'I am the God of Abraham, and the God of Isaac, and the God of Jacob'? He is not God of the dead, but of the living'" (vv. 29, 31–32).

Both the stricter Shammai and more lenient Hillel schools of the Pharisees knew that Herod and the Romans stood in the way of the messianic age, but believed that through a wide-scale rededication to the temple and Torah, the true Messiah would arrive, liberating Israel. This action would culminate in the resurrection of the just and the messianic reign of peace.[4] Other sects abandoned the temple and leadership in Jerusalem altogether, establishing desert communities. Most notable among these was the Essene community. Some Essenes required celibacy and an extremely ascetic life and were especially given to studying the prophets, interpreting current events as harbingers of the last days. Josephus claimed, "It is but seldom that they miss in their predictions."[5]

John the Baptist and his disciples represent one of these desert communities, warning of imminent judgment and the arrival of the Messiah. Not even this community seems to have thought of the end-times in terms of two distinct advents of Messiah, but expected the resurrection of the dead *and* the final judgment to occur in the earthly ministry of Jesus. This is suggested by the question that John's disciples were sent to ask Jesus: "Are you the one who is to come, or shall we look for another?" (Mt 11:3). Jesus answered, "Go and tell John what you hear and see: the blind receive their sight and the lame walk, lepers are cleansed and the deaf hear, and the dead are raised up, and the poor have good news preached to them. And blessed is the one who is not offended by me" (vv. 4–6). Perhaps this was not the scale that John was expecting. Yes, the dead are raised—but only here and there; it is hardly the general resurrection. Yet these were signs, prolepses of the consummation at the end of the age. Jesus went on to tell that crowds that in spite of John's significance, "the one who is least in the kingdom of heaven is greater than he" (v. 11). John prepared the way for the kingdom, but it was only now dawning in Christ—as John himself prophesied at Jesus' baptism (Mt 3).

Together with the resurrection of the dead and the last judgment, belief in the literal restoration of Israel's theocratic kingdom, under the leadership of the Messiah, has continued to be a hallmark of orthodox Jewish belief through the centuries. The prophetic and apocalyptic writings of the New Testament—especially Jesus' Olivet Discourse (Mt 24), Paul's references to the end-times events, and John's Apocalypse (the book of Revelation)—reflect the messianic orientation of Jewish

---

4. Luke reports a seminal moment in Paul's ministry before the council of chief priests, with the council divided between Sadducees and Pharisees. Invoking his high credentials as a Pharisee, he said, "It is with respect to the hope and the resurrection of the dead that I am on trial." With this, the council erupted in dissension, with some Pharisees even defending Paul. The tribunal became so violent that Paul was taken away to his barracks (Ac 23:6–11).

5. Josephus, *Wars of the Jews*, 2.8.12 [159].

hopes. However, as I will argue in elaborating my own view below, they interpret the fulfillment of Old Testament prophecy in Jesus Christ's person and work rather than in events that culminate in a restored theocratic kingdom with a renewed temple and sacrificial system.

Throughout the last days of Jesus on earth, his disciples failed to understand the purpose of his mission. They imagined that they were going to Jerusalem for an inaugural ball rather than a bloody crucifixion. Even at Christ's ascension the last question that the disciples ask is, "Lord, will you at this time restore the kingdom to Israel?" (Ac 1:6). Jesus' answer is crucial for Christian eschatology: "It is not for you to know times or seasons that the Father has fixed by his own authority. But you will receive power when the Holy Spirit has come upon you, and you will be my witnesses in Jerusalem and in all Judea and Samaria, and to the ends of the earth" (vv. 7–8). This was Jesus' last statement on the subject—and indeed, on the earth.

B. ANCIENT AND MEDIEVAL ESCHATOLOGIES

In the main, the ancient church seems to have held that the kingdom had been inaugurated with Christ's first advent, yet awaited its full consummation in the future: the position associated today with amillennialism.[6] The first widespread millenarian movement was associated with the Montanists, named after Montanus, who claimed to have received revelations in which Christ promised to return within his lifetime. With two young women, Prisca and Maximilla, Montanus led a popular movement that included Tertullian among its number. The failure of the alleged prophecies, the eccentric asceticism associated with the movement, and the condemnation of its views by the church eventually extinguished Montanism, but its apocalyptic spirit would be revived at various points throughout church history.[7]

At the same time, the "amillennialism" of the early church underwent alteration as the church transitioned from being a persecuted minority to receiving imperial favor with the conversion of Constantine in the fourth century. Historical circumstances rendered more plausible the belief that Christ is presently reigning on the earth through his earthly representative, the emperor. Gradually, the earlier type of amillennialism, which recognized the precariousness of the church's existence in this clash between the two ages, surrendered to a more triumphalistic version. How could the visibility of Christ's kingdom be considered ambiguous or mostly hidden

---

6. Although Justin Martyr held something close to what we would call historical premillennialism, he acknowledged that this was not the most widely held view of his day. For one of the best treatments of patristic perspectives on eschatology, see Charles E. Hill, *Regnum Caelorum: Patterns of Millennial Thought in Early Christianity* (2nd ed.; Grand Rapids: Eerd-

mans, 2001). For his treatment of Martyr's views, see especially pages 194–95.

7. See Ronald Knox, *Enthusiasm: A Chapter in the History of Religion, with Special Reference to the XVII and XVIII Centuries* (New York: Oxford Univ. Press, 1950).

in this age when its teachings, rites, symbols, and ministers now received secular approval? At this point, amillennialism became more like what we refer to today as postmillennialism: the view that an earthly geopolitical kingdom will be brought about by the gradual success of the church and its mission in the world. Church historian Eusebius, in fact, celebrated his patron Constantine as Christ's earthly image. "Our divinely favored emperor," said Eusebius, "receiving, as it were, a transcript of the divine sovereignty, directs, in imitation of God himself, the administration of this world's affairs." With divine mandate, therefore, the emperor "subdues and chastens the open adversaries of the truth in accordance with the usages of war."[8]

Because of various factors (including the shift of the political center from Rome to Constantinople), the significance and power of the bishop of Rome grew to the point where he claimed supremacy over the whole church and, eventually, over the whole world. Like the Caesars before them, the bishops of Rome were considered the high priests of the empire. Whether embodied in the emperor or in the pope, Christendom confused the present reign of Christ in grace with his everlasting reign in glory. In other words, it assumed not only that Christ's kingdom was already present in the world, but that it was fully realized in the Holy Roman Empire.

A more nuanced version of ancient amillennialism was advocated by Augustine in the fifth century.[9] Discerning the thread of Christ's kingdom throughout redemptive history, and recognizing its varied manifestations and administrations, Augustine's *City of God* distinguished clearly the "two cities" of this present age—each with its own commission, purpose, destiny, and means.[10] Nevertheless, Augustine reluctantly conceded the use of the secular sword in the suppression of the Donatists, a schismatic and apocalyptic group that sought to usher in the kingdom by the use of force.

After Augustine, the fusion of the kingdom of Christ with the empire in the Middle Ages virtually extinguished the already–not yet tension of earlier amillennialism. Monarchs fancied themselves King David *redivivus*, driving out the Canaanites with their holy knights. On a cold November day in 1095, Pope Urban II roused a Christendom plagued by internal wars to take up the cause of holy war against Islam. "If you must have blood," he exhorted, "bathe in the blood of infidels."[11] Much as in early Judaism, apocalyptic eschatologies (i.e., predictions of imminent judgment and

---

8. Eusebius, *Oration in Praise of Constantine* 1.6–2.5 (see *NPNF2*, 1:583), quoted in Douglas Farrow, *Ascension and Ecclesia* (Edinburgh: T&T Clark, 1999), 115.

9. See the excellent study by Robert Markus, *Saeculum: History and Society in the Theology of St. Augustine* (Cambridge: Cambridge Univ. Press, 1989), as well as his more recent (and slightly revised) reflections in *Christianity and the Secular* (South Bend, Ind.: Univ. of Notre Dame Press, 2006).

10. Paradoxically, an Augustinian soteriological "dualism" between those within the covenant community and those outside

of it—yet not outside of God's common grace—together with its suspicion of Christian perfectionism and an overrealized eschatology, feeds respect for the other *as* other. Cain may be exiled from the City of God, but God has provided richly for his earthly sojourn nonetheless. The same point has often been drawn from the examples of Ishmael and Esau. They may be exiled from the cultic community, but they cannot be exiled from the common community of creation and the law of our very humanity.

11. Cited in Robert Payne, *The Dream and the Tomb: A History of the Crusades* (New York: Stein & Day, 1985), 34.

renewal from outside of the present system) erupted from time to time in the medieval era in sharp criticism of the reigning establishment. Thus, the Constantinian distortion of amillennialism fostered a conservative temperament, reducing Christ's kingdom to a historical institution, while millenarian movements encouraged radical criticism of the status quo, understanding Christ's kingdom as an apocalyptic and anti-institutional reality. The story of Christendom reminds us that the attempt to Christianize the empires of this age is as easily described as the secularization of the church.

Among many apocalyptic movements in the Middle Ages, one is especially noteworthy for its long-term influence. Sicilian monk Joachim of Fiore (1132–1202) wrote a commentary on the book of Revelation that interpreted prophecy in literal, historical, and futuristic terms. Dividing history into three periods, Joachim advanced the thesis that the Age of the Father (from the time of Adam to the time of Christ) was the era of law, the Age of the Son (from Christ to Joachim's day) was the era of grace, and the coming Age of the Spirit (which he predicted would begin in 1260) would bring an end to the church and the necessity of all external aids (such as preaching and sacrament). Everyone would know God directly and immediately in that age, producing a complete spiritual unity of the human race.[12] Although the categories we employ today are somewhat anachronistic as applied to that age, Joachim's views are closest to what we would call "postmillennial."

Apocalyptic millenarianism fueled various medieval sects, including neo-Gnostic groups such as the Albigensians and Cathari, as well as less extreme movements such as the Spiritual Franciscans (following in Joachim's wake) and the Brethren of the Common Life. Yet the most significant flowering of this legacy is seen in the rise of Anabaptism. While most Anabaptists were pacifists, Thomas Müntzer and John of Leyden led violent revolutions in an effort to establish the kingdom of the Spirit. Taking over the German city of Münster, radical Anabaptists established a communist and polygamous regime.[13]

C. REFORMATION ESCHATOLOGIES

Like Augustine, Luther and Calvin defended in theory a two-kingdoms approach that they did not always follow in practice. More clearly than Augustine, Luther and Calvin articulated the distinction between the heavenly and earthly kingdoms. The former proceeds by the Word alone, not by the secular sword, they insisted. The Reformers went a long way toward recovering, at least in principle,

12. Marjorie Reeves, *Joachim of Fiore and the Prophetic Future: A Medieval Study in Historical Thinking* (London: SPCK, 1976); Bernard McGinn, *The Calabrian Abbot: Joachim of Fiore in the History of Western Thought* (New York: Harper & Row, 1985); Delno C. West and Sandra Zimdars-Swartz, *Joachim of Fiore: A Study in Spiritual Perception and History* (Bloomington: Indiana Univ. Press, 1983).

13. Eugene F. Rice Jr. and Anthony Grafton, *The Foundations of Early Modern Europe, 1460–1559* (2nd ed.; New York: Norton, 1994), 163–68, 178–83.

the sense of the church's precariousness in this present age—its ambiguity as an already–not yet reality, simultaneously justified and sinful. Douglas Farrow correctly observes that Calvin, more than any other figure in this period, focused attention again on the historical economy of Christ's advent, ascension, and return in the flesh.[14] Because Christ inaugurated his kingdom and poured out his Spirit as a harbinger of the last days, this reign is partially realized and becomes visible through the gospel ministry. However, it will not be consummated until Christ returns physically to the earth. The church cannot substitute itself for Christ's earthly presence in the flesh.

If Rome had confused the kingdom of Christ with the political kingdoms of this age, the Reformers believed that the Anabaptists had set the two kingdoms in dangerous opposition. Instead, the Reformers insisted, believers must live as citizens of two kingdoms, each with its own distinct sources, ends, and means.[15] Patiently awaiting the final separation and judgment by Christ, believers live under various secular regimes as dutiful citizens and neighbors. In fact, Calvin counseled, "it makes no difference what your condition among men may be or under what nation's laws you live, since the Kingdom of Christ does not at all consist in these things."[16] "In short," Calvin exhorted, "when any one of us hears that Christ's kingship is spiritual, aroused by this word let him attain to the hope of a better life; and since it is now protected by Christ's hand, let him await the full fruit of this grace in the age to come."[17] All attempts to transform this spiritual kingdom under the cross into a geopolitical kingdom of pomp and glory are really driven by the same eschatological misunderstanding of Christ's disciples, expressed in their expectation of a recovery of the theocracy even when the messianic King had himself arrived. Christians continue to repeat this error, Calvin argues.[18]

Like their predecessors in the ancient church, the churches of the Reformation identified millenarian enthusiasm with the apocalyptic expectations of first-century Judaism: identifying God's end-time kingdom with a political regime—a restoration of the Sinai theocracy. The Reformers believed that it was precisely this misunderstanding that left Jesus' contemporaries (even his disciples) disillusioned

---

14. Farrow, *Ascension and Ecclesia*, 176–77.

15. See David VanDrunen, *Natural Law and the Two Kingdoms: A Study in the Development of Reformed Social Thought* (Grand Rapids: Eerdmans, 2010).

16. Calvin, *Institutes* 4.20.1; cf. 4.20.8.

17. Ibid., 2.15.3.

18. Ibid., 4.5.17.

19. The *Augsburg Confession* (art. 17) (in *The Book of Concord: The Confessions of the Evangelical Lutheran Church* [ed. and trans. Theodore G. Tappert; Philadelphia: Fortress, 1959]) rejected chiliasm, identifying it with the Anabaptists "who now scatter Jewish opinions that, before the resurrection of the dead, the godly shall occupy the kingdom of the world, the wicked being everywhere suppressed." The Reformed concurred, as in the *Second Helvetic Confession*'s rejection of "the Jewish dream of a millennium, or golden age on earth, before the last judgment" (in *The Book of Confessions* [Louisville: PCUSA General Assembly, 1991]). Calvin similarly dismissed millenarian views (*Institutes* 4.25.5), and Archbishop Cranmer rejected such views as a "fable of Jewish dotage" (*Anglican Articles*, art. 41). The repeated references to "Jewish opinions" were therefore not an anti-Semitic slur, but a comparison of chiliastic movements of their day to the misunderstanding of Jesus' contemporaries. See Philip Schaff, *History of the Christian Church* (Peabody, Mass.: Hendrickson, n.d.), 2:381.

when his triumphal entry into Jerusalem was followed by his crucifixion.[19] Therefore, the Reformers rejected both the "Christendom" version of amillennialism and the millennial literalism of radical sects. Both versions in their own way reflected an overrealized eschatology: an attempt to seize the kingdom of glory rather than receive the kingdom of grace. However, it should be noted that practice was not always consistent with theory in the Reformation, any more than it was in the case of Augustine's counsel concerning Donatism.[20]

D. EARLY MODERN ESCHATOLOGIES: POSTMILLENNIALISM AND PROGRESS

The myth of Western Christendom persisted as God's favoritism in Roman Catholic (Spanish, Portuguese, and French) and Protestant (especially British) colonial expansion as well. Many Protestants interpreted the surprising British defeat of the Spanish Armada in 1588 as the destruction of the dragon and the beginning of the end of Antichrist's rule. Cromwell's Commonwealth was rife with millennial fanaticism, enlivened by appeals to Joachim of Fiore's speculations about a Third Age of the Spirit. References to Joachim's prophecies are abundant in the writings of the rationalists, idealists, revolutionaries, and romantics. The Age of the Spirit became secularized as the Age of Enlightenment.

From this penchant for interpreting current events as the literal fulfillment of biblical prophecy arose the dominance of a postmillennial eschatology (especially in Britain and America). From John Winthrop's announcement of Puritan New England as "a shining city upon a hill" to the presidency of Woodrow Wilson, the expectation of a golden age fueled foreign missions and a proliferation of church-sponsored voluntary societies, moral reforms, and service agencies. At last, the kingdoms of this world would become the kingdom of Christ, it was consistently argued, and America would be at the headwaters of this millennial age before Christ's return. This view was widely held by many American Protestants at the turn of the twentieth century. Meanwhile, in Roman Catholic countries, the pope continued to require absolute obedience of all states and rulers. In fact, the First Amendment to the U.S. Constitution was identified as the "Americanist heresy" by the Vatican until the mid-twentieth century.[21]

---

20. Luther's counsel to the princes in the Peasant's War and Calvin's consent to the execution of Servetus serve as cautionary examples of inconsistency.

21. The remarkable American Jesuit theologian John Courtney Murray was formative in developing a Roman Catholic social doctrine that was compatible with liberal democracy. See his *We Hold These Truths: Catholic Reflections on the American* *Proposition* (New York: Sheed and Ward, 1960). Although he met staunch opposition by the Vatican, his views made a strong impression at the Second Vatican Council, as is especially evident in the Council's *Dignitatis Humanae* (see *Patristic Sources and Catholic Social Teaching* [ed. Brian J. Matz; Leuven: Peeters, 2008], 35–40).

E. LATER MODERN ESCHATOLOGIES: PREMILLENNIAL PESSIMISM

After the failure of "the war to end all wars" (World War I) to deliver the promised reign of peace, dreams of paradise turned to visions of Armageddon. Even among some traditional Protestants premillennialism experienced a revival during this era as a growing number of Christians in Britain and the United States interpreted Daniel's prophecies as having been fulfilled in the French and American revolutions. Although initially enamored of Charles Finney's social activism, evangelist D. L. Moody became increasingly pessimistic about the extent to which earthly empires could become the kingdom of God. "I look upon this world as a wrecked vessel," he would later write. "God has given me a lifeboat and said to me, 'Moody, save all you can.'"[22] Whereas revival was usually regarded as an instrument of Christianizing society through evangelism and social action, Moody saw it as a means of converting individuals: "soul-saving."

John Nelson Darby (1800–1882), an Anglo-Irish lawyer who became ordained in the (Anglican) Church of Ireland, became convinced that the prophecies of Isaiah, Daniel, and Revelation referred to a future kingdom that was utterly distinct from the church. In 1832 he formally severed his ties with the Church of Ireland and articulated his belief in a "secret rapture" of believers prior to the tribulation, return, and millennial kingdom of Christ. A founding figure in the rise of the Plymouth Brethren, Darby is the father of *dispensational premillennialism*.[23]

Distinguished from historic premillennialism by its belief in a stark separation of Israel and the church and a secret rapture of believers prior to a seven-year tribulation, dispensationalism also divided history into seven distinct periods. These are the dispensations of (1) innocence (prefall), (2) conscience (postfall to Noah), (3) human government (Noah to Abraham), (4) promise (Abraham to Moses), (5) law (Moses to Christ), (6) grace (the church age), (7) kingdom (the millennial age).[24] Just as postmillennial eschatology played a significant role in the formation of United States foreign and domestic policy in the nineteenth century, which to some extent endures in more liberal social and political circles, dispensationalism has shaped the eschatological horizon of evangelical conservatives in the public square.

More recently, some dispensationalists, such as Craig Blaising and Darrell Bock,

---

22. D. L. Moody, as quoted in George Marsden, *Fundamentalism and American Culture* (New York: Oxford Univ. Press, 1980), 38.

23. See Michael Williams, *This World Is Not My Home: The Origins and Development of Dispensationalism* (Fearn, Ross-shire, Scotland: Mentor, 2003).

24. Dispensationalism spread rapidly, especially through a series of annotated reference Bibles from C. I. Scofield to

Charles Ryrie to John MacArthur Jr., and the founding of Bible colleges and seminaries, such as the Moody Bible Institute and Dallas Theological Seminary. It has been popularized by numerous Bible prophecy conferences, the most successful television and radio evangelists, and national best sellers, from Hal Lindsey's *Late Great Planet Earth* to the recent *Left Behind* series by Tim LaHaye and Jerry Jenkins.

have formulated *progressive dispensationalism*, which moves away from the sharp distinction between Israel and the church and affirms that the kingdom of Christ is in some sense present although it will be fully realized in the millennium.[25] This position is therefore much closer to *historic premillennialism*.[26]

While classic dispensationalism represents an extreme version of the thesis that most biblical prophecies are still future, an extreme view at the opposite end, known as *full preterism*, holds that every biblical prophecy has already been fulfilled (including the Second Coming, the general resurrection, and the final judgment). There is no resurrection of the body, according to full preterists. However, partial preterists hold that the second coming of Christ to raise the dead and judge the world is still future.[27]

F. BROADER TRENDS IN CONTEMPORARY ESCHATOLOGY

After centuries of assimilating the kingdom of Christ to the progress of secular culture, liberal Protestantism was shaken from within by the "consistent eschatology" of Albert Schweitzer (1875–1965). In sharp contrast to the idea of a gradual evolution of the kingdom of love (widely assumed by liberal Protestants), Schweitzer argued that Jesus expected an imminent kingdom arriving from above, bringing cataclysm and judgment. However, when this kingdom did not materialize, Jesus surrendered himself to death in the hope that it would somehow provoke the Father to act on his behalf. After his death, Jesus' followers transformed his apocalyptic anticipation of an imminent dawn of the kingdom into a steady growth of the church. This perspective was short lived, however, soon to be replaced by the dialectical circle (early Bultmann, Barth, Gogarten, and Brunner) of the 1920s and 1930s, with its tendency to set history and eschatology in antithesis as virtually synonymous with a time-eternity dualism.

However, by midcentury interest in history flowered anew, even among some of Bultmann's students. Associated with a working group at Heidelberg University that included Oscar Cullmann and Gerhard von Rad (Old Testament), Günther Bornkamm (New Testament), and Hans von Campenhausen (Historical Theology/Systematic Theology), renewed attention to the history of Israel and its covenant theology challenged a century of anti-Jewish (and therefore, anti-Old Testament) presuppositions of

---

25. Craig A. Blaising and Darrell L. Bock, *Progressive Dispensationalism* (Grand Rapids: BridgePoint, 2000).

26. George Eldon Ladd's work remains the ablest statement of historic premillennialism. See his *The Blessed Hope* (Grand Rapids: Eerdmans, 1956) and his *Commentary on Revelation* (Grand Rapids: Eerdmans, 1987).

27. Full preterism is defended in the 1878 book by J. S. Russell, *Parousia: The New Testament Doctrine of Our Lord's*

Second Coming (Grand Rapids: Baker, 1999). Partial preterism is defended in R. C. Sproul, *The Last Days According to Jesus* (Grand Rapids: Baker, 1998), and Kenneth Gentry Jr., "The Preterist View," in *Four Views of the Book of Revelation* (ed. Marvin Pate; Grand Rapids: Zondervan, 1998). An outstanding rebuttal of the full preterist view is found in Keith A. Mathison, ed., *When Shall These Things Be? A Reformed Response to Hyper-Preterism* (Phillipsburg, N.J.: P&R, 2004).

biblical scholarship, especially in Germany. A young member of this circle, Wolfhart Pannenberg, sought to relate eschatology to history in developing his theology of the kingdom.[28] Pannenberg's eschatology is future oriented. Only in the end is the meaning of the whole of history finally revealed. However, as the prolepsis of the end, Christ's resurrection is the fully realized aspect of eschatology that warrants the Christian hope.

Jürgen Moltmann joined this broader trajectory, but with a more radical expectation of the power of Christ's future to transform the present. Indeed, eschatology is the principal theme of Moltmann's work. However, it is shaped explicitly by Joachim of Fiore's vision of the Age of the Spirit, the panentheistic ontologies of German mysticism and idealism (especially Böhme, Schelling, and Hegel), and democratic socialism. It offers a staunch defense of what he refers to as premillennialism but is more postmillennial in orientation.[29] Where Barth tended to see eschatology as a hope beyond history in an eternity-time dualism, Moltmann sees eschatology as the hope within history that propels us toward the future. Timothy Gorringe has pointed out, "In terms of cultural background, Barth's theology begins in apocalypse and ends with relative stability; Moltmann begins with relative stability and moves increasingly into the insecurity signified by the preoccupation of present-day culture with apocalypse."[30] Moltmann's *Theology of Hope* is especially directed against Barth's "epiphany of the eternal present," Gorringe notes.[31] However, dispensationalism is dangerously attached to a negative apocalypticism, anticipating the destruction of the world in a violent conflagration rather than its consummation in a kingdom of peace. "Christian eschatology—eschatology, that

28. Wolfhart Pannenberg, *Theology and the Kingdom of God* (Philadelphia: Westminster Press, 1969).

29. Richard Bauckham, "The Millennium," in *God Will Be All in All: The Eschatology of Jürgen Moltmann* (ed. Richard Bauckham; Edinburgh: T&T Clark, 1999), 132–33.

30. Timothy Gorringe, "Eschatology and Political Radicalism," in Bauckham, ed., *God Will Be All in All*, 92.

31. Gorringe, "Eschatology and Political Radicalism," 104. Similarly, Miroslav Volf observes, "Eschatology was the heartbeat of Barth's theology. But it was an eschatology that managed to posit itself, so to speak, only by denying itself. It was an 'eternalized' eschatology, which had much to do with the present (the transcendent 'eternal Moment' in the early Barth) or with the past (the 'hour' of Christ's coming in the later Barth), but little with the future—either the future of God or the future of God's world (CoG 15)" (Miroslav Volf, "After Moltmann," in Bauckham, ed., *God Will Be All in All*, 233–34).

32. Jürgen Moltmann, *The Coming of God*: *Christian Eschatology* (trans. Margaret Kohl; Minneapolis: Fortress, 1996), 202. For an interesting reflection on how he developed his early foci, see Moltmann, "Can Christian Eschatology Become Post-Modern? Response to M. Volf," in Bauckham, ed., *God Will Be All in All*: "What next? is a typically modern question—generally an American one. So what comes 'after' the modern? We have it: the post-modern. What comes after the post-modern? We have it: the ultra-modern. Or are these merely further instalments of modernity, which is always out to outstrip itself—a kind of post-ism? If we look at the ever-shorter 'shelf-life' of what is produced, and the speeding up of time, then the post- and ultra-modern are no more than modernity in new packaging" (259). After writing *Theology of Hope*, Moltmann says, he came as a visiting professor at Duke and found that the book was being used to bolster American optimism. Thereafter, "I promised friends that if I were to come back I would only talk about 'the theology of the cross.' This is what I then did in 1972 with my book, *The Crucified God*, which appeared in English in 1974" (260). The Reformation attack on millenarianism as a "Jewish dream" caught his attention. "The Reformation critics no doubt grasped the fact: anyone who banishes the millennium from the Christian hope has no further interest in Israel and no positive relationship to the Jews" (262). The fervent interest in the outpouring of the Spirit on Jews, inspiring early missions to ethnic Jews among Reformed churches, is entirely overlooked by Moltmann.

is, which is messianic, healing and saving—is millenarian eschatology," Moltmann insists.[32]

Mark C. Mattes has observed that in Moltmann's view of the kingdom, believers are regarded almost exclusively as actors rather than receivers, building the kingdom rather than receiving it. "In Luther's view," remarks Mattes, "the kingdom is promised. It is Jesus Christ in action.... For Luther, the kingdom is realized linguistically, not existentially, metaphysically, or politically, in the gift-word of the gospel as sheer promise."[33] In other words, the triune God is speaking a new creation into existence, not merely directing human aspirations and activities. This is not quietism, but the liberation of the church to fulfill the Great Commission and of believers in their worldly callings to fulfill their cultural obligations alongside unbelievers. By contrast, says Mattes,

> Along with Engels and Bloch, who maintained that communism was indebted to [Thomas] Müntzer (1490–1525), Moltmann believes that the human is always an agent (*homo semper agens*), not a recipient.... The paradoxes that help preserve faith, described by Luther (that one is simultaneously lord and servant, sinful and righteous, that God is hidden and revealed, and that Jesus Christ is human and divine), are flattened out into a "Christ transforming culture" perspective, effected, strangely enough, by means of a counterculture—"Christ against culture," to use the helpful typology of H. Richard Niebuhr (1894–1962).... Here, the gospel is given within the matrix of law.[34]

But Moltmann's view misses the important fact that "misplaced trust" is the root cause of ethical problems and can be challenged only by proclamation of the gospel.[35] In fact, Mattes goes so far as to call Moltmann's approach a "post-tribulation premillennialist of the 'left.' "[36]

Moltmann rightly judges that Aquinas's eschatology is completely vertical (consistent with the eternity-time dialectic and the ascent from time to eternity), whereas Joachim's is linear (historical). Aquinas "loses the remembrance of the biblical history: the Old Testament and Israel are forgotten." And hope is lost too. In the end, Moltmann judges, this eschatology is basically Gnostic.[37] However, it is not amillennialism, as Moltmann argues, but a Neoplatonist ontology and an overrealized eschatology of ecclesiastical pretension, that led to this state of affairs. Overcoming an overrealized amillennialism, Moltmann properly distinguishes the church from

---

33. Mark C. Mattes, *The Role of Justification in Contemporary Thought* (Grand Rapids: Eerdmans, 2004), 89–90.

34. Ibid., 91.

35. Ibid., 92.

36. Ibid., 95.

37. Richard Bauckham, "Eschatology in *The Coming of God*," in *God Will Be All in All*, 37–41. Moltmann explores the contrast between Joachim of Fiore and Thomas Aquinas

in "Christliche Hoffnung Messianisch oder transzendental? Ein theologisches Gespräch mit Joachim von Fiore und Thomas von Aquin,' " *Münchner Theologische Zeitschrift* 33 (1982): 241–60. He calls the Thomist (Balthasarian) version a "presentative" or "vertical" eschatology, which "loses ... their sense of disruption of history, but restores the future to an eschatological category" (Bauckham, "Eschatology in *The Coming of God*," 27).

the kingdom. However, he often transfers this overrealized status of the church as the fully realized kingdom to the moral activity of believers in building a social-democratic political order.

Moltmann's interpretations are susceptible to challenge on various counts, both historical and exegetical. First, as Richard Bauckham observes, "The pre-Constantinian church was by no means unanimously millenarian," as Moltmann claims.[38] Furthermore, those who did not hold millenarian views (i.e., amillennialists) in this period certainly did not hold a triumphalist view of church or empire. "The popular view that the martyrs ascend at death to be with Christ in his heavenly kingdom may have seemed incompatible with the expectation of an earthly kingdom and may have led to a non-millenarian reading of Revelation 20 already in the pre-Constantinian period, anticipating Augustine's exegesis of the reign of the martyrs as their present rule in heaven (*De Civ. Dei* [*City of God*] 20.9)."[39] If Augustine and his colleagues believed in the resurrection of the dead, they can hardly be scolded for embracing amillennialism because of a "spiritualizing" tendency. Such "spiritualizing" is not due to amillennialism but to "the strong Platonic influence in the tradition...."[40]

Second, Moltmann collapses premillennialism and postmillennialism into a single eschatology, erroneously identifying Joachim's (as well as his own) as premillennial.[41] Third, Moltmann assumes that an amillennial perspective negates the renewal of the present creation in favor of a "hope for souls in the heaven of a world beyond this one."[42] However, Bauckham finds this an odd claim, totally unsupported by the history of amillennial interpretation. In fact, amillennialists expect a total renewal of creation at Christ's return and not simply in a thousand-year reign. If this is the case, "The question we must ask is: what theological function does the millennium fulfill which the new creation cannot?"[43] Moltmann argues, as Bauckham points out, that, "before the millennium there is no rule of the saints," but only the church: "the brotherly and sisterly, charismatic, non-violent fellowship of those who wait for the coming of the Lord ...(CoG 184)."[44] However, this argument is "in danger of suggesting that while it is premature for Christians to attempt to exercise absolutist and violent domination over the world now, they will exercise such domination in the coming millennium."[45] If this is so, the Anabaptist radicals

---

38. Bauckham, "The Millennium," 129, citing the important work by Hill, *Regnum Caelorum*, 194–95.

39. Bauckham, "The Millennium," 129.

40. Ibid., 130–31.

41. Ibid., 131–32. "This is not just terminologically confusing; it also deprives him of a distinction between two kinds of futurist millenarianism which is essential to an accurate reading of the Christian millenarian tradition and its relationship to the secular eschatologies of the modern period." See Moltmann, *The*

Coming of God, 147, 153, 194.

42. Bauckham, "The Millennium," 135, citing Moltmann, *The Coming of God*, 147.

43. Bauckham, "The Millennium," 135–36.

44. Ibid., 136.

45. Ibid., 137.

46. Ibid., 138. For his statement concerning radical Anabaptists Bauckham refers to Norman Cohn, *The Pursuit of the Millennium* (2nd ed.; London: Paladin, 1970), ch. 13.

were not wrong in principle but only in their timing.[46] Furthermore, "according to Revelation, it is not only in the millennium that the saints rule (20:4) but also in the New Jerusalem (22:5)." Why substitute a penultimate for an ultimate realization of the restoration of creation? "Once the new creation is understood in this way, it is not clear why a millennium is necessary."[47] "According to Moltmann, only the millennium supplies a 'goal of history' (CoG 133–134, 137, 193, 197)."[48] However, is not this goal just as certainly realized—even more so—after the end of this age, as amillennialism argues, as within it? "Why should it not have its goal in the new creation?"[49]

Fourth, for those who deny a literal millennium in the future, Moltmann insists, the end of history can be anticipated only as "an abrupt Big Bang," to which he attaches the terms "Hiroshima images" and "catastrophe."[50] However, Bauckham replies, this is far from the view held by amillennialists for whom God's act of new creation "redeems and renews and transfigures" rather than destroys creation in catastrophe. On the other hand, "Even the world history that reaches its goal in Moltmann's millennium would end with 'an abrupt Big Bang,' if that were the appropriate way to conceptualize the end."[51] Baukham writes,

> "Only the new earth offers possibilities for the new embodiment of human beings" (CoG 104). Yet in Moltmann's millennium there are precisely human beings risen to new embodiment *without the new earth* ... Moltmann's millenarianism here has the problem which all millenarianism has: how to characterize the millennium in such a way as to make it intelligible as transitional rather than final. (emphasis added)[52]

Moltmann is rightly concerned to see that our anticipation of the renewal of all things in the future guides our reflection and action in the present. However, this can be as fully maintained with or without a literal millennium. No less than millenarianism does an amillennial position anticipate the consummation of Christ's kingdom in the future. Yet it does so without an expectation either of final destruction of the cosmos (as in some popular versions of dispensationalism) or of a reduction of this wonderful condition of everlasting peace to a millennial era. In fact, Miroslav Volf argues that, "understood as transition, the millennium is not only unnecessary but *detrimental*."[53]

---

47. Bauckham, "The Millennium," 137.

48. Ibid.

49. Ibid., 139.

50. Ibid., 139, quoting Moltmann, *The Coming of God*, 201–2.

51. Bauckham, "The Millennium," 140–41.

52. Ibid., 141–42. It should be noted that Moltmann himself makes even further problems for himself on this score when he says, "Theological tradition has always related the word consummatio to the created world: De consummatione mundi is the title given to the relevant article in seventeenth-century Lutheran and Reformed theology: the old heaven and the old earth are to become a new imperishable heaven and a new imperishable earth" ("Can Christian Eschatology Become Post-Modern?" 262). If this is so, then everything that he has said thus far in criticism of the tradition is at least in need of qualification to avoid obvious contradiction.

53. Volf, "After Moltmann," 243.

II. Evaluating Millennial Perspectives Exegetically

Historic premillennialism has much to commend it. First, if Revelation 20 is to be interpreted literally, then the clear reference to a thousand-year period in which Satan is bound seems well founded. Second, as Wayne Grudem observes, Isaiah prophesies a period in which "The wolf shall dwell with the lamb, and the leopard shall lie down with the young goat," and "the earth shall be full of the knowledge of the Lord as the waters cover the sea" (Isa 11:6–9). According to Grudem, these prophecies envision "a momentous renewal of nature that takes us far beyond the present age," when a remnant of the nations will be drawn to the Lord (vv. 10–11).[54] Third, Grudem observes that those raised to reign with Christ in Revelation 20 had refused to worship the beast or receive his mark (Rev 20:4).

> But if the severity of the persecution described in Revelation 13 leads us to conclude that the beast *has not yet come* on the world scene, but is yet future, then the persecution by this beast is still future as well. And *if this persecution is still future, then the scene in Revelation 20* where those "who had not worshiped the beast ... and had not received its mark on the foreheads or their hands" (Rev. 20:4) *is still future as well.* This means that Revelation 20:1–6 does not describe the present church age but is best understood to refer to a future millennial reign of Christ.[55]

Grudem's conclusion follows logically if one grants the premise that the persecution envisioned in chapter 13 is in fact future—a premise that seems to me to run counter at least to the contemporary relevance of this Apocalypse for the suffering church under the Roman Empire.

A final exegetical argument that Grudem offers concerns the reference in Revelation 20 to those who "came to life and reigned with Christ for a thousand years" (v. 4). Does this not suggest a bodily resurrection of saints prior to the millennium and general resurrection of the dead? "Some amillennialists argue that the phrase 'came to life' refers to a coming of heavenly existence or coming into the presence of God. But it must be asked, Where does the Greek term *zaō* ('live') ever take that meaning? No other examples of that word in the New Testament take the sense, 'come into the presence of God.'" Furthermore, "resurrection" never means "going to heaven," as in the amillennial interpretation of this coming to life as a "first resurrection."[56]

Grudem observes that premillennialists and postmillennialists are talking about a radically different "millennium." For the latter, Christ is not bodily present as

---

54. Wayne Grudem, *Systematic Theology: An Introduction to Bible Doctrine* (Grand Rapids: Zondervan, 1994), 1128.

55. Ibid., 1131.

56. Ibid., 1119.

king; the earth is not completely restored with glorified saints reigning with him. Rather, there is a massive conversion of the nations to Christ, *after which* he will return in glory to raise the dead and personally reign in glory.[57] Far from expecting a wide-scale conversion of humanity, the New Testament speaks of "few" finding the narrow gate (Mt 7:13–14). "When the Son of man comes, will he find faith on earth?" (Lk 18:8). Paul describes life in "the last days" as mired in selfishness, materialism, hatred of God, and violence (2Ti 3:1–5).

However, postmillennialism also adduces passages in its favor. Messianic Psalms (like Psalm 2) envision an era in which the rulers of the earth serve the Lord and his Messiah. Certainly the Great Commission (Mt 28:18–20) suggests a gradual progress of the gospel. Everything now has been put in subjection to Christ (Heb 2:5–9). Jesus likened the kingdom to the smallest seed that grows into a great tree (Mt 13:31–32).

In my view, amillennialism provides the most satisfying account of the passages adduced by pre- and postmillennialists. Let me attempt then a brief summary and defense of this claim.

First, the term itself is something of a misnomer. Amillennialism does not deny the reality of the millennium; rather, it interprets that age as a present reality with a future consummation.[58] Jay Adams prefers the term "realized millennialism," stressing that amillennialism does not offer a spiritualized interpretation of Revelation 20 and does not reduce the period of which it speaks to unreality.[59] However, we must qualify this "realized millennialism" as a "*semi*realized millennialism," in order to avoid the dangers into which "Constantinian" versions fell. Not until Christ returns in glory at the end of the age will the kingdoms of this age become the kingdom of Christ. This brings at least the Reformed and Lutheran versions of amillennialism in closer proximity with historic premillennialism. Yet in agreement with postmillennialists, amillennialism argues that the kingdom was inaugurated by Christ's earthly ministry and will continue to flourish until he returns in glory.

Second, and related to the first point, the key to an amillennial understanding of the kingdom is the "already" and "not yet" dialectic. Jesus spoke of the kingdom as a present ("already") reality (Mk 1:15; Mt.11:5–6; 12:28; 13:1–46; Lk 11:5–6, 20; 17:20–23; 15:4–32), but also as something "not yet," belonging to the future (Mt 6:10; 16:28; Mk 9:1; Lk 6:20–26; 9:27; 11:2; 13:28–29). The kingdom is coming, but also has come (Mt 12:28–29; Lk 11:20).

In Luke 10 and 11 Jesus claims that in his earthly ministry he is binding Satan and looting his treasure, toppling his empire. It is in the light of these historical events and

---

57. Ibid., 1323.

58. Geerhardus Vos, *Redemptive History and Biblical Interpretation: The Shorter Writings of Geerhardus Vos* (ed. Richard

B. Gaffin Jr.; Phillipsburg, N.J.: P&R, 1980), 54.

59. Jay Adams, *The Time Is at Hand* (Phillipsburg, N.J.: P&R, 1970), 7–11.

their interpretation by Jesus in the Gospels that we should interpret the highly symbolic language of the book of Revelation. Against both premillennial and traditional postmillennial tendencies to reduce the kingdom to an exclusively visible regime of geopolitical power and glory, Jesus answered the question of the Pharisees concerning when the kingdom would come, "The kingdom of God is not coming with signs to be observed, nor will they say, 'Look, here it is!' or 'There!' for behold, the kingdom of God is in the midst of you" (Lk 17:20–21). Premillennialism fails adequately to appreciate the "already," while postmillennialism undervalues the "not yet" of Christ's kingdom.[60]

Third, an amillennial perspective is more consistent with the way in which the New Testament itself interprets the Old. Extreme versions of premillennialism (i.e., dispensationalism) and postmillennialism (i.e., preterism) seem to follow the assumption of early Jewish eschatology: namely, that Christ's kingdom will be fully realized in *one* coming. The key difference between dispensationalist premillennialists and postmillennial preterists is whether the millennium belongs to his second or first advent. The problem with both views, then, is that they tend to flatten out biblical prophecy. Either all of the significant end-time events *have* occurred (full preterism) or they all *will* occur (dispensationalism).

However, biblical prophecy exhibits a "telescoping" effect. Kim Riddlebarger uses the analogy of a mountainous horizon off in the distance. Approaching the initial range, one often discovers another one behind it.[61] Many of the messianic Psalms obviously refer to David, and yet he fails as an adequate fulfillment. Similarly, many of the prophecies in Isaiah are partly fulfilled in Cyrus king of Persia, and yet they never receive their complete fulfillment until Christ. Only his foot fits the glass slipper perfectly. Jesus himself applied these prophecies to himself. The question therefore, especially concerning the prophecies in the New Testament, is not whether they refer to Christ and his kingdom but whether they refer to his reign in grace or to his reign in glory. Because of the "already"/"not yet" dialectic, we should not be surprised that they refer to both. Christ's kingdom is simultaneously powerful in the eyes of God and weak in the eyes of the world.

In the Olivet Discourse (Matthew 24), Jesus prepares his disciples for imminent upheavals. Verses 1–2 introduce the topic, as Jesus is provoked by the disciples' awe at the grandeur of the temple's buildings: "Truly, I say to you, there will not be left here one stone upon another that will not be thrown down." In the following verses, Jesus explains the signs of the end of the age. There will be false messiahs and false

---

60. Although postmillennialism acknowledges that the kingdom has not yet been fully consummated, it holds that this is merely in degree. In principle, the kingdoms of this age already belong to Christ's heavenly kingdom, even if they have not yet submitted to it and realized its benefits. Amillennialists hold, however, that this is not even true in principle yet. Only when Christ returns will the two kingdoms become one.

61. Kim Riddlebarger, *A Case for Amillennialism* (Grand Rapids: Baker, 2003), 56.

prophets, deceiving many, along with natural disasters. "All these are but the beginning of the birth pains" (vv. 3–8). Then will follow tribulation and hatred "by all nations," tempting many followers to turn aside. "But the one who endures to the end will be saved" (vv. 9–13). Crucially, Jesus adds, "And this gospel of the kingdom will be proclaimed throughout the whole world as a testimony to all nations, and then the end will come" (v. 14). This is consistent with his response to the disciples' last question before his ascension concerning the coming of the kingdom, in which Jesus directs them to Pentecost and the universal mission to spread the gospel.

Here once again we recognize the paradox of the kingdom that is stressed by an amillennial perspective: the gospel will be preached to all nations, yet the witnesses will be held in derision by all nations. Jesus is "telescoping" all of the events between his two advents, since he concludes that during this whole period the gospel will be preached to all nations "and *then* the end will come." Since the gospel was obviously not preached to all nations by AD 70, it is impossible to conclude with preterists that the "end" to which Jesus refers is a past event. At the same time, Jesus speaks of the period of tribulation and success of the gospel as occurring simultaneously over an extended period of time. This fits well with the interpretation of the book of Revelation as a series of apocalyptic snapshots of the whole history of Christ's kingdom from its inauguration to its consummation at his return.[62]

Contrary to dispensationalism, Jesus says that the events to which he is referring will already begin to take place within the lifetime of his hearers (v. 34); yet contrary to preterism, he does not teach that they all took place in the lifetime of his hearers. In verses 15–28, Jesus recapitulates and elaborates the message of verses 3–14. Jesus warns his followers that during this entire period they must not be seduced by those who claim that he has returned. "For as the lightning comes from the east and shines as far as the west, so will be the coming of the Son of Man" (v. 27). Employing stark apocalyptic imagery, Jesus adds,

> Immediately after the tribulation of those days the sun will be darkened, and the moon will not give its light, and the stars will fall from heaven, and the powers of the heavens will be shaken. Then will appear in heaven the sign of the Son of Man, and then all the tribes of the earth will mourn, and they will see the Son of Man coming on the clouds of heaven with power and great glory. And he will send out his angels with a loud trumpet call, and they will gather his elect from the four winds, from one end of heaven to the other. (vv. 29–31)

This coming of the Son of Man in glory and power immediately follows the era of tribulation. Jesus does not mention a secret rapture or a millennium, but only a second coming to gather his elect. The last judgment follows this second coming (vv. 48–51).

---

62. See Dennis E. Johnson, *Triumph of the Lamb: A Commentary on Revelation* (Phillipsburg, N.J.: P&R, 2001), 1–48.

After telling two parables illustrating the unexpectedness of his coming, Jesus says, "When the Son of Man comes in his glory, and all the angels with him, then he will sit on his glorious throne," judging the nations and separating the sheep from the goats (Mt 25:31–32). After the period of tribulation and gospel advance, all of these events occur in one sweeping event: the second coming, the gathering of the elect, and the judging of the nations.

Jesus' apocalyptic imagery is taken from the prophets, where we discover both the telescoping pattern and the symbolic character of this genre. Issuing the judgment against Babylon, Yahweh declares, "Behold, the day of the LORD comes, cruel, with wrath and fierce anger, to make the land a desolation and to destroy its sinners from it. For the stars of the heavens and their constellations will not give their light; the sun will be dark at its rising, and the moon will not shed its light" (Isa 13:9–10). A similar vision of God's wrath is prophesied for the whole earth in chapter 24. When Yahweh comes to judge, "the moon will be confounded and the sun ashamed" (vv. 22–23). In the prophecy against Pharaoh and Egypt in Ezekiel 32 we encounter similarly vivid imagery. Although Egypt prowls like a sea monster in the deep for nations to devour, God will catch the proud empire in his net and fling it on an open field where the birds will gather and the beasts will pick its bones (vv. 2–4). "I will strew your flesh upon the mountains and fill the valleys with your carcass.... When I blot you out, I will cover the heavens and make their stars dark; I will cover the sun with a cloud, and the moon shall not give its light. All the bright lights of heaven will I make dark over you, and put darkness on your land, declares the Lord GOD" (vv. 5, 7–8).

The day of the LORD is similarly described in terms of earthquakes, trembling heavens, and the eclipse of sun, moon, and stars (Joel 2:10, 31; 3:15; cf. Zep 1:15). As we have seen, the coming of the Son of Man in the clouds, of which Jesus speaks, is prophesied in Daniel 7:13–14. There is no more reason to interpret the apocalyptic imagery literally in Matthew 24 than in the prophetic texts that Jesus cites. In both cases, *historical-apocalyptic* turning points of dramatic moment can be signified only by appeal to cataclysmic *natural and cosmic* phenomena.

In the light of this seminal discourse, the teaching of the rest of the New Testament can be seen to anticipate the following end-time scenario. At this point, amillennialists will agree with postmillennialists (specifically, *partial* preterists) in concluding that some of the apocalyptic images of Matthew 24:29–31 are fulfilled in the events to which Jesus in fact directly refers: namely, the destruction of the temple in AD 70, an event that Jesus explicitly says will be witnessed by some of his hearers.[63]

---

63. R. T. France, *The Gospel According to Matthew* (Tyndale New Testament Commentaries; Leicester, U.K.: Inter-Varsity Press, 1985), 343–46.

Peter's Pentecost sermon itself seems to point in this direction, as he quotes Joel's prophecy (Ac 2:16–21). In a premillennialist interpretation, it would have made sense for Peter to end his quotation from Joel 2:28–32 at verse 18, with the Spirit being poured out on all flesh. However, he continues: "And I will show wonders in the heavens above and signs on the earth below, blood, and fire, and vapor of smoke; the sun shall be turned to darkness and the moon to blood, before the day of the Lord comes, the great and magnificent day. And it shall come to pass that everyone who calls upon the name of the Lord shall be saved'" (Ac 2:19–21). This whole series of events is encompassed, according to Peter, in Christ's crucifixion and exaltation to the right hand of God with continuing effects in the present (vv. 22–36). Here once more it may be possible to understand this as "telescoping," with an immediate fulfillment followed by an ultimate and greater one, but this would require at least some break in thought between the first and second halves of Peter's quotation from Joel. In Ezekiel 32:7, Joel 2:10, and Amos 8:9, similar apocalyptic imagery is used for the fall of the first temple—even though we have no reason to take such imagery literally in that case.

With Grudem, I am not persuaded by R. T. France's interpretation of Christ's "coming on the clouds" as fulfilled in his ascension and the gathering of "his elect from the four corners of the earth" as referring to the witnesses he sent to preach the gospel to the nations during his earthly ministry.[64] This interpretation (also adopted by partial preterists) faces the challenge of the angel's promise to the disciples at Jesus' ascension: "This Jesus, who was taken up from you into heaven, will come in the same way as you saw him go into heaven" (Ac 1:11). The angel does not speak of Jesus coming on the clouds of glory, but as being taken up into heaven. Just as they visibly witnessed his departure in clouds of glory, the families of the earth "will see the Son of man coming on the clouds of heaven with power and great glory" (Mt 24:30). I agree with France's interpretation of the apocalyptic imagery as referring to a cataclysmic turn of historical events rather than to meteorological phenomena, but the scope is not limited to first-century events. It is a period of great tribulation that separates these two comings of the Son of Man in Matthew 24.

Accordingly, we should not assume that biblical prophecy is weighted toward the past or the future. Rather, it is part of the "already"/"not yet" dialectic of redemptive history. Since Christ's ascension and the descent of the Spirit at Pentecost, we have been living in "the/these last days" (Ac 2:17; 1Ti 4:1; 2Ti 3:1; Heb 1:2; Jas 5:3; 2Pe 3:3; Jude 18; 1Pe 1:20; 1Jn 2:18), before the "last day" (Jn 6:39, 40, 44, 54; 11:24; 12:28). Paul says that "the end of the ages has come" (1Co 10:11). Nevertheless, there is more still to come. Christ appeared "at the end of the ages" (Heb 9:26), yet

---

64. Grudem, *Systematic Theology*, 1126.

spoke of "the coming age" that even now is breaking in upon us through preaching and sacrament (Heb 6:5). It is a period in which the kingdom has been inaugurated by Christ's earthly ministry, empowered by the Spirit, advanced through witness to the gospel, consistently opposed by the world even to the point of great tribulation for the saints. Christ is reigning in grace from heaven by his Word and Spirit. Yet he will return in power and glory on the earth. With his second coming will arrive the resurrection of all the dead and the last judgment as one single and sweeping event. In fact, in spite of our experience now in the middle of it all, on that day we will look back to the whole history of the church from Christ's resurrection to his return as a single event — namely, "the end of the age" that is dominated by sin and death. In this perspective, believers are not awaiting a series of intervening events and regimes, but Christ's return in judgment and resurrection power. As Grudem recognizes, "This scheme is quite simple because all of the end time events happen at once, immediately after Christ's return."[65]

Paul understood Christ's reign as "already" and "not yet": "For he must reign until he has put all his enemies under his feet. The last enemy to be destroyed is death" (1Co 15:25–26). According to Hebrews, even now we "[taste of] the powers of the age to come" through baptism, preaching, and the Supper (Heb 6:5). The presence of the Spirit in our hearts as a pledge (*arrabōn*) of the consummation assures that what he has begun in us he will complete. The Spirit brings the blessings of the age to come into the present, which fills us not only with unspeakable joy but also with unutterable longing for the "more" still up ahead. The strong man is bound (Mt 12:28–29; Lk 10:18), so that the veil of unbelief may be torn from the eyes of Satan's prisoners. Christ has triumphed over Satan at the cross, and in his resurrection and ascension led captivity captive. According to the epistles, Christ is now reigning (1Co 15:25; Heb 1:3, 8, 13; 8:1; 10:12–13; Ac 2:24–25; 3:20–21). For this reason, Jesus can assure his persecuted saints, "Fear not, I am the first and the last, and the living one. I died, and behold I am alive forevermore, and I have the keys of Death and Hades" (Rev 1:17–18).

In this interim period, the kingdom advances alongside the suffering and even martyrdom of its witnesses. Yet Christ "will appear a second time, not to deal with sin but to save those who are eagerly waiting for him" (Heb 9:28; cf. 10:37). As we have seen, the regeneration of all things works in concentric circles, beginning with the inner person and then, at the consummation, including the resurrection of the body and the complete renewal of creation. Wherever the New Testament treats the complex of Christ's return, the resurrection, and the last judgment, no intervening raptures, resurrections, or judgments are mentioned. Grudem believes

---

65. Ibid., 1110.

that in John 5:28–29 Jesus refers to two resurrections, with "those who have done good *to the resurrection of life*, and those who have done evil to *the resurrection of judgment*."[66] However, Jesus' reference here is not to two separate *events* but to two separate *destinies*.

If Revelation 20 were straightforward historical narrative—or even prophecy—we would follow the dictum of dispensationalism to interpret it "literally wherever possible." However, the apocalyptic genre of the entire book is to be taken seriously on its own terms. Dispensationalists certainly recognize that there is much in Revelation that is symbolic. In fact, symbolic interpretations sometimes border on the fanciful, as biblical prophecies are interpreted in the light of daily headlines in the news.[67] However, especially in the light of the straightforward statements of Jesus and the rest of the New Testament, it makes better sense to interpret the thousand years of Revelation 20 (like the measurements of the heavenly temple) as symbolizing the present reign of Christ. In this perspective, the part of John's vision that we find in Revelation 20 happens in heaven, not on earth, and in the present day, not simply in a future event. The whole book is meant to be read not chronologically but as snapshots of the current age of the church from a heavenly point of view.[68]

How then do we respond to Grudem's objections above? If the New Testament itself speaks of Satan as having *blinded* unbelievers, how can we speak of his being *bound*?

First, from an amillennial perspective, *belief* is a greater problem for premillennialism than is the problem of *unbelief* for amillennialism. If Satan were not bound, there could not be a church—much less one that endures through the centuries despite heresy and schism. Yet Christ promised that he would build his church and that not even the gates of Hades would be able to withstand its assaults (Mt 16:18). Of greater difficulty for premillennialism to explain is how Christ's glorious reign for a thousand years can conclude with another "falling away."

It is true, as Grudem observes, that Revelation 20 speaks not only of Satan being bound but of his being thrown into the bottomless pit.[69] Yet here again it is quite consistent with prophecy, especially apocalyptic, to understand this as a telescop-

66. Ibid., 1119.

67. For example, Hal Lindsey identifies the "two wings of the great eagle" in Revelation 12 with a massive airlift of Jews fleeing the Antichrist's pursuit. "Since the eagle is the national symbol of the United States, it's possible that the airlift will be made available by aircraft from the U. S. Sixth Fleet in the Mediterranean" (*There's a New World Coming: A Prophetic Odyssey* [Santa Ana, Calif.: Vision House, 1973], 179). Similarly, Lindsey offers the conjecture that the locusts in Revelation 9 may be Cobra helicopters, especially since "they also make the sound of 'many chariots.'" The means of torment described may even be "a kind of nerve gas sprayed from its tail" (*New World Coming,*

138–39). For decades, classic dispensationalists have identified the Antichrist and other end-times figures with contemporary individuals, movements, and nations. In spite of the fact that these predictions prove erroneous, the same author often finds a willing audience for a new set of predictions.

68. On this interpretation, see Richard Bauckham, *The Theology of the Book of Revelation* (Cambridge: Cambridge Univ. Press, 1993), 7. In Revelation John was "taken up into heaven in order to see the world from the heavenly perspective. In fact, John mentions that it was 'on the Lord's day,' which highlights the Christian Sabbath as the sign participating in the reality."

69. Grudem, *Systematic Theology*, 1118.

ing of this action, encompassing both the period of his being bound (now) and the consummation of his judgment (destruction in the future). Hebrews 2:14 speaks of Satan as having been "destroyed" through Christ's death, and yet we know that Satan will be cast into the lake of fire at the end of history.[70] He still "prowls around like a roaring lion, seeking someone to devour" (1Pe 5:8), but this is consistent with an amillennial interpretation of Revelation 12, where Satan is cast out of the heavenly sanctuary, unable to affect the outcome of redemption, and yet persecutes the church. This interpretation underscores the point that it is the ministry in the heavenly courtroom that is decisive and that whatever Satan is allowed to do on earth is finally nothing more than the desperate and angry struggle of a defeated foe.

Grudem refers also to 2 Corinthians 4:4, where it is said that "the god of this world has blinded the minds of the unbelievers, to keep them from seeing the light of the gospel of the glory of Christ."[71] Yet it is precisely Satan's being bound that finally thwarts this effort. To the ends of the earth, the blind see (vv. 3,6). Grudem also refers to 1 John 5:19, where it is said that "the whole world lies in the power of the evil one."[72] However, when read together with the many passages indicating that the kingdom has been inaugurated and is progressing through the gospel, and that all authority now belongs to Christ in heaven and on earth, such passages reveal that the imprisonment of the world is precisely *the condition that Christ's kingdom of grace is overturning*. At present, he is looting Satan's kingdom, liberating captive hosts in his train. The world lies in darkness, but it has seen a great Light. Not only in spite of but even through the suffering testimony of the church, the gates of hell will not prevail against it.

For amillennialists, the already–not yet tension will not be resolved until Christ returns. Just as Christ's life was both humiliation and exaltation, the church suffers even as it fulfills its mission to bring the gospel to the ends of the earth. Neither a kingdom for which we are still waiting nor a kingdom that we must bring about, Christ's reign in grace is a kingdom that we are even now receiving from heaven.

Second, in response to Grudem's argument that the Old Testament prophecies (such as the wolf dwelling with the lamb) anticipate "a momentous renewal of nature that takes us far beyond the present age," we may again appeal to principles of prophetic interpretation. Apocalyptic language draws on natural images to express the force of major turning points in redemptive history. Wolves and lambs, serpents and doves, routinely describe the violent and peaceful condition of nations. Furthermore, the telescoping pattern of prophecy anticipates penultimate (semirealized) and ultimate (fully realized) fulfillments.

---

70. I am grateful to Keith Mathison for suggesting this reference.

71. Grudem, *Systematic Theology*, 1118.
72. Ibid.

Third, Grudem argues that Revelation 20 must be yet future on the basis that the persecution described in Revelation 13 has not yet occurred. However, I have indicated why I think that this entire era between Christ's two advents can be identified with the scenes in both chapters. The book of Revelation gives us snapshots of simultaneous realities in history, not a chronology of events. Exactly as Jesus foretold in his Olivet Discourse, this era is marked by simultaneous suffering and success.

I confess that the most difficult exegetical challenge is Grudem's final objection, namely, that those who "came to life" during the period described in Revelation 20 represent the souls of saints in heaven in the present rather than the resurrection of the dead in the future. However, the passage does speak of these who came to life as "the *souls* of those who had been beheaded for the testimony of Jesus and for the word of God ..." (v. 4). If the use of the Greek term *zaō* ("live") here cannot take the meaning of coming into the presence of God (prior to the resurrection of the body), then the explicit reference to *souls* is a larger problem. Surely the souls of the martyrs were not dead and so could not have come to life in a literal sense. Does it not make better sense to regard this as a reference to their coming into the presence of God upon their martyrdom? Are these not the same martyr-souls who cry out for vindication in Revelation 6:10?

As John's visions attest, Christ is certainly reigning in heaven even while there is great suffering and martyrdom of his people on earth. It would have been a source of great encouragement (the goal of this series of visions) for those facing persecution to know that they were among those who "came to life and reigned with Christ for a thousand years"—that is, during the present era of the church's continuing struggle below (symbolized as "a thousand years"). Although Grudem is correct that the Greek term *zaō* ("live") does not means "coming into the presence of God" elsewhere in the New Testament, it is not inconceivable that this is what is intended here. If this is so, the point being stressed is that martyrs can be assured that although they die, they will immediately come to life in heaven and reign with Christ awaiting his return.

Yet Grudem understandably asks how this could constitute a "first resurrection."[73]

We have to recall the context and purpose of the Apocalypse. John's strange visions were given first of all for the comfort of early Christians who were suffering extreme persecution under the Roman Empire. The book begins, "The revelation of Jesus Christ, which God gave [John] to show to his servants *the things that must soon take place*.... Blessed is the one who reads aloud the words of this prophecy, and blessed are those who hear, and who keep what is written in it, *for the time is near*"

---

73. Ibid., 1119.

(Rev 1:1, 3, emphasis added). A greeting is then offered to the seven churches in Asia Minor.[74] These are actual churches in John's day. They are to be comforted by the fact that Christ is now already "the firstborn of the dead and the ruler of kings on earth," who "has freed us from our sins by his blood and made us a kingdom, priests to his God and Father.... Behold, he is coming with the clouds, and every eye will see him, even those who pierced him, and all tribes of the earth will wail on account of him. Even so. Amen" (1:5–7).

On one hand, this repetition of Jesus' prophecy in Matthew 24:30 challenges the postmillennial (at least preterist or partial preterist) view that this event has already occurred—particularly given that John probably wrote the Apocalypse in the last decade of the first century, probably under Domitian's reign, sixty years after Christ's ascension and more than twenty years after the destruction of the temple. Nevertheless, it challenges also the premillennial view that the events described in John's visions are exclusively future for us when they were even in John's day "the things that must soon take place ..., for the time is near." Jesus was preparing his flock for imminent slaughter, assuring them that he is now already king over all powers and authorities and that he will, in due time, return to set everything right (Rev 1:17–18).

Great persecution did come upon the church and has continued uninterrupted in various parts of the world ever since. It may be more difficult for those of us in Western democracies to appreciate, but our brothers and sisters in other parts of the world recognize that the persecutions under Nero and Domitian are merely representative of the suffering church through the centuries.[75] Therefore, the visions that unfold are not successive reportage but are rather like snapshots of the kingdom in both its heavenly and its earthly, its triumphant and its militant, form: a kingdom of grace on earth now, which will one day be revealed as a kingdom of glory. In this context, the visions encompass the whole history of the church from the first century until the return of Christ and the church's entrance into the everlasting Sabbath. The visions in Revelation, through their stirring episodes of this present age from the heavenly perspective, highlight the "already"/"not yet" tension. Present persecution of the saints and the proud oppression of the masses by earthly empires is real, but so too is Christ's victory which lies in the past and the promised future yet to be consummated. This is the comfort of all believers in this time between Christ's two advents.

---

74. In many popular versions of dispensational teaching, these seven churches are taken to represent different periods of church history. So, ironically, the nonapocalyptic introduction to Revelation is in some sense "spiritualized," while the apocalyptic visions that follow are largely interpreted according to a more literalistic hermeneutic.

75. Millions of Christians have died for their witness to Christ over the last century. As I write, nearly 200 million Christians face arrest, imprisonment, and even death in many parts of the world. At most, 100,000 Christians were martyred under the Roman Empire.

According to an amillennial interpretation, then, we are presently living in the "thousand years" of Revelation 20, longing not for a literal millennium with yet another fall into sin but for the everlasting kingdom of righteousness and peace that will dawn with Christ's return in judgment and restoration. Borrowing imagery from the natural world, God promises a state of affairs in which erstwhile enemies (wolves, lambs, and lions) will be at peace.

Amillennialism has space, therefore, for a kingdom now (in grace) and its ultimate consummation (in glory). For now, it is at work within individuals, bringing them into a fellowship with Christ and therefore with each other that establishes peace. This, in fact, is "the mystery of Christ, which was not made known to the sons of men in other generations as it has now been revealed to his holy apostles and prophets by the Spirit. This mystery is that the Gentiles are fellow heirs, members of the same body, and partakers of the promise in Christ Jesus through the gospel" (Eph 3:4–6). Although once "separated from Christ, alienated from the commonwealth of Israel and strangers to the covenants of promise, having no hope and without God in the world," believing Gentiles "have been brought near by the blood of Christ. For he himself is our peace, who has made us both one and has broken down in his flesh the dividing wall of hostility" (Eph 2:12–14). Unless Christ is reigning now, Gentiles still have no hope in the world—and neither do Jews, since they too lie under the law's condemnation. Nevertheless, the kingdom is not yet revealed in glory, as it will be when Christ returns. Then his kingdom will indeed be entirely visible, complete, unopposed, and fully realized in the public sphere. The peace that reconciles us to God and to each other will be realized in a global peace that will never again be disturbed by violence. There is little place for confidence in a golden age prior to Christ's return, especially in the light of Paul's description of these last days in 2 Timothy 3:1–9 and Jesus' query, "Nevertheless, when the Son of Man comes, will he find faith on the earth?" (Lk 18:8). And yet these passages occur alongside Christ's promise to build and preserve his church to the end of the age. Measured by the progress of the gospel across all times and places, ours is a golden age indeed.

III. Israel and the End Times

The apostle Paul posed the question, "I ask, then, has God rejected his people?"—referring, of course, to ethnic Jews—and answered, "By no means!" (Ro 11:1). Before returning to this argument in Romans 9–11, it is important to examine its wider biblical-theological horizon and the interpretive options.

Many premillennialists, especially dispensationalists, distinguish sharply between the end-time events that culminate God's program with Israel and others that culminate his program with the church. Is it not "spiritualizing" to interpret promises and prophecies made to Israel as fulfilled in Christ's expanded Israel composed of "people ... from every tribe and language and people and nation," (Rev 5:9) who form his "holy nation" (1Pe 2:9)?

We may consider Amos 9:11 – 12, for example, a key passage on the restoration of Israel: "'In that day I will raise up the booth of David that is fallen and repair its breaches, and raise up its ruins and rebuild it as in the days of old, that they may possess the remnant of Edom and all the nations who are called by my name,' declares the LORD who does this." In that day, Israel's fortunes will be restored, and "they shall plant vineyards and drink their wine, and they shall make gardens and eat their fruit" (v. 14). They will never again be uprooted (v. 15). This is a vision of an everlasting paradise. Premillennialists (especially dispensational premillennialists) treat this as referring exclusively to the restoration of the nation of Israel, in its geopolitical land, with the restoration of the temple sacrifices, and the earthly kingship of Messiah.[76] The amillennial interpretation — namely, that it refers to this present age of the church's mission under Christ's reign — is regarded as a "spiritualizing" exegesis that does not take such prophecies at face value. However, there are several difficulties with the dispensational approach to a passage such as Amos 9.

First, Amos 9 speaks of a condition of everlasting, uninterrupted, unconditional blessing, whereas dispensationalism interprets this as pertaining merely to a millennial age. Second, and most decisive, is the fact that the apostles typically interpreted these prophecies as being fulfilled now in Jesus Christ and his gathering of a remnant from Israel and the nations by his Spirit. In fact, Amos 9 is quoted by James in his defense of Gentile inclusion in the church:

> Simeon [Peter] has related how God first visited the Gentiles, to take from them a people for his name. And with this the words of the prophets agree, just as it is written, "After this I will return, and I will rebuild the tent of David that has fallen; I will rebuild its ruins, and I will restore it, that the remnant of mankind may seek the Lord, and all the Gentiles who are called by my name, says the Lord, who makes these things known from of old." (Ac 15:14 – 18)

For James, the application of this passage is not future but present: Do not make the entrance requirements of the church depend on Jewish distinctives (v. 19).

James's interpretation is typical of the christocentric reading of the whole of Scripture that Jesus Christ himself taught his disciples (Lk 24:25 – 27, 31 – 32, 44 – 49). In fact, it is clear enough from such passages that the disciples' confusion and despair after Christ's death was due to their assumption that these Old Testament prophecies referred to the restoration of an earthly kingdom. "But we had

---

76. According to the Scofield Reference Bible (1917), Amos 9:11 – 15 (like Ps 72:1) teaches that "it is through restored Israel that the kingdom is to be extended over the earth."

hoped that he was the one to redeem Israel," the sorrowful disciples said on the road to Emmaus (Lk 24:21). Jesus explained that he had in fact redeemed Israel, far beyond her expectations, but through the cross and the resurrection. Even at his ascension the disciples asked, "Lord, will you at this time restore the kingdom to Israel?" and Jesus tells them simply to go to Jerusalem and wait for the descent of the Spirit (Ac 1:6–8).

From Peter's Pentecost sermon on, the apostles proclaimed that in Jesus Christ, through the progress of his gospel and the growth of his church, the Old Testament prophecies were being fulfilled. Now the core designations of the people of Israel — "a chosen race, a royal priesthood, a holy nation, a people for his own possession" (Ex 19:6; Dt 7:6; 10:15; Isa 43:20; 61:6; 66:21; Mal 3:17) are applied to all who have faith in Christ (1Pe 2:9). In fact, the inclusion of Gentiles in this identification is explicit in verse 10: "Once you were not a people, but now you are God's people; once you had not received mercy, but now you have received mercy."

Paul's contrast between the heavenly and earthly Jerusalem in the allegory of Sarah and Hagar (Gal 4:21–31) redraws the boundaries of Israel around Jesus Christ. Earthly descent no longer means anything, since the Mosaic covenant is no longer in force and could never annul or revise the earlier Abrahamic covenant, which promised blessing to the nations through the seed of Abraham and Sarah. As a result, the Jew-Gentile distinction no longer has any religious or ecclesial significance (Gal 3:15–4:7). It is the promise, not the law, that determines inheritance — and this is true now for everyone. "This means that it is not the children of the flesh who are the children of God, but the children of the promise are counted as offspring" (Ro 9:8).

Jesus would not have raised the ire of the religious leaders by claiming that he was about to overthrow Rome and reconsecrate the theocratic economy, but the charges of blasphemy are heard when Jesus presumes to forgive sins in his own person. The kingdom becomes partly visible in this age through this advent of the forgiveness of sins and release from the bondage of death. It is recognized not in the patriotic fervor of the zealots, but in Peter's confession of Jesus as the Christ/Messiah (Mt 16:16) and in the mission that leads to Jerusalem (the cross and resurrection). Similarly, the preaching of the kingdom in Acts concentrates on fulfillment of the messianic prophecies concerning the forgiveness of sins through the cross and resurrection of Christ (Ac 2:14–36; 3:12–16; 17:2–3). If this is so, then the binding of the strong man (Satan) in Luke 11 corresponds to the binding of Satan during the thousand years in Revelation 20, allowing for the progress of the gospel.

It can hardly be denied that this too is the core of Paul's message (as he summarizes in 1 Corinthians 15:3–4 what is likely an earlier formula). Still waiting for the *parousia* (Ro 8:19, 23–25; Php 3:20; 1Th 1:10), Paul nevertheless maintains that the new creation/kingdom has been inaugurated in Christ's conquest: the righteousness of God has been revealed from heaven (Ro 1:16–17), including justification of sinners and new birth, the Spirit and his gifts poured out (Ro 5:5). In Matthew 28:18, the climax is that all kingdom authority is in Christ's hands, which the Pauline corpus also emphasizes (Ro 1:3–4; Eph 1:18–22; Php 2:9–11; Col 1:15–20).

We find the same emphasis in the catholic epistles, and Hebrews 1:1–4 hails the ascended Christ as "heir of all things" and the ruler of all, "at present, we do not yet see everything in subjection to him" (Heb 2:8). The ascension of Christ to the place of dominion and rule assures us that although we do not yet see everything in subjection to him, the kingdom is present and will one day be universally manifested. If the preaching of the gospel, no less than the miracles, is the sign that the kingdom has come, Paul's message and ministry can only serve as confirmation of the kingdom's arrival. All of the realities that the Gospels announce as evidence of the messianic kingdom—judgment and justification, forgiveness, a new birth, the gift of the Spirit, and the gathering of a people for the end-time feast—are central in the Pauline corpus. Only if we have a different sort of kingdom in mind will the kingdom motif be thought to have fallen off of Paul's horizon.

Given the contrast between Jews and (mostly Jewish) Christians in the first century, it is not surprising that the Protestant Reformers referred to the millenarian concept of a revived theocracy as "a Jewish error." In our day, classic dispensationalism teaches that the millennium will consist of a renewed theocracy with a rebuilt temple and sacrifices. According to Lewis Sperry Chafer and John Walvoord, "a millennial temple is described in Ezekiel 40–46." "In this temple sacrifices are offered which differ somewhat from the Mosaic sacrifices.... There is no solid reason for not accepting both the temple and the sacrificial system as literal prophecy. Although the death of Christ has brought to an end the Mosaic law and its system of sacrifices, the sacrifices mentioned by Ezekiel seem to be memorial in character, looking back to the cross even as the Old Testament sacrifices looked forward to the cross."[77] However, the authors do not offer any passages that teach either a revival of the sacrificial system or the possibility of a merely memorial sacrifice.

Equating the role of sacrifices in the millennium with that of those in the old covenant only deepens the impression that this view stands in contradiction to the emphatic New Testament claim that Christ's fulfillment has rendered the entire Levitical system obsolete (see especially Hebrews 8–10). It also deepens the impression among some amillennialists (at least the present writer) that classic dispensationalism's pattern of two peoples and two programs requires two objects of

---

77. Lewis Sperry Chafer, *Major Bible Doctrines* (rev. by John Walvoord; Grand Rapids: Zondervan, 1974), 357–58.

fulfillment: Jesus Christ and the nation of Israel. However, if we recognize the basic unity of Scripture and God's covenant of grace (as progressive dispensationalism is more willing to acknowledge), the millennium as envisaged by classic dispensationalism represents a regression in redemptive history from fulfillment back to the types and shadows.

Now we return to Paul's argument in Romans 9–11. First, Paul points out that neither mere physical descent from Abraham and Sarah, nor mere physical circumcision (cf. 2:25–29), has ever determined one's salvation. God has always maintained his prerogative of election even with respect to those within the visible covenant community (9:1–21). This election of a remnant includes Gentiles as well as Jews (vv. 24–29). Paul's brothers and sisters according to the flesh are for the most part pursuing the eternal inheritance according to the law, while many Gentiles are inheriting the promises made to the patriarchs through faith in Christ (vv. 30–33). Chapter 10 elaborates this contrast, and we reach the summit of Paul's argument: "I ask, then, has God rejected his people? By no means!" (11:1). But he explains his answer by referring to himself as part of the remnant now being saved by grace. God has always preserved an elect remnant, like the seven thousand who refused to bow the knee to Baal. "So too at the present time there is a remnant, chosen by grace" (vv. 4–5). Throughout the history of God's covenant faithfulness, Israel was saved through a remnant, just as the world was saved through Noah and his family. The same is true today.

Nevertheless, the second half of chapter 11 seems to argue that although this era is dominated by the widespread ingrafting of Gentiles and only a small remnant of Jews, there will be a widespread reingrafting of Jews at the end of the age: "Lest you be wise in your own sight, I want you to understand this mystery, brothers: a partial hardening has come upon Israel, until the fullness of the Gentiles has come in. And in this way all Israel will be saved" (vv. 25–26).[78]

However, it is difficult to account for the classic dispensationalist view, articulated by Charles Ryrie, that "the Church is not fulfilling in any sense the promises to Israel.... The Church age is not seen in God's program for Israel. It is an intercalation."[79]

So while some amillennialists regard all of the saving promises to Israel as fulfilled in the new covenant church without remainder and dispensationalists treat them as fulfilled only in a revived theocracy of Israel in the millennium, Paul's argu-

---

78. Although in the minority among amillennialists on this matter, Geerhardus Vos, Herman Ridderbos, and John Murray are among defenders of the view that there will be a massive ingathering of Jews at the end of history. I have especially been persuaded by the arguments in David E. Holwerda, *Jesus and Israel: One Covenant or Two?* (Grand Rapids: Eerdmans, 1994).

A good defense of the amillennial majority report is offered by Robert Reymond, *A New Systematic Theology of the Christian Faith* (Nashville: Nelson, 1988), 1027–30.

79. Charles C. Ryrie, *The Basis of the Premillennial Faith* (New York: Loizeaux Bros., 1953), 136.

ment in Romans 9–11 seems more complicated. While Israel is the church and the church is Israel, this spiritual nation will be enlarged in the last days—this time, with a great influx of ethnic Jews. As I have argued, I do not believe that the New Testament teaches that the church is a replacement for Israel but rather that Gentiles have been grafted onto the vine of the true Israel, from which the original nucleus of new covenant disciples emerged. Salvation has come to the world through the Jews; Jesus was sent to the Jews; the gospel was first brought to the Jews, and the kingdom grew from Jerusalem to the ends of the earth. In the end, it will be brought full circle, from the ends of the earth back to Jerusalem again.

IV. Antichrist and the Secret Rapture

According to the classic dispensationalist scenario of end times, the "seventy sevens" of Daniel's vision in Daniel 9 should be interpreted as 490 years, 483 of which are from the command to restore and rebuild Jerusalem (Da 9:25) to the Messiah.[80] "The day of the Lord" "refers to that lengthened period extending from the rapture of the church and the judgments following this event on the earth, to the end of His millennial reign (Isa. 2:10–22; Zech. 14)."[81] After the secret rapture, the primary role of evangelizing those who are alive during the tribulation will be given to Jewish converts. The tribulation itself will be led by a revived Roman Empire (the feet stage of Da 2 and ten-horn stage of fourth beast of 7:7).[82] After a seven-year period of peace, the Antichrist—a Middle Eastern dictator in league with Russia—will break his treaty with Israel. The Great Tribulation will last for forty-two months, "leading up to the second coming of Christ."[83]

With respect to the rapture, Chafer and Walvoord write,

> The tendency has been, on the part of those who spiritualize prophecies relating to a future kingdom on earth, to merge the prophecies of the Rapture and the prophecies of Christ's second coming into one event, occurring at the same time, thereby making the Rapture a posttribulational event.... Those who interpret prophecy literally, and who consistently take into consideration the details of prophecy, can support adequately the conclusion that the second coming of Christ is posttribulational and premillennial.[84]

Once again it is important to bear in mind that amillennialists do not "spiritualize prophecies relating to a future kingdom on earth"; rather, they simply do not find a chronological gap in the relevant texts between the "catching up" of believers and Christ's second coming.

---

80. Chafer and Walvoord, *Major Bible Doctrines*, 305–6.
81. Ibid., 309.
82. Ibid., 315.
83. Ibid., 321.
84. Ibid., 332.

According to dispensationalism, however, the rapture is distinguished sharply from the second coming—and is, in fact, separated by the Great Tribulation. "In contrast with the Rapture, where there is no evidence that the world as a whole will see the glory of Christ, the second coming to the earth will be both visible and glorious."[85] After the total destruction of the cosmos, God will create a new heaven and earth.[86] There are seven resurrections in all.[87] "Beginning at this point in the prophetic program, approximately forty-two months before the second coming of Christ (cf. Rev. 12:6), Satan and the wicked angels are at long last excluded from heaven."[88]

In summary, then, classic dispensationalism anticipates a secret rapture, followed by the tribulation, the second coming, and the judgment of the nations regarding their treatment of Israel (the Great White Throne Judgment), followed by the destruction of heaven and earth, the resurrection of the unrighteous, the judgment of believers' works (the Bema Seat Judgment), and finally the creation of new heavens and a new earth.[89]

A. THE ANTICHRIST

One of the most explicit references to the Antichrist or "man of lawlessness" is found in 2 Thessalonians 2:1–12:

> Now concerning the coming of our Lord Jesus Christ and our being gathered together to him, we ask you, brothers, not to be quickly shaken in mind or alarmed, either by a spirit or a spoken word, or a letter seeming to be from us, to the effect that the day of the Lord has come. Let no one deceive you in any way. For that day will not come, unless the rebellion comes first, and the man of lawlessness is revealed, the son of destruction, who opposes and exalts himself against every so-called god or object of worship, so that he takes his seat in the temple of God, proclaiming himself to be God. Do you not remember that when I was still with you I told you these things? And you know what is restraining him now so that he may be revealed in his time. For the mystery of lawlessness is already at work. Only he who now restrains it will do so until he is out of the way. And then the lawless one will be revealed, whom the Lord Jesus will kill with the breath of his mouth and bring to nothing by the appearance of his coming. The coming of the lawless one is by the activity of Satan with all power and false signs and wonders, and with all wicked deception for those who are perishing, because they refused to love the truth and so be saved. Therefore God sends them a strong delusion, so that they

---

85. Ibid., 333.
86. Ibid., 353: "In this discussion it will be assumed that prophecy should be interpreted in the same literal sense as any other theme of divine revelation." However, interpreting prophetic and apocalyptic literature—or, for that matter, parables and poetry—as if they were historical narrative results in violence to the actual intention of the text.
87. Ibid., 340–43.
88. Ibid., 362.
89. Ibid., 366–69.

may believe what is false, in order that all may be condemned who did not believe the truth but had pleasure in unrighteousness.

From this passage we notice that the revealing of "the man of lawlessness" occurs as a precursor to Christ's return and gathering of his saints—with no intervening periods of tribulation or a millennium mentioned. At the same time, Paul explicitly warns against the teaching of some "that the day of the Lord has come." It is a future event, with the Antichrist taking "his seat in the temple of God, proclaiming himself to be God." If we are to take this straightforward prophecy literally, it could not have been fulfilled after the destruction of the temple in AD 70, nor is there any reference here (or elsewhere) to his taking his seat in a rebuilt temple.

In an amillennial interpretation, Paul (writing most likely in the early 50s) may have been prophesying any number of future Caesars: the reign of Nero or perhaps Titus, who sacked Jerusalem in AD 70, offered a pig on the altar, and burned the city to the ground (with not one stone left upon another, as Jesus prophesied). The Arch of Titus was built in Rome to commemorate the deified emperor's sacking of Jerusalem. Although he (like Satan himself) is being restrained, "the mystery of lawlessness is already at work." At the same time, the apostle seems to indicate that this satanic figure will be destroyed by Christ's return. Given the telescoping pattern of biblical prophecy, it does not seem unreasonable to conclude that this antichrist figure, truly mimicking Christ, appears in two advents: first as the self-deifying Roman emperor and then as a climactic figure at the end of the age. In the meantime, such antichrists come and go on the world stage as echoes and foreshadowings.[90]

This interpretation seems also to fit with the references in John's epistles. "Children," warns John, "it is the last hour, and as you have heard that antichrist is coming, so now many antichrists have come. Therefore we know that it is the last hour" (1Jn 2:18). The apostle then speaks of apostasy then occurring: "They went out from us, but they were not of us; for if they had been of us, they would have continued with us" (v. 19). Here the antichrist is anyone spreading heresy. "This is the antichrist, he who denies the Father and the Son" (v. 22). Specifically, those who deny that "Jesus Christ has come in the flesh" are "not from God." "This is the spirit of the antichrist, which you heard was coming and now is in the world already" (1Jn 4:2–3). Just as the antichrist is spoken of by Paul and John as "coming" and yet as "in the world already" (1Jn 4:2–3), the tribulation is coming and is already present. In the upper room Jesus prepared his disciples for immediate persecution (Jn 15–16). Again he stresses the paradox and tension of being, on the one hand, benefi-

---

90. See Kim Riddlebarger, *Man of Sin: Uncovering the Truth about the Antichrist* (Grand Rapids: Baker, 2006).

ciaries of a far richer benefit than the saints of the past, since the Father and the Son will send the Spirit to indwell them, and, on the other hand, targets of the world's hatred. "I have said all these things to you to keep you from falling away. They will put you out of the synagogues. Indeed, the hour is coming when whoever kills you will think he is offering service to God.... But I have said these things to you, that when their hour comes you may remember that I told them to you" (Jn 16:1–2, 4).

Various groups throughout the medieval period (most notably, Joachim of Fiore) identified the Antichrist with a pope or with the papal office more generally. The Protestant Reformers shared this view. As John R. Stephenson explains, "Luther lays his finger on the sacrilegious expression of the papal claims set forth in Boniface VIII's *Unam Sanctam* of 1302: 'Furthermore, we declare, say, define, and proclaim to every human creature that they by necessity for salvation are entirely subject to the Roman Pontiff.' "[91] Luther thunders, "This is a powerful demonstration that the pope is the real Antichrist who has raised himself over and set himself against Christ, for the pope will not permit Christians to be saved except by his own power, which amounts to nothing, since it is neither established nor commanded by God."[92]

This interpretation is difficult to sustain, however, for various reasons. Most evidently, as Kim Riddlebarger observes, such a view would mean that John's Apocalypse was addressed not to the first-century witnesses and martyrs "but to Christians living centuries later."[93] Although it was the dominant Protestant interpretation (among advocates of all three millennial positions), it finds little support among serious commentators today.[94] Nevertheless, if these passages refer generally to a series of rulers who exalt themselves in God's sanctuary and persecute the saints, the Reformers may well have been right to include the cruelty of the Inquisition with the unfolding "mystery of lawlessness" that uses secular power to effect its idolatrous ends.

B. THE SECRET RAPTURE

Many Christians today believe that believers will be secretly caught up to heaven before a seven-year tribulation period and then return with Christ in judgment.

---

91. John R. Stephenson, *Eschatology: Confessional Lutheran Dogmatics XII* (Fort Wayne, Ind.: The Luther Academy, 1993), 79.

92. *The Schmalkaldic Articles* II.iv.10, quoted in Stephenson, *Eschatology*, 80. These articles are more commonly known as *The Smalcald Articles*.

93. Riddlebarger, *A Case for Amillennialism*, 22.

94. With Riddlebarger (ibid.) I would recommend the commentaries on Revelation by G. K. Beale, *The Book of Revelation: A Commentary on the Greek Text* (Grand Rapids: Eerdmans, 1980), and Dennis Johnson, *Triumph of the Lamb: A Commentary on Revelation* (Phillipsburg, N.J.: P&R, 2001), which regard the Apocalypse as a series of snapshots that characterize the entire era between Christ's two advents. Although the Roman Empire is in the immediate foreground, Babylon (like its precursor, Babel) represents all of the Promethean regimes that oppose Yahweh and his Messiah, persecuting the saints.

The concept of a secret rapture was first formulated by John Nelson Darby in the nineteenth century, on the basis of 1 Thessalonians 4:13–18:

> But we do not want you to be uninformed, brothers, about those who are asleep, that you may not grieve as others do who have no hope. For since we believe that Jesus died and rose again, even so, through Jesus, God will bring with him those who have fallen asleep. For this we declare to you by a word from the Lord, that we who are alive, who are left until the coming of the Lord, will not precede those who have fallen asleep. For the Lord himself will descend from heaven with a cry of command, with the voice of an archangel, and with the sound of the trumpet of God. And the dead in Christ will rise first. Then we who are alive, who are left, will be caught up together with them in the clouds to meet the Lord in the air, and so we will always be with the Lord. Therefore encourage one another with these words.

Several problems arise with the dispensationalist reading of this passage. First, Paul expresses his purpose to comfort those who mourn the death of loved ones in the Lord. Second, he does this by assuring them that their fellow saints are already with the Lord and will return with him at "the coming of the Lord"—and only one "coming" is mentioned here. Third, he says that those who are alive at this coming will *not* precede those who have died, and his reference is not to a secret rapture before the resurrection but to the latter itself: "And the dead in Christ will rise first," followed by the resurrection of those who are still alive, so that all of the elect may join Christ's retinue as he comes on the clouds of the final judgment. Fourth, far from being a secret event that is only discovered after millions of earth's inhabitants are unaccounted for, this event is described by Paul in the most public terms. Compare this passage with Matthew 24:30–31, which Jesus not only identifies with his second coming "with power and great glory," but describes as an event that will provoke the mourning of "all the tribes of the earth." Jesus even refers here to "a loud trumpet call," at which the angels "will gather his elect from the four winds, from one end of heaven to the other." Finally, Paul says that this event—the second coming, the resurrection, and the last judgment—will culminate in the final state: "and so we will always be with the Lord." There does not appear to be any room in this series for the insertion of a secret rapture.

CONCLUSION

At least in its Reformed expression, amillennialism is as opposed in principle to allegorizing exegesis as are rival views. It is a mistake to think that there is anything particularly intrinsic to an amillennial viewpoint that requires allegorical exegesis. As Richard Bauckham helpfully points out, for example, a rejection of a literal millennium with Christ personally reigning in the flesh from the actual city of Jerusalem does not suggest a docetic or spiritualizing ("Platonizing") alternative to embodied restoration of the human and nonhuman creation. In fact, premillennialism grounds the "earthiness" of this vision in its *millennial* hope, while amillennialists look for an *everlasting* reign of Christ in the flesh with a restored cosmos. The only real difference between premillennialism and amillennialism with respect to the concrete and literal restoration of creation, therefore, is whether it is a one-thousand-year epoch followed by another "fall" (apostasy), resurrection, and judgment, or whether it is the final consummation that will characterize Christ's kingdom of glory into eternity.

The main problems with the kind of amillennialism identified by Moltmann are intrinsic to any theory that confuses Christ with the church and the church with a secular culture. As we have seen, the assimilation of Christ to culture can occur in any eschatological system when we look away from the ascended Savior who promised to return at the end of the age. On the other hand, as Ridderbos points out, the "eschatological" view of Bultmann and even Barth "leaves no room for the kingdom in its real and beneficent presence." It represents a docetic view of the kingdom.[95] The main problem with Augustinian amillennialism is its tendency to exchange the eschatological tension between the "already" and "not yet" for an ontological binary of time and eternity, which is even more thorough in Barth's eschatology.

Often in our day, in reaction against Barth, the tendency is toward overrealized eschatologies again, with constant appeals to make the church into a society of moral transformers and to bring into being the kingdom of Christ. Resisting both extremes, New Testament eschatology keeps us located at that disorienting and precarious intersection of the two ages. Affirming together the "already" and "not yet" aspects of the kingdom is, as Ridderbos concludes, "one of the fundamental presuppositions for understanding the gospel."[96] Richard Bauckham rightly concludes, "The challenge to the contemporary church is to formulate the Christian hope in a way which (with the postmillennial tradition) promotes responsible and hopeful activity, but (with the premillennial tradition) avoids the dangerous Utopianism of believing that humanity can design and build the kingdom of God itself."[97]

Believers are neither simply waiting for Christ's kingdom to dawn nor building his kingdom through their own efforts. Rather, it is descending *from heaven* (Rev 21:2) as those who are spiritually dead are raised and receive a new birth *from above* that makes them citizens of the new age (Jn 3:3–6; Eph 2:1–10). The writer to the Hebrews reminds us in chapter 12 that the whole system of world powers and

---

95. Herman Ridderbos, *The Coming of the Kingdom* (ed. Raymond O. Zorn; trans. H. de Jongste; Philadelphia: P&R, 1962), 104.

96. Ibid., 106.

97. Richard Bauckham, "Millenarianism," in *Dictionary of Ethics, Theology and Society* (ed. P. B. Clarke and A. Linzey; London: Routledge, 1996), 568.

kingdoms will be shaken when Christ returns. At the same time, the kingdom of Christ is a present reality: "Therefore let us be grateful for receiving a kingdom that cannot be shaken, and thus let us offer to God acceptable worship, with reverence and awe, for our God is a consuming fire" (Heb 12:27–28).

DISCUSSION QUESTIONS

1. What are the different positions on the millennium? Discuss the evolution of these views in history and contemporary options. Do historical circumstances sometimes play a role in the popularity of one view over others?

2. Discuss the millennial views of Jürgen Moltmann. What are some of his influences?

3. Does the amillennial view actually deny that there is a millennium — that is, an actual reign of Christ?

4. Relate your own understanding of this question to the "already"/"not yet" character of Christ's kingdom that we see in the New Testament.

5. Discuss Revelation 20 in the light of Jesus' teaching on the kingdom in the Gospels.

6. How should we understand the place of Israel in the last days?

7. Does Scripture teach that there will be a literal Antichrist? What about a secret rapture of believers?

Chapter Twenty-Nine

THE LAST
BATTLE AND
LIFE EVERLASTING

Particularly in an era when there is so much talk of holy war, clarity on the Last Judgment—and the difference between the present era and Christ's return in glory—is critical for Christian faith and practice. On one hand, there are those who regard any concept of divine wrath as repugnant to the moral imagination. In an era of religious terrorism, many people—including theologians and ministers—argue that the Old Testament's "texts of terror" must simply be repudiated. On the other hand, some appeal to these texts as if they were still in force and could be invoked for their own national, moral, or political causes. A proper interpretation of the holy war theme in Scripture, however, refuses both options.

I. HOLY WAR AND THE HISTORY OF REDEMPTION

The concept of holy war cannot be understood apart from its relation to holiness. In fact, the Hebrew word *ḥērem* means "to devote to destruction" or "to place under the ban." Thus, we encounter yet another covenantal term, this time in relation to God's enemies. It is inextricably tied to the structure of the treaty itself: its sanctions of curse and blessing. Even among evangelical scholars there has been a wide spectrum of interpretation on this subject.[1] Some verge on a Marcionite

---

[1] C. S. Cowles, Eugene H. Merrill, Daniel L. Gard, Tremper Longman III, *Show Them No Mercy: Four Views on God and Canaanite Genocide* (Grand Rapids: Zondervan, 2003). Referring to these holy wars as "genocide" already prejudices the discussion, however. Genocide is a crime of wiping out a people simply because of its ethnic/racial background. The Bible represents the holy wars as God's judgment of violent and immoral idolaters who have occupied his holy land and threaten his holy people. Regardless of one's evaluation of these texts, genocide is not the appropriate category.

opposition between the Old and New Testaments, between the God of Israel and the God and Father of our Lord Jesus Christ.[2] According to C. S. Cowles, the Old Testament texts of holy war are "pre-Christ, sub-Christ, and anti-Christ."[3]

Cowles's interpretation requires a "canon-within-a-canon" hermeneutic. The authoritative passages of Scripture must be only those (like the Sermon on the Mount) that call believers to nonviolence in their witness to the Lamb of God. To maintain consistency, he would have to judge as noncanonical (at least as not canonically binding) Jesus' own teaching concerning a final judgment. After all, Jesus said that his return in judgment on the last day will make the destruction of Sodom pale in comparison (Lk 10:12). Responding to Cowles's antithesis between Joshua (warrior) and Jesus (Prince of Peace), Eugene Merrill judges, "Not only does this claim ignore texts that portray Yahweh as warrior (e.g., Ex. 15:3), but it overlooks eschatological descriptions of this same Prince of Peace as one who 'judges and makes war,' who is 'dressed in a robe dipped in blood,' and from whose mouth 'comes a sharp sword with which to strike down the nations' (Rev. 19:11 – 15)."[4] Further, Jesus identifies his Father (and our God) as the God of the patriarchs and prophets (Mt 22:32), as does Peter in Acts 3:13 (cf. 7:32).[5] At the end of the day, it does not seem that even such passages of nonviolence are themselves the ultimate canon in Cowles's interpretation. Rather, the canon becomes *our* moral sense of what constitutes violence and peace.

As Jewish theologian Michael Wyschogrod reminds us,

> Immanuel Kant, in commenting on Psalm 79:11 – 14, in which he finds "a prayer for revenge which goes to tarrying extremes," can dismiss with contempt a writer who comments, "The Psalms are inspired; if in them punishment is prayed for, it cannot be wrong, and we must have no morality holier than the Bible," and instead hurl the following rhetorical question which, for Kant, obviously settles the issue: "I raise the question as to whether morality should be expounded according to the Bible or whether the Bible should not rather be expounded according to morality."[6]

"Expounding the Bible according to morality, the choice of Kant," Wyschogrod properly concludes, makes our natural (indeed, perverted) judgment the measure of justice.[7]

At the other extreme are many conservative Christians (especially in the United States) who seem to think that such Old Testament passages can be invoked by us against whatever nations or groups we regard as external or internal threats to

2. See C. S. Cowles's essay in Cowles et al., *Show Them No Mercy*, 11 – 44.

3. Ibid., 36.

4. Eugene H. Merrill, "Response to C. S. Cowles," in Cowles et al., *Show Them No Mercy*, 49.

5. Ibid.

6. Michael Wyschogrod, *Abraham's Promise: Judaism and Jewish-Christian Relations* (ed. R. Kendall Soulen; Grand Rapids: Eerdmans, 2004), 216 – 17, citing Immanuel Kant's *Religion within the Limits of Reason Alone* (trans. T. M. Greene and H. H. Hudson; New York: Harper and Row, 1960), 101.

7. Ibid., 217.

the "American way of life." Although Israel alone was taken into God's care as a covenant nation, and the theocracy was a temporary regime typological of Christ's kingdom, these texts of national blessing and curse are often applied directly to the United States or to Israel — or both. Neither view does justice to the different redemptive-historical contexts in which this theme emerges in Scripture.

In recent decades, M. G. Kline has offered a helpful category, which he calls *intrusion ethics*, for defining the nature and role of *ḥērem* (or holy) war in the Bible.[8] At various points in redemptive history, God's heavenly kingdom has descended to earth. Under these conditions, the stipulations governing the covenant people have encompassed the totality of life: both cult and culture, and the sanctions (life and death) were carried out immediately and directly by God himself. Yahweh was Israel's great king, ruling in the midst of his people. Just as God's miraculous acts in redemptive history suspend the ordinary course of natural processes, they also suspend the ordinary course of common law that God has ordained for the nations.

A. From Adam until Moses

In Eden, the covenantal representative of humanity — prophet, priest, and king of the earthly sanctuary — was called to "work it and keep [or guard]" it (Ge 2:15). (The same verbs are used for the vocation of the Levitical priests.) After the disobedience of the covenant servant, God approaches: "And they heard the sound of the LORD God walking in the garden in the cool of the day, and the man and his wife hid themselves from the presence of the LORD God among the trees of the garden" (Ge 3:8). Although *rûaḥ* — here translated "cool" — can mean "wind," it is the usual term for "spirit," including the Holy Spirit. It makes little sense in the context — especially with the trial and sentencing of Adam and Eve in the verses that follow — to imagine God entering the garden caressed by a gentle morning breeze. Rather, as Kline suggests, "This passage must be played fortissimo."[9] The Covenant Lord comes in judgment to prosecute the servant who defiled his sanctuary instead of guarding and keeping it. Since the servant did not expel the beguiling serpent but instead succumbed to his seductions, the man and woman will be exiled from the holy land.

Thus, "the Spirit of the day" refers to the arrival of Yahweh coming in the day of judgment. We have seen in chapter 17 that the Spirit's presence is judicial: judging and justifying. The Spirit is sent to convict the ungodly and to give them faith to embrace the forgiveness of sins. The Spirit's indwelling presence is an *arrabōn* (legal

8. M. G. Kline, *The Structure of Biblical Authority* (Grand Rapids: Eerdmans, 1972), 154–71. This view is defended in Cowles et al., *Show Them No Mercy*, in the essays by Daniel Gard (111–49) and Tremper Longman III (159–87).

9. M. G. Kline, *Images of the Spirit* (S. Hamilton, Mass.: self-published, 1986), 98.

pledge) guaranteeing the final vindication of believers at the resurrection of the dead. The Spirit separates, as he did the waters in creation. Already at the arraignment of Adam and Eve, then, we encounter the Spirit of judgment. In *The Structure of Biblical Authority*, Kline argues,

> It was not the fall in itself that delayed the consummation. According to the conditions of the Covenant of Creation the prospective consummation was either/or. It was either eternal glory by covenantal confirmation of original righteousness or eternal perdition by covenant-breaking repudiation of it. The fall, therefore, might have been followed at once by a consummation of the curse of the covenant. The delay was due rather to the principle and purpose of divine compassion by which a new way of arriving at the consummation was introduced, the way of redemptive covenant with common grace as its historical corollary.[10]

However, at various points later in Genesis, cult and culture once again become fused as God's heavenly kingdom becomes identified with a particular family (Noah and the ark) and then Israel. In these cases, God again separates the waters, exercising judgment on the ungodly while delivering his people.

In the creation narrative, seven times the declaration resounds, three times in the first triad of days and four in the second triad, twice each in the third and sixth days (one of the marks of their correspondence in the parallelism of the two triads). In the seventh, summarizing occurrence the pronouncement is heightened to "very good." In the land of Canaan there is the contest between David and the Philistines. "On that occasion," as Kline observes, "David's advance on earth was matched by (or better, corresponded to) Yahweh's advance above, the latter signalized by the 'voice' of marching over the tree-tops (II Sam. 5:24)."[11] Seven acts of "seeing" by the Spirit-Creator are recorded, and here, it would seem, is the ultimate source of the imagery of "the seven eyes, which are the seven Spirits of God sent out into all the earth" (Rev 5:6) on judicial missions, the seven eyes which are seven torches of fire burning before the Glory-throne of judgment (Rev 4:5).[12] "And the prophet attributes to the Glory-Spirit the guidance of Israel through the depths of the sea (Isa 63:13; cf. Deut. 32:10; Gen. 1:2) on to the Sabbath-rest in the land of their inheritance: 'The Spirit of the Lord brought him to rest' (Isa 63:14; cf. Deut. 12:9)."[13] The seventh day is the Day of the Lord: a day of deliverance and judgment.

Similarly, the prophets often receive their commission and visions "in the Spirit," as they are—in their visions—caught up in the heavenly courtroom where Yahweh, arrayed in majesty, prepares for judgment (for example, compare the scenes in Eze 1:4–28 and Rev 1:10–19; 4:1–11). The Day of the Lord/Spirit is a day of judicial verdict.

---

10. M. G. Kline, *The Structure of Biblical Authority* (rev. ed.; self-published, 1989), 155.

11. Kline, *Images of the Spirit*, 99.

12. Ibid., 109–10.

13. Ibid., 112.

The concept of *ḥērem* war is not left behind when we cross the threshold of the testaments. "Baptism is a sign of the *parousia* of the Spirit in judgment."[14] "At Jesus' birth, his identifying sign (*sēmeion*) was his clothing, the swaddling clothes, the garment of his humiliation, and his position, lying in a manger (Lk 2:12). At his coming again, the identifying (name-) sign of his exaltation will be the Glory-robe in which he is arrayed, his Spirit-clothing, and his position, standing in the heavens."[15] In fact, "invested with the Glory-Name, he comes in the day of the Lord as the Spirit of the day."[16]

Intrusions, like sacraments, are prolepses of realized eschatology. Beyond merely pointing to the reality, these intrusions are previews of the last judgment and the age to come. However, these old covenant types are never the full realization of the consummation. "The identification of the new covenant with the consummation keeps pace with the stages in the exaltation of the Son of Man; and while we see him sitting on the right hand of power, we have not yet seen him coming in the clouds of heaven. Hence, there is not yet a corresponding antitype [fulfillment] for every element of Old Testament typology." Some types (namely, the sacrifices) are fulfilled, but others (e.g., the final judgment) are not.[17]

Already now, the kingdom of God is present, but it is not identified with any nation or ethnic people. For now, it is manifested as a kingdom of grace, bringing the forgiveness of sins, not yet as the kingdom of glory, bringing final justice, righteousness, and peace to the earth. Because Christ alone — with his body — is the temple, holy land, and society of prophets, priests, and kings, there is no nation, building complex, or plot of land to which we may point as the locus of God's kingdom. All places are common — cathedrals no less than public parks. In whatever buildings God's people are gathered around the world on the Lord's day, they are the place, the living stones being built into a holy sanctuary filled with the Spirit of Glory. Since there is no holy land, there can be no holy war. Christ himself has driven the serpent from the archetypal sanctuary, toppled his kingdom, and looted his prisons, and now dispenses the treasury of his kingdom by his Spirit.

Therefore, the believer's attitude toward unbelieving neighbors is determined by common grace, not by either taking judgment into our own hands or basing this neighbor-love on any illusion of universal salvation. For now, James and John are rebuked for wanting to call down God's judgment on unbelievers (Lk 9:53–55), but not if they make the same request in the age to come. The imprecatory Psalms, invoking God's judgment on enemies, are appropriate on the lips of David and the martyrs in heaven. However, they are entirely out of place on the lips of Christians today, guided as we are not by the ethics of intrusion but by the ethics of common

---

14. Ibid., 125.
15. Ibid., 128–29.

16. Ibid., 131.
17. Ibid., 157.

grace.[18] Therefore, moderns are wrong for *dismissing* such episodes as immoral, and fundamentalists are wrong for *invoking* them as if they were in effect during this intermission between Christ's two advents.

Once again, therefore, we recognize the precariousness, and often the ambiguity, of this era of redemptive history in which we must live as the church. It is an in-between time. We are living in neither the typological theocracy of Canaan nor its consummated realization at the last judgment. Israel's conquest of its promised land was a prolepsis of this last judgment, directly commanded by God, as a suspension of the laws of common grace. However, we are living in a different era, when God patiently endures the injustice, idolatry, and immorality of the nations so that his gospel can be brought peacefully to the ends of the earth. When God commanded Abraham to place Isaac on the altar of sacrifice or called his prophet Hosea to marry a prostitute as a vivid illustration of his relationship to Israel, they must obey. "When our Father shall say, 'It is done,' we must listen to his voice. But if we are listening to him today, we are still seeking by his grace to be good Samaritans."[19]

Lutheran biblical scholar Daniel L. Gard properly concludes, "Kline's 'intrusion ethics' and its understanding of the Old Testament destruction of the Canaanites as the final judgment foreshadowed is extraordinarily helpful in coming to grips with what is for many an ethical quandary." Gard adds,

> God's justice will be manifested before the universe on the Last Day, just as it was against the Canaanites. But those with whom God has established his covenant of grace will live. Is God unjust in preserving the Israelites and destroying the Canaanites, especially since all have sinned and equally deserve condemnation? If it appears so, the issue is not only of God's justice but of human fallibility and inability to fully comprehend the ways of God.[20]

It makes a great deal of difference whether we treat the old covenant holy wars as simply another attempt by one ethnic group to eliminate others or as periodic and localized divine judgments that could easily have been final and universal were it not also for God's mercy.

In light of the preceding discussion, I will summarize what I take to be the general plot within which the theme of holy war must be situated. The dual themes of election and common grace can be observed side by side in the stories of Seth ("Appointed") and Cain, over whom God proclaims a providential rather than redemptive benediction (Ge 4:15–16). Similarly, although Isaac is chosen, Ishmael and his mother Hagar are, like Cain, sent away from the covenant community, yet God promises Hagar that he will make a great nation of Ishmael, confirming

---

18. Ibid., 157.
19. Ibid., 171.

20. Gard, in Cowles et al., *Show Them No Mercy*, 202.

this oath by providing mother and child with water to drink in the desert (Ge 21:18 – 19). In fact, "God was with the boy, and he grew up. He lived in the wilderness and became an expert with the bow" (v. 20).

Yet the warfare between the "two seeds" promised to Eve in Genesis 3:15 intensifies with the calling of Abraham and especially with the liberation from Egypt and conquest of Canaan. Each of the Old Testament judgments is based on ethical rather than ethnic considerations. Therefore, to refer to these as examples of "ethnic cleansing" is misleading. Even God's promise to bring Abraham's descendants to the land presupposes that it is God's land. It does not belong to Israel any more than it belongs to the pagan nations that occupied it (Lev 25:23 – 24). Israel was not using God to justify its own policy of ethnic cleansing. Rather, God was using Israel for the *ethical* cleansing of his holy garden. In fact, the delay of occupation of Canaan by the long sojourn of Abraham's descendants in Egypt was based on the fact that "the iniquity of the Amorites is not yet complete" (Ge 15:16). It was because they were thoroughly corrupt, not because they were Amorites, that God exercised his judgment through Israel his servant.

After Yahweh liberates his people from Egypt — described repeatedly in the Old Testament (especially the Psalms and prophets) as a new creation — he brings them to Sinai to receive the terms of his suzerainty treaty. As a new Adam, Israel must drive the serpent from God's temple and guard and keep it. The land is not simply a gift to be enjoyed, but a task to be fulfilled; the land must be subdued and brought under God's lordship. It is significant that the first holy war legislation appears in the Book of the Covenant itself (Ex 23:20 – 33). It is not added but intrinsic to the covenant. Yahweh alone is to be worshiped — by anyone, anywhere. Delbert Hillers observes that "the covenant framework served to set in its place a potentially dangerous notion, the idea of election, the affirmation that Israel was the chosen people."[21] The nations deified themselves (the king) and had the gods as witnesses, but only Israel had a covenant with its God.

In the federation, each family unit is to pledge loyalty (Dt 6:6 – 7), while in the monarchy it is the king who represents the nation's pledge before Yahweh. Israel's commission in the land (a land which belongs to Yahweh, not ultimately to Israel) is to cleanse it from idols and make it a luxurious habitation for God's presence in their midst. Echoes of Eden are explicit (especially in the prophets). Israel's holy wars are echoes from the past failure of Adam to cleanse God's garden, finally succumbing (along with his wife) to the serpent's treason. And they are also echoes from the future, anticipating the day when the Last Adam would rid the world of

---

21. Delbert Hillers, *Covenant: The History of a Biblical Idea* (Baltimore: Johns Hopkins Press, 1969), 65.

sin and evil "in one day" — the "last day" before the Sabbath, when the whole earth will be filled with God's glory. In Judges 5 we see the Spirit who clothed creation now clothing the trumpeter and saying, "Follow after me!" "Before the battle the word is: 'Yahweh has delivered them into your hands.' "[22] As suzerain, Yahweh lays out the terms of Israel's holy wars on his behalf (Dt 20:1–20). "The spoils belong to Yahweh, too. This is especially clear from the story of Achan's theft (Joshua 7)."[23]

The rules of holy war are explicitly set forth in Deuteronomy 20. The priest is to prepare the troops by reminding them that Yahweh, the Great King, is the leader of the campaign, "to give you victory" (v. 4). After the officers have invited the soldiers to return to dedicate new homes and enjoy the fruit of them, as well as marry and enjoy their wives (in case they die in battle), the troops assemble to receive their battle instructions. Upon entering a town, they are to offer it terms of peace and, upon acceptance, take the inhabitants as slaves. If the town does not submit but instead fights, it must be besieged and its male inhabitants "put to the sword," although the women, children, livestock, and goods must be preserved and taken as a tribute to the Great King.

More stringent commands are given with respect to those towns that God has marked out for judgment. Reminiscent of the story of the flood, Deuteronomy 20 continues, "But in the cities of these peoples that the LORD your God is giving you for an inheritance, you shall save alive nothing that breathes." Again, it is ethical, not ethnic, cleansing: "that they may not teach you to do according to all their abominable practices that they have done for their gods, and so you sin against the LORD your God" (vv. 16–18).[24] The tribes mentioned in Deuteronomy 20 to be given over into Israel's hand are explicitly mentioned in Genesis 15 (vv. 16, 19–21), where God deeds the land to Abraham. What is significant here is that the holy war being adumbrated in Deuteronomy 20 presupposes the radical corruption of the inhabitants. From what we know of Hittite and Canaanite practices, child sacrifice was part of the cultus, as were prostitution and draconian measures against the surrounding peoples who were victims of their perpetual thirst for blood and land. However, from a theocentric perspective, idolatry alone was sufficient to justify the sentence of death.

It will not be adequate to dismiss such Old Testament passages in favor of an ostensibly milder Jesus, since he says himself that the judgment awaiting all who reject him will be greater than that which fell on Sodom and Gomorrah (Lk 10:12; cf. Mt

---

22. Ibid., 83–84.

23. Ibid., 85; cf. 150, where Hillers observes the suzerainty structure of Deuteronomy.

24. Interestingly, if we continue with the rules of holy war in Deuteronomy 20, Yahweh decrees that the trees of a besieged town must be spared. "You may eat from them, you shall not cut them down. *Are trees in the field human, that they should be besieged by you?*" (vv. 19–20; emphasis added). This further underscores the point that these were holy wars, divine judg-

ments, against rebels of God and his kingdom. The natural creation, as the psalmist will remind us, is still "[declaring] the glory of God," pouring "out speech" in testimony to God's majesty, goodness, and power (Ps 19:1–4). God lodges no complaint against creation as such, which "was subjected to futility, not willingly, but because of him who subjected it" (Ro 8:20), and which groans because of human sin (v. 22). God's action through Israel is a focused campaign.

11:20–24). In fact, it is significant that Jesus speaks these ominous warnings to the religious leaders of Israel. It is on the basis of the covenant, not ethnicity, that God distinguishes between friends and foes. The same covenant code that commanded holy war against the idolatrous Gentiles threatened exactly the same measures against Israel itself should it violate its terms (esp. Dt 28:1–68; cf. 30:11–20). In fact, this sentence was prophesied and carried out, as God used pagan nations as his instruments of judgment upon Israel and Judah. God's "firstborn," Israel, was given the same commission as Adam, as a type of things to come. Yet "like Adam, Israel broke my covenant" (Hos 6:7), as the Angel of the LORD underscores when he recounts the failure of those whom he brought up from Egypt to fulfill his commission in the land (Jdg 2:1–5).

If this interpretive path is taken, then these passages that provoke such offense can actually be seen to reveal divine forbearance and mercy as well as justice. Given the verdict of universal sinfulness (Ge 8:21), it might be reasonably asked why God limited the focus of this campaign to the Amorites, Hittites, Canaanites, and Jebusites. If the kingdom of God could only come with such a thorough housecleaning, might it not have been more thorough? Furthermore, throughout its history in the land, Israel displayed a halfhearted commitment to this commission, and the prophets will point to the failure to fully cleanse the land as one of the reasons for the apostasy of Israel and Judah, as the covenant people adopted the civil and cultic practices of the Gentiles. Then, as now, the victims of injustice and oppression protest against God's delay of such sweeping judgment, while oppressors (or at least those whose relative peace, prosperity, and security numbs them to injustice) deny any final reckoning.

Although Israel often refused to carry out the thorough judgment that its covenant Lord required, there were instances of *un*holy and unauthorized warfare that are frankly judged as such. For example, we recall the reaction of Dinah's brothers after she was raped by Shechem, prince of the Hivite region. Although there was treachery on both sides after this incident, Dinah's brothers hatched an elaborate plot for vengeance and slaughtered the males and plundered the city. "All their wealth, all their little ones and their wives, all that was in the houses, they captured and plundered" (Ge 34:29). What is especially interesting about this incident is that Shechem was in fact on God's list for a holy war that would eventually be waged (Ex 23:27–31; Dt 20:16–20); nevertheless, the brothers were executing their own vengeance, on their own timetable, rather than divine judgment, on God's schedule. They were acting in the absence of any divine warrant. In his last words to his sons, in effect reading his last will and testament, Jacob pronounced on these brothers,

Simeon and Levi are brothers;
  weapons of violence are their swords.
Let my soul not come into their council;
  O my glory, be not joined to their company.

> For in their anger they killed men,
> and in their willfulness they hamstrung oxen.
> Cursed be their anger, for it is fierce,
> and their wrath, for it is cruel!
> I will divide them in Jacob
> and scatter them in Israel. (Ge 49:5–7)

In another example of unholy war, the Gibeonites (a remnant of the Amorites) were given sworn protection by Israel (Jos 9:14–19), but "Saul had sought to strike them down in his zeal for the people of Israel and Judah" (2Sa 21:2). This "zeal," however, was self-determined and self-motivated, a nationalistic rather than religious zeal. God tells David, "There is bloodguilt on Saul and on his house, because he put the Gibeonites to death" (v. 1). Israel's story is that David therefore made an atonement to the Gibeonites by fulfilling their request for the representative execution of seven of Saul's own sons. David's own blood-stained hands, as well as those of his house, were thoroughly recounted in Israel's scriptures (2Sa 11).

When God acts in judgment, it is righteous and serves the purpose ultimately of establishing justice, righteousness, and peace in an otherwise violent and hostile environment. Yet when humans arrogate to themselves the right to execute this divine judgment, they only perpetuate violence and become part of that very bloody fabric of hatred that has provoked God's holy wars against the godless. The recurring implication is that such judgment must be seen in God-centered rather than in human-centered terms. God's justice must neither be ignored when Yahweh speaks nor be executed when Yahweh is silent. Interestingly, holy war is described as "vengeance for the covenant" (Lev 26:25). It is nothing like ethnic cleansing.

Christians interpret the "war songs" of the Psalter in light of the messianic king greater than David. Jesus Christ, then, is the King whom God has installed on his holy hill, requiring all rulers to do him homage, even demanding that they "kiss the Son, lest he be angry, and you perish in the way; for his wrath is quickly kindled. Blessed are all who take refuge in him" (Ps 2:11). In Psalm 144, attributed to David, we read, "Blessed be the LORD, my rock, who trains my hands for war, and my fingers for battle; he is my steadfast love and my fortress, my stronghold and my deliverer, my shield and he in whom I take refuge, who subdues peoples under me" (vv. 1–2). How we interpret these messianic references, however, makes all the difference, as we will see below.

The themes of salvation and holy war are inextricably bound in the Psalter. The messianic reign, as in Psalm 99, observes Oliver O'Donovan, draws together such themes as "'judgment' (*mišpāṭ*), 'equity' (*mêšārîm*) and 'right' (*ṣᵉdāqâ*)...."[25] Salva-

---

25. Oliver O'Donovan, *Desire of the Nations* (Cambridge: Cambridge Univ. Press, 1996), 33.

tion is identified with military victory.[26] The group of words formed on the root *ṣdq* are traditionally translated "righteousness" or "justice"; but their sense is often better caught by "vindication" or "justification," as Luther famously discovered. If with *ḥesed* we are in a relation known only from within, inscrutable to the outside world and private to Yahweh and his people, with *ṣedeq* we are in the fully public realm of a world court. When Yahweh's right hand and holy arm have effected a victory for his people, it is a matter of international notice (Ps 98:2).[27] Zion "is to be 'redeemed by *mišpāṭ* ([Is.] 1:26f)."[28] The Levites were without property. "Yhwh himself was their possession (Deut. 8:1f. etc.) ...," a theme that is also picked up elsewhere: "The LORD is my portion" (La 3:24, with Ps 73:26). "The LORD is my portion; I promise to keep your words" (Ps 119:57). To say that Yahweh is king is to say that "he gives Israel victory; he gives judgment; he gives Israel its possession," with Mount Zion as its security.[29]

Therefore, O'Donovan concludes, the result of the divine victory in battle is the restoration of that worship that is God's due, a political act on the part of the covenant people, renouncing their allegiances to other lords and taking Yahweh alone as their great king:

> "Gather us from the nations, that we may give thanks to your holy name and glory in your praise" (Ps. 106:47). The community is a political community by virtue of being a worshipping community; while the worship of the single believer, restored from some affliction and desiring to thank God, must, as it were, be politicised by being brought into the public arena of "the great congregation" (Pss. 35:18; 40:9f.) in "the gates of the daughter of Zion" (Ps. 9:14). Otherwise, the poet says, Yhwh's righteousness, faithfulness, salvation, love and truth would be "hidden" and "concealed" (Ps. 40:10).[30]

Given such moral complexity, Israel's story simply cannot be reduced to yet another attempt to legitimize nationalistic ambitions by religious justifications. The same Scriptures that called for holy war in the name of the covenant Lord brought the same judgment upon Israel itself for executing violence. This becomes especially obvious in the prophetic literature.

B. FROM THE PROPHETS UNTIL CHRIST

One of the interesting interpretive paradoxes in the prophets is the indictment against Israel for both failing to thoroughly discharge the duty of holy war (thus making the people prey to idolatry) and failing to refrain from the shedding of

26. Ibid., 36.
27. Ibid., 37.
28. Ibid., 39.
29. Ibid., 45.
30. Ibid., 47.

innocent blood. If the interpretive line I have suggested is about right, this twofold indictment fully coheres.

"Generally, the other cultures of the biblical world were, by comparison to Israel, remarkably tolerant," according to Jon D. Levenson. "Their pantheons absorbed gods with ease."[31] "The radicalism of this aspect of covenant theology must not be missed. The covenant with YHWH is here presented as the alternative to conventional political relations."[32] In the tradition of the judges, YHWH alone is king. "In the theo-politics of this stream of tradition, there is no room for earthly government. The state is not part of the solution to the problems inherent in human society, but itself one of the problems."[33]

Israel itself has now thoroughly violated the terms of its covenant with Yahweh. The land of promise, typological of the everlasting Sabbath, has been made desolate not by the invading armies but by the judgment that Israel's sin deserves. Having driven out the bloodthirsty nations and oppressors in order to establish a regime of justice for the poor, the orphan, the widow, and the alien, Yahweh now drives out his own bride from his defiled land. The tables are turned and God executes holy war on the apple of his eye.

Once again, this points up the fact that, whatever one finally makes of it, this story is not about justifying national aims but about loyalty to God's covenant: righteousness, love, justice, peace, and integrity. Israel's God is not a national mascot nor a respecter of persons: unrighteousness, idolatry, and violence will not go unpunished. The covenant Israel made with God at Sinai is her source of both security and danger. Yet, Levenson notes, Hosea 2:20 prophesies a new covenant: "All threats, whether from nature or from war, will vanish. Lurking behind these great promises are the blessings of the covenant formulary. *But we hear nothing of the curses, for the vision is one of redemption through covenant, and the assumption seems to be that, where God mediates and thus guarantees covenant, the stipulations will be fulfilled as a matter of course*" (emphasis added).[34] Interpreting the Sinai covenant in the light of the New Testament, we see that the geopolitical theocracy could only anticipate the everlasting blessing of the Sabbath; it could never bring it about. Only on the basis of God's own unchangeable oath and faithfulness could there be forgiveness of sins and a genuine renewal of creation.

Already in the prophets attention turns from the theocracy (including its holy wars), as a typological kingdom pointing forward to the everlasting city, to the desacralization (desecration in the most literal sense) of that earthly kingdom as the reality it anticipates draws near. When the Messiah comes, his people are not to be

---

31. Jon D. Levenson, *Sinai and Zion: An Entry into the Jewish Bible* (San Francisco: HarperSanFrancisco, 1985), 65.
32. Ibid., 72.
33. Ibid., 73.
34. Ibid., 78.

active in holy war, but to "be still." Levenson relates Psalm 46 to Isaiah 30:15 in this regard: "In quietness and trust shall be your strength," the prophet declared, "in calm and confidence shall be your heroism." In that day, it will be time for Israel to simply stand back and watch God work salvation in all the earth.[35]

Although the returning exiles from Babylon sought to reinstitute the Sinai covenant, Israel never recovered from exile, but remained under the oppressive dominion of foreign powers. Not by looking back to Sinai and Israel's oath, but forward to Zion, and God's unfailing promise, could redemption be fully and finally expected.

Whereas Sinai represents everything that is conditional, violable, threatened by human disobedience, and subject to political intrigues from within and without, Zion is the "unshakable kingdom" because it is Christ's throne:

> For you have not come to what may be touched, a blazing fire and darkness and gloom and a tempest and the sound of a trumpet and a voice whose words made the hearers beg that no further messages be spoken to them.... Indeed, so terrifying was the sight that Moses said, "I tremble with fear." But you have come to Mount Zion and to the city of the living God, the heavenly Jerusalem, and to innumerable angels in festal gathering, and to the assembly of the firstborn who are enrolled in heaven, and to God, the judge of all, and to the spirits of the righteous made perfect, and to Jesus, the mediator of a new covenant, and to the sprinkled blood that speaks a better word than the blood of Abel.
>
> See that you do not refuse him who is speaking. For if they did not escape when they refused him who warned them on earth, much less will we escape if we reject him who warns from heaven. At that time his voice shook the earth, but now he has promised, "Yet once more I will shake not only the earth but also the heavens." This phrase, "Yet once more," indicates the removal of things that are shaken—that is, things that have been made—in order that the things that cannot be shaken may remain. Therefore let us be grateful for receiving a kingdom that cannot be shaken, and let us offer to God acceptable worship, with reverence and awe, for our God is a consuming fire. (Heb 12:18–29)

Everything that belongs to "this present age," including the church to the extent that it is not yet the kingdom of Christ, is exposed to this divine shaking that will leave only the immovable and eternal standing. Both the shadows of Sinai and the Gentile parodies of the kingdom of God will belong to the past, and Zion will remain forever, in a state of perpetual festival.

II. HOLY WAR AND THE MESSIANIC KINGDOM

The theme of holy war hardly disappears in the New Testament. Rather, it reaches its fulfillment—of which the Old Testament examples were merely

---

35. Ibid., 154–55.

previews. In his Sermon on the Mount (paralleling Moses' delivery of the law at Mount Sinai), Jesus issues his famous decrees: "You have heard it said, '...,' but I say,...." He is not here condemning the law of Moses. In fact, he repeatedly affirms and interprets the law, adding nothing to the law, for example, in his conversation with the rich young ruler and also with the religious leaders in Mark 7:1–13. The moral law (summarized in the Ten Commandments) remains in full force, but the ceremonial and civil laws that governed the "intrusion ethics" of the theocracy are now being fulfilled and are therefore passing away. There was a time when there was a holy land and there were holy wars, when pagan nations were to be driven from the land, but now is the era of forgiveness, good news, and grace. Yet the same Jesus clearly—more clearly than any biblical figure—warns of the day when he will come in the clouds to judge, separating the sheep from the goats, issuing in the blessing of everlasting life for all who believe in him and the sentence of everlasting death for those who reject him.

The holy war theme is drawn upon by the New Testament, but within a distinct politics. The overtly military recognition of Yahweh, "Through you we push back our enemies" (Ps 44:4), can now be heard in the light of Jesus' declaration that "the gates of Hades will not prevail against" the church to whom Christ has given the keys to bind and loose (Mt 16:18–19). Similarly, Paul's appeal to believers to put on "the whole armor of God" prepares them for the real battle that the holy wars foreshadowed:

> For we do not wrestle against flesh and blood, but against the rulers, against the authorities, against the cosmic powers over this present darkness, against the spiritual forces of evil in the heavenly places. Therefore take up the whole armor of God, that you may be able to withstand in the evil day, and having done all, to stand firm. Stand therefore, having fastened on the belt of truth, and having put on the breastplate of righteousness, and, as shoes for your feet, having put on the readiness given by the gospel of peace. In all circumstances take up the shield of faith, with which you can extinguish all the flaming darts of the evil one; and take the helmet of salvation, and the sword of the Spirit, which is the word of God. (Eph 6:12–17)

On one hand, there is a tendency to interpret such passages in quasignostic fashion, as a purely internal battle within the individual to conquer the body and its passions and aspire to pure spirit. On the other, we may so identify the "spiritual forces of evil in the heavenly places" with certain political and economic systems that the claim that "our struggle is not against enemies of blood and flesh" is muted.

The cosmic struggle that dominates the story from Genesis 3 to the Apocalypse is that war between the serpent and his seed on the one hand and the woman and hers on the other. In fact, Revelation 12 can be seen as a snapshot of that redemptive-historical battle, with the "woman clothed with the sun, with the moon under her feet, and on her head a crown of twelve stars" (v. 1). Crying out in the agony of childbirth, she is threatened, as "another sign appeared in heaven: behold, a great red dragon, with seven heads and ten horns, and on his heads seven diadems."

> His tail swept down a third of the stars of heaven and cast them to the earth. And the dragon stood before the woman who was about to give birth, so that when she bore her child he might devour it. She gave birth to a male child, one who is to rule all the nations with a rod of iron, but her child was caught up to God and to his throne, and the woman fled into the wilderness, where she has a place prepared by God, in which she is to be nourished for 1,260 days. (vv. 4–6)

At this point, we read, "war arose in heaven," with the devil and his angels defeated. "And I heard a loud voice in heaven, saying, 'Now the salvation and the power and the kingdom of our God and the authority of his Christ have come, for the accuser of our brothers has been thrown down, who accuses them day and night before our God'" (vv. 7–10). The martyrs triumph by their testimony to the Lamb. "Therefore, rejoice, O heavens and you who dwell in them! But woe to you, O earth and sea, for the devil has come down to you in great wrath, because he knows that his time is short!" (vv. 11–12). Verses 13–17 then capture something of this persecution of the enraged, if overthrown, enemy, who "went off to make war on the rest of her offspring, on those who keep the commandments of God and hold to the testimony of Jesus."

Once we see what these stories were prefiguring—the kingdom of Christ— they no longer can be seen as belonging to the bleak history of the will to power among nations and empires. When Christ wages war, the blind see, the deaf hear, the poor have the gospel preached to them, the weak are made strong, and the victims are liberated. The entire order of Gentile power and submission in the fallen world no longer obtains in the kingdom of Christ, as Jesus not only taught and exemplified but brought about in his own humiliation and exaltation. He proved that in this story at least, we have a Lord—the only lord who really *is* Lord of all— as a servant of all. Thus, Luther's famous paradox of the freedom of the Christian, which can happen for the Christian only because of union with Christ, the Lord who is Servant. When *this* King declares war, the whole earth leaps for joy. It is the Year of Jubilee, the liberation day of the world from its bondage to decay, oppression, and violence. We should be cynical about the pretensions of the City of Man to bring peace through violence, but we have already seen too much in Christ's first advent to allow us to entertain the same logic for the church's mission here and now.

In the Olivet Discourse, Jesus explains that the Son of Man will come in glory and power at the end of the age. "You will see the son of man seated at the right hand of Power and coming on the clouds of heaven" (Mt 26:64, with Lk 22:69; Mk 14:62). There was a partial realization of this in the vision of Stephen the Martyr

(Ac 7:56), whose execution the preconversion Paul approved (8:1), as also in the vision of Paul on his way to another campaign against the believers in Damascus (9:1–6). Yet they saw Christ enthroned in heaven; we still await his "coming on the clouds of heaven," which marks the transition from a kingdom of grace to the kingdom of glory.

That the cosmic warfare envisioned by the New Testament is not ethereal or irrelevant to earthly realities is clear enough already in the history of this battle between the serpent and the woman inaugurated in Genesis 3:15, running from Cain's murder of Abel to the flood, Israel's exodus, conquest, and captivity, until finally reaching its climax at the cross. The story behind all of these stories is that of one cosmic battle commenced in Eden and reaching its climax in the massacre of the male infants by Herod (Mt 2:13–23). The "exile" in Egypt and repatriation to Nazareth already announce that this singular child is recapitulating Israel's history and, in so doing, bringing about the triumph of the "seed of the woman" over the serpent and his human agents. In fact, in Jesus' outlook, the opposition of his own people to the kingdom that belonged to them was really a playing out of this cosmic battle:

> You serpents, you brood of vipers, how are you to escape being sentenced to hell? Therefore I send you prophets and wise men and scribes, some of whom you will kill and crucify, and some you will flog in your own synagogues and persecute from town to town, so that on you may come all the righteous blood shed on earth, from the blood of innocent Abel to the blood of Zechariah son of Barachiah, whom you murdered between the sanctuary and the altar. (Mt 23:33–35)

Belonging to the right (covenant) line and performing the right worship, Abel by faith brought the sacrifice God had commanded, while Cain did not (Ge 4:4–8 with Heb 11:4). Even Peter's attempt to dissuade Jesus from the cross can be treated by Jesus as the voice of Satan (Mt 16:23).

For Jesus, then, the story behind the stories is not ethnic cleansing or even the restoration of an earthly theocracy. Good and evil cannot be easily classified in the static categories of ethnic, national, or political allegiance. "Outsiders" and "insiders" are redefined in exclusive reference to him. Exorcisms and healing in the New Testament, therefore, are not odd habits of an ancient people lacking the proper tools of psychological and medical analysis, but are redemptive-historical signposts, harbingers of the new creation: Jesus' contest with the powers of the age. *Christus Victor* meets *Agnus Dei*; the conquering King and the substitutionary Lamb are one and the same in this unique person and his kingdom. Jesus responds to the elation of the seventy at being able to subdue even the demons (in the language of treading on serpents, redolent of Genesis 3:15) with the even greater news that their names are written in heaven.

While the strong man may be bound, and consequently the extraordinary ministry of Jesus and his disciples may be succeeded by the ordinary ministry of Word and sacrament, our warfare "against the rulers, against the authorities, against the cosmic powers over this present darkness, against the spiritual forces of evil in the heavenly places" (Eph 6:12) continues unabated. Discovered especially wherever the progress of the gospel most threatens the kingdom of Satan, such pernicious forces are also recognized in the arrogance and rebellion of the nations and in heresy and schism in the church. As throughout the history recounted above, the cosmic battle is waged through earthly agents, both personal and institutional, religious and social, cultic and cultural, rhetorical and political. Wherever human beings are seduced into deeper self-confidence and away from the proclamation of Christ and his kingdom, the battle lines are drawn.

Thus, the kingdom of grace is not a geopolitical entity, like the empires and nations of this age. Neighbor love, inscribed on the human conscience in creation, still governs all laws and constitutions. God still protects Cain and his rebellious city by his common grace. It is not the era of intrusion ethics, but of the rule of common law measured by equity (justice tempered by love), to which believers and unbelievers are bound in secular friendship.[36] The heresy of Constantinianism, old and new, is to imagine that the church or the nations of this age can invoke the holy land and holy war passages from the Sinai covenant for our own time and place. Whatever wars may be waged among nations and powers in this present evil age, Christians may appeal to general principles of justice and love of neighbor, but not to Israel's national covenant.

Nevertheless, Christ is King and he is building his kingdom. It is composed of citizens from every nation and tongue, is founded in the blood of its King rather than his subjects, and expands by the Word and Spirit rather than by the sword. As O'Donovan comments, the kingdom of Christ in its present manifestation unmasks the powers of darkness arrayed against God and his Christ. "Unmasking supposes a theological point of vantage, essentially an eschatological one. Christ has led captivity captive; he has disarmed the principalities and powers; the Kingdom of Heaven is at hand. When we claim to have seen through the appearances of political power, we act, as King Lear says (v.3), 'as if we were God's spies.'"[37]

III. HEAVEN AND HELL

In this era, Christ's kingdom does not overthrow the kingdoms of this age. Nor does it execute God's wrath. However, when Christ returns, he will judge and reign in glory over all the earth.

The idea of heaven as a place where souls are forever freed from their bodily

---

36. See Eric Gregory, *Politics and the Ethic of Democratic Citizenship* (Chicago: Univ. of Chicago Press, 2008).

37. O'Donovan, *Desire of the Nations*, 7.

carapace to enjoy a dreamlike existence is far from the biblical understanding. I have already pointed out that the Christian hope is oriented not to the intermediate state (going to heaven when we die), but to the renovation of creation, including our natural bodies. In this light, heaven is not so much a place as it is a condition of God's Sabbath, where (and when) he sits enthroned in the midst of his people. The whole earth will be raised from death to life when the children of God are revealed (Ro 8:19 – 21).[38] When the covenant of peace is consummated, "the mountains and the hills before you shall break forth into singing, and all the trees of the field shall clap their hands" (Isa 55:12).

Biblical eschatology has always run counter to the prevailing assumptions of paganism, Eastern and Western, affirming liberation of rather than from creation. Heaven is a real place, not just a state of mind (Lk 24:51; Jn 14:2 – 4; Ac 1:11; 7:55 – 56). Nevertheless, the biblical vision of a new heaven and a new earth is not the abolition of the old creation, but describes the new condition of the world that the Father has made and remade in his Son and by his Spirit.

Heaven and hell appear together, affirmed side by side, in the New Testament as well (Mt 25:31 – 46; 1Pe 3:22; 2Pe 3:13; Rev 20:11 – 21:3). As we have seen, the most detailed and frequent references to the reality of hell come from the mouth of Jesus himself. Even in John's vision Jesus announces, "Fear not, I am the first and the last, and the living one. I died, and behold I am alive forevermore, and I have the keys of Death and Hades" (Rev 1:17 – 18). Christ gives Death and Hades the power to devour a fourth of the earth (Rev 6:8). "Then Death and Hades were thrown into the lake of fire. This is the second death, the lake of fire. And if anyone's name was not found written in the book of life, he was thrown into the lake of fire" (Rev 20:14 – 15). The term that Jesus often used, *Gehenna*, has its origins in the perpetually burning fire of the Ben Hinnom valley, where Israel imitated the pagan practices of its neighbors in child sacrifice (Jer 19:5; 32:35). The wicked will find themselves facing the same fate.

A. ETERNAL PUNISHMENT

We are now living in an era of common grace, in which neither salvation nor judgment has been fully consummated. For now, wheat and weeds grow together, awaiting the final separation. However, the era of God's patience will come to an

---

38. To be sure, 2 Peter 3:10 and Revelation 20:1, 11 speak of a "passing" of the old creation and creation of the new world, but in both instances the apocalyptic language of the prophets is borrowed. In this genre, natural "signs in the heavens" are employed to refer to historical turning points of cosmic significance. Although Grudem does not favor the view that the creation will be destroyed, he interprets 2 Peter 3:10 as referring to "the surface things on the earth (that is, much of the ground and the things on the ground)" (Wayne Grudem, *Systematic Theology: An Introduction to Bible Doctrine* [Grand Rapids: Zondervan, 1994], 1161). However, if my interpretation of the genre is correct, there is no reason even to go this far in assuming a catastrophic natural disaster, since the goal is redemption rather than destruction of creation.

end. From the beginning of Jesus' ministry, he was announced as the judge who baptizes with the Spirit and also with fire (Mt 3:11–12). In fact, Jesus speaks more directly and vividly of the reality of hell than any Old Testament prophet or New Testament apostle (Mt 5:30; 8:10–12; 13:40–42, 49–50; 22:13; 24:51; 25:30, and parallels; cf. Lk 16:19–31). In his Olivet Discourse Jesus explained, "When the Son of Man comes in his glory, and all the angels with him, then he will sit on his glorious throne." Echoing Isaiah 2 (as well as chapter 11), Jesus says that the nations will appear before the Son of Man in judgment and all will be separated, as sheep and goats, "into eternal life" and "into eternal punishment" (Mt 25:31, 41, 46). If we have trouble with Joshua and his campaigns, we should be more unsettled still by Jesus.

The epistles reveal the same solemn expectation. God is not ignoring human rebellion. "But because of your hard and impenitent heart you are storing up wrath for yourself on the day of wrath when God's righteous judgment will be revealed." For the wicked and unbelieving, "there will be wrath and fury ... tribulation and distress" (Ro 2:5, 8–9). First Thessalonians 5 warns that "the day of the Lord will come like a thief in the night," just when everyone is proclaiming peace and security (vv. 1–3). This event of salvation-and-judgment will be as final as it is sudden,

> when the Lord Jesus is revealed from heaven with his mighty angels in flaming fire, inflicting vengeance on those who do not know God and on those who do not obey the gospel of our Lord Jesus. They will suffer the punishment of eternal destruction, away from the presence of the Lord and from the glory of his might, when he comes on that day to be glorified by his saints, and to be marveled at among all who have believed, because our testimony to you was believed. (2Th 1:7–10)

Elsewhere we read that Sodom and Gomorrah "serve as an example by undergoing a punishment of eternal fire," and false teachers are "wandering stars, for whom the gloom of utter darkness has been reserved forever" (Jude 7, 13). Second Peter 3:7 speaks of "the day of judgment and destruction of the ungodly."

The Apocalypse deserves its own special treatment of the theme of holy war, but a few examples will suffice. With the opening of the sixth seal, the powerful and wealthy of all the earth who have feared neither God nor mortals call "to the mountains and rocks, 'Fall on us and hide us from the face of him who is seated on the throne, and from the wrath of the Lamb, for the great day of their wrath has come, and who can stand?'" (Rev 6:15–17). This is followed by the vision of the bowls of wrath and of the fall of the great Babylon, symbol of the earthly city in all of its infamous pride, injustice, and immorality, not to mention its persecution of the saints (chs. 16–18). Finally, Babylon—symbolic of the human attempt to rise up in pride against the Lord and his Messiah—is judged and destroyed, with the saints singing, "'Hallelujah! The smoke from her goes up forever and ever'" (Rev

19:1–3). The marriage feast of the Lamb is contrasted with "the great supper of God," as the angel calls the birds of prey to feast on "the flesh of all men, both free and slave, both small and great" (19:6–18).

After this the rider on the white horse defeats the beast and its armies, and then there is a thousand-year interim, which I take (in amillennial fashion) to refer symbolically to the present era between Christ's advents. At the end of history, Satan is "thrown into the lake of fire and sulfur, where the beast and the false prophet were, and they will be tormented day and night forever and ever" (Rev 19:11–20:10). The dead are then judged. "This is the second death, the lake of fire" (20:14–15). It is the finality of this holy war that ushers in the finality of the new heavens and earth, where there is no longer any judgment, war, pain, suffering, or oppression. And it is there, finally, where the Tree of Life yields its fruit for the healing of the nations (chs. 21–22).

It is certainly true that the images of the last day and heaven and hell are communicated in an apocalyptic form. Therefore, such images are not meant to be read like a morning newspaper. Nevertheless, they are also not meant to be ignored. They indicate realities that are beyond our conceptual grasp, yet are certain to come to fruition. Ours is not the first age to have found the doctrine of everlasting punishment difficult to accept. In recent decades, contemporary views have been classified as (1) *pluralist* (all religions are paths to God), (2) *inclusivist* (salvation comes by Christ alone but not exclusively through explicit faith in Christ), and (3) *particularist* (also identified, usually by critics, as exclusivism or restrictivism, holding that salvation comes only through faith in Christ). Affirming a pluralist view, John Hick represents a wide agreement of liberal Protestants.[39]

Most evangelical positions today that reject particularism/exclusivism (salvation through explicit faith in Christ) embrace various forms of inclusivism rather than pluralism. Generally speaking, inclusivism tends toward universalism without foreclosing the possibility that some may be lost. Some inclusivists defend their position as an affirmation of God's sovereign grace, while others follow a more synergistic (Arminian) line of argumentation. Two varieties should especially be mentioned.

1. *APOKATASTASIS* AND INCLUSIVISM

The concept of universal restoration (*apokatastasis*) was taught by the ancient Gnostics and also by the church father Origen, but was condemned at the Fifth Council of Constantinople in 553. Nevertheless, it has had its admirers throughout the ages, including John Scotus Erigena and some Anabaptist leaders (Hans Denck and Hans Hut), and continues to inspire universalist speculations in our own day.[40]

---

39. John Hick, "The Pluralist View," in *Four Views on Salvation in a Pluralist World* (ed. Dennis L. Ockholm and Timothy R. Phillips; Grand Rapids: Zondervan, 1996), 27–59.

According to Origen's barely disguised Platonizing of Christian eschatology, all spiritual essences (including human souls) will be at last freed from the body and reunited with their origin, but only after passing through successive cycles of educative purgation through reincarnation in other worlds. Even Satan and his hosts will be at last reunited with God.

Unwilling to endorse an absolute principle of universal salvation, many Roman Catholic and Protestant theologians in the modern era have embraced *inclusivism*: the belief that although Jesus Christ is the only Savior, people may be saved without explicit faith in Christ.

The logical consequence of Karl Barth's doctrine of election is universal salvation. One may continue to object, to refuse to be defined by one's election and reconciliation in Christ, but that rejection is not finally decisive. "God does not permit [the human person] to execute this No of his, this contradiction and opposition."[41] Even God's No is overtaken by God's Yes; hence, Law must always be finally subsumed under Gospel.[42] "*This* No is really Yes. *This* judgment is grace. *This* condemnation is forgiveness. *This* death is life. *This* hell is heaven."[43] It might be suggested that for Barth human existence under the reign of sin, death, unbelief, and condemnation is finally like the existence of the prisoners in Plato's cave. It is not the truth of their reality, but a terrible dream from which they need to be awakened. "There is no one who does not participate in [Christ] in this turning to God.... There is no one who is not raised and exalted with him to true humanity."[44] Nevertheless, according to Barth, we cannot say with certainty that every person will be saved, because this would compromise the absolute freedom of God in grace. Barth insists, "The Church ought not to preach Apokatastasis."[45]

---

40. Like Origen himself, some Roman Catholic theologians seek to revive *apokatastasis* by way of the dogma of purgatory, suggesting that after various levels of "suffering love," the souls of all will be finally educated in spiritual ascent. In 1983 the Roman Catholic theologian Hans Urs von Balthasar wrote a foreword and afterword commending a new edition of a 1967 book by Valentin Tomberg, *Meditations on the Tarot: A Journey into Christian Hermeticism* (New York: Tarcher/Penguin, 2002). Balthasar commends Tomberg's reflections for weaving together ancient Babylonian and Indian religion, Gnosticism, Hermeticism, Cabbala, magic, and astrology as "veiled presentiments of the Logos" (659). Acknowledging that Origen's views of reincarnation and *apokatastasis* were condemned by the church, Balthasar nevertheless sees these reflections of secret gnosis as leading believers more deeply into the wisdom of the Catholic Mystery (659). Although this particular form of universalism finds some support among liberal Protestants, most evangelicals reject it. It was taught by Herbert W. Armstrong (founder of the World Wide Church of God). In 2004, television evangelist Carlton Pearson became a staunch advocate of this view, but the Joint College of African-American Pentecostal Bishops concluded that this position was heretical. Clark Pinnock finds the concept of purgatory consistent with Arminian theology, while insisting on the possibility of some being finally annihilated in merciful love out of respect for their free will. See John Walvoord, William Crockett, Zachary Hayes, and Clark Pinnock, *Four Views on Hell* (Grand Rapids: Zondervan, 1996), 119–66.

41. Barth, *Church Dogmatics*, vol. 4, pt. 3.1, p. 3.

42. Ibid., vol. 2, pt. 2, 13: "The Yes cannot be heard unless the No is also heard. But the No is said for the sake of the Yes and not for its own sake. In substance, therefore, the first and last word is Yes and not No."

43. Karl Barth, *The Word of God and the Word of Man* (trans. Douglas Horton; New York: Harper & Brothers, 1956, 1957), 120.

44. Barth, *Church Dogmatics*, vol. 4, pt. 2, p. 271. A helpful discussion of Barth's view on this point is found in George Hunsinger, *How to Read Karl Barth: The Shape of His Theology* (New York and Oxford: Oxford Univ. Press, 1991), 128–35.

45. Barth, *Church Dogmatics*, vol. 2, pt. 2, 417.

Jürgen Moltmann follows a similar interpretation, although he seems less reticent than Barth to affirm universal salvation.[46] Like Barth, he bases his inclusivism on God's grace rather than on human goodness, but unlike Barth, he makes God's "suffering love" necessary to God's being and therefore compromises the very idea of grace as a free decision and act. It is difficult to resist the impression that both theologians reflect a nearly fatalistic interpretation of God's sovereign grace. In fact, Moltmann criticizes the notion of annihilation (see below) for making human free will ultimate rather than God's grace. Taking aim at a 1995 statement by the Church of England in defense of annihilation, Moltmann writes,

> The logic of hell is nothing other than the logic of human free will, in so far as this is identical with freedom of choice.... Does God's love preserve our free will, or does it free our enslaved will, which has become un-free through the power of sin? Does God love free men and women, or does he seek the men and women who have become lost? It is apparently not Augustine who is the Father of Anglo-Saxon Christianity; the Church Father who secretly presides over it is his opponent Pelagius. And it is Erasmus who is the saint of modern times, not Luther or Calvin.... The first conclusion, it seems to me, is that it is inhumane, for there are not many people who can enjoy their free will where their eternal fate in heaven or hell is concerned.[47]

"God is merely the accessory who puts that will into effect."[48] Rather, "the Christian doctrine of hell is to be found in the gospel of Christ's descent into hell, not in a modernization of hell into total non-being."[49] "The true universality of God's grace is not grounded in 'secular humanism'" but in "the theology of the cross."[50] Like Barth, Moltmann is attracted to the Christian Socialist preacher, Christoph Blumhardt: "Jesus can judge but not condemn."[51] "Judgment is not God's last word.... From this [new creation] no one is excepted.... Transforming grace is God's punishment for sinners. It is not the right to choose that defines the reality of human freedom. It is the doing of the good."[52] This form of inclusivism is therefore more "Augustinian," but with God's electing grace encompassing every person.

Evangelical Arminians like Clark Pinnock and John Sanders share the presupposition that all of God's attributes are subservient to his love and that his purpose is to save every person. In fact, Pinnock recognizes that these theses function as presuppositions or "axioms" by which exegesis must be tested.[53] However, these

46. Jürgen Moltmann, "The Logic of Hell," in *God Will Be All in All: The Eschatology of Jürgen Moltmann* (ed. Richard Bauckham; Edinburgh: T&T Clark, 1999), 43–48.

47. Moltmann, "The Logic of Hell," 44, reviewing the Doctrine Commission of the Church of England, *The Mystery of Salvation: The Story of God's Gift* (London: Church House Publishing, 1995).

48. Ibid., 45.

49. Ibid., 46.

50. Ibid., 47.

51. Christoph Blumhardt, as quoted in ibid.

52. Ibid.

53. Clark Pinnock, "Overcoming Misgivings about Evangelical Inclusivism," *Southern Baptist Journal of Theology* 2, no. 2 (Summer 1998): 33–34. He adds, "I agree that inclusivism is not a central topic of discussion in the Bible and that the evidence for it is less than one would like. But the vision of God's love there is so strong that the existing evidence seems sufficient to me" (35).

theologians differ sharply from the inclusivism of theologians like Barth and Moltmann in at least two crucial respects. First, they argue that salvation is dependent on the free will of individuals. Second, they believe that the content of saving revelation is mediated apart from the gospel, even in and through other religions as "means of grace."[54] Therefore, where Barth and Moltmann ground inclusivism in a notion of God's universal electing grace, Pinnock's inclusivism is grounded in a notion of God's making grace universally accessible to those who respond to the offer of it even apart from explicit faith in Christ. As Pinnock acknowledges, his version is especially indebted to the "anonymous Christian" concept of Karl Rahner and the Second Vatican Council.[55] Pinnock appeals to the examples of Melchizedek and Job and to Paul's quotation of pagan poets in Acts 17 to defend the idea that God reveals himself in a saving way outside of biblical revelation.[56]

2. Annihilation

Other Christians have concluded that the exegetical evidence for the reality of hell is impossible to reconcile with universal salvation. The question addressed by

---

54. These theses are defended in the following works by Clark H. Pinnock: "An Inclusivist View," in *Four Views on Salvation in a Pluralistic World* (ed. Dennis L. Okholm and Timothy R. Phillips; Grand Rapids: Zondervan, 1995), 251–54; *A Wideness in God's Mercy: The Finality of Jesus Christ in a World of Religions* (Grand Rapids: Zondervan, 1992); "Acts 4:12 — No Other Name under Heaven," in *Through No Fault of Their Own? The Fate of Those Who Have Never Heard* (ed. William Crockett and James Sigountos; Grand Rapids: Baker, 1991), 114ff. See also John Sanders, *No Other Name: An Investigation into the Destiny of the Unevangelized* (Grand Rapids: Eerdmans, 1992); "Inclusivism," in *What about Those Who Have Never Heard? Three Views on the Destiny of the Unevangelized* (Downers Grove, Ill.: InterVarsity Press, 1995). Sanders's position, however, is less inclusivist than Pinnock's. See also Amos Yong, *Beyond the Impasse: Toward a Pneumatological Theology of Religions* (Grand Rapids: Baker, 2003); Stanley J. Grenz, "Toward an Evangelical Theology of Religions," *Journal of Ecumenical Studies* 31 (Winter–Spring 1995): 49–65. None of the major theses and presuppositions of inclusivism is original with Pinnock or other evangelicals. It has been defended and assumed within much of mainline Protestantism as well as post-Conciliar Roman Catholicism. This view is distinguished from religious pluralism by its affirmation that while saving truth is present in other religions, all truth derives from Christ and its fullness is found in special revelation. Within evangelical circles, a more Augustinian (and guarded) interpretation of inclusivism is argued by John Stackhouse, *What Does It Mean to Be Saved? Broadening Evangelical Horizons of Salvation* (Grand Rapids: Baker Academic, 2002), and by Terrance L. Tiessen, *Who Can Be Saved? Reassessing Salvation in Christ and World Religions* (Downers Grove, Ill.: InterVarsity Press, 2004). Nevertheless, even these last two proposals reflect the tendency (much more

pronounced in the previously cited volumes) to identify the revelation of God in creation (and therefore in other religions) as differing in degree rather than in kind from the revelation of God in the gospel.

55. Pinnock, "Overcoming Misgivings about Evangelical Inclusivism," 34: "Scripture speaks in different ways about how people are saved subjectively. For example, it says that God loves seekers and rewards them, even if they are not Jews or Christians (Heb 11:6). It says that Christ will save some people who have no idea who Jesus is but who showed by their deeds that they love God's kingdom (Mt 25:37)." It should be noted that neither of these passages even implies that the subjects are outside of the covenant community. On the contrary, for example, in Matthew 25 Jesus speaks of a final separation of sheep and goats, with the former told, " 'Come, you who are blessed by my Father, inherit the kingdom *prepared for you from the foundation of the world*' " (v. 34, emphasis added). The good deeds that Jesus then goes on to describe are consequences and evidences of these persons' being in Christ, not the means, and the context is the imminent threat of persecution, when believers will be cast into prison for their faith in Christ. Pinnock appeals to "Declaration on the Relationship of the Church to Non-Christian Religions," par. 2, in *The Documents of Vatican II* (ed. Walter M. Abbott; trans. Joseph Gallagher; New York: Herder & Herder, 1966), 662.

56. Pinnock, "Overcoming Misgivings about Evangelical Inclusivism," 35–36: "I find support in Paul's statement that people may search for God and find him from anywhere in the world (Ac 17:27). I appreciate him saying that the gentiles have God's law written on their hearts (Ro 2:16) and may be given eternal life when, by patiently doing good, they seek for glory and honor and immortality (Ro 2:7). As a Catholic might put it, there are people with a desire for baptism who have not been able to be baptised."

annihilationism is not the scope of God's mercy, but the nature of hell. Some annihilationists (such as Philip E. Hughes) could be considered exclusivists (i.e., salvation through explicit faith in Christ alone), while others (such as Clark Pinnock) are inclusivists. At the same time, they interpret various passages as teaching that unbelievers are raised on the last day for destruction (the second death) rather than for everlasting, conscious torment. Because they are destroyed forever, Scripture can still speak in apocalyptic terms of "their smoke going up forever" and their being eternally destroyed. However, this need not entail conscious punishment.[57]

Historically, this view has not gained adherents except among the Adventists, Jehovah's Witnesses, Christadelphians, and other groups. More recently, however, it has gained ground especially in British evangelicalism, including (possibly) C. S. Lewis, as well as John Wenham, Philip E. Hughes, and, more tentatively, John Stott.[58] It has also been defended, in more emotional language, by Clark Pinnock and Edward Fudge.[59] Proponents of this view cite the emotional difficulty of accepting the idea of conscious punishment that lasts forever, but most finally defend their view as most consistent with Scripture.

Annihilationists claim that the notion of eternal, conscious torment is based on the Greek doctrine of the immortality of the soul. In its place, they argue for conditional immortality. At the final resurrection and judgment, the immortal God will grant immortality to believers and condemn unbelievers to destruction. Satan and the false prophet are said to suffer eternal consciousness in hell, but no one else (Rev 14:9–11; 20:10). Jesus' description of the fire as "eternal" and "unquenchable" (Mt 3:12; 18:8; 25:41; Lk 3:17) can be interpreted as annihilation. Positively, advocates of this view appeal to passages that speak of unbelievers perishing (Jn 3:16) and being destroyed (Mt 10:28), and believe that the reference in Revelation 20 to the "second death" can only refer to this annihilation. In Matthew 10:28, Jesus warns hearers to "fear him who can destroy both soul and body in hell."

---

57. One of the most extensive treatments of eternal punishment from this perspective is Edward W. Fudge, *The Fire That Consumes: A Biblical and Historical Study of the Doctrine of Final Punishment* (Houston, Tex.: Providential Press, 1982). Various studies interact thoughtfully with Fudge's thesis, including Robert A. Peterson, *Hell on Trial: The Case for Eternal Punishment* (Phillipsburg, N.J.: P&R, 1995). Cf. Edward W. Fudge and Robert A. Peterson, *Two Views on Hell: A Biblical and Theological Dialogue* (Downers Grove, Ill.: InterVarsity Press, 2000); Christopher W. Morgan and Robert A. Peterson, eds., *Hell under Fire: Modern Scholarship Reinvents Eternal Punishment* (Grand Rapids: Zondervan, 2004).

58. It is difficult to discern exactly what Lewis held on this matter. In *The Problem of Pain* (San Francisco: HarperSanFrancisco, 1940, 2001) C. S. Lewis writes, "The characteristic of lost souls is 'their rejection of everything that is not simply themselves.' Our imaginary egoist has tried to turn everything he meets into a province or appendage of the self. The taste for the other, that is, the very capacity for enjoying good, is quenched in him except in so far as his body still draws him into some rudimentary contact with an outer world. Death removes this last contact. He has his wish—to lie wholly in the self and to make the best of what he finds there. And what he finds there is Hell" (124–25). For Stott's view, see David L. Edwards and John Stott, *Essentials: A Liberal-Evangelical Dialogue* (Downers Grove, Ill.: InterVarsity Press, 1988), 314–20.

59. Clark Pinnock, "The Conditional View," in *Four Views on Hell* (ed. William Crockett; Grand Rapids: Zondervan, 1997), 135–66; Fudge, *The Fire That Consumes*.

3. EVALUATING THESE ALTERNATIVES

Any notion of a final restoration of all spiritual beings, including Satan and his demonic forces, is dispelled by the clear teaching of Scripture that they will be destroyed. In offering a brief response to the inclusivist position I would direct readers to earlier places in this volume where I have defended (1) God's simplicity against the tendency to assimilate God's character to a single attribute, (2) God's sovereign election of many but not all sinners and his grace in Christ alone, received through faith alone, and (3) the distinction between law and gospel (and the corollary distinction between general and special revelation).[60]

While Origen's doctrine may be characterized as somewhat Pelagian as well as Platonic, the view of Barth and Moltmann might be better described as "Augustinian universalism."[61] In fact, given that according to this view even those who do not wish to be saved are saved against their will, it might be justly reckoned a "Hyper-Calvinistic universalism." However, Scripture clearly gives decisive importance to faith in Christ, apart from which no one can be saved. This hardly represents a "Pelagian" triumph of human will over divine grace, since Scripture also teaches that faith is a gift of God. Whatever the plausibility of Moltmann's quarrel with Arminian accounts, an Augustinian interpretation of salvation through faith in Christ is just as committed to *sola gratia*. The question is not whether God's "Yes" overcomes our "No," but whether God is free to show this mercy to whomever he will and whether the nonelect are responsible for their rejection of the gospel.

According to Barth and his school, one practical outcome of his view is a strongly objective doctrine of God's sovereign, electing, and irresistible grace. Everyone is elect in Christ, the Elect One, and therefore there is no place for questioning this fact. Everyone is already saved in Christ, at least *de jure*.[62] At the same time, as we have seen, Barth explicitly rejected Origen's view, and he thought that any absolute denial of the possibility that some human beings may finally be lost compromised God's sovereign freedom. This seems quite strange, since it means that for the first time in church history it has been suggested that it is possible that some whom God

60. In addition, the following resources are recommended: Ronald Nash, *Is Jesus the Only Savior?* (Grand Rapids: Zondervan, 1994); R. Douglas Geivett, "Is Jesus the Only Way?" in *Jesus under Fire: Modern Scholarship Reinvents the Historical Jesus* (ed. Michael J. Wilkins and J. P. Moreland; Grand Rapids: Zondervan, 1995); and R. Douglas Geivett and W. Gary Phillips, "A Particularist View: An Evidentialist Approach," in Okholm and Phillips, eds., *Four Views on Salvation in a Pluralistic World*; D. A. Carson, *The Gagging of God: Christianity Confronts Pluralism* (Grand Rapids: Zondervan, 1996); Ajith Fernando, *The Supremacy of Christ* (Wheaton, Ill.: Crossway, 1995); Paul R. House and Gregory A. Thornbury, eds., *Who*

Will Be Saved?: Defending the Biblical Understanding of God, Salvation, and Evangelism (Wheaton, Ill.: Crossway, 2000); Douglas Moo, "Romans 2: Saved Apart from the Gospel?" in *Through No Fault of Their Own: The Fate of Those Who Have Never Heard* (ed. William V. Crockett and James G. Sigountos; Grand Rapids: Baker, 1991), 137–45; Daniel Strange, *The Possibility of Salvation among the Unevangelized: An Analysis of Inclusivism in Recent Evangelical Theology* (Carlisle, U.K.: Paternoster Press, 2002).

61. See Oliver D. Crisp, "Augustinian Universalism," *International Journal for Philosophy of Religion* 53 (2003): 127–45.

62. Barth, *Church Dogmatics*, vol. 4, pt. 3, p. 811.

has eternally and unconditionally included in Christ as elect, justified and sanctified may nevertheless be finally condemned.

Barth's position is only as persuasive as his exegesis of the relevant passages. Contrary to Barth's interpretation of "sheep" and "goats" as the dialectical truth about every person, Jesus speaks clearly of the one group being welcomed into heaven and the other group being cast into hell. Although Brunner objected as strongly as Barth to the doctrine of particular election, he recognized that according to the New Testament, only the elect are "in Christ" and they are "those who believe."[63] Barth mistakes human responsibility for synergism.[64] Brunner suggests that, besides ignoring the conditions in Scripture, Barth eliminates "the vital tension, based on the dialectic of God's Holiness and Love, by means of a monistic *schema*."[65] We do recognize in Jesus Christ the consistency of God's love and holiness. "But outside of Jesus Christ, outside of faith, God's Holiness is not the same as His Love, but *there* it is His wrath; *there* what God is 'in Himself' is not the same as that which He is 'for us,' *there* it is the unfathomable, impenetrable mystery of the '*nuda majestas*'; *there* is no election, but rejection, judgment, condemnation...."[66] God's wrath is not a form of grace. Apostolic preaching in the New Testament announces forgiveness for all who believe, but it also warns that apart from faith there is the fearful expectation of wrath, not merely a lack of awareness of being saved.

If the decisiveness of history—and the decisions that human beings make within it—are treated too lightly by Barth, human willing and acting become *ultimately* determinative in the synergistic versions of inclusivism.

With respect to the inclusivist position, with its notion of the "anonymous Christian" (see p. 979 above), it should be noted that although revelation progresses from Old Testament shadows to New Testament reality, the object of faith is the same. However, the religions of the nations are regarded as idolatrous throughout this history. Ever since Justin Martyr, some Christians have claimed that the pagan philosophers prepared the way for Christ among the Gentiles as Moses and the prophets prepared the Jews. But this is to confuse general revelation with special revelation and the law with the gospel.

Pinnock's examples cited above do not demonstrate that there can be a saving knowledge of God apart from his revelation to Israel. From what little we know about Melchizedek, he could not have been a "noble pagan."[67] He was "king of

---

63. Emil Brunner, *Dogmatics*, vol. 1, *The Christian Doctrine of God* (trans. Olive Wyon; Philadelphia: Westminster Press, 1946), 315.

64. Ibid., 316.

65. Ibid., 334, 336.

66. Ibid., 337. Brunner adds (in my concluded ellipsis), "... but no eternal decree."

67. James L. Kugel, *Traditions of the Bible: A Guide to the Bible as It Was at the Start of the Common Era* (Cambridge, Mass.: Harvard Univ. Press, 1988), 276–78.

Salem" (proto-Jerusalem), "priest of God Most High," "God Most High" (*ʾēl ʿelyôn*) being identified as none other than "the LORD [Yahweh], God Most High" (Ge 14:18–22). He brought Abram bread and wine, blessed him, and received a tributary tithe—all of these actions reflecting a covenantal context in which Abram recognized Melchizedek as his high priest. Nor can Job qualify as an anonymous believer. Whatever his precise relationship to Abraham, Job's allusion to Psalm 8:4 (Job 7:17–18) and direct quotations of Psalm 107:40 and Isaiah 41:11–12 in Job 12 (vv. 21–24) place him squarely in God's covenant community.[68]

Paul quotes pagan poets to his audience of Athenian philosophers in Acts 17 for the express purpose of demonstrating that they are not even living consistently with general revelation. In any case, Paul declares, "The times of ignorance God overlooked, but now he commands all people everywhere to repent, because he has fixed a day on which he will judge the world in righteousness by a man whom he has appointed; and of this he has given assurance to all by raising him from the dead" (Ac 17:30–31). However lenient God may have been in "the times of ignorance," the appearance of Christ in these last days leaves everyone without excuse. It is the universal-public character of Christ's decisive work and coming judgment that gives to the missionary enterprise the kind of urgency that is found throughout the book of Acts.

At the same time, I do not believe that we can conclude that no one can be saved apart from explicit faith in Christ. First, it is precisely because God is sovereign and free in his grace that he can have mercy on whomever he chooses. From first to last, "Salvation is of the LORD" (Jnh 2:9). Second, since the children of believers are comprehended with their parents in the covenant of grace, in the words of the *Canons of Dort*, "godly parents ought not to doubt the election and salvation of their children whom it pleases God to call out of this life in their infancy (Gen. 17:7; Acts 2:39; 1 Cor. 7:14)."[69] Third, we are not told what God does in extraordinary cases: e.g., those who are physically or mentally incapable of understanding God's Word. As in all theological questions, we must restrain our curiosity and refuse to speculate beyond God's own instruction. Apart from God's self-disclosure in Scripture, we do not know what God has ordained from all of eternity. Whatever God *might choose to do* in any given case, he has *promised* to save all of those—and only those—who call on the name of his Son.

Finally, with respect to annihilationism, Jesus' teaching concerning the final separation of the saved and the lost seems to treat punishment and life as equally

---

68. These examples, often put forward by inclusivists, as well as other principal arguments from this camp, are treated respectfully and carefully in *Faith Comes by Hearing: A Response to Inclusivism* (ed. Christopher W. Morgan and Robert A. Peterson; Downers Grove, Ill.: InterVarsity Press, 2008).

69. *Canons of Dort*, ch. 1, art. 17, in *Psalter Hymnal: Doctrinal Standards and Liturgy of the Christian Reformed Church* (Grand Rapids: CRC Publications, 1976), 95. There is also the example of the death of David's week-old son. "I shall go to him," David said, "but he will not return to me" (2Sa 12:23).

eternal: "And these will go away into eternal punishment, but the righteous into eternal life" (Mt 25:46). If it is generally assumed that "eternal life" means unending, conscious joy, then it would seem that annihilationists bear the burden of proof in treating "eternal punishment" as otherwise in duration. Regardless of how one finally interprets these passages, it cannot be decided on the basis of our fallen moral judgment of God and his ways and our consequent emotional revulsion at the admittedly difficult idea of conscious punishment forever. Nor, indeed, can it be decided out of concern to protect the missionary imperative, as if the motive for our evangelism were to be based on the fear of conscious eternal punishment. The only decisive question is whether Scripture teaches it. Furthermore, we must be careful to distinguish scriptural teaching from the popular images of hell that we have inherited from popular mythology, whether pagan or Christian. We must admit candidly that the elaborate descriptions of hell from Dante's *Inferno* to Billy Sunday are as speculative as they are evocative. The critical point to be made from Scripture with regard to eternal punishment is not its degree or duration, but its horrifying reality as God's personal judgment that is final and forever.

B. Everlasting *Šālôm*

I have argued that in the old covenant *some* places were holy, and that in the present phase of Christ's kingdom there are *no* holy places. However, when Christ returns, cleansing the land in a final judgment, *everything* will be holy. Zechariah prophesies the day when the true temple will be cleansed of all traders and everything that defiles. The most common household pots and pans—even the bells on the horses—will bear the inscription, "Holy to the Lord!" (Zec 14:20–21). The wasteland will again become a lush garden, from which the violent and the oppressor is banished (Isa 35). One last time the world will be shaken and the nations will come to the Desire of All Nations, the end-time Temple filled with the glory of the Spirit (Hag 2:6–7). "The latter glory of this house shall be greater than the former, says the Lord of hosts. And in this place I will give peace, says the Lord of hosts" (v. 9).

Undoubtedly, 1 Kings 6 sets the compass for the theocracy and its later developments of this theme of the temple, as we transition from the movable tabernacle to the stationary sanctuary. It was sixty cubits long, twenty cubits wide, and thirty cubits high (v. 2), with the inner sanctuary being the perfect cube (v. 20). Following the specific commands he was given, Solomon relates detailed orders, "in order that the whole house might be perfect" (v. 22 NRSV). The foundation was made of "costly stones" (7:10).

After the destruction of the first temple, Ezekiel received a vision of the new one (Eze 40–42), and he relates the return of the Glory-Cloud to the temple in chapter 43. A man "whose appearance was like bronze" stood with a measuring rod, six cubits long (40:3, 5). Detailed measurements were taken, along with specific instructions for its construction and furnishings. "He measured the court, a hundred cubits long and a hundred cubits broad, a square. And the altar was in front of the temple" (v. 47). More detailed measurements follow, with the final measurement of the entire new temple, each of the four sides measuring five hundred cubits, with a wall separating the holy from the common (42:16–20). Recalling that cherubim were posted at the eastern gate of Eden, barring reentry to the sanctuary after the fall, as was the case when the Glory evacuated Israel's first temple, Ezekiel is now taken in his vision to the gate that faces east: "and it was shut. And the LORD said to me: 'This gate shall remain shut; it shall not be opened, and no one shall enter by it, for the LORD, the God of Israel, has entered by it. Therefore it shall remain shut. Only the prince may sit in it to eat bread before the LORD. He shall enter by way of the vestibule of the gate, and shall go out by the same way'" (44:1–3). Nothing "uncircumcised" will be allowed to enter its sacred precincts (vv. 4–9).

Finally, in Revelation 21 and 22 we have a similar description of the temple. First, it will be the ultimate dwelling place of God among his covenant people, bringing a final end to suffering, sin, pain, and injustice. "And he who was seated on the throne said, 'Behold, I am making all things new'" (21:5). The inhabitants will drink freely of the water of life, just as they are finally allowed to eat from the Tree of Life. "The one who conquers will have this heritage, and I will be his God and he will be my son. But as for the cowardly, the faithless, the detestable, as for murderers, the sexually immoral, sorcerers, idolaters, and all liars, their portion will be in the lake that burns with fire and sulfur, which is the second death" (vv. 7–8). John is then shown "the Bride, the wife of the Lamb," which is none other than "the holy city Jerusalem coming down out of heaven from God" (vv. 9–10). Rare jewels, high walls, twelve gates and twelve foundations are mentioned. And once more the angel appears with a measuring rod. "The city lies foursquare, its length the same as its width. And he measured the city with his rod, 12,000 stadia. Its length and width and height are equal" (v. 16). In fact, it becomes increasingly clear that the temple is not something within the city, but the city itself. "I saw no temple in the city, for its temple is the Lord God the Almighty and the Lamb" (v. 22). Unlike the temples of Eden and Jerusalem, it will remain unpolluted forever, for "nothing unclean will ever enter it," and therefore this Sanctuary's gates "will never be shut," so that all whose names "are written in the Lamb's book of life" may enter (vv. 25–27). There is no sea there, which surely means that just as the wild beasts no longer threaten on land, the chaos monster of the dark and turbulent depths no longer has a home from which to assault the citizens of Zion.

In his remarkable treatment of this theme, G. K. Beale articulates "a biblical theology of the dwelling place of God," as the subtitle of his book indicates.[70]

> Our thesis is that Israel's temple was composed of three main parts, each of which symbolized a major part of the cosmos: (1) the outer court represented the habitable world where humanity dwelt; (2) the holy place was emblematic of the visible heavens and its light sources; (3) the holy of holies symbolized the invisible dimension of the cosmos, where God and his heavenly hosts dwelt.... The identification of the outer court as the visible earth and sea is suggested further by the Old Testament description, where the large molten wash-basin and altar in the temple courtyard are called respectively the "sea" (1 Kgs. 7:23–26) and the "bosom of the earth" (Ezek. 43:14; the altar also likely was identified with the "mountain of God" in Ezek. 43:16). The altar was also to be an "altar of earth" (in the early stages of Israel's history) or an "altar of [uncut] stone" (Exod. 20:24–25), thus identifying it even more with the natural earth.[71]

It is not too fanciful to suggest that the movement from the inner court, entered only by the High Priest once a year, to the surrounding precincts of the Holy Place, and finally to the outer court of the Gentiles is typological of Jesus' answer to the disciples' query at his ascension, " 'Lord, will you at this time restore the kingdom to Israel?' He said to them, 'It is not for you to know times or season that the Father has fixed by his own authority. But you will receive power when the Holy Spirit has come upon you, and you will be my witnesses in *Jerusalem* in all *Judea and Samaria*, and to the *ends of the earth*" (Ac 1:7–8).

In its typological-theocratic form, Israel was a centripetal community, separated from the nations; in its fulfillment, it becomes a centrifugal community, sent out from the Holy of Holies, through the Holy Place, out to the court of the Gentiles. This is the force of Christ's Great Commission: "All authority in heaven and on earth has been given to me. Go therefore and make disciples of all nations, baptizing them in the name of the Father and of the Son and of the Holy Spirit ..." (Mt 28:18–19). "Go into all the world and proclaim the gospel to the whole creation" (Mk 16:15).

The end-time sanctuary, made without hands, has finally appeared in Christ. Far greater than the rending of the temple curtain at Jesus' crucifixion is the rending of Jesus' own body on the cross, opening up direct access to all believers. There our High Priest has entered the heavenly sanctuary of which the earthly temple was merely a type, and he enters bearing his own blood as the complete and final sacrifice for sin. There will be no renewal of the Sinai covenant, no going back to the shadows now that the reality has come. Now believers, Jew and Gentile, are being

---

70. G. K. Beale, *The Temple and the Church's Mission: A Biblical Theology of the Dwelling Place of God* (Downers Grove, Ill.: InterVarsity Press, 2004).

71. Ibid., 32–33.

built up into Christ as living stones. The people have become the place of God's dwelling, robed in the glorious robes of Christ's righteousness.

The city and the temple in the book of Revelation encompass the whole cosmos. "Not only does the horizontal demarcation between the old temple and city disappear in the New Jerusalem," notes Kline, "but the vertical distinction between heavenly and earthly temples as well."[72] Not only the prophets and apostles, but the whole people of God are now "caught up in the Spirit" to stand in the heavenly council, covered in priestly vestments, sent from the throne-room as witnesses.[73] In the New Testament, the glory of Christ's face (2Co 4:5–6) reveals judgment from heaven. "It is a *parousia*-glory, as Jesus returns on the last day (Mt 16:27; Mk 8:38; Lk 9:26)."[74] In Hebrews 12, this parousia-glory is identified with his voice (cf. Rev 1:10–15).[75] In John's account of his vision of the heavenly worship, he describes how, amid flashes of lightning and peals of thunder, the twenty-four elders were seated around God's throne, with flaming torches burning before each throne. And behind the thrones hangs the rainbow of peace (Rev 4:2–5). The flaming torches in Revelation are reminiscent of the flame of fire above each Spirit-endowed witness at Pentecost. The new temple is not built "by human hands" (Ac 7:48), and Christ's witnesses are "circumcised by a circumcision without human hands, by the circumcision [death] of Christ" (Col 2:11).[76]

The new creation is therefore entirely the work of God, and the end-time sanctuary is the temple that God has built for himself. "Judaism highlighted this by saying that God would 'build the temple [of Exod. 15:17] … with his two hands' (*Mekilta de-Rabbi Ishmael, Tractate Shirata* 10.40–42)."[77] It is not built by us but by God, whose indwelling presence is not conditioned on the nation's faithfulness but on his own covenant faithfulness; it is erected not from inanimate blocks that may be pulled down but from living stones taken from every tribe under heaven, with Christ as the cornerstone (1Pe 2:4–8).

Far from the vision of disembodied spirits floating on ethereal clouds with harps, Isaiah 65 speaks of a "new heavens and a new earth" (v. 17), with buildings and vineyards, trees, labor, and fellowship with all of creation. What is gone are not emotions, but "the sound of weeping and the cry of distress" (v. 19). Its inhabitants "shall build houses and inhabit them; they shall plant vineyards and eat their fruit," enjoying the fruit of their labor rather than building and planting only to have their homes occupied by invaders (vv. 21–22a). Not work itself, but the curse of tiresome, frustrating, and meaningless labor, will be no more (vv. 22b). Children will be a blessing rather than a cause for distress over their future (v. 23). No one will need

---

72. Kline, *Images of the Spirit*, 35.
73. Ibid., 94.
74. Ibid., 121–22.

75. Ibid., 122.
76. Beale, *The Temple and the Church's Mission*, 233–34.
77. Ibid., 235n66.

to cry to the Lord, for "while they are yet speaking I will hear" (v. 24), and it is not the absence of wildlife but of danger that will characterize this Sabbath land (v. 25). The book of Isaiah closes with this prophecy:

> For as the new heavens and the new earth that I make shall remain before me, says the Lord, so shall your offspring and your name remain. From new moon to new moon, and from Sabbath to Sabbath, all flesh shall come to worship before me, declares the Lord. And they shall go out and look on the dead bodies of the men who have rebelled against me. For their worm shall not die, their fire shall not be quenched, and they shall be an abhorrence to all flesh. (Isa 66:22–24)

The resurrection of the body underscores the anticipation of the final state as redemption of nature rather than its oblivion.

In the New Testament as well, the final heavenly abode is a created place (Lk 24:51; Jn 14:2–4; Ac 1:11; 7:55–56; 1Pe 3:22). To be sure, the renewal is so radical that it can be described only in apocalyptic terms (2Pe 3:12–13), as passing away (Rev 21:2–3). Nevertheless, we should think not in terms of the end of God's creation itself but of the end of creation *in its current condition*. Steven Prediger-Bouma observes, "An orthodox Christian eschatology speaks not of the annihilation of the earth but of its renewal and restoration."[78] Our heavenly hope is not only of saved souls but of a saved creation (Ro 8:19–21). Just as Jesus ate and drank after his resurrection, there will be eating and drinking in the new creation, although this time at the consummated marriage supper of the Lamb (Rev 19:9), with Jesus drinking wine with us (Lk 22:18). The theme of eating and drinking in the presence of the Lord that we find throughout the Old Testament narratives and again so prominently in Luke's Gospel will be fully realized in that day.

Revelation 22 employs the imagery of a river flowing through the city, with the tree of life "yielding its fruit each month" (Rev 22:2). Again, it is apocalyptic imagery, but the purchase of such imagery is lost if there is no physical creation. Just as the imagery of fire, outer darkness, and the grave seem contradictory if taken literally and yet, taken together, indicate the horrible condition of hell, the imagery of wedding feasts, rivers, trees, and a city with streets of gold is richly suggestive of a condition that we cannot conceive of apart from such analogies. This does not mean that these are "mere metaphors," since the value of metaphors is to actually convey

---

78. Steven Prediger-Bouma, *For the Beauty of the Earth* (Grand Rapids: Baker, 2001), 125. It is worth noting that although Moltmann is sharply critical of dispensationalist emphases on apocalyptic catastrophe, his tendency to allow the new creation (eschatology) to swallow the original creation (protology) may lead in the same direction. Peter Macek has raised this question: "Does not Moltmann's *creatio nova*, interpreted as a *novum ex nihilo*, rather than 'restoration,' presuppose total and active *annihilatio mundi* and not only *annihilatio nihil*? Or, to put it differently, does not the necessity of 'new creation' undercut the goodness of *creatio orginalis* and does it not in this sense fail to account for the biblical distinction between 'creation' and 'fall'?" (Peter Macek, "The Doctrine of Creation in the Messianic Theology of Jürgen Moltmann," *Communio Viatorum* 49, no. 2 [2007]: 180).

truth. Whatever the condition of "the life everlasting," it is more, certainly not less, than the embodied joy that such imagery suggests. We are creatures of time and space, and we will transcend not our humanity but the bondage of our humanity to the conditions of sin and death.

Interpreting the apocalyptic imagery of 2 Peter 3:12–13 literally, classic dispensationalism anticipates a complete annihilation of the cosmos.[79] The title of Hal Lindsey's classic bears this point: *The Late Great Planet Earth*. Lewis Sperry Chafer and John Walvoord write, "The day of the Lord, which begins at the Rapture and includes in its introduction the judgments preceding and immediately following the Second Coming, concludes with the end of the millennium and with the final destruction of the present heaven and earth."[80] After the great white throne judgment, "the old creation is destroyed.... Because of the destruction of the present earth and heaven, the judgment of the great white throne apparently takes place in space."[81] The heavenly Jerusalem coming down from heaven, beautifully described in Revelation 21, is apparently uncreated: "It is most significant that the city is not said to be created, and it apparently was in existence during the preceding period of the millennial kingdom, possibly as a satellite city above the earth; as such, it may be the millennial home of the resurrected and translated saints."[82]

Although Grudem does not favor the view that the creation will be destroyed, he interprets 2 Peter 3:10–13 as referring to "the surface things on the earth (that is, much of the ground and the things on the ground)."[83] While I appreciate his attempt to limit the effects of a literalized interpretation, these verses seem to encompass the whole created order. Furthermore, if what is eliminated is "much of the ground and the things on the ground," such destruction leaves little of creation left. If, however, such apocalyptic language in 2 Peter is to be interpreted like apocalyptic language elsewhere, there is no reason to interpret these verses as communicating anything more than a complete transition from one condition of existence to another. "This present age" versus "the age to come," not this present world versus another world, reflects the consistent emphasis of New Testament eschatology. This whole creation will be wholly saved, and yet wholly new.

If our goal is to be liberated *from* creation rather than the liberation *of* creation, we will understandably display little concern for the world that God has made. If, however, we are looking forward to "the restoration of all things" (Ac 3:21) and

---

79. Lewis Sperry Chafer, *Major Bible Doctrines* (ed. John Walvoord; rev. ed.; Grand Rapids: Zondervan, 1974), 353: "In this discussion it will be assumed that prophecy should be interpreted in the same literal sense as any other theme of divine revelation." However, interpreting prophetic and apocalyptic literature — or, for that matter, parables and poetry — as if they were historical narrative results in violence to the actual intention of the text.

80. Ibid., 334–35.
81. Ibid., 367.
82. Ibid., 370.
83. Grudem, *Systematic Theology*, 1161.

the participation of the whole creation in our redemption (Ro 8:18–21), then our actions here and now pertain to the same world that will one day be finally and fully renewed.

DISCUSSION QUESTIONS

1. Explore the theme of "holy war" from Genesis to Revelation.
2. Distinguish "just war" from "holy war." God is sovereign over history and reveals his moral will in this matter, but in different ways at different times. How would you explain this difference? Can we invoke Israel's "holy war" passages against our enemies today? Can nations?
3. Does the New Testament also teach this theme of holy war? How is it different from the holy wars of the Old Testament?
4. What are the different views concerning eternal punishment? Which do you think is most biblical?
5. Describe the biblical promise of *šālôm*. How was Israel's theocracy a type of this condition? How will the consummation transcend it? Is this final peace something that we can bring about? How does this hope transform our lives today?

GLOSSARY

Active obedience of Christ: term used to express Jesus Christ's fulfillment of the law on behalf of his people

Adoptionism: Christological heresy that Jesus of Nazareth was conceived as merely a natural human being, but was later adopted as the Son of God at his baptism

Apokotastasis: the concept of the universal restoration (universal salvation) for all of creation, humanity, and fallen angels alike. Ancient Gnostics and the early church theologian Origen (c. 185–254) taught this view, but it was condemned at the Fifth Council of Constantinople in 553.

Apostles' Creed: Although dating in its final form from the eighth century, most of the elements are present already in second-century creedal affirmations. Along with the Nicene (also known as the Nicene-Constantinopolitan) Creed (325/381), it is the most widely used ecumenical creed in Christian churches.

Analogical: the epistemological position that creaturely knowledge is a copy (an analogue) of divine knowledge. This type of knowledge is both similar and dissimilar (cf. equivocal, univocal).

Archetypal knowledge: the knowledge that only God possesses. It is the original whereas all else is the copy (cf. ectypal knowledge).

Arianism (also, Subordinationism): Only the Father is God in the fullest sense; the Son and the Spirit are ontologically inferior. According to Arianism, the Son is the first created being.

Arminians: Initiated in the seventeenth century, this movement follows the teachings of Jacobus Arminius (1560–1609), who emphasized that God's election is conditioned upon foreseen faith, his grace can be resisted, and Christ's atonement was made on behalf of all humanity. The first confessional statement of Arminian theology is in the *Remonstrance* (1610), to which the Synod of Dordt responded with its "Canons," later known as the Five Points of Calvinism.

Baptists: those who believe that only professing believers should be baptized (credobaptism), in contrast to those who believe professing believers and their children should be baptized (paedobaptism)

Barthians: theologians continuing (to varying degrees) the work of Swiss-German theologian Karl Barth, who was one of the most significant twentieth-century theologians

Beatific vision: Roman Catholic and Eastern Orthodox teaching that the angels and souls in heaven will see and experience God face-to-face, with the result perfect and supreme blessedness

Calvinists: named after Protestant Reformer John Calvin (1509–1564). Calvinism is often associated with the five heads of doctrine articulated at the Synod of Dordt: Total Depravity, Unconditional Election, Limited Atonement, Irresistible Grace, and Perseverance of the Saints.

Canon: The Bible is a canon, which is a collection of varied texts that are united by their divine source (the Father's speaking), their content (the Son's work of redemption), and their power to generate the world of which they speak (the Spirit's work of inspiration, illumination, and regeneration).

Cappadocian fathers: Basil the Great (330–379), bishop of Caesarea; Gregory of Nyssa (c. 330–395), bishop of Nyssa and Basil's brother; Gregory Nazianzus (329–389), patriarch of Constantinople. They were influential theologians in the development of Christian theology in the East and West, in such areas as the doctrine of the Trinity, theological terminology, and Christology.

Common grace: God's bestowal of a variety of gifts and blessings on Christians and non-Christians alike, such as health, intelligence, friendship, vocation, family, government, art, science, etc. Common grace upholds fallen humanity, but it is not saving.

Communicable attributes: those attributes that may be predicated of God and humans (though only analogically), such as love, mercy, and justice

Concursus (or, concurrence): the simultaneity of divine and human agency in specific actions and events

Council of Trent: One of the most important Roman Catholic councils. Meeting between 1545–1563, this council discussed Reformation teachings and defined Roman Catholic doctrine on theological topics, such as Scripture and tradition, original sin, justification, and the sacraments. Many of these central Christian doctrines had not received official Roman Catholic statements until this council. It sought not only to state clearly the Roman Catholic position on various topics but also to renew the church in its polity and practice.

Covenant: an oath-based union under given stipulations and sanctions

Covenant of creation (also, covenant of works; covenant of nature): covenant between the triune Lord and humanity in Adam, with Adam as its covenantal representative (federal head). With disobedience, Adam (and humanity whom he represented) would die (Gen. 2:15–17; Rom. 5:12–18).

Covenant of grace: post-fall covenant between the triune God and Christ with the church, with Christ as its head and mediator. It began with God's promise of salvation to Adam and Eve and continued through the family of faith leading from Seth to Noah and on to Abraham and Sarah all the way to the new covenant as inaugurated by Christ's death. In this covenant, God promises to be our God and to make believers and their children his own redeemed family, with Christ—the Last Adam—as its federal representative, head, and mediator. It is the historical unfolding of the eternal plan of God in the covenant of redemption.

Covenant of redemption (also, *pactum salutis*; covenant of peace): covenant entered into by the persons of the Trinity in the councils of eternity, with the Son mediating its benefits to the elect. This covenant is the basis for all of God's purposes in nature and history, and it is the foundation and efficacy of the covenant of grace.

Deism: God created the world but does not intervene miraculously within it.

Demythologization: term coined by Rudolf Bultmann (1884–1976), referring to his project of removing what he regarded as the first-century mythic elements of the New Testament, which alienated modern thinkers from Christian faith

Descartes' *ego cogito*: René Descartes, the father of modern philosophy, proved his existence through doubting everything. He realized that he doubted, so there must be a doubting thing. His famous phrase, "I think, therefore I am" (*cogito ergo sum*), represents the foundation on which he builds the rest of his knowledge.

Dispensationalism: a system of theology that sees God's relationship to humans under distinct economies (dispensations) through history. Dispensationists hold to a distinction between Israel and the church and a premillennial return of Christ, and many argue for a pretribulation rapture. John Nelson Darby (1800–1882) and C. I. Scofield (1843–1921) were significant writers in the formation and development of dispensationalism.

Docetism: early church heresy that denied Jesus Christ as fully human

Dogmatics: a deeper analysis of Christian doctrines than systematic theology, including more exegesis and engagement with alternative views

Dominicans: Roman Catholic order named after St. Dominic, which began in the thirteenth century. The most famous Dominican is Thomas Aquinas (c.1225–1274). Its emphasis was predominantly education and preaching.

Donatism: Similar to the Novatianists, the Donatists sought a church of saints, not sinners. They declared invalid all baptisms that had been performed by bishops and pastors who had apostatized. Augustine (354–430) opposed them by arguing that the validity of the ministry of Word and sacraments in no way depends on the piety or sincerity of the administrator.

Economic Trinity: the revealed activity of the Triune God in creation and redemption, distinguished from the immanent Trinity. This parallels the distinction between our knowledge of God-in-himself (to which we do not have access), and God-for-us (given by God's revelation).

Ectypal knowledge: creaturely knowledge that is revealed by God and accommodated to our finite capacities. Creaturely knowledge is always imperfect, incomplete, and dependent on God's perfect and complete knowledge.

Effectual call (also, inward call, irresistible grace): occurs when through the hearing of the gospel the Spirit illumines an individual's heart and gives them faith

Epistemology: branch of philosophy that deals with questions about knowledge, answering the question, "How do we know?"

Equivocal (also, equivocity): the epistemological position that God's knowledge and creaturely knowledge have nothing in common (cf. analogical, univocal)

Erastianism: political theory that the church's outward administration, worship, and discipline function under the state

Essence-energies distinction: the Cappadocian fathers' and Eastern Orthodox distinction between the essence of God (which we cannot know) and his energies (which we can know). Eastern Orthodoxy has appealed to Exodus 33 for this distinction between God's inaccessible glory (his essence) and his gracious acts (his energies). Reformation theologians utilized this distinction in a variety of ways: theologies of glory or the cross; archetypal or ectypal theology; or knowing God's being or his acts.

Existentialism: philosophical view that emphasizes authentic individual existence. Significant existentialists have been Søren Kierkegaard (1813–1855), Friedrich Nietzsche (1844–1900), Martin Heidegger (1889–1976), and Jean-Paul Sartre (1905–1980).

Ex opere operato: medieval sacramental formulation meaning, "By doing it, it is done."

Extracalvinisticum (the "Calvinistic extra"): Lutheran critics used this term of derision against Reformed theologians who taught that even in the incarnation the eternal Son who nursed at Mary's breast continued to fill the heavens. Following the patristic consensus, Reformed theologians argued that the finite could not contain the infinite (*finitum non capax infiniti*).

Fact-value dilemma: deals with the question of what *is* (fact) and what *ought to be* (value). Fact is often seen as deduced from reason (and is therefore objective), whereas value comes from collective experience and agreement (and is therefore subjective).

Federal theology (also, covenant theology): interpretative framework with the biblical idea of "covenant" as an organizing principle. It utilizes the covenantal and representative (federal) headship of Adam and Jesus Christ (the Second and Last Adam) to understand the flow, continuity, and discontinuity in redemptive history.

Fideism: literally, "faith-ism," which is a Christian apologetic approach that refuses to offer any arguments or evidence for Christian claims, usually assuming that faith is opposed to reason

Fides qua creditur: the personal act of believing

Fides quae creditur: the faith (the content) that is believed

Filioque (Latin: "and from the Son"): addition to the Nicene Creed at the Third Council of Toledo (589), affirming the eternal procession of the Holy Spirit from both the Father and the Son. This additional clause created tensions between Western and Eastern Christendom and is considered to be one of the fundamental points of disagreement that led to their split in 1054.

Five Points of Calvinism: based on the five canons given by the Synod of Dordt (1618–19), which sought to answer Remonstrant (early Arminian) positions by affirming the following: Unconditional Election, Limited Atonement, Total Depravity, Irresistible Grace, and Perseverance of the Saints. The acronym used to remember these points is TULIP.

Formula of Concord: Lutheran confessional statement that sought to unite Lutheran churches. Jakob Andreä (1528–1590) and Martin Chemnitz (1522–1586) were the main writers of the Formula in 1577.

Franciscans: Roman Catholic order following the life and teachings of St. Francis of Assisi (c. 1181–1226). Its emphasis was on literal obedience to the biblical commands of selling possessions and serving the poor.

Geneva Catechism: catechism produced by John Calvin (1509–1564) in 1541, organized under the topics Faith, Law, Prayer, and the Sacraments

Gnosticism: a diverse group of writers and beliefs in the first and later centuries. Its primary underpinning was dualism. Two examples of this dualism are the Gnostic contrast between the God of the Old Testament and the loving God of the New Testament and the Gnostic contrast between matter being evil and spirit being good. The Gnostics sought redemption from this evil, material creation through secret knowledge (*gnosis*) possessed only by the spiritually elite. This heresy was decisively challenged by Irenaeus (115–202 AD), bishop of Lyons, in his *Against Heresies*, from which comes much of the information we have about Gnosticism.

Hasmonean Dynasty: the kingdom in Israel under descendents of the family of the Maccabees from c. 143 to 37 BC, arising out of the rebellion against Antiochus IV (215–164 BC) during the Maccabean wars. It fell to the Herodian dynasties in 37 BC.

Heidelberg Catechism: Reformation document with a question-and-answer format used to teach Christian doctrine and practice. It was written by Zacharius Ursinus (1534–1583) and approved by the Synod of Heidelberg in 1563.

Heilsgeschichte: a German term for the history of redemption

Hermeneutics: the study and practice of interpretation

Herodian Dynasty: kingdom in Israel from 37 BC to 92 AD led by rulers who were descendants from Herod the Great (74 BC–c. 4 BC)

Historia salutis: literally, the history of salvation. It refers to the historical events of Christ's life, death, resurrection, ascension, and the coming of the Spirit.

Hyper-Calvinism: theological position that so emphasizes the sovereignty of God that it minimizes (or denies) the place of creaturely means and secondary causation (thereby rejecting the need for evangelism)

Hypostatic union: theological term used in the early church to describe the union of the divine and human natures in the one person (hypostasis) of Jesus Christ

Idealism: philosophical theory that the center and origin of all knowledge is based on mind and ideas. With sources in Plato and Platonism, modern German idealism has exercised enormous influence through Kant, Hegel, Schelling, and others.

Illocutionary act: level of a speech act that is the force or intended meaning of a communicative act (the locutionary act)

Immanence: being entirely within creation

Immanent Trinity: the hidden intratrinitarian communion (distinguished from the economic Trinity)

Incommunicable attributes: those attributes that belong to God alone, such as simplicity, omnipresence, and omniscience

Infinite-qualitative distinction (also, Creator-creature distinction): the theological teaching that God and creation are qualitatively different

Infralapsarianism: the theological position that God's decree to save *follows* logically (not temporarily) the decision to create and permit the fall

Kabbalah: an esoteric school of thought within Judaism based on mystical interpretations of the Hebrew Scriptures

Kenosis: from a Greek verb in Philippians 2:7 (*kenoō*), meaning "to empty." Nineteenth-century theologians understood this verse and others to argue that the Son of God emptied himself of some (or all) of his divine attributes when he became a human.

Lessing's ugly ditch: the epistemological dilemma that G. E. Lessing (1729–1781) expressed, that contingent historical truths could not be used to verify necessary truths of reason; one could not cross from one side of the ditch (contingent history) to the other (necessary truths)

Locutionary act: level of a speech act that is the act of speaking itself

Logos asarkos: literally, "Word without flesh"; term for the second person of the Trinity, *before* he took on flesh

Maccabean wars: a Jewish rebellion against the Seleucid dynasty (part of Alexander the Great's empire) that ruled over the land of Israel from 198 to 63 BC. These wars were named after the Maccabee family, who led the rebellion and later ruled as the Hasmonean Dynasty.

Manicheanism: materialistic dualist group in the early centuries of the church, which separated the God of creation (of the Old Testament) from the God of redemption (of the New Testament)

"Meeting a stranger": the ontological paradigm articulated by Protestant theologian Paul Tillich (1886–1965) in contrast to the "overcoming estrangement" paradigm. Central to this paradigm are an ontology of difference (God and the creation) and an epistemology of hearing (God condescends and speaks to us).

Metanarrative: a story (narrative) that pretends it is not a narrative. It claims that it is "beyond" (*meta*) grand-overarching narratives that sought to explain all of reality and human existence.

Method of correlation: theological paradigm of Paul Tillich (1886–1965), which seeks to correlate Christian theology to the philosophical and existential questions of the contemporary world. Philosophers determine the questions and theologians provide the answers.

Modalism (also, Sabellianism): There is only one person in God who represents himself in the roles of three persons.

Montanism: early church sect founded by Montanus, who emphasized the work of the Spirit through continuing prophecy and speaking in tongues

Moral ability: the power to approve, delight in, and fulfill God's moral will

Mortification: Latin term used by Reformer theologians to refer to the dying of the old self in sanctification

Mutatis mutandis: Latin phrase meaning "the necessary changes having been made" or "with particular differences taken into consideration"

Narrative theology (also, the Yale School; postliberal theology): begun by professors Hans Frei (1922–1988) and George Lindbeck (1923-) of Yale Divinity School, with a focus on the centrality of narrative for the church's confession and as the governing paradigm for theology. Postliberal theology has also brought renewed attention to the connection between a community's practices with its beliefs.

Natural ability: humans having the necessary faculties and abilities to fulfill God's commands, but since these faculties have been marred by sin, they lack the moral ability to fulfill these commands

Natural law: the law of God written on the conscience of every person (Rom. 2:14–15)

Neo-Platonism: the revival and recasting of Platonism in the third century mainly through writers such as Plotinus and Porphyry, which influenced theologians such as Origen, Augustine, Boethius, and Bonaventure

Nicene Creed: the result of the first ecumenical (universal) church council in 325 A.D., in the midst of orthodox and Arian debates over the divinity of Jesus Christ. The Council of Constantinople later revised the Nicene Creed in 381, which is the text commonly used today, although the East retains its original language of the Spirit proceeding from the Father and the West added "from the Father and the Son" (see *Filioque*).

Noetic: of or related to the mind

Noumena: term used by Immanuel Kant (1724–1804), meaning "things as they are in themselves," in contrast to phenomena. According to Kant, noumena are unknowable to us.

Novatianists: Followers of Novatius (c. 200–258), who would not allow people readmission into the church if they had recanted of their faith during the time of the Decian persecution (c. 250 AD). The church deemed this teaching heretical.

Occasionalism: school of thought founded by philosopher Nicolas Malebranche (1638–1715), who argued that every event was an *ex nihilo* creation (a direct and immediate act of God), in an effort to affirm God's active role in every aspect of creation

Ontology: branch of philosophy that seeks to answer questions dealing with reality and existence

Onto-theology: "being-theology" or "a theology of being." Beginning with Kant, "onto-theology" became increasingly a term of derision for the synthesis of theology and philosophy in Western metaphysics.

Open theism: twentieth-century theological movement seeking to affirm the free will of humanity and the openness of the future, which since it has yet to happen, cannot be known by anyone (including God). Open theists reject the classical attributes of God, such as omniscience, omnipotence, omnipresence, immutability, and impassibility. Main proponents include Clark Pinnock, John E. Sanders, and Gregory Boyd.

Ordo salutis: literally, the order of salvation. It refers to the logical order as to how the Spirit applies the benefits of Christ to individuals.

Original sin: the guilt and corruption brought on the human race as a result of Adam's sin

Outward call (also, external call): occurs anytime when God summons the world to Christ through the preaching of the gospel

"Overcoming estrangement": The ontological paradigm articulated by Protestant theologian Paul Tillich (1886–1965) in contrast to the "meeting a stranger" paradigm, to categorize various philosophies of religion. This paradigm emphasizes hyper-immanence, an ontology of emanation, and an epistemology of vision. God reveals himself from within the human, rather than from outside.

Over-realized eschatology: the assumption that the new creation and its benefits have already been realized fully in the present, without the recognition of the "not yet" dimension in which we wait and struggle

Panentheism: literally, "all-within-God." This view holds that God (or the divine principle) transcends the world, although God and the world exist in mutual dependence.

Pantheism: literally, "all is divine." It is the theological belief that all of reality is God.

Passive obedience of Christ: term used to express Jesus Christ's suffering the penalty of sin and death on behalf of his people

Pelagianism: school of thought named after Pelagius (354–418?) and promulgated by Julian of Eclanum (c. 386-c. 455). They taught that the human will was capable of spiritual good without the aid of God's grace, and that sinless perfection was possible in this life. Augustine and Jerome were chief critics of Pelagianism, and it was condemned by church councils in 418 and 431.

Penal substitution: Jesus Christ's sacrifice was the payment of a debt to divine justice as a substitute for his people

Perfectionism: theological position that teaches that believers can live above sin. The Pelagian view assumed believers can (and must) attain absolute perfection in this life to be acceptable to God. The Arminian version of John Wesley (1703–1791) argues for the possibility of believers living without known sin through grace-perfected love.

Perichoresis: a term first used by the Cappadocian fathers, referring to the mutual indwelling and fellowship of the persons of the Trinity

Perlocutionary act: the level of a speech act that is the effect of the intended meaning (illocution) of one's speech (locutionary act)

Phenomena: term used by Immanuel Kant (1724–1804), meaning "things as they appear to us." According to Kant's epistemology, we can know only phenomena, not noumena, though the latter provide the categories for knowing and interpreting the former.

Postmodernity: a term with a variety of meanings, whether one is speaking of architecture, literature, music, philosophy, theology, etc. In many ways it is both reaction to and rejection of modern thought, yet can also be seen as its culmination.

Poststructuralism: associated especially with the French thinkers Emmanuel Levinas (1906–1995), Jacques Derrida (1930–2004), and Michel Foucault (1926–1984). Poststructuralism arises from the tradition of (and often in reaction to) German idealism, phenomenology (especially Husserl), and existentialism (Heidegger).

Prelapsarian: literally, "before the fall"

Premodernity: in philosophy, a term usually referring to the period in Western intellectual history before the work of René Descartes (1596–1650)

Process theology: theological school that holds that just as the universe changes and evolves, so also part of God is changeable. Alfred North Whitehead (1861–1947) and his process philosophy is an important precursor to process theology.

Propitiation: Jesus Christ's death propitiated (satisfied) God's justice and wrath against sin

Protestant scholasticism (also, Protestant orthodoxy; Post-Reformation dogmatics): the post-Reformation period in which the Reformation insights and theology were refined, and which produced the evangelical confessions, catechisms, liturgies, church orders, and hymns

Qumran community: Qumran is located near the shore of the Dead Sea in Israel. A community lived in this area in the first century BC and AD and hid scrolls of biblical texts and other works in nearby caves. These caves were first discovered in 1947 and the scrolls were known as "the Dead Sea Scrolls," one of the most significant archaeological findings in the twentieth century.

Rationalism: epistemological theory that attempts to base theological beliefs on universal principles of innate reason, with absolute certainty as the only legitimate form of knowing

Regeneration: the Spirit's sovereign work of raising those who are spiritually dead to life in Christ through the announcement of the gospel

Regulative principle of worship: the Reformed and Presbyterian teaching that only what Christ commands is obligatory for faith, practice, and church worship

Romanticism: cultural and intellectual movement in the late eighteenth century and early nineteenth century, seeking aesthetic experience and emotion as a reaction to Enlightenment thought and the mechanization of nature brought about through the rise of science

Sacrament: a visible sign and seal of a spiritual grace

Schleitheim Confession: statement of faith of early Anabaptists in 1527, who met in Schleitheim, Switzerland. The confession has seven articles, including a rejection of infant baptism, the use of the ban (excommunication), and pacifism

Scots Confession: statement of faith written by John Knox (c. 1510–1572) and others in 1560, which became the Church of Scotland's confessional standard until the *Westminster Confession of Faith* was accepted in 1648

Second Helvetic Confession: Reformation statement of faith written by Heinrich Bullinger (1504–1575) in 1562, which became popular in many Reformed congregations in and geographical areas such as Switzerland, Scotland, and France

Second Vatican Council: significant twentieth-century (1962–1965) Roman Catholic Church council that discussed issues such as the relation between Scripture and tradition, ecclesiology, ecumenism, and the liturgy. It was the twenty-first ecumenical council of the Roman Catholic Church.

Semi-Pelagianism: term coined in the sixteenth century for the teaching that human beings are affected by sin but can still choose the good and, in the common formulation of the late medieval period, "God will not deny his grace to those who do what lies within them." Salvation is attained by human cooperation with grace.

Simil iustus et peccator: Reformation slogan meaning "both saint and sinner," which points out that the believer in Christ is simultaneously righteous before God, yet also still sins

Socinianism: radical Protestant heresy starting in the sixteenth-century, named after Laelius Socinus (d. 1562) and his nephew Faustus (d. 1604). They denied the Trinity, original sin, the deity of Christ, his substitutionary atonement, and justification by faith alone. In many ways, the thought and criticisms of Socinianism anticipated those of the Unitarianism and Enlightenment rationalism.

Speech-act theory: linguistic theory analyzing the content, intention, and effect of language by speakers and on listeners. The most significant writers on speech-act theory have been J. L. Austin (1911 – 1960) and John R. Searle (1932-). Cf. illocutionary, locutionary, and perlocutionary acts.

Stoicism: a school of philosophy founded around the third-century BC in Athens. It valued indifference and a lack of emotion.

"The stranger we never meet": a third ontological paradigm in addition to Paul Tillich's (1886 – 1965) "overcoming estrangement" and "meeting a stranger." This hyper-transcendence paradigm has an epistemology of equivocity, denying any possibility of access to or knowledge of the divine stranger.

Sufficient grace: grace that is enough to enable sinners to respond positively to God if they choose to do so

Sufi Islam (Sufism): the mystical aspect of Islamic practice that seeks inner renewal and experience of the divine

Supralapsarianism: The theological position that God's decree to save is logically *prior to* his decree to create and permit the fall

Suzerainty treaty: a treaty imposed unilaterally by the great king (the suzerain) on the lesser ruler (the vassal), which required strict obedience to specific commands or else the vassal would die (cf. royal grant)

Synergism (meaning "working together"): the view that salvation is attained through a cooperative process between God and human beings

Systematic theology: an organized and detailed summary of important topics in theology (cf. dogmatics)

Theology of the cross: Phrase used by Protestant Reformer Martin Luther (1483 – 1546) to emphasize that human knowledge and experience must be based on the foolishness of the cross, not human abilities or human ascent to God (theology of glory)

Theology of glory: Phrase used by Protestant Reformer Martin Luther (1483–1546) to criticize medieval theologians who sought direct access to God without the need of mediation

Theōsis: deification

Theotokos: term used of Mary ("the mother of God") at the Council of Ephesus in 431 to affirm the divinity of Jesus Christ

Thomists: followers of the teaching of Thomas Aquinas (c. 1225–1274)

The Three Forms of Unity: The three most widely accepted confessional standards of the Reformed church. It includes the *Belgic Confession* (1563), the *Heidelberg Catechism* (1565), and the *Canons of Dordt* (1618–1619).

Total depravity: theological position that every aspect of human nature has been corrupted by the fall—body, soul, mind, heart, and will

Transcendence: being entirely above and outside of creation

Transubstantiation: the Roman Catholic teaching that in the Eucharist the physical elements of bread and wine materially change into the body and blood of Christ, although the accidents of the bread and wine (their appearance, taste, and smell, for instance) remain unchanged

Tritheism: a denial of the essential unity of the Trinity in favor of three Gods

Ubiquity: ability to be omnipresent. "Ubiquitarianism" teaches that the human nature of the resurrected Christ is omnipresent and is therefore possible to be in the elements of the Lord's Supper simultaneously around the world.

Unconditional election: God election based entirely on his own good pleasure, dependent on no condition in the one he elects

Under-realized eschatology: any theological viewpoint that too heavily underrates the present (already) reality of the presence of Christ through his Spirit and too one-sidedly affirms the not-yet of salvation and the kingdom of Jesus Christ

Union with Christ: phrase referring to the way in which believers share in Christ in eternity (by election), in past history (by redemption), in the present (by effectual calling, justification, and sanctification), and in the future (by glorification). This union is mystical, legal, and organic.

Univocal (also, univocity): the view that there is only one kind of reality or existence; in epistemology, that the knowledge of God and creatures are identical (cf. analogical, equivocal)

Univocity of being: everything that truly exists is one

Vivification: Latin-based term used by Reformed theologians to refer to the making alive of the new man in sanctification

Voluntarism: school of thought with its emphasis on the will (whether human or divine), which determines what is good, true, and beautiful. It is contrasted with intellectualism, where what is good determines the will. This debate is associated especially with the Franciscans (Scotus) and Dominicans (Thomas), who emphasized the primacy of the will and the intellect, respectively. Nineteenth-century voluntarism finds its source in Immanuel Kant (1724–1804), who elevated the practical reason (the will) over pure reason.

Westminster standards: confessional statements and catechisms developed and written by the Westminster Assembly in England during the years 1643–1648. These standards include the *Westminster Confession of Faith*, the *Westminster Larger Catechism*, and the *Westminster Shorter Catechism*. These documents are the doctrinal standards (subordinate to the Scriptures) in Presbyterian churches throughout the world.

SCRIPTURE INDEX

JAMES

1 PETER

2 Peter

1 John

2 John

3 John

Jude

Revelation

APOCRYPHAL LITERATURE

1 ENOCH

2 ESDRAS

2 MACCABEES

4 EZRA

SUBJECT INDEX

Bold page ranges indicate entire units of the traditional categories of theology.

NAME INDEX

CONFESSION INDEX

RECOMMENDED RESOURCES: AN ANNOTATED BIBLIOGRAPHY

Scores of books could be recommended for closer study of topics treated in this volume. Many valuable works cited in the footnotes throughout this volume do not appear in this bibliography. This reduced bibliography offers at least a few suggestions for further reading; they are grouped under topics and have levels attached: Beginner, Intermediate, and Advanced.

THE HISTORY OF THE REFORMED AND PRESBYTERIAN CHURCHES

Benedict, Philip. *Christ's Churches Purely Reformed: A Social History of Calvinism.* New Haven: Yale University Press, 2010. *Advanced.*

Clark, R. Scott. *Recovering the Reformed Confession: Our Theology, Piety, and Practice.* Phillipsburg, NJ: P&R, 2008. *Intermediate.*

Cunningham, William. *The Reformers and the Theology of the Reformation.* Edinburgh: Banner of Truth, 1979. *Intermediate.*

Dickens, A. G. *The English Reformation.* New York: Schocken, 1964. *Intermediate.*

Dillenberger, John, ed. *John Calvin: Selections from His Writings.* Missoula, MT: Scholars Press, 1975. *Intermediate.*

———. *Martin Luther: Selections from His Writings.* New York: Anchor, 1961. *Beginner.*

Ganoczy, Alexandre. *The Young Calvin.* Philadelphia: Westminster, 1987. *Advanced.*

Godfrey, W. Robert. *John Calvin: Pilgrim and Pastor.* Phillipsburg, NJ: P&R, 2010. *Beginner.*

Hillerbrand, Hans, ed. *The Reformation: A Narrative History Related by Contemporary Observers and Participants.* Grand Rapids: Baker, 1978. *Intermediate.*

Lull, Timothy, ed. *Martin Luther's Basic Theological Writings.* Minneapolis: Fortress, 1989. *Intermediate.*

McNeill, John Thomas. *The History and Character of Calvinism.* Oxford: Oxford University Press, 1979. *Intermediate.*

Muller, Richard. *The Unaccommodated Calvin: Studies in the Foundations of a Theological Tradition.* Oxford Studies in Historical Theology. New York: Oxford University Press, 2001. *Advanced.*

———. *After Calvin: Studies in the Development of a Theological Tradition.* Oxford Studies in Historical Theology. New York: Oxford University Press, 2003. *Advanced.*

Neill, Stephen. *Anglicanism.* 4th edition. New York: Oxford University Press, 1978. *Advanced.*

Noll, Mark A., ed. *Confessions and Catechisms of the Reformation.* Grand Rapids: Baker, 1991. *Beginner.*

Oberman, Heiko A. *Forerunners of the Reformation: The Shape of Late Medieval Thought.* Philadelphia: Fortress, 1981. *Intermediate.*

Olin, John C., ed. *A Reformation Debate: Sadoleto's Letter to the Genevans and Calvin's Reply.* Grand Rapids: Baker, 1976. *Beginner.*

Parker, T. H. L. *John Calvin: A Biography.* Philadelphia: Westminster, 1975. *Beginner.*

Pauck, Wilhelm, ed. *Melanchthon and Bucer.* Philadelphia: Westminster, 1969. *Advanced.*

Reid, W. Stanford, and Paul Woolley, eds. *John Calvin: His Influence in the Western World.* Grand Rapids: Zondervan, 1982. *Beginner.*

Rupp, E. Gordon, and Philip S. Watson, ed. and trans. *Luther and Erasmus: Free Will and*

Salvation. Philadelphia: Westminster, 1969. *Intermediate*.

Ryken, Leland. *Worldly Saints: The Puritans As They Really Were*. Grand Rapids: Zondervan, 1986. *Beginner*.

Spitz, Lewis W. *The Renaissance and Reformation Movements*. The Rand McNally History Series. Chicago: Rand McNally, 1971. *Intermediate*.

Wallace, Ronald S. *Calvin, Geneva and the Reformation*. Grand Rapids: Baker, 1988. *Intermediate*.

Wells, David F., and Roger R. Nicole, eds. *Reformed Theology in America: A History of Its Modern Development*. Grand Rapids: Eerdmans, 1985. *Beginner*.

GENERAL STUDIES OF REFORMED THEOLOGY

Bavinck, Herman. *Reformed Dogmatics*. Ed. John Bolt; trans., John Vriend, volumes 1-4. Grand Rapids: Baker Academic, 2003-2008. *Intermediate-Advanced*.

―――. *Our Reasonable Faith*. Grand Rapids: Eerdmans, 1956. *Intermediate*.

Berkhof, Louis. *Systematic Theology*. 2nd rev. and enlarged ed. Grand Rapids: Eerdmans, 1996. *Intermediate*.

Calvin, John. *The Institutes of the Christian Religion*. Ed. John T. McNeill, trans. by Lewis Ford Battles. 2 volumes. Library of Christian Classics. Philadelphia: Westminster, 1960. *Intermediate*.

Calvin, John. *The Institutes of the Christian Religion*. Ed. Tony Lane and Hilary Osborne. Grand Rapids: Baker, 1987. An abridged edition. *Beginner*.

Hodge, Charles. *Systematic Theology*. 3 vols. Peabody, MA: Hendrickson, 1999. *Intermediate*.

Horton, Michael S. *Putting Amazing Back into Grace*. Rev. ed. Grand Rapids: Baker, forthcoming. *Beginner*.

―――. *Introducing Covenant Theology*. Grand Rapids: Baker, 2009. *Beginner/Intermediate*.

Godfrey, W. Robert, and Jess L. Boyd, III, eds. *Through Christ's Word: Festschrift for Philip E. Hughes*. Phillipsburg, NJ: P&R, 1985. *Advanced*.

Meeter, H. Henry. *The Basic Ideas of Calvinism*. 6th ed., rev. by Paul A. Marshall. Grand Rapids: Baker, 1990. *Beginner*.

Murray, John. *Redemption Accomplished and Applied*. Grand Rapids: Eerdmans, 1984. *Intermediate*.

Packer, J. I. *God's Words: Studies of Key Bible Themes*. Downers Grove, IL: InterVarsity Press, 1981. *Beginner*.

Reymond, Robert L. *A New Systematic Theology of the Christian Faith*: 2nd ed. Nashville: Nelson, 1998. *Intermediate*.

Sproul, R. C. *What Is Reformed Theology?* Grand Rapids: Baker, 2005. *Beginner*.

THEOLOGICAL METHOD AND SCRIPTURE

Carson, D. A., and Woodbridge, John. *Scripture and Truth*. Downers Grove, IL: InterVarsity Press, 1992. *Intermediate*.

Kelly, Douglas F. *Systematic Theology*; Vol. 1: *Grounded in Holy Scripture and Understood in the Light of the Church*. Rothshire, Scotland: Mentor, 2008. *Intermediate*.

Kline, M. G. *The Structure of Biblical Authority*. Eugene, OR: Wipf & Stock, 1997. *Intermediate*.

Thompson, Mark D. *A Clear and Present Word: The Clarity of Scripture*. Downers Grove, IL: InterVarsity Press, 2006. *Intermediate/Advanced*.

Vanhoozer, Kevin. *The Drama of Doctrine*. Louisville: Westminster John Knox, 2005. *Advanced*.

Young, E. J. *Thy Word Is Truth*. Edinburgh: Banner of Truth, 1963. *Intermediate*.

GOD AND HUMANITY

Bray, Gerald. *The Doctrine of God*. Contours of Christian Theology. Downers Grove, IL: InterVarsity Press, 1993. *Intermediate*.

Fesko, John V. *Last Things First: Unlocking Genesis with the Christ of Eschatology*. Rothshire, Scotland: Mentor, 2007. *Intermediate*.

Hoekema, Anthony A. *Created in God's Image*. Grand Rapids: Eerdmans, 1986. *Beginner/Intermediate*.

Letham, Robert. *The Holy Trinity*. Phillipsburg, NJ: P&R, 2005. *Intermediate*.

Packer, J. I. *Knowing God.* Downers Grove, Ill.: InterVarsity Press, 1979. *Beginner.*

———. *Knowing Man.* Westchester, IL: Cornerstone, 1978. *Beginner.*

Sanders, Fred. *The Deep Things of God: How the Trinity Changes Everything.* Westchester, IL: Crossway, 2010. *Beginner.*

Sproul, R. C. *The Holiness of God.* 2nd ed. Wheaton: Tyndale, 2000. *Beginner.*

Zizioulas, John. *Being as Communion.* Crestwood, NY: St. Vladimir's Seminary Press, 1997. *Advanced.*

CHRIST'S PERSON AND WORK

Athanasius. *On the Incarnation.* Trans. and ed. by Sister Penelope Lawson. New York: Macmillan, 1946. *Intermediate.*

Bray, Gerald. *Creeds, Councils and Christ.* Downers Grove, IL: InterVarsity Press, 1984. *Beginner.*

Hoekema, Anthony. *Saved by Grace.* Grand Rapids: Eerdmans, 1989. *Beginner.*

Kuiper, R. B. *For Whom Did Christ Die?* Grand Rapids: Baker, 1982. *Beginner.*

Morris, Leon. *The Atonement.* Downers Grove, IL: InterVarsity, 1983. *Beginner/Intermediate.*

Muller, Richard A. *Christ and the Decree: Christology and Predestination in Reformed Theology from Calvin to Perkins.* Grand Rapids: Baker, 1986. *Advanced.*

Murray, John. *Redemption Accomplished and Applied.* Grand Rapids: Eerdmans, 1955. *Beginner.*

Owen, John. *The Death of Death in the Death of Christ.* Edinburgh: Banner of Truth, 1983. *Advanced.*

Pinnock, Clark. *The Grace of God and the Will of Man: A Case for Arminianism.* Grand Rapids: Zondervan, 1989. *Intermediate.*

Valdes, Juan de, and Don Benedetto. *The Benefit of Christ.* Ed. James Houston. Portland, OR: Multnomah, 1984. *Beginner.*

Warfield, B. B. *The Person and Work of Christ.* Phillipsburg, NJ: P&R, 1958. *Advanced.*

———. *Studies in Perfectionism.* Phillipsburg, NJ: P&R. *Advanced.*

———. *Biblical and Theological Studies.* Phillipsburg, NJ: P&R, 1958. *Advanced.*

———. *The Plan of Salvation.* Grand Rapids: Eerdmans, 1980. *Intermediate.*

THE DOCTRINE OF JUSTIFICATION

Billings, J. Todd. *Calvin, Participation, and the Gift.* New York: Oxford University Press, 2008. *Advanced.*

Buchanan, James. *The Doctrine of Justification.* Edinburgh: Banner of Truth, 1961. *Intermediate.*

Fesko, J. V. *Justification: Understanding the Classic Reformed Doctrine.* Phillipsburg, NJ: P&R, 2008. *Beginner/Intermediate.*

Horton, Michael. *Covenant and Salvation: Union with Christ.* Louisville: Westminster John Knox, 2007. *Advanced.*

Luther, Martin. *Commentary on Galatians.* Grand Rapids: Baker, 1975. *Beginner.*

SANCTIFICATION, THE CHURCH, AND THE CHRISTIAN LIFE

Alexander, Donald L., ed. *Christian Spirituality: Five Views of Sanctification.* Downers Grove, IL: InterVarsity Press, 1988. *Intermediate.*

Bromiley, Geoffrey W. *Children of Promise.* Grand Rapids: Eerdmans, 1979. *Beginner.*

Clowney, Edmund P. *The Church.* Contours in Christian Theology. Downers Grove, IL: InterVarsity Press, 1995. *Intermediate.*

Ferguson, Sinclair. *The Holy Spirit.* Contours in Christian Theology. Downers Grove, IL: InterVarsity Press, 1996. *Intermediate.*

Hooker, Thomas. *The Poor Doubting Christian Drawn to Christ.* Grand Rapids: Baker, 1981. *Beginner.*

Horton, Michael. *People and Place: A Covenantal Ecclesiology.* Louisville: Westminster John Knox, 2009. *Advanced.*

Knox, D. Broughton. *The Lord's Supper from Wycliffe to Cranmer.* London: Paternoster, 1983. *Intermediate.*

Marcel, Pierre Ch. *The Biblical Doctrine of Infant Baptism.* Trans. Philip Hughes. Greenwood, SC: Attic, 1981. *Intermediate.*

Mathison, Keith A. *Given For You: Reclaiming*

Calvin's Doctrine of the Lord's Supper. Phillipsburg, NJ: P&R, 2002. *Intermediate.*

Packer, J. I. *Keep in Step with the Spirit*. Old Tappan, NJ: Revell, 1984. *Intermediate.*

———. *A Quest for Godliness*. Wheaton, IL: Crossway, 1991. *Intermediate.*

Sartelle, John. *What Every Christian Parent Should Know about Infant Baptism*. Phillipsburg, NJ: P&R, 1989. *Beginner.*

VanDrunen, David. *Living in God's Two Kingdoms*. Westchester, IL: Crossway, 2011. *Beginner.*

Last Things

Clouse, Robert, ed. *The Meaning of the Millennium: Four Views*. Downers Grove, IL: InterVarsity Press, 1977. *Beginner.*

Davis, John Jefferson. *Christ's Victorious Kingdom: Postmillennialism Reconsidered*. Grand Rapids: Baker, 1987. *Intermediate.*

Erickson, Millard J. *Contemporary Options in Eschatology*. Grand Rapids: Baker, 1983. *Advanced.*

Hendriksen, William. *More Than Conquerors*. Grand Rapids: Baker, 1940. *Beginner.*

Hoekema, Anthony. *The Bible and the Future*. Grand Rapids: Eerdmans, 1979. *Beginner.*

Johnson, Dennis E. *The Triumph of the Lamb: A Commentary on Revelation*. Phillipsburg, NJ: P&R, 2001. *Beginner/Intermediate.*

Ladd, George. *The Blessed Hope*. Grand Rapids: Eerdmans, 1956. *Intermediate.*

Ridderbos, Herman. *The Coming of the Kingdom*. Phillipsburg, NJ: P&R, 1962. *Intermediate.*

Riddlebarger, Kim. *A Case for Amillennialism*. Grand Rapids: Baker, 2003. *Beginner/Intermediate.*

Vos, Geerhardus. *The Pauline Eschatology*. Phillipsburg, NJ: P&R, 1979. *Intermediate/Advanced.*

textbook*plus*⁺

Equipping Instructors and Students with
FREE RESOURCES for Core Zondervan Textbooks

Available Resources for The Christian Faith

Instructor Resources

- Instructor's manual
- Chapter quizzes
- Presentation slides
- Reading schedule
- Chapter summaries

Student Resources

- Flashcards
- Quizzes
- Chapter videos

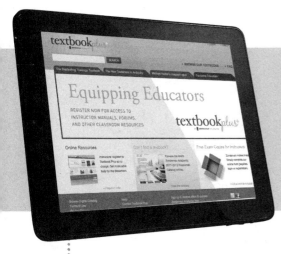

*How To Access Resources

- Go to www.TextbookPlus.Zondervan.com
- Click "Register Now" button and complete registration process
- Find books using search field or "Browse Our Textbooks" feature
- Click "Instructor Resources" or "Student Resources" tab once you get to book page to access resources

www.TextbookPlus.Zondervan.com

A Place for Weakness

Preparing Yourself for Suffering

Michael S. Horton

In a world of hype, we may buy into the idea that, through Jesus, we'll be healthier and wealthier as well as wiser. So what happens when we become ill, or depressed, or bankrupt? Did we do something wrong? Has God abandoned us?

As a child, Michael Horton would run up the down escalator, trying to beat it to the top. As Christians, he notes, we sometimes seek God the same way, believing we can climb to him under our own steam. We can't, which is why we are blessed that Jesus descends to us, especially during times of trial.

In *A Place for Weakness*, formerly titled *Too Good to Be True*, Horton exposes the pop culture that sells Jesus like a product for health and happiness and reminds us that our lives often lead us on difficult routes we must follow by faith. This book offers a series of powerful readings that demonstrate how, through every type of earthly difficulty, our Father keeps his promises from Scripture and works all things together for our good.

Available in stores and online!

Four Views on Eternal Security

Stanley N. Gundry, Series Editor;
J. Matthew Pinson, General Editor

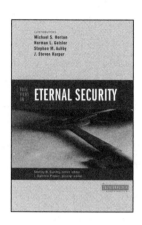

Does the Bible support the concept of "once saved, always saved," or can a person lose his or her salvation? How do the Scriptures portray the complex interplay between grace and free will? These and related questions are explored from different angles in this thought-provoking Counterpoints volume.

The contributors each state their case for one of four prominent views on eternal security: classical Calvinist (Michael S. Horton), moderate Calvinist (Norman L. Geisler), reformed Arminian (Stephen M. Ashby), and Wesleyan Arminian (J. Stephen Harper). In keeping with the forum approach of the Counterpoints series, each view is first presented by its proponent, then critiqued and defended. This fair and respectful approach allows you to weigh for yourself the strengths and weaknesses of the different doctrinal stances. By furnishing you with scholarly and thoughtful perspectives on the topic of eternal security, this book helps you sift through opposing views to arrive at your own informed conclusions.

The Counterpoints series provides a forum for comparison and critique of different views on issues important to Christians. Counterpoints books address two categories: Church Life and Bible and Theology. Complete your library with other books in the Counterpoints series.

Available in stores and online!